FIFTH EDITION

Understanding Psychology

Charles G. Morris
University of Michigan

Albert A. Maisto
University of North Carolina at Charlotte

Prentice Hall

Upper Saddle River, New Jersey 07458

Library of Congress Cataloging-in-Publication Data

Understanding psychology / Charles G. Morris with Albert A. Maisto.—5th ed.
    p.   cm
Includes bibliographical references and index.
ISBN 0-13-018934-0
  1. Psychology.   I. Morris, Charles G.   II. Maisto, Albert A. (Albert Anthony)
BF139.U53 2000
150—dc21   00-037495

VP/Editorial Director: *Laura Pearson*
Executive Editor: *Bill Webber*
Development Editor: *Robert Weiss*
AVP/Director of Production
  and Manufacturing: *Barbara Kittle*
Project Manager: *Maureen Richardson*
Managing Editor: *Mary Rottino*
Manufacturing Manager: *Nick Sklitsis*
Prepress and Manufacturing Buyer: *Tricia Kenny*
Creative Design Director: *Leslie Osher*

Interior Design: *Ximena Tamvakopoulos*
Cover Design: *Ximena Tamvakopoulos*
Cover Art: *Susan LeVan*
Photo Researcher: *Linda Sykes*
Image Specialist: *Beth Boyd*
Manager, Rights & Permissions: *Kay Dellosa*
Director, Image Resource Center: *Melinda Reo*
Production/Formatting/Art Manager: *Guy Ruggiero*
Marketing Manager: *Sharon Cosgrove*

Photo credits appear on pp. C-1–C-2, which constitute a continuation of the copyright page.

This book was set in 10/12.5 Janson by TSI Graphics and was printed and bound by Von Hoffman Press. Inc.
The cover was printed by Phoenix Color Corp.

Copyright © 2001, 1999, 1996, 1993, 1991 by Prentice-Hall, Inc.
A Division of Pearson Education
Upper Saddle River, New Jersey 07458

Printed in the United States of America
10 9 8 7 6 5 4 3 2

ISBN 0-13-018934-0
ISBN 0-13-029073-4 (Without Mind Matters)

Prentice-Hall International (UK) Limited, London
Prentice-Hall of Australia Pty. Limited, Sydney
Prentice-Hall Canada Inc., Toronto
Prentice-Hall Hispanoamericana, S.A., Mexico
Prentice-Hall of India Private Limited, New Delhi
Prentice-Hall of Japan, Inc., Tokyo
Pearson Education Asia Pte. Ltd., Singapore
Editora Prentice-Hall do Brasil, Ltda., Rio de Janeiro

BRIEF CONTENTS

CONTENTS

7 COGNITION AND MENTAL ABILITIES 228

8 MOTIVATION AND EMOTION 274

9 LIFE SPAN DEVELOPMENT 310

10 PERSONALITY   360

11 STRESS AND HEALTH PSYCHOLOGY   390

12 PSYCHOLOGICAL DISORDERS   418

FEATURE BOXES

FEATURE BOXES

PREFACE

I T IS ALWAYS AN EXCITING CHALLENGE to capture recent developments in psychology and report them in a brief form that is accurate, interesting, and understandable. The field of psychology has changed so much over the years, and so many of the recent discoveries are truly exciting, that it's still fun to be able to pull it all together every three years in interesting, readable prose. The challenge is made more exciting as electronic media become more prevalent. For this edition especially, a great deal of time was spent locating and evaluating electronic resources that complement the text material. Electronic resources are so important to this revision that in conversations the publisher and the authors refer to this edition as the "media edition." Read on to discover what is new and exciting about *Understanding Psychology*, Fifth Edition!

New in this Edition

Electronic Resources

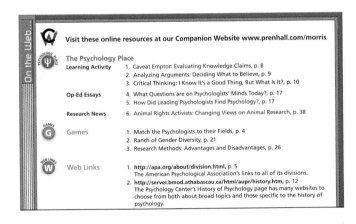

On the Web...

Visit these online resources at our Companion Website www.prenhall.com/morris

The Psychology Place

Learning Activity
1. Caveat Emptor: Evaluating Knowledge Claims, p. 8
2. Analyzing Arguments: Deciding What to Believe, p. 9
3. Critical Thinking: I Know It's a Good Thing, But What Is It?, p. 10

Op-Ed Essays
4. What Questions are on Psychologists' Minds Today?, p. 17
5. How Did Leading Psychologists Find Psychology?, p. 17

Research News
6. Animal Rights Activists: Changing Views on Animal Research, p. 38

Games
1. Match the Psychologists to their Fields, p. 4
2. Ranch of Gender Diversity, p. 21
3. Research Methods: Advantages and Disadvantages, p. 26

Web Links
1. **http://apa.org/about/division.html**, p. 5
   The American Psychological Association's links to all of its divisions.
2. **http://server.bmod.athabascau.ca/html/aupr/history.htm**, p. 12
   The Psychology Center's History of Psychology page has many websites to choose from both about broad topics and those specific to the history of psychology.

A major objective of the media edition has been to expand from the text to a number of online and electronic sources, taking maximum advantage of the new media that are increasingly becoming part of students' lives. To accomplish this we have added to the end of each chapter a new feature titled "On the Web" that lists relevant electronic materials including the following:

 Learning activities and essays from *The Psychology Place*;

 Readings from journals, magazines, and newspapers that relate to chapter material;

 Games that incorporate psychological information;

 Interactive exercises and demonstrations from James Hilton and Charles Perdue's *Mind Matters* CD-ROM;

 Links to websites devoted to the study of psychology

All these features contain page references to show students where they fall within the chapter. In addition, icons in the page margins indicate the appropriate locations for these features. All these elements can be accessed through the Morris/Maisto companion website at **http://www.prenhall.com/Morris** or on the *Mind Matters* CD-ROM. Taken together with the text, they constitute an outstanding and thoroughly modern learning package.

Significant New Information

Significant new information has been added on the Decade of Behavior, the Human Genome Project, neural plasticity and neurogenesis, ESP, sleep and dreaming, procedural memory, context-dependent and state-dependent memory, the biological basis of memory, emotional intelligence,

---

HIGHLIGHTS

In Search of the Human Genome

The term *genome* refers to the full complement of an organism's genetic material. Thus the genome for any particular organism contains a complete blueprint for building all the structures and directing all the living processes for the lifetime of that organism. The **human genome** refers to the complete set of genes that define the human being. Scientists estimate that the human genome is made up of 80,000 to 100,000 individual genes, located on the 23 pairs of chromosomes that make up human DNA. These genes, contained within every cell of our body, distinguish us from other forms of life. Surprisingly minute variations in the human genome are responsible for the individual differences we see in the world's 6 billion people. Experts believe that the average variation in the human genetic code from any two different people is much less than 1 percent.

In 1990 the National Institutes of Health and the U.S. Department of Energy began an ambitious project to isolate and catalog every gene contained on the human genome. Originally conceived as a 15-year endeavor, the Human Genome Project seeks to identify and locate all

> Knowledge about variations in the genetic code is expected to lead to revolutionary new ways to diagnose, treat, and prevent illnesses.

the genes contained on human DNA, to store this information and make it available for researchers, and to address the ethical, social, and legal issues that may arise from possessing this knowledge.

The practical benefits of the information derived from the Human Genome Project are enormous. For example, because genes play an important role in a wide variety of human disorders, knowledge about variations in the genetic code is expected to lead to revolutionary new ways to diagnose, treat, and prevent illnesses. Researchers have already begun to identify specific genes that contribute to the development of disorders such as cystic fibro-

sis, mental retardation, and some forms of cancer.

Although rich with promise, the Human Genome Project raises many social and ethical questions. For example, will predicting the likelihood of cancer in an individual lead to discrimination from potential employers and insurers? Will the knowledge that a person has a 25 percent chance of producing a child with Parkinson's disease affect the choice of having children? How will the products of the Human Genome Project, such as medicines and diagnostic techniques, be shared by the international community, patented, and commercialized? Fortunately, committees made up of ethicists, physicians, researchers, and other concerned professionals have already begun to confront many of these issues. As our understanding of human genetic inheritance continues to grow, it will not, we hope, outpace our understanding of how to apply this knowledge in ways that are both effective and socially responsible. To learn more visit the Human Genome Web site at **http://www.ornl.gov/TechResources/Human_Genome/home.html**

human sexuality, the impact of peers and non-shared environments, teenage killers, the Big Five personality theory, gender and coping with stress, biological basis of stress, subjective well-being, non-specific factors in therapy, and ethnic violence. And of course, throughout the text statistics have been carefully updated to correspond to the most recent data available. By any measure, that is a substantial amount of new material that reflects the most up-to-date developments in the field of psychology. But there is more!

New Chapter-Opening Vignettes

Our approach to teaching has always been to start with the familiar and use that as a platform from which to explore the unfamiliar. With that in mind, each chapter in the book starts with an opening vignette that sets the stage for what is to come. In a continuing effort to make these vignettes as effective and timely as possible, several of them—based on real-life cases—are new to this edition.

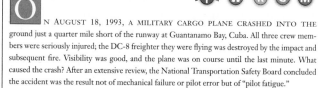

O N AUGUST 18, 1993, A MILITARY CARGO PLANE CRASHED INTO THE ground just a quarter mile short of the runway at Guantanamo Bay, Cuba. All three crew members were seriously injured; the DC-8 freighter they were flying was destroyed by the impact and subsequent fire. Visibility was good, and the plane was on course until the last minute. What caused the crash? After an extensive review, the National Transportation Safety Board concluded the accident was the result not of mechanical failure or pilot error but of "pilot fatigue."

This was the first (and only) time an aviation accident has been officially attributed to pilot fatigue. But the problem of fatigue is more common than most of us realize. According to NASA and federal aviation experts, one in seven pilots nods off in the cockpit. The problem is most acute on overnight international trips, but it can happen on any flight. Off the record, many pilots admit to suddenly waking up and not knowing where they are. This isn't dangerous if the co-pilot is awake. But flight attendants report going into the cabin and finding both pilots sleeping, which is why they regularly knock on the door and offer the crew refreshments. In the 1980s a cargo plane missed the Los Angeles airport and flew out over the Pacific for nearly an hour before air controllers were able to rouse the sleeping pilots and bring them back. Even when pilots remain awake, they may be too groggy to react efficiently in an emergency, as at Guantanamo Bay. Estimates are that pilot fatigue contributes to as many as one-third of aviation accidents; fortunately most are minor.

Sleep and wakefulness are both states of **consciousness.** In everyday conversation, we use the word *consciousness* to describe being alert. Psychologists, however, define *consciousness* more broadly, as our awareness of various mental processes. On any given day, we engage in a great variety of cognitive activities—making decisions, planning, remembering, concentrating, daydreaming, reflecting, sleeping, and dreaming are but a few. Sleep is a state of consciousness that, although different from waking consciousness, is vital to our survival.

Continuing Unifying Themes

Although there is much that is new in this edition, the original goals for this book remain unchanged: to present a scientific, accurate, and thorough overview of the essential concepts of psychology in engaging language that the average student can easily comprehend; to be current without being trendy; and to write clearly about psychology and its applications without being condescending. Three unifying themes continue to run throughout the text:

- **Psychology is a science.** Every edition of this text has reflected the fact that psychology is the scientific study of behavior and mental processes, and this new edition is no exception. Key topics are presented in a balanced, scientific manner, incorporating both classic studies and the most recent developments.

- **Human behavior and thought are diverse, varied, and affected by culture.** For today's students and instructors of introductory psychology, diversity is more than simply an issue for discussion and debate; it is a daily reality. The challenge confronting any textbook author is to satisfy a heterogeneous audience without becoming trendy or unscientific. Over the last several years, the body of research examining issues of diversity has grown to significant levels. As a result, consideration of diversity is expanded in every new edition, both diversity within the North American population and diversity across cultures worldwide. For example, the Fifth Edition contains new boxes on the universality of the Big Five personality traits and ethnic violence throughout the world. Material relating to diversity is incorporated throughout the text.

- **The study of psychology involves active thinking, questioning, and problem solving.** Education involves far more than just memorizing information. A successful course in general psychology (and, for that matter, in most other disciplines) helps students develop their ability to analyze, to ask questions, to evaluate the ideas of others, and ultimately to form their own judgments. Encouraging active, critical thinking has long been a major objective of the courses we teach and of this text, and it remains a basic theme in the Fifth Edition.

Accessible to Students

Writing Style

Throughout every edition of this text we have kept in mind that our final audience consists primarily of college undergraduates. Having taught undergraduates for decades, we realize that it is essential to make a textbook as accessible and helpful as possible. We have retained the clear, straightforward writing style to which students and reviewers have responded so positively over the years. Once again the text contains plenty of examples relevant to today's undergraduates. The tone is conversational without resorting to slang.

Pedagogy

The teaching pedagogy integrated in every chapter has made this book a student favorite. A chapter-opening **Overview** provides students with a road map for each chapter. **Summary Tables** provide concise reviews of the most important concepts (for example, defense mechanisms, types of memory, theories of personality, and the structures and functions of the brain). **Key terms** are printed in boldface and defined in the margin where they first appear. The result is that students don't just process lists of unrelated facts, but instead have a cognitive map with which to contextualize, better understand, and more effectively relate and recall concepts. By answering the **Review Questions** at the end of each major section, students can test themselves before moving ahead.

SUMMARY TABLE

Parts of the Brain and Their Function

Hindbrain	Medulla	Sensory and motor nerves crossover
	Pons	Regulation of sleep–wake cycle
	Cerebellum	Reflexes (e.g., balance)
		Coordinates movement
Midbrain		Hearing, vision relay point
		Pain registered
Forebrain	Thalamus	Major message relay center
		Regulates higher brain centers and peripheral nervous system
	Hypothalamus	Emotion and motivation
		Stress reactions
	Cerebral hemispheres	
	Occipital lobe	Receives and processes visual information
	Temporal lobe	Complex vision
		Hearing and smell
		Balance and equilibrium
		Emotions and motivations
		Some language comprehension
	Parietal lobe	Processing sensory information
		Visual/spatial abilities
	Frontal lobe	Goal-directed behavior, concentration
		Emotional control and temperament
		Voluntary movement
		Coordinates messages from other lobes

Art and Design

Finally, the Fifth Edition has been completely redesigned to complement the goals and features of the text. It is colorful and engaging without being busy or distracting. New figures and photographs have been carefully selected to complement the text material.

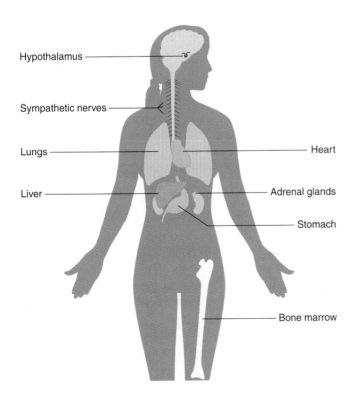

Supplements

It is increasingly true today that, as valuable as a good textbook is, it is still only one element of a comprehensive learning package. Throughout the many editions of this book, we have labored to produce not only a well-written text but also a full range of supplemental learning tools. The supplements package that accompanies the Fifth Edition is the most comprehensive and impressive yet.

Multimedia, Internet, and World Wide Web Materials for Instructors and Students

Prentice Hall and Peregrine Publishers are proud to present a melding of two acclaimed interactive learning resources: Prentice Hall's *Companion Website* with Peregrine's *The Psychology Place*. Both are accessible at http://www.prenhall.com/morris.

The Companion Website portion of this new resource provides materials to help students review chapter content and prepare for tests. Practice tests and matching/labeling exercises can be submitted for immediate grading to help students know where they need to spend the most time in review. In addition, chat rooms and message boards allow students to share their ideas about psychology with students from their own classroom or from colleges across the country.

Other materials are referenced by icons in the margins of the text and can be found in *The Psychology Place*, which is accessible through each chapter of the Companion Website. Interactive exercises, reports of interesting research, articles from *Scientific American*, and Op-ed pieces are provided that will enhance the course for motivated students. The Instructor's Resource Manual, the Practice Test and Review Manual, and our new Media User's Guide reference these materials, which can be made a part of the classroom experience or used as homework assignments.

On-Line Course Management. For instructors interested in distance learning, Prentice Hall and Pearson Education are proud to offer a fully customizable, on-line course with www links, on-line testing, and many other course management tools. See your local Prentice Hall representative or visit our special Demonstration Central website at **http://www.prenhall.com/demo** for more information.

For Instructors

Instructor's Resource Manual (0-13-027990-0) by Alan Swinkels, St. Edward's University, and Tracy Giuliano, Southwestern University. For each chapter the manual contains a Chapter Outline; a list of Learning Objectives which correspond to the exercises in the Practice Test and Review Manual; Lecture Suggestions describing additional topics of interest; suggested Demonstrations and Activities such as class projects and experiments; and Student Assignments including reports and out-of-class exercises. Each chapter also contains a list of the ABC News videos, multimedia resources, and transparencies available to accompany the text plus Handouts for use with the Demonstrations and Activities. Finally, each chapter ends with suggestions on how to use the associated multimedia materials in either classroom presentations or as homework assignments.

Test Item File   (0-13-027996-X) by Gary Piggrem, DeVry Institute of Technology. Contains over 4000 multiple-choice, true/false, and essay questions. To facilitate instructors in creating tests, each question is page-referenced to the textbook, is described as either factual, conceptual, or applied, and is identified as being new, from the previous edition, or revised. We will continue our effort to improve and expand the Test Item File for future editions, and as always we welcome your comments, suggestions, and teaching feedback. Send them directly to: Charles G. Morris, Department of Psychology, University of Michigan, Ann Arbor, MI 48109-1109.

Prentice Hall Custom Test for Windows and Macintosh platforms.   The questions in the Test Item File are available on both platforms and allow instructors complete personal flexibility in building and editing their own customized tests. Advances in the most recent version of this software now allow instructors to load their tests onto the World Wide Web or a Local Area Network in an online testing format.

Windows PH Custom Test (0-13-027998-6)
Macintosh PH Custom Test (0-13-027999-4)

Toll-Free Telephone Test Preparation Services.   Prentice Hall offers a telephone test preparation service through which instructors an call a special, toll-free number and select up to 200 questions from the printed Test Item File available with the text. The test and an alternate version (if requested), and answer key are mailed or faxed within hours of the initial request.

PH Color Acetate Transparencies for Introductory Psychology Series V   (0-13-095708-9) contains illustrations, figures, and graphs from the text as well as images from a variety of other sources.

PowerPoint Slides.   Scores of illustrations, figures, and graphs from the text have been made accessible via the popular PowerPoint programs from Microsoft. Instructors can download these images from the Faculty Section on the Companion Website (**http://www.prenhall.com/morris**), edit them, and project them onto a screen while delivering lectures, or clip them for inclusion on web-based learning systems.

ABCNEWS **ABC News/PH Video Library.**   Prentice Hall has assembled a collection of feature segments from award-winning news programs. The following libraries are currently available to qualified adopters:

Introductory Psychology Series III (0-13-886235-4) consists of segments from award-winning news programs such as "ABC Nightly News," "Nightline," "20/20/" "Prime Time Live," and "The Health Show." Summaries of questions, designed to stimulate critical thinking for each segment, are included in the Instructor's Resource Manual.

The Alliance Series: The Annenberg/CPB Collection. The Alliance Series is the most extensive collection of professionally produced videos available with any introductory psychology textbook. Selections include videos in the following Annenberg series: The Brain, The Brain Teaching Modules, Discovering Psychology, The Mind, and The Mind Teaching Modules. Contact your local Prentice Hall representative for details.

Teaching Psychology, 3/E   (0-13-028990-6) by Fred Whitford of Montana State University. Serves as a guide for new instructors or teaching assistants to help them manage the myriad complex tasks required to teach effectively from the start. The Third Edition has been updated to reflect the explosive growth of technology for the classroom and provides many excellent suggestions for integrating the Web into the course.

For Students

Practice Test and Review Manual   (0-13-028001-1) by Joyce Bishop, Golden West College. Each chapter contains an Overview to introduce students to the chapter; Class Notes Outline with space for students to take notes from the text and during lecture; a Learning Objectives exercise to test students' understanding of the main themes; a multiple choice Pretest and Posttest for gauging students' progress; Short Essay Questions to develop writing skills; Language Support Section for extra support in English; and Flash Cards of vocabulary terms. Each chapter also reviews the multimedia materials available with this edition with special exercises relating these resources to material in the text.

The New York Times **Themes of the Times Supplement for Introductory Psychology**. Prentice Hall and the New York Times have joined forces to bring students a complimentary newspaper supplement containing recent articles pertinent to introductory psychology. These articles augment the text material and provide real-world examples. They are updated twice a year.

Supplementary Texts

Any one of these texts can be packaged with *Understanding Psychology, Fifth Edition* at a reduced price:

The Psychology Major: Careers and Strategies for Success by Eric Landrum (Idaho State University), Stephen Davis (Emporia State University), and Terri Landrum (Idaho State University). This 160-page paperback provides valuable information on career options available to psychology majors, tips for improving academic performance, and a guide to the APA style of research reporting.

Experiencing Psychology by Gary Brannigan (State University of New York at Plattsburgh). This hands-on activity book contains thirty-nine active learning experiences corresponding to major topics in psychology to provide students with hands-on experience in "doing" psychology.

Forty Studies that Changed Psychology, Third Edition by Roger Hock (Mendocino College). Presenting the seminal research studies that have shaped modern psychological study, this brief supplement provides an overview of the environment that gave rise to each study, its experimental design, its findings, and its impact on current thinking in the discipline.

How to Think Like a Psychologist by Donald McBurney (University of Pittsburgh). This unique supplementary text uses a question-answer format to explore some of the most common questions students ask about psychology.

Acknowledgments

We are deeply grateful for the assistance we received from the many people who reviewed the previous edition and suggested improvements for this edition:

Bobby Hutchinson, Modesto Junior College
Cheryl McFadden, York Technical College
Anita Rosenfield, DeVry Institute of Technology
Denys deCatanzaro, McMaster University
John Jahnke, Miami University
Philip S. Lasiter, Florida Atlantic University

Stephen Mayer, Oberlin College
Ronald Nowaczyk, Clemson University
Wesley Schultz, California State University, San Marcos
Steve Arnold, Northeast Community College
Susan K. Johnson, University of North Carolina, Charlotte
Don McCoy, University of Kentucky
Jerald S. Marshall, University of Central Florida
Michael Ruchs, Baker College
Morgan Slusher, Essex Community College
Harold G. Souheaver, East Arkansas Community College

We would also like to express our deep gratitude to the outstanding team of people at Prentice Hall, all of whom made major contributions. We are immensely grateful to Bob Weiss who served as development editor on this edition. Bob's good judgment, writing skills, and eye for details have led to countless improvements from the previous edition. Bill Webber, Executive Editor, continued to bring invigorating dedication and commitment to this edition, not to mention his excellent ideas for new features. Editorial assistant, Deborah Fenster, helped with many of the administrative details involved in this project. The multimedia elements were prepared by John Jordan with considerable help from Dennis Thompson (Georgia State University) and Michael D'Angelo. Al Maisto's former graduate assistant, Sherri McKee, provided invaluable help with many research tasks. The production of the Fifth Edition was managed by Mary Rottino and directly supervised by Maureen Richardson, whose dedication, expertise, and quiet persistence assured an end product of very high quality, delivered on schedule! Thanks also to manufacturing buyer Tricia Kenny, and to Cyndy Taylor, who coordinated various aspects of the ancillary program for this edition. Ximena Tamvakopoulos did a super job on the design of both the interior and the cover. Photo researcher Linda Sykes supplied the Fifth Edition with many new and interesting photographs. Finally, special thanks to Sharon Cosgrove for directing the marketing campaign for the book.

Charles G. Morris
Albert A. Maisto

TO THE STUDENT

Getting the Most from *Understanding Psychology, Fifth Edition*

WITH MORE THAN 500 PAGES OF TEXT IN 14 chapters on topics ranging from brain physiology to social psychology, this text can appear daunting, but embedded throughout are tools to help you master the material in each chapter. But before we review these features, we strongly recommend that you read the two boxes listed below.

Read These First

Throughout *Understanding Psychology, Fifth Edition* you will find a series of boxes that apply concepts in psychology to real-life situations. Two of these *Applying Psychology* boxes can help you to do your best in this or any other course. We urge you to read these boxes before you begin Chapter 1.

■ Improving Your Memory for Textbook Material, page 222
■ Coping with Stress at College, p. 399

Study Tools

Every chapter starts with an **Overview,** which is your road map to the chapter. Read through the overview to get a sense of the structure and major topics discussed in the chapter. The **preview questions** under each major heading can help you organize your thoughts in advance about the material that follows.

As you read a chapter, a list of **key terms** and definitions appears in the margin of every page. Study these as you go along rather than waiting until you have finished reading the chapter. You will be actively learning the important concepts in each chapter as you move from section to section. Focus too on the **summary tables** that organize concepts into a manageable format. At the end of every major section, answer the **review questions,** and review any concepts you are unsure of before moving on to the next section. After you have read a chapter, answer the **critical thinking questions.** Then see if you can define the key terms that appear on the **list of key terms.**

The next few pages are a guide to using these tools to enhance your learning. Begin by previewing the first chapter. These techniques will help you to study any subject. Please turn to Chapter 1.

Preview the Chapter   Previewing prepares your brain to receive information in an organized way. Properly done, it will help you read faster and comprehend better. To preview a chapter, read the outline, the preview questions under each major head, all the key terms, and the chapter review.

Ask Questions   Then, ask yourself the preview questions as you read the chapter. This technique stimulates thinking and learning, as you actively search for answers while you read.

Use Charts, Graphs, Summary Tables, and Photographs   In every chapter, charts, graphs, and summary tables will help you to organize information, and photographs will help you visualize concepts.

Study in Chunks   Researchers have discovered that we remember the first and last things we learn far better than the material in the middle. Breaking up your studying into many short sessions creates many more beginnings and endings, and it also reduces fatigue.

Take Study Breaks   You need time to process information. Taking study breaks every 20 to 40 minutes gives you the time you need to process the new information. Without this time for processing, the information may disappear quickly, long before you need to recall it for an exam. Begin with short breaks of about 5-10 minutes each, adding a longer break of about 30 minutes after a couple of hours.

Review Often   One of the earliest memory researchers, Hermann Ebbinghaus, discovered that the rate of forgetting is highest during the first hour after learning new information. Reviewing often, then, allows your memory to relearn material you may have forgotten earlier. In fact, if you review your class notes immediately after leaving a class, you will retain the information longer and actually save time later on. This isn't always possible, but when you can, schedule classes with some time in between to allow you to review your notes. You also need time to process the material you just learned; rushing from class to class each hour sharply limits your ability to process new information effectively.

You can review material in many ways: reread your notes and the summary, complete the review questions again, define each of the key terms, and answer the review questions. Rewriting your notes in a format that is easiest for you to learn is a good way to review. For example, *visual learners* like to organize their notes with adequate white space left on the page. People who *learn through doing* like the physical involvement of rewriting their notes.

THE SCIENCE OF PSYCHOLOGY

OVERVIEW

Rey Ramos graduated from Harvard University, magna cum laude, and was accepted by Harvard Medical School—against all odds. Rey grew up in the South Bronx, an urban ghetto where young males are more likely to go to jail than they are to graduate from high school, and where early, violent death is not uncommon. All anyone asked of Rey was that he stay out of trouble and stay alive. As a young boy, he was considered a problem child, out of control. In eighth grade, Rey's principal told his mother that her son was being expelled and reassigned to a program for students with learning problems.

Rey: *"My Mom just started crying, you know, in front of him, and I saw that. And I felt ashamed of myself."*

Rey entered ninth grade determined to turn his life around. His math teacher recognized his change in attitude—and his ability in math.

Math teacher: *"When he got here, I knew he wasn't joking around anymore. He knew this was it. This was where it starts new."*

Rey: *"And I started feeling good about this one teacher who said good things about me, and that made me feel good."*

Rey also excelled in science. But the high school he attended, considered one of the worst in New York City and since shut down, offered little. Rey enrolled in a special science program at a local college and graduated first in his class. It was his biology teacher who first suggested to Rey that he might be "Harvard material."

Biology teacher: *"I was trying to push him to believe in himself and do something, because I felt he was incredible."*

Rey accepted the challenge. In his Harvard application he wrote, "The four years I invest in Harvard will probably be the most important four years of my life. I will waste no time while I attend Harvard University." True to his word, Rey maintained a 3.4 grade point average, enlisted in ROTC, joined a Latino fraternity, and worked part time. At graduation, he looked back.

Rey: *"My father always said you can't change anything; destiny has everything written for you. And I told him no. I rebelled against that, and I told him I was going to make my own destiny, and so far I've never heard him say that line to me again."*

Rey planned to marry Maiysha, his childhood sweetheart, that summer; to enter Harvard Medical School in the fall; and to fulfill his lifelong dream of returning to the South Bronx as a doctor.

Rey Ramos's story is the American Dream. Indeed, he was chosen to represent "The American Spirit" on *NBC Nightly News* (June 13, 1997). How did Rey Ramos escape from the "mean streets" to the Ivy League and a future as a physician? What can psychology tell us about his success story? about intelligence and motivation in general? about the many factors that shape who we become?

What is Psychology?

Psychology is the scientific study of behavior and mental processes. Some people might think that psychologists are interested only in problem or abnormal behaviors. In fact, they are interested in every aspect of human thought and behavior. One way to grasp the breadth and depth of psychology is to look at several major subdivisions of the field (see Table 1-1).

The Fields of Psychology

What are the major subdivisions of psychology?

Developmental Psychology   Developmental psychologists study human mental and physical growth from the prenatal period through childhood, adolescence, adulthood, and old age. *Child psychologists* focus on infants and

TABLE 1-1	AMERICAN PSYCHOLOGICAL ASSOCIATION DIVISIONS (2000)

The two major organizations of psychologists in the United States are the American Psychological Association (APA), founded more than 100 years ago, and the American Psychological Society (APS), founded in 1988. Members of both groups work in a wide variety of areas. This list of divisions of the APA reflects the enormous diversity of the field of psychology.

Division*

1. General Psychology	30. Psychological Hypnosis
2. Society for the Teaching of Psychology	31. State Psychological Association Affairs
3. Experimental Psychology	32. Humanistic Psychology
5. Evaluation, Measurement, and Statistics	33. Mental Retardation and Developmental Disabilities
6. Behavioral Neuroscience and Comparative Psychology	34. Population and Environmental Psychology
7. Developmental Psychology	35. Society for the Psychology of Women
8. Society for Personality and Social Psychology	36. Psychology of Religion
9. Society for the Psychological Study of Social Issues (SPSSI)	37. Child, Youth, and Family Services
10. Psychology and the Arts	38. Health Psychology
12. Society of Clinical Psychology	39. Psychoanalysis
13. Consulting Psychology	40. Clinical Neuropsychology
14. The Society for Industrial and Organizational Psychology	41. American Psychology—Law Society
15. Educational Psychology	42. Psychologists in Independent Practice
16. School Psychology	43. Family Psychology
17. Counseling Psychology	44. Society for the Psychological Study of Lesbian, Gay and Bisexual Issues
18. Psychologists in Public Service	45. Society for the Psychological Study of Ethnic Minority Issues
19. Military Psychology	46. Media Psychology
20. Adult Development and Aging	47. Exercise and Sport Psychology
21. Applied Experimental and Engineering Psychology	48. Society for the Study of Peace, Conflict, and Violence
22. Rehabilitation Psychology	49. Group Psychology and Group Psychotherapy
23. Society for Consumer Psychology	50. Addictions
24. Theoretical and Philosophical Psychology	51. Society for the Psychological Study of Men and Masculinity
25. Experimental Analysis of Behavior	52. International Psychology
26. History of Psychology	53. Clinical Child Psychology
27. Society for Community Research and Action	54. Society of Pediatric Psychology
28. Psychopharmacology and Substance Abuse	
29. Psychotherapy	

*There are no divisions 4 or 11.

For information on a division, e-mail the APA at division@apa.org, or consult its Web site, http://www.apa.org/division.html.

Source: Copyright © 1997 by the American Psychological Association. Reprinted by permission.

children. They are concerned with such issues as whether babies are born with distinct personalities and temperaments, how infants become attached to their parents and caretakers, the age at which sex differences in behavior emerge, and changes in the meaning and importance of friendship during childhood. *Adolescent psychologists* specialize in the teenage years, and how puberty, changes in relationships with peers and parents, and the search for identity can make this a difficult period for some young people. *Life-span psychologists* focus on the adult years, and the different ways individuals adjust to partnership and parenting, middle age, retirement, and eventually death.

Developmental psychologists would see Rey Ramos's change of direction in eighth grade in part as a reflection of his level of cognitive and emotional development. At earlier ages, the same experience would have not had the same impact. At

Psychology
The scientific study of behavior and mental processes.

age 3, he probably would have been frightened by his mother bursting into tears. If he had been assigned to a slow-learner class at age 8, he might have known that he'd been "bad," but he would not have understood how or why. By age 12, his ability to analyze the connection between actions and consequences was much sharper. As a young adult now, Rey seems to have a strong sense of identity and purpose; he is ready to make a commitment to his girlfriend. But development does not suddenly stop at this point. Many chapters of his life story—establishing himself in his profession, parenthood, evaluating what he has made of his life in middle age, and facing the challenges of old age—have not yet been written.

Physiological Psychology Physiological psychologists investigate the biological basis of human behavior, thoughts, and emotions. *Neuropsychologists* are primarily interested in the brain and the nervous system. Why can't you taste food when you have a stuffy nose? What happens when a person has a stroke? *Psychobiologists* specialize in the body's biochemistry, and how hormones, psychoactive medications (such as antidepressants), and "social drugs" (such as alcohol, marijuana, and cocaine) affect people. Do changes in hormone levels—at puberty, before menstruation, at menopause—cause mood swings? Exactly how does alcohol act on the brain? *Behavioral geneticists* investigate the impact of heredity on both normal and abnormal traits and behavior. To what degree is intelligence hereditary? What about shyness? Do illnesses such as alcoholism and depression run in families? To what extent are differences in the way men and women think, act, and respond to situations rooted in biology?

Some of the most exciting work in contemporary psychobiology concerns the effect of stress on health. We know that Rey Ramos grew up in a dangerous neighborhood; we can imagine that he faced many frustrations in his struggle to change directions as a teenager and that he had to adjust to an almost totally new environment at Harvard—all sources of stress. Will this stress eventually take a toll on his health? Research shows that some racial and ethnic groups are more vulnerable to certain conditions than others. For example, African Americans are at high risk for hypertension (high blood pressure). Is this because of a genetic weakness (as is sickle-cell anemia, also more prevalent among African Americans)? because African Americans are more likely than other groups in the United States to be poor and live in unsafe neighborhoods like Rey's? or because even middle-class African-American professionals are viewed with suspicion and have direct experience of prejudice—ranging from small insults to police brutality—and so may live in a state of constant vigilance?

Experimental Psychology Experimental psychologists conduct research on basic psychological processes, including learning, memory, sensation, perception, cognition, motivation, and emotion. They are interested in answering such questions as: "How do people remember, and what makes them forget?" "How do people make decisions and solve problems?" "Do men and women go about solving complex problems in different ways?" "Why are some people more motivated than others?"

Rey Ramos apparently has a "flair for numbers," and he clearly excels at science. Experimental psychologists might be interested in discovering exactly how his style of thinking differs from that of other people. Does he process mathematical and scientific information in an unusual way? Does he perhaps have an unusually good memory for such information, and if so, how does his memory differ from yours and mine? During childhood and adolescence, Rey probably was given a number of aptitude, achievement, and intelligence tests. Do such tests actually measure important cognitive skills such as the ability to make decisions and solve problems, or are they more a measure of cultural knowledge? And finally, what motives drive Rey to achieve and excel?

A psychologist talking with a client. About half of all psychologists specialize in clinical or counseling psychology.

Personality Psychology

Personality psychologists study the differences among individuals in such traits as anxiety, sociability, self-esteem, the need for achievement, and aggressiveness. Psychologists in this field attempt to determine what causes some people to be optimists and others to be pessimists, and why some people are outgoing and sociable whereas others are more reserved. They also study whether there are consistent differences between men and women in such characteristics as friendliness, anxiety, and conscientiousness.

From our brief introduction to Rey Ramos, we can infer that he is sociable: At Harvard, he made friends and deepened his relationship with his fiancée, Maiysha. He appears to have a strong need to achieve and a healthy level of self-esteem. Where did these characteristics come from? His early childhood experiences? The realization, in ninth grade, that he could take control of "his destiny"? Is he as competitive in sports as he is in academics? as self-confident in an art gallery as he is in a laboratory? If he realizes his dream by returning to the Bronx with his M.D. and spends years trying to deal with the desperate needs of his patients, on the one hand, and the lack of adequate funding and up-to-date facilities, on the other, will he remain an optimist? A major issue for personality psychologists is whether a given characteristic is a stable personality trait or simply a response to the social situation.

Clinical and Counseling Psychology

When asked to describe a "psychologist," most people think of a therapist who sees patients (or "clients") in his or her office, a clinic, or a hospital. This popular view is half-correct. About half of all psychologists specialize in clinical or counseling psychology. *Clinical psychologists* are interested primarily in the diagnosis, cause, and treatment of psychological disorders. Counseling psychologists are concerned primarily with "normal" problems of adjustment that most of us face at some point, such as choosing a career or coping with marital problems. Clinical and counseling psychologists often divide their time between treating patients and conducting research on the causes of psychological disorders and the effectiveness of different types of psychotherapy and counseling.

One of the deepest controversies in psychological treatment today pits drug therapy against psychotherapy. The development of new medications—beginning with antipsychotic drugs such as Thorazine, anti-anxiety drugs or tranquilizers such as Valium, and most recently antidepressive medications such as Prozac—reflects advances in our knowledge of the genetic or biochemical basis of many psychological disorders. No one debates that these drugs can be highly effective in relieving symptoms, especially with schizophrenia (delusions, hallucinations, disorganized speech, and extreme withdrawal) and depression (feelings of hopelessness, lethargy, having difficulty thinking, and being preoccupied with death or suicide). Advocates of drug therapy foresee a day when psychotherapy will become obsolete. But many others disagree. Opponents argue, first, that drug therapy addresses the symptoms of psychological disorder, but not the causes. Even if a biochemical imbalance triggered the disturbance, psychotherapy is needed to help individuals understand the events surrounding the onset and to deal with marital problems, strained family relationships, broken friendships, and disrupted work histories caused by the disorder. Second, all medications have side effects; the more powerful the medication, the more likely that some individuals will have extreme reactions. Third, severely disturbed patients often stop taking medication. Conversely, patients may overrequest and doctors may overprescribe antidepressive and anti-anxiety medication for normal, temporary problems in living. Most mental health professionals agree that drug therapy is not a substitute for psychotherapy; rather, the two work best in combination.

As a child, Rey Ramos was described as "out of control." A clinical psychologist who saw him at age 8 or 10 might have diagnosed his problem as "hyperactivity" (now called attention-deficit/hyperactivity disorder, or ADHD), a childhood disorder seen mostly in boys and characterized by restlessness, impulsive behavior, and inability to focus on one subject or activity for very long. In the 1970s, the treatment of choice might have been the drug Ritalin, a stimulant that—paradoxically—slows down hyperactive children, apparently by increasing their powers of concentration (Barkley, 1990). Hailed as a "miracle cure" when first introduced, Ritalin soon drew criticism. Short-term use may help some children diagnosed with ADHD, but long-term use does not sustain improvements. Critics (for example, McGuinness, 1985) ask if many children were medicated simply because they were acting like boys (and found school more restrictive than girls do), or because they had not learned middle-class concepts of proper classroom decorum.

Social Psychology   Social psychologists study how people influence one another. They explore such issues as first impressions and interpersonal attraction; how attitudes are formed, maintained, or changed; prejudice; conformity; and whether people behave differently when they are part of a group or crowd than they would on their own.

As a teenager living in a tough, urban neighborhood, Rey Ramos no doubt experienced considerable peer pressure to become a member of a gang. Gangs seem to be an institution in poor neighborhoods. Why? Many of Rey's contemporaries probably gave in to this pressure; Rey didn't. Again, why? As a Latino at one of America's most prestigious universities, Rey probably encountered prejudice. Classmates may have assumed that, because he was a member of a minority group, he was admitted to Harvard as part of an affirmative action program, not because of his academic achievements. The Latino fraternity Rey joined probably helped him to maintain ethnic pride in the face of such prejudice. Do ethnically based social organizations promote mutual tolerance, or do they contribute to maintaining social distance?

Industrial and Organizational (I/O) Psychology   Industrial and organizational (I/O) psychologists are concerned with such practical issues as selecting and training personnel, improving productivity and working conditions, and the impact of computerization and automation on workers. Is it possible to determine in advance who will be an effective salesperson or airline pilot, and who will not? Do organizations tend to operate differently under female as opposed to male leadership? Research shows that work groups with high morale usually are more productive than those with low morale: Are there specific strategies that managers can use to improve group morale?

In medical school, Rey Ramos will spend much of his time in hospitals, on rotations, as an intern, and finally as a resident. Hospitals and other large organizations frequently hire I/O psychologists as consultants to advise them on ways to increase efficiency, humanize a sterile environment, boost the morale of patients as well as staff, and so on.

Enduring Issues

What are the principal issues common to many subfields of psychology?

Given this wide array of interests, what holds psychology together? What do psychologists who study organizations, psychological disorders, memory and cognition, behavioral genetics, or attachment in infants have in common? What distinguishes psychologists from other scientists (and nonscientists) who observe and seek to understand human beings?

In part, psychologists are drawn together by their common interest in a number of fundamental questions about behavior that cut across their areas of specialization. We identify five of these enduring issues.

An industrial and organizational psychologist might study a work scene like this computer factory to discover ways to increase productivity or improve relations among workers.

Person–Situation To what extent is behavior caused by processes that occur inside the person (such as thoughts, emotions, motives, attitudes, values, personality, and genes)? In contrast, to what extent is behavior controlled, caused, or triggered by factors outside the person (such as incentives, cues in the environment, and the presence of other people)? We will encounter these questions most directly in our consideration of behavior genetics, learning, emotion and motivation, personality, and social psychology, though they will arise elsewhere as well.

Heredity–Environment For decades, psychologists have been debating the degree of influence that heredity (genetics) and environment or experience have on behavior. This is the famous "nature versus nurture" debate. This issue appears in our discussions of behavior genetics, intelligence, development, personality, and psychological disorders, though it will arise elsewhere as well.

Stability–Change To what extent do people stay relatively unchanged throughout their lives? How much do they change? Can you "teach old dogs new tricks"? Is the child "father to the man"? Or is each day a new beginning with the possibility for significant change? Developmental psychologists are especially interested in these questions, though their interest is shared by psychologists who specialize in personality, adjustment, psychological disorders, and therapy as well as other areas.

Diversity Another topic of increasing interest to many psychologists is diversity—the extent to which "Every person is in certain respects (a) like all other people, (b) like some other people, (c) like no other man" (Kluckhohn & Murray, 1961, p. 53). Throughout the book we encounter these questions: "Does our understanding of behavior apply equally well to every human being, or does it apply only to men or women, or only to particular racial or ethnic groups, or particular societies?" "Do we perhaps need 'different psychologies' to account for the wide diversity of human behaviors?"

Mind–Body Finally, many psychologists are fascinated by the relationship between what we experience (such as thoughts and feelings) and biological processes (such as activity in the nervous system). This mind–body issue will arise most clearly in our discussions of psychobiology, sensation and perception, altered states of consciousness, emotion and motivation, adjustment/health psychology, and disorders/therapy, though you will find it in other chapters as well.

So despite their apparent differences, psychologists are drawn together in part because of their common interest in enduring questions such as these. In addition, psychologists share a common belief that the scientific method is the most promising way to gain insight into the causes of behavior, as we see in the next section.

Psychology as Science

What does psychology have in common with other sciences?

As we saw on p. 3, psychology is the science of behavior and mental processes. The key word in this definition is *science*. Although psychologists share the average person's interest in behavior and the unseen mental processes that shape it, they rely on the **scientific method** when searching for answers to psychological questions. They collect data through careful, systematic observation; attempt to explain what they have observed by developing theories; make new predictions based on those theories; and then systematically test those predictions through additional observations and experiments to determine whether they are correct. Thus, like all scientists, psychologists use the scientific method to *describe, under-*

Scientific method
An approach to knowledge that relies on collecting data, generating a theory to explain the data, producing testable hypotheses based on the theory, and testing those hypotheses empirically.

"Your father's a suit, and when you grow up you'll be just a suit, too."

stand, predict, and eventually, to achieve some measure of *control* over what they study. (The scientific method is not for scientists only; see *Applying Psychology*).

Take, for example, the issue of males, females, and aggression. Some people believe that males are naturally more aggressive than females. Others contend that this is merely a stereotype, or at least that it is not always true. How would psychologists approach this issue? First, they would want to find out whether men and women actually differ in aggressive behavior. A number of research studies have addressed this question, and the evidence seems conclusive: Males do behave more aggressively than females, particularly when we're talking about physical aggression (Eagly & Steffen, 1986; Wright, 1994). Perhaps girls and women make nasty remarks or yell, but boys and men are far more likely to fight. Having established that there are sex differences in physical aggression, and having described those differences, the next step is to explain them. A number of explanations are possible. Physiological psychologists would probably ascribe these differences to genetics or body chemistry, developmental psychologists might look to the ways in which a child is taught to behave "like a boy" or "like a girl," and social psychologists might explain the differences as a function of cultural constraints against aggressive behavior in women.

Each of these explanations stands as a **theory** about the causes of sex differences in aggression; each attempts to distill a few principles from a large number of facts. And each theory allows us to make a number of new **hypotheses,** or predictions, about the phenomenon in question—in this case, aggressive behavior. For example, if gender differences in aggression arise because males have a greater amount of the male hormone testosterone than females do, then we would predict that extremely violent men have higher levels of testosterone than do men who are generally nonviolent. If sex differences in aggression stem from early training, then we would predict that there would be fewer sex differences in aggression in families in which parents did not stress gender differences. Finally, if sex differences in aggression reflect cultural constraints against aggression in women, then we would predict that removing or reducing those prohibitions would result in higher levels of aggressive behavior among women.

A number of research studies have shown that males behave more aggressively than females. Different psychologists might propose different reasons for this finding, depending on their field of specialization.

Theory
Systematic explanation of a phenomenon; it organizes known facts, allows us to predict new facts, and permits us to exercise a degree of control over the phenomenon.

Hypotheses
Specific, testable predictions derived from a theory.

APPLYING PSYCHOLOGY

Critical Thinking: A Fringe Benefit of Studying Psychology

■ Gifted children are less well adjusted than other children.

■ Opposites attract.

■ Subliminal messages on self-help audiotapes have beneficial effects.

Do you agree with these statements? Many people answer yes without a moment's hesitation on the grounds that "Everybody knows that." Critical thinkers, however, question common knowledge.

What exactly is critical thinking? It is the process of examining the information we have and then, based on this inquiry, making judgments and decisions. When we think critically, we define problems, examine evidence, analyze assumptions, consider alternatives, and ultimately find reasons to support or reject an argument. To think critically, you must

adopt a certain state of mind, one characterized by objectivity, caution, a willingness to challenge other people's opinions, and—perhaps most difficult of all—a willingness to subject your deepest beliefs to scrutiny. In other words, you must think like a scientist.

The ability to think critically is learned behavior. Many people, including quite a few introductory psychology students, view psychology as nothing more than common sense "dressed up" with fancy jargon. In fact, however, psychology is based on data resulting from carefully designed research. Reading about the research in this text, some of which questions common knowledge, will sharpen your own critical thinking skills. You don't have to take our word for this (in fact, you

shouldn't). Several studies of graduate students in psychology, medicine, law, and chemistry found that psychology students improved their reasoning abilities the most during their first 2 years of study (Lehman, Lempert, & Nisbett, 1988; Nisbett et al., 1987).

Psychologists use a number of strategies in questioning assumptions and examining data. Here, we use the rules of psychological investigation to judge whether the second statement earlier, "Opposites attract," is correct.

1. *Define the problem or the question you are investigating.* Do opposites attract each other?

2. *Suggest a theory or a reasonable explanation for the problem.* People who are dissimilar balance each other out in a relationship.

Each of these predictions or hypotheses can be tested through research, and the results should indicate whether one theory is better than another at accounting for known facts and predicting new facts. If one or more of the theories is supported by research evidence, it should be possible to control aggressive behavior to a greater degree than was possible before. For example, if people with higher levels of testosterone are indeed more aggressive, then, theoretically, it should be possible to make a highly aggressive person less aggressive by lowering the overall level of testosterone in that person's body.

REVIEW QUESTIONS

1. Match each of the following major themes in psychology with its appropriate description.

____ personal–social

____ heredity–environment

____ stability–change

____ diversity

____ mind–body

a. How much do we stay the same as we develop, and how much do we change?

b. In what ways do people differ in how they think and act?

c. What is the relationship between our internal experiences and our biological processes?

d. Is behavior caused more by inner traits or by external situations?

e. How do genes and experiences interact to influence people?

3. *Collect and examine all the available evidence.* In doing so, be skeptical of people's self-reports, as they may be subjectively biased. If data conflict, try to find more evidence. Research on attraction yields no support for the idea that opposites attract, whereas many studies confirm that people of similar looks, interests, age, family background, religion, values, and attitudes seek each other out.

4. *Analyze assumptions.* Because balancing different people's strengths and weaknesses is a good way to form a group, it is probably a good basis for personal relationships as well, and that is why people of opposite temperaments are naturally attracted to each other. Yet research evidence shows that this assumption is false. Why should similars attract? One important reason is that they often belong to the same social circles. Research suggests proximity is a big factor in attraction.

5. *Avoid oversimplifying.* Don't overlook the evidence that people of similar temperaments find living together rather difficult in some ways. For example, living with someone who is as tense as you are may be harder than living with someone of calm temperament—your opposite.

6. *Draw conclusions carefully.* It seems safe to conclude that, in general, opposites don't attract, but there are specific exceptions to this general rule.

7. *Consider every alternative interpretation.* People may cite cases that conflict with your conclusion. Remember, however, that their arguments are based on subjective observations and a far narrower database than attraction researchers have used.

8. *Recognize the relevance of research to events and situations.* If you have been thinking of dating someone whose temperament seems quite different from yours, you may decide, on the basis of what you now know, not to rush into things but to go more slowly, testing your own observations against your knowledge of research findings.

By the way, psychological research has demonstrated that the other two statements are also false.

---

2. Indicate if the following statements are true (T) or false (F).

_____ a. Psychologists collect data through careful, systematic observation.

_____ b. Psychologists try to explain their observations by developing theories.

_____ c. Psychologists form hypotheses or predictions based on theories.

_____ d. Psychologists appeal to common sense in their arguments.

_____ e. Psychologists systematically test hypotheses.

_____ f. Psychologists base their conclusions on widely shared values.

The Growth of Psychology

What does it mean to say that psychology has a long past but a short history?

Psychology has a long past but a short history. Dating back to the time of Plato and Aristotle, people have wondered about human behavior and mental processes. But not until the late 1800s did they begin to apply the scientific method to questions that had puzzled philosophers for centuries. Only then did psychology come into being as a formal, scientific discipline separate from philosophy.

Charles Darwin (1809–1882) was not a psychologist. Yet more than any other individual, he was responsible for the idea that human behavior and thinking

Charles Darwin

might be subjects for scientific inquiry. Before Darwin, human beings had considered themselves separate from all other creatures, occupying a special place between the angels and the beasts; as such, they were above the laws of nature. Science was the study of the natural world. In contrast to planets, plants, and cells, human beings possess consciousness and exercise free will and self-determination. Hence the study of human beings belonged to the realm of philosophy and metaphysics. In *Origin of Species* (1859) and *The Descent of Man* (1871), Darwin marshaled evidence that, like all other forms of life on our planet, human beings *evolved* through a process of natural selection. If human beings are a product of evolution, maybe we, too, are subject to the laws of nature and therefore can be studied, analyzed, and understood scientifically.

Looking back, more than a century later, it is difficult to grasp just how radical Darwin's ideas were. Darwin developed his theory of evolution as a young man, but he did not publish his "dreadful secret" for 20 years. Darwin feared—correctly, as it turned out—that he would be vilified, ridiculed, and misinterpreted. More than 2 decades would pass before the theory of evolution gained widespread acceptance among scientists, much less among the public. We discuss Darwin's theory in more detail in Chapter 2, "The Biological Basis of Behavior." The key point here is that he inspired a number of young thinkers to apply the scientific method to our own species, paving the way for modern psychology.

Wilhelm Wundt and Edward Bradford Titchener: Structuralism

How did Wundt and Titchener apply scientific procedures to psychology?

The first formal psychological laboratory was founded in 1879 by Wilhelm Wundt, a physiologist and philosopher at the University of Leipzig in Germany. His goal was to develop techniques for uncovering the natural laws of the human mind. At the outset, Wundt did not attract much attention; only four students attended his first lecture. By the mid-1890s, however, his classes were filled to capacity.

Wilhelm Wundt

Wundt's primary interest was perception. When we look at a banana, for example, we immediately think, "Here is a fruit, something to peel and eat." But these are associations based on past experience. All we really see is a long, yellow object. Wundt and his students set out to strip perception of all its associations to find the most fundamental elements, or "atoms," of thought. They trained themselves in the art of objective introspection, recording in minute detail their thoughts, feelings, heartbeat, and respiration rates when listening to a metronome, for example. This may sound crude today, but Wundt's insistence on measurement and experimentation marked psychology as a science from the beginning.

Perhaps the most important product of the Leipzig lab was its students, who carried the new science to universities around the world. Among them was Edward Bradford Titchener, who was appointed professor of psychology at Cornell University, a post that he held until his death in 1927.

Psychology, Titchener wrote, is the science of consciousness—"physics with the observer kept in." In physics, an hour or a mile is an exact measure. To the observer, however, an hour may seem to pass in seconds, whereas a mile may seem endless. Titchener broke consciousness down into three basic elements: physical sensations (what we see), feelings (such as liking or disliking bananas), and images (memories of other bananas). Even the most complex thoughts and feelings can be reduced to these simple elements. Titchener saw psychology's role as identifying these elements and showing how they can be combined and integrated. Because it stresses the basic units of experience and the combinations in which they occur, this school of psychology is called **structuralism.**

William James: Functionalism

What was the focus of James's functionalist theory?

William James was the first American-born psychologist. As a young man, James earned a degree in physiology and studied philosophy in his spare time, unable to decide which interested him more. In psychology he found the link between the two. In 1875, James offered a class in psychology at Harvard. He later commented that the first lecture he ever heard on the subject was his own. James held that Wundt's "atoms of experience"—pure sensations without associations—simply do not exist in real-life experience. Our minds are constantly weaving associations, revising experience, starting, stopping, jumping back and forth in time. Perceptions, emotions, and images cannot be separated, James argued; consciousness flows in a continuous stream. If we could not recognize a banana, we would have to figure out what it was each time we saw one. Mental associations allow us to benefit from previous experience. When we get up in the morning, get dressed, open a door, or walk down the street, we don't have to think about what we are doing; we act out of habit. James suggested that when we repeat something, our nervous systems are changed so that each repetition is easier than the last.

With these insights, James arrived at a theory of mental life and behavior known as **functionalism.** Functionalist theory goes beyond mere sensation and perception to explore how an organism learns to function in its environment.

Sigmund Freud: Psychodynamic Psychology

What major contributions did Freud make to psychology?

Sigmund Freud, unlike the other figures we have introduced, was a doctor. Although his first love was research, he also maintained a private medical practice. A neurologist by training, Freud noticed that many of his patients' nervous ailments appeared to be psychological rather than physiological in origin. He came to believe that unconscious desires and conflicts lie at the root of their symptoms. Freud's clinical discoveries led him to develop a comprehensive theory of mental life that differed radically from the views of American psychologists.

Freud held that human beings are not as rational as they imagine and that "free will" is largely an illusion. Rather, we are motivated by unconscious instincts and urges that are not available to the rational, conscious part of our mind. To uncover the unconscious, he developed a technique (called *psychoanalysis*) in which the patient lies on a couch, recounts dreams, and says whatever comes to mind (free association). Somewhat like an archaeologist, the psychoanalyst sorts through half-remembered scenes, broken trains of thought, and the like and attempts to reconstruct the past experiences that shape the patient's present behavior. Freud maintained that personality develops in a series of critical stages during the first few years of life. If we successfully resolve the conflicts that we encounter at each of these stages, we can avoid psychological problems in later life. But if we become "fixated" at any one of these stages, we may carry related feelings of anxiety or exaggerated fears with us into adulthood. Freud maintained that many unconscious desires and conflicts have their roots in sexual repression. A 5-year-old boy, Freud argued, desires his mother and dreams of destroying his father, whom he sees as his rival for her affection. Yet at the same time, he loves—and fears—his father. These two feelings give rise to the "Oedipal conflict" (so named for the Greek myth in which Oedipus unknowingly murders his father and marries his

William James

Sigmund Freud

Structuralism
School of psychology that stresses the basic units of experience and the combinations in which they occur.

Functionalism
Theory of mental life and behavior that is concerned with how an organism uses its perceptual abilities to function in its environment.

mother, and becomes king). Ideally the boy is able to repress these feelings, to push them out of consciousness, but they may resurface later, for example, when he selects a marriage partner.

Freud's **psychodynamic theory** was as controversial at the turn of the century as Darwin's theory of evolution was 25 years earlier. Freud's Victorian contemporaries were shocked, not only by his emphasis on sexuality, but also by his suggestion that we are often unaware of our true motives and thus are not entirely in control of our thoughts, desires, and behavior. Yet Freud's lectures and writings attracted considerable attention in both the United States and Europe; he had a profound impact on twentieth-century arts and philosophy, not just on psychology.

The view that unconscious conflicts within the individual influence much human thought and action is known today as psychodynamic psychology. Psychodynamic theory, as expanded and revised by Freud's colleagues and successors, laid the foundation for the study of personality and psychological disorders, and remains influential today.

John B. Watson: Behaviorism

How did Watson approach the study of psychology?

Challenging structuralist, functionalist, and psychodynamic theories, the American psychologist John B. Watson argued that the whole idea of mental life was superstition, a relic left over from the Middle Ages. In "Psychology as a Behaviorist Views It" (1913), Watson contended that you cannot define consciousness any more than you can define a soul. And if you cannot locate or measure something, it cannot be the object of scientific study. For Watson, psychology was the study of observable, measurable behavior—and nothing more.

Watson's view of psychology, known as **behaviorism,** was based on well-known experiments conducted by the Russian physiologist Ivan Pavlov. Pavlov had noticed that the dogs in his laboratory began to drool (or salivate) as soon as they heard their feeder coming, even before they could see their dinner. He decided to find out whether salivation, which appeared to be an automatic reflex to food, could be shaped by learning. He succeeded by first pairing the sound of a bell with the presence of food and then eventually ringing the bell without introducing any food. Pavlov found that dogs that had experienced several pairings of the food and the bell together now salivated in response to the bell alone. Pavlov concluded that all behavior is a learned response to some stimulus in the environment. He called this training *conditioning*.

Could the same type of conditioning be applied to people? In a famous experiment, Watson worked with "Little Albert," a secure, happy baby who had no reason to fear soft, furry white rats. Each time the child reached out to pet the rat that Watson offered him, Watson made a loud, frightening noise. Before long, Albert became terrified of white rats (Watson & Rayner, 1920). Watson came to the conclusion that an infant is a *tabula rasa* (Latin for "blank slate") on which experience may write virtually anything:

> Give me a dozen healthy infants, well-formed, and my own specialized world to bring them up in, and I'll guarantee to take any one at random and train him to become any type of specialist I might select—doctor, lawyer, artist, merchant, chief and, yes, even beggar man, and thief, regardless of his talents, penchants, tendencies, abilities, vocations, and race. (Watson, 1924, p. 104)

When first published in the 1920s, Watson's orthodox scientific approach (if you cannot see it and measure it, then forget about it) found a receptive audience. Watson was also interested in showing that fears could be eliminated by conditioning. Mary Cover Jones (1924), one of his graduate students, suc-

John B. Watson

Psychodynamic theories
Personality theories contending that behavior results from psychological factors that interact within the individual, often outside conscious awareness.

Behaviorism
School of psychology that studies only observable and measurable behavior.

cessfully reconditioned a boy who showed a fear of rabbits (not caused by laboratory conditioning) to overcome this fear. Her technique, which involved presenting the rabbit at a great distance and then gradually bringing it closer while the child was eating, is similar to conditioning techniques used by psychologists today.

B. F. Skinner: Behaviorism Revisited

How did Skinner expand behaviorism?

B. F. Skinner became one of the leaders of the behaviorist school of psychology. Like Watson, Skinner fervently believed that psychologists should study only observable and measurable behavior (Skinner, 1938, 1987, 1989, 1990). He, too, was primarily interested in changing behavior through conditioning—and in discovering natural laws of behavior in the process. But Skinner added a new element to the behaviorist repertoire: *reinforcement.* He rewarded his subjects for behaving the way he wanted them to behave. For example, an animal (rats and pigeons were Skinner's favorite subjects) was put into a special cage and allowed to explore it. Eventually, the animal reached up and pressed a lever or pecked at a disk on the wall, whereupon a food pellet dropped into the box. Gradually, the animal learned that pressing the bar or pecking at the disk always brought food. Why did the animal learn this? Because it was reinforced, or rewarded, for doing so. Skinner thus made the animal an active agent in its own conditioning. Behaviorism dominated academic psychology in the United States well into the 1960s.

Gestalt Psychology

On what did the Gestalt psychologists focus?

Meanwhile, a group of psychologists in Germany was attacking structuralism from another direction. Max Wertheimer, Wolfgang Köhler, and Kurt Koffka were all interested in perception, but particularly in certain tricks that the mind plays on itself. Why, they asked, when we are shown a series of still pictures flashed at a constant rate (for example, movies or "moving" neon signs), do the pictures seem to move? The eye *sees* only a series of still pictures. What makes us *perceive* motion?

Phenomena like these launched a new school of thought, **Gestalt psychology.** Roughly translated from German, *Gestalt* means "whole" or "form." When applied to perception, it refers to our tendency to see patterns, to distinguish an object from its background, to complete a picture from a few cues. Like William James, the Gestalt psychologists rejected the structuralists' attempt to break down perception and thought into their elements. When we look at a tree, we see just that, a tree, not a series of isolated leaves and branches. Gestalt psychology paved the way for the modern study of perception (see Chapter 3).

Existential and Humanistic Psychology

How might existential psychology help modern individuals to feel less alienated? What aspects of life do humanistic psychologists stress?

Existential psychology draws on the philosophy put forward in the 1940s by the French philosopher, playwright, and novelist Jean-Paul Sartre and others. Existential psychologists are concerned with the search for meaning in an indifferent or hostile world—one in which religion and tradition have lost the authority to define the purpose of life, which leads to alienation and apathy.

Mary Cover Jones

B. F. Skinner

Gestalt psychology
School of psychology that studies how people perceive and experience objects as whole patterns.

Existential psychology
School of psychology that focuses on the meaninglessness and alienation of modern life, and how these factors lead to apathy and psychological problems.

Psychoanalyst Rollo May, for example, held that modern Americans are lost souls—a people without myths and heroes. R. D. Laing, another existentialist, believed that we must reevaluate our attitude toward psychotic behavior. Such behavior, he felt, constituted a reasonable, normal response to an abnormal world. Existential psychology guides people toward an inner sense of identity, which allows them to take responsibility for their actions and, in the process, to achieve freedom.

Humanistic psychology is closely related to existential psychology. Both schools insist that people must learn how to realize their human potential. But where existential psychology emphasizes restoring an inner sense of identity and willpower, humanistic psychology focuses on the possibilities of non-verbal experience, the unity of mind, altered states of consciousness, and "letting go."

The existential and humanistic viewpoints have not been widely accepted in American psychology, but they raise questions that are still relevant to explanations of personality and the treatment of psychological disorders.

Cognitive Psychology

What is the "cognitive revolution" in psychology?

One of the newest fields in psychology, which began to grow in the 1960s, has also been one of the most influential. **Cognitive psychology** is the study of our mental processes in the broadest sense: thinking, feeling, learning, remembering, making decisions and judgments, and so on. Thus cognitive psychologists are especially interested in the ways in which people "process"—that is, perceive, interpret, store, and retrieve—information.

In contrast to the behaviorists, cognitive psychologists believe that mental processes can and should be studied scientifically. Although we cannot observe cognitive processes directly, we can observe behavior and make inferences about the kinds of cognitive processes that underlie that behavior. For example, we can read a lengthy story to people and then observe the kinds of things that they remember from that story, the ways in which their recollections change over time, and the sorts of errors in recall they are prone to make. On the basis of systematic research of this kind, we can gain insight into the cognitive processes of human memory.

Although relatively young, cognitive psychology has already had an enormous impact on almost every area of psychology (Sperry, 1988, 1995). Even the definition of psychology has changed. Psychology is still the study of human "behavior," but psychologists' concept of "behavior" has been expanded to include thoughts, feelings, and states of consciousness.

Evolutionary Psychology

What Is Evolutionary Psychology?

The most recent addition to psychology is the evolutionary perspective. **Evolutionary psychology,** as the name suggests, focuses on the evolutionary origins of behavior patterns and mental processes, exploring what adaptive value they have and what functions they serve (DeKay & Buss, 1992; Wright, 1994). All of the views introduced so far seek to explain modern humans, or *Homo sapiens;* evolutionary psychologists ask how human beings got to be the way we are. They study such diverse topics as helping others (altruism), mate selection, and jealousy. By studying such phenomena in different species, different habitats, different cultures, and different times, and by comparing males and females, evolutionary psychologists have expanded our under-

Humanistic psychology
School of psychology that emphasizes nonverbal experience and altered states of consciousness as a means of realizing one's full human potential.

Cognitive psychology
School of psychology devoted to the study of mental processes in the broadest sense.

Evolutionary psychology
An approach to, and subfield of, psychology that is concerned with the evolutionary origins of behaviors and mental process, their adaptive value, and the purposes they continue to serve.

standing of cultural and gender differences in particular (DeKay & Buss, 1992; Scarr, 1993). The basic principle underlying evolutionary biology and psychology is called reproductive success; simply put, all species are genetically "programmed" to produce offspring who successfully reproduce themselves. Biologists have identified two basic reproductive strategies. One is to produce a very large number of offspring and leave them to mature on their own, with the possibility that a few will survive (as fish and turtles do). The other is to have a small number of offspring and to protect and nurture them so that most will survive (the pattern among mammals, especially humans and their close relatives the great apes).

These basic principles help to explain jealousy, for example. People in all cultures experience jealousy. How is jealousy adaptive? Evolutionary psychologists link jealousy to reproductive success, which explains why men and women experience jealousy somewhat differently. Because men cannot be certain that they are the biological fathers of their children, they are more likely to experience jealousy regarding their partner's sexual fidelity. They are also more likely to be promiscuous, because the more liaisons they have, the more likely they will father offspring. In contrast, women, as childbearers, know for certain which children are their own. As a rule, women bear only one offspring at a time, and devote years to rearing that child. Hence they are more likely to experience jealousy regarding the potential loss of their partner's commitment and investment in raising offspring (Daly & Wilson, 1988; Symonds, 1979, cited in DeKay & Buss, 1992).

Evolutionary psychology does not seek to replace or supplant other theories of human thought and behavior; rather, it adds another dimension to our understanding (Archer, 1996). The evolutionary perspective may become increasingly important as advances in behavioral genetics add to our scientific understanding of human beings.

Multiple Perspectives of Psychology Today

Does any single perspective dominate contemporary psychology?

For many years, psychologists clashed over the merits of the various approaches to psychology. Contemporary psychologists are less likely to advocate one theoretical perspective to the exclusion of all others (Friman et al., 1993). Rather, psychologists today tend to see the various perspectives as complementary, with each approach contributing in its own way to our understanding of human behavior.

Consider the study of aggression. Psychologists no longer limit their explanations to the behavioral view (aggressive behavior is learned as a consequence of reward and punishment) or the Freudian perspective (aggression is an expression of unconscious hostility toward a parent). Instead, most contemporary psychologists trace aggression to a number of factors, including long-standing adaptations to the environment (evolutionary psychology) and the influences of culture, gender, and socioeconomic status on how people perceive and interpret events—"That guy is making fun of me" or "She's asking for it"—(cognitive psychology). Likewise, physiological psychologists no longer limit themselves to identifying the genetic and biochemical roots of aggression. Instead they study how heredity and the environment *interact*.

Sometimes these theoretical perspectives mesh beautifully, with each one enhancing the others; at other times adherents of one approach challenge their peers, arguing for one viewpoint over all the others. But all psychologists agree that the field advances only with the addition of new evidence to support or challenge existing theories.

Missing: Women in Psychology

In 1906, James McKeen Cattell published *American Men of Science*, which, despite its title, included a number of women, among them 22 female psychologists. Cattell rated three of these women as among the 1,000 most distinguished scientists in the country: Mary Whiton Calkins (1863–1930), Christine Ladd-Franklin (1847–1930), and Margaret Floy Washburn (1871–1939).

Their accomplishments were particularly impressive at a time when discrimination kept women and their work in the background. Ladd-Franklin and Calkins were admitted to all-male graduate schools only after men interceded on their behalf. Washburn transferred from Columbia to Cornell, where the opportunities for women were greater (Furumoto & Scarborough, 1986). Only Calkins and Washburn went on to have academic careers. Though both taught at distinguished schools (Calkins at Wellesley and Washburn at Wells and Vassar), neither gained a place on the faculty of

> Although women are increasing in number and influence in psychology, women's experiences as psychologists are still considerably different from those of men.

a major research institution. All three grappled with the competing demands of family and career. Denied a doctorate from Harvard because of her sex—although the university's most eminent psychologist, William James, described her as his brightest student—Mary Whiton Calkins developed an influential system of self-psychology (Furumoto, 1980). She also developed a significant research tool used in the study of memory, and in 1891 she inaugurated the psychology laboratory at Wellesley College.

Unlike Calkins, Christine Ladd-Franklin received a Ph.D., but only in 1926—more than 40 years after she had completed the degree requirements—when Johns Hopkins finally lifted its restrictions against granting doctoral degrees to women. Although she developed an influential theory of color vision, Ladd-Franklin never received a permanent academic position, largely because of the prevailing prejudice against women combining a professional career with marriage and

The Decade of Behavior

What do psychologists mean by "The Decade of Behavior"?

The beginning of the twenty-first century and the third millennium provides a unique opportunity for the behavioral and social sciences to inform the public about the importance of behavioral and social research. Though psychology is a young science, it is in an ideal position to help solve some of our pressing and perplexing problems, from ensuring the health and well-being of people throughout the life span to reducing such persistent problems as domestic violence, ethnic conflict, and drug abuse. According to psychologist Martin Seligman, "Human behavior and misbehavior are at the root of seven out of ten deaths, and an even larger proportion of mental illness. If we can get the government and the American people to focus on behavior, solving many of our problems will be within our grasp" (quoted in Azar, 1998).

With this in mind, the American Psychological Association has declared the beginning of the new millennium "The Decade of Behavior: 2000–2010." With enthusiasm, dozens of scientific organizations and federal agencies have joined this initiative. Their goal is to improve health, safety, and education within a more prosperous democratic society by (1) promoting the application of behavioral and social science research to understand and address major national challenges; (2) increasing funding for research and formulating a strategy for training the next generation of social scientists; and (3) educating the public—including federal policymakers and lawmakers—on the value of the behavioral

motherhood (Furumoto & Scarborough, 1986).

In contrast to Calkin and Ladd-Franklin, Margaret Floy Washburn received her Ph.D. in psychology from Cornell soon after completing her degree requirements. She subsequently taught at Wells and Vassar for 34 years. Washburn went on to write several important books, including *Movement and Mental Imagery* (1916), which anticipated current research on the role of imagery in directing thought and activity.

Today women receive more than half of the Ph.D.s granted in psychology (Chronicle of Higher Education 1995; Pion et al., 1996) and perform key research in all of psychology's subfields. You will find their work referred to throughout this text. Terry Amabile has studied creativity, in particular the positive effect exposure to creative role models can have on people. Elizabeth Loftus studies memory; her work has uncovered how unreliable eyewitness accounts of a crime can be. Carol Nagy Jacklin has studied the role that parents' expectations can play in girls' (and boys') perceptions of the value of mathematics. Judith Rodin's research examines eating behavior, in particular bulimia and obesity. Eleanor Maccoby, Alice Eagly, and Jacqueline Eccles are prominent among the growing number of women and men who are studying sex differences in a variety of areas, such as emotionality, math and verbal ability, and helping behavior. Throughout this text we look at this work to see what part biology and society play in differences in the behavior of women and men.

Although women are increasing in number and influence in psychology, women's experiences as psychologists are still considerably different from those of men (Pion et al., 1996). Women graduate students tend to receive less financial support from their institutions than men do (Cohen & Gutek, 1991; Pion et al., 1996). After graduation, men are more likely to secure full-time employment in psychology and to be employed by the government and business, whereas women more often work in schools (APA, 1991a; Stapp & Fulcher, 1984, cited in Cohen & Gutek, 1991). The most recent available statistics indicate that the median annual salary for male psychologists is $58,700, whereas that for female psychologists is $50,300 (National Science Foundation, 1994, cited in Pion et al., 1996). Encouragingly, salary differences are smaller among more recent graduates (Cohen & Gutek, 1991).

and social sciences. For further information, visit their Web site at **http://www.decadeofbehavior.org/**.

Where Are the Women?

What problems did early women psychologists face?

As you read the brief history of modern psychology, you may have concluded that the founders of the new discipline were all men. But did psychology really have only fathers and no mothers? If there were women pioneers, why are their names and accomplishments missing from historical accounts?

In fact, psychology has profited from the contributions of women from its beginnings. Women presented papers and joined the national professional association as soon as it was formed in 1892 (Furumoto & Scarborough, 1986). Often, however, they faced discrimination. Some colleges and universities did not grant degrees to women, professional journals were reluctant to publish their work, and teaching positions were often closed to them (O'Connell & Russo, 1990; Russo & Denmark, 1987; Stevens & Gardner, 1982). Despite these barriers, a number of early women psychologists made important contributions and were acknowledged by at least some of the men in the growing discipline of psychology (see *Highlights*).

The apparent absence of women from the history of psychology is only one aspect of a much bigger and more troubling concern: the relative inattention to human diversity that has characterized psychology through most of the twentieth century. Only recently have psychologists looked closely at the ways in which culture, gender, race, and ethnicity can affect virtually all aspects of human behavior. In the next section, we begin our examination of this important topic.

REVIEW QUESTIONS

1. It was not until the late _____ that psychology came into its own as a separate discipline.

2. Match the following schools of thought in psychology with the appropriate description.

___ structuralism	a. Explores the origins of human behavior and establishes links to the behavior of other animals.
___ functionalism	b. Stresses the whole character of perception.
___ behaviorism	c. Is concerned with alienation in modern life and resulting psychological problems.
___ psychodynamic psychology	d. Studies only observable and measurable behavior.
___ existential psychology	e. Stresses the basic elements of experience and how they combine.
___ humanistic psychology	f. Emphasizes realizing one's full potential.
___ Gestalt psychology	g. Studies mental processes in the broadest sense.
___ cognitive psychology	h. Maintains that hidden motives and unconscious desires govern much of our behavior.
___ evolutionary psychology	i. Is concerned with how an organism uses its perceptual abilities to function in its environment.

3. Match the following famous psychologists with their accomplishment.

___ Wilhelm Wundt	a. Developed psychoanalysis and explored unconscious conflicts.
___ William James	b. An early psychologist at Harvard who developed a functionalist theory.
___ Sigmund Freud	c. Established the first psychological laboratory.
___ John B. Watson	d. Extensively studied the effects of rewards on behavior.
___ B. F. Skinner	e. Used conditioning principles to instill a fear of rats in "Little Albert".

Answers: 1. 1800s or nineteenth century. **2.** structuralism (e); functionalism (i); behaviorism (d); psychodynamic psychology (h); existential psychology (c); humanistic psychology (f); Gestalt psychology (b); cognitive psychology (g); evolutionary psychology (a). **3.** Wundt (c); James (b); Freud (a); Watson (e); Skinner (d).

Human Diversity

Why should students learn about human diversity?

Most contemporary psychologists agree that appreciating the rich diversity in behavior and mental processes that exists within the human species will lead to a fuller understanding of human behavior and mental processes.

Let us suppose you accept the foregoing argument. Still you may ask, Why should I be interested in learning about human diversity? The answer is all around you. Our major cities are populated by people from diverse backgrounds, with diverse values and goals, living side by side. But proximity does not always produce harmony; sometimes it leads to aggression, prejudice, and conflict. Understanding the behavior of people from diverse backgrounds gives us the tools to reduce some of these interpersonal tensions. The differences between males and females are also important to understand. Advertisers' images of the sexes are widely accepted, yet they may have little basis in fact. For example, stereotypes about how the "typical male" looks and acts or the "accepted social roles" for females often lead to confusion and misunderstandings between the sexes. Knowing the scientific bases of human diversity will enable you to separate fact from fiction in your daily interactions with people. Moreover, once you understand how and why groups differ in their values, behaviors, approaches to the world, thought processes, and responses to situations, you will savor the diversity around you. Finally, the more you comprehend the extent of human diversity, the more you will appreciate the many universal features of humanity.

Throughout this book we explore similarities and differences among *individuals* and among *groups* of people. For example, we examine differences in personality characteristics, intelligence, and levels of motivation; we look at similarities in biological functioning and developmental stages. We also consider the research on males and females and members of different cultural and ethnic groups.

Our expectations about gender roles often reflect traditional gender stereotypes. What were your first reactions to these photos?

Gender

How are psychologists trying to explain gender differences?

Male and *female* refer to one's biological makeup, the physical and genetic facts of being one sex or the other. Some people (e.g., Unger & Crawford, 1992) use the term *sex* to refer exclusively to biological differences in anatomy, genetics, or physical functioning and **gender** to refer to the psychological and social meanings attached to being biologically male or female. This distinction can be difficult to maintain, however, as we are all biological beings interacting in a social world. Because distinguishing what is biologically produced from what is socially influenced is almost impossible, in our discussion of these issues we use the terms *sex* and *gender* interchangeably.

In contrast, the terms *masculine* and *feminine* have distinct psychological and social meanings. "Masculine" preferences, attributes, and interests are those that are typically associated with being a male in our society, whereas "feminine" preferences, attributes, and interests are those associated with being a female. These terms are based on people's perceptions about the sexes (and indeed, about themselves) rather than on biological facts.

Gender Stereotypes Many popular beliefs concerning differences between the sexes are based on *gender stereotypes*: characteristics that are assumed to be typical of each sex. For example, in most cultures, men are seen as dominant, strong, and aggressive, whereas women are viewed as affectionate, emotional, and soft-hearted (Williams & Best, 1990).

Beyond our stereotypes about what males and females "typically" are like, we have general beliefs about *gender roles*, behaviors that we expect males and females to engage in. For example, some common gender roles for women in many cultures are to take care of children and family, to cook meals, and to do laundry. Men, in contrast, are expected to hold a paying job, to provide resources, and to drive the car whenever the family goes somewhere.

Generalizations are undeniably an important "cognitive shorthand"; the point about stereotypes is that they are overgeneralizations. Habitually relying on stereotypes rather than paying attention to an individual's personal characteristics can lead to mistaken impressions, false beliefs, and misbegotten conclusions about a person. Because our stereotypes about men and women are so firmly fixed and so potentially damaging, they need to be examined scientifically.

Gender
The psychological and social meanings attached to being biologically male or female.

To understand human behavior fully, we must appreciate the rich diversity of human beings throughout the world.

One group of psychologists has been doing exactly that. We discuss the work of feminist psychologists later in this section.

Culture

How does culture contribute to human diversity?

Culture refers to the tangible goods produced in a society, such as art, inventions, literature, and consumer goods. But it also refers to *intangible* processes such as shared beliefs, values, attitudes, traditions, and behaviors that are communicated from one generation to the next within a society (Barnouw, 1985). These cultural values, traditions, and beliefs in turn give rise to characteristic rules or norms that govern the behavior of people in that society, including what foods they eat, whom they may marry, and what they do on Saturday nights.

Even within a dominant culture, diversity exists in the form of *subcultures*, "cultural patterns that distinguish some segment of a society's population" (Macionis, 1993, p. 75). Texans, psychology professors, persons with AIDS, African-American women, homeless people, and teenagers all form subcultures within U.S. society. These subcultures have their own norms, values, and rituals, which may or may not be similar to those of the dominant culture. Moreover, many nations (such as the United States) are composed of various peoples with different backgrounds and traditions. Although we identify certain ideas, products, and behaviors as distinctly "American," we are actually a nation of great diversity—within our borders there are many well-formed subcultures of immigrants and their families. In later chapters, we discuss how cultural differences affect psychological processes, including our motivation to achieve, the way we express emotion, and a whole range of social behaviors.

Race and Ethnicity

Do race and ethnicity affect behavior?

Most people (including some psychologists) speak of Asians, Latinos, Native Americans, African Americans, Caucasians, and Pacific Islanders as distinct races, implying fundamental differences among these peoples. A **race** is usually defined as a subpopulation of a species (in this case, humans) who share some biological and genetic similarities and who have reproduced among themselves

Culture
The tangible goods and the values, attitudes, behaviors, and beliefs that are passed from one generation to another.

Race
A subpopulation of a species, defined according to an identifiable characteristic (that is, geographic location, skin color, hair texture, genes, facial features, and so forth).

(Betancourt & López, 1993; Diamond, 1994; Macionis, 1993). Furthermore, members of different races generally have distinct physical characteristics, such as hair color or type, skin pigmentation, and facial features. At one time it might have been reasonable to talk about races as distinct groups, given the isolated geographic regions some peoples occupied and the identifiable physical characteristics they developed in adapting to those regions. Today, however, many scientists do not consider race a valid scientific concept because humans have so frequently migrated, intermarried, and commingled. Consequently, genetic characteristics that were once specific to a group of individuals in a particular region were spread widely across a much larger area. All contemporary societies are populated by people with rich genetic mixtures, so it is difficult to argue that human beings now differ substantially on a genetic basis. Furthermore, the physical characteristics that were once thought to "define" membership in a racial group are somewhat arbitrary. Race classification has often been based on melanin (the substance that produces differences in the color of skin, hair, and eyes), but humans could just as easily be classified along several other dimensions. For example, some people have a genetic resistance to malaria and others do not; some people can digest milk products and others cannot; and some people have fingerprint patterns that form spirals, whereas others have patterns that form loops and still others exhibit patterns that form arches (Diamond, 1994). We could posit any number of different "races" based on these other classification schemes.

Because it is so difficult to define "race" exactly, most psychologists have abandoned the term as a fundamental scientific concept (e.g., Dole, 1995), although social scientists and public officials still use racial categories for demographic purposes or for purposes of formulating public policy. (Think of the many forms you've completed that asked you to check off a box identifying yourself as a member of one racial group or another.) Race still has a role in psychology, however, because it can form an important part of a person's self-identity. Identifying with a socially or politically recognized racial group—for example, feeling strongly about oneself as an Asian American—can affect an individual's behavior, attitudes, and cognitive processes. This type of self-identification is even more apparent in the related concept of ethnicity.

Whereas race refers to an individual's biological heritage, **ethnicity** refers to a common cultural heritage that is shared by a group of people. Members of an ethnic group may have common ancestors, language, or religion or feel a kinship based on traditional social practices. For example, a person of Cuban ancestry living in Florida may share the traditions and viewpoints of her compatriots in Cuba (the ethnic group to which she belongs), all the while residing in Florida (the cultural setting in which these behaviors are taking place).

What effect does ethnicity have on behavior? *Ethnic identity* refers to that aspect of one's self-concept that is based on identifying oneself as a member of a particular ethnic group. Our Cuban American friend may feel strongly about her ethnic background and build on that identification as a foundation for her overall self-concept. In turn, this view of herself can influence her choice of friends (she may seek out other Cubans), the activities she engages in (she may participate in activities associated with her ethnic group), and her cognitions about herself (seeing herself as a person who is Cuban first and a resident of the United States second). Research shows that a strong sense of ethnic identity is linked to high self-esteem (Phinney, 1996), but only when the individual also feels a positive association with the mainstream culture he or she is living in. In other words, holding a strong ethnic identity and being assimilated to the larger culture (for example, seeing oneself as a Cuban in the United States) is a positive combination.

Members of an ethnic group can have many things in comon, including dress. A person's ethnic identity can have a major influence on his or her behavior.

Ethnicity
A common cultural heritage—including religion, language, or ancestry—that is shared by a group of individuals.

Psychology and Human Diversity

In what ways has psychology become sensitive to issues involving human diversity?

In recent years psychologists have taken steps to ensure that psychology reflects the richness and diversity of the human population (Phinney, 1996). To meet this end, the American Psychological Association established a number of divisions (see Table 1–1) to promote the representation and appreciation of diverse perspectives.

Feminist Challenges   Division 35, *The Psychology of Women*, was founded to promote feminist research, theories, education, and practice to improve the lives of girls and women. Psychologists who have embraced the feminist perspective have challenged many of the accepted theories of human behavior. Many feminist psychologists have argued that before the emergence of **feminist theory**, psychology reflected only a male perspective of human behavior—essentially excluding the views of half the human species (Rabinowitz & Sechzer, 1993).

As the number of female psychologists has grown, so have their questions about psychological theories, research, and clinical practices. Feminist psychologists make three main points. First, much of the research supporting key psychological theories, such as moral development, was based on all-male samples. Measured against "universal male" standards, females often were found "lacking." Thus on tests of moral development, adolescent boys usually score higher than girls. The reason, as Carol Gilligan (1982) has pointed out, may be that they think about moral issues in different ways: Males tend to emphasize impartial rules and principles, whereas females are more concerned with people's feelings. Second, reports of gender differences tend to focus on the extremes, exaggerating small differences and ignoring much greater similarities (Tavris, 1992). For example, boys and girls score about the same on tests of mathematical ability (Hyde & Linn, 1988; Lumis & Stevenson, 1990). Only when one looks at mathematically gifted students do boys come out ahead. But this finding has received far more attention than the overlap in male/female ability. Third, the questions psychologists ask and the topics they study reflect what they consider to be important. Because psychology was dominated by men for so long, many issues of primary concern to women—including domestic violence, pregnancy, and childbirth—received little attention (DeAngelis, 1991a). For example, developmental psychology was long considered a "stepchild" of general psychology; indeed, courses in child development were usually taught in departments of home economics or education (Kessen, 1965). Not until the late 1950s and early 1960s was development recognized as an important branch of psychology. As another example, researchers have found that the rate of depression soars among adolescent girls (but not boys); this phenomenon has received very little attention from researchers.

Beyond research and theory, contemporary feminist psychology has begun to influence every facet of psychological practice by seeking mechanisms to empower women in the community, by advocating action to establish policies that advance equality and social justice, and by increasing women's representation in global leadership.

Sexual Orientation   Division 44, *Society for the Psychological Study of Lesbian and Gay Issues*, focuses psychological research on the diversity of human *sexual orientations*—that is, on whether one's sexual interest is directed toward members of the same sex, the other sex, or both sexes. Psychologists have only begun to investigate the many sensitive issues associated with this dimension of human diversity—including such topics as the origins of sexual orientation (LeVay & Hamer, 1994), brain differences between heterosexual and homosexual men

Psychologist Carol Gilligan has argued that adolescent girls may think about moral issues in different ways than boys.

Feminist theory
Feminist theories offer a wide variety of views on the social roles of women and men, the problems and rewards of those roles, and prescriptions for changing those roles.

(Swaab & Hoffman, 1995), and the impact of allowing gays and lesbians in the military (Jones & Koshes, 1995).

Ethnic and Minority Issues   Division 45, *The Society for the Psychological Study of Ethnic Minority Issues*, was founded to encourage research and promote the application of psychological knowledge to our understanding of ethnic and minority issues. This increased sensitivity toward issues of ethnic minorities has enabled psychologists to develop a better appreciation for the unique challenges faced by individuals from various ethnic backgrounds. For example, research has shown that African Americans are more likely to be unnecessarily admitted to psychiatric hospitals than are whites (Friedman, Paradis, & Hatch, 1994), while other research has shown that some forms of mental disorders are more prevalent among ethnic minorities (Beidel, Turner, & Trahger, 1994; Brown, Eaton, & Sussman, 1990). Although researchers have only begun to identify the psychological processes associated with ethnicity (Betancourt & Lopez, 1993), simply increasing awareness can help psychologists be more sensitive and knowledgeable in the treatment of clients from diverse ethnic backgrounds (Rogler, Cortes, & Malgady, 1991).

Unfortunately most ethnic minorities are still underrepresented among the ranks of psychologists. For example, African Americans receive only about 3 percent of the Ph.D.s in psychology, with a similar percentage being earned by Hispanic Americans (Smith & Davidson, 1992). To alleviate this problem, the American Psychological Association is currently examining mechanisms aimed at increasing minority representation among psychologists (*Trends in Education*, 1995).

The relatively small number of ethnic minorities in psychology has not stopped minorities from achieving prominence and making significant contributions to the field. Kenneth Clark, for example, an African American who served as president of the American Psychological Association, received national recognition for his important work on the effects of segregation on black children. The Supreme Court cited his research in the *Brown v. Board of Education* decision of 1954 that outlawed school segregation in the United States. More than 50 years later, psychologists are still exploring the effects of racial prejudice.

Very little research has been done on differences in psychological processes from one society and culture to another, but this neglect is also beginning to be remedied. A special effort has been made in this text to address concerns about gender, sexual orientation, race, and culture and to report on research that bears on these issues. For example, we consider findings on the influence of culture on academic achievement (in Chapter 7, "Cognition and Mental Abilities"), on emotional expression (in Chapter 8, "Motivation and Emotion"), and on how gender and culture combine to affect many aspects of development (Chapter 9, "Life Span Development").

In the next section, we see how psychologists are also working to uncover and overcome biases in psychological research that are related to gender, race, and ethnicity. The field of psychology is broadening its scope to probe the full range and richness of human diversity, and this text mirrors that expansive and inclusive approach.

Unintended Biases   The gender, race, or ethnicity of the experimenter (in the past, usually a white male) may introduce subtle, unintended biases. For example, some early research concluded that women were more likely than men to conform to social pressure in the laboratory (e.g., Crutchfield, 1955). When the experimenter is female (Eagly & Carli, 1981), however, research now reveals no gender difference in this area. Similarly, evidence suggests that the results of research with African-American participants may be significantly affected by the race of the experimenter (Graham, 1992). Data on race and IQ scores have been widely misinterpreted as "demonstrating" innate racial inferiority. Advocates of this view rarely note that African Americans score higher on IQ and other tests when the person administering the test is also African American (Graham, 1992). Similarly, do feminist theories, developed by and tested primarily with white, college-educated women, apply to women of color (Yoder & Kahn, 1993)?

Biases, intended or not, also influence clinical psychologists. As we noted earlier, African Americans are far more likely to be unnecessarily admitted to psychiatric hospitals than are whites (Friedman, Paradis, & Hatch, 1994). When health care professionals are shown identical case studies, they are more likely to diagnose alcoholism or schizophrenia if the patient is identified as black and depression if the patient is identified as white.

The systematic reappraisal of research studies and the methods used in conducting them have caused many psychologists to question the view of the scientist as an impartial or value-free observer (Riger, 1992). Although research methods and the scientific process strive for objectivity, subjective values—whether they derive from race, gender, or cultural background—influence human behavior, whether the human in question is the designer of or the participant in research. We look now at the methods psychologists use to study human behavior.

REVIEW QUESTIONS

1. Which of the following are reasons for studying human diversity?
   _____ a. Because our society is made up of so many different kinds of people.
   _____ b. As a way of helping to solve interpersonal tensions based on misunderstandings of others.
   _____ c. To help define what humans have in common.
   _____ d. Because diversity psychology is one of the major subdivisions of psychology.
2. "A subculture is a group within a larger society that shares a certain set of values, beliefs, outlooks, and norms of behavior." True or false.
3. Subcultures that contribute to diversity in our own society include
   _____ a. African Americans
   _____ b. gay men and women
   _____ c. teenagers
   _____ d. blue-eyed blondes
   _____ e. the homeless
4. People who have ancestors from the same region of the world and who share a common language, religion, and set of social traditions are said to be part of the same _____ group.
5. "Minority groups are seriously underrepresented among psychologists". True or false.

Answers: 1. a, b, and c. 2. T. 3. a, b, c, and e. 4. ethnic. 5. T.

Research Methods in Psychology

What are some of the research methods psychologists use in their work?

Because psychology is a science, psychologists must collect data systematically and objectively. To accomplish this, they use a variety of research methods, each of which has advantages and disadvantages as compared with the others. In this section we examine some of the techniques psychologists frequently use in their research, including naturalistic observation, case studies, surveys, correlational research, and experimental research.

Naturalistic Observation

How would you go about studying behavior in a natural setting?

Psychologists rely on **naturalistic observation** to study human or animal behavior in its natural context instead of under imposed conditions in the laboratory. One psychologist with this real-life orientation might observe behavior in a school or a factory; another might actually join a family to study the behavior of its members; still another might observe monkeys in their natural habitats instead of in cages. The primary advantage of naturalistic observation is that the behavior observed in everyday life is likely to be more natural, spontaneous, and varied than that observed in a laboratory.

For example, W. H. Whyte (1956) wanted to learn how people living in a suburban community chose their friends. By reading the social column in the local newspaper, he learned when parties were being given and who was invited to each one. After collecting such data for some time, Whyte noticed that there were definite friendship patterns in the community. *Proximity*—people's nearness to one another—seemed to be important in determining which people became friends. Whyte concluded that all things being equal, people are more likely to make friends with those who live nearby—something he could not have discovered in a laboratory.

Whyte restricted his observations to one specific behavior: going to parties. It is not always possible, however, to make such restrictions. Psychologists using naturalistic observation have to take behavior as it comes. They cannot suddenly yell "Freeze!" when they want to study what is going on in more detail. Nor can psychologists tell people to stop what they are doing because it is not what the psychologists are interested in researching.

Another potential problem with naturalistic observation is **observer bias.** Any police officer will tell you how unreliable eyewitnesses can be. Even psychologists who are trained observers may subtly distort what they see to make it conform to what they were hoping to see. For this reason, contemporary observational studies often use videotapes that can be analyzed and scored by researchers who do not know what the study is designed to find out. Another potential problem is that psychologists may not observe or record behavior that seems to be irrelevant. Therefore, it is sometimes preferable to rely on a team of

The world-famous primatologist Jane Goodall has spent most of her adult life observing chimpanzees in their natural environment in Africa.

When people are unaware that they are being watched, they behave naturally. A one-way mirror is therefore sometimes used for naturalistic observation.

Naturalistic observation
Research method involving the systematic study of animal or human behavior in natural settings rather than in the laboratory.

Observer bias
Expectations or biases of the observer that might distort or influence his or her interpretation of what was actually observed.

trained observers who pool their notes. This strategy often generates a more complete picture than one observer could draw alone.

Unlike laboratory experiments that can be continually repeated, each natural situation is a one-time-only occurrence. Therefore psychologists prefer not to make general statements based on information from naturalistic studies alone. They would rather test the information under controlled conditions in the laboratory before they apply it to situations other than the original.

Despite these disadvantages, naturalistic observation is a valuable tool. After all, real-life behavior is what psychology is all about. Naturalistic observation often provides new ideas and suggests new theories, which can then be studied more systematically and in more detail in the laboratory. This method also helps researchers keep their perspective by reminding them of the larger world outside the lab.

Case Studies

When is it useful to conduct a case study?

Another research method, similar to naturalistic observation, is the **case study** method. A researcher using this method observes the real-life behavior of one person or just a few people at a time. Case studies helped Sigmund Freud develop his psychological theories and refine his therapeutic techniques. One of his patients was a 5-year-old boy whom he called "Little Hans" (Freud, 1909). Little Hans had a terrible fear of horses, which, Freud later concluded, stemmed from his fear of his father and his sexual longing for his mother. This case not only confirmed Freud's suspicion that even very young children have sexual desires but also his belief that strong emotions that are pushed out of consciousness may surface in disguised form and cause psychological distress. Another famous psychologist, Jean Piaget, developed a comprehensive theory of cognitive development by carefully studying each of his three children as they grew and changed during childhood; his theory of cognitive development is described in Chapter 9, "Life Span Development."

Like naturalistic observation, case studies can provide valuable insights but also have some significant drawbacks. Observer bias is as much a problem here as it is with naturalistic observation. Moreover, because each person is unique, it is impossible to know whether we can confidently draw general conclusions from a single case. Nevertheless, case studies figure prominently in psychological research. For example, the famous case of Phineas Gage, who suffered severe and unusual brain damage, led researchers to identify the front portion of the brain as important for the control of emotions and the ability to plan and carry out complex tasks (see Chapter 2).

Surveys

What are some of the advantages of survey research?

In some respects, surveys address some of the shortcomings of naturalistic observation and case studies. In **survey research,** a carefully selected group of people is asked a set of predetermined questions in face-to-face interviews or in questionnaires. Perhaps the most familiar surveys are the polls taken before major elections: For weeks or months before the election, we are bombarded with estimates of the percentage of people likely to vote for each candidate. But surveys are used for other purposes as well. For example, a 1991 survey determined that 61 percent of the adults questioned by telephone believed that advertisers embedded subliminal messages in their ads, and 56 percent were convinced that such messages make people buy things they do not want (Lev,

Case study
Intensive description and analysis of a single individual or just a few individuals.

Survey research
Research technique in which questionnaires or interviews are administered to a selected group of people.

1991). (There is no scientific evidence to support these beliefs.) According to another 1991 survey, 38 percent of the American women polled said they had been "the object of sexual advances, propositions, or unwanted sexual discussions from men who supervised [them] or could affect [their] position at work" and that only 10 percent of that group had reported the incident at the time (Kolbert, 1991). This survey—and others more recently—indicates that sexual harassment in the workplace is both widespread and underreported.

Surveys may generate a great deal of interesting and useful information at relatively low cost, but to be accurate, the survey questions must be unambiguous and clear, and the people surveyed must be selected with great care. Moreover, the results can be seriously distorted if people are reluctant to talk about or admit to certain feelings, beliefs, or behaviors.

Naturalistic observations, case studies, and surveys can provide a rich set of raw data that describes behaviors, beliefs, opinions, and attitudes. But these research methods are not ideal for making predictions, and they are not at all well suited to explaining, or determining, the causes of behavior.

Correlational Research

What is correlational research?

A psychologist, under contract to the Air Force, is asked to predict which applicants for a pilot training program will make good pilots. An excellent approach to solving this problem would be **correlational research.** The psychologist might select several hundred trainees, give them a variety of aptitude and personality tests, then compare the results to their performance in training school. This approach would tell him whether there is some characteristic or set of characteristics that is closely related to, or correlated with, eventual success as a pilot.

Suppose he finds that the most successful trainees score higher than the unsuccessful trainees on mechanical aptitude tests and that they are also cautious people who do not like to take unnecessary risks. The psychologist has discovered that there is a *correlation*, or relationship, between these traits and success as a pilot trainee: High scores on tests of mechanical aptitude and caution predict success as a pilot trainee. If these correlations are confirmed in new groups of trainees, then the psychologist could recommend with some confidence that the Air Force consider using these tests to select future trainees.

This psychologist has *described* a relationship between skill as a pilot and two other characteristics, and as a result he is able to use those relationships to predict with some accuracy which trainees will and will not become skilled pilots. But he has no basis for drawing conclusions about cause and effect. Does the tendency to shy away from risk-taking make a trainee a good pilot? Or is it the other way around: Learning to be a skillful pilot makes people cautious? Or is there some unknown factor that causes people to be both cautious and capable of acquiring the different skills needed in the cockpit? Correlational data do not permit the researcher to *explain* cause and effect.

Despite limitations, correlational research often sheds light on important psychological phenomena. In this book you will come across many examples of correlational research: People who are experiencing severe stress are more prone to develop physical illnesses than people who are not; children whose parent(s) have schizophrenia are more likely to develop this disorder than are other children; and when someone needs help, the more bystanders, the less likely it is that any one of them will come forward to offer to help.

These interesting findings allow us to make some predictions, but most psychologists eventually want to move beyond simply making predictions. They want to understand the causes of phenomena. To explain psychological phenomena, psychologists most often use experimental research.

Surveys can generate a great deal of useful data, but only if the questions are clear and the people surveyed are carefully selected and answer the questions honestly.

Correlational research
Research technique based on the naturally occurring relationship between two or more variables.

Experimental Research

When is an experiment called for?

A psychology instructor notices that on Monday mornings most students in her class do not remember material as well as they do later in the week. This psychologist has discovered a correlation between the day of the week and memory for course-related material. Based on this correlation, she could predict that next Monday and every Monday after that the students in her class will not absorb material as well as on other days. But she wants to go beyond simply predicting her students' behavior; she wants to understand or explain why their memories are poorer on Mondays than on other days of the week.

Based on her own experiences and some informal interviews with students, she suspects that students stay up late on weekends and their difficulty remembering facts and ideas presented on Mondays is due to lack of sleep. This hypothesis appears to make sense, but the psychologist wants to prove that it is correct. To gather evidence that lack of sleep actually causes memory deficits, she turns to the **experimental method.**

Her first step is to pick **subjects** or **participants,** people whom she can observe to find out whether her theory is correct. She decides to use student volunteers. To keep her results from being influenced by sex differences or intelligence levels, she chooses a group made up of equal numbers of men and women who scored between 520 and 550 on the verbal section of their college entrance exams.

Next, she designs a memory task. She needs something that none of her participants will know in advance. If she chooses a chapter in a history book, for example, she runs the risk that some of her participants will be history buffs. Given the various possibilities, the psychologist decides to print a page of geometric shapes, each labeled with a nonsense word. Circles are "glucks," triangles are "rogs," and so on. She will give the students half an hour to learn the names, and then she will take the pages away and ask the students to assign those same labels to geometric shapes on a new page.

The psychologist also needs to know which participants are sleep-deprived. Simply asking people whether they have slept well is not ideal: Some may say "no" so that they will have an excuse for doing poorly on the test, whereas others may say "yes" because they do not want a psychologist to think they are so unstable they cannot sleep. And two people who both say they "slept well" may not mean the same thing by that phrase. So the psychologist decides to intervene—that is, to control the situation more closely. Everyone in the experiment, she decides, will spend the night in the same dormitory. They will be kept awake until 4 A.M., and then they will be awakened at 7 A.M. sharp. She and her colleagues will patrol the halls to make sure that no one falls asleep ahead of schedule. By *manipulating* the amount of time the participants sleep, the psychologist is introducing and controlling an essential element of the experimental method: an independent variable. The psychologist believes that the students' ability to learn and remember labels for geometric shapes will depend on their having had a good night's sleep. Performance on the memory task (the number of correct answers) thus becomes the dependent variable. According to the hypothesis, changing the **independent variable** (the amount of sleep) should also change the **dependent variable** (performance on the memory task). Her prediction is that this group of participants, who get no more than 3 hours of sleep, should do quite poorly on the memory test.

At this point, the experimenter begins looking for loopholes in her experimental design. How can she be sure that poor test results mean that the participants did less well than they would have done had they had more sleep? For example, their poor performance could be the result simply of knowing that

Experimental method
Research technique in which an investigator deliberately manipulates selected events or circumstances and then measures the effects of those manipulations on subsequent behavior.

Subjects or participants
Individuals whose reactions or responses are observed in an experiment.

Independent variable
In an experiment, the variable that is manipulated to test its effects on the other, dependent variables.

Dependent variable
In an experiment, the variable that is measured to see how it is changed by manipulations in the independent variable.

they were being closely observed. To be sure that her experiment measures only the effects of inadequate sleep, the experimenter creates two groups, containing equal numbers of males and females of the same ages and with the same college entrance exam scores. One of the groups, the **experimental group,** will be kept awake, as described, until 4 A.M. That is, they will be subjected to the experimenter's manipulation of the independent variable—amount of sleep. Members of the other group, the **control group,** will be allowed to go to sleep whenever they please. If the only consistent difference between the two groups is the amount of sleep they get, the experimenter can be much more confident that if the groups differ in their test performance, the difference is due to the length of time they slept the night before.

Finally, the psychologist questions her own objectivity. Because she believes that lack of sleep inhibits students' learning and memory, she does not want to prejudice the results of her experiment; that is, she wants to avoid **experimenter bias.** So she decides to ask a neutral person, someone who does not know which participants did or did not sleep all night, to score the tests.

The experimental method is a powerful tool, but it, too, has limitations. First, many intriguing psychological variables, such as love, hatred, and grief, do not readily lend themselves to experimental manipulation. And even if it were possible to induce such strong emotions as part of a psychological experiment, this would raise serious ethical questions. In some cases, psychologists may use animals rather than humans for experiments. For example, an experimenter might study the effects on infant monkeys of separation from their mothers (Harlow, 1958). But some subjects, such as the emergence of language in children or the expression of emotions, cannot be studied with other species. Second, because experiments are conducted in an artificial setting, participants—whether human or nonhuman animals—may behave differently from the way they would in real life.

Multimethod Research

What are the benefits of multimethod research?

Each of the research methods we have discussed has advantages and disadvantages. Therefore most psychologists use several methods to study a single problem. For example, someone interested in studying creativity might begin her research by giving a group of college students a creativity test that she invented to measure their capacity to discover or produce something new. Next she would compare the students' scores with their scores on intelligence tests and with their grades to see if there is a *correlation* between them. Then she would spend several weeks *observing* a college class and *interviewing* teachers, students, and parents to correlate classroom behavior and the adults' evaluations with the students' scores on the creativity test. She would go on to test some of her ideas with an *experiment* using a group of students as participants. Finally, her findings might prompt her to revise the test, or they might give the teachers and parents new insight into particular students.

Interestingly, there are some indications that male and female researchers have somewhat different preferences in their choice of research methods (Moses, 1991). Many women researchers report that they feel uncomfortable conducting laboratory experiments that isolate psychological processes and study them out of their natural context. Moreover, some issues of special interest to many female psychologists—rape, incest, sexual abuse, and domestic violence—cannot be studied effectively in a laboratory; they are best understood in context. Thus, traditionally, many female researchers have been drawn more to naturalistic observation, case study, and correlational research methods than to laboratory experiments.

Experimental group
In a controlled experiment, the group subjected to a change in the independent variable.

Control group
In a controlled experiment, the group not subjected to a change in the independent variable; used for comparison with the experimental group.

Experimenter bias
Expectations by the experimenter that might influence the results of an experiment or its interpretation.

SUMMARY TABLE

Basic Methods of Research

Research Method	Advantages	Limitations
Naturalistic Observation Behavior is observed in the environment in which it occurs naturally.	Provides a great deal of firsthand behavioral information that is more likely to be accurate than reports after the fact. The subject's behavior is more natural, spontaneous, and varied than behaviors taking place in the laboratory. A rich source of hypotheses as well.	The presence of an observer may alter the participants' behavior; the observer's recording of the behavior may reflect a pre-existing bias; and it is often unclear whether the observations can be generalized to other settings and other subjects.
Case Studies Behavior of one person or a few people is studied in depth.	Yields a great deal of detailed descriptive information. Useful for forming hypotheses.	The case(s) studied may not be a representative sample. Can be time-consuming and expensive. Observer bias is a potential problem.
Surveys A large number of participants are asked a standard set of questions.	Enables an immense amount of data to be gathered quickly and inexpensively.	Sampling biases can skew results. Poorly constructed questions can result in answers that are ambiguous, so data are not clear. Accuracy depends on ability and willingness of participants to answer questions accurately.
Correlational Research Employs statistical methods to examine the relationship between two or more variables.	May clarify relationships between variables that cannot be examined by other research methods. Allows prediction of behavior.	Does not permit researchers to draw conclusions regarding cause-and-effect relationships.
Experimental Research One or more variables are systematically manipulated, and the effect of that manipulation on other variables is studied.	Strict control of variables offers researchers the opportunity to draw conclusions about cause-and-effect relationships.	The artificiality of the lab setting may influence participants' behavior; unexpected and uncontrolled variables may confound results; many variables cannot be controlled and manipulated.

The Importance of Sampling

Why is proper sampling so critical?

One obvious drawback to every form of research is that it is usually impossible, or at least impractical, to measure every single occurrence of a characteristic. No one could expect to measure the memory of every human being, to study the responses of all individuals who suffer from phobias (irrational fears), or to record the maternal behavior of all female monkeys. No matter what research method is used, whenever researchers conduct a study, they examine only a relatively small number of people or animals of the population they seek to understand. In other words, researchers almost always study a small *sample* and then use the results of that limited study to generalize about larger populations. For example, the psychologist who was trying to predict success in pilot training assumed that the trainees he was studying were representative of future groups of trainees. The psychology instructor who studied the effect of lack of sleep on memory assumed that her results would apply to other students in her classes (past and future), as well as to students in other classes and at other colleges.

How realistic are these assumptions? How confident can researchers be that the results of research conducted on a relatively small sample of people apply to the much larger population from which the sample was drawn (see *Highlights*)? A classic example of faulty generalization involves a national magazine that predicted the election of a certain candidate, who then lost the election. The magazine had based its prediction on a postcard survey of people who were listed in the phonebook. They failed to realize, however, that a large number of voters did not have telephones due to economic hardships, and many of these people voted for the other candidate. This famous blunder has become a beacon—a flashing yellow light—warning researchers to avoid biased samples and faulty generalizations.

Social scientists have developed several techniques to deal with sampling error. One is to select participants at random from the larger population. For example, the researcher studying pilot trainees might begin with an alphabetical list of all trainees and then select every third name or every fifth name on the list to be in his study. These participants would constitute a **random sample** from the larger group of trainees, because at the outset every trainee had an equal chance of being chosen for the study.

Another way to make sure that conclusions apply to the larger population is to pick a **representative sample** of the population being studied. For example, researchers looking for a representative cross-section of Americans would want to ensure that the proportion of males and females in the study matched the national proportion, that the number of participants from each state matched the national population distribution, and so on.

Even with these precautions, however, unintended bias may influence psychological research. This issue has received a great deal of attention recently, particularly in relation to women and African Americans, as discussed in the next section (for example, Denmark, 1994; Gannon et al., 1992; Graham, 1992; Riger, 1992).

Human Diversity and Research

Can we generalize about research findings from one group to another?

Historically, most psychological researchers have been white American males, and most participants used in psychological research have been white American male college students. For decades, hardly anyone thought about the underlying assumption that the results of these studies would also apply to women, to people of other racial and ethnic groups, and to people of different cultures. Psychologists have now begun to question that assumption explicitly. Are women more likely to help a person in distress than men are? Are African Americans more vulnerable to certain types of mental illness than white people, and vice versa? Do the Japanese view children's ability to learn in the same way that Americans do?

Research indicates that the answer to such questions often is "no"; people's gender, race, ethnic background, and culture often have a profound effect on their behavior. Research has found consistent cultural differences in aggression (Triandis, 1994), memory (Mistry & Rogoff, 1994), some forms of nonverbal communication (Johnson, Ekman, & Friesen, 1975), and other behaviors. Similarly, men and women display differences in a variety of traits, including aggression (Eagly & Steffen, 1986) and their skill at perceiving or reading another person's expressions of emotion (Hall, 1984).

Avoiding Cultural Bias   A major concern for clinical psychologists is how to avoid cultural bias in diagnosing mental disorders. Behavior that is considered abnormal in one culture may be considered normal in others. A woman tells a

Random sample
Sample in which each potential participant has an equal chance of being selected.

Representative sample
Sample carefully chosen so that the characteristics of the participants correspond closely to the characteristics of the larger population.

HIGHLIGHTS

Internet Users: A Flawed Study?

"Sad, Lonely World Discovered in Cyberspace"

"Isolation Increases with Internet Use"

"Online and Bummed Out"

What's behind these headlines that appeared in various publications during the fall of 1998? If you had read the stories, you would have learned that a Carnegie Mellon University study (Kraut et al., 1998) showed that—as these publications phrased it—"using the Internet can cause isolation, loneliness, and depression"; "the Internet is actually bad for some people's psychological well-being"; and "greater use of the Internet leads to shrinking social support and happiness."

As a critical thinker, you would raise a number of questions about these headlines. Who was studied? How did the researchers determine Internet use? How did they measure such things as isolation, loneliness, depression, social support, and happiness? Did the researchers actually conduct a genuine experiment, manipulating the independent variable of Internet use and observing its effect on the dependent variables, or did they use some other, less powerful research design? If the latter, how do they know that Internet use caused any changes they might have observed?

These are all excellent questions, and the answers to them should cause you to be far more cautious than the headline writers about what the research actually showed. To begin with, the researchers studied 256 people from only 93 families in Pittsburgh, and 20 of the families and 87 of the people dropped out before the study was completed. The families were selected either because they had teenagers enrolled in high school journalism classes or because an adult

was on the board of directors of a community development organization. Households with pre-existing Internet connections were excluded. Thus, for most of the households, this was their first experience with a home computer. Would you consider this a representative sample of the population? Are you confident that the results from this sample can be generalized as broadly as the mass media did? Is it possible that the Internet users were already unusually lonely or isolated or depressed? If so, how might Internet use affect these individuals?

The most that could be said is that heavier users of the Internet showed very slight declines in some (but not all) aspects of social involvement

---

Going further, the researchers actually tracked Internet usage through software on the computer. To measure social involvement and psychological well-being, however, they relied entirely on *self-report measures;* that is, the participants themselves supplied all the relevant data. The participants were asked to estimate the amount of time they spent communicating with other family members as well as the number of people they socialized with, talked to, or visited during an average month. In addition, they filled out questionnaires on social support, loneliness, stress, and depression in their lives. Does this reliance on self-reports cause you to be cautious about the results of the

research? How do we know whether these reports were accurate? For example, did loneliness actually increase as a result of Internet use, or did people simply become more willing to *say* that they were lonely as time went on? Did actual depression increase, or did people's *reports* of being depressed increase? Does Internet usage "cause isolation, loneliness, and depression," or does it cause people to *say* that they are more "isolated, lonely, and depressed"?

If you relied solely on the headlines, you might conclude that the study found dramatic differences between Internet users and nonusers. In fact, the changes in the dependent variable were *not* very large. The most that could be said is that heavier users of the Internet showed very slight declines in some (but not all) aspects of social involvement and only slight increases in self-reported feelings of loneliness and depression.

Finally, you might ask whether anything happened during the period from March 1995 to March 1997 that might have increased Internet use and also caused people to report more loneliness, isolation, and depression. For example, some of the participants were adolescents. Is it possible that they made greater use of the Internet and also withdrew somewhat from their families simply as part of growing up? In other words, could another variable have caused *both* greater Internet use and increased social withdrawal? We don't know the answer to this question, but it should be explored.

These are the kinds of questions you should ask yourself when you read accounts of psychological research in the mass media. And in fairness, they are among the questions the researchers themselves raised in their article.

psychologist that she was up all night caring for her second baby by her spirit husband. (her children are grown, and there is no baby in her home.) Is this woman hallucinating? If she were American, or French, or Japanese, a psychologist would conclude she was. In the Saora tribe of India, however, people take for granted that some women are wooed, wed, and impregnated by supernatural lovers (Elwin, 1955). Suckled at night, the children are never seen. In her own culture this woman may be no more "mentally ill" than we are in our culture for believing that germs, which we never see, cause disease.

The most recent edition of the American Psychiatric Association's *Diagnostic and Statistical Manual of Mental Disorders*, the DSM-IV, addresses the issue of cultural bias. A "Glossary of Culture-Bound Syndromes" identifies behavior that is considered normal in other cultural contexts, such as "ghost sickness" in many Native American tribes and "the evil eye" in Mediterranean cultures. The diagnosis of schizophrenia includes a warning that "in some cultures, visual or auditory hallucinations with a religious content may be a normal part of religious experience (e.g., seeing the Virgin Mary or hearing God's voice)" (American Psychiatric Association, 1994, p. 847) and should not automatically be treated as symptoms.

REVIEW QUESTIONS

1. A method of research known as _____ allows psychologists to study behavior as it occurs in real-life settings.

2. Psychologists use _____ research to examine relationships between two or more variables without manipulating any variable.

3. The experimental method is associated with all of the following except
   a. hypotheses.
   b. variables.
   c. experimenter bias.
   d. subjects or participants.

4. "Difficulty generalizing from observations is a major shortcoming of the case study method." True or false.

5. The method of research best suited to explaining behavior is _____ research.

6. The _____ variable in an experiment is manipulated to see how it affects a second variable; the _____ variable is the one observed for any possible effects.

7. To ensure that the results of a particular study apply to a larger population, researchers use _____ or _____ samples.

Answers: 1. naturalistic observation. 2. correlational. 3. c. 4. T. 5. experimental. 6. independent, dependent. 7. random, representative.

Ethics and Psychology

Are there ethical guidelines for conducting psychological research?

Almost all psychological research involves people—often college students—or live animals. What responsibilities do psychologists have toward their human and nonhuman animal research subjects?

Ethics in Research on Humans

What ethical issues are central to studies involving human participants?

If the school you attend has a research facility, it is likely that you will have a chance to become a participant in an experiment in your psychology department. You will probably be offered a small sum of money or class credit to participate.

But you may not learn the true purpose of the experiment until after it's over. Is this deception necessary to the success of psychology experiments? And what if the experiment causes you discomfort? Before answering, consider the ethical debate that flared up in 1963 when Stanley Milgram published the results of several experiments he had conducted.

Milgram hired people to participate in what he said was a learning experiment. When a participant arrived at the laboratory, he was met by a stern-faced researcher in a lab coat; another man in street clothes was sitting in the waiting room. The researcher explained that he was studying the effects of punishment on learning. When the two men drew slips out of the hat, the participant's slip said "teacher." The teacher watched as the "learner" was strapped into a chair and an electrode attached to his wrist. Then the teacher was taken into an adjacent room and seated at an impressive looking "shock generator" with switches from 15 to 450 volts, labeled "Slight Shock," "Very Strong Shock" up to "Danger: Severe Shock" and finally "XXX." The teacher's job was to read a list of paired words, which the learner would attempt to memorize and repeat. The teacher was instructed to deliver a shock whenever the learner gave a wrong answer and to increase the intensity of the shock each time the learner made a mistake. At 90 volts the learner began to grunt; at 120 volts he shouted, "Hey, this really hurts!"; at 150 volts he demanded to be released; at 270 volts his protests became screams of agony. Beyond 330 volts, the learner appeared to pass out. If the teacher became concerned and asked if he could stop, the experimenter politely but firmly replied that he was expected to continue, that this experiment was being conducted in the interests of science.

In reality, Milgram was studying obedience, not learning. He wanted to find out whether ordinary people would obey orders to cause another person pain. As part of his research, Milgram (1974) described the experiment to 110 psychiatrists, college students, and middle-class adults and asked them at what point they thought participants would stop. Members of all three groups guessed that most people would refuse to continue beyond 130 volts, and no one would go beyond 300 volts. The psychiatrists estimated that only one in a thousand people would continue to the XXX shock panel. Astonishingly, 65 percent of Milgram's participants administered the highest level of shock, even though many worried aloud that the shocks might be causing the learners serious damage.

To find out what he wanted to know, Milgram had to deceive his participants. The stated purpose of the experiment—to test learning—was a lie. The "learners" were Milgram's accomplices, who had been trained to act as though they were being hurt; the machines were fake; and the learners received no shocks at all (Milgram, 1963). But, critics argued, the "teachers"—the real subjects of the study—were hurt. Most not only voiced concern, but they showed clear signs of stress: They sweated, bit their lips, trembled, stuttered, or in a few cases broke into uncontrollable nervous laughter. Critics also worried about the effect of the experiment on the participants' self-esteem. How would you like to be compared with the people who ran the death camps in Nazi Germany (*60 Minutes*, 1979)?

Although the design of this experiment was not typical of the vast majority of psychological experiments, it sparked such a public uproar that the American Psychological Association (APA) reassessed its ethical guidelines, first published in 1953 (APA, 1953). A new code of ethics on psychological experimentation was approved. The code is assessed each year and periodically revised to ensure that it adequately protects participants in research studies. In addition to outlining the ethical principles guiding research and teaching, the code spells out a set of ethical standards for psychologists who offer therapy and other professional services, such as psychological testing.

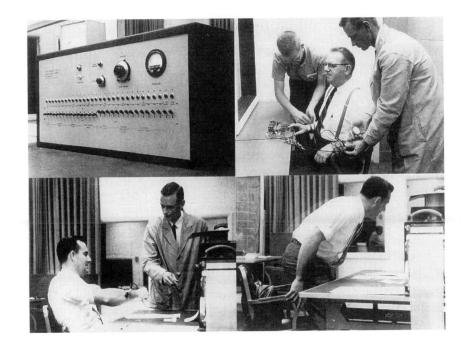

Stanley Milgram's Obedience Experiment. (A) The shock generator used in the experiment. (B) With electrodes attached to his wrists, the learner provides answers by pressing switches that light up on an answer box. (C) The subject administers a shock to the learner. (D) The subject breaks off the experiment. Milgram's study yielded interesting results, but it also raised serious questions about the ethics of such experimentation.

The APA code of ethics requires that researchers obtain informed consent from participants and stipulates that:

- Participants must be informed of the nature of research in clearly understandable language.
- Informed consent must be documented.
- Risks, possible adverse effects, and limitations on confidentiality must be spelled out in advance.
- If participation is a condition of course credit, equitable alternative activities must be offered.
- Participants cannot be deceived about aspects of the research that would affect their willingness to participate, such as risks or unpleasant emotional experiences.
- Deception about the goals of the research can be used only when absolutely necessary to the integrity of the research.

In addition, psychological researchers are required to follow the government's Code of Federal Regulations, which includes an extensive set of regulations concerning the protection of human participants in all kinds of research. Failure to abide by these federal regulations may result in the termination of federal funding for the researcher and penalties for the research institution.

Despite these formal ethical and legal guidelines, controversy still rages about the ethics of psychological research on humans. Some people contend that research procedures should never be emotionally or physically distressing (Baumrind, 1985). Others assert that ethical guidelines that are too strict may undermine the scientific value of research or cripple future research (Gergen, 1973; Sears, 1994). Still others maintain that psychology, as a science, should base its ethical code on documented evidence about the effects of research procedures on participants, not on conjecture about what is "probably" a good way to conduct research (Holmes, 1976b; Trice, 1986). Still another view is that the explanations necessary to produce informed consent may foster a better understanding of the goals and methods of research (Blanck et al., 1992).

Ethics in Research on Nonhuman Animals

What objections have been raised in regard to research on animal subjects?

In recent years questions have been raised about the ethics of using nonhuman animals in psychological research (Herzog, 1995; Plous, 1996; Rowan & Shapiro, 1996; Shapiro, 1991).

Psychologists study animal behavior in order to shed light on human behavior. Crowding mice into small cages, for example, has yielded valuable insights into the effects of overcrowding on humans. Animals are used in experiments in which it would be clearly unethical to use human participants—for instance, studies involving brain lesions (requiring cutting into the brain) or electric stimulation of parts of the brain. In fact, much of what we know about sensation, perception, drugs, emotional attachment, and the neural basis of behavior is derived from animal research (Domjan & Purdy, 1995). Yet animal protectionists and others question whether it is ethical to use nonhuman animals, which cannot give their consent to serve as subjects, in psychological research.

At the heart of this debate is the pain and suffering that some experiments can cause animals. A number of animal rights groups, including Psychologists for the Ethical Treatment of Animals (PsyETA), are urging legislators to place stricter limits on experimentation with animals on the grounds that it is inhumane (Shapiro, 1991). Their opponents contend that the goals of scientific research—in essence, to reduce or eliminate human suffering—justify the means, even though they agree that animals should be made to suffer as little as possible (Gallistel, 1981; Novak, 1991). They argue that procedures now in place, including the use of anesthesia in many experiments, already minimize animal suffering.

What is the public's attitude toward the use of animals in research? Not surprisingly, vegetarians oppose animal research more strongly than do people who eat meat. People who are highly skeptical toward science are also more likely to oppose animal research than are people who have great faith in science (Skrzycki, 1995). In addition, females tend to oppose animal research more than males do (Broida et al., 1993). How do psychologists themselves feel about this issue? Results from a national survey showed that the majority of psychologists support animal studies involving observation and confinement but generally disapprove of animal studies involving pain or death (Plous, 1996).

The APA has addressed this issue in its ethical guidelines, noting that psychologists using animals in research must ensure "appropriate consideration of [the animal's] comfort, health, and humane treatment." Under these guidelines, animals may not be subjected to "pain, stress, or privation" when an alternative procedure is available (APA, 1992). Significantly, the National Institute of Health (NIH), which opposes animal protectionists' views and funds about 40 percent of biomedical research in the United States, has instituted more stringent policies governing animal research. A project cannot receive NIH funding unless it has been sanctioned by an animal-research committee. This committee must include someone not affiliated with the institution conducting the research, as well as the research institutions' attending veterinarian and a scientist experienced in laboratory animal medicine. Nevertheless, opponents still argue that the only ethical research on nonhuman animals is naturalistic observation, such as Jane Goodall's ongoing study of the chimpanzees at Gombe Stream (1986) or Roger Fout's study of communication among chimpanzees who have learned sign language (Fouts, Fouts, & Schoenfeld, 1974).

REVIEW QUESTIONS

1. "Controversy over ethical standards in psychology has almost disappeared." True or false.
2. "The APA code of ethics used today is unchanged since 1953." True or false."
3. "Ethical questions in psychological research apply only to laboratory experiments." True or false.
4. "Getting the informed consent of participants in studies is central to the ethics of doing research on humans." True or false.
5. "Researchers who fail to follow the federal code of regulations are subject to penalties." True or false.
6. "Psychologists are much less concerned about ethical guidelines pertaining to animal research." True or false.

Answers: 1. F. 2. F. 3. F. 4. T. 5. T. 6. F.

Careers in Psychology

What can you do with a background in psychology?

Some readers may be studying psychology out of general interest; others may be considering careers in psychology. What kinds of careers are open to psychology graduates? People holding bachelor's degrees in psychology may find jobs assisting psychologists in mental-health centers, vocational rehabilitation, and correctional centers. They may also take positions as research assistants, teach psychology in high school, or land jobs as trainees in government or business.

Community college graduates with associates degrees in psychology are well qualified for paraprofessional positions in state hospitals, mental health centers, and other human service settings. Job responsibilities may include screening and evaluating new patients, record keeping, and assisting in consultation sessions.

Many careers outside psychology draw on a person's knowledge of psychology without requiring postgraduate study. For example, personnel administrators deal with employee relations; vocational rehabilitation counselors help people with disabilities find employment; directors of volunteer services recruit and train volunteers; probation officers work with parolees; and supervisors of day care centers oversee the care of preschool children of working parents. Indeed, employers in areas such as business and finance seek out psychology majors because of their knowledge of the principles of human behavior and their skills in experimental design and data collection and analysis.

Academic and Applied Psychology

What careers are open to those with advanced degrees in psychology?

For those who pursue advanced degrees in psychology—a master's degree or a doctorate—career opportunities span a wide range. Many doctoral psychologists join the faculties of colleges and universities. Others work in applied settings such as school, health, industrial, commercial, and educational psychology. Nearly half of doctoral psychologists are clinicians or counselors who treat people experiencing mental, emotional, or adaptational problems. Master's graduates in psychology often work as researchers, collecting and analyzing data, at universities, in government, or for private companies. Others work in health, industry,

About one-third of psychologists work in colleges and universities. Here, Al Maisto, co-author of this text, talks with a student at the University of North Carolina, Charlotte.

and education. APA standards require that master's graduates who work in clinical, counseling, school, or testing and measurement settings be supervised by a doctoral-level psychologist.

Clinical Settings

What specific opportunities exist in the field of mental health?

Many students who major in psychology want to become therapists. For these students, there are five main career paths. A *psychiatrist* is a medical doctor who, in addition to 4 years of medical training, has completed 3 years of residency training in psychiatry, most of which is spent in supervised clinical practice. Psychiatrists specialize in the diagnosis and treatment of abnormal behavior. They are the only mental health professionals who are licensed to prescribe medications, in addition to providing psychotherapy. A *psychoanalyst* is a psychiatrist (or psychologist) who has received additional specialized training in psychoanalytic theory and practice, usually at a psychoanalytic institute that requires him or her to undergo psychoanalysis before practicing.

Clinical psychologists assess and treat mental, emotional, and behavioral disorders, ranging from short-term crises to chronic disorders such as schizophrenia. They hold advanced degrees in psychology (a Ph.D. or Psy.D.)—the result of a 4- to 6-year graduate program, plus a 1-year internship in psychological assessment and psychotherapy and at least one more year of supervised practice. *Counseling psychologists* help people to cope with situational problems, such as adjusting to college, choosing a vocation, resolving marital problems, or dealing with the death of a loved one.

Finally, *social workers* may also offer treatment for psychological problems. Typically they have a master's degree (M.S.W.) or doctorate (D.S.W.). Social workers often work under psychiatrists or clinical psychologists, though in some states they may be licensed to practice independently.

A free booklet, *Psychology: Scientific Problem Solvers, Careers for the Twenty-first Century*, is available by calling the Order Department of the American Psychological Association at 1-800-374-2721. The APA also maintains a Web site, **http://www.apa.org/,** that provides up-to-date information about employment opportunities, as well as a vast array of related material of interest to psychology students.

REVIEW QUESTIONS

1. "Careers in psychology are largely limited to people with Ph.D.s." True or false.
2. "Almost all the careers related to a knowledge of psychology are in the mental health field." True or false.
3. Which of the following are also medical doctors?
   _____ a. psychiatrists
   _____ b. some psychoanalysts
   _____ c. clinical psychologists
4. Psychologists can be found working in which of the following settings?
   _____ a. research laboratories
   _____ b. schools
   _____ c. government
   _____ d. corporations and other businesses
   _____ e. hospitals and clinics

Answers: 1. F. 2. F. 3. a and b. 4. a, b, c, d, and e.

KEY TERMS

CHAPTER REVIEW

☐ What are the major subdivisions of psychology?

Psychology is the science of behavior and mental processes, which makes it an extremely broad discipline. It seeks to both describe and explain every aspect of human thought, feelings, perceptions, and actions. Psychology has many major subdivisions. *Developmental psychology* is concerned with processes of growth and change over the life course, from the prenatal period through old age and death. *Physiological psychology* focuses on the body's neural and chemical systems, studying how these affect thought and behavior. *Experimental psychology* investigates basic psychological processes, such as learning, memory, sensation, perception, cognition, motivation, and emotion. *Personality psychology* looks at differences among people in traits such as anxiety, aggressiveness, and self-esteem. *Clinical and counseling psychology* specializes in diagnosing and treating psychological disorders, while *social psychology* focuses on how people influence one another's thoughts and actions. Finally, *industrial and organizational psychology* studies problems in the workplace and other kinds of organizations.

☐ What are the principal issues common to many subfields of psychology?

A number of fundamental questions cut across the various subfields of psychology, unifying them with similar themes. Five fundamental questions are: (1) Is behavior caused more by inner traits or by external situations? (2) How do genes and experiences interact to influence people? (3) How much do we stay the same as we develop and how much do we change? (4) In what ways do people differ in how they think and act? (5) What is the relationship between our internal experiences and our biological processes?

☐ What does psychology have in common with other sciences?

Psychology is a science because it relies on the **scientific method** to find answers to questions. This method involves careful observation and collection of data, efforts to explain observations by developing **theories** about relationships and causes, and the systematic testing of **hypotheses** (or predictions) to rule out theories that aren't valid.

☐ What does it mean to say that psychology has a long past but a short history?

As a subject of interest to people, psychology has a long past because humans have wondered about behavior and mental processes since ancient times. As a scientific discipline, however, psychology has a short history, dating back only to the late-nineteenth century.

☐ How did Wundt and Titchener apply scientific procedures to psychology?

Two leading structuralists in psychology were Wilhelm Wundt and Edward Titchener. Wundt established the first psychology laboratory in 1879 at the University of Leipzig in Germany. His use of experiment and measurement marked the beginnings of psychology as a science. Wundt and one of his students, Edward Titchener, established a perspective called **structuralism,** which was based on the belief that psychology's role was to identify the basic elements of experience and how they combine.

☐ What was the focus of James's functionalist theory?

The American psychologist William James criticized structuralism, arguing that sensations cannot be separated from the mental associations that allow us to benefit from past experiences. Our rich storehouse of ideas and memories is what enables us to function in our environment, James believed. His perspective became known as **functionalism.**

What major contributions did Freud make to psychology?

The theories of Sigmund Freud added another new dimension to psychology: the idea that much of our behavior is governed by unconscious conflicts, motives, and desires. Freud's work gave rise to **psychodynamic theories.**

How did Watson approach the study of psychology?

John B. Watson, a spokesman for the school of thought called **behaviorism,** argued that psychology should concern itself only with observable, measurable behavior. Watson based much of his work on the conditioning experiments of Ivan Pavlov.

How did Skinner expand behaviorism?

B. F. Skinner's beliefs were similar to Watson's, but he added the concept of reinforcement or rewards. In this way, he made the learner an active agent in the learning process. Skinner's views dominated American psychology into the 1960s.

On what did the Gestalt psychologists focus?

According to **Gestalt psychology,** perception depends on the human tendency to see patterns, to distinguish objects from their backgrounds, and to complete pictures from a few clues. In this emphasis on wholeness the Gestalt school radically differed from structuralism.

How might existential psychology help modern individuals to feel less alienated? What aspects of life do humanistic psychologists stress?

Existential psychology is a school of thought that attributes psychological problems to feelings of alienation in modern life. The goal of existentialist psychology is to guide people toward an inner identity and the freedom to exercise their personal will. **Humanistic psychology** is another perspective, one that emphasizes the goal of reaching one's fullest potential.

What is the "cognitive revolution" in psychology?

Cognitive psychology is the study of mental processes in the broadest sense, focusing on how people perceive, interpret, store, and retrieve information. Unlike behaviorists, cognitive psychologists believe that mental processes can and should be studied scientifically. This view has dramatically changed American psychology from its previous behaviorist focus.

What is evolutionary psychology?

Evolutionary psychology focuses on the functions and adaptive values of various human behaviors, trying to understand how they have evolved. In this way it seeks to add a new dimension to psychological research.

Does any single perspective dominate contemporary psychology?

Most contemporary psychologists do not adhere to just one school of thought. They believe that different theories can often complement one another and together enrich our understanding of human behavior.

What do psychologists mean by "The Decade of Behavior"?

The APA has declared the beginning of the new millennium "The Decade of Behavior: 2000–2010." During these years the APA will work with scientific organizations and government agencies to improve health, safety, and education throughout society by applying psychology and other behavioral sciences.

What problems did early women psychologists face?

Although psychology has profited from the contributions of women from its beginnings, women often faced discrimination: Some colleges and universities did not grant degrees to women, professional journals were often reluctant to publish their work, and teaching positions were often closed to them.

Why should students learn about human diversity?

A rich diversity of behavior and thought exists in the human species, among individuals and groups. A knowledge of this diversity can help reduce the tensions that arise when people misunderstand one another. It can also help us to define what humans have in common.

How are psychologists trying to explain gender differences?

One area of research on diversity involves differences in thought and behavior between the two sexes or **genders.** Popular beliefs regarding these differences are called *gender stereotypes.* Psychologists are trying to determine the causes of gender differences—both the contributions of heredity to them and those of culturally learned *gender roles.*

How does culture contribute to human diversity?

The intangible aspects of **culture**—the beliefs, values, traditions, and norms of behavior that a particular people share—make an important contribution to human diversity. In a society as large and diversified as ours, there are also many subcultural groups with their own subcultural identities.

☐ Do race and ethnicity affect behavior?

Race and ethnicity are two traditional dimensions of diversity in humans. Because it is so difficult to define **race,** most psychologists have abandoned the term as a scientific concept. **Ethnicity** and *ethnic identity*, however, remain meaningful. They involve a shared cultural heritage based on common ancestry, a shared heritage that can affect norms of behavior.

☐ In what ways has psychology become sensitive to issues involving human diversity?

In recent years psychologists have taken steps to ensure that psychology reflects the richness and diversity of the human population. The American Psychological Association (APA), for example, has established a number of divisions, including the *Psychology of Women*, which embraces **feminist theory;** the *Society for the Psychological Study of Lesbian and Gay Issues*, which focuses its research on the diversity of human sexual orientations; and the *Society for the Psychological Study of Ethnic Minority Issues*.

☐ What are some of the research methods psychologists use in their work?

Psychologists use a variety of methods to study behavior and mental processes. These include naturalistic observation, case studies, surveys, correlational research, and experiments. Each method has its own advantages and limitations.

☐ How would you go about studying behavior in a natural setting?

Psychologists use **naturalistic observation** to study behavior in natural settings. Because there is minimal interference from the researcher, the behavior observed is likely to be more accurate, spontaneous, and varied than behavior studied in a laboratory. Researchers using this method must be careful to avoid **observer bias.**

☐ When is it useful to conduct a case study?

Researchers conduct a **case study** to investigate the behavior of one person or a few persons in depth. This method can yield a great deal of detailed, descriptive information that is useful for forming hypotheses.

☐ What are some of the advantages of survey research?

Survey research generates a large amount of data quickly and inexpensively by asking a standard set of questions of a large number of people. Great care must be taken, however, in how the questions are worded.

☐ What is correlational research?

Correlational research investigates the relation, or correlation, between two or more variables. Correlational research is useful for clarifying relationships between preexisting variables that can't be examined by other means.

☐ When is an experiment called for?

An **experiment** is called for when a researcher wants to draw conclusions about cause and effect. In an experiment, the impact of one factor can be studied while all other factors are held constant. The factor whose effects are being studied is called the **independent variable** because the researcher is free to manipulate it at will. The factor on which there is apt to be an impact is called the **dependent variable.** Usually an experiment includes both an **experimental group** of **subjects** or **participants** and a **control group** for comparison purposes. Often a neutral person records data and scores results, so **experimenter bias** doesn't creep in.

☐ What are the benefits of multimethod research?

Because each research method has benefits as well as limitations, many psychologists use multiple methods to study a single problem. Together they can give much fuller answers to questions.

☐ Why is proper sampling so critical?

Regardless of the particular research method used, psychologists almost always study a small *sample* of subjects and then generalize their results to larger populations. Proper sampling is critical to ensure that results have broader application. **Random samples,** in which subjects are chosen randomly, and **representative samples,** in which subjects are chosen to reflect the general characteristics of the population as a whole, are two ways of doing this.

☐ Can we generalize about research findings from one group to another?

Because of differences among people based on age, sex, ethnic background, culture, and so forth, findings from studies that use white, male, American college students as participants cannot always be generalized to other groups. In addition, the gender, race, and ethnic background of a psychologist can have a biasing impact on the outcome of research.

☐ Are there ethical guidelines for conducting psychological research?

The American Psychological Association (APA) has a code of ethics for conducting research involving human participants or animal subjects. Still, controversy over ethical guidelines continues, with some critics thinking they are too strict and impede psychological research, and others thinking they are not strict enough to protect subjects from harm.

☐ What ethical issues are central to studies involving human participants?

A key part of the APA code regarding research on humans is the requirement that researchers obtain informed consent from participants in their studies. Participants must be told in advance about the nature of the research and the possible risks involved. People should not feel pressured to participate if they do not want to.

◻ What objections have been raised in regard to research on animal subjects?

Although much of what we know about certain areas of psychology has come from animal research, the practice of experimenting on animals has strong opponents because of the pain and suffering that is sometimes involved. APA and federal guidelines govern the humane treatment of laboratory animals, but animal rights advocates argue that the only ethical research on animals is naturalistic observation.

◻ What can you do with a background in psychology?

Psychology is one of the most popular majors in colleges and universities. A background in it is useful in a wide number of fields because so many jobs involve a basic understanding of people.

◻ What careers are open to those with advanced degrees in psychology?

Careers for those with advanced degrees in psychology include teaching, research, jobs in government and private business, and a number of occupations in the mental health field.

◻ What specific opportunities exist in the field of mental health?

Opportunities in the mental health field depend on one's degree of training. They include the occupations of psychiatrist which requires medical training; the job of clinical psychologist, which involves getting a doctoral degree; and the jobs of counseling psychologist and social worker.

CRITICAL THINKING AND APPLICATIONS

1. What do we mean when we say that psychology is a science?
2. Choose an aspect of human behavior such as kindness, intelligence, or aggressiveness and describe how a contemporary psychologist might use multiple perspectives to understand it.
3. You notice that some students in your psychology class take many more notes than others, and you wonder whether the amount of note taking ultimately affects grades. What research methods might you use to find out? What would each of these methods tell you about the issue? What are the drawbacks of each? Be specific about the procedures you suggest.
4. How do you feel about animal research and experimentation in psychology? When, if ever, do you think that animal research is justified? Do you approve of the current regulations concerning it? Why or why not?

On the Web...

Visit these online resources at our Companion Website www.prenhall.com/morris

The Psychology Place

Learning Activity
1. Caveat Emptor: Evaluating Knowledge Claims, p. 8
2. Analyzing Arguments: Deciding What to Believe, p. 9
3. Critical Thinking: I Know It's a Good Thing, But What Is It?, p. 10

Op-Ed Essays
4. What Questions are on Psychologists' Minds Today?, p. 17
5. How Did Leading Psychologists Find Psychology?, p. 17

Research News
6. Animal Rights Activists: Changing Views on Animal Research, p. 38

Games
1. Match the Psychologists to their Fields, p. 4
2. Ranch of Gender Diversity, p. 21
3. Research Methods: Advantages and Disadvantages, p. 26

Web Links
1. **http://apa.org/about/division.html**, p. 5
   The American Psychological Association's links to all of its divisions.
2. **http://server.bmod.athabascau.ca/html/aupr/history.htm**, p. 12
   The Psychology Center's History of Psychology page has many websites to choose from both about broad topics and those specific to the history of psychology.
3. **http://www.geocities.com/Athens/Delphi/6061/en_linha.htm**, p. 12
   History of Psychology Timeline from early civilization to the present.
4. **http://www.yorku.ca/dept/psych/classics**, p. 12
   Compilations of important documents pertaining to the history of psychology.
5. **http://www.columbia.edu/barnard/psych/b_museum.html**, p. 13
   Consists of links to historical psychological documents, photographs, and apparatus.
6. **http://www.slu.edu/colleges/AS/PSY/510Guide.html**, p. 13
   Complete and detailed resource guide to the history of psychology.
7. **http://trochim.human.cornell.edu/ck/kbhome.htm**, p. 26
   The Knowledge Base: An Online Research Methods Textbook
   Online textbook about how to conduct research.
8. **http://www.apa.org/ethics/code.html**, p. 35
   American Psychological Association's Ethical Principles of Psychologists and Code of Conduct.
9. **http://www.psych.bangor.ac.uk/deptpsych/Ethics/HumanResearch.html**, p. 35
   Human Subjects/Participants and Research Ethics, including links to policy documents and position papers, and ethics committees and Institutional Review Boards.
10. **http://www.apa.org/students/brochure/contents.html**, p. 39
    Job Outlook for the Next Two Decades.

Explore these topics on the Mind Matters CD-ROM

Mind Matters
1. The Science of Psychology, p. 9
2. Psychology's Roots, p. 11
3. Recent Trends in Psychology, p. 17

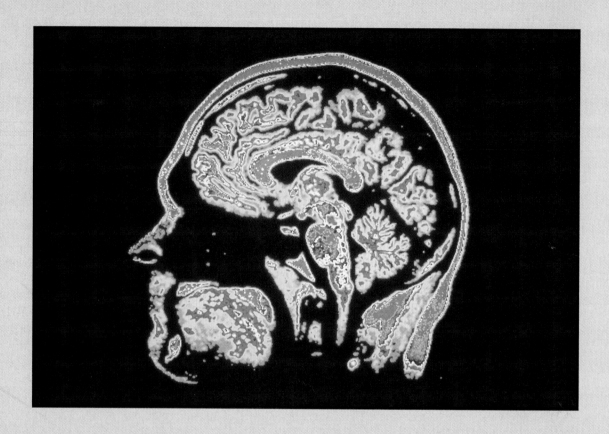

THE BIOLOGICAL BASIS OF BEHAVIOR

OVERVIEW

WHEN ALEX WAS BORN, THE LEFT SIDE OF HIS BRAIN, WHICH CONTROLS speech, was smothered by a tangle of abnormal blood vessels that left him mute, half-blind, semi-paralyzed, and prone to epileptic seizures. As Alex got older, the seizures became increasingly frequent and severe. Unable to control his epilepsy with medication, Alex's doctors recommended surgery to remove the entire left side of his brain. They were reasonably sure that this procedure would reduce Alex's seizures, but they warned his parents not to expect much other improvement. He was long past the age when a mute child can learn to talk.

The operation was a success; the seizures stopped. Then, 10 months later, Alex stunned everyone by beginning to speak, first in single words and then in complete sentences. At age 11 he still pronounced some words incorrectly, as if he had a foreign accent; by age 16 he was fluent. To date, more than 50 epileptic children have undergone successful "hemispherectomies" (removal of the left or right half of the brain). All are expected to be able to lead normal lives.

Because the brain is the master control center of everything we say and do, you might think that removing half of a child's brain would leave him or her severely disabled. But Alex and others have shown that just the opposite is true. Children emerge from the operation with their memory, personality, and sense of humor intact. Like Alex, some show dramatic improvement in speech, coordination, and other areas. How can this be?

One reason is that the human brain—the product of millions of years of evolution—is an extremely complex organ. Our brains contain billions of cells, arranged in countless overlapping pathways and networks, with many backup systems—far more "mental equipment" than we need. In addition, the two hemispheres of the brain are similar though not identical, like our right and left hands. Normally, the two work together. But if the left hemisphere is removed, the right hemisphere takes over most of its functions. Alex's sudden ability to speak suggests that during the years he was mute, the right side of his brain stored the language he heard around him. When the confused signals from his damaged left brain were eliminated, the backup store of language in his right hemisphere began to function.

Moreover, the human brain demonstrates extraordinary *plasticity*, or ability to adapt to new environmental conditions. While the brain may be the command center of our bodies, it also responds to feedback from the senses and surrounding environment, and it changes as a result. One reason why children like Alex improve after a hemispherectomy is that their environment changes when their seizures stop and they no longer need antiseizure medications (powerful sedatives that make children groggy). Before the operation, the internal environment of their bodies is chaotic, and their ability to respond to the external environment is dulled. After the operation, their internal environment is calmer, and their awareness of the external environment is enhanced. All of the organs of our body—and all of our behaviors—depend on intricate feedback-and-control patterns. We live surrounded by objects and events, and our biological systems are geared to make adjustments that keep us in tune with our surroundings.

This chapter focuses on **psychobiology**, the ways in which biological processes affect our behavior. We explore the two major systems that integrate and coordinate our behavior, keeping us in constant touch with what is going on "out there." One is the nervous system, of which the brain is a part. The other is the endocrine system, made up of glands that secrete chemicals called hormones into the blood. We begin by putting under a microscope the nervous system's smallest unit: the nerve cell, or **neuron**.

Neurons: The Nervous System's Messengers

How is a neuron different from other types of cells?

There may be as many as 100 billion neurons in the brain of an average person, and there are many more in other parts of the body, including the spinal cord and the complex network of nerves that radiates from it. Like most other cells, a neuron has a cell body, which contains a nucleus where metabolism takes place. Unlike other cells, however, a neuron has tiny fibers extending from it. These fibers enable it to receive messages from surrounding cells and pass them on to other cells. Figure 2–1 contains a photograph of a neuron, as well as a drawing of its parts.

The many short fibers that branch out from a neuron's cell body are called **dendrites.** Dendrites pick up messages coming in from surrounding areas and carry them to the cell body. Also extending from the cell body is a single long fiber called an **axon.** The axon is very thin and is usually much longer than the dendrites. In adults the axons that run from the brain to the base of the spinal cord or from the spinal cord to the tip of the thumb may be as long as 3 feet. Most axons, however, are only 1 to 2 inches long. A group of axons bundled together like parallel wires in an electrical cable is called a **nerve** or **tract.** An axon carries outgoing messages from the cell body and either relays them to neighboring neurons or directs a muscle or gland to act. Although there is just one axon per neuron, near its end the axon splits into many terminal branches. Because there may be hundreds or thousands of dendrites on a single neuron, as well as a great many axon terminal branches, one neuron can be in touch with a large number of other cells.

Look at the neuron in Figure 2–1. Its axon is surrounded by a white fatty covering called a **myelin sheath.** Not all axons are covered by myelin sheaths, but myelinated axons are found throughout the body. The myelin sheath appears pinched at intervals, which makes the axon resemble a string of microscopic sausages. Because myelin is white, tissues made up of many myelinated axons are often referred to as "white matter," whereas tissues with many unmyelinated axons look gray and are called "gray matter." Myelin sheaths have two purposes: to help neurons act with greater efficiency, and to provide insulation for neurons.

The nervous system also contains a vast number of **glial cells,** or **glia.** (Some glial cells form the myelin sheaths.) Glial cells support neurons in a number of ways. They hold the neurons in the nervous system together (the word *glia* actually means "glue"), they remove neural waste products, and they block the passage of harmful substances from the bloodstream into the brain. Glial cells may even influence learning and memory (Roitbak, 1993). An autopsy of Albert Einstein's brain found that it contained an exceptional number of glia.

The Neural Impulse

What form does a neural message take?

A neuron's messages are partly electrical in nature. The semiliquid solutions inside and outside a neuron contain electrically charged particles called **ions.** When a neuron is resting (not being stimulated), the membrane around it keeps many positively charged ions from entering the cell's interior. As a result, there is a greater concentration of positively charged ions on the outer surface of the membrane than on the inner surface. The membrane is said to be **polarized—** that is, the electrical charge inside it is negative relative to its outside. This electrical imbalance across the neural membrane, called the **resting potential,** is illustrated in Figure 2–2A. The resting potential is like a spring that has been compressed. All that is needed to generate a neural signal is the release of the electrical tension stored in the polarized state.

When a small area on an axon's membrane is adequately stimulated by an incoming message, channels in the membrane at the stimulated area open, allowing positively charged ions to rush inside. For an instant the inside is positively charged relative to the outside—that is, the membrane becomes *de*polarized. Then the channels close, positively charged ions are pumped out of the axon, and the resting potential is restored.

GAMES
G

Psychobiology
The area of psychology that focuses on the biological foundations of behavior and mental processes.

Neuron
Individual cell that is the smallest unit of the nervous system.

Dendrites
Short fibers that branch out from the cell body and pick up incoming messages.

Axon
Single long fiber extending from the cell body; it carries outgoing messages.

Nerve or tract
Group of axons bundled together.

Myelin sheath
White fatty covering found on some axons.

Glial cells or glia
Cells that insulate and support neurons by holding them together, removing waste products, and preventing harmful substances from passing from the bloodstream into the brain.

Ions
Electrically charged particles found both inside and outside the neuron.

Polarized
The condition of a neuron when the inside is negatively charged relative to the outside; for example, when the neuron is at rest.

Resting potential
Electrical charge across a neuron membrane owing to excess positive ions concentrated on the outside and excess negative ions on the inside.

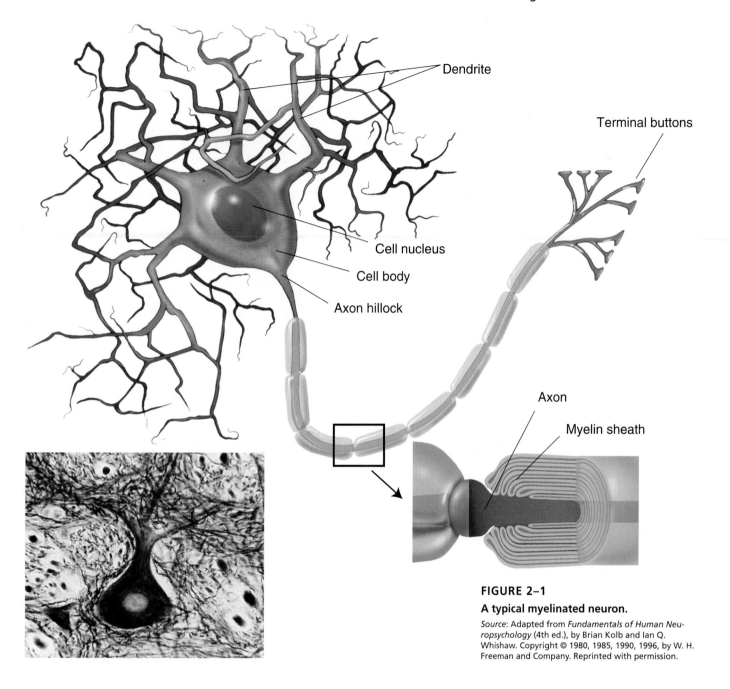

Dendrite

Terminal buttons

Cell nucleus

Cell body

Axon hillock

Axon

Myelin sheath

FIGURE 2–1

A typical myelinated neuron.

Source: Adapted from *Fundamentals of Human Neuropsychology* (4th ed.), by Brian Kolb and Ian Q. Whishaw. Copyright © 1980, 1985, 1990, 1996, by W. H. Freeman and Company. Reprinted with permission.

This depolarization and repolarization of the axon membrane does not occur at just one point. As soon as the membrane allows positively charged ions to enter the axon at one point, the next point on the membrane also opens up channels. More positively charged ions flow into the axon at the second spot, depolarizing this part of the membrane, and so on. The process is repeated along the length of the axon, creating a **neural impulse,** or **action potential,** that travels down the axon, much like a fuse burning from one end to the other (see Figure 2–2B). When this happens, we say that the neuron has "fired."

As a general rule, single impulses received from neighboring neurons do not make a neuron fire. Incoming impulses cause temporary small shifts in electrical charge in areas of the neuron that receive the impulse. These **graded potentials** are transmitted along the cell membrane and may simply fade away, leaving the membrane in its normal polarized state. If, however, the graded potentials caused by impulses from many neighboring neurons—or even from one other

Neural impulse or action potential
The firing of a nerve cell.

Graded potentials
A shift in the electrical charge in a tiny area of a neuron.

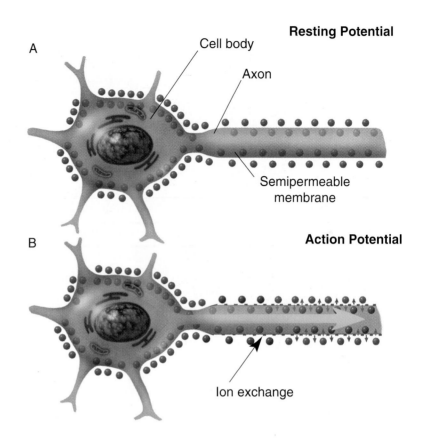

A — Resting Potential
Cell body
Axon
Semipermeable membrane

B — Action Potential
Ion exchange

FIGURE 2–2

The neural impulse—communication within the neuron. At rest (A) there is an excess of negative ions inside the neuron compared to the outside. When a point on the neural membrane is adequately stimulated by an incoming message, the membrane opens at that point, and positively charged ions flow in. (B) This process is repeated along the length of the membrane, creating the neural impulse that travels down the axon, causing the neuron to fire.

Source: Adapted from *Psychology* (2d ed.), by John G. Seamon and Douglas Kenrick. Copyright © 1994, p. 45. Reprinted by permission of Prentice Hall, Inc.

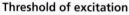

Threshold of excitation
The level that graded potentials must reach to cause a neuron to fire.

Absolute refractory period
A period after firing when a neuron will not fire again no matter how strong the incoming messages may be.

Relative refractory period
A period after firing when a neuron is returning to its normal polarized state and will fire again only if the incoming message is much stronger than usual.

All-or-none law
Principle that the action potential in a neuron does not vary in strength; the neuron either fires at full strength or it does not fire at all.

Terminal button or axon terminal
Structure at the end of an axon terminal branch.

Synaptic space or synaptic cleft
Tiny gap between the axon terminal of one neuron and the dendrites or cell body of the next neuron.

Synapse
Area composed of the terminal button of one neuron, the synaptic space, and the dendrite or cell body of the next neuron.

neuron firing repeatedly—combine to exceed a certain minimum **threshold of excitation,** the neuron will fire. Just as a light switch requires a minimum amount of pressure to be activated, an incoming message must be above the minimum threshold to make a neuron fire.

Immediately after firing, during the **absolute refractory period,** a neuron will not fire again, no matter how strong the incoming messages may be. In the **relative refractory period,** when positively charged ions are leaving the axon, the neuron will fire, but only if the incoming message is considerably stronger than is normally needed. Not until the neuron is returned to its resting state is it ready to fire again in its usual way.

Interestingly, stronger incoming signals do not cause stronger neural impulses. Neurons either fire or they do not, and every firing of a particular neuron produces an impulse of the same strength. This is called the **all-or-none law.** A neuron is likely to fire *more often,* however, when stimulated by a strong signal. Rapid neural firing communicates the message "There's a very strong stimulus out here."

The Synapse

Why is it important for psychologists to understand how synapses function?

At the end of each branch of an axon is a tiny knob called a **terminal button** or **axon terminal.** In most cases a tiny gap separates this knob and the next neuron. This tiny gap is called a **synaptic space** or **synaptic cleft.** The entire area composed of the terminal button of one neuron, the synaptic space, and the dendrite or cell body of the next neuron is called a **synapse** (see Figure 2–3).

If a neural impulse is to move on to the next neuron, it must somehow cross the synaptic space. It is tempting to imagine that the neural impulse simply leaps

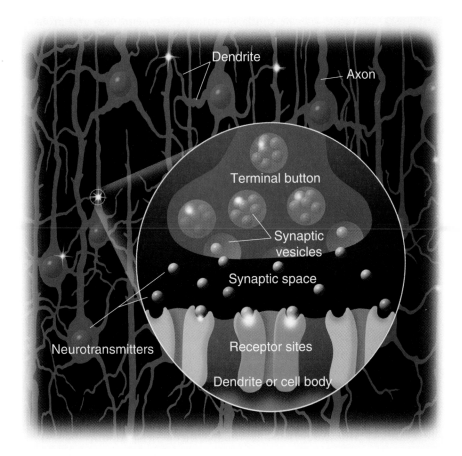

Dendrite

Axon

Terminal button

Synaptic vesicles

Synaptic space

Neurotransmitters

Receptor sites

Dendrite or cell body

FIGURE 2–3

Synaptic transmission—communication between neurons. When a neural impulse reaches the end of an axon, tiny oval sacs, called synaptic vesicles, release varying amounts of chemical substances called neurotransmitters. These substances travel across the synaptic space and affect the next neuron.

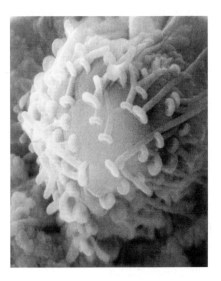

A photograph taken with a scanning electron microscope, showing the terminal buttons at the ends of axons. Inside the buttons or knobs are the vesicles that contain neurotransmitters.

across the gap like an electric spark, but in reality the transfer is made by chemicals. What happens is this: Most terminal buttons contain a number of tiny oval sacs called **synaptic vesicles** (see Figure 2–3). When a neural impulse reaches the end of an axon, it causes these vesicles to release chemicals called **neurotransmitters.** The neurotransmitters diffuse into the synaptic space, where they can affect the next neuron.

There are many different neurotransmitters, and their functions are still being investigated. Each one has matching **receptor** (or hookup) **sites** on the other side of the synaptic space. The neurotransmitter molecules fit into their corresponding receptor sites just as keys fit into locks. Some neurotransmitters "excite" the next neuron, making it more likely to fire. For example, *acetylcholine* (ACh) acts as an excitatory transmitter wherein neurons meet skeletal muscles. It also appears to play a critical role in arousal, attention, memory, and motivation (Panksepp, 1986). Alzheimer's disease, which involves loss of memory and severe language problems, is thought to be due to a reduction in ACh and a corresponding loss of cells that respond to it in certain parts of the brain.

Other neurotransmitters "inhibit" the next neuron, making it less likely to fire. *Dopamine* is one inhibitory transmitter that seems to play an important part in the severe mental disorder known as schizophrenia; in Parkinson's disease, which affects movement; and also in Tourette's syndrome. *Serotonin,* another inhibitory neurotransmitter, affects emotions, arousal, and sleep.

Synaptic vesicles
Tiny sacs in a terminal button that release chemicals into the synapse.

Neurotransmitters
Chemicals released by the synaptic vesicles that travel across the synaptic space and affect adjacent neurons.

Receptor site
A location on a receptor neuron into which a specific neurotransmitter fits like a key into a lock.

Endorphins, which are released into the brain and body during exercise, are neurotransmitters that act as natural painkillers.

Norepinephrine similarly influences wakefulness and arousal, as well as learning, memory, and mood. (See the Summary Table for a more detailed list of major neurotransmitters and their effects.)

Some neurochemicals have more widespread effects than just exciting or inhibiting certain neurons. These chemicals seem to regulate or adjust the sensitivity of large numbers of synapses, in effect "turning up" or "turning down" the activity level of whole portions of the nervous system. A good example are the *endorphins*, involved in the body's relief of pain. Endorphins appear to reduce pain by "turning down" the neurons that transmit pain messages in the brain. One endorphin was found to be 48 times more potent than morphine when injected into the brain, and 3 times more potent when injected into the bloodstream (S. H. Snyder, 1977).

Once a neurochemical has been released into the synaptic space and has performed its job, what happens to it? If it remains loose or if it continues to occupy receptors, it will affect neurons indefinitely, long after the initial signal is over. There are two ways that its action can be ended. First, some neurochemicals are broken down by other chemicals. In some cases the by-products are recycled; in other cases they are treated as wastes and removed from the body. Second, many neurochemicals are simply reabsorbed into axon terminals to be used again. In either case, the synapse is cleared up and returned to its normal state.

Because synapses are where communication between neurons takes place, scientists believe they must play a major role in the processes of learning and remembering. How neurons in the brain change in response to new experiences is an active area of research. The *Highlights* box discusses some of the intriguing findings.

SUMMARY TABLE

Major Neurotransmitters and Their Effects

Acetylcholine (ACh)	Generally excitatory	Affects arousal, attention, memory, motivation, movement. Too much: spasms, tremors. Too little: paralysis, torpor.
Dopamine	Inhibitory	Inhibits wide range of behavior and emotions, including pleasure. Implicated in schizophrenia and Parkinson's disease.
Serotonin	Inhibitory	Inhibits virtually all activities. Important for sleep onset, mood, eating behavior.
Norepinephrine	Generally excitatory	Affects arousal, wakefulness, learning, memory, mood.
Endorphins	Inhibitory	Inhibit transmission of pain messages.

New Connections for Old Neurons: Experience and Plasticity

How do the neurons of your brain change as a result of new experiences? Although it may seem strange to think that the cells in your brain are constantly changing, some changes take place every time you learn new information, adjust to new conditions or, as we saw in the beginning of this chapter, recover function following massive brain surgery. This ability of the brain to be shaped by its environment is called **plasticity** (Kolb & Whishaw, 1999).

In a classic study demonstrating brain plasticity, Rosenzweig (1984) raised young rats in either an impoverished or an enriched environment. The enriched environments contained several small objects providing a variety of opportunities for manipulation and exploration. In the impoverished environments, rats had little opportunity for either exploration or manipulation. Rosenzweig discovered that the brains of the rats raised in the enriched environments had larger neurons with more synaptic connections than those of rats reared in the impoverished environments. More recent experiments by Rosenzweig (1996) have shown that similar changes can be produced in rats of any age if they are placed in stimulating environments.

Research has also shown that experience can alter human brains. For example, one study found that when the left hand of string musicians was stimulated, a strong increase in neural activity occurred in the area of the brain associated with left-hand sensations (Elbert, Pantev, Wienbruch, Rockstroh, & Taub, 1995). Stimulating the left hands of nonmu-

> **Research has also shown that experience can alter human brains.**

sicians resulted in a comparatively weaker response. No doubt the years of practice that string musicians devote to developing precise left-hand sensitivity and movement was responsible for producing this difference. Interestingly, this effect was most pronounced for string musicians who began playing their instrument before the age of 12. In another study involving humans, psychotherapy aimed at treating patients with obsessive-compulsive behavior (see Chapter 12) produced changes in brain function (Schwartz, Stoessel, Baxter, Martin, & Phelps, 1996).

Experience can also cause changes in the strength of communication across synapses. One such change, called *long-term potentiation (LTP)*, was demonstrated in a study in which researchers used a single electrical pulse to stimulate certain neurons in the hippocampus (a brain structure involved in memory formation) and then measured the resulting current in nearby neurons (Bliss & Collingridge, 1993). Although the current measured was initially very weak, subsequent stimulation of the same pathway with a series of high-frequency pulses caused the nearby neurons to respond vigorously. Weeks later they retained this ability. This long-term effect on synaptic transmission appears to help the brain learn and store new information (Martinez, Barea-Rodriguez, & Derrick, 1998).

Research on brain plasticity has important implications for early childhood education as well as for designing programs to overcome the effects of poverty and abuse (Joseph, 1999).

Synapses and Drugs

How do drugs change behavior?

Most drugs and toxins have their effects at synapses. Some impede the release of neurotransmitters into the synaptic space. For example, the toxin produced by the microorganism that causes botulism prevents the release of ACh. The result is paralysis and even death. Drugs such as reserpine cause neurotransmitters to leak out of synaptic vesicles and to be rapidly broken down, creating a shortage of transmitters and decreased activity at the synapse. Reserpine is often prescribed to reduce blood pressure because it decreases the activity of neurons that excite the circulatory system. The powerful hallucinogen LSD is another drug that inhibits the release of a neurotransmitter—in this case serotonin. It does so by attaching to receptor sites on serotonin-releasing neurons, preventing these

Plasticity
The ability of the brain to change its structure and function in response to the environment.

neurons from firing. Some psychologists speculate that under normal waking conditions some of these neurons deter us from dreaming (N. Carlson, 1994). So perhaps when LSD inhibits or interferes with those neurons, they are no longer able to suppress dreaming, even though the user is awake, thus producing the bizarre sensations of an LSD "trip."

In contrast to toxins or drugs that *reduce* the quantity of neurotransmitters, some drugs speed up the release of neurotransmitters into synaptic spaces. For example, the poison of the black widow spider causes an outpouring of ACh. As a result, neurons leading to muscles fire repeatedly, causing spasms and tremors. Caffeine increases the release of excitatory neurotransmitters by blocking the action of adenosine, a transmitter that normally inhibits the release of these excitatory chemicals (Nehlig, Daval, & Debry, 1992). Two or three cups of coffee contain enough caffeine to block half the adenosine receptors for several hours, producing a high state of arousal. The arousal can be so intense that we say the person is suffering from "coffee nerves."

Curare and Paralysis Yet another way that drugs have their effects is by blocking receptors on the targets of neurotransmitters. For example, curare, the poison with which some native peoples of South America traditionally have tipped their arrows, blocks the ACh receptors that control skeletal muscles, producing paralysis. Still other drugs interfere with the removal of neurotransmitters from the synapse after they have done their job. Cocaine, for instance, prevents dopamine from being reabsorbed. As a result, excess quantities of dopamine accumulate in the nervous system, producing heightened arousal.

Natural Painkillers Sometimes investigations of drug effects lead to surprising discoveries about the brain and its neurotransmitters. For example, in attempting to explain the effects of *opiates*—painkilling drugs such as morphine and heroin, which are derived from the opium plant—researchers discovered that the central nervous system contained receptor sites for these substances (Pert & Snyder, 1973). Why would these receptor sites exist unless the body produced its own natural painkillers? The brain's natural painkillers—the endorphins—were discovered. Morphine and other narcotics lock into the receptors for endorphins and have the same painkilling effects. Similarly, researchers investigating the effects of marijuana found brain receptors for a chemical called tetrahydrocannabinal (THC), the active ingredient in marijuana (Herkenham et al., 1990; Howlett, Evans, & Houston, 1992; Matsuda et al., 1990; Restak, 1993). Afterward, other researchers discovered a natural transmitter, called *anandamide*, that binds to these same receptors (Devane et al., 1992). Although its natural functions are not yet known, anandamide should have at least some of the effects of marijuana.

Neurotransmitters and Mental Illness Another fascinating discovery is that imbalances in some neurotransmitters may contribute to certain kinds of mental illness. Schizophrenia, for example, seems to be associated with an overabundance of dopamine. Some drugs that have been developed to treat schizophrenia seem to reduce its symptoms by blocking dopamine receptors. Similarly, some theories link depression to reduced serotonin activity. Antidepressant drugs such as Prozac alleviate the symptoms of depression by blocking reabsorption of serotonin, thus increasing the overall level of serotonin in synapses. We explore these intriguing discoveries more fully in the chapters on psychological disorders and therapies (Chapters 12 and 13).

REVIEW QUESTIONS

Match each term with the appropriate definition.

_D_ neuron	a. long cellular fibers carrying outgoing messages
_F_ dendrites	b. when a nerve cell cannot fire again
_A_ axons	c. affects emotions, arousal, and sleep
_H_ neural impulse	d. cell that transmits information
_J_ resting potential	e. chemicals that carry messages across synapses
_B_ absolute refractory period	f. short cellular fibers that pick up incoming messages
_I_ synapse	g. neurotransmitter with a role in schizophrenia
_e_ neurotransmitters	h. action potential
_G_ dopamine	i. terminal button, synaptic space, and dendrite of neighboring neuron
_C_ serotonin	j. electrical imbalance across a neural membrane at rest

Answers: neuron (d); dendrites (f); axons (a); neural impulse (h); resting potential (j); absolute refractory period (b); synapse (i); neurotransmitters (e); dopamine (g); serotonin (c)

The Central Nervous System

What are the two main parts of the nervous system?

If the brain alone has as many as 100 billion neurons, and if each neuron can be "in touch" with thousands of other neurons, then our bodies must contain trillions of synapses through which each neuron is indirectly linked to every other neuron. Within this immense system of interconnected neurons, there is an overall structure. The nervous system consists of two main parts: the **central nervous system (CNS),** made up of the brain and spinal cord, and the **peripheral nervous system (PNS),** which connects the brain and spinal cord to everything else in the body (see Figure 2–11, p. 68).

The Spinal Cord

Why does a break in the spinal cord cause paralysis below the break?

The cable of long nerve fibers that runs up through the backbone to the brain is known as the **spinal cord.** One function of the spinal cord is to enable reflex movements. For instance, when you burn your finger on a match, a message is transmitted from receptors in your skin to your spinal cord, which then relays instructions to the muscles of your hand and arm to pull the finger away. A pain message also travels up the spinal cord to your brain, but even before it gets there, your hand is being jerked to safety. Most spinal reflexes are protective: They enable the body to avoid serious damage and to maintain proper muscle tone and position. The reflex reaction that occurs when a doctor taps your knee with a rubber mallet is illustrated in Figure 2–4.

Another function of the spinal cord is to carry messages to and from the brain. People who have accidentally severed their spinal cords by breaking their necks or backs provide tragic evidence of how important this spinal cord function is. When the cord is severed, parts of the body are literally disconnected from the brain, and the victim loses all sensations from, and control over, them.

Central nervous system (CNS)
Division of the nervous system that consists of the brain and spinal cord.

Peripheral nervous system (PNS)
Division of the nervous system that connects the central nervous system to the rest of the body.

Spinal cord
Complex cable of neurons that runs down the spine, connecting the brain to most of the rest of the body.

Severing the spinal cord at the neck typically causes paralysis of everything below the head because nerves connecting to the body's muscles no longer have a cable to the brain. Actor Christopher Reeve suffered this tragedy after being thrown from a horse. He and others may someday benefit from research on neurogenesis. (See the *Highlights* box on neurogenesis on p. 65.)

FIGURE 2–4

The spinal cord and reflex action. Simple reflexes are controlled by the spinal cord. The message travels from the sense receptors near the skin through the afferent nerve fibers to the spinal cord. In the spinal cord, the messages are relayed through association neurons to the efferent nerve fibers, which carry them to the muscle cells that cause the reflex movement.

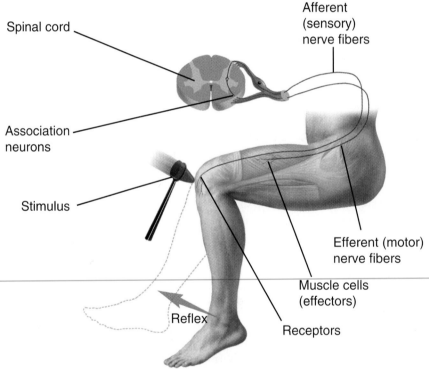

Spinal cord

Afferent (sensory) nerve fibers

Association neurons

Stimulus

Efferent (motor) nerve fibers

Muscle cells (effectors)

Reflex

Receptors

The Brain

Which areas of the brain process or control breathing, balance, sexual behavior, and visual information?

How does the brain allow us to analyze a situation and respond emotionally to it?

Containing more than 90 percent of the body's neurons, the brain is the seat of awareness and reason, the place where learning, memory, and emotions take place. It is the part of us that decides what to do—and it also imagines how things might have turned out differently if we had acted in some other way. How the brain manages such complex tasks with such apparent ease is a scientific mystery that is still being solved.

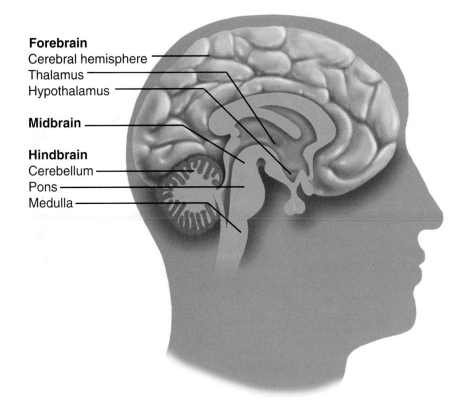

Forebrain
Cerebral hemisphere
Thalamus
Hypothalamus

Midbrain

Hindbrain
Cerebellum
Pons
Medulla

FIGURE 2–5

A cross section of the brain. This diagram shows the areas that make up the hindbrain, the midbrain, and the forebrain.

The brain contains many parts that serve specific functions (see Figure 2–5), but they all work together as an integrated whole. The lowermost part of the brain, which resembles a stalk leading up from the spinal cord, is called the **brain stem.** Its first functional region is the **medulla,** a narrow structure about 1.5 inches long. The medulla controls breathing, heart rate, and blood pressure. It is also where many of the nerves from the body cross over on their way to and from higher brain centers; axons from neurons on the left part of the body cross to the right side of the brain and vice versa. Above the medulla lies the **pons,** which produces chemicals that help maintain our sleep–wake cycle (discussed in Chapter 4, States of Consciousness). Near the pons but projecting out the back of the brain stem is the **cerebellum.** It is composed of two halves, or hemispheres, and it performs a wide range of functions. It handles certain reflexes, especially those that have to do with balance, and it coordinates the body's actions to ensure that movements go together in smooth, efficient sequences. Above the pons the brain stem widens to form the **midbrain.** The midbrain is especially important for hearing and sight. It is also one of several places in the brain where pain is registered.

Lying above the top of the brain stem are two egg-shaped structures that make up the **thalamus.** Parts of the thalamus relay and translate incoming messages from the body's sense receptors (except those for smell). Other parts are relay stations for certain messages that travel from one area of the brain to another. The thalamus also seems to be important for regulating the activity of centers in the brain's outermost layer (the cortex), where all our higher-order thinking takes place.

Located directly below the thalamus is a smaller structure called the **hypothalamus.** The hypothalamus exerts an enormous influence on many kinds of motivation. Portions of it govern eating, drinking, sexual behavior, sleeping, and temperature control (Winn, 1995). The hypothalamus is also directly involved in emotions such as rage, terror, and pleasure, and it appears to play a central role in times of stress, coordinating and integrating the activities of the nervous system.

Brain stem
The top of the spinal column; it widens out to form the hindbrain and midbrain.

Medulla
Part of the hindbrain that controls such functions as breathing, heart rate, and blood pressure.

Pons
Part of the hindbrain that connects the cerebral cortex at the top of the brain to the cerebellum.

Cerebellum
Structure in the hindbrain that controls certain reflexes and coordinates the body's movements.

Midbrain
Region between the hindbrain and the forebrain; it is important for hearing and sight, and it is one of several places in the brain where pain is registered.

Thalamus
Forebrain region that relays and translates incoming messages from the sense receptors, except those for smell.

Hypothalamus
Forebrain region that governs motivation and emotional responses.

Figure 2–6

The limbic system.   A ring of structures that work together to play an essential role in the formation of new memories as well as to influence motivation and emotion.

Cingulate gyrus

Midbrain

Corpus callosum

Thalamus

Fornix

Thalamus

Septal area

Hypothalamus

Amygdala

Hippocampus

Spinal cord

Hypothalamus

Cerebellum

Pons

Medulla

Running through the brain stem and up to the thalamus is a netlike bundle of neurons called the **reticular formation.** Its main job seems to be to send alert signals to the higher parts of the brain in response to incoming messages. Anesthetics work largely by shutting down the reticular formation. Permanent damage to it can induce a coma.

Deep in the brain, surrounding the thalamus, is a ring of structures known as the **limbic system** (see Figure 2–6). Two of its parts—the *amygdala* and the *hippocampus*—play an essential role in the formation of new memories. People with severe damage in these regions cannot form new memories, though they can still remember names, faces, places, and events that they learned before they were injured. The limbic system also influences emotion and motivation. For instance, the amygdala and the hippocampus are critical to emotions related to self-preservation (MacLean, 1970). When portions of these structures are damaged or removed, hostile animals become docile, and when the structures are electrically stimulated, animals may either attack or show signs of panic, depending on the particular areas receiving the stimulation. Two other limbic structures are involved in the experience of pleasure and the inhibition of aggression. Destruction of areas in these two structures can prompt high levels of aggression, and electrical stimulation of other areas results in intensely pleasurable sensations. Animals given the opportunity to electrically stimulate themselves in these "pleasure centers" will do so endlessly, even to the point of ignoring all food and water. Humans, too, experience pleasure when some of these areas are stimulated, though apparently it is not as intense an experience as it is for nonhumans. The limbic system is also closely connected to the hypothalamus, which, as we said earlier, plays a central role in a wide variety of motivations and emotions, such as hunger, thirst, sexual motivation, fear, anger, and stress (Kupfermann, 1991; Olds & Forbes, 1981).

The Cerebral Hemispheres   Above the brain stem, thalamus, hypothalamus, and limbic system are the two **cerebral hemispheres.** These are what most people think of first when they talk about the brain. The two cerebral hemi-

Reticular formation
Network of neurons in the hindbrain, midbrain, and part of the forebrain, the primary function of which is to alert and arouse the higher parts of the brain.

Limbic system
Ring of structures that plays a role in learning and emotional behavior.

Cerebral hemispheres
The largest part of the brain, developed more in humans than in any other animal.

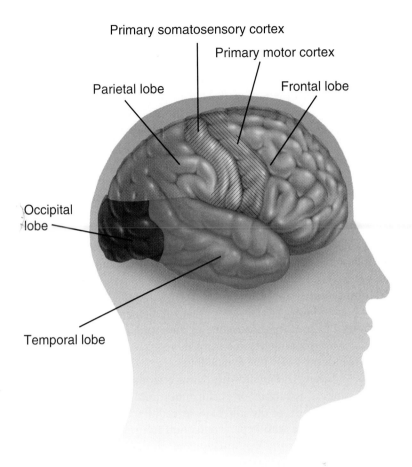

Primary somatosensory cortex

Primary motor cortex

Parietal lobe

Frontal lobe

Occipital lobe

Temporal lobe

FIGURE 2–7
The four lobes of the cerebral cortex.
Deep fissures in the cortex separate these areas or lobes. Also shown are the primary sensory and motor areas.

spheres take up most of the room inside the skull (see Figure 2–5). They balloon out over the brain stem, fold down over it, and actually hide most of it from view. The cerebral hemispheres are the most recently evolved part of the nervous system, and they are more highly developed in humans than in any other animal. They account for about 80 percent of the weight of the human brain, and they contain about 70 percent of the neurons in the central nervous system.

The outer layer of the cerebral hemispheres (a layer about six cells deep) is called the **cerebral cortex.** If the cerebral cortex were spread out, it would cover 2 to 3 square feet and would be about as thick as the letter "I" at the start of this sentence. To fit inside the skull, the cerebral cortex has developed intricate folds—hills and valleys called convolutions. In each person these convolutions form a pattern that is as unique as a fingerprint.

Each cerebral hemisphere can be divided into four large parts, or lobes, which are partially separated from one another by deep *fissures* or cracks (see Figure 2–7). Because the same four lobes are on each hemisphere and the brain has two hemispheres, there are two of each kind of lobe. On all of the lobes there are regions, called **association areas,** that integrate information from diverse parts of the cortex and are involved in mental processes such as learning, thinking, and remembering.

To a great extent the lobes of the brain are responsible for different functions. For instance, the **occipital lobes,** located at the back of the cerebral hemispheres, have areas for receiving and processing visual information. It is in the occipital lobes that we visually experience shapes, colors, and motion. Damage to the occipital lobes can produce blindness, even though the eyes and their neural connections to the brain are perfectly healthy and intact.

Cerebral cortex
The outer surface of the two cerebral hemispheres that regulate most complex behavior.

Association areas
Areas of the cerebral cortex that integrate information from diverse parts of the cortex and are involved in mental processes such as learning, thinking, and remembering.

Occipital lobes
Part of each cerebral hemisphere that receives and interprets visual information.

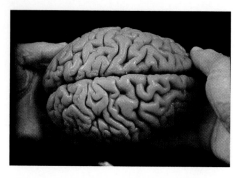

The human brain, viewed from the top. Its relatively small size belies its enormous complexity.

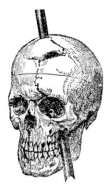

The skull of Phineas Gage, showing where the tamping iron passed through it, severely damaging his frontal lobes.

Temporal lobes
Part of each cerebral hemisphere that helps to regulate hearing, balance and equilibrium and certain emotions and motivations.

Parietal lobes
Part of the cerebral cortex that receives sensory information from throughout the body.

Frontal lobes
Part of the cerebral cortex that is responsible for voluntary movement; it is also important for attention, goal-directed behavior, and appropriate emotional experiences.

The **temporal lobes,** located in front of the occipital lobes, roughly behind the temples, handle complex visual tasks such as recognizing faces. They are also the primary smell centers in the brain, and they receive and process information from the ears as well. Other parts of the temporal lobes help to regulate balance and equilibrium, while still others are involved in motivations and emotions such as anxiety, pleasure, and anger. In addition, the ability to understand language is thought to be concentrated primarily in the rear portion of the left temporal lobe, though some language comprehension may also occur in the parietal and frontal lobes (Ojemann et al., 1989).

The **parietal lobes** sit on top of the temporal and occipital lobes and occupy the top back half of the brain. These lobes receive sensory information from all over the body—from sense receptors in the skin, muscles, and joints. Messages from these sense receptors are directed ultimately to the *primary somatosensory cortex* (see Figure 2–7). The parietal lobes also play a role in spatial abilities, such as the ability to follow a map or to tell someone how to get from one place to another (A. Cohen & Raffal, 1991).

The **frontal lobes,** located just behind the forehead, account for about half of the volume of the human brain. When you make a voluntary movement of your body, such as turning a page of this book, the response messages start in the *primary motor cortex* of your frontal lobes and from there go to the various skeletal muscles involved (see Figure 2–7). The frontal lobes also seem to permit and anticipate goal-directed behavior. People with damage to the frontal lobes have trouble following complex directions or performing tasks in which the directions change during the course of the job. Low levels of activity in portions of the frontal lobes are associated with hyperactivity and attention deficits in some people (Zametkin et al., 1990), and abnormalities in frontal lobes are often observed in people with schizophrenia (Raine et al., 1992).

The Case of Phineas Gage   Scientists are still uncertain of all the functions the frontal lobes perform. Insights from experimental animals are limited because their frontal lobes are relatively undeveloped, and cases of people with frontal lobe damage are rare. One famous case involved a bizarre accident that happened in 1848 to a man named Phineas Gage. Gage, who was the foreman of a railroad construction gang, made a careless mistake while using some blasting powder and a tamping iron. As a result, the tamping iron tore through his cheek, skull, and brain, severely damaging his frontal lobes. Gage remained conscious and walked part of the way to a doctor. To the amazement of those who witnessed the accident, his memory and skills seemed as good as ever. He did, however, undergo major personality changes. Once a steady worker, congenial and polite, he lost interest in work and drifted from job to job. He also became obstinent, impatient, rude, and profane. In the view of his friends, Gage was no longer the same man.

Such personality changes are not uncommon in cases of frontal lobe damage. The frontal lobes figure prominently in the ability to lead a normal, mature emotional life. People whose frontal lobes have been severed often seem apathetic and capable of only shallow emotions, although this apathy may be interrupted by periods of boastful and silly behavior. Other people with injuries to the frontal lobes experience explosive anger: They react with inappropriate, purposeless, and instantaneous rage to the slightest provocation (Damasio, Tranel, & Damasio, 1990b). The frontal lobes may also be linked to emotional temperament—being cheerful and optimistic or melancholy and alarmist (Tomarken, Davidson, & Henriques, 1990). Much more research needs to be done before psychologists can understand how this part of the cortex contributes to such a wide and subtle range of activities. (See the Summary Table for a list of the parts of the brain and their functions.)

SUMMARY TABLE

Parts of the Brain and Their Function

Hindbrain	Medulla	Sensory and motor nerves crossover
	Pons	Regulation of sleep–wake cycle
	Cerebellum	Reflexes (e.g., balance)
		Coordinates movement
Midbrain		Hearing, vision relay point
		Pain registered
Forebrain	Thalamus	Major message relay center
		Regulates higher brain centers and peripheral nervous system
	Hypothalamus	Emotion and motivation
		Stress reactions
	Cerebral hemispheres	
	Occipital lobe	Receives and processes visual information
	Temporal lobe	Complex vision
		Hearing and smell
		Balance and equilibrium
		Emotions and motivations
		Some language comprehension
	Parietal lobe	Processing sensory information
		Visual/spatial abilities
	Frontal lobe	Goal-directed behavior, concentration
		Emotional control and temperament
		Voluntary movement
		Coordinates messages from other lobes

Hemispheric Specialization

Why might it be advantageous for each cerebral hemisphere to specialize in certain functions?

Because we have two separate cerebral hemispheres, we have, in a sense, a right half-brain and a left half-brain. These two halves are connected at several locations, but the primary connection is a thick band of nerve fibers across the center of the brain, called the **corpus callosum.** Under normal conditions the left and right cerebral hemispheres are in close communication through the corpus callosum, and they work together as a coordinated unit (Hellige, 1993; Hoptman & Davidson, 1994; Semrud-Clikeman & Hynd, 1990). The cerebral hemispheres are not really equivalent, however (see Figure 2–8). Although there is much overlap between the tasks of the two hemispheres, each one also specializes in certain functions that the other does not. For example, damage to the left hemisphere often results in severe language problems, whereas similar damage to the right hemisphere seldom has this effect.

Dramatic evidence for hemispheric specialization comes from research performed in the early 1960s on people with epilepsy. In some cases of severe epilepsy, surgeons cut the corpus callosum in an effort to stop the spread of epileptic seizures from the cortex of one hemisphere to the other. But this operation also cuts the only direct communication link between the two hemispheres, thus making it possible to watch each hemisphere work on its own (Sperry, 1964, 1968, 1970). The results are startling.

Corpus callosum
A thick band of nerve fibers connecting the left and right cerebral cortex.

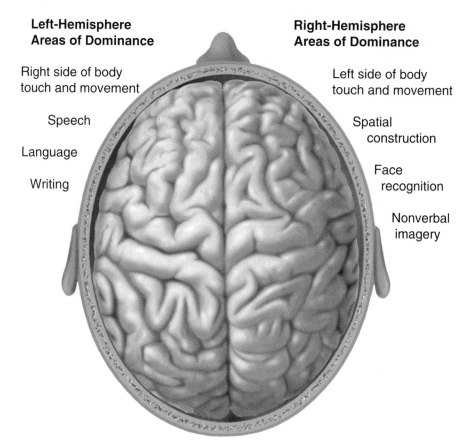

Left-Hemisphere Areas of Dominance

Right side of body touch and movement

Speech

Language

Writing

Right-Hemisphere Areas of Dominance

Left side of body touch and movement

Spatial construction

Face recognition

Nonverbal imagery

FIGURE 2–8

The two cerebral hemispheres. The left hemisphere controls touch and movement of the right side of the body; the right hemisphere controls the left side of the body. The left hemisphere is usually dominant in verbal tasks, whereas the right hemisphere is typically superior at nonverbal, visual, and spatial tasks.

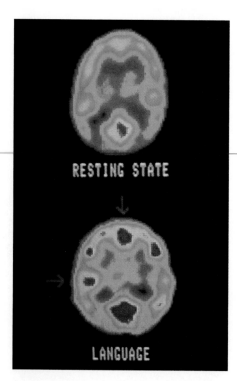

RESTING STATE

LANGUAGE

PET scans of a person at rest (*top*) and using language (*bottom*). The "hot" colors (red and yellow) indicate greater brain activity. These scans show that language activity is located primarily, but not exclusively, in the brain's left hemisphere.

When such "split-brain patients" are asked to stare at a spot on a projection screen while pictures of various objects are projected to the *right* of that spot, they are able to identify the objects verbally, and they are also able to pick them out of a group of hidden objects using their right hands (see Figure 2–9). When pictures of objects are shown on the *left* side of the projection screen, however, split-brain patients can pick out the objects by feeling them with their left hands, yet they are unable to say what the objects are. In fact, when objects are projected on the left side of the screen, split-brain patients report verbally that they see nothing on the screen, even though they can accurately identify the objects when given a chance to touch and feel them with their left hands (see Figure 2–10).

The explanation for these unusual results is found in the way each hemisphere of the brain operates. When the corpus callosum is cut, the *left hemisphere* receives information only from the right side of the body and the right half of the visual field. As a result, it can match an object shown in the right visual field with information received by touch from the right hand, but it is unaware of (and thus unable to identify) objects shown in the left visual field or touched by the left hand. Conversely, the *right hemisphere* receives information only from the left side of the visual field and the left side of the body. Consequently, the right hemisphere can match an object shown in the left visual field with information received by touch from the left hand, but it is unaware of any objects shown in the right visual field or touched with the right hand.

But why can't the right hemisphere verbally identify an object that is shown in the left visual field? The answer is that for the great majority of people (even for most left-handers), language ability is concentrated primarily in the *left* hemisphere (Hellige, 1990, 1993). As a result, when an object is in the left visual field, the nonverbal right hemisphere can see the object but can't name it. The

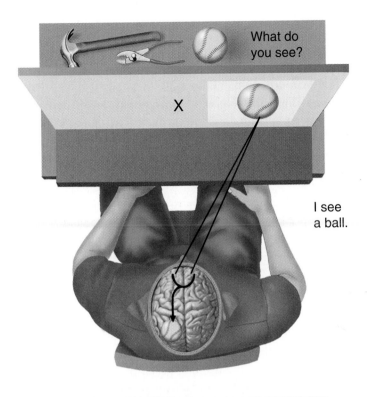

What do you see?

X

I see a ball.

FIGURE 2–9
When split-brain patients stare at the "X" in the center of the screen, visual information projected on the *right* side of the screen goes to the patient's *left* hemisphere, which controls language. When asked what they see, patients can reply correctly.

Source: Adapted from Carol Ward, © *Discover* magazine, 1987.

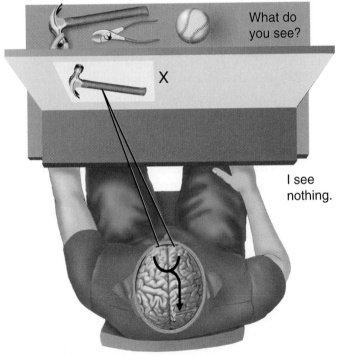

What do you see?

X

I see nothing.

FIGURE 2–10
When split-brain patients stare at the "X" in the center of the screen, visual information projected on the *left* side of the screen goes to the patient's *right* hemisphere, which does not control language. When asked what they see, patients cannot name the object, but they can pick it out by touch with the *left* hand.

verbal left hemisphere, in contrast, can't see an object in this location, so when asked what it sees, it answers that nothing is on the screen.

Does the left hemisphere specialize in any other tasks besides language? Some researchers think that it may also operate more analytically, logically, rationally, and sequentially than the right hemisphere does (Kingstone, Enns Mangun, & Gazzaniga, 1995). In contrast, the right hemisphere excels at visual and spatial tasks—nonverbal imagery, including music, face recognition, and the perception of emotions (Hellige, 1990, 1993; Metcalfe, Funnell, & Gazzaniga, 1995; Semrud-Clikeman & Hynd, 1990).

The frontal lobes of the two hemispheres may also influence temperament in distinctive ways. People whose left frontal lobe is more active than the right tend to be more cheerful, sociable, ebullient, and self-confident, whereas people with more right frontal lobe activity are more easily stressed, frightened, and upset by unpleasant things. They also tend to be more suspicious and depressed than people with predominantly left frontal lobe activity (Henriques & David-son, 1990; Tomarken et al., 1990). In keeping with these findings, people whose right hemisphere is anesthetized for medical reasons frequently laugh and express positive emotions, while anesthetizing the left hemisphere often produces crying (Lee et al., 1993).

Although such research is fascinating and fun to speculate about, it is necessary to be cautious in interpreting it. First, not everyone shows the same pattern of differences between the left and right hemispheres. In particular, the differences between the hemispheres may be greater in men than in women (Hellige, 1993; Seamon & Kenrick, 1992; Semrud-Clikeman & Hynd, 1990). Second, it is easy to oversimplify and exaggerate differences between the two sides of the brain. Under normal conditions the right and left hemispheres are in close communication through the corpus callosum and so work together in a coordinated, integrated way (Hoptman & Davidson, 1994).

Split-brain patients may shed light on the different abilities of the two sides of the brain, but serious injuries to the brain and spinal cord restrict the mobility and lifestyles of thousands of people each year. Some new research is now offering hope of actually regenerating damaged neurons in people who have been paralyzed through accidents or those severely impaired by degenerative diseases (see *Highlights*).

New Tools for Studying the Brain

What tools are used for studying the brain?

How can brain imaging help people with psychological disorders?

For centuries our understanding of the brain depended entirely on observing people who had suffered brain damage or by examining the brains of cadavers. Then, in 1929, Hans Berger developed the *electroencephalograph* (EEG), which provided the first window into the electrical activity of a living brain. Since that time, science has produced a virtual explosion of brain research techniques, including microelectrode recordings, macroelectrode recordings, structural imaging, and functional imaging.

Microelectrode Techniques *Microelectrode recording techniques* are used to study single neurons. A microelectrode is a tiny pipette (smaller in diameter than a human hair) that is filled with conducting liquid. When researchers place the tip of a microelectrode on the surface of a neuron (or even inside a neuron), they can study that neuron's electrical activity. Microelectrode techniques have been used to understand action potentials and the effects of drugs or toxins on neurons.

Macroelectrode Techniques An EEG is an example of a *macroelectrode* technique to study the brain. Macroelectrode techniques involve large recording devices placed on the surface of the scalp, where they detect the collective electrical activity of millions of neurons in the underlying cortex. These so-called brain waves measure both the intensity and rhythm of neural firing. An EEG presents a continuous picture of the brain over an extended period; the patterns vary depending on what the person being studied is doing at the time. *Alpha waves* are commonly found when someone is relaxing with his or her eyes closed. Alphas change to higher-frequency *beta waves* when someone is awake

HIGHLIGHTS

Growing New Neurons

Each year thousands of people suffer injuries to the brain and spinal cord. Traditionally, such injuries were considered permanent, and treatment options were limited to rehabilitation. Today, however, research is providing exciting new options for treating these injuries as well as for medical disorders such as Parkinson's disease, Alzheimer's disease, and stroke.

Before birth, human fetuses have a large supply of cells known as *stem cells* that are capable of becoming neurons in a process known as **neurogenesis.** For many years scientists believed that new neurons could not form in adult brains because no stem cells were left. Studies in birds, however, gave researchers the first clues that neurogenesis might be possible in mature humans. Fernando Nottebohm and Stephen Goldman (1983) discovered that in canaries, new neurons grow in the regions of the brain associated with song learning. The mechanism for this neural regrowth appeared to involve *precursor cells* that are similar in many ways to stem cells but have a reduced capacity for differentiation (Lois & Alvarez-Buylla, 1994). To discover if precursor cells exist in adult human brains, Goldman obtained tissue from the brains of patients undergoing surgery for severe epilepsy (Altman, 1995). When the brain tissue

from these patients was placed in a supportive environment, it produced functional mature neurons, demonstrating that neurogenesis is indeed possible in adult human brains.

In November 1998 a dramatic breakthrough occurred when a group of American and Swedish researchers examined the brains of deceased patients who had been treated prior to their death with a substance that was thought to stimulate neurogenesis

---

Researchers have found evidence of neurogenesis in humans and the existence of stem cells in the adult brains.

(Eriksson et al., 1998). These researchers found that new neurons had indeed developed, thus indicating that living human adult brains could make new neurons. Since this initial finding, other researchers have found evidence of neurogenesis in humans and the existence of stem cells in the adult brains (Gage, 1998; Johansson et al., 1999). Because stem cells can replicate indefinitely and can also give rise

to more specialized cells, they can be used to repair brain damage. Hence, the adult brain, once thought to be almost incapable of repair, is now believed to harbor enormous potential to generate new neurons.

These findings give rise to the possibility of exciting new treatment options (McMillian, Robertson, & Wilson, 1999). Once the chemicals that regulate neurogenesis are more fully understood, it may be possible to increase the amounts of these substances in areas of the central nervous system where neural growth needs to occur. Some researchers have already begun to identify substances that show promise at stimulating neural regrowth (Rasika, Alvarez-Buylla, & Nottebohm, 1999).

Growing neurons in the laboratory and transplanting them into patients with neurological damage is yet another avenue being explored (McKay, 1997). Remarkably, there is some evidence that when stem cells are transplanted into the brain or spinal cord, they spontaneously migrate to damaged areas and begin to generate specialized neurons for replacement. It is as if stem cells move through the brain, going from one neuron to the next looking for damage. If damage is found, the stem cells begin to divide, producing specialized neurons that are appropriate for that area of the brain.

---

and still, but with his or her eyes open. At the other extreme are low-frequency *delta waves*, which occur during deepest sleep. As you will see in Chapter 4, States of Consciousness, the changes in brain waves during sleep have provided valuable insights into the biology of sleep and dreaming.

Structural Imaging   *Computerized axial tomography* (CT) *scanning* is one technique that allows scientists to create three-dimensional images of the structure of a human brain. To create a CT scan, an X-ray photography unit rotates around a person's head from the top to the bottom. A computer then combines the resulting images. Even more successful at producing pictures of the inner regions of the brain—its ridges, folds, and fissures—is a technique called *magnetic resonance imaging* (MRI). Here the person's head is placed in a magnetic field,

Neurogenesis
The growth of new neurons.

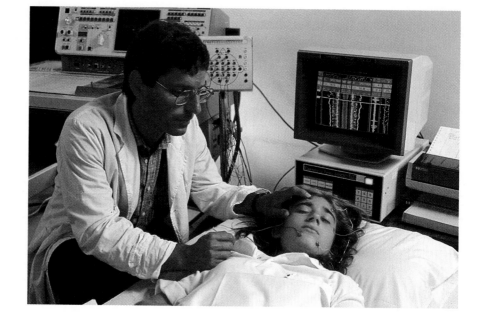

In an EEG, electrodes attached to the scalp are used to create a picture of neural activity in the brain.

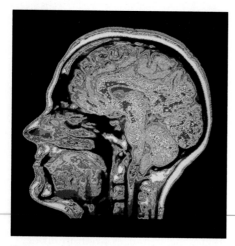

MRI image of the human head.

and the brain is exposed to radio waves; this causes hydrogen atoms in the brain to release energy. The energy released by different structures in the brain generates an image that appears on a computer screen.

Functional Imaging   Both CT scanning and MRI permit unparalleled mapping of the brain's structures in a living person, but neither technique can provide a picture of the brain at work. This is the goal of several functional imaging methods. In one of them, called *EEG imaging*, more than two dozen electrodes, placed at important locations on the scalp, record the brain's electrical activities every thousandth of a second (Fischman, 1985). These recordings are then converted by a computer into colored images on a television screen. EEG imaging has been extremely useful in detecting abnormal cortical activity such as that occurring during an epileptic seizure.

Two related techniques, called *magnetoencephalography* (MEG) and *magnetic source imaging* (MSI), are helping biopsychologists to determine exactly which parts of the brain do most of the work in such processes as memory (Gabrieli et al., 1996), language processing (Tulving et al., 1994), and reading. This research is shedding new light on such disorders as amnesia and dyslexia (a reading disorder). Using these functional imaging techniques, scientists also hope to pinpoint the areas of the brain affected by particular drugs, such as those used to treat severe psychological disorders such as schizophrenia. This knowledge would be valuable in understanding the negative side effects these drugs sometimes induce.

Another family of functional imaging techniques uses radioactive energy to map brain activity. Some of the findings produced by these techniques have been surprising. For example, the brains of people with higher IQ scores are actually *less* active than those of people with lower IQ scores, perhaps because they process information more efficiently (Haier, 1988). These techniques have also provided important medical insights. For instance, they have helped locate the damaged brain region involved in Parkinson's disease.

More recent techniques measure the movement of blood and water molecules as brain neurons work. Because these methods collect images rapidly and do not use radioactive chemicals, they are especially promising as research tools. By combining them with other techniques, neuroscientists are now able to study the brain in greater detail than ever before (Sarter, Berntson, & Cacioppo, 1996).

REVIEW QUESTIONS

1. Which brain structure is a vital center for the control of temperature, eating, drinking, and sexual behavior?

   a. cerebral cortex   b. pons   c. cerebellum   d. hypothalamus

2. Match the lobes of the cerebral cortex with their functions.

   ____ frontal lobes   a. process language and information from the ears

   ____ occipital lobes   b. process body sensations and spatial information

   ____ temporal lobes   c. plan goal-directed behavior

   ____ parietal lobes   d. process visual information

3. Label each technique as either structural imaging (S) or functional imaging (F).

   ____ EEG imaging   ____ CT   ____ MRI

Answers: 1. D. 2. frontal lobes (c); occipital lobes (d); temporal lobes (a); parietal lobes (b). 3. EEG imaging (F); CT (S); MRI (S).

The Peripheral Nervous System

How does the brain communicate with the rest of the body? How is the autonomic branch of the peripheral nervous system involved in controlling emotions?

The peripheral nervous system (PNS) links the brain and spinal cord to the rest of the body, including the sensory receptors, glands, internal organs, and skeletal muscles (see Figure 2–11). It consists of both **afferent neurons,** which carry messages *to* the central nervous system (CNS), and **efferent neurons,** which carry messages *from* the CNS. The afferent neurons carry sensory information. All the things that register through your senses—sights, sounds, smells, temperature, pressure, and so on—travel to your brain via afferent neurons. The efferent neurons carry signals to the body's muscles and glands.

Some neurons belong to a part of the PNS called the **somatic nervous system.** Neurons in this system are involved in making voluntary movements of the skeletal muscles. Every deliberate action you make, from pedaling a bike to scratching a toe, involves neurons in the somatic nervous system. Other neurons belong to a part of the PNS called the **autonomic nervous system.** Neurons in the autonomic nervous system govern involuntary activities of your internal organs, from the beating of your heart to the hormone secretions of your glands.

The autonomic nervous system is of special interest to psychologists because it is involved not only in vital body functions, such as breathing and blood flow, but in important emotions as well. To understand the workings of the autonomic nervous system, you must know about the system's two parts: the *sympathetic* and the *parasympathetic* divisions (see Figure 2–12).

The nerve fibers of the **sympathetic division** are busiest when you are intensely aroused, such as being enraged or very frightened. For example, if you were hiking through a woods and suddenly encountered a large, growling bear, your sympathetic division would be instantaneously triggered. In response to messages from it, your heart would begin to pound, your breathing would quicken, your pupils would enlarge, and your digestion would stop. All these changes would help direct your energy and attention to the emergency you faced, giving you the keen senses, stamina, and strength needed to flee from the danger or to stand and fight it. Your sympathetic division would also tell your glands to start pumping hormones into your blood to further

When you are in a frightening situation, such as being confronted with an angry dog, the sympathetic division of the autonomic nervous system triggers a number of responses within your body. These responses give you the strength and stamina to either fight the danger or flee from it.

Afferent neurons
Neurons that carry messages from sense organs to the spinal cord or brain.

Efferent neurons
Neurons that carry messages from the spinal cord or brain to the muscles and glands.

Somatic nervous system
The part of the peripheral nervous system that carries messages from the senses to the central nervous system and between the central nervous system and the skeletal muscles.

Autonomic nervous system
The part of the peripheral nervous system that carries messages between the central nervous system and the internal organs.

Sympathetic division
Branch of the autonomic nervous system; it prepares the body for quick action in an emergency.

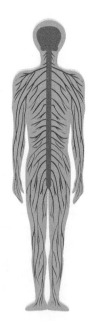
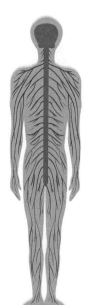
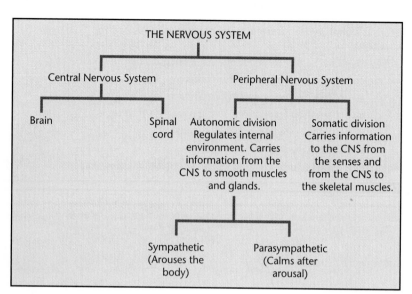

FIGURE 2–11
A diagram of the divisions of the nervous system and their various subparts.

strengthen your body's reactions. Sympathetic nerve fibers connect to every internal organ—a fact that explains why the body's response to sudden danger is so widespread.

Sympathetic division reactions are often sustained for quite some time after a danger has passed. If the bear you meet turns and lumbers harmlessly away, you will still feel pumped up and ready for action for quite a while after you know you are safe. Because dangers in the wild may suddenly return, it made sense for our early ancestors to stay "on alert" a bit longer than was deemed necessary. This sustained response is probably not so essential today, but it remains with us as part of our evolutionary heritage.

Eventually even the most intense sympathetic division reaction fades, and the body calms down, returning to normal. This calming effect is promoted by the **parasympathetic division** of the autonomic nervous system. Parasympathetic nerve fibers connect to the same organs as sympathetic nerve fibers do, but they cause just the opposite reaction. The parasympathetic division says, in effect, "OK, the heat's off, back to normal." The heart then goes back to beating at its regular rate, the stomach muscles relax, digestion resumes, breathing slows down, and the pupils contract. So while the sympathetic division arouses the body in response to danger and stress, the parasympathetic division calms the body once the threat has passed.

Both parts of the autonomic nervous system have traditionally been considered automatic. You could not, it was believed, tell your autonomic nervous system when to speed up or slow down your heartbeat or when to stop or start digesting food. We may have more control over the autonomic nervous system than previously thought, however. For example, people can be taught to moderate the severity of high blood pressure, migraine headaches, and ulcers. Some have even learned to regulate their own heart rate and brain waves. These are all cases in which the autonomic nervous system is brought under voluntary control. We look more closely at these possibilities when we discuss biofeedback in Chapter 5, Learning.

Parasympathetic division
Branch of the autonomic nervous system; it calms and relaxes the body.

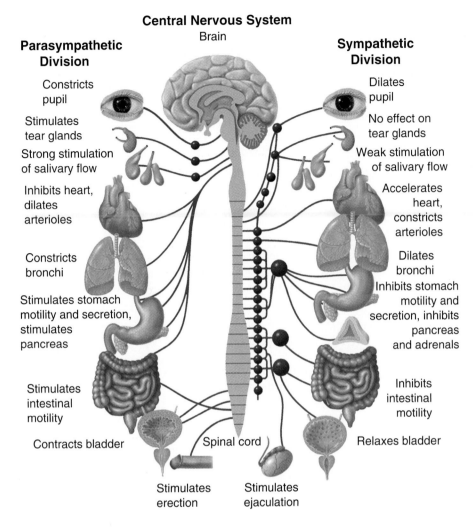

Central Nervous System
Brain

Parasympathetic Division

Constricts pupil

Stimulates tear glands

Strong stimulation of salivary flow

Inhibits heart, dilates arterioles

Constricts bronchi

Stimulates stomach motility and secretion, stimulates pancreas

Stimulates intestinal motility

Contracts bladder

Spinal cord

Stimulates erection

Stimulates ejaculation

Sympathetic Division

Dilates pupil

No effect on tear glands

Weak stimulation of salivary flow

Accelerates heart, constricts arterioles

Dilates bronchi

Inhibits stomach motility and secretion, inhibits pancreas and adrenals

Inhibits intestinal motility

Relaxes bladder

FIGURE 2–12

The sympathetic and parasympathetic divisions of the autonomic nervous system. The sympathetic division generally acts to arouse the body, preparing it for "fight or flight." The parasympathetic division follows with messages to relax.

Source: Adapted from *General Biology*, (rev. ed.), by Willis Johnson, Richard A. Laubengayer, and Louis E. Delanney, Copyright © 1961 by Holt, Rinehart, and Winston, Inc., and renewed 1989 by Willis H. Johnson and Louis E. Delanney. Reproduced by permission.

REVIEW QUESTIONS

Match each function with the sympathetic (S) or the parasympathetic (P) division of the autonomic nervous system.

_____ a. heartbeat increases

_____ b. the stomach starts digesting food

_____ c. breathing speeds up

_____ d. the body recovers from an emergency situation

Answers: a. (S). b. (P). c. (S). d. (P).

The Endocrine System

Why are hormones of interest to psychologists?

When you encountered that bear, your body's response didn't end with your nervous system's reaction. Chemical substances called **hormones** were also released into your bloodstream, by internal organs called **endocrine glands.** These hormones travel throughout your body and have effects on many organs. Together they form a second major communications system.

Hormones
Chemical substances released by the endocrine glands; they help regulate bodily activities.

Endocrine glands
Glands of the endocrine system that release hormones into the bloodstream.

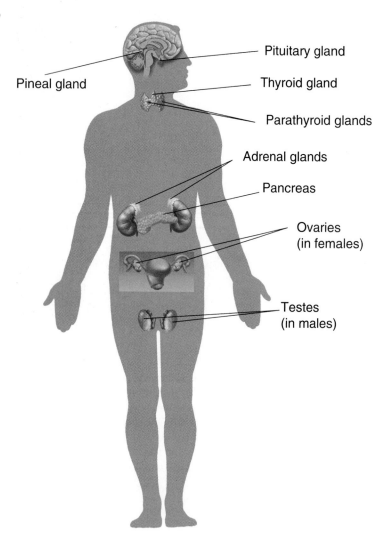

Pineal gland

Pituitary gland

Thyroid gland

Parathyroid glands

Adrenal glands

Pancreas

Ovaries
(in females)

Testes
(in males)

FIGURE 2–13
The glands of the endocrine system.

Hormones are of interest to psychologists for two reasons. First, hormones *trigger changes* that occur in our bodies at certain stages of development. The dramatic hormone-induced changes of puberty and menopause are two examples. Second, hormones *activate behavioral responses*. They affect such things as alertness or sleepiness, excitability, sexual behavior, the ability to concentrate, aggressiveness, reactions to stress, and even the desire for companionship. Hormones can also have dramatic effects on mood, emotional reaction, the ability to learn, and the ability to resist disease. Radical changes in some hormones may contribute to serious psychological disorders such as depression.

The locations of the endocrine glands are shown in Figure 2–13. Our discussion focuses on those glands whose functions are best understood and whose effects are most involved in human behavior.

The Thyroid Gland

What are the symptoms of an overactive and an underactive thyroid?

The **thyroid gland,** located just below the voice box, produces the hormone *thyroxin*. This hormone regulates the body's rate of metabolism; that is, it determines how fast or how slowly the foods we eat are transformed into energy. An overactive thyroid can produce anxiety, insomnia, tension, reduced attention span, impulsivity, and agitation. Too little thyroxin leads to the other extreme: lethargy, constant fatigue, reduced muscle tone, and a sluggish metabolism.

The Parathyroid Glands

Where are the parathyroid glands, and what substances do they regulate?

Embedded in the thyroid gland are the **parathyroids**—four tiny, pea-shaped organs. They secrete the hormone *parathormone*, which controls and balances the levels of calcium and phosphate in the blood and tissue fluids. The level of calcium in the blood has a direct effect on the excitability of the nervous system. A person with too little parathormone is hypersensitive and may have muscle spasms. Too much parathormone leads to lethargy and poor physical coordination.

The Pineal Gland

What is the function of the pineal gland?

The **pineal gland** is a pea-sized gland that regulates the general activity level over the course of a day. Increased levels of light in the morning stimulate the pineal gland, which in turn reduces the amount of the hormone *melatonin* it releases. As a result, body temperature rises and the organism "wakes up." At the end of the day, as light levels decrease, the pineal gland releases more melatonin, which lowers body temperature and prepares the organism for sleep. We examine these effects in greater detail in Chapter 4, States of Consciousness.

Thyroid gland
Endocrine gland located below the voice box; it produces the hormone thyroxin.

Parathyroids
Four tiny glands embedded in the thyroid; they secrete parathormone.

Pineal gland
A gland located roughly in the center of the brain that appears to regulate activity levels over the course of a day.

The Pancreas

What two disorders are caused by imbalances in pancreatic hormones?

The **pancreas** lies in a curve between the stomach and the small intestine. It controls the level of sugar in the blood by secreting two hormones: *insulin* and *glucagon*. When the pancreas secretes too little insulin, an excess of sugar accumulates in the blood, and the person suffers *diabetes*. Oversecretion of insulin leads to too little blood sugar and the chronic fatigue of *hypoglycemia*.

The Pituitary Gland

Why is the pituitary often called the "master gland"?

The endocrine gland that regulates the largest number of different activities in the body is the **pituitary gland.** It is located on the underside of the brain and is connected to the hypothalamus, with which it interacts. The pituitary influences blood pressure, thirst, uterine contractions in childbirth, milk production, sexual behavior and interest, and the amount and timing of body growth, among other functions. It is often called the "master gland" because it affects the output of other endocrine glands.

The Gonads

What are the gonads, and what are their functions?

The **gonads**—the *testes* in males and the *ovaries* in females—secrete *androgens* and *estrogens*. Although both sexes produce both types of hormone, androgens predominate in males, and estrogens predominate in females. A high concentration of the androgen testosterone during prenatal development causes the fetus to become a boy; otherwise, a female develops. Traditionally, testosterone has been associated with aggression, but recent evidence seems to point to an excess of estrogen rather than testosterone as a source of aggressive behavior. Other interesting links exist between estrogen and the performance on certain tests of manual dexterity, verbal skills, and perceptual speed. Women do better at these sorts of tasks during the ovulatory phase of their menstrual cycles, when estrogen levels are high, and postmenopausal women show improvement in them when they undergo estrogen replacement therapy (E. Hampson & Kimura, 1992; Kimura & Hampson, 1994).

The Adrenal Glands

What is the role of the adrenal glands in our reactions to stress?

The two **adrenal glands** are located just above the kidneys. Each adrenal gland has two parts: an outer covering, called the *adrenal cortex*, and an inner core, called the *adrenal medulla*. Both affect our reactions to stress, although the adrenal cortex affects other body functions, too. One stress-related hormone of the adrenal medulla is *epinephrine*, which amplifies the effects of the sympathetic nervous system: The heart beats faster, digestion stops, the pupils of the eyes enlarge, more sugar is released into the blood, blood pressure rises, and the blood is prepared to clot fast if needed. The result is a body pulsing with energy, ready to deal with the threat. The endocrine system, then, functions hand in hand with the nervous system to keep the body in tune with what is going on in its surroundings. You will see other examples of this in Chapter 8, Motivation and Emotion.

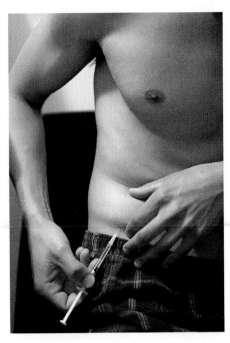

A diabetic man injecting himself with insulin. People with diabetes must take insulin because their pancreas secretes too little of the hormone.

Pancreas
Organ lying between the stomach and small intestine; it secretes insulin and glucagon to regulate blood-sugar levels.

Pituitary gland
Gland located on the underside of the brain; it regulates the largest number of behaviors and affects the output of the other endocrine glands.

Gonads
The reproductive glands—testes in males and ovaries in females.

Adrenal glands
Two endocrine glands located just above the kidneys.

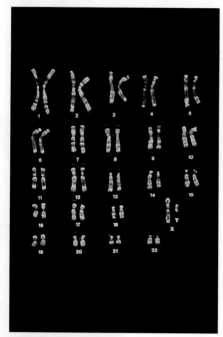

21

The 23 pairs of chromosomes found in every normal human cell. The two members of 22 of these pairs look exactly alike. The two members of the 23rd pair, the sex chromosomes, may or may not look alike. Females have equivalent X chromosomes, whereas males have one X and one Y, which look very different. Shown in the inset is the chromosome pattern that causes Down syndrome—the presence of 3 chromosomes number 21.

Genes
Elements that control the transmission of traits; they are found on the chromosomes.

Nature versus nurture debate
A debate surrounding the relative importance of heredity (nature) and environment (nurture) in determining behavior.

Heredity
The transmission of traits from one generation to the next.

Genetics
Study of how traits are transmitted from one generation to the next.

Chromosomes
Pairs of threadlike bodies within the cell nucleus that contain the genes.

Behavior Genetics and Our Human Heritage

What is the nature versus nurture debate?

At the moment that a sperm from your father united with an egg from your mother, the first cell that was to become you was created. In its nucleus was packed a set of chemically encoded messages, called **genes,** that would help to guide the development and functioning of your body. Most important to psychologists, these genes have influenced the workings of your nervous and endocrine systems, which in turn have affected how you tend to think and act. Genes, in other words, are at least partly responsible for some of your behavior.

Although the idea of genes influencing human behavior seems simple enough, in the past it has sparked much controversy. The impact of genes on behavior represents one side of the **nature versus nurture debate.** Supporters of the nature side of the debate argue that genes play the major role in determining such characteristics as intelligence, personality, and temperament. Advocates of the nurture side argue that the environment, including our daily experiences, upbringing, and education, are the prime determinants of these characteristics. Today no psychologist takes either a pure nature or pure nurture view. Nonetheless, there still is strong disagreement about the relative importance of genetic and environmental influences on human behavior. To understand this disagreement, you first need to know a little about genetics.

Genetics

How is genetic information transmitted to the next generation?

Every year in Twinsburg, Ohio, a twin convention takes place. Hundreds of identical twins from across the country descend on this small midwestern town, like a horde of identically dressed clones of every size, shape, color, and age. So many twins together is a powerful reminder of the influence of genes on human development. The transmission of genes from one generation to the next is known as **heredity.** Identical twins have inherited exactly the same genes from their parents because they began life as a single fertilized egg cell that split to form two separate embryos, each carrying a faithful copy of the genes contained in the original cell.

The study of genes and how they work is called **genetics.** Today many genetic mysteries have already been solved. We know, for example, that within a cell nucleus genes are lined up on tiny threadlike bodies called **chromosomes,** which are visible under an electron microscope. The chromosomes are arranged in pairs, and each species has a constant number of pairs. Mice have 20 pairs, monkeys have 27, peas have 7, and humans have 23.

The main ingredient of chromosomes and genes is **deoxyribonucleic acid (DNA),** a complex molecule that looks like two chains, connected between their lengths and twisted around each other to form what resembles a spiral staircase. The order of the "rungs" on this staircase forms a code that carries our genetic information. Individual genes, which are the message units of DNA, carry instructions for the building of proteins. The structure and function of proteins, in turn, are the foundation for an organism's basic **traits,** from size, shape, and coloring to behavioral tendencies. To learn more about human genetics and our current efforts to understand how genes work, see the *Highlights* box titled "In Search of the Human Genome."

Each pair of chromosomes carries a complete set of genes. Because each pair provides the coding for the same kinds of traits, a gene for a given trait may be present in two alternate forms—one inherited from the mother and the other from the father. We can think of a gene for eye color, for example, as having one form, *B*, which will result in brown eyes, and another form, *b*, which will result in blue eyes. If a girl receives *b* genes from both parents, her eyes will be blue. But if she inherits a *b* gene from one parent and *B* gene from the other, her eyes will be brown (see Figure 2–14). The *B* form is said to be the **dominant gene** (its trait is expressed), whereas the *b* form is the **recessive gene** (its trait is masked). But though the girl with one *B* gene and one *b* gene has brown eyes, the recessive *b* gene is still present in her and can be passed on to her children, thus producing a blue-eyed baby if it is paired with a recessive *b* gene from the baby's father.

A trait such as eye color is controlled by a single pair of genes, but this is not true of most other important characteristics, such as intelligence, height, and weight. These traits are influenced by a number of genes, each making a small or moderate contribution in a process known as **polygenic inheritance** (*poly* means "many"). Just as each of the instruments in an orchestra contributes separate notes to a symphony, each of the genes in a polygenic system contributes separately to the total characteristic (McClearn et al., 1991).

The effects of genes need not be fully apparent in childhood. In some cases expression of a trait is delayed until later in life. For example, many men inherit "male-pattern baldness" that does not show up until middle age. Moreover, genes may predispose a person to develop a particular trait, but environmental factors alter or suppress its expression. Having certain genes gives a person the *potential* for a trait, but that trait may not appear unless the environment cooperates. People with an inherited tendency to gain weight, for instance, may or may not become obese, depending on their diet, amount of exercise, and overall health. Both nature *and* nurture are required for the development of most traits.

Genetics and Behavior

What methods do psychologists use to study the effects of genes on behavior?

We have examined the role of genes in determining physical characteristics, such as eye color and weight. But there is increasing evidence that heredity also has a significant impact on many behavioral differences between people, including activity level, emotions, stress response, nervousness, shyness, aggressiveness, intelligence, and susceptibility to certain psychological disorders (Brunner et al., 1993; D. Johnson, 1990; Loehlin, Willerman, & Horn, 1988; Plomin, De-Fries, & McClearn, 1990; Plomin & Rende, 1991). Of course, genes do not directly cause any behavior. Rather, they affect the development and operation of the nervous and endocrine systems, which in turn influence the likelihood that a certain behavior will occur when circumstances encourage or allow it.

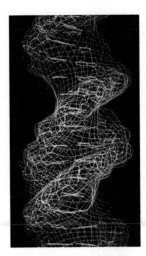

The twisted chain of the long DNA molecule contains the genetic code.

Deoxyribonucleic acid (DNA)
Complex molecule in a double-helix configuration that is the main ingredient of chromosomes and genes and forms the code for all genetic information.

Traits
Characteristics on which organisms differ.

Dominant gene
Member of a gene pair that controls the appearance of a certain trait.

Recessive gene
Member of a gene pair that can control the appearance of a certain trait only if it is paired with another recessive gene.

Polygenic inheritance
Process by which several genes interact to produce a certain trait; responsible for our most important traits.

HIGHLIGHTS

In Search of the Human Genome

The term *genome* refers to the full complement of an organism's genetic material. Thus the genome for any particular organism contains a complete blueprint for building all the structures and directing all the living processes for the lifetime of that organism. The **human genome** refers to the complete set of genes that define the human being. Scientists estimate that the human genome is made up of 80,000 to 100,000 individual genes, located on the 23 pairs of chromosomes that make up human DNA. These genes, contained within every cell of our body, distinguish us from other forms of life. Surprisingly minute variations in the human genome are responsible for the individual differences we see in the world's 6 billion people. Experts believe that the average variation in the human genetic code for any two different people is much less than 1 percent.

In 1990 the National Institutes of Health and the U.S. Department of Energy began an ambitious project to isolate and catalog every gene contained on the human genome. Originally conceived as a 15-year endeavor, the Human Genome Project seeks to identify and locate all the genes contained on human DNA, to store this information and make it available for researchers, and to address the ethical, social, and legal issues that may arise from possessing this knowledge.

The practical benefits of the information derived from the Human Genome Project are enormous. For

> Knowledge about variations in the genetic code is expected to lead to revolutionary new ways to diagnose, treat, and prevent illnesses.

example, because genes play an important role in a wide variety of human disorders, knowledge about variations in the genetic code is expected to lead to revolutionary new ways to diagnose, treat, and prevent illnesses. Researchers have already begun to identify specific genes that contribute to the development of disorders such as cystic fibro-sis, mental retardation, and some forms of cancer.

Although rich with promise, the Human Genome Project raises many social and ethical questions. For example, will predicting the likelihood of cancer in an individual lead to discrimination from potential employers and insurers? Will the knowledge that a person has a 25 percent chance of producing a child with Parkinson's disease affect the choice of having children? How will the products of the Human Genome Project, such as medicines and diagnostic techniques, be shared by the international community, patented, and commercialized? Fortunately, committees made up of ethicists, physicians, researchers, and other concerned professionals have already begun to confront many of these issues. As our understanding of human genetic inheritance continues to grow, it will not, we hope, outpace our understanding of how to apply this knowledge in ways that are both effective and socially responsible. To learn more visit the Human Genome Web site at **http://www.ornl.gov/TechResources/Human_Genome/home.html**

Human genome
The full complement of genes within a human cell.

Behavior genetics
Study of the relationship between heredity and behavior.

Evolutionary psychology
A subfield of psychology concerned with the origins of behaviors and mental processes, their adaptive value, and the purposes they continue to serve.

Heritability
The extent to which variations in a trait can be attributed to genetic factors.

Two different but related fields address the influence of heredity on human behavior—**behavior genetics** and **evolutionary psychology**. Behavior genetics is concerned with how specific behavioral traits are transmitted from parents to their children. Evolutionary psychology looks at the evolutionary mechanisms that account for the origins of various behaviors and mental processes. In the remainder of this chapter we examine both of these areas and see how research has contributed to contemporary psychology.

Animal Behavior Genetics   Several methods using experimental animals can help determine the **heritability** of a behavioral trait—that is, the extent to which variations in that trait can be attributed to genetic factors (Plomin, De-Fries, & McClearn, 1990). One example is a strain study in which close relatives (such as siblings) are intensively inbred over many generations to create strains

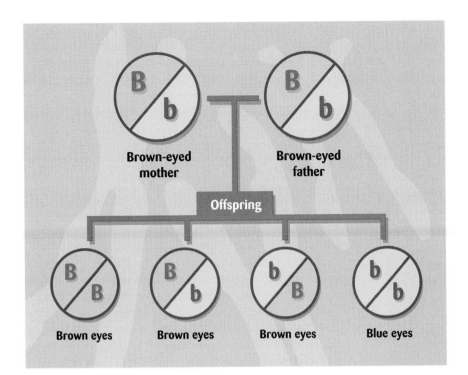

FIGURE 2–14

Transmission of eye color by dominant (*B*) and recessive (*b*) genes. This figure represents the four possible combinations of eye-color genes in these parents' offspring. Because 3 out of the 4 combinations result in brown-eyed children, the chance that any child will have brown eyes is 75 percent.

of animals that are genetically very similar to one another and different from other strains. Mice are often used because they breed quickly and yet have relatively complex behavioral patterns. When animals from different strains are raised together in the same environment, differences between them largely reflect genetic differences. Strain studies have shown that differences between mice regarding such traits as sense of smell, susceptibility to seizures, and performance on a number of learning tasks are all affected by heredity.

Animal selection studies can also be used to assess heritability. In this procedure animals having a trait in common are bred with one another to see the extent to which the trait appears in the next generation. By measuring changes in the proportion of successive generations that have the trait, scientists can estimate the trait's heritability. Such selective breeding has been carried out for thousands of years to create strains of plants and animals with desirable traits. Dogs, for example, have been bred to herd sheep, flush out small animals from their burrows, point in the direction of hidden prey, and retrieve a hunter's kill. Because dog breeds differ greatly in many behavioral characteristics—including excitability, trainability, and social relationships—scientists conclude that variations in these characteristics are, at least to some extent, governed by genes (Plomin, DeFries, & McClearn, 1990).

Human Behavior Genetics For ethical reasons, neither strain nor selection studies can be used to explore human genetics, but scientists have developed a number of molecular genetic techniques that are making it possible to examine the human genetic code directly. Scientists participating in the Human Genome Project have set out to map all 23 pairs of human chromosomes, hoping to learn which genes are associated with which characteristics (D. Johnson, 1990; Plomin & Rende, 1991). The human genome is the complete set of chromosomes with all their associated genes. Researchers have identified an individual gene on chromosome 19 that is associated with some forms of Alzheimer's disease (Corder et al., 1993), while other chromosome sites have been implicated in alcoholism (Uhl, Blum, Nobel, & Smith, 1993) and intelligence (Plomin et al., 1994). Researchers expect that eventually we will be able to determine the role of heredity in even the most complex behaviors (Plomin et al., 1990).

Dogs have been bred over the years to assist humans in such activities as hunting. Selective breeding provides evidence for the heritability of certain behavioral characteristics.

People clearly do inherit physical traits from their parents. Whether—and to what extent—they also inherit behavioral traits remains uncertain.

Identical twins develop from a single ovum and consequently start out with the same genetic material. Fraternal twins develop from two different fertilized ova and so are as different in genetic makeup as any two children of the same parents.

Family studies
Studies of heritability in humans based on the assumption that if genes influence a certain trait, close relatives should be more similar on that trait than distant relatives.

Twin studies
Studies of identical and fraternal twins to determine the relative influence of heredity and environment on human behavior.

Identical twins
Twins developed from a single fertilized ovum and therefore identical in genetic makeup at the time of conception.

Fraternal twins
Twins developed from two separate fertilized ova and therefore different in genetic makeup.

Adoption studies
Research carried out on children, adopted at birth by parents not related to them, to determine the relative influence of heredity and environment on human behavior.

In the meantime, behavior geneticists have learned a great deal about the heritability of human behaviors by analyzing the behavioral similarities of members of the same family. Such **family studies** are based on the assumption that if genes influence differences in some trait, close relatives should be more similar regarding that trait than distant relatives are, because close relatives have more genes in common. Family studies have uncovered strong evidence that heredity plays a role in whether or not people develop certain psychological disorders. Siblings of people with schizophrenia, for example, are about eight times more likely to develop schizophrenia than someone chosen randomly from the general population. And children of schizophrenic parents are about ten times more likely to develop schizophrenia than are other children. Similarly, a controversial study found a link in one family between highly aggressive, violent behavior and the mutations in a gene involved in the activities of certain neurotransmitters (Brunner et al., 1993). Of course, such findings do not rule out the influence of environment. Growing up in a household in which both parents have schizophrenia might cause a child to develop the disorder even if that child does not have a genetic predisposition for the illness (Plomin et al., 1990). Similarly, we cannot rule out the behavioral effects of growing up in a family in which violence is common.

In an effort to separate more clearly the influences of heredity and environment, psychologists often use **twin studies.** Twins can be either identical or fraternal. Because **identical twins** develop from a single fertilized egg, they have identical genes, so any differences between them should be due to environmental differences. **Fraternal twins,** in contrast, develop from two separate fertilized eggs and are no more similar genetically than are other brothers and sisters. The differences between fraternal twins thus stem from both heredity *and* environment. Assuming that the various pairs of twins studied have experienced similar environments, if identical twins are no more alike regarding a particular characteristic than are fraternal twins, then heredity cannot be a very important contributor to variations in that trait. If, on the other hand, identical twins are much more similar on some trait than are fraternal twins, we have reason to suspect that heredity is at least partly the cause.

Some basic assumptions of twin studies have been questioned, however. Identical twins may be treated more alike than fraternal twins, so experience may cause them to be more similar than fraternal twins. Even studies of identical twins reared apart cannot rule out the influence of similar environments, because adoption agencies usually try to place siblings in similar homes. If these twins turn out to be similar regarding certain behavioral traits, how do we know whether the similarity is due to genetics or to the similarities of the homes in which the twins were raised? Moreover, people with a certain characteristic (such as intelligence or attractiveness) are likely to be treated in similar ways by other people. How can we tell with confidence whether their similarities are due to genetics or to the ways in which others have reacted to them during the course of their lives? Do studies of twins raised separately really eliminate environmental variables and focus exclusively on heredity? Or do they demonstrate the extent to which similar environments and life experiences interact with similar genetic codes to produce similar traits and behaviors?

Adoption studies are another way of trying to find answers to questions about the heritability of traits. Adoption studies focus on children who were adopted at birth and brought up by parents not genetically related to them. Adoption studies provide additional evidence for the heritability of intelligence and some forms of mental illness (J. Horn, 1983; Scarr & Weinberg, 1983). By combining the results of *twin, adoption,* and *family* studies, psychologists have obtained an even clearer picture of the role of heredity in schizophrenia. The average risk of schizophrenia steadily increases in direct relation to the closeness of one's biological relationship to a person with the disorder.

In recent years behavior geneticists have begun to probe a wide array of human behaviors once thought to be solely determined by environment. These include sexual orientation (Bailey & Bell, 1993; Bailey & Benishay, 1993; King & McDonald, 1992; Whitam et al., 1993), smoking (Boomsma et al., 1994; Heath & Martin, 1993), chronic alcoholism (Health et al., 1994), and even suicide. Human differences in all these behaviors may have much more of a genetic basis than ever before believed.

Evolutionary Psychology

How might the process of natural selection influence human social behaviors?

While behavior geneticists try to explain the individual differences in human behavior, evolutionary psychologists try to explain the behavioral traits that people have in common. The key to these shared characteristics, they feel, is the process of evolution by **natural selection,** first described by Charles Darwin in *Origin of Species* (1859). The modern theory of evolution contains four assumptions:

1. Variations exist among the individual members of a species.
2. Some of these variations have a genetic basis, and the genes involved may be passed on from one generation to the next.
3. Individuals with traits that give them an advantage over others in surviving and reproducing will leave more offspring, who are apt to inherit the genes that contribute to their parents' fitness.
4. The advantaged offspring are also more likely to survive and reproduce, resulting in an increase in individuals with those characteristics and an increase in the genes responsible for them within the population.

Natural selection therefore promotes the survival and reproduction of individuals who are genetically well adapted to their particular environment. If the environment changes or the individual moves into a new environment, the survival and reproductive value of inherited characteristics may also change, and so eventually may the frequency of genes in the population's gene pool.

Evolutionary psychologists are especially interested in the origins of social behaviors such as aggression, jealousy, number of sexual partners, and criteria for choosing a mate. These behaviors may have been adaptive in our evolutionary past, so the genes related to them may have been perpetuated. For example, different criteria used by the two sexes in selecting a mate might be explained by the influence of natural selection. Consider what historically has been most adaptive for men versus women in choosing a mate. Women have a much greater investment in reproduction than men do. Carrying a fetus through pregnancy and nourishing the baby after birth are biologically a female's responsibility. So from an evolutionary standpoint it is adaptive for females to look for males who will give them support in these tasks: healthy genes, good economic resources, and long-term help in parental care. Men, on the other hand, are limited reproductively only by the number of prospective mates they can attract, because sperm are plentiful and quickly replaced. Mating with younger women at the peak of a woman's fertility, however, will generally increase a man's chances of causing pregnancy and therefore contributing his genes to the next generation. Men, therefore, find it adaptive to mate with as many highly fertile females as they can and to compete with other males for access to these women.

Studies have found that men and women do indeed take different approaches to mate selection, as predicted by evolutionary psychology. For example, one

Natural selection
The mechanism proposed by Charles Darwin in his theory of evolution, which states that organisms best adapted to their environment tend to survive, transmitting their genetic characteristics to succeeding generations, whereas organisms with less adaptive characteristics tend to vanish from the earth.

researcher surveyed more than 10,000 people from 37 cultures to determine what they considered desirable characteristics in mates (Buss, 1989, 1992). In every culture the men put greater emphasis on youth and attractiveness than the women did. In addition, in almost every culture women found men with higher earning capacity to be more desirable. The women in most cultures also considered ambition and industriousness in a mate to be more important traits than did the men.

Evolutionary psychology has its critics, however. Some opponents argue that science is being used to justify perpetuating unjust social policies. These critics claim that simply by saying a trait is adaptive implies that it is both genetically determined and good. In the past, racists and fascists have misused biological theories to promote social injustices. In Nazi Germany, for example, Jews were considered genetically inferior, a view that was used to justify their extermination. Similarly, the evolutionary theory of male–female differences in mate selection could be seen as endorsing male promiscuity because it is biologically adaptive. In response, evolutionary psychologists are quick to point out that their aim is not to shape social policy but to understand the origins of human behavior. They argue further that behaviors that may have contributed to our adaptive success during the early years of human evolution may no longer be adaptive in our current environment and should not be viewed as good and right simply because at one time they may have served an important adaptive function.

Other critics chide evolutionary psychologists for too hastily explaining behaviors from an evolutionary perspective rather than investigating other plausible origins of them. Just because a behavior occurs to some degree across a wide variety of cultures does not necessarily mean that it has evolutionary roots, they argue. Evolutionary psychologists answer that their goal is not to propose evolutionary theories that exclude all other possible explanations; instead, their aim is to offer an evolutionary perspective that may complement other points of view.

The evolutionary perspective is relatively new in psychology and has yet to become one of the field's major approaches. Given the central role that evolutionary theory plays in the other life sciences, however, it is difficult to imagine that it will ever fully disappear from psychology. But only the results of empirical research, which compares it with competing theories of behavior, will determine how widely accepted this intriguing perspective becomes.

Social Implications

What are some of the ethical issues that arise as society gains more control over genetics?

Science is not simply a process that takes place in a laboratory; it can also have widespread effects on society at large. To the extent that we can trace individual differences in human behavior to chromosomes and genes, we have a potential to biologically control people's lives. This potential raises new ethical issues.

Modern techniques of prenatal screening now make it possible to detect many genetic defects even before a baby is born. *Chorionic villus sampling* and *amniocentisis* are two procedures for obtaining samples of cells from fetuses in order to analyze their genes. In the first, the cells are taken from membranes surrounding the fetus; in the second, they are harvested from the fluid in which the fetus grows. Using these procedures, genetic problems are detected in about 2 percent of pregnancies. Does the child in these cases nonetheless have a right to live? Do the parents have a right to abort the fetus? Should society protect all life no matter how imperfect it is in the eyes of some? If not, which defects are so unacceptable that abortion is justified? Most of these questions have a long history, but recent progress in behavior genetics and medicine has given them a new urgency. We are reaching the point at which we will be able to intervene in a fetus's development by replacing some of its genes with others. For which traits might this procedure be considered justified, and who has the right to make those decisions? If in tampering with genes we significantly change our society's gene pool, are future generations harmed or benefited? Such questions pose major ethical dilemmas.

These ethical issues cause many people concern about the future application of new genetic knowledge, but to some extent these concerns may be exaggerated. Far from finding human behavior to be genetically predetermined, the recent work of behavior geneticists actually shows just how important the environment is in determining whether and how genetic predispositions are expressed (Rutter, 1997). In other words, we may inherit biological predispositions, but we do not inherit destinies. Simply by manipulating genes we do not create a certain kind of person. Both heredity *and* environment (nature *and* nurture) play an important role in shaping most significant human behaviors and traits.

REVIEW QUESTIONS

1. "Individual differences in intelligence, emotional reactivity, and susceptibility to schizophrenia and depression may all be influenced by genes." True or false.

2. Match each term with the appropriate definition.

   _____ nature
   a. the study of how traits are passed from one generation to another

   _____ nurture
   b. genetic influences on development and behavior

   _____ DNA
   c. environmental influences on development and behavior

   _____ genetics
   d. the total amount of genetic material in a cell

   _____ genome
   e. complex molecule that carries genetic information

Answers: 1. T. **2.** nature (b); nurture (c); DNA (e); genetics (a); genome (d).

KEY TERMS

psychobiology, p. 48

Neurons: The nervous system's messengers
neuron, p. 48
dendrites, p. 48
axon, p. 48
nerve or tract, p. 48
myelin sheath, p. 48
glial cells/glia, p. 48
ions, p. 48
polarized, p. 48
resting potential, p. 48
neural impulse or action potential, p. 49
graded potentials, p. 49
threshold of excitation, p. 50
absolute refractory period, p. 50
relative refractory period, p. 50
all-or-none law, p. 50
terminal button or axon terminal, p. 50
synaptic space or synaptic cleft, p. 50

synapse, p. 50
synaptic vesicles, p. 51
neurotransmitters, p. 51
receptor site, p. 51
plasticity, p. 53

The central nervous system
central nervous system (CNS), p. 55
peripheral nervous system (PNS), p. 55
spinal cord, p. 55
brain stem, p. 57
medulla, p. 57
pons, p. 57
cerebellum, p. 57
midbrain, p. 57
thalamus, p. 57
hypothalamus, p. 57
reticular formation, p. 58
limbic system, p. 58
cerebral hemispheres, p. 58
cerebral cortex, p. 59
association areas, p. 59
occipital lobes, p. 59
temporal lobes, p. 60

parietal lobes, p. 60
frontal lobes, p. 60
corpus callosum, p. 61
neurogenesis, p. 65

The peripheral nervous system
afferent neurons, p. 67
efferent neurons, p. 67
somatic nervous system, p. 67
autonomic nervous system, p. 67
sympathetic division, p. 67
parasympathetic division, p. 68

The endocrine system
hormones, p. 69
endocrine glands, p. 69
thyroid gland, p. 70
parathyroids, p. 70
pineal gland, p. 70
pancreas, p. 71
pituitary gland, p. 71
gonads, p. 71
adrenal glands, p. 71

Behavior genetics and our human heritage
genes, p. 72
nature versus nurture debate, p. 72
heredity, p. 72
genetics, p. 72
chromosomes, p. 72
deoxyribonucleic acid (DNA), p. 73
traits, p. 73
dominant gene, p. 73
recessive gene, p. 73
polygenic inheritance, p. 73
human genome, p. 74
behavior genetics, p. 74
evolutionary psychology, p. 74
heritability, p. 74
family studies, p. 76
twin studies, p. 76
identical twins, p. 76
fraternal twins, p. 76
adoption studies, p. 76
natural selection, p. 77

CHAPTER REVIEW

Biological processes are the basis of our thoughts, feelings, and actions. All of our behaviors are kept in tune with our surroundings and coordinated with one another through the work of two interacting systems: the nervous system and the endocrine system.

▢ How is a neuron different from other types of cells?

The basic building block of the nervous system is the **neuron,** or nerve cell. Neurons have several characteristics that distinguish them from other cells. Neurons receive messages from other neurons through short fibers, called **dendrites.** A longer fiber, called an **axon,** carries outgoing messages from the cell. A group of axons bundled together forms a **nerve** or **tract.** Some axons are covered with a **myelin sheath,** made up of **glial cells;** this increases neuron efficiency and provides insulation.

▢ What form does a neural message take?

When a neuron is at rest, a state called the **resting potential,** there is a slightly higher concentration of negatively charged **ions** inside its membrane than there is outside. The membrane is said to be **polarized**—that is, the electrical charge inside it is negative relative to its outside. When an incoming message is strong enough, this electrical imbalance abruptly changes (the membrane is depolarized), and an **action potential (neural impulse)** is generated. Incoming messages cause **graded potentials,** which, when combined, may exceed the minimum **threshold of excitation** and make the neuron "fire." After firing, the neuron briefly goes through the **absolute refractory period,** when it will not fire again, and then through the **relative refractory period,** when firing will occur only if the incoming message is much stronger than usual. According to the **all-or-none law,** every firing of a particular neuron produces an impulse of equal strength. More rapid firing of neurons is what communicates the strength of a message.

▢ Why is it important for psychologists to understand how synapses function?

Neurotransmitter molecules, released by **synaptic vesicles,** cross the tiny **synaptic space** (or **cleft**) between an **axon terminal** (or **terminal button**) of a sending neuron and a dendrite of a receiving neuron. Here they latch on to **receptor sites,** much as keys fit into locks, and pass on their excitatory or inhibitory messages. Psychologists need to understand how synapses function because neurotransmitters affect an enormous range of physical and emotional responses.

▢ How do drugs change behavior?

Certain drugs produce psychological effects by increasing or decreasing the amount of neurotransmitters at **synapses.** Other drugs work on receptor sites, blocking the receptors or interfering with the removal or reabsorption of neurotransmitters.

▢ What are the two main parts of the nervous system?

The nervous system is organized into two parts: the **central nervous system (CNS),** which consists of the brain and spinal cord, and the **peripheral nervous system (PNS),** made up of nerves that radiate throughout the body, linking all of the body's parts to the CNS.

▢ Why does a break in the spinal cord cause paralysis below the break?

The **spinal cord** is a complex cable of nerves that connects the brain to most of the rest of the body. It is made up of bundles of long nerve fibers and has two basic functions: to permit some reflex movements and to carry messages to and from the brain. A break in the cord disrupts the flow of impulses from the brain below that point, causing paralysis.

▢ Which areas of the brain process or control breathing, balance, sexual behavior, and visual information? How does the brain allow us to analyze a situation and respond emotionally to it?

The brain contains many regions that serve specific functions, but they all work together as an integrated whole. The lowermost part of the brain is called the **brain stem.** Its first functional region is the **medulla,** a narrow structure nearest the spinal cord, where many of the nerves from the left part of the body cross to the right side of the brain and vice versa. The medulla controls breathing, heart rate, and blood pressure. The **pons** is located just above the medulla. Chemicals produced there help maintain our sleep–wake cycle. The **cerebellum,** which projects out the back of the brain stem, is divided into two hemispheres. It handles certain reflexes, especially those related to balance, and it coordinates body movements into smooth sequences. At the top of the brain stem is the **midbrain,** which is important for hearing and sight.

Lying above the top of the brain stem is the **thalamus,** parts of which relay and translate incoming messages from the sense receptors (except those for smell). Other parts are relay stations for certain messages that travel from one area of the brain to another. The **hypothalamus,** located below the thalamus, is involved in many motivations and emotions and plays a central role in times of stress.

Running through the brain stem and up to the thalamus is a netlike bundle of neurons called the **reticular formation,** which serves to arouse higher brain centers in response to incoming messages. Surrounding the thalamus is a ring of structures known as the **limbic system.** These structures serve various functions, including involvement in emotion and motivation, as well as in memory formation.

The **cerebral hemispheres,** located above the brain stem, thalamus, hypothalamus, and limbic system, take up most of the room inside the skull. The thin outer layer of the cerebral hemispheres is known as the **cerebral cortex.** It is the most recently evolved portion of the human brain, and it regulates our most complex behaviors.

Each cerebral hemisphere is divided into four lobes, partially delineated by deep fissures. Because the same four lobes are on each hemisphere, the brain has two of each kind of lobe. All the lobes have regions, called **association areas,** that integrate information from diverse parts of the cortex, but in addition, all of the lobes have regions with functions that differ from one another. The **occipital lobes,** located at the back of the brain, receive and process basic visual information. The **temporal lobes,** located roughly behind the temples, are important in smell, hearing, and certain complex visual tasks, such as recognizing faces. The left temporal lobe, specifically, has a region that is central to understanding language. The **parietal lobes** sit on top of the temporal and occipital lobes and receive sensory information in the *primary somatosensory cortex* from all over the body. They also play a role in spatial abilities. The **frontal lobes** are responsible for voluntary movements, and they are involved in attention, goal-directed actions, and emotion as well.

☐ Why might it be advantageous for each cerebral hemisphere to specialize in certain functions?

The two cerebral hemispheres are linked by the **corpus callosum,** through which they communicate and coordinate their activities. Nevertheless, each hemisphere appears to specialize in certain tasks (although they also have overlapping functions). The right hemisphere excels at visual and spatial tasks, nonverbal imagery, and the perception of emotion, whereas the left hemisphere excels at language and perhaps analytical thinking, too. The right hemisphere controls the left side of the body, and the left hemisphere controls the right side.

☐ What tools are used for studying the brain? How can brain imaging help people with psychological disorders?

An increasingly sophisticated technology exists for investigating the brain. Among the most important tools are microelectrode techniques, macroelectrode techniques (BEG and ERP), structural imaging (CT scanning and MRI), and functional imaging (EEG imaging, MEG and MSI). Scientists often combine these techniques to study brain activity in unprecedented detail—information that can help in the treatment of schizophrenia and other psychological disorders.

☐ How does the brain communicate with the rest of the body? How is the autonomic branch of the PNS involved in controlling emotions?

The peripheral nervous system (PNS) contains two types of neurons: **afferent neurons,** which carry sensory messages *to* the central nervous system, and **efferent neurons,** which carry messages *from* the CNS. Neurons involved in making voluntary movements of the skeletal muscles belong to a part of the PNS called the **somatic nervous system,** while neurons involved in governing the actions of internal organs belong to a part of the PNS called the **autonomic nervous system.** The autonomic nervous system is itself divided into two parts: the **sympathetic division,** which acts primarily to arouse the body when it is faced with threat, and the **parasympathetic division,** which acts to calm the body down, restoring it to normal levels of arousal.

☐ Why are hormones of interest to psychologists?

The endocrine system is the other communication system in the body. It is made up of **endocrine glands** that produce **hormones,** chemical substances released into the bloodstream to either trigger developmental changes in the body or to activate certain behavioral responses.

☐ What are the symptoms of an overactive and an underactive thyroid?

The **thyroid gland** secretes thyroxin, a hormone involved in regulating the body's rate of metabolism. Symptoms of an overactive thyroid are agitation and tension, while an underactive thyroid produces lethargy.

☐ Where are the parathyroid glands, and what substances do they regulate?

The **parathyroids** secrete parathormone to control and balance the levels of calcium and phosphate in the blood and tissue fluids. This in turn affects the excitability of the nervous system.

☐ What is the function of the pineal gland?

The **pineal gland,** by responding to light, regulates activity levels over the course of the day.

☐ What are two disorders caused by imbalances in pancreatic hormones?

The **pancreas** controls the level of sugar in the blood by secreting insulin and glucagon. When the pancreas secretes too much insulin, the person can suffer *hypoglycemia*. Too little insulin can result in *diabetes*.

☐ Why is the pituitary often called the "master gland"?

Of all the endocrine glands, the **pituitary gland** regulates the largest number of different activities in the body. It affects blood pressure, thirst, uterine contractions in childbirth, milk production, sexual behavior and interest, and the amount and timing of body growth, among other functions. Because of its influences on other glands, it is often called the "master gland."

☐ What are the gonads, and what are their functions?

These reproductive glands—the testes in males and the ovaries in females—secrete hormones called androgens (including testosterone) and estrogens.

☐ What is the role of the adrenal glands in our reactions to stress?

Each of the two **adrenal glands** has two parts: an outer covering, the *adrenal cortex*, and an inner core, the *adrenal medulla*. Both affect our response to stress, although the adrenal cortex affects other body functions, too. One stress-related hormone of the adrenal medulla is epinephrine, which amplifies the effects of the sympathetic nervous system.

☐ What is the nature-versus-nurture debate?

The related fields of **behavior genetics** and **evolutionary psychology** explore the influences of heredity on human behavior. Both are helping to settle the **nature-versus-nurture debate** over the relative contributions of genes and the environment to human similarities and differences.

☐ How is genetic information transmitted to the next generation?

Genetics is the study of how **traits** are passed on from one generation to the next via **genes.** This process is called **heredity.** Each gene is lined up on tiny threadlike bodies called **chromosomes,** which in turn are made up predominantly of **deoxyribonucleic acid (DNA).** Each member of a gene pair can be either **dominant** or **recessive.** In **polygenic inheritance** a number of genes interact to produce a trait.

☐ What methods do psychologists use to study the effects of genes on behavior?

Psychologists use a variety of methods to study **heritability**—that is, the contribution of genes in determining variations in certain traits. Strain studies approach the problem by observing strains of highly inbred genetically similar animals, while selection studies try to determine the extent to which an animal's traits can be passed on from one generation to another. In the study of humans, **family studies** tackle heritability by looking for similarities in traits as a function of biological closeness. Also useful in studying human heritability are **twin studies** and **adoption studies.**

☐ How might the process of natural selection influence human social behaviors?

The theory of evolution by **natural selection** states that organisms best adapted to their environment tend to survive, transmitting their genetic characteristics to succeeding generations, while organisms with fewer adaptive characteristics tend to die off. **Evolutionary psychology** analyzes human behavioral tendencies by examining their adaptive value from an evolutionary perspective. It has proved useful in helping to explain some of the commonalities in human behavior that occur across cultures.

☐ What are some of the ethical issues that arise as society gains more control over genetics?

Manipulating human genes in an effort to change how people develop is a new technology that makes many people uneasy. But their concerns may be exaggerated because genes are not all-powerful. Both heredity and environment play a part in shaping most significant human behaviors and traits. Ethical issues regarding pregnancy, fetal development, and the nature of the human gene pool arise as scientists develop the technology to alter the basic processes of human heredity.

CRITICAL THINKING AND APPLICATIONS

1. Why are withdrawal symptoms from cocaine the opposite of the drug's effects?
2. Brain scans of men and women communicating show very different patterns of brain activity. What impact might these differences have on relationships between the sexes?
3. Because the sympathetic division of the ANS is designed to help us deal with stress, why does long-term stimulation of it cause so many health problems?
4. A clinical psychologist refers a new client to a medical doctor because the client's psychological symptoms could indicate a problem with the thyroid gland. What symptoms might the psychologist be responding to?
5. How do twin studies help determine the relative contribution of genes and environment to human differences?

Visit these online resources at our Companion Website www.prenhall.com/morris

The Psychology Place

Learning Activities	1. Action at the Synapse, p. 51
Research News	2. Planum Temporale: Brain Structure behind Language Evolution?, p. 63
	3. Evolutionary Change before Your Eyes, p. 77
Op-Ed Forum	4. Are We Hostages to Our Brains?, p. 79

Readings

1. Thinking Will Make It So, p. 56
2. Split Brain Revisited, p. 61
3. New Nerve Cells for the Adult Brain, p. 64

Games

1. Label the Neuron, p. 48
2. The Brain Matching Game, p. 57

Web Links:

1. **http://server.bmod.athabascau.ca/html/aupr/biological.htm**, p. 47
   Biological and physiological psychology links.
2. **http://mentalhelp.net/guide/pro02.htm**, p. 47
   Comprehensive Behavioral and Cognitive Sciences; Includes theory and therapy. These are Web links with descriptions and ratings of each source.
3. **http://psych.hanover.edu/Krantz/neurotut.html**, p. 56
   Basic Neural Processes Tutorials to learn about basic brain functioning.
4. **http://uta.maymt.edu/~psychol/brain.html**, p. 58
   The Human Brain: A Learning tool; allows students to view close-up pictures of the brain's lobes.
5. **http://www.neuropat.dote.hu/caud.gif**, p. 59
   Cross-sectional image of the human brain.

Explore these topics on the Mind Matters CD-ROM

Mind Matters

1. Physiological Psychology: Neurons and the Endocrine System, p. 47
2. Physiological Psychology: The Brain, p. 55
3. Evolution and Behavior, p. 72

3

SENSATION AND PERCEPTION

OVERVIEW

SHIRL JENNINGS LOST HIS SIGHT AT AGE 3. SENT TO THE STATE INSTITUTE for blind and deaf children, he studied massage therapy and eventually got a job as a masseur at the DeKalb YMCA, outside Atlanta. Then, at age 51, Shirl underwent an operation to restore his vision. The operation was a success, but his life became a nightmare. For as long as Shirl could remember, he had lived in a "cocoon" of sound, touch, and smell. After years of seeing nothing, suddenly seeing everything was overwhelming. Because he had no visual memory, the images bombarding his mind were strange and often terrifying. Facial expressions confused him. He found the sight of the bodies he had massaged with his hands disgusting. His own shadow frightened him: What was it? Why was it following him? With no experience of depth perception, Shirl found himself stumbling over curbs and falling on stairs—a stranger in a world he had navigated successfully with a cane. Eight years have passed since Shirl had the operation; his sight is deteriorating and he is not upset. "It's really more easy to be blind than see," he told a reporter (*News-Press* 1999, p. 10A).

Ian Waterman, in contrast, is totally dependent on sight. At age 19, Ian suffered a rare viral infection that destroyed part of his nervous system. He has no feeling or sense of touch below his neck, nor can he tell how his body is positioned without looking. Ian's nervous system does register pain, temperature, and fatigue, and his motor muscles respond to messages from his brain. But if the lights suddenly go out, Ian collapses to the floor and cannot move until they're turned back on. Other people with Ian's condition remain in wheelchairs, dependent on others for almost everything. But Ian was determined to use the senses he has to make up for those he'd lost. With much effort, he taught himself to monitor his body with his eyes. For instance, to judge the weight of an object he watches his body. The faster and higher his arms move picking the object up, the lighter the object must be. But he cannot *feel* weight or even where his arms are, a condition most people cannot even imagine. Ian says that before his problem was diagnosed, "I often thought I might be mad" (*Monitor* 1998, p. 18).

The cases of Shirl and Ian demonstrate the resilience of the human body—and spirit. They illustrate the remarkable ability of the human brain to use backup systems when one or another part of the nervous system malfunctions. And they remind us how dependent we are on sensation and perception to provide us with information about the world. We are constantly bombarded with sensory data—images, sounds, smells and so on. But to make sense of these raw data we rely on perception. In Shirl's case, an operation restored his sight, but after a lifetime in darkness he hadn't developed the perceptual capacity to interpret the unfamiliar visual images flooding his brain.

For the most part we take our sensation and perception for granted. Without much conscious thought, we focus on a book or computer screen, tune in when we hear our name spoken, or look for the source of a noxious odor. Although our brain receives a steady stream of information about our body's position and movement (the senses Ian lost), we notice this only when we are uncomfortable or when we are trying to improve our tennis serve or learn a new dance step. Yet our brains are constantly receiving and processing vast amounts of information.

This chapter explores just how we interpret the raw data picked up by our senses. First we examine **sensation**— that is, the basic experience of stimulation of the body's senses: sight, hearing, smell, taste, balance, touch, and pain. We describe how each of the body's senses converts physical energy—light or sound waves, for example—into nerve impulses. Then, by investigating how our brains organize and interpret elementary sensations, we see how we arrive at our **perception** of meaningful events. In the process we discuss how we perceive patterns, distance, and movement, as well as how we are able to identify an object despite changing or even contradictory information. Finally, we examine how our personal characteristics influence the way we perceive the world.

The Nature of Sensory Processes

What causes us to have sensory experiences?

The Character of Sensation

How is energy, such as light or sound, converted into a message to the brain?

The sequence of events that produces a sensation seems quite simple: Initially, some form of energy, either from an external source or from inside the body, stimulates a **receptor cell** in one of the sense organs, such as the eye or the ear. Each receptor cell responds to one particular form of energy—light waves in the case of vision, or vibration in the case of hearing. When there is sufficient energy, the receptor cell sends to the brain a coded signal that varies according to the characteristics of the stimulus. For instance, a very bright light might be coded by the rapid firing of a set of nerve cells, but a dim light would set off a much slower firing sequence. The neural signal is coded still further as it passes along the sensory nerves to the central nervous system, so the message that reaches the brain is precise and detailed. Thus the coded signal that the brain receives from a flashing red light differs significantly from the message signaling a soft yellow haze. And both of these signals are coded in a much different way from a loud, piercing noise.

In a way, each sensory experience is an illusion created in the brain by neural signals. The brain, isolated inside the skull, is bombarded by the "clicks" of coded neural signals arriving on millions of nerve fibers. The one-to-one relationship between stimulation of a specific nerve and the resulting sensory experience is known as the *doctrine of specific nerve energies*: The clicks on the optic nerve reliably produce an experience we call vision, just as clicks moving along an auditory nerve produce the experience we call hearing, or audition. Even if the clicks on the optic nerve are caused by something other than light, the result is still a visual experience. Gentle pressure on an eye, for instance, results in signals from the optic nerve that the brain interprets as visual patterns—the visual pattern of "seeing stars" when we're hit in the eye is so familiar that even cartoons depict it.

Sensory Thresholds

What is the dimmest light or softest sound that we can sense?

To produce any sensation at all, the physical energy reaching a receptor cell must achieve a minimum intensity, or **absolute threshold.** Any stimulation below the absolute threshold will not be experienced. But how much sensory stimulation is enough? How loud must a sound be, for example, for a person to hear it? How bright does a blip on a radar screen have to be for the operator to see it?

To answer such questions, psychologists present a stimulus at different intensities and ask people whether they sense anything. You might expect that there would come a point at which people would suddenly say, "Now I see the flash," or "Now I hear a sound." But actually there is a range of intensities over which a person sometimes—but not always—can sense a stimulus. The absolute threshold is defined as the point at which a person can detect the stimulus 50 percent of the time that it is presented (see Figure 3–1).

Sensation
The experience of sensory stimulation.

Perception
The process of creating meaningful patterns from raw sensory information.

Receptor cell
A specialized cell that responds to a particular type of energy.

Absolute threshold
The least amount of energy that can be detected as a stimulation 50 percent of the time.

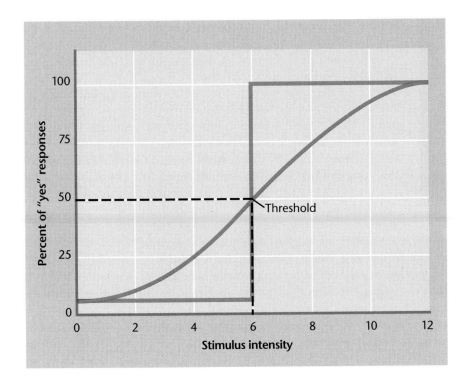

FIGURE 3–1

Determining a sensory threshold. The red line represents an ideal case: At all intensities below the threshold, the person reports no sensation or no change in intensity; at all intensities above the threshold, the person reports a sensation or a change in intensity. In actual practice, however, we never come close to the ideal of the red line. The blue line shows the actual responses of a typical person. The threshold is taken as the point where the person reports a sensation or a change in intensity 50 percent of the time.

Although there are differences among people—and even from moment to moment for the same person—the absolute threshold for each of our senses is remarkably low. According to McBurney and Collings (1984), the approximate absolute thresholds *under ideal circumstances* are as follows:

- Taste: 1 gram (0.0356 ounce) of table salt in 500 liters (529 quarts) of water
- Smell: One drop of perfume diffused throughout a 3-room apartment
- Touch: The wing of a bee falling on the cheek from a height of 1 centimeter (0.39 inch)
- Hearing: The tick of a watch from 6 meters (20 feet) in very quiet conditions
- Vision: A candle flame seen from 50 kilometers (30 miles) on a clear, dark night

Under normal conditions, absolute thresholds vary according to the level and nature of *ongoing* sensory stimulation. For example, your threshold for the taste of salt would be considerably higher after you eat salted peanuts, and your vision threshold would be much higher in the middle of a sunny day than at midnight on a moonless night. In both cases the absolute threshold would rise because of sensory **adaptation,** in which our senses automatically adjust to the overall average level of stimulation in a particular setting. When confronted by a great deal of stimulation, they become much less sensitive than when the overall level of stimulation is low. Similarly, when the level of stimulation drops, our sensory apparatus becomes much more sensitive than under conditions of high stimulation. This process of adaptation allows all of our senses to be keenly attuned to a multitude of environmental cues without getting overloaded. We can hear the breathing of a sleeping dog when we enter a quiet room, but if we are on a city street during rush hour, the noise would be deafening if our ears did not become less sensitive to stimulation. Similarly, we can go from a dark room into bright sunshine without experiencing great pain. (Later in this chapter we look more closely at adaptation.)

Imagine now that you can hear a particular sound. How much stronger must the sound become before you notice that it has grown louder? The smallest change in stimulation that you can detect 50 percent of the time is called the

Adaptation
An adjustment of the senses to the level of stimulation they are receiving.

Adding 1 pound to this barbell would not produce a noticeable difference because 1 pound would fall below the difference threshold for this amount of weight.

difference threshold, or the **just noticeable difference (jnd).** Like the absolute threshold, the difference threshold varies from person to person and from moment to moment for the same person. And like absolute thresholds, difference thresholds tell us something about the flexibility of sensory systems. For example, adding 2 pounds to a 10-pound load will certainly be noticed, so we might assume that the difference threshold must be considerably less than 2 pounds. Yet adding 2 pounds to a 100-pound load probably would not make much of a difference, so we might conclude that the difference threshold must be considerably more than 2 pounds. But how can the difference threshold (jnd) be both less than and greater than 2 pounds? It turns out that the difference threshold varies according to the strength or intensity of the original stimulus. The greater the stimulus, the greater the change necessary to produce a jnd.

In the 1830s Ernst Weber concluded that the difference threshold is a constant *fraction or proportion* of the original stimulus, a theory known as **Weber's law.** It is important to note that the values of these fractions vary significantly for the different senses. Hearing, for example, is very sensitive: We can detect a change in sound of 0.3 percent (⅓ of 1 percent). By contrast, producing a jnd in taste requires a 20 percent (⅕) change. To return to our earlier example of weight, a change in weight of 2 percent (1/50) is necessary to produce a jnd. So adding 1 pound to a 50-pound load would produce a noticeable difference half of the time; adding 1 pound to a 100-pound load would not.

Subliminal Perception

Under what circumstances might messages outside our awareness nevertheless affect our behavior?

The idea of a threshold implies that some events occur *subliminally*—below our level of awareness. Can subliminal messages used in advertisements and self-help tapes, for example, change people's behavior? For decades the story has circulated that refreshment sales increased dramatically when a movie theater in New Jersey flashed subliminal messages to "Drink Coca-Cola" and "Eat Popcorn." In fact, sales of Coke and popcorn did not change.

Similarly, audiotapes with subliminal self-help messages (which make up between one-quarter and one-third of all spoken-word audiocassette sales) often promise more than they deliver. In one series of studies, volunteers used such tapes for several weeks. About half said they had improved as a result of listening to the tapes, but objective tests detected no measurable change. Moreover, the perceived improvement had more to do with the label on the tape than its subliminal content: About half the people who received a tape labeled "Improve Memory" said that their memory had improved even though many of them had actually received a tape intended to boost self-esteem, and about one-third of the people who listened to tapes labeled "Increase Self-Esteem" said their self-esteem had gone up, though many of them had actually been listening to tapes designed to improve memory (Greenwald et al., 1991).

Nevertheless, there is some evidence that under carefully controlled conditions people can be influenced by information outside their awareness. In one study, for example, a group of people was shown a list of words related to competition, while a second group was exposed to a list of neutral words (Nuberg, 1988). Later, when playing a game, participants who had been shown the subliminal list of words with competitive overtones became especially competitive. In another study, one group of subjects was subliminally exposed to words conveying honesty (a positive trait), whereas other subjects were subliminally exposed to words conveying hostility (a negative trait). Subsequently, all the

Difference threshold or just noticeable difference (jnd)
The smallest change in stimulation that can be detected 50 percent of the time.

Weber's law
The principle that the jnd for any given sense is a constant fraction or proportion of the stimulation being judged.

HIGHLIGHTS

Extrasensory Perception

Some people claim to have an extra power of perception, one beyond those of the normal senses. This unusual power, known as *extrasensory perception*, or *ESP*, has been defined as "a response to an unknown event not presented to any known sense" (McConnell, 1969). The term *ESP* actually refers to a number of different phenomena, including *clairvoyance* (awareness of an unknown object or event), *telepathy* (knowledge of someone else's thoughts or feelings), and *precognition* (foreknowledge of future events). The operation of ESP and other psychic phenomena is the focus of a field of study called *parapsychology*.

Much of the research into ESP has been criticized for poor experimental design, failure to control for dishonesty, selective reporting of results, or inability to obtain repeatable results (Hansel, 1969). Nevertheless, psychologists continue to explore the possibility of psychic phenomena using increasingly sophisticated procedures. For instance, Bem and Honorton (1994), using what has come to be known as the *autoganzfeld* procedure, reported encouraging results in their initial investigations of telepathy. In this procedure, a "sender," isolated in a soundproof room, concentrates on a picture or video segment randomly selected (by a computer) from a set of 80 photos or 80 videotape segments. A "receiver" is placed alone in another soundproof room. The receiver engages in deep relaxation while wearing half of a Ping-Pong ball over each eye

---

Surveys indicate that psychologists and other scientists do not discount ESP entirely.

---

and headphones playing a hissing sound (to provide uniform visual and auditory stimulation). The receiver then tries to experience any message or image coming from the sender. The experiment concludes with a test in which a computer displays four photos or videotape segments to the receiver, who rates them for similarity to impressions or images received during the sending phase of the experiment. Although receivers did not identify all the actual photos and videos that the senders were looking at, they performed significantly better than would be expected by chance alone.

Unfortunately, recent attempts to replicate Bem and Honorton's original findings have not generally met with success. Indeed, an extensive review of 30 studies involving more than 1,100 participants concluded that no convincing evidence for psychic functioning had emerged from the majority of studies that have used the autoganzfeld procedure (Milton & Wiseman, 1999).

Surveys indicate that psychologists and other scientists do not discount ESP entirely. In fact, one survey (Wagner & Monnet, 1979) indicated that 34 percent of psychologists accepted ESP as either an established fact or a likely possibility. Even many of those who remain skeptical do not dismiss ESP out of hand but rather point out that experimentation has not yet given scientific credence to these phenomena.

---

subjects read a description of a woman whose behavior could be looked at as either honest or hostile. When asked to assess various personality characteristics of the woman, the participants who had been subliminally exposed to "honest" words rated her as more honest, and those who had been subliminally exposed to "hostile" words judged her as being hostile (Erdley & D'Agostino, 1988).

Studies like these indicate that in a controlled laboratory setting people can process and respond to information outside of awareness. But the fact remains that there is no independent scientific evidence that subliminal messages in advertising or self-help tapes have any appreciable effect (Beatty & Hawkins, 1989; Greenwald et al., 1991; T. G. Russell, Rowe, & Smouse, 1991; Smith & Roger, 1994; Underwood, 1994).

So far we have been talking about the general characteristics of sensation, but each of the body's sensory systems works a little differently. Individual sensory systems contain receptor cells that specialize in converting a particular kind of energy into neural signals. The threshold at which this conversion occurs varies from system to system. So do the mechanisms by which sensory data are sent to the brain for additional processing. We now turn to the unique features of each of the sensory systems.

Review Questions

Match the following terms with the appropriate definition.

1. ___ receptor cell
2. ___ absolute threshold
3. ___ difference threshold
4. ___ jnd
5. ___ Weber's law
6. ___ subliminal perception

a. just noticeable difference

b. perception of sensory information that is below the threshold of awareness

c. smallest stimulus detected 50 percent of the time

d. difference threshold is a constant fraction of the stimulus

e. smallest change in stimulus detectable 50 percent of the time

f. converts energy into a neural signal

Answers: 1. f, 2. c, 3. a or e, 4. a or e, 5. d, 6. b.

Vision

Why have psychologists studied vision more than any other sense?

Different animal species depend more on some senses than on others. Dogs rely heavily on the sense of smell, bats on hearing, some fish on taste. But for humans, vision is the most important sense, so it has received the most attention from psychologists. To understand vision, we need to look first at the parts of the visual system, beginning with the structure of the eye.

The Visual System

How does light create a neural impulse?

The structure of the human eye, including the cellular path to the brain, is shown in Figure 3–2. Light enters the eye through the **cornea,** the transparent protective coating over the front part of the eye. It then passes through the **pupil,** the opening in the center of the **iris,** the colored part of the eye. In very bright light the muscles in the iris contract to make the pupil smaller and thus protect the eye from damage. This contraction also helps us to see better in bright light. In dim light the muscles relax to open the pupil wider and let in as much light as possible.

Inside the pupil light moves through the **lens,** which focuses it onto the **retina,** the light-sensitive inner lining of the back of the eyeball. Normally the lens is focused on a middle distance and changes shape to focus on objects that are closer or farther away. To focus on a very close object, tiny muscles contract and make the lens rounder. To focus on something far away, the muscles flatten the lens. On the retina and directly behind the lens is a depressed spot called the **fovea** (see Figure 3–3). The fovea occupies the center of the visual field, and images that pass through the lens are in sharpest focus here. Thus the words you are now reading are hitting the fovea, while the rest of what you see—a desk, walls, or whatever—is striking other areas of the retina.

The Receptor Cells   The retina contains the *receptor cells* responsible for vision. These cells are sensitive to only a fraction of the spectrum of electromagnetic energy, which includes *light* along with other energies (see Figure 3–4). Energies in the electromagnetic spectrum are referred to by their **wavelength.** The shortest wavelengths that we can see are experienced as violet-blue colors; the longest appear as reds.

There are two kinds of receptor cells in the retina—**rods** and **cones**—named for their characteristic shapes (see Figure 3–5). About 120 million rods and 8 million cones are present in the retina of each eye. Rods and cones differ from

Cornea
The transparent protective coating over the front part of the eye.

Pupil
A small opening in the iris through which light enters the eye.

Iris
The colored part of the eye.

Lens
The transparent part of the eye inside the pupil that focuses light onto the retina.

Retina
The lining of the eye containing receptor cells that are sensitive to light.

Fovea
The area of the retina that is the center of the visual field.

Wavelengths
The different energies represented in the electromagnetic spectrum.

Rods
Receptor cells in the retina responsible for night vision and perception of brightness.

Cones
Receptor cells in the retina responsible for color vision.

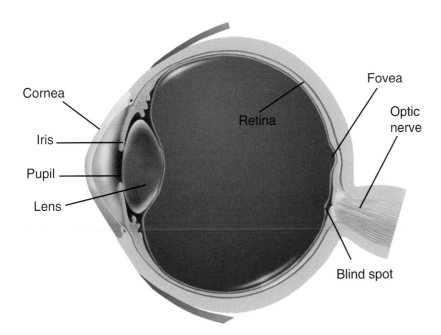

FIGURE 3–2

A cross section of the human eye. Light enters the eye through the cornea, passes through the pupil, and is focused by the lens onto the retina.

Source: Adapted from Hubel, 1963.

FIGURE 3–3

The retina. A view of the retina through an ophthalmoscope, an instrument used to inspect blood vessels in the eye. The small dark spot is the *fovea*. The yellow circle marks the *blind spot*, where the optic nerve leaves the eye.

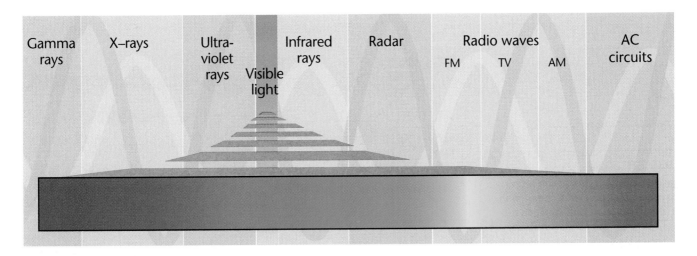

FIGURE 3–4

The electromagnetic spectrum. The eye is sensitive to only a very small segment of the spectrum, known as *visible light*.

each other in a number of ways. Rods, chiefly responsible for *night vision*, respond only to varying degrees or intensities of light and dark. Cones, in contrast, allow us to see colors. Operating chiefly in daylight, cones are also less sensitive to light than rods are (MacLeod, 1978). In this regard, cones, like color film, work best in relatively bright light. The more sensitive rods, like black-and-white film, respond to much lower levels of illumination.

Cones are found mainly, but not exclusively, in the fovea, which contains no rods. The greatest density of cones is in the very center of the fovea, where images are projected onto the retina in sharpest focus. Rods predominate just outside the fovea. The greater the distance from the fovea, the sparser both rods and cones become until at the extreme edges of the retina there are almost no cones and only a few rods.

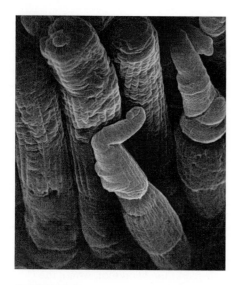

FIGURE 3–5

Rods and cones.   As you can see from this photomicrograph, the rods and cones are named for their shape.

Rods and cones also differ in the ways that they connect to the nerve cells leading to the brain. Both rods and cones connect to specialized neurons called **bipolar cells,** which have only one axon and one dendrite (see Figure 3–6). In the fovea, cones generally connect with only one bipolar cell—a sort of "private line" arrangement. In contrast, it is normal for several rods to share a single bipolar cell.

These characteristics of rods and cones explain some of our more common visual experiences. For example, the location of the rods and cones means that at night you can best see a dimly lit object if you look slightly to one side of it. When you look directly at an object, its image falls on the fovea, which has only the relatively light-insensitive cones. When you look slightly to one side of an object, however, its image falls next to the fovea, onto the highly light-sensitive rods. Moreover, a weak stimulus may not prompt the cones to fire their bipolar cells. But because many rods usually converge on a single bipolar cell, that neuron is much more likely to fire—initiating a sensory message to the brain—in dim light.

Our ability to see improves as light intensity increases: For "close" activities such as reading, sewing, and writing, the more light the better. If you cannot make out the details of an object, moving it into direct sunlight or under a lamp enables you to see it better. The stronger the illumination, the greater the number of cones stimulated; the greater the number of cones stimulated, the more likely that bipolar cells will start a message to the brain.

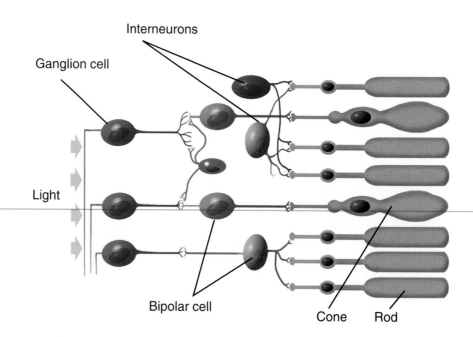

FIGURE 3–6

A close-up of the layers of the retina. Light must pass between the *ganglion cells* and the *bipolar cells* to reach the rods and cones. The sensory messages then travel back out from the receptor cells, through the bipolar cells, to the ganglion cells. The axons of the ganglion cells gather together to form the *optic nerve*, which carries the messages from both eyes to the brain (see Figure 3–2).

Bipolar cells
Neurons that have only one axon and one dendrite; in the eye, these neurons connect the receptors on the retina to the ganglion cells.

Visual acuity
The ability to distinguish fine details visually.

For related reasons, vision is sharpest—even in normal light—whenever you look directly at an object and its image falls on the fovea. In the fovea the one-to-one connection between cones and bipolar cells allows for maximum **visual acuity**—the ability to visually distinguish fine details. You can easily see how acuity works by conducting the following experiment: Hold this book about 18 inches from your eyes and look at the "X" in the center of the line below. Notice how your vision drops off for words and letters toward the left and right ends of the line.

This is a test to show how visual X acuity varies across the retina.

Your fovea picks up the "X" and about four letters to each side. This is the area of greatest visual acuity. The letters at the left and right ends of the line fall well outside the fovea, where there are many more rods than cones. Because rods normally pool their signals to their bipolar cells, the signal that goes to the brain is less detailed. Outside the fovea acuity drops by as much as 50 percent.

Adaptation Earlier in the chapter we introduced the term *adaptation*, the process by which our senses adjust to different levels of stimulation. In the case of vision, adaptation occurs as the sensitivity of rods and cones changes according to how much light is available. When you go from bright sunlight into a dimly lit theater, your cones are initially fairly insensitive to light, and you can see little as you look for a seat. During the first 10 minutes in the dark, the cones become increasingly sensitive to the dim light, and you will be able to see things directly in front of you, at least as well as you are going to: After about 10 minutes the cones do not become any more sensitive. But the rods continue adapting until they reach their maximum sensitivity, about 30 minutes after you enter a darkened room. The process by which rods and cones become more sensitive to light in response to lowered levels of illumination is called **dark adaptation.** But even with dark adaptation there is usually not enough energy in very dim light to stimulate many cones, so you see only a black-and-white-and-gray world of different brightnesses.

Problems with dark adaptation account in part for the much greater incidence of highway accidents at night (Leibowitz & Owens, 1977). When people drive at night, their eyes shift from the darkened interior of the car, to the road area illuminated by headlights, to the darker areas at the side of the road. Unlike the situation in a darkened movie theater, these changing night-driving conditions do not permit complete adaptation of either rods or cones, so neither system is operating at maximum efficiency. Thus at night people may be able to focus fairly well on the location of an object—say, a bicyclist in the middle of the road—but may not be able to determine how far away the bicyclist is or how fast the bicyclist is moving. Because most drivers are generally unaware of the deterioration of their vision at night, they may overestimate their ability to stop in time to avoid an accident.

In the reverse process, **light adaptation,** the rods and cones become less sensitive to light. By the time you leave a movie theater, your rods and cones have grown very sensitive, and all the neurons fire at once when you go into bright outdoor light. You squint and shield your eyes, and your irises contract—all of which reduces the amount of light entering your pupils and striking your retinas. As light adaptation proceeds, the rods and cones become less sensitive to stimulation by light. Within about a minute both rods and cones are fully adapted to the light, and you no longer need to shield your eyes.

You can observe the effects of dark and light adaptation by staring continuously at the dot in the center of the upper square in Figure 3–7 for about 20 seconds, then shifting your gaze to the dot in the lower square. A gray-and-white pattern should appear in the lower square. (When looking at the lower square, if you blink your eyes or shade the book from bright light, the illusion will be even stronger.) When you look at the lower square, the striped areas that were black in the upper square will now seem to be white, and the areas that were white in the upper square will now appear gray. This **afterimage** appeared because the part of the retina that was exposed to the dark stripes of the upper square became more sensitive (it dark-adapted), and the area exposed to the white part of the upper square became less sensitive (it light-adapted). When you shifted your eyes to the lower square, the less sensitive parts of the retina produced the sensation of gray rather than white. This afterimage fades within a minute as the retina adapts again, this time to the solid white square.

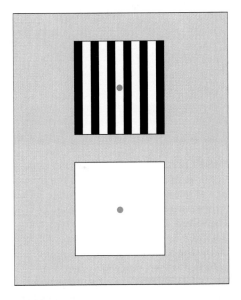

FIGURE 3–7

An afterimage. First stare continuously at the center of the upper square for about 20 seconds, then look at the dot in the lower square. Within a moment, a gray-and-white afterimage should appear inside the lower square.

Dark adaptation
Increased sensitivity of rods and cones in darkness.

Light adaptation
Decreased sensitivity of rods and cones in bright light.

Afterimage
Sense experience that occurs after a visual stimulus has been removed.

FIGURE 3–8

Finding your blind spot. To locate your blind spot, hold the book about a foot away from your eyes. Then close your right eye, stare at the "X," and slowly move the book toward you and away from you until the red dot disappears.

These examples show how visual adaptation is a partial back-and-forth process. The eyes adjust, but they never adapt completely. If stimulation somehow remained constant and the eyes did adapt completely, all the receptors would gradually become totally insensitive and we would be unable to see anything at all. In the real world our eyes do not adapt completely, because light stimulation is rarely focused on the same receptor cells long enough for them to become totally insensitive. Rather, small involuntary eye movements keep the image moving slightly on the retina, so the receptor cells never have time to adapt completely.

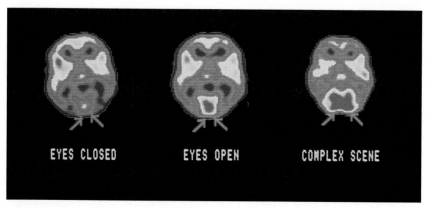

Nerve fibers from each eye cross to opposite sides of the brain, enabling the optic nerves to carry visual information to different parts of the brain. As these PET scans show, the more complex the scene, the more the visual areas of the brain (primarily the occipital lobes to the rear of both hemispheres, as shown by the arrows) are engaged in active processing. (High levels of brain activity are shown as yellow and red; low levels of activity are shown as green and blue.)

Ganglion cells
Neurons that connect the bipolar cells in the eyes to the brain.

Optic nerve
The bundle of axons of ganglion cells that carries neural messages from each eye to the brain.

Blind spot
The place on the retina where the axons of all the ganglion cells leave the eye and where there are no receptors.

Optic chiasm
The point near the base of the brain where some fibers in the optic nerve from each eye cross to the other side of the brain.

From Eye to Brain We have so far directed our attention to the eye, but messages from the eye must travel along multiple pathways to the brain in order for a visual experience to occur (see Figure 3–6). To begin with, rods and cones are connected to bipolar cells in many different numbers and combinations. In addition, sets of neurons called *interneurons* link receptor cells to one another and bipolar cells to one another. Eventually these bipolar cells hook up with the **ganglion cells,** leading out of the eye. The axons of the ganglion cells join to form the **optic nerve,** which carries messages from each eye to the brain. Although there are more than 100 million rods and cones in each retina, there are only about 1 million ganglion cells in the optic nerve. Thus a single ganglion cell must transfer to the brain a "summary" of information from a large number of individual receptor cells.

The place on the retina where the axons of all the ganglion cells join to form the optic nerve is called the **blind spot.** This area contains no receptor cells, so even when light from a small object is focused directly on the blind spot, the object will not be seen (see Figure 3–8). After the nerve fibers that make up the optic nerves leave the eyes, they separate, and some of them cross to the other side of the head at the **optic chiasm** (see Figure 3–9). The nerve fibers from the right side of each eye travel to the right hemisphere of the brain; those from the left side of each eye travel to the left hemisphere. Thus, as shown in Figure 3–9, visual information about any object in the left visual field, the area to the left of the viewer, will go to the right hemisphere (the pathway traced by the red line in Figure 3–9). Similarly, information about any object in the right visual field, the area to the right of the viewer, will go to the left hemisphere (the pathway traced by the blue line). (You can

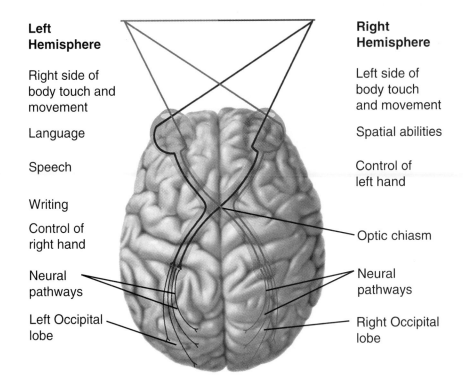

Left visual field   Right visual field

Left Hemisphere

Right side of body touch and movement

Language

Speech

Writing

Control of right hand

Neural pathways

Left Occipital lobe

Right Hemisphere

Left side of body touch and movement

Spatial abilities

Control of left hand

Optic chiasm

Neural pathways

Right Occipital lobe

FIGURE 3–9

The neural connections of the visual system. Messages about the red-colored area in the left visual field of each eye travel to the right occipital lobe; information about the blue area in the right visual field of each eye goes to the left occipital lobe. The crossover point is the *optic chiasm.*

Source: Adapted from "The Split Brain of Man," by Michael S. Gazzaniga. Copyright © 1967 by Scientific American, Inc.

refer back to Figures 2–9 and 2–10 in Chapter 2, The Biological Basis of Behavior, to recall how researchers took advantage of the split-processing of the two visual fields to study split-brain patients.)

The optic nerves carry their messages to various parts of the brain. Some messages reach the area of the brain that controls the reflex movements that adjust the size of the pupil. Others go to the region that directs the eye muscles to change the shape of the lens. But the main destinations for messages from the retina are the visual projection areas of the cerebral cortex (see Figure 2–7, the occipital lobe), where the complex coded messages from the retina are registered and interpreted.

Knowledge about the way in which visual information is coded and relayed to the brain has valuable practical applications. For example, people in the early stages of *glaucoma*, a condition that can cause permanent loss of vision, tend to lose their dim-light vision before any permanent damage is done to the optic nerve or to daylight vision. Thus researchers hope to use loss of dim-light vision as an early warning sign of glaucoma (Dadona, Hendrickson, & Quigley, 1991).

Color Vision

How do we see color?

Humans, like most mammals, can see a range of colors. In the following pages we first explore characteristics of color vision and then consider how the eyes convert light energy into sensations of color.

Properties of Color   Look at the color solid in Figure 3–10. What do you see? Most people report that they see some oranges, some yellows, some reds—

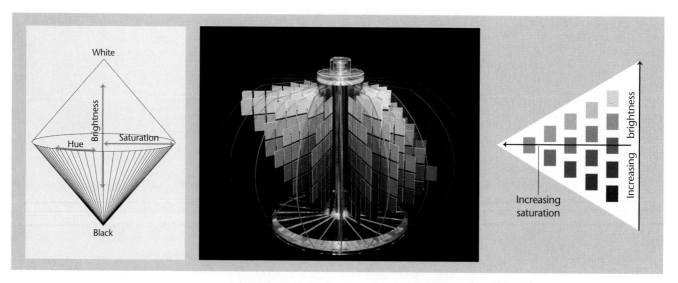

FIGURE 3–10

The color solid. In the center portion of the figure, known as a color solid, the dimension of *hue* is represented around the circumference. *Saturation* ranges along the radius from the inside to the outside of the solid. *Brightness* varies along the vertical axis. The drawing at the left illustrates this schematically. The illustration at the right shows changes in saturation and brightness for the same hue.

a number of different colors. We call these different colors **hues,** and to a great extent the hues you see depend on the wavelength of the light reaching your eyes (see Figure 3–4).

Now look at the triangle of green colors on the right side of Figure 3–10. Although each color patch on the triangle is the same hue, the green color is deepest or richest toward the left side of the triangle. The vividness or richness of a hue is its **saturation.**

Finally, notice that the colors near the top of the color patches are almost white, while those close to the bottom are almost black. This is the dimension of **brightness,** which depends largely on the strength of the light entering your eyes. If you squint and look at the color solid, you will reduce the apparent brightness of all the colors in the solid, and many of them will appear to become black.

Hue, saturation, and brightness are three separate aspects of our experience of color. Although people can distinguish only about 150 hues (Coren, Porac, & Ward, 1984), gradations of saturation and brightness within those 150 hues allow us to see more than 300,000 different colors (Hochberg, 1978; Kaufman, 1979). Some of this variety is captured in Figure 3–10.

Theories of Color Vision   If you look closely at a color television screen, you will see that the picture is actually made up of tiny red, green, and blue dots that blend together to give all possible hues. The same principle is at work in our own ability to see thousands of colors.

For centuries scientists have known that they could produce all 150 basic hues by mixing together only a few lights of different colors (see Figure 3–11). Specifically, red, green, and blue lights—the primary colors for light mixtures—can be combined to create any hue. For example, red and green lights combine to give yellow; red and blue lights combine to make magenta. Combining red, green, and blue lights in equal intensities produces white. The process of mixing lights of different wavelengths is called **additive color mixing,** because each light adds additional wavelengths to the overall mix.

Hue
The aspect of color that corresponds to names such as red, green, and blue.

Saturation
The vividness or richness of a hue.

Brightness
The nearness of a color to white as opposed to black.

Additive color mixing
The process of mixing lights of different wavelengths to create new hues.

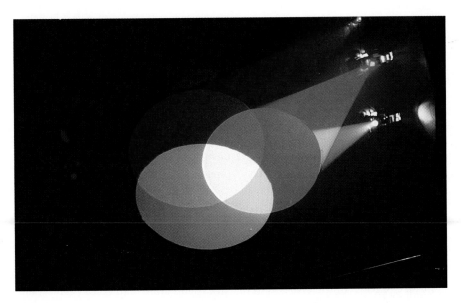

FIGURE 3–11

Additive color mixing. Mixing light waves is an *additive process*. When red and green lights are combined, the resulting hue is yellow. Adding blue light to the other two yields white light.

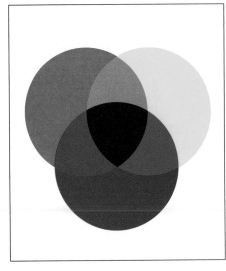

FIGURE 3–12

Subtractive color mixing. The process of mixing paint pigments rather than lights is a *subtractive process,* because the pigments absorb some wavelengths and reflect others. A mixture of the three primary pigments (red, yellow, and blue) absorbs all wavelengths, producing black.

The rules for mixing paints (or pigments) differ from those for lights (see Figure 3–12). For example, when you mix red and blue paints, you get violet, not magenta: Red paint absorbs light from the blue end of the spectrum and reflects light from the red end, whereas blue paint absorbs light from the red end of the spectrum and reflects light from the blue end (see Figure 3–4). Thus, when mixed, these pigments reflect only the red and blue wavelengths, giving violet. This process is called **subtractive color mixing,** because each paint subtracts or absorbs light from various portions of the spectrum. For paint pigments the primary colors are red, yellow, and blue. Graphic designers working on computers must be very attentive to the difference between additive and subtractive color mixing. They work with the "RGB" (red, green, blue) color system if their work is going to be displayed only on the computer screen, but they must change to subtractive color mixing if their work is to be printed.

In the 1800s the German physiologist Hermann von Helmholtz drew on his knowledge of additive color mixing to propose that the eye contains some cones that are sensitive to reds, some that pick up greens, and still others that respond most strongly to blue-violet. According to Helmholtz's hypothesis, known as the **trichromatic theory,** color experiences in the brain come from mixing the signals from the three receptors. But trichromatic theory accounts for only some kinds of **colorblindness**—the partial or total inability to perceive hues (see Figure 3–13). Because Helmholtz's hypothesis falls short of explaining all color-vision experiences, including afterimages (see Figure 3–14), another German scientist, Ewald Hering, proposed an alternative theory in 1878. Hering's **opponent-process theory** postulated that our visual response system is made up of three pairs of color receptors: a yellow-blue pair and a red-green pair that determine the hue a person sees, and a black-white pair that assesses the brightness of colors. The members of each pair work in opposition to each other. The yellow-blue pair cannot relay messages about yellow and blue light at the same time, nor can the red-green pair send both red and green messages at the same time. This explains why we never

Subtractive color mixing
The process of mixing pigments, each of which absorbs some wavelengths of light and reflects others.

Trichromatic theory
The theory of color vision that holds that all color perception derives from three different color receptors in the retina (usually red, green, and blue receptors).

Colorblindness
Partial or total inability to perceive hues.

Opponent-process theory
Theory of color vision that holds that three sets of color receptors (yellow-blue, red-green, black-white) respond to determine the color you experience.

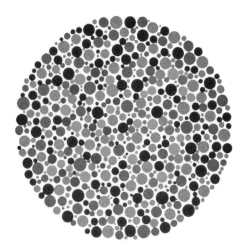

FIGURE 3–13

Experiencing colorblindness. Perceiving the number 96 embedded in the mass of green circles is easy, except for people who have red-green colorblindness.

Source: Ishiharo, *Test for Color Deficiency.* Courtesy Kanehara Shuppan Co., Ltd. Offered exclusively in the USA by Graham-Field, Inc., Hauppauge, New York.

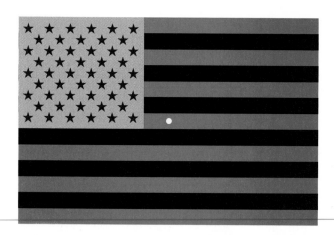

FIGURE 3–14

Afterimage. Stare at the white spot in the center of the flag for about 30 seconds. Then look at a blank piece of white paper and you will see an *afterimage* in complementary colors.

Trichromats
Organisms that have normal color vision.

Dichromats
Organisms that are blind to either red-green or yellow-blue.

Monochromats
Organisms that are totally colorblind.

see yellowish-blue or reddish-green. It also explains afterimages, in which receptor pairs have adapted to stimulation: While you were looking at the green bars in Figure 3–14, the red-green receptors were sending "green" messages to your brain but were also adapting to the stimulation by becoming less sensitive to green light. When you then looked at the white page (made up of light from all parts of the spectrum), the red-green receptors responded vigorously to the red wavelengths.

Contemporary research has established that both the trichromatic and the opponent-process theories of color vision are valid, although at two different stages in the visual process. As trichromatic theory asserts, there are three kinds of cones for color (some are most sensitive to violet-blue light, others are most responsive to green light, and still others are most sensitive to yellow light—not red light, as Helmholtz contended). Thus trichromatic theory corresponds fairly closely to the types of color receptors that actually exist in the retina. The opponent-process theory corresponds closely to neurons that exist between the eye and the brain. Taken together, trichromatic and opponent mechanisms in the visual system can explain almost all color phenomena for humans.

Color Vision in Other Species   Many animals have some color vision. Primates—including humans, monkeys, and apes—are **trichromats** and are able to see all hues. Most other mammals are **dichromats,** experiencing the world in terms of only reds and greens or blues and yellows (Abramov & Gordon, 1994; G. H. Jacobs, 1993). Rodents such as hamsters, mice, and squirrels are **monochromats,** completely colorblind. Some reptiles, fish, insects, and shellfish can also distinguish colors (Neitz, Geist, & Jacobs, 1989; Rosenzweig & Leiman, 1982).

But although animals can see colors, the colors they see differ from animal to animal. For example, human infants appear to be insensitive to violet, pigeons cannot see indigo and violet, and dogs don't have green-sensitive cones. Just knowing that an animal is sensitive to light of a certain wavelength, however, does not tell us how that light is experienced by the animal. For instance, deer—to their benefit—can distinguish the fluorescent orange that hunters wear. But they probably see it as a brightness that somehow just doesn't belong in the environment. In other words, "Run!"

Review Questions

Match the following terms with the appropriate definitions.

1. ____ cornea   a. colored part of the eye
2. ____ pupil   b. center of the visual field
3. ____ iris   c. receptor cell responsible for color vision
4. ____ lens   d. protective layer over front part of the eye
5. ____ fovea   e. contains the receptor cells that respond to light
6. ____ retina   f. focuses light onto the retina
7. ____ rod   g. receptor cell most responsible for night vision
8. ____ cone   h. opening in the iris through which light enters
9. The place on the retina where the axons of all the ganglion cells come together to leave the eye is called the ____.
10. Trichromats can mix ____, ____, and ____ lights to create virtually any hue.

Hearing

If a tree falls in the forest and no one is there, does the tree make a sound?

A psychologist would answer this ancient question about the tree falling in the forest by saying, "There are sound waves, but there is no sound or noise." Sounds and noise are psychological experiences created by the brain in response to stimulation. In this section we examine our important sense of hearing by first determining what kinds of stimuli cause us to hear sounds and then exploring how those stimuli are converted into neural signals.

Sound

How do the characteristics of sound waves cause us to hear different sounds?

The physical stimuli that prompt the sense of hearing are sound waves—changes in pressure caused when molecules of air or fluid collide, then move apart again, transmitting energy at every collision. The simplest sound wave—what we hear as a pure tone—can be pictured as a sine wave (see Figure 3–15). The tuning fork vibrates, causing the molecules of air first to contract and then to expand. The **frequency** of the waves is measured in cycles per second, expressed in a unit called **hertz (Hz).** Frequency primarily determines the **pitch** of the sound—how high or how low it is. The human ear responds to frequencies from approximately 20 Hz to 20,000 Hz. A double bass can reach down to about 50 Hz; a piano can reach as high as 5,000 Hz.

The height of the sound wave represents its **amplitude** (Figure 3–15), which, together with frequency, determines the perceived loudness of a sound. Loudness is measured in **decibels** (see Figure 3–16). As we grow older, we lose some of our ability to hear soft sounds, but we can hear loud sounds as well as ever.

The sounds that we hear seldom result from pure tones. Unlike a tuning fork, which can produce a tone that is almost pure, musical instruments produce **overtones**—accompanying sound waves that are different multiples of the frequency of the basic tone. A violin string, for example, not only vibrates as a whole, but it also vibrates in halves, thirds, quarters, and so on—all at the same time. This complex pattern of overtones determines the **timbre,** or texture, of the sound. Music synthesizers can mimic different instruments electronically because they produce not only pure tones but also the overtones that produce the timbre of different musical instruments.

Like our other senses, hearing undergoes adaptation and can function optimally under a wide variety of conditions. City residents enjoying a weekend in the country, for example, may be struck at first by how quiet everything seems. But after a while they may find that the country starts to sound very noisy.

The Ear

What path does sound follow in the ear?

For us to hear, a sound must travel through the outer, middle, and inner ear, where it finally is transmitted along the **auditory nerve** to the brain. Hearing begins in the *outer ear* when sound waves strike the eardrum (see Figure 3–17) and cause it to vibrate. These vibrations are then magnified during their trip through the *middle ear:* The quivering of the eardrum causes three tiny bones in the middle ear—called the *hammer,* the *anvil,* and the *stirrup*—to hit one another in sequence. The stirrup is attached to a membrane called the **oval window.** When the oval window starts to vibrate in response to the stirrup, the vibrations

Frequency
The number of cycles per second in a wave; in sound, the primary determinant of pitch.

Hertz (Hz)
Cycles per second; unit of measurement for the frequency of sound waves.

Pitch
Auditory experience corresponding primarily to frequency of sound vibrations, resulting in a higher or lower tone.

Amplitude
The magnitude of a wave; in sound, the primary determinant of loudness.

Decibel
Unit of measurement for the loudness of sounds.

Overtones
Tones that result from sound waves that are multiples of the basic tone; primary determinant of timbre.

Timbre
The quality of texture of sound; caused by overtones.

Auditory nerve
The bundle of axons that carries signals from each ear to the brain.

Oval window
Membrane across the opening between the middle ear and inner ear that conducts vibrations to the cochlea.

FIGURE 3–15

Sound waves. As the tuning fork vibrates, it alternately compresses and expands the molecules of air, creating a *sound wave*.

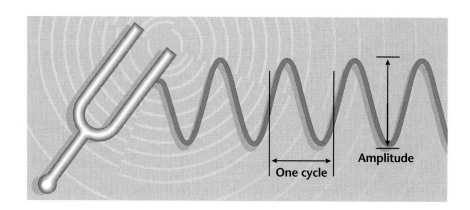

Amplitude

One cycle

FIGURE 3–16

A decibel scale for several common sounds. Prolonged exposure to sounds above 85 decibels can cause permanent damage to the ears, as can even brief exposure to sounds near the pain threshold.
Source: Adapted from Dunkle, 1982.

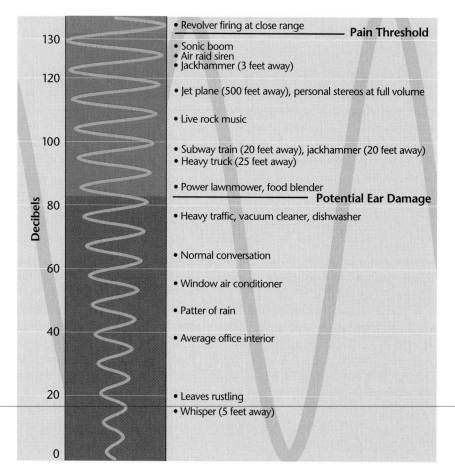

Decibels		
130	• Revolver firing at close range	**Pain Threshold**
	• Sonic boom	
120	• Air raid siren	
	• Jackhammer (3 feet away)	
	• Jet plane (500 feet away), personal stereos at full volume	
	• Live rock music	
100	• Subway train (20 feet away), jackhammer (20 feet away)	
	• Heavy truck (25 feet away)	
	• Power lawnmower, food blender	**Potential Ear Damage**
80	• Heavy traffic, vacuum cleaner, dishwasher	
	• Normal conversation	
60	• Window air conditioner	
	• Patter of rain	
40	• Average office interior	
20	• Leaves rustling	
	• Whisper (5 feet away)	
0		

Cochlea
Part of the inner ear containing fluid that vibrates, which in turn causes the basilar membrane to vibrate.

Basilar membrane
Vibrating membrane in the cochlea of the inner ear; it contains sense receptors for sound.

are transmitted to the *inner ear*—to the fluid inside a snail-shaped structure called the **cochlea**. The cochlea is divided lengthwise by the **basilar membrane.** The basilar membrane is stiffer near the oval and round windows and becomes gradually more flexible toward its other end. When the fluid in the cochlea begins to move, the basilar membrane is pushed up and down, rippling in response to the movement of the cochlear fluid and undulating tiny hair cells topped by bundles of hair fibers, or hair bundles (see Figure 3–18). When these fibers move, the receptor cells send a signal through the auditory nerve to the brain. The brain pools the information from thousands of hair cells to create sounds.

Scientists now know that each hair cell not only sends messages to the brain but also receives messages from the brain. The brain apparently can send signals that reduce the sensitivity of hair cells to sound in general or to sound waves of

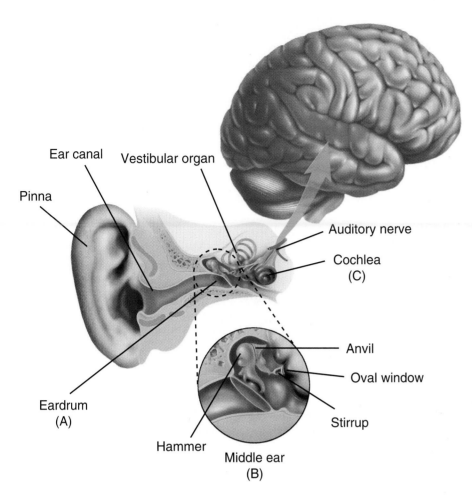

FIGURE 3–17

How we hear. The first stage of the hearing process is a series of vibrations: (A) Sound waves enter the outer ear and travel to the eardrum, causing it to vibrate. The vibrating eardrum causes the bones of the middle ear (B) (the hammer, anvil, and stirrup) to hit one another, amplifying and carrying the vibrations to the oval window and on to the fluid in the coiled cochlea of the inner ear (C). Now the moving fluid sets the basilar membrane, inside the cochlea, moving. The organ of Corti, on top of the basilar membrane, moves, too. Inside the organ of Corti, thousands of tiny receptor cells are topped by a bundle of hairlike fibers. As the basilar membrane vibrates, the fibers bend, stimulating the receptor cells to send a signal through afferent nerve endings that join to form the auditory nerve to the brain. There the impulses are interpreted as sounds.

particular frequencies. The brain can in effect "shut down" the ears somewhat, but for what purpose remains one of the mysteries of research on hearing (Hudspeth, 1983; Kim, 1985).

Neural Connections The sense of hearing is truly bilateral: Each ear sends messages to both cerebral hemispheres. The switching station where the nerve fibers from the ears cross over is in the medulla, part of the brain stem (see Figure 2–6). From the medulla other nerve fibers carry the messages from the ears to the higher parts of the brain. Some messages go to the brain centers that coordinate the movements of the eyes, head, and ears. Others travel through the reticular formation (which we examined in Chapter 2). But the primary destinations for these auditory messages are the auditory areas in the temporal lobes of the two cerebral hemispheres (see Figure 2–7). En route to the temporal lobes, auditory messages pass through at least four lower brain centers where auditory information becomes more precisely coded.

Theories of Hearing

How do we distinguish low-frequency and high-frequency sounds?

Thousands of tiny hair cells send messages about the infinite variations in the frequency, amplitude, and overtones of sound waves. But how are the different sound-wave patterns coded into neural messages? One aspect of sound—loudness—seems to depend primarily on how many neurons are activated: The more cells that fire, the louder the sound seems to be. The coding of messages regarding

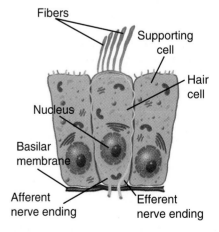

FIGURE 3–18

A detailed drawing of a hair cell. At the top of each hair cell is a bundle of fibers. If the fibers bend as much as 100 trillionths of a meter, the receptor cells transmit a sensory message to the brain.

Source: Adapted from "The Hair Cells of the Inner Ear," by A. J. Hudspeth, © 1983. Illustrated by Bunji Tagawa for Scientific American.

pitch is more complicated. There are two basic views of pitch discrimination—place theory and frequency theory. According to **place theory,** the brain determines pitch by noting the place on the basilar membrane at which the message is strongest. High-frequency sounds cause the greatest vibration at the stiff base of the basilar membrane; low-frequency sounds resonate most strongly at the opposite end (Zwislocki, 1981). The brain detects the location of the most intense nerve-cell activity and uses this to determine the pitch of a sound.

The **frequency theory** of pitch discrimination holds that the frequency of vibrations of the basilar membrane as a whole—not just parts of it—is translated into an equivalent frequency of nerve impulses. Thus if a hair bundle is pulled or pushed rapidly, its hair cell sends a high-frequency message to the brain. Because neurons cannot fire as rapidly as the frequency of the highest-pitched sound that can be heard, however, theorists have modified the frequency theory to include a **volley principle.** According to this view, auditory neurons can fire in sequence: One neuron fires, then a second one, then a third. By then the first neuron has had time to recover and can fire again. In this way, a set of neurons together, firing in sequence, can send a more rapid series of impulses to the brain than any single neuron could send by itself.

Because neither place theory nor frequency theory alone fully explains pitch discrimination, some combination of the two is necessary. Frequency theory appears to account for the ear's responses to frequencies up to about 4,000 Hz; above that, place theory provides a better explanation of what is happening.

Hearing Disorders   Because the mechanisms that allow us to hear are so complicated, there is a large number of possible problems that can interfere with hearing. Deafness, one of the most common concerns, may result from defects in the outer or middle ear—for instance, the eardrum may be damaged, or the small bones of the middle ear may not work properly. Deafness may also occur because the basilar membrane or the auditory nerve has been damaged, or it could be due to disease, infections, and even long-term exposure to loud noise. In fact, of the estimated 28 million Americans with some loss of hearing, approximately 10 million are the victims of protracted loud noise on the job or at home, with the chief culprits being leaf blowers, chain saws, snowmobiles, and personal stereo systems (Leary, 1990). Even high-impact aerobics has been known to contribute to hearing loss (Weintraub, 1990).

Far from not hearing enough sound, some people hear too much of the wrong kind of sound and therefore suffer greatly. Most of us at some time have heard a steady, high-pitched hum that seems to come from inside our head. But for about 1 percent of the population this sound, called tinnitus, becomes unbearably loud (Dunkle, 1982). In most cases tinnitus is due to irritation or permanent damage to the hair cells—usually caused by prolonged exposure to loud sound or toxins, including some antibiotics.

Repeated exposure to loud noises such as a chainsaw can lead to hearing disorders.

Place theory
Theory that pitch is determined by the location of greatest vibration on the basilar membrane.

Frequency theory
Theory that pitch is determined by the frequency with which hair cells in the cochlea fire.

Volley principle
Refinement of frequency theory; it suggests that receptors in the ear fire in sequence, with one group responding, then a second, then a third, and so on, so that the complete pattern of firing corresponds to the frequency of the sound wave.

Review Questions

Number the following terms in the order in which a sound wave would reach them when traveling from the outer ear to the inner ear.

____ 1. oval window

____ 2. anvil

____ 3. cochlea

____ 4. auditory nerve

____ 5. eardrum

Match the following theories with the appropriate definitions.

6. ____frequency theory

    a. pitch is determined by groups of receptor cells firing in sequence, not individually

7. ____volley principle

    b. pitch is determined by the rate at which hair cells in the cochlea fire

8. ____place theory

    c. pitch is determined by the location of the greatest vibration on the basilar membrane

Answers: 1. 3rd. 2. 2nd. 3. 4th. 4. 5th. 5. 1st. 6. b. 7. a. 8. c.

The Other Senses

What are the chemical senses?

Researchers have focused most of their attention on vision and hearing because people rely primarily on these two senses to gather information about their environment. Our other senses—smell, taste, balance, motion, pressure, temperature, and pain—are also at play, even when we are less conscious of them. We turn first to the chemical senses: smell and taste.

Smell

What activates the sense of smell?

According to one estimate, the sense of smell in humans is about 10,000 times as acute as that of taste (Moncrieff, 1951). Despite this great sensitivity, the sense of smell undergoes adaptation much like the other senses. A person can no longer smell his or her cologne after a few hours, for example, though others continue to notice it.

Our sense of smell for common odors is activated by a complex protein produced in a nasal gland. As we breathe, a fine mist of this protein, called *odorant binding protein (OBP)*, is sprayed through a duct in the tip of the nose. The protein binds with airborne molecules that then activate receptor cells for this sense, located high in each nasal cavity (see Figure 3–19). The axons from these millions of receptors go directly to the **olfactory bulb,** where some recoding takes place. Then messages are routed to the brain, resulting in our awareness of the smells.

Most mammals, including humans, have a second sensory system devoted to the sense of smell—which some animals use for communicating sexual, aggressive, or territorial signals. Receptors located in the roof of the nasal cavity detect chemicals called **pheromones,** which can have quite specific and powerful effects on behavior. For example, many animals, including dogs and wolves, use pheromones to mark their territory. Although humans have receptors for pheromones (Takami et al., 1993), no one has conclusively established what role—if any—pheromones play in human behavior.

Certain animal species rely more on their sense of smell than humans do. This dog has been trained to use its keen sense of smell to detect bombs hidden in luggage at an airport.

Taste

What are the most basic tastes?

To understand taste, we must distinguish it from flavor—a complex interaction of taste and smell. Try holding your nose when you eat. You will notice that most of the food's flavor will disappear, and you will experience only the *four primary taste qualities*: sweet, sour, salty, and bitter. All other tastes are derived from combinations of these four.

The receptor cells for the sense of taste are housed in the **taste buds,** most of which are found on the tip, sides, and back of the tongue. The tip of the tongue

Olfactory bulb
The smell center in the brain.

Pheromone
Chemical that communicates information to other organisms through smell.

Taste buds
Structures on the tongue that contain the receptor cells for taste.

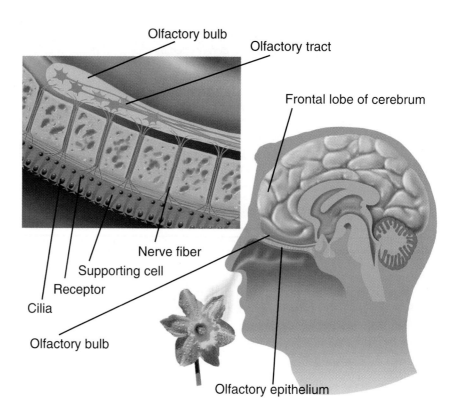

FIGURE 3–19

The human olfactory system. The sense of smell is triggered when odor molecules in the air reach the olfactory receptors located inside the top of the nose. Inhaling and exhaling odor molecules from food does much to give food its flavorful "taste."

Source: From *Human Anatomy and Physiology* by Anthony J. Gaudin and Kenneth C. Jones. Copyright © 1989 by Holt, Rinehart, and Winston, Inc. Reprinted by permission.

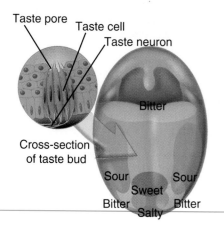

FIGURE 3–20

The structure of a taste bud. The sensory receptors for taste are found primarily on the tongue. Taste cells can detect only sweet, sour, salty, and bitter qualities. All other tastes result from different combinations of these taste sensations.

Kinesthetic senses
Senses of muscle movement, posture, and strain on muscles and joints.

Stretch receptors
Receptors that sense muscle stretch and contraction.

Golgi tendon organs
Receptors that sense movement of the tendons, which connect muscle to bone.

is most sensitive to sweetness and saltiness; the back, to bitterness; and the sides, to sourness (see Figure 3–20). But recent studies have shown that each area can distinguish all four qualities to some degree (Bartoshuk & Beauchamp, 1994). Because the number of taste buds decreases with age, older people often lose interest in food—they simply cannot taste it as well as they used to.

The taste buds are embedded in the tongue's *papillae*, bumps that you can see if you look at your tongue in the mirror. When we eat something, the chemical substances in the food dissolve in saliva and go into the crevices between the papillae, where they come into contact with the taste receptors. The chemical interaction between food substances and the taste cells causes adjacent neurons to fire, sending a nerve impulse to the parietal lobe of the brain and to the limbic system. This process is very fast: People can accurately identify a taste within $\frac{1}{10}$th of a second after something salty or sweet has touched the tongue (Cain, 1981). Interestingly, the same nerves that carry messages about taste also conduct information about chewing, swallowing, and the temperature and texture of food.

Taste, like the other senses, experiences adaptation. When you first start eating salted peanuts or potato chips, the saltiness is quite strong, but after a while it becomes less noticeable. Furthermore, exposure to one quality of taste can modify other taste sensations—after brushing your teeth in the morning, for instance, you may notice that your orange juice has lost its sweetness.

Kinesthetic and Vestibular Senses

How do we know which way is up and whether we are moving or standing still?

The **kinesthetic senses** provide information about the speed and direction of our movement in space. More specifically, they relay information about muscle movement, changes in posture, and strain on muscles and joints. Specialized nerve endings called **stretch receptors** are attached to muscle fibers, and different nerve endings called **Golgi tendon organs** are attached to the tendons, which connect muscle to bones. Together these two types of receptors provide constant feedback from the stretching and contraction of individual muscles. The information from these receptors travels via the spinal cord to the brain, where it is ultimately represented on the cortex of the parietal lobes, the same area of the cortex where the sense of touch is represented.

The **vestibular senses** provide information about our orientation or position in space (Leigh, 1994). We use this information to determine which way is up and which way is down. Birds and fish also rely on these senses to determine in which direction they are heading when they cannot see well. Like hearing, the vestibular senses originate in the inner ear, where hair cells serve as the sense organs. There are actually two kinds of vestibular sensation. The first one, which relays messages about the speed and direction of body rotation, arises in the three *semicircular canals* of the inner ear. Like the cochlea, each canal is filled with fluid that shifts hair bundles, which in turn stimulate hair cells, sending a message to the brain about the speed and direction of body rotation.

The second vestibular sense gives us information about gravitation and movement forward and backward, up and down. This sense arises from the two *vestibular sacs* that lie between the semicircular canals and the cochlea. Both sacs are filled with a jellylike fluid that contains millions of tiny crystals. When the body moves horizontally or vertically, the crystals bend hair bundles, prompting a sensory message.

The nerve impulses from both vestibular organs travel to the brain along the auditory nerve, but their ultimate destinations in the brain are still something of a mystery. Certain messages from the vestibular system go to the cerebellum, which controls many of the reflexes involved in coordinated movement. Others reach the areas that regulate the internal body organs, and some find their way to the parietal lobe of the cerebral cortex for analysis and response.

This dancer is utilizing information provided by both her kinesthetic and her vestibular senses. Her kinesthetic senses are relaying messages pertaining to muscle strain and movements; her vestibular senses are suppplying feedback about her body position in space.

Sensations of Motion

What causes motion sickness?

Riding in cars, or ships, and even on camels and in space ships can trigger motion sickness in some people and in laboratory animals (Daunton, 1990; Davis et al., 1988; Stern & Koch, 1996). Motion sickness arises in the vestibular organs, and susceptibility appears to be related to both race and genetics: People of Asian ancestry are particularly susceptible to motion sickness, which also seems to be inherited (Muth et al., 1994).

According to one theory, motion sickness stems from discrepancies between visual information and vestibular sensations (Stern & Koch, 1996)—as happens, for example, when you read a book while your body is being jolted up and down in a bus. Occasionally the vestibular sense can be completely overwhelmed by visual information: When we watch an automobile chase scene that was filmed from inside a moving car, we may feel a sensation of movement because our eyes are telling our brain that we are moving, even though the organs in our inner ear insist that we are sitting still. In fact, some people experience motion sickness while sitting absolutely still as they watch a movie filmed from an airplane or a boat. This effect does have an advantage: People who have had one or even both vestibular organs removed can function normally as long as they have visual cues on which to rely.

The Skin Senses

What are the three cutaneous sensations?

Our skin is our largest sense organ—a person 6 feet tall has about 21 square feet of skin. Our skin protects us from the environment, holds in body fluids,

Vestibular senses
The senses of equilibrium and body position in space.

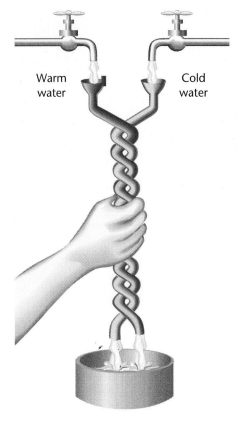

FIGURE 3–21

Paradoxical heat. Touching a warm pipe and a cold pipe at the same time causes two sets of skin receptors to signal at once to the brain. The brain reads their combined pattern of firings as "hot," a phenomenon known as *paradoxical heat.*

regulates our internal temperature, and affects our physical and mental well-being as we develop.

The skin's numerous nerve receptors, distributed in varying concentrations throughout its surface, send nerve fibers to the brain by two routes. Some information goes through the medulla and the thalamus and from there to the sensory cortex in the parietal lobe of the brain—which is presumably where our experiences of touch, pressure, and so on arise (see Figure 2–7). Other information goes through the thalamus and then on to the reticular formation, which, as we saw in Chapter 2, is responsible for arousing the nervous system or quieting it down.

Skin receptors give rise to what are called the *cutaneous sensations* of pressure, temperature, and pain, but the relationship between the receptors and our sensory experiences is a subtle one. Researchers believe that our brains draw on complex information about the *patterns* of activity received from many different receptors to detect and discriminate among skin sensations. For example, the "cold fibers" increase their firing rate as the skin cools down, and they slow their firing when the skin heats up. Conversely, the "warm fibers" accelerate their firing rate when the skin gets warm, and they slow down when the skin cools. The brain may use the combined information from these two sets of fibers as the basis for determining skin temperature. If both sets are activated at once, the brain may read their combined pattern of firings as "hot" (Craig & Bushnell, 1994). Thus you might sometimes think that you are touching something hot when you are really touching something warm and something cool at the same time, a phenomenon known as *paradoxical heat* (see Figure 3–21).

The skin senses are remarkably sensitive. For example, skin displacement of as little as 0.00004 of an inch can result in a sensation of pressure. Moreover, various parts of the body differ greatly in their sensitivity to pressure: Your face and fingertips are extremely sensitive, whereas your legs, feet, and back are much less so (Weinstein, 1968). It is no wonder, then, that when we examine things with our hands, we tend to do so with our fingertips. It is this remarkable sensitivity in our fingertips that makes possible Braille touch reading, which requires identifying patterns of tiny raised dots distributed over a very small area.

Like other senses, the skin senses undergo various kinds of sensory adaptation. When we first get into a bath, it may be uncomfortably hot, but in a few minutes we adapt to the heat, just as our eyes adapt to darkness. Similarly, when we put on an article of clothing that is a bit tight, we may feel uncomfortable at first but not even notice it later. How soon this adaptation occurs—or whether it occurs at all—appears to depend on how large an area of the skin is being stimulated and the intensity of the pressure (Geldard, 1972). The larger the area and the more intense the pressure, the longer it takes for us to adapt.

Pain

What differences among people have an effect on the degree of pain they experience?

An old adage holds that pain is nature's way of telling you that something is wrong. It does seem reasonable to assume that damage to the body causes pain, but in many cases actual physical injury is not accompanied by pain. Conversely, people may feel pain even though they have not suffered any physical harm.

We might also assume that pain occurs when some kind of pain receptor is stimulated, but there is no simple relationship between pain receptors and the experience of pain. In fact, scientists have had great difficulty even *finding* pain receptors.

The sensation of pain is an extraordinarily complex sensory event. Because there are such great differences in how people react to it, some psychologists question whether pain should even be considered a basic sensation, like pressure and temperature (Melzack, 1992). One extreme variation is that certain people appear to be completely insensitive to pain (Manfredi et al., 1981). In one famous case a young Canadian girl felt nothing when she inadvertently bit off part of her tongue and suffered third-degree burns as a result of kneeling on a hot radiator (Baxter & Olszewski, 1960; McMurray, 1950). Moreover, people perceive and react to pain in strikingly different ways. If you burn your hand, you might calmly run cold water over the burn; someone else might scream loudly.

Our beliefs about pain can affect our experience of it. One study found that hospital patients who believed that a particular medical procedure was not painful actually reported experiencing less pain (DiMatteo & Friedman, 1982). Emotional or motivational conditions also have an impact on our perception of pain. One researcher noted that only 25 percent of soldiers wounded during a battle requested pain medication, whereas more than 80 percent of surgical patients asked for painkillers for comparable "wounds" (Beecher, 1972). Athletes injured during a game often feel no pain until the excitement of competition has passed.

As a rite of initiation in the Asian nation of Indonesia, this man is inserting wooden needles into a boy's arm. How much pain people actually experience can vary depending on their cultural background.

Culture and Pain   Culture and belief systems play a dramatic role in how we respond to bodily injury (Bates & Rankin-Hill, 1994). For instance, in a religious ceremony practiced in parts of India, a young man swings from a ceremonial platform, supported by hooks embedded in his back, seemingly without pain (Melzack, 1973). It should not be surprising, then, that in cases of serious injury the perception of pain is not related to the amount of tissue damage sustained (Schiffman, 1982). Because of the great variability in the ways that people experience pain, scientists encounter difficulty in measuring typical pain thresholds and in studying how individuals adapt to pain (Irwin & Whitehead, 1991).

Gate Control   How do psychologists explain our varying sensitivities to pain? One commonly accepted view is the **gate control theory** of pain (Melzack, 1980; Wall & Melzack, 1989). According to this theory, a "neurological gate" in the spinal cord controls the transmission of pain impulses to the brain. If the gate is open, we experience more pain than we do if it is closed. Whether the gate is closed or open depends on a complex competition between two different types of sensory nerve fibers—large fibers that tend to "close the gate" and small fibers that "open the gate" when they are stimulated, letting the pain messages get through to the brain. Moreover, certain areas of the brain stem can also close the gate from above by sending down signals to fibers in the spinal cord to close the gate. Finally, by focusing our attention away from pain (as in certain forms of meditation), we may also experience greatly diminished feelings of pain. All these mechanisms may be at work when, in the same circumstances, one person experiences excruciating pain while another feels no pain at all.

Despite its complexities, gate control theory is already being used to develop new techniques for the control of pain (Aronoff, 1993). For example, some dentists are experimenting with devices that electrically stimulate large nerve fibers and block the action of small fibers, thus closing the gate on pain. Patients can adjust the amount of stimulation based on their own needs.

Studies of pain relief suggest that there are two other pain-controlling systems that may be independent of or in some way related to the spinal pain gate.

Gate control theory
The theory that a "neurological gate" in the spinal cord controls the transmission of pain messages to the brain.

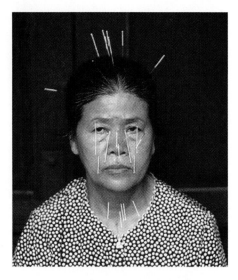

Traditional Asian medicine has used acupuncture to reduce or eliminate pain. Studies indicate that acupuncture works by releasing endorphins into the body.

In the first case, if you give pain sufferers a chemically neutral pill, or *placebo*, but tell them that it is an effective pain reducer, they will often experience less pain after taking it. No doubt many home remedies and secret cures rely on the *placebo effect*. In addition, traditional Chinese and Korean medicine have demonstrated that acupuncture treatments, involving the insertion of thin needles into parts of the body, can reduce or eliminate pain. Research indicates that both placebos and acupuncture work through the release of endorphins, the pain-blocking neurotransmitters that we examined in Chapter 2. Some other pain-reduction techniques, however—such as hypnosis or related concentration exercises (as in the Lamaze birth technique)—have nothing to do with endorphins.

Review Questions

Match the following senses with the appropriate description.

1. ___ smell   a. awareness of body position
2. ___ taste   b. detected in vestibular organs
3. ___ kinesthetic   c. includes sweet, sour, salty, and bitter
4. ___ vestibular   d. pressure, temperature, and pain
5. ___ motion   e. gate control theory
6. ___ skin senses   f. activated by airborne molecules
7. ___ pain   g. muscle movement

Answers: 1. f. 2. c. 3. g. 4. a. 5. b. 6. d. 7. e.

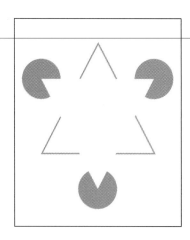

FIGURE 3–22

An illusory triangle. When sensory information is incomplete, we tend to create a complete perception by supplying the missing details. In this figure we fill in the lines that let us perceive a white triangle in the center of the pattern.

WEB LINKS

Perception

How is perception different from sensation?

Our senses provide us with raw data about the external world. But unless we *interpret* this raw information, it is nothing more than what William James (1890) called a "booming, buzzing confusion." The eye records patterns of lightness and darkness, but it does not "see" a bird flittering from branch to branch. The eardrum vibrates in a particular fashion, but it does not "hear" a symphony. Deciphering *meaningful* patterns in the jumble of sensory information is what we mean by *perception*. But how does perception differ from sensation?

Ultimately, it is the brain that interprets the complex flow of information from the various senses. Using sensory information as raw material, the brain creates perceptual experiences that go beyond what is sensed directly. For example, looking at Figure 3–22, we tend to perceive a white triangle in the center of the pattern, although the sensory input consists only of three circles from which "pie slices" have been cut and three 60-degree angles. Or take Figure 3–23. At first glance most people see only an assortment of black blotches. If you are told that the blotches represent a person riding a horse, suddenly your perceptual experience changes. What was meaningless sensory information now takes shape as a horse and rider.

Sometimes, as in certain optical illusions, you perceive things that could not possibly exist. The trident shown in Figure 3–24 exemplifies such an "impossible" figure; on closer inspection, you discover that the object that you "recognized" is not really there. In all these cases, the brain actively creates and organizes perceptual experiences out of raw sensory data—sometimes even from data we are not aware of receiving. We now explore how perceptual processes organize sensory experience.

Perceptual Organization

How do we organize our perceptual experiences?

Early in this century a group of German psychologists, calling themselves *Gestalt psychologists*, set out to discover the principles through which we interpret sensory information. The German word *Gestalt* has no exact English equivalent, but essentially it means "whole," "form," or "pattern." The Gestalt psychologists believed that the brain creates a coherent perceptual experience that is more than simply the sum of the available sensory information and that it does so in predictable ways.

In one important facet of the perceptual process, we distinguish *figures* from the *ground* against which they appear. A colorfully upholstered chair stands out from the bare walls of a room. A marble statue is perceived as a whole figure separate from the red brick wall behind it. The illusory trident in Figure 3–24 stands out from the white page. In all these cases, we perceive some objects as figures and other sensory information as background.

The figure–ground distinction pertains to all of our senses, not just vision. We can distinguish a violin solo against the ground of a symphony orchestra, a single voice amid cocktail-party chatter, and the smell of roses in a florist's shop. In all these instances, we perceive a figure apart from the ground around it.

Sometimes, however, there are not enough cues in a pattern to permit us to easily distinguish a figure from its ground. The horse and rider in Figure 3–23 illustrate this problem, as does Figure 3–25, which shows a spotted dog investigating shadowy surroundings. It is hard to distinguish the dog because it has few visible contours of its own, and as a result, it seems to have no more form than

FIGURE 3–23

Perceiving a pattern. Knowing beforehand that the black blotches in this figure represent a person riding a horse changes our perception of it.

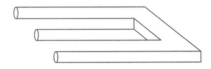

FIGURE 3–24

An optical illusion. In the case of the trident, we go beyond what is sensed (blue lines on flat white paper) to perceive a three-dimensional object that isn't really there.

FIGURE 3–25

Random dots or something more? This pattern does not give us enough cues to allow us to easily distinguish the *figure* of the Dalmatian dog from the *ground* behind it.

Source: Gregory, 1970.

FIGURE 3–26 The reversible figure and ground in this M. C. Escher woodcut cause us to see first black devils and then white angles in each of the rings.

Do you see a vase or the silhouettes of a man and a woman? Both interpretations are possible, but not at the same time. Reversible figures like this work because it is unclear which part of the stimulus is the figure and which is the neutral ground against which the figure is perceived.

Perceptual constancy
A tendency to perceive objects as stable and unchanging despite changes in sensory stimulation.

the background. This is the principle behind camouflage—to make a figure blend into its background.

Sometimes a figure with clear contours can be perceived in two very different ways because it is unclear which part of the stimulus is the figure and which is the ground (see Figure 3–26). At first glance you perceive figures against a specific background, but as you stare at the illustrations, you will discover that the figures eventually dissolve into the ground, making for two very different perceptions of the same illustration.

Figure 3–27 demonstrates some other important principles of perceptual organization. In every case our perceptual experience makes a leap beyond the raw sensory information available to us. In other words, we use sensory information to create a perception that is more than just the sum of the parts. While sometimes this can cause problems, the perceptual tendency to "fill in the blanks" usually broadens our understanding of the world. As creatures searching for meaning, we tend to fill in the missing information, to group various objects together, to see whole objects and hear meaningful sounds rather than just random bits and pieces of raw sensory data.

Perceptual Constancies

How do we perceive things as unchanging despite changing sensory information?

Without **perceptual constancy**—the tendency to perceive objects as relatively unchanging despite changing sensory information—we would find the world very confusing. But once we have formed a stable perception of an object, we can recognize it from almost any position, at almost any distance, under almost

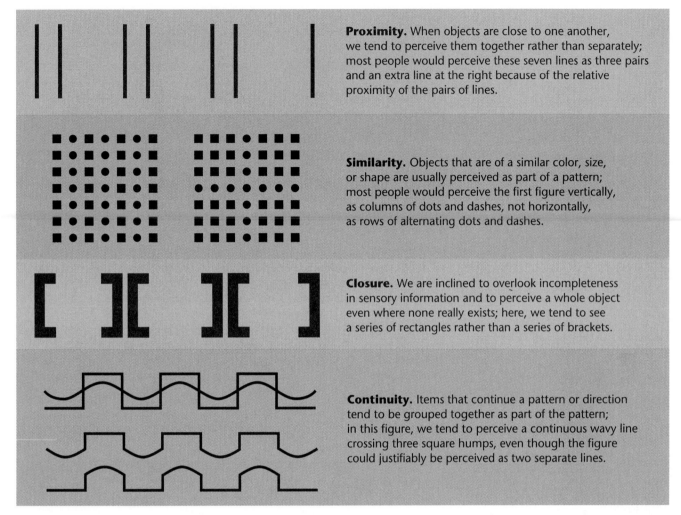

FIGURE 3–27
Gestalt principles of perceptual organization.   Size constancy

any illumination. A white house looks like a white house by day or by night and from any angle. The sensory information may change as illumination and perspective change, but the object is perceived as constant.

Memory and experience play important roles in perceptual constancy. For example, look at Figure 3–28A, a slightly altered photograph of former British prime minister Margaret Thatcher. Before reading further, turn the book upside down and look at the picture again. An essentially normal face has taken on a gruesome aspect. Your experience in recognizing people and interpreting their facial expressions has accustomed you to focus on certain perceptual cues (particularly eyes and mouths). When you look at the upside-down picture, the eyes and mouth are normal, so you perceive the entire face as normal. In other words, you use your experience in perceiving normal human faces to perceive this (very unusual) face, and as a result you do not perceive it as grossly distorted until you look at the face rightside up.

Size constancy, too, depends partly on experience—information about the relative sizes of objects is stored in memory—and partly on distance cues. We tend to perceive objects as their true size regardless of the size of the image that they cast on the retina. As Figure 3–29 shows, the farther away an object is

Size constancy
The perception of an object as the same size regardless of the distance from which it is viewed.

FIGURE 3–28

A. Look at the picture and then turn the book upside down so that the picture is rightside up. Based on experience, you use certain perceptual cues to recognize facial expressions, so the upside-down picture looks fairly normal. Those same cues make the rightside-up picture look grossly distorted.

B. Context, hair style, and head shape lead us to believe that this is a picture of President Clinton and Vice President Gore when, in reality, President Clinton's face is superimposed over the face of Vice President Gore.

Source: APA Monitor, 1997.

FIGURE 3–29

The relationship between distance and the size of the retinal image. Object A and object B are the same size, but A, being much closer to the eye, casts a much larger image on the retina.

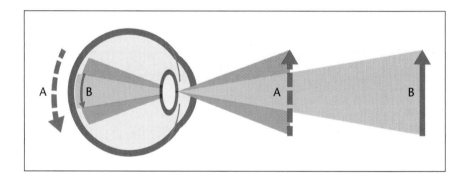

Shape constancy
A tendency to see an object as the same shape no matter what angle it is viewed from.

Brightness constancy
The perception of brightness as the same, even though the amount of light reaching the retina changes.

Color constancy
An inclination to perceive familiar objects as retaining their color despite changes in sensory information.

from the lens of the eye, the smaller the retinal image it casts. For example, a 6-foot-tall man standing 20 feet away casts a retinal image that is only 50 percent of the size of the retinal image he casts at a distance of 10 feet. Yet he is not perceived as having shrunk to 3 feet. When there are no distance cues, size constancy has to rely solely on what we have learned from our previous experience with an object.

Familiar objects also tend to be seen as having a constant shape, even though the retinal images that they cast change as they are viewed from different angles. A dinner plate is perceived as a circle even when it is tilted and the retinal image is oval. A rectangular door will project a rectangular image on the retina only when it is viewed directly from the front. From any other angle, it casts a trapezoidal image on the retina, but it is not perceived as having suddenly become a trapezoidal door (see Figure 3–30). These are examples of **shape constancy.**

Two other important perceptual constancies are **brightness constancy** and **color constancy.** Brightness constancy means that even though the amount of light available to our eyes varies greatly over the course of a day, the perceived brightness of familiar objects hardly varies at all. We perceive a sheet of white

FIGURE 3–30
Examples of shape constancy.   Even though the image of the door on the retina changes greatly as the door opens, we still perceive the door as being rectangular.
Source: Boring, Langfeld, & Weld, 1976.

paper as brighter than a piece of coal whether we see these objects in candlelight or under bright sunlight. Brightness constancy occurs because an object reflects the same percentage of the light falling on it whether that light is from a candle or the sun. Rather than basing our judgment of brightness on the *absolute* amount of light that the object reflects, we assess how the *relative* reflection compares to the surrounding objects.

Similarly, we tend to perceive familiar objects as keeping their colors, regardless of information that reaches the eye. If you own a red automobile, you will see it as red whether it is on a brightly lit street or in a dark garage, where the small amount of light may send your eye a message that the color is closer to brown or black than red. But when objects are unfamiliar or there are no customary color cues to guide us, color constancy may be distorted, as when we buy a pair of pants in a brightly lit store, only to discover that in ordinary daylight they are not the shade we thought they were.

In exploring these constancy principles, we have noted that perceptual experiences rarely if ever correspond exactly to the information that we receive through our senses. We have already seen how neural structures organize sensory information. Now we turn to the ways certain "personal" variables also influence and organize sensation.

Observer Characteristics

What personal factors influence our perceptions?

We clearly draw on past experience and learning when it comes to perception, but our own motivations, values, expectations, cognitive style, and cultural preconceptions can also affect our perceptual experiences. In this section we probe how these sorts of variables influence the perceptual organization of sensory information.

Motivation   Often our desires and needs strongly shape our perceptions. People in need are likely to perceive something that they think will satisfy that need. For example, if people are deprived of food for some time and are then shown vague or ambiguous pictures, they are apt to perceive the pictures as being related to food (McClelland & Atkinson, 1948; Sanford, 1937).

Values   In an experiment that revealed how strongly perceptions can be affected by a person's values, nursery schoolchildren were shown a poker chip. Each child was asked to compare the size of the chip to the size of an adjustable circle of light until the child said the chip and the circle of light were the same size. The children were then brought to a machine with a crank that, when turned, produced a poker chip that could be exchanged for candy.

Thus, the children were taught to value the poker chips more highly than they had before. After the children had been rewarded with candy for the poker chips, they were again asked to compare the size of the chips to a circle of light. This time the chips seemed larger to the children (Lambert, Solomon, & Watson, 1949).

Expectations Preconceptions about what we are supposed to perceive can influence perception by causing us to *delete, insert, transpose,* or otherwise *modify* what we see (Lachman, 1996). For example, in a well-known children's game a piece of cardboard with a red stop sign is flashed in front of you. What did the sign say? Nearly everyone says that the sign read STOP. In fact, however, the sign was misprinted and read STOPP. Because we are accustomed to seeing stop signs reading STOP, we tend to perceive the familiar word rather than the misprint. Lachman (1984) demonstrated this phenomenon by asking people to copy a group of stimuli similar to this one:

PARIS
IN THE
THE SPRING

When the expressions were flashed briefly on a screen, the vast majority of subjects tended to omit the "extra" words and to report seeing more familiar (and more normal) expressions, such as PARIS IN THE SPRING. This phenomenon of *perceptual familiarization* or *perceptual generalization* reflects a strong tendency to see what we expect to see, even if our expectation conflicts with external reality.

Cognitive Style As we mature, we develop a cognitive style—our own way of dealing with the environment—which also affects how we see the world. Some psychologists distinguish between two general approaches that people use in perceiving the world (Witkin et al., 1962). People taking the *field-dependent approach* tend to perceive the environment as a whole and do not clearly delineate in their minds the shape, color, size, or other qualities of individual items. If field-dependent people are asked to draw a human figure, they generally draw it so that it blends into the background. By contrast, people who are *field independent* are more likely to perceive the elements of the environment as separate and distinct from one another and to draw each element as standing out from the background.

Cognitive styles can also be viewed from the perspective of "levelers" and "sharpeners"—those who level out the distinctions among objects and those who magnify them. To investigate the differences between these two cognitive styles, G. S. Klein (1951) showed people sets of squares of varying sizes and asked them to estimate the size of each one. One group, the levelers, failed to perceive any differences in the size of the squares. The sharpeners, however, picked up the differences in the size of the squares and made their size estimates accordingly.

Experience and Culture Cultural background also influences people's perceptions. As we will see in Chapter 7, Cognition and Mental Abilities, to some extent the language that people speak affects the ways in which they perceive their surroundings. Cultural differences in people's experiences can also influence how people use perceptual cues. Historically, for example, the Mbuti pygmies of Zaire seldom left the Ituri Rain Forest and rarely encountered objects that were more than a few feet away. On one occasion anthropologist Colin Turnbull (1961) took a pygmy guide named Kenge on a trip onto the

African plains. When Kenge looked across the plain and saw a herd of buffalo, he asked what kind of insects they were. He refused to believe that the tiny black spots he saw were buffalo. As he and Turnbull drove toward the herd, Kenge believed that magic was making the animals grow larger. Because he had no experience of distant objects, he could not perceive the buffalo as having constant size.

Personality   A number of researchers have shown that even our personalities influence perception (for a review of the research, see Greenwald, 1992). In two studies healthy college students were compared with depressed students or students with an eating disorder in terms of their ability to identify words related to depression and food (von Hippel, Hawkins, & Narayan, 1994). All the words in this study were exposed very quickly (generally less than ⅒oth of a second). In general, people with an eating disorder were faster at identifying words that referred to foods they commonly thought about than they were at identifying foods they rarely thought about. Similarly, depressed people were faster at identifying adjectives describing personality traits they commonly thought about (such as "quiet," "withdrawn," "hesitant," and "timid") than adjectives that described traits they rarely thought about (such as "extrovert," "lively," and "bold").

Next we look at a basic perceptual phenomenon—distance and depth—to see how we use both stimulus information and past experience to create perceptual experiences.

Perception of Distance and Depth

How do we know how far away something is?

We are constantly judging the distance between ourselves and other objects. When we walk through a classroom, our perception of distance helps us to avoid bumping into desks or tripping over the wastebasket. If we reach out to pick up a pencil, we automatically judge how far to extend our hand. And as a matter of course, we also assess the depth of objects—how much total space they occupy. We use many cues to determine the distance and the depth of objects. Some of these cues depend on visual messages that one eye alone can transmit; these are called **monocular cues.** Others, known as **binocular cues,** require the use of both eyes. Having two eyes allows us to make more accurate judgments about distance and depth, particularly when objects are relatively close. But monocular cues alone are often sufficient to allow us to judge distance and depth quite accurately, as we see in the next section.

Monocular Cues   One important monocular distance cue that provides us with information about relative position is called **superposition.** Superposition occurs when one object partly blocks a second object. The first object is perceived as being closer, the second as more distant (see Figure 3–31).

As art students learn, there are several ways in which perspective can help in estimating distance and depth. In **linear perspective** two parallel lines that extend into the distance seem to come together at some point on the horizon. In **aerial perspective** distant objects have a hazy appearance and a somewhat blurred outline. On a clear day mountains often seem to be much closer than on a hazy day, when their outlines become blurred. The **elevation** of an object also serves as a perspective cue to depth: An object that is on a higher horizontal plane seems to be farther away than one on a lower plane (see Figure 3–32). Another useful monocular cue to distance and depth is **texture gradient.** An object that is close seems to have a rough or detailed texture. As distance

Monocular cues
Visual cues requiring the use of one eye.

Binocular cues
Visual cues requiring the use of both eyes.

Superposition
Monocular distance cue in which one object, by partly blocking a second object, is perceived as being closer.

Linear perspective
Monocular cue to distance and depth based on the fact that two parallel lines seem to come together at the horizon.

Aerial perspective
Monocular cue to distance and depth based on the fact that more distant objects are likely to appear hazy and blurred.

Elevation
Monocular cue to distance and depth based on the fact that the higher on the horizontal plane an object is, the farther away it appears.

Texture gradient
Monocular cue to distance and depth based on the fact that objects seen at greater distances appear to be smoother and less textured.

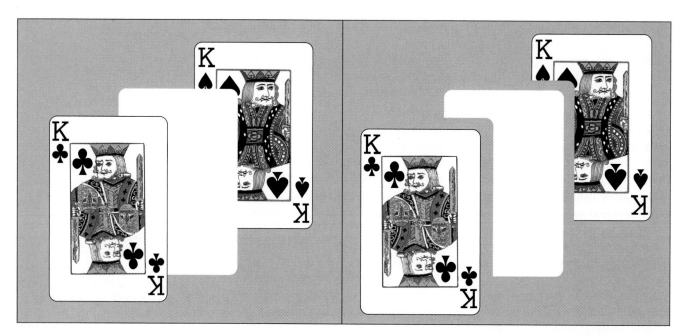

FIGURE 3–31

Superposition. (*left panel*) Because the king of clubs appears to have been superimposed on the blank card, we perceive it as being closer to us than the king of spades (*right panel*). When the cards are spaced out, however, we can see that the king of spades is actually no farther away than the king of clubs. It appears to be farther away because the other two cards seem to be superimposed on it.

FIGURE 3–32

Elevation as a visual cue. Because of the higher elevation and the suggestion of depth provided by the road, the tree on the right is perceived as being more distant and about the same size as the tree at lower left. Actually, it is appreciably smaller, as you can see if you measure the heights of the two drawings.

increases, the texture becomes finer, until finally the original texture cannot be distinguished clearly, if at all. For example, when standing on a pebbly beach, you can distinguish among the gray stones and the gravel in front of your feet. As you look down the beach, however, the stones appear to become smaller and finer until eventually you cannot make out individual stones at all.

Shadowing provides another important cue to the distance, depth, and solidity of an object. Because shadows normally appear on the parts of objects that are more distant, the shadowing of the outer edges of a spherical object, such as a ball or a globe, gives it a three-dimensional quality (see Figure 3–33). Without this shadowing, the object might be perceived as a flat disk.

Shadowing
Monocular cue to distance and depth based on the fact that shadows often appear on the parts of objects that are more distant.

In addition to serving as cues of three-dimensionality, shadows serve as cues to the direction of depth—whether an object rises above or rests below the surface. The shadow that an object casts behind itself also gives a cue to its depth. The presence of shadows either before or behind objects indicates how far away they are.

People traveling on buses or trains often notice that nearby trees or telephone poles seem to flash past the windows, while buildings and other objects farther away seem to move slowly. These differences in the speeds of movement of images across the retina as you move give an important cue to distance and depth. You can observe the same effect if you stand still and move your head from side to side. Also, if you move your head from side to side and focus your gaze on something in the middle distance, objects close to you seem to move in the direction opposite to the direction in which your head is moving, while objects far away seem to move in the same direction as your head. This distance cue is know as **motion parallax.**

Binocular Cues   All the visual cues examined so far depend on the action of only one eye. Many animals—such as horses, deer, and fish—rely entirely on monocular cues. Although they have two eyes, the two visual fields do not overlap, because their eyes are located on the sides of the head rather than in front. Humans, apes, and many predatory animals—such as lions, tigers, and wolves—have a distinct physical advantage over these animals. Because both eyes are set in the front of the head, the visual fields overlap. The **stereoscopic vision** derived from combining the two retinal images makes the perception of depth and distance more accurate.

Because our eyes are set approximately 2½ inches apart, each one has a slightly different view of things. The difference between the two images that the eyes receive is known as **retinal disparity.** The left eye receives more information about the left side of an object, and the right eye receives more information about the right side. You can easily prove that each of your eyes receives a different image. Close one eye and line up a finger with some vertical line, like the edge of a door. Then open that eye and close the other one. Your finger will appear to have moved a great distance. When you look at the finger with both eyes, however, the two different images become one.

One binocular cue to distance comes from the muscles that control the **convergence** of the eyes. When we look at objects that are fairly close to us, our eyes tend to converge—to turn slightly inward toward each other. The sensations from the muscles that control the movement of the eyes thus provide another cue to distance. If the object is very close, such as at the end of the nose, the eyes cannot converge, and two separate images are perceived. If the object is more than a few yards (meters) away, the sight lines of the eyes are more or less parallel, and there is no convergence.

Location of Sounds   Just as we use monocular and binocular cues to establish visual depth and distance, we draw on **monaural** (single-ear) and **binaural** (two-ear) **cues** to locate the source of sounds (see Figure 3–34). In one monaural cue, loud sounds are perceived as closer than faint sounds, with changes in loudness translating into changes in distance. Binaural cues work on the principle that because sounds off to one side of the head reach one ear slightly ahead of the other (in the range of ¹⁄₁,₀₀₀th of a second), the time difference between sound waves reaching the two ears registers in the brain and helps us to make accurate judgments of location.

In a second binaural cue, sound signals arriving from a source off to one side of you are slightly louder in the nearer ear than in the ear farther from the source. The slight difference occurs because your head, in effect, blocks

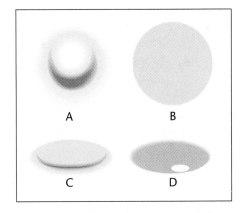

FIGURE 3–33

Shadowing.   Shadowing on the outer edges of a spherical object, such as a ball or globe, gives it a three-dimensional quality (A). Without shadowing (B), it might be perceived as a flat disk. Shadowing can also affect our perception of the direction of depth. In the absence of other cues, we tend to assume overhead lighting, so image C appears to be a bump because its top edge is lit, whereas image D appears to be a dent. If you turn the book upside down, the direction of depth is reversed.

Motion parallax
Monocular distance cue in which objects closer than the point of visual focus seem to move in the direction opposite to the viewer's moving head, and objects beyond the focus point appear to move in the same direction as the viewer's head.

Stereoscopic vision
Combination of two retinal images to give a three-dimensional perceptual experience.

Retinal disparity
Binocular distance cue based on the difference between the images cast on the two retinas when both eyes are focused on the same object.

Convergence
A visual depth cue that comes from muscles controlling eye movement as the eyes turn inward to view a nearby stimulus.

Monaural cue
Cue to sound location that requires just one ear.

Binaural cue
Cue to sound location that involves both ears working together.

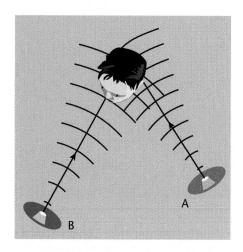

FIGURE 3–34
Cues used in sound localization.   Sound waves coming from source B will reach both ears simultaneously. A sound wave from source A reaches the left ear first, where it is also louder. The head casts a "shadow" over the other ear, thus reducing the intensity of the delayed sound in that ear.
Source: Langfeld & Weld, 1976.

Autokinetic illusion
The perception that a stationary object is actually moving.

the sound, reducing the intensity of sound in the opposite ear. This relative loudness difference between signals heard separately by the two ears is enough for the brain to locate the sound source and to judge its distance. When sound engineers record your favorite musical group, they may place microphones at many different locations. On playback the two speakers or headphones project sounds at slightly different instants to mimic the sound patterns you would hear if you were actually listening to the group perform right in front of you.

Most of us rely so heavily on visual cues that we seldom pay much attention to the rich array of auditory information available around us. Blind people, who often compensate for their lack of vision by sharpening their awareness of sounds (Arias, Curet, Moyano, Joekes, & Blanch, 1993), can figure out where obstacles lie in their paths by listening to the echoes from a cane, their own footsteps, and their own voices. In one notable case a blind boy had grown so adept at avoiding obstacles by sound that he could safely ride a bicycle in public places. Many blind people can judge the size and distance of one object in relation to another using nothing more than sound cues. They can also discriminate between contrasting surfaces, such as glass and fabric, by listening to the difference in the echo produced when sound strikes them.

Perception of Movement

How do we perceive movement?

The perception of movement is a complicated process involving both visual information from the retina and messages from the muscles around the eyes as they follow an object. On occasion our perceptual processes play tricks on us, and we think we perceive movement when the objects that we are looking at are in fact stationary. We must distinguish, therefore, between real and apparent movement.

Real movement refers to the physical displacement of an object from one position to another. The perception of real movement depends only in part on movement of images across the retina of the eye. If you stand still and move your head to look around you, the images of all the objects in the room will pass across your retina. Yet you will probably perceive all of the objects as stationary. Even if you hold your head still and move only your eyes, the images will continue to pass across your retina. But the messages from the eye muscles seem to counteract those from the retina, so the objects in the room will be perceived as motionless.

The perception of real movement seems to be determined less by images moving across the retina than by how the position of objects changes in relation to a background that is perceived as stationary. When we perceive a car moving along a street, for example, we see the street, the buildings, and the sidewalk as a stationary background and the car as a moving object. Remarkably, the brain can distinguish these retinal images of an object moving against an immobile background from all the other moving images of the retina.

Apparent movement occurs when we see movement in objects that are actually standing still. One form of apparent movement is referred to as the **autokinetic illusion**—the perceived motion created by a single stationary object. If you stand in a room that is absolutely dark except for one tiny spot of light and stare at the light for a few seconds, you will begin to see the light drift. In the darkened room your eyes have no visible framework; there are no cues telling you that the light is really stationary. The slight movements of the eye muscles, which go unnoticed most of the time, make the light appear to move.

Another form of illusory movement is **stroboscopic motion**—the apparent motion created by a rapid series of still images. This form of apparent movement is illustrated best by a motion picture, which is not in motion at all. The film consists of a series of still pictures showing people and objects in slightly different positions. When the separate images are projected sequentially onto a screen at a specific rate of speed, the people and objects seem to be moving because of the rapid change from one still picture to the next.

Another common perceptual illusion, known as the **phi phenomenon,** occurs as a result of stroboscopic motion. When a light is flashed on at a certain point in a darkened room, then flashed off, and a second light is flashed on a split second later at a point a short distance away, most people will perceive these two separate lights as a single spot of light moving from one point to another. This perceptual process causes us to see motion in neon signs or theater marquees, where words appear to move from one side to the other as the different combinations of stationary lights are flashed on and off.

When we look at an electronic marquee such as this one, we see motion, even though the sign consists of stationary lights that are flashed on and off.

Visual Illusions

What causes visual illusions?

Visual illusions graphically demonstrate the ways in which we use a variety of sensory cues to create perceptual experiences that may (or may not) correspond to what is out there in the real world. By understanding how we are fooled into "seeing" something that isn't there, psychologists can figure out how perceptual processes work in the everyday world and under normal circumstances.

Psychologists generally distinguish between physical and perceptual illusions. One example of a *physical illusion* is the bent appearance of a stick when it is placed in water—an illusion easily understood because the water acts like a prism, bending the light waves before they reach our eyes. Other illusions depend primarily on our own perceptual processes—of which we are not ordinarily aware—and as a result can be quite startling. *Perceptual illusions* occur because the stimulus contains misleading cues that give rise to inaccurate or impossible perceptions.

Figure 3–35 presents several false and misleading depth cues. In Figure 3–35E the top line is perceived as shorter than the bottom, when in reality both lines are the same length. Our experience tells us that objects appear smaller when they are far away. In Figure 3–35F both monsters cast the same size image on the retina in our eyes. But the depth cues in the tunnel suggest that we are looking at a three-dimensional scene and that therefore the top monster is much farther away. In the real world this would mean that the top monster is actually much larger than the bottom monster. Therefore we "correct" for the distance and actually perceive the top monster as larger, despite other cues to the contrary. We know that the image is actually two-dimensional, but we still respond to it as if it were three-dimensional.

There are also "real world" illusions that illustrate how perceptual processes work, such as the illusion of *induced movement*. When you are sitting in a stationary train and the train next to you begins to move forward, you seem to be moving backward. Because you have no reference point by which to tell if you are standing still, you are confused as to which train is actually moving. However, if

Stroboscopic motion
Apparent movement that results from flashing a series of still pictures in rapid succession, as in a motion picture.

Phi phenomenon
Apparent movement caused by flashing lights in sequence, as on theater marquees.

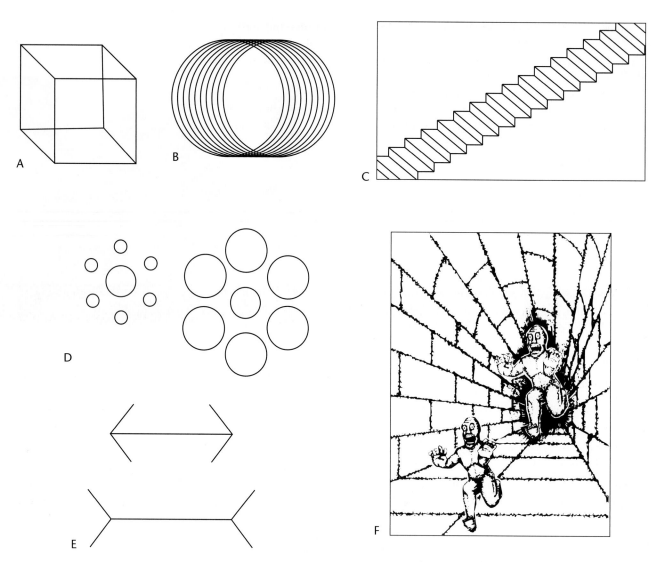

FIGURE 3–35

Reversible figures and misleading depth cues. Images A, B, and C are examples of reversible figures—drawings that we can perceive two different ways, but not at the same time. Images D, E, and F show how, through the use of misleading *depth cues*, we misjudge the size of objects. The middle circles in image D are exactly the same size, as are the lines in image E and the monsters in image F.

you look down at the ground, you can establish an unambiguous frame of reference and make the situation clear to yourself.

Artists rely on many of these perceptual phenomena both to represent reality accurately and to distort it deliberately. In paintings and sketches drawn on a two-dimensional surface, it is almost always necessary to distort objects for them to be perceived correctly by viewers. For example, in representational art, the railroad tracks, sidewalks, and tunnels are always drawn closer together in the distance. Three-dimensional movies also work on the principle that the brain can be deceived into seeing three dimensions if slightly different images are presented to the left and right eyes (working on the principle of retinal disparity). Thus our understanding of perceptual illusion enables us to manipulate images for deliberate effect—and to delight in the results.

REVIEW QUESTIONS

1. The process by which we create meaningful experiences out of the jumble of sensory information is called ____.

Match the following principles of perception with the appropriate definitions.

2. ____ similarity   a. tendency to perceive a whole object even where none exists

3. ____ continuity   b. elements that continue a pattern are likely to be seen as part of the pattern

4. ____ proximity   c. objects that are like one another tend to be grouped together

5. ____ closure   d. elements found close together tend to be perceived as a unit

Answers: 1. perception. 2. c. 3. b. 4. d. 5. a.

KEY TERMS

sensation, p. 86
perception, p. 86

The nature of sensory processes
receptor cell, p. 86
absolute threshold, p. 86
adaptation, p. 87
difference threshold or just noticeable difference (jnd), p. 88
Weber's law, p. 88

Vision
cornea, p. 90
pupil, p. 90
iris, p. 90
lens, p. 90
retina, p. 90
fovea, p. 90
wavelengths, p. 90
rods, p. 90
cones, p. 90
bipolar cells, p. 92
visual acuity, p. 92

dark adaptation, p. 93
light adaptation, p. 93
afterimage, p. 93
ganglion cells, p. 94
optic nerve, p. 94
blind spot, p. 94
optic chiasm, p. 94
hue, p. 96
saturation, p. 96
brightness, p. 96
additive color mixing, p. 96
subtractive color mixing, p. 97
trichromatic theory, p. 97
colorblindness, p. 97
opponent-process theory, p. 97
trichromats, p. 98
dichromats, p. 98
monochromats, p. 98

Hearing
frequency, p. 99
hertz (Hz), p. 99

pitch, p. 99
amplitude, p. 99
decibel, p. 99
overtones, p. 99
timbre, p. 99
auditory nerve, p. 99
oval window, p. 99
cochlea, p. 100
basilar membrane, p. 100
place theory, p. 102
frequency theory, p. 102
volley principle, p. 102

The other senses
olfactory bulb, p. 103
pheromone, p. 103
taste buds, p. 103
kinesthetic senses, p. 104
stretch receptors, p. 104
Golgi tendon organs, p. 104
vestibular senses, p. 105
gate control theory, p. 107

Perception
perceptual constancy, p. 110
size constancy, p. 111
shape constancy, p. 112
brightness constancy, p. 112
color constancy, p. 112
monocular cues, p. 115
binocular cues, p. 115
superposition, p. 115
linear perspective, p. 115
aerial perspective, p. 115
elevation, p. 115
texture gradient, p. 115
shadowing, p. 116
motion parallax, p. 117
stereoscopic vision, p. 117
retinal disparity, p. 117
convergence, p. 117
monaural cue, p. 117
binaural cue, p. 117
autokinetic illusion, p. 118
stroboscopic motion, p. 119
phi phenomenon, p. 119

CHAPTER REVIEW

☐ What causes us to have sensory experiences?

Humans have sensory experiences of sight, hearing, smell, taste, touch, pain, and balance, which are known as **sensations.** These experiences begin when the body's sensory receptors are stimulated. In each case some form of physical energy is converted into neural impulses that are carried to the brain.

☐ How is energy, such as light or sound, converted into a message in the brain?

The process of sending a sensory message to the brain begins when energy stimulates **receptor cells** in one of the sense organs. The receptor cells then send the brain a coded neural signal that varies according to the characteristics of the stimulus. Further coding occurs as the signal passes along sensory nerve fibers, so that the message finally reaching the brain is very detailed and precise.

What is the dimmest light or softest sound that we can sense?

The amount of physical energy that reaches sensory receptors must be of a minimal intensity to produce a detectable sensation. The least amount of energy needed to produce a sensation 50 percent of the time is called the **absolute threshold.** For hearing the absolute threshold is roughly the tick of a watch from 6 meters (20 feet) away in a very quiet room, and for vision it is a candle flame seen from 50 kilometers (30 miles) on a clear, dark night.

Under what circumstances might messages outside our awareness nevertheless affect our behavior?

When people respond to sensory messages that are below their threshold level of awareness, they are said to be responding subliminally. Such subliminal processing can occur in controlled laboratory settings, but there is no scientific evidence that subliminal messages have any effect in everyday life.

Why have psychologists studied vision more than any other sense?

Different animal species depend more on some senses than others. In bats hearing is particularly important; in dogs it is the sense of smell. In humans vision is probably the most important sense, which is why it has received the most research attention.

How does light create a neural impulse?

Light enters an eye through the **cornea** (a transparent protective coating) and passes through the **pupil** (the opening in the **iris**) as well as the **lens,** which focuses it onto the eye's light-sensitive inner lining called the **retina.** Neural impulses are generated in the retina by receptor cells known as **rods** and **cones.** The rods and cones connect to nerve cells called **bipolar cells,** which in turn connect to **ganglion cells.** The axons of ganglion cells converge to form the **optic nerve,** which carries to the brain the neural impulses triggered in the retina.

How do we see colors?

One theory of color vision, the **trichromatic theory,** is based on the principles of **additive color mixing.** It holds that the eyes contain three different kinds of color receptors, one of which is most responsive to red, another to green, and another to blue. By combining signals from these three types of receptors, the brain can detect a wide range of shades. In contrast, the **opponent-process theory** of color vision maintains that receptors in the eyes are specialized to respond to one member of three basic color pairs: red-green, yellow-blue, and black-white (or light-dark). Research gives some support for both these theories. There are indeed three kinds of color receptors in the retinas, but the messages they initiate are coded by other neurons into opponent-process form.

If a tree falls in the forest and no one is there, does the tree make a sound?

A psychologist's answer to this age-old question is no; there isn't a sound. Although sound waves are produced by a falling tree, no sound can be heard without an ear to detect it.

How do the characteristics of sound waves cause us to hear different sounds?

The physical stimuli for the sense of hearing are sound waves, which produce vibration in the eardrums. **Frequency,** the number of cycles per second in a sound wave, is the primary determinant of **pitch** (how high or low the tones seems to be). **Amplitude,** the magnitude of a wave, largely determines the loudness of a sound.

What path does sound follow in the ear?

When sound waves strike an eardrum and cause it to vibrate, three bones in the middle ear—the hammer, the anvil, and the stirrup—are stimulated to vibrate in sequence. These vibrations are magnified in their passage through the middle ear and into the inner ear beyond it. In the inner ear, movement of the **basilar membrane** stimulates sensory receptors, which are called hair cells because of the bundles of tiny fibers at their tops. This stimulation of the hair cells produces auditory signals that travel to the brain through the **auditory nerve.**

How do we distinguish low-frequency and high-frequency sounds?

The **place theory** holds that the brain distinguishes low-frequency from high-frequency sounds by noting the place on the basilar membrane at which the greatest stimulation is occurring. For high-frequency sounds this is the base of the basilar membrane; for low-frequency sounds it is the membrane's opposite end. Another theory of pitch discrimination is the **frequency theory.** According to this theory, the frequency of vibrations on the basilar membrane as a whole is translated into an equivalent frequency of nerve impulses that travel to the brain. The frequency theory can account for pitch detection up to frequencies of about 4,000 Hz. Above that, the place theory seems to provide a better explanation.

What are the chemical senses?

Two of our senses are designed to detect the presence of various chemical substances in the air and in things that we eat. These two chemical senses are smell and taste.

☐ What activates the sense of smell?

Substances carried by airborne molecules into the nasal cavities activate highly specialized receptors for smell. From here messages are carried directly to the **olfactory bulb** in the brain, where they are sent to the brain's temporal lobe, resulting in our awareness of smell.

☐ What are the most basic tastes?

The overall flavor of something is a complex blend of taste and smell. When we consider taste alone, there are only four basic ones: sweet, sour, salty, and bitter. All other tastes derive from combinations of these four. The receptors for taste are housed in the **taste buds** on the tongue. When these receptors are activated by the chemical substances in food, their adjacent neurons fire, sending nerve impulses to the brain.

☐ How do we know which way is up and whether we are moving or standing still?

The **vestibular senses** provide information about our orientation or position in space, such as whether we are rightside up or upside down. The receptors for these senses are in two vestibular organs in the inner ear—the semicircular canals and the vestibular sacs. The kinesthetic senses provide information about the speed and direction of our movements. They rely on feedback from two sets of specialized nerve endings—**stretch receptors,** which are attached to muscle fibers, and **Golgi tendon organs,** which are attached to the tendons that connect muscle to bone.

☐ What causes motion sickness?

The vestibular organs are responsible for motion sickness. This queasy feeling may be triggered by discrepancies between visual information and vestibular sensations.

☐ What are three cutaneous sensations?

The skin is the largest sense organ, and sensations that arise from the receptors embedded in it are called cutaneous sensations. The three cutaneous sensations are pressure, temperature, and pain. Research has not yet established a simple, direct connection between these three sensations and the various types of skin receptors whose nerve fibers lead to the brain.

☐ What differences among people have an effect on the degree of pain they experience?

People have varying degrees of sensitivity to pain based partly on their physiological makeup but also on their current mental and emotional state, their expectations about what they will experience, and their cultural beliefs and values. The most commonly accepted explanation of pain is the **gate control theory,** which holds that a "neurological gate" in the spinal cord controls the transmission of pain messages to the brain.

☐ How is perception different from sensation?

Sensation refers to the raw sensory data the brain receives from the senses of sight, hearing, smell, taste, balance, touch, and pain. **Perception** is the process of organizing, interpreting, and giving meaning to that raw data in order to understand what is going on around us.

☐ How do we organize our perceptual experiences?

Early in the twentieth century a group of Gestalt psychologists in Germany set out to discover the principles through which we interpret sensory information. They believed that the brain creates a coherent perceptual experience that is more than simply the sum of the available sensory data. The brain imposes order on the data it receives partly by distinguishing patterns such as figure and ground, proximity, similarity, closure, and continuity.

☐ How do we perceive things as unchanging despite changing sensory information?

Perceptual constancy is our tendency to perceive objects as unchanging even given many changes in sensory stimulation. Once we have formed a stable perception of something, we see it as essentially the same regardless of differences in viewing angle, distance, lighting, and so forth. These **size, shape, brightness,** and **color constancies** help us to understand and relate to the world better.

☐ What personal factors influence our perceptions?

In addition to past experience and learning, several personal factors color our perceptions. For example, familiarity with an object affects our expectations about how that object should look, even if we observe subtle changes in its appearance. Our perceptions are also influenced by our individual ways of dealing with the environment and by our cultural background, values, motivation, personality, and cognitive style.

☐ How do we know how far away something is?

We perceive distance and depth through both **monocular cues** (which can be received even by one eye alone) and **binocular cues** (which depend on the interaction of both eyes). Some monocular cues are **superposition** (in which one object partly covers another), **linear perspective, elevation** (or closeness of something to the horizon), **texture gradient** (from coarser to finer depending on distance), **shadowing,** and **motion parallax** (differences in the relative movement of close and distant objects as we change position). An important binocular cue is **stereoscopic vision,** which is derived from combining our two retinal images to produce a 3-D effect. Two other binocular cues are **retinal disparity** (the fact that each eye receives a slightly different view from the other) and **convergence** of the eyes as viewing distance decreases.

☐ How do we perceive movement?

Perception of movement is a complicated process involving both visual messages from the retina and messages from the muscles around the eyes as they shift to follow a moving object. At times our perceptual processes trick us into believing that an object is moving when in fact it is not. There is a difference, then, between real movement and apparent movement. Examples of apparent movement are the **autokinetic illusion** (caused by the absence of visual cues surrounding a stationary object), **stroboscopic motion** (produced by rapidly flashing a series of pictures), and the **phi phenomenon** (produced by a pattern of flashing lights).

☐ What causes visual illusions?

Visual illusions occur when we use a variety of sensory cues to create perceptual experiences that do not actually exist. Some are *physical illusions*, such as the bent appearance of a stick in water. Others are *perceptual illusions*, which occur because a stimulus contains misleading cues that lead to inaccurate perceptions.

CRITICAL THINKING AND APPLICATIONS

1. Research on the effectiveness of subliminal perception is inconsistent. Suggest several explanations for those inconsistencies.
2. When we look directly at an object, the image is focused on each eye's fovea. Why is this advantageous?
3. When we are reading or studying, we often seem to be very aware of movements off to our sides. Why is it so easy to sense these events?
4. Why do you get different colors when you mix colored lights as compared to when you mix colored inks?
5. What is the difference between the vestibular sense and the kinesthetic sense? What kinds of activities require both?
6. "Flavor" is thought of as the combination of the taste sense with the sense of smell. How could you demonstrate the difference between flavor and taste? between flavor and smell?
7. Why do people have such differences in pain tolerance?
8. In what ways can emotional or motivational factors affect our sense of pain? Do these same factors have similar effects on other senses?
9. Examine a few passages of your favorite song. Explain how the Gestalt principles of organization (proximity, similarity, closure, and so on) operate in the perception of music.
10. What principles do artists rely on to make a realistic drawing of a person?

On the Web...

Visit these online resources at our Companion Website www.prenhall.com/morris

The Psychology Place

| Learning Activities | 1. Seeing with Your Auditory Cortex, p. 95 |

| Research News | 2. Brain Area Represents Local Visual Environments, p. 95 |
| | 3. Investigating Depth Perception, p. 115 |

Games

1. Label the Eye, p. 91
2. Color Afterimage, p. 97
3. Label the Ear, p. 100
4. Stroboscopic Motion, p. 119

Web Links

1. **http://psych/hanover.edu/Krantz/scn_tut.html,** p. 86
   Sensation and Perception Tutorials and demonstrations related to human senses.
2. **http://mentalhelp.net/guide/pro20.htm,** p. 86
   Sensation and Perception Web site links that are described and rated by Mental Help Net.
3. **http://www.socsci.uci.edu/cogsci/vision.html,** p. 90
   Vision Research WWW Servers provides an alphabetized list of vision research Web sites.
4. **http://insight.med.utah.edu/Webvision/index.html,** p. 91
   Webvision shows and discusses the organization of the retina in great detail.
5. **http://www.accessexcellence.org/AE/AEC/CC/vision_background.html,** p. 95
   How We See: The First Steps in Human Vision. This is a detailed text Web site complemented by helpful diagrams that explain the nature of human vision.
6. **http://online.anu.edu.au/ITA/ACAT/drw/PpofM/INDEX.html,** p. 99
   Outlines and describes the physics and psychophysics of sound and the physiology of hearing.
7. **http://coglab.psych.purdue.edu/coglab/,** p. 108
   Coglab offers demonstrations for various perception and imagery concepts.
8. **http://www.vision3d.com/,** p. 119
   Contains links to 3-D Eye Exercises, Vision therapy, Optical Illusions, and Magic Eye 3D and explains some disorders related to vision.

Explore these topics on the Mind Matters CD-ROM

Mind Matters

1. Sensory Transduction, p. 86
2. Sensory Adaptation, p. 87
3. Sensory Coding, p. 95
4. Introduction to Perception, p. 109
5. Perceptual Constancy, p. 111
6. Perceptions as Decisions, p. 115
7. Perceptual Illusions, p. 119

4

STATES OF
CONSCIOUSNESS

O N AUGUST 18, 1993, A MILITARY CARGO PLANE CRASHED INTO THE ground just a quarter mile short of the runway at Guantanamo Bay, Cuba. All three crew members were seriously injured; the DC-8 freighter they were flying was destroyed by the impact and subsequent fire. Visibility was good, and the plane was on course until the last minute. What caused the crash? After an extensive review, the National Transportation Safety Board concluded the accident was the result not of mechanical failure or pilot error but of "pilot fatigue."

This was the first (and only) time an aviation accident has been officially attributed to pilot fatigue. But the problem of fatigue is more common than most of us realize. According to NASA and federal aviation experts, one in seven pilots nods off in the cockpit. The problem is most acute on overnight international trips, but it can happen on any flight. Off the record, many pilots admit to suddenly waking up and not knowing where they are. This isn't dangerous if the co-pilot is awake. But flight attendants report going into the cabin and finding both pilots sleeping, which is why they regularly knock on the door and offer the crew refreshments. In the 1980s a cargo plane missed the Los Angeles airport and flew out over the Pacific for nearly an hour before air controllers were able to rouse the sleeping pilots and bring them back. Even when pilots remain awake, they may be too groggy to react efficiently in an emergency, as at Guantanamo Bay. Estimates are that pilot fatigue contributes to as many as one-third of aviation accidents; fortunately most are minor.

Sleep and wakefulness are both states of **consciousness.** In everyday conversation, we use the word *consciousness* to describe being alert. Psychologists, however, define *consciousness* more broadly, as our awareness of various mental processes. On any given day, we engage in a great variety of cognitive activities—making decisions, planning, remembering, concentrating, daydreaming, reflecting, sleeping, and dreaming are but a few. Sleep is a state of consciousness that, although different from waking consciousness, is vital to our survival.

Human beings need sleep as much as we need food and water; indeed, we can go without food and water for longer than we can go without sleep. For this reason the FAA has established rules limiting the number of hours a pilot can fly and requiring time off for sleep between flights. The problem is that FAA rules are based on numbers of hours (say, 15 hours on, 9 hours off), whereas our need for sleep is regulated by biological rhythms. What counts is not the number of hours we sleep, but the quality of that sleep. Our brains and bodies are programmed for a 24- to 25-hour cycle, known as a *circadian* cycle. To be fully alert and function at our peak when awake, most adults need 8 hours of sleep (though individual needs vary from 6 to 10 hours). Moreover, we need a good *night's* sleep: An afternoon siesta and naps here and there do not meet our sleep requirements. We can reprogram ourselves to get by with less sleep on different schedules, but our adaptability is limited. Extended periods with too little regular sleep lead to slower reaction times, difficulty processing information and making decisions, and unplanned, involuntary naps lasting a few minutes—or even hours. We experience jet lag when we travel to a different time zone because our biological clock is out of synch with the world around us. Pilots, who work variable shifts and cross and recross time zones, are especially vulnerable to both sleep deprivation and jet lag.

Air travel is still remarkably safe—much safer, statistically, than traveling by car. Ironically, the technological advances that have made it possible to fly larger planes greater distances safely contribute to pilot fatigue. Today's jetliners virtually fly themselves. Once a plane reaches cruising altitude and the autopilot turns on, pilots face long hours with little to do. Boredom and inactivity trigger daydreaming and drowsiness. A psychologist who studies pilot fatigue warns, "If we ignore this, it's going to get worse and worse" (Merzer, 1998, p. 4).

Just why we need sleep to be alert when we are awake is unknown. For centuries, philosophers, theologians, artists, and most recently, scientists have all tried to grasp the elusive nature of consciousness. In the late nineteenth century the psychologist William James characterized consciousness as a kaleidoscope that transforms internal and external information into a coherent and continuous stream. Only recently have scientists begun to consider exactly how this binding takes place and to establish links between conscious processes and neurological mechanisms. For example, Rodolfo Llinás (1996) hypothesizes that individual pieces of information received from the various sensory modalities are first forwarded to specific areas on the cerebral cortex, where they are analyzed and processed as the elements of our perceptual experience (see Chapter 3, "Sensation and Perception"). At the same time, the thalamus, deep in the center of the brain, is "sweeping or scanning" all of these centers at a rate of 40 times per second (Contreras, Destexhe, Sejnowski, & Steriade, 1996; Pedroarena & Llinás, 1997). Each sweep produces a single image or "moment of consciousness." Because the data from all the senses are bound together so quickly, they appear as a continuous flow of consciousness. According to this theory, then, consciousness represents a dialogue between the thalamus and the cerebral cortex. But considerably more research is needed before this provocative theory is either confirmed or rejected.

Contemporary psychologists generally divide consciousness into two broad areas. **Waking consciousness**—or conscious awareness—includes all the thoughts, feelings, and perceptions that occur when we are awake and reasonably alert: sensation and perception, learning, memory, thinking, problem solving, decision making, intelligence, and creativity. Waking consciousness is action- or plan-oriented and is tuned into the external environment.

Altered states of consciousness (ASC) differ from our normal waking consciousness in that we're detached, in varying degrees, from our external environment. Some altered states—such as sleep, daydreaming, and dreaming—occur routinely, even spontaneously. Other ASC are induced by hypnosis, meditation, and mind-altering substances such as alcohol. We begin this chapter by examining natural variations in consciousness; we then turn to the strategies people use to deliberately bring about altered states of consciousness.

Natural Variations in Consciousness

What problems could arise if we were constantly aware of all external and internal sensations?

Even when we are fully awake and alert, we are usually conscious of only a small portion of what is going on around us. At any given moment we are exposed to a great variety of sounds, sights, and smells from the outside world. At the same time, we experience all sorts of internal sensations, such as heat and cold, touch, pressure, pain, and equilibrium, as well as an array of thoughts, memories, emotions, and needs. Normally, however, we are not aware of all these competing stimuli. To make sense of our environment, we must select only the most important information to attend to and then filter out everything else. At times we pay such close attention to what we are doing that we are oblivious to what is going on around us. How the process of attention works is examined at some length in Chapter 6, Memory. Here it is enough to note that the hallmark of normal waking consciousness is the highly selective nature of attention.

The selective nature of attention can be seen in the number of processes that go on without drawing our conscious attention. We are rarely attuned to such vital bodily processes as blood pressure and respiration, for example, and we can walk down the street or ride a bicycle without consciously thinking about every movement. In fact, we carry out certain tasks, such as signing our name, better when we are *not* consciously aware of performing each movement. Similarly, when we drive or walk along a familiar route that we always take to work or school, the process may be so automatic that we remain largely unaware of our surroundings.

Consciousness
Our awareness of various cognitive processes, such as sleeping, dreaming, concentrating, and making decisions.

Waking consciousness
Mental state that encompasses the thoughts, feelings, and perceptions that occur when we are awake and reasonably alert.

Altered states of consciousness (ASC)
Mental states that differ noticeably from normal waking consciousness.

Many psychologists believe that certain key mental processes, such as recognizing a word or a friend's face, also go on outside of normal waking consciousness. As we saw in the first chapter, Sigmund Freud thought that many of the most important influences on our behavior—such as erotic feelings for our parents—are screened from our consciousness and may be accessible only through states such as dreaming. We explore the notion of nonconscious mental processes as we consider various ASC, beginning with natural ones such as daydreaming, and we return to them when we discuss behavioral disorders in Chapter 12.

Daydreaming and Fantasy

Do daydreams serve any useful function?

It takes a deliberate effort to enter an altered state of consciousness via hypnosis, drugs, or meditation, but daydreaming is a universal ASC that occurs seemingly without effort. Typically, we daydream when we would rather be somewhere else or be doing something else; it is a momentary escape from the demands of the real world. You may reminisce about a pleasant vacation while doing a tedious chore or mentally flee a boring class to fantasize about your future as a business tycoon. Your daydreams give you the opportunity to write, star in, and stage-manage a private drama for which you are the only audience.

Are daydreams random paths your mind travels? Not at all. Psychologists have discovered that people's daydreams fall into several distinct categories and that different people prefer particular kinds of daydreams (Singer, 1975). People who score high on measures of anxiety often have fleeting, loosely connected daydreams related to worrying, which give them little pleasure. In contrast, people who are achievement oriented tend to replay in their daydreams recurring themes of achievement, guilt, fear of failure, and hostility, reflecting the self-doubt and competitive envy that accompanies great ambition. Still other people derive considerable enjoyment from their daydreams and use them to solve problems, think ahead, or distract themselves. These "happy daydreamers" stage for themselves pleasant fantasies uncomplicated by guilt or worry. Finally, people who have unusual curiosity and who also value objective thinking tend to experience daydreams filled with scenes from the objective world and marked by controlled lines of thought. Although the frequency of daydreaming varies, about 4 percent of us—generally highly creative people (Lynn & Rhue, 1988)—are considered *fantasy-prone*, meaning that we spend more than half our time not merely daydreaming but lost in elaborate reveries.

Does daydreaming serve any useful function? Some psychologists regard daydreaming as nothing more than a retreat from the real world, especially when that world is not meeting our needs, but others stress the positive value of daydreaming and fantasy (Klinger, 1990). According to Freudian theorists, daydreams allow us to express and deal with desires—generally relating to sex or hostility—that would otherwise make us feel guilty or anxious (Giambra, 1974). It has also been suggested that daydreaming builds cognitive and creative skills, especially among artists and writers (Pulaski, 1974). Daydreaming also helps people endure difficult situations; prisoners of war have used it to survive torture and deprivation. Daydreaming and fantasy do provide relief from everyday—often unpleasant—reality while serving the important functions of reducing internal tension and external aggression (Pulaski, 1974).

Daydreams may also be more than just a substitute for reality or a means of relieving tension (Singer, 1975). They are also an important way of dealing with

Prisoners of war in a prison camp in Bosnia. Such prisoners often use daydreaming to help themselves endure their captivity and deprivation.

information (see Chapter 6, Memory). Every day we process a vast, potentially overwhelming array of information received through the senses. When the chance arises—either during a dull moment in the day or in dreams at night—we reshape some of this information into new and more useful forms. Daydreams and dreams, then, may provide a forum for us to handle "unfinished business." Although daydreaming temporarily distracts us from the real world, this pause allows us to take a step back and reassess things, perhaps enhancing our ability to cope with reality (Singer, 1975).

Cycles of Waking, Sleeping, and Dreaming

What is the purpose of sleep?

We spend about one-third of our lives in the altered state of consciousness known as sleep. Throughout history, cultures have paid varying degrees of respect to sleep and the dreams that inhabit it. In some societies people believe that universal truths are revealed in dreams; members of other societies view sleep as a nonproductive, though essential, activity. Only recently have sleep researchers started to analyze the fascinating complexity of sleep, its functions, and its psychological and biological value.

Circadian Cycles: The Biological Clock   Many of our biological functions—including sleeping and waking, alertness, body temperature, blood pressure, and the level of most hormones—vary predictably over the course of a day. Together these rhythms are often referred to as our *biological clock*.

Like many other physiological functions, sleeping and waking follow a daily, or *circadian*, cycle (Moore-Ede, Czeisler, & Richardson, 1983). The time we spend asleep and awake depends on a 24-hour cycle influenced by the sun, and sleep–wake cycles change as the days grow longer or shorter with the seasons. Not all body cycles follow exactly the same pattern. For example, the level of the hormone epinephrine (which causes the body to "go on alert") reaches a peak in the late morning, then steadily declines until around midnight, when it suddenly drops to a very low level and remains there until morning. By contrast, levels of melatonin (which figures in the onset of sleep) surge at night and drop off during the day—in fact, researchers and medical doctors have used small doses of melatonin to adjust sleep cycles.

Normally, the rhythms and chemistry of all these different cycles interact smoothly, so that a shift in one brings about a corresponding shift in others (Moore-Ede, Czeisler, & Richardson, 1983). In fact, we rarely notice these circadian rhythms until they are disturbed, such as when we fly long distances and undergo jet lag. In another example, when people who work shifts are transferred from the day shift to the midnight shift, they often experience weight loss and suffer from irritability, health problems, insomnia, and extreme drowsiness around the clock for a very long time (Richardson, Miner, & Czeisler, 1989–90). Such disruptions of the biological clock can pose a threat to safety in the case of pilots or workers operating dangerous equipment.

Even the change from standard time to daylight saving time and back again creates temporary problems of adjustment for most people, though the artificial lights in our homes and offices seem to suppress our natural response to seasonal light changes (Wehr et al., 1995). In one study even a moderate change in the sleep–wake cycle—a 28-hour sleep–wake schedule for 33 to 36 days—produced profound effects on the moods of a group of healthy young college students (Boivin et al., 1997). But what is sleep, and why is it so important to us?

Sleep   No one who has tried to stay awake longer than 20 hours or so can doubt the necessity of sleep. When we are sleep-deprived, we crave sleep just as

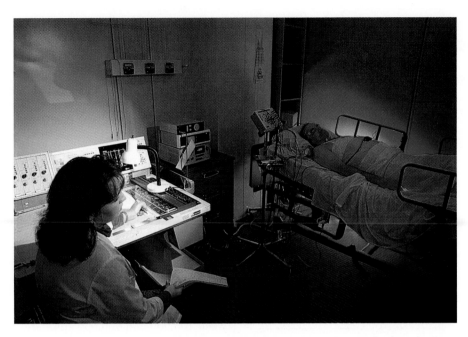

Sleep researchers monitor volunteers' brain waves, muscle tension, and other physiological changes during a night's sleep.

strongly as we would food or water after a period of deprivation (see *Highlights*). Merely resting doesn't satisfy us. But nobody knows exactly why we—and the rest of the animal kingdom—need to sleep.

Many scientists believe that sleep restores effective functioning of the body and brain. Some psychologists, working from an evolutionary perspective, conclude that sleep evolved to encourage organisms to remain inactive and conserve energy during times of the day when their food supplies were low or their predators were especially numerous. In fact, the manner in which many organisms sleep does appear to have become adapted to specific needs and environments. For instance, dolphins, which must come to the surface to breathe, sleep with only one hemisphere of their brain at a time (Borbely, 1986), whereas lions—which have few predators—sleep undisturbed for extended periods of the day. Despite such provocative examples, scientists so far have been unable to piece together a satisfactory explanation of *why* sleep functions as it does, but they are learning a great deal more about *how* sleep occurs.

A recent study suggests that the naturally occurring chemical adenosine may play a pivotal role in what causes us to need sleep (Porkka-Heiskanen et al., 1997). In this study cats kept awake an abnormally long time had an increased amount of adenosine in their brains. When the cats were finally permitted to sleep, the adenosine levels dropped. To determine if the adenosine buildup actually caused sleepiness, investigators injected it into well-rested cats, who immediately became sleepy and began to exhibit the brain patterns typical of drowsiness. Exactly why the level of adenosine appears to trigger sleepiness is not known, but additional research along this line may soon provide us with a better understanding of the neurological processes that cause us to need sleep.

Sleep researchers do not usually enter people's homes to study how they sleep. Typically, they recruit volunteers to spend one or more nights in a "sleep lab." With electrodes painlessly attached to their skulls, the volunteers sleep comfortably as their brain waves, eye movements, muscle tension, and other physiological functions are monitored.

HIGHLIGHTS

Most of Us Need More Sleep than We Get

Inadequate sleep has become a "national epidemic" in the United States (Angier, 1990). Between one-third and one-half of all adults regularly fail to get enough sleep, and the problem is getting worse: Americans were sleeping an average of 8 to 12 hours a night in the 1950s, but by 1990 they were down to only 7 hours a night. In the 1980s more than one-quarter of American adults said they felt unrested in the morning (Bliwise, 1996). The problems associated with inadequate sleep are not limited to adults. Recent estimates indicate that high school and college students average only about 6 hours of sleep a night, with 30 percent of high school students reporting that they fall asleep in class about once a week (Maas, 1998). Moreover, the number of accredited sleep-disorder clinics in the United States has risen from 25 in 1980 to more than 337 in 1997 with still more on the way (Angier, 1990; Dotto, 1990; Grady, 1997).

Between one-third and one-half of all adults regularly fail to get enough sleep.

Extensive research shows that losing an hour or 2 of sleep every night, week after week, month after month, makes it more difficult for people to pay attention (especially to monotonous tasks) and to remember things. Reaction time slows down, behavior becomes unpredictable, and accidents and errors in judgment increase, while productivity and the ability to make decisions decline (Angier, 1990; Babkoff et al., 1991; Borbély, 1984; C. Evans, 1983; Webb & Levy, 1984). These findings have important implications. For example, experts estimate that sleep loss is a contributing factor in between 200,000 and 400,000 automobile accidents each year, resulting in approximately 1,500 deaths. This makes *sleep deprivation* the most common contributing factor to automobile accidents after alcohol (Brody, 1994; Richardson et al., 1989–90; Wald, 1995).

Data from sleep-lab studies show that although there are significant individual differences in sleep behavior, almost everyone goes through several stages of sleep (Anch et al., 1988) and that each stage is marked by characteristic patterns of brain waves, muscular activity, blood pressure, and body temperature (see Figure 4–1). "Going to sleep" means losing awareness and failing to respond to a stimulus that would produce a response in the waking state. As measured by an electroencephalograph (EEG), brain waves during this "twilight" state are characterized by irregular, low-voltage *alpha waves*. This brain-wave pattern mirrors the sense of relaxed wakefulness that we experience while lying on a beach or resting after a big meal. In this twilight state, with the eyes closed, people often report seeing flashing lights and colors, geometric patterns, and visions of landscapes. Sometimes they also experience a floating or falling sensation, followed by a quick jolt back to consciousness.

After this initial twilight phase the sleeper enters Stage 1 of sleep. Stage 1 brain waves are "tight" and of very low amplitude, resembling those recorded when a person is alert or excited. But in contrast to normal waking consciousness, Stage 1 of the sleep cycle is marked by a slowing of the pulse, muscle relaxation, and side-to-side rolling movements of the eyes—the last being the most reliable indication of this first stage of the sleep process (Dement, 1974). Stage 1 usually lasts only a few moments. The sleeper is easily aroused at this stage and, once awake, may be unaware of having slept at all.

Stages 2 and 3 are characterized by progressively deeper sleep. Brain waves increase in amplitude and become slower. At these stages the sleeper is hard to awaken and does not respond to stimuli such as noises or lights. Heart rate, blood pressure, and temperature continue to drop.

Sleep deprivation may also routinely affect the performance of people in high-risk positions, such as pilots (as we saw in the opening of this chapter). Hospital staff and nuclear power–plant operators, who often have to make critical decisions on short notice, are also at risk. A dramatic example of the effects of sleep deprivation on the ability to cope is the 1979 accident at the nuclear power plant at Three Mile Island, Pennsylvania, in which human error transformed a minor mishap into a major nuclear disaster.

Awareness of the relationship between sleep deprivation and accidents has led to changes in the working patterns of people whose jobs can have life-and-death consequences. Several states have short-ened the shifts of hospital residents to prevent errors caused by sleep deprivation. Similarly, the FAA has restricted the number of hours a pilot can fly without having time off to sleep.

Unfortunately, people do not always know when they are not getting enough sleep. In one recent study by the National Transportation Safety Board, most truck drivers involved in accidents that clearly resulted from their falling asleep at the wheel claimed they felt rested at the time (Wald, 1995). In a laboratory study one group of healthy college students who were getting 7 to 8 hours of sleep a night showed no apparent signs of sleep deprivation. Yet 20 percent of them fell asleep immediately when they were put into a dark room, a symptom of chronic sleep loss. Another group for a period of time went to bed 60 to 90 minutes earlier than their normal bedtime. These students reported that they felt much more vigorous and alert—indeed, they performed significantly better on tests of psychological and mental acuity (Carskadon & Dement, 1982).

According to a well-known sleep researcher, Dr. William Dement, one way to reduce your sleep debt is to take short naps. Unfortunately, while in many cultures mid-afternoon is seen as siesta time, in America we often reach for a cup of coffee to keep us going. Even a 20-minute nap can increase alertness, reduce irritability, and improve efficiency.

In Stage 4 sleep the brain emits very slow *delta waves*. Heart rate, breathing rate, blood pressure, and body temperature are as low as they will become during the night. In young adults delta sleep occurs in 15- to 20-minute segments—interspersed with lighter sleep—mostly during the first half of the night. Delta sleep time lessens with age but continues to be the first sleep to be made up after sleep has been lost.

About an hour after falling asleep, the sleeper begins to ascend from Stage 4 sleep to Stage 3, Stage 2, and back to Stage 1—a process that takes about 40 minutes. The brain waves return to the low-amplitude, saw-toothed shape characteristic of Stage 1 sleep and waking alertness. Heart rate and blood pressure also increase, yet the muscles of the body are more relaxed than at any other point in the sleep cycle and the person is very difficult to awaken. The eyes move rapidly under closed eyelids. This **rapid eye movement (REM)** sleep stage is distinguished from all other stages of sleep—called **non-REM** or **NREM**—that precede and follow it.

REM sleep is also called **paradoxical sleep,** because while measures of brain activity, heart rate, blood pressure, and other physiological functions closely resemble those recorded during waking consciousness, the person in this stage appears to be deeply asleep and is incapable of moving, because the body's voluntary muscles are essentially paralyzed. Some research suggests that REM sleep is also the stage when most vivid dreaming occurs, so inhibition of movement through muscle paralysis makes REM sleep safer for all of us. When researchers surgically prevented this paralysis in cats, the results were spectacular. After the cats entered the REM stage, although otherwise sound asleep, they raised their heads, tried to stand up, and in some cases even searched for and attacked prey (Morrison, 1983).

REM (paradoxical) sleep
Sleep stage characterized by rapid eye movement and increased dreaming.

Non-REM (NREM) sleep
Non-rapid-eye-movement stages of sleep that alternate with REM stages during the sleep cycle.

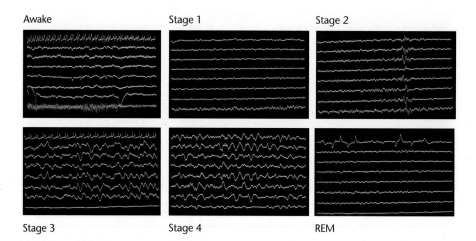

Awake   Stage 1   Stage 2

Stage 3   Stage 4   REM

FIGURE 4–1

Waves of sleep. This series of printouts illustrates electrical activity in the brain, heart, and facial muscles during the various stages of sleep. Note the characteristic delta waves that begin to appear during Stage 3 and become more pronounced during Stage 4.

The first Stage 1–REM period lasts about 10 minutes, then is followed by Stages 2, 3, and 4 of NREM sleep. This sequence of sleep stages is repeated all night long, averaging 90 minutes from Stage 1–REM to Stage 4 and back again. Normally a night's sleep consists of 4 to 5 sleep cycles of this sort, but the pattern of sleep changes as the night progresses. At first, Stages 3 and 4 dominate, but as time passes, the Stage 1–REM periods gradually become longer and Stages 3 and 4 become shorter, eventually disappearing altogether. Over the course of a night, then, about 45 to 50 percent of the sleeper's time is spent in Stage 2, whereas REM sleep takes up another 25 percent of the total.

Sleep requirements and patterns vary considerably from person to person and from age to age. Although some people claim that they never sleep, when they are observed under laboratory conditions, some actually sleep soundly without being aware of it, while others engage in short periods of "microsleep," dozing for a second or two at a time. But researchers have documented the cases of some adults who need hardly any sleep (Rosenzweig & Leiman, 1982).

Sleep patterns change with age (see Figure 4–2). Infants sleep much more than adults—13 to 16 hours during the first year—and a greater proportion of their sleep is REM sleep (see Figure 4–3). Unlike adults, infants enter the REM stage immediately after falling asleep and change sleep stages often. The elderly, on the other hand, tend to sleep less than younger adults, wake up more often during the night, and spend much less time in the deep sleep of Stages 3 and 4. Finally, men generally sleep less well than women do: During early adulthood they awaken more often and sleep less restfully; after age 60 their sleep patterns are more disturbed, and they engage in less Stage 3 and 4 sleep than women do (Paulson, 1990).

Dreams *Dreams* are visual and auditory experiences that our minds conjure up during sleep. Although most dreams are quickly forgotten, people typically have 4 or 5 dreams a night. Collectively these dreams account for about 2 hours of our total time spent sleeping every night.

People awakened during REM sleep report graphic dreams about 80 to 85 percent of the time (Berger, 1969). Less striking dreamlike experiences that resemble the thinking done during normal wakeful consciousness are reported 50 percent of the time during NREM sleep. At times dreams can be so vivid that it is hard to distinguish them from reality. In some cultures, in fact, dreams are considered to be real experiences of a world that is inaccessible to us in our waking lives. Similarly, most young children have great difficulty distinguishing between dreams and waking experiences.

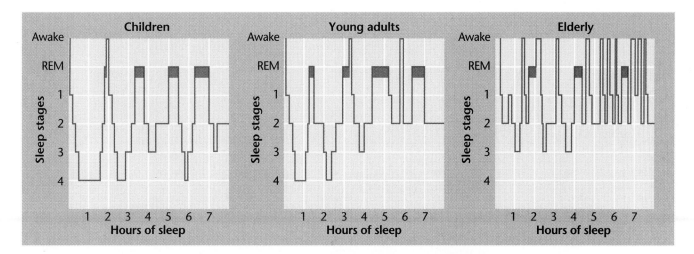

FIGURE 4–2

A night's sleep across the life span.   Sleep patterns change from childhood to young adulthood to old age. The red areas represent REM sleep, the stage of sleep that varies most dramatically across age groups.

Source: Adapted by permission of *The New England Journal of Medicine, 290,* 487, 1974.

Sigmund Freud (1900), whose theories are explored more comprehensively in Chapter 10, Personality, called dreams the "royal road to the unconscious." Freud believed that dreams represent our wishes and that they can reveal the motives guiding our behavior—motives of which we are often unaware. Freud distinguished the *manifest,* or *surface,* content of dreams from their latent content—the hidden, unconscious thoughts or desires that he thought were expressed indirectly through dreams.

In dreams, according to Freud, people permit themselves to express primitive desires that are relatively free of moral controls. For example, someone who is not consciously aware of hostile feelings toward a loved one (say, a sister) may have dreams about murdering her. Even in a dream, however, such hostile feelings may be "censored" and transformed into a highly symbolic form. For instance, the desire to terminate one's sister (the dream's latent content) may be recast into the dream image of seeing her off at a train "terminal" (the dream's manifest content). According to Freud, this process of censorship and symbolic transformation explains the highly illogical nature of many dreams. Deciphering the disguised meanings of dreams is one of the principal tasks of psychoanalysts in their work with clients. Although researchers have found little evidence to support Freud's theory of manifest and latent dream content (Fisher & Greenberg, 1996), his pioneering work, focused on exploring the meaning of dreams, paved the way for contemporary investigations of dream content (Domhoff, 1996).

Whatever the ultimate explanation for dream content, we do know that it is related to several factors, including where you are in your sleep cycle, what you were doing before you went to sleep, your gender, your age, and even your socioeconomic status. For example, women not only tend to recall more dreams than men do, but they are also more likely to report dreams with characters, emotions, and friendly interaction as well as dreams that take place indoors and deal with home and family. By contrast, men more often remember dreams about aggression and overt hostility as well as successful striving for achievement (Brenneis, 1970; Cohen, 1973; Hall & Van de Castle, 1966; Winger, Kramer, & Whitman, 1972). Before the onset of menstruation, women often dream about waiting; before childbirth, they generally dream more about babies

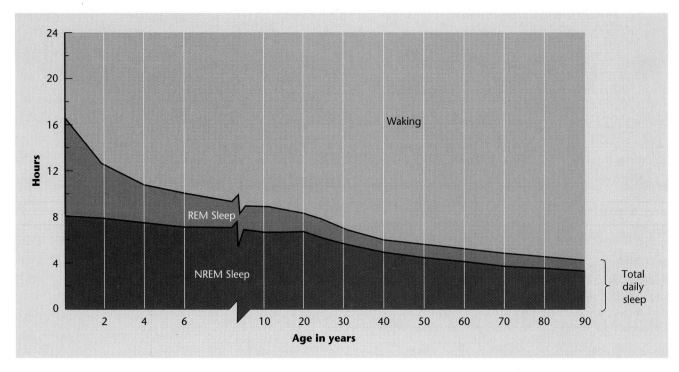

FIGURE 4–3

Changes in REM and NREM sleep. The amount of REM sleep people need declines sharply during the first few years of life. Newborns spend about 8 hours, or almost half of their total sleep time in REM sleep, whereas older children and adults spend just 1–2 hours or about 20–25 percent of their total sleep time in REM sleep.

Source: Adapted from H. P. Roffwarg, "Ontogenetic development of the human sleep-dream cycle," *Science, 152,* p. 60. Copyright © 1966 by the American Association for the Advancement of Science. Reprinted with permission.

or their mothers than about their husbands. Women are also more likely to dream about being the victims of aggression (Domhoff, 1996).

Dream content also varies by age (Foulkes, 1982). Very young children (ages 2 to 5) tend to have brief dreams, many of which involve animals, but the images are usually unrelated to one another, and there is seldom any emotion, narrative, or story line. In children between the ages of 5 and 9, dreams become considerably longer. A few narrative, storylike dreams appear around ages 5 to 7, but it is not until the child is 7 to 9 years old that most dreams take this narrative, sequential form. Also between ages 7 and 9 feelings and emotions appear in dreams, and children more often appear as a character in their own dreams. In children aged 9 to 15, dreams become more adultlike: Narratives follow well-developed story lines, other people play important roles, and there are many verbal exchanges in addition to motor activity (Anch et al., 1988).

A few studies have examined differences in dream content across social classes or racial groups. One such study (Winger et al., 1972) found that individuals from lower-income groups reported more dreams involving people as well as more dreams involving misfortune than upper-middle-class people did. The latter reported fewer dreams involving death anxiety. This study, like earlier studies, found only negligible differences in dream content among racial groups. Similarly, cross-cultural studies have shown that people from different cultures report dream content consistent with the unique cultural patterns inherent in their respective cultures (Domhoff, 1996).

Dream content also displays some degree of continuity with a person's waking activities. Research has shown that what people dream about is generally

The fanciful images of Marc Chagall's paintings capture the quality of many of our dreams. Is a dream of an entwined man and woman floating high above a city symbolic of some subconscious sexual desire, as Freud would have suggested? Or is it just an illogical image caused by random brain cell activity during sleep? As yet psychologists have no conclusive answer. Perhaps both views have merit.

similar to what they think about and do while they are awake. That is, dream content commonly reflects an individual's unique conceptions, interests, and concerns. For example, things that concern an individual while he or she is awake may also appear in his or her dreams. Dream content also appears to be relatively consistent for most individuals, displaying similar themes across years and even decades (Domhoff, 1996).

Some evidence suggests that dream content is also modified by presleep events, so that it complements and compensates for waking experiences (Hauri, 1970). Volunteers who had exercised strenuously for 6 hours before sleep tended to have dreams with relatively little physical activity. People who had been socially isolated during the day had dreams filled with social interaction (Wood, 1962). Volunteers who had been deprived of water during the day dreamed of drinking (Bokert, 1970). These compensatory effects seem to be only temporary, however. People who were recently paralyzed reported more physical activity in their dreams than did long-term paralyzed people (Newton, 1970). This kind of evidence suggests that compensatory dreams die out when they are not supported by reality.

One neurophysiological explanation for dreaming holds that in our dreams we reprocess information gathered during the day as a way of strengthening the memory of information crucial to survival (Winson, 1990). Others think that REM sleep may be related to brain "restoration" and growth (Oswald, 1973, 1974), and that this biochemical activity "serves as the organic basis for new developments in the personality" (Rossi, 1973). How would this process work? Because protein synthesis proceeds at a faster rate during REM sleep than during NREM sleep, protein synthesis may be the neurophysiological process that enables us to combine new and old information into imaginatively restructured patterns. Research has demonstrated that both human and nonhuman subjects spend more time in REM sleep after learning difficult material, but also that interfering with their REM sleep immediately afterward severely disrupts their memory for the newly learned material (C. T. Smith, 1985; C. T. Smith & Lapp, 1986; C. T. Smith & Kelly, 1988). Thus if you study hard during the week and then stay up all night on Friday and Saturday, you are likely to forget up to one-third of the material you would have remembered had you had a more restful weekend.

If these neurological explanations prove to be accurate, does it mean that you can learn while you're asleep? If you set up a tape recorder to play information while you sleep, will you painlessly absorb this material? Unfortunately, research has never confirmed that people can learn complex material while sleeping. Even experiments designed to teach sleepers simple pairs of words have failed. Very rudimentary forms of learning may be possible, however. The first time a stimulus such as a loud noise is presented to a sleeper, it produces signs of arousal. Repetition of the stimulus causes less and less arousal, suggesting that the sleeper has learned that the stimulus is not a cause for alarm.

Most dreams last about as long as the events would in real life; they do not flash on your mental screen just before waking. Generally, dreams consist of a sequential story or a series of stories. External stimuli, such as an alarm clock going off, may modify an ongoing dream, but they do not initiate dreams.

Are all the dreams from a single night related? Unfortunately, experimenters encounter a methodological problem when they try to answer this question: Each time the subject is awakened to be asked about a dream, the natural course of the dream is interrupted and is usually lost forever. If one particular problem or event weighs heavily on the dreamer's mind, however, it will often show up in dreams throughout the night (Dement, 1974).

Do We *Need* to Dream?

Scientists are even more uncertain about why we dream than they are about why we need to sleep. Freud suggested that dreams serve as a psychic safety valve. If his theory is correct, depriving people of the opportunity to dream should significantly affect their waking lives, and to some extent research has supported this idea.

In early experiments designed to study the effects of dream deprivation, people were awakened just as they entered REM sleep. (Early investigators targeted the REM period because they believed at the time that dreams occurred almost exclusively during REM sleep.) The participants became anxious, testy, and hungry. They had difficulty concentrating and even hallucinated during their waking hours. All of these ill effects vanished as soon as the people experienced REM sleep again (Dement, 1965; May & Kline, 1987).

In addition, when the people deprived of REM sleep were finally allowed to sleep undisturbed, the amount of REM sleep nearly doubled—a phenomenon called *REM rebound*. Unfortunately, because the researchers did not control for the dreaming that takes place outside the REM period, we cannot be certain whether the changes they observed were due simply to the denial of REM sleep or to the decrease in dreaming associated with the REM period.

Dreams may help us process emotional information. In dreams, emotionally significant events may be assimilated with previous experiences (Farthing, 1992). For example, a child's first experience of a carnival or amusement park is usually a blend of terror and excitement. Later in life, whenever he or she experiences something that is exciting but also somewhat frightening, carnival rides or images may dominate his or her dreams. That we do not yet know exactly why we need dreams may only reflect the great variability in both dreams themselves and in their uses.

Sleeptalking, Sleepwalking, and Night Terrors

Sleeptalking and *sleepwalking* usually occur during deep sleep (Stage 4). Both are more common among children than adults: About 20 percent of children have at least one episode of either sleepwalking or sleeptalking. Boys are more likely to walk in their sleep than girls, and contrary to popular belief, waking a sleepwalker is not dangerous. But because sleepwalking commonly takes place during a very deep stage of sleep, waking a sleepwalker is not easy (Hobson, 1994).

Some children also experience *sleep terrors*, or *night terrors*, a form of nocturnal fright that makes them suddenly sit up in bed, often screaming out in fear. Sleep terrors are altogether different from *nightmares*. Children generally cannot be awakened from sleep terrors and will push away anyone trying to comfort them. Unlike nightmares, sleep terrors cannot be recalled the next morning. They also occur more often if the child is very tired. Though sleep terrors are usually seen in children between 4 and 12 years old, they may continue into adulthood (Hartmann, 1984). Adults who have them are more likely to suffer from a personality disorder (Kales et al., 1980) or to abuse drugs or alcohol. Brain injuries associated with epilepsy may also contribute to night terrors in adults.

Neither nightmares nor night terrors alone indicate psychological problems. Anxious people have no more nightmares than other people do. And like night terrors, nightmares diminish with age (J. M. Wood & Bootzin, 1990). People whose nightmares stem from a traumatic experience, however, may be plagued by these terrifying nighttime episodes for years.

Sleep Disorders   The scientific study of typical sleep patterns—our focus so far—has also resulted in new insights into sleep disorders. **Insomnia**—difficulty in falling asleep or remaining asleep during the night—afflicts as many as 35 million Americans. Most episodes of insomnia stem from stressful events and are temporary (see *Applying Psychology*). But for some sufferers insomnia is a persistent life disruption. Taking sleeping pills is often counterproductive: Many such drugs lose their effectiveness over time. One of the most widely prescribed medications for insomnia, Halcion, frequently causes severe side effects, including anxiety, memory loss, hallucinations, and violent behavior.

For some people insomnia is a symptom of psychological problems, such as depression (A. Kales et al., 1976), so its cure requires treating the underlying disorder. For others insomnia results from an abnormally aroused biological system. A physical predisposition to insomnia may combine with associated distress over the sleeplessness, creating a cycle in which biological and emotional factors reinforce one another. People may worry so much about not sleeping that their bedtime rituals, such as brushing teeth and getting dressed for bed, "become harbingers of frustration, rather than stimuli for relaxation" (Hauri, 1982). Furthermore, bad sleep habits, such as varying bedtimes and distracting sleep settings, may aggravate or even cause insomnia.

Another sleep disorder, **apnea,** affects 2 to 4 percent of the population. This condition is associated with breathing difficulties at night. In severe cases, the victim actually stops breathing after falling asleep (Vgontzas & Kales, 1999). When the level of carbon dioxide in the blood rises to a certain point, apnea sufferers are spurred to a state of arousal just short of waking consciousness. Because this may happen hundreds of times a night, apnea patients typically feel exhausted and fall asleep repeatedly the next day.

People suffering from insomnia and apnea may envy those who have no trouble sleeping. But too much sleep has serious repercussions as well. **Narcolepsy** is a hereditary disorder whose victims nod off without warning in the middle of a conversation or other activity. People with narcolepsy often experience a sudden loss of muscle tone upon expression of any sort of emotion; laughter, anger, or sexual arousal may bring on a feeling of weakness. Another symptom of the disorder is immediate entry into REM sleep, which produces frightening hallucinations that are, in fact, dreams that the person is experiencing while still

Insomnia
Sleep disorder characterized by difficulty in falling asleep or remaining asleep throughout the night.

Apnea
Sleep disorder characterized by breathing difficulty during the night and feelings of exhaustion during the day.

Narcolepsy
Hereditary sleep disorder characterized by sudden nodding off during the day and sudden loss of muscle tone following moments of emotional excitement.

APPLYING PSYCHOLOGY

Coping with Occasional Insomnia

If you are like most people, you probably have had at least a few nights when you found it difficult to fall asleep. Episodes of even temporary or occasional insomnia can impair your ability to function during the day. So what can you do if you suddenly find yourself going through a period when you are unable to get a good night's sleep? Here are some tips that may help:

■ Maintain regular bedtime hours; don't sleep late on weekends.

■ Establish a regular bedtime routine that you follow each night before retiring, such as a warm bath, followed by a little reading or writing a letter.

■ Abstain from drugs (including alcohol, caffeine, and nicotine, as well as the routine use of sleeping pills). Tryptophan, a substance that promotes sleep, may be taken as a sleep aid in the form of warm milk, confirming a folk remedy for sleeplessness.

■ Adjust the temperature of the room if it is too cold or too warm.

■ Avoid foods that may cause sleeplessness, such as chocolate.

■ Establish a regular exercise program during the day, but never exercise within several hours of bedtime.

■ Avoid anxious thoughts while in bed. Set aside regular times during the day—well before bedtime—to mull over your worries. This technique may be supplemented by relaxation training, using such methods as biofeedback, self-hypnosis, or meditation (Morin et al., 1994).

■ Don't fight insomnia when it occurs. The old saying "If I can't sleep, I mop the kitchen floor" makes sense to sleep researchers, who counsel their clients to get out of bed and engage in an activity for an hour or so until they feel sleepy again.

To learn more about coping with insomnia, visit our Web site at **www.prenhall.com/morris.**

---

partly awake. Narcolepsy is believed to arise from a defect in the central nervous system (Bassetti & Aldrich, 1996).

REVIEW QUESTIONS

1. Our awareness of the mental processes of our everyday life is called _Consciousness_

2. Technological innovations such as ____ (____) enable scientists to study brain activity during various states of consciousness.

3. The major characteristic of waking consciousness is _Selection attention_

4. In humans, sleeping and waking follow a ____ cycle.

5. Most vivid dreaming takes place during the ____ stage of sleep.

6. We normally spend about ____ hours each night dreaming.

7. Freud distinguished between the ____ and ____ content of dreams.

True or false:

_T_ 8. The content of men's and women's dreams differs.

_F_ 9. We do not really need to dream.

_T_ 10. Sleep depreviation has been implicated in both industrial and driving accidents.

Match the following terms with the correct definition:

11. _C_ circadian cycle   a. relaxed wakefulness
12. _a_ alpha waves   b. hidden meaning
13. _b_ latent content   c. daily cycle
14. _f_ sleep deprivation   d. trouble getting to sleep or staying asleep
15. _d_ insomnia   e. suddenly falling asleep during the day
16. _e_ narcolepsy   f. national epidemic

Answers: 1. consciousness. 2. electroencephalography (EEG). 3. selective attention. 4. circadian. 5. REM. 6. two. 7. manifest, latent. 8. true. 9. false. 10. true. 11. c. 12. a. 13. b. 14. f. 15. d. 16. e.

Artificial Alterations in Consciousness

What are the ways in which we can intentionally and artificially alter consciousness?

Daydreams and dreams are the most common alterations of normal consciousness, and both are most likely to occur when sensory stimulation is reduced—for example, when the eyes are closed or the environment is quiet. This raises an intriguing question for scientists: What would happen if we were deprived of all sensory stimulation? Would we feel deeply rested? Or would sensory deprivation affect our consciousness in more profound ways?

Sensory Deprivation

What happens when people are deprived of sensory stimulation?

In the 1950s and 1960s experimenters explored the effects of **sensory deprivation**—the radical reduction of sensory stimuli—on human participants. In the initial study, student volunteers at McGill University were put into sensory-deprivation chambers that severely restricted their visual, auditory, and tactile stimulation; they were released from their constraints only for meals and trips to the bathroom. The results were dramatic. The volunteers were increasingly unable to do mental tasks such as studying. They grew more and more irritable, and eventually they began to hallucinate. When they were released from their cubicles, they performed poorly on a number of tests in comparison with a control group (Heron, 1957).

Later research modified the techniques for studying sensory deprivation used in the McGill study, and as a result, some of the findings changed. Nevertheless, no matter how deprivation was induced, its effects were similar. The volunteers hallucinated, although not as often as in the McGill study. They also experienced altered perceptions, both similar to and different from those found among the participants in the McGill study. Finally, they dreamed, daydreamed, and fantasized. Within a few hours of entering the chamber, most volunteers began to experience alternating states of drowsiness, sleep, and wakefulness. The distinctions among these states became so blurred that the volunteers found it difficult to distinguish between waking hallucinations and dreams (Suedfeld, 1975). They reported seeing flashes of light, geometrical forms, and various complex images of objects or living beings, as well as hearing various noises. Some of the participants also described smelling nonexistent odors, such as tobacco smoke, and feeling that the room or they themselves were moving.

When the volunteers emerged from solitary confinement, both their perception of color and reaction time were impaired. Their vision and ability to perceive brightness were relatively unimpaired. Pain and taste sensitivity had actually been heightened by the experience. Some of the effects described lasted for up to a day after the end of the experiment.

Meditation

What are the effects of meditation?

For centuries people have used various forms of **meditation** to experience an alteration in consciousness (Benson, 1975). Each form of meditation focuses the meditator's attention in a slightly different way. *Zen meditation* concentrates on respiration, for example, while *Sufism* relies on frenzied dancing and prayer (G. E. Schwartz, 1974). In *transcendental meditation (TM)* practitioners recite or chant a mantra, which is a sound specially selected for a student by the teacher

Sensory deprivation
Extreme reduction of sensory stimuli.

Meditation
Any of the various methods of concentration, reflection, or focusing of thoughts undertaken to suppress the activity of the sympathetic nervous system.

of TM to keep all other images and problems at bay and to allow the meditator to relax more deeply (Deikman, 1973; Schwartz, 1974).

In all its forms, meditation suppresses the activity of the sympathetic nervous system, the part of the nervous system that prepares the body for strenuous activity during an emergency. Meditation lowers the rate of metabolism and reduces heart and respiratory rates. Alpha brain waves (which accompany relaxed wakefulness) increase noticeably during meditation, while blood lactate, a chemical linked to stress, decreases. Not surprisingly, then, meditation can reduce high blood pressure (Benson, Alexander, & Feldman, 1975; R. A. Stone & DeLeo, 1976).

Meditation has been used to treat certain medical problems, including drug abuse. Some studies have found that a high percentage of people who used drugs stopped doing so after taking up meditation. For example, among people who practiced TM, marijuana use fell from 78 percent to 22 percent after 21 months; of those taking LSD, 97 percent stopped using the drug after an average of 22 months of meditation. The participants in this study, however, were already committed to TM when they were surveyed; among other populations the effects are not always so dramatic (Benson et al., 1979).

Besides physiological benefits, people who practice some form of meditation may gain certain emotional and even spiritual advantages: They often report increased sensory awareness, euphoria, strong emotions, and a sense of timelessness (Deikman, 1973). Peace of mind, a sense of well-being, and total relaxation have also been reported by meditators (S. R. Dean, 1970). Some investigators question whether meditation significantly alters normal states of consciousness, because the same physical changes can be brought about simply by deep relaxation (D. S. Holmes, 1984). Advocates of meditation reply that this fact does not rule out the possibility that meditation produces some uniquely beneficial psychological effects. And, in fact, a meta-analysis comparing TM with other forms of meditation and physical relaxation techniques, such as biofeedback (see Chapter 5, Learning), did demonstrate that TM is superior when it comes to reducing anxiety (Eppley, Abrams, & Shear, 1989).

Hypnosis

What possible clinical uses have been found for hypnosis?

In mid-eighteenth-century Europe, Anton Mesmer, a Viennese physician, fascinated audiences by putting patients into trances in order to cure their illnesses. Mesmerism—now known as **hypnosis**—was initially discredited by a French commission chaired by Benjamin Franklin. But some respectable nineteenth-century physicians revived interest in hypnosis when they discovered it could be used to treat certain forms of mental illness. Nevertheless, even today considerable disagreement persists about how to define hypnosis and even about whether it is a valid ASC.

One reason for the controversy is that from a behavioral standpoint, there is no simple definition of what it means to be hypnotized. Different people believed to have undergone hypnosis describe their experiences in very different ways (Farthing, 1992, p. 349):

> "Hypnosis is just one thing going on, like a thread . . . focusing on a single thread of one's existence. . . ."

> "I felt as if I were 'inside' myself; none of my body was touching anything. . . ."

> "I was very much aware of the split in my consciousness. One part of me was analytic and listening to you (the hypnotist). The other part was feeling the things that the analytic part decided I should have."

Hypnosis
Trancelike state in which a person responds readily to suggestions.

Given such variations among hypnotized individuals, it is difficult to arrive at a single definition for the state of hypnosis. It appears that consciousness has been altered, though how hypnosis occurs, the ways it is experienced, and even susceptibility vary from one person to another.

Hypnotic Susceptibility   People differ greatly in their susceptibility to hypnosis. If you're easily carried away by a book or a movie, you're probably extremely susceptible to hypnosis. Hypnotic susceptibility appears to be partly learned and partly inherited. Growing up with parents who have fertile imaginations and who encourage imaginative play in their children seems to contribute to hypnotic susceptibility (Kihlström, 1985). But so does growing up with severely strict parents, perhaps because such a childhood makes people highly obedient to instructions from authority, including a hypnotist's suggestions. Susceptibility also varies according to age. Children are generally more susceptible to hypnotic induction than adults are (Banyai & Hilgard, 1976). Finally, scientists have established that hypnotic behavior is greatly affected by contextual cues, including the setting in which the hypnosis occurs and the exact words used by the hypnotist (Kihlström & McConkey, 1990; Spanos, 1986; Spanos & Chaves, 1989).

Inducing Hypnosis and Making Suggestions   To induce hypnosis, the hypnotist usually begins by focusing a willing subject's attention on the hypnotist's voice. The subject may also be asked to concentrate on a specific object or to visualize a particular scene, such as a relaxing day at the beach. Guided imagery may be used to bring the scene into sharp focus—for example, a subject imagining himself or herself stretching out at the beach might be told to think about becoming progressively more relaxed. As a subject enters the hypnotic trance, its effects may be heightened and tested by some preliminary suggestions. For instance, the subject may be told that at the count of 10 it will be impossible to open his or her eyes. Sometimes these suggestions are put in "paradoxical" form. Subjects are told, for example, that the harder they try to open their eyes, the more tightly shut their eyes will remain. More suggestions of relaxation follow until eventually the subject appears to be in a state of complete relaxation.

The effect of a hypnotist's suggestions vary from person to person. Some people who are told that they cannot move their arms or that their pain has vanished do, in fact, experience paralysis or anesthesia. Some who are told that they are hearing a certain piece of music or are unable to hear anything may hallucinate or become deaf temporarily. Some remember events from their early childhood and say they feel as though they are experiencing those events all over again. After instructions such as "You will remember nothing that happened under hypnosis until I tell you," some have amnesia, which lingers even when they are no longer hypnotized. In still other cases, instructions received while under hypnosis may temporarily diminish a person's desire to smoke or overeat.

Some of these results are easier to achieve than others. It is usually relatively easy to convince suggestible people that they cannot open their eyes or that their arms are too heavy to lift. It is more difficult to produce anesthesia so that people become insensitive to pain (Spiegel, Bierre, & Rootenberg, 1989). And it is still more difficult to coax people to recall lost memories or to generate hallucinations (Hilgard, 1965). Hypnotic suggestion, it seems, is most effective with simpler behaviors or mental processes.

Clinical Applications of Hypnosis   Because hypnotic susceptibility varies greatly from one person to another, hypnosis in clinical and therapeutic settings

A hypnotist and his patient. Although hypnosis is often applied in clinical situations, psychologists disagree as to whether it really is an altered state of consciousness.

is difficult to assess and is not universally effective. Nevertheless, hypnosis is used in a variety of medical and counseling situations (Rhue, Lynn, & Kirsch, 1993). Some research suggests that it can enhance the effectiveness of traditional forms of psychotherapy (Kirsch, Montgomery, & Sapirstein, 1995), but psychologists do not agree on this issue. Hypnosis has been found more effective as an anesthetic than morphine for certain types of pain. Dentists, for example, have been using it as an anesthetic for years, and some doctors use it to alleviate pain in children with leukemia who have to undergo repeated—and very painful—bone-marrow biopsies (Hilgard, Hilgard, & Kaufmann, 1983).

Can hypnosis change or eliminate bad habits? Researchers disagree. Critics point out that if people really want to change a behavior, they are likely to do so without hypnosis. Hypnosis may strengthen their will, but so might joining a support group such as Weight Watchers. In other words, posthypnotic suggestions may be no more effective than other kinds of supportive help. Psychologists also disagree over whether hypnosis creates a separate, definable state of consciousness or whether suggestibility alone explains "hypnotic" behavior. In fact, most current explanations of hypnotic phenomena incorporate elements of both perspectives (Kirsch & Lynn, 1995).

REVIEW QUESTIONS

Match the following terms with the appropriate description:

1. _A_ sensory deprivation
2. _D_ meditation
3. _C_ hypnosis
4. _B_ hypnotic susceptibility

a. sometimes results in hallucinations
b. varies tremendously over time
c. controversial altered state of consciousness
d. suppresses sympathetic nervous system

5. Many psychologists believe that the effects of hypnosis can be accounted for by the variable of ____.

Answers: 1. a. 2. d. 3. c. 4. b. 5. suggestibility.

Drug-Altered Consciousness

Historically, what substances have been used—and for what reasons—to alter consciousness?

Meditation, hypnosis, daydreams, sleep, dreaming—so far our discussion has focused on altered states of consciousness produced naturally, without drugs. But since ancient times, people have continuously used various drugs for social, religious, and personal reasons. Wine is mentioned often in the Bible and today plays a sacramental role in several major religions. Marijuana is alluded to in the herbal recipe book of a Chinese emperor in 2737 B.C. The Jivaro Indians of Ecuador, who consider the world of the senses an illusion, habitually use drugs to contact the "real world" of supernatural forces. In our own culture the use of some substances to alter mood or behavior is, under certain circumstances, regarded as normal—including moderate intake of alcohol and of the caffeine in coffee, tea, or cola, although smoking tobacco is increasingly becoming unpopular. In some circles illegal substances such as marijuana, cocaine, and amphetamines are also common.

For as long as people have recorded using drugs, the problems associated with abusing them have also been recognized. About 2,500 years ago one of the earliest precepts of the Buddha was to avoid using intoxicants to cloud the mind. The Greeks advocated moderation in all things, including the drinking of wine, and the Bible preaches against the sin of alcohol abuse. A national survey showed that more than 60 percent of adult Americans believe that all nonprescription drug use is immoral and should be illegal ("61% of Americans," 1990). These concerns about drug abuse are not without foundation: Substance abuse among employees, for example, costs U.S. businesses more than $100 billion a year through absenteeism, lost productivity, and medical expenditures (Freudenheim, 1988). But the cost to human lives is even more startling. More than 15,000 Americans die every year and more than a million are injured in alcohol-related car accidents. And smoking is at least partly responsible for the deaths of more than a quarter of a million people each year—which is more than 1 out of every 6 deaths in the United States.

We turn now to altered states of consciousness induced by **psychoactive drugs,** chemical substances that change moods and perceptions. We'll first look broadly at the effects that sustain the use of drugs and at how researchers study these effects; then we'll focus on some of the most commonly used drugs. In examining the effects of particular drugs, it is useful to group them into the categories of *depressants, stimulants,* and *hallucinogens.* Even though these are not rigid categories, this division helps to organize our knowledge about drugs.

Substance Use, Abuse, and Dependence

How can we tell if someone is dependent on a substance?

If we define drugs broadly, as we did earlier, to include caffeine, tobacco, and alcohol, then most people throughout the world use some type of drug on an occasional or regular basis. The majority of these people use such drugs in moderation and do not suffer ill effects. But for many, substance use escalates into **substance abuse**—a pattern of drug use that diminishes a person's ability to fulfill responsibilities, that results in repeated use of the drug in dangerous situations, or that leads to legal difficulties related to drug use (Oltmanns & Emery, 1995). For example, people whose drinking causes ill health and problems within their families or on their jobs are abusing alcohol.

The ongoing abuse of drugs, including alcohol, may lead to compulsive use of the substance, or **substance dependence** (also known as *addiction*) (see Table 4–1). Although not everyone who abuses a substance develops dependence, dependence usually follows a period of abuse. Dependence often includes *tolerance,* the phenomenon whereby higher doses of the drug are required to produce its original effects or to prevent *withdrawal symptoms,* the unpleasant physical or psychological effects following discontinuance of the substance.

The causes of substance abuse and dependence are a complex combination of biological, psychological, and social factors that varies for each individual and for each substance. Also, the development of substance dependence does not follow an established timetable. One person might drink socially for years before abusing alcohol, whereas someone else might become addicted to cocaine in a matter of days. Before we examine specific drugs and their effects, we first look at how psychologists study drug-related behaviors.

How Drug Effects Are Studied
The effects of particular drugs are studied under carefully controlled scientific conditions. In most cases experimenters compare people's behavior before the administration of the drug with their behavior afterward, taking special precautions to ensure that any observed changes in behavior are due to the drug alone.

To eliminate research errors based on subject or researcher expectations, most drug experiments use the **double-blind procedure,** in which some participants

---

Psychoactive drugs
Chemical substances that change moods and perceptions.

Substance abuse
A pattern of drug use that diminishes the ability to fulfill responsibilities at home or at work or school, that results in repeated use of a drug in dangerous situations, or that leads to legal difficulties related to drug use.

Substance dependence
A pattern of compulsive drug taking that results in tolerance, withdrawal symptoms, or other specific symptoms for at least a year.

Double-blind procedure
Experimental design, useful in studies of the effects of drugs, in which neither the subject nor the researcher knows at the time of administration which subjects are receiving an active drug and which are receiving an inactive substitute.

TABLE 4-1	Signs of Substance Dependence

The most recent clinical definition of *dependence* (APA, 1994) describes a broad pattern of drug-related behaviors characterized by at least three of the following seven symptoms over a 12-month period.

1. Developing tolerance: needing increasing amounts of the substance to gain the desired effect or experiencing a diminished effect when using the same amount of the substance. For example, the person might have to drink an entire six-pack to get the same effect formerly experienced after drinking just one or two beers.

2. Experiencing withdrawal symptoms—physical and psychological problems that appear if the person tries to stop using the substance. Withdrawal symptoms range from anxiety and nausea to convulsions and hallucinations.

3. Using the substance for a longer period or in greater quantities than intended.

4. Having a persistent desire or making repeated efforts to cut back on the use of the substance.

5. Devoting a great deal of time to obtaining or using the substance.

6. Giving up or reducing social, occupational, or recreational activities as a result of drug use.

7. Continuing to use the substance even in the face of ongoing or recurring physical or psychological problems likely to be caused or made worse by use of the substance.

receive the active drug, while others take a neutral, inactive substance called a **placebo.** Neither the researchers nor the participants know who took the active drug and who got the placebo. If the behavior of the participants who actually received the drug differs from the behavior of those who got the placebo, the cause is likely to be the active ingredient in the drug.

Studying drug-altered consciousness is complicated by the fact that most drugs not only affect different people in different ways but also produce different effects in the same person at different times or in different settings. For example, some people are powerfully affected by even small amounts of alcohol, while others are not. And drinking alcohol in a convivial family setting usually produces somewhat different effects than does consuming alcohol under the watchful eyes of a scientist.

Recently, sophisticated neuroimaging procedures have proved useful for studying drug effects. Techniques such as PET imaging have enabled researchers to isolate specific differences between the brains of addicted and non-addicted people. For example, the "addicted brain" has been found to differ qualitatively from the nonaddicted brain in a variety ways, including metabolism and responsiveness to environmental cues (Leshner, 1996). Investigators have also focused on the role played by neurotransmitters in the addictive process—noting that every addictive drug causes dopamine levels in the brain to increase (Glassman & Koob, 1996). Results like these may lead to not only better understanding of the biological basis of addiction but also more effective treatments.

Depressants: Alcohol, Barbiturates, and the Opiates

Why does alcohol, a depressant, lead to higher rates of violence?

Depressants are chemicals that retard behavior and thinking by either speeding up or slowing down nerve impulses. Generally speaking, alcohol, barbiturates, and the opiates have depressant effects.

Alcohol   Our society recognizes many appropriate occasions for the consumption of alcohol—to celebrate milestone events, to break down social isola-

Placebo
Chemically inactive substance used for comparison with active drugs in experiments on the effects of drugs.

Depressants
Chemicals that slow down behavior or cognitive processes.

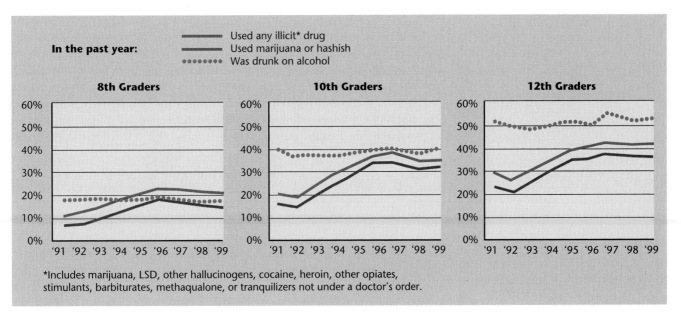

In the past year:
——— Used any illicit* drug
——— Used marijuana or hashish
•••••••• Was drunk on alcohol

8th Graders   **10th Graders**   **12th Graders**

*Includes marijuana, LSD, other hallucinogens, cocaine, heroin, other opiates, stimulants, barbiturates, methaqualone, or tranquilizers not under a doctor's order.

FIGURE 4–4

Teenage drug use. A national survey found that the use of illegal drugs and alcohol by American teenagers held fairly steady in 1999. Prior to that year it had diminished slightly after years of growth. Among high school seniors, 42 percent reported that they used an illegal drug in the previous year. More than 20 percent of 8th graders admitted to drug use, up from 11 percent in 1991 but down slightly from the previous year. In this group, 18.5 percent reported getting drunk during the past year. Among 12th graders, that number rises to 53 percent.

Source: L. D. Johnston, P. M. O'Malley, & J. G. Bachman. (December, 1999). *Drug trends in 1999 are mixed.* University of Michigan News and Information Services: Ann Arbor, MI. [On-line]. Available: **www.monitoringthe-future.org;** accessed 01/14/00.

tion and inhibitions, and to promote group harmony. Perhaps because of its social acceptability and legality, alcohol is widely used in our society: About 500 million gallons of alcoholic beverages are consumed annually in the United States. Unfortunately, despite age restrictions on the purchase and consumption of alcohol, much of this drinking is done by American youth. Rates of alcohol consumption among students are illustrated in Figure 4–4.

The social costs of abusing alcohol are high. Alcohol is implicated in more than two-thirds of all fatal automobile accidents, two-thirds of all murders, two-thirds of all spouse beatings, and more than half of all cases of violent child abuse. Moreover, the use of alcohol during pregnancy is related to a variety of birth defects, the most notable being *fetal alcohol syndrome*, which will be discussed more fully in Chapter 9, Life Span Development.

A study conducted by the National Institute on Alcohol Abuse and Alcoholism (NIAAA) found that more than 40 percent of all "heavy drinkers" die before the age of 65 (compared with less than 20 percent of nondrinkers). Even light to moderate drinking is associated with shorter life spans ("Study Links," 1990). In addition, there is the untold cost for the nearly 30 million children of alcohol abusers. One person, whose experience growing up in an alcoholic household was in many ways typical, wrote, "I lived with a daily dread—about how bad the drinking would be that day, about how much shouting, crying or fighting there might be and about when, or if, it was ever going to end. I never knew what to expect next. I lived with constant fear and worry. I felt ashamed and confused. But more than anything else, I felt alone" (cited in Brody, 1987).

Despite its dangers, alcohol continues to be a popular drug because of its short-term effects. As a depressant, it calms down the nervous system very much like a general anesthetic (McKim, 1986, 1997). Thus some people consume alcohol to relax, to enhance their mood, to put them at ease in social situations, and to relieve the stress and anxiety of everyday living (Steele & Josephs, 1990). Paradoxically, although it is a depressant, alcohol is often experienced subjectively as a stimulant because it inhibits centers in the brain that govern critical judgment and impulsive behavior. To the drinker the long-term negative consequences of alcoholism pale beside the short-term positive effects, such as the sense that alcohol makes them feel more courageous, less inhibited, and more spontaneous (Steele & Josephs, 1990).

A study by Muriel Vogel-Sprott demonstrated just how strong these short-term effects of alcohol are (1967). In the experiment, participants received both painful shocks and money for engaging in certain behaviors. Some of the participants were given alcohol before the experiment began, while others received only a placebo. The people who received a placebo sharply reduced the behaviors that caused them to receive shocks—the money just wasn't worth the pain. But the subjects under the influence of alcohol showed no such inhibition—they weathered the shocks to get the money. Apparently, the negative consequences of their behavior (the shocks) were no longer important to them. The term *alcohol myopia* was coined to describe the alcohol-induced shortsightedness that makes drinkers oblivious to many behavioral cues in the environment and less able to make sense of those cues they do perceive (Steele & Josephs, 1990). Several dozen research studies that clearly demonstrate the correlation between alcohol use and increased aggression, hostility, violence, and abusive behavior found that alcohol dulls the effects of environmental cues to proper behavior and makes drinkers less aware of and less concerned about the negative consequences of their actions (Bushman, 1993; Bushman & Cooper, 1990; Ito, Miller, & Pollock, 1996).

Physiologically, alcohol first affects the frontal lobes of the brain (Adams & Johnson-Greene, 1995), which figure prominently in inhibitions, impulse control, reasoning, and judgment. As consumption continues, alcohol affects the cerebellum, the center of motor control and balance (Johnson-Greene et al., 1997). Eventually, alcohol consumption affects the spinal cord and medulla, which regulate such involuntary functions as breathing, body temperature, and heart rate. A blood-alcohol level of 0.25 percent severely impairs functionality, and slightly higher levels can cause death from alcohol poisoning (see Table 4–2).

TABLE 4-2	The Behavioral Effects of Blood-Alcohol Levels
Levels of Alcohol in the Blood	**Behavioral Effects**
0.05%	Feels good; less alert
0.10%	Slower to react; less cautious
0.15%	Reaction time much slower
0.20%	Sensory-motor abilities suppressed
0.25%	Staggering (motor abilities severely impaired); perception is limited as well
0.30%	Semistupor
0.35%	Level for anesthesia; death is possible
0.40%	Death is likely (usually as a result of respiratory failure)

Source: Data from Oakey Ray (1983), *Drugs, Society, and Human Behavior* (3d ed.). St. Louis: The C. V. Mosby Co.

Alcohol compromises perception, motor processes, and memory. It diminishes the ability to see clearly, to perceive depth, and to distinguish the differences between bright lights and colors. Alcohol also impairs the spatial-cognitive functioning necessary for driving (Matthews et al., 1996). Some aspects of hearing, such as the perception of loudness, are not affected by alcohol, but the ability to discriminate between different rhythms and pitches is impaired by even a small quantity of the drug. Smell and taste perception are uniformly diminished, and the perception of time also becomes distorted. Most people report that time seems to pass more quickly when they are "under the influence" (National Commission on Marijuana and Drug Abuse [NCMDA], 1973b).

Alcohol also interferes with memory storage: People find it difficult to recall what happened after having only two or three drinks (Parker, Birnbaum, & Noble, 1976). Prolonged drinking impairs retrieval of memories—that is, heavy drinkers have difficulty recalling memories they once could retrieve easily. In heavy drinkers, alcohol may also produce blackouts, after which the person is unable to remember anything that occurred during certain periods—from a few minutes in some cases to whole days in others—when he or she was drinking.

Exactly how alcohol affects the brain and memory at the neurological level is still unclear, but at least one recent study suggests that alcohol "disconnects" the fibers that link the cells to one another. This theory, if proved, is very significant because the brain does not normally grow large quantities of new brain cells, it readily strengthens existing synapses and creates new ones (see Chapter 2, *Highlights:* "New Connections for Old Neurons"). Thus if the person stops drinking, it may be possible for the brain to heal, to some extent, the physiological damage often caused by alcohol abuse (Pakkenberg, 1993).

Statistics show that alcohol is a major cause of automobile accidents.

Although many of the effects of drinking can be traced to the ways in which alcohol operates on the central nervous system, they also reflect people's *expectations* about how alcohol will affect them (Critchlow, 1986; Goldman et al., 1991; Leigh, 1989; Leigh & Stacy, 1991). For example, experimental evidence indicates that men become more aggressive, more sexually aroused, and less anxious in social situations when they *believe* they are drinking alcohol, even if they are not actually doing so (Marlatt & Rohsenow, 1980).

Does alcohol have stronger effects on women than on men? Yes, partly because the same quantity of alcohol will have a greater impact on a lighter person than on a heavier person, and women generally weigh less than men (York & Welte, 1994). But research has also shown that even when the effect of weight is equalized, alcohol has a more pronounced effect on women than on men. It turns out that most women have less of the stomach enzyme that regulates the amount of alcohol reaching the bloodstream than do men. (In similar fashion, drinking alcohol on an empty stomach has more pronounced effects because less of this enzyme is present in an empty stomach [Frezza et al., 1990].) For these reasons, one drink is likely to have the same biological and psychological effects on the average woman as two drinks on the average man.

Despite its social and legal acceptance, alcohol is a highly addictive drug with potentially devastating long-term effects. One study found the rate of alcohol dependence among men between the ages of 18 and 44 to be 27 percent. Overall, approximately 13 percent of U.S. adults (about 20 million people) either abuse alcohol or are dependent on it, making alcohol abuse and dependence the most serious substance-abuse problem in the United States. (See *Applying Psychology*.)

Long-term abuse of alcohol can cause memory loss, decreased sexual drive or impotence, menstrual problems, liver and kidney damage, damage to the

APPLYING PSYCHOLOGY

What Are the Signs of Alcoholism?

The following test is excerpted from a comprehensive self-test published by the National Council on Alcoholism. It will help you determine if you or someone you know needs to find out more about alcoholism, *but it should not be used to establish the diagnosis of alcoholism.*

1. Do you ever drink heavily when you are disappointed, under pressure, or when you have had a quarrel with someone?

2. Can you handle more alcohol now than when you first started to drink?

3. Have you ever been unable to remember part of the previous evening, even though your friends say you didn't pass out?

4. When drinking with other people, do you try to have a few extra drinks the others won't know about?

5. Has a family member or close friend ever expressed concern or complained about your drinking?

6. Have you been having memory "blackouts"?

7. Do you often want to continue drinking after your friends say they've had enough?

8. Do you usually have a reason for the occasions when you drink heavily?

9. When you're sober, do you sometimes regret things you did or said while drinking?

10. Have you tried switching brands or drinks or following different plans to control your drinking?

11. Have you sometimes failed to keep promises you made to yourself about controlling or cutting down on your drinking?

If your answer to any of these questions is yes, you may be at risk for alcoholism. More than one yes may signal an alcohol-related problem and the need to consult with an alcoholism counselor. To find out more, contact the National Council on Alcoholism and Drug Dependence in your area.

For further information about drug dependence, call or e-mail the following organizations:

National Council on Alcoholism and Drug Dependence:
(800) 622-2255

Psychiatric Institutes of America:
(800) COCAINE

Alcoholics Anonymous:
http://www.alcoholics-anonymous.org

National Institute on Drug Abuse:
(301) 443-6245
6001 Executive Boulevard
Bethesda, MD 20892
http://www.nida.nih.gov

American Cancer Society (nicotine): (800) 227-2345
http://www.cancer.org/index_4up.html

Additional resources are listed in the box on getting help in Chapter 13, Therapies.

stomach and intestine, cancers of the mouth and esophagus, anxiety, insomnia, and brain damage. Long-term heavy use may also bring on a form of mental illness known as Korsakoff's syndrome, which is characterized by hallucinations, confusion, and severe memory problems (Bowden, 1990; see the discussion in Chapter 6, Memory). Chronic abuse of alcohol may lead to institutionalization in a hospital or prison or ultimately to death: Approximately 100,000 Americans die each year as a result of using alcohol with other drugs or from alcohol-related breathing difficulties, heart failure, pneumonia, automobile accidents, and suicide (Van Natta et al., 1985).

Are some people especially prone to alcohol abuse? Researchers have no clear answers (Newlin & Thomson, 1990). Alcoholism does run in families: Children whose parents do not use alcohol tend to abstain or to drink only moderately; to a lesser extent, children whose parents abuse alcohol also tend to drink heavily (Cotton, 1979; Harburg, DiFranceisco, Webster, Gleiberman, & Schork, 1990; Harburg, Gleiberman, DiFranceisco, Schork, & Weissfeld, 1990; Gordis, 1996; Webster, Harburg, Gleiberman, Schork, & DiFranceisco, 1989). Moreover, there is some direct evidence of a genetic basis for alcohol abuse. For example, identical twins are far more likely to have similar drinking patterns than are fraternal twins. And people whose biological parents have alcohol-abuse problems are likely to abuse alcohol even if they are adopted and raised by people who do not abuse alcohol (Gordis, 1996; McGue, 1993; Shields, 1977).

Although alcoholism runs in families, psychologists have reached no consensus on the exact role heredity plays in the tendency to alcoholism. Some researchers point to hereditary differences in levels of the stomach enzyme mentioned earlier, whereas others note that people differ genetically in their tolerance for alcohol in the blood and in the ways that they react to alcohol, although a specific genetic mechanism that may put people at risk for developing alcoholism has not been identified (Bolos et al., 1990; Gordis, 1996). There was a flurry of excitement in the spring of 1990 when it was reported that a single gene that puts people at risk for alcoholism had been identified (Blum et al., 1990), but subsequent research failed to confirm the finding. Instead, it appears that the genetic basis of alcoholism is considerably more complex (Bolos et al., 1990).

Others cite nonbiological factors as the keys in determining who is likely to abuse alcohol. Some researchers have identified an "alcoholic personality," one that is emotionally immature and needy, low in self-esteem, and unable to tolerate frustration well (Coleman et al., 1984). But this personality profile cannot be the whole answer, because many people who have these characteristics do not abuse alcohol. Another line of research holds that specific psychological disorders underlie the propensity for addiction to alcohol and other drugs. According to this view, people who are so removed from their own feelings that they are unable to form relationships with others are likely to be attracted to alcohol because it helps them experience and express affection, aggression, and closeness. By contrast, people who are depressed or hyperactive are more likely to be drawn to stimulants such as amphetamines, and people who have difficulty controlling their anger and hostility favor the opiates (Khantzian, 1990).

Culture, too, may steer people toward or away from alcoholism. Parents and spouses may introduce people to a pattern of heavy drinking. Alcohol is also more acceptable in some ethnic cultures than in others—for example, Orthodox Jews frown on the use of alcohol, and Muslims prohibit it.

Many researchers believe that a full understanding of the causes of alcoholism and other drug addictions will not be achieved unless we take account of a wide variety of factors: heredity, personality, social setting, and culture (Zucker & Gomberg, 1990). In Chapter 14, Social Psychology, we look at social influences on binge drinking, a major concern on college campuses across the United States.

Barbiturates   **Barbiturates** commonly known as "downers"—include such medications as Amytal, Nembutal, and Seconal. Discovered about a century ago, this class of depressants was first prescribed for its sedative and anticonvulsant qualities. But after researchers recognized in the 1950s that barbiturates had potentially deadly effects—particularly in combination with alcohol—their use declined, though they are still sometimes prescribed to treat such diverse conditions as insomnia, anxiety, epilepsy, arthritis, and bedwetting (Reinisch & Sanders, 1982). Though barbiturates are often prescribed to help people sleep, they actually disrupt the body's natural sleep patterns and cause dependence when used for long periods. Frequently prescribed for elderly people, who tend to take them chronically along with their other medications, barbiturates may produce significant side effects such as confusion and anxiety (Celis, 1994).

The general effects of barbiturates are strikingly similar to those of alcohol: Taken on an empty stomach, a small dose causes lightheadedness, silliness, and poor motor coordination (McKim, 1986, 1997), while larger doses may bring on slurred speech, loss of inhibition, and increases in aggression (Aston, 1972). As with alcohol, the effect of the drug varies from one setting to another: A dose that prompts aggressive behavior at a party may cause only drowsiness when taken in

Barbiturates
Potentially deadly depressants, first used for their sedative and anticonvulsant properties, now used only to treat such conditions as epilepsy and arthritis.

the privacy of one's home. In addition, when taken during pregnancy, barbiturates, like alcohol, produce such birth defects as a cleft palate and malformations of the heart, skeleton, and central nervous system (Wilder & Bruni, 1981).

Strangely enough, barbiturates sometimes enhance memory. While barbiturates may cause amnesia (as alcohol does, in the form of blackouts), in smaller doses these drugs are the "truth serums" of contemporary spy thrillers.

The Opiates   The use of **opiates**—a group of substances derived from the opium poppy or synthetic substances resembling it—may go back as far as 6,000 years, though the best-known opiate, heroin, is a relative newcomer. Used as a medicine by ancient physicians and as a poison by ancient kings, opium quickly replaced tobacco when it was banned in China in 1644—and the use of opiates to produce an altered state of consciousness was firmly established.

In the United States during most of the nineteenth century and into the early part of this century, opium was a widely used ingredient in a variety of over-the-counter (patent) medicines marketed under such innocuous names as "Mrs. Winslow's Soothing Syrup" and "Street's Infant Quietness." In this same period the drug morphine was chemically isolated from opium, and it was relatively easy to obtain with a prescription. By the latter part of the nineteenth century, people realized that opiates are highly addictive. Ironically, heroin—a further refinement of opium, discovered in 1898—was originally proposed as a cure for morphine addiction. Although the nonmedicinal distribution of opiates was banned early in this century, opiate dependence remained a social problem and appears to be on the rise today (Kantrowitz et al., 1993).

Generally the opiates produce subjective feelings of euphoria, well-being, and relaxation. Controlled studies reveal, however, that these pleasant effects are short-lived and are quickly replaced by undesirable changes in mood and behavior.

In advanced stages of addiction, heroin becomes less a means to alter consciousness than a painkiller to stave off withdrawal symptoms. The first symptom of withdrawal is restlessness, accompanied by fits of yawning, chills, and hot flashes. The skin often breaks out into goose bumps, resembling the texture of a plucked turkey (hence the term *cold turkey*). This is generally followed by periods of prolonged sleep lasting up to 12 hours. When awake, the addict experiences severe cramps, vomiting, and diarrhea, along with convulsive shaking and kicking, as well as profuse sweating. In about a week the withdrawal symptoms diminish and then disappear.

Because heroin is illegal and expensive, addicts must spend a great deal of time—often engaged in criminal activities—obtaining the money to buy it. The increasing need for the drug and the severe withdrawal without it, the tendency to violence, and the crimes committed to pay for it all underlie policymakers' concerns about heroin as a social problem.

Stimulants: Caffeine, Nicotine, Amphetamines, and Cocaine

How does someone feel after a stimulant wears off?

The drugs classified as **stimulants**—caffeine, nicotine, amphetamines, and cocaine—have legitimate uses, but because they produce feelings of optimism and boundless energy, the potential for abuse is high.

Caffeine   Caffeine, which occurs naturally in coffee, tea, and cocoa, belongs to a class of drugs known as *xanthine stimulants*. The primary ingredient in over-the-counter stimulants, caffeine is popularly believed to maintain wakefulness and alertness, but many of its stimulant effects are illusory. In one study, subjects performing motor and perceptual tasks thought they were doing better when

Opiates
Drugs, such as opium and heroin, derived from the opium poppy, that dull the senses and induce feelings of euphoria, well-being, and relaxation. Synthetic drugs resembling opium derivatives are also classified as opiates.

Stimulants
Drugs, including amphetamines and cocaine, that stimulate the sympathetic nervous system and produce feelings of optimism and boundless energy.

they were on caffeine, but their actual performance was no better than without it. In terms of wakefulness, caffeine reduces the total number of sleep minutes and increases the time it takes to fall asleep. Interestingly, it is the only stimulant that does not appear to alter sleep stages or cause REM rebound, making it much safer than amphetamines.

Caffeine is found in many beverages and nonprescription medications, including pain relievers and cold and allergy remedies (see Figure 4–5). It is generally considered a benign drug, although large doses—more than five or six cups of strong coffee, for example—may cause *caffeinism*, or "coffee nerves": anxiety, headaches, heart palpitations, insomnia, and diarrhea. Caffeine interferes with prescribed medications, such as tranquilizers and sedatives, and appears to aggravate the symptoms of many psychiatric disorders. It is not clear what percentage of coffee drinkers are dependent on caffeine. Those who are dependent experience tolerance, difficulty in giving it up, and physical and psychological distress, such as headaches, lethargy, and depression, whether the caffeine is in soda, coffee, or tea (Blakeslee, 1994).

Nicotine Nicotine is far more dangerous than caffeine. It occurs naturally only in tobacco. Like caffeine, it has stimulant effects, but at higher doses it acts as a depressant. Besides the immediate effects of increased heart rate and constricted blood cells, over time it places users at increased risk for lung and other cancers, as well as for cardiovascular disease and blindness (Seddon, Willett, Speizer, & Hankinson, 1996). Links between the biochemical and behavioral effects of nicotine are difficult to pinpoint. We know that nicotine causes an elevation in mood, increases the activity of a number of neurotransmitters affecting different areas of the brain, and produces a craving for the drug.

Recent studies have found that nicotine shares several neurobiological traits with such other highly addictive drugs as cocaine, amphetamines, and morphine (Glassman & Koob, 1996; Pontieri, Orzi, & Chiara, 1996). When ingested through smoking, nicotine tends to arrive at the brain all at once, following each puff. This rush, similar to the "high" experienced by heroin users, makes the brain crave more nicotine, and users tend to become highly dependent. The power of this craving was seen dramatically in one study in which a participant pulled a plunger 14,000 times over 45 minutes to get just two puffs of tobacco (T. Adler, 1993a).

Caffeine and nicotine are both widely used stimulants. Although heavy use of caffeine can have adverse health effects, nicotine is far more dangerous than caffeine.

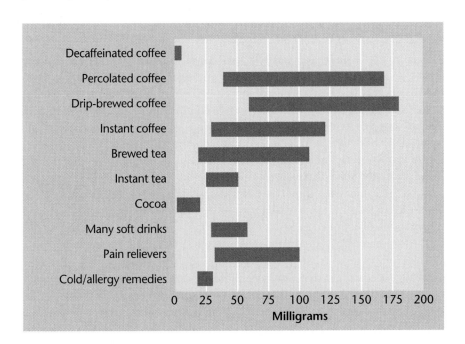

FIGURE 4–5

The amount of caffeine in some common preparations. Caffeine occurs in varying amounts in coffee, tea, soft drinks, and many nonprescription medications. On average, Americans consume about 200 mg of caffeine each day.

Source: Copyright © 1991 by the New York Times Company. Reprinted by permission.

The withdrawal symptoms for nicotine users include nervousness, insomnia and drowsiness, headaches, irritability, and an intense craving for nicotine (Brandon, 1994). Research on treatment outcomes indicates that as few as 15 percent of smokers manage to quit permanently. Certain conditions and behaviors increase a user's likelihood of quitting. Nicotine patches and nicotine gum, which deliver smaller doses of the drug, may lessen the physical addiction while also helping to break the habit of lighting up. Those who have quit previously and started smoking again also have a higher success rate. But nicotine is so highly addictive that the majority of smokers do not succeed in giving up smoking for good. There are no miracle cures for smokers who want to quit.

Amphetamines   Reports of amphetaminelike substances date back more than 5,000 years, but the medicinal value of amphetamines was not recognized until the early part of the twentieth century. Chemically, **amphetamines** resemble epinephrine, a neurotransmitter that stimulates the sympathetic nervous system (see Chapter 2, The Biological Basis of Behavior). Because of this chemical similarity, amphetamines are used to treat asthma; they have also been prescribed for narcolepsy because of their stimulant qualities.

The popularity of amphetamines stems from their wide use by the military during World War II. Soon truck drivers and students also came to rely on amphetamines to stay awake and alert. And because amphetamines tend to suppress the appetite, they were widely used for a time as "diet pills." Until recently, it was easy to get prescriptions for these medications. In fact, amphetamines became so easy to obtain that by the 1970s, an estimated 10 percent of the U.S. population over the age of 14 had used an amphetamine (Greaves, 1980). This represented 10 billion pills per year, or 50 pills a year for every man, woman, and child in the United States.

These drugs have a tremendous potential for abuse, however, because of their effects on consciousness and behavior. One side effect is the ability to make people feel happy. Higher doses amplify this effect, and users who inject amphetamines report "rushes" of euphoria. But after euphoria wears off, users may experience a "crash" and subsequent severe depression (Gunne & Anggard, 1972). To head off this unpleasant experience, users tend to take more amphetamines, leading to a condition called *amphetamine psychosis*, similar to paranoid schizophrenia and characterized by delusions, hallucinations, and paranoia. Habitual amphetamine use can also prompt aggressive and violent behavior, caused not so much by the drug itself as by the profound personality changes—particularly paranoia—that accompany excessive use (Leccese, 1991).

Recently the *methamphetamines*—illegal derivatives known on the street as *MDMA* or *Ecstasy*—have shown a marked increase in use among college students. Users report an extraordinary loss of inhibition in addition to the euphoria and increased energy associated with amphetamine use. Unfortunately, evidence suggests that even short-term excessive use of the methamphetamines may produce *long-term* harmful effects on sleep, mood, appetite, and impulsiveness by damaging the neuroconnections between lower brain centers and the cortex (McCann, Slate, & Ricaurte, 1996).

To a large extent the old phrase "dope fiend" is a more appropriate description of the amphetamine addict than of the heroin addict. Because of the addictive potential of amphetamines, their medicinal use is now restricted to the treatment of narcolepsy and hyperactivity in children.

Cocaine   A stimulant that, like the amphetamines, can cause euphoric moods, **cocaine** is extracted from the leaves of the South American coca bush. Sixteenth-century Spanish conquistadors in Peru discovered the power of this drug and paid native laborers with it because the conquerors could extract more labor

Amphetamines
Stimulant drugs that initially produce "rushes" of euphoria often followed by sudden "crashes" and, sometimes, severe depression.

Cocaine
Drug derived from the coca plant that, while producing a sense of euphoria by stimulating the sympathetic nervous system, also leads to anxiety, depression, and addictive cravings.

from workers who chewed coca leaves for the stimulant effects. At the same time, they could cut down on food rations, because the drug suppresses the appetite (McKim, 1997).

The drug remained generally unknown among other Europeans until the mid-nineteenth century, when it became popular to blend coca into wine and other drinks. The Coca-Cola Company used chemically active coca leaves in its original formula, but today Coca-Cola—and other colas—are blended with coca leaves from which the active ingredient has been removed. Among the more famous users of cocaine was Sigmund Freud, who recommended it to friends and relatives and promoted it as a cure for alcoholism and morphine addiction. Eventually, Freud became disillusioned with the drug, but one of his colleagues developed what is still the only legitimate medical use for cocaine—as a local anesthetic (Novocain is the familiar form).

The use of cocaine as a recreational drug gradually declined in the first half of the twentieth century, partly because cocaine was associated in the popular culture with the opiates, even though it is chemically quite distinct from them. In recent decades, however, cocaine use has become more widespread, particularly in its crystalline form, known as "crack," which can be smoked. What makes crack such a serious problem is that many users report becoming dependent on the drug almost immediately; because of the way the drug acts on the brain, the craving for it is difficult to break.

The effects of cocaine mirror those of the amphetamines, although they don't last as long. In addition to the feelings of euphoria, energy, and perceived clarity of thought, physiological effects include stimulation of the sympathetic nervous system, an increase in heart rate and blood pressure, and constriction of the blood vessels. Large doses also raise the body temperature and dilate the pupils. After relatively large doses wear off, some users experience a "crash" characterized by anxiety, depression, and a strong craving for more cocaine. R. K. Siegel (1982) surveyed habitual users and discovered that one-third to one-half also experienced such mood and behavioral symptoms as paranoia, visual hallucinations, cravings for the drug, and attention and concentration problems.

The effects of crack are even faster and more intense than those produced by amphetamines. When smoked as crack, molecules of cocaine reach the brain in less than 10 seconds, producing a high that lasts from 5 to 20 minutes, followed by a swift and equally intense depression. Crack and cocaine stimulate a pleasure center in the base of the brain that is responsible for our emotions. As the levels

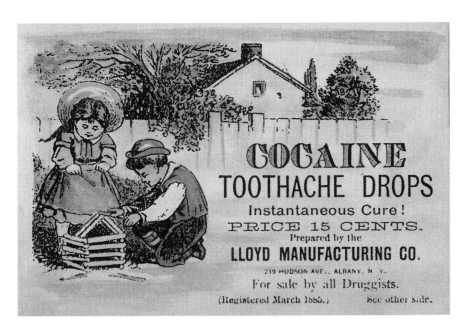

An 1885 American advertisement for Cocaine Toothache Drops, obviously intended for young children as well as adults. The addition of cocaine to everyday products, including Coca-Cola, was quite common in the nineteenth century.

A man snorting cocaine. Cocaine is a stimulant that produces feelings of euphoria followed by a pleasureless "crash" that fosters even greater craving for, and dependency on, the drug.

of cocaine in the brain drop, users begin to feel depressed and anxious. With crack this pleasureless state begins to set in within 30 minutes. Because cocaine interferes with the chemistry of this pleasure center in the brain—and subsequently with the brain's ability to reestablish emotional balance—the craving for the drug is doubly painful and difficult to overcome.

Cocaine use creates problems not only for users but also for their unborn children. Women addicted to crack and cocaine often give birth to premature, low-birthweight babies because these drugs often prevent them from carrying their babies to term (Zuckerman & Frank, 1994). The agitation and shaking these babies experience are typical of premature babies in general (Coles, 1992).

Hallucinogens and Marijuana

What are the cognitive effects of using marijuana?

The **hallucinogens** include lysergic acid diethylamide (LSD, also known as "acid"), mescaline, peyote, psilocybin, and phencyclidine (PCP, or "angel dust"). Marijuana is sometimes included in this group, although its effects are usually less powerful. Even in very small doses, these drugs often produce striking visual effects that resemble hallucinations, giving rise to the term *hallucinogen*. Large enough doses of many drugs bring on hallucinatory or delusional experiences, mimicking those that occur in severe mental illnesses, but hallucinogens do so in far less than toxic quantities.

Hallucinogens Many of the hallucinogens occur in natural forms, such as mushrooms and other fungi. In natural form they share with other consciousness-altering drugs an ancient history. Mescaline, for example, occurs in the peyote cactus, and historians believe that it has been used for at least 8,000 years by Native Americans.

By contrast, the story of **lysergic acid diethylamide (LSD),** the drug that triggered the current interest in the hallucinogens, began in 1943, when the American pharmacologist who synthesized it reported experiencing "an uninterrupted stream of fantastic pictures and extraordinary shapes with an intense, kaleidoscopic play of colors" after ingesting it. His report led others to experiment with LSD as a means of altering normal consciousness in the 1960s. There was a steady decline in use after the 1970s, but LSD and marijuana have recently become popular again with high school and college students (Janofsky, 1994).

The use of LSD changes peoples' auditory perceptions in a variety of ways. Some people report hearing imaginary conversations, fully orchestrated original symphonies, or foreign languages previously unknown to them. Auditory acuity may be increased, making the person keenly aware of low sounds such as breathing, heartbeat, and the light rustle of leaves in the wind.

Unlike depressants and stimulants, LSD and the other hallucinogens seem to produce no withdrawal effects. But tolerance builds up rapidly. If LSD is taken repeatedly, after a few days no amount of the drug will produce its usual effects until administration is halted for about a week (McKim, 1986, 1997). This rapid development of tolerance is a built-in deterrent to continuous use—a fact that helps explain why LSD is generally taken episodically rather than habitually. After a time, users seem to get tired of the experience and decrease or discontinue taking the drug, at least for a period of time.

One strong negative effect of some hallucinogens is "bad trips," or unpleasant experiences during which the user may not realize that the experiences are being caused by the drug and panic may set in. More serious are the stories of users who kill themselves because the drug makes them think they can fly out a window, or users who commit murders while under the influence of the drug. *Flashbacks*, or recurrences of hallucinations that occur weeks after ingesting

Hallucinogens
Any of a number of drugs, such as LSD and mescaline, that distort visual and auditory perception.

Lysergic acid diethylamide (LSD)
Hallucinogenic or "psychedelic" drug that produces hallucinations and delusions similar to those occurring in a psychotic state.

LSD, are also relatively common. In rare cases people have developed enduring mental illnesses from repeated use of hallucinogens, apparently because the drug triggers a powerful emotional response that in turn sets off a pre-existing tendency toward disturbed behavior. Other consequences include memory loss, paranoia, panic attacks, nightmares, and aggression (Seligmann et al., 1992).

Marijuana Produced from the *cannabis* plant, **marijuana** has a lengthy history in China, Greece, and India. Only in this century did it become popular in the United States. Its spreading use generated alarm during the 1920s, and by the end of the 1930s, marijuana had all but disappeared. It was revived by the youth culture of the 1960s. Since then an estimated 50 million Americans have tried it at least once. In recent years marijuana use by adolescents has increased again (see Figure 4–4), and it currently is the fourth most popular drug among students, after alcohol, caffeine, and nicotine (Treaster, 1994). The percentage of high school seniors who reported having used marijuana rose from 24 percent in 1991 to 38 percent in 1999, according to Figure 4–4.

These Native American women in Mexico are grinding dry peyote that will be mixed with water and drunk during an upcoming festival. Many Native American peoples have traditionally included peyote in their religious ceremonies.

Although the active ingredient in marijuana, *tetrahydrocannabinol (THC)*, shares some chemical properties with hallucinogens like LSD, it is far less potent and affects consciousness much less profoundly. The marijuana "high" is often marked by euphoric feelings and a sense of well-being, accompanied by swings from gaiety to relaxation—but sometimes also to anxiety and paranoia. Whether the user is suffused with happiness or filled with anxiety depends on the overall setting and the mood of others there. One study found that users' initial experience with marijuana is predictive of their continued use (Davidson & Schenk, 1994).

Marijuana has a number of physiological effects. It dilates the blood vessels in the eyes, making the eyes appear bloodshot. Because it is generally smoked, users frequently experience a dry mouth and coughing, as well as increased thirst and hunger and mild muscular weakness, often in the form of drooping eyelids (Donatelle & Davis, 1993). The major negative physiological effects of marijuana are potential respiratory and cardiovascular damage (Wu, Tashkin, Djahed, & Rose, 1988; Sridhar, Ruab, & Weatherby, 1994)—effects found in smokers of any substance.

Among the drug's psychological effects is a distortion of time, which has been confirmed under experimental conditions (Chait & Pierri, 1992). In addition, marijuana may produce alterations in attention and memory, including an inability to concentrate on many types of tasks—a fact that contributes to concern about people's ability to drive a car after using marijuana (Chait & Pierri, 1992; DeLong & Levy, 1974). One-third of car-accident victims admitted to the trauma unit of one hospital had noticeable levels of THC in their blood (Donatelle & Davis, 1993). The drug has also been shown to interfere with short-term memory: Users often cannot retain information for later use, which brings on anxiety and even panic (Hollister, 1986; Leccese, 1991). While under the influence of marijuana, people even lose the ability to coordinate information in the moment—a phenomenon called *temporal disintegration*—and frequently forget what they are talking about in the middle of a sentence. One recent study found that heavy marijuana use—which was defined as smoking marijuana at least 2 out of every 3 days—continued to affect performance even after the immediate effects of the drug had worn off (Block, 1996).

Finally, some studies have observed "apathy, loss of effectiveness, and diminished capacity to carry out complex, long-term plans, endure frustration, concentrate for long periods, follow routines, or successfully master new material" in marijuana users (McGothlin & West, 1968). It is difficult to determine from

Marijuana
A mild hallucinogen that produces a "high" often characterized by feelings of euphoria, a sense of well-being, and swings in mood from gaiety to relaxation; may also cause feelings of anxiety and paranoia.

SUMMARY TABLE

Drugs: Characteristics and Effects

Depressants	Typical Effects	Effects of Overdose	Tolerance/Dependence
Alcohol	Biphasic; tension-reduction "high," followed by depressed physical and psychological functioning.	Disorientation, loss of consciousness, death at extremely high blood-alcohol levels.	Tolerance; physical and psychological dependence; withdrawal symptoms.
Barbiturates Tranquilizers	Depressed reflexes and impaired motor functioning, tension reduction.	Shallow respiration, clammy skin, dilated pupils, weak and rapid pulse, coma, possible death.	Tolerance; high psychological and physical dependence on barbiturates, low to moderate physical dependence on such tranquilizers as Valium, although high psychological dependence; withdrawal symptoms.
Opiates	Euphoria, drowsiness, "rush" of pleasure, little impairment of psychological functions.	Slow, shallow breathing; clammy skin; nausea; vomiting; pinpoint pupils; convulsions; coma; possible death.	High tolerance; physical and psychological dependence; severe withdrawal symptoms.

Stimulants

	Typical Effects	Effects of Overdose	Tolerance/Dependence
Amphetamines Cocaine Caffeine Nicotine	Increased alertness, excitation, euphoria, increased pulse rate and blood pressure, sleeplessness.	For amphetamines and cocaine: agitation and, with chronic high doses, hallucinations (e.g., "cocaine bugs"), paranoid delusions, convulsions, death. For caffeine and nicotine: restlessness, insomnia, rambling thoughts, heart arrhythmia, possible circulatory failure. For nicotine: increased blood pressure.	For amphetamines, cocaine and nicotine: tolerance, psychological and physical dependence. For caffeine: physical and psychological dependence; withdrawal symptoms.

Hallucinogens

	Typical Effects	Effects of Overdose	Tolerance/Dependence
LSD PCP (dissociative anesthetic)	Illusions, hallucinations, distortions in time perception, loss of contact with reality.	Psychotic reactions.	No physical dependence for LSD; degree of psychological dependence unknown for LSD.
Marijuana	Euphoria, relaxed inhibitions, increased appetite, possible disorientation.	Fatigue, disoriented behavior, possible psychosis.	Psychological dependence.

such reports whether these changes are produced by marijuana in normal people or whether people who are predisposed toward apathy are more likely to select and use marijuana for a long period of time. Nevertheless, when all the effects of marijuana are considered, this "recreational drug" clearly has the potential to seriously interfere with the goals—especially educational—of the young people who are currently embracing it in such large numbers.

REVIEW QUESTIONS

1. _____ _____ are chemical substances that change moods and perceptions.
2. The three major substances categorized as depressants are ____, ____, and ____.
3. The four major substances categorized as stimulants are ____, ____, ____, and ____.

True or false:

____ 4. Alcohol is implicated in more than two-thirds of all automobile accidents.

____ 5. Caffeine is not addictive.

____ 6. Many users become dependent on crack cocaine almost immediately after beginning to use it.

____ 7. Recurring hallucinations are common among users of hallucinogens.

____ 8. Marijuana interferes with short-term memory.

9. Although alcohol is a ____, it is sometimes experienced subjectively as a ____.

Match the following categories of drugs with the appropriate descriptions:

10. ____ alcohol   a. produce feelings of optimism and boundless energy

11. ____ amphetamines   b. addictive drugs that dull the senses

12. ____ barbiturates   c. can produce euphoria, followed by anxiety, depression, and a craving for more

13. ____ opiates   d. its use is associated with the most serious drug problem in the United States today

14. ____ cocaine   e. profoundly affect visual and auditory perception

15. ____ hallucinogens   f. depressants that affect memory and perception of time

Answers: 1. psychoactive drugs. 2. alcohol, barbiturates, opiates. 3. caffeine, nicotine, amphetamines, cocaine. 4. true. 5. false. 6. true. 7. true. 8. true. 9. depressant, stimulant. 10. d. 11. a. 12. f. 13. b. 14. c. 15. e.

KEY TERMS

consciousness, p. 128
waking consciousness, p. 128
altered states of consciousness (ASC), p. 128

Natural variations in consciousness
REM (paradoxical) sleep, p. 133
non-REM (NREM) sleep, p. 133

insomnia, p. 139
apnea, p. 139
narcolepsy, p. 139

Artificial alterations in consciousness
sensory deprivation, p. 141
meditation, p. 141
hypnosis, p. 142

Drug-altered consciousness
psychoactive drugs, p. 145
substance abuse, p. 145
substance dependence, p. 145
double-blind procedure, p. 145
placebo, p. 146
depressants, p. 146

barbiturates, p. 151
opiates, p. 152
stimulants, p. 152
amphetamines, p. 154
cocaine, p. 154
hallucinogens, p. 156
lysergic acid diethylamide (LSD), p. 156
marijuana, p. 157

CHAPTER REVIEW

☐ **What problems could arise if we were constantly aware of all external and internal sensations?**

If we were aware of all the external sounds, sights, and smells, all the internal sensations of temperature, pressure, pain, and equilibrium—as well as all the thoughts, memories, emotions, and needs—we simply could not make sense of our environment. We must select only the most important information and then filter out the rest.

☐ **Do daydreams serve any useful function?**

Psychologists' opinions about the use of daydreams differ widely. Some argue that daydreams are only retreats from the real world and serve no useful functions. Freudian theorists say that daydreams allow us to deal with desires that could make us guilty or anxious. Still other researchers speculate that daydreaming builds cognitive and creative skills, is involved in our processing the huge amount of information we receive through our senses, and temporarily gives us a respite that allows us to better cope with real-world crises.

☐ **What is the purpose of sleep?**

Many scientists believe that sleep restores effective functioning of the body and the brain. From an evolutionary perspective, some psychologists see sleep as an adaptive mechanism that encouraged organisms to remain inactive and to conserve energy during the times of day when their food supplies were low or their predators were especially numerous.

□ **What are the ways in which we can intentionally and artificially alter our consciousness?**

Sensory deprivation, often resulting in sleep and dreaming, is the most common natural cause of **altered consciousness. Meditation, hypnosis,** and taking drugs such as **depressants, stimulants,** and **hallucinogens** can be used to induce altered states.

□ **What happens when people are deprived of sensory stimulation?**

Prolonged sensory deprivation induces **hallucinations,** altered perceptions, dreaming, daydreaming, and fantasizing. After experiencing alternating states of drowsiness, sleep, and wakefulness, it is difficult to distinguish between waking hallucinations and dreams. Many sensory perceptions arise without stimulation, including flashes of light, images of objects or living beings, noises, odors, the sense of being in motion, and impaired color perception and reaction time. Pain and taste sensitivity may be heightened.

□ **What are the effects of meditation?**

Meditation suppresses the activity of the sympathetic nervous system, lowers the rate of metabolism, and reduces heart and respiratory rates. Alpha brain waves—which accompany relaxed wakefulness—increase, and blood lactate, a chemical linked to stress, decreases.

□ **What possible clinical uses have been found for hypnosis?**

Although there are no universally accepted applications, hypnosis has been tried in diverse situations such as to relieve certain types of physical pain—for instance, that deriving from dental work—and to change or eliminate habits such as smoking and overeating.

□ **Historically, what substances have been used—and for what reasons—to alter consciousness?**

Since ancient times, people have used drugs to alter their consciousness for social, religious, and personal reasons. Wine and hallucinogenic substances, for example, have played a sacramental role in many religions. In our own culture, practices—including drinking alcohol and caffeine, smoking tobacco, and using illegal drugs such as **marijuana** and **cocaine**—are used by some people to alter their mood or behavior.

□ **How can we tell if someone is dependent on a substance?**

A broad pattern of drug-related behaviors is characterized by at least three of the following seven symptoms over a 12-month period: (a) developing tolerance; (b) experiencing withdrawal symptoms; (c) using the substance for a longer period or in greater quantities than intended; (d) persistently desiring to cut back on use of the substance; (e) devoting a great deal of time to getting or using the substance; (f) reducing social, occupational, or recreational activities as a result of drug use; and (g) continuing to use the substance even when use causes recurring physical or psychological problems.

□ **Why does alcohol, a depressant, lead to higher rates of violence?**

Although alcohol is a depressant, it is often experienced subjectively as a stimulant because it inhibits centers in the brain that govern critical judgment and impulsive behavior. The phenomenon called *alcohol myopia*—the alcohol-induced shortsightedness that makes drinkers less sensitive to behavioral cues in the environment—is correlated with increased aggression, hostility, violence, and abusive behavior.

□ **How does someone feel after a stimulant wears off?**

Withdrawal symptoms for **nicotine** include nervousness, **insomnia** and drowsiness, headache, irritability, and an intense craving for nicotine. After the drug effects wear off, users of **amphetamines,** cocaine, and crack cocaine may experience a "crash" characterized by anxiety, depression, and a strong craving for more of the drug.

□ **What are the cognitive effects of using marijuana?**

The **hallucinogens** are a number of drugs that distort visual and auditory perception. **Lysergic acid diethylamide (LSD)** is an artificial hallucinogen that was popular in the 1960s. **Marijuana** is sometimes included among the hallucinogens, although its effects are usually less powerful. The cognitive effects of using marijuana often include euphoric feelings and a sense of well-being, but some users experience anxiety and paranoia. Use of marijuana can also interfere with short-term memory.

CRITICAL THINKING AND APPLICATIONS

1. Why is—or why isn't—consciousness a valid subject for scientific research?
2. Why should—or why shouldn't—the controversial technique of using hypnosis to alter consciousness be an acceptable medical practice and an acceptable form of obtaining legal testimony?
3. What in your opinion are the major causes of substance abuse?

On the Web...

Visit these online resources at our Companion Website www.prenhall.com/morris

The Psychology Place

Learning Activities
1. Tick Tock Goes the Social and Biological Clock, p. 130
2. Are We Chronically Sleep-Deprived?, p. 133

Research News
3. Drug Use, Abuse, and Addictions: Focus on Alcohol, p. 146

Op-Ed Forum
4. Cigarette Smoking and Genetics: A Not So Unlikely Combination, p. 153

Games
1. Alcohol and Its Effects, p. 148
2. Blood Alcohol Content, p. 148

Web Links
1. **http://ura1195-6.univ-lyon1.fr/main_e.html**, p. 130
   Sleep, Dreams and Wakefulness site has links to documents, discussion, and Internet sites about sleep.
2. **http://www.users.cloud9.net/~thoryp/**, p. 130
   Sleep Medicine Home Page has links to sleep-related newsgroups and discussion groups, sleep disorders, professional associations, professional journals, sleep research and education sites, medications, and lists sleep disorders clinics.
3. **http://www.psywww.com/asc/asc.html**, p. 142
   States of Consciousness Web site provides links about hypnosis, out-of-body experiences, and dreams.
4. **http://www.rxlist.com/**, p. 144
   RxList - The Internet Drug Index
5. **http://www.healthtouch.com/levell/p_dri.htm**, p. 144
   Health Touch - Drug Information
6. **http://www.rci.rutgers.edu/~1wh/drugs/**, p. 145
   Drugs, brains, and behavior
7. **http://www.well.com/user/woa/**, p. 145
   Web of Addictions offers a variety of links to sites associated with addiction facts, meetings, topics, and help.
8. **http://www.habitsmart.com/**, p. 145
   HabitSmart Home Page has links to sites for the treatment or coping strategies one may use for an addiction, and it has links to a variety of other addiction-related Web sites.
9. **http://orion.it.luc.edu/~pcrowe/375link.htm**, p. 145
   Drug abuse and addiction-related links about prevention/treatment, research on addictions/substance use, organizations, and drugs and social policy.

5

LEARNING

TO FELICIA, A CITY KID, THE OUTDOORS USED TO MEAN CONCRETE, smog, and traffic. Now, after 6 weeks at summer camp in the mountains, she thinks of the outdoors as a playground for swimming, boating, hiking, and having fun.

On completing a course at the National Zoo, the star students show off their new skills. Junior, a young orangutan, cleans up his cage for the chance to blow a whistle, and two 18-inch-long lizards jump several feet into the air to snatch insects from the tip of a pair of forceps.

While driving through his hometown, a middle-aged man feels a sudden flood of emotion as he passes the park gate where he and his high school sweetheart used to meet years ago.

As unlikely as it may seem, all these incidents have something in common. That elusive something is learning, the topic of this chapter. Although most people associate **learning** with classrooms and studying for tests, psychologists define it more broadly. To them learning occurs whenever experience or practice results in a relatively permanent change in behavior or in potential behavior. This definition includes all the preceding incidents, plus a great deal more. When you remember which way to put the key into your front door lock, when you recall how to execute a turn on skis or where the library water fountain is, you are showing just a small part of your enormous capacity for learning.

Human life would be impossible without learning. Learning is involved in virtually everything we do. You could not communicate with other people, recognize yourself as human, or even know what substances are appropriate to eat if you were unable to learn. In this chapter we explore several kinds of learning. One type is learning to associate one event with another. When lizards associate jumping and receiving food, when a man associates a certain place and a certain strong emotion, they are engaging in two forms of learning called *operant* and *classical conditioning*. Because psychologists have studied these forms of learning so extensively, much of this chapter is devoted to them. But learning associations isn't all there is to human learning. Our learning also involves the formation of concepts, theories, ideas, and other mental abstractions. Felicia's new mental image of what the outdoors is like is just one example. Psychologists call this *cognitive learning*, and we discuss it at the end of this chapter.

Our tour of learning begins in another time and place: the laboratory of a Nobel prize–winning Russian scientist at the turn of the twentieth century. His name is Ivan Pavlov, and his work is helping to revolutionize the study of learning. He has discovered classical conditioning.

Classical Conditioning

How did Pavlov discover classical conditioning?

Pavlov (1849–1936) discovered **classical conditioning** almost by accident. He was studying digestion, which begins when saliva mixes with food in the mouth. While measuring how much saliva dogs produce when given food, he noticed that they began to salivate even before they tasted the food. The mere sight of food made them drool. In fact, they even drooled at the sound of the experimenter's footsteps. This aroused Pavlov's curiosity. What was causing these responses? How had the dogs learned to salivate to sights and sounds?

To answer this question, Pavlov sounded a bell just before presenting his dogs with food. A ringing bell does not usually make a dog's mouth water, but after hearing the bell many times right before getting fed, Pavlov's dogs began to salivate as soon as the bell rang. It was as if they had learned that the bell signaled the appearance of food, and their mouths watered on cue even if no food followed. The dogs had been conditioned to salivate in response to a new

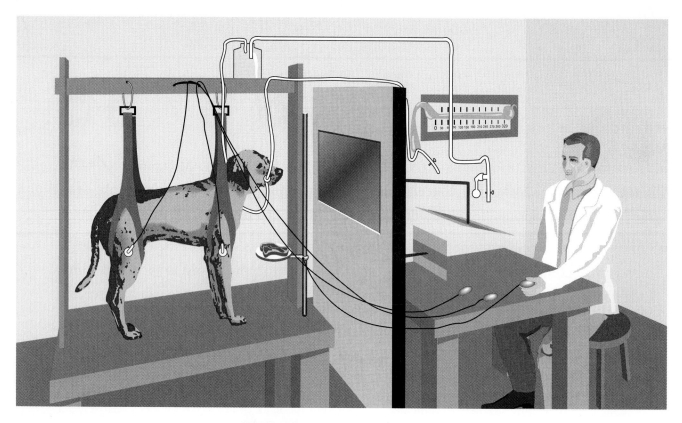

FIGURE 5–1

Pavlov's apparatus for classically conditioning a dog to salivate.   The experimenter sits behind a one-way mirror and controls the presentation of the conditioned stimulus (touch applied to the leg) and the unconditioned stimulus (food). A tube runs from the dog's salivary glands to a vial, where the drops of saliva are collected as a way of measuring the strength of the dog's response.

Learning
The process by which experience or practice results in a relatively permanent change in behavior or potential behavior.

Classical (or Pavlovian) conditioning
The type of learning in which a response naturally elicited by one stimulus comes to be elicited by a different, formerly neutral stimulus.

Unconditioned stimulus (US)
A stimulus that invariably causes an organism to respond in a specific way.

Unconditioned response (UR)
A response that takes place in an organism whenever an unconditioned stimulus occurs.

Conditioned stimulus (CS)
An originally neutral stimulus that is paired with an unconditioned stimulus and eventually produces the desired response in an organism when presented alone.

Conditioned response (CR)
After conditioning, the response an organism produces when a conditioned stimulus is presented.

stimulus—the bell—that normally would not prompt salivation (Pavlov, 1927). Figure 5–1 shows one of Pavlov's procedures in which the bell has been replaced by a touch to the dog's leg just before food is given.

Elements of Classical Conditioning

How might you classically condition a pet?

Figure 5–2 diagrams the four basic elements in classical conditioning: (1) the unconditioned stimulus, (2) the unconditioned response, (3) the conditioned stimulus, and (4) the conditioned response. The **unconditioned stimulus (US)** is an event that automatically triggers a certain reflex reaction, which is the **unconditioned response (UR)**. In Pavlov's studies, food in the mouth was the unconditioned stimulus, and salivation to it was the unconditioned response. The third element in classical conditioning, the **conditioned stimulus (CS)**, is an event that is repeatedly paired with the unconditioned stimulus. For a conditioned stimulus Pavlov often used a bell. At first the conditioned stimulus does not elicit the desired response. But eventually, after repeatedly being paired with the unconditioned stimulus, the conditioned stimulus alone comes to trigger a reaction similar to the unconditioned response. This learned reaction is the **conditioned response (CR)**.

Classical conditioning has been demonstrated in virtually every animal species, even squid and spiders (Krasne & Glanzman, 1995). You yourself may have inadvertently classically conditioned one of your pets. For instance, you

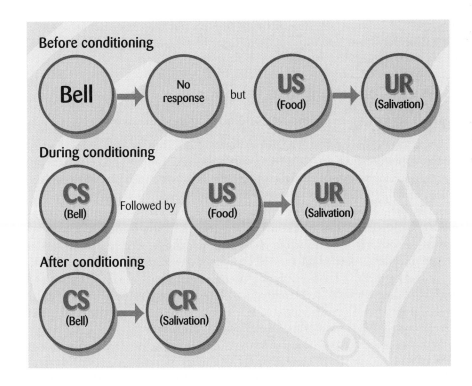

FIGURE 5–2
A paradigm of the classical conditioning process.

may have noticed that your cat begins to purr when it hears the sound of the can opener running. For a cat the taste and smell of food are unconditioned stimuli for a purring response. By repeatedly pairing the can opener whirring with the delivery of food, you have turned this sound into a conditioned stimulus that triggers a conditioned response.

Establishing a Classically Conditioned Response

If you once burned your finger on a match while listening to a certain song, why doesn't that song now make you reflexively jerk your hand away?

Certain procedures make it easier to establish a classically conditioned response. One is repeated pairings of the unconditioned stimulus and the cue that will eventually become the conditioned stimulus. The likelihood or strength of the conditioned response increases each time these two stimuli are paired. This learning, however, eventually reaches a point of diminishing returns. The amount of each increase gradually becomes smaller until finally no further learning occurs. The conditioned response is now fully established.

It is fortunate that *repeated* pairings are usually needed for classical conditioning to take place (Schwartz, 1989). There are always a lot of environmental stimuli present whenever an unconditioned stimulus triggers an unconditioned response. If conditioning occurred on the basis of single pairings, all these usually irrelevant stimuli would generate some type of CR. Soon we would be overwhelmed by learned associations. Because a number of pairings are usually needed to produce a conditioned response, only a cue consistently related to the unconditioned stimulus typically becomes a conditioned stimulus.

The spacing of pairings is also important in establishing a classically conditioned response. If pairings of the CS and US follow each other very rapidly, or if they are very far apart, learning the association is slower. If the spacing of pairings is moderate—neither too far apart nor too close together—learning occurs more quickly. It is also important that the CS and

US rarely, if ever, occur alone. Pairing the CS and US only once in a while, called **intermittent pairing**, reduces both the rate of learning and the final strength of the learned response.

Classical Conditioning in Humans

What is an example of classical conditioning in your own life?

Classical conditioning is as common in humans as it is in other animals. For instance, some people learn phobias through classical conditioning. Phobias are intense, irrational fears of particular things or situations, such as spiders, snakes, flying, or being in enclosed places (claustrophobia). In a now classic study, psychologist John Watson and his assistant Rosalie Rayner used classical conditioning to instill a phobia of white rats in a 1-year-old baby named Albert. They started by showing Albert a white rat, which he happily tried to play with. But every time he approached the rat, the experimenters made a loud noise by striking a steel bar behind the baby's head. After a few attempts at pairing the rat and the frightening noise, Albert would cry in fear at the sight of the rat alone. By being paired with the unconditioned stimulus of the loud noise, the rat had become a conditioned stimulus for a conditioned fear response.

Several years later psychologist Mary Cover Jones demonstrated a way that fears can be unlearned by means of classical conditioning (Jones, 1924). Her subject was a 3-year-old boy named Peter who, like Albert, had a fear of white rats. Jones paired the sight of a rat with an intrinsically pleasant experience— eating candy. While Peter sat alone in a room, a caged white rat was brought in and placed far enough away so that the boy would not be frightened. At this point Peter was given plenty of candy to eat. On each successive day the cage was moved closer to Peter, after which he was given candy. Eventually he showed no fear of the rat, even without any candy. By being repeatedly paired with a stimulus that evokes a pleasant emotional response, the rat had become a conditioned stimulus for pleasure.

In more recent times psychiatrist Joseph Wolpe (1915–1997) adapted Jones's method to the treatment of certain kinds of anxiety (Wolpe, 1973, 1982). Wolpe reasoned that it is not possible to be both fearful and relaxed at the same time. Therefore if people could be taught to relax in fearful or anxious situations, their anxiety should disappear. Wolpe's **desensitization therapy** begins by teaching a system of deep-muscle relaxation. Then the person constructs a list of situations that prompt various degrees of fear or anxiety, from intensely frightening to only mildly so. A person with a fear of heights, for example, might construct a list that begins with standing on the edge of the Grand Canyon and ends with climbing two rungs on a ladder. While deeply relaxed, the person imagines the least distressing situation on the list first. If he or she succeeds in remaining relaxed, the person proceeds to the next item on the list, and so on until no anxiety is felt, even when imagining the most frightening situation. In this way, classical conditioning is used to change an undesired reaction: A fear-arousing thought is repeatedly paired with a muscular state that produces calmness until eventually the formerly fearful thought no longer triggers anxiety.

Classical conditioning has even been applied to the treatment of medical conditions, such as disorders in which the immune system attacks and destroys healthy tissue. Drugs that suppress the immune system and help alleviate these disorders must be used sparingly because of their dangerous side effects. So researchers have paired doses of these drugs with a harmless, neutral stimulus, such as a distinctive odor. Soon the distinctive odor alone begins to suppress the immune system without the drugs being given. The odor has become a conditioned stimulus without harmful side effects.

Intermittent pairing
Pairing the conditioned stimulus and the unconditioned stimulus on only a portion of the learning trials.

Desensitization therapy
A conditioning technique designed to gradually reduce anxiety about a particular object or situation.

Classical Conditioning Is Selective

Why are people more likely to develop a phobia of snakes than of flowers?

If people can develop phobias through classical conditioning, as Little Albert did, why don't we acquire phobias of virtually everything that is paired with harm? For example, many people get shocks from electric sockets, but almost no one develops a socket phobia. Why should this be? Why shouldn't most carpenters have phobias of hammers because they have accidentally pounded their fingers with them?

Psychologist Martin Seligman has offered an answer. The key, he says, lies in the concept of **preparedness.** Some things readily become conditioned stimuli for fear responses because we are biologically prepared to learn those associations. Among the common objects of phobias are heights, snakes, and the dark. In our evolutionary past, fear of these potential dangers probably offered a survival advantage, and so a readiness to form such fears may have become "wired into" our species.

Preparedness also underlies **conditioned taste aversion,** a learned association between the taste of a certain food and a feeling of nausea and revulsion. Conditioned taste aversions are acquired very quickly. It usually takes only one pairing of a distinctive flavor and subsequent illness to develop a learned aversion to the taste of that food. Seligman calls this the "sauce béarnaise effect," because he once suffered severe nausea after eating sauce béarnaise and ever since has abhorred the flavor. In one study more than half the college students surveyed reported at least one such conditioned taste aversion (Logue, Ophir, & Strauss, 1981). Readily learning connections between distinctive flavors and illness has clear benefits. If we can quickly learn which foods are poisonous and avoid those foods in the future, we greatly increase our chances of survival. Other animals with a well-developed sense of taste, such as rats and mice, also readily develop conditioned taste aversions, just as humans do.

Even knowing that a certain food paired with nausea wasn't the cause of the illness doesn't spare us from developing a conditioned taste aversion. Seligman knew that his nausea was due to stomach flu, not to something he ate, but he acquired an aversion to sauce béarnaise just the same. Similarly, cancer patients often develop strong taste aversions to foods eaten right before nausea-inducing chemotherapy, even though they know it is the drug that triggered their nauseous reaction. These patients can't prevent themselves from automatically learning a connection they are biologically prepared to learn (Jacobsen et al., 1994).

Seligman's theory of *preparedness* argues that we are biologically prepared to associate certain stimuli, such as heights, the dark, and snakes, with fear responses. In our evolutionary past, fear of these potential dangers probably offered a survival advantage.

REVIEW QUESTIONS

1. The simplest type of learning is called ____. It refers to the establishment of fairly predictable behavior in the presence of well-defined stimuli.

2. Match the following in Pavlov's experiment with dogs:

   ____ unconditioned stimulus   a. bell

   ____ unconditioned response   b. food

   ____ conditioned stimulus   c. salivating to bell

   ____ conditioned response   d. salivating to food

3. Which of the following are examples of classical conditioning?

   a. eating when not hungry just because we know it is lunchtime

   b. a specific smell triggering a bad memory

   c. a cat running into the kitchen to the sound of a can opener

   d. all of the above are examples of classical conditioning

____ 4. The intense, irrational fears we call phobias can be learned through classical conditioning. T/F

Preparedness
A biological readiness to learn certain associations because of their survival advantages.

Conditioned taste aversion
Conditioned avoidance of certain foods even if there is only one pairing of conditioned and unconditioned stimuli.

5. You have a cat that runs to the sound of the kitchen cabinet opening. The sound of the cabinet is the

a. US

b. CS

c. CR

6. A learned association between the taste of a certain food and a feeling of nausea is called ____ ____ ____.

7. Teaching someone to relax even when he or she encounters a distressing situation is called ____ ____ ____.

8. In the experiment with Little Albert, the unconditioned stimulus was ____ ____.

Answers: 1. classical conditioning. 2. unconditioned stimulus –b; unconditioned response–d; conditioned stimulus–a; conditioned response–c. 3. d. 4. T. 5 b. 6. conditioned taste aversion. 7. systematic desensitization therapy. 8. loud noises.

Operant Conditioning

How are operant behaviors different from the responses involved in classical conditioning?

Around the turn of the century, while Pavlov was busy with his dogs, the American psychologist Edward Lee Thorndike was using a "puzzle box," or simple wooden cage, to study how cats learn (Thorndike, 1898). As illustrated in Figure 5–3, Thorndike confined a hungry cat in the puzzle box, with food just outside where the cat could see and smell it. To get to the food, the cat had to figure out how to open the latch on the box door, a process Thorndike timed. In the beginning it took the cats quite a while to discover how to open the door. But on each trial it took them less time, until eventually they could escape from the box in almost no time at all. Thorndike was a pioneer in studying this kind of learning, which involves making a certain response because of the consequences it brings. This form of learning has come to be called **operant** or **instrumental conditioning.**

Elements of Operant Conditioning

What two essential elements are involved in operant conditioning?

One essential element in operant conditioning is *emitted behavior.* This is one way in which operant conditioning is different from classical conditioning. In classical conditioning a response is automatically triggered by some stimulus. Food in the mouth automatically triggers salivation; a loud noise automatically triggers fear. In this sense, classical conditioning is passive. The behaviors are *elicited* by stimuli. This is not true of the behaviors involved in operant conditioning. Thorndike's cats *spontaneously* tried to undo the latch on the door of the box. You *spontaneously* wave your hand to signal a taxi or bus to stop. You *voluntarily* study your teacher's assignments *by choice* in an effort to earn a good grade. You *voluntarily* put money into machines to obtain food, sodas, entertainment, or a chance to win a prize. These and similar actions are called **operant behaviors** because they involve "operating" on the environment.

A second essential element in operant conditioning is a *consequence* following a behavior. Thorndike's cats gained freedom and a piece of fish for escaping from the puzzle boxes; your dog may receive a food treat for sitting on command; a child may receive praise or a chance to watch television for helping to clear the table. Consequences like these that *increase* the likelihood that a behavior will be repeated are called **reinforcers.** In contrast, consequences that *decrease* the chances that a behavior will be repeated are called **punishers.** Imagine how Thorndike's cats might have acted had they been greeted by a large,

---

Operant (or instrumental) conditioning
The type of learning in which behaviors are emitted (in the presence of specific stimuli) to earn rewards or avoid punishments.

Operant behavior
Behavior designed to operate on the environment in a way that will gain something desired or avoid something unpleasant.

Reinforcer
A stimulus that follows a behavior and increases the likelihood that the behavior will be repeated.

Punisher
A stimulus that follows a behavior and decreases the likelihood that the behavior will be repeated.

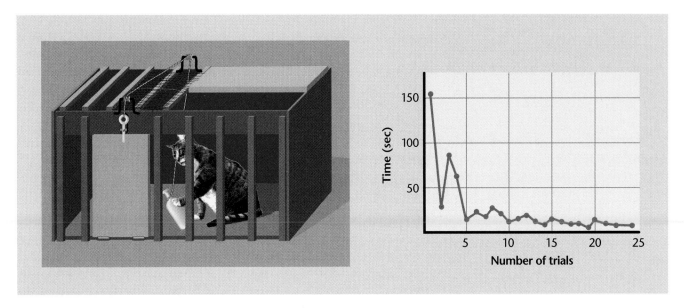

FIGURE 5–3

A cat in a Thorndike "puzzle box." The cat can escape and be rewarded with food by tripping the bolt on the door. As the graph shows, Thorndike's cats learned to make the necessary response more rapidly after an increasing number of trials.

snarling dog when they escaped from the puzzle boxes. Or what might happen if a dog that sits on command is scolded for doing so, or if a child who has helped to clear the table is sent to sit in a "time out" corner. Thorndike summarized the influence of consequences in his **law of effect:** Behavior that brings about a satisfying effect (reinforcement) is apt to be performed again, whereas behavior that brings about a negative effect (punishment) is apt to be suppressed. Contemporary psychologists often refer to the **principle of reinforcement** rather than the law of effect, but the two terms mean the same thing.

It is sometimes hard to tell whether a particular consequence will be reinforcing or punishing. We must wait to see if that consequence increases or decreases

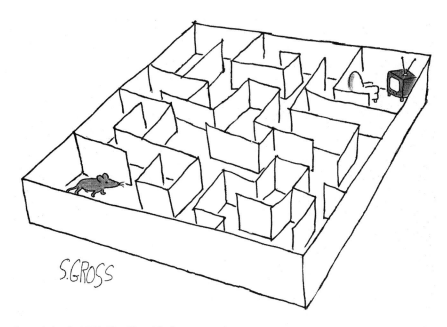

Law of effect (principle of reinforcement)
Thorndike's theory that behavior consistently rewarded will be "stamped in" as learned behavior, and behavior that brings about discomfort will be "stamped out" (also known as the principle of reinforcement).

the behavior that precedes it. For instance, you might assume that candy is always reinforcing for children, but some children don't like candy, so for them it isn't an effective reward. Moreover, children for whom candy is initially reinforcing may eat too much of it, until it becomes neutral to them or even punishing. We must be careful, therefore, when identifying consequences as reinforcers or punishers.

Establishing an Operantly Conditioned Response

How might a speech therapist teach the sound of "s" to a child with a lisp?

Because the behaviors involved in operant conditioning are voluntary behaviors, it is not always easy to establish an operantly conditioned response. The desired behavior must first be performed spontaneously in order for it to be rewarded and strengthened. Sometimes you can simply wait for this to happen. Thorndike, for example, waited for his cats to trip the latch that opened the door to his puzzle boxes. Then he rewarded them with fish.

But when there are many opportunities for making irrelevant responses, waiting can be slow and tedious. If you were an animal trainer for a circus, imagine how long you would have to wait for a tiger to decide to jump through a flaming hoop so you could reward it. One way to speed up the process is to increase motivation, as Thorndike did by allowing his cats to become hungry and placing a piece of fish outside the box. Even without food in sight a hungry animal is more active than a well-fed one and so is more likely, just by chance, to make the response you're looking for. Another strategy is to reduce opportunities for irrelevant responses, as Thorndike did by making his puzzle boxes small and bare. Many researchers do the same thing by using Skinner boxes to train small animals in. A **Skinner box,** named after B. F. Skinner, another pioneer in the study of operant conditioning, is a small cage with solid walls that is relatively empty, except for a food cup and an activating device, such as a bar or a button (see Figure 5–4). In this simple environment it doesn't take long for an active, hungry rat or pigeon to press the bar or peck the button that releases food into the cup, thereby reinforcing the behavior.

Another way to speed up operant conditioning is to reinforce successive approximations of the desired behavior. This approach is called **shaping.** In a Skinner box, for example, we might first reward a rat for turning toward the bar, then for moving toward it, then for touching the bar with its paw, and so on until it performs the desired behavior. The circus is a wonderful place to see the results of shaping. To teach a tiger to jump through a flaming hoop, the trainer might first reinforce the animal simply for jumping up on a pedestal. After that behavior has been learned, the tiger might be reinforced only for leaping from that pedestal to another. Next, the tiger might be required to jump through a hoop between the pedestals to gain a reward. And finally, the hoop is set on fire and the tiger must leap through it to be rewarded. In much the same way, a speech therapist might reward a child with a lisp for closer and closer approximations of the correct sound of "s."

As in classical conditioning, the learning of an operantly conditioned response eventually reaches a point of diminishing returns. If you look back at Figure 5–3, you'll see that the first few reinforcements produced quite large improvements in performance, as indicated by the rapid drop in time required to escape from the puzzle box. But each successive reinforcement produced less of an effect until, eventually, continued reinforcement brought no evidence of further learning. After 25 trials, for instance, Thorndike's cats were escaping from the box no more quickly than they had been after 15 trials. The operantly condi-

Skinner box
A box often used in operant conditioning of animals; it limits the available response and thus increases the likelihood that the desired response will occur.

Shaping
Reinforcing successive approximations to a desired behavior.

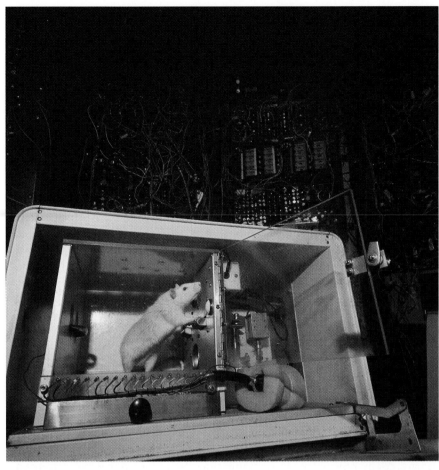

FIGURE 5–4
A rat in a Skinner box. By pressing the bar, the rat releases food pellets into the box; this reinforces its bar-pressing behavior.

tioned response has now been fully established. Can operant conditioning influence human behavior? See the *Highlights* box to learn about its uses in regulating biological responses.

A Closer Look at Reinforcement

What is the difference between positive and negative reinforcement? What are some of the unintentional effects that reinforcement can have?

We have been talking about reinforcement as if all reinforcers are alike, but in fact this is not the case. Think about the kinds of consequences that would encourage you to perform some behavior. Certainly these include consequences that give you something positive, like praise, recognition, or money. But the removal of some negative stimulus is also a good reinforcer of behavior. When new parents discover that rocking a baby will stop the child's persistent crying, they often sit there rocking deep into the night; the removal of the infant's crying is a powerful reinforcer.

These examples show that there are two kinds of reinforcers. **Positive reinforcers,** such as food, praise, or money, add something rewarding to a situation, whereas **negative reinforcers,** such as stopping an aversive noise, subtract something unpleasant. You might find it helpful to use a plus sign (+) to refer to

How does an animal trainer get a tiger to jump through a flaming hoop so that behavior can be rewarded? The answer is usually through shaping. The trainer reinforces closer and closer approximations of the desired response until eventually the tiger leaps through the hoop on command.

Positive reinforcer
Any event whose presence increases the likelihood that ongoing behavior will recur.

Negative reinforcer
Any event whose reduction or termination increases the likelihood that ongoing behavior will recur.

Shaping Better Health through Biofeedback

For 20 of her 29 years, Janet B. had suffered from tension headaches. The dull ache would begin in the morning and last all day. Her doctor referred her to a psychologist who traced the headaches to excessive contraction of the frontalis muscle, the main muscle in the forehead. The psychologist then taught Janet to relax this muscle by providing her with biofeedback. Electrodes attached to Janet's forehead enabled a biofeedback machine to monitor the degree of contraction in her frontalis muscle, signaling it with a tone. The milder the contraction, the lower the tone's pitch. Janet worked to relax the muscle more and more, using the dropping pitch of the tone as her guide. Over the course of several dozen 30-minute training sessions, she became increasingly adept at controlling the muscle. Three months after therapy began, she reported virtually no tension headaches (Budzynski, Stoyva, & Adler, 1970).

Biofeedback training is an operant conditioning technique in which

> Biofeedback has become a well-established treatment for a number of medical problems, but some still reject it as quackery.

instruments are used to give feedback about the strength of some biological response over which a person seeks to gain control. That biological response—such as heart rate, blood pressure, or contraction of the frontalis muscle—normally occurs outside of conscious awareness. Variations in the strength of the response are indicated by some signal, such as a tone that gets higher or lower, or a light that gets brighter or dimmer. Through this feedback information the response is learned, little by little, as with other shaping techniques.

Biofeedback has become a well-established treatment for a number of medical problems, including tension headaches, migraine and posttraumatic headaches, and peptic ulcers (Ham & Packard, 1996; Wauquier et al., 1995). It has also been used to treat a painful bowel condition in infants (Cox et al., 1994) and incontinence in adults (Keck et al., 1994). Biofeedback does require effort, patience, and discipline. But it has the advantage of giving a person

Biofeedback
A technique that uses monitoring devices to provide precise information about internal physiological processes, such as heart rate or blood pressure, to teach people to gain voluntary control over these functions.

a positive reinforcer that *adds* something rewarding and a minus sign (–) to refer to a negative reinforcer that *subtracts* something noxious. Animals will learn to press bars and open doors not only to obtain food and water (positive reinforcement) but also to turn off a loud buzzer or to avoid an electric shock (negative reinforcement).

Both positive and negative reinforcement result in the learning of new behaviors or the strengthening of existing ones. Remember, in everyday conversation when we say that we have "reinforced" something, we mean that we have strengthened it. "Reinforced concrete" is strengthened by the addition of steel rods or steel mesh; generals strengthen armies by sending in "reinforcements"; arguments are strengthened by being "reinforced" with facts. Similarly, in operant conditioning, reinforcement—whether positive or negative—always strengthens or encourages a behavior. A child might practice the piano because he receives praise for it (positive reinforcement) or because it gives him a break from doing tedious homework (negative reinforcement), but in either case the end result is a higher incidence of piano playing.

But what if a particular behavior is just *accidentally* reinforced because it happens by chance to be followed by some rewarding incident? Will the behavior still be more likely to occur again? B. F. Skinner showed that the answer is yes. He put a pigeon in a Skinner box and at random intervals dropped a few grains of food into the food cup. The pigeon began repeating whatever it had been doing just before the food was given: standing on one foot, hopping around, or strutting with its neck stretched out. None of these actions had anything to do

control over treatment, and when it works well, the results can be impressive (Olton & Noonberg, 1980).

In addition to serving as a medical aid, biofeedback has been used in many other contexts. Musicians and other performers sometimes use it to control the anxiety that can hamper their performance. Athletes use it, too. Marathon runners, for instance, often find biofeedback helpful to overcome the tight shoulders and shallow breathing that can prevent them from finishing a race. While the effectiveness of biofeedback in sports has not been extensively studied using controlled experiments, personal accounts by athletes suggest that it offers real benefits (Peper, 1990). Biofeedback has even found usefulness in space. NASA has combined a program of biofeedback with cognitive therapy (such as mental messages) to reduce

the motion sickness astronauts experience at zero gravity (Cowlings, 1989).

Despite its successes, however, some people still reject biofeedback as quackery (National Institute of Health Consensus Development Conference, 1996). Critics challenge the scientific rigor of studies that have evaluated biofeedback and the professional caliber of the technicians who operate the various biofeedback instruments (Middaugh, 1990). In addition, some conditions, such as high blood pressure, do not always respond well to biofeedback training (McGrady, 1996; Weaver & McGrady, 1995). Further research may reveal other conditions for which biofeedback is not appropriate.

Still, advocates of biofeedback contend that it plays a valuable role when viewed properly. It must be looked at not as a medical therapy equivalent to drug treatments but as a way of helping

A person attached to a biofeedback machine. Biofeedback has become a well-established treatment for a number of medical problems, even though some people still reject it as quackery.

people gain some control over biological processes that are causing them problems. When evaluated in these terms, they argue, biofeedback can stand up to the most rigorous scientific scrutiny (Norris, 1986).

with getting the food, of course. But still the bird repeated them over and over again. Skinner called the bird's behavior *superstitious*, because it was learned in a way that is similar to how some human superstitions are learned. If you happen to be wearing an Albert Einstein T-shirt when you get your first A on an exam, you may come to believe that wearing this shirt was a factor. Even though the connection was pure coincidence, you may keep on wearing your "lucky" shirt to every test thereafter.

In the case of forming superstitions, reinforcement has an illogical effect on behavior, but that effect is generally harmless. Are there any more negative results that rewards can sometimes inadvertently have? Some psychologists think there may be. They believe that offering certain kinds of reinforcers (candy, money, play time) for a task that could be intrinsically rewarding can undermine the intrinsic motivation to perform it. People may begin to think that they are working only for the reward and lose enthusiasm for what they are doing. They may no longer see their work as an intrinsically interesting challenge in which to invest creative effort and strive for excellence. Instead they may see it as a chore that must be done to earn some tangible payoff. This warning can be applied to many situations, such as offering tangible rewards to students for their work in the classroom, or giving employees a "pay for performance" incentive to meet company goals (Kohn, 1993; Tagano, Moran, & Sawyers, 1991). Concern about tangible reinforcers may be exaggerated, however. While the use of rewards may sometimes produce negative outcomes, this is not always the case. In fact, one extensive review of more than 100 studies showed that when used appropriately, rewards do not compromise intrinsic motivation, and they may even help to encourage creativity (Eisenberger & Cameron, 1996).

A Closer Look at Punishment

What problems can punishment create?

Although we all hate to be subjected to it, **punishment** is a powerful controller of behavior. After receiving a heavy fine for failing to report extra income to the IRS, we are less likely to make that mistake again. After being rudely turned down when we ask someone for a favor, we are less apt to ask that person for another favor. In both cases an unpleasant consequence reduces the likelihood that we will repeat a behavior. This is the definition of punishment.

Punishment is different from negative reinforcement. Reinforcement of whatever kind *strengthens* (reinforces) behavior. Negative reinforcement strengthens behavior by removing something unpleasant from the environment. In contrast, punishment *adds* something unpleasant to the environment, and as a result, it tends to *weaken* the behavior that caused it. If going skiing for the weekend rather than studying for a test results in getting an F, the F is an unpleasant consequence (a punisher) that makes you less likely to give more importance to skiing than to homework again.

Is punishment effective? Does it always work? We can all think of instances where it doesn't seem to. Children often continue to misbehave even after they have been punished repeatedly for that misbehavior. Some drivers persist in driving recklessly despite repeated fines. The family dog may sleep on the couch at night despite being punished for being on the couch every morning. Why these seeming exceptions to the law of effect? Why, in these cases, isn't punishment having the result it is supposed to?

For punishment to be effective, it must be imposed properly. First, punishment should be *swift*. If it is delayed, it doesn't work as well. Sending a misbehaving child immediately to a time-out seat (even when it is not convenient to do so) is much more effective than waiting for a "better" time to punish. Punishment should also be *sufficient* without being cruel. If a parent briefly scolds a child for hitting other children, the effect will probably be less pronounced than if the child is sent to his room for the day. At the same time, punishment should be *consistent*. It should be imposed for all infractions of a rule, not just for some. If parents allow some acts of aggression to go unpunished, hitting and bullying other children is likely to persist.

Punishment is particularly useful in situations where a behavior is dangerous and must be changed quickly. A child who likes to poke things into electric outlets must be stopped immediately, so punishment may be the best course of action. Similarly, punishment may be called for to stop severely disturbed children from repeatedly banging their heads against walls or hitting themselves in the face with their fists. Once this self-destructive behavior is under control, other forms of therapy can be more effective.

But even in situations like these, punishment has drawbacks (Skinner, 1953). First, it only *suppresses* the undesired behavior; it doesn't prompt someone to "unlearn" the behavior, and it doesn't teach a more desirable one. If the threat of punishment is removed, the negative behavior is likely to recur. This is apparent on the highway. Speeders slow down when they see a police car (the threat of punishment) but speed up again as soon as the threat is passed. Punishment, then, rarely works when long-term changes in behavior are wanted. Second, punishment often stirs up negative feelings (frustration, resentment, self-doubt),

Incarceration is a major form of punishment that is practiced throughout the world.

Punishment
Any event whose presence decreases the likelihood that ongoing behavior will recur.

which can impede the learning of new, more desirable behaviors. For example, when a child who is learning to read is scolded for every mispronounced word, the child may become very frustrated and unsure of himself. This frustration and doubt about ability can prompt more mispronunciations, which lead to more scolding. In time the negative feelings that punishment has caused can become so unpleasant that the child avoids reading. A third drawback of punishment, when it is harsh, is the unintended lesson that it teaches: Harsh punishment may encourage the learner to copy that same harsh and aggressive behavior toward other people. In laboratory studies monkeys that are harshly punished tend to attack other monkeys, pigeons other pigeons, and so on (B. Schwartz, 1989). In addition, punishment often makes people angry, and angry people frequently become more aggressive and hostile.

Because of these drawbacks, punishment should be used carefully, and always together with reinforcement of desirable behavior. Once a more desirable response is established, punishment should be removed to negatively reinforce that new behavior. Positive reinforcement (praise, rewards) should also be used to strengthen the desired behavior. This approach is more productive than punishment alone, because it teaches an alternative behavior to replace the punished one. Positive reinforcement also makes the learning environment less threatening.

Sometimes, after punishment has been administered a few times, it needn't be continued, because the mere threat of punishment is enough to induce the desired behavior. Psychologists call this **avoidance training** because the person is learning to avoid the possibility of a punishing consequence. Avoidance training is responsible for many everyday behaviors. It has taught you to carry an umbrella when it looks like rain to avoid the punishment of getting wet, and to keep your hand away from a hot iron to avoid the punishment of a burn. Avoidance training, however, doesn't always work in our favor. For instance, a child who has been repeatedly criticized for poor performance on math may learn to shun difficult math problems in order to avoid further punishment. Unfortunately, because of this avoidance, the child fails to develop his math skills and therefore improve the capabilities he has, and so a vicious cycle has set in. The avoidance must be unlearned through some positive experiences with math in order for this cycle to be broken.

Learned Helplessness

In what ways do some college students exhibit learned helplessness?

Through avoidance training, people learn to prevent themselves from being punished, but what happens when such avoidance of punishment for some reason isn't possible? The answer is often a "giving up" response that can generalize to other situations. This response is known as **learned helplessness.**

Martin Seligman and his colleagues first studied learned helplessness in experiments with dogs (Maier, Seligman, & Soloman, 1969). They placed two groups of dogs in chambers that delivered a series of electric shocks to their feet at random intervals. The dogs in the control group could turn off (escape) the shock by pushing a panel with their nose. The dogs in the experimental group could not turn off the shock—they were, in effect, helpless. Next, both the experimental and control animals were placed in a different situation, one in which they could escape shock by jumping over a hurdle. A warning light always came on 10 seconds before each 50-second shock was given. The dogs in the control group quickly learned to jump the hurdle as soon as the warning light flashed, but the dogs in the experimental group didn't. These dogs, which had previously experienced unavoidable shocks, didn't even jump the hurdle *after* the shock started. They just lay there and accepted the pain. Also, many of these dogs were generally listless, suffered loss of appetite, and displayed other symptoms associated with depression.

Avoidance training
Learning a desirable behavior to prevent the occurrence of something unpleasant such as punishment.

Learned helplessness
Failure to take steps to avoid or escape from an unpleasant or aversive stimulus that occurs as a result of previous exposure to unavoidable painful stimuli.

Many subsequent studies have shown that learned helplessness can occur both in animals and in humans (Maier & Seligman, 1976). Once established, it generalizes to new situations and can be very persistent, even given evidence that an unpleasant circumstance can now be avoided (Peterson, Maier, & Seligman, 1993). For example, when faced with a series of unsolvable problems, a college student may eventually give up trying and make only half-hearted efforts to solve new problems, even when the new problems *are* solvable. Moreover, success in solving new problems has little effect on the person's behavior. He or she continues to make only halfhearted tries, as if never experiencing *any* success at all. Similarly, children raised in an abusive family, where punishment is unrelated to behavior, often develop a feeling of helplessness. Even in relatively normal settings outside their home, they often appear listless, passive, and indifferent. They make little attempt either to seek rewards or to avoid discomfort.

REVIEW QUESTIONS

1. Match the following terms with their appropriate definition:

   ____ reinforcement
   a. any event whose reduction or termination increases the likelihood that ongoing behavior will recur

   ____ positive reinforcement
   b. any event whose presence increases the likelihood that ongoing behavior will recur

   ____ negative reinforcement
   c. anything that decreases the likelihood that a behavior wil recur

   ____ punishment
   d. anything that increases the likelihood that a behavior will recur

2. A type of learning that involves reinforcing the desired response is known as ____ ____.

3. When a threat of punishment induces a change to more desirable behavior, it is called ____ ____.

4. Superstitious behavior can result when a behavior is rewarded by pure ____.

5. Which of the following is *not* an example of operantly learned behavior?
   a. eye blinking after a flash of light is presented
   b. a child studying in order to get a teacher's approval
   c. a rat pressing a bar after receiving food for this behavior
   d. a rat pressing a bar to avoid a shock for this behavior

6. Any stimulus that follows a behavior and decreases the likelihood that the behavior will be repeated is called ____.
   a. cue
   b. situational stimulus
   c. punishment
   d. higher-order conditioner

7. Which of the following problems may result from avoidance training?
   a. a person may continue to avoid something that no longer needs to be avoided
   b. the effects of avoidance training tend to last for only a short time
   c. avoidance training may produce latent learning
   d. avoidance training tends to take effect when it is too late to make a difference in avoiding the problem situation

Answers: 1. reinforcement–d; positive reinforcement–b; negative reinforcement–a; punishment–c. **2.** operant conditioning. **3.** avoidance training. **4.** coincidence. **5.** a. **6.** c. **7.** a.

Factors Shared by Classical and Operant Conditioning

Can you think of any similarities between classical and operant conditioning?

Despite the differences between classical and operant conditioning, these two forms of learning have many things in common. First, they both involve the learning of associations. In classical conditioning it is a learned association between one stimulus and another (between food and a bell, for instance), while in operant conditioning it is a learned association between some action and a consequence. Second, the responses in both classical and operant conditioning are under the control of stimuli in the environment. A classically conditioned fear might be triggered by the sight of a white rat; an operantly conditioned jump might be cued by the flash of a red light. In both cases, moreover, the learned responses to a cue can generalize to similar stimuli. Third, neither classically nor operantly conditioned responses will last forever if they aren't periodically renewed. This doesn't necessarily mean that they are totally forgotten, however. Even after you think these responses are long extinguished, either can suddenly reappear in the right situation. And fourth, in both kinds of learning—classical *and* operant conditioning—new behaviors can build on previously established ones.

The Importance of Contingencies

How can changes in the timing of a conditioned stimulus lead to unexpected learning? Why does intermittent reinforcement result in such persistent behavior?

Because classical and operant conditioning are both forms of associative learning, they both involve perceived contingencies. A **contingency** is a relationship in which one event *depends* on another. Graduating from college is *contingent* on passing a certain number of courses. Earning a paycheck is *contingent* on having a job. In both classical and operant conditioning, perceived contingencies are very important.

Contingencies in Classical Conditioning   In classical conditioning a contingency is perceived between the CS and the US. The CS comes to be viewed as a signal that the US is about to happen. This is why, in classical conditioning, the CS must not only occur in close proximity to the US, but it should also precede the US and provide predictive information about it (Rescorla, 1966, 1967, 1988).

Imagine an experiment in which animals are exposed to a tone (the CS) and a mild electric shock (the US). One group always hears the tone a fraction of a second before they are shocked. Another group sometimes hears the tone first, but other times the tone sounds a fraction of a second *after* the shock, and still other times the tone and shock occur together. Soon the first group will show a fear response upon hearing the tone alone, but the second group will not. This is because the first group has learned a contingency between the tone and the shock. For them the tone has always preceded the shock, so it has come to mean that the shock is about to be given. For the second group, in contrast, the tone has signaled little or nothing about the shock. Sometimes it has meant that a shock is coming, sometimes it has meant that the shock is here, and sometimes it has meant that the shock is over and "the coast is clear." Because the meaning of the tone has been ambiguous for the members of this group, they have not developed a conditioned fear response to it.

Contingency
A reliable "if–then" relationship between two events such as a CS and a US.

Although scientists once believed that no conditioning would occur if the CS *followed* the US, this turns out not to be true. The explanation again lies in contingency learning. Imagine a situation in which a tone (the CS) always follows a shock (the US). This is called *backward conditioning*. After a while, when the tone is sounded alone, the learner will not show a conditioned fear response to it. After all, the tone has never predicted that a shock is about to be given. But what the learner *does* show is a conditioned *relaxation* response to the sound of the tone. This is because the tone has served as a signal that the shock is over and will not occur again for some time. Again we see the importance of contingency learning. The learner responds to the tone on the basis of the information it gives about what will happen next.

Other studies similarly show that predictive information is crucial in establishing a classically conditioned response. In one experiment with rats, for instance, a noise was repeatedly paired with a brief electric shock until the noise soon became a conditioned stimulus for a conditioned fear response (Kamin, 1969). Then a second stimulus—a light—was added right before the noise. You might expect that the rat came to show a fear of the light as well, because it, too, preceded the shock. But this is not what happened. Apparently, the noise–shock contingency that the rat had already learned had a **blocking** effect on additional learning. Once the rat had learned that the noise signaled the onset of shock, adding yet another cue (a light) provided no new predictive information about the shock's arrival, and so the rat paid little attention to it. Classical conditioning, then, occurs only when a stimulus tells the learner something *new* or *additional* about the likelihood that a US will occur.

Contingencies in Operant Conditioning   Contingencies also figure prominently in operant conditioning. The learner must come to perceive a connection between performing a certain voluntary action and receiving a certain reward or punishment. If no contingency is perceived, there is no reason to increase or decrease the behavior.

But once a contingency is perceived, does it matter how often a consequence is actually delivered? When it comes to rewards, the answer is yes. Fewer rewards are often better than more. In the language of operant conditioning, *partial* or *intermittent reinforcement* results in behavior that will persist longer than behavior learned by *continuous reinforcement*. Why would this be so? The answer has to do with expectations. When people receive only occasional reinforcement, they learn not to expect reinforcement with every response, so they continue responding in the hopes that eventually they will gain the desired reward. Vending machines and slot machines illustrate these different effects of continuous versus partial reinforcement. A vending machine offers continuous reinforcement. Each time you put in the right amount of money, you get something desired in return (reinforcement). If a vending machine is broken and you receive nothing for your coins, you are unlikely to put more money in it. In contrast, a casino slot machine pays off intermittently; only occasionally do you get something back for your investment. This intermittent payoff has a compelling effect on behavior. You might continue putting coins into a slot machine for a very long time even though you are getting nothing in return.

Psychologists refer to a pattern of reward payoffs as a **schedule of reinforcement.** Partial or intermittent reinforcement schedules are either fixed or variable and may be based on either the number of correct responses or the time elapsed between correct responses. Table 5–1 gives some everyday examples of different reinforcement schedules.

On a **fixed-interval schedule** learners are reinforced for the first response after a certain amount of time has passed since that response was previously rewarded. That is, they have to wait for a set period before they will be reinforced

Blocking
A process whereby prior conditioning prevents conditioning to a second stimulus even when the two stimuli are presented simultaneously.

Schedule of reinforcement
In operant conditioning, the rule for determining when and how often reinforcers will be delivered.

Fixed-interval schedule
A reinforcement schedule in which the correct response is reinforced after a fixed length of time since the last reinforcement.

TABLE 5-1	Examples of Reinforcement in Everyday Life
Continuous reinforcement (reinforcement every time the response is made)	Putting money in the parking meter to avoid getting a ticket. Putting coins in a vending machine to get candy or soda.
Fixed-ratio schedule (reinforcement after a fixed number of responses)	Being paid on a piecework basis. In the garment industry, for example, workers may be paid a fee per 100 dresses sewn.
Variable-ratio schedule (reinforcement after a varying number of responses)	Playing a slot machine. The machine is programmed to pay off after a certain number of responses have been made, but that number keeps changing. This type of schedule creates a steady rate of responding, because players know that if they play long enough, they will win. Sales commissions. You have to talk to many customers before you make a sale, and you never know whether the next one will buy. The number of sales calls you make, not how much time passes, will determine when you are reinforced by a sale, and the number of sales calls will vary.
Fixed-interval schedule (reinforcement of first response after a fixed amount of time has passed)	You have an exam coming up, and as time goes by and you haven't studied, you have to make up for it all by a certain time, and that means cramming. Picking up a salary check, which occurs every week or every two weeks.
Variable-interval schedule (reinforcement of first response after varying amounts of time)	Surprise quizzes in a course cause a steady rate of studying because you never know when they'll occur; you have to be prepared all the time. Watching a football game, waiting for a touchdown. It could happen anytime. If you leave the room, you may miss it, so you have to keep watching continuously.

Source: From Landy, 1987, p. 212. Adapted by permission.

again. With a fixed-interval schedule, performance tends to fall off immediately after each reinforcement and then tends to pick up again as the time for the next reinforcement draws near. For example, when exams are given at fixed intervals—like midterms and finals—students tend to decrease their studying right after one test is over and then increase studying as the next test approaches (see Figure 5–5).

A **variable-interval schedule** reinforces correct responses after varying lengths of time following the last reinforcement. One reinforcement might be given after 6 minutes, the next after 4 minutes, the next after 5 minutes, and the next after 3 minutes. The learner typically gives a slow, steady pattern of responses, being careful not to be so slow as to miss all the rewards. For example, if exams are given during a semester at unpredictable intervals, students have to keep studying at a steady rate, because on any given day there might be a test.

On a **fixed-ratio schedule** a certain number of correct responses must occur before reinforcement is provided. This results in a high response rate because making many responses in a short time yields more rewards. Being paid on a piecework basis is an example of a fixed-ratio schedule. Farmworkers might get $3 for every 10 baskets of cherries they pick. The more they pick, the more money they make. Under a fixed-ratio schedule a brief pause after reinforcement is followed by a rapid and steady response rate until the next reinforcement.

On a **variable-ratio schedule** the number of correct responses needed to gain reinforcement is not constant. The casino slot machine is a good example of a variable-ratio schedule. It will eventually pay off, but you have no idea when. Because there is always a chance of hitting the jackpot, the temptation to keep playing is great. Learners on a variable-ratio schedule tend not to pause after reinforcement and have a high rate of response over a long period of time. Because they never know when reinforcement may come, they keep on testing for a reward.

Variable-interval schedule
A reinforcement schedule in which the correct response is reinforced after varying lengths of time following the last reinforcement.

Fixed-ratio schedule
A reinforcement schedule in which the correct response is reinforced after a fixed number of correct responses.

Variable-ratio schedule
A reinforcement schedule in which a varying number of correct responses must occur before reinforcement is presented.

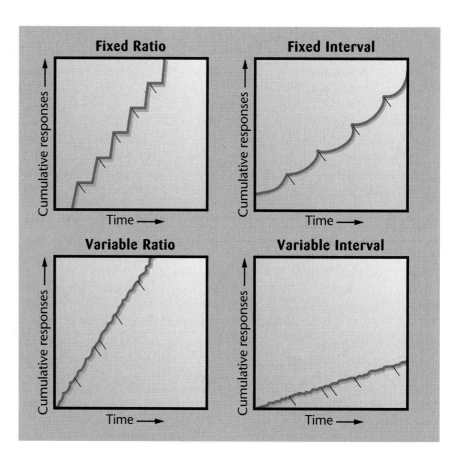

FIGURE 5–5

Response patterns to schedules of reinforcement. The *fixed-ratio* schedule is characterized by a high rate of response and a pause after each reinforcement. On a *fixed-interval* schedule, as the time for reinforcement approaches, the number of responses increases, and the slope becomes steeper. A *variable-ratio* schedule produces a high rate of response with little or no pause after each reinforcement. On a *variable-interval* schedule, the response rate is moderate and relatively constant. Notice that each tick mark on the graph represents one reinforcement.

Extinction
A decrease in the strength or frequency of a learned response because of failure to continue pairing the US and CS (classical conditioning) or withholding of reinforcement (operant conditioning).

Spontaneous recovery
The reappearance of an extinguished response after the passage of time, without further training.

Extinction and Spontaneous Recovery

Can you ever get rid of a conditioned response? Under what circumstances might old learned associations suddenly reappear?

Another factor shared by classical and operant conditioning is that learned responses sometimes weaken and may even disappear. If a CS and a US are *never* paired again, or if a consequence *always* stops following a certain behavior, the learned association will begin to fade until eventually the effects of prior learning are no longer seen. This is called **extinction** of a conditioned response.

Extinction and Spontaneous Recovery in Classical Conditioning

For an example of extinction in classical conditioning, let's go back to Pavlov's dogs, which had learned to salivate upon hearing a bell. What would you predict happened over time when the dogs heard the bell (the CS) but food (the US) was no longer given? The conditioned response to the bell—salivation—gradually decreased until eventually it stopped altogether. The dogs no longer salivated when they heard the bell. Extinction had taken place. Extinction of classically conditioned responses also occurs in your own life. If scary music in films (a CS) is no longer paired with frightening events on the screen (a US), you will eventually stop becoming tense and anxious (a CR) when you hear that kind of music. Your classically conditioned response to the music has undergone extinction.

Once such a response has been extinguished, is the learning gone forever? Pavlov trained his dogs to salivate when they heard a bell, then extinguished this conditioned response. A few days later the dogs were exposed to the bell again in the laboratory setting. As soon as they heard it, their mouths began to water. The response that had been learned and then extinguished reappeared on its own with no retraining. This phenomenon is known as **spontaneous recovery.**

The dogs' response was now only about half as strong as it had been before extinction, and it was very easy to extinguish a second time. Nevertheless, the fact that the response occurred at all indicated that the original learning was not completely forgotten. Similarly, if you stop going to the movies for a while, you may find that the next time you go, that scary music once again makes you tense and anxious. A response that was extinguished has returned spontaneously after the passage of time.

How can extinguished behavior disappear, then reappear later? According to Mark Bouton (1993, 1994), the explanation is that extinction does not erase learning. Rather, extinction occurs because *new* learning interferes with a previously learned response. New stimuli in other settings come to be paired with the conditioned stimulus, and these new stimuli may elicit responses different from (and sometimes incompatible with) the original conditioned response. For example, if you take a break from watching the latest horror movies in theaters and instead watch reruns of classic horror films on television, these classic films may seem so amateurish that they make you laugh rather than scare you. Here you are learning to associate the scary music in such films with laughter, which in effect opposes your original fear response. The result is interference and extinction. Spontaneous recovery consists of overcoming this interference. For instance, if you return to the theater to see the latest Stephen King movie, the conditioned response of fear to the scary music may suddenly reappear. It is as if the unconditioned stimulus of watching "up-to-date" horror acts as a reminder of your earlier learning and renews your previous classically conditioned response. Such "reminder" stimuli work particularly well when presented in the original conditioning setting.

Extinction and Spontaneous Recovery in Operant Conditioning

Extinction and spontaneous recovery also occur in operant conditioning. In operant conditioning, extinction happens as a result of withholding reinforcement. The effect usually isn't immediate. In fact, when reinforcement is first discontinued, there is often a brief *increase* in the strength or frequency of responding before a decline sets in. For instance, if you put coins in a vending machine and it fails to deliver the goods, you may pull the lever more forcefully and in rapid succession before you finally give up.

Just as in classical conditioning, extinction in operant conditioning doesn't completely erase what has been learned. Even though much time has passed since a behavior was last rewarded and the behavior seems extinguished, it may suddenly reappear. This spontaneous recovery may again be understood in terms of interference from new behaviors. If a rat is no longer reinforced for pressing a lever, it will start to engage in other behaviors—turning away from the lever, biting at the corners of the Skinner box, attempting to escape, and so on. These new behaviors will interfere with the operant response of lever pressing, causing it to extinguish. Spontaneous recovery is a brief victory of the original learning over interfering responses. The rat decides to give the previous "reward" lever one more try, as if testing again for a reward.

The difficulty of extinguishing an operantly conditioned response depends on a number of factors. One is the strength of the original learning. The stronger the original learning, the longer it takes the response to extinguish. If you spend many hours training a puppy to sit on command, you will not need to reinforce this behavior very often once the dog grows up. The pattern of reinforcement matters also, however, as you learned earlier. Responses that were reinforced only occasionally when acquired are usually more resistant to extinction than responses that were reinforced every time they occurred. Another important factor is the variety of settings in which the original learning took place. The greater the variety of settings, the harder it is to extinguish the

The slot machine is a classic example of a variable-ratio schedule of reinforcement. Because people keep hoping that the next play will be rewarded, they maintain a high rate of response over a long period of time.

A person who learned to feel anxious over math tests in school might come to feel anxious about balancing a checkbook. This is an example of stimulus generalization in classical conditioning.

response. Rats trained to run several different types of alleys in order to reach a food reward will keep running longer after food is withdrawn than will rats trained in a single alley. Complex behavior, too, is much more difficult to extinguish than simple behavior is. Complex behavior consists of many actions put together, and each of those actions must be extinguished in order for the whole to be extinguished. Finally, behaviors learned through punishment rather than reinforcement are especially hard to extinguish. If you avoid jogging down a particular street because a vicious dog there attacked you, you may never venture down that street again, so your avoidance of the street may never extinguish.

One way to speed up the extinction of an operantly conditioned response is to put the learner in a situation that is different from the one in which the response was originally learned. The response is likely to be weaker in the new situation, and therefore it will extinguish more quickly. Of course, when the learner is returned to the original learning setting after extinction has occurred elsewhere, the response may undergo spontaneous recovery, just as in classical conditioning. But now it is likely to be weaker than it was initially, and it should be relatively easy to extinguish once and for all. You may have experienced this yourself when you returned home for the holidays after your first semester in college. A habit that you thought you had outgrown at school may have suddenly reappeared. The home setting worked as a "reminder" stimulus, encouraging the response, just as we mentioned when discussing classical conditioning. Because you have already extinguished the habit in another setting, however, extinguishing it here shouldn't be difficult.

Stimulus Control, Generalization, and Discrimination

How can anxiety about math in grade school affect a college student? Why do people often slap the wrong card when playing a game of slapjack?

The home setting acting as a "reminder" stimulus is just one example of how conditioned responses are influenced by surrounding cues in the environment. This is called **stimulus control,** and it occurs in both classical and operant conditioning. In classical conditioning the conditioned response (CR) is under the control of the conditioned stimulus (CS) that triggers it. Salivation, for example, might be controlled by the sound of a bell. In operant conditioning the learned response is under the control of whatever stimuli come to be associated with delivery of reward or punishment. A leap to avoid electric shock might come under the control of a flashing light, for instance. In both classical and operant conditioning, moreover, the learner may respond to cues that are merely similar (but not identical) to the ones that prevailed during the original learning. This tendency to respond to similar cues is known as **stimulus generalization.**

Generalization and Discrimination in Classical Conditioning   There are many examples of stimulus generalization in classical conditioning. One is the case of Little Albert, who was conditioned to fear white rats. When the experimenters later showed him a white rabbit, he cried and tried to crawl away, even though he had not been taught to fear rabbits. He also showed fear of other white, furry objects—cotton balls, a fur coat, even a bearded Santa Claus mask. Similarly, Pavlov noticed that after his dogs had been conditioned to salivate when they heard a bell, their mouths would often water when they heard a buzzer or the ticking of a metronome. Both Pavlov's dogs and Albert had generalized their learned reactions from rats and bells to similar stimuli. In much the same way, a person who learned to feel anxious over math tests in grade school might come to feel anxious about any task involving numbers, even balancing a checkbook.

Stimulus control
Control of conditioned responses by cues or stimuli in the environment.

Stimulus generalization
The transfer of a learned response to different but similar stimuli.

Stimulus generalization is not inevitable, however. Through a process called **stimulus discrimination,** learners can be trained not to generalize but rather to make a conditioned response only to a single specific stimulus. This process involves presenting several similar stimuli, only one of which is followed by the unconditioned stimulus. For instance, Albert might have been shown a rat, a rabbit, cotton balls, and other white, furry objects, but only the rat would be followed by a loud noise (the US). Given this procedure, Albert would have learned to discriminate the white rat from the other objects, and the fear response would not have generalized as it did.

Learning to discriminate is essential in everyday life. We prefer for children to learn not to fear *every* loud noise, *every* insect, *every* dog, and so forth, but only those that are potentially harmful. Through stimulus discrimination, behavior becomes more finely tuned to the demands of our environment.

Generalization and Discrimination in Operant Conditioning

Stimulus generalization also occurs in operant conditioning. A baby who is hugged and kissed for saying "Mama" when he sees his mother may begin to call everyone "Mama"—males and females alike. Although the person whom the baby sees—the stimulus—changes, he responds with the same word. Similarly, the skills you learn when playing tennis may be generalized to badminton, Ping-Pong, and squash.

In operant conditioning, responses, too, can be generalized, not just stimuli. For example, the baby who calls everyone "Mama" may also call people "Nana." His learning has generalized to other sounds that are similar to the correct response, "Mama." This is called **response generalization.** Response generalization doesn't occur in classical conditioning. If a dog is taught to salivate when it sees an orange light, it will salivate less when it sees a red or a yellow light, but the response is still salivation.

Just as discrimination is useful in classical conditioning, it is also useful in operant conditioning. Learning *what* to do has little value if you do not know *when* to do it. Learning that a response is triggered is pointless if you do not know which response is right. Discrimination training in operant conditioning consists of reinforcing *only* a specific, desired response and *only* in the presence of a specific stimulus. With this procedure, pigeons have been trained to peck at a red disk but not at a green one. First they are taught to peck at a disk. Then they are presented with two disks, one red and one green. They get food when they peck at the red one but not when they peck at the green. Eventually they learn to discriminate between the two colors, pecking only at the red. In much the same way, children learn to listen to exactly what the teacher is asking before they raise their hands.

New Learning Based on Original Learning

How might you build on a conditioned response to make an even more complex form of learning? Why is money such a good reinforcer for most people?

There are other ways, besides stimulus generalization and discrimination, that original learning can serve as the basis for new learning. In classical conditioning an existing conditioned stimulus can be paired with a new stimulus to produce a new conditioned response. This is called **higher-order conditioning.** In operant conditioning, objects that have no intrinsic value can nevertheless become reinforcers because of their association with other, more basic reinforcers. These learned reinforcers are called *secondary reinforcers.*

Higher-order Conditioning

Pavlov demonstrated higher-order conditioning with his dogs. After the dogs had learned to salivate when they heard a bell, Pavlov used the bell (*without* food) to teach the dogs to salivate at the sight of a

The skills a person learns in playing tennis may also be utilized in such sports as Ping-Pong, squash, and badminton. This is an example of stimulus generalization in operant conditioning.

Stimulus discrimination
Learning to respond to only one stimulus and to inhibit the response to all other stimuli.

Response generalization
Giving a response that is somewhat different from the response originally learned to that stimulus.

Higher-order conditioning
Conditioning based on previous learning; the conditioned stimulus serves as an unconditioned stimulus for further training.

black square. Instead of showing them the square and following it with food, he showed them the square and followed it with the bell until the dogs learned to salivate when they saw the square alone. In effect, the bell served as a substitute unconditioned stimulus and the black square became a new conditioned stimulus. This procedure is known as higher-order conditioning, not because it is more complex than other types of conditioning or because it incorporates any new principles. It is called higher-order simply because it is conditioning based on previous learning.

Higher-order conditioning is difficult to achieve because it is battling against extinction of the original conditioned response. The unconditioned stimulus no longer follows the original conditioned stimulus, and that is precisely the way to extinguish a classically conditioned response. During higher-order conditioning, Pavlov's dogs were exposed to the square followed by the bell, but no food was given. So the square became a signal that the bell would not precede food, and soon all salivation stopped. For higher-order conditioning to succeed, the unconditioned stimulus must be occasionally reintroduced. Food must be given once in a while after the bell sounds so that the dogs will continue to salivate when they hear the bell.

Secondary Reinforcers   Some reinforcers, such as food, water, and sex, are intrinsically rewarding in and of themselves. These are called **primary reinforcers.** No prior learning is required to make them reinforcing. Other reinforcers have no intrinsic value. They have only acquired value through association with primary reinforcers. These are the **secondary reinforcers** we mentioned earlier. They are called secondary not because they are less important, but because prior learning is needed before they will function as reinforcers. Suppose a rat learns to get food by pressing a bar; then a buzzer is sounded every time food drops into the dish. Even if the rat stops getting the food, it will continue to press the bar for a while just to hear the buzzer. Although the buzzer by itself has no intrinsic value to the rat, it has become a secondary reinforcer through association with food, a primary reinforcer.

Note how, in creating a secondary reinforcer, classical conditioning is involved. Because it has been paired with an intrinsically pleasurable stimulus, a formerly neutral stimulus comes to elicit pleasure, too. This stimulus can then serve as a reinforcer to establish an operantly conditioned response.

Money is one of the best examples of a secondary reinforcer. Although money is just paper or metal, through its exchange value for food and other primary reinforcers it becomes a powerful reinforcer. Tokens, such as poker chips, can serve the same function if they can ultimately be exchanged for primary reinforcers. Chimpanzees will learn to work for poker chips that they insert into a vending machine to obtain a primary reinforcer: raisins. Tokens have also been used successfully as reinforcers for schoolchildren, prisoners, and patients suffering from chronic schizophrenia. In the classroom, for example, students can be reinforced for remaining quiet during study periods or for paying attention to a teacher's lesson by receiving a token for good behavior that can later be exchanged for candy or privileges (Packard, 1970). These *token economies* have proved especially effective in encouraging institutionalized mental patients to improve their personal hygiene and to engage in more social interaction (Schaefer & Martin, 1966).

Summing Up

Does operant conditioning ever look like classical conditioning?

Classical and operant conditioning both entail forming associations between stimuli and responses and perceiving contingencies between one event and another. Both are subject to extinction and spontaneous recovery, as well as to stimulus control, generalization, and discrimination. The main difference be-

Primary reinforcer
A reinforcer that is rewarding in itself, such as food, water, and sex.

Secondary reinforcer
A reinforcer whose value is acquired through association with other primary or secondary reinforcers.

tween the two is that in classical conditioning the learner is passive and the behavior involved is usually involuntary, whereas in operant conditioning the learner is active and the behavior involved is usually voluntary. Some psychologists downplay these differences, however, suggesting that classical and operant conditioning are simply two different ways of bringing about the same kind of learning. For example, once an operant response becomes linked to a stimulus, it looks very much like a conditioned response in classical conditioning. If you have been reinforced repeatedly for stepping on the brake when a traffic light turns red, the red light comes to elicit braking just as the sound of a bell elicited salivation in Pavlov's dogs. Classical and operant conditioning, then, may simply be two different procedures for achieving the same end (Hearst, 1975). If so, psychologists may have overstressed the differences between them and paid too little attention to what they have in common.

REVIEW QUESTIONS

1. Identify the following schedules of reinforcement as fixed interval (FI), variable interval (VI), fixed ratio (FR), and variable ratio (VR).
   a. Reinforcement comes on the first correct response after 2 minutes have passed since the last reinforcement. ____
   b. Reinforcement comes on every sixth correct response. ____
   c. Reinforcement comes after 4 correct responses, then after 6 more, then after 5 more. ____
   d. Reinforcement comes after varying lengths of time following the last reinforcement. ____
2. To extinguish a classically conditioned response, you must break the association between which pair?
   a. CS and US
   b. US and UR
   c. US and CR
3. After extinction and a period of rest, a conditioned response may suddenly reappear. This is called ____ ____.
4. The process by which a learned response to a specific stimulus comes to be associated with different but similar stimuli is known as ____ ____.
5. Classify the following as primary (P) or secondary (S) reinforcers.
   a. food ____
   b. money ____
   c. college diploma ____
   d. sex ____

Answers: 1. a. (FI). b. (FR). c. (VR). d. (VI). 2. a. 3. spontaneous recovery. 4. stimulus generalization. 5. a. (P). b. (S). c. (S). d. (P).

Cognitive Learning

How would you study the kind of learning that occurs when you memorize the layout of a chessboard?

Some psychologists insist that because classical and operant conditioning can be *observed* and *measured*, they are the only legitimate kinds of learning to study scientifically. But others contend that mental activities are crucial to learning and so can't be ignored. How do you grasp the layout of a building from someone else's description of it? How do you know how to hold a tennis racket just from watching a game of tennis being played? How do you enter into memory abstract concepts like *conditioning* and *reinforcement*? You do all these things and many others through **cognitive learning**—the mental

Cognitive learning
Learning that depends on mental processes that are not directly observable.

processes that go on inside us when we learn. Cognitive learning is impossible to observe and measure directly, but it can be *inferred* from behavior, and so it is also a legitimate topic for scientific study.

Latent Learning and Cognitive Maps

Did you learn your way around campus solely through operant conditioning (rewards for correct turns, punishments for wrong ones), or was something more involved?

Interest in cognitive learning began shortly after the earliest work in classical and operant conditioning. In the 1930s Edward Chace Tolman, one of the pioneers in the study of cognitive learning, argued that we do not need to show our learning in order for learning to have occurred. Tolman called learning that isn't apparent because it is not yet demonstrated **latent learning.**

Tolman studied latent learning in a famous experiment (Tolman & Honzik, 1930). Two groups of hungry rats were placed in a maze and allowed to find their way from a start box to an end box. The first group found food pellets (a reward) in the end box; the second group found nothing there. According to the principles of operant conditioning, the first group would learn the maze better than the second group—which is, indeed, what happened. But when Tolman took some of the rats from the second, unreinforced group and started to give them food at the goal box, almost immediately they ran the maze as well as the rats in the first group (see Figure 5–6). Tolman argued that the unrewarded rats had actually learned a great deal about the maze as they wandered around inside it. In fact, they may have even learned *more* about it than the rats that had been trained with food rewards, but their learning was *latent*—stored internally but not yet reflected in their behavior. It was not until they were given a motivation to run the maze that they put their latent learning to use.

Since Tolman's time, there has been much work on the nature of latent learning regarding spatial layouts and relationships. From studies of how animals or humans find their way around a maze, a building, or a neighborhood with many available routes, psychologists have proposed that this kind of learning is stored in the form of a mental image, or **cognitive map.** When the proper time comes, the learner can call up the stored image and put it to use.

In response to Tolman's theory of latent learning, Thorndike proposed an experiment to test whether a rat could learn to run a maze and store a cognitive image of the maze without experiencing the maze firsthand. He envisioned researchers carrying each rat through the maze in a small wire-mesh container and then rewarding the rat at the end of each trial as if it had run the maze itself. He predicted that the rat would show little or no evidence of learning as compared to rats that had learned the same maze on their own through trial and error. Neither he nor Tolman ever conducted the experiment.

Two decades later, however, researchers at the University of Kansas did carry out Thorndike's idea (McNamara, Long, & Wike, 1956). But instead of taking the passive rats through the "correct" path, they carried them over the same path that a free-running rat had taken in that maze. Contrary to Thorndike's prediction, the passenger rats learned the maze just as well as the free-running rats. They did, however, need visual cues to learn the maze's layout. If carried through the maze only in the dark, they later showed little latent learning.

More recent research confirms this picture of cognitive spatial learning. Animals show a great deal more flexibility solving problems like mazes than can be explained by simple conditioning (Domjan, 1987). In a series of experiments with rats in a radial maze, the rats consistently recalled which arms they had previously traveled down and which they hadn't, even when scent cues were re-

Latent Learning
Learning that is not immediately reflected in a behavior change.

Cognitive map
A learned mental image of a spatial environment that may be called on to solve problems when stimuli in the environment change.

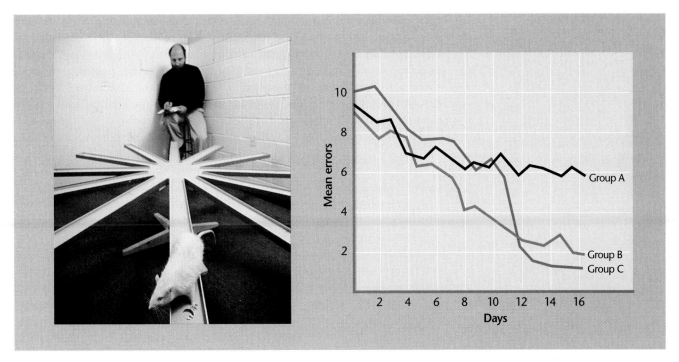

FIGURE 5–6

Maze used to study latent learning in rats.　The results of the classic Tolman-Honzik study are revealed in the graph. Group A never received a food reward; Group B was rewarded each day. Group C was not rewarded until the eleventh day, but note the significant change in the rats' behavior on Day 12. The results suggest that Group C had been learning all along, although this learning was not reflected in their performance until they were rewarded with food for demonstrating the desired behaviors.
Source: From Tolman and Honzik, 1930.

moved and all arms contained a reward. These rats had developed a cognitive map not only of the maze's layout but of their experiences in it, too (Olton & Samuelson, 1976). Even in rats, learning involves more than just a new behavior "stamped in" through reinforcement. It also involves the formation of new mental images and constructs that may be reflected in future behavior.

Insight and Learning Sets

Do you have a learning set for writing a term paper?

During World War I the German Gestalt psychologist Wolfgang Köhler conducted a series of studies into another aspect of cognitive learning—sudden **insight** into a problem's solution. Outside a chimpanzee's cage Köhler placed a banana on the ground, not quite within the animal's reach. When the chimp realized it couldn't reach the banana, it reacted with frustration. But then it started looking at what was in the cage, including a stick left there by Köhler. Sometimes quite suddenly the chimp would grab the stick, poke it through the bars of the cage, and drag the banana within reach. The same kind of sudden insight occurred when the banana was hung from the roof of the cage, too high for the chimp to grasp. This time the cage contained some boxes, which the chimp quickly learned to stack up under the banana so it could climb up to pull the fruit down. Subsequent studies have shown that even pigeons can solve the box-and-banana problem through insight if they are properly motivated, given the right tools, and taught how to use them (R. Epstein et al., 1984).

Insight
Learning that occurs rapidly as a result of understanding all the elements of a problem.

Köhler's experiments with chimpanzees illustrate learning through insight. In this photo one of the chimps has arranged a stack of boxes to reach bananas hanging from the ceiling. Insights gained in this problem-solving situation may transfer to similar ones.

Learning set
The ability to become increasingly more effective in solving problems as more problems are solved.

Observational (or vicarious) learning
Learning by observing other people's behavior.

Social learning theorists
Psychologists whose view of learning emphasizes the ability to learn by observing a model or receiving instructions, without firsthand experience by the learner.

Previous learning can often be used to help solve problems through insight. This was demonstrated by Harry Harlow in a series of studies with rhesus monkeys (Harlow, 1949). Harlow presented each monkey with two boxes—say, a round green box on the left side of a tray and a square red box on the right side. A morsel of food was put under one of the boxes. The monkey was permitted to lift just one box; if it chose the correct box, it got the food. On the next trial the food was put under the same box (which had been moved to a new position), and the monkey again got to choose just one box. Each monkey had six trials to figure out that the same box covered the food no matter where that box was located. Then the monkeys were given a new set of choices—say, between a blue triangular box and an orange oval one—and another six trials, and so on with other shapes and colors of boxes. The solution was always the same: The food was invariably under only one of the boxes. Initially the monkeys chose boxes randomly, sometimes finding the food, sometimes not. After a while, however, their behavior changed: In just one or two trials they would find the correct box, which they chose consistently thereafter until the experimenter changed the boxes. They seemed to have learned the underlying principle—that the food would always be under the same box—and they used that learning to solve almost instantly each new set of choices given.

Harlow concluded that the monkeys had established a **learning set** regarding this problem: Within the limited range of choices available to them, they had discovered how to tell which box would give the reward. Similarly, Köhler's chimps could be said to have established a learning set regarding how to get food that was just out of reach. When presented with a new version of the problem, they simply called upon past learning in a slightly different situation (reaching a banana on the ground versus reaching one hanging from the ceiling). In both Harlow's and Köhler's studies the animals seemed to have learned more than just specific behaviors—they had apparently learned *how* to learn. Whether this means that animals can think is an issue still being debated.

Learning by Observing

Why would it be harder to learn to drive a car if you had never been in one before? Why is it hard for deaf children to learn spoken language when they can easily be reinforced for correct speech sounds?

The first time you drove a car, you successfully turned the key in the ignition, put the car in gear, and pressed the gas pedal without having ever done any of those things before. How were you able to do that without step-by-step shaping of the correct behaviors? The answer is that you had often watched other people driving, which made all the difference. There are countless things we learn by watching other people and listening to what they say. This is called **observational** or **vicarious learning,** because while we are learning, we don't have to do the learned behaviors firsthand; we merely look or listen. Observational learning is a form of "social learning" because it involves interaction with other people. Psychologists who study it are known as **social learning theorists.**

Observational learning is very common. By watching other people who model new behaviors, we can learn such things as how to start a lawn mower and how to saw wood. We also learn how to show love or respect or concern, as well as how to show hostility and aggression. We can even learn bad habits, such as smoking. When the Federal Communications Commission (FCC) banned cigarette commercials on television, it was acting on the belief that providing models of smokers would prompt people to imitate smoking. They removed the models to discourage the behavior.

Of course, we do not imitate *everything* that other people do. Why are we selective in our imitation? There are several reasons (Bandura, 1977, 1986). First, we don't pay attention to everything going on around us. The behaviors we are most

In observational or vicarious learning, we learn by watching a model perform a particular action and then trying to imitate that action correctly. Some actions would be very difficult to master without observational learning.

apt to imitate are those that are modeled by someone who commands our attention (as does a famous or attractive person or an expert). Second, we must remember what a model does in order to imitate it. If a behavior isn't memorable, it won't be learned. Third, we must make an effort to convert what we see into action. If we have no motivation to perform an observed behavior, we probably won't show what we've learned. This is a distinction between *learning* and *performance*, which is crucial to social learning theorists: We can learn without any change in overt behavior that demonstrates our learning. Whether or not we act depends on our motivation.

One important motivation for acting is the kind of consequences associated with an observed behavior—the rewards or punishments it appears to bring. These consequences do not necessarily have to happen to the observer. They may happen simply to the other people the observer is watching. This is called **vicarious reinforcement** or **vicarious punishment,** because the consequences aren't experienced firsthand by the learner; they are experienced *through* other people. If a young teenager sees adults drinking and they seem to be having a great deal of fun, the teenager is experiencing vicarious reinforcement of drinking and is much more likely to imitate it.

The foremost proponent of social learning theory is Albert Bandura, who refers to his perspective as a *social cognitive theory* (Bandura, 1986). In a classic experiment, Bandura (1965) showed that people can learn a behavior without being reinforced directly for it and that learning a behavior and performing it are not the same thing. Three groups of nursery schoolchildren watched a film in which an adult model walked up to an adult-size plastic inflated doll and ordered it to move out of the way. When the doll failed to obey, the model became aggressive, pushing the doll on its side, punching it in the nose, hitting it with a rubber mallet, kicking it around the room, and throwing rubber balls at it. The film ended differently for children in each of the three groups. Those in the *model-rewarded condition* saw the model showered with candies, soft drinks, and praise by a second adult (vicarious reinforcement). Those in the *model-punished condition* saw the second adult shaking a finger at the model, scolding, and spanking him (vicarious punishment). And those in the *no-consequences condition* saw nothing happen to the model as a result of his aggressive behavior.

Immediately after seeing the film, the children were individually escorted into another room where they found the same large inflated doll, rubber balls, and mallet, as well as many other toys. Each child played alone for 10 minutes, while observers behind a one-way mirror recorded the number of imitated aggressive

Vicarious reinforcement or vicarious punishment
Reinforcement or punishment experienced by models that affects the willingness of others to perform the behaviors they learned by observing those models.

Photos from Bandura's experiment in learned aggressive behavior. After watching an adult behave aggressively toward an inflated doll, the children in Bandura's study imitated many of the aggressive acts of the adult model.

behaviors the child spontaneously performed in the absence of any direct reinforcement for those actions. After 10 minutes an experimenter entered the room and offered the child treats in return for imitating things the model had done. This was a measure of how much the child had previously learned from watching the model but perhaps hadn't yet displayed.

The green bars in Figure 5–7 show that *all* the children had learned aggressive actions from watching the model, even though they were not overtly reinforced for that learning. When later offered treats to copy the model's actions, they all did so quite accurately. In addition, the yellow bars in the figure show that the children tended to suppress their inclination to spontaneously imitate an aggressive model when they had seen that model punished for aggression. This was especially true of girls. Apparently, vicarious punishment provided the children with information about what might happen to them if they copied the "bad" behavior. Vicarious reinforcement similarly provides information about likely consequences, but in this study its effects were not large. For children this age (at least those not worried about punishment), imitating aggressive behavior toward a doll seems to have been considered "fun" in its own right, even without being associated with praise and candy. This was especially true for boys.

This study has important implications regarding how not to teach aggression unintentionally to children. Suppose you want to get a child to stop hitting other children. You might think that slapping the child as punishment would change the behavior, and it probably would suppress it to some extent. But slapping the child also demonstrates that hitting is an effective means of getting one's way. So slapping not only provides a model of aggression; it also provides a model associated with vicarious reinforcement. You and the child would both be better off if the punishment given for hitting was not a similar form of aggression and if the child could also be rewarded for showing appropriate interactions with others (Bandura, 1973, 1977).

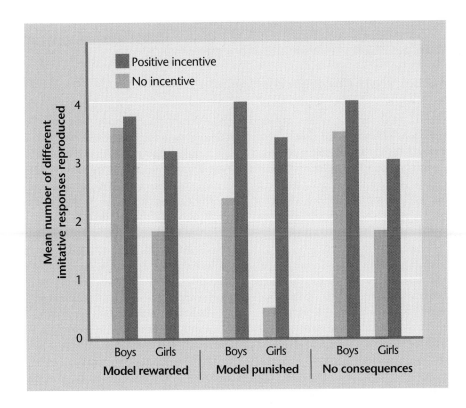

FIGURE 5–7

Results of Bandura's study. As the graph shows, even though all the children in Bandura's study of imitative aggression learned the model's behavior, they *performed* differently depending on whether the model they saw was rewarded or punished.

Source: A. Bandura, "Influence of models' reinforcement contingencies on the acquisition of imitative responses, *Journal of Personality and Social Psychology, 1*, 592. Copyright © 1965 by the American Psychological Association. Reprinted by permission.

Social learning theory's emphasis on expectations, insights, and information broadens our understanding of how people learn. According to social learning theory, humans use their powers of observation and thought to interpret their own experiences and those of others when deciding how to act (Bandura, 1962). This important perspective can be applied to the learning of many different things, from skills and behavioral tendencies to attitudes, values, and ideas.

REVIEW QUESTIONS

1. An ape examines a problem and the tools available for solving it. Suddenly the animal leaps up and quickly executes a successful solution. This is an example of

   a. insight.

   b. operant conditioning.

   c. trial-and-error learning.

2. Match the following terms with the appropriate definition.

   ____ latent learning   a. new, suddenly occurring idea to solve a problem

   ____ insight   b. learning by watching a model

   ____ observational learning   c. learning that has not yet been demonstrated in behavior

3. The view of learning that emphasizes the ability to learn through watching what happens to other people or by hearing about something is called ____ ____ ____.

4. If a person increases her behavior because she saw someone rewarded for that behavior, the reward is called ____ ____.

5. "Social learning theory broadens our understanding of how people learn skills and gain abilities by emphasizing expectations, insight, information, self-satisfaction, and self-criticism." True or false.

6. "Social learning theory supports spanking as an effective way to teach children not to hit." True or false.

Answers: 1. a. 2. latent learning (c); insight (a); observational learning (b). 3. social learning theory. 4. vicarious reinforcement. 5. T. 6. F.

APPLYING PSYCHOLOGY

Modifying Your Own Behavior

Can you modify your own undesirable behaviors using operant conditioning techniques? Yes, but first you must observe your own actions, think about their implications, and plan a strategy of intervention.

Begin by *identifying the behavior you want to acquire*—called the "target" behavior. You will be more successful if you focus on acquiring a new behavior rather than on eliminating an existing one. For example, instead of setting a target of being less shy, you might define the target behavior as becoming more outgoing or more sociable. Other possible target behaviors might include behaving more assertively, studying more, and getting along better with your roommates. In each case, you have spotlighted the behavior that you want to acquire rather than the behavior that you want to eliminate.

The next step is *defining the target behavior precisely*: What exactly do you mean by "assertive" or "sociable"? Imagine situations in which the target behavior could be performed. Then describe in writing the way in which you now respond to these situations. For example, in the case of shyness, you might write, "When I am sitting in a lecture hall, waiting for class to begin, I don't talk to the people around me." Next, write down how you would rather act in that situation: "In a lecture hall before class I want to talk to at least one other person. I might ask the person sitting next to me how he or she likes the class or the professor, or simply comment on some aspect of the course."

The third step is *monitoring your present behavior* by keeping a daily log of activities related to the target behavior. This will establish your current "base rate" and give you something concrete against which to gauge improvements. At the same time, try to figure out if your present, undesirable behavior is being reinforced in some way. For example, if you find yourself unable to study, record what you do instead (Get a snack? Watch television?) and determine if you are inadvertently rewarding your failure to study.

The next step—the basic principle of self-modification—is *providing yourself with a positive reinforcer that is contingent on specific improvements* in the target behavior. You may be able to use the same reinforcer that now maintains your undesirable behavior, or you may want to pick a new reinforcer. For example, if you want to in-

crease the amount of time you spend studying, you might reward yourself with a token for each 30 minutes of study. Then, if your favorite pastime is watching movies, you might charge yourself three tokens for an hour of television, while the privilege of going to a movie might cost six.

Remember that the new, more desirable behavior need not be learned all at once. You can use shaping or successive approximations to change your behavior bit by bit. A person who wants to become more sociable might start by giving rewards just for sitting next to another person in a classroom rather than picking an isolated seat. The person could then work up to rewarding increasingly sociable behaviors, such as first saying hello to another person, then striking up a conversation.

If you would like to try a program of self-improvement, a book by David Watson and Roland Tharp, *Self-Directed Behavior: Self-Modification for Personal Adjustment* (1997), is a good place to start. It contains step-by-step instructions and exercises that provide a useful guide.

To learn more about behavior modification, visit our Web site at **www.prenhall.com/morris**

KEY TERMS

learning, p. 164
classical (or Pavlovian) conditioning, p. 164

Classical conditioning
unconditioned stimulus (US), p. 164
unconditioned response (UR), p. 164
conditioned stimulus (CS), p. 164
conditioned response (CR), p. 164

intermittent pairing, p. 166
desensitization therapy, p. 166
preparedness, p. 167
conditioned taste aversion, p. 167

Operant conditioning
operant (or instrumental) conditioning, p. 168
operant behavior, p. 168
reinforcer, p. 168

punisher, p. 168
law of effect (principle of reinforcement), p. 169
Skinner box, p. 170
shaping, p. 170
positive reinforcer, p. 171
negative reinforcer, p. 171
biofeedback, p. 172
punishment, p. 174
avoidance training, p. 175
learned helplessness, p. 175

Factors shared by classical and operant conditioning
contingency, p. 177
blocking, p. 178
schedule of reinforcement, p. 178
fixed-interval schedule, p. 178
variable-interval schedule, p. 179
fixed-ratio schedule, p. 179
variable-ratio schedule, p. 179

CHAPTER REVIEW

◻ How did Pavlov discover classical conditioning?

Learning is the process by which experience or practice produces a relatively permanent change in behavior or potential behavior. One basic form of learning involves learning to associate one event with another. **Classical conditioning** is a type of associative learning that Pavlov discovered while studying digestion. He trained a dog to salivate at the sound of a bell by ringing the bell just before food was given. The dog learned to associate the bell with food and began to salivate at the sound of the bell alone.

◻ How might you classically condition a pet?

Suppose you wanted to classically condition salivation in your own dog. You know that food is an **unconditioned stimulus (US)** that automatically evokes the **unconditioned response (UR)** of salivation. By repeatedly pairing food with a second, initially neutral stimulus (such as a bell) that doesn't at first cause salivation, the second stimulus would eventually become a **conditioned stimulus (CS)** for a **conditioned response (CR)** of salivation.

◻ If you once burned your finger on a match while listening to a certain song, why doesn't that song now make you reflexively jerk your hand away?

It is usually easier to establish a classically conditioned response if the US and CS are paired with each other repeatedly, rather than just being paired a single time, or even once in a while (**intermittent pairing**). That is why a single burn to your finger is not usually enough to produce a classically conditioned response. It is also important that the spacing of pairings be neither too far apart nor too close together.

◻ What is an example of classical conditioning in your own life?

John Watson conditioned a little boy, Albert, to fear white rats by making a loud, frightening noise every time the boy was shown a rat. In your own life you may have acquired a classically conditioned fear or anxiety (to the sound of a dentist's drill, for instance) in much the same way. Perhaps you have also unlearned a conditioned fear by repeatedly pairing the feared object with something pleasant. Mary Cover Jones pioneered this procedure by pairing the sight of a feared rat (at gradually decreasing distances) with a child's pleasant experience of eating candy. This procedure evolved into **desensitization therapy.**

◻ Why are people more likely to develop a phobia of snakes than of flowers?

Martin Seligman has used the concept of **preparedness** to account for the fact that certain conditioned responses are acquired very easily. The ease with which we develop **conditioned taste aversions** illustrates preparedness. Because animals are biologically prepared to learn them, conditioned taste aversions can occur with only one pairing of the taste of a tainted food and later illness, and even when there is a lengthy interval between eating the food and becoming ill. A fear of snakes may also be something that humans are prepared to learn.

◻ How are operant behaviors different from the responses involved in classical conditioning?

Operant or **instrumental conditioning** is learning to make or withhold a certain response because of its consequences. **Operant behaviors** are different from the responses involved in classical conditioning because they are voluntarily emitted, whereas those involved in classical conditioning are elicited by stimuli.

◻ What two essential elements are involved in operant conditioning?

One essential element in operant conditioning is an operant behavior, or a behavior performed by one's own volition while "operating" on the environment. The second essential element is a consequence associated with that operant behavior. When a consequence increases the likelihood of an operant behavior being emitted it is called a **reinforcer.** When a consequence decreases the likelihood of an operant behavior it is called a **punisher.** These relationships are the basis of the **law of effect,** or **principle of reinforcement:** Consistently rewarded behaviors are apt to be repeated, while consistently punished behaviors are apt to be suppressed.

◻ How might a speech therapist teach the sound of "s" to a child with a lisp?

To speed up establishing an operantly conditioned response in the laboratory, the number of potential responses may be reduced by restricting the environment, as in a **Skinner box.** For behaviors outside the laboratory, which cannot be controlled so conveniently, the process of **shaping** is often useful. In shaping, reinforcement is given for successive approximations to the desired response. A speech therapist might use shaping to teach a child to pronounce a certain sound correctly.

▢ What is the difference between positive and negative reinforcement? What are some of the unintentional effects that reinforcement can have?

There are several kinds of reinforcers, all of which strengthen behavior. **Positive reinforcers** (like food) increase the likelihood of a behavior by adding something rewarding to a situation. **Negative reinforcers** (such as stopping an electric shock) increase the likelihood of a behavior by subtracting something unpleasant. When an action is followed closely by a reinforcer, we tend to repeat it, even if it did not actually produce the reinforcement. Such behaviors are called *superstitious.*

▢ What problems can punishment create?

Punishment is any event that decreases the likelihood that the behavior that precedes it will occur again. Whereas negative reinforcement strengthens behavior, punishment weakens it. Although punishment can be effective, it also has drawbacks, such as stirring up negative feelings and sometimes modeling aggressive behavior. Punishment also doesn't teach a more desirable response; it only suppresses an undesirable one. Sometimes, after punishment has been given a few times, it needn't be continued because the threat of it is enough. This is called **avoidance training.**

▢ In what ways do some college students exhibit learned helplessness?

When people or other animals are unable to escape from a punishing situation, they may acquire a "giving up" response, called **learned helplessness.** Learned helplessness can generalize to new situations, causing resignation in the face of unpleasant outcomes, even when they can be avoided. A college student who gives up trying to do well in school after a few poor grades on tests is exhibiting learned helplessness.

▢ Can you think of any similarities between classical and operant conditioning?

A number of factors characterize both classical conditioning and operant conditioning: (1) both involve learned associations; (2) in both cases responses come under control of stimuli in the environment; (3) in both cases the responses will extinguish if they are not periodically renewed; and (4) in both cases new behaviors can build upon previously established ones.

▢ How can changes in the timing of a conditioned stimulus lead to unexpected learning? Why does intermittent reinforcement result in such persistent behavior?

In both classical and operant conditioning an "if–then" relationship, or **contingency,** exists either between two stimuli or between a stimulus and a response. In both these kinds of learning, perceived contingencies are very important.

In classical conditioning the contingency is between the CS and the US. The CS comes to be viewed as a signal that the US is about to happen. That is why the CS must not only occur in close proximity to the US, but it must also precede the US and provide predictive information about it. If the CS occurs *after* the US it will come to serve as a signal that the US is over, not that the US is imminent.

In operant conditioning contingencies exist between responses and consequences. Contingencies between responses and rewards are called **schedules of reinforcement.** *Partial reinforcement,* in which rewards are given for some correct responses but not for every one, generates behavior that persists longer than behavior learned by continuous reinforcement. This is because partial reinforcement encourages learners to keep "testing" for a reward. The type of partial reinforcement schedule also matters. A **fixed-interval schedule,** by which reinforcement is given for the first correct response after a fixed time period, tends to result in a flurry of responding right before a reward is due. A **variable-interval schedule,** which reinforces the first correct response after an unpredictable period of time, tends to result in a slow but steady pattern of responding as the learner keeps testing for the next payoff. In a **fixed-ratio schedule** behavior is rewarded after a fixed number of correct responses, so the result is usually a high rate of responding because faster responses yield quicker payoffs. Finally, **a variable-ratio schedule** provides reinforcement after a varying number of correct responses. It encourages a high rate of response that is especially persistent because the person keeps harboring the hope that the next response will bring a reward.

▢ Can you ever get rid of a conditioned response? Under what circumstances might old learned associations suddenly reappear?

Another factor shared by classical and operant conditioning is that learned responses sometimes weaken and may even disappear, which is called **extinction.** The learning is not necessarily completely forgotten, however. Sometimes the learned response suddenly reappears on its own, with no retraining. This is known as **spontaneous recovery.**

Extinction is produced in classical conditioning by failure to continue pairing the CS and the US. The CS no longer serves as a signal that the US is about to happen, and so the conditioned response dies out. An important contributing factor is often new learned associations that interfere with the old one. In situations where you are reminded of the old association, spontaneous recovery may occur.

Extinction occurs in operant conditioning when reinforcement is withheld until the learned response is no longer emitted. The ease with which an operantly conditioned behavior is extinguished varies according to several factors: the strength of the original learning, the variety of settings in which learning took place, and the schedule of reinforcement used during conditioning. Especially hard to extinguish is behavior learned through punishment.

☐ How can anxiety about math in grade school affect a college student? Why do people often slap the wrong card when playing a game of slapjack?

Conditioned responses are influenced by surrounding cues in the environment. This is called **stimulus control.** The tendency to respond to cues that are similar, but not identical, to those that prevailed during the original learning is known as **stimulus generalization. Stimulus discrimination** enables learners to perceive differences among cues so as not to respond to all of them.

In classical conditioning the conditioned response (CR) is under the control of the conditioned stimulus (CS) that triggers it. An example of stimulus generalization in classical conditioning is a student feeling anxious about studying math in college because he or she had a bad experience learning math in grade school.

In operant conditioning the learned response is under the control of whatever cues come to be associated with delivery of reward or punishment. Learners often generalize about these cues, responding to others that are broadly similar to the ones that prevailed during the original learning. An example is slapping any face card in a game of slapjack. Learners may also generalize their responses by performing behaviors that are similar to the ones that were originally reinforced. This is called **response generalization.** Discrimination in operant conditioning is taught by reinforcing only a certain response and only in the presence of a certain stimulus.

☐ How might you build on a conditioned response to make an even more complex form of learning? Why is money such a good reinforcer for most people?

In both classical and operant conditioning original learning serves as a building block for new learning. In classical conditioning an earlier conditioned stimulus can be used as an unconditioned stimulus for further training. For example, Pavlov used the bell to condition his dogs to salivate at the sight of a black square. This is called **higher-order conditioning** and is difficult to achieve because of extinction. Unless the original unconditioned stimulus is presented occasionally, the initial conditioned response will die out.

In operant conditioning, initially neutral stimuli can become reinforcers by being associated with other reinforcers. A **primary reinforcer** is one that, like food and water, is rewarding in and of itself. A **secondary reinforcer** is one whose value is learned through its association with primary reinforcers or with other secondary reinforcers. Money is such a good secondary reinforcer because it can be exchanged for so many different primary and secondary rewards.

☐ Does operant conditioning ever look like classical conditioning?

Despite their differences, classical and operant conditioning share many similarities: Both involve associations between stimuli and responses; both are subject to extinction and spontaneous recovery as well as generalization and discrimination; in both new learning can be based on original learning. Many psychologists now wonder whether classical and operant conditioning aren't just two ways of bringing about the same kind of learning.

☐ How would you study the kind of learning that occurs when you memorize the layout of a chessboard?

Cognitive learning refers to the mental processes that go on inside us when we learn. Some kinds of learning, such as memorizing the layout of a chessboard, seem to be purely cognitive, because the learner does not appear to be "behaving" while the learning takes place. Cognitive learning, however, can always affect future behavior, such as reproducing the layout of a memorized chessboard after it is cleared away. It is from such observable behavior that cognitive learning is inferred.

☐ Did you learn your way around campus solely through operant conditioning (rewards for correct turns, punishments for wrong ones), or was something more involved?

Latent learning is any knowledge we acquire that has not yet been demonstrated in behavior. Your knowledge of psychology is latent if you have not yet displayed it in what you say, write, and do. One kind of latent learning is knowledge of spatial layouts and relationships, which is usually stored in the form of a **cognitive map.** Rewards or punishments aren't essential for latent learning to take place. You did not need rewards and punishments to learn the layout of your campus, for example. You acquired this cognitive map simply by storing your visual perceptions.

☐ Do you have a learning set for writing a term paper?

A **learning set** is a concept or procedure that provides a key to solving a problem even when its demands are slightly different from those of problems you have solved in the past. As a student, you probably have a learning set for writing a term paper that allows you to successfully develop papers on many different topics. A learning set can sometimes encourage **insight,** or the sudden perception of a solution even to a problem that at first seems totally new. In this case you are perceiving similarities between old and new problems that weren't initially apparent.

☐ **Why would it be harder to learn to drive a car if you had never been in one before? Why is it hard for deaf children to learn spoken language when they can easily be reinforced for correct speech sounds?**

Social learning theorists argue that we learn much by observing other people who model a behavior, or by simply hearing about something. This is called **observational (or vicarious) learning.** It would be harder to learn to drive a car without ever having been in one because you would lack a model of "driving behavior." It is hard for deaf children to learn spoken language because they have no auditory model of correct speech.

The extent to which we imitate behaviors learned through observation depends on our motivation to do so. One important motivation is any reward or punishment we have seen the behavior bring. When a consequence isn't experienced firsthand, but only occurs to other people, it is called **vicarious reinforcement** or **vicarious punishment.**

CRITICAL THINKING AND APPLICATIONS

1. Imagine biting into a slice of lemon. Your mouth probably starts to pucker, and you begin to secrete saliva, even though you are not actually experiencing the sour lemon taste. Use classical conditioning principles to explain this reaction.
2. Imagine that you want to keep your dog from barking and annoying the neighbors. What kind of reinforcement would you use to do this?
3. Think about your daily schedule. What kinds of things do you do every day that can be called operant behaviors?
4. Are secondary reinforcers the same for everyone? Explain your answer.
5. What attitudes about introductory psychology have you learned from observing your instructor?
6. Based on what you have read, would you recommend biofeedback to someone who suffers from motion sickness or headaches? Why or why not?

On the Web...

Visit these online resources at our Companion Website www.prenhall.com/morris

The Psychology Place

Learning Activities   1. Principles of Learning in the Real World, p. 163

Research News   2. Songbird Brain: Cell Count Predicts Learning, p. 163
3. Beyond Pavlov's Dogs, p. 164
4. Giving Children Rewards: A Right Way and a Wrong Way, p. 173
5. Should Creativity Be Rewarded?, p. 174

Games

1. You're the Duck, p. 163
2. Train the Chicken, p. 165
3. Consequences Matching Game, p. 177

Web Links

1. **http://www.usq.edu.au/users/rogerscl/learning/index.htm**, p. 163
Learning Web site about a variety of related sites.
2. **http://www.pigeon.psy.tufts.psy.tufts.edu/psych26/classical.htm**, p. 165
Animal Cognition Home Page offers a good explanation of classical conditioning.
3. **http://www.vams.edu/department_of_psychiatry/slides/html/learning/index.htm**, p. 168
Memory, Learning and Behavior Modification Web site has slides and examples and explains types of memory, reinforcement, habituation, sensitization, conditioning, punishment, and generalization.
4. **http://www.pigeon.psy.tufts.psy.tufts.edu/psych26/operant.htm**, p. 168
Animal Cognition Home Page offers a good explanation of operant conditioning.
5. **http://mmg2.im.med.umich.edu/~klueug/training.html**, p. 170
Use of Operant Conditioning in Dog Training describes theories of reinforcement and shaping and then gives examples of implementing these theories.
6. **http://www-anw.cs.umass.edu/~mharmon/rltutorial/frames.html**, p. 172
Reinforcement Learning: A Tutorial.
7. **http://dutch.nl/bart/sitemap.htm & http://dutch.nl/bart/abcframe.htm**, p. 177
Behavior Is What Business Is All About explains antecedents, behavior, and consequences as they relate to reinforcement.
8. **http://www.brembs.net/learning/general_introduction.html**, p. 185
Compares and contrasts operant and classical conditioning with helpful diagrams.

Explore these topics on the Mind Matters CD-ROM

Mind Matters

1. Learning Through Association: Classical Conditioning, p. 163
2. Learning from Consequences: Operant Conditioning, p. 168
3. Opening the Black Box: Cognitive Learning, p. 185

6

MEMORY

ALL OF US ARE ABLE TO REMEMBER PAST EXPERIENCES, THOUGHTS, AND images, as well as previously learned information and skills. This is probably why we tend to take memory for granted. Only when confronted with people whose memories are exceptionally good—or exceptionally bad—do we begin to realize how much we rely on this multifaceted mental faculty. Consider these examples of people with unusual memories:

- The world-renowned conductor Arturo Toscanini memorized every single note written for every instrument in some 250 symphonies and all the music and lyrics for more than 100 operas. Once, when he could not locate a score of Joachim Raff's Quartet No. 5, he sat down and wrote it out entirely from memory—even though he had not seen or played the score for decades. With the exception of a single note, Toscanini reproduced the score perfectly (Neisser, 1982).

- A young man known as HM who had parts of his brain removed to treat his epilepsy could not remember anything that occurred after his surgery. If he mowed the lawn on Monday, for example, he didn't know where to look for the lawn mower on Tuesday. He read the same magazine over and over, each time, as if for the first time (Milner, Corkin, & Teuber, 1968).

- Before being stricken with a viral illness, a 29-year-old woman known as MZ told researchers she could remember "the exact day of the week of future or past events of almost anything that touched my life . . . all personal telephone numbers . . . colors of interiors and what people wore . . . pieces of music. . . . [R]ecalling a picture, as a painting in a museum, was like standing in the museum looking at it again" (Klatzky, 1980).

Accounts of people with such extraordinary or dysfunctional memories raise many questions about the nature of memory. Why are some people so much better at remembering things than others are? Are they born with this ability, or do they hone the skill of precise recall? How do we account for people whose memories don't function properly? And why is it that remembering may sometimes be so easy (think of how effortlessly baseball fans remember the batting averages of their favorite players) and other times so difficult (as when we grope for answers on an exam)? Why do we find it so hard to remember something that happened only a few months back, yet we can recall in vivid detail some other event that occurred decades ago? Just how does memory work, and what makes it fail?

Among the first to seek scientific answers to these questions was the nineteenth-century German psychologist Hermann Ebbinghaus. Using himself as a subject, Ebbinghaus composed lists of "nonsense syllables," meaningless combinations of letters, such as PIB, WOL, or TEB. He memorized lists of 13 nonsense syllables each. Then, after varying amounts of time, he tried to relearn each list of syllables. He found that the longer he waited after first learning a list, the longer it took to learn the list again. Most of the information was lost in the first few hours. Ebbinghaus's contributions dominated memory research for many years.

Today many psychologists find it useful to view memory as a series of steps in which we process information, much like a computer stores and retrieves data (Massaro & Cowan, 1993). Together these steps form what is known as the **information-processing model** of memory (see Figure 6–1). In this chapter you will find terms like *encoding*, *storage*, and *retrieval*—convenient ways of comparing human memory to computers. But the social, emotional, and biological factors that make us human also separate our memories from computers; our senses would be bombarded with far more information than our senses could possibly process. The first stage of information processing, then, involves selecting some of this material to think about and remember.

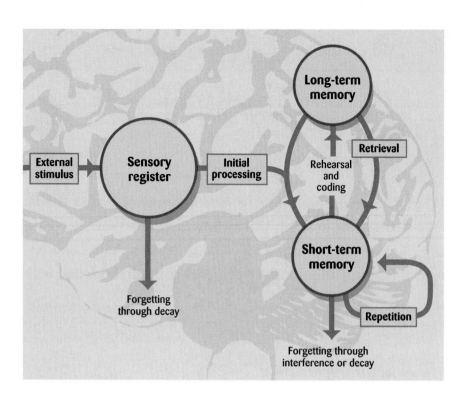

FIGURE 6–1

The sequence of information processing. Raw information flows from the senses into the sensory registers, where it fades away or is processed in terms of existing knowledge and information. Information that is determined to be meaningful is passed on for further processing in short-term memory; the rest is discarded. Once in short-term memory, information is either forgotten or transferred into long-term memory, where it can be stored and retrieved when necessary.

The Sensory Registers

What is the role of sensory registers?

Look slowly around the room. Each glance takes in an enormous amount of visual information, including colors, shapes, textures, relative brightness, and shadows. At the same time you pick up sounds, smells, and other kinds of sensory data. All of this raw information flows from your senses into what are known as the **sensory registers.** These registers are like waiting rooms in which information enters and stays for only a short time. Whether we remember any of this information depends on which operations we perform on it, as you will see throughout this chapter. Although there are registers for each of our senses, the visual and auditory registers have been studied most extensively.

Visual and Auditory Registers

What would happen if auditory information faded as quickly as visual information does?

Although the sensory registers have virtually unlimited capacity (Cowan, 1988), information disappears from them quite rapidly. A simple experiment can demonstrate how much visual information we take in—and how quickly it is lost. Bring an instant camera into a darkened room, and take a photograph using a flash. During the split second that the room is lit up by the flash, your visual register will absorb a surprising amount of information about the room and its contents. Try to hold on to that visual image, or *icon*, as long as you can. You will find that in a few seconds it is gone. Then compare your remembered image of the room with what you actually saw, as captured in the photograph. You will discover that your visual register took in far more information than you were able to retain for even a few seconds.

Information-processing model
A computerlike model used to describe the way humans encode, store, and retrieve information.

Sensory registers
Entry points for raw information from the senses.

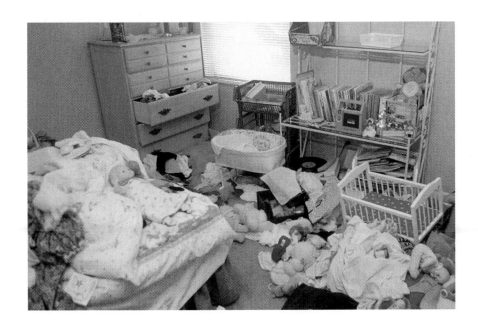

Look quickly at this photo of a cluttered room, and then try to recall as many details as you can. Your visual register will take in far more information than you can remember from a quick glance.

Experiments by George Sperling (1960) clearly demonstrate how quickly information disappears from the visual register. Sperling flashed groups of letters, organized into three rows, on a screen for just a fraction of a second. When the letters were gone, he sounded a tone to tell his participants which row of letters to recall: A high-pitched tone indicated that they should try to remember the top row of letters, a low-pitched tone meant that they should recall the bottom row, and a medium-pitched tone signaled them to recall the middle row. Using this *partial-report technique*, Sperling found that if he sounded the tone immediately after the letters were flashed, his subjects could usually recall 3 or 4 of the letters in any of the three rows; that is, they seemed to have at least 9 of the original 12 letters in their visual registers. But if he waited for even 1 second before sounding the tone, his participants were able to recall only 1 or 2 letters from any single row—in just 1 second, then, all but 4 or 5 of the original set of 12 letters had vanished from their visual registers.

Visual information may actually disappear from the visual register even more rapidly than Sperling thought (Cowan, 1988). In everyday life new visual information keeps coming into the register, and this new information replaces the old information almost immediately, a process often called *masking*. Under normal viewing conditions, visual information is erased from the sensory register in about a quarter of a second and is replaced by new information—fortunately, because otherwise the visual information would simply pile up in the sensory register and become hopelessly scrambled.

Auditory information fades more slowly than visual information. The auditory equivalent of the icon, the *echo*, tends to last for several seconds, which, given the nature of speech, is certainly lucky for us. Otherwise, "*You* did it!" would be indistinguishable from "You *did* it!" because we would be unable to remember the emphasis on the first words by the time the last words were registered.

Initial Processing

Why does some information capture our attention, whereas other information goes unnoticed?

If information disappears from the sensory registers so rapidly, how do we remember anything for more than a second or two? Through **attention**—the

Attention
The selection of some incoming information for further processing.

When having a conversation with someone in a crowded environment, we filter out the other conversations, a behavior known as the *cocktail-party phenomenon.*

process of *selective* looking, listening, smelling, tasting, and feeling—we choose some of the incoming information for further processing (see Figure 6–1). In the process of attending, we also give meaning to the information that is coming in. Look at the page in front of you. You will see a series of black lines on a white page. Until you recognize these lines as letters and words, they are just meaningless marks. For you to make sense of this jumble of data, the information in the sensory registers must be processed for meaning.

How do we select what we are going to pay attention to at any given moment, and how do we give that information meaning? Donald Broadbent (1958) suggested that a filtering process at the entrance to the nervous system allows only those stimuli that meet certain requirements to pass through. Those stimuli that do get through the filter are compared with what we already know, so that we can recognize them and figure out what they mean. If you and a friend are sitting in a restaurant talking, you filter out all other conversations taking place around you, a process known as the *cocktail-party phenomenon* (Cherry, 1966; Wood & Cowan, 1995). Although you later might be able to describe certain characteristics of those other conversations, such as whether the people speaking were men or women and whether the words were spoken loudly or softly, according to Broadbent you normally cannot recall what was being discussed, even at neighboring tables. Because you filtered out those other conversations, the processing of that information did not proceed far enough for you to understand what you heard.

Broadbent's filtering theory helps explain some aspects of attention, but sometimes unattended stimuli do capture our attention. To return to the restaurant example, if someone nearby were to mention your name, your attention probably would shift to that conversation. Anne Treisman (1960, 1964) modified the filter theory to account for phenomena like this. She contended that the filter is not a simple on/off switch but rather a variable control, like the volume control on a radio, which can "turn down" unwanted signals without rejecting them entirely. According to this view, although we may be paying attention to only some incoming information, we monitor the other signals at a low volume. In this way we can shift our attention if we pick up something particularly meaningful. This automatic processing works even when we are asleep: Parents often wake up immediately when they hear their baby crying but sleep through other, louder noises.

To summarize, we consciously attend to very little of the information in our sensory registers; instead we select some information and process those signals further as we work to recognize and understand them. Unattended information receives at least some initial processing, however, so that we can shift our attention to any element of our surroundings that strikes us as potentially meaningful. The information that we *do* attend to enters our short-term memory.

REVIEW QUESTIONS

1. Raw information from the senses reaches the ____ ____ before it disappears or is further processed.

2. Auditory information fades from the registers more slowly than ____ information.

3. The selection process that allows us to retain information after it has arrived from the senses is termed ____.

4. We are able to focus on some information while ignoring other information. This is called the ____ ____ phenomenon.

5. We tend to shift our attention when we pick up on something that is particularly ____.

Indicate whether the following statements are true (T) or false (F).

6. The sensory registers have virtually unlimited capacity. ____

7. Some kinds of information are stored permanently in the sensory registers. ____

8. New visual information replaces old almost immediately through masking. ____

9. The filter theory as modified by Treisman holds that attention is like an on/off switch. ____

Answers: 1. sensory registers. 2. visual. 3. attention. 4. cocktail-party. 5. meaningful. 6. T. 7. F. 8. T. 9. false.

Short-Term Memory

What are the two primary tasks of short-term memory?

Short-term memory (STM) holds the information we are thinking about or are aware of at any given moment (Stern, 1985). When you listen to a conversation or a song on the radio, when you watch a television show or a football game, when you become aware of a leg cramp or a headache—in all these cases you are using STM both to hold on to and to think about new information coming in from the sensory registers. STM has two primary tasks: to store new information briefly and to work on that (and other) information. STM is sometimes called *working memory* to emphasize the active or working component of this memory system (Baddeley, 1986; Baddeley & Hitch, 1994).

Capacity of STM

How does chunking improve the capacity of STM?

The video game fanatic is oblivious to the outside world. Chess masters at tournaments demand complete silence. You shut yourself in a quiet room to study for final exams. All these examples illustrate that STM can handle only so much information at any given moment. Some 40 years ago psychologists proposed that STM could hold at most five to ten bits of information at the same time (Miller, 1956; Sperling, 1960). More recently, research suggests that STM can hold as much information as can be repeated or rehearsed in 1.5 to 2 seconds (Baddeley, 1986; Schweickert & Boruff, 1986).

Short-term memory (STM)
Working memory; briefly stores and processes selected information from the sensory registers.

Chess players demand complete silence as they consider their next move. This is because there is a definite limit to the amount of information STM can handle at any given moment.

To get a better idea of the limits of STM, read the first row of letters in the following list just once. Then close your eyes and try to remember the letters in the correct sequence before going on to the next row.

1. C X W
2. M N K T Y
3. R P J H B Z S
4. G B M P V Q F J D
5. E G Q W J P B R H K A

Like most people, you probably found rows 1 and 2 fairly easy, row 3 a bit harder, row 4 extremely difficult, and row 5 impossible to remember after just one reading. You have just experienced the relatively limited capacity of STM.

Now try reading through the following set of 12 letters just once and see if you can repeat them.

TJYFAVMCFKIB

How many letters were you able to recall? In all likelihood, not all 12. But what if you had been asked to remember the following 12 letters instead?

TV FBI JFK YMCA

Could you do it? Almost certainly the answer is yes. These are the same 12 letters as before, but here they are grouped into four separate "words." This way of grouping and organizing information so that it fits into meaningful units is called **chunking.** The 12 letters have been chunked into four meaningful elements that can readily be handled by STM—they are well below the 5- to 10-item limit of STM, and they can be repeated in less than 2 seconds. Try to remember this list of numbers:

106619451812

Remembering 12 separate digits is usually very difficult, but try chunking the list into 3 groups of 4:

1066 1945 1812

For those who take an interest in military history, these three chunks will be much easier to remember than 12 unrelated digits.

By chunking words into sentences or sentence fragments, we can process an even greater amount of information in STM (Aaronson & Scarborough, 1976, 1977; Baddeley, 1994; Tulving & Patkau, 1962). For example, suppose you want to remember the following list of words: tree, song, hat, sparrow, box, lilac, cat. One strategy would be to cluster as many of them as possible into phrases or sentences: "The sparrow in the tree sings a song"; "a lilac hat in the box"; "the cat in the hat." But isn't there a limit to this strategy? Would 5 sentences be as easy to remember for a short time as 5 single words? No. As the size of any individual chunk increases, the number of chunks that can be held in STM declines (Simon, 1974). STM can easily handle 5 unrelated letters or words at once, but 5 unrelated sentences are much harder to remember.

The limit of STM, then, might better be conceived as a 2-second limit rather than a 5- to 10-item limit: In both cases there are only 5 items of information to be remembered, but it takes longer to repeat 5 sentences than it does to repeat 5 words. If there is a 5- to 10-item limit on STM, the sentences should be just as easy to remember as the individual words. But if there is a 2-second limit on information in STM, the sentences should be more difficult to remember than the individual words—and this is what research confirms.

Keep in mind that STM usually has to perform more than one task at a time (Baddeley & Hitch, 1994). During the brief moments you spent memorizing the

Chunking
The grouping of information into meaningful units for easier handling by short-term memory.

preceding rows of letters, you probably gave them your full attention. But normally you have to attend to new incoming information while you work on whatever is already present in short-term memory. Competition between these two tasks for the limited work space in STM means that neither task will be done as well as it could be.

Encoding in STM

Is material stored in short-term memory as it sounds or as it looks?

Just how do we *encode* information for storage in STM? This question has sparked controversy for years. Research confirms that strings of letters or numbers are stored in STM *phonologically*—that is, in a manner based on speech (Baddeley, 1986). We encode verbal information according to how it sounds, even if we see the word, letter, or number on a page rather than hear it spoken. Numerous experiments have shown that when people try to retrieve material from STM, they generally mix up items that sound alike and that are spoken alike, even if they look different (Sperling, 1960). For example, a list of words such as *mad, man, mat,* and *cap* is much tougher for most people to recall accurately than is a list like *pit, day, cow,* and *bar* (Baddeley, 1986).

Not all material in short-term memory is stored phonologically, however. At least some material is stored in visual form, while other information is retained based on its meaning (Cowan, 1988; Matlin, 1989). For example, we don't have to convert visual data such as maps, diagrams, and paintings into sound before we can code them into STM and think about them. And deaf people rely primarily on shapes rather than sounds to retain information in STM (Conrad, 1972; Frumkin & Ainsfield, 1977). In fact, it appears that the capacity for visual encoding in STM actually exceeds that for phonological coding (Reed, 1992). A good illustration of the superiority of visual encoding in STM is an experiment conducted by Nielsen and Smith (1973). They asked their participants to pay close attention to either a verbal description of a face or an actual picture of a face for 4 seconds. The participants were then asked to match features of a test face with the features they had just seen or heard described. Because it took much longer to recognize the face from the verbal description ("large ears," "small eyes," and so on), researchers concluded that visual images tend to be more efficiently encoded and decoded than verbal ones.

Retention and Retrieval in STM

Why do we forget information from STM?

Why do we forget material stored in short-term memory? According to the **decay theory,** the mere passing of time causes the strength of memory to decrease, thereby making the material harder to remember. Most of the evidence supporting the decay theory comes from experiments known as *distracter studies.* For example, Peterson and Peterson (1959) first asked participants to learn a sequence of letters, such as *PSQ*. Next, the participants were given a 3-digit number, such as *167*, and were asked to count backward from 167 by threes: 167, 164, 161, and so on, for up to 18 seconds. At the end of that period they were asked to recall the three letters. The results of this test astonished the experimenters. The subjects showed a rapid decline in their ability to remember the letters. Counting backward was assumed not to interfere with remembering, so the researchers concluded that the forgotten letters had faded from short-term memory in a matter of seconds. Decay, then, seems to be at least partly responsible for forgetting in short-term memory.

Decay theory
The theory that the passage of time causes forgetting.

"Hold on a second, Bob. I'm putting you on a stickie."

Interference may also lead to forgetting in STM (Shiffrin & Cook, 1978). **Interference theory** holds that information gets mixed up with, or pushed aside by, other information, becoming harder to remember. Some of this forgetting may be due to the limited capacity of STM, as new information pushes out old. Interference is strongest when the new information resembles the old in some way. If you are counting items, keeping a running total in your head or repeating a phone number over and over to remember it, you may not lose your train of thought if some friends start talking to you about a movie. But if someone begins counting another set of items or calls your attention to some other group of numbers, you will quickly become confused about which set of digits was yours.

Now, without looking back, try to recall the 5 rows of letters you learned on page 204. You probably have forgotten them, because material in short-term memory disappears in 15–20 seconds unless it is rehearsed or practiced (Bourne et al., 1986).

Losing much of what is initially stored in STM provides space for new information and keeps us from being overwhelmed with a jumble of irrelevant, trivial, or unrelated data. But sometimes we want to hold on to some information for longer than 15 or 20 seconds, and at other times we want to remember a new piece of information permanently. How do we keep from forgetting in these cases?

Rote Rehearsal

Is repeating something over and over again a good way to remember it?

The best way to hold on to information for only a minute or two is through **rote rehearsal**, also called *maintenance rehearsal*, in which you repeat information over and over, silently or out loud (Greene, 1987). This is not the most efficient way to remember something permanently, but it is useful for a short time—perhaps until you can dial a telephone number you've just looked up. In fact, if you repeat something to yourself but cannot recall it later, you may still *recognize* the

Interference theory
The theory that interference from other information causes forgetting.

Rote rehearsal
Retaining information in STM simply by repeating it over and over.

FIGURE 6–2

A penny for your thoughts. Which of these accurately illustrates a real U.S. penny? The answer is on page 208.

information when you hear or use it again. If, for example, someone asks you 20 minutes later for that telephone number you looked up, you are not likely to recall it. But if someone asks instead, "Were you dialing 555-1356?" you might recognize the number if you had repeated it often enough (Glenberg, Smith, & Green, 1977).

Rote rehearsal is a very common memory strategy. Millions of students have learned the alphabet and multiplication tables by doggedly repeating letters and numbers, but mere repetition usually does not lead to subsequent recall (Greene, 1987). Stop here and try to draw from memory the front side of a U.S. penny. Now look at Figure 6–2 and pick the illustration that matches your memory of a real penny. For most people this task is surprisingly difficult: We see tens of thousands of pennies, but most of us cannot accurately draw one or even pick one out from among other, similar objects (Nickerson & Adams, 1979).

If you simply repeat something more often than something else, will that improve later recall? Not necessarily (Craik & Watkins, 1973). It is not so much the *amount* of rehearsal that increases memory but the *type* of rehearsal—and rote memorizing is unlikely to be very effective over the long term.

Elaborative Rehearsal

What is the best way to go about remembering something?

If simple rote repetition is not sufficient, what do we have to do to ensure that information in STM will be remembered for a long time? Most researchers believe that we need to practice **elaborative rehearsal,** a method of relating new information to something that we already know (Postman, 1975). Suppose that you had to remember that the French word *poire* means "pear." You are already familiar with *pear,* both as a word and as a fruit. *Poire,* however, means nothing to you. To remember what it means, you have to connect it to *pear,* either by telling yourself that "*pear* and *poire* both begin with *p*" or by associating *poire* with the familiar taste and image of a pear.

Clearly elaborative rehearsal calls for a deeper and more meaningful processing of new information than does simple rote repetition (Craik & Lockhart, 1972). Unless we rehearse in this way, we will probably forget new information quickly. People who suffer concussions, for example, cannot remember things that happened just before the injury, even though they *can* remember what happened some time earlier. This condition is known as **retrograde amnesia.** The events right before the accident were at the short-term memory level and had not been rehearsed enough to be remembered for more than a brief time. Therefore they were forgotten.

Another example of rehearsal failure may be familiar to you. Have you ever been part of a group in which people were taking turns speaking up—perhaps introducing themselves briefly on the first day of class or at the beginning of a panel discussion in front of an audience? Did you notice that you forgot virtually

Elaborative rehearsal
The linking of new information in short-term memory to familiar material stored in long-term memory.

Retrograde amnesia
The inability to recall events immediately preceding an accident or injury, but without loss of earlier memory.

everything that was said by the person who spoke just before you did? According to recent research, you failed to remember because you did not elaboratively rehearse what that person was saying (Bond, Pitre, & Van Leeuwen, 1991). As the time for your own introduction approached, your attention shifted increasingly to what you yourself were going to say, and as a result you spent little or no time elaboratively rehearsing what the person before you was saying. That person's comments simply "went in one ear and out the other" while you were preoccupied with thinking about your own remarks.

Trying to remember dreams also involves the rehearsal process. Dreams take place in STM, and unless they are elaboratively rehearsed, they are likely to be forgotten quickly. Cohen (1974) asked one group of experimental participants to telephone for the weather report immediately after they woke up and to write down the day's expected temperature. This task effectively prevented them from rehearsing their dreams. A second group of participants was instructed to lie still for 90 seconds upon waking—the approximate time it took the first group to call for the weather report—and then to write down their dreams. This group could think about and rehearse their dreams while waiting. Only 33 percent of the first group could recall their dreams, while 63 percent of the second group remembered theirs.

Elaborative rehearsal is crucial to future recall. Before we look further into the nature of this process, we need to know more about long-term memory. (The accurate illustration of a penny in Figure 6–2 is the third from the left.)

REVIEW QUESTIONS

1. ____ memory is what we are thinking about at any given moment. Its function is to briefly store new information and to work on that and other information.

2. ____ enables us to group items into meaningful units.

3. Strings of letters and numbers are encoded in short-term memory ____.

4. Which of the following explain(s) why we forget material stored in short-term memory?

   a. decay theory

   b. interference theory

   c. cocktail-party phenomenon

   d. chunking

5. "STM can hold, at most, 7 bits of information." True or false.

6. ____ rehearsal, or simply repeating information over and over, is an effective way of retaining information for just a minute or two.

7. To ensure that information in short-term memory will be remembered for a long time, the best strategy to use is ____ rehearsal, which involves relating new information to something that we already know.

8. When people cannot remember events immediately before an accident, they are experiencing ____ ____.

Answers: 1. short-term. 2. chunking. 3. phonologically 4. a, b. 5. F. 6. rote. 7. elaborative. 8. retrograde amnesia.

Long-Term Memory

How do semantic memory, episodic memory, and procedural memory differ?

Long-term memory (LTM)
The portion of memory that is more or less permanent, corresponding to everything we "know."

Everything that we "know" is stored in **long-term memory (LTM)**—the words to a popular song; the results of the last election; the meaning of "justice"; the fact that George Washington was the first president of the United States; the meaning of abbreviations such as TV, FBI, JFK, and YMCA; what you ate for dinner last night; the date you were born; and what you are supposed to be doing tomorrow at 4 P.M. Endel Tulving (1972, 1985) of the University of Toronto contended that LTM should be divided into separate memory systems. One system, called **semantic memory,** is much like a dictionary or encyclopedia, filled with *general* facts and information, such as the first 5 examples in this paragraph. When you see the words *George Washington*, you call up all sorts of additional information from LTM: 1776, the first president, "father of our country," Mount Vernon, crossing the Delaware. This kind of information is stored in semantic memory.

But other information in LTM is more personal and specific. This personal memory system, known as **episodic memory,** encompasses specific events that have personal meaning for us, like the last three examples in the first paragraph (Tulving, 1972, 1985). If semantic memory is like an encyclopedia or dictionary, then episodic memory is like a diary, even though it may include events that we did not participate in but that are important to us. Episodic memory lets you go back in time to a childhood birthday party, to the day you got your driver's license, to the story of how your parents met.

More recently, a third memory system, called **procedural memory,** has also been proposed. Procedural memory refers to our ability to learn skills, complex perceptual-motor tasks, and habits. Riding a bicycle, driving a car, swimming, playing a musical instrument, and typing are all examples of procedural memory. Information stored in procedural memory usually consists of a precise sequence of coordinated movements that are often difficult to describe in words. While repetition, and in some cases extended practice, are required to master such skills, once learned they are rarely lost.

Information in LTM is highly organized and cross-referenced, like a cataloging system in a library. The more carefully we organize information, the more likely we will be to retrieve it later.

Encoding in LTM

How are long-term memories encoded?

Can you picture the shape of Florida? Do you know what a trumpet sounds like? Can you imagine the smell of a rose or the taste of coffee? When you answer the telephone, can you sometimes identify the caller immediately, just from the sound of the voice? Your ability to do most or all of these things means that at

---

SUMMARY TABLE

Types of Long-Term Memory Systems

Memory System	Definition	Example
Semantic memory	Portion of long-term memory that stores general facts and information	Recalling the capital of Ohio
Episodic memory	Portion of long-term memory that stores specific information that has personal meaning	Recalling where you went on your first date
Procedural memory	Portion of long-term memory that stores information relating to skills, habits, and complex perceptual-motor tasks	Riding a bicycle, driving a car, playing a musical instrument, typing, ice-skating

Semantic memory
The portion of long-term memory that stores general facts and information.

Episodic memory
The portion of long-term memory that stores more specific information that has personal meaning.

Procedural memory
The portion of long-term memory that stores information relating to skills, habits, and other complex perceptual-motor tasks.

Once skills such as playing tennis have been stored in our procedural memory, they are seldom lost.

least some long-term memories are encoded in terms of nonverbal images: shapes, sounds, smells, tastes, and so on (Cowan, 1988).

Yet most of the information in LTM seems to be encoded in terms of meaning. If material is especially familiar (the national anthem, say, or the opening of the Gettysburg Address) you may have stored it verbatim in LTM, and often you can retrieve it word for word when you need it. Generally speaking, however, we do not use verbatim storage in LTM. If someone tells you a long, rambling story, you may listen to every word, but you certainly will not try to remember the story verbatim. Instead you will extract the main points and try to remember those. Even simple sentences are usually encoded in terms of their meaning. Thus when people are asked to remember that "Tom called John," they often find it impossible to remember later whether they were told "Tom called John" or "John was called by Tom." They usually remember the meaning of the message but not the exact words (Bourne et al., 1986).

Information in STM gets transferred to LTM when, through *elaborative rehearsal*, you first extract and then link its meaning to as much of the material already in LTM as possible. The more links or associations you can make, the more likely you are to remember the new information later, just as it is easier to find a book in the library if it is cataloged under many headings rather than just one or two. We tend to remember semantic material better than episodic material because episodic material is quickly dated, so we code few cross-references for it. For instance, you may remember that you ate a hamburger last night, but normally there is no good reason to relate that piece of information to anything else in LTM, so it is not something you are likely to remember for very long. But if you had been a vegetarian for years and had found the very thought of eating beef repulsive, then eating that hamburger was a very meaningful event, and it is probably linked to many other facts in your LTM. As a result, you are unlikely to forget it for quite some time.

There are many different ways of rehearsing material. Think for a moment about how you might study for an examination in this course. Your approach will depend on whether you expect a multiple-choice test or an essay exam. Research confirms that the way we encode material for storage in LTM affects the ease with which we can retrieve it later (Flexser & Tulving, 1978; Leonard & Whitten, 1983). We examine this principle in greater detail later in the chapter when we look at how to improve memory.

Implicit Memory

Do we sometimes remember things we never intended to remember?

Most of the memories we've considered so far are things that you intended to remember, at least at one time. Psychologists call such memories **explicit memory.** But you also acquire a great deal of information that you never intended to remember. For example, have you ever misplaced something, like eyeglasses, and then retraced your steps trying to find them? "I came in the door, put down my keys; then I went to the kitchen, where I put down the packages . . ." Then you go to the kitchen and find your glasses, although you may not actually recall having left them there. Or perhaps you have had the experience of recalling exactly where on a page a particular piece of information appeared, even though you did not try to remember the item or its placement. If you stop to think about it, the fact that you have such memories is really quite remarkable. You made no deliberate effort to remember either of these things, yet in each case memories were apparently formed outside your awareness and without any conscious elaborative processing on your part (Adler, 1990; Cowan, 1988). Similarly, memories are sometimes called up spontaneously (Roediger, 1990). The smell of a particular perfume or the taste of a distinctive cake may bring back a flood of memories. In these cases, too, you first stored and then retrieved information without any conscious intention to do so. Moreover, the recall of stored information does not include any conscious awareness of the occasion when it was acquired. Psychologists call such unintentional memories **implicit memory** (Graf & Schacter, 1985; Jacoby & Witherspoon, 1982; Squire, Knowlton, & Musen, 1993; Tulving & Schacter, 1990).

The importance of implicit memory might become clearer if you think about the following experiment. Schab (1990) presented a group of students with a list of 40 adjectives; he asked them to write down the opposite of each word and informed them that the next day he would ask them to recall the words they had written. The smell of chocolate permeated the air surrounding one group of students while they were writing their list of words. The next day, adding a chocolate smell to the air significantly increased the number of words these students recalled from the previous day. In other words, the smell of chocolate somehow became linked to the words they wrote, and the smell then became an effective cue or "hint" that helped them find and recall the correct words. This kind of thing happens all the time: Whenever we try (explicitly) to memorize something, we are also unintentionally (implicitly) picking up facts about the context in which the learning occurs. Those facts, now in implicit memory, become useful cues when we later try to retrieve the corresponding information from explicit memory.

When contextual or environmental cues, like the smell of chocolate in the preceding example, enhance or hinder our ability to recall information, it is referred to as a *context-dependent memory* effect. Context-dependent memory effects have been demonstrated in a wide variety of both common and unusual circumstances. For instance, scuba divers were shown to recall a list of words better if learned underwater and recalled underwater, than if learned underwater and recalled on the beach (Baddeley, 1975). Similar context effects have been demonstrated with background music (Balch & Lewis, 1996), odors (Herz, 1997), and even classrooms (Smith, Glenberg, & Bjork, 1978). Unfortunately, context-dependent memory effects tend to be small, so studying in the same classroom where you are

Looking into a bakery window, perhaps smelling the aromas of the cakes inside, may trigger distinct memories associated with those sights and smells, formed many years ago. Anyone who has read Marcel Proust's *Remembrance of Things Past* will recall the famous scene in which the main character dips a madeleine, a kind of French cookie, into a cup of tea and is flooded with memories.

Explicit memory
Memory for information that was intentionally committed to memory or intentionally retrieved from memory.

Implicit memory
Memory for information that was either unintentionally committed to memory or unintentionally retrieved from memory.

scheduled to take an exam will probably not do too much to improve your grade (although it probably won't hurt). Nevertheless, contextual cues are occasionally used by police who sometimes take witnesses back to the scene of a crime in the hope that they will recall crucial details that can be used to solve the crime.

In addition to being influenced by external cues (like odors or sounds), our ability to accurately recall information is also affected by internal cues in what is known as *state-dependent memory*. State-dependent memory refers to the intriguing finding that people who learn material in a particular physiological or mental state tend to recall that material better if they return to that same state.

Understanding the workings of implicit memory has concrete implications for ordinary life. Say you are having difficulty remembering something. If possible, return to the setting in which you first learned it, or try to re-create the setting vividly in your mind in as much detail as possible, including the thoughts and feelings you were having at the time. Your implicit memory of the setting should help trigger your memory of the information you are trying to recall.

Storage and Retrieval in LTM

Are memories accurate, or do they change over time?

We saw earlier that information in short-term memory disappears in less than 20 seconds unless it is rehearsed, but under the proper circumstances we can often recall an astonishing amount of information from LTM. Adults who had graduated from high school more than 40 years earlier were still able to recognize the names of 75 percent of their classmates (Bahrick, Bahrick, & Wittlinger, 1974). Not everything stored in LTM can be remembered when we need it, however. A classic example of this is the *tip-of-the-tongue phenomenon*, or *TOT* (Brown & McNeil, 1966). Everyone has had the experience of knowing that he or she knows a word but is not quite able to recall it. We say that such a word is "right on the tip of my tongue." If you want to experience TOT yourself, try naming Snow White's Seven Dwarfs (Meyer & Hilterbrand, 1984).

The TOT phenomenon has several intriguing characteristics (Brown, 1991; Brown & McNeil, 1966). While everyone experiences TOT episodes, these experiences become more frequent during stressful situations and as people get older. Moreover, other words—with a sound or meaning similar to the word you are seeking—occur to you while you are in the TOT state and interfere with your attempt to recall the desired word. The harder you try, the worse the TOT state gets. The best way to recall a blocked word, then, is to stop trying to recall it. The word you were searching for may just pop into your head minutes, or even hours, after you stopped consciously searching for it (Norman & Bobrow, 1976).

Such TOT episodes demonstrate the power of interference to disrupt memory. The TOT phenomenon occurs most often with words that are seldom used. The infrequent use of these words may weaken the link between their meaning and their pronunciation (Burke, McKay, Worthley, & Wade, 1991).

The effects of interference are not limited to TOT episodes. In fact, interference often explains why people cannot retrieve information from long-term memory. Interference can come from two directions. First, new material may interfere with material already in long-term memory, a phenomenon known as **retroactive interference.** If you learn a new way of doing something, for example, you may find it difficult to recall how you had done it for years. Second, interference may also proceed the other way, with old information blocking a similar, new memory through **proactive interference.** These two processes are illustrated in Figure 6–3.

Because interference strains our ability to retrieve information from long-term memory, knowing how to reduce or overcome interference is useful. As the TOT phenomenon suggests, similarity is the primary determinant of interfer-

Retroactive interference
The process by which new information interferes with old information already in memory.

Proactive interference
The process by which old material already in memory interferes with new information.

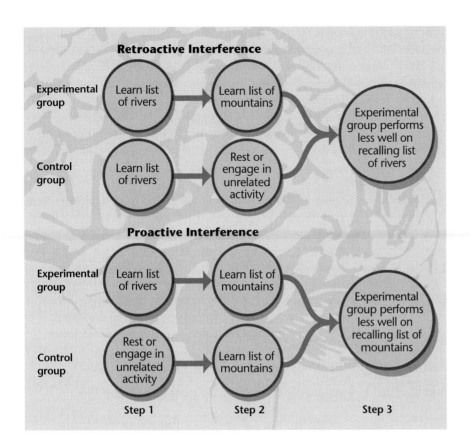

FIGURE 6–3
Diagram of experiments measuring retroactive and proactive interference. In the case of retroactive interference, the experimental group usually does not perform as well on tests of recall as those in the control group, who experience no retroactive interference from a list of words in Step 2. In the case of proactive interference, people in the experimental group suffer the effects of proactive interference from the list in Step 1; when asked to recall the list from Step 2, they perform less well than those in the control group.

ence: Items are likely to interfere with one another to the extent that they are similar to one another.

In this light consider the following experiment, conducted by Bower & Mann (1992). Participants learned two lists of 21 letters each: SOJFNUGPAHWM-SELICBQTA and YADILOHSREKNABYHTLAEW. Then the participants were asked to recall the first list. Retroactive interference occurred because the second list consists of a sequence of letters just like the first list and thus interferes with it. But when some of the participants were told that the second list spells WEALTHY BANKERS HOLIDAY backward, interference dropped significantly. With the new information, the second list could be distinguished from the first list, so there was less interference between the two lists. You can see that to learn something successfully, you should try to avoid interference—or at least keep it to a minimum—by making the new material as distinctive as possible. The more dissimilar something is from other things you have already learned, the less likely it will be to mingle and interfere with other material in memory.

The Effects of Cues on Retrieval from LTM   Two other factors also affect retrieval from long-term memory: The more extensively the information was linked to other material when it was first entered into LTM and the more cues we have to work with at the time of retrieval, the more likely we are to recall the information. If you are asked, "Who was the twenty-second president of the United States?" you might have difficulty recalling his name, as the only useful retrieval cue is "twenty-second." But if you are also told, "His name is the same as that of a large city in Ohio," the additional cue might help you to recall his name. But if you are then asked, "Was it John Sherman, Thomas Bayard, or Grover Cleveland?" you will probably recognize the correct answer as Grover Cleveland immediately. His name is a powerful retrieval cue.

Reconstructive Memory   If memory is so malleable, can it be trusted in a courtroom or even in private psychotherapy? That is a topic of considerable controversy among psychologists, lawyers, and psychotherapists. Psychologist Frederic Bartlett believed that people "reconstruct memories" as time passes—a phenomenon well documented in the accounts of witnesses to, or victims of, crimes and accidents (see *Highlights*). People also unknowingly rewrite their memories of past events to fit their current image or their desired image of themselves. Such reconstruction can actually be very helpful. For example, when children whose home life had been very troubled "rewrote" their memories of early childhood, their disadvantaged life was less of a liability. Interviewed 30 years later, those who incorrectly recalled their childhood as fairly normal were the ones who had been able to develop a basically stable, conventional life as adults (Robins et al., 1985).

Like the children from troubled homes in this study, any of us may reconstruct memories for social or personal self-defense. Each time you tell someone the story of an incident, you may unconsciously make subtle changes in the story's details, and these changes are encoded as part of your memory. When an experience does not fit our view of the world or of ourselves, we unconsciously tend to adjust it or to blot it out of memory altogether. Freud called this phenomenon *repression*.

Autobiographical Memory

What kinds of events are most likely to be remembered?

One researcher contends that our *autobiographical memory*—the recollection of events in our life and when they took place—"is central to self, to identity, to emotional experience, and to all those attributes that define an individual" (Conway, 1996, p. 295). Long-term memory enables us to recall the events that have occurred throughout our lifetime, although we are most likely to recall events from particular periods.

In a classic study of autobiographical memory, researchers presented 20 words to young adults and asked that they report the earliest personal memory that came to mind when they saw each of the words, then to estimate how long ago each event had occurred. The words were all common nouns, such as *hall* and *oven*, for which people can easily create images. In general, most personal memories concerned relatively recent events: The longer ago an event occurred, the less likely that people were to report it (Crovitz & Schiffman, 1974). Research reviewed by Holland and Rabbitt (1990), however, shows that people over 50 years of age have a tendency to recall events—though not necessarily important ones—from relatively early in life.

You might like to try Crovitz and Schiffman's technique yourself. You and a friend should each make up a list of 20 nouns—such as *table*, *robin*, and *dog*—whose image can easily be pictured, then generate one personal memory for each of the other person's words. Try to date each memory as accurately as possible. Did you have more memories for recent events than for events early in your life? Did you have any memories for events in the first 3 or 4 years of your life? In most cases our earliest personal memories tend to date back to between 3 and 4 years of age (Kihlstrom & Harackiewicz, 1982).

Certain kinds of events are more likely to be remembered than others from the first few years of life. Generally, the earliest memories are those for events that significantly change one's life story or are particularly frightening. College students, for example, recalled as early as age 2 the birth of a sibling or being hospitalized, while the death of a family member or making a family move could be recalled as early as age 3 (Usher & Neisser, 1993). It is extremely rare, however, for people to recall events that occurred before they were 2 years old. This phenomenon, sometimes called *infantile amnesia*, is still not well understood.

Older people are likely to think about the people and events in their young adulthood, when they made the choices that shaped their lives.

One hypothesis holds that the brain is not fully developed at birth and that immature brain structures are incapable of efficiently processing and storing information in memory. Another explanation is that very young children lack the prior experiences necessary to build *schemata*, the framework to organize and interpret new information for memory storage (Neisser, 1992).

In contrast to these positions, Patricia Bauer (1996) has recently argued that infantile amnesia is not a genuine phenomenon at all. Using carefully controlled procedures, her research has shown that infants as young as 13 months have the capacity to construct and maintain memories of specific events over extended periods of time. Bauer contends that the availability of appropriate cues and repetition—not age—are the primary determinants of efficient recall.

In examining personal memories of the entire life span, Mackavey, Malley, and Stewart (1991) analyzed the autobiographies of 49 well-known psychologists, written when the psychologists were between 54 and 86 years of age. These researchers discovered that 80 percent of the psychologists' autobiographically consequential experiences or decisions occurred between the ages of 18 and 35; very few occurred during early childhood or after age 50. They concluded that because the most pivotal life choices (such as those concerning marriage and career) are typically made in late adolescence and young adulthood and the outcomes of these choices shape the rest of our lives, it makes sense for us to focus on this period when we look back to summarize and evaluate our lives.

We have seen that long-term memory offers a vast storage space for information that we can retrieve in a variety of ways. Its capacity is immense, and material stored in LTM never seems to decay, although it may be transformed. By comparison, short-term memory has a sharply limited capacity; information may disappear from STM as a result of decay or interference or simply because the storage space is full. To keep information in STM, we must refresh it constantly through rote rehearsal. If we want to retain information for a long period of time, we must transfer it to long-term memory through the process of elaborative rehearsal. The sensory registers can take in an enormous volume of less permanent information, but they have no ability to process memories. Together these three stages of memory—the sensory registers, STM, and LTM—make up the information-processing view of memory (see Table 6–1 on p. 218). Let us now take a brief look at some special topics in memory, including ways in which memory might be improved.

HIGHLIGHTS

Eyewitness Testimony and Recovered Memories: Can We Trust Them?

Jurors in court cases tend to believe eyewitnesses. Faced with conflicting or ambiguous testimony, they are tempted to put their faith in people who actually "saw" an event. This faith in eyewitnesses may be misplaced, however (McCloskey & Egeth, 1983). Although eyewitness accounts are essential to courtroom testimony, studies clearly show that people who say, "I know what I saw," often mean, "I know what I *think* I saw." And these people may be wrong.

Consider this scenario. Two women enter a bus station and leave their belongings unattended on a bench while they check the bus schedule. A man enters, reaches into their baggage, stuffs something under his coat, and leaves. One of the women returns to her baggage and, after checking its contents, exclaims, "My tape recorder was stolen!" Eyewitnesses sitting nearby confirm her story when contacted by insurance investigators; many of the eyewitnesses provide a description of the missing tape recorder, including its color, size, and shape. In fact, there never was a tape recorder. The "thief" and the women "travelers" were assisting psychologist Elizabeth Loftus in a study of the fallibility of eyewitness testimony (Loftus, 1983).

When eyewitnesses to actual crimes make mistakes, the results are devastating. In more than 1,000 cases in which innocent people were convicted of crimes, errors made by eyewitnesses were the single most persuasive element leading to false conviction (Wells, 1993).

For more than 20 years Elizabeth Loftus has been the most influential researcher into eyewitness memory (1993a; Loftus & Hoffman, 1989; Loftus & Pickrell, 1995). In a classic study, Loftus and Palmer (1974) showed participants a film depicting a traffic accident. Some of the participants were asked "About how fast were the cars going when they hit each other?" Other participants were asked the same question, but with the words *smashed into, collided with, bumped into,* and *contacted* in place of *hit.* The researchers discovered that

---

People who say, "I know what I saw," often mean, "I know what I *think* I saw." And these people may be wrong.

---

people's reports of the cars' speed depended on which word was inserted in the question. Those asked about cars that "smashed into" each other reported that the cars were going faster than if they were asked simply about cars that "contacted" each other.

In another experiment, participants were also shown a film of a collision and then asked either "How fast were the cars going when they hit each other?" or "How fast were the cars going when they smashed into each other?" One week later the participants were asked some additional questions about the accident they had

seen on film the week before. One of the questions was "Did you see any broken glass?" Of the participants who originally had been asked the speed of the cars that had "smashed into" each other, more reported that they had seen broken glass than did the participants who simply had been asked the speed of the cars that had "hit" each other.

These findings illustrate how police, lawyers, and other investigators may, often unintentionally, sway witnesses and influence subsequent eyewitness accounts. Based on studies like these, Loftus and Palmer concluded that eyewitness memory is unreliable because witnesses cannot disentangle their memory of the original event from information and suggestions they receive after the event.

The impact of subsequent information seems to be particularly strong when it is repeated several times (Zaragoza & Mitchell, 1996), as is often the case with extensive media coverage. Many psychologists contend that if people paid more attention to the source of their memories, eyewitness accounts and memories in general would be less biased by information and suggestions picked up after an event (Lindsay, 1993; Zaragoza et al., 1997).

Inaccuracies in eyewitness testimony present a challenge to both cognitive and forensic psychologists. Forensic psychologists are interested in the practical question of how to improve the accuracy of eyewitness testimony, whereas memory researchers work to understand the processes that lead to errors in memory (Pezdek & Roe, 1995).

Eyewitness research may have implications for the study of recovered memories of traumatic events, such as childhood sexual abuse. The veracity of such memories has been hotly debated by psychologists in recent years (Freyd, 1996; Pope, 1996). Nobody denies the severity of the problem of sexual abuse of children or the intensity of the suffering of incest survivors. And because of repression, memories of such events sometimes do not surface until many years later. The phenomenon of repressed memories has legal as well as psychological repercussions: Individuals who recover memories may accuse other people of abuse or other criminal behavior that allegedly occurred far in the past.

Some observers, including Loftus, question the accuracy of memories recovered so many years after the original event (Loftus, 1993b, 1996, 1997). Although Loftus does not doubt that many such memories accurately reflect actual incidents, she also notes that in at least some instances other sources (such as the media and even psychotherapists) may *shape* people's recollections of early childhood experiences (Loftus, Milo, & Paddock, 1995). For example, in some cases well-meaning psychotherapists may unwittingly create false memories by leading patients to vividly imagine incidents that never happened (Garry, Loftus, & Brown, 1994; Hyman & Pentland, 1996). In addition, some evidence suggests that in children false memories may be more persistent than true memories (Brainerd, Reyna, & Brandse, 1995).

Other researchers, however, argue that false accusations are rare and that it is destructive to lead incest survivors to doubt the reality of their memories (Byrd, 1994; Berlinger & Williams, 1994; Olio, 1994). Research has shown that children can be the victims of abuse and later forget the experience (Feldman-Summers & Pope, 1994; Williams, 1994). For example, one study used a sample of 129 girls with hospital records of *verified* sexual abuse that took place during the 1970s (Williams, 1994). After contacting these girls almost 20 years later, Williams found that more than one-third of them did not "remember" the incident of abuse shown in the hospital records. Interestingly, however, over two-thirds of these "nonreporters" described other episodes of childhood sexual abuse.

Similarly, a national survey that asked psychologists whether they had ever been sexually abused as children and, if so, had they ever forgotten the event, found that more than 20 percent recalled being abused as children and about 40 percent of this group had forgotten the incident at some time during their life (Feldman-Summers & Pope, 1994).

In light of such studies, no expert would claim that all recovered memories of childhood abuse are false. Solid research evidence does suggest, however, that at least some recollections of childhood traumatic events are either untrue or distort what really may have happened. This volatile issue will only be resolved as we learn more about long-term memory and the extent to which it changes over time.

Father Bernard Pagano (*right*) was identified as an armed robber by seven eyewitnesses and was nearly convicted for crimes actually committed by the man on the left.

TABLE 6-1	Memory as an Information-Processing System				
System	Means by Which Information Is Encoded	Storage Organization	Storage Duration	Means by Which Information Is Retrieved	Factors in Forgetting
Sensory Registers	Visual and auditory registers	None	From less than 1 second to only a few seconds	Reconsideration of registered information	Decay or masking
Short-Term Memory	Visual and phonological representation	None	Usually 15 to 20 seconds	Rote or maintenance rehearsal	Interference or decay
Long-Term Memory	Comprehension of meaning, elaborative rehearsal	Logical frameworks, such as hierarchies or categories	Perhaps for an entire lifetime	Retrieval cues linked to organized information	Retrieval failure or interference

REVIEW QUESTIONS

1. Long-term memory includes ____ memory, which is filled with general facts and information; ____ memory, which is made up of events that have personal meaning for us; and ____ memory, which stores information relating to skills, habits, and other complex perceptual-motor tasks.

Indicate whether the following are true (T) or false (F).

2. Information in STM gets transferred to LTM if it is elaboratively rehearsed. ____

3. We remember only the explicit memories that we intend to remember. ____

4. The context in which learning takes place can provide useful cues for retrieval. ____

5. Most psychologists agree that the tip-of-the-tongue phenomenon is due to ____.

6. In long-term memory we tend to store the ____ ____ ____ ____ rather than the verbatim information.

7. ____ memories are unintentional.

Match the following terms with the appropriate definitions.

8. retroactive interference ____   ____ a. old material in memory interferes with new information

9. proactive interference ____   ____ b. new information interferes with old information already in memory

10. autobiographical memory ____   ____ c. recollection of events that happened in our life and when they took place

Answers: 1. semantic, episodic, procedural. 2. T. 3. F. 4. T. 5. interference. 6. main points or meaning. 7. implicit. 8. b. 9. a. 10. c.

Special Topics in Memory

What factors can influence how well you remember a specific incident?

Cultural Influences on Memory

Are the memory tasks in Western schools different from those in cultures that pass on oral traditions?

Remembering has practical consequences for our daily life and takes place within a particular context. So it's not surprising that many researchers believe that the values and customs of a given culture have a profound effect on what people remember and how easily they recall it (Mistry & Rogoff, 1994). In many

Western cultures, for example, being able to recite a long list of words or numbers, to repeat the details of a scene, and to provide facts and figures about historical events are all signs of a "good memory." In fact, tasks such as these are often used to test people's memory abilities. What we should realize is that these kinds of memory tasks reflect the type of learning, memorization, and categorization skills taught in *Western* schools. Members of other cultures often perform poorly on such memory tests because the exercises seem so odd to them.

In contrast, consider the memory skills of a person living in a society in which cultural information is passed on from one generation to the next through a rich oral tradition. An individual here may be able to recite the deeds of the culture's heroes in verse or rattle off the lines of descent of families, larger lineage groups, and elders. Or perhaps the individual has a storehouse of information about the migration of animals or the life cycles of plants that help people obtain food and know when to harvest crops.

Our memories of the traditional information of our particular culture are far different from a memory of a sudden and traumatic event.

Culture influences our reconstructive memory. People who are not Chinese rarely have an accurate memory of a Chinese New Year celebration. Because of their lack of familiarity with the traditions and ceremony that give meaning to this holiday, they will distort or drop certain details of the event in their memories.

Flashbulb Memories

How can we explain the enduring vividness of flashbulb memories?

"I was standing by the stove getting dinner; my husband came in and told me." "I was fixing the fence. . . . Mr. W. came along and told me. It was 9 or 10 o'clock in the morning." "It was in the forenoon; we were at work on the road by K's mills: A man driving past told us." These were three responses to the question "Do you recall where you were when you heard that Abraham Lincoln was shot?" Other accounts were even more detailed. In fact, of 179 people interviewed, 127 recalled precisely the time and place at which they first heard of the assassination. That is a very high proportion, considering that the question was asked 33 years after the event (Colegrove, 1982).

A **flashbulb memory** is the experience of remembering vividly a certain event and the incidents surrounding it even after a long time has passed. Events that are shocking or otherwise highly significant are often remembered in this way. The death of a close relative, a birth, a graduation, or a wedding day may all elicit flashbulb memories. So can dramatic events in which we were not personally involved, such as the assassination of President John F. Kennedy, in November 1963, or the explosion of the space shuttle *Challenger* in January 1986.

How do people form flashbulb memories? Some researchers have proposed the *now-print* theory: When something especially significant, shocking, or noteworthy is at hand, a mechanism in the brain captures the entire event, then "prints" it, much like a photograph. The "print" is then stored, like a photograph in an album, for long periods, perhaps a lifetime. It is periodically reinforced, because such an important event is bound to be remembered and discussed many times throughout the years.

This theory raises some questions, however. Why are all sorts of insignificant features remembered along with the main event—"standing by the stove," "fixing the fence"? The answer given by the now-print theory is that the entire event is registered—not just the primary subject—like a photograph. It's as if you decided to photograph your mother sitting on the couch on her silver wedding anniversary. Your mother is the main subject, but that same picture may also capture the arrangement of the living-room furniture, the antics of the family dog, and a small crack in the plaster of the back wall. You did not intend to include those things in your picture, but because they were there in the background, they, too, were registered on film (Brown & Kulik, 1977).

The now-print theory implies, among other things, that flashbulb memories are accurate, that they are created at the time of an event, and that they are

Flashbulb memory
A vivid memory of a certain event and the incidents surrounding it even after a long time has passed.

Uniformed Horse Guards bearing the coffin of Princess Diana. Many years from now, you may remember where you were and what you were doing when you heard the news of her death. This is an example of a flashbulb memory.

remembered better because of their highly emotional content. All of these implications have come under criticism. First, flashbulb memories are certainly not always accurate. Although this is a difficult contention to test, let's consider just one case. Psychologist Ulric Neisser clearly recalled what he was doing on the day in 1941 when the Japanese bombed Pearl Harbor. He distinctly remembered that he was listening to a baseball game on the radio, which was interrupted by the shocking announcement. But baseball is not played in December, when the attack took place, so this sharp flashbulb memory simply was incorrect (Neisser, 1982).

Moreover, even if an event is registered accurately, it may undergo periodic revision, just like other long-term memories. We are bound to discuss and rethink a major event many times, and we probably also hear a great deal of additional information about that event in the weeks and months after it occurs. As a result, the flashbulb memory may undergo reconstruction and become less accurate over the years until it sometimes bears little or no resemblance to what actually occurred.

Improving Your Memory

What can you do to improve your memory?

It's the active decision to get better and the number of hours you push yourself to improve that makes the difference. *Motivation* is much more important than innate ability (Singular, 1982). One researcher's answer to this question may encourage you. Regardless of innate ability, anyone can improve memory by doing the following:

1. **Develop motivation for remembering.** Without a strong desire to learn or to remember something, you probably won't. But if you find a way to keep yourself alert and interested, you will have an easier time learning and remembering things.

2. **Practice memory skills.** To stay sharp, memory skills, like all skills, must be practiced and used. Memory experts recommend exercises such as crossword puzzles, acrostics, anagrams, Scrabble, Monopoly, Trivial Pursuit, and bridge. Or you might learn Japanese, join a chess club, or make a point of discussing news events regularly with friends.

3. **Be confident about your ability to remember.** If you're convinced that you won't remember something, you probably won't. Self-doubt often leads to anxiety, which in turn interferes with the ability to retrieve information from

memory. Relaxation exercises may substantially boost your ability to retrieve information from memory.

4. **Minimize distractions.** Although some people can study for an exam and listen to the radio simultaneously, most people find that outside distractions interfere with both learning and remembering. If you are being distracted, look for a quiet, even secluded, setting before attempting to commit something to memory.

5. **Focus on what you want to remember.** Paying close attention to details and focusing on your surroundings, emotions, and other elements associated with an event will help you to remember it clearly.

6. **Make connections between new material and other information already stored in your long-term memory.** One key to improving memory lies in organizing and encoding material more effectively when it first enters LTM. Discuss things you want to remember with other people. Think about or write down ways in which the new information is related to things you already know. The more links you forge between new information and old information already in LTM, the more likely you are to remember the new material.

In some situations **mnemonics** (pronounced new-MON-iks) may help you to tie new material to information already in LTM. Mnemonics are techniques that make material easier to remember. Some of the simplest mnemonic techniques are the rhymes and jingles that we often use to remember dates and other facts. "Thirty days hath September, April, June, and November . . ." enables us to recall how many days are in a month. We are also familiar with other simple mnemonic devices in which we make up words or sentences out of the material to be recalled. The colors of the visible spectrum—red, orange, yellow, green, blue, indigo, and violet—are easily remembered by using their first letters to form the name ROY G. BIV. Use mnemonics whenever you can.

7. **Use mental imagery.** Imagery works wonders as an aid to recalling information from memory. Whenever possible, form mental pictures of the items, people, words, or activities you want to remember. If you have a sequence of stops to make, picture yourself leaving each place and heading for the next. To memorize long speeches, Greek and Roman orators would go through the rooms of a building they knew well, placing images of material to be remembered in sequence at different spots. During a speech the orators imagined themselves going through the rooms in order, and by association they would recall each point of the speech.

8. **Use retrieval cues.** As we saw earlier, the more retrieval cues you have, the more likely it is that you will remember something. One way to establish automatic retrieval cues is to create routines and structure. For example, when you come in the door, put your keys in the same place every time. Then when you ask yourself, "Where did I put my keys?" the fact that you have a special place for the keys serves as a retrieval cue. Similarly, if you want to remember to do something before you go to bed, leave something unusual on your bed (perhaps a shoe or a sock); when it's time to go to bed, you'll see the unusual object, and that should help you remember what you wanted to do.

9. **Rely on more than memory alone.** Human memory is less than perfect, so it's wise not to rely entirely on memory when there are alternatives. Write down the things you need to remember, and then post a note or list of those things somewhere obvious, such as on your bulletin board or refrigerator door. Put all the dates you want to remember on a calendar, then put the calendar in a conspicuous place. If you witness an accident, immediately write down everything you saw and heard in as much detail as you can.

Most memory-improvement books are filled with suggestions and techniques such as these, and they do work if you are willing to devote the time and energy to learning how to use them. To learn more about how to improve your

The key to storing new material in LTM is to study actively. Simply reading a textbook chapter is not the same as learning it. To do that requires active participation, outlining, making notes, questioning, and reviewing as you go along.

Mnemonics
Techniques that make material easier to remember.

APPLYING PSYCHOLOGY

Improving Your Memory for Textbook Material

How can you use the principles spelled out in this chapter to help you remember material from textbooks like this one? We have seen that the key to storing new material in long-term memory is making associations between that material and information that is already in LTM. If you simply passively reread a chapter over and over, you are not likely to store, retain, or retrieve information effectively (McDaniel, Waddill, & Shakesby, 1996). Highlighting or underlining passages makes for a slight improvement, if only because you are at least thinking about which material is most important.

A more effective technique is to prepare an outline of the chapter before reading it so that you have associations and links ready to be made when you actually read the material. Some textbooks (including this one) provide you with a ready-made outline at the beginning of the chapter, but you are better off putting one together for yourself, because that forces you to start thinking about the content of the chapter and how one section relates to another. How would you compose a chapter outline? You might scan the various headings in the chapter or read the first few sentences of each paragraph or look at the end-of-chapter summary for ideas to insert in your outline. Then, as you read, enter brief comments under the various headings of your outline as a way of summarizing each portion of the chapter. Not only will your personal summary help you to remember material, but it will also prove useful when you are reviewing the material for a test.

Another simple technique is to engage actively in a form of elaborative rehearsal of the material as you read the chapter. As an example, you might write in the margin of the text as you go along, recording your reactions, questions, and ideas about how the new material may relate to other material, thoughts about how you might apply what you are learning in your own life, and so on. Try to relate the new material to all sorts of things you already know and to express this relationship in your own words. You can also work with a friend, taking turns challenging each other with questions that draw on material from different sections or paragraphs. However you go about it, integrating and elaborating on the textual material forces you to process it and to form new associations among the pieces of information that you are storing. This approach to learning offers two distinct benefits: It ties the new material to information already in memory, and it generates a multitude of retrieval cues to help you put your finger on the material when you need it.

A more ambitious—but even more effective—system for studying is known by the letters of its five stages: *SQRRR* (or *SQ3R*). SQRRR involves the following steps:

1. **Survey.** Before you even start to read, look quickly at the chapter

memory, especially for textbook material, see *Applying Psychology*. You may learn some techniques that improve not only your memory but also your grades.

REVIEW QUESTIONS

1. ____ memory is the experience of vividly remembering a certain event.
2. ____ are techniques that help us to learn new material by relating it to something already in LTM.

Indicate whether the following are true (T) or false (F).

3. The now-print theory holds that entire events are recorded in memory. ____
4. Flashbulb memories are always accurate. ____
5. Linking new material to things already in LTM can cause confusing memories. ____
6. Lack of motivation can interfere with memory. ____

Answers: 1. flashbulb. 2. mnemonics. 3. T. 4. F. 5. F. 6. T.

Biology and Memory

According to current research, where in the brain are memories located?

Studies have shown that some memories may be localized in certain portions of the brain. For example, some of the learning that takes place in classical condi-

outline, the headings of the various sections in the chapter, and the chapter summary. This gives you an overview of what you will be reading and helps you to organize and integrate the material as you go along.

2. **Question.** Before you start to read, translate each chapter heading into questions about the text to follow, as a way to compare the new material with what you already know. This process gets you actively involved in thinking about the topic and helps to bring the main points into sharp relief. Before reading this chapter, for example, you might have recast the heading "Short-Term Memory" on page 203 into questions such as "Why is it called short-term?" "Is there another type of memory that lasts longer?" "What good is memory if it's only short-term?" "Why do memories fade?" It is usually helpful to write these questions down.

3. **Read.** Now read the first section in the chapter, looking for answers to the questions you have posed. If you discover major points not directly related to your questions, either revise or refine your old questions to encompass the new material or make up new questions more specifically targeted to the new material.

4. **Recite.** After you finish reading the section, close the book and recite from memory the answers to your questions and any other major points that you can remember. You may want to jot down your answers in outline form or even recite them aloud to someone else. Then open the book and check to make sure that you have covered all the key points raised in the section. Repeat steps 2, 3, and 4 for each section of the chapter.

5. **Review.** After reading through the chapter, review your notes, then recite your questions and answers from memory. Relate the material to other ideas, to experiences in your life, or to things with which you are familiar. Try to think of particularly good examples or illustrations of the points brought out in the chapter. Get involved.

The SQRRR method forces you to react—to enter into a dialogue with the text. This interaction makes the material more interesting and meaningful and improves your chances of recalling it. It also organizes the material and relates it to what you already know. Although this method may strike you as too time-consuming, you will probably spend less time studying overall if you use it, because studying for exams later on should go much more quickly.

To learn more about techniques to enhance your studying, visit our Web site at **www.prenhall.com/morris**.

tioning (see Chapter 5, Learning) is stored in the cerebellum (McCormick et al., 1982). Research also reveals, however, that in many cases memories are not stored in any single part of the brain (Logan & Grafton, 1995).

Why is this so? One reason may be that several different senses usually contribute to any one memory. That is, a single memory may be stored in the brain's centers for vision, smell, and touch—all at the same time. Consistent with this idea of multiple memory storage sites is the recent finding that an area of the brain known as the *basal forebrain* (see Figure 6–4) may be involved in binding together information stored in different sites throughout the brain (Tranel, 1994). This binding together of different sensory experiences probably enriches the quality of many of our memories.

Although memories are *stored* throughout the brain, they are *formed* by activity in certain areas. We know, for example, that the *hippocampus* helps to transfer information from short-term to long-term memory. If the hippocampus is damaged, we can remember events that have just occurred (STM), but our long-term memory of those events would be disrupted (Gluck & Myers, 1997). Memories already stored, however, are not lost even if the hippocampus is destroyed.

The role of various neurotransmitters, especially acetylcholine, in our memory system is also being studied. The importance of acetylcholine to normal memory functioning has also been implicated in studies involving Alzheimer's patients (Coyle, 1987), but the precise role of neurotransmitters

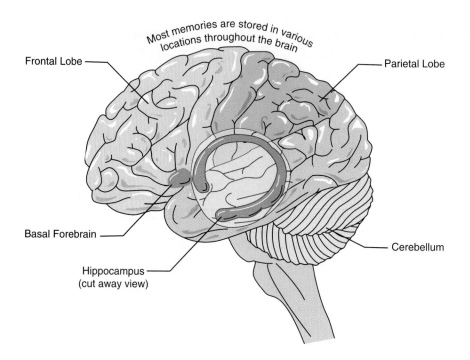

Most memories are stored in various locations throughout the brain

Frontal Lobe

Parietal Lobe

Basal Forebrain

Cerebellum

Hippocampus
(cut away view)

FIGURE 6–4
The biological basis of memory.

in the memory process is complex. Research on the biological basis of memories promises to increase our understanding of how memory works.

Memory Loss

What biological factors can cause memory loss?

Brain damage caused by accidents, surgery, poor diet, or disease can lead to severe memory loss. As we saw earlier, head injuries often result in *retrograde amnesia*, a condition in which people cannot remember what happened to them immediately before their injury. Researchers think that information that was being processed at the time of the injury vanishes from memory.

In older people who are having trouble remembering new material, tests often show that a part of the brain (the hippocampus) is smaller than its normal size (Golomb et al., 1994). Brain scans also reveal a diminished hippocampus in people suffering from *Alzheimer's disease*, an untreatable neurological disorder that causes severe memory loss. About 10 percent of people over 65 and nearly half of those over 85 have this disorder (Bennett & Knopman, 1994). Alzheimer's patients show both the atrophy of some brain structures (including the hippocampus) and the abnormal growth of others (Haberlandt, 1997).

Another disease, chronic alcoholism, can lead to another form of amnesia. In this case memory loss is caused by a vitamin deficiency in the poor diet typical of people who abuse alcohol (Baddeley, 1987).

REVIEW QUESTIONS

1. Damage to one area of the brain may diminish a particular memory but not destroy it entirely. That is because memory is stored in ____ ____ areas of the brain.
2. Images of the brains of Alzheimer's patients show that a region of the brain involved with memory, the hippocampus, has ____ ____.
3. In people with chronic alcoholism, memory loss can result from ____ ____.
4. "All of memory is stored in the cerebral cortex." True or false.
5. "Neurotransmitters influence memory functioning." True or false.

Answers: 1. several different. 2. gotten smaller. 3. a vitamin deficiency. 4. F. 5. T.

KEY TERMS

CHAPTER REVIEW

☐ What is the role of sensory registers?

Many psychologists view memory as a series of steps in which we encode, store, and retrieve information, much like a computer does. This is called the **information-processing** model of memory. The first step in the model is inputting data through our senses into temporary holding bins, called **sensory registers.** These registers give us a brief moment to decide whether something deserves our attention.

☐ What would happen if auditory information faded as quickly as visual information does?

Information entering a sensory register disappears very quickly if it isn't processed further. Information in the visual register lasts for only about a quarter of a second before it is replaced by new information. If sounds faded from our auditory register as rapidly as this, spoken language would be more difficult. Information in the auditory register can linger for several seconds.

☐ Why does some information capture our attention while other information goes unnoticed?

The next step in the memory process is **attention**—selectively looking at, listening to, smelling, tasting, or feeling what we deem to be important. The nervous system seems to automatically filter out peripheral information, allowing us to zero in on what is essential at a particular time. Unattended information receives at least some processing, however, so we can quickly shift attention to it if it suddenly strikes us as significant.

☐ What are the two primary tasks of short-term memory?

Short-term memory (STM) holds whatever information we are actively attending to at any given time. Its two primary tasks are to store new information briefly and to "work" on information that we currently have in mind. This second function is why STM is also called *working memory*.

☐ How does chunking improve the capacity of STM?

Short-term memory can hold only as much information as can be repeated or rehearsed in 1-1/2 to 2 seconds. This is usually somewhere between 5 and 10 items. By clustering bits of related information into larger groups (called **chunking**), however, the amount of information held in STM can be expanded even though the 5-to-10-item limit still holds true. Each item is simply larger.

☐ Is material stored in short-term memory as it sounds or as it looks?

Information can be stored in STM according to the way it sounds or the way it looks. Verbal information is encoded by sound, even if we see the words written rather than hear them spoken. Interestingly, the capacity for visual encoding in STM seems to be greater than for encoding by sound.

☐ Why do we forget information from STM?

Information in short-term memory disappears in 15–20 seconds unless it is rehearsed or practiced. **Decay theory** holds that material that is not actively renewed simply fades away with the passage of time. **Interference theory** adds to this the idea of new information following old and pushing it out of the way. Both theories have merit.

☐ Is repeating something over and over again a good way to remember it?

Repeating something over and over, known as **rote rehearsal,** is useful for remembering something for a brief time, but it is not the most efficient way to remember something permanently.

☐ What is the best way to go about remembering something?

The best way to remember something is to practice elaborative rehearsal in which you think about the meaning of new information and link it to information you already know. This kind of processing is deeper than simple rote repetition and more likely to transfer data from short-term to **long-term memory (LTM).**

How do semantic memory, episodic memory, and procedural memory differ?

In discussing long-term memory, psychologists sometimes distinguish among semantic memory, episodic memory, and procedural memory. **Semantic memory** stores general facts and information, much as an encyclopedia or dictionary does, with numerous cross-references to related ideas. In contrast, **episodic memory** stores memories of events that have happened, much as a diary might. **Procedural memory** stores information relating to skills, habits, and other complex perceptual-motor tasks.

How are long-term memories encoded?

There are several ways we encode information in long-term memory. Sometimes memories are encoded in terms of nonverbal images, such as shapes, sounds, smells, tastes, and touch sensations. More commonly, however, memories are encoded by their meaning. You extract the significant highlights from what you read, hear, or experience, and lodge those in LTM, linking them to other material already stored there. In this way, your long-term memories become categorized and interrelated, much like information in an elaborate filing system.

Do we sometimes remember things we never intended to remember?

Human memory is filled with information not deliberately placed there. This is called **implicit memory,** or memory for things that were either not deliberately encoded into long-term storage or were retrieved without conscious intention. In contrast, **explicit memory** is memory for information that is intentionally committed to and retrieved from LTM, such as the facts you learn when studying for a test.

Are memories accurate, or do they change over time?

Not everything stored in LTM is recalled with precision. One reason is interference from bits of information that are similar to the one we want to retrieve. This can cause confusion and sometimes lead to the *tip-of-the-tongue phenomenon*. In addition, people may unknowingly reconstruct their memories over time. For instance, they may recast negative memories to make them less painful, or they may embellish the past to fit a desired self-image.

What kinds of events are most likely to be remembered?

Autobiographical memory refers to recollection of events from one's life. Not all of these events are recalled with equal clarity, of course, and some are not recalled at all. People generally cannot remember events that occurred before age 2 (a phenomenon called *infantile amnesia*), and our memories are typically strongest for events that had a major impact on our lives or that aroused strong emotion.

What factors can influence how well you remember a specific incident?

The values and customs of a given culture have a profound effect on what people remember and how easily they recall it. So do the emotions we attach to a memory, with some emotion-laden events being remembered for life. Also affecting how well we remember are the strategies we use to store and retrieve information.

Are memory tasks in Western schools different from those in cultures that pass on oral traditions?

Many Western schools stress being able to recall long lists of words, facts, and figures that are divorced from everyday life. In contrast, societies in which cultural information is passed on through a rich oral tradition may instead emphasize memory for events that directly affect people's lives.

How can we explain the enduring vividness of flashbulb memories?

Vivid **flashbulb memories** sometimes form for events that are linked to some powerful emotion, such as shock, terror, grief, or joy. Such memories can remain highly detailed and unchanged throughout the years because of the strong emotion that prevailed when they were formed.

What can you do to improve your memory?

The key to improving long-term memory lies in organizing and encoding information more effectively. Techniques called **mnemonics** can sometimes help you to do this. Examples of mnemonics are rhymes and jingles for remembering particular dates or other facts. Other mnemonics rely on mental imagery to provide retrieval cues. You can also improve your memory by developing a strong motivation to remember and by practicing memory skills in a deliberate way.

According to current research, where in the brain are memories located?

Some memories may be localized in certain parts of the brain. The cerebellum, for example, stores some of the learning that occurs in classical conditioning. In many cases, however, memories are stored more diffusely. This is shown by the fact that damage to one part of the brain may diminish but not erase many of our memories.

What biological factors can cause memory loss?

Accidents, surgery, poor diet, and disease can lead to brain damage and memory loss. For instance, head injury often causes *retrograde amnesia*, an inability to remember what happened right before the accident. The condition called Alzheimer's disease is an example of memory loss due to disease, one that involves both atrophy and abnormal growth of brain structures. Interestingly, the memory loss associated with chronic alcoholism may be caused by a vitamin deficiency due to poor diet.

CRITICAL THINKING AND APPLICATIONS

1. How could our psychological state influence our attention?

2. What are three examples of elaborative rehearsal for course material you need to learn now?

3. What impact can the phenomenon of reconstructive memory have on our judicial system? Do you think that recovered memories should be admissible in court? Why or why not?

On the Web...

Visit these online resources at our Companion Website www.prenhall.com/morris

The Psychology Place

Learning Activities	1. Emotion, Memory and the Brain, p. 200
Scientific American Connection	2. Another Measure of Intelligence: Working Memory, p. 203
	3. Creating False Memories, p. 214
Research News	4. The Repressed Memory Debate, p. 214
	5. Test Your Memory, p. 215
Op-Ed Essays	6. Recovered-Memory Experiences: Explaining True and False Delayed Memories of Childhood Sexual Abuse, p. 217

Games

1. Types of Memory, p. 218
2. Memory Test, p. 220

Web Links

1. **http://www.valdosta.edu/~whuitt/psy702/cogsys/infoproc.html**, p. 199
   Offers in-depth description of the Stage Model of Information Processing, organization of knowledge, and concept formation.

2. **http://www.psy.ulaval.ca?~arvid/R1e.html**, p. 209
   Cognitive Psychology Research Laboratory. This research group is particularly interested in working and long-term memory.

3. **http://www.exploratorium.edu/memory/magnani/index.html**, p. 214
   A Memory Artist: An artist paints his childhood home from memory.

4. **http://www.selfgrowth.com/memory.html**, p. 220
   Self-Improvement Online's Recommended and Reviewed "Memory Improvement and Training: Related Web sites."

5. **http://www.memory.uva.nl/memory_improvement/mnemonics.htm**, p. 221
   Online Memory Improvement Course: Basic mnemonic, Peg mnemonic, and advanced mnemonic strategies.

6. **http://www.psywww.com/mtsite/memory.html**, p. 221
   Mind Tools: Memory Techniques and Memories: Introduction to memory techniques, memory techniques explained, and applications of mnemonic techniques.

Explore these topics on the Mind Matters CD-ROM

Mind Matters

1. The Process of Remembering, p. 203

COGNITION AND MENTAL ABILITIES

7

PERHAPS YOU KNOW THIS RIDDLE: "A MAN MARRIED 20 DIFFERENT women in the same small town. All these women are still alive, and he never divorced a single one of them. How could this be if he broke no law against bigamy?" The solution: The man was a minister. When you hear the answer for the first time, you are liable to groan because the answer is so obvious *once you know it*. In this chapter we explore the processes that enable you to solve little puzzles, such as this one, as well as bigger, more important problems.

The term **cognition** refers to all the processes we use to acquire and apply information. We have already considered the cognitive processes of perception, learning, and memory. In later chapters we examine cognition's crucial relation to coping and adjustment, abnormal behavior, and interpersonal relations. In this chapter we focus on three cognitive processes we think of as characteristically human: thinking, problem solving, and decision making. We also discuss two mental abilities that psychologists have tried to measure: intelligence and creativity.

If you had taken this course a generation ago, you probably would not have studied most of the topics in this chapter. Cognitive psychology is a relatively recent field, as you learned in Chapter 1. It developed partly as a reaction to the behaviorists, who believed that only directly *observable* processes could be studied scientifically. Today this belief is no longer widely accepted, and cognitive psychology has grown greatly in popularity.

Building Blocks of Thought

What are the three most important building blocks of thought?

When you think about a close friend, you may have in mind complex statements about her, such as "I'd like to talk to her soon" or "I wish I could be more like her." You may also have an image of her—probably her face, but perhaps the sound of her voice as well. Or you may think of your friend by using various concepts or categories such as *woman, kind, strong, dynamic, gentle*. When we think, we make use of all these things—language, images, and concepts—often simultaneously. These are the three most important building blocks of thought.

Language

What steps do we go through to turn a thought into a statement?

Human *language* is a flexible system of symbols that enables us to communicate our ideas, thoughts, and feelings. Spoken language is based on units of sound called **phonemes.** The sounds of *t, th,* and *k,* for instance, are all phonemes in English. There are about 45 phonemes in the English language and as many as 85 in some other languages (Bourne, Dominowski, Loftus, & Healy, 1986). By themselves, phonemes are meaningless and seldom play an important role in helping us to think. The sound *b,* for example, has no inherent meaning. But phonemes can be grouped together to form words, prefixes (such as *un-* and *pre-*), and suffixes (such as *-ed, -ing*). These meaningful combinations of phonemes are known as **morphemes**—the smallest meaningful units in a language. Morphemes play a key role in human thought. They can represent important ideas such as "red" or "calm" or "hot." The suffix *-ed* captures the idea of "in the past" (as in *visited* or *liked*). The prefix *pre-* conveys the idea of "before" or "prior to" (as in *preview* or *predetermined*).

We can combine morphemes to create words that represent quite complex ideas, such as *pre-exist-ing, un-excell-ed, psycho-logy*. In turn, we can put words together to form phrases and sentences that represent even more complex thoughts. When we think about something—say, the ocean or a sunset—our thoughts rarely reflect the single ideas

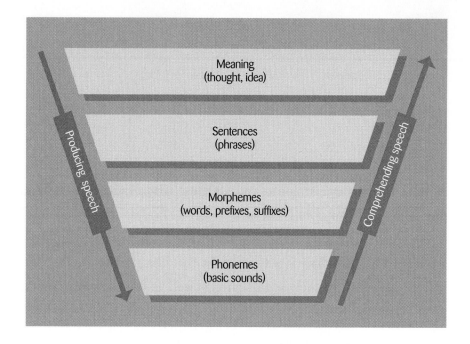

expressed by morphemes like *red* or *calm*. Instead, our ideas usually consist of phrases and sentences, such as "The ocean is unusually calm tonight."

Sentences have both a **surface structure**—the particular words and phrases—and a **deep structure,** or underlying meaning. The same deep structure can be conveyed by different surface structures, as in this example:

The ocean is unusually calm tonight.

Tonight the ocean is particularly calm.

Compared to most nights, tonight the ocean is calm.

When you wish to communicate an idea, you start with a thought, then choose words and phrases that will express the idea, and, finally, produce the speech sounds that make up those words and phrases. This is sometimes called *top-down processing*, and you can see from the left arrow in Figure 7–1 that the movement is indeed from top to bottom. When you want to understand a sentence, your task is reversed. You must start with speech sounds and work your way up to the meaning of those sounds. This is sometimes called *bottom-up processing*, as shown by the right arrow in Figure 7–1.

Just as there are rules for combining phonemes and morphemes, there are also rules for structuring sentences and their meanings. These rules—called **grammar**—exist for both spoken and sign languages, but we focus here on spoken language. Linguist Noam Chomsky (1957) pioneered the study of how grammar enables speakers and listeners to go from surface to deep structure. The two major components of grammar are semantics and syntax. *Semantics* is the system by which we assign meaning to the morphemes we use. Some semantic rules describe how a word may refer to an object—for example, that a large, striped cat is a *tiger*. Other semantic rules explain how different combinations of morphemes affect meaning, such as adding the suffix *-ed* to a verb like *play* to put the action in the past, or adding the prefix *un-* to *necessary* to reverse its meaning. *Syntax* is the system of rules that governs how we combine words to form grammatical sentences. Syntax is crucial, because a random jumble of individually meaningful words doesn't communicate very much. In English, for example, a syntax rule specifies that adjectives come before nouns. In some European languages adjectives come after nouns.

Cognition
The processes whereby we acquire and use knowledge.

Phonemes
The basic sounds that make up any language.

Morphemes
The smallest meaningful units of speech, such as simple words, prefixes, and suffixes.

Surface structure
The particular words and phrases used to make up a sentence.

Deep structure
The underlying meaning of a sentence.

Grammar
The language rules that determine how sounds and words can be combined and used to communicate meaning within a language.

Images

What role do images play in thinking?

Think for a moment about Abraham Lincoln. Then think about being outside in a summer thunderstorm. Your thoughts of Lincoln may have included such phrases as "wrote the Gettysburg Address," "president during the Civil War," and "assassinated by John Wilkes Booth." You probably also had some mental images about him: bearded face, lanky body, or log cabin. When you thought about the thunderstorm, you probably formed mental images of wind, rain, and lightning—perhaps even the smell of wet leaves and earth. An **image** is a mental representation of some sensory experience, and it can be used to think about things. We can visualize the Statue of Liberty; we can smell Thanksgiving dinner or the scent of a Christmas tree; we can hear Martin Luther King, Jr., saying, "I have a dream!" In short, we can think by using images.

Images allow us to think about things in nonverbal ways. Albert Einstein relied heavily on his powers of visualization to understand phenomena he would later describe using complex mathematical formulas. Einstein believed that his extraordinary genius resulted in part from his skill in visualizing possibilities (Shepard, 1978). Although few of us can match Einstein's brilliance, we all use images to think about and solve problems. We have seen a teacher clarify a difficult concept by drawing a quick, simple sketch on a blackboard. Many times, when words make a tangled knot of an issue, a graphic image drawn on paper straightens out the confusion. Images also allow us to use concrete forms to represent complex and abstract ideas, as when newspapers use pie charts and graphs to illustrate how people voted in an election.

Concepts

How do concepts help us think more efficiently?

Concepts are mental categories for classifying specific people, things, or events (Komatsu, 1992). *Dogs*, *books*, and *mountains* are all concepts for classifying things, while *fast*, *beautiful*, and *interesting* can classify things, events, or people. When you think about a specific thing—say, Mt. Everest—you usually think of the concepts that apply to it, such as *highest* and *dangerous to climb*. Concepts can also be used to create and organize hierarchies or groups of subordinate categories. For example, the general concept of *plants* can be broken down into the subordinate categories of *trees*, *bushes*, and *grasses*, just as the subordinate concept of *trees* can be further subdivided into *oaks*, *maples*, *pines*, and so forth (Reed, 1996). If we could not form concepts, we would need a different name for every object. Thus concepts help us to think efficiently about things and how they relate to one another.

Concepts also give meaning to new experiences. We do not stop and form a new concept for every new experience we have. We draw on concepts that we have already formed and place the new event into the appropriate categories. As we do, we may modify some of our concepts to better match our experiences. Consider the concept of job interview. You probably have some concept of this process even before your first interview, but your concept will probably change somewhat after you actually look for a job. Once you have formed a concept of *job interview*, you will not have to respond to each interview as a totally new experience; you will know what to expect and how you are expected to behave. Conceptualizing, whether *job interview* or anything else, is a way of organizing experiences.

Although it is tempting to think of concepts as simple and clear-cut, most of the concepts that we use are rather "fuzzy": They overlap one another and are often

When you think about the concept *bird*, you don't think about every different kind of bird you know, nor do you imagine a list of features that all birds share (wings, feathers, beak, two feet, egg-laying). Instead you think of a prototype of a "typical" bird. A penguin doesn't match this prototype very well, but you can still tell it is a bird by its degree of category membership.

"Well, you don't look like an experimental psychologist to me."
©1994 *The New Yorker* magazine

Image
A mental representation of a sensory experience.

Concept
A mental category for classifying objects, people, or experiences.

poorly defined. For example, most people can tell a mouse from a rat, but listing the critical differences between the two would be difficult (Rosch, 1973, 1978).

If we cannot explain the difference between mouse and rat, how can we use these *fuzzy concepts* in our thinking? We may construct a model, or **prototype**, of a representative mouse and one of a representative rat and then use those prototypes in our thinking (Rosch, 1978). Our concept of bird, for example, does not consist of a list of a bird's key attributes, like *feathered, winged, two feet*, and *lives in trees*. Instead, most of us have a model bird, or prototype, in mind—such as a robin or a sparrow—that captures for us the essence of *bird*. When we encounter new objects, we compare them with this prototype to determine if they are in fact birds. And when we think about birds, we usually think about our prototypical bird.

Concepts, then, like words and images, help us to formulate thoughts. But human cognition involves more than just passively thinking about things. It also involves actively using words, images, and concepts to fashion an understanding of the world, to solve problems, and to make decisions. In the next three sections we see how this is done.

Review Questions

1. ____, ____, and ____ are the three most important building blocks of thought.

2. In language, units of sound, called ____, are combined to form the smallest units of meaning, called ____. These smallest meaningful units can then be combined to create words, which in turn can be used to build phrases and whole ____.

3. Language rules that specify how sounds and words can be combined into meaningful sentences are called rules of ____.

4. According to Chomsky, language users employ rules to allow them to go from the surface structure to the ____ ____ of language.

5. Categories for classifying specific people, things, or events are called
   a. concepts.   b. images.   c. phonemes.   d. morphemes.

Indicate whether the following statements are true (T) or false (F).

6. Images help us to think about things because images use concrete forms to represent complex ideas.____

7. People decide which objects belong to a concept by comparing the object's features to a model or prototype of the concept. ____

8. Concepts help us give meaning to new experiences. ____

Answers: 1. language, images, concepts. **2.** phonemes, morphemes, sentences. **3.** grammar. **4.** deep structure. **5.** a. **6.** T. **7.** T. **8.** T.

Language and Thought

How does language affect the way we think?

Language is closely tied to the expression and understanding of thoughts. Many English words—such as *friend, family, airplane*, and *love*—correspond to concepts that are among the building blocks of thought. By combining words into sentences, we can link concepts to other concepts and express complex ideas. Because language determines not only the words we use but also the ways in which we combine those words into sentences, is it possible that language also determines how we think and what we can think about?

Some theorists believe that it does. For instance, that language can facilitate memory was shown in a study in which people gave names to color patches and then were asked to recall them (R. W. Brown & Lenneberg, 1954). Colors that were quickly and easily named (like blue) were more readily coded and retrieved than were those that took longer to name and were given less common labels

Prototype
According to Rosch, a mental model containing the most typical features of a concept.

(like sky blue or pale blue). Apparently, the ease with which we process and remember an experience is closely related to the ease and speed with which we name it using language.

If language affects our ability to store and retrieve information, it should also affect our ability to think about things. Benjamin Whorf (1956) was the strongest spokesperson for this view. According to Whorf's **linguistic relativity hypothesis,** the language that a person speaks determines the pattern of that person's thinking and his or her view of the world. For Whorf, if a language lacks a particular expression, the thought to which the expression corresponds will probably not occur to the people who speak that language. For example, the Hopi, a Native American people of the southwestern United States, have only two nouns for things that fly. One noun refers to birds; the other is used for everything else. A plane and a dragonfly, for instance, are both referred to with the same noun. According to Whorf, Hopi speakers would not see as great a difference between planes and dragonflies as we do, because their language labels the two similarly.

Think how linguistic relativity might apply to what you are learning in this course. Phrases like *linguistic relativity hypothesis*, *surface structure*, and *deep structure* capture very complex ideas. To the extent that you understand those terms, you probably find it easier to think about the relationship between language and thought, or between words and sentences and their underlying meaning. The technical vocabulary of any field of study permits people to think and communicate more easily, more precisely, and in more complex ways about the content of that field. In this way, language can help us to organize our thoughts into concepts that serve as a kind of shorthand for a whole array of meanings.

But this example also illustrates some of the criticisms of Whorf's hypothesis. The *idea* of deep structure had to occur before someone thought up that particular term. Similarly, you were able to identify and think about basic speech sounds before you learned that they are called phonemes. And you certainly recognize the difference between what someone says and what that person means without having to know that these are called surface structure and deep structure, respectively.

In the same vein, some critics say it is more likely that the need to think about things differently changes a language than the mere fact that language changes the way we think. For example, if the Hopi had been subjected to air raids, they would probably have created a word to distinguish a butterfly from a bomber. In fact, the more complex a society is, the more terms its language contains (Berlin & Kay, 1969). As a society becomes more complex, people simply add new words to accommodate their expanded concepts.

Moreover, although language efficiently organizes human thought, it doesn't necessarily capture all of human experience. For example, the Dani people of New Guinea have only two words for colors—"dark" and "light"—yet they can easily see and learn to label basic colors like red, yellow, and green. They can also judge the similarity of colors much as English-speaking people do (E. R. Heider, 1972; E. R. Heider & Oliver, 1972; Rosch, 1973). Thus the ability to think about colors is quite similar across cultures regardless of how many color terms a culture's language has.

The Dani of New Guinea can perceive and remember the many colors of their world just as readily as you can, even though their language has only two color terms—"light" and "dark." Human thought is not limited to the words in a person's language. Language may indeed influence thought, but it doesn't seem to restrict thought to the extent that Whorf believed.

Linguistic relativity hypothesis
Whorf's idea that patterns of thinking are determined by the specific language one speaks.

In summary, language and thought are intertwined, but thought doesn't totally depend on language (Matsumoto, 1996). People create words to capture important aspects of their experiences, and once created, the words may indeed shape how people think and what they think about. Experience shapes language, and language in turn affects subsequent experience. But people can also think about things for which they have no words, so thinking is not limited to the words in one's language.

We also use language in creative ways, known as *figurative language*. Metaphors and irony are two examples. A *metaphor* compares two things, such as saying that someone was "a lion in combat." This expression doesn't mean that the person really was a lion, but rather draws attention to the soldier's courage and ferocity. *Irony* involves saying one thing but meaning the opposite, as in "What a great day!" when it is pouring rain. In both these cases, language expresses an idea that is different from what the words literally mean. Interestingly, people can often comprehend figurative language as quickly as they comprehend literal language, suggesting again a very flexible relationship between language and thought (Gibbs, 1986).

Review Questions

1. According to Whorf's ____ ____ hypothesis, the language we speak shapes our thinking.

2. Critics of Whorf's hypothesis argue that
   a. when we think of a word we know, the corresponding idea comes to mind.
   b. the need to think about particular things changes our language as much as, if not more than, language shapes our thoughts.
   c. there is no relationship between language and thought.

3. Indicate whether the following statements are true (T) or false (F).
   a. Many words in our language correspond to concepts. ____
   b. The more complex a society is, the more words its language contains.
      ____
   c. Thoughts are not limited to the words in the language a person speaks.
      ____

4. The fact that people can often comprehend figurative language as quickly as they comprehend literal language suggests that the relationship between language and thought is (rigid/flexible).

Answers: 1. linguistic relativity. **2.** b. **3.** a. T. b. T. c. T. **4.** flexible.

Problem Solving

What are three general aspects of the problem-solving process?

Solve the following problems:

Problem 1   You have three measuring spoons (see Figure 7–2). One is filled with 8 teaspoons of salt; the other two are empty but have a capacity of 2 teaspoons each. Divide the salt among the spoons so that only 4 teaspoons of salt remain in the largest spoon.

Problem 2   You have a 5-minute hourglass and a 9-minute hourglass (see Figure 7–3). How can you use them to time a 14-minute barbecue? (Adapted from Sternberg, 1986.)

Most people find these problems very easy. But now try solving more elaborate versions of them (the answers are at the end of this chapter):

Problem 3   You have three measuring spoons (see Figure 7–4). One (spoon A) is filled with 8 teaspoons of salt. The second and third spoons are both empty. The second spoon (spoon B) can hold 5 teaspoons, and the third (spoon C) can hold 3 teaspoons. Divide the salt among the spoons so that spoon A and spoon B each have exactly 4 teaspoons of salt and spoon C is empty.

Problem 4   You have a 5-minute hourglass and a 9-minute hourglass. How can you use them to time a 13-minute barbecue? (Adapted from Sternberg, 1986.)

Most people find these two problems much more difficult than the first two. Why? The answer lies in *interpretation, strategy,* and *evaluation.* Problems 1 and 2 are considered trivial because it's so easy to interpret what is called for, the strategies for solving them are simple, and you can effortlessly verify that each step you take moves you closer to a solution. Problems 3 and 4, in contrast, require some thought to interpret what is called for, the strategies for solving them are not immediately apparent, and it is harder to evaluate whether any given step has actually made progress toward your goal. These three aspects of problem solving—interpretation, strategy, and evaluation—provide a useful framework for investigating this topic.

The Interpretation of Problems

Why is representing the problem so important to finding an effective solution?

The first step in solving a problem is called **problem representation,** which means interpreting or defining the problem. It is tempting to leap ahead and try to solve a problem just as it is presented, but this impulse often leads to poor solutions. For example, if your business is losing money, you might define the problem as deciphering how to cut costs. But by defining the problem so narrowly, you have ruled out other options. A better representation of this problem would be to figure out ways to boost profits—by cutting costs, by increasing income, or both.

To see the importance of problem representation, consider these two problems:

Problem 5   You have four pieces of chain, each of which is made up of 3 links (see Figure 7–5). All links are closed at the beginning of the problem. It costs 2 cents to open a link and 3 cents to close a link. How can you join all 12 links together into a single, continuous circle without paying more than 15 cents?

Problem 6   Arrange six kitchen matches into four equilateral triangles (see Figure 7–6). Each side of every triangle must be only one match in length.

These two problems are difficult because people tend to represent them in ways that impede solutions. For example, in Problem 5 most people assume that the best way to proceed is to open and close the end links on the pieces of chain. As long as they persist with this "conceptual block," they will be unable to solve the problem. If the problem is represented differently, the solution is almost immediately obvious. Similarly, for the kitchen match problem, most people assume that they can work only in two dimensions—that is, that the triangles must lie flat on a surface—or that one match cannot serve as the side of two triangles. When the problem is represented differently, the solution becomes much easier. (The solutions to both of these problems appear at the end of this chapter.)

FIGURE 7–2

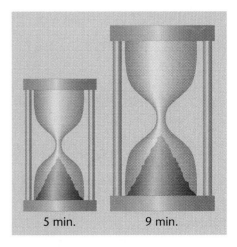

5 min.   9 min.

FIGURE 7–3

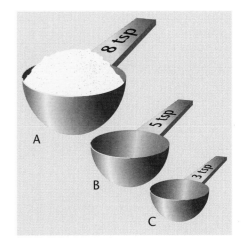

FIGURE 7–4

Problem representation
The first step in solving a problem; it involves interpreting or defining the problem.

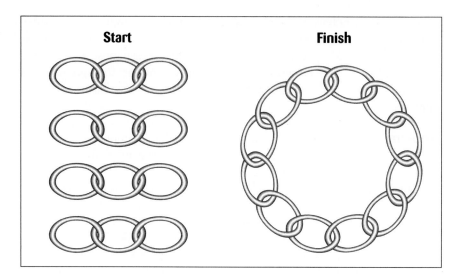

FIGURE 7–5

FIGURE 7–6

The six-match problem. Arrange the six matches so that they form four equilateral triangles. The solution is given in Figure 7–12.

If you have successfully interpreted Problems 5 and 6, give number 7 a try:

Problem 7 A monk wishes to get to a retreat at the top of a mountain. He starts climbing the mountain at sunrise and arrives at the top at sunset of the same day. During the course of his ascent, he travels at various speeds and stops often to rest. He spends the night engaged in meditation. The next day he starts his descent at sunrise, following the same narrow path that he used to climb the mountain. As before, he travels at various speeds and stops often to rest. Because he takes great care not to trip and fall on the way down, the descent takes as long as the ascent. And he does not arrive at the bottom until sunset. Prove that there is one place on the path that the monk passes at exactly the same time of day on the ascent and on the descent.

This problem is extremely difficult to solve if it is represented verbally or mathematically. It is considerably easier to solve if it is represented visually, as you can see from the explanation that appears at the end of this chapter.

Another aspect of successfully representing a problem is deciding which category the problem belongs to. Properly categorizing a problem can provide clues about how to solve it. In fact, once a problem has been properly categorized, its solution may be very easy. Quite often, people who seem to have a knack for solving problems are actually just very skilled at categorizing them in effective ways. Star chess players, for example, can readily categorize a game situation by comparing it to various standard situations stored in their long-term memories. This strategy helps them interpret the current pattern of chess pieces with greater speed and precision than the novice chess player can. Similarly, a seasoned football coach may quickly call for a particular play because he has interpreted a situation on the field in terms of familiar categories. Gaining expertise in any field, from football to physics, consists primarily of increasing your ability to represent and categorize problems so that they can be solved quickly and effectively (Haberlandt, 1997).

Producing Strategies and Evaluating Progress

Why is an algorithm often better for solving a problem than is the process of trial and error?

Once you have properly interpreted a problem, the next steps needed are selecting a solution strategy and evaluating progress toward your goal. A solution strategy can be anything from simple trial and error, to information retrieval based on similar problems, to a set of step-by-step procedures guaranteed to work (called an algorithm), to rule-of-thumb approaches known as heuristics.

Trial and Error   *Trial and error* is a strategy that works best when there are only limited choices. For example, if you have only three or four keys to choose from, trial and error is the best way to find out which one unlocks your friend's garage door. In most cases, however, trial and error wastes time because there are so many different options to test. It is better to eliminate unproductive approaches and zero in on an approach that will work. Let's consider some alternative strategies.

Information Retrieval   One approach is to retrieve from long-term memory information about how such a problem was solved in the past. *Information retrieval* is an especially important option when a solution is needed quickly. For example, pilots simply memorize the slowest speed at which a particular airplane can fly before it stalls.

Algorithms   More complex problems require more complex strategies. An **algorithm** is a problem-solving method that guarantees a solution if it is appropriate for the problem and is properly carried out. For example, to calculate the product of 323 and 546, we multiply the numbers according to the rules of multiplication (the algorithm). If we do it accurately, we are guaranteed to get the right answer. Similarly, to convert temperatures from Fahrenheit to Celsius, we use the algorithm $C = 5/9(F - 32)$.

Heuristics   Because we don't have algorithms for every kind of problem, we often turn to **heuristic,** or rules of thumb, approaches. Heuristics do not guarantee a solution, but they may bring it within reach. Part of problem solving is to decide which heuristic is most appropriate for a given problem (Bourne et al., 1986).

A very simple heuristic is **hill climbing:** We try to move continually closer to our goal without going backward. At each step we evaluate how far "up the hill" we have come, how far we still have to go, and precisely what the next step should be. On a multiple-choice test, for example, one useful hill-climbing strategy is first to eliminate the alternatives that are obviously incorrect. In trying to balance a budget, each reduction in expenses brings you closer to the goal and leaves you with a smaller deficit.

Another problem-solving heuristic is to create **subgoals.** By setting subgoals, we break a problem into smaller, more manageable pieces, each of which is easier to solve than the problem as a whole (Reed, 1996). Consider the problem of the Hobbits and the Orcs:

Problem 8   Three Hobbits and 3 Orcs are on the bank of a river. They all want to get to the other side, but their boat will carry only 2 creatures at a time. Moreover, if at any time the Orcs outnumber the Hobbits, the Orcs will attack the Hobbits. How can all the creatures get across the river without danger to the Hobbits?

The solution to this problem may be found by thinking of it in terms of a series of subgoals. What has to be done to get just one or two creatures across the river safely, temporarily leaving aside the main goal of getting everyone across? We could first send two of the Orcs across and have one of them return. That gets 1 Orc across the river. Now we can think about the next trip. It's clear that we can't then send a single Hobbit across with an Orc, because the Hobbit would be outnumbered as soon as the boat landed. So that means we have to

An experienced football coach can analyze a situation on the field in terms of familiar categories. The coach can then call plays based on this knowledge. This is an example of how expertise can contribute to problem solving.

Algorithm
A step-by-step method of problem solving that guarantees a correct solution.

Heuristics
Rules of thumb that help in simplifying and solving problems, although they do not guarantee a correct solution.

Hill climbing
A heuristic problem-solving strategy in which each step moves you progressively closer to the final goal.

Subgoals
Intermediate, more manageable goals used in one heuristic strategy to make it easier to reach the final goal.

send either 2 Hobbits or 2 Orcs. By working on the problem in this fashion—concentrating on subgoals—we can eventually get everyone across.

Once you have solved Problem 8, you might want to try Problem 9, which is considerably more difficult (the answers to both problems are at the end of the chapter):

Problem 9   This problem is identical to Problem 8, except that there are 5 Hobbits and 5 Orcs and the boat can carry 3 creatures at a time.

Subgoals are often helpful in solving a variety of everyday problems. For example, a student whose goal is to write a term paper might set subgoals by breaking the project into a series of separate tasks: choosing a topic, doing research and taking notes, preparing an outline, writing the first draft, editing, rewriting, and so on. Even the subgoals can sometimes be broken down into separate tasks: Writing the first draft of the paper might break down into the subgoals of writing the introduction, describing the position to be taken, supporting the position with evidence, drawing conclusions, writing a summary, and writing a bibliography. Subgoals make problem solving more manageable because they free us from the burden of having to "get to the other side of the river" all at once. Although the overall purpose of setting subgoals is still to reach the ultimate goal, this tactic allows us to set our sights on closer, more manageable objectives.

One of the most frequently used heuristics, called **means-end analysis,** combines hill climbing and subgoals. Like hill climbing, means-end analysis involves analyzing the difference between the current situation and the desired end, and then doing something to reduce that difference. But in contrast to hill climbing—which does not permit detours away from the final goal in order to solve the problem—means-end analysis takes into account the entire problem situation. It formulates subgoals in such a way as to allow us temporarily to take a step that appears to be backward in order to reach our goal in the end. One example is the pitcher's strategy in a baseball game when confronted with the best batter in the league. The pitcher might opt to walk this batter intentionally even though doing so moves away from the major subgoal of keeping runners off base. Intentional walking might enable the pitcher to keep a run from scoring and so contribute to the ultimate goal of winning the game. This flexibility in thinking is a major benefit of means-end analysis.

But means-end analysis also poses the danger of straying so far from the end goal that the goal disappears altogether. One way of avoiding this is to use the heuristic of **working backward** (Bourne et al., 1986). With this strategy the search for a solution begins at the goal and works backward toward the "givens." Working backward is often used when the goal has more information than the givens and when the operations involved can work in two directions. For example, if you wanted to spend exactly $100 on clothing, it would be difficult to reach that goal simply by buying some items and hoping that they totaled exactly $100. A better strategy would be to buy one item, subtract its cost from $100 to determine how much money you have left, then purchase another item, subtract its cost, and so on, until you have spent $100.

Obstacles to Solving Problems

How can a "set" both help and hinder problem solving?

In everyday life many factors can either help or hinder problem solving. One is a person's level of motivation, or emotional arousal. Generally, we must generate a certain surge of excitement to motivate ourselves to solve a problem, yet too much arousal can hamper our ability to find a solution (see Chapter 8, Motivation and Emotion).

Means-end analysis
A heuristic strategy that aims to reduce the discrepancy between the current situation and the desired goal at a number of intermediate points.

Working backward
A heuristic strategy in which one works backward from the desired goal to the given conditions.

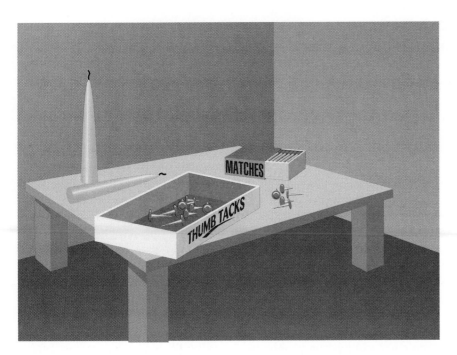

FIGURE 7–7
To test the effects of functional fixedness, participants might be given the items shown on the table and asked to mount a candle on the wall. See Figure 7–15 for a solution.

Another factor that can either help or hinder problem solving is **set**—our tendency to perceive and to approach problems in certain ways. Set determines which information we tend to retrieve from memory to help us find a solution. Set can be helpful if we have learned operations that we can apply to the present situation. Much of our formal education involves learning sets and ways to solve problems (that is, learning heuristics and algorithms). But sets can also create obstacles, especially when a novel approach is needed. The most successful problem solvers have many different sets to choose from and can judge when to change sets or when to abandon them entirely. Great ideas and inventions come out of such flexibility.

One type of set that can seriously hinder problem solving is called **functional fixedness.** Consider Figure 7–7. Do you see a way to mount the candle on the wall? If not, you are probably stymied by functional fixedness. The more you use an object in only one way, the harder it is to see new uses for it, because you have "assigned" the object to a fixed function. To some extent part of the learning process is to assign correct functions to objects—this is how we form concepts. But we need to be open to seeing that an object can be used for an entirely different function. (The solution to this problem appears at the end of the chapter.) See *Applying Psychology* for techniques that will improve your problem-solving skills.

Because creative problem solving requires thinking up original ideas, deliberate strategies don't always help. Solutions to many problems rely on *insight*, often a seemingly arbitrary flash "out of the blue." (See Chapter 5, Learning.) Psychologists have only recently begun to investigate such spontaneous and unplanned problem-solving processes as insight and intuition (Bechara et al., 1997; see also Underwood, 1996).

You can't always sit back and wait for a flash of insight to solve a problem. When you need a quick solution, you can do some things that encourage creative answers. Sometimes we get so enmeshed in the details of a problem that we

Set
The tendency to perceive and to approach problems in certain ways.

Functional fixedness
The tendency to perceive only a limited number of uses for an object, thus interfering with the process of problem solving.

A P P L Y I N G   P S Y C H O L O G Y

Becoming a More Skillful Problem Solver

Even the best problem solvers occasionally get stumped, but you can do some things that will help you find a solution. These tactics encourage you to discard unproductive approaches and find strategies that are more effective.

1. **Eliminate poor choices**

   When we are surer of what won't work than what will, the *tactic of elimination* can be very helpful. First, list all the possible solutions you can think of, and then discard all the solutions that seem to lead in the wrong direction. Now examine the list more closely. Some solutions seem to be ineffective but on closer examination may turn out to be good.

2. **Visualize a solution**

   Sometimes people who are stumped by a problem can find a solution by using a basic building block of thought: visual images. *Visualizing* often involves diagramming courses of action (J. L. Adams, 1980). For example, in the Hobbit and Orc problem draw a picture of the river and show the Hobbits and Orcs at each stage of the solution as they are ferried across. Drawing a diagram can help you grasp what a problem calls for. You also can visualize mentally.

3. **Develop expertise**

   People get stumped on problems because they lack the knowledge to find a quick solution. Experts not only know more about a particular subject, but they also organize their information in larger "chunks" that are extensively interconnected, much like a cross-referencing system in a library.

4. **Think flexibly**

   Striving to be more flexible and creative is an excellent tactic for becoming a better problem solver. Many problems require some original thinking. For example, how many unusual uses can you think of for a brick? Problems that have no single correct solution and that require a flexible, inventive approach call for **divergent thinking**—or thinking that involves generating many different possible answers. In contrast, **convergent thinking** is thinking that narrows its focus in a particular direction, assuming that there is only one, or at most a limited number of right solutions (Guilford, 1967). Many business and engineering schools stress divergent thinking skills to encourage more creative problem solving (Kaplan & Simon, 1990).

lose sight of the obvious. If we stop thinking about the problem for a while, we may return to it from a new angle (H. G. Murray & Denny, 1969). Then we may be able to *redefine* the problem, circumventing an unproductive mind-set.

The value of looking for new ways to represent a difficult problem cannot be overstressed. Ask yourself, "What is the real problem here? Can the problem be interpreted in other ways?" Also be open to potential solutions that at first seem unproductive. The solution may turn out to be more effective, or it may suggest related solutions that *will* work. This is the rationale behind the technique called **brainstorming:** When solving a problem, generate a lot of ideas before you review and evaluate them (Haefele, 1962).

Finally, people often become more creative when exposed to creative peers and teachers (Amabile, 1983). Although some creative people work well alone, many others are stimulated by working in teams with other creative people.

Divergent thinking
Thinking that meets the criteria of originality, inventiveness, and flexibility.

Convergent thinking
Thinking that is directed toward one correct solution to a problem.

Brainstorming
A problem-solving strategy in which an individual or a group produces numerous ideas and evaluates them only after all ideas have been collected.

Review Questions

1. Match each problem-solving strategy with the appropriate definition.

   algorithm _____

   heuristic _____

   hill climbing _____

   a. rule-of-thumb approach that helps in simplifying and solving problems, although it doesn't guarantee a correct solution

   b. strategy in which each step moves you closer to a solution

   c. step-by-step method that guarantees a solution

means-end analysis ____   d. strategy in which one moves from the goal to the starting point

working backward ____   e. strategy that aims to reduce the discrepancy between the current situation and the desired goal at a number of intermediate points

subgoal creation ____   f. breaking down the solution to a larger problem into a set of smaller, more manageable steps

2. Which of the following can sometimes be an obstacle to problem solving?

  a. sets   c. functional fixedness

  b. overexcitement   d. all of the above

3. Match each form of thinking with its definition and the kind of problems to which it is suited.

  ____ divergent thinking

    a. suited to problems for which there is one correct solution or a limited number of solutions

    b. thinking that involves generating many different ideas

  ____ convergent thinking

    c. suited to problems that have no one right solution and require an inventive approach

    d. thinking that limits its focus to a particular direction

4. The first step in problem solving is problem ____.

5. ____ and ____ is a problem-solving strategy based on the successive elimination of incorrect solutions.

6. The simplest and fastest way to produce a solution to a problem is through ____ ____.

7. Producing many ideas without evaluating them prematurely is called ____.

Answers: 1. Algorithm–c; heuristic–a; hill climbing–b; means-end analysis–e; working backward–d; subgoal creation–f. 2. d. 3. divergent thinking–b and c; convergent thinking–a and d. 4. representation (or interpretation). 5. trial and error. 6. information retrieval. 7. brainstorming.

Decision Making

How does decision making differ from problem solving?

Decision making is a special kind of problem solving in which we already know all the possible solutions or choices. The task is not to come up with new solutions but rather to identify the best available one based on whatever criteria we are using. This might sound like a fairly simple process, but sometimes we have to juggle a large and complex set of criteria as well as many possible options. For example, suppose you are looking for an apartment and there are hundreds available. A reasonable rent is important to you, but so are good neighbors, a good location, a low noise level, and cleanliness. If you find a noisy apartment with undesirable neighbors but at a cheap rent, should you take it? Is it a better choice than an apartment in a better location with less noise but a higher rent? How can you weigh your various criteria and make the best choice?

Logical Decision Making

How would you go about making a truly logical decision?

The logical way to make a decision is to rate each of the available choices on all the criteria you are using, arriving at some overall measure of the extent to which each choice matches your criteria. For each choice the attractive features

TABLE 7-1	Compensatory Decision Table for Purchase of a New Car			
	Price (weight = 4)	Gas Mileage (weight = 8)	Service Record (weight = 10)	Weighted Total
Car 1	5 (20)	2 (16)	1 (10)	(46)
Car 2	1 (4)	4 (32)	4 (40)	(76)
Ratings: 5= excellent; 1= poor				

can offset or compensate for the unattractive features, which is why this approach to decision making is called a **compensatory model.**

Table 7–1 illustrates one of the most useful compensatory models. The various criteria are listed across the top, and each one is assigned a weight according to its importance. Here the decision involves the purchase of a new car, and only three criteria are considered: price (which is not weighted heavily), gas mileage (weighted twice as heavily as price), and service record (weighted more heavily than mileage). Each car is then rated from 1 (poor) to 5 (excellent) on each of the criteria. You can see that Car 1 has an excellent price (rated 5) but relatively poor gas mileage (rated 2) and service record (rated 1); Car 2 has a less desirable price but fairly good mileage and service record. Each rating is then multiplied by the weight for that criterion (for example, for Car 1 the price rating of 5 is multiplied by the weight of 4), and the result is put in parentheses next to the rating. The numbers in parentheses are added to give a total for each car. Clearly, Car 2 is the better choice. It has a less desirable price, but that is offset by its well-rated mileage and service record, and to this particular buyer mileage and service record are more important than price.

A table like this allows evaluation of a large number of choices using a large number of criteria. It can be extremely helpful in making choices such as which college to attend, which job offer to accept, which career to pursue, where to take a vacation, which apartment to rent. If you have properly weighted each criterion and correctly rated each alternative, the option with the highest total score is in fact the most rational choice, given the information available to you.

Alternative Approaches

How are most everyday decisions made?

Most people do not follow a precise and logical system of making most decisions. Rather, they use various **noncompensatory models** in which shortcomings on one criterion are not offset by strengths on others. Especially popular is the *elimination-by-aspects* tactic (Reed, 1988). In this case you toss out specific choices if they do not meet one or two of your requirements, regardless of how good they are on other criteria. For example, you might eliminate Car 2, regardless of all its advantages, because "it costs too much." As this example illustrates, noncompensatory models tend to be shortsighted. They do not help us weigh the values of particular features, nor do they invite us to compare all the alternatives. As a result, such a decision-making model can lead to a decision that is adequate, but not the best.

If you were shopping for a new car, would you use a compensatory or a noncompensatory approach to decision making?

Compensatory model
A rational decision-making model in which choices are systematically evaluated on various criteria.

Noncompensatory model
A decision-making model in which weaknesses in one or more criteria are not offset by strengths in other criteria.

Sometimes mixing compensatory and noncompensatory strategies can lead to a decision. When there are many alternatives and many criteria, a noncompensatory approach can eliminate any choices that are especially weak on one or more key criteria, even though they may be strong on other criteria. When we've narrowed the field to a few alternatives, all of which are at least average on the various criteria, we might then use a compensatory decision model to identify the best choice from the remaining alternatives. For example, when buying a car, we can eliminate all the choices that are too expensive or all those with especially poor service records (noncompensatory strategy). We could then evaluate and choose from the remaining choices based on a number of weighted criteria (compensatory strategy).

Choosing an appropriate decision-making model often depends on how much is at stake. We are more likely to use a compensatory model when the stakes are high: buying a home or choosing a college, for example. When the stakes are low, as in deciding which pair of shoes to wear, a noncompensatory model can help us decide quickly.

When Heuristics Lead Us Astray

What are some factors that can lead to poor choices?

Just as we use rule-of-thumb approaches in solving problems, we use them in making decisions. These decision-making heuristics can save us a great deal of time and effort, but they do not always produce the best choices. Heuristics can sometimes lead us astray.

One example is errors in judgment based on the **representativeness heuristic** (Kahneman & Tversky, 1996; Rottenstreich & Tversky, 1997). We use representativeness whenever we make a decision based on information that matches our model of the "typical" member of a category. Representativeness can help simplify the decision-making process. For example, if every time you went shopping you bought the least expensive items, and if all of these items turned out to be poorly made, you might eventually decide not to buy anything that is low-priced because you assume that it will be representative of "cheap and shoddy."

One potential flaw of representativeness is our tendency to *stereotype*; that is, to attribute certain characteristics to all members of a particular group. For example, many people will not hire elderly workers because they hold a stereotype of the elderly as suffering cognitive and physical declines. They then judge *all* elderly people as being representative of their general model. (Stereotypes are discussed in more detail in Chapter 14.)

Another rule-of-thumb approach that can lead decision making astray is the **availability heuristic.** Without full and accurate information, we often make decisions based on whatever information we can easily retrieve from memory, even though this information may be wrong. In one experiment people were asked whether the letter *r* appears more frequently as the first or third letter in English words. The correct answer is third, but most said it appears more frequently as the first letter because words with an initial *r* are more readily available in memory. Examples of the availability heuristic affecting choices are plentiful (Gilovich, 1991). For example, after a widely publicized plane crash some people avoid flying and instead travel by car, even though serious accidents are far more common on the highways than in the air. The reason for this faulty judgment is that the plane disaster is so easily recalled. People are using the availability heuristic to make a faulty choice.

Another faulty heuristic, closely related to availability, is **confirmation bias**—the tendency to seek evidence in support of our existing beliefs and to ignore evidence that contradicts them (Myers, 1996). Confirmation bias helps maintain stereotypes. For example, if you consider elderly people to be cognitively slow,

Representativeness heuristic
A heuristic by which a new situation is judged on the basis of its resemblance to a stereotypical model.

Availability heuristic
A heuristic by which a judgment or decision is based on information that is most easily retrieved from memory.

Confirmation bias
The tendency to look for evidence in support of a belief and to ignore evidence that would disprove a belief.

you are apt to selectively remember times when elderly people seemed confused or forgetful. But you are also apt to ignore the many instances when elderly people were just as cognitively able as you are. If you ignore this disconfirming evidence, your stereotype of the elderly will remain.

Culture and Decision Making

Can culture affect our decisions?

Psychologists have only recently begun to explore the influence of culture on decision making (Radford, 1996). For example, a study that compared university students from Australia, China, and Japan found that when coping with the pressure of making a difficult decision, Japanese students experienced more *decisional stress* and tended to be more complacent than Australian students (Radford et al., 1990). In addition, the Japanese felt it was important to involve the members of an entire team in a decision-making process, whereas the Australian students tended to be more self-reliant and to focus on their own personal ability. As the world's cultures become increasingly interdependent, psychologists will need to learn more about the influence of culture on decision making.

Review Questions

1. Matt is trying to decide between going camping in the Rockies or hiking in the Grand Canyon. To make the choice, he sets up some criteria for a good vacation and then rates the two alternatives on each criterion to see how they stack up against each other. Matt is using a _____ model of decision making.

2. Decision-making models that do not try to systematically weigh comparisons among alternatives are _____ models.

3. People are most likely to use a compensatory model when
   a. the stakes are low.
   b. the stakes are high.
   c. others are observing them.
   d. the problem is simple.

4. Match each decision-making heuristic with the appropriate definition.

representativeness heuristic _____   a. making judgments based on whatever information can be most readily retrieved from memory

availability heuristic _____   b. attending to evidence that supports your existing beliefs and ignoring other evidence

confirmation bias _____   c. making decisions based on information that matches your model of what is "typical" of a certain category

Answers: 1. compensatory. 2. noncompensatory. 3. b. 4. representativeness heuristic–c; availability heuristic–a; confirmation bias–b.

Intelligence and Mental Abilities

What questions are asked by psychologists who study intelligence?

Answer the following questions:

1. Describe the difference between *laziness* and *idleness*.
2. Which direction would you have to face so that your right hand would be pointing north?
3. What does *obliterate* mean?
4. In what way are an hour and a week alike?

5. Select the item that completes the following series of four figures:

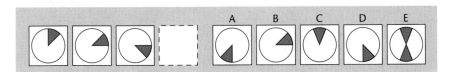

6. Choose the lettered block that best completes the pattern in the following figure.

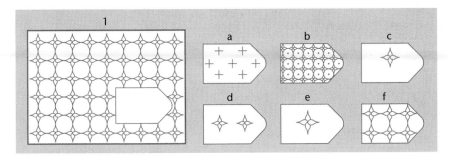

7. If three pencils cost 25 cents, how many pencils can you buy for 75 cents?

8. Choose the word that is most nearly *opposite* in meaning to the word in capital letters:
   SCHISM: (a) majority;　(b) union;　(c) uniformity;　(d) conference;
   　　　　　(e) construction

9. Choose the set of words that, when inserted in the sentence, best fits in with the meaning of the sentence as a whole: From the first, the islanders, despite an outward _____, did what they could to _____ the ruthless occupying power.
   (a) harmony . . . assist
   (b) enmity . . . embarrass
   (c) rebellion . . . foil
   (d) resistance . . . destroy
   (e) acquiescence . . . thwart

10. Select the lettered pair that best expresses a relationship similar to that expressed in the original pair:
    CRUTCH: LOCOMOTION: (a) paddle: canoe;　(b) hero: worship;
    (c) horse: carriage;　(d) spectacles: vision;　(e) statement: contention

11. The first three items in the following figure are alike in some way. Find the item at the right that goes with the first three.

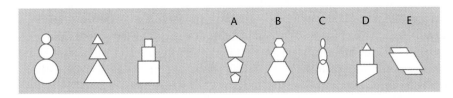

12. Decide how the first two items in the following figure are related to each other. Then find the one item at the right that goes with the third item in the same way that the second item goes with the first.

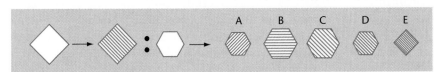

13. For each item in the following figure, decide whether it can be completely covered by using some or all of the given pieces without overlapping any.

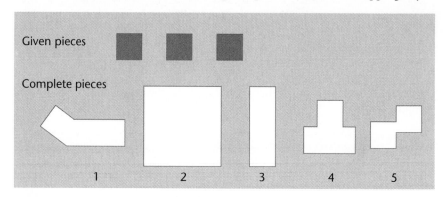

These questions were taken from various tests of **intelligence,** or general intellectual ability (the answers appear at the end of the chapter). An *ability* is a skill; an *aptitude* is a *potential* ability. Do intelligence tests accurately reflect what intelligence is all about? What exactly is intelligence, and how is it related to creativity?

Theories of Intelligence

What are some of the major theories of intelligence?

For more than a century, psychologists have argued about what constitutes general intelligence—or even if "general" intelligence actually exists. One of their most basic questions is whether intelligence is a single, general mental ability or whether it is composed of many separate abilities.

Early Theorists   Charles Spearman, an early-twentieth-century British psychologist, maintained that intelligence is quite general—a kind of well, or spring, of mental energy that flows through every action. Spearman believed that people who are bright in one area are often bright in other areas as well. The intelligent person understands things quickly, makes sound decisions, carries on interesting conversations, and tends to behave intelligently in a variety of situations.

The American psychologist L. L. Thurstone disagreed with Spearman. Thurstone argued that intelligence is composed of seven distinct kinds of mental abilities (Thurstone, 1938): *spatial ability, memory, perceptual speed, word fluency, numerical ability, reasoning,* and *verbal meaning.* Unlike Spearman, Thurstone believed that these abilities are relatively independent of one another. Thus a person with exceptional spatial ability (the ability to perceive distance, recognize shapes, and so on) might lack word fluency. To Thurstone these primary mental abilities, taken together, make up general intelligence.

In contrast to Thurstone, the American psychologist R. B. Cattell (1971) identified just two clusters of mental abilities. The first cluster—*crystallized intelligence*—includes abilities such as reasoning and verbal and numerical skills. These are the kinds of abilities stressed in school, and they tend to be greatly affected by experience and formal education. Cattell's second cluster of abilities—*fluid intelligence*—is made up of skills such as spatial and visual imagery, awareness of visual details, and a capacity for rote memory. Scores on tests of fluid intelligence are much less influenced by experience and education.

Contemporary Theorists   More recently, two American psychologists have proposed alternative theories of intelligence. Robert Sternberg's *triarchic theory of intelligence* concludes that human intelligence encompasses a much broader variety of skills than imagined by earlier theorists and that skills necessary for effective performance in the world are just as important as the more

Intelligence
A general term referring to the ability or abilities involved in learning and adaptive behavior.

limited skills assessed by traditional intelligence tests (Sternberg, 1985, 1986). Sternberg illustrates his theory by comparing three graduate students he worked with at Yale, whom he calls Alice, Barbara, and Celia. Alice fit the standard definition of intelligence perfectly: She scored high on tests of intelligence and achieved nearly a 4.0 average as an undergraduate. Her analytical abilities were excellent. Alice excelled in her first year of graduate work, but in the second year she was having trouble developing her own research ideas and dropped from the top of the class to the lower half. In contrast, Barbara's undergraduate record was poor, and her admission test scores were well below Yale's standards. Nevertheless, professors who had worked with her as an undergraduate described her as highly creative and able to do good research. Barbara proved to be the associate Sternberg had hoped for. In fact, he believes that some of his most important work has been done in collaboration with her. The third graduate student, Celia, was somewhere between the other two: She had good recommendations and fairly good admission test scores. She did skillful (but not great) research work, yet she had the easiest time finding a good job after graduate school.

These three students represent the three aspects of Sternberg's triarchic theory of intelligence. Alice was high in **componential intelligence,** which refers to the mental abilities emphasized in most theories of intelligence, such as the ability to learn how to do things or acquire new knowledge and carry out tasks effectively. Barbara was particularly strong in what Sternberg calls **experiential intelligence**—the ability to adjust to new tasks, to use new concepts, to respond effectively in new situations, to gain insight, and to think creatively. Celia had the easiest time finding a job because of her strong **contextual intelligence**—her ability to capitalize on her strengths and compensate for her weaknesses. People like Celia make the most of their talents by seeking situations that match their skills, by shaping those situations so they can use those skills to best advantage, and by knowing when to change situations to better fit their talents.

An influential alternative to Sternberg's theory of intelligence is the *theory of multiple intelligences,* advanced by Howard Gardner and his associates at Harvard (Gardner, 1983a, 1993, 1997). Like Thurstone, Gardner argues that intelligence consists of many separate abilities, each relatively independent of the others. He lists seven: *logical-mathematical intelligence, linguistic intelligence, spatial intelligence, musical intelligence, bodily kinesthetic intelligence, interpersonal intelligence,* and *intrapersonal intelligence* (Gardner, 1993). The first two are included in the other theories of intelligence we have discussed. Spatial intelligence, the ability to imagine the relative location of objects in space, is particularly prominent in people with artistic talent. Exceptional musical intelligence is demonstrated by people with an outstanding gift for music, while outstanding athletes and dancers show strong bodily kinesthetic intelligence. People who are extraordinarily talented at understanding and communicating with others, such as exceptional teachers and parents, have strong interpersonal intelligence. Intrapersonal intelligence reflects the ancient adage "Know thyself." People who rank high in it understand themselves and use this knowledge effectively to reach their goals. Daniel Goleman has recently expanded on the concepts of interpersonal and intrapersonal intelligence with his notion of *emotional intelligence.* (see *Highlights*).

Author Toni Morrison, whose vivid, compelling prose has been likened to poetry, possesses an abundance of what Howard Gardner calls linguistic intelligence. In recognition of her exceptional talent, she was awarded a Nobel Prize in Literature.

Intelligence Tests

What kinds of intelligence tests are used today?

Formal theories of intelligence shape the content of intelligence tests and other measures of mental abilities. These tests are used to help evaluate the abilities of millions of people, including students. How are these tests developed and administered, and do they accurately measure intelligence?

Componential intelligence
According to Sternberg, the ability to acquire new knowledge, to solve problems effectively.

Experiential intelligence
Sternberg's term for the ability to adapt creatively in new situations, to use insight.

Contextual intelligence
According to Sternberg, the ability to select contexts in which you can excel, to shape the environment to fit your strengths.

Emotional Intelligence

Why do people with high IQs sometimes fail, while those with more modest intellectual skills prosper? Psychologist Daniel Goleman suggests that differences in emotional intelligence may be responsible. **Emotional intelligence** refers to how effectively people perceive and understand their own emotions and the emotions of others, and can regulate and manage their emotional behavior. Goleman contends that one of the reasons that IQ tests sometimes fail to accurately predict success is that they do not take into account an individual's emotional competency. According to Goleman, "The brightest among us can flounder on the shoals of unbridled passions and unruly impulses; people with high IQs can be stunningly poor pilots of their private lives" (Goleman, 1997, p. 34).

Five characteristics are generally recognized as contributing to emotional intelligence (Goleman, 1997; Mayer & Salovey, 1997):

- **Knowing your own emotions.** The ability to monitor and recognize our own feelings *as we experience them* is of central importance to self-awareness and all other dimensions of emotional intelligence. Knowing your emotions helps you to make better decisions about important things such as whom to marry, what job to take, and what your *real* goals are.

- **Managing your emotions.** Managing emotions refers to the ability to control impulses, to cope effectively with sadness, depression, and minor setbacks, and to control how long emotions last. Handling emotions responsibly builds on the capacity for self-awareness.

- **Using emotions to motivate yourself.** This component of emotional intelligence refers to the capacity to marshal emotions toward achieving personal goals. People who are effective at appropriately directing their emotions are more likely to lead personally satisfying and productive lives.

- **Recognizing the emotions of other people.** To be sensitive to the emotions of others, we must be able to read subtle, nonverbal cues that reveal what other people really want and need. Recognizing how other people feel makes us more effective in all social situations.

> Because the concept of emotional intelligence is relatively new, researchers have only begun to evaluate its scientific merit.

- **Managing relationships.** To manage relationships effectively you must be able to accurately acknowledge and *display* your emotions while being sensitive to the emotions of others. Socially competent people generally inspire, persuade, and influence other people, as well as enjoy satisfying intimate relationships.

Goleman contends that many of today's social problems—including senseless violence, depression, and the escalating divorce rate—reflect our failure to nurture emotional skills. While acknowledging the contribution of genetics to the development of emotional character, Goleman emphasizes that education and early experience also play an important role in establishing emotional competency. He argues that our schools should teach more than academic skills; they should also nurture basic emotional skills such as self-awareness, self-control, empathy, and cooperation. Schools that have incorporated Goleman's suggestions have reported some success in teaching students to get along better with one another (Mitchell, Sachs, & Tu, 1997). Parents can help, too, by teaching children to identify, understand, and manage their emotions more effectively (Kuebli, 1999).

Because the concept of emotional intelligence is relatively new, researchers have only begun to evaluate its scientific merit (Sternberg & Kaufman, 1998). Thus we must approach this concept with skepticism. Nevertheless, initial studies have shown promising results. For example, Mayer & Gehr (1996) found that the ability to accurately identify emotions in other people correlates positively with SAT scores. Other investigators, however, remain skeptical. In a series of three studies aimed at identifying the unique nature of emotional intelligence, Davies, Stankov, and Roberts (1998) concluded that emotional intelligence might not be a new concept at all. Instead they argue that emotional intelligence is already assessed by more traditional measures of intelligence and personality. More research is obviously needed before we can fully understand the scientific validity and usefulness of this intriguing, and potentially important, new theory of intelligence.

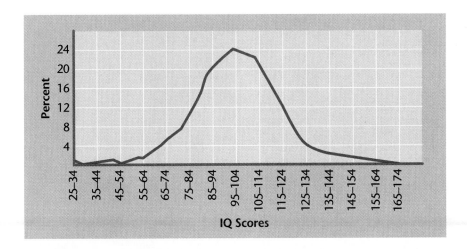

FIGURE 7–8

The approximate distribution of IQ scores in the population. Note that the greatest percentage of scores fall around 100. Very low percentages of people score at the two extremes of the curve.

The Stanford–Binet Intelligence Scale

The first intelligence test was designed by two Frenchmen, Alfred Binet and Theodore Simon. The test, first used in Paris in 1905, was designed to identify children who might have difficulty in school.

The first *Binet–Simon Scale* consisted of 30 tests arranged in order of increasing difficulty. With each child the examiner started at the top of the list and worked down until the child could no longer answer questions. By 1908 enough children had been tested to predict how the average child would perform at each age level. From these scores Binet developed the concept of *mental age*. A child who scores as well as an average 4-year-old has a mental age of 4; a child who scores as well as an average 12-year-old has a mental age of 12.

A well-known adaptation of the Binet–Simon Scale, the *Stanford–Binet Intelligence Scale*, was prepared at Stanford University by L. M. Terman and published in 1916. Terman introduced the now famous term **intelligence quotient (IQ)** to establish a numerical value of intelligence, setting the score of 100 for a person of average intelligence. Figure 7–8 shows an approximate distribution of IQ scores in the population.

The latest version of the Stanford–Binet, released in 1986, replaced items that had been found to have cultural or gender bias with neutral items. New items were added that permitted testers to identify mentally retarded and intellectually gifted people, as well as people with specific learning disabilities (Sattler, 1992). Questions 1 and 2 on page 244 were drawn from an early version of the Stanford–Binet.

The current Stanford–Binet Intelligence Scale is designed to measure four kinds of mental abilities that are almost universally considered to be part of intelligence: *verbal reasoning, abstract/visual reasoning, quantitative reasoning,* and *short-term memory.* Test items vary with the subject's age. For example, a 3-year-old might be asked to describe the purpose of a cup and to name objects such as a chair and a key. A 6-year-old might be asked to define words such as *orange* and *envelope* and to complete a sentence such as "An inch is short; a mile is ____." A 12-year-old might be asked to define *skill* and *juggler* and to complete the sentence: "The streams are dry ____ there has been little rain" (Cronbach, 1990).

The Stanford–Binet test is given individually by a trained examiner. It is best suited for children, adolescents, and very young adults.

The Wechsler Intelligence Scales

The most commonly used individual test of intelligence for adults is the **Wechsler Adult Intelligence Scale–Third Edition (WAIS-III)**, originally developed in the late 1930s by David Wechsler, a psychologist. The Stanford–Binet emphasizes verbal skills, but Wechsler felt

Emotional intelligence
According to Goleman, a form of intelligence that refers to how effectively people perceive and understand their own emotions and the emotions of others and can regulate and manage their emotional behavior.

Intelligence quotient (IQ)
A numerical value given to intelligence that is determined from the scores on an intelligence test; based on a score of 100 for average intelligence.

Wechsler Adult Intelligence Scale-Third Edition (WAIS–III)
An individual intelligence test developed especially for adults; measures both verbal and performance abilities.

The Wechsler Intelligence Scales, developed by David Wechsler, are individual intelligence tests administered to one person at a time. There are versions of the Wechsler Scales for both adults and children. Here a child and an adult are being asked to copy a pattern using blocks.

that adult intelligence consists more of the ability to handle life situations than to solve verbal and abstract problems.

The WAIS-III is divided into two parts, one stressing verbal skills, the other performance skills. The verbal scale includes tests of information ("Who wrote *Paradise Lost?*"), tests of simple arithmetic ("Sam had three pieces of candy, and Joe gave him four more. How many pieces of candy did Sam have then?"), and tests of comprehension ("What should you do if you see someone forget a book on a bus?"). The performance scale also measures routine tasks. People are asked to "find the missing part" (buttonholes in a coat, for example), to copy patterns, and to arrange 3 to 5 pictures so that they tell a story. Questions 3 and 4 on page 244 resemble questions on the WAIS–III.

Although the content of the WAIS-III is somewhat more sophisticated than that of the Stanford–Binet, Wechsler's chief innovation was in scoring. His test gives separate verbal and performance scores as well as an overall IQ score. On some items one or two extra points can be earned, depending on the complexity of the answer given. This unique scoring system gives credit for the reflective qualities that we expect to find in intelligent adults. On some questions both speed and accuracy affect the score.

Wechsler also developed a similar intelligence test for use with school-age children. Like the WAIS-III, the 1991 version of the **Wechsler Intelligence Scale for Children–Third Edition (WISC-III)** yields separate verbal and performance scores as well as an overall IQ score.

Group Tests   The Stanford–Binet, the WAIS-III, and the WISC-III are individual tests. The examiner takes a person to an isolated room, spreads the materials on a table, and spends from 30 to 90 minutes administering the test. The examiner may then take another hour or so to score the test according to detailed instructions in the manual. This is a time-consuming, costly operation, and the examiner's behavior may greatly influence the score. For these reasons test makers have devised **group tests.** These are written tests that a single examiner can administer to a large group of people at the same time. Instead of sitting across the table from a person who asks you questions, you receive a test booklet that contains questions for you to answer within a certain amount of time. Questions 5–9 on page 245 are from group tests.

There are group tests not only for intelligence but also for aptitudes and other mental abilities. Schools are among the biggest users of group tests. From

Wechsler Intelligence Scale for Children-Third Edition (WISC–III)
An individual intelligence test developed especially for school-aged children; measures verbal and performance abilities and also yields an overall IQ score.

Group tests
Written intelligence tests administered by one examiner to many people at one time.

fourth grade through high school, tests such as the *School and College Ability Tests (SCAT)* and the *California Test of Mental Maturity (CTMM)* are used to measure students' abilities. The *SAT*—Questions 10–13 on pages 245–246—and the *American College Testing Program (ACTP)* are designed to measure a student's potential to do college-level work. The *Graduate Record Examination (GRE)* performs the same function on the graduate level. Group tests are also widely used in different industries, the civil service, and the military.

Group tests have some distinct advantages over individualized tests. They eliminate bias on the part of the examiner, and answer sheets can be scored quickly and objectively. But group tests also have some distinct disadvantages. The examiner is unlikely to notice people who are tired, ill, or confused by the directions. People who are not used to being tested tend to do less well on group tests than on individual tests. Finally, emotionally disturbed children seem to do better on individual tests than on group tests (Anastasi & Urbina, 1997).

Performance and Culture-Fair Tests To perform well on the intelligence tests we have discussed, people must be adept at the language in which the test is given. Standard intelligence tests simply cannot accurately assess cognitive abilities in children who are not fluent in English. How, then, can we test these people? Psychologists have designed two general forms of tests for such situations: performance tests and culture-fair tests.

Performance tests consist of problems that minimize or eliminate the use of words. One of the earliest performance tests, the *Seguin Form Board*, was devised in 1866 to test people with mental retardation. The form board is essentially a puzzle. The examiner removes specifically designed cutouts, stacks them in a predetermined order, and asks the person to replace them as quickly as possible. A more recent performance test, the *Porteus Maze*, consists of a series of increasingly difficult printed mazes. Subjects trace their way through the maze without lifting the pencil from the paper. Such tests require the test taker to pay close attention to a task for an extended period and to continuously plan ahead in order to make the correct choices.

Culture-fair tests are designed to measure the intelligence of people who are outside the culture in which the test was devised. Like performance tests, culture-fair tests minimize or eliminate the use of language. Culture-fair tests also try to downplay skills and values—such as the need for speed—that vary from culture to culture. In the *Goodenough–Harris Drawing Test*, subjects are asked to draw the best picture of a person they can. Drawings are scored for proportions, correct and complete representation of the parts of the body, detail in clothing, and so on. An example of a culture-fair item from Cattell's *Culture-Fair Intelligence Test* is Question 5 on page 245. Another culture-fair test is the *Progressive Matrices* (Question 6 on page 245). This test consists of 60 designs, each with a missing part. The person is given 6 to 8 possible choices to replace the part. The test involves various logical relationships, requires discrimination, and can be given to one person or to a group.

What Makes a Good Test?

What are some important characteristics of a good test?

How can we tell if intelligence tests will produce consistent results no matter when they are given? And how can we tell if they really measure what they claim to measure? Psychologists address these questions by referring to a test's reliability and validity. Issues of reliability and validity apply equally to all psychological tests, not just to tests of mental abilities. In Chapter 10, for example, we re-examine these issues as they apply to personality assessment.

Performance tests
Intelligence tests that minimize the use of language.

Culture-fair tests
Intelligence tests designed to eliminate cultural bias by minimizing skills and values that vary from one culture to another.

Reliability   By **reliability** psychologists mean the dependability and consistency of the scores that a test yields. If your alarm clock is set for 8:15 A.M., and it goes off at that time every morning, it is reliable. But if it is set for 8:15 and rings at 8:00 one morning and 8:40 the next, you cannot depend on it; it is unreliable. Similarly, a test has reliability when it yields consistent results.

How do we know if a test is reliable? The simplest way to find out is to give the test to a group and then, after a short time, give the same people the same test again. If they score approximately the same each time, the test is reliable.

There is a drawback, however. How do we know that people have not simply remembered the answers from the first testing and repeated them the second time around? To avoid this possibility, psychologists prefer to give two equivalent tests, both designed to measure the same thing. If people score the same on both forms, the tests are considered reliable. One way to create alternate forms is to split a single test into two parts—for example, to assign odd-numbered items to one part and even-numbered items to the other. If scores on the two halves agree, the test has **split-half reliability.** Most intelligence tests do in fact have alternate equivalent forms, just as each college admission test often has many versions.

How reliable are intelligence tests? In general, people's IQ scores on most intelligence tests are quite stable. Performance and culture-fair tests are somewhat less reliable. Scores on even the best tests, however, vary somewhat from one day to another. Therefore many testing services now report a person's score along with a range of scores that allows for some day-to-day variation.

Validity   We have seen that many intelligence tests are reliable, but do these tests really measure "intelligence"? When psychologists ask this question, they are concerned with test validity. **Validity** refers to a test's ability to measure what it has been designed to measure. How do we know if a given test actually measures what it claims to measure?

One measure of validity is known as **content validity**—whether the test contains an adequate sample of the skills or knowledge that it is supposed to measure. Most widely used intelligence tests, such as those from which Questions 1–13 were taken, seem to measure at least some of the mental abilities that we think of as part of intelligence. These include planning, memory, understanding, reasoning, concentration, and the use of language. Although they may not adequately sample all aspects of intelligence equally well, they at least seem to have some content validity.

Another way to measure a test's validity is to see if a person's score on that test closely matches his or her score on another test designed to measure the same thing. The two different scores should be correlated if they are both measures of the same ability. In fact, various intelligence test scores do relate well with one another despite the differences in test content: People who score high on one test tend to score high on another.

Still, this doesn't necessarily mean that the two tests measure intelligence. Conceivably they could both be measuring the same thing, but that thing is not intelligence. To demonstrate that the tests are valid, we need an independent measure of intelligence against which to compare intelligence test scores. Determining test validity in this way is called **criterion-related validity.** Ever since Binet invented the intelligence test, the criterion against which intelligence test scores have been compared has been school achievement. Even the strongest critics agree that IQ tests predict school achievement well (Aiken, 1988).

Criticisms of IQ Tests   What is it about IQ tests, then, that makes them controversial? One major criticism concerns the narrowness of their content. Many critics believe that intelligence tests assess only a very limited set of skills:

Reliability
Ability of a test to produce consistent and stable scores.

Split-half reliability
A method of determining test reliability by dividing the test into two parts and checking the agreement of scores on both parts.

Validity
Ability of a test to measure what it has been designed to measure.

Content validity
Refers to a test's having an adequate sample of questions measuring the skills or knowledge it is supposed to measure.

Criterion-related validity
Validity of a test as measured by a comparison of the test score and independent measures of what the test is designed to measure.

passive verbal understanding, the ability to follow instructions, common sense, and at best scholastic aptitude (Ginsberg, 1972; Sattler, 1975). One critic observes, "Intelligence tests measure how quickly people can solve relatively unimportant problems making as few errors as possible, rather than measuring how people grapple with relatively important problems, making as many productive errors as necessary with no time factor" (Blum, 1979, p. 83).

If there is one thing that all intelligence tests measure, it is the ability to take tests. This could explain why people who do well on one IQ test also tend to do well on others. And it could also explain why intelligence test scores correlate so closely with school performance: Academic grades also depend heavily on test-taking ability. This criticism of intelligence tests challenges the assumption that academic achievement depends on intelligence. It proposes that neither academic achievement nor intelligence tests measure the capacity to successfully handle real-life situations.

Still other critics maintain that the content and administration of IQ tests discriminate against minorities. High scores on most IQ tests require considerable mastery of standard English, which biases the tests in favor of middle- and upper-class white people (Blum, 1979). Moreover, white middle-class examiners may not be familiar with the speech patterns of lower-income African-American children or children from homes in which English is not the primary language, a complication that may hamper good test performance (Sattler, 1992). In addition, certain questions may have very different meanings for children of different social classes. The WISC-III, for instance, asks, "What are you supposed to do if a child younger than you hits you?" The "correct" answer is, "Walk away." But for a child who lives in an environment where survival depends on being tough, the "correct" answer might be, "Hit him back." This answer, however, receives zero credit.

Even presumably culture-fair tests may accentuate the very cultural differences that they were designed to minimize, to the detriment of test takers (Linn, 1982). For example, when given a picture of a head with the mouth missing, one group of Asian-American children responded by saying that the body was missing, thus receiving no credit. To them the absence of a body under the head was more remarkable than the absence of the mouth (Ortar, 1963).

If IQ tests were used only for obscure research purposes, the issue of their fairness would not matter much. But because they are used for so many significant purposes, it is critical that we understand their strengths and their weaknesses. In particular, to what extent can they accurately predict a person's future performance, and how can we explain whatever correlations exist between IQ and performance?

Some people argue that intelligence tests largely measure test-taking skills, not a person's underlying mental capabilities. Others contend that the content of these tests and the ways in which they are administered discriminate against minorities.

The IQ-Performance Connection

Alfred Binet developed the first IQ test to help the Paris public school system identify students who needed to be put in special classes. But the practice of using IQ tests to put a person into a "track" or "slot" in school may backfire. To the extent that children get low scores on IQ tests because of test bias, language handicap, or their own lack of interest in test taking, putting them in special classes apart from "normal" students can lead them to doubt their abilities. Tracking may also have the opposite effect on high IQ scorers. In a self-fulfilling prophecy, such children may come to believe that they will be high achievers, and this expectation may figure prominently in their subsequent success (Dahlstrom, 1993). Teachers, too, may come to expect particular students to do well or poorly on the basis of IQ scores and so encourage or neglect those students. IQ scores, then, may not simply predict future achievement or failure; they may also contribute to it.

Of course, self-fulfilling prophecies are not the only reason why IQ tests can predict future school performance. It isn't surprising that scores on these tests correlate well with academic achievement since both involve some intellectual activity and both stress verbal ability. Moreover, both academic achievement and high IQ scores require similar kinds of motivation, attention, perseverance, and test-taking ability.

Whatever the reason, IQ scores do predict success in school with some accuracy. In addition, people with high IQ scores tend to enter high-status occupations: Physicians and lawyers tend to have higher IQs than truck drivers and janitors. Critics point out, however, that this pattern can be explained in various ways. For one thing, because people with higher IQs tend to do better in school, they stay in school longer and earn advanced degrees, which in turn opens the door to high-status jobs. Moreover, children from wealthy families are more likely to have the money needed for graduate school and advanced occupational training. They also tend to have helpful family connections. Perhaps most important, they grow up in environments that encourage academic success and reward good performance on tests (Blum, 1979).

It is important to remember, however, that despite a link between IQ scores and future performance, an IQ score is not the same as intelligence. Tests measure a person's ability level at a certain point in time and in relation to the norms for his or her age group. Furthermore, the abilities measured will vary to some extent from culture to culture. Those abilities a culture considers important will tend to be brought to the fore; those abilities deemed less important will tend to be downplayed (McAndrew, 1993). These are some of the limitations of tests.

Review Questions

1. Indicate whether the following statements are true (T) or false (F).
   a. Intelligence is synonymous with problem-solving ability. _____
   b. Cattell maintained that visual–spatial abilities were part of crystallized intelligence. _____
   c. Intrapersonal intelligence reflects the adage "Know thyself." _____
   d. Sternberg's and Gardner's theories of intelligence both emphasize practical abilities. _____

2. In 1916 the Stanford psychologist L. M. Terman introduced the term _____ _____ or _____ and set the score of _____ for a person of average intelligence.

3. _____ tests eliminate or minimize the use of words in assessing mental abilities. Like these tests, _____-_____ tests minimize the use of language, but they also include questions that minimize skills and values that vary across cultures.

4. If you take a test several times and score about the same each time you take it, your results suggest that the test has _____.

5. _____ is a test's ability to measure what it was designed to measure.

Answers: 1. a–F; b–F; c–T; d–T. 2. intelligence quotient, I.Q., 100. 3. performance, culture-fair. 4. reliability 5. validity.

Heredity, Environment, and Intelligence

What determines individual differences in intelligence?

Is intelligence level inherited, or is it more a product of environment? This is a question many people have asked. Scientists often use studies of identical twins to measure the contributions of heredity and environment to individual differences in intelligence. They begin by comparing the IQ scores of identical twins who have been raised together. As Figure 7–9 shows, the correlation between their IQ scores is very high. These twins grew up in very similar environments: They shared parents, home, teachers, vacations, and probably friends. To check the effects of environment, researchers have tested identical twins who were separated early in life—generally before they were 6 months old—and raised in

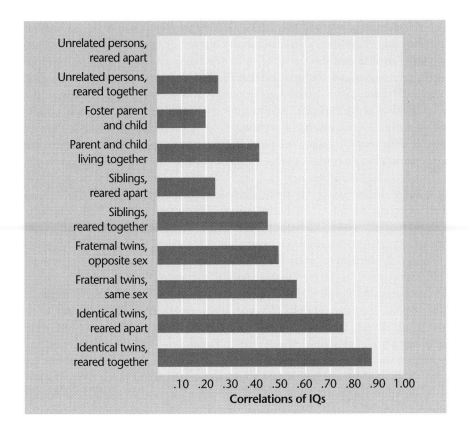

FIGURE 7–9

Correlations of IQ scores and family relationships. Identical twins who grow up in the same household have IQ scores that are almost identical to each other. Even when they are reared apart, their scores are highly correlated.

Source: Adapted from "Genetics and intelligence: A review," by Erlenmeyer-Kimling and L. F. Jarvik 1963, *Science, 142,* pp. 1477–79. Copyright © 1963 by the American Association for the Advancement of Science.

different families. You can see in Figure 7–9 that even when identical twins are raised apart, they tend to have similar IQ scores. In fact, the similarity is much greater than that between nontwin siblings who grew up in the same home.

Adoption studies have also shown the influence of heredity on IQ. Adopted children have IQs that are more similar to their biological mothers than to the mothers who are raising them (Loehlin, Horn, & Willerman, 1997). Researcher John Loehlin finds these results particularly interesting because they reflect "genetic resemblance in the absence of shared environment: These birth mothers had no contact with their children after the first few days of life" (Loehlin et al., 1997, p. 113).

But proponents of the environment's influence on differences in intelligence are not put off by such findings. Heredity, they say, may establish a range of potentials, but that is only the beginning. Each of us inherits the tendency toward a certain body build, for example, but actual weight is primarily determined by what we eat and how much we exercise. Similarly, even though we inherit the potential for a certain range of mental abilities, the *development* of those abilities depends on what we see around us as infants, how our parents respond to our first attempts to talk, the schools we attend, the books we read, the television programs we watch—and even what we eat.

Environment affects children before birth as well, such as through prenatal nutrition (Hack et al., 1991). In one study of pregnant women who were economically deprived, half were given a dietary supplement and half were given placebos. At ages 3 and 4, the children of the mothers who had taken the supplement scored significantly higher on intelligence tests than the other children (Harrell, Woodyard, & Gates, 1955). During infancy, malnutrition can lower IQ scores—in one study by an average 20 points (Stock & Smythe, 1963). Conversely, vitamin supplements can increase young children's IQ scores, possibly even among children who are not experiencing malnutrition (Benton & Roberts, 1988; Schoenthaler et al., 1991).

Quite by chance, psychologist H. M. Skeels found evidence in the 1930s that IQ scores among children also depend on environmental stimulation. While investigating orphanages for the state of Iowa, Skeels observed that the children lived in very overcrowded wards and that the few adults there had almost no time to play with them, to talk to them, or to read them stories. Many of these children were classified as "subnormal" in intelligence. Skeels followed the cases of two girls who, after 18 months in an orphanage, were sent to a ward for women with severe retardation. Originally the girls' IQs were in the range of retardation, but after a year on the adult ward, as if by magic, their IQs had risen to normal (Skeels, 1938). Skeels regarded this fact as quite remarkable—after all, the women with whom the girls had lived were themselves severely retarded. When he placed 13 other "slow" children as houseguests in such adult wards, within 18 months their mean IQ rose from 64 to 92 (within the normal range)—all because they had had someone (even someone of below-normal intelligence) to play with them, to read to them, to cheer them on when they took their first steps, and to encourage them to talk (Skeels, 1942). During the same period, the mean IQ of a group of children who had been left in orphanages dropped from 86 to 61. Thirty years later Skeels found that all 13 of the children raised on adult wards were self-supporting, their occupations ranging from waiting on tables to real-estate sales. Of the contrasting group, half were unemployed, 4 were still in institutions, and all of those who had jobs were dishwashers (Skeels, 1966).

A French study reinforces Skeels's findings on the importance of intellectually stimulating surroundings as well as the value of good nutrition (Capron & Duyme, 1989). The researchers found that the socioeconomic status (SES) of adoptive parents had an effect on their adopted children's IQs. Regardless of the socioeconomic status of the child's biological parents, those children adopted by high-SES parents had higher IQs than did those children adopted by low-SES parents, because high-SES families tend to provide children with better nutrition and heightened stimulation. Do such findings mean that intervention programs that enhance the environments of impoverished children can have a positive impact on their IQ?

Intervention Programs: How Much Can We Boost IQ?   In 1961 the so-called Milwaukee Project was launched. Its purpose was to learn if intervening in a child's family life could offset the negative effects of cultural and socioeconomic deprivation on IQ scores (Garber & Heber, 1982; Heber et al., 1972). The 40 women in the study, all from the Milwaukee area, were poor, pregnant, and primarily African American. As a group, they averaged less than 75 on the Wechsler intelligence scale. They were split into two groups: One received no special education or training; the other was sent to school, given job training, and instructed in child care, household management, and personal relationships.

After all 40 women had their babies, the research team began to concentrate on the children. Starting when they were 3 months old and continuing for the next 6 years, the children in the experimental group—those whose mothers were being given special training—spent most of each day in an infant-education center, where they received nourishing meals, participated in an educational program, and were cared for by paraprofessionals who behaved like nonworking mothers in affluent families. The children in the control group—whose mothers were not receiving any special training—did not attend the education center.

Periodically all the children were tested for IQ. The children in the experimental group achieved an average IQ score of 126—51 points higher than their mothers' average scores. In contrast, the children in the control group had an average IQ of 94—not as high as the experimental group but still much higher than their mothers' average scores, perhaps in part because they had become accustomed to taking tests, an experience their mothers never had.

Individual differences in intelligence can be partly explained by differences in environmental stimulation and encouragement. The specific forms of stimulation given vary from culture to culture. Because our culture assigns importance to developing academic skills, the stimulation of reading and exploring information in books can give children an IQ edge over those who are not so encouraged.

Head Start, the nation's largest intervention program, began in 1965. By the mid-1990s it provided "comprehensive services for 721,000 children lasting at least a half a day for 128 days a year" (Kassebaum, 1994). Head Start focuses on preschoolers between the ages of 3 and 5 from low-income families and has two key goals: to provide the children with some educational and social skills before they go to school, and to provide information about nutrition and health to both the children and their families. Head Start involves parents in all its aspects, from daily activities to administration of the program itself. This parental involvement may be crucial to Head Start's success (Cronan, Walen, & Cruz, 1994).

Several studies evaluating the long-term effects of Head Start have found that it boosts cognitive abilities (B. Brown & Grotberg, 1981), but some experts are concerned that these improvements may be modest or impermanent. Nevertheless, children leaving Head Start are in a better position to profit from schooling than they would be otherwise (Zigler & Styfco, 1994). Head Start graduates followed until age 27 show several benefits, including higher academic achievement (Schweinhart, Barnes, & Weikart, 1993), a tendency to stay in school longer, and a greater likelihood of graduating from college. Even if the IQ gains owing to Head Start are temporary, then, the program still seems to provide long-term practical benefits.

Overall, the effectiveness of early intervention appears to depend on the quality of the particular program (Collins, 1993; Zigler & Muenchow, 1992; Zigler & Styfco, 1993). Intervention programs with clearly defined goals that take into account the broad context of human development, including health care and other social services, achieve the most significant and long-lasting results. Also, interventions that begin in the preschool years and include a high degree of parental involvement, ensuring continuity after the official program terminates, are generally more successful (Cronan, Walen, & Cruz, 1994; Hart & Risley, 1995; Jaynes & Wlodkowski, 1990).

Summing Up: The IQ Debate   Both heredity and environment have important effects on individual differences in intelligence, but is one of these factors more important than the other? The answer depends on whose IQs you are comparing. A useful analogy comes from studies of plants (Turkheimer, 1991). Suppose you grow one group of randomly assigned plants in enriched soil, and another group in poor soil. The enriched group will grow to be taller and

Head Start is a program designed to do just what its name implies: to give children from disadvantaged environments a head start in acquiring the skills and attitudes needed for success in school. Although researchers debate whether Head Start produces significant and lasting boosts in IQ, it does have many school-related benefits for those who participate in it.

stronger than the nonenriched group; the difference between the two groups in this case is due entirely to differences in their environment. *Within* each group of plants, however, differences among individual plants are likely to be due primarily to genetics, because all plants in the same group share essentially the same environment. The height and strength of any single plant, then, reflects both heredity *and* environment.

Similarly, group differences in IQ scores might be due to environmental factors, but differences among people *within* groups could be due primarily to genetics. At the same time, the IQ scores of particular people would reflect the effects of both heredity *and* environment. Robert Plomin, an influential researcher in the field of human intelligence, concludes that "the world's literature suggests that about half of the total variance in IQ scores can be accounted for by genetic variance" (Plomin, 1997, p. 89). This means that environment accounts for the other half. Heredity and environment both contribute to human differences.

Mental Abilities and Human Diversity

Do gender and culture influence mental abilities?

Many people believe that males and females are innately different in their verbal and mathematical abilities. Others believe that people from certain cultures have a natural tendency to excel at academic skills. Is there any truth to these common assumptions?

Gender Differences   Many occupations are dominated by one gender or the other. Engineering, for example, has traditionally been a predominantly male domain. Does this occupational difference and others like it reflect underlying gender differences in mental abilities?

In 1974 psychologists Eleanor Maccoby and Carol Jacklin published a review of psychological research on gender differences. They found no differences at all between males and females in most of the studies they examined. However, a few differences did appear in the area of cognitive abilities: Girls tended to display greater verbal ability and boys tended to exhibit stronger spatial and mathematical abilities. Largely as a result of this research, gender differences in the areas of verbal, spatial, and mathematical abilities became so widely accepted that they were often cited as established facts (Hyde, Fennema, & Lamon, 1990; Hyde & Linn, 1988).

Yet a closer examination of research, including more recent work, indicates that gender differences in math and verbal ability may be virtually nonexistent. For example, Janet Shibley Hyde and her colleagues analyzed 165 research studies of gender differences in verbal abilities, involving more than 1 million people. They concluded that "there are no gender differences in verbal ability, at least at this time, in American culture, in the standard ways that verbal ability has been measured" (Hyde & Linn, 1988, p. 62). In a similar analysis of studies on mathematical ability, Hyde and her colleagues concluded that "females outperformed males by only a negligible amount. . . . Females are superior in computation, there are no gender differences in understanding of mathematical concepts, and gender differences favoring males do not emerge until the high school years" (Hyde et al., 1990, pp. 139, 151).

But why, if gender differences in math ability are so slight, do relatively few women pursue careers in mathematics and science? One study found that women avoid these careers because of *mathematics anxiety* (Chipman, Krantz, & Silver, 1992), perhaps owing to subtle messages from parents and teachers that math is for males. So maybe different career choices among men and women simply result from differences in the socialization of boys and girls.

Why do more males than females pursue careers in science? The reason is not that males have more innate aptitude for mathematics, because gender differences in math ability are negligible during childhood. The answer probably has more to do with cultural stereotypes about what girls are "good at" and what they are not.

Males, however, apparently do have an advantage over females in spatial ability (Halpern, 1992; Voyer, Voyer, & Bryden, 1995). Spatial tasks include mentally rotating an object and mentally estimating horizontal and vertical dimensions. These skills are particularly useful in solving certain engineering, architecture, and geometry problems.

Although the average male and female IQ is about the same, there seem to be higher proportions of men with mental retardation or with superior IQs. In one review of several large studies, males accounted for 7 out of 8 people both with extremely high IQ scores (top 1 percent) and with IQs in the mentally retarded range (Hedges & Nowell, 1995).

What should we conclude from these findings? First, the cognitive differences between males and females appear to be restricted to specific skills. Scores on tests such as the Stanford–Binet or the WAIS–III reveal *no* gender differences in general intelligence (Halpern, 1992). Second, gender differences in specific cognitive abilities typically are small and in some cases appear to be diminishing—even when studied cross-culturally (Skaalvik & Rankin, 1994). Finally, we do not know whether the differences that do exist are a result of biological or cultural factors.

Cultural Diversity and Academic Performance

U.S. educators, policymakers, and parents are concerned that American students are falling behind students in other countries. Is this concern valid? And if it is, how can we explain it? Could it be, as some have suggested, that these differences in academic performance reflect underlying differences in mental abilities (Herrnstein & Murray, 1994; Jensen, 1969)?

In a series of comprehensive studies, a team of researchers led by Harold Stevenson investigated differences in academic performance among members of various cultures (Stevenson, 1992, 1993; Stevenson, Chen, & Lee, 1993). They began their research in 1980 by examining the performance of first- and fifth-grade children in American, Chinese, and Japanese schools (Stevenson, Lee, & Stigler, 1986). At that time the Japanese and Chinese students at both grade levels far surpassed the American students in mathematics, and the Chinese were also more proficient readers. A decade later, when the study was repeated with a new group of fifth-graders, the researchers discovered an even larger difference in mathematical proficiency. The reading vocabulary scores of the three groups also showed changes. In 1980 Chinese fifth-graders scored the highest on vocabulary, whereas Japanese students scored the lowest. By 1990, however, the Japanese fifth-graders performed the best, and American students had dropped to the lowest position. In 1990 the research team also studied the original first-graders from all three cultures, now in the eleventh grade. The results? American students retained their low standing in mathematics.

A scene from a Japanese schoolroom. Studies have shown that Japanese students outperform their American peers on tests of mathematical proficiency. Some psychologists believe that cultural attitudes toward ability and effort might be partially responsible for these findings.

To test their hypothesis that cultural attitudes toward ability and effort might be partly responsible for these findings, Stevenson and his colleagues (1993) asked students, their parents, and their teachers whether they thought effort or ability had a greater impact on academic performance. From the first through the eleventh grade, American students disagreed with the statement "Everyone in my class has about the same natural ability in math." They also thought that "studying hard" had little to do with performance. Apparently, American children believe they are born with or without the ability to succeed in math. So, too, do their mothers and teachers. Asian students, parents, and teachers believe just the opposite: Effort and "studying hard," not innate ability, determined success in math.

Such culturally influenced views of the relative importance of effort and innate ability may have profound consequences for the way children, their parents, and their teachers approach the task of learning. Students who believe that learning is based on natural ability see little value in working hard to learn a difficult subject. In contrast, students who believe that academic success comes from studying are more likely to work hard, and in so doing to succeed.

Attitudes toward what constitutes a sufficiently "good" education may also affect student performance in these cultures. For instance, 79 percent of the American mothers thought their schools were doing a "good" or "excellent" job of educating their children. Asian mothers were far more critical of their schools' performance, which could lead them to lobby for more challenging curriculums. Also, American mothers and students were generally satisfied with the students' academic performance, even though it was comparatively low. Such complacency does not contribute to high achievement.

Extremes of Intelligence

What do psychologists know about the two extremes of human intelligence: very high and very low?

The average IQ score on intelligence tests is 100. Nearly 70 percent of all people have IQs between 85 and 115, and all but 5 percent of the population have IQs between 70 and 130. In this section we focus on people who score at the two extremes of intelligence—those with mental retardation and those who are intellectually gifted.

Mental Retardation   **Mental retardation** encompasses a vast array of mental deficits with a wide variety of causes, treatments, and outcomes. The American Psychiatric Association (1994) defines mental retardation as "significantly subaverage general intellectual functioning . . . that is accompanied by significant limitations in adaptive functioning" and that appears before the age of 18 (p. 39). There are also various degrees of mental retardation. Mild retardation corresponds to Stanford–Binet IQ scores ranging from a high of about 70 to a low near 50. Moderate retardation corresponds to IQ scores ranging from the low 50s to the mid 30s. People with IQ scores between the mid-30s and 20 are considered severely retarded, and the profoundly retarded are those whose scores are below 20 (see Table 7–2).

But a low IQ is not in itself sufficient for diagnosing mental retardation. The person must also be unable to perform the daily tasks needed to function independently (Wielkiewicz & Calvert, 1989). So evaluations of people with mental retardation usually include tests of motor skills and social adaptation as well as tests of intelligence. Motor-skill tests, such as the widely used *Oseretsky Tests of Motor Proficiency*, measure the control of facial muscles, hand and finger coordination, and posture. Measures of social adaptation, such as the *Adaptive Behavior Scale (ABS)* and the *Vineland Adaptive Behavior Social Maturity Scale*, are based on observations of the person's behavior in everyday situations. People are scored in such areas as language development, understanding and use of number and time concepts, domestic activity, responsibility, and social action. Another portion of the ABS focuses on the person's maladaptive behaviors, such as withdrawal, hyperactivity, and disturbing interpersonal behaviors.

What causes mental retardation? In most cases the causes are unknown (Beirne-Smith, Patton, & Ittenbach, 1994)—especially in cases of mild retardation, which account for nearly 90 percent of all retardation. When causes can be

Down syndrome is a common biological cause of mental retardation, affecting 1 in 600 newborns. The prognosis for Down syndrome children today is much better than it was in the past. With adequate support, many children with the affliction can participate in regular classrooms and other childhood activities.

Mental retardation
Condition of significantly subaverage intelligence combined with deficiencies in adaptive behavior.

TABLE 7-2	Levels of Mental Retardation	
Type of Retardation	**IQ Range**	**Level of Functioning**
Mild retardation	Low 50s–70s	People may be able to function adequately in society and learn skills comparable to a sixth-grader, but they need special help at times of unusual stress.
Moderate retardation	Mid-30s–low 50s	People profit from vocational training and may be able to travel alone. They learn on a second-grade level and perform skilled work in a sheltered workshop under supervision.
Severe retardation	Low 20s–mid-30s	People do not learn to talk or to practice basic hygiene until after age 6. They cannot learn vocational skills but can perform simple tasks under supervision.
Profound retardation	Below 20 or 25	Constant care is needed. Usually people have a diagnosed neurological disorder.

Source: Based on APA, DSM-IV, 1994.

identified, most often they stem from a wide variety of environmental, social, nutritional, and other risk factors (Scott & Carran, 1987).

About 25 percent of cases—especially the more severe forms of retardation—appear to involve genetic or biological disorders. Scientists have identified more than 100 forms of mental retardation caused by single defective genes (Plomin, 1997). One is the genetically based disease *phenylketonuria,* or *PKU,* which occurs in about 1 person out of 25,000 (Minton & Schneider, 1980). In people suffering from PKU, the liver fails to produce an enzyme necessary for early brain development. Fortunately, placing a PKU baby on a special diet can prevent mental retardation from developing. Another form of hereditary mental retardation is *fragile-X syndrome,* which affects about 1 in every 1,250 males and 1 in every 2,500 females (Plomin, 1997). A defect in the X chromosome, passed on between generations, seems to be caused by a specific gene (M. Hoffman, 1991). In the disorder known as *Down syndrome,* which affects 1 in 600 newborns, an extra 21st chromosome is the cause (see the photo on page 72 in Chapter 2). Down syndrome, named for the physician who first described its symptoms, is marked by moderate to severe mental retardation.

Biologically caused mental retardation can be moderated through education and training. The prognosis for those with no underlying physical causes is even better. People whose retardation is due to a history of social and educational deprivation may respond dramatically to appropriate interventions.

Today the majority of children with physical or mental disabilities are educated in local school systems (Lipsky & Gartner, 1996; Schroeder, Schroeder, & Landesman, 1987), a process called *mainstreaming,* which helps these students to socialize with their nondisabled peers. The principle of mainstreaming has also been applied to adults with mental retardation, by taking them out of large, impersonal institutions and placing them in smaller community homes that provide more normal life experiences (Conroy, 1996; Landesman & Butterfield, 1987; Maisto & Hughes, 1995; Stancliffe, 1997).

When evaluating children for mental retardation, we must watch for possible biases in measuring techniques. Like intelligence, mental retardation is a highly complex phenomenon. Just as intelligence tests do not measure certain abilities, such as artistic talent, people with mental retardation sometimes display exceptional skills in areas other than general intelligence. Probably the most dramatic and intriguing examples involve *savant performance*, in which a person with mental retardation displays remarkable abilities in some specialized area, such as numerical computation, memory, art, or music (O'Connor & Hermelin, 1987).

Giftedness   At the other extreme of the intelligence scale are "the gifted"—those with exceptional mental abilities, as measured by scores on standard intelligence tests. As with mental retardation, the causes of **giftedness** are largely unknown.

The first and now-classic study of giftedness was begun by Lewis Terman and his colleagues in the early 1920s. They defined giftedness in terms of academic talent and measured it by an IQ score in the top 2 percentile (1925). More recently, some experts have sought to broaden the definition of giftedness beyond that of simply high IQ (Csikszentmihalyi, Rathunde, & Whalen, 1993; Subotnik & Arnold, 1994). One view is that giftedness is often an interaction of above-average general intelligence, exceptional creativity, and high levels of commitment (Renzulli, 1978). Congress has defined gifted children as those with demonstrated achievement or potential ability in any of the following areas, singly or in combination: (1) general intellectual ability, (2) specific academic aptitude, (3) creative or productive thinking, (4) leadership ability, and (5) fine arts.

Various criteria are used to identify gifted students, including scores on intelligence tests, achievement tests, and other diagnostic tests, teacher recommendations, interviews, and evaluation of the student's academic and creative work (Sattler, 1992). These selection methods seem to work well for identifying those with a broad range of talents, but they do not do the best job of distinguishing those with specific abilities, such as a talent for mathematics or music. This fact has led to the development of specialized programs, such as the *Study of Mathematically Precocious Youth (SMPY)*, to identify children who are gifted in some area without necessarily exhibiting general intellectual superiority (L. H. Fox, 1981). Another criticism of current methods of identifying gifted students is that they may be biased against members of minority groups (Baldwin, 1985). To address this concern, experts have devised alternative tests and multiple screening methods that take into account a child's sociocultural group.

Giftedness
Refers to superior IQ combined with demonstrated or potential ability in such areas as academic aptitude, creativity, and leadership.

REVIEW QUESTIONS

1. Indicate whether the following statements are true (T) or false (F).

   a. When identical twins are raised apart, their IQ scores are not highly correlated. ____

   b. Environmental stimulation has no effect on IQ. ____

   c. Head Start graduates are more likely than their peers to graduate from college. ____

   d. IQ scores in the population as a whole have declined in recent years. ____

2. Mental retardation and very high IQs are (more/less) common in males than in females.

3. Only about ____ percent of the population have IQs below 70 and above 130.

4. As psychologists learn more about giftedness, the definition of it has become (broader/narrower).

Answers: 1. a–F; b–F; c–T; d–F. 2. more 3. 5. 4. broader.

Special effects such as these from *Star Wars: The Phantom Menace* show a great deal of creativity. It seems as though a certain minimum level of intelligence must be reached for high creativity to develop.

Creativity

What is creativity?

Creativity is the ability to produce novel and socially valued ideas or objects ranging from philosophy to painting, from music to mousetraps (Mumford & Gustafson, 1988; Sternberg, 1996). Sternberg included creativity and insight as important elements in the experiential component of human intelligence. Most IQ tests, however, do not measure creativity, and many researchers would argue that intelligence and creativity are not the same thing. What, then, is the relationship between intelligence and creativity? Are people who score high on IQ tests likely to be more creative than those who score low?

Intelligence and Creativity

How is creativity related to intelligence?

Early studies typically found little or no relationship between creativity and intelligence (for example, Getzels & Jackson, 1962; Wing, 1969), but these studies examined only bright students. Perhaps creativity and intelligence are indeed linked, but only until IQ reaches a certain threshold level, after which higher intelligence isn't associated with higher creativity. There is considerable evidence for this threshold theory (Barron, 1963; Yamamoto & Chimbidis, 1966). All the research supporting it, however, has relied heavily on tests of creativity, and perhaps real-life creativity isn't the same as what these tests measure. Still, it makes sense that a certain minimum level of intelligence might be needed for creativity to develop but that other factors underlie creativity as well.

Interestingly, creative people are often *perceived* as being more intelligent than less creative people who have equivalent IQ scores. Perhaps some characteristic that creative people share—possibly "effectiveness" or some quality of social competence—conveys the impression of intelligence even though it is not measured by intelligence tests (Barron & Harrington, 1981).

Factors Promoting Creativity

Are you more creative at some times than other times?

What factors tend to spur the imagination? Mild mood swings may figure in the creative process. Interviews with well-known writers and artists have

Creativity
The ability to produce novel and socially valued ideas or objects.

revealed that their most creative periods occurred when they were in a mildly elated mood (Jamison, 1989). Why does a mild emotional high spark creativity? First, it may give people the energy needed to create. Second, a person may be more imaginative and productive in an elated mood, then use the following, more sober phase to evaluate the work produced (Richards, Kinney, Lunde, & Benet, 1988b). Also, exposure to novel circumstances, such as travel, may stimulate creativity, as may choosing and enjoying the tasks one is engaged in.

If certain circumstances encourage creativity, others inhibit it. When parents reject or discourage their children's accomplishments—both imaginative and otherwise—the children grow up to be less creative adults (Harrington, Black, & Black, 1987). Requiring children to perform on command or in competition with others, or even watching them work also can inhibit creativity. To be creative, people must be willing to take risks—and competition, surveillance, and evaluation promote safety over risk, thereby stifling creativity (Amabile, Hennessey, & Grossman, 1986).

In general, creative people are *problem finders* as well as problem solvers (Getzels, 1975; Mackworth, 1965). The more creative people are, the more they like to work on problems they have set for themselves. Creative scientists (such as Charles Darwin and Albert Einstein) often work for years on a problem that has sprung from their own curiosity. Beyond talent or genius, great scientists, artists, and writers have intense dedication, ambition, and perseverance.

Creativity Tests

Can creativity be measured?

Opinions differ about the best way to test creativity. Because creativity involves original responses to situations, questions that can be answered *true* or *false* or *a* or *b* are not good measures. More open-ended tests are better. Instead of asking for one predetermined answer to a problem, the examiner asks the test takers to let their imaginations run free. Scores are based on the originality of a person's answers and often on the number of responses, too.

In one such test, the *Torrance Test of Creative Thinking*, people must explain what is happening in a picture, how the scene came about, and what its consequences are likely to be. In the *Christensen–Guilford Test*, they are to list as many words containing a given letter as possible, to name things belonging to a certain category (such as liquids that will burn), and to write four-word sentences beginning with the letters *RDLS*—"Rainy days look sad, Red dogs like soup, Renaissance dramas lack symmetry," and so on. One of the most widely used creativity tests, S. A. Mednick's (1962) *Remote Associates Test (RAT)*, asks people to relate three apparently unrelated words. For example, the three stimulus words might be *poke*, *go*, and *molasses*, and one response is to relate them through the word *slow*: "slowpoke, go slow, slow as molasses." In the newer *Wallach and Kogan Creative Battery*, people form associative groupings. For instance, children are asked to "name all the round things you can think of" and to find similarities between objects, such as between a potato and a carrot.

Although people who do not have high IQs can score well on the Wallach and Kogan test, the Torrance test seems to require a reasonably high IQ for adequate performance. This raises the question of which of these tests is a valid measure of creativity. In general, current tests of creativity do not show a high degree of validity (Feldhusen & Goh, 1995), so measurements derived from them must be interpreted with caution.

Review Questions

1. The ability to produce novel and unique ideas or objects, ranging from philosophy to painting, from music to mousetraps, is termed
   a. creativity
   b. IQ
   c. fluid intelligence
   d. contextual intelligence
2. Two important features of creative people are that
   a. they take risks and like to work on problems they invent themselves.
   b. they are perceived as less intelligent and more irresponsible than other people.
   c. they excel at art but are poor at science.
3. ____–____ tests are the best type for measuring creativity.
4. Indicate whether the following statements are true (T) or false (F).
   a. Most IQ tests do not measure creativity. ____
   b. Highly intelligent people are always highly creative. ____
   c. An elevated mood sometimes sparks creativity. ____
   d. Encouraging children to compete with one another enhances their creativity. ____
   e. Newly developed tests of creativity show a high degree of validity. ____

Answers: 1. a. 2. a. 3. open-ended. 4. a–T; b–F; c–T; d–F; e–F.

Answers to Problems in the Chapter

Problem 1   Fill each of the smaller spoons with salt from the larger spoon. That will require 4 teaspoons of salt, leaving exactly 4 teaspoons of salt in the larger spoon.

Problem 2   Turn the 5-minute hourglass over; when it runs out, turn over the 9-minute hourglass. When it runs out, 14 minutes have passed.

Problem 3   As shown in Figure 7–10, fill spoon C with the salt from spoon A (now A has 5 teaspoons of salt and C has 3). Pour the salt from spoon C into spoon B (now A has 5 teaspoons of salt and B has 3). Again fill spoon C with the salt from spoon A (leaving A with only 2 teaspoons of salt, while B and C each have 3). Fill spoon B with the salt from spoon C (this leaves 1 teaspoon of salt in spoon C, while B has 5 teaspoons and A has only 2). Pour all of the salt from spoon B into spoon A (now A has 7 teaspoons of salt and C has 1). Pour all of the salt from spoon C into spoon B, and then fill spoon C from spoon A (this leaves 4 teaspoons of salt in A, 1 teaspoon in B, and 3 teaspoons in C). Finally, pour all of the salt from spoon C into spoon B (this leaves 4 teaspoons of salt in spoons A and B, which is the solution).

Problem 4   Start both hourglasses. When the 5-minute hourglass runs out, turn it over to start it again. When the 9-minute hourglass runs out, turn over the 5-minute hourglass. Because there is 1 minute left in the 5-minute hourglass when you turn it over, it will run for only 4 minutes. Those 4 minutes, together with the original 9 minutes, add up to the required 13 minutes for the barbecue.

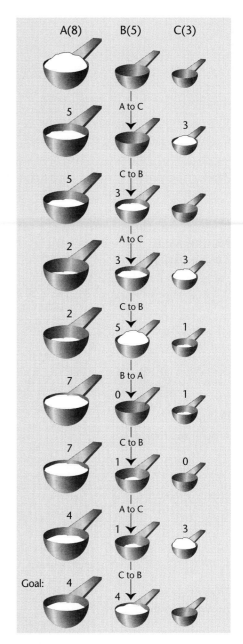

FIGURE 7–10
Answer to Problem 3.

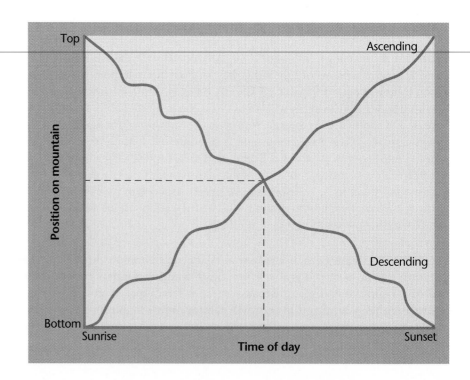

Step 1: cut one piece of chain into three open links

Step 2: use three links to join three remaining pieces of chain

FIGURE 7–11
Answer to Problem 5.

FIGURE 7–12
Answer to Problem 6.

Problem 5   Take one of the short pieces of chain shown in Figure 7–11, and open all three links (this costs 6 cents). Use those three links to connect the remaining three pieces of chain (closing the three links costs 9 cents).

Problem 6   Join the matches to form a pyramid as seen in Figure 7–12.

Problem 7   One way to solve this problem is to draw a diagram of the ascent and the descent, as in Figure 7–13. From this drawing, you can see that indeed there is a point that the monk passes at exactly the same time on both days. Another way to approach this problem is to imagine that there are two monks on the mountain; one starts ascending at 7 A.M. while the other starts descending at 7 A.M. on the same day. Clearly, sometime during the day the monks must meet somewhere along the route.

Problem 8   This problem has four possible solutions, one of which is shown in Figure 7–14 (the other three differ only slightly from this one).

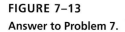

FIGURE 7–13
Answer to Problem 7.

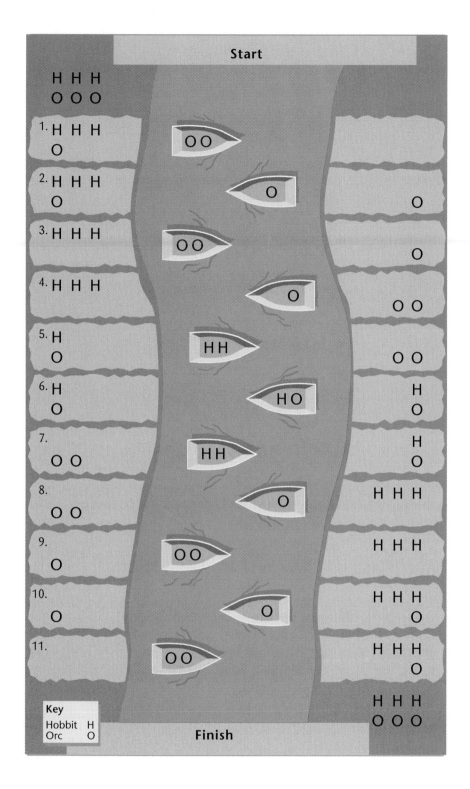

FIGURE 7–14
Answer to Problem 8.

Problem 9   There are 15 possible solutions to this problem, of which this is one: One Hobbit and one Orc cross the river in the boat; the Orc remains on the opposite side while the Hobbit rows back. Next, three Orcs cross the river; two of those Orcs remain on the other side (making a total of three Orcs on the opposite bank) while one Orc rows back. Now three Hobbits and one Orc row the boat back. Again three Hobbits row across the river, at which point all five Hobbits are on the opposite bank with only two Orcs. One of the Orcs then rows back and forth across the river twice to transport the remaining Orcs to the opposite side.

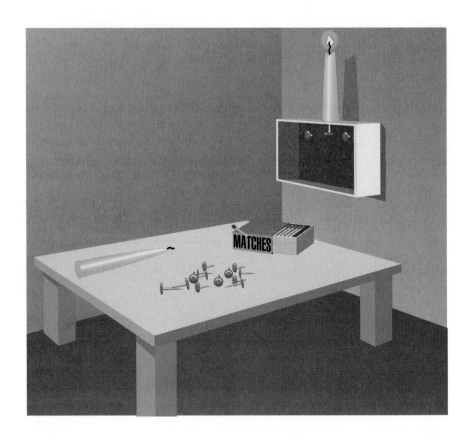

FIGURE 7–15
Solution to Figure 7–7.

Solution to Figure 7–7 In solving the problem given in Figure 7–7, many people have trouble realizing that the box of tacks can also be used as a candleholder, as shown in Figure 7–15.

Answers to Intelligence Test Questions

1. *Idleness* refers to the state of being inactive, not busy, unoccupied; *laziness* means an unwillingness or reluctance to work. Laziness is one possible cause of idleness, but not the only cause.

2. If you face west, your right hand will point north.

3. *Obliterate* means to erase or destroy something completely.

4. Both an hour and a week are measures of time.

5. Alternative D is correct. Each sector starts where the previous sector left off and extends 45 degrees clockwise around the circle.

6. Alternative (f) is the correct pattern.

7. 75 cents will buy 9 pencils.

8. Union (b) is most nearly opposite in meaning to schism. *Union* means a uniting or joining of several parts into a whole; *schism* means a splitting apart or dividing of something that was previously united.

9. Alternative (e) makes the most sense. The phrase "despite an outward" implies that the words in the blanks should form a contrast of some sort. *Acquiescence* (agreeing, consenting without protest) certainly contrasts with thwarting (opposing, hindering, obstructing).

10. Alternative (d) is correct. A crutch is used to help someone who has difficulty with locomotion; spectacles are used to help someone who has difficulty with vision.

11. Alternative B is correct. In each case the figure is made up of three shapes that are identical except for size; the largest shape goes on the bottom and the smallest on top, with no overlap between the shapes.

12. Alternative D is correct. The second figure is the same shape and size but with diagonal crosshatching from upper left to lower right.

13. Figures 3, 4, and 5 can all be completely covered by using some or all of the given pieces.

KEY TERMS

cognition, p. 230

Building blocks of thought
phonemes, p. 230
morphemes, p. 230
surface structure, p. 230
deep structure, p. 230
grammar, p. 230
image, p. 231
concept, p. 231
prototype, p. 232

Language and thought
linguistic relativity
hypothesis, p. 233

Problem solving
problem representation,
p. 235
algorithm, p. 237

heuristics, p. 237
hill climbing, p. 237
subgoals, p. 237
means-end analysis, p. 238
working backward, p. 238
set, p. 239
functional fixedness, p. 239
brainstorming, p. 240
divergent thinking, p. 241
convergent thinking, p. 241

Decision making
compensatory model, p. 242
noncompensatory model,
p. 242
representativeness heuristic,
p. 243
availability heuristic, p. 243
confirmation bias, p. 243

**Intelligence and mental
abilities**
intelligence, p. 246
componential intelligence,
p. 247
experiential intelligence,
p. 247
contextual intelligence,
p. 247
emotional intelligence,
p. 249
intelligence quotient (IQ),
p. 249
Wechsler Adult Intelligence
Scale–Third Edition, (WAIS-
III) p. 249
Wechsler Intelligence Scale
for Children–Third Edition
(WISC-III), p. 250

group tests, p. 250
performance tests, p. 251
culture-fair tests, p. 251
reliability, p. 252
split-half reliability, p. 252
validity, p. 252
content validity, p. 252
criterion-related validity,
p. 252

**Heredity, environment, and
intelligence**
mental retardation, p. 260
giftedness, p. 262

Creativity
creativity, p. 263

CHAPTER REVIEW

▢ What are the three most important building blocks of thought?

The three most important building blocks of thought are language, images, and concepts. Whatever we think about, we invariably use words, sensory "snapshots," and categories that classify things.

▢ What steps do we go through to turn a thought into a statement?

Language is a flexible system of symbols that allows us to communicate ideas to others. When we express thoughts as statements, we must conform to our language's rules. Every language has rules as to which sounds (or **phonemes**) are part of that particular language, how those sounds can be combined into meaningful units (or **morphemes**), and how those meaningful units can be ordered into phrases and sentences (rules of **grammar**). When we wish to communicate an idea, we start with a thought, then choose sounds, words, and phrases that will express the idea in an understandable way. To understand the speech of others, the task is reversed.

▢ What role do images play in thinking?

Images are mental representations of sensory experiences. Visual images in particular can be powerful aids in thinking about the relationships between things. Picturing things in our mind's eye can sometimes help us solve problems.

▢ How do concepts help us to think more efficiently?

Concepts are categories for classifying objects, people, and experiences based on their common elements. Without the ability to form concepts, we would need a different name for every new thing we encountered. Concepts also help clarify new experiences, as we can draw on them to anticipate what new experiences will be like.

☐ How does language affect the way we think?

According to Benjamin Whorf's **linguistic relativity hypothesis,** thought is greatly influenced by the language a person speaks. If a language lacks a particular expression, the thought to which that expression corresponds rarely, if ever, occurs to the people who speak that language, according to Whorf. But critics contend that Whorf overstated his case. Thought, they say, can shape and change a language as much as a language can shape and change thought.

☐ What are three general aspects of the problem-solving process?

Interpreting a problem, formulating a strategy, and evaluating progress toward a solution are three general aspects of the problem-solving process. Each in its own way is critical to success at the task.

☐ Why is representing the problem so important to finding an effective solution?

Problem representation—defining or interpreting the problem—is the first step in problem solving. We must decide whether to view the problem verbally, mathematically, or visually, and we must decide what category of problems it belongs to in order to get clues about how to solve it. Representing a problem in an unproductive way can block progress completely.

☐ Why is an algorithm often better for solving a problem than is the process of trial and error?

Selecting a solution strategy and evaluating progress toward the goal are also important steps in the problem-solving process. A solution strategy can be anything from simple trial and error, to information retrieval based on similar problems, to a set of step-by-step procedures guaranteed to work (called an **algorithm**), to rule-of-thumb approaches known as **heuristics.** An algorithm is often preferable over trial and error because it guarantees a solution and does not waste time. But because there are so many things for which we don't have algorithms, heuristics are vital to human problem solving. Some useful heuristics are **hill climbing,** creating **subgoals,** and **working backward.**

☐ How can a "set" both help and hinder problem solving?

A **set** is a tendency to perceive and approach a problem in a certain way. Although sets can enable us to draw on past experience to help solve problems, a strong set can also prevent us from using essential new approaches. One set that can seriously hamper problem solving is **functional fixedness**—the tendency to perceive only traditional uses for an object.

☐ How does decision making differ from problem solving?

Decision making is a special kind of problem solving in which we already know all the possible solutions or choices. The task is not to come up with new solutions but rather to identify the best available one based on whatever criteria we are using.

☐ How would you go about making a truly logical decision?

The logical way to make a decision is to rate each of the available choices in terms of criteria you have weighted based on how important they are to you. Then total the ratings for each choice to arrive at a "best" option. Because heavily weighted attractive features can compensate for lightly weighted unattractive ones, this decision-making approach is called a **compensatory model.**

☐ How are most everyday decisions made?

Most people do not use a precise and logical system for making most decisions. Rather, they use various **noncompensatory models,** in which shortcomings on one criterion are not offset by strengths on others. Especially popular is the *elimination-by-aspects* tactic in which you toss out certain choices if they don't meet one or two of your requirements, regardless of how good they are on other criteria.

☐ What are some factors that can lead to poor choices?

When people use heuristics or rule-of-thumb approaches to help them make decisions, they can save a great deal of time and effort, but they do not always make the best choices. One example is errors in judgment based on the **representativeness heuristic,** which involves making decisions based on information that matches our model of the "typical" member of a category. Other examples are overreliance on the **availability heuristic** (making choices based on whatever information we can most easily retrieve from memory, even though it may not be accurate) and the **confirmation bias** (the tendency to seek evidence in support of our existing beliefs and to ignore evidence that contradicts them).

☐ Can culture affect our decisions?

Although psychologists have only recently begun to explore the influence of culture on decision making, there do seem to be cross-cultural differences related to it. For instance, in some cultures people tend to favor group-made decisions, while in others decision makers tend to be more self-reliant. Greater knowledge of cultural differences in decision making can encourage greater understanding between cultures.

What questions are asked by psychologists who study intelligence?

Psychologists who study **intelligence** ask what intelligence entails and how it can be measured. They also wonder about the relationship between intelligence and creativity.

What are some of the major theories of intelligence?

Intelligence theories fall into two categories: those that argue in favor of a "general intelligence," which affects all aspects of cognitive functioning, and those that say intelligence is composed of many separate abilities, with a person not necessarily scoring high in all of them. Spearman's theory of intelligence is an example of the first category. The theories of Thurstone and Cattell are examples of the second category, as are Sternberg's triarchic theory of intelligence and Gardner's theory of multiple intelligences.

What kinds of intelligence tests are in use today?

The *Binet–Simon Scale*, developed in France by Alfred Binet and Theodore Simon, was adapted by Stanford University's L. M. Terman to create a test of **intelligence quotient (IQ)** called the *Stanford–Binet Intelligence Scale*. The **Wechsler Adult Intelligence Scale** was developed by David Wechsler especially for adults. He also created the **Wechsler Intelligence Scale for Children.** In contrast to these individual intelligence tests, there are also **group tests** of intelligence, which are administered by one examiner to many people at a time. In addition, some psychologists who criticize traditional IQ tests have developed alternatives to them. Some are **performance tests** of mental abilities, which don't involve the use of language, and others are **culture-fair tests** that reduce cultural bias in a variety of ways.

What are some important characteristics of a good test?

Reliability, the ability of a test to produce consistent and stable scores, and **validity,** the ability of a test to measure what it has been designed to measure, are two important characteristics of a good test. Although the reliability of IQ tests is seldom questioned, their validity is. Critics charge that these tests assess only a very limited set of mental skills—for instance, passive verbal understanding, the ability to follow instructions, and the ability to give correct answers in a limited time frame.

What determines individual differences in intelligence?

Many experts say that about 50 percent of the differences in intelligence that IQ tests measure are due to genetic differences, with the other half being due to differences in environment and education. With such a sizable percentage being accounted for by experience, many psychologists are strongly in favor of compensatory education programs for young children from disadvantaged homes. One such program is Head Start. Although it may not boost IQ scores greatly in the long run, it does seem to have significant educational benefits.

Do gender and culture influence mental abilities?

Many people believe that males and females are innately different in their verbal and mathematical abilities. Others believe that people from certain cultures have a natural tendency to excel at academic skills. Neither of these beliefs holds up under scientific scrutiny.

What do psychologists know about the two extremes of human intelligence: very high and very low?

The IQs of nearly 70 percent of the general population fall between 85 and 115, and all but 5 percent of the population have IQs between 70 and 130. **Mental retardation** and **giftedness** are the two extremes of intelligence. About a quarter of the cases of mental retardation can be traced to biological causes, including Down syndrome, but the causes of the other 75 percent of cases are not fully understood. Neither are the causes of giftedness. Gifted people do not necessarily excel in all mental abilities. Sometimes they are gifted in one area without being gifted in others.

What is creativity?

Creativity is the ability to produce novel and socially valued ideas or objects, from philosophy to painting, from music to mousetraps.

How is creativity related to intelligence?

The threshold theory holds that a certain minimum level of intelligence is needed for creativity, but above that threshold level, higher intelligence doesn't necessarily make for greater creativity. Apparently other factors, besides intelligence, contribute to creativity.

Are you more creative at some times than other times?

People are more creative in some situations than others. A moderately elated mood can spur creativity, just as belittlement of one's accomplishments can inhibit it. Also putting a damper on creativeness are performing on command or in competition with others, or being watched while working.

Can creativity be measured?

A number of tests of creativity have been developed. These tests are scored on the originality of answers and frequently on the number of responses (divergent thinking). Some psychologists question how valid these tests are, however.

CRITICAL THINKING AND APPLICATIONS

1. Einstein believed his extraordinary genius resulted in part from his skill in visualizing the possibilities of abstract ideas. Could anyone become a genius by developing skills of visualization?

2. Think for a moment of the last time you were confronted with an important decision. What approach did you use in making your choice? Now that you have read this chapter, would you respond differently if you were faced with a similar decision today?

3. Because a performance test does not rely on language skills, it is necessarily culture-fair. Is this statement accurate? Why or why not?

4. In what ways has intelligence testing had a profound influence on our lives? Do you think this influence has been predominantly positive or negative? What could be done to improve intelligence tests and make their impact more positive?

Visit these online resources at our Companion Website www.prenhall.com/morris

The Psychology Place

Learning Activities	1. Understanding Mental Models, p. 232
Research News	2. The Growing Popularity of "Emotional Intelligence", p. 247
	3. How Stereotypes Affect Test Performance, p. 253
	4. Another Explanation for Differences in Intellectual Performance: Stereotype Threat, p. 255

Games

1. Building Blocks of Cognition, p. 229
2. Problem Solving, p. 234
3. Subtests of the Stanford–Binet, p. 249

Web Links

1. **http://casper.beckman.uiuc.edu/~c-tsai4/cogsci/,** p. 229
   Cognitive sciences resources on the Internet.
2. **http://www.surfaquarium.com/micrit.htm,** p. 247
   Gardner's Eight Criteria for Identifying an Intelligence: List and explanation of the eight criteria for identifying intelligence.
3. **http://www.homearts.com:80/depts/relat/01eggab5.htm,** p. 249
   Emotional intelligence quiz.
4. **http://maple.lemoyne.edu/~hevern/psychref4-11.html,** p. 250
   Psychological Testing, Assessment, and Psychometrics: Intelligence. Links to related Web sites.
5. **http://ericae.net/intbod.stm,** p. 250
   Assessment and evaluation on the Internet: Offers definitions, descriptions, resources, and other detailed information about a wide range of assessment measures.
6. **http://www.hbem.com/library/parents/htm,** p. 252
   Some things parents should know about testing: A series of questions and complete answers to questions related to testing.
7. **http://www.Ldonline.org/,** p. 261
   LD Online: Learning disabilities information & resources.
8. **http://www.thearc.org/fags/mrga.html,** p. 261
   Introduction to mental retardation. Provides complete answers to common questions one may have about mental retardation.
9. **http://home8.swipnet.se/~w-80790/Index.htm,** p. 262
   Estimated IQs of some of the greatest geniuses. Explains IQ and then offers estimated IQs of the greatest geniuses.
10. **http://www.ozemail.com.au/~caveman/Creative/index2.html,** p. 263
    Creativity Web: Resources for creativity and innovation.

8

MOTIVATION AND EMOTION

CLASSIC DETECTIVE STORIES ARE USUALLY STUDIES OF MOTIVATION and emotion at a sophisticated level. In the beginning all we know is that a murder has been committed: After eating dinner with her family, sweet old Amanda Jones collapses and dies of strychnine poisoning. "Now, why would anyone do a thing like that?" everyone wonders. The police ask the same question, but in different terms: "Who had a motive for killing Miss Jones?" In a good mystery the answer is "Practically everybody."

The younger sister—now 75 years old—still bristles when she thinks of that tragic day 50 years ago when Amanda stole her sweetheart. The next-door neighbor, a frequent dinner guest, has been heard to say that if Miss Jones's poodle tramples his peonies one more time, he intends to . . . The nephew, who stands to inherit a fortune from the deceased, is deeply in debt. The parlor maid has a guilty secret that Miss Jones knew. All four people are in the house when Amanda Jones is poisoned. All four have easy access to strychnine, which is used to kill rats in the basement. All had strong emotional reactions to Amanda Jones—envy, anger, shame, guilt. All had a motive for killing her.

Motivation and emotion also play a role in some of the less dramatic events in the story. Motivated by hunger, the family sits down together to eat a meal. The poodle, motivated by curiosity or the call of nature, is attracted on repeated occasions to the neighbor's peonies. The next-door neighbor visits because he is lonely and longs for company. The parlor maid's guilt stems from activities engaged in to satisfy sexual urges. The tragedy of Amanda Jones's death brings the four suspects closer together out of a need for affiliation, but the fear generated by the murder makes each of them suspicious of the others.

In this story motivation and emotion are closely intertwined. A **motive** is an inner directing force—a specific need or want—that arouses the organism and directs its behavior toward a goal. When one or more stimuli create a motive, the result is goal-directed behavior (see Figure 8–1). Like motives, **emotions**—the experience of such feelings as fear, joy, surprise, and anger—may activate and affect behavior, but it is more difficult to predict the *kind* of behavior that a particular emotion will prompt. If people are hungry, we can be reasonably sure that they will seek food. If, however, the same people experience feelings of joy or surprise, we cannot know exactly how they will act or whether they will act at all.

It is important to remember that motives and emotions push us to take some kind of action—from an act as drastic as murder to one as mundane as drumming our fingers. Motivation occurs whether we are aware of it or not. We do not have to think about being hungry to head for the refrigerator, or focus on our need for achievement to study for an exam. We do not have to consciously recognize that we are afraid to step back from a growling dog or know that we are angry before raising our voice. Moreover, the same motivation or emotion may produce different behaviors in different people. Ambition might motivate one person to go to law school and another to join a crime ring. Feeling sad might lead one person to cry alone and another to talk to a friend. On the other hand, the same behavior might arise from different motives or emotions: You may buy liver because you like it, because it is inexpensive, or because you know that your body needs the iron it contains. You may go to a movie because you are happy, bored, or lonely. The workings of motives and emotions are very complex.

In this chapter we look first at specific motives that play an important role in human behavior. Then we turn to emotions and the various ways in which they are expressed.

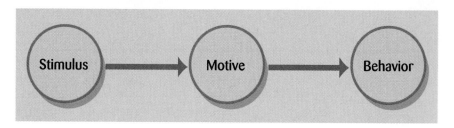

FIGURE 8–1
How motivation works.   A *motive* is triggered by some kind of *stimulus*—a bodily need or a cue in the environment. A motive, in turn, activates and directs *behavior*.

Perspectives on Motivation

How can you use intrinsic and extrinsic motivation to help you achieve your goals in school?

Early in the twentieth century psychologists were inclined to attribute behavior to **instincts**—specific behavior patterns characteristic of an entire species. Animal instincts include salmon swimming upstream to spawn and spiders spinning webs. In 1890 William James proposed that humans have such diverse instincts as hunting, rivalry, fear, curiosity, shyness, love, shame, and resentment. Instinct theory lost favor as an explanation of human behavior for two reasons: (1) Most significant human behavior is not inborn but is learned through experience; and (2) human behavior is rarely rigid, inflexible, unchanging, and characteristic of the species. In addition, ascribing every conceivable human behavior to a corresponding instinct really explains nothing. (Calling a person's inclination to be alone an "antisocial instinct," for example, simply describes the behavior without pinpointing its origins.) By the 1920s psychologists started looking for more credible explanations of human behavior.

One alternative view of motivation holds that bodily needs (such as the need for food or for water) create a state of tension or arousal called a **drive** (such as hunger or thirst). According to **drive-reduction theory,** motivated behavior is an attempt to reduce this unpleasant state of tension in the body and to return the body to a state of **homeostasis,** or balance. When we are hungry we look for food to reduce the hunger drive. When we are tired we go to sleep. When we are thirsty we find something to drink. In each of these cases behavior is directed toward reducing a state of bodily tension or arousal.

Drive reduction doesn't explain all motivated behavior, however. When we are bored, for instance, we may actually seek out activities that *heighten* tension and arousal. Some people go to horror movies, take up skydiving, and pursue new challenges just to raise their level of arousal. These thrill seekers enjoy a higher-than-normal level of stimulation; they feel especially alive when they are taking part in some dangerous activity. Human beings strive to maintain an optimal state of arousal: If arousal is too high, we will make efforts to reduce it; if arousal is too low, we will take steps to increase it.

To complicate matters further, some behavior isn't triggered by internal states at all. For example, the smell from a bakery may prompt us to eat, even if we have just finished a satisfying meal; an inviting advertisement or a store window display may lead us to buy something we would not otherwise have bought. In other words, objects in the environment—called **incentives**—can also motivate behavior (Bolles, 1972; Rescorla & Solomon, 1967).

Psychologists sometimes distinguish between **intrinsic** and **extrinsic motivation.** For example, when a child spontaneously picks up a pencil and paper

Motive
Specific need, desire, or want, such as hunger, thirst, or achievement, that prompts goal-oriented behavior.

Emotion
Feeling, such as fear, joy, or surprise, that underlies behavior.

Instincts
Inborn, inflexible, goal-directed behavior that is characteristic of an entire species.

Drive
State of tension or arousal brought on by biological needs.

Drive-reduction theory
Theory that motivated behavior is aimed at reducing a state of bodily tension or arousal and returning the organism to homeostasis.

Homeostasis
State of balance and stability in which the organism functions effectively.

Incentives
External stimuli that prompt goal-directed behavior.

Intrinsic motivation
A desire to perform a behavior that originates within the individual.

Extrinsic motivation
A desire to perform a behavior to obtain an external reward or to avoid punishment.

and writes a letter to her grandparents, we say that her behavior is intrinsically motivated because the motivation apparently comes from *within*. Climbing trees and finger painting are other examples of behavior in children that are often intrinsically motivated—just as doing crossword puzzles and tinkering in a garden or workshop may be for adults. In contrast, when a child writes a letter to her grandparents because she hopes to receive some reward (such as a gift) or as a requirement to receive her allowance, her behavior is extrinsically motivated: The child performs this behavior to receive some *external* reward or to avoid some threat of punishment. Whether behavior is intrinsically or extrinsically motivated can have important consequences:

> When people pursue activities for their intrinsic interest they are especially likely to become and remain fascinated and absorbed by them and feel happy. Conversely, when people concentrate on the external rewards of particular tasks, they experience decreased emotional involvement and negative feelings. . . . Higher intrinsic motivation is linked to higher school achievement and psychological adjustment in children, adolescents and college students. (National Advisory Mental Health Council, 1995, p. 843)

We look next at a motive that is primarily guided by internal biological states—hunger. Then we turn to sexual behavior, which is responsive to both internal states and external incentives. We then examine several behaviors, such as curiosity and manipulation, that depend heavily on external environmental cues. Finally, we describe several additional motives that figure prominently in human social relationships.

Thrill-seeking behaviors cannot be explained by drive-reduction theory, because thrill seekers are trying to *increase* arousal, not reduce it. Everyone sometimes seeks to increase arousal, but thrill seekers seem to desire higher levels of arousal than most people do.

REVIEW QUESTIONS

Match the following terms with the appropriate definition.

1. drive	____	a. external stimulus that prompts goal-directed behavior
2. drive reduction	____	b. state of balance in which the organism functions effectively
3. homeostasis	____	c. theory that motivated behavior is focused on reducing bodily tension
4. incentive	____	d. performs behavior to receive some external reward or avoid punishment
5. intrinsic motivation	____	e. state of tension brought on by biological needs
6. extrinsically motivated	____	f. motivation arising from within an individual

Indicate whether the following statements are true (T) or false (F).

7. Most significant human behavior is learned, not inborn. ____

8. Human behavior is rigidly unchanging and characteristic of our species. ____

9. Drive-reduction theory explains our attempts to increase arousal when we are bored. ____

Answers: 1. e. 2. c. 3. b. 4. a. 5. f. 6. d. 7. T. 8. F. 9. F.

Primary Drives

What activates primary drives?

Biological needs that trigger a corresponding state of psychological arousal or tension (a drive) are called **primary drives.** These unlearned drives—principally, hunger, thirst, and sex—are common to every animal, including humans. Primary drives are strongly influenced by stimuli within the body that are part

Primary drive
Physiologically based unlearned motive, such as hunger.

of the biological programming for survival of the organism (or, in the case of sex, for survival of the species).

Hunger

Why is it so difficult for some people to lose weight while others have no trouble maintaining their weight?

When you are hungry, you eat. If you don't, your need for food—but not necessarily your appetite—will increase the longer you are deprived of it. If you skip lunch, your need for food will increase throughout the day, but your hunger will come and go. You will probably be hungry around lunchtime; then your hunger will likely abate. But by dinnertime no concern will seem as pressing as eating. The psychological state of hunger, then, is not the same as the biological need for food, although the psychological state is often triggered by biological processes.

Early research established the importance of the hypothalamus as the brain center involved in hunger and eating. Initially, researchers identified two regions in the hypothalamus as controlling our experience of hunger and satiety (*satiety* means being full to satisfaction). One of these centers, the *lateral hypothalamus*, appeared to act as the feeding center because when it was stimulated animals began to eat, but when it was destroyed the animals stopped eating to the point of starvation. The *ventromedial hypothalamus*, in contrast, was thought to be the satiety center because when it was stimulated animals ceased eating, but when it was destroyed animals ate to the point of extreme obesity. More recent studies, however, have challenged this simple "on-off" explanation for the control of eating by showing that a number of other areas of the brain are also involved (Winn, 1995). For instance, a third center in the hypothalamus called the *paraventricular nucleus* appears to influence the drive to eat specific foods. Studies have also shown that regions of the cortex and spinal cord play an important role in regulating food intake. Moreover, the connections among brain centers that control hunger are now known to be considerably more complex than was once thought, involving more than a dozen different neurotransmitters (Flier & Maratos-Flier, 1998; Woods, Seeley, Porte, & Schwartz, 1998). Some of these neurotransmitters act to increase the consumption of specific foods such as carbohydrates or fats, while others suppress the drive for these foods (Blundell & Halford, 1998; Lin, Umahara, York, & Bray, 1998).

How do these areas of the brain know when to signal hunger? The brain monitors the blood levels of substances like *glucose* (a simple sugar used by the body for energy), fats, and carbohydrates as well as hormones like insulin that are released into the blood in response to these nutrients. Changes in the blood levels of these substances then signal the need for food to the brain (Seeley & Schwartz, 1997).

The brain also monitors the amount and kind of food that you have eaten. Receptors in the stomach sense not only how much food the stomach is holding but also how many calories that food contains. Signals from these receptors travel to the brain. In addition, when food enters the small intestine, a hormone is released into the bloodstream and carried to the brain, where it serves as an additional source of information about the body's nutritional needs (Albus, 1989; Takaki et al., 1990).

These hunger mechanisms regulate our day-to-day intake of food. But there appears to be yet another hunger regulator, one that operates on a long-term basis to regulate the body's weight. Have you ever noticed that very few animals besides humans and some domesticated animals become grossly overweight? The body seems to have a way of monitoring its own fat stores and regulating the intake of food to provide just enough energy to maintain normal activities without storing excessive fat deposits.

How and when you satisfy hunger and thirst depends on social, psychological, environmental, and cultural influences as well as on physiological needs. For example, the Japanese tea ceremony is concerned more with restoring inner harmony than with satisfying thirst. Do you think the office worker is drinking coffee because she is thirsty?

Although hunger often is triggered by a biological need for food, external cues, like the smell of a cake baking in the oven, may also trigger the desire to eat at almost any hour. Sometimes merely looking at the clock and realizing that it is dinnertime makes us feel hungry. One intriguing line of research suggests that such external cues may set off internal biological processes that mimic real internal needs. The mere sight, smell, or thought of food causes an increase in insulin production, which in turn lowers glucose levels in the body's cells, mirroring the body's response to a physical need for food (Rodin, 1985).

With all of these mechanisms for monitoring the body's need for food and the many ways of controlling hunger, why do some people eat so much that they become overweight or even obese? Researchers have identified a mechanism in the brain that may be responsible for obesity (Chua et al., 1996; Leroy et al., 1996; Vaisse et al., 1996). Fat cells produce a hormone called *leptin* that travels in the bloodstream and is sensed by the hypothalamus (Carlson, 1998). In response to high levels of leptin, the brain signals a reduction in appetite or an increase in the rate at which fat is burned, both of which serve to reduce the amount of fat in the body. Research with mice suggests that a defective gene may in part be responsible for obesity by failing to regulate the level of leptin in the brain (Reed et al., 1996). Increasing the level of leptin in obese animals results in a rapid loss of body fat. Because leptin also appears to be involved in the human response to hunger, this finding may someday lead to the development of safe and effective treatments for obesity in humans (Ravussin et al., 1997).

The hunger drive may be affected by emotions as well. Suppose you are very hungry, but in the midst of preparing dinner, you have a serious argument with your boyfriend or girlfriend. If you become extremely upset by the argument, you may not want to eat for hours. In contrast, some people *become* hungry whenever they are anxious or nervous.

Social influences also affect our motivation to eat. If you are intent on impressing a prospective client over lunch, you may not feel very hungry even though it is an hour past your usual lunchtime. Social situations may also prompt you to eat when you are not hungry, so as not to appear rude, or simply to do what everyone else is doing.

Cultural Differences in Eating Behavior   How you respond when you are hungry will vary according to your experiences with food, which are mostly governed by learning and social conditioning. The majority of Americans eat three meals a day at regular intervals. A typical American family eats breakfast at 7 A.M., lunch around noon, and dinner about 6 P.M. In Italy people rarely eat dinner before 9 P.M.

This photo of gymnast Christy Henrich was taken about a year before her death in June 1994. Henrich suffered from the eating disorder known as *anorexia nervosa*, as her gaunt appearance shows.

How much and what we choose to eat are also influenced by our culture. Most Americans will not eat horse meat, but it is very popular in Europe. Some preindustrial peoples traditionally ate insect larvae, the thought of which would disgust most Americans. Yet many Americans eat pork, which violates both Islamic and Orthodox Jewish dietary laws (Scupin, 1995).

So although hunger is basically a biological drive, it is more than an internal state that we satisfy when our body tells us to. Both the motivation to eat and eating behavior itself are influenced by psychological, cultural, and environmental factors.

Weight Loss   The body interprets weight loss as a danger signal and responds to protect itself against further weight loss. So if you significantly reduce the number of calories in your diet, you will probably lose weight, but your body will respond by lowering your metabolism so that you need fewer calories to maintain your weight. This explains why some dieters, after losing 10 or 15 pounds, reach a plateau at which further weight loss is very difficult to achieve (see *Applying Psychology*). How does this process occur?

According to one theory, a homeostatic mechanism in the body known as the **set point** regulates metabolism, fat storage, and food intake (Bennett & Gurin, 1982). Set-point theory argues that the body is programmed for a certain weight. If you regularly weigh about 150 pounds and gain 10 pounds on vacation, you can easily lose the additional pounds because you will be returning to a weight consistent with your body's set point. Set-point theory helps to explain plateauing and backsliding among dieters, as well as why a thin person can consume the same number of calories as an overweight person and stay thin. It may also offer insights into how genes influence weight.

Set-point theory directly challenges the idea that there is one *ideal* body type for everyone. For some of us our natural set point is geared to being thin; for others it is geared to being stocky. When achieving an ideal body becomes an obsession, serious—sometimes life-threatening—eating disorders such as *anorexia* and *bulimia* can result. Sometimes, too, the desire to lose weight and become fit may reflect a lack of self-esteem more than a real need to lose weight.

Eating Disorders   "When people told me I looked like someone from Auschwitz [the Nazi concentration camp], I thought that was the highest compliment anyone could give me," confessed a young woman who as a teenager suffered from a serious eating disorder known as **anorexia nervosa.** She was 18 years old, 5 feet 3 inches tall, and weighed 68 pounds. She was lucky—she managed to overcome the disorder and has since maintained normal body weight. Others are less fortunate. In 1983 the singer Karen Carpenter died of cardiac arrest following a long battle with anorexia. More recently the world-class gymnast Christy Henrich succumbed to the disease, weighing just 61 pounds at her death (Pace, 1994).

People with anorexia nervosa perceive themselves as overweight and strive to lose weight, usually by severely limiting their intake of food. Even after they become very thin, they constantly worry about weight gain. The following four symptoms are used in the diagnosis of anorexia nervosa (APA, 1994):

1. Intense fear of becoming obese, which does not diminish as weight loss progresses.

2. Disturbance of body image (for example, claiming to "feel fat" even when emaciated).

3. Refusal to maintain body weight at or above a minimal normal weight for age and height.

4. In females the absence of at least three consecutive menstrual cycles.

Set point
A homeostatic mechanism in the body that regulates metabolism, fat storage, and food intake so as to maintain a pre-programmed weight.

Anorexia nervosa
A serious eating disorder that is associated with an intense fear of weight gain and a distorted body image.

APPLYING PSYCHOLOGY

Losing Weight: More than Just Dieting

A successful weight-control program must be long-term and must work with, rather than against, the body's normal tendency to maintain weight. It should be undertaken only after consultation with a doctor. Based on studies of the hunger drive and the relationship between eating and body weight, how should you go about losing excess weight?

1. Increase the body's metabolism through regular exercise. The most effective metabolism raiser is 20–30 minutes of moderate activity several times a week in which only 200–300 calories are burned off during each session (Craighead, 1990). Exercise coupled with dietary changes does reduce weight (Wadden et al., 1997).

2. Modify what you eat. A moderate reduction in calories is beneficial, but even more important is reducing the consumption of fats (particularly saturated fats) and substances such as table sugars and syrups that trigger an increase in the body's level of insulin. High levels of fat and insulin in the blood stimulate hunger, and dietary fats are more easily stored by the body as fat than as muscle.

3. Reduce, as much as possible, external cues that trigger hunger or encourage you to eat undesirable foods. The mere sight or smell of food can increase the amount of insulin in the body, thus triggering the hunger drive. If possible, don't bring foods high in calories or fat into your home. Many people find that if they do their food shopping on a full stomach, they are less tempted to buy foods high in calories and fat.

4. Set realistic goals for weight loss and focus at least as much on *maintaining* the lower weight as on losing more weight. If you need to lose weight, try to shed just 1 pound a week for 2 or 3 months, then concentrate on maintaining that new, lower weight for the rest of the year before moving on to further weight loss.

5. Reward yourself—in ways unrelated to food—for small improvements. Use some of the behavior-modification techniques described in Chapter 5: Reward yourself not only for each pound of weight lost but also for each day or week that you maintain that weight loss.

To learn more about weight control visit our Web site at **www.prenhall. com/morris.**

Approximately 1 percent of all adolescents suffer from anorexia nervosa; about 90 percent of these are white upper- or middle-class females (Brumberg, 1988; E. H. Gilbert & DeBlassie, 1984; Romeo, 1984). Generally people suffering from anorexia enjoy an otherwise normal childhood and adolescence. They are usually successful students and cooperative, well-behaved children. They have an intense interest in food but view eating with disgust. They also have a very distorted view of their own body.

Anorexia is frequently compounded by another eating disorder, **bulimia** (Fairburn & Wilson, 1993; Yanovski, 1993). The following criteria are used for the diagnosis of bulimia (APA, 1994):

1. Recurrent episodes of binge eating (rapid consumption of a large amount of food in a discrete period of time, usually less than 2 hours).

2. Recurrent inappropriate behaviors to try to prevent weight gain, such as inducing vomiting, using laxatives, or exercising excessively.

3. Binge eating and compensatory behaviors that occur at least twice a week for 3 months.

4. The person's self-image is excessively influenced by body shape and weight.

These behaviors do not occur only during episodes of anorexia. It is estimated that 4–8 percent of all adolescent females and up to 2 percent of adolescent males suffer from bulimia (Gwirtsman, 1984; Heatherton & Baumeister, 1991; C. Johnson et al., 1984).

Bulimia
An eating disorder characterized by binges of eating followed by self-induced vomiting.

Society places a great deal of pressure on women to remain thin, like these fashion models. This pressure may contribute to such eating disorders as anorexia and bulimia.

Binge-eating behavior usually begins at about age 18, when adolescents are facing the challenge of new life situations. Not surprisingly, living on a college campus is associated with a higher incidence of bulimia (S. Squire, 1983). Part of the reason is that the socioeconomic group at high risk for bulimia—again, primarily white upper- and middle-class women—is highly represented on college campuses. College campuses also foster social as well as academic competition; there is some evidence that bulimia is more prevalent on campuses where dating is emphasized than on those where it is not (Rodin, Striegel-Moore, & Silberstein, l985).

Although anorexia and bulimia are apparently much more prevalent among females than males (Turnbull, 1996), newer evidence suggests that many more men are affected by these disorders than was once suspected (Tanofsky et al., 1997). For example, a 1992 survey of people who had graduated from Harvard University in 1982 reported that eating disorders dropped by half for women over the decade but doubled for men (J. Seligman, Rogers, & Annin, 1994). The increase in reported eating disorders among men most likely was due to their greater willingness to admit to such disorders in the 1990s as compared with the 1980s. Because attempts to understand the causes of eating disorders have focused almost entirely on females, we know very little about what might predispose males to develop such disorders. Among adolescent women, several factors appear to contribute to the likelihood of eating disorders (Brooks-Gunn, 1993). Most visibly, the media promote the idea that a woman must be thin to be attractive (Crandall, 1994). Rarely do fashion magazine covers feature a well-proportioned woman of normal weight for her height. Perhaps because of the media's emphasis on weight, American women are prone to overestimate their body size (Bruch, 1980; Fallon & Rozin, 1985). More than 95 percent of female participants in one study believed they were about one-fourth larger than they actually were in the waist, thighs, and hips (Thompson et al., 1986).

Psychological factors also contribute to the risk of eating disorders (Walters & Kendler, 1995). The general portrait of the adolescent with an eating disorder (again, based mostly on women) is of an individual with an obsessive-compulsive disorder (see Chapter 12) who feels personally ineffective and depends on others (Phelps & Bajorek, 1991). Women with bulimia commonly have lowered self-esteem and have experienced some form of clinical depression before developing the eating disorder (Klingenspor, 1994). Feelings of vulnerability and helplessness apparently dispose some people to adopt inappropriate ways of controlling the world around them.

There is considerable disagreement on the most effective treatment for eating disorders (Garfinkel & Garner, 1982). Of course, the first step in cases of anorexia is to get the victim to gain weight, because the disorder can be life-threatening. Cognitive-behavior modification therapy (see Chapter 13) has been successful in increasing food intake and somewhat successful in treating physical stress in cases of anorexia (Telch et al., 1990). Some forms of cognitive-behavior therapy have also helped people with bulimia, especially when coupled with techniques to prevent vomiting. Often the biggest difficulty in beginning treatment is overcoming the patients' insistence that "nothing is wrong" (Rastam, 1994). In many developing countries such as Taiwan, Singapore, and China, where dieting is becoming a fad, these once little-known eating disorders are now becoming a serious problem (Hsu, 1996).

Sex

How do biology, experience, and culture influence the human sex drive?

Sex is the primary drive that motivates reproductive behavior. Like the other primary drives, it can be turned on and off by biological conditions in the body and by environmental cues. But it differs from them in one important way:

Hunger and thirst are vital to the survival of the individual, but sex is vital only to the survival of the species.

Describing the physiology of sexual behavior, sex researchers William Masters and Virginia Johnson identified a *sexual response cycle* that consists of four phases: excitement, plateau, orgasm, and resolution (Masters & Johnson, 1966). In the *excitement phase*, the man's penis becomes engorged with blood and erect, and the woman's breasts and clitoris swell. This engorgement of the sexual organs continues into the *plateau phase*, in which sexual tension levels off as breathing becomes more rapid and genital secretions and muscle tension increase. During *orgasm*, the male ejaculates and the woman's uterus contracts, as both men and women experience a loss of muscle control. The *resolution phase* is one of relaxation in which muscle tension decreases and the engorged penis and clitoris return to normal. Heart rate, breathing, and blood pressure also return to normal.

Biological Factors in Sexual Arousal   Biology clearly plays a major role in sexual motivation. At one time the level of hormones like *testosterone*—the male sex hormone—was believed to *determine* sex drive. Today scientists recognize that hormonal influences on human sexual arousal are considerably more complex. As we have seen in earlier chapters, testosterone does play a role in early sexual development (such as the onset of puberty), in differentiating male and female sex organs and, to some extent, in establishing characteristic patterns of adult sexual behavior (Kalat, 1988). But moment-to-moment fluctuations in testosterone levels are not necessarily linked to sex drive. In fact, adult males who have been castrated (resulting in a significant decrease in testosterone levels) often report little decrease in sex drive (Persky, 1983). Unlike lower animals whose sexual activity is largely controlled by hormones and is tied to the female's reproductive cycle, humans are capable of sexual arousal at any time.

Scientists suspect that as in other animals, the sex drive in humans may also be affected by subtle smells. Many animals secrete substances called *pheromones* that, when smelled by the other sex, promote sexual readiness. Some indirect evidence suggests that pheromones may influence human sexual attraction as well (Wedekind, Seebeck, Bettens, & Paepke, 1995).

The brain exerts a powerful influence on the sex drive. In particular, the limbic system (see Chapter 2), located deep within the brain, is involved in sexual excitement (R. C. Heath, 1972; Hyde, 1982).

Psychological and Cultural Influences on Sexual Motivation   Although hormones and the nervous system figure in the sex drive, human sexual motivation—especially in the early stages of excitement and arousal—is much more dependent on experience and learning than on biology.

What kind of stimuli activate the sex drive in humans? Erotic fantasies, the sight of one's lover, the smell of perfume or after-shave lotion—all of these can stimulate sexual excitement (Laan et al., 1995). As with the other drives, experience also shapes human sexual arousal. Soft lights and music often have an aphrodisiac effect. One person may be unmoved by a sexually explicit movie but aroused by a romantic love story, while another may respond in just the opposite way. The human sexual drive is also affected by social experience, sexual experience, nutrition, emotions—particularly feelings about one's sex partner—and age. Just thinking about or having fantasies about sex can lead to sexual arousal in humans (Leigenberg & Henning, 1995). Ideas about what is moral, appropriate, and pleasurable also influence the kinds of things that are sexually arousing. Interestingly, men and women tend to be aroused in different ways (see *Highlights*).

Just as society dictates standards for sexual conduct, culture guides our views of sexual attractiveness. Culture and experience may influence the extent to which we find particular articles of clothing or body shapes sexually arousing. In

Do his elongated ear lobes and other bodily adornments enhance this young man's sexual attractiveness? It all depends on your cultural point of view. In the Samburu society of Kenya in which he lives, these particular adornments are considered highly attractive.

HIGHLIGHTS

Gender Differences in Human Sexuality

Although both men and women are sexual beings, research has shown that they tend to be sexually aroused in different ways. In general, men are more aroused by visual cues, whereas women respond more to touch (Schulz, 1984). A man may be aroused to erection simply by watching his partner undress, but a woman may need to have her body caressed to achieve the same state of arousal. In addition, although descriptions or scenes of sexual activity are arousing to both men and women, the rate of arousal in women is slow compared with the instantaneous response that often occurs in males (Christensen, 1986). The focus of interest also differs for males and females: Men tend to favor viewing close-ups of sexual acts, whereas women respond more to style, setting, and mood (Masters, Johnson, & Kolodny, 1982).

Men and women also differ somewhat in sexual experiences, although

---

Men and women also differ somewhat in sexual experiences, although these differences are less pronounced than we might expect.

---

these differences are less pronounced than we might expect. According to one survey by the National Opinion Research Center (NORC), women are more likely to have had only one sexual partner since age 18 (31 percent of women as compared with only 20 percent of men), yet roughly the same proportion of women (22 percent) and men (23 percent) reported having from 5 to 10 sexual partners since age 18. Women were somewhat less likely than men to be satisfied sexually, however. The survey found that 95 percent of men, single or married, said they usually or always had an orgasm, as compared with 75 percent of married women and 62 percent of single women. When it came to thinking about sex, more than 50 percent of the men surveyed said that they thought about sex every day or several times a day, whereas only 19 percent of women reported thinking about sex so often (Lewin, 1994b).

---

some cultures most men prefer women with large breasts, while in other cultures small breasts are preferred. Among some African cultures elongated earlobes are considered very attractive. In our own culture what we find attractive often depends on the styles of the time.

Sexual Orientation   As described in Chapter 1, *sexual orientation* refers to the direction of an individual's sexual interest. A person with a *heterosexual orientation* is sexually attracted to members of the other sex. People with a *homosexual orientation* are sexually attracted to members of their own sex. *Bisexuals* are attracted to members of both sexes. Early surveys (Kinsey, 1948, 1953) estimated that approximately 10 percent of the population was homosexual. More recent statistics, however, indicate that only about 2.8 percent of males and 1.4 percent of females have a homosexual orientation (Laumann, 1994; Sell, Wells, & Wypij, 1995).

Why people display different sexual orientations, and in particular homosexuality, has been argued for decades in the form of the classic nature-versus-nurture debate. Those on the nature (or biological) side hold that sexual orientation has its roots in biology and is primarily influenced by genetics. They point out that homosexual men and women generally know before puberty that they are "different" and often remain "in the closet" regarding their sexual orientation for fear of recrimination. They cite evidence from family and twin studies that shows a higher incidence of male homosexuality in families with other gay men, as well as a higher rate of homosexuality among men with a homosexual twin, even when the twins were raised separately (LeVay & Hamer, 1994). The nature position also derives support from studies that have suggested that the sizes of specific brain structures may differ between homosexual and heterosexual men (Allen & Gorski, 1992; LeVay, 1991; Swaab & Hoffman, 1995).

On the nurture (or environmental) side are those who hold that sexual orientation is primarily a learned behavior influenced by early experience and largely under voluntary control. They argue that the research supporting the biological position is methodologically flawed and sometimes confuses what causes homosexuality with what results from homosexuality (Byne, 1994). They contend that early socialization determines sexual orientation and point out that the frequency of different sexual orientations differs significantly from one culture to another.

To date, neither the biological view nor the environmental view can completely explain the origin of sexual orientation. As with most complex behaviors, it is likely that both nature and nurture play significant roles (Kelley & Dawson, 1994).

REVIEW QUESTIONS

1. Unlearned drives based on biological needs and common to all animals are called ____ ____.
2. The three principal primary drives that ensure survival of the organism or species are ____, ____, and ____.
3. The level of ____ in the blood signals hunger.
4. Hunger can be stimulated by both ____ and ____ cues.
5. ____ ____ theory maintains that the body is "programmed" for a certain weight.
6. ____ is the primary drive necessary for the survival of the species.

Match the following terms with the appropriate definition.

7. hypothalamus ____ a. homeostatic mechanism that regulates metabolism, fat storage, and food intake
8. leptin ____ b. recurrent episodes of binge eating, followed by vomiting, taking laxatives, or excessively exercising
9. set point ____ c. contains both a hunger center and a satiety center
10. anorexia nervosa ____ d. hormone produced by fat cells
11. bulimia ____ e. intense fear of obesity, disturbance of body image, and very little intake of food, with resulting weight well below normal minimums
12. testosterone ____ f. scents that may cause sexual attraction
13. pheromones ____ g. male sex hormone

Answers: 1. primary drives. 2. hunger, thirst, sex. 3. glucose. 4. internal, external. 5. set-point. 6. sex. 7. c. 8. d. 9. a. 10. e. 11. b. 12. g 13. f.

Other Important Motives

How do stimulus motives and social motives differ from primary drives?

Stimulus Motives

What motives cause people to explore and change their environment?

Like the primary drives, **stimulus motives** are largely unlearned, but in all species these motives are more dependent than primary drives on external stimuli—things in the world around us. Whereas primary drives are associated with the survival of the organism or the species, stimulus motives are

Stimulus motives
Unlearned motives, such as curiosity or contact, that prompt us to explore or change our world.

This infant is exhibiting curiosity, a stimulus motive.

associated with obtaining information about the environment. Motives such as *curiosity*, *exploration*, *manipulation*, and *contact* push us to investigate and often to change our environment.

Exploration and Curiosity

Exploration and curiosity are motives sparked by the new and unknown and are directed toward no more specific goal than "finding out." Even rats, when given a choice, will opt to explore an unknown maze rather than run through a familiar one.

Psychologists disagree about the nature and causes of curiosity (Loewenstein, 1994). William James viewed it as an emotion; Freud considered it a socially acceptable expression of the sex drive. Others have seen it as a response to the unexpected and as evidence of a human need to find meaning in life. Curiosity has been linked to creativity, but studies attempting to establish a positive correlation between curiosity and intelligence have been inconclusive.

Curiosity can vary according to our familiarity with events and circumstances. At times we have all perceived the unknown as more distressing than stimulating or have found something—an argument, a symphony, a chess game—too complex for us. A young child accustomed only to her parents may withdraw from a new face and scream with terror if that face has a beard. But greater familiarity and understanding may change the face, clothing, or symphony from something unacceptable to something interesting and praiseworthy.

As we continually explore and learn from our environment, we raise our threshold for the new and complex, and in turn our explorations and our curiosity become much more ambitious. In this respect, curiosity is linked to cognition. A gap in our understanding may stimulate our curiosity. But as our curiosity is satisfied and the unfamiliar becomes familiar, boredom prompts us to explore our surroundings further (Loewenstein, 1994).

Manipulation

The urge to touch is sometimes nearly irresistible. Unlike curiosity and exploration, manipulation focuses on a specific object that must be touched, handled, played with, and felt before we are satisfied. Manipulation is a motive limited to primates, which have agile fingers and toes.

Psychologists trace the desire to manipulate to two things: the need to know about something at the tactile level and the need to be soothed. Greek "worry beads"—beads that are moved back and forth on a short string during a conversation—exemplify manipulation as a calming action. The brighter the object, the more vivid its colors, the more irregular its shape, the more appealing it is as a potential object for manipulation.

Contact

The need for *contact* is more universal than the need for manipulation. In a classic series of experiments, Harry Harlow demonstrated how important our need for contact is (Harlow, 1958; Harlow & Zimmerman, 1959). Newborn baby monkeys were separated from their mothers and given two "surrogate mothers." Both "mothers" were the same shape, but one was made of wire mesh and had no soft surfaces. The other was cuddly—layered with foam rubber and covered with terry cloth. A nursing bottle was put in the wire-mesh mother, and both mothers were warmed by means of an electric light placed inside them. Thus the wire-mesh mother fulfilled two physiological needs for the infant monkeys: the need for food and the need for warmth. But baby monkeys most often gravitated to the terry-cloth mother, which did not provide food: When they were frightened, they would run and cling to it as they would to a real mother. Because both mothers were warm, the researchers concluded that the need for affection, cuddling, and closeness goes deeper than a need for mere warmth. More recently, the importance of contact has been demonstrated with premature infants. Low-birthweight babies who were held and massaged gained weight faster and were calmer than those who were touched only minimally (Field, 1986).

Aggression

Is aggression a biological or a learned response?

We are not born with all of our motives intact. In fact, as we have seen, some motives that appear to be innate—such as hunger, thirst, and sex—are actually partly learned. As we develop our behavior is governed by new motives that are even more strongly influenced by learning. Some of these motives, such as aggression, may exert just as much influence over our behavior as unlearned drives and motives do. We first look at aggression; then we consider some of the most crucial social motives, which center on our relationships with other people.

Aggression in human beings encompasses all behavior that is intended to inflict physical or psychological harm on others. *Intent* is a key element of aggression (R. Beck, 1983). If you accidentally hit a pedestrian with your car, you have inflicted harm, but without intent to do so. If, however, you spot the person who mugged you last week and try to hit him with your car as he crosses the street, you are doing something intentionally harmful. This is an act of aggression.

Some studies have linked aggression to frustration, but frustration does not always produce aggression. In fact, individuals have very different responses to frustration: Some seek help and support, others withdraw from the source of frustration, and some choose to escape into drugs or alcohol. In other words, frustration seems to generate aggression only in people who have learned to be aggressive as a means of coping with unpleasant situations (Bandura, 1973). Moreover, aggression may be a learned response to a number of different stimuli quite apart from frustration. Almost any unpleasant event may prompt an aggressive outburst. Foul odors, high room temperature, frightening information, and exposure to cigarette smoke have all been found to increase hostility in humans (L. Berkowitz, 1983). Frustration, then, is only one of many stimuli that may provoke aggression.

One way we learn aggression is by observing aggressive models. For example, in contact sports, acts of aggression are frequent and are often praised (Bredemeier & Shields, 1985). In professional hockey, fights between players may elicit as much fan fervor as goal scoring does.

Does it make a difference if the aggressive model does not come out ahead or even is punished? The old customs of public executions and painful punishments like flogging arose from the notion that punishing a person for aggressive acts would deter others from committing those acts. As we saw in Chapter 5, however, children who viewed aggressive behavior learned aggressive behavior regardless of whether the aggressive model was rewarded or punished. The same results were obtained when children were shown films of aggressive behavior. Those children who saw the aggressive model being punished were less aggressive than those who saw the aggressive model rewarded, but both groups of children were more aggressive than those who saw no aggressive model at all. So simply seeing an aggressive model seems to increase aggressive behavior among children, whether the model is punished or rewarded and whether the model is live or is shown on film. These data are consistent with research showing that exposure to cinematic violence of any sort causes a small to moderate increase in naturally occurring aggressive behavior among children and adolescents (Wood, Wong, & Chachere, 1991).

This research has implications for children growing up in homes where aggression and violence are prevalent. Domestic violence is rampant in the United States: One survey found that in a 12-month period more than 3 percent of women (1.8 million) had been severely assaulted, with many of these assaults occurring at home (Browne, 1993). In addition, more than 1 million cases of child abuse are reported each year (National Research Council Panel on Child Abuse

An infant monkey with Harlow's surrogate "mothers"—one made of bare wire, the other covered with soft terrycloth. The baby monkey clings to the terrycloth "mother," even though the wire "mother" is heated and dispenses food. Apparently, there is contact comfort in the cuddly terrycloth that the bare wire "mother" can't provide.

& Neglect, 1993), and more than 1,000 children die annually as a result of abuse. Children who witness domestic violence learn aggressive behavior and are more likely to behave aggressively in the future whenever they believe that violence will serve their purposes (Feldman et al., 1995).

Aggression and Culture   Some cultures—such as the Semai of Malaysia, the Tahitian Islanders of the Pacific, the Zuni and Blackfoot of North America, the Pygmy of Africa, the Japanese, and the Scandinavian—place a premium on resolving conflicts peacefully (Moghaddam, Taylor, & Wright, 1993; P. B. Smith & Bond, 1994; Triandis, 1994). People in these cultures tend to withdraw from confrontation in order to reduce hostility. In contrast, cultures such as the Yanomamö of South America and the Simbu of New Guinea encourage aggressive behavior among their members, particularly the males. But we need not travel to exotic, far-away lands to find such diversity. Within the United States, subcultures such as Quakers, the Amish, the Mennonites, and the Hutterites have traditionally valued nonviolence and peaceful coexistence—in marked contrast to attitudes and practices in the larger American culture.

Cultural differences in aggressiveness are reflected in statistics on violent crimes. Despite the presence of a few nonviolent subcultures, the United States struggles with violent crime rates that are shockingly high as compared with those of other nations. The murder rate in Norway, for example, is estimated at 0.9 per 100,000 people; in Finland and China it is 1.1 per 100,000. In contrast, in the United States the murder rate is 8.6 per 100,000 people—more than 7 times higher than China and almost 10 times higher than Norway (Triandis, 1994). The United States also reports higher rates of rape and vandalism.

These striking cultural differences in aggressive behavior suggest that aggression is very much influenced by the learning that takes place within a particular cultural context and by cultural norms and values. Most of the relatively nonaggressive cultures we just described are *collectivist* societies, which emphasize the good of the group over the desires of the individual. Members of collectivist societies are more likely to seek compromise or to withdraw from a threatening interaction because of their concern for maintaining group harmony. In contrast, members of *individualist* societies are more likely to follow the adage "Stand up for yourself."

Individualism/collectivism is an important and widely used dimension to describe cultures. Cultures high in individualism, such as the United States, see the individual person as the basic unit of society and thus foster individual decision

The Amish are an example of an American subculture that traditionally has valued nonviolence.

making and action. Members of individualist societies have social relationships with many different individuals and groups. In contrast, cultures high in collectivism see the group as the basic unit of society and foster group cohesion and input. Members of collectivist societies have close relationships only with others in similar circumstances who share their goals and fate. Although there are some exceptions, the United States and most European societies emphasize individualism, whereas societies in Latin America, Asia, and Africa tend to be collectivist.

Gender and Aggression   Across cultures and at every age, males are more likely than females to behave aggressively. Moreover, men are more likely than women to murder, to favor capital punishment, to use force to achieve their goals, and to prefer aggressive sports such as hockey, football, and boxing.

Reviews of more than 100 studies of aggression concluded that males are more aggressive than females both verbally—through taunts, insults, and threats, for example—and especially physically, through acts such as hitting, kicking, and fighting (Eagly & Steffen, 1986; Hyde, 1986). These gender differences tend to be greater in real-life and naturalistic settings than in controlled laboratory settings, and their incidence appears to have remained remarkably stable in recent years (Hyde, 1986; Knight, Fabes, & Higgins, 1996). Indeed, even historical data that go back to sixteenth-century Europe show that males committed more than three times as many serious crimes than did females (see Ellis & Coontz, 1990).

Is the gender difference in aggression biological or social in origin? The answer is not simple. On the one hand, certain biological factors appear to contribute to aggressive behavior. As we saw in Chapter 2, some research suggests that testosterone (a sex hormone found predominantly in males) may play a role in the expression of aggression and violence. Consistent with this hypothesis, research has noted that increases in crime rates in the United States closely parallel increases in the population of 14- to 24-year-old males, the ages at which testosterone levels in males are at their highest levels (Goldstein & Segall, 1983). More recent research, however, disputes the link between testosterone and aggression (Albert, Walsh, & Jonik, 1993). This evidence suggests that human aggression has its roots in evolution and can be traced to defensive behaviors characteristic of our nonprimate ancestors.

It also seems clear that our society encourages and even expects greater aggressiveness in boys than in girls (Sommers-Flanagan, Sommers-Flanagan, & Davis, 1993; Bettencourt & Miller, 1996). Boys are more likely than girls to be given toy guns or to be rewarded for behaving aggressively; girls are more likely than boys to feel guilty for behaving aggressively or to expect parental disapproval for their aggressive behavior (Perry, Perry, & Weiss, 1989). While early socialization strongly affects the way in which boys and girls express aggression, it is likely that *both* biological and social factors contribute to these differences. In short, like most complex behaviors, aggressive behavior reflects the interaction of nature and nurture.

Achievement

Is being highly competitive important to high achievement?

Climbing Mt. Everest "because it is there," sending rockets into space, making the dean's list, rising to the top of a giant corporation—all these achievements may have mixed underlying motives. But in all of them there is a desire to excel, "to overcome obstacles, to exercise power, to strive to do something difficult as well and as quickly as possible" (H. A. Murray, 1938, pp. 80–81). It is this desire for achievement for its own sake that leads psychologists to suggest that there is a separate **achievement motive.**

As with all learned motives, the need for achievement varies widely from person to person. Researchers discovered three separate but interrelated aspects of

Achievement motive
The need to excel, to overcome obstacles; a social motive.

HIGHLIGHTS

Sexual Coercion and Its Effects

The term *sexual coercion* is used to describe a variety of behaviors. Rape, or sexual assault, is the most serious form of sexual coercion and the most widely studied. Every 5 minutes somewhere in the United States a woman reports being raped. In approximately 80 percent of rapes the victim knows the rapist; about half the rapes take place on a date; and about one-third of the time rape occurs in the victim's home. It is important to note that these figures refer only to *reported* cases of violent rape. Because many rapes go unreported, the actual numbers are undoubtedly considerably higher.

Sexual coercion also encompasses the less extreme forms of pressure to have sex, known as *sexual harassment*. Harassment includes demands for sexual favors in the workplace as well as unwanted and unceasing sexual advances, both verbal and physical (Fitzgerald, 1993). It also includes sexual activity in response to pressure from partners or peers. What are the motives behind sexual coercion? Are perpetrators driven primarily by sexual desires or by power and aggression?

Early research focusing on rapists in prison cited power, anger, and

---

What are the motives behind sexual coercion? Are perpetrators driven primarily by sexual desires or by power and aggression?

---

sadism as the principal motives in rape. More recent research, however, based on a more representative cross section of the population, disputes those conclusions. One study found that anger and the desire to inflict pain played a prominent role in only about 20 percent of the most violent rapes (Prentky, Knight, & Rosenberg, 1988). In another 30 percent of rapes the motivation sprang from a general hatred of women; the rapists sought to degrade and humiliate their victims as a way of exacting revenge for perceived wrongs committed against them by other women.

In nearly half the cases the predominant motives seemed to be sexual: Roughly one-quarter of the rapists impulsively raped a date or an acquaintance when the opportunity arose, their primary motivation being sexual. Another 25 percent of the rapists were obsessed with a sexual fantasy that they sought to act out in the rape; many of these men seemed to believe that their victims would eventually enjoy the experience and perhaps even fall in love with them. It is possible that many more than half of all rapes are motivated by sexual impulsiveness and sexual fantasies.

---

achievement-oriented behavior: *work orientation*, the desire to work hard and to do a good job; *mastery*, the preference for difficult or challenging feats, with an emphasis on improving one's past performance; and *competitiveness*, the enjoyment of pitting one's skills against those of other people (Helmreich & Spence, 1978).

How do individual differences in the three aspects of achievement motivation relate to people's attainment of goals? Being highly competitive may actually interfere with achievement. In one study students with the highest grades were those who had high work and mastery scores but *low* competitiveness scores. The counterproductive effect of competitiveness curbs achievement in other groups of participants as well, including businesspeople, elementary school students, and scientists. What accounts for this phenomenon? Researchers think that highly competitive people alienate the very people who would otherwise help them to achieve their goals, or that preoccupation with winning distracts them from taking the actions necessary to attain their goals. Or perhaps, as we will see later in this chapter, the overwhelming need to succeed produces a level of arousal that is too high for optimum performance on complex tasks.

From psychological tests and personal histories, psychologists have developed a profile of people with a high level of achievement motivation. These people do best in competitive situations and are fast learners. They enjoy the

Laboratory research tends to confirm that there is a close connection among rape, aggression, and sexuality. For most men sexual violence is not at all arousing. In fact, viewing films simulating forced sex in which the victim was clearly in distress and experiencing pain decreased sexual arousal in most men so much that they would not be able to engage in intercourse at all (Barbaree & Marshall, 1991). Many of these same men, however, became aroused by scenes of sexual violence if they had been drinking, if they had had an argument with a woman before viewing the film, or if the victim seemed to them to be "asking for it."

Like rape, harassment is often an expression of anger and aggression toward women (Fitzgerald, 1993). In some cases of sexual harassment, crude and sexually explicit graffiti are deliberately placed where women will see them. In others women are subjected to unwanted caresses or comments about their dress or anatomy. In extreme cases women are pressured or forced into having sex by male colleagues or supervisors. Over one 2-year period, for example, approximately 12,000 female federal employees reported that they were victims of rape or attempted rape by their supervisors or coworkers (U.S. Merit Systems Protection Board, 1993).

Sexual coercion exacts a severe emotional toll. Though the victims of sexual harassment do not necessarily experience the same trauma as rape victims, many of the aftershocks experienced by those who have been raped apply to victims of sexual harassment as well. Sexual coercion places a woman in a state of great conflict. She must first decide whether to report the incident. Women who do report a rape are often treated insensitively, even though the treatment of rape victims by police and hospital personnel has improved in recent years. Women who file charges of sexual harassment risk being demoted, fired, or shunned. Their accounts are often regarded with indifference or skepticism or are ignored altogether (Fitzgerald, 1993).

From an emotional standpoint, women who have been sexually coerced frequently experience symptoms of *posttraumatic stress disorder (PTSD)*, a serious psychological disorder first identified in soldiers returning from the horrors of the battlefield. (We examine PTSD in greater depth in Chapter 11.) People suffering from PTSD have difficulty readjusting to normal life and continue to relive the traumatic event. They become alienated and unable to trust or form close bonds with others. In addition, they feel guilty and often blame themselves for what has happened. Women who have been raped may become unable to feel parts of their bodies or experience sexual pleasure. They also suffer from depression and lowered self-esteem (Gruber & Bjorn, 1986).

opportunity to develop new strategies when confronted with unique and challenging tasks as compared to people with a low need for achievement, who rarely deviate from methods that worked for them in the past. Driven less by the desire for fame or fortune than by the need to live up to a high, self-imposed standard of performance (Carr, Borkowski, & Maxwell, 1991), they are self-confident, willingly take on responsibility, and do not readily bow to outside social pressures. They are energetic and allow few things to stand in the way of their goals, but they are also apt to be tense and to suffer from psychophysiological disorders—that is, real physical ailments, such as stomachaches and headaches, with psychological origins. They may also feel like impostors even—or especially—when they achieve their goals.

Power

What kinds of careers or activities appeal to people with a strong need for power?

Another principally learned motive is the **power motive**, which may be defined as the need to win recognition or to influence or control other people or groups. College students who score high on the need for power tend to occupy "power

Power motive
The need to win recognition or to influence or control individuals or groups; a social motive.

A scene from a rape crisis center. Many rape victims experience posttraumatic stress disorder and have difficulty readjusting to normal life.

positions," such as offices in student organizations, residence counseling positions, and membership on key committees. They are inclined to participate in contact sports and to pursue careers in teaching, psychology, and business (Beck, 1983).

David Winter (1973) studied the power motives of 12 American presidents, from Theodore Roosevelt through Richard Nixon, by scoring each president's concerns, aspirations, fears, and plans for action as revealed in each of their inaugural speeches. Those found to have the greatest power drives were Theodore Roosevelt, Franklin Roosevelt, Harry Truman, Woodrow Wilson, John Kennedy, and Lyndon Johnson. All six men were action-oriented presidents and, except for Theodore Roosevelt, all were Democrats. All the presidents also scored high in the need for achievement.

Affiliation

What complex factors influence our motivation to be with other people?

Simply put, the need for affiliation is the need to be with other people. Being isolated from social contact for a long time can make us anxious. Why do human beings seek out one another? How are groups formed, and how does a handful of isolated people become a group?

For one thing, the **affiliation motive** is aroused when people feel threatened. *Esprit de corps*—the feeling of being part of a sympathetic group—is critical among troops going into a battle and among a football team going into a game. Both the troops and the football players must feel they are working for a common cause or against a common foe, and a coach's pregame pep talk is intended to fuel this team spirit.

But affiliative behavior often results from other motives entirely. For example, you may give a party to celebrate landing a job because you want to be praised for your achievement. Fear and anxiety may also be closely tied to the affiliation motive. When rats, monkeys, or humans are placed in anxiety-producing situations, the presence of a member of the same species who remains calm will reduce the fear of the anxious ones. If you are nervous on a plane during a bumpy flight, you may strike up a conversation with the calm-looking woman sitting next to you because the agitation of the plane does not seem to be worrying her. Because affiliation behavior (like most behavior) stems from a subtle interplay of internal and external factors, whether you begin that conversation depends on how friendly you normally are, as well as on how scared you feel at the moment, how calm or nervous your neighbor appears to be, and how turbulent the flight is.

A Hierarchy of Motives

Must basic needs be satisfied before a person can develop self-esteem?

You probably have noticed that our narrative has gradually moved from primitive motives, shared by all animals, to motives that are more sophisticated, complex, and specifically human. A number of years ago Abraham Maslow (1954), a humanistic psychologist, arranged all motives in such a hierarchy, from lower to higher (see Figure 8–2). The lower motives are relatively simple: They spring from physical needs that must be satisfied. As we move higher on Maslow's hierarchy of needs, the motives have more subtle origins: the desire to live as comfortably as possible, to deal as well as we can with other human beings, and to make the best possible impression on others. Maslow believed that the most highly "evolved" motive in the hierarchy is *self-actualization*—the drive to realize one's full potential. According to Maslow, on both an evolutionary and an individual scale higher motives emerge only after the more basic ones have largely

Affiliation motive
The need to be with others; a social motive.

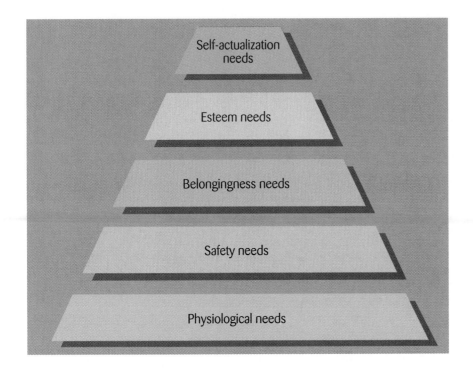

FIGURE 8–2

A pyramid representing Maslow's hierarchy of needs. From bottom to top, the stages correspond to how fundamental the motive is for survival and how early it appears in both the evolution of the species and the development of the individual. According to Maslow, the more basic needs must largely be satisfied before higher motives can emerge.

Source: From *Motivation and Personality* by A. H. Maslow. Copyright © 1954 by Harper & Row.

been satisfied. Someone who literally is starving doesn't care what people think of her table manners.

Although Maslow's model offers an appealing way to organize a wide range of motives into a coherent structure, recent research challenges the universality of his views. Maslow based his hierarchical model on observations of historical figures, famous living individuals, and even friends whom he admired greatly—mostly white males living in Western society. In many simpler societies, however, people often live on the very edge of survival, yet they form strong and meaningful social ties and possess a firm sense of self-esteem (Neher, 1991). In fact, difficulty in meeting basic needs can actually foster the satisfaction of higher needs: A couple struggling financially to raise a family may grow closer as a result of the experience. Such findings have caused many contemporary psychologists to view Maslow's model with some skepticism.

REVIEW QUESTIONS

1. The category of wants or needs that is activated by external stimuli and pushes us to investigate our environment is called ____ motives.
2. ____ is all behavior in humans intended to inflict harm on others.
3. ____ societies emphasize the good of the group, whereas ____ societies emphasize the good of the individual.
4. A high degree of ____ may interfere with achievement.
5. A person who is willing to contend with the high risks of a career in sales is probably motivated by a high ____ motive.
6. The ____ motive is sometimes aroused when a person needs to be consoled or supported by a group of peers.

Indicate whether the following are true (T) or false (F).

7. Curiosity has been linked to creativity. ____
8. Research shows that low-birthweight babies gain weight faster with frequent physical contact. ____
9. Aggression may be a learned response to numerous stimuli. ____

Answers: 1. stimulus. 2. aggression. 3. collectivist, individualistic. 4. competitiveness. 5. achievement. 6. affiliation. 7. T. 8. T. 9. T.

Perspectives on Emotion

Does intense emotional arousal improve performance?

In the first part of this chapter we saw that motives can both arouse and direct our behavior. Emotions can also. "She shouted for joy," we say, or "I was so angry I could have strangled him."

In the past, emotions were often viewed as a "base instinct"—a vestige of our evolutionary heritage that needs to be repressed. More recently, however, scientists have begun to see them as safeguards for survival that are capable of enriching our experience (National Advisory Mental Health Council, 1995). At the simplest level, we can classify emotions according to whether they make us turn toward or away from objects or situations. Imagine that you overhear this conversation among three people whose television has just gone out during a thunderstorm:

A: "Just when the movie was getting good! I've wanted to see it for years, and now this happens. Things like this always happen at the worst time. It makes me furious!"

B: "I *hate* thunderstorms—I always have. Don't you think we ought to shut off all the lights so we won't attract the lightning?"

C: "Look at it! It's fantastic—the way the blue flashes light up everything! I've always loved thunderstorms—they're so wild. They make me feel alive!"

A is frustrated and angry. These emotions move us to *approach* something, but in an aggressive or hostile way. *B* is fearful and anxious. These emotions make us want to *avoid* something. *C* is happy and exhilarated, experiencing a sense of release and joy. These emotions prompt us to *approach* something in a positive way.

But emotions, like motives, can trigger a chain of complex behavior that goes far beyond simple approach or avoidance reactions. For example, if we are anxious about something, we may collect information about it, ask questions, and then decide whether to approach it, flee from it, or stay and fight it. Imagine a family faced with an anxiety-provoking situation: The husband and wife both have been temporarily laid off from their jobs. Faced with uncertainties and the anxiety they create, the family decides on a series of positive strategies. The husband, who is knowledgeable about cars, gets a job at an automobile repair shop. The wife accepts a former employer's offer of a part-time job. Their daughter accepts a scholarship at a local campus of the state university instead of attending a more expensive private college. In short, the anxiety created by the crisis triggered a complex sequence of goal-directed behaviors in much the same way that motives do.

Sometimes, however, emotions can overwhelm good sense. Most of us have found ourselves in situations in which we desperately wanted to think rationally but could not because our emotions were interfering with our ability to concentrate. Whether emotion blocks us or helps us to act is related to the strength of the emotion and the difficulty of the task. The **Yerkes–Dodson law** puts it this way: The more complex the task, the lower the level of arousal that can be tolerated without interfering with performance. You may feel very angry while washing the dishes, but your anger may not make much difference in how well you perform that task. The same degree of emotional arousal though, could interfere with your ability to drive safely.

Yerkes–Dodson law
States that there is an optimal level of arousal for the best performance of any task; the more complex the task, the lower the level of arousal that can be tolerated before performance deteriorates.

Basic Emotional Experiences

Do people in different cultures experience the same basic emotions?

As we saw, emotions can be broadly grouped according to whether they motivate us to approach or to avoid something. But within these broad groups, how many different emotions are there?

A number of attempts have been made to identify and describe the basic emotions experienced by humans (Ekman, 1980; Plutchik, 1980; also see Cornelius, 1996). Robert Plutchik (1980), for example, proposes that animals and human beings experience 8 basic categories of emotions that motivate various kinds of adaptive behavior: *fear, surprise, sadness, disgust, anger, anticipation, joy,* and *acceptance.* Each of these emotions helps us adjust to the demands of our environment, although in different ways. Fear, for example, underlies flight, which helps to protect animals from their enemies, while anger propels animals to attack or destroy.

Emotions adjacent to each other on Plutchik's emotion "circle" (see Figure 8–3) are more alike than those situated opposite each other or that are farther away from each other. Surprise is more closely related to fear than to anger; joy and acceptance are more similar to each other than either is to disgust. Moreover, according to Plutchik's model, different emotions can combine to produce an even wider and richer spectrum of experience. Occurring together, anticipation and joy, for example, yield optimism; surprise and sadness make for disappointment. Within any of Plutchik's 8 categories, emotions vary in intensity.

Some researchers have questioned the universality of Plutchik's model, arguing that it may apply only to the emotional experience of English-speaking people. Anthropologists report enormous differences in the ways that different cultures view and categorize emotions. Some languages, in fact, do not even have a word for emotion (J. A. Russell, 1991a). Other languages differ in the number of words they have to name emotions. While English includes more than 2,000 words to describe emotional experiences, Taiwanese Chinese has only 750 such descriptive words. Moreover, the English language has many terms for self-focused emotions, such as anger and sadness, whereas the Japanese language has many terms for other-focused emotions, such as sympathy and empathy (Markus & Kitayama, 1991). Interestingly, words used to name or describe an emotion may influence how that emotion is experienced. For example, the Tahitian language has no direct translation for "sadness." Instead, Tahitians experience sadness in terms of physical illness. Whereas we would feel sad if a close friend moved to another country, a Tahitian would describe that feeling as exhaustion. Some cultures lack words for anxiety, depression, or guilt. Samoans have one word encompassing love, sympathy, pity, and liking—all distinct emotions in Western culture (J. A. Russell, 1991a).

Despite these differences, cross-culture research has generally confirmed Plutchik's model of 8 basic emotions (Ekman, 1987; Izard, 1994). For example, Paul Ekman and his colleagues asked participants from 10 countries to interpret photographs depicting facial expressions of emotions (Ekman et al., 1987). (We consider this research in more detail later in the chapter.) In *each* country, 60 to 98 percent of participants correctly identified the emotions expressed in the photographs. Across the 10 cultures, agreement was high as well.

This and other evidence argues for the *universality* of at least 6 emotions: *happiness, surprise, sadness, fear, disgust,* and *anger.* These correspond closely to Plutchik's 8 basic emotions; only "anticipation" and "acceptance" are missing. What about love? Isn't it a basic emotion? Psychologists disagree on this question (Hazan & Shaver, 1987). Ekman did not find a universally recognized facial expression for love. Cultural conventions could explain this fact. For example, when American college students participating in a study were asked to display a facial expression for love, they performed like Hollywood actors, sighing deeply, gazing skyward, and placing a hand over their heart (Cornelius, 1996).

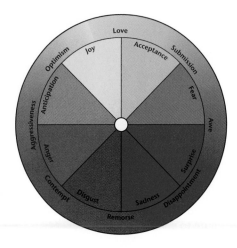

FIGURE 8–3

Plutchik's 8 basic categories of emotion. Emotions adjacent to each other on Plutchik's emotion "circle" are more alike than those that lie opposite each other or are farther apart. When adjacent emotions are combined, they yield new but related emotions. For example, sadness mixed with surprise leads to disappointment.

Source: Plutchik, 1980.

Psychologists disagree as to the ways that cognition and physiological processes contribute to emotions such as fear.

Theories of Emotion

Are emotions based on biological reactions or thoughts?

Why can we feel happy and confident one day and sad and uncertain the next? What causes emotional experiences?

In the 1880s the American psychologist William James formulated the first modern theory of emotion, and the Danish psychologist Carl Lange reached the same conclusions. According to the **James–Lange theory,** stimuli in the environment (say, seeing a large growling dog running toward us) cause physiological changes in our bodies (accelerated heart rate, enlarged pupils, deeper or shallower breathing, increased perspiration, goosebumps), and emotions arise from those physiological changes. The emotion of fear, then, is simply the *almost instantaneous and automatic awareness of physiological changes.*

If physiological changes alone *cause* specific emotions, we should be able to pinpoint different body changes for each emotion. Perhaps butterflies in the stomach make us afraid, and blushing causes shame or guilt. Indeed, there is some evidence that the physiological changes associated with fear and anxiety are somewhat different from those that accompany anger and aggression (McGeer & McGeer, 1980). Similarly, fear and anger appear to be distinguishable from happiness by subtle changes in heart-rate acceleration (Levenson, 1992). Different emotions also appear to be processed on different sides of the brain. Positive emotions are accompanied by increased electrical activity on the left side of the brain, whereas negative emotions generate more activity on the right side (Davidson, 1992). Beyond these findings, however, psychologists have not discovered distinct bodily states that account for all of our various emotions. Moreover, as we saw in Chapter 2, sensory information about bodily changes flows to the brain through the spinal cord. If physical reactions cause emotions, then people with severe spinal cord injuries should experience fewer and less intense emotions, but that is not the case (Chwalisz, Diener, & Gallagher, 1988). Thus it appears that bodily changes do not directly cause specific emotions and may not even be necessary for emotional experience.

An alternative theory of emotions, the **Cannon–Bard theory,** dating back nearly 70 years, holds that *emotions and bodily responses occur simultaneously,* not one after another. Thus when you see the growling dog, you feel afraid and you may start running—neither of these precedes the other. What you see or otherwise perceive strongly affects your emotional experience.

Today cognitive psychologists argue that our perception or judgment of situations (cognition) is absolutely essential to our emotional experience of those situations (Lazarus, 1982, 1991a, 1991b, 1991c). All emotional states involve arousal of the nervous system, but according to the **cognitive theory** of emotion, the situation that we are in when we are aroused—the environment—provides clues as to how we should respond to this general state of arousal. Therefore, our cognitions tell us how to label our diffuse feelings in a way that suits our current thoughts and ideas about our surroundings. (See Figure 8–4 for a comparison of these three theories of emotion.)

Although the cognitive theory of emotion makes a great deal of sense, some critics reject the idea that feelings always stem from cognitions. Quoting the poet e. e. cummings, Zajonc (1980) argues that "feelings come first." Human infants, he points out, can imitate emotional expressions at 12 days of age, well before they acquire language. Animals rely on their sense of danger to survive: A rabbit doesn't evaluate the possibilities that might account for a rustle in the bushes before it runs away. Zajonc notes that the affective (emotional) system has the ability to respond instantaneously to the situations in which we find ourselves, without taking time to interpret and evaluate those situations. According

James–Lange theory
States that stimuli cause physiological changes in our bodies, and emotions result from those physiological changes.

Cannon–Bard theory
States that the experience of emotion occurs simultaneously with biological changes.

Cognitive theory
States that emotional experience depends on one's perception or judgment of the situation one is in.

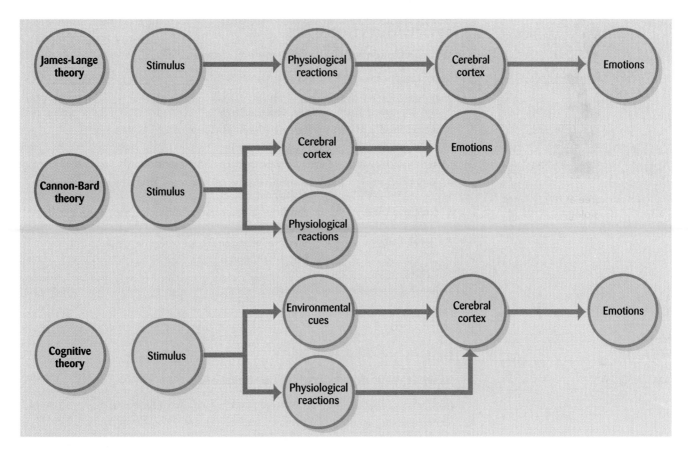

FIGURE 8–4

The three major theories of emotion.　According to the *James–Lange theory,* the body first responds physiologically to a stimulus, and then the cerebral cortex determines which emotion is being experienced. The *Cannon–Bard theory* holds that impulses are sent simultaneously to the cerebral cortex and the peripheral nervous system; thus the response to the stimulus and the processing of the emotion are experienced at the same time but independently. *Cognitive theorists* assert that the cerebral cortex interprets physiological changes in the light of information about the situation to determine which emotions we feel.

to this view, we invent explanations to label feelings: Cognition thus comes *after* emotion.

Another challenge to the cognitive theory of emotions comes from C. E. Izard (1971), who claims that emotions can be experienced without any accompanying thoughts. In Izard's view, a situation such as separation or pain provokes a unique pattern of unlearned facial movements and body postures that may be completely independent of conscious thought (Trotter, 1983). When information about our facial expressions and posture reaches the brain, we automatically experience the corresponding emotion. According to Izard, then, the James–Lange theory was essentially right in suggesting that emotional experience follows physical reactions. In Izard's theory, facial expression and body posture are crucial to experiencing emotion, while the James–Lange theory emphasizes muscles, skin, and internal organs.

Considerable evidence supports Izard's view that facial expressions influence emotions (Adelmann & Zajonc, 1989; Cappella, 1993; Ekman & Davidson, 1993; Zajonc, Murphy, & Inglehart, 1989). If further research bolsters Izard's theory, we will be able to say with certainty that a key element in determining our emotional experience is our own expressive behavior, the topic we turn to now.

1. According to the ____ ____ law, there is a relationship between the complexity of a task and the level of emotional arousal that can be tolerated while performing that task.

2. Robert Plutchik asserts that emotions vary in ____, a fact that accounts in part for the great range of emotions we experience.

3. Izard's theory of emotion stresses the importance of which element?

   a. cognition   b. expressive behavior

Match the following theories with the appropriate description.

4. Cannon–Bard   a. states that physical reactions directly cause experienced emotions

5. cognitive theory   b. contends that emotions and bodily responses occur simultaneously

6. James–Lange   c. says that emotional experience depends on the perception of a given situation

Answers: 1. Yerkes–Dodson. 2. intensity 3. b. 4. b. 5. c. 6. a.

Expressing Emotion

In what ways do we express our emotions?

Sometimes you are vaguely aware that a person makes you uncomfortable. When pressed to be more precise, you might say, "You never know what she is thinking." But you don't mean that you never know her opinion of a film or what she thought about the last election. It would probably be more accurate to say that you do not know what she is feeling. Almost all of us conceal our emotions to some extent to protect our self-image or to conform to social conventions. But usually we give off some clues that help others determine what we are feeling. We communicate emotions verbally, nonverbally (through facial expressions, body posture, tone of voice, hand gestures, and eye contact), or with both verbal and nonverbal cues. Facial expressions seem to communicate the most specific nonverbal information. Hand gestures or posture can communicate general emotional states, but the complexity of the muscles in the face allows facial expressions to communicate very particular feelings, such as sadness, anger, and fear.

Verbal Communication

How accurately do people describe their emotions?

The simplest way to find out what someone is feeling is to ask. But sometimes people don't express verbally what they are feeling. If your roommate finishes washing the dishes and says acidly, "I hope you are enjoying your novel," the literal meaning of his words is quite clear, but you know very well that he is not expressing pleasure at your choice of reading material. If he were to say, "I'm angry that you didn't offer to help clean up after dinner," he would be giving you an accurate report of his emotions at that moment.

For many reasons we may be unable or unwilling to report our emotions accurately. In some situations people simply cannot pinpoint what they are feeling. A father who abuses his child may sincerely profess affection for the child but act in ways that reflect emotions far removed from tenderness—feelings that are hidden from his own awareness. Even when we are aware of our emotions, we sometimes minimize the degree of emotion that we are feeling: We may say we are "a little worried" about an upcoming exam when in fact we are terrified. Or we may deny the emotion entirely, especially if it is negative (hatred toward a parent or sibling, for example). And as we saw earlier, cultures differ greatly in the variety of words to express emotions. So what people say may not mirror exactly what they are feeling, and we must turn to other cues to understand their feelings fully.

Nonverbal Communication

In the emotional arena, do "actions speak louder than words"?

"Actions speak louder than words," the saying goes, and people are often more eloquent with their bodies than they realize or intend. We transmit a good deal of information to others through our facial expressions, body postures, and physical distance. In fact, our bodies often send emotional messages that contradict our words. Because these kinds of physiological changes are not normally under our control, they tend to function independently of our will—indeed, often against it (see *Highlights*).

Facial expressions are the most obvious emotional indicators and, as we saw earlier, may actually cause some emotional experiences. We can tell a good deal about a person's emotional state by observing whether that person looks as if he or she is laughing, crying, smiling, or frowning. Many facial expressions are innate, not learned (Ekman, 1994), and children who are born deaf and blind use the same facial expressions as other children do to express the same emotions.

Body language is another way that we communicate nonverbally. Slouching and straightness of the back, for example, supply clues about whether someone is feeling relaxed or tense.

Body communication is also reflected in *personal distance*. Within every culture there is a generally accepted distance between two people during normal conversation, but it differs from culture to culture. Two Swedes conversing, for example, would ordinarily stand much farther apart than would two Arabs or two Greeks. If someone is standing closer than usual, it may indicate

Working from Charles Darwin's theory that certain emotional and facial expressions have an evolutionary basis, psychologist Caroll Izard believes he has isolated 10 universal emotions that can be seen in the facial expressions of infants. Four are illustrated here.

Sadness: Brows' inner corners raised, mouth drawn out and down.

Interest: Brows raised or knit, mouth softly rounded, lips pursed.

Distress: Eyes tightly closed; mouth as in anger, squared and angular.

Joy: Mouth forms smile, cheeks lifted, twinkle in eyes.

HIGHLIGHTS

The Lie Detector: What Does It Tell Us?

Lie detectors (also called polygraphs) do not register lies. Their readings are based on the fact that lying causes inner emotional conflict that is typically accompanied by specific, uncontrollable physiological changes in blood pressure, in breathing, and in the resistance of the skin to electrical current, known as galvanic skin response. It is these physiological changes the polygraphs measure. Nevertheless, there is no set of responses that definitively indicates that a person has been lying; the pattern of responses varies from person to person (Saxe, 1994). Further, in the typical lie detector situation, failing the test has serious consequences, so subjects generally are quite nervous before the test even begins.

Polygraphs are far from error-free in determining whether someone is lying or telling the truth. Figures vary widely, but according to one estimate, polygraphs correctly identify only about 75 percent of those who are lying. Unfortunately, about 49 percent of people telling the truth are falsely branded as liars (Horvath, 1977). One major source of error is that galvanic skin response changes in reaction to many kinds of emotions—not just those associated with deception (Lykken, 1975). When someone is asked if he committed a murder, the lie detector is likely to surge. Although this reaction *may* reflect guilt, it may also signal anxiety, fear, or loathing—all possible reactions to being suspected of murder. Similarly, if a subject were questioned about marital problems, relationships with parents, or even attitudes toward work, the polygraph might register a similar sharp peak, indicating an emotional response regardless of whether the subject was telling the truth (Stern et al., 1981). Subjects'

Unfortunately, about 49 percent of people telling the truth are falsely branded as liars.

---

feelings about the accuracy of the test also have an impact on the strength of their physiological reactions. The more accurate that subjects believe the polygraph to be, the more arousal they are likely to experience when responding deceptively (Saxe, 1994).

It is fairly easy to fool the polygraph machine. In one experiment subjects counted backward by 7s during their polygraph examination to distract themselves from the questions, and their lies were undetectable more often than the norm would have predicted (Waid, Orne, & Orne, 1981).

Personal and social factors can also affect the physiological signs monitored by the machine. The galvanic skin response of some people changes quickly and spontaneously, making it more likely that their truthful answers will appear to be lies. Finally, the degree to which examiner and subject are matched in terms of sex, age, race, and ethnicity also seems to have an impact on polygraph results. In one study the lie detector failed most often when examiner and subjects shared the same ethnicity, possibly because the subjects felt most at ease in this situation (Waid & Orne, 1981).

Because polygraph results are often inaccurate, many people are convinced that polygraph examinations pose more risks to individuals than benefits for society.

A person taking a polygraph test. How much faith should we put in the results of lie detector tests?

---

aggressiveness or seductiveness; if farther away than usual, it may indicate withdrawal or repugnance.

Explicit acts can also serve as nonverbal clues. We slam a door when we are angry. Gestures, such as a pat on the back or an embrace, can also indicate feelings. A word of caution: Although overt behavior may offer a clue to a person's feelings, it is not an *infallible* clue. Laughing and crying sound alike, for example, and we bare our teeth in smiles as well as in snarls. Crying may "mean" sorrow, joy, anger, nostalgia—or that you are slicing an onion. Moreover, as with verbal reports, it is always possible that someone is projecting false cues. We all have done something thoughtlessly—turned our backs, frowned because we were thinking about something else, laughed at the wrong time—that was misinterpreted as an expression of an emotion we were not in fact feeling. In all of these cases nonverbal cues do not correspond well to the actual emotions being felt.

R. Rosenthal and his colleagues (1974, 1979) studied both gender and age differences in sensitivity to nonverbal cues by showing people a film in which an actress or actor portrayed various emotional states. Sometimes the portrayal was accompanied by spoken phrases, but the tones and rhythms that identify distinct words had been removed. The viewer then picked one of two possible interpretations of the scene. Women were consistently better than men at accurately deciphering nonverbal cues, although men in the "nurturing" professions—psychiatrists, psychologists, mental hospital aides, and teachers—along with artists, actors, and designers, scored as high as women. The study also showed that sensitivity to nonverbal cues increases with age, most likely because we accumulate more experience in judging vocal tones and observing body movements as we grow older.

Closely related to the ability to read other people's emotions is *empathy*—the arousal of emotion in an observer that is a vicarious response to another person's situation (Parke & Asher, 1983). Empathy depends on one's ability to identify someone else's emotions, to put oneself in the other person's place, and to experience an appropriate emotional response. Just as sensitivity to nonverbal cues increases with age, so do the cognitive and perceptual abilities required for empathy.

Gender Differences in Emotional Expression

Do men feel emotions differently from women, or do they just express them differently?

Experience tells us that males and females differ considerably in how they express emotion and in the emotions they choose to express. Men are often perceived as being less emotional than women, but do men feel less emotion, or are they simply less likely to express the emotions they feel? And are there some emotions that men are more likely to express than are women?

Research sheds some light on these questions. In one study, when men and women saw depictions of people in distress, the men showed little emotion but the women expressed concern (Eisenberg & Lennon, 1983). Physiological measures of emotional arousal (such as heart rate and blood pressure), however, showed that the men in the study were just as affected as the women were. The men simply inhibited the *expression* of their emotions, while the women were more open about their feelings. Also, emotions such as sympathy, sadness, empathy, and distress are often considered to be "unmanly," and boys are trained from an early age to suppress those emotions in public (V. E. O'Leary & Smith, 1988). It would seem, then, that perhaps men and women do experience emotions similarly.

But in certain circumstances men and women clearly react with very different emotions. In one study, for example, participants responded to hypothetical situations in which they were betrayed or criticized by another person (L. Brody, 1985). Males usually said that they would feel angry, but females were likely to report that they would feel hurt, sad, or disappointed. Moreover, when men get angry, they tend to interpret the source of their anger as something or someone in the environment around them, and they generally turn their anger outward, against other people and against the situation in which they find themselves. Women, as a rule, are more likely to see themselves as the source of the problem and turn their anger inward, against themselves. Given these gender-specific reactions, it is not surprising that men are four times more likely than women to become violent in the face of life crises, whereas women are much more likely than men to become depressed.

Men, in general, often have less skill than women at decoding the emotional expressions of others. One reason may be that men aren't usually the primary caregivers of children who are too young to speak, and so they get less practice "reading" emotion in the face and body. As traditional sex roles in our society change and fathers take a larger role in the care of young children, many men may become more attuned to the subtleties of emotional expression.

Apart from possible differences in emotional experiences, do men and women differ in the ways they communicate emotions? At the most basic level, there are two aspects to communicating emotion: (1) sending an emotional message (through facial expressions, tone of voice, posture, and so on) and (2) perceiving the emotional content of a message sent by someone else. According to the stereotype, women are more expressive than men, which suggests that they should be better "senders" of emotional information. Furthermore, the popular notion of "women's intuition" suggests that women should be better than men at perceiving or "decoding" the emotional expressions of others—for instance, figuring out what is being communicated by a brief facial expression.

Research indicates that these stereotypes have a kernel of truth. After reviewing many similar studies in this area, Judith Hall (1984) concluded that women are indeed more skilled than men at decoding the facial expressions, body cues, and tones of voice of others. Several explanations could account for these gender differences (Taylor, Peplau, & Sears, 1994). One is that many women are the primary caregivers for preverbal infants, and as such they need to become more attuned than men to the subtleties of emotional expressions. Consistent with an evolutionary perspective, some have even suggested that this skill may be genetically programmed into females. Another explanation is based on the social power held by women and men. Because women historically have occupied less powerful positions in society, they may have felt the need to become acutely attuned to the emotional displays of others, particularly those in more powerful positions (namely, men). Indeed, one researcher found that regardless of gender, followers are more sensitive to the emotions of leaders than vice versa (Snodgrass, 1992).

Cultural Differences in Emotional Expression

What is the difference between the universalist and culture-learning explanations for the facial expression of emotion?

Because facial expressions are so precise and because they are independent of language, researchers studying cultural differences in emotional communication have focused on these outward expressions of emotion. As we saw earlier, some researchers have argued that across cultures the face looks the same whenever certain emotions are expressed—the *universalist* position. Charles Darwin subscribed to this view and argued that as part of our common evolutionary heritage, all people used the same expressions to convey the same emotions. In contrast, other researchers support the *culture-learning* position, which holds that we learn facial expressions of emotion as part of our culture, and therefore these expressions may differ greatly from one culture to the next. In sum, the universalist position predicts that the same emotion will elicit the same facial response from people in many different cultures, whereas the culture-learning position predicts that the facial responses will be quite different. Which view is more accurate?

Paul Ekman and Wallace Friesen, who have been studying this question for decades, have concluded that the 6 primary emotions we discussed earlier—happiness, sadness, anger, surprise, fear, and disgust—are indeed accompanied by universal facial expressions (Ekman, 1993; Ekman & Friesen, 1986; Ekman et al., 1987). In one set of studies, for example, Ekman & Friesen (1969) showed photographs of faces expressing these 6 emotions to people in Argentina, Brazil, Japan, Chile, and the United States. They found very high rates of agreement across cultures about which emotion was being displayed.

Carroll Izard (1980) conducted similar studies in England, Germany, Switzerland, France, Sweden, Greece, and Japan with similar results. These studies seem to support the universalist position: Regardless of culture, people tend to agree on which emotions other people are expressing facially. This research does not completely rule out the culture-learning view, however. Because the research participants were all members of developed countries that likely had been exposed to one another through movies, magazines, and tourism, they might simply have become familiar with the facial expressions seen in other cultures. A test was needed that reduced or eliminated this possibility.

This test was made possible by the discovery of several contemporary cultures that had been totally isolated from Western culture for most of their existence. Members of the Fore and the Dani cultures of New Guinea, for example, had their first contact with anthropologists only a few years before Ekman's research took place, so they provided a nearly perfect opportunity to test the universalist/culture-learning debate. If members of these cultures—who had had little or no experience with Western peoples—gave the same interpretation of facial expressions and produced the same expressions on their own faces as people in Western cultures, there would be much stronger evidence for the universality of facial expressions of emotion.

Ekman and his colleagues (Ekman & Friesen, 1971; Ekman, Sorenson, & Friesen, 1969) presented members of the Fore culture with three photographs of people from outside their culture and asked them to point to the picture that represented how they would feel in a certain situation. For example, if a person was told "Your child has died and you feel very sad," he or she would have the opportunity to choose which of the three pictures most closely corresponded to sadness. The results indicated very high rates of agreement regarding which facial expressions showed which emotions. So even members of these isolated groups were able to identify correctly the emotional expressions of people with whom they had had virtually no previous contact. Moreover, when photographs of the Fore and Dani's posing the primary emotions were shown to college students in the United States, the same high agreement was found: Americans, who had had no prior experience with these groups, were able to identify the emotional expressions on their faces with considerable accuracy (Ekman & Friesen, 1975). Consequently it appears that facial expressions of at least some emotions are indeed universal.

If this is true, then why are people so often confused about the emotions being expressed by people in other cultures? Consider, for example, the experience of an American exchange student in Japan who sometimes had difficulty figuring out what her hosts were feeling. She might sense that they were disappointed about some decision she had made, yet they continued to smile. If facial expressions reliably convey basic emotional states, why did her Japanese hosts appear to be pleased at her mistakes?

The answer lies in what Ekman and Friesen (1975) called **display rules:** the circumstances under which it is appropriate for people to show emotion on their faces. In essence, display rules help govern which emotions are displayed, by whom, to whom, and under what conditions. Depending on the situation, some

Display rules
Culture-specific rules that govern how, when, and why facial expressions of emotion are displayed.

Can you identify the emotions being expressed by this man from New Guinea? The finding that U.S. college students could recognize the emotional expressions of people who had been largely isolated from Western cultures—and vice versa—lent support to the *universalist* position of facial expression.

Source: From P. Ekman and W. V. Friesen, *Unmasking the Face,* Englewood Cliffs, N.J., Prentice Hall, 1975, p. 27.

common display rules would be to intensify, to deintensify, to mask, or to neutralize your expression. You practice *intensification* when you exaggerate your facial expression and *deintensification* when you mute your facial expression. For example, when showing greater joy than you are actually experiencing at a surprise party your friends have thrown for you, you are following the intensification display rule that dictates "Look happy and thrilled when people unexpectedly do nice things for you." *Masking* is a quite different display rule: Here you are feeling one emotion but showing a completely different one. Smiling when you are feeling sad is an example. Finally, *neutralizing* means keeping a "poker face," or showing a blank expression regardless of what you are feeling. Following this rule might be appropriate in situations that require you to be "strong and silent."

Although facial expressions of primary emotions appear to have a universal quality, display rules differ substantially from culture to culture. Ekman demonstrated these differences in a study of Japanese and American college students (Ekman, Friesen, & Ellsworth, 1972). While these students watched graphic films of surgical procedures, either by themselves or in the presence of an experimenter, their facial expressions were secretly videotaped. The videos revealed that when the students were alone, both the Japanese and the Americans showed facial expressions of disgust (precisely the emotion the films were intended to elicit). But when the students watched the film with an experimenter present, the two groups displayed different responses. American students continued to show disgust on their faces, but the Japanese students showed facial expressions that were more neutral, even somewhat pleasant.

Why the switch? The answer lies in the different use of display rules by members of the two cultures. The Japanese norm is "Don't display strong negative emotion in the presence of a respected elder" (in this case, the experimenter). Americans typically don't honor this display rule, so they expressed their true emotions whether they were alone or with someone else. In order to understand what people in a different culture are feeling, we need to understand both the universal expression of emotions *and* the particular rules operating in a culture.

Unlike facial expressions of primary emotions, which have a universal quality, forms of nonverbal communication vary from culture to culture—especially *emblems*, or hand gestures that have a specific meaning (H. G. Johnson, Ekman, & Friesen, 1975). Giving someone the "thumbs up," for example, or circling your thumb and index finger in an "OK" sign, or flashing a friend two fingers in a "V" shape all have well-defined meanings within American culture. Outside this cultural context, however, these emblems may either be meaningless or take on very different meanings.

Cultures also differ in the amount of touching that takes place among people, the distance between people who are interacting, and the amount of eye contact that is appropriate between friends, business partners, loved ones, and strangers. There is one form of eye contact that is almost universal, however: the "brow raise" greeting used when a friend approaches (Irenäus Eibl-Eibesfeldt, 1972). The next time a friend approaches you, watch to see if he or she uses this greeting.

REVIEW QUESTIONS

1. Cultural differences, particularly ____, influence how we experience emotion.
2. Two important nonverbal cues to emotions are ____ ____ and ____ ____.
3. Men tend to interpret the source of their anger to be in their ____.
4. Research shows that some ____ ____ are recognized universally.
5. _____ _____ are the cultural circumstances under which it is appropriate to show emotions on the face.

Indicate whether the following statements are true (T) or false (F).

6. Overt behavior is an infallible clue to emotions. ____
7. Women are better than men at deciphering nonverbal cues. ____
8. Women experience emotions more deeply than men do. ____
9. Women express emotions more openly than men do. ____
10. Men are more likely than women to express violence in the face of life crises. ____

Answers: 1. language. 2. facial expression, body language. 3. environment. 4. facial expressions. 5. display rules. 6. F. 7. T. 8. F. 9. F. 10. T.

KEY TERMS

motive, p. 276
emotion, p. 276

Perspectives on motivation
instincts, p. 276
drive, p. 276
drive-reduction theory, p. 276
homeostasis, p. 276
incentives, p. 276

intrinsic motivation, p. 276
extrinsic motivation, p. 276

Primary drives
primary drive, p. 277
set point, p. 280
anorexia nervosa, p. 280
bulimia, p. 281

Other important motives
stimulus motives, p. 285
achievement motive, p. 289
power motive, p. 291
affiliation motive, p. 292

Perspectives on emotion
Yerkes-Dodson law, p. 294

James-Lange theory, p. 296
Cannon-Bard theory, p. 296
cognitive theory, p. 296

Expressing emotion
display rules, p. 303

CHAPTER REVIEW

☐ How can you use intrinsic and extrinsic motivation to help you achieve your goals in school?

There are many ways of viewing human motivation. The idea that our motivations are largely based on **instincts** was popular in the early twentieth century but has since fallen out of favor. Human motivation has also been viewed as an effort toward **drive reduction** and **homeostasis** or balance in the body, as well as an effort to maintain an optimum level of arousal. Another perspective is that of motivational inducements or **incentives.** When inducements come from outside the person they are called **extrinsic motivation,** and when they originate from within they are called **intrinsic motivation.** Extrinsic motivation can certainly help you to achieve your goals in school, as when your parents offer to buy you an expensive present for good grades. Developing intrinsic motivation to succeed in college, however, will have a greater, more long-lasting effect.

☐ What activates primary drives?

A biological need can trigger a state of psychological tension called a **primary drive.** Two principal primary drives are hunger and sex.

☐ Why is it so difficult for some people to lose weight while others have no trouble maintaining their weight?

Hunger is regulated by several centers within the brain. These centers are stimulated by receptors that monitor stomach contents, as well as by receptors that monitor the contents of the blood, especially its levels of glucose, fat, and the hormone leptin. The body may also have a particular **set point** for "appropriate" weight, with metabolism and fat storage being automatically regulated to maintain that set point even when food intake varies. Differences in biologically based set point could explain why some obese people can't lose weight even with heroic dieting, while some very thin people can't gain weight even when they gorge.

☐ How do biology, experience, and culture influence the human sex drive?

Sex is a primary drive that gives rise to reproductive behavior essential for the survival of the species. Although hormones are involved in human sexual responses they don't play as dominant a role as they do in some other species. In humans, psychological factors that involve learning are very important as well. Because people have different experiences they also have different preferences for sexually arousing stimuli. Men tend to be aroused by visual cues, while women tend to respond more to touch. In both sexes, what is sexually appealing is also influenced by culture.

☐ How do stimulus motives and social motives differ from primary drives?

In contrast to primary drives, stimulus motives and social motives are less obviously associated with the survival of the organism or the species, even though they often help human beings adapt successfully to their environments. **Stimulus motives,** such as the urge to explore and manipulate things, are associated with obtaining information about the world. **Social motives,** such as the desire to affiliate with other people, center on human interactions with one another.

☐ What motives cause people to explore and change their environment?

The motives to investigate our surroundings and manipulate objects are two human motivations that encourage us both to explore our environment and often to change it. Without these two important stimulus motives, human discovery and inventiveness would be greatly reduced. Another important stimulus motive in humans and other primates is to seek various forms of tactile stimulation. This contact motive can be seen in the child's urge to cling and cuddle.

☐ Is aggression a biological or learned response?

Any behavior intended to inflict physical or psychological harm on others is an act of **aggression.** Some psychologists see aggression as an innate drive in humans that must be channeled to constructive ends, but others see it more as a learned response that is greatly influenced by modeling. The fact that levels of aggression differ markedly across cultures tends to support the view of human aggression as encouraged and shaped by learning. There are also gender differences in aggression, with males generally being more inclined than females to strike out at others and commit acts of violence. These gender differences probably depend on an interaction of nature and nurture.

☐ Is being highly competitive important to high achievement?

People who display a desire to excel, to overcome obstacles, and to accomplish difficult things score high in what psychologists call **achievement motive.** Although hard work and a strong desire to master challenges both contribute to achievement, competitiveness toward others often does not. In fact, competitiveness can actually interfere with achievement—perhaps by alienating other people, perhaps by becoming a preoccupation that distracts from the attainment of goals.

□ What kinds of careers or activities appeal to people with a strong need for power?

The **power motive** is the need to win recognition or to influence or control individuals or groups. Those who score high in the power motive are inclined to seek out positions of power, such as major political offices. And yet not all of those in powerful positions have a strong power motive; some are more driven by a need for achievement. In one study of 12 U.S. presidents, only half were strongly motivated by a desire for power.

□ What complex factors influence our motivation to be with other people?

The **affiliation motive,** or need to be with other people, is especially pronounced when we feel threatened or anxious. Affiliation with others in this situation can counteract fear and bolster spirits. Other factors contributing to the affiliation motive include a desire to receive acknowledgment and positive regard from others.

□ Must basic needs be satisfied before a person can develop self-esteem?

Abraham Maslow suggested that human motives can be arranged in a hierarchy, with primitive ones based on physical needs positioned at the bottom, and higher ones such as self-esteem positioned toward the top. Maslow believed that the higher motives don't emerge until the more basic ones have been met, but recent research challenges his view. In some societies, difficulty in meeting basic needs can actually foster the satisfaction of higher motives.

□ Does intense emotional arousal improve performance?

Emotions, like motives, both arouse and direct our behavior. They tend to prompt us to move toward or away from things. But also like motives, emotions may trigger a complex chain of thoughts and behaviors that can sometimes interfere with the accomplishment of goals. According to the **Yerkes–Dodson law,** the more complex the task, the lower the level of emotional arousal that can be tolerated without interfering with performance.

□ Do people in different cultures experience the same basic emotions?

Robert Plutchik's classification system for emotions uses a circle to position 8 basic emotional categories. But not all cultures categorize emotions the way Plutchik does. Some do not even have a word for emotion. Others describe feelings by their physical sensations. A cross-cultural analysis of emotional expression has led Paul Ekman to argue for the universality of at least 6 emotions—happiness, surprise, sadness, fear, disgust, and anger. Many psychologists add love to this list.

□ Are emotions based on biological reactions or thoughts?

According to the **James–Lange theory,** certain stimuli in the environment can bring on physiological changes in the body, and emotions then arise from our awareness of those changes. In contrast, the **Cannon–Bard theory** holds that emotions and bodily responses occur simultaneously, not one after the other. A third perspective, the **cognitive theory** of emotion, contends that our perceptions and judgments of situations are essential to our emotional experiences. Without these cognitions we would have no idea how to label our feelings. Not everyone agrees with this view, however, because emotions sometimes seem to arise too quickly to depend on mental evaluations. C. E. Izard argues that it may not be cognitive assessments that give rise to emotions but rather certain inborn facial expressions and body postures that are automatically triggered in emotion-arousing situations and then "read" by the brain as particular feelings.

□ In what ways do we express our emotions?

People sometimes express their emotions verbally through their words, tone of voice, exclamations, and other sounds. They also express their feelings nonverbally through their facial expressions, body postures, direction of gaze, hand gestures, and other actions.

□ How accurately do people describe their emotions?

What people say about what they are feeling often doesn't accurately reflect their emotions. In some cases they may not know or be aware of what they are feeling; in others they may choose to minimize or conceal their emotions.

□ In the emotional arena, do "actions speak louder than words"?

People often reveal more emotions with their bodies than they realize or intend. In fact, our bodies can send out emotional messages that contradict our words and are more genuine than words are. Facial expressions are the most obvious nonverbal indicators of emotion. Other indicators involve body language—our posture, the way we move, our preferred personal distance from others when talking to them, our degree of eye contact. Explicit acts, such as slamming a door, express emotions, too. People vary in their skill at reading these nonverbal cues.

□ Do men feel emotions differently from women, or do they just express them differently?

Research confirms some gender differences in expressing and perceiving emotions. For instance, when confronted with a person in distress, women are more likely than men to express emotion, even though the levels of physiological arousal are the same for the two sexes. Also, in some stressful situations, such as being betrayed or criticized, men tend to report more anger and women more disappointment and hurt. There is also some truth to the common stereotype that women are generally better than men at reading other people's emotions. This skill may be sharpened by their role as caretakers of infants and their traditional subordinate status to men.

□ **What is the difference between the universalist and the culture-learning explanations for the facial expressions of emotion?**

The facial expressions associated with certain basic emotions appear to be universal: The expressions are the same regardless of a person's cultural background. This cross-cultural finding contradicts the culture-learning view, which suggests that facial expressions of emotion are learned within a particular culture. This is not to say that there are no cultural differences in emotional expression, however. Overlaying the universal expression of certain emotions are culturally varying **display rules** that govern when it is appropriate to show emotion—to whom, by whom, and under what circumstances. Other forms of nonverbal communication of emotion vary more from culture to culture than facial expressions do.

CRITICAL THINKING AND APPLICATIONS

1. People who get low grades in school or do poorly on the job are often viewed as lacking motivation. What are some other possible explanations for their substandard performance?
2. What would you recommend to someone who wanted to lose weight but had failed many times to do so?
3. Some research reveals that boredom inspires curiosity; other studies show that curiosity is piqued by the new and unknown. Explain why these findings do not contradict each other. How would you apply these concepts in a classroom?
4. Which theory of emotions do you prefer the most, and why?
5. Think about how you experience and handle feelings of love, anger, and sadness. Do you express all these emotions with equal ease? Do any of these emotions make you uncomfortable? Are your responses to these feelings typical of your gender and culture? In what ways?

On the Web...

Visit these online resources at our Companion Website www.prenhall.com/morris

The Psychology Place:

Research News
1. Giving Children Rewards: A Right Way and a Wrong Way, p. 277
2. Should Creativity Be Rewarded?, p. 277
3. Eating Disorders and Sudden Death, p. 280
4. When "Harmless" Flirtation Hurts, p. 291
5. Is Embarrassment a Distinct Emotion?, p. 295

Games

1. Maslow's Hierarchy of Motives, p. 293

Web Links

1. **http://www.vanguard.edu/psychology/webemotion.html**, p. 276
   AmoebaWeb: Emotion and Motivation. Web resources related to emotion and motivation.
2. **http://www.carleton.ca/~tpychyl/**, p. 276
   Procrastination research group: History of procrastination, intervention strategies, and related Web site links.
3. **http://www.ozemail.com.au/~jsip/instinct.htm**, p. 277
   A Review of the Freudian perspective on human motivation.
4. **http://www.kathy-on the-edge.com/**, p. 281
   Eating disorders online. Links to news and resources, and many relevant topics related to eating disorders.
5. **http://www.popcouncil.org/gfd/scoer/scandrh.html**, p. 291
   Sexual coercion and reproductive health: A focus on research.
6. **http://www.fas.org/sgp/othergov/polygraph/ota/analog.html**, p. 300
   Review and analysis of polygraph analog studies: Online chapter on the scientific validity of polygraph testing.
7. **http://mambo.ucsc.edu/ps1/fanl.html**, p. 303
   Facial Analysis: Offers pictures, descriptions, and theories of facial analysis.
8. **http://nirc.com/cgi-bin/db2www.exe/citations.mac/report**, p. 303
   Online documents, home pages of people, and links relevant to facial emotion expression and analysis of faces.

9

LIFE SPAN
DEVELOPMENT

KAY'S WAS A VERY UNUSUAL CHILDHOOD. BORN THE FOURTH OF FIVE children in a very wealthy family, she grew up in palatial houses tended by large staffs of servants. Yet oddly enough, she had no sense of being wealthy. Money was never talked about in her home, and she and her brother and sisters were never showered with expensive toys. From her earliest days she saw herself as shy, passive, lacking self-assurance, and never quite "measuring up." She envied her second sister's rebellious nature, but she didn't have the courage to be rebellious herself. Her mother did nothing to nurture greater self-confidence. She set such high expectations for her children that reaching those heights seemed an impossible goal. The man Kay married was brilliant, witty, charming, and extremely successful. He dominated all the decisions in their family life. He was the creative thinker, she the implementer. He was the provider of excitement and zest, she the dutiful follower. And yet, after quietly suffering her husband's bouts of heavy drinking, his unpredictable anger, his long struggle with manic-depressive illness, and his eventual violent suicide, she went on to take over the family business and become the talented and powerful head of a highly influential newspaper. This poor little rich girl so burdened with self-doubts is none other than Katharine Graham, former publisher of the *Washington Post* (Graham, 1997). Now in her eighties, she won the Pulitzer Prize in 1998 for her autobiography.

The study of how people change from birth to old age is called **developmental psychology.** Because virtually everything about a person changes over the life span, developmental psychology includes all the other topics that psychologists study, such as thinking, language, intelligence, emotions, and social behavior. But developmental psychologists focus only on a certain aspect of these topics: how and why changes in them occur as people grow older.

In trying to understand both the "what" and the "why" of human development, psychologists focus on three of the major themes we introduced in Chapter 1. One is the theme of individual characteristics versus shared human traits. While there are many common patterns to human development, each person's development is also in some ways unique. Katharine Graham's life illustrates this well. Like so many other women, she progressed through the stages of childhood, adolescence, and adulthood; she married, had children, worked at a job, and eventually became a grandmother. These are all common developmental milestones. In other ways, however, Katharine Graham's development was *not* like everyone else's. Far from every woman is born into such a wealthy family, feels the shyness and insecurity that she did, has to cope with the early death of a husband, or achieves such heights in the business world. This combination of shared and distinctive elements is characteristic of all human development. We all take essentially the same developmental journey, but each of us travels somewhat different roads and experiences events in different ways.

A second theme in the study of human development is stability versus change. Development is characterized by both major life transitions *and* continuities with the past. Again, Katharine Graham's life is an excellent example. The death of her husband and her takeover of his job at the family-owned *Post* was a major turning point in her development. She went from being the dutiful, subordinate wife to the accomplished head of a major American newspaper. And yet with all the changes this transition brought, she still had ties to the person she had been. Self-doubts about her job performance plagued her endlessly, even at the pinnacle of her success. She would lie awake at night reliving how she handled situations, wondering how she might have done better. The little girl fearful of never being "good enough" still lingered on inside her.

Katharine Graham, former publisher of the *Washington Post*. To what extent did Graham change over the course of her lifetime, and to what extent did she maintain certain traits and behaviors?

Finally, the theme of heredity versus environment is central to developmental psychology. Human development can be explained by a combination of biological forces and environmental experiences. These two constantly interact to shape how people grow. What made Katharine Graham into the person she became? She herself has said that she lacked the "proper instincts" to be self-assured and daring, that what she was to some extent stemmed from her inherited makeup. And yet she also recognizes the crucial importance of her environment. How different might she have been had she been born into a different family, married a different husband, or chosen a different life's work? People, she writes, are "molded by the way they spend their days." This is an important concept in developmental psychology.

You will encounter these three major themes often as we journey through the human life course. We begin with the development of the embryo.

Prenatal Development

How can a drug cause devastating effects at one point in prenatal development but not at others?

During the earliest period of **prenatal development**—the stage of development from conception to birth—the fertilized egg divides, embarking on the process that will transform it in just 9 months from a one-celled organism into a complex human being. The dividing cells form a hollow ball, which implants itself in the wall of the uterus. Two weeks after conception the cells begin to specialize. Some will form the baby's internal organs; others will form muscles and bones; and still others will form the skin and the nervous system. No longer an undifferentiated mass of cells, the developing organism is now called an *embryo*.

The embryo stage ends 3 months after conception, when the stage of the **fetus** begins. At this point, although it is only 1 inch long, the fetus roughly resembles a human being, with arms and legs, a large head, and a heart that is beating and pumping blood through tiny arteries and veins.

The embryo and the fetus are nourished by an organ called the *placenta*. Within the placenta the mother's blood vessels transmit substances to the embryo or fetus and carry waste products away from it. Although the mother's blood never actually mingles with that of her unborn child, almost anything the mother eats, drinks, or inhales can be transmitted through the placenta. If she develops an infection such as syphilis, rubella (German measles), or HIV, the microorganisms involved can cross the placenta and infect the fetus, often with disastrous results. If she inhales nicotine, drinks alcohol, or uses other drugs during pregnancy, these, too, can cross the placenta, compromising the baby's development (Harris & Liebert, 1991).

Even seemingly harmless over-the-counter drugs can have adverse effects on an embryo or fetus. For instance, a pregnant woman who takes an aspirin to alleviate a headache runs the risk of causing bleeding in her fetus. More potent drugs can do even greater harm, as we learned in the 1950s when a drug called thalidomide, sometimes used to combat morning sickness, was found to inhibit development of an embryo's arms and legs. More recently, the use of cocaine has taught a similar lesson. Babies whose mothers take cocaine are often born addicted, and they are often smaller and thinner than normal, prone to serious respiratory troubles and sometimes even seizures, and likely to suffer cognitive and social difficulties in childhood (Lewis & Bendersky, 1995).

Alcohol is the drug most often abused by pregnant women, and with devastating consequences (Steinhausen, Willms, & Spohr, 1993). Pregnant women who consume large amounts of alcohol risk giving birth to a child with *fetal alco-*

Developmental psychology
The study of the changes that occur in people from birth through old age.

Prenatal development
Development from conception to birth.

Fetus
A developing human between 3 months after conception and birth.

hol syndrome (FAS), a condition characterized by facial deformities, heart defects, stunted growth, and cognitive impairments. Even smaller amounts of alcohol can be harmful (Hunt et al., 1995). Taking just two drinks a day during pregnancy is associated with having a child who functions more poorly than others both mentally and behaviorally (Shriver & Piersel, 1994). To be safest, pregnant women and those who are trying to become pregnant should not drink alcohol.

Smoking during pregnancy is also risky. Smoking restricts the oxygen supply to the fetus, slows its breathing, and speeds up its heartbeat. These changes are associated with a significantly increased risk of miscarriage. In the United States alone more than 100,000 miscarriages a year are thought to be caused by smoking. Babies of mothers who smoke are also more apt to suffer low birthweight, which puts the child at risk for developmental problems (DiFranza & Lew, 1995; Feng, 1993).

For many potentially harmful substances there is a **critical period** during which their presence is most likely to have detrimental effects. At other times the same substance may have no effect at all. For example, if a woman contracts rubella during the first 3 months of pregnancy, the effects can range from death of the embryo to a child who is born deaf. If the woman contracts rubella during the final 3 months of her pregnancy, however, severe damage to the fetus is unlikely because the critical period for the formation of major body parts has passed.

Pregnancy is most likely to have a favorable outcome when the mother gets good nutrition and good medical care and when she avoids exposure to substances that could be harmful to her baby. One of the most important things a pregnant woman can do is to eat a well-balanced diet. Women who eat a variety of highly nutritious foods during pregnancy are apt to have fewer complications, an easier delivery, and a healthier child, both physically and mentally (Morgane et al., 1993; Sigman, 1995). Unfortunately, good nutrition is not so readily available around the globe. The United Nations has estimated that there are 555 million hungry people in the world and 1 billion who are vulnerable to hunger (United Nations, 1994). Dietary supplements can do a great deal to help pregnant women with inadequate diets (Prentice, 1991). Differences in access to good nutrition and health care help to explain why the infant death rate for African Americans in this country is more than double what it is for whites (see Figure 9–1) (Singh & Yu, 1995). Because of high poverty rates, African Americans often have poor diets and receive inadequate medical care during pregnancy (Aved et al., 1993).

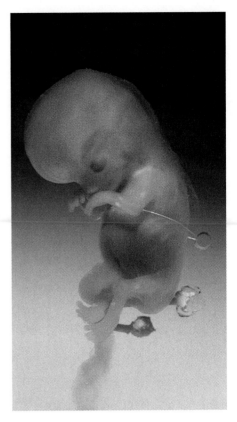

The human fetus can be affected by anything its mother eats, drinks, or inhales.

FIGURE 9–1

Mortality rates for white and African-American infants.

Source: National Center for Health Statistics, 1995.

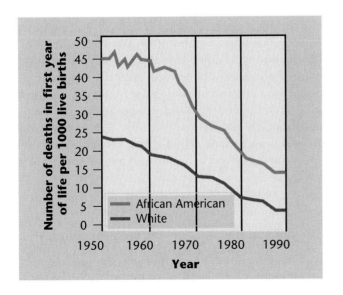

Critical period
Time when certain internal and external influences have a major effect on development; at other periods the same influences will have little or no effect.

REVIEW QUESTIONS

1. The stage of development from conception to birth is called ____ ____.
2. During the first 3 months of human prenatal development, when all the major body parts are forming, the developing organism is called an ____.
3. During the final 6 months of human prenatal development, when rapid growth in size and weight occurs and the body is readied for life outside the womb, the developing organism is called a ____.
4. The organ that nourishes the developing embryo and fetus is known as the ____.
5. A time when an organism is especially susceptible to environmental influences related to a particular aspect of development is called a ____ period.

Answers: 1. prenatal development. 2. embryo. 3. fetus. 4. placenta. 5. critical.

The Newborn Baby

What early reflexes enable newborns to respond to their environment?

Research has disproved the old idea that **neonates,** or newborn babies, do nothing but eat, sleep, and cry, while remaining oblivious to the world. True, newborns can sleep up to 16 or 20 hours a day (depending on the baby), but when they are awake they are much more aware and competent than they may seem at first glance.

For one thing, newborns come equipped with a number of useful reflexes. Many of these reflexes, such as those that control breathing, are essential to life outside the uterus. Some reflexes enable babies to nurse. The *rooting reflex* causes them to turn the head toward the touch of a nipple on the cheek and grope around with the mouth. The *sucking reflex* causes them to suck on anything that enters the mouth, and the *swallowing reflex* enables them to swallow milk and other liquids without choking.

Other reflexes have purposes that are less obvious. The *grasping reflex* causes newborns to cling vigorously to an adult's finger or to any object placed in their hands. The *stepping reflex* causes very young babies to take what looks like walking steps if they are held upright with their feet just touching a flat surface. These reflexes normally disappear after 2 or 3 months, re-emerging later as voluntary grasping (at around 5 months of age) and real walking (at the end of the first year).

Very young babies are also capable of a surprisingly complex kind of behavior: imitating the facial expressions of adults. If an adult opens his mouth or sticks out his tongue, newborn babies often respond by opening their mouths or sticking out their tongues (McCall, 1979; A. N. Meltzoff & Moore, 1985). This early imitation appears to be only a primitive reflex, like the grasping and stepping reflexes. The behavior disappears after a few weeks and then re-emerges in more complex form many months later (Bjorklund, 1989; Wyrwicka, 1988).

Almost all newborns respond to the human face, the human voice, and the human touch. This improves their chances of survival. After all, babies are totally dependent on the people who take care of them, so it is essential that their social relationships get off to a good start. From the very beginning they have a means of communicating their needs to those they live with: They can cry. And very soon—in only about 6 weeks—they have an even better method of communication, one that serves as a thank-you to the people who are working so hard to keep them happy: They can smile.

Temperament

Is your temperament the same as it was when you were a newborn?

It is tempting to talk about babies as if they are all the same, but babies display individual differences in **temperament** (Goldsmith & Harman, 1994; Piontelli,

---

Neonate
Newborn baby.

Temperament
Term used by psychologists to describe the physical/emotional characteristics of the newborn child and young infant; also referred to as personality.

1989). Some cry much more than others; some are much more active. Some babies love to be cuddled; others seem to wriggle uncomfortably when held. Some are highly reactive to intense sights and sounds, while others are quite placid no matter what they see or hear.

In a classic study of infant temperament Alexander Thomas and Stella Chess (1977) identified three types of babies: "easy," "difficult," and "slow-to-warm-up." Easy babies are good-natured and adaptable, easy to care for and please. Difficult babies are moody and intense, reacting to new people and new situations both negatively and strongly. Slow-to-warm-up babies are relatively inactive and slow to respond to new things, and when they do react, their reactions are mild. To these three types Jerome Kagan and his associates (Kagan et al., 1988; Kagan & Snidman, 1991) have added a fourth: the "shy child." Shy children are timid and inhibited, fearful of anything new or strange. Their nervous systems react to stimuli in a characteristically hypersensitive way (Kagan, 1994). Kagan and his colleagues have discovered interesting differences in the frequency with which various behaviors related to temperament appear in babies from different cultures. They speculate that such differences may be due in large part to the effects of different gene pools and genetic predispositions (Kagan et al., 1993).

Regardless of what initially causes a baby's temperament, it often remains quite stable over time. In one study that asked mothers to describe their children's temperaments, characteristics such as degree of irritability, flexibility, and persistence were all quite stable from infancy through age 8 (Pedlow, Sanson, Prior, & Oberklaid, 1993). Other studies have found that fussy or difficult infants are likely to become "problem children" who are aggressive and have difficulties in school (Guerin, 1994; Patterson & Bank, 1989; Persson-Blennow & McNeil, 1988). A longitudinal study of shy children and some of their less-inhibited peers showed that most shy infants continue to be relatively shy and inhibited in middle childhood, just as most uninhibited infants remained relatively outgoing and bold (Kagan & Snidman, 1991).

A combination of biological and environmental factors generally contributes to this stability in behavior. For instance, if a newborn has an innate predisposition to cry often and react negatively to things, the parents may find themselves tired, frustrated, and often angry. These reactions in the parents may serve to reinforce the baby's difficult behavior, and so it tends to endure.

This is not to say that the temperament a baby is born with destines a child for life. Not all difficult infants become problem children, and not all children who are easy as infants sail through childhood without any trouble. Each child's predispositions interact with his or her experiences, and how the child turns out is the result of that interaction (Kagan, 1989, 1994).

The Perceptual Abilities of Infants

Which senses are the most developed at birth, and which are the least developed?

Newborn babies can see, hear, and understand far more than previous generations gave them credit for. Their senses work fairly well at birth and rapidly improve to near-adult levels. They begin to absorb and process information from the outside world as soon as they enter it—or, in some cases, even before.

Vision Unlike puppies and kittens, human babies are born with their eyes open and functioning, even though the world looks a bit fuzzy to them at first. They see most clearly when faces or objects are only 8 to 10 inches away from them. Visual acuity (the clarity of vision) improves rapidly, however, and so does the ability to focus on objects at different distances. By 6 or 8 months of age, babies can see almost as well as the average college student, though their visual system takes another 3 or 4 years to develop fully (Maurer & Maurer, 1988).

Even very young babies already have visual preferences. They would rather look at a new picture or pattern than one they have seen many times before. If given a choice between two pictures or patterns, both of which are new to them, they generally prefer the one with the clearest contrasts. This is why they choose to look at a black-and-white pattern more than a colored one, even though they are able to distinguish primary colors from gray. For a young baby, however, the pattern shouldn't be too complex. For example, a baby would prefer a large black-and-white checkerboard to one with smaller squares, because the smaller squares tend to blur from the baby's point of view. As babies get older and their vision improves, they prefer more and more complex patterns, perhaps reflecting their need for an increasingly complex environment (Acredolo & Hake, 1982; Fantz, Fagan, & Miranda, 1975).

Depth Perception   Depth perception is the ability to see the world in three dimensions, with some objects or surfaces nearer and others farther away. Although researchers have been unable to find evidence of depth perception in babies younger than 4 months (Aslin & Smith, 1988), the ability to see the world in three dimensions is well developed by the time a baby learns to crawl at between 6 and 12 months of age.

This was demonstrated in a classic experiment using a device called a *visual cliff* (Walk & Gibson, 1961). Researchers divided a table into three parts. The center was a solid runway, raised above the rest of the table by about an inch. On one side of this runway was a solid surface decorated in a checkerboard pattern and covered with a sheet of clear glass. The other side was also covered with a thick sheet of clear glass, but on this side—the visual cliff—the checkerboard surface was not directly under the glass but 40 inches below it. An infant of crawling age was placed on the center runway, and the mother stood on one side or the other, encouraging the baby to crawl toward her across the glass. All of the 6- to 14-month-old infants tested refused to crawl across the visual cliff, even though they were perfectly willing to cross the shallow side of the table. When the deep side separated the baby from the mother, some of the infants cried; others peered down at the surface below the glass or patted the glass with their hands. Their behaviors clearly showed that they could perceive depth.

Other Senses   Even before birth, ears are in working order. Babies can hear sounds in the uterus and will startle at a sudden, loud noise. After they are born, they may even show signs that they remember sounds they heard in the womb. In one study babies modified their rate of sucking on a pacifier in order to hear a recording of the children's book *The Cat in the Hat*, which their mothers had read aloud twice a day in their last 6 weeks of pregnancy. The babies made no such effort to hear a recording of another children's story to which they had never been exposed (DeCasper & Spence, 1986).

Infants are particularly adept at differentiating speech sounds. One-month-olds can distinguish between similar speech sounds such as "pa-pa-pa" and "ba-ba-ba" (Eimas & Tartter, 1979). In some ways, young infants are even better at distinguishing speech sounds than older children and adults are. As children grow older, they often lose their ability to hear the difference between two very similar speech sounds that are not distinguished in their native language (Werker & Desjardins, 1995). For example, young Japanese infants have no trouble hearing the difference between "ra" and "la," sounds that are not distinguished in the Japanese language. By the time they are a year old, however, Japanese infants can no longer tell these two sounds apart (Werker, 1989).

With regard to taste and smell, newborns have clear-cut likes and dislikes. They like sweet flavors, a preference that persists through childhood. Babies only a few hours old will show pleasure at the taste of sweetened water but will screw up their

When placed on the visual cliff, babies of crawling age (about 6 to 14 months) will not cross the deep side, even to reach their mothers. This classic experiment tells us that by the time they can crawl, babies can also perceive depth.

Cross-sectional study
A method of studying developmental changes by examining groups of subjects who are of different ages.

Cohort
A group of people born during the same period in historical time.

HIGHLIGHTS

Methods in Developmental Psychology

Developmental psychologists use the same research methods that psychologists in other areas use: naturalistic observations, correlational studies, and experiments (see Chapter 1). But because developmental psychologists are interested in processes of change over time, they use these methods in three special types of studies: cross-sectional, longitudinal, and biographical.

In a **cross-sectional study,** researchers examine developmental change by observing or testing people of different ages at the same point in time. For example, they might study the development of logical thought by testing a group of 6-year-olds, a group of 9-year-olds, and a group of 12-year-olds, and then looking for differences among the age groups. Or, if they are interested in cognitive changes during adulthood, they might study 40-year-olds, 60-year-olds, and 80-year-olds simultaneously. One problem with cross-sectional studies, however, is that they don't distinguish age differences from *cohort differences.* A **cohort** is a group of people born during the same period of history: All Americans born in 1940, for example, form a cohort. Cohort differences are differences between individuals stemming from the fact that they were born and grew up at different historical times. If we found that 40-year-olds were able to solve harder math problems than

80-year-olds, we wouldn't know whether this difference was due to better cognitive ability in younger people (an age difference) or to better math education 40 years ago than 80 (a cohort difference).

Longitudinal studies overcome this problem by testing the same people two or more times as they grow older. For instance, researchers who are interested in the development of logical thought might begin their

---

Developmental psychologists are interested in processes of change.

---

study by testing a group of 6-year-olds, then wait 3 years and test the same children again at age 9, then wait another 3 years to test them again at age 12. One problem with longitudinal studies, however, is that they don't distinguish age differences from differences that arise from improved assessment or measurement tools. For example, researchers retesting a cohort at age 9 might have access to a more sensitive measure of logical thought than they did when they tested that cohort at age 6. So if they found significant improvement

in logical thought over this 3-year period, they wouldn't know to what extent it reflected the advance in age and to what extent it reflected the more sensitive measuring tool.

Another drawback to a longitudinal study is that it takes considerable time even when investigating childhood alone. And when studying the entire course of adulthood, a longitudinal study can require 50 years or more. To avoid the huge expense of such a long study, researchers have devised a third way of studying adulthood: the **biographical** or **retrospective study.** Whereas a longitudinal study might start with some 20-year-olds and follow them as they grew older, a biographical approach might start with some 70-year-olds and pursue their lives backward. That is, the researchers would try to reconstruct their subjects' past by interviewing them and consulting various other sources, much as a biographer does when writing about someone's life. Biographical data are less trustworthy than either longitudinal or cross-sectional data, however, because people's recollections of the past are not always accurate. Each research method is highly useful in its way, and together they provide a wealth of information about human development. You will come across examples of all three in this chapter.

---

faces in disgust at the taste of lemon juice (Steiner, 1979). Babies also seem to prefer many of the smells that adults find pleasant, although some things that smell good to most adults (shrimp, for example) provoke expressions of disgust in babies.

As infants grow older, their perceptions of the world become keener and more meaningful. Two factors are important in this development. One is physical maturation of the sense organs and the nervous system. The other is gaining more experience in the world. As babies learn about people and objects, they encounter a growing variety of sights, sounds, textures, smells, and tastes. As a result, their perceptions are increasingly enriched by a growing fund of memories and understandings. (See *Highlights* for an overview of the research methods used by developmental psychologists.)

GAMES
G

Longitudinal study
A method of studying developmental changes by examining the same group of subjects two or more times as they grow older.

Biographical (or retrospective) study
A method of studying developmental changes by reconstructing subjects' past through interviews and investigating the effects of past events on current behaviors.

REVIEW QUESTIONS

1. Put an X next to each reflex found in human newborns and circle whether that particular reflex is essential (E) or nonessential (NE) to survival.

____ the rooting reflex (E/NE)

____ the sucking reflex (E/NE)

____ the swallowing reflex (E/NE)

____ the smiling reflex (E/NE)

____ the grasping reflex (E/NE)

____ the crawling reflex (E/NE)

____ the stepping reflex (E/NE)

2. Put an X next to each sensory or perceptual ability that definitely functions at birth in humans.

____ sight (the ability to see an object held in front of the baby's face)

____ depth perception

____ hearing

____ taste

____ smell

3. Stability in a baby's temperament over time is probably due to

____ a. the influence of genetic predispositions that can't be changed.

____ b. the influence of predispositions interacting with environment.

Answers: 1. rooting (E); sucking (E); swallowing (E); grasping (E); stepping (NE); 2. sight; hearing; taste; smell; 3. b.

Infancy and Childhood

What kinds of developmental changes do infants and children undergo?

During the first dozen or so years of life, a helpless baby becomes a competent member of society. Many important kinds of developments occur during these early years. Among them are physical and motor changes as well as cognitive and social ones.

Physical Development

Do children grow at a steady pace?

In the first year of life the average baby grows 10 inches and gains 15 pounds. By 4 months birthweight has doubled, and by 1 year it has tripled. During the second year physical growth slows considerably. Rapid increases in height and weight will not occur again until early adolescence.

Interestingly, an infant's growth does not occur in the smooth, continuous fashion depicted by growth charts. Rather, growth takes place in fits and starts (Lampl, Veidhuis, & Johnson, 1992). When babies are measured daily over their first 21 months, most show no growth 90 percent of the time, but when they do grow, they do so rapidly—sometimes startlingly so. Incredible though it may sound, some children gain as much as 1 inch in height overnight.

Changes in the baby's size are accompanied by marked changes in body proportions (see Figure 9–2). During the first 2 years after birth, babies and toddlers have heads that are large relative to their bodies. This rapid growth of the head reflects that rapid development of the central nervous system: An infant's brain reaches three-quarters of its adult size by about the age of 2, at which point head growth slows down and the body does most of the growing. Head growth is virtually complete by age 10, but the body continues to grow for several more years.

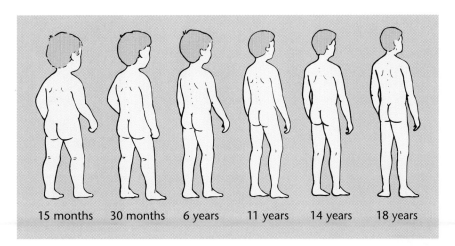

FIGURE 9–2

Body proportions at various ages. Young children are top-heavy: They have large heads and small bodies. As they get older the body and legs become longer, and the head becomes proportionately smaller.

Source: Adapted from Bayley, 1956. Copyright Society for Research in Child Development, Inc., University of Michigan, Center for Human Growth and Development. Reprinted by permission.

Motor Development

Is walking at an early age a sign of future athletic ability?

Motor development refers to the acquisition of skills involving movement, such as grasping, crawling, and walking. During infancy these skills are acquired in fairly predictable ways. For example, by about 9 months the average infant can stand up while holding onto something. Crawling occurs, on average, at 10 months, and walking at about 1 year. Some normal infants develop much faster than average, however, while others develop more slowly. A baby who is 3 or 4 months behind schedule may be perfectly normal, and one who is 3 or 4 months ahead is not necessarily destined to become a star athlete. To some extent, parents can accelerate the acquisition of motor skills in children by providing them with ample training, encouragement, and practice. Differences in these factors seem largely to account for cross-cultural differences in the average age at which certain milestones in motor development are reached (Hopkins & Westra, 1989, 1990).

Much early motor development consists of substituting voluntary actions for reflexes (Clark, 1994). The newborn grasping and stepping reflexes, for instance, give way to voluntary grasping and walking in the older baby. Motor development proceeds in a *proximodistal fashion*—that is, from nearest the center of the body (proximal) to farthest from the center (distal). For example, the infant initially has much greater control over gross arm movements than over movements of the fingers. Babies start batting at nearby objects as early as 1 month, but they cannot reach accurately until they are about 4 months old. It takes them another month or 2 before they are consistently successful in grasping objects they reach for (von Hofsten & Fazel-Zandy, 1984). At first they grasp with the whole hand, but by the end of the first year they can pick up a tiny object with the thumb and forefinger.

Maturation refers to biological processes that unfold as a person grows older and contribute to orderly sequences of developmental changes, such as the progression from crawling to toddling to walking. Psychologists used to believe that maturation of the central nervous system largely accounted for many of the

Maturation
An automatic biological unfolding of development in an organism as a function of the passage of time.

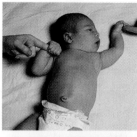

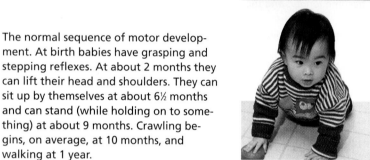

The normal sequence of motor development. At birth babies have grasping and stepping reflexes. At about 2 months they can lift their head and shoulders. They can sit up by themselves at about 6½ months and can stand (while holding on to something) at about 9 months. Crawling begins, on average, at 10 months, and walking at 1 year.

changes in early motor skills—that environment and experience played only a minor part in their emergence. But in recent years this view has been changing (Thelen, 1994, 1995). Many researchers now see early motor development as arising from a combination of factors both within and outside the child. The child is viewed as playing an active part in the process by exploring, discovering, and selecting solutions to the demands of new tasks. A baby who is learning to crawl, for example, must figure out how to position his body with belly off the ground and coordinate arm and leg movements to maintain balance while managing to proceed forward (Bertenthal et al., 1994). What doesn't work must be discarded or adapted; what does work must be remembered and called upon for future use. This is a far cry from seeing the baby as one day starting to crawl simply because he has reached the point of maturational "readiness."

As children's coordination improves, they learn to run, skip, and climb. At 3 and 4 they begin to use their hands for increasingly complex tasks, first learning how to put on mittens and shoes, then grappling with buttons, zippers, shoelaces, and pencils. Gradually, through a combination of practice and the physical maturation of the body and the brain, they acquire increasingly complex motor abilities, such as bike riding, roller-skating, and swimming. By about age 11 some begin to be highly skilled at such tasks (Clark, 1994).

Cognitive Development

How does a child's ability to reason change over time?

Early cognitive development consists partly of changes in how children think about the world. The most influential theorist in this area was the Swiss psychologist Jean Piaget (1896–1980). Piaget became interested in cognitive development while working as a research assistant in the laboratory of Alfred Binet and Theodore Simon, creators of the first standardized intelligence test for children. Piaget became intrigued by the reasons young children gave for answering certain questions incorrectly (Brainerd, 1996). Later he observed and studied other children, including his own three. He watched them play games, solve problems, and perform everyday tasks, and he asked them questions and devised tests to learn how they thought. His early training as a biologist had an important influence on his views.

Piaget believed that cognitive development is a way of adapting to the environment. Unlike other animals, human children do not have many built-in responses. This gives them more flexibility to adapt their thinking and behavior to "fit" the world as they experience it at a particular age. In Piaget's view children are intrinsically motivated to explore and understand things. They are active participants in creating their own understandings of the world. This view is one of Piaget's major contributions (Fischer & Hencke, 1996; Flavell, 1996). Others are the four basic stages of cognitive development that he proposed.

Piaget's Stages of Cognitive Development   According to Piaget, babies spend the first 2 years of life in the **sensory-motor stage** of development. They start out simply by applying the skills they are born with—primarily sucking and grasping—to a broad range of activities. Young babies delight in taking things into their mouths—their mother's breast, their own thumb, or anything else within reach. Gradually they divide the world into what they can and cannot suck on. Similarly, young babies will grasp a rattle reflexively. When they eventually realize that the noise comes from the rattle, they begin to shake everything they can get hold of in an effort to reproduce the sound. Eventually they distinguish between things that make noise and things that do not. In this way infants begin to organize their experiences, fitting them into rudimentary categories such as "suckable" and "not suckable," "noise-making" and "not noise-making."

Another important outcome of the sensory-motor stage, according to Piaget, is the development of **object permanence,** an awareness that objects continue to exist even when out of sight. For newborns objects that disappear simply cease to exist—"out of sight, out of mind." But as children gain experience with the world, they develop a sense of object permanence. By the time they are 18 to 24 months old, they can even imagine the movement of an object that they do not actually see move. This last skill depends on the ability to form **mental representations** of objects and to manipulate those representations mentally. This is a major achievement of the late sensory-motor stage.

By the end of the sensory-motor stage, toddlers have also developed a capacity for self-recognition—that is, they are able to recognize the child in the mirror as "myself." In one famous study mothers put a dab of red paint on their child's nose while pretending to wipe the child's face. Then each child was placed in front of a mirror. Babies under 1 year of age stared in fascination at the red-nosed baby in the mirror; some of them even reached out to touch the nose's reflection. But babies between 21 and 24 months reached up and touched their *own* reddened noses, showing that they knew the red-nosed baby in the mirror was "me" (Brooks-Gunn & Lewis, 1984).

When children enter the **preoperational stage** of cognitive development (from 2 to 7 years of age) their thought is still tightly bound to their physical and perceptual experiences. But their increasing ability to use mental representations lays the groundwork for the development of language—using words as symbols to represent events and to describe, remember, and reason about experiences. (We will say much more about language development shortly.)

Sensory-motor stage
In Piaget's theory, the stage of cognitive development between birth and 2 years of age in which the individual develops object permanence and acquires the ability to form mental representations.

Object permanence
The concept that things continue to exist even when they are out of sight.

Mental representation
Mental images or symbols (such as words) used to think about or remember an object, a person, or an event.

Preoperational stage
In Piaget's theory, the stage of cognitive development between 2 and 7 years of age in which the individual becomes able to use mental representations and language to describe, remember, and reason about the world, though only in an egocentric fashion.

In Piaget's famous experiment, the child has to judge which glass holds more liquid: the tall, thin one or the short, wide one. Although both glasses hold the same amount, children in the preoperational stage say that the taller glass holds more, because they focus their attention on only one thing—the height of the column of liquid.

Representational thought also lays the groundwork for two other hallmarks of this stage—engaging in *fantasy play* (a cardboard box becomes a castle) and using *symbolic gestures* (slashing the air with an imaginary sword to slay an imaginary dragon).

But although children this age have made advances over sensory-motor thought, in many ways they don't yet think like older children and adults. For example, preschool children are often **egocentric.** They may have difficulty seeing things from another person's point of view or putting themselves in someone else's place. They also find it hard to distinguish between things as they appear to be and things as they really are (Flavell, 1986). This is partly because they have trouble focusing on two things simultaneously. They tend to concentrate on the most obvious features, ignoring everything else. As a result, they are easily misled by appearances.

In a famous experiment that illustrated this important limitation, Piaget showed preoperational children two identical glasses filled to the same level with juice. The children were asked which glass held more juice, and they replied (correctly) that both had the same amount. Then Piaget poured the juice from one glass into a taller, narrower glass. Again the children were asked which glass held more juice. They looked at the two glasses, saw that the level of the juice in the tall, narrow one was much higher, and replied that the narrow glass had more. According to Piaget, children at this stage can't consider the past and the present (equal versus taller) at the same time, nor can they consider a container's height and width simultaneously. Thus they can't understand how an increase in one dimension (height) might be offset by a decrease in another dimension (width).

During the **concrete-operational stage** (from ages 7 to 11), children become able to consider more than one dimension of a problem at a time and to look at a situation from someone else's point of view. This is the age at which they grasp **principles of conservation,** such as the idea that the volume of a liquid stays the same regardless of the size and shape of the container into which it is poured. Other related conservation concepts have to do with number, length, area, and mass. All involve an understanding that basic amounts remain constant despite superficial changes in appearance, which can always be reversed. Another accomplishment of this stage is the ability to grasp complex classification schemes such as those involving superordinate and subordinate classes. For instance, if you show a preschooler four toy dogs and two toy cats and ask if there are more dogs or more animals present, the child will almost always answer "more dogs." It is not until age 7 or 8 that children are able to think about objects as being simultaneously members of *two* classes, one more

Egocentric
Unable to see things from another's point of view.

Concrete-operational stage
In Piaget's theory, the stage of cognitive development between 7 and 11 years of age in which the individual can attend to more than one thing at a time and understand someone else's point of view, though thinking is limited to concrete matters.

Principles of conservation
The concept that basic amounts remain constant despite superficial changes in appearance, such as the idea that the volume of a liquid stays the same regardless of the size and shape of the container into which it is poured.

SUMMARY TABLE

Piaget's Stages of Cognitive Development

Stage	Approximate Age	Key Features
Sensory-motor	0 – 2 years	Object permanence Mental representations
Preoperational	2 – 7 years	Representational thought Fantasy play Symbolic gestures Egocentricism
Concrete-operational	7 – 11 years	Conservation Complex classification
Formal-operational	Adolescence – adulthood	Abstract and hypothetical thought

inclusive than the other. Yet even well into the elementary school years, children's thinking is still very much stuck in the "here and now." Often they are unable to solve problems without concrete reference points that they can handle or imagine handling.

This limitation is overcome in the **formal-operational stage** of cognitive development, which is often reached during adolescence. Youngsters at this stage can think in abstract terms. They can formulate hypotheses, test them mentally, and accept or reject them according to the outcome of these mental experiments. This makes them capable of going beyond the here-and-now to understand things in terms of cause and effect, to consider possibilities as well as realities, and to develop and use general rules, principles, and theories.

Criticisms of Piaget's Theory   Piaget's work has produced a great deal of controversy. Many question his assumption that there are distinct stages in cognitive development that always progress in an orderly, sequential way and that a child must pass through one stage before entering the next (Brainerd, 1978; L. Siegel, 1993). Some see cognitive development as a more gradual process, resulting from the slow acquisition of experience and practice rather than the abrupt emergence of distinctly higher levels of thinking (Paris & Weissberg, 1986).

Piaget's theory has also been criticized for assuming that young infants understand very little about the world, such as the permanence of objects in it. When young babies are allowed to reveal their understanding of object permanence without being required to conduct a search for a missing object, they often seem to know perfectly well that objects continue to exist when hidden by other objects (Baillargeon, 1994). They also show other quite sophisticated knowledge that Piaget thought they lacked, such as a rudimentary grasp of numbers (Wynn, 1995). At older ages, too, children seem to reach milestone cognitive achievements much sooner than Piaget believed (Gopnik, 1996).

Other critics have argued that Piaget underplayed the importance of social interaction in cognitive development. For instance, the influential Russian psychologist Lev Vygotsky contended that critical opportunities for cognitive growth are provided by other people who are more advanced in their thinking than the particular child they are interacting with (Vygotsky, 1978). The nature

Formal-operational stage
In Piaget's theory, the stage of cognitive development beginning at about age 11, in which the individual becomes capable of abstract thought.

of these learning experiences greatly depends on a society's culture, another factor that Piaget ignored (Daehler, 1994).

Finally, although Piaget's theory gives us a schematic road map of cognitive development, the interests and experiences of a particular child may influence the development of cognitive abilities in ways not accounted for in the theory. Piaget's theory, in other words, does not adequately address human diversity.

Moral Development

How do gender and ethnic background affect moral development?

One of the important changes in thinking that occurs during childhood and adolescence is the development of moral reasoning. Lawrence Kohlberg (1979, 1981) studied this kind of development by telling his participants stories that illustrate complex moral issues. The "Heinz dilemma" is the best known of these stories:

> In Europe, a woman was near death from cancer. One drug might save her, a form of radium that a druggist in the same town had recently discovered. The druggist was charging $2,000, ten times what the drug cost him to make. The sick woman's husband, Heinz, went to everyone he knew to borrow the money, but he could only get together about half of what it cost. He told the druggist that his wife was dying and asked him to sell it cheaper or let him pay later. But the druggist said, "No." The husband got desperate and broke into the man's store to steal the drug for his wife. (Kohlberg, 1969, p. 379)

The children and adolescents who heard this story were asked, "Should the husband have done that? Why?"

On the basis of his subjects' replies to these questions (particularly the second one, "Why?"), Kohlberg theorized that moral reasoning develops in stages, much like Piaget's account of cognitive development. Pre-adolescent children are at what Kohlberg called the *preconventional level* of moral reasoning: They tend to interpret behavior in terms of its concrete consequences. Younger children at this level base their judgments of "right" and "wrong" behavior on whether it is rewarded or punished. Somewhat older children, still at this level, guide their moral choices on the basis of what satisfies needs, particularly their own.

With the arrival of adolescence and the shift to formal-operational thought, the stage is set for progression to the second level of moral reasoning, the *conventional level*. At this level the adolescent at first defines right behavior as that which pleases or helps others and is approved by them. Around mid-adolescence there is a further shift toward considering various abstract social virtues, such as being a good citizen and respecting authority. Both forms of conventional moral reasoning require an ability to think about such abstract values as "duty" and "social order," to consider the intentions that lie behind behavior, and to put oneself in the "other person's shoes."

The third level of moral reasoning, the *postconventional level*, requires a still more abstract form of thought. This level is marked by an emphasis on abstract principles such as justice, liberty, and equality. Personal and strongly felt moral standards become the guideposts for deciding what is right and wrong. Whether these decisions correspond to the laws of a particular society at a particular time is irrelevant. For the first time, people may become aware of discrepancies between what they judge to be moral and what society has determined to be legal.

Kohlberg's views have been criticized on several accounts. First, research indicates that many people in our society, adults as well as adolescents, never progress beyond the conventional level of moral reasoning (Conger & Petersen, 1991). Does this mean that these people are morally "underdeveloped," as Kohlberg's theory implies?

Second, Kohlberg's theory does not take account of cultural differences in moral values. Kohlberg put considerations of "justice" at the highest level of moral reasoning. In Nepal, however, researchers discovered that a group of adolescent Buddhist monks placed the highest moral value on alleviating suffering and showing compassion, concepts that have no place in Kohlberg's scheme of moral development (Huebner, Garrod, & Snarey, 1990).

Third, Kohlberg's theory has been criticized as sexist. Kohlberg found that boys usually scored higher than girls on his test of moral development. According to Carol Gilligan (1982, 1992), this was because boys are more inclined to base their moral judgments on the abstract concept of justice, while girls tend to base theirs more on the criteria of caring about other people and the importance of maintaining personal relationships. In Gilligan's view there is no valid reason to assume that one of these perspectives is morally superior to the other. Although subsequent research has found that gender differences in moral thinking tend to diminish in adulthood (Cohn, 1991), concerns about gender bias in Kohlberg's theory remain.

More recent research on moral development has moved in the direction of broadening Kohlberg's focus on changes in moral reasoning. These researchers are interested in the factors that influence moral choices in everyday life and the extent to which those choices are put into action. In other words, they want to understand moral behavior as much as moral thinking (Power, 1994).

Language Development

How does a child develop language skills?

The development of language follows a predictable pattern. At about 2 months of age an infant begins to coo (a nondescript word for nondescript sounds). In another month or 2 the infant enters the *babbling* stage and starts to repeat sounds such as *da* or even meaningless sounds that developmental psychologists refer to as "grunts"; these sounds are the building blocks for later language development (Dill, 1994). A few months later the infant may string together the same sound, as in *dadadada*. Finally, the baby will form combinations of different sounds, as in *dabamaga* (Ferguson & Macken, 1983).

Deaf babies with deaf parents who communicate with sign language also engage in a form of babbling (Pettito & Marentette, 1991). Like hearing infants, these babies begin to babble before they are 10 months old—but they babble with their hands. Just as hearing infants utter sounds over and over, deaf babies make repetitive movements of their hands, like those of sign language.

Gradually an infant's babbling takes on features of adult speech. At about age 4 to 6 months it begins to show signs of intonation, the rising and lowering of pitch that allows adults to distinguish, for example, between questions ("You're tired?") and statements ("You're tired"). By around their first birthday, babies are using intonation to indicate questions and commands, even though the sounds they make may not yet be real words (Greenfield & Smith, 1976). At about the same age, they show signs of understanding what is said to them, and they begin to imitate what they hear others say (for instance, saying "bye-bye" while waving a hand). Parents facilitate language development by speaking to their babies in what is called *parentese:* slow, high-pitched speech that uses simple sentences and exaggerated intonations to engage the baby's attention and to help distinguish the elements of speech (J. Hampson & Nelson, 1993).

All this preparation leads up to the first word at about 12 months. During the next 6 to 8 months children build a vocabulary of one-word sentences called *holophrases:* "Up!"; "Out!"; "More!" Children may also use compound words such as *awgone* ("all gone"). To these holophrases they add words used to address people—*Hi* is a favorite—and a few exclamations, such as *Ouch!*

In the second year of life children begin distinguishing between themselves and others. Possessive words become a big part of their vocabulary: "[The shoes are] Daddy's." But the overwhelming passion of children from 12 to 24 months old is naming. With little or no prompting they will name virtually everything they see, though not always correctly. If they don't know the name of an object, they simply will invent one or use another word that is almost right. Feedback from parents ("No, that's not a dog; it's a cow") expands vocabulary and helps children understand what names can and cannot be assigned to classes of things ("dog" is not used for big four-legged animals that live on farms and moo rather than bark).

From 12 to 24 months babies typically point at and name, although not always correctly, whatever object interests them.

During the third year of life children begin to form simple two- and three-word sentences such as "See daddy," "Baby cry," "My ball," and "Dog go woof-woof." They typically leave out auxiliary verbs and verb endings ("[Can] I have that?"; "I [am] eat[ing] it up"), as well as prepositions and articles ("Time [for] Sarah [to] take [a] nap") (Bloom, 1970). Apparently children this age seize on the most important parts of speech—those that contain the most meaning.

After 3 years of age children begin to fill in their sentences ("Nick school" becomes "Nick goes to school"), and language production increases dramatically. Children start to use the past tense as well as the present. Sometimes they *overregularize* the past tense by applying the regular form when an irregular one is called for (saying "goed" instead of "went," for example). Such mistakes are signs that the child has implicitly grasped the basic rules of language (Marcus, 1996). Preschoolers also ask more questions and learn to use "Why?" effectively (sometimes monotonously so). By the age of 5 or 6 most children have a vocabulary of more than 2,500 words and can construct fairly complex sentences, such as those with subordinate clauses.

Theories of Language Development   Children readily pick up the vocabulary of their native language, as well as the complex rules for putting words together into sentences. Two very different theories explain how language develops. B. F. Skinner (1957) believed that parents and other people listen to the infant's babbling and reinforce, or reward, the baby for making sounds that resemble adult speech. If the infant says something that sounds like *mama*, its mother reinforces the behavior with smiles and attention. In the same way, Skinner believed, children are systematically reinforced to learn where words belong in a sentence, how to use prefixes and suffixes, and so on.

Most psychologists and linguists believe that reinforcement alone cannot explain the speed, accuracy, and originality with which children learn to use language. Noam Chomsky (1965) has been the most influential critic of the notion that children must be *taught* language. Instead he argues that children are born with a **language acquisition device,** an internal mechanism for processing speech that is "wired into" the human brain, facilitating language learning and making it universal (Kuhl, Kuhl, & Williams, 1992). This language acquisition device is like an internal "map" of language: All the child has to do is to fill in the blanks with specific words and rules supplied by the environment. An American child fills in the blanks with English words and grammar, a Mexican child with Spanish ones, and so on.

Language acquisition device
An internal mechanism for processing speech that is "wired into" all humans.

Of course, the environment should do more than simply provide examples of a language being spoken. Without caring people to talk to, children are slow to pick up words and grammatical rules. Babies reared in institutions, without smiling adults around to reward their efforts, babble like other children but take much longer to begin talking than children reared in families (R. Brown, 1958). The greater attention paid to firstborn children may explain why these children tend to be more advanced in their language development than those born later (C. P. Jones & Adamson, 1987).

Social Development

How can parents help their children to become both securely attached and independent?

One of the central aspects of human development is the process whereby a child learns to interact with other people. Early in life children's most important relationships are with their parents and other caregivers. But by the time they are 3, their important relationships have usually expanded to include siblings, playmates, and adults outside the family. When they start school, their social world expands even further. As you will see, social development involves both established relationships and new ones.

Parent–Child Relationships in Infancy: Development of Attachment   Young animals of many species follow their mothers around because of **imprinting.** Shortly after they are born or hatched, they form a strong bond to the first moving object they see. In nature this object is normally the mother, the first source of nurturing and protection. But in laboratory experiments certain species of animals, such as geese, have been hatched in incubators and have imprinted on decoys, mechanical toys, and even humans (H. S. Hoffman & De-Paulo, 1977; Lorenz, 1935). These goslings faithfully follow their human "mother," showing no interest whatever in adult females of their own species (see photo).

Human newborns do not imprint on first-seen moving objects, but they do gradually form an **attachment,** or emotional bond, to the people who care for them (regardless of the caretakers' gender). As we saw in Chapter 8, classic studies of baby monkeys suggest that the sense of security engendered by physical contact and closeness is one important root of attachment (Harlow, 1958; Harlow & Zimmerman, 1959).

In humans, of course, attachment is based on more than just tactile sensations. It is built on many hours of interaction from which baby and parent come to form a close relationship. Signs of attachment are evident by the age of 6 months or even earlier. The baby will react with smiles and coos at the caregiver's appearance and with whimpers and doleful looks when the caregiver goes away. At around 7 months, attachment behavior becomes more intense. The infant will reach out to be picked up by the caregiver and will cling to the caregiver, especially when tired, frightened, or hurt. The baby will also begin to be wary of strangers, sometimes reacting with loud wails at even the friendliest approach by an unfamiliar person. If separated from the caregiver even for a few minutes in an unfamiliar place, the baby usually will become quite upset.

Parents are often puzzled by this new behavior in their previously nonchalant infants, but it is perfectly normal. In fact, anxiety over separation from the mother indicates that the infant has developed a sense of "person permanence" along with a sense of object permanence. For the 5-month-old it's still "out of sight, out of mind" when Mother leaves the room, but for the 9-month-old the memory of Mother lingers, and he announces at the top of his lungs that he wants her to come back.

Konrad Lorenz discovered that goslings will follow the first moving object they see, regardless of whether it is their mother, a mechanical toy, or a human. Here Lorenz is trailed by ducklings who have imprinted on him.

Imprinting
A form of primitive bonding seen in some species of animals; the newborn animal has a tendency to follow the first moving thing (usually its mother) it sees after it is born or hatched.

Attachment
Emotional bond that develops in the first year of life that makes human babies cling to their caregivers for safety and comfort.

A scene from a day-care center. Studies have shown that working parents can instill feelings of trust and attachment in their infant children even when the infants are in full-time day care.

Ideally, infants eventually learn that Mother and other primary caregivers can be counted on to be there when needed. Psychologist Erik Erikson (1902–94) called this the development of *basic trust*. In his theory of psychosocial development, which spanned the entire life course from birth until old age, each stage of life presents a major task or challenge regarding the self and others, which people must somehow deal with, successfully or not (Erikson, 1963). The challenge of the first stage, which encompasses the first year of life, is to develop a basic trust in the world, especially of the people in it. If babies' needs are generally met, they come to acquire this view. They develop faith in other people and also in themselves. They see the world as a secure, dependable place and have optimism about the future. In contrast, babies whose needs are not usually met grow to be fearful and overly anxious about their own security. Erikson referred to these two possible outcomes as *trust versus mistrust*.

There has been concern that putting infants in full-time day care may interfere with the development of basic trust and secure attachment (Barglow, Vaughn, & Molitor, 1987; Belsky & Rovine, 1988). But according to the findings of a recent large-scale longitudinal study (NICHD, 1996), full-time day care even in the first few months of life doesn't in itself undermine attachment. Working parents and their babies still have ample opportunity to engage in the daily give-and-take of positive feelings on which trust and attachment are built.

As infants develop basic trust and secure attachment, they begin to venture away from the caregiver, exploring objects and other people. This exploration is a first sign of children's developing **autonomy**, or a sense of independence. Autonomy and attachment may seem to be opposites, but they are actually closely related. The child who has formed a secure attachment to a caregiver can explore the environment without fear. Such a child knows that the caregiver will be there when needed, and so the caregiver serves as a "secure base" from which to venture forth (Ainsworth, 1977).

Unfortunately, not all children form secure attachments. Perhaps the primary caregiver is under too much stress to be responsive to the child's needs, or perhaps the caregiver is absent almost all of the time. Whatever the reason, children who are insecurely attached to their mothers are less likely to explore an unfamiliar environment, even when their mother is present. Moreover, if temporarily left alone in a strange place, they are likely to continue crying even after the mother returns, either pushing her away angrily or ignoring her altogether. In contrast, a securely attached 12-month-old is apt to rush to the returning mother for a hug and words of reassurance and then happily begin to play (Ainsworth et al., 1978).

Autonomy
Sense of independence; a desire not to be controlled by others.

The importance of secure attachment early in life is evident for many years afterward. Studies of children from 1 through 6 years of age show that those who form a secure attachment to their mothers by the age of 12 months later tend to be more at ease with other children, more interested in exploring new toys, and more enthusiastic and persistent when presented with new tasks (Harris & Liebert, 1991). Some researchers believe that a secure attachment instills in children a positive *inner working model* of the self and others (Bowlby, 1969, 1982; Belsky et al., 1996). These children come to see themselves as basically lovable and competent, and others as trustable and supportive (Thompson & Ganzel, 1994). This inner working model then positively colors the children's responses toward much that they encounter as they grow older.

At about 2 years of age children begin to assert their growing independence, becoming very negative when interfered with by parents. They refuse everything: getting dressed ("No!"), going to sleep ("No!"), using the potty ("No!"). The usual outcome is that the parents begin to discipline the child. Children are told they must eat and go to bed at a particular time, they must not pull the cat's tail or kick their sister, and they must respect other people's rights. The conflict between the parents' need for peace and order and the child's desire for autonomy often creates tension. But it is an essential first step in **socialization,** the process by which children learn the behaviors and attitudes appropriate to their family and their culture.

Erik Erikson saw two possible outcomes of this early conflict: *autonomy versus shame and doubt.* If a toddler fails to acquire a sense of independence and separateness from others, self-doubt may take root. The child may begin to question his or her ability to act effectively in the world. If parents and other adults belittle a toddler's efforts, the child may begin to feel ashamed. The need for both autonomy and socialization can be met if parents allow the child a reasonable amount of independence, while still insisting that the child follow certain social rules.

Parent–Child Relationships in Childhood

As children enter the pre-school years, their newfound autonomy encourages them to take initiative in trying out new tasks. But these initiatives may not always please their parents. This is why Erik Erikson saw the stage between ages 3 and 6 as one of growing initiative surrounded by a potential for guilt (*initiative versus guilt*). Children this age become increasingly involved in independent efforts to accomplish goals—making plans, undertaking projects, and mastering new skills, from bike riding, to table setting, to drawing, painting, and writing simple words. Parents' support and encouragement of these initiatives leads to a sense of joy in taking on new tasks. But

According to Erik Erikson, children between the ages of 3 and 6 take the initiative to try to master new skills.

Socialization
Process by which children learn the behaviors and attitudes appropriate to their family and culture.

if children are repeatedly criticized and scolded for things they do wrong, they may develop strong feelings of unworthiness, resentment, and guilt. According to Erikson, avoiding these negative feelings is the major challenge of this stage.

How parents interact with their children and the demands they place on them appears to have an important influence on children's outlooks and behavior. Diana Baumrind (1972), who has done extensive research on parenting styles, found that *authoritarian* parents, who control their children's behavior rigidly and insist on unquestioning obedience, are likely to produce children who are withdrawn and distrustful. But *permissive* parenting can also have negative effects: When parents exert too little control, their children tend to be overly dependent and lacking in self-control. The most successful parenting style is what Baumrind calls *authoritative*. Authoritative parents provide firm structure and guidance without being overly controlling. They listen to their children's opinions and give explanations for their decisions, but it is clear that they are in charge. Parents who use this approach are most likely to have children who are self-reliant and responsible.

Of course, a parent–child relationship is not determined solely by the parent: Children also affect it. Parents do not act the same way toward every child in the family (even though they may say they try to), because each child is a different individual. A thoughtful, responsible child is more likely to encourage authoritative parenting, whereas an impulsive child who is difficult to reason with is more likely to elicit an authoritarian style. For instance, children with conduct disorders have been found to elicit controlling responses from a great many adults, even from those who do not behave toward their own children in a controlling way (O'Leary, 1995). Thus children influence their caregivers at the same time that the caregivers are influencing them (see *Highlights*).

Researchers have identified several characteristics that can make child abuse more likely. Children who in some way are difficult to care for have an increased risk of being abused. Included in this group are children who are premature, colicky, physically and behaviorally handicapped, or temperamentally irritable or overactive. Such children are even more likely to be abused if the mother is depressed or if a stepparent lives in the home (Carlson, 1994; Daly & Wilson, 1996; Knutson, 1995). This is not to say that children are responsible for their own mistreatment. Child abuse is solely the responsibility of the adults involved. But certain circumstances seem to make it more difficult for parents to care appropriately for their children. These include being young, unmarried (or in a conflict-ridden marriage), relatively less educated, financially troubled, living in overcrowded conditions, having health problems (physical or mental), and having a history of being abused as a child themselves (Carlson, 1994). Child abuse, in other words, is partly the product of a stressful environment, which is why programs aimed at preventing it often focus on offering various forms of support for high-risk parents. Educating these parents about more effective approaches to child rearing is another widely used tactic (Fagot, 1994).

Relationships with Other Children   At a very early age infants begin to show an interest in other children, but the social skills required to play with these children develop only gradually (Pellegrini & Galda, 1994). Children first play alone, called *solitary play*. Then, between ages 1½ and 2, they begin to engage in *parallel play*—that is, they play side by side doing the same things, but not interacting much with each other. Around the age of 2 imitation becomes a game: One child throws a toy into the air, the other does the same, and then they both giggle. At around age 2½ children begin to use language to communicate with their playmates, and their play becomes increasingly imaginative. By age 3 or 3½ they are engaging in *cooperative play*, including games that involve group imagination, such as playing "house" (Eckerman, Davis, & Didow, 1989).

HIGHLIGHTS

Shaping Personality: What Families Don't Share May Matter Most

How much of your personality can be attributed to your genes and how much to your early childhood environment? Although there is no exact answer to this question, studies suggest that these factors are approximately equal in importance (Plomin & Rende, 1991; Rutter, 1997). Significantly, researchers have found that identical twins raised in the same home are no more alike in personality than identical twins separated during infancy and reared in different homes (Bouchard, Lykken, McGue, Segal, & Tellegren, 1990; Saudino, 1998). This finding makes it appear that the home environment has little or no effect on personality.

This is the position taken in a controversial book titled *The Nurture Assumption*, by Judith Rich Harris (1998). Harris contends that parents have little influence on their children's personalities (except for their genetic contribution). Instead she argues that peers, not parents, are the key factor in shaping adult personality. Adopting an evolutionary perspective, Harris argues that children logically are more likely to imitate the behaviors of their peers because peers are their future collaborators and are responsible for creating the culture in which they ultimately will live. To support her position, she cites studies showing that the best predictor of an adolescent becoming a smoker is whether her peers smoke, not the smoking habits of her parents. She also draws support from research that shows that the children of immigrants adopt the language and culture of their peers, not that of their parents.

Many psychologists, however, are skeptical of Harris's oversimplified and extreme position that parents don't matter (Parke & O'Neil, 1999; Williams, 1999). They point to studies that have shown that parents can

---

Studies have shown that the non-shared environment has the power to shape personalities.

---

affect a child's personality even in the face of strong peer influence by monitoring (Ary, Duncan, Duncan, & Hops, 1999) and by buffering the negative effects of peers (Voydanoff & Donnelly, 1999). While most developmental psychologists believe that peer influence is also important, they consider it just one type of a much broader class of environmental factors called the *nonshared environment* (Plomin, 1999). The nonshared environment refers to the unique aspects of the environment that are experienced differently by siblings even though they are raised in the same family with the same parents. Studies have shown that the non-shared environment has the power to shape personalities.

To illustrate the concept of a non-shared environment, consider a child who was an "easy" baby and is now a "good girl," who is not very pretty, and who has a younger brother who is always getting into trouble. The girl gets along well with her mother, who relies on her help and cooperation, but her father wishes he had a prettier daughter. Compare this child's environment to that of her brother, who was a "difficult" baby (and has been typecast as the "bad one" ever since) but who gets along well with his father because the father admires the boy's energy, athletic talent, and good looks. These children are growing up in the same home, with the same parents, but their human relationships and day-to-day experiences are very different.

"The message is not that family experiences are unimportant," concludes one review. But the crucial environmental influences that shape personality development are non-shared—"specific to each child, rather than general to an entire family" (Plomin & Rende, 1991, p. 180).

Among the first peers that children encounter are their siblings. The quality of sibling relationships can have a major impact, especially on how children learn to relate to other peers. Sibling relations are usually most compatible when other relationships within the family are good, including good relationships between husband and wife and between parents and children (Brody, 1995). Siblings also influence one another indirectly, simply by their order of birth. In general firstborn children tend to be more anxious and fearful of physical injury, but also more intellectually able and more achievement-oriented than their later-born siblings. Among boys, firstborns also tend to be more creative. These differences probably have to do with the extra attention (both negative and positive) that parents tend to give their firstborn children (Eisenman, 1994).

Peer influences outside the family increase greatly when children start school. Now they are under a great deal of pressure to be part of a **peer group** of friends. In peer groups children learn many valuable things, such as how to engage in cooperative activities aimed at collective goals and how to negotiate the social roles of leader and follower (Rubin et al., 1994). Inability to get along well with classmates has long-lasting consequences. Children whose classmates actively dislike them are more likely to drop out of school, to engage in criminal behavior, and to become mentally ill. This is particularly true of children who are disliked because they are aggressive (J. G. Parker & Asher, 1987).

As children get older, they develop a deeper understanding of the meaning of friendship (Rubin et al., 1994). For preschoolers a friend simply is "someone I play with," but around age 7 children begin to realize that friends "do things" for one another. At this still egocentric age, however, friends are defined largely as people who "do things for *me.*" Later, at about age 9, children come to understand that friendship is a two-way street and that, while friends do things for us, we are also expected to do things for them. By late childhood or early adolescence children see friendship as a stable and continuing social relationship, requiring mutual support, trust, and confidence (Selman, 1981).

Successfully making friends is one of the tasks that Erik Erikson saw as centrally important to children between the ages of 7 and 11, the stage of *industry versus inferiority.* At this age children must master many increasingly difficult skills, social interaction with peers being only one of them. Others have to do with mastering academic skills at school, meeting growing responsibilities placed on them at home, and learning to do various tasks that they will need as independent adults. If children become stifled in their efforts to prepare themselves for the adult world, they may conclude that they are inadequate or inferior and lose faith in their power to become self-sufficient. In Erikson's view, those whose industry is rewarded by a successful outcome to this challenge develop a sense of competence and self-assurance.

Sex-Role Development

By about age 3 both boys and girls have developed a **gender identity**—that is, a little girl knows that she is a girl, and a little boy knows that he is a boy. At this point, however, children have little understanding of what it means to be a girl or a boy. A 3-year-old boy might think that he can grow up to be a mommy or that if you put a dress on him and a bow in his hair, he will turn into a girl. By the age of 4 or 5 most children know that gender depends on what kind of genitals a person has (Bem, 1989). They have acquired **gender constancy,** the realization that gender cannot be changed.

At quite a young age children also start to acquire **gender-role awareness,** a knowledge of what behaviors are expected of males and of females in their society (Lewin, 1996). As a result they develop **gender stereotypes,** or oversimplified beliefs about what the "typical" male and female are like (Sinnott, 1994). Girls are supposed to be clean, neat, and careful, whereas boys are supposed to like rough, noisy, physical play. Women are kind, caring, and emotional, whereas men are strong, dominant, and aggressive. Interestingly, there is much consistency across cultures regarding the gender stereotypes that children develop (Williams & Best, 1990). This is partly because gender roles tend to be similar in many different cultures, and gender stereotypes tend to "match" the tasks thought appropriate for the sexes.

At the same time that children acquire gender-role awareness and gender stereotypes, they also develop their own **sex-typed behavior:** Girls play with dolls, whereas boys play with trucks; girls put on pretty clothes and fuss with their hair, whereas boys run around and wrestle with one another. Although the behavioral differences between boys and girls are minimal in infancy, quite major differences tend to develop as children grow older (Prior et al., 1993).

By school age boys and girls tend to play by the rules of sex-typed behavior. Typically girls play nonaggressive games like hopscotch in pairs or small groups, while boys prefer more active group games.

Peer group
A network of same-aged friends and acquaintances who give one another emotional and social support.

Gender identity
A little girl's knowledge that she is a girl, and a little boy's knowledge that he is a boy.

Gender constancy
The realization by a child that gender cannot be changed.

Gender-role awareness
Knowledge of what behavior is appropriate for each gender.

Gender stereotypes
General beliefs about characteristics that men and women are presumed to have.

Sex-typed behavior
Socially prescribed ways of behaving that differ for boys and girls.

Boys become more active and aggressive and tend to play in larger groups. Girls talk more, shove less, and tend to interact in pairs. Of course, there are some active, aggressive girls and some quiet, polite boys, but they are not in the majority. The source of such sex-typed behavior is a matter of considerable debate.

Because gender-related differences in styles of interaction appear very early in development (even before the age of 3), Eleanor Maccoby, a specialist in this area of research, believes that they are at least partly biological in origin, perhaps being influenced to some extent by prenatal sex hormones (Collaer & Hines, 1995). But Maccoby thinks that biologically based differences are small at first and later become exaggerated because of the different kinds of socialization experienced by boys and girls when they play with members of their own sex. Undoubtedly, popular culture—especially as portrayed on television—also influences the norms of gender-appropriate behavior that develop in children's peer groups. And parents, too, can sometimes add input, especially during critical transitions in the child's life when parents feel it is important to behave in more sex-stereotyped ways (Fagot, 1994). The end result is substantial sex-typed behavior by middle childhood. While research on this topic continues, there is growing consensus that biology and experience probably both contribute to gender differences in behavior (Collaer & Hines, 1995).

Television and Children   American children spend more time watching television than they do engaging in any other activity besides sleeping (Huston, Watkins, & Kunkel, 1989). On average, children between 2 and 5 years of age watch about 4 hours of television each day (Lande, 1993). What are they getting and giving up by watching so much television?

One concern regards the violence that pervades much television entertainment (Carter, 1996). Children who watch 2 hours of television daily (well below our national average) will see about 8,000 murders and 100,000 other acts of violence by the time they leave elementary school (American Psychological Association, 1992). Does witnessing this violence make children more aggressive, and if so, does television violence account, at least in part, for the rapid rise in violent crime among adolescents (Lande, 1993)? Children themselves think the answers may be yes. In one recent survey most young people between the ages of 10 and 16 felt that television violence was a factor in aggressive acts among their peers (Puig, 1995). Some data on copycat crimes of violence seem to bear this out (W. Wilson & Hunter, 1983), but scientific answers concerning the effects of television violence are still uncertain, because the causal links aren't clear. Although there is convincing evidence that children who frequently watch television violence *are* more aggressive than other children (Eron, 1982; Singer & Singer, 1983), does this simply mean that children who are prone to aggression are also drawn to violent shows?

Perhaps the best evidence that supports that watching television violence can encourage violent behavior comes from a study that compared rates of violence in three similar towns, one of which did not have television until 1973 (Will, 1993). Two years after television was introduced into that remote community, the rate of physical aggression soared by 45 percent for both boys and girls, while it did not change in the two other towns that already had television.

The most convincing theoretical argument that violent behavior is linked to television watching is based on social learning theory, which we discussed in Chapter 5. Social learning theory leads us to expect that children who see fictional characters on television being rewarded for their violent behaviors will not only learn those behaviors but will also be more likely to perform them when given the opportunity. Children need not be personally rewarded for a behavior in order to be encouraged to imitate it. They need only see an admired model being so rewarded.

Studies confirm that watching television is associated with aggressive behavior in children, but only if the content of the shows is violent. There is no evidence linking television watching to lower IQ scores.

Another concern about the effects of television viewing on children involves the extent to which it affects their cognitive development, IQs, and academic achievement. A study of television viewing by preschoolers found no correlation between their IQ scores and how much television they watched (Plomin et al., 1990). Also, despite the general increase in television viewing over the past few decades, IQ scores haven't declined. Rather, they have increased—all over the world (Flynn, 1987).

There is evidence that children can learn worthwhile things from watching television. In one study 12- to 18-month-old babies learned new words by hearing them used on a television show, making television a kind of "talking picture book" for them (Lemish & Rice, 1986). In another study children who watched the PBS program *Mr. Rogers* exhibited increased prosocial behavior (Tower et al., 1979). In addition, the content of some children's shows has been shown to promote good health and nutrition (Calvert & Cocking, 1992).

Television is a significant influence on children's development. It presents both "good" and "bad" models for them to copy, and it provides vast amounts of information. On the downside, children who watch a lot of television spend less time doing other productive and useful things, and they may learn undesirable behaviors, including acts of violence.

REVIEW QUESTIONS

1. Early motor development in children (acquiring and refining the abilities to grasp, crawl, walk, and so forth) can best be explained

   a. entirely by biological maturation of the muscles and nervous system.

   b. by a combination of factors both within and outside the child.

2. Match each of Piaget's stages of cognitive development with the appropriate description(s).

   ____ sensory-motor stage
   ____ preoperational stage
   ____ concrete operations
   ____ formal operations

   a. the ability to use representational thought expands
   b. thinking is still egocentric in many ways
   c. the ability to think abstractly emerges
   d. begins with applying reflex actions
   e. the ability to consider two dimensions at once emerges
   f. the ability to classify things in complex ways emerges
   g. awareness of object permanence emerges

3. Number the following language developments in the order in which they emerge.

   ____ a. holophrases
   ____ b. babbling
   ____ c. overregularization of verbs
   ____ d. two- and three-word sentences

4. Match each phase of childhood with its major challenge, according to Erik Erikson's theory.

   ____ infancy
   ____ toddlerhood
   ____ preschool years
   ____ elementary school years

   a. industry versus inferiority
   b. trust versus mistrust
   c. autonomy versus shame and doubt
   d. initiative versus guilt

Answers: 1. b. **2.** sensory-motor stage: d and g; preoperational stage: a and b; concrete operations: e and f; formal operations: c. **3.** b, a, d, c. **4.** infancy: b; toddlerhood: c; preschool years: d; elementary school years: a.

Adolescence

Is adolescence characterized only by physical changes?

Adolescence is the period of life between roughly age 10 and 20, when a person is transformed from a child into an adult. This involves not just the physical changes of a body maturing but many cognitive and social–emotional changes as well.

Physical Changes

What are the consequences of going through puberty early or late?

Adolescence is ushered in by a series of dramatic physical milestones. The most obvious is the growth spurt, a rapid increase in height and weight that begins, on average, at about age 10½ in girls and 12½ in boys and reaches its peak at age 12 in girls and 14 in boys (see Figure 9–2). The typical adolescent attains his or her adult height about 6 years after the start of the growth spurt (Tanner, 1978).

The growth spurt begins with a lengthening of the hands, feet, arms, and legs, which produces the awkward, gangly look of young adolescents. This stage is followed by the growth of the torso, which brings the body back into proportion. In boys the final stage of growth results in a broadening of the chest and shoulders and the development of heavier muscles. For girls, changes in body shape occur as the hips widen and fat is deposited on the breasts, hips, buttocks, and thighs. All these changes result from an increase in hormones, which, as we saw in Chapter 2, are chemicals released by the endocrine system (Dyk, 1993).

In both sexes changes also occur in the face. The chin and nose become more prominent, and the lips get fuller. Increases in the size of oil glands in the skin can contribute to acne; sweat glands produce a more odorous secretion. The heart, lungs, and digestive system all expand.

Sexual Development   The visible signs of **puberty**—the onset of sexual maturation—occur in a different sequence for boys and girls. In boys the initial sign is growth of the testes, which starts on average at around 11½, about a year before the beginning of the growth spurt in height. Along with the growth spurt comes enlargement of the penis. Development of pubic hair takes a little longer, and development of facial hair longer still. Deepening of the voice is one of the last noticeable changes of male maturation.

In females the beginning of the growth spurt is typically the first sign of approaching puberty. Shortly thereafter the breasts begin to develop; some pubic hair appears at around the same time. **Menarche**, the first menstrual period, occurs about a year or so later—between 12½ and 13 for the average American girl (Powers, Hauser, & Kilner, 1989). Health and nutrition affect the timing of menarche, with fatter girls maturing earlier than thinner ones.

The onset of menstruation does not necessarily mean that a girl is biologically capable of becoming a mother, for it is uncommon (though not unheard of) for a girl to become pregnant during her first few menstrual cycles. Female fertility increases gradually during the first year after menarche. The same is true of male fertility. Boys achieve their first ejaculation at an average age of 13½, often during sleep. But first ejaculations contain relatively few sperm (Tanner, 1978). Nevertheless, adolescents are capable of producing babies long before they are mature enough to take care of them.

Psychologists used to believe that the beginnings of sexual attraction and desire in young people coincided with the physical changes of puberty, but recent research may be changing this view. Hundreds of case histories that researchers

Puberty
The onset of sexual maturation, with accompanying physical development.

Menarche
First menstrual period.

have collected tend to put the first stirrings of sexual interest in the fourth and fifth grade. The cause may be increases in an adrenal sex hormone that begin at age 6 and reach a critical level around age 10 (McClintock & Herdt, 1997). Other pubertal hormones may also begin their rise much earlier than we formerly knew (Marano, 1997). If so, the onset of the obvious physical changes that we now call puberty may actually be more of an ending to a process than they are a start.

Early and Late Developers   Individuals differ greatly in the age at which they go through the changes of puberty. Some 12-year-old girls and 14-year-old boys still look like children, while others their age already look like young women and men. Among boys, early maturing has psychological advantages. Boys who mature earlier do better in sports and in social activities and receive greater respect from their peers (Conger & Petersen, 1991). At least one study (Peskin, 1967), however, found that late-maturing boys develop a stronger sense of identity during early adulthood, perhaps because they do not feel pressured to "grow up" too quickly. For girls, early maturation appears to be a mixed blessing. A girl who matures early may be admired by other girls but is likely to be subjected to embarrassing treatment as a sex object by boys (Clausen, 1975).

Adolescent Sexual Activity   The achievement of the capacity to reproduce is probably the single most important development in adolescence. But sexuality is a confusing issue for adolescents in our society. Fifty years ago young people were expected to postpone expressing their sexual needs until they were responsible, married adults. Since then, major changes have occurred in sexual customs. Approximately two-thirds of all boys and half of all girls have had intercourse by the time they are 17 (Alan Guttmacher Institute, 1990).

There are significant differences between the ways boys and girls tend to view their early sexual behavior (T. Lewin, 1994a). Significantly fewer high school girls than boys report feeling good about their sexual experiences (46 percent versus 65 percent). Similarly, more girls than boys say they should have waited until they were older before having sex (65 percent compared to 48 percent).

Cognitive Changes

Are there fallacies to adolescent thinking as well as advances in thought?

Just as bodies mature during adolescence, so do patterns of thought. Piaget (1969) saw the cognitive advances of adolescence generally as an increased ability to reason abstractly, called formal operational thought. Adolescents can understand and manipulate abstract concepts, speculate about alternative possibilities, and reason in hypothetical terms. This allows them to debate such problematic issues as abortion, sexual behavior, and AIDS. Of course, not all adolescents reach the stage of formal operations, and even among those who do, many fail to apply formal operational thinking to the everyday problems they face (H. Gardner, 1982). Younger adolescents especially are unlikely to be objective about matters concerning themselves and have not yet achieved a deep understanding of the difficulties involved in moral judgments.

Moreover, in those who do achieve formal operational thinking, this advance has its hazards. Among them are overconfidence in their new mental abilities and a tendency to place too much importance on their own thoughts. Some adolescents also fail to realize that everyone does not share their mental processes and that other people may hold different views (Harris & Liebert, 1991).

Adolescent self-centeredness may account for two types of fallacies of thought often found in this age group (Elkind, 1968, 1969). The first is the *imaginary audience*—the tendency of teenagers to feel that they are constantly being observed and judged by others. This feeling of being perpetually "on stage" may be the source of much self-consciousness, concern about personal appearance, and showing off in adolescence.

The other fallacy of adolescent thinking is the *personal fable*—adolescents' unrealistic sense of their own uniqueness. For instance, a teenager might feel that others can't possibly understand the love that he or she feels toward a boyfriend or girlfriend because that love is so unique and special. This view is related to the feeling of invulnerability we mentioned earlier. Many teenagers believe that they are so different from other people that they won't be touched by the negative things that happen to others. This feeling of invulnerability explains much of the reckless risk taking among people in this age group (Arnett, 1991). Of course, cultures vary in the degree to which they allow reckless behavior in teenagers. Those cultures that strongly inhibit it may create a safer, more orderly society, but they may also stifle some of the liveliness and spontaneity of adolescence (Arnett, 1995).

Personality and Social Development

What important tasks do adolescents face in their personal and social lives?

Adolescents are eager to establish independence from their parents, but at the same time they fear the responsibilities of adulthood. They have many important tasks ahead of them and many important decisions to make. Particularly in a technologically advanced society like ours, this period of development is bound to involve some stress.

How "Stormy and Stressful" Is Adolescence?
Early this century many people saw adolescence as a time of great instability and strong emotions. For example, G. Stanley Hall (1904), one of the first developmental psychologists, portrayed adolescence as a period of "storm and stress" fraught with suffering, passion, and rebellion against adult authority. Recent research, however, suggests that the "storm and stress" view greatly exaggerates the experiences of most teenagers. True, adolescence is accompanied by some stress, related to school, family, and peers, and this stress can at times be difficult to manage (Crystal et al., 1994). But the great majority of adolescents do not describe their lives as filled with turmoil and chaos (J. Eccles et al., 1993).

Nonetheless, between 15 and 30 percent of adolescents drop out of high school, many regularly abuse drugs, and some are repeatedly in trouble with the law (teenagers have the highest arrest record of any age group) (Office of Educational Research and Improvement, 1988). Those whose prior development has been stressful are more likely to experience a stressful adolescence. So are teenagers who suffer serious emotional problems or who live in chaotic environments. Still, there are individual differences in the ability to cope with even the worst conditions. Some young people are particularly *resilient* and are able to overcome great odds, partly because of a strong belief in their own ability to make things better (Werner, 1995). Thus the degree of struggle that any given adolescent faces in growing up is due to an interaction of developmental challenges and factors that promote resilience (Compas, Hinden, & Gerhardt, 1995).

Forming an Identity
To make the transition from dependence on parents to dependence on oneself, the adolescent must develop a stable sense of self. This process is called **identity formation,** a term derived from Erik Erikson's

Identity formation
Erikson's term for the development of a stable sense of self necessary to make the transition from dependence on others to dependence on oneself.

"Is everything all right, Jeffrey? You never call me 'dude' anymore."

Source: Leo Cullum © 1997 from The New Yorker collection.

theory, which sees the major challenge of this stage of life as *identity versus role confusion* (Erikson, 1968). The overwhelming question for the young person becomes "Who am I?" In Erikson's view the answer comes by integrating a number of different roles—talented math student, athlete, artist, political liberal, aspiring architect—into a coherent whole that seems to comfortably "fit." Failure to form this coherent sense of identity leads to confusion about roles.

James Marcia (1980) believes that finding an identity requires a period of intense self-exploration called an **identity crisis.** He sees four possible outcomes regarding identity formation. One is *identity achievement.* Adolescents who have reached this status have passed through the identity crisis and succeeded in making personal choices about their beliefs and goals. In contrast are adolescents who experience *identity foreclosure:* They have prematurely settled on an identity that others provided for them. Other adolescents are in *moratorium* regarding their identity. They are in the process of actively exploring various role options, but they have not yet committed to any of them. Finally, there are teens who are experiencing *identity diffusion.* They avoid considering role options in any conscious way. Many are dissatisfied with this condition but are unable to start a search to "find themselves." Some resort to escapist activities such as drug or alcohol abuse (G. R. Adams & Gullota, 1983). Of course, any given adolescent's identity status can change over time as the person matures or even regresses. Identity development may also tend to vary depending on such factors as social class or ethnic background. For instance, teens from poor families are often less likely to experience a period of identity moratorium, probably because financial constraints make it harder for them to explore many different role options (Holmbeck, 1994).

Relationships with Peers

For most adolescents the peer group provides a network of social and emotional support that helps them move toward greater independence from adults and search for a personal identity. By choosing to associate with a particular group of friends, adolescents define themselves and create their own social style (P. R. Newman, 1982). Young teenagers feel an almost desperate need for their friends to approve of their choices, views, and behavior. The result is often a rigid conformity to peer-group values that peaks around the ninth grade (Perry, 1990).

The nature of peer relationships changes during the adolescent years. Friendship groups in early adolescence tend to be small unisex groups, called **cliques,** of three to nine members. Especially among girls, these unisex friendships increasingly deepen and become more mutually self-disclosing as the teens develop the cognitive abilities to better understand themselves and one another (Holmbeck, 1994). Then, in mid-adolescence, unisex cliques generally break down and are replaced by mixed-sex groups. These in turn are usually replaced by groups consisting of couples. At first adolescents tend to have short-term heterosexual relationships within the group that fulfill short-term needs without exacting the commitment of "going steady" (Sorensen, 1973). Such relationships do not demand love and can dissolve

Identity crisis
Period of intense self-examination and decision making; part of the process of identity formation.

Cliques
Groups of adolescents with similar interests and strong mutual attachment.

Peer groups help adolescents to develop identities apart from family influences. Cliques are small groups of friends that offer closeness but can also exert significant control over adolescents' lives.

overnight. But between the ages of 16 and 19 most adolescents settle into more stable dating patterns.

Relationships with Parents   While they are still searching for their own identity, striving toward independence, and learning to think through the long-term consequences of their actions, adolescents require guidance and structure from adults, especially from their parents. In their struggle for independence, adolescents question everything and test every rule. Unlike young children who believe that their parents know everything and are all-powerful and good, adolescents are all too aware of their parents' shortcomings. It takes many years for adolescents to see their mothers and fathers as real people with their own needs and strengths as well as weaknesses (Smollar & Youniss, 1989). In fact, the renewed perception of strengths may come as a bit of a shock. Many young adults find themselves surprised that their parents have gotten so much smarter in the past 7 or 8 years.

The low point of parent–child relationships generally occurs in early adolescence, when the physical changes of puberty are occurring. Then the warmth of the parent–child relationship ebbs, and conflict rises. Warm and caring relationships with adults outside the home, such as those at school or at a supervised community center, are valuable to adolescents during this period (Eccles et al., 1993). Conflicts with parents, however, tend to be over minor issues and are usually not intense (Holmbeck, 1994). In only a small minority of families does the relationship between parents and children show a marked deterioration in adolescence (Paikoff & Brooks-Gunn, 1991).

Some Problems of Adolescence

What are some major problems among adolescents in our society?

Adolescence is a time of experimentation, whether it be with sex, drugs, hair color, or various kinds of rule breaking. It is also a time when certain kinds of developmental problems are apt to arise, especially problems that have to do with self-perceptions, feelings about the self, and negative emotions in general.

Declines in Self-esteem   Teenagers are acutely aware of the changes taking place in their bodies. Many become anxious about whether they are the "right" shape or size and obsessively compare themselves with the models and actors they see on television and in magazines. Because few adolescents can match these ideals, it is not surprising that when young adolescents are asked what they most dislike about themselves, physical appearance is mentioned more often than anything else (Conger & Petersen, 1991). Satisfaction with one's appearance tends to be tied to satisfaction with oneself. Adolescents who are least satisfied with their physical appearance have the lowest self-esteem (G. R. Adams & Gullota, 1983; Altabe & Thompson, 1994). Among girls, however, there are major racial differences in the extent to which American adolescents are dissatisfied with their bodies and suffer a consequent drop in self-esteem. In general, white girls tend to be more critical of their bodies than are African-American girls (Ingrassia, 1995; Nichter, 1995).

Of course, negative body image is not the only thing that can cause self-esteem to drop in adolescence. Another is a negative view of one's school performance. In one study that found a sharp drop in self-esteem among girls during adolescence, the girls said that they felt this way largely because they were ignored by teachers, believed they were not being given an equal chance at intellectual challenges, and found it hard to compete in the classroom with their more assertive male classmates. Boys' self-esteem dropped, too, during adolescence, but not nearly as much. The result was that by mid-adolescence the average boy had a much better opinion of himself than the average girl had of herself. For example, while 46 percent of high school boys reported being "happy the way I am," only 29 percent of high school girls did (Daley, 1991).

The reasons for a significant decline in female self-esteem during adolescence are unclear (J. Block & Robbins, 1993). In one recent longitudinal study of 25,000 adolescents conducted by the U.S. Department of Education, more girls than boys reported feeling that teachers are interested in them, and by the tenth grade nearly three-quarters of girls said that teachers listened to what they had to say (Sommers, 1994). Apparently school concerns may be less important to the drop in self-esteem among young women than earlier research suggested. More studies are needed to sort out the reasons for these differences in survey results.

Depression and Suicide   The rate of suicide among adolescents has increased more than 600 percent since 1950. Suicide is now the third leading cause of death among adolescents, (Centers for Disease Control and Prevention, 1999; Hoyert, Kochanek, & Murphy, 1999). According to one survey, 27 percent of high school students had thought seriously about suicide. A smaller proportion (16 percent) had made a specific plan for killing themselves, and a still smaller percentage (8 percent) had actually attempted suicide. One-quarter of the attempts were serious enough to require medical attention. Although successful suicide is more common in males than in females, more females attempt suicide (Centers for Disease Control, 1991a). There is also a disturbing trend in our society toward suicide at younger ages. Between 1980 and 1992 the suicide rate among adolescents ages 10 to 14 rose by 120 percent and was especially high among black males in this age group (an increase of 300 percent) (Leary, 1995). A growing culture of youth violence and an increased accessibility of guns may contribute to these statistics.

Research shows that suicidal behavior in adolescents (including thinking about suicide as well as actually attempting it) is often linked to other psychological problems, such as depression, drug abuse, and disruptive behaviors (Andrews & Lewinson, 1992). One study of more than 1,700 adolescents revealed that a set of related factors put an adolescent at higher-than-average risk for attempting suicide. Among these are being female, thinking about suicide, having a mental disorder (such as depression), and having a poorly educated father who is absent from the home.

But it is hard to tell which adolescents at higher-than-average risk will actually attempt suicide. For example, depression in and of itself rarely leads to suicide: Although 3 percent of adolescents suffer severe depression at any one time, the annual suicide rate among adolescents is only 0.01 percent (Connelly et al., 1993). Apparently a combination of depression and other risk factors makes suicide more likely, but exactly which factors are most important and what kinds of intervention might reduce adolescent suicides are still unclear.

Youth Violence   In April 1999 two boys, one 17 and the other 18, opened fire on their classmates at Columbine High School in Littleton, Colorado. Armed with two sawed-off shotguns, a semi-automatic rifle, and a semi-automatic pistol, they killed 13 fellow students and a teacher and wounded 23 others before killing themselves. Fortunately, 30 bombs filled with shrapnel and planted throughout the school were found and defused before they exploded. One of the shooters arrived at school that day wearing a favorite shirt that read "SERIAL KILLER."

In the days after the shootings, people throughout the country expressed their shock and outrage and offered different theories as to the reasons for the tragedy. But well before these shootings took place, surveys had repeatedly shown that violence and crime are the issues of greatest concern to most Americans. And, despite an overall decrease in criminal activities in the 1990s, juvenile crime continues to rise (Waldman, 1996) (see *Highlights*).

People gather outside Columbine High School in Littleton, Colorado, after two students opened fire on their classmates in April 1999. Youth violence has become an emotionally charged issue in the United States.

REVIEW QUESTIONS

1. The most obvious indication that adolescence is starting is a rapid increase in height and weight, known as the ____ ____. This is combined with a series of physical changes leading to sexual maturation, the onset of which is called ____.

2. Which of the following are common fallacies of adolescent thinking?

   a. role confusion

   b. the appearance/reality problem

   c. the personal fable

   d. the imaginary audience

3. Match each status regarding identity formation with the appropriate definition.

   ___ identity achievement   a. prematurely settling on an identity that others provide

   ___ identity foreclosure   b. success in making personal choices about beliefs and goals

   ___ identity moratorium   c. avoiding consideration of role options

   ___ identity diffusion   d. exploring role options but not yet committing to any

4. Indicate whether the following statements are true (T) or false (F).

   a. The most difficult time in the relationship between a teenager and parents is usually in late adolescence, when the young person is anxious to leave the family "nest." ____

   b. The suicide rate among American adolescents has increased more than 600 percent since 1950. ____

Answers: 1. growth spurt; puberty. 2. c and d. 3. identity achievement: b; identity foreclosure: a; identity moratorium: d; identity diffusion: c. 4. a. F; b. T.

Kids Who Kill

Redlands, California . . . Blackville, South Carolina . . . Lynnville, Tennessee . . . Moses Lake, Washington . . . Bethel, Alaska . . . Pearl, Mississippi . . . West Paducah, Kentucky . . . Stamps, Arkansas . . . Jonesboro, Arkansas . . . Springfield, Oregon . . . Littleton, Colorado . . .

It is hard to imagine what such far-flung communities have in common, but they share at least one feature: They were the sites of killings by teenagers with guns between October 1995 and April 1999. When the gunfire ended, more than 40 people were dead, and many more were wounded.

Why did it happen? What causes boys as young as 11 to kill other people and, equally often, to kill themselves? Were they just "bad kids" from the start, or was their environment to blame? And if it was their environment, then why do other children *not* become violent when exposed to the same events? Although it is tempting to look for simple answers to these questions, in reality the causes of violence are quite complex. Our genes may affect the likelihood of violence. Our brain chemistry certainly does. And so does our environment. All of these factors influence one another in complex ways to lead to explosive violence.

All the killers indicated that they felt isolated from their family and from girls, outcast and abandoned by those who should have loved them.

Biology certainly plays a role. There may be something as simple as a "murderer gene," but more likely the genetic component, if any, is related to a lack of compassion or an inability to control strong emotions. Apart from genetics, the constant in-terplay between the brain and the environment actually "rewires" the brain, sometimes with disastrous effects (Niehoff, 1999). For example, Bruce Perry and his colleagues at Baylor College of Medicine point out that repeated stress in the first 3 years of life gives rise to a steady flow of "stress chemicals" that can have two consequences. First, the normal "fight or flight" response may go on "hair-trigger alert," which can result in impulsive aggression. Alternatively, the person may become unresponsive and unfeeling, which leads in turn to a lack of empathy or sensitivity to the surrounding world, including an unresponsiveness to punishment (Perry & Pollard, 1998; Schwarz & Perry, 1994). In a similar vein, Daniel Amen has provided evidence that early trauma may cause a part of the brain called the cingulate gyrus to become hyperactive, leading individuals to become obsessed with a single thought (such as violence) at the same time that the prefrontal cortex becomes less able to control impulsive behavior

Young and Middle Adulthood

How predictable is the course of adult development?

Compared with adolescent development, development during adulthood is much less predictable and much more a function of the individual's decisions, circumstances, and even luck. In adulthood, unlike in childhood and adolescence, developmental milestones do not occur at a particular age, although there are certain experiences and changes that take place sooner or later in nearly everyone's life and certain needs that nearly every adult tries to fulfill.

Partnerships, Sex, and Parenting

Is a sense of personal identity needed to form a long-term, intimate relationship?

Nearly all adults form a long-term intimate partnership with another adult at some point in their lives. This can happen at any stage in the life course, but it is especially common in young adulthood. According to Erik Erikson, the major challenge of young adulthood is *intimacy versus isolation*. Failure to form an intimate

(Amen, Stubblefield, Carmicheal, & Thisted, 1996).

But biology is only part of the story. Most psychologists also believe that an important factor in youth killings is the "gun culture" in which most of the youths were raised, along with the relatively easy availability of guns in their environments (Bushman & Baumeister, 1998; Jones & Krisberg, 1994). Most of the killers had extensive experience with guns. One relentlessly begged his parents for guns until they finally gave in. Another had a map over his bed with the slogan "One Nation under My Gun" (Cloud, 1998).

Another environmental factor mentioned by many psychologists is severe neglect or rejection. All the killers indicated that they felt isolated from their family and from girls, outcast and abandoned by those who should have loved them. In turn this led to feelings of powerlessness and injustice. Violence became a way of asserting power and saying "I matter." Luke Woodham, an overweight youth who at age 16 killed three people (including his mother) and injured seven others, said, "[My mother] always told me that I wouldn't amount to anything. She always told me that I was fat and stupid and lazy." Other rationales include "The world has wronged me and I couldn't take it anymore." "I killed because people like me are mistreated every day. My whole life I felt outcasted, alone" (Cloud, 1998, p. 60; Lacayo, 1998, p. 38; Begley, 1999, p. 35). In other cases, a contributing factor appears to be a lack of adult supervision and support, often to the point of having no real attachment to at least one loving and reliable adult (Garbarino, 1999). With parents missing owing to work or divorce or other factors, and with no extended family to fill in the gap, increasing numbers of youths are "left to the mercies of a peer culture shaped by the media, the ultimate in crazed nannies" (Lacayo, 1998, p. 38).

Many youthful killers had also been exposed to a culture of violence reflected in role-playing games such as Doom and Mortal Kombat and music by such artists as Nirvana, Rammstein, and Marilyn Manson (Bok, 1999). The American Psychiatric Association concluded in 1993 that media violence can promote not only desensitization and callousness but also aggression and an appetite for violence.

Are there any warning signs that might alert family and friends to potential violence? Indeed there are. Lack of connection, masking emotions, withdrawal (being habitually secretive and antisocial), silence, rage, increased lying, trouble with friends, hypervigilance, cruelty toward other children and animals—these should all be a cause for concern. This is especially true if they are exhibited by a boy who comes from a family with a history of criminal violence, who has been abused, who belongs to a gang, who abuses drugs or alcohol, who has previously been arrested, or who has experienced problems at school.

partnership with someone else can cause a young adult to feel painfully lonely and incomplete. Erikson believed that a person is not ready to commit to an intimate relationship until he or she has developed a firm sense of personal identity.

Carol Gilligan (1982) doesn't agree that a sense of identity is a prerequisite to forming a loving relationship. She argues that the path to love is different for males and females. Young men, she says, tend to find intimacy and commitment frightening. Before they can take such risks, they must first develop a sense of identity as separate individuals. Young women, on the other hand, fear most the isolation of not having an intimate relationship. Because they are often more concerned about finding love than answering the question of "Who am I?," they need not follow Erikson's rule of "identity before intimacy."

Forming Partnerships   More than 90 percent of Americans eventually get married (Doherty & Jacobson, 1982), but those who marry are waiting longer to do so. In 1970 only 15 percent of men and women ages 25 to 29 had never married; by 1988 the percentage had increased to 36 percent (U.S. Bureau of the Census, 1990). Apparently many Americans are taking more time before they commit to marriage. This postponement of marriage is even greater among African Americans than among whites (Balaguer & Markman, 1994).

Most people marry someone of similar age, race, religion, education, and background (Gagnon, Laumanm, Michael, & Kolata, 1994). This is because people with similar characteristics and backgrounds are more likely to meet, and once they meet they are more likely to discover shared interests and compatibility (Murstein, 1986). Choice of a partner for cohabitation (living together) seems to proceed in much the same way. Often there is a spoken or unspoken assumption among couples that "If things work out, then we'll marry." Interestingly, couples who live together before marriage are generally less satisfied with their marriages and more likely to later divorce as compared with couples who married without first living together (DeMaris & Rao, 1992). One reason may be that many of those who decide to live together first are more tentative about their relationships than those who proceed directly to marriage (Balaguer & Markman, 1994).

While heterosexual marriage is still the statistical norm in our society, other types of partnerships are increasingly meeting the needs of a diverse population. Long-term cohabiting relationships are one example. Contrary to popular belief, the greatest recent increase in cohabiting couples is not among the very young but rather among people over age 35 (Steinhauer, 1997). Among elderly widows and widowers, cohabitation is increasingly seen as a way of enjoying a shared life together without financial complications and tax penalties.

Homosexual couples are another example of intimate partnerships outside the tradition of heterosexual marriage. Studies show that most gays and lesbians seek the same loving, committed, and meaningful partnerships as most heterosexuals do (Peplau & Cochran, 1990). Moreover, successful relationships among them have the same characteristics as successful relationships in the heterosexual world: high levels of mutual trust, respect, and appreciation, shared decision making, good communication, and good skills at resolving conflicts (Birchler & Fals-Stewart, 1994; Edwards, 1995; Kurdek, 1991, 1992) (see *Applying Psychology*, p. 346).

Adult Sexual Behavior   Until recently the only comprehensive studies conducted on the sexual behavior of adults were the Kinsey Report, completed in 1948, and the work of Masters and Johnson in the 1960s. Both of these studies involved a generally nonrandom and therefore unrepresentative sample of all adults.

Now we have a report (Gagnon et al., 1994) based on 3,432 randomly selected men and women, ages 18 to 59, who were interviewed at length about their sexual behaviors. Some of the results obtained from this more representative study are surprising. For example, contrary to the popular view that extramarital affairs and casual sex are the norm in contemporary America, 85 percent of the married women and 74 percent of the married men reported being faithful to their spouses. And contrary to the common belief that many single people have very active and exciting sex lives, only 23 percent of single persons reported having sex 2 or more times weekly, with roughly equal percentages reporting rates of a few times monthly, a few times yearly, or not at all. In contrast, 41 percent of all married couples said they had sex 2 or more times weekly, as did 56 percent of unmarried couples who were living together.

Parenthood   For most adults, loving and being loved by their children is an unparalleled source of fulfillment. The birth of the first child, however, is also a major turning point in a couple's relationship, one that requires many adjustments. Romance and fun often give way to duty and obligations. Young children demand a lot of time and energy, which may leave parents with little time or energy for each other.

Parenthood can also heighten conflicts between pursuit of careers and responsibilities at home. This is especially likely among women who have had an

Parenthood can bring deep fulfillment and pride, but it also requires major adjustments by both partners.

active career outside the home. They may be torn between feelings of loss and resentment at the prospect of leaving their job, and anxiety or guilt over the idea of continuing to work. This conflict is added to the usual worries about being an adequate wife and mother (Warr & Perry, 1982). No wonder women feel the need for their partner's cooperation more strongly during this period of life than men do (Belsky, Lang, & Rovine, 1985). But while today's fathers spend more time with their children than their fathers did, mothers still bear the greater responsibility for both child rearing and housework. Interestingly, although homosexual couples as a group believe more strongly in equally dividing household duties than do heterosexual couples, homosexuals tend to make an exception when it comes to child rearing. After the arrival of a child (through adoption or artificial insemination), child-care responsibilities tend to fall more heavily on one member of a homosexual couple, while the other spends more time in paid employment (Patterson, 1994, 1995).

Given the demands of child rearing, marital satisfaction tends to decline after the arrival of the first child (Ruble et al., 1988). But once children leave home, many parents experience renewed satisfaction in their relationship as a couple. For the first time in years the husband and wife can be alone together and enjoy each other's company.

Divorce   Intimate relationships frequently break up. Although this is true for all types of couples—married and unmarried, heterosexual and homosexual—most of the research on ending relationships has focused on divorced couples. The U.S. divorce rate has risen substantially since the 1960s, as it has in many other developed nations (Lewin, 1995). The good news is that our divorce rate now appears to have stabilized (Darnton, 1992). The bad news is that it has stabilized at quite a high level. Almost half of American marriages today eventually end in divorce.

Rarely is the decision to separate a mutual one. In most cases one partner takes the initiative in ending the relationship after a long period of slowly increasing unhappiness. Making the decision does not necessarily bring relief. Usually, in the short term it brings turmoil, animosity, and apprehension. In the longer term, however, most divorced adults report that the divorce was a positive step that eventually resulted in greater personal contentment and healthier psychological functioning. A substantial minority, however, seem to suffer long-term negative effects (Kelly, 1982; Stack, 1994).

Divorce can have serious and far-reaching effects on children—especially on their school performance, self-esteem, gender-role development, emotional adjustment, relationships with others, and attitudes toward marriage (Barber & Eccles, 1992; Vaughn, 1993). Children adapt more successfully to divorce when they have good support systems, when the divorcing parents maintain a good relationship, and when sufficient financial resources are made available to them (Ahrons, 1994; Davies & Cummings, 1994; Edwards, 1995; Miller, Kliewer, & Burkeman, 1993).

The divorce rate in the United States has risen dramatically since the 1960s. Divorce can have serious and far-reaching effects on both the couple and the couple's children.

The World of Work

What are the satisfactions and stresses of adult work?

Three or four generations ago, choosing a career was not an issue for most young adults. Men followed in their fathers' footsteps or took whatever apprenticeships were available in their communities. Women were occupied in child care, housework, and helping with the family farm or business. Those who worked outside the home generally pursued such "female" careers as secretarial work, nursing, and teaching. Today career choices are far more numerous for both men and women. In 1990, for example, women constituted 25 percent of

APPLYING PSYCHOLOGY

Resolving Conflicts in Intimate Relationships

Even the closest, most loving couples have disagreements. People, after all, are different. They have different desires, different approaches, different priorities, different points of view. This makes conflict inevitable in every intimate relationship. But conflict does not necessarily mean destructive forms of fighting. Conflict can be resolved in constructive ways that don't tear a couple apart. Constructive fighting can actually bring people closer together in search of mutually satisfactory solutions.

Psychologists who have studied intimate relationships often suggest a number of steps that lead to constructive conflict resolution:

1. *Carefully choose the time and place for an argument.* People who start airing a grievance at some inappropriate time shouldn't be surprised when the outcome is unsatisfactory. Try not to begin a major disagreement while your partner is in the middle of completing some important task or is ready to fall asleep after a long, tiring day. Bring up the subject when there is ample time to discuss it fully.

2. *Be a good listener.* Don't go on the defensive as soon as your partner brings up a concern or complaint. Listen carefully without interrupting. Try to understand what your partner is saying from his or her point of view. Listening calmly, without anger, will help to get the discussion off to a good start. Don't let your body give nonverbal cues that contradict good listening. For instance, don't continue to do chores or watch television while your partner is speaking. Don't shrug your shoulders or roll your eyes as if discounting your partner's view.

3. *Give feedback regarding your understanding of the other person's grievance.* Restate what your partner has told you in your own words. Ask questions about anything you're not sure of. For instance, if a wife says she is fed up with the amount of time her husband spends watching television sports, he might respond by saying, "I know you don't like me watching sports a lot, but do you expect me to stop entirely?" Such feedback helps to clarify and avoid misunderstandings.

4. *Be candid.* Level with your partner about your feelings. Say what you really think. If you are angry, don't make your partner guess your feelings by giving the silent treatment or showing anger in indirect ways. Of course, being candid does not mean being tactless or hurtful. Don't engage in name calling, sarcasm, mockery, or insults. Such tactics are counterproductive.

5. *Use "I" rather than "you" statements.* For instance, if you're angry with your partner for being late, say, "I've been really worried and upset for the last hour" rather than "You're a whole hour late!

full-time employed physicians, 27 percent of lawyers, and 30 percent of college professors. All told, women accounted for about 39 percent of the labor force (Gilbert, 1994). On average, however, women get paid 30 percent less than men for doing the same job. Moreover, many women experience discrimination or sexual harassment at work. And women typically have fewer opportunities to change jobs or receive a promotion, two ways by which men tend to get out of an unsatisfactory job (Aranya, Kushnir, & Valency, 1986). The vast majority of workers are moderately or highly satisfied with their jobs and would continue to work even if they didn't have to, because work gives meaning to their lives. Jobs also provide economic independence and self-esteem. In addition, people in all occupational groups say they value the relationships they form with their colleagues at work. For these and other reasons, men and women who are employed are healthier than those who are not.

Dual-Career Families Over the past 50 years the number of married women in the paid labor force has increased dramatically: 71 percent of married women with school-age children and 60 percent of women with children under 6 now have jobs outside the home (Gilbert, 1994; Harris & Liebert, 1991). The two-paycheck family is not always a matter of choice. With increasingly unstable

Why couldn't you get here on time?" "You" statements sound like accusations and tend to put people on the defensive. "I" statements sound more like efforts to communicate feelings in nonjudgmental ways.

6. ***Focus on behavior, not on the person.*** For example, focus on your partner's lateness as a problem, don't accuse your partner of being thoughtless and self-centered. People respond defensively to broadside attacks on their character. Such attacks threaten their self-esteem.

7. ***Don't overstate the frequency of a problem or overgeneralize about it.*** Don't tell your partner that he's *always* late or that she's *exactly* like her mother. Such exaggerations are annoying and tend to lead discussions away from legitimate complaints.

8. ***Focus on a limited number of specific issues.*** Don't overwhelm your partner with a barrage of grievances.

Stick to current concerns of high priority. Don't get distracted by trivial matters that waste emotional energy. Don't dredge up a long list of complaints from the past.

9. ***Don't find scapegoats for every grievance against you.*** We all tend to explain away our shortcomings by blaming them on circumstances or sometimes on other people. Resist the temptation to offer excuses designed to get you "off the hook." Take responsibility for your actions, and encourage your partner to do the same.

10. ***Suggest specific, relevant changes to solve a problem.*** Both participants in the conflict should propose at least one possible solution. A proposed solution should be reasonable and take into account the other person's viewpoint as well as your own.

11. ***Be open to compromise.*** Settling disputes successfully often involves negotiation. Both people must be willing to give in a little. Don't

back your partner into a corner by giving an ultimatum: "Do what I want *or else!*" Partners need to be willing to change themselves to some extent in response to each other's feelings. This is the essence of being in an intimate relationship. Being loved by your partner doesn't necessarily mean being accepted *exactly* as you are.

12. ***Don't think in terms of winner and loser.*** Popular books have been written on how always to *win* arguments. This competitive approach to conflict resolution is unfortunate in intimate relationships. If one partner is repeatedly the winner and the other repeatedly the loser, their relationship inevitably suffers. Strive for solutions that are satisfactory to both parties. Think of each other as allies attacking a mutual problem. In this way your relationship will become stronger.

To learn more about resolving interpersonal conflicts, visit our Web site at **www.prenhall.com/morris.**

economic conditions and the rising costs of essentials such as health care and education, it is not unusual for both adults in a family to have to work simply to make ends meet. This increasing role of women as economic providers is a trend found worldwide (Lewin, 1995).

Balancing the demands of career and family is a problem in many families, especially for women. Even when the wife has a full-time job outside the home, she is likely to end up doing far more than half of the housework and child care. She is also likely to be aware of this imbalance and to resent it (Benin & Agostinelli, 1988). The "double shift"—one at paid work outside the home and another at unpaid household labor—is the common experience of millions of women throughout the world (Mednick, 1993). True equality—the goal of the dual-career movement—has yet to be achieved (Gilbert, 1994).

Despite the pressures associated with the "double shift," most women report increases in self-esteem when they have a paid job (Baruch & Barnett, 1986). They also tend to experience less anxiety and depression than childless working women do (Barnett, 1994). The vast majority say they would continue to work even if they didn't need the money (Schwartz, 1994). Those women most apt to feel stressed by a "double shift" are those who do not find satisfaction in their various roles (Barnett, 1994).

Cognitive Changes

In what ways do adults and adolescents think differently?

Only recently have researchers begun to explore the ways in which an adult's thinking differs from that of an adolescent. Whereas adolescents are able to test alternatives and to arrive at what they see as the "correct" solution to a problem, adults gradually come to realize that there isn't a single correct solution to every problem—there may, in fact, be no correct solution, or there may be several. Adolescents rely on authorities to tell them what is "true," but adults realize that "truth" often varies according to the situation and one's point of view. Adults are also more practical: They know that a solution to a problem must be realistic as well as reasonable (Cavanaugh, 1990). No doubt these changes in adult thinking derive from greater experience of the world. Dealing with the kinds of complex problems that arise in adult life requires moving away from the literal, formal, and somewhat rigid thinking of adolescence and young adulthood (Labouvie-Vief, 1986).

Just as physical exercise is necessary for optimal physical development, mental exercise—*using* cognitive skills—is necessary for optimal cognitive development (Denney, 1984). In one study adults who received training in spatial orientation skills improved their performance by 40 percent (Schaie, 1994). Although some decline in cognitive skills is inevitable as we age, staying mentally active can minimize the decline.

Personality Changes

In terms of personality development, are any patterns evident in adulthood?

Research shows that we experience certain broad patterns of personality change through adulthood. Both men and women tend to become less self-centered and develop better coping skills with age (Neugarten, 1977). One longitudinal study found that people are more sympathetic, giving, productive, and dependable at 45 than they were at 20 (Block, 1971). Another study found that people in their middle years develop new ways of adapting, are more comfortable in interpersonal relationships, and feel an increasing commitment to and responsibility for others (Vaillant, 1977). Such findings suggest that the majority of people are successfully meeting what Erik Erikson saw as the major challenge of middle adulthood: *generativity versus stagnation.* Generativity refers to the ability to continue being productive and creative, especially in ways that guide and encourage future generations. For those who fail to achieve this state, life becomes a drab and meaningless routine, causing feelings of stagnation and boredom.

These feelings may be part of what is called a **midlife crisis.** The person in midlife crisis feels painfully unfulfilled, ready for a radical, abrupt shift in career, personal relationships, or lifestyle. Research shows, however, that the midlife crisis is not typical; most people do not make sudden, dramatic changes in their lives in mid-adulthood (Martino, 1995). In fact, many use this time to make renewed commitments to marriage, work, and family (B. M. Newman, 1982).

Daniel Levinson, who has studied personality development in men and women throughout adulthood (Levinson, 1978, 1986, 1987, 1996), preferred the term **midlife transition** for the period when people tend to take stock of their lives. This is the time when many of the people in his studies, confronted with the first signs of aging, began to think about the finite nature of life. They realized that they may never accomplish all that they had hoped to do, and they questioned the value of some of the things they had accomplished so far, won-

As people experience middle age, they frequently undergo physical changes such as hair loss.

Midlife crisis
A time when adults discover that they no longer feel fulfilled in their jobs or personal lives and attempt to make a decisive shift in career or lifestyle.

Midlife transition
According to Levinson, a process whereby adults assess the past and formulate new goals for the future.

dering how meaningful they were. As a result, some gradually reset their life priorities, establishing new goals based on their new insights.

The "Change of Life"

What is menopause, and what changes accompany it?

During middle age the function of the reproductive organs declines. In women the amount of estrogen (the principal female hormone) produced by the ovaries drops sharply at around age 45. Breasts, genital tissues, and the uterus begin to shrink, and menstrual periods become irregular and then cease altogether at around age 50. The cessation of menstruation is called **menopause.**

The hormonal changes that accompany menopause often cause certain physical symptoms, of which the most noticeable are "hot flashes." In some women menopause also leads to a serious thinning of the bones, making them more vulnerable to fractures. Both of these symptoms can be prevented by estrogen replacement therapy (a pill or a skin patch that must be prescribed by a physician). Although this therapy may slightly increase a woman's risk for breast and uterine cancer (Steinberg et al., 1991), it appears to significantly decrease her risk for heart disease (Barrett-Connor & Bush, 1991). Some women are apprehensive about the "change of life," but others revel in their newfound freedom from fear of pregnancy.

Experts disagree about whether there is such a thing as a "male menopause." Men never experience as severe a drop in testosterone (the principal male hormone) as women do in estrogen. Instead, studies have found a more gradual decline—perhaps 30 to 40 percent—in testosterone in men between ages 48 and 70 (Angier, 1992). In any case, there is much disagreement as to whether older men should be treated, as menopausal women commonly are, with hormones. Some experts are concerned that hormone therapy could increase men's risk of prostate cancer and heart disease.

REVIEW QUESTIONS

1. According to Erik Erikson, the major challenge of young adulthood is ____ versus ____, while the major challenge of middle adulthood is ____ versus ____.

2. Indicate whether the following statements are true (T) or false (F).

   a. The old saying "opposites attract" is an accurate description of how most people choose someone to marry. ____

   b. Marital satisfaction generally increases with the arrival of the first child. ____

   c. Working women who also have children to care for tend to experience more anxiety and depression than childless working women do. ____

   d. A significant decline in cognitive skills is inevitable after young adulthood. ____

   e. The vast majority of middle-age people experience a midlife crisis in which they feel painfully unfulfilled. ____

3. The cessation of menstruation in middle-age women is called ____.

Answers: 1. intimacy versus isolation; generativity versus stagnation. 2. a–F; b–F; c–F; d–F; e–F. 3. menopause.

Late Adulthood

What are two factors related to life expectancy in the United States?

Older adults constitute the fastest-growing and one of the most politically powerful segments of the U.S. population. There are currently 35 million Americans over age 65; by the year 2030 there may be more than 70 million in this age

Menopause
The time in a woman's life when menstruation ceases.

group, or about a quarter of the population (Kolata, 1992). This dramatic rise in the numbers of older adults stems from the aging of the large baby-boom generation, coupled with increases in life expectancy owing primarily to better health care and nutrition (Downs, 1994).

There is, however, a sizable gender gap in life expectancy. The average woman lives 7 years longer than the average male. The reasons for this gender gap are still unclear, but factors suspected of contributing to it include differences in hormones, exposure to stress, health-related behaviors, and genetic makeup. We know more about the reasons for the gap in life expectancy between whites and African Americans in this country. While the average white American child is likely to live to age 76, the average African American child is apt to live only to age 71. This difference stems largely from the social and economic disadvantages that African Americans as a group face.

Physical Changes

Why does the body deteriorate with age?

Although physical changes are inevitable during late adulthood, how people respond to these changes has a major effect on their quality of life.

Beginning in middle adulthood and continuing through late adulthood, physical appearance and the functioning of every organ change. The hair thins and turns white or gray. The skin wrinkles. Bones become fragile and more easily broken. Muscles lose power, and joints stiffen or wear out. Circulation slows, blood pressure rises, and because the lungs hold less oxygen, the older adult has less energy. Body shape and posture change, and the reproductive organs atrophy. Difficulties in falling asleep and staying asleep become more common, and reaction times are slower. Vision, hearing, and the sense of smell all become less acute (Cavanaugh, 1990; LaRue & Jarvik, 1982). Most people are at first unaware of these changes because they occur gradually. But the decline eventually becomes undeniable.

We do not yet know why physical aging happens (DiGiovanna, 1994). One explanation is that genes may program our cells to eventually deteriorate and die. This programming might occur through "death genes" that guide the onset, speed, and course of the body's decline. Alternatively, the genetic instructions for running the body may be capable of being read only a limited number of times before they begin to degrade and instructional errors (aging) result. Eventually the genetic instructions become so illegible and confused that the body can no longer live. Another explanation for aging is that the parts of the body simply wear out through repeated use, much as the parts of a car ultimately wear out after so many miles. Contributing to this wearing-out process may be toxins that the body is exposed to, both external toxins in the environment (radiation, chemicals, viruses, and so forth) and toxins that accumulate as inevitable by-products of the body's own activities.

Still, the physical changes of aging need not be incapacitating for most or even all of late adulthood. In fact, older people can to some extent control the speed at which these changes happen. In contrast to the physical changes that occurred in adolescence, the changes of middle and late adulthood are only loosely controlled by a person's biological clock. The physical well-being of older adults is affected by many factors, some of which they can influence, such as diet (including type and amount of food), exercise, health care, smoking, drug use, and overexposure to the sun (Levenson & Aldwin, 1994; Roth, 1996). Attitude and interests also matter. People who have a continuing sense of usefulness, maintain old ties, investigate new ideas, take up new activities, and feel in control of their lives have the lowest rates of disease and the highest survival rates (Butler & Lewis, 1982; Caspi & Elder, 1986).

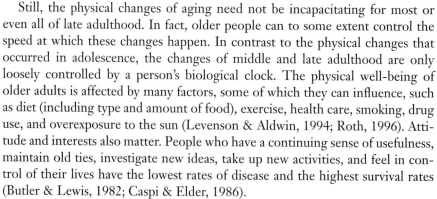

Social Development

What kind of lifestyle and sex life can you expect after 65?

One common myth about older adults is that many are lonely and helpless, often dependent on others for support. In fact, most men and women over 65 live autonomous lives apart from their children and outside of nursing homes, and most are very satisfied with their lifestyles. In one survey of people 65 years and older, more than half reported being just as happy as they were when they were younger. Three-quarters said they were involved in activities that were as interesting to them as any they had engaged in during their younger years (Birren, 1983).

Still, gradual social changes do take place in late adulthood. These changes have been described as occurring in three stages (Cumming & Henry, 1961). The first stage is shrinkage of life space: The older person starts to interact with fewer people and perform fewer social roles. The second stage is increased individuality: Behavior becomes less influenced by social rules and expectations than it was earlier in life. The third and final stage involves acceptance of the changes in the first two stages: The person steps back and assesses life, realizes there is a limit to the capacity for social involvement, and learns to live comfortably with those restrictions. This process does not necessarily entail a psychological "disengagement" with the social world, as some researchers have contended. Instead, older people simply may be making choices that suit their more limited time frames (Carstensen, 1995).

Retirement   Another major change that most people experience in late adulthood is retiring from paid employment. People's reactions to retirement differ greatly, partly because society has no clear idea of what retirees are supposed to do.

Of course, the nature and quality of retired life depend in part on financial status. If retirement means a major decline in a person's standard of living, that person will be less eager to retire and will lead a more limited life after retirement. Another factor in people's attitudes toward retirement is their feelings about work. People who are fulfilled by their jobs are usually less interested in retiring than people whose jobs are unrewarding (Atchley, 1982). Similarly, people who have very ambitious, hard-driving personalities tend to want to stay at work longer than those who are more relaxed.

Sexual Behavior   A common misconception about the aged is that they have outlived their sexuality. This myth reflects our stereotypes. To the extent that we see the elderly as physically unattractive and frail, we find it difficult to believe that they are sexually active. True, older people respond more slowly and are less sexually active than younger people, but the majority of older adults can enjoy sex and have orgasms. One survey revealed that 37 percent of married people over 60 have sex at least once a week, 20 percent have sex outdoors, and 17 percent swim in the nude (Woodward & Springen, 1992). Another study of people ages 65 to 97 found that about half the men still viewed sex as important, and slightly over half of those in committed relationships were satisfied with the quality of their sex lives (Mark Clements Research, 1995).

Nonetheless, several factors work against sexual satisfaction in old age. First, some older adults accept the myth that they should no longer be interested in sex and, as a result, they deny their sexual urges. Second, because women tend to outlive men, many older women do not have an available partner. Poor health is another factor that can curb sexual activity. Furthermore, while menopause does not halt a woman's sexual interests, the physical effects of declining hormones can produce bodily changes that require some adjustment in technique or timing (Brody, 1990). Finally, there are cohort differences to consider. Today's older adults grew up in the early part of this century, when attitudes toward sexuality were quite different from what they are now. Thus their sexual attitudes and behaviors are likely to reflect generational differences as well as age.

Cognitive Changes

Is memory loss inevitable in old age?

Healthy people who remain intellectually involved maintain a high level of mental functioning in old age (Schaie, 1984; Shimamura et al., 1995). Far from the common myth that the brain cells of elderly people are rapidly dying off, the brain of the average person shrinks only about 10 percent in size between the ages of 20 and 70 (Goleman, 1996). This means that for a sizable number of older adults, cognitive abilities remain largely intact. For instance, interviews with men, now in their seventies, who are part of a long-running longitudinal study of "gifted children," found that those who had remained mentally active and healthy showed no noticeable declines in intellect or vocabulary (Shneidman, 1989). True, the aging mind works a little more slowly (Birren & Fisher, 1995; Salthouse, 1991), and certain types of memories are a little more difficult to store and retrieve (Craik, 1994). These changes, however, are not serious enough to interfere with the ability to enjoy an active, independent life. Furthermore, training and practice can greatly reduce the decline in cognitive performance in later adulthood (Willis, 1985; Willis & Schaie, 1986).

The psychologist K. Warner Schaie found that different abilities decline at different rates (1994). For example, the sharpest decline is in the area of mathematics: At age 74 men tested about one-third lower than they had in their fifties. The smallest decline is in spatial ability (for example, reading a map): At age 80 men tested only about one-eighth lower than they had at age 50.

Because people with Alzheimer's disease suffer memory loss, signs can remind them to perform ordinary activities.

Alzheimer's Disease   For people suffering **Alzheimer's disease,** the picture is quite different. They forget the names of their children or are unable to find their way home from the store. Some even fail to recognize their husband or wife. Named for the German neurologist Alois Alzheimer, the disease causes progressive loss of the ability to communicate and reason resulting from changes in the brain (Glenner, 1994).

Alzheimer's is a common disorder, typically the cause of what used to be called "senility" when it appears in older people. According to current estimates, 5 to 7 percent of adults over 65 (some 4 million people) and at least 20 percent of adults 85 or older suffer from Alzheimer's disease (Anthony & Aboraya, 1992). Factors that put people at risk for developing the disorder are having a family history of *dementia* (a general decline in physical and cognitive abilities), having Down syndrome or Parkinson's disease, being born to a woman over the age of 40, suffering a head trauma (especially one that caused unconsciousness), and having a specific genetic defect (Kokmen, 1991; Myers, 1996).

As Alzheimer's progresses—and this may take anywhere from 2 to 20 years— it frequently leads to personality changes. First, victims may exhibit a kind of emotional withdrawal or flatness. They become confused and may not know where they are or what time of day it is. Eventually they lose the ability to speak, to care for themselves, and to recognize family members. If they do not die of other causes, Alzheimer's will eventually prove fatal, as the body "forgets" how to swallow and how to breathe.

Of course, Alzheimer's disease is not the only cause of mental impairment in older people. Depression, deafness, alcoholism, stroke, anemia, kidney failure, reactions to certain prescription drugs, and even a vitamin deficiency can all

Alzheimer's disease
A disorder of late adulthood that is characterized by progressive losses in memory and cognition and changes in personality that is believed to be caused by a deterioration of the brain's structure and function.

produce symptoms that resemble those of Alzheimer's disease. These other conditions, however, are often treatable and may be reversed (Gruetzner, 1988). At present there is no known cure for Alzheimer's, but breakthroughs in research are now occurring so fast that a drug to slow the progress of the disorder may be developed in the near future (Henry, 1996).

Facing the End of Life

How well do most elderly people cope with the end of life?

Fear of death is seldom a central concern for people in later adulthood. In fact, such fear seems to be a greater problem in young adulthood or in middle age, when the first awareness of mortality coincides with a greater interest in living (Kimmel, 1974). Older people spend more time taking stock of past accomplishments than worrying about death (Butler, 1963). This does not mean that the elderly are constantly brooding about the past. Rather, review of one's life goes on alongside concerns about the present.

But the elderly do have some major fears associated with dying. They fear the pain, indignity, and depersonalization they might experience during a terminal illness, as well as the possibility of dying alone. They also worry about burdening their relatives with the expenses of their hospitalization or nursing care. As for their relatives, they have their own fears about dying, and these fears, combined with the psychological pain they feel watching a loved one die, sometimes makes them depersonalize the loved one just at the time when that person most needs comfort and compassion (Kübler-Ross, 1975).

Stages of Dying   Psychiatrist Elisabeth Kübler-Ross (1969) interviewed more than 200 dying people of all ages to try to understand the psychological aspects of dying. From these interviews, she described a sequence of 5 stages through which she believed people pass as they react to their own impending death.

Denial: The person denies the diagnosis, refuses to believe that death is approaching, insists that an error has been made, and seeks other, more acceptable opinions or alternatives.

Anger: The person now accepts the reality of the situation but expresses envy and resentment toward those who will live to fulfill a plan or dream. The question becomes "Why me?" Anger may be directed at the doctor or randomly in all directions. The patience and understanding of other people are particularly important at this stage.

Bargaining: The person desperately tries to buy time, negotiating with doctors, family members, clergy, and God in a healthy attempt to cope with the realization of death.

Depression: As bargaining fails and time is running out, the person may succumb to depression, lamenting failures and mistakes that can no longer be corrected.

Acceptance: Tired and weak, the person at last enters a state of "quiet expectation," submitting to fate.

According to Kübler-Ross, Americans have a greater problem coping with death than people in some other cultures, because we fear and deny it (1975).

Some observers have found fault with Kübler-Ross's model of dying. Most of the criticisms have focused on her methodology. She studied only a relatively small sample of people and provided little information about how they were selected and how often they were interviewed. Also, all her patients were suffering from cancer, leading some critics to wonder whether Kübler-Ross's model applies as well to people dying from other causes. Finally, some critics question whether her model is universal, noting that different cultures have very different

The loss of loved ones is one of the major challenges people face in late adulthood.

ways of thinking about death. Death itself is universal, but reactions to dying may differ greatly from one culture to another.

Despite these legitimate questions, there is nearly universal agreement that Kübler-Ross deserves credit for pioneering the study of the transitions people undergo during the dying process. She was the first to investigate an area long considered taboo, and her research has made dying a more "understandable" experience and perhaps one that is easier to deal with.

Widowhood   The death of one's spouse may be the most severe challenge people face during late adulthood. Especially if it was unexpected, people respond to such a loss with initial disbelief, followed by numbness. Only later is the full impact of the loss felt, and that can be severe. The incidence of depression rises significantly following the death of a spouse (F. H. Norris & Murrell, 1990). Moreover, a long-term study of several thousand widowers 55 years of age and older revealed that nearly 5 percent of them died in the 6-month period following their wife's death, a figure that is well above the expected death rate for men that age. Thereafter the mortality rate of these men fell gradually to a more normal level (Butler & Lewis, 1982).

Perhaps because they are not as used to taking care of themselves, men seem to suffer more than women from the loss of a mate. But because women have a longer life expectancy, there are many more widows than widowers. Thus men have a better chance of remarrying. More than half the women over 65 are widowed, and half of them will live another 15 years without remarrying. For somewhat different reasons, then, the burden of widowhood is heavy for both men and women (Feinson, 1986).

REVIEW QUESTIONS

1. Indicate whether the following statements are true (T) or false (F).
   a. The average man lives as long as the average woman. ____
   b. The physical changes of aging inevitably become incapacitating. ____
   c. Most elderly people are dependent on their adult children. ____
   d. Healthy people who remain intellectually involved maintain a high level of mental functioning in old age. ____

2. Match the following stages of dying with the appropriate definition.

   ____ denial   a. person submits to fate
   ____ anger   b. person expresses resentment toward others
   ____ bargaining   c. person refuses to believe the diagnosis
   ____ depression   d. person may lament mistakes
   ____ acceptance   e. person tries to buy time

Answers: 1. a. F; b. F; c. F; d. T. 2. denial: c; anger: b; bargaining: e; depression: d; acceptance: a.

KEY TERMS

developmental psychology, p. 312

Prenatal development
prenatal development, p. 312
fetus, p. 312

critical period, p. 313

The newborn baby
neonate, p. 314
temperament, p. 314
cross-sectional study, p. 316

cohort, p. 316
longitudinal study, p. 317
biographical study or retrospective study, p. 317

Infancy and childhood
maturation, p. 319

sensory-motor stage, p. 321
object permanence, p. 321
mental representation, p. 321
preoperational stage, p. 321
egocentric, p. 322

CHAPTER REVIEW

☐ How can a drug cause devastating effects at one point in prenatal development but not at others?

The period of development from conception to birth is called **prenatal development.** During this time disease-producing organisms or potentially harmful substances such as drugs can pass through the placenta and cause irreparable harm to the embryo or **fetus.** This harm is greatest if the drug or other substance is introduced just at the time when some major developmental process that it interferes with is occurring. If the same drug is introduced outside this **critical period,** little or even no harm may result.

☐ What early reflexes enable newborns to respond to their environment?

Newborns come equipped with a number of reflexes that help them to respond to their environments. Those that help them to breathe and nurse are critical to survival. For instance, the *rooting reflex* causes newborns, when touched on the cheek, to turn their head in that direction and grope around with their mouth. This helps them to locate a nipple. Nursing is further facilitated by the *sucking reflex,* which causes newborns to suck on anything placed in their mouth, and the *swallowing reflex,* which enables them to swallow liquids without choking.

☐ Is your temperament the same as it was when you were a newborn?

Babies are born with individual differences in personality called **temperament** differences. Often a baby's temperament remains quite stable over time due to a combination of genetic and environmental influences. But stability in temperament is not inevitable; changes in temperament can also take place. Your own temperament, therefore, may be both similar to and different from the temperament you displayed as a newborn.

☐ Which senses are the most developed at birth, and which are the least developed?

All of a baby's senses are functioning at birth: sight, hearing, taste, smell, and touch. Although it is hard to tell exactly what a baby's sensory world is like, newborns seem particularly adept at discriminating speech sounds, which suggests that their hearing is quite keen. Their least developed sense is probably vision, which takes 6 to 8 months to become as good as the average college student's.

☐ What kinds of developmental changes do infants and children undergo?

During the first dozen years of life a helpless infant becomes a competent older child. This transformation encompasses many important kinds of changes, including physical, motor, cognitive, and social developments.

☐ Do children grow at a steady pace?

Growth of the body is most rapid during the first year, with the average baby growing approximately 10 inches and gaining about 15 pounds. It then slows down considerably until early adolescence.

☐ Is walking at an early age a sign of future athletic ability?

This is a question about motor development, the acquisition of skills involving movement. Babies tend to reach the major milestones in early motor development at broadly similar ages, give or take a few months. Those who are somewhat ahead of their peers are not necessarily destined for athletic greatness. Motor development that is slower or faster than the norm tells us little or nothing about a child's future characteristics.

☐ How does a child's ability to reason change over time?

According to the Swiss psychologist Jean Piaget, children undergo qualitative changes in thinking as they grow older. Piaget depicted these changes as a series of stages. During the **sensory-motor stage** (from birth to age 2) children acquire object permanence, the understanding that things continue to exist even when they are out of sight. In the **preoperational stage** (ages 2 to 7) they become increasingly adept at using mental representations, and language assumes an important role in describing, remembering, and reasoning about the world. Children in the **concrete-operational stage** (ages 7 to 11) are able to pay attention to more than one factor at a time and can understand someone else's point of view. Finally, in the **formal-operational stage** (age 11 and older) teenagers acquire the ability to think abstractly and test ideas mentally using logic. Not all psychologists agree with Piaget's theory, however. His is one of several perspectives on children's cognitive development.

How do gender and ethnic background affect moral development?

Like Piaget, Lawrence Kohlberg developed a stage theory about the development of thinking, but his focused exclusively on moral thinking. He proposed that children at different levels of moral reasoning base their moral choices on different factors: first a concern about physical consequences, then a concern about what other people think, and finally a concern about abstract principles. One problem with Kohlberg's view, however, is that it doesn't consider how gender and ethnic background affect moral development. The cultural values associated with being female, African American, Japanese, and so on may affect the ways in which people determine what is right and wrong, good and bad.

How does a child develop language skills?

Some psychologists believe that childhood is a critical period for acquiring language, during which it is much easier to build a vocabulary, master the rules of grammar, and form intelligible sentences. If so, this would explain why learning a second language is also easier for children than for adults.

How can parents help their children to become both securely attached and independent?

Developing a sense of independence is just one of the tasks that children face in their social development. It comes to the fore especially during the toddler period, when a growing awareness of being a separate person makes developing some **autonomy** from parents a very important issue. Parents can encourage independence in their children by allowing them to make choices and do things on their own within a framework of reasonable and consistently enforced limits. Other major social issues during the childhood years include forming a secure **attachment** toward and trust in other people (infancy), learning to take initiative in tackling new tasks (the preschool years), and mastering some of the many skills that will be needed in adulthood (middle and later childhood).

Is adolescence characterized only by physical changes?

The physical changes of adolescence—rapid growth and sexual **maturation**—are just part of the transformation that occurs during this period. The child turns into an adult not only physically but also cognitively, socially, and personally.

What are the consequences of going through puberty early or late?

Although **puberty,** the onset of sexual maturation, starts earlier in girls than in boys, there are substantial individual differences in exactly when it begins. Very early maturing girls face both advantages and disadvantages. They may like the admiration they get from other girls but dislike the embarrassing sexual attention given to them by boys. Boys who mature early do better in sports and in social activities and receive greater respect from their peers, so it may seem that early maturation is preferable in males. Many late-maturing boys, however, may eventually develop a stronger sense of self-identity, perhaps because they don't feel pressured to "grow up" too quickly.

Are there fallacies to adolescent thinking as well as advances in thought?

In terms of cognitive development, teenagers often reach the level of formal-operational thought, in which they can reason abstractly and speculate about alternatives. These newfound abilities may make them overconfident that their own ideas are right, turning adolescence into a time of cognitive **egocentrism.** Frequent focus on the self may also make teens prone to feeling constantly watched and judged by others, a phenomenon called the **imaginary audience.** In addition, adolescents may think of themselves as so unique as to be untouched by the negative things that happen to other people. This **personal fable** may encourage them to take needless risks.

What important tasks do adolescents face in their personal and social lives?

Many adolescents undertake a search for personal identity in which they ideally acquire a solid sense of who they are. In Erik Erikson's theory, identity versus role confusion is the major challenge of this period. Teenagers also work toward developing romantic interests that can build a foundation for strong, intimate relationships in adulthood. Parent–child relationships may become temporarily rocky during adolescence as teenagers become aware of their parents' faults and question parental rules. These conflicts are most common during early adolescence and tend to resolve themselves by the later adolescent years.

What are some major problems among adolescents in our society?

Psychiatric disorders often show up for the first time during adolescence. A sizable number of adolescents think about committing suicide; a much smaller number attempt it. Statistics reflect a common decline in self-esteem during adolescence, especially among girls. In addition, teenagers have to cope with the demands of their new sexuality, the potential for early pregnancy, and the threat of violence in their **peer groups.**

□ How predictable is the course of adult development?

Reaching developmental milestones in adulthood is much less predictable than in earlier years, much more a function of the individual's decisions, circumstances, and even luck. Still, there are certain experiences and changes that take place sooner or later in nearly everyone's life and certain needs that nearly every adult tries to fulfill.

□ Is a sense of personal identity needed to form a long-term, intimate relationship?

Almost every adult forms a long-term loving partnership with at least one other adult at some point in life. According to Erik Erikson, the task of finding intimacy versus being isolated and lonely is especially important during young adulthood. Erikson believed that people are not ready for love until they have formed a firm sense of identity. But other psychologists, such as Carol Gilligan, suggest that intimacy can sometimes come before identity, especially in young women.

□ What are the satisfactions and stresses of adult work?

The vast majority of adults are moderately or highly satisfied with their jobs and would continue to work even if they didn't need to for financial reasons. Balancing the demands of job and family is often difficult, however, especially for women, because they tend to have most of the responsibility for housework and child care. Yet despite this stress of a "double shift," a job outside the home is a positive, self-esteem–boosting factor in most women's lives.

□ In what ways do adults and adolescents think differently?

An adult's thinking is more flexible and practical than an adolescent's. Whereas adolescents search for the one "correct" solution to a problem, adults realize that there may be several "right" solutions or none at all. Adults also place less faith in authorities than adolescents do.

□ In terms of personality development, are any patterns evident in adulthood?

Certain broad patterns of personality change occur in adulthood. As people grow older, they tend to become less self-centered and more comfortable in interpersonal relationships. They also develop better coping skills and new ways of adapting. By middle age many adults feel an increasing commitment to, and responsibility for, others.

This suggests that many adults are successfully meeting what Erik Erikson saw as the major challenge of middle adulthood: generativity (the ability to continue being productive and creative, especially in ways that guide and encourage future generations) versus stagnation (a sense of boredom or lack of fulfillment, sometimes called a **midlife crisis**).

□ What is menopause, and what changes accompany it?

Middle adulthood brings a decline in the functioning of the reproductive organs. In women this is marked by **menopause,** the cessation of menstruation, accompanied by a sharp drop in estrogen levels. Without estrogen-replacement therapy, some negative symptoms such as thinning bones and "hot flashes" can result. Men experience a slower decline in testosterone levels.

□ What are two factors related to life expectancy in the United States?

Over the past century life expectancy in America has increased mainly because of improved health care and nutrition. There is, however, a sizable gender gap, with women living an average of 7 years longer than men. There is also a sizable racial gap, with white Americans living an average of 5 years longer than blacks.

□ Why does the body deteriorate with age?

The physical changes of late adulthood affect outward appearance and the functioning of every organ. We don't yet know why these changes happen. Perhaps our genes program cells to eventually deteriorate and die, or perhaps genetic instructions simply degrade over time. Another possible explanation is that body parts wear out after repeated use, with environmental toxins contributing to the wearing-out process. Whatever the reason for it, physical aging is inevitable, although it can be slowed by a healthy lifestyle.

□ What kind of lifestyle and sex life can you expect after 65?

Most older adults have an independent lifestyle and engage in activities that interest them. Although their sexual responses may be slowed, most continue to enjoy sex in their sixties and seventies. Still, gradual social changes occur in late adulthood. Older adults start to interact with fewer people and perform fewer social roles. They may also become less influenced by social rules and expectations. Realizing that there is a limit to the capacity for social involvement, they learn to live with some restrictions.

□ Is memory loss inevitable in old age?

The aging mind works a little more slowly, and certain kinds of memories are more difficult to store and retrieve, but these changes are generally not extensive enough to interfere with most everyday tasks. Healthy older adults who engage in intellectually stimulating activities usually maintain a high level of mental functioning.

□ **How well do most elderly people cope with the end of life?**

Most elderly people fear death less than younger people do. What they do fear are the pain, indignity, depersonalization, and loneliness associated with a terminal illness. They also worry about becoming a financial burden to their families. The death of a spouse may be the most severe challenge the elderly face.

CRITICAL THINKING AND APPLICATIONS

1. Does watching violent television lead to more violent behavior?

2. To what degree do you think people maintain a stable and consistent identity throughout their lifetime? To what degree do people change at each developmental stage of their life?

On the Web...

Visit these online resources at our Companion Website www.prenhall.com/morris

The Psychology Place

Learning Activities
1. Nature vs. Nurture: Genes Win Again!, p. 312
2. Challenging the Nurture Assumption, p. 312

Scientific American Connection
3. Light Maternal Drinking Affects the Unborn Child, p. 312
4. Babies, Phonetics, and Mastering Language, p. 325

Research News
5. The Power of Parents, p. 327
6. Childhood Attachment Style: How Stable Over the Life Span?, p. 328
7. Daycare: What's a Parent to Do?, p. 328
8. Is a Male Role Model Essential to Positive Child Development?, p. 329
9. The Social Usefulness of Self-esteem: A Skeptical View, p. 340
10. Teen Suicide — Symptom of a Changing World or Exaggerated Suggestibility of Adolescence, p. 340
11. Who or What is to Blame for the Littleton Massacre?, p. 341
12. Tick Tock Goes the Social and Biological Clock, p. 342
13. Regrets? ... I've Heard a Few: Women's Midlife Review and Well-being, p. 349
14. The Oldest Old, p. 350

Op-Ed Forum
15. Successful Aging: A Matter of Control?, p. 350
16. Aging Brain, Aging Mind, p. 352
17. Searching the Web: Investigating Alzheimer's Disease, p. 352
18. Fear of Death: Our Final Developmental Crisis, p. 353

Games
1. Research Methods in Life Span Development, p. 317

Web Links:
1. **http://www.psych.ucr.edu/Div7/Div7.html**, p. 311
   American Psychological Association Division 7: Developmental psychology
2. **http://server.bmod.athabascau.ca/html/aupr/developmental.htm**, p. 311
   Psychology Center — Developmental Psychology. Links to Web sites related to developmental psychology.
3. **http://ecdgroup.harvard.net/cdt/html**, p. 314
   Child development theory. The child: Key needs from conception through early years.
4. **http://www.ecdgroup.com**, p. 318
   Early childhood care and development: International resources in support of young children (up to age 8) and their families.
5. **http://www.wpi.edu/~isg_501/nsuchkin.html**, p. 321
   Development Theories: Development theories of Piaget, Perry, Belenky, Kohlberg, Loevinger, and Kagan.
6. **http://idealist.com/children/cdw.html**, p. 328
   The Child Development Website: Classic Theories of Child Development (Margaret Mahler, Sigmund Freud, and Erik Erikson: A Hypertext Overview).
7. **http://maple.lemoyne.edu/~hevern/psychref4-4.html**, p. 335
   PsychREF: Developmental psychology: Childhood and adolescence. Links to Web sites related to the care and development of children and adolescents.
8. **http://education.indiana.edu/cas/adol.adol.html**, p. 335
   ADOL: Adolescence Directory Online. Resource guide for teens, counselors, educators, health practitioners, and researchers on adolescent issues.

PERSONALITY

W E TALK ABOUT PERSONALITY ALL THE TIME. WE DESCRIBE OUR BEST friend as a "fun-loving but quiet personality," or "kind of a jock, but really gentle." Acquaintances we know less well may elicit a one-dimensional assessment: "He's really arrogant" or "She's a snob." These brief characterizations of people do not define their personalities, however, because personality is made up of not one or two outstanding characteristics or abilities but a whole range of them.

Many psychologists define **personality** as an individual's unique pattern of thoughts, feelings, and behaviors that persists over time and across situations. Notice that there are two important parts to this definition. On the one hand, *personality* refers to *unique differences*—those aspects that distinguish a person from everyone else. On the other hand, the definition asserts that personality is relatively *stable* and *enduring*—that these unique differences persist through time and across situations. If you have had the chance to view yourself at various ages in home movies or videos, you've probably noticed that at each age some of the same characteristics are evident. Maybe you are a natural "ham," always showing off for the camera, or you might be a director type who, at age 4 as well as at age 14, was telling the camera operator what to do. Because we expect people's personalities to be relatively consistent, we generally suspect that something is wrong with a person when that is not so.

Psychologists approach the study of personality in a number of ways. Some set out to identify the most important characteristics of personality. Others seek to understand why there are differences in personality. Among the latter group, some psychologists identify the family as the most important factor in the development of the individual's personality. Others emphasize environmental influences outside the family, and still others see personality as the result of how we learn to think about ourselves and our experiences. Out of these various approaches have come four major categories of personality theories:

- *Psychodynamic theories* place the origins of personality in unconscious, often sexual, motivations and conflicts.
- *Humanistic theories* spotlight positive growth motives and the realization of potential in shaping personality.
- *Trait theories* categorize and describe the ways in which people's personalities differ.
- *Cognitive–social learning theories* find the roots of personality in the ways people think about, act on, and respond to their environment.

To varying degrees each of these theoretical approaches contributes to our overall understanding of personality.

In this chapter we explore the four approaches by examining some representative theories that each one has produced. We see how each theoretical paradigm sheds light on the personality of Jaylene Smith, a young doctor who is having trouble forming close and lasting relationships and who is described in the case that follows. Finally, we evaluate the strengths and weaknesses of each approach to understanding personality.

The Case of Jaylene Smith

Jaylene Smith is a single 30-year-old physician with a promising career. She has entered therapy because she is troubled by certain aspects of her social life. Acquaintances describe Jay in glowing terms—as highly motivated, intelligent, attractive, and charming—though she herself feels terribly insecure and anxious. When asked by a psychologist to pick out some self-descriptive adjectives, Jay selected *introverted*, *shy*, *inadequate*, and *unhappy*—far from an enviable self-image.

Jay was the firstborn in a family of two boys and one girl. Her father is a quiet and gentle medical researcher who married when he was 35 years old. Dr. Smith often worked at home, so he had extensive contact with his children when they were young. He loved all his children but clearly favored Jay. His ambitions for her were extremely high, and as she matured he responded to her every need and demand almost immediately and with full conviction. He wanted to instill in her a strong desire for achievement. Their relationship remains as close today as it was during Jay's childhood.

Jay's mother, who was 30 years old when she married, worked long hours away from home as a store manager and consequently saw her children primarily at night and on an occasional free weekend. When she came home, Mrs. Smith was tired and had little energy for "nonessential" interactions with her children; instead she devoted her efforts to feeding them (especially the younger ones) and to putting the house in order. The competing demands of her roles as mother, homemaker, and employee caused her considerable conflict. Mrs. Smith was usually amiable toward all her children but tended to argue more with Jay than with the others—at least until Jay was about 6 or 7 years old, when the bickering subsided. Today their relationship is cordial but lacks the closeness that exists between Jay and her father.

Dr. and Mrs. Smith's relationship was not a tranquil one. Stormy outbursts over seemingly trivial matters were followed by periods of mutual silence lasting for days. Jay was very jealous of her first brother, born when she was 2 years old. Her parents recall that Jay sometimes staged temper tantrums when the new infant demanded and received a lot of attention (especially from Mrs. Smith). The tantrums intensified when Jay's second brother was born, just 1 year after the first. As children, the brothers formed an alliance to try to undermine Jay's supreme position with their father. Jay only became closer to her father, while her relationships with her brothers were marked by greater-than-average jealousy and rivalry from early childhood to the present.

Throughout elementary, junior high, and high school Jay was popular and did well academically. When asked once by a favorite teacher about future goals, she replied confidently, "I plan on going into medicine because I enjoy helping people, particularly when they are sick and must be taken care of." Yet despite Jay's stated lofty goals and ambitions, off and on between the ages of 8 and 17 she had strong feelings of loneliness, depression, insecurity, and confusion—feelings common enough during this age period, but stronger than in most youngsters and very distressing to Jay.

Jay's college days, when she was away from home for the first time, proved exciting and challenging. This was a period of great personal growth for her, but it also caused her much pain. While having new friends and responsibilities increased Jay's self-confidence and zeal for pursuing a medical career, several unsuccessful romantic involvements led her to concentrate even more on her studies. The failure to achieve a lasting relationship persisted after college and troubled Jay greatly.

Although even-tempered in most circumstances, Jay has had explosive fits of anger that have ended each important heterosexual relationship she has cultivated. Her friendships with other women, while more stable than those with men, are usually casual, uncommitted, and of short duration.

When Jay was 13, she became good friends with a male classmate named Mark. They had many interesting hours of conversation, even though Jay was never able "to be myself" or "really express my feelings" to Mark. The relationship thrived, nevertheless, until one day when a minor disagreement suddenly erupted into a major argument. Jay ran away and tearfully said that she did not want to see Mark again. Despite his persistent efforts to talk with her, she would have nothing further to do with him.

Much later, while finishing her undergraduate education, Jay met Ted, a graduate student 15 years older than she. At 21 Jay felt that she was falling in love, but their relationship was over in just 2 months. Although Jay and Ted were close and trusted each other, an innocent conversation between Ted and a

Personality
An individual's unique pattern of thoughts, feelings, and behaviors that persists over time and across situations.

female classmate triggered Jay's rage. When Jay caught sight of the two together, she turned and hurried away. Ted finally caught up with her, but she screamed angrily that she never wanted to see him again. And she never did.

Jay was admitted to medical school, but after her initial excitement, she realized that she was in for years of difficult work, intense competition, and the always present possibility of failure. Feeling the intense pressures of medical school, Jay passed up potential romantic involvements, although she had many casual friends. While she tried not to dwell on her feelings during this period, they crept into her consciousness periodically: "I don't deserve to be a doctor"; "I won't pass my exams"; "Who am I, and what do I want from life?"; "Why can't I meet that special person?" At graduation Dr. Jaylene Elizabeth Smith was at the top of her class—but far from satisfied.

How can we describe and understand Jaylene Smith's personality? How did she become who she is? Why does she feel insecure and uncertain despite her obvious success? Why do her friends see her as charming and attractive, while she describes herself as introverted and inadequate? Each of the several theoretical perspectives on personality provides somewhat different answers to these questions.

Psychodynamic Theories

According to psychodynamic theorists, how is personality determined?

Psychodynamic theories view behavior as the end product of psychological dynamics that interact within the individual, often outside conscious awareness. Freud drew on the physics of his day to coin the term *psychodynamics:* As thermodynamics is the study of heat and mechanical energy and how one may be transformed into the other, psychodynamics is the study of psychic energy and how it is transformed and expressed in behavior. Psychodynamic theorists disagreed among themselves about the exact nature of this psychic energy. Some, like Freud, traced it to sexual and aggressive urges; others, like Karen Horney, saw it as rooted in the individual's struggle to deal with dependency. But all psychodynamic theorists share the sense that personality is primarily determined by unconscious processes and can best be understood within the context of life span development.

Sigmund Freud

When Freud stated that the sexual instinct is the basis of behavior, how was he defining "sexual instinct"?

To this day, Sigmund Freud (1856–1939) is the best known and most influential of the personality theorists (see Chapter 1). Freud created an entirely new perspective on the study of human behavior. Before Freud, psychology had focused on consciousness—that is, on those thoughts and feelings of which we are aware. Freud, however, stressed the **unconscious**—all the ideas, thoughts, and feelings of which we are *not* normally aware. The term **psychoanalysis** is used for both the theory of personality that Freud developed and the form of therapy that he invented (discussed in Chapter 13).

According to Freud, human behavior is based on unconscious instincts, or drives. Some instincts are aggressive and destructive; others—such as hunger, thirst, self-preservation, and sex—are necessary to the survival of the individual and the species. Freud used the term *sexual instinct* to refer not just to erotic sexuality but also to the desire for virtually any form of pleasure. In this broad sense, Freud regarded the sexual instinct as the most critical factor in the development of personality.

Psychodynamic theories
Personality theories contending that behavior results from psychological dynamics that interact within the individual, often outside conscious awareness.

Unconscious
In Freud's theory all the ideas, thoughts, and feelings of which we are not and normally cannot become aware.

Psychoanalysis
The theory of personality that Freud developed as well as the form of therapy he invented.

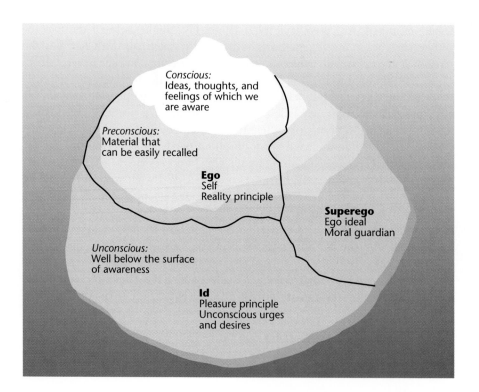

FIGURE 10–1

The structural relationship formed by the id, ego, and superego. Freud's conception of personality is often depicted as an iceberg to illustrate how the vast workings of the mind occur beneath its surface. Notice how the ego is partly conscious, partly unconscious, and partly preconscious; it derives knowledge of the external world through the senses. The superego also works at all three levels. But the id is an entirely unconscious structure.

Source: Adapted from *New Introductory Lectures on Psychoanalysis,* by Sigmund Freud (New York: Carleton House, 1933).

Id
In Freud's theory of personality, the collection of unconscious urges and desires that continually seek expression.

Pleasure principle
According to Freud, the way in which the id seeks immediate gratification of an instinct.

Ego
Freud's term for the part of the personality that mediates between environmental demands (reality), conscience (superego), and instinctual needs (id); now often used as a synonym for "self."

Reality principle
According to Freud, the way in which the ego seeks to satisfy instinctual demands safely and effectively in the real world.

How Personality Is Structured According to Freud, personality is formed around three structures: the *id*, the *ego*, and the *superego*. The **id** is the only structure present at birth and the only one that is completely unconscious (see Figure 10–1). In Freud's view the id consists of unconscious urges and desires that continually seek expression. It operates according to the **pleasure principle**—that is, it tries to obtain immediate pleasure and to avoid pain (see Figure 10–2). As soon as an instinct arises, the id seeks to gratify it. But because the id is not in contact with the real world, it has only two ways of obtaining gratification. One is by reflex actions, such as coughing, which relieve unpleasant sensations at once. The other is through fantasy, or what Freud referred to as *wish fulfillment*: A person forms a mental image of an object or situation that partially satisfies the instinct and relieves the uncomfortable feeling. This kind of thought occurs most often in dreams and daydreams, but it may take other forms. For instance, if someone insults you and you spend the next half hour imagining all the things you might say or do to get even with that person, you are engaging in a form of wish fulfillment.

Mental images of this kind provide fleeting relief, but they cannot fully satisfy most needs. Just thinking about being with someone you love may be gratifying, but it is a poor substitute for actually being with that person. Therefore the id by itself is not very effective at gratifying instincts. It must link up with reality if it is to relieve its discomfort. The id's link to reality is the ego.

Freud conceived of the **ego** as the psychic mechanism that controls all thinking and reasoning activities. The ego operates partly consciously, partly *preconsciously*, and partly unconsciously. (Preconscious refers to material that is not currently in awareness but can easily be recalled.) The ego learns about the external world through the senses and sees to the satisfaction of the id's drives in the external world. In seeking to replace discomfort with comfort, the id acts according to the pleasure principle, while the ego operates by the **reality principle:** By means of intelligent reasoning, the ego tries to delay satisfying the id's desires until it can do so safely and successfully (see Figure 10–2). For example,

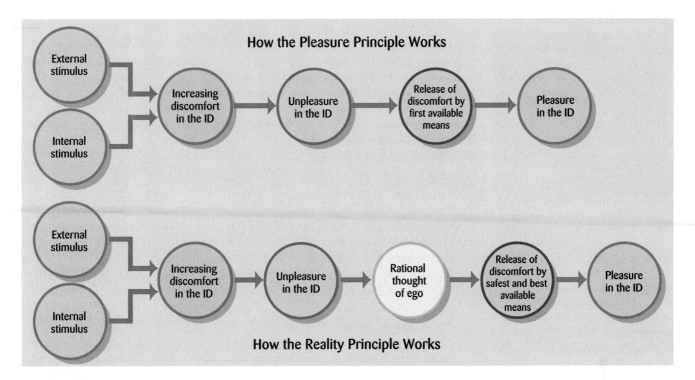

FIGURE 10–2

How Freud conceived the workings of the pleasure and reality principles. Note that according to the reality principle, the ego uses rational thought to postpone the gratification of the id until its desires can be satisfied safely.

if you are thirsty, your ego will attempt to determine how best to obtain something to quench your thirst effectively and safely.

A personality that consisted only of ego and id would be completely selfish. It would behave effectively but unsociably. Fully adult behavior is governed not only by reality but also by morality—that is, by the individual's conscience or the moral standards that the individual develops through interaction with parents and society. Freud called this moral watchdog the **superego.**

The superego is not present at birth. In fact, as young children we are amoral and do whatever is pleasurable. As we mature, however, we assimilate, or adopt as our own, the judgments of our parents about what is "good" and "bad." In time the external restraint applied by our parents is completely replaced by our own internal self-restraint. The superego, eventually acting as conscience, takes over the task of observing and guiding the ego, just as the parents once observed and guided the child. Like the ego, it works at both the conscious and the unconscious level.

According to Freud, the superego also compares the ego's actions with an **ego ideal** of perfection and then rewards or punishes the ego accordingly. Unfortunately, the superego is often harsh in its judgments. An artist dominated by such a punishing superego, for example, may realize the impossibility of ever equaling Rembrandt or Michelangelo and give up painting in despair.

Ideally, our id, ego, and superego work in harmony, the ego satisfying the demands of the id in a reasonable, moral manner approved by the superego. We are then free to love and to hate and to express our emotions sensibly and without guilt. When our id is dominant, our instincts are unbridled, and we are apt to endanger both ourselves and society. When our superego dominates, our behavior is checked too tightly, and we are inclined to judge ourselves so harshly or quickly that we impair our ability to act on our own behalf and enjoy ourselves.

Superego
According to Freud, the social and parental standards that the individual has internalized; the conscience and the ego ideal.

Ego ideal
The part of the superego that consists of standards of what one would like to be.

Freud believed that during the oral stage, when babies are dependent on others to fulfill their needs, they derive pleasure from the mouth, lips, and tongue. Lack of confidence is among the traits he attributed to fixation at this stage.

Libido
According to Freud, the energy generated by the sexual instinct.

Fixation
According to Freud, a partial or complete halt at some point in the individual's psychosexual development.

Oral stage
First stage in Freud's theory of personality development, in which the infant's erotic feelings center on the mouth, lips, and tongue.

Anal stage
Second stage in Freud's theory of personality development, in which a child's erotic feelings center on the anus and on elimination.

Phallic stage
Third stage in Freud's theory of personality development, in which erotic feelings center on the genitals.

Oedipus complex and Electra complex
According to Freud, a child's sexual attachment to the parent of the opposite sex and jealousy toward the parent of the same sex; generally occurs in the phallic stage.

How Personality Develops   Freud's theory of personality development gives center stage to the way in which the sexual instinct—broadly, the craving for sensual pleasure of all kinds—is satisfied during the course of life. Freud called the energy generated by the sexual instinct **libido.** As infants mature, their libido becomes focused on different sensitive parts of the body. During the first 18 months of life the dominant source of sensual pleasure is the mouth. At about 18 months sensuality shifts to the anus, and at about age 3 it shifts again, this time to the genitals. According to Freud, children's experiences at each stage stamp their personality with tendencies that endure into adulthood. If a child is deprived of pleasure (or allowed too much gratification) from the part of the body that dominates a certain stage, some sexual energy may remain permanently tied to that part of the body instead of moving on in normal sequence to give the individual a fully integrated personality. This is called **fixation,** and as we shall see, Freud believed that it leads to immature forms of sexuality and to certain characteristic personality traits. Let's look more closely at the psychosexual stages that Freud identified and their presumed relationship to personality development.

In the **oral stage** (birth to 18 months) infants, who depend completely on others to satisfy their needs, relieve sexual tension by sucking and swallowing; when their baby teeth come in, they obtain oral pleasure from chewing and biting. According to Freud, infants who receive too much oral gratification at this stage grow into overly optimistic and dependent adults. Conversely, those who receive too little may turn into pessimistic and hostile people later in life. Freud suggested that fixation at this stage is linked to such personality characteristics as lack of confidence, gullibility, sarcasm, and argumentativeness.

During the **anal stage** (roughly 18 months to 3½ years) the primary source of sexual pleasure shifts from the mouth to the anus. Just about the time children begin to derive pleasure from holding in and excreting feces, toilet training takes place, and they must learn to regulate this new pleasure. According to Freud, if parents are too strict in toilet training, their children may become obstinate, stingy, and excessively orderly. If parents are too lenient, their children may become messy, unorganized, and sloppy.

When children reach the **phallic stage** (after age 3) they discover their genitals, develop a marked attachment to the parent of the opposite sex, and become jealous of the same-sex parent. In males Freud called this phenomenon the **Oedipus complex,** after the character in Greek mythology who killed his father and married his mother. Girls go through a corresponding **Electra complex,** involving possessive love for their fathers and jealousy toward their mothers. Most children eventually resolve these conflicts by identifying with the parent of the same sex. Freud contended, however, that fixation at this stage leads to vanity and egotism in adult life, with men boasting of their sexual prowess and treating women with contempt, and women becoming flirtatious and promiscuous. Phallic fixation may also prompt feelings of low self-esteem, shyness, and worthlessness.

At the end of the phallic period, Freud believed, children lose interest in sexual behavior and enter a **latency period.** During this period, which begins at about age 5 or 6 and lasts until 12 or 13, boys play with boys, girls play with girls, and neither sex takes much interest in the other.

At puberty the individual enters the last psychosexual stage, which Freud called the **genital stage.** At this time sexual impulses reawaken. In lovemaking the adolescent and the adult are able to satisfy unfulfilled desires from infancy and childhood. Ideally, immediate gratification of these desires is replaced by mature sexuality, in which postponed gratification, a sense of responsibility, and caring for others all play a part.

Freud's male-centered phallic view of personality development has been assailed by feminists, especially because he also hypothesized that all little girls feel inferior because they do not have a penis. The tendency today is to see *penis*

According to Carl Jung, we all inherit from our ancestors collective memories or "thought forms" that people have had in common since the dawn of human evolution. The image of a motherlike figure with protective, embracing arms is one such primordial thought form that stems from the important, nurturing role of women throughout human history. This thought form is depicted here in this Bulgarian clay figure of a goddess that dates back some six or seven thousand years. It is also captured in this contemporary painting, *In Communication,* by the artist Bharati Chaudhuri.

envy as much less central to female personality development than Freud thought it was (Gelman, 1990). In fact, the whole view that male and female personality development proceed along similar lines is being challenged. It may be, for example, that the developmental tasks facing boys are quite different from those facing girls. If this is the case, then the unique developmental tasks encountered by girls may leave them with important skills and abilities that were overlooked or minimized in Freud's theory.

Freud's beliefs, particularly his emphasis on sexuality, were not completely endorsed even by members of his own psychoanalytic school. Carl Jung and Alfred Adler, two early associates of Freud, eventually broke with him and formulated their own psychodynamic theories of personality. Jung accepted Freud's stress on unconscious motivation but expanded the scope of the unconscious well beyond the selfish satisfactions of the id. Adler believed that human beings have positive—and conscious—goals that guide their behavior. Other psychodynamic theorists put greater emphasis on the ego and its attempts to gain mastery over the world. These neo-Freudians, principally Karen Horney and Erik Erikson, also focused more on the influence of social interaction on personality.

Carl Jung

How did Carl Jung's view of the unconscious differ from Freud's?

Carl Jung (1875–1961) embraced many of Freud's tenets, but his beliefs differed from Freud's in novel ways. Jung contended that libido, or psychic energy, represents *all* the life forces, not just the sexual ones. Both Freud and Jung emphasized the role of the unconscious in determining human behavior, but whereas Freud viewed the id as a "cauldron of seething excitations" that the ego has to control, Jung saw the unconscious as the ego's source of strength and vitality. Jung also believed that the unconscious can be divided into the personal unconscious and

Latency period
In Freud's theory of personality development a period in which the child appears to have no interest in the other sex; occurs after the phallic stage.

Genital stage
In Freud's theory of personality development the final stage of normal adult sexual development, which is usually marked by mature sexuality.

Stevie Wonder, a blind man who became a highly successful musician, illustrates what Alfred Adler referred to as *compensation*.

Personal unconscious
In Jung's theory of personality one of the two levels of the unconscious; it contains the individual's repressed thoughts, forgotten experiences, and undeveloped ideas.

Collective unconscious
In Jung's theory of personality the level of the unconscious that is inherited and common to all members of a species.

Archetypes
In Jung's theory of personality thought forms common to all human beings, stored in the collective unconscious.

Persona
According to Jung, our public self, the mask we put on to represent ourselves to others.

Anima
According to Jung, the female archetype as it is expressed in the male personality.

Animus
According to Jung, the male archetype as it is expressed in the female personality.

Compensation
According to Adler, the person's effort to overcome imagined or real personal weaknesses.

the collective unconscious. Within the realm of the **personal unconscious** fall our repressed thoughts, forgotten experiences, and undeveloped ideas, which may rise to consciousness if an incident or sensation triggers their recall.

The **collective unconscious,** Jung's most original concept, comprises the memories and behavior patterns inherited from past generations. Just as the human body is the product of millions of years of evolution, so, too, according to Jung, has the human mind developed over the millennia "thought forms," or collective memories, of experiences that people have had in common since prehistoric times. These thought forms, which he called **archetypes,** appear as typical mental images or mythical representations. Because all people have mothers, for example, the archetype of "mother" is universally associated with the image of one's own mother, with Mother Earth, and with a protective presence.

Jung felt that specific archetypes play special roles in shaping personality. The **persona** (an archetype whose meaning stems from the Latin word for "mask") is the element of our personality by which we are known to other people—a "shell" that grows around our inner self. For some people the public self so predominates that they lose touch with their inner feelings, leading to personality maladjustments.

Because Jung saw men and women as each having aspects of both sexes in their personalities, two other important archetypes are the **anima,** the female archetype as it is expressed in a man, and the **animus,** the male archetype as expressed in a woman. Thus Jung considered aggressive behavior in females and nurturant behavior in males to be manifestations of the animus and the anima, respectively.

Jung also divided people into two general attitude types: extroverts and introverts. *Extroverts* turn their attention to the external world; they are "joiners" who take an active interest in other people and in the events going on around them. *Introverts* are more caught up in their own private worlds; they tend to be unsociable and lack confidence in dealing with other people. Everyone, Jung felt, possesses some aspects of both attitude types, but one is usually dominant while the other remains largely submerged.

While Freud emphasized the primacy of the sexual instinct, Jung stressed people's rational and spiritual qualities. Jung brought a sense of historical continuity to his theories, tracing the roots of human personality back through our ancestral past. Yet he also contended that a person moves constantly toward self-realization—toward blending all parts of the personality into a harmonious whole.

Alfred Adler

What did Alfred Adler believe was the major determinant of personality?

Alfred Adler (1870–1931) disagreed sharply with Freud's concept of the personality emerging out of the conflict between the id's desire to gratify instinctual impulses and the superego's morality-based restrictions. Adler believed that we all possess innate positive motives that strive for personal and social perfection. As a child, Adler was frail and almost died of pneumonia at the age of 5. This early brush with death led him to the concept that personality develops through the individual's attempt to overcome physical weaknesses, an effort he called **compensation.** The blind person who, like Stevie Wonder, cultivates particularly acute auditory abilities, and the disabled child who, like the late Wilma Rudolph, surmounts the crippling effects of a disease to become an athlete illustrate Adler's theory of compensation.

Later on Adler modified and broadened his views, contending that people seek to overcome *feelings* of inferiority that may or may not have a basis in reality. Such feelings may spring from a child's sense of being inferior to parents, siblings, teachers, or peers. To Adler, birth order made a crucial difference in this sense of inferiority. That is, it does not matter whether second or third children are, in fact, inferior to their older siblings at athletics; what matters is that they *believe* they are. Adler held that the attempt to overcome such feelings of inferiority drives much of human behavior and strongly shapes adult personality. Inferiority feelings often spark personal growth, but some people become so fixated on their feelings of inferiority that they become paralyzed, developing what Adler called an **inferiority complex.**

Late in life Adler again shifted his thinking to a more positive direction when he concluded that strivings for superiority and perfection were more important to personality development than overcoming feelings of inferiority. He suggested that people strive both for personal perfection and for the perfection of society. As they do so, they set goals that guide their behavior. Adler's emphasis on positive, socially constructive goals and on striving for perfection contrast sharply with Freud's vision of the selfish person locked into conflict with society. Adler re-introduced into psychology the idea that striving toward personally positive and socially beneficial goals is an important part of human personality and development.

Unlike Freud, Adler believed that we are not controlled by our environment. Instead he argued that we have the capacity to master our own fate. Because of this emphasis on voluntary striving toward positive goals, Adler has been hailed by many psychologists as the father of humanistic psychology.

Karen Horney

Freud's theory emphasized unconscious conflicts. What external factors did Horney add to this theory?

Karen Horney (1885–1952), another psychodynamic personality theorist who was greatly indebted to Freud, disagreed with some of his most prominent ideas, especially his analysis of women and his emphasis on sexual instincts. Based on her experience as a practicing therapist in Germany and the United States, Horney concluded that environmental and social factors are the most important influences in shaping personality, and among these, the most critical are the relationships we have as children.

Horney believed that Freud overemphasized the sex drive, leading him to a distorted picture of human relationships. While sexuality does figure in the development of personality, Horney thought that nonsexual factors—such as the need for a sense of basic security and the response to real or imagined threats—play an even larger role. For example, all people share the need to feel loved and nurtured by their parents, regardless of any sexual feelings they might have about them. Conversely, parents' protective feelings toward their children emerge not only from biological forces but also from the value society places on the nurturance of children.

For Horney, *anxiety*—an individual's reaction to real or imagined dangers—is a powerful motivating force. Whereas Freud believed that anxiety usually emerges from sexual conflicts, Horney stressed that feelings of anxiety also originate in a variety of nonsexual contexts. In childhood, anxiety arises because children depend on adults for their very survival. Anxious because they are insecure about receiving continued nurturance and protection, children develop inner protections, or defenses, that provide both satisfaction and security. They experience more anxiety when those defenses are threatened.

As adults, according to Horney (1937), we adopt one of three coping strategies, or **neurotic trends,** that help us to deal with emotional problems and ensure safety, albeit at the expense of personal independence: moving toward

"I'm only a <u>good</u> dane."

Inferiority complex
In Adler's theory the fixation on feelings of personal inferiority that results in emotional and social paralysis.

Neurotic trends
Horney's term for irrational strategies for coping with emotional problems and minimizing anxiety.

Karen Horney, a psychotherapist during the first half of the twentieth century, disagreed with Freud's emphasis on sexual instincts. She considered environmental and social factors, especially the relationships we have as children, to be the most important influences on personality.

people (submission), moving against people (aggression), and moving away from people (detachment). Each person's characteristic reliance on one or another of these strategies is reflected in his or her patterns of behavior, or *personality type.* For Horney a compliant type is an individual who has an overriding need to give in or submit to others and feels safe only when receiving their protection and guidance. This is neurotic, according to Horney, because the resultant friendliness is superficial and masks feelings of aggression and anxiety. In contrast, the aggressive type masks his or her submissive feelings and relates to others in a hostile and domineering manner. The aggressive type, however, is also hiding basic feelings of insecurity and anxiety. Finally, the detached type copes with basic anxiety by withdrawing from other people. This person seems to be saying, "If I withdraw, nothing can hurt me." Well-adjusted people also experience anxiety and threats to their basic security, but because their childhood environment enabled them to satisfy their basic emotional needs, they were able to develop without becoming trapped in neurotic lifestyles.

Parting company with Freud again, Horney held that cultural forces—including social status and social roles—shape our development more than do biological imperatives. She believed that adults can continue to develop and change throughout life. And if biology is not destiny, then personality differences between men and women would have more to do with culture than anatomy. Horney was a forerunner of contemporary thinkers who believe that culture and society can be changed and, in the process, transform human relationships as well.

Erik Erikson

Erikson's theory focused less on unconscious conflict and more on what factors?

Erik Erikson (1902–1994), who studied with Freud in Vienna, was another psychodynamic theorist who held a socially oriented view of personality development. Erikson agreed with much of Freud's thinking on sexual development and the influence of libidinal needs on personality. He also stressed the quality of parent–child relationships, and he shifted the focus of Freud's personality theory to ego development: Within the family, the child's first contact with society, Erikson believed that children can be treated in ways that make them feel loved or hated. The key is that children should feel their own needs and desires to be compatible with those of society as embodied in their family. Only if children feel competent and valuable, in their own eyes and in society's, will they develop a secure sense of identity.

In Chapter 9, Life Span Development, we examined how some aspects of Erikson's theory have been incorporated in the contemporary view of human development. Erikson (1963) outlined 8 stages of personality development (see Figure 10–3). Each stage involves its own developmental crisis, whose resolution is crucial to adjustment in successive stages.

1. *Trust versus mistrust.* During the first year of life, babies are torn between trusting and not trusting their parents. If their needs are generally met, infants come to trust the environment and themselves. This leads to faith in the predictability of the environment and optimism about the future. Frustrated infants become suspicious, fearful, and overly concerned with security.

2. *Autonomy versus shame and doubt.* During their first 3 years, as physical development proceeds, children gain increasing autonomy and begin to explore their surroundings. They learn to walk, hold on to things, and control their excretory functions. A child who repeatedly fails to master these skills may develop self-doubt. One response to self-doubt is the practice of abiding compulsively by fixed routines. At the other extreme is the hostile rejection of

Erik Erikson, another psychodynamic theorist, also stressed the influence of parent–child relationships on development. His 8-stage theory of personality development is still influential today.

Erikson's stages of personality development

Stage	1	2	3	4	5	6	7	8
Oral	Basic trust vs. mistrust							
Anal		Autonomy vs. shame, doubt						
Phallic			Initiative vs. guilt					
Latency				Industry vs. inferiority				
Genital					Identity vs. role confusion			
Young adulthood						Intimacy vs. isolation		
Adulthood							Generativity vs. stagnation	
Maturity								Ego integrity vs. despair

(Left axis label: Freud's stages of personality development — brackets Oral through Genital)

FIGURE 10–3

Erikson's 8 stages of personality development. Each stage involves its own developmental crisis, whose resolution is crucial to adjustment in successive stages. The first 5 of the 8 stages correspond to Freud's stages of personality development.

Source: From *Childhood and Society,* by Erik H. Erikson. Copyright © 1950, 1963 by W. W. Norton & Company, Inc. Renewed 1978 by Erik H. Erikson. Used by permission of W. W. Norton & Company, Inc.

all controls, both internal and external. If parents and other adults belittle a child's efforts, the child may begin to feel shame and acquire a lasting sense of inferiority.

3. *Initiative versus guilt.* Between the ages of 3 and 6, children become increasingly active, undertaking new projects, manipulating things in the environment, making plans, and conquering new challenges. Parental support and encouragement for these initiatives lead to a sense of joy in exercising initiative and taking on new challenges. If the child is scolded for these initiatives, however, strong feelings of guilt, unworthiness, and resentment may take hold and persist.

4. *Industry versus inferiority.* During the next 6 or 7 years, children encounter a new set of expectations at home and at school. They must learn the skills needed to become well-rounded adults, including personal care, productive work, and independent social living. If children are stifled in their efforts to become part of the adult world, they may conclude that they are inadequate, mediocre, or inferior and lose faith in their power to become self-sufficient.

5. *Identity versus role confusion.* At puberty, childhood ends, and the responsibilities of adulthood loom just ahead. The critical problem at this stage is to find one's identity. In Erikson's view, identity is achieved by integrating a number of roles—student, sister or brother, friend, and so on—into a coherent pattern that gives the young person a sense of inner continuity or identity. Failure to forge an identity leads to role confusion and despair.

According to Erikson, gaining some autonomy from parents is the central challenge of the toddler years. The sense of being able to do simple things "by myself" is a major source of joy and pride for children this age. If adults belittle these efforts toward early independence, the child may come to feel shame and self-doubt.

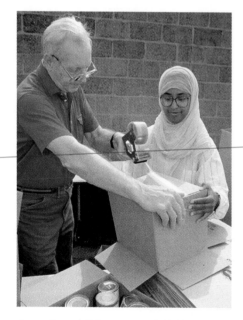

According to Erikson, people in late adulthood can achieve a sense of ego integrity in which they view their life as complete and satisfactory.

6. *Intimacy versus isolation.* During young adulthood, men and women must resolve a critical new issue: the question of intimacy. To love someone else, Erikson argued, we must have resolved our earlier crises successfully and feel secure in our own identities. To form an intimate relationship, lovers must be trusting, autonomous, and capable of initiative, and must exhibit other hallmarks of maturity. Failure at intimacy brings a painful sense of loneliness and the feeling of being incomplete.

7. *Generativity versus stagnation.* During middle adulthood, roughly between the ages of 25 and 60, the challenge is to remain productive and creative in all aspects of one's life. People who have successfully negotiated the 6 earlier stages are likely to find meaning and joy in all the major activities of life—career, family, community participation. For others life becomes a drab routine, and they feel dull and resentful.

8. *Ego integrity versus despair.* With the onset of old age, people must try to come to terms with their approaching death. For some this is a period of despair at the loss of former roles, such as employee and parent. Yet, according to Erikson, this stage also represents an opportunity to attain full selfhood. By this he meant an acceptance of one's life, a sense that it is complete and satisfactory. People who have gained full maturity by resolving the conflicts in all the earlier stages possess the integrity to face death with a minimum of fear.

A Psychodynamic View of Jaylene Smith

Psychodynamic theorists would consider Jaylene Smith's personality the result of what unresolved issues?

According to Freud, personality characteristics such as insecurity, introversion, and feelings of inadequacy and worthlessness often arise from fixation at the phallic stage of development. Thus, had Freud been Jaylene's therapist, he would probably have concluded that Jay has not yet effectively resolved her Electra complex. Working from this premise, he might have hypothesized that Jay's relationship with her father was either very distant and unsatisfying or unusually close and gratifying. As we know, it was the latter.

Freud might also have asserted that at around age 5 or 6 Jay had become aware that she could not actually marry her father and do away with her mother, as he would say she wished to do. On this point it is interesting that the arguments and fights between Jay and her mother subsided when Jay was about 6 or 7 years of age. Moreover, we know that shortly thereafter, Jay began to experience strong feelings of loneliness, depression, insecurity, and confusion. Clearly, something important happened in Jay's life when she was 6 or 7.

Finally, the continued coolness in Jay's relationship with her mother and the unusual closeness with her father would probably have confirmed Freud's suspicion that Jay has still not satisfactorily resolved her Electra complex. Thus Freud would have predicted Jay's problems making the progression to mature sexual relationships with other men.

Erikson maintained that success in dealing with developmental crises depends on how effectively one has resolved earlier crises. Jay's difficulty in dealing with intimacy (Stage 6) would have suggested that she is still struggling with problems from earlier stages. Erikson would have looked for the source of these problems in the quality of Jay's relationships with others. Her mother's "subtly" communicated feelings of dissatisfaction and pattern of spending little time on "nonessential" interactions with her children would not have instilled the sense of basic trust and security essential to the first stage and, in turn, later stages of development. In addition, her relationship with her mother and brothers continued to be less than fully satisfactory. It is not surprising, then, that Jay had some difficulty working through subsequent developmental crises. Although she developed a close and caring relationship with her father, Jay was surely aware that his affection partly depended on her fulfilling his dreams, ambitions, and goals for her.

Evaluating Psychodynamic Theories

What are the major criticisms of psychodynamic theories?

Freud's insight that we are often unaware of the real causes of our behavior has fundamentally changed the way we view ourselves and others and has had a lasting impact on history, literature, and the arts. Nevertheless, Freud was a product of his time and place. He apparently was unable to imagine a connection between his female patients' sense of inferiority and their subordinate position in their society.

Psychodynamic views have been criticized because they are based largely on retrospective (backward-looking) accounts of people who have sought treatment rather than on experimental research with "healthy" individuals. Freud's theory has received some limited support from research, however. For example, people who eat and drink too much do tend to report oral images when interpreting inkblot tests (Bertrand & Masling, 1969; Masling, Rabie, & Blondheim, 1967). Orally fixated people also seem to depend heavily on others, as Freud predicted (Fisher & Greenberg, 1985). Research has not confirmed that such personality characteristics stem from the kinds of early childhood experiences described by Freud, but some support for Freud's theory has come from experiments that use stimuli designed to "trigger" particular unconscious processes (Cloninger, 1993).

Although the effectiveness of psychoanalysis as a therapy has been cited as evidence supporting Freud's theories, it does not seem to be any more or less effective than therapies based on other theories (Stiles, Shapiro, & Elliott, 1986). Whatever their merit as science, psychodynamic theories attempt to explain the root causes of all human behavior, and the sheer magnitude of this undertaking helps to account for their lasting attractiveness.

REVIEW QUESTIONS

1. Personality is the pattern of thoughts, feelings, and behaviors that persists over ____ and ____ and that distinguishes one person from another.

Match the following of Freud's terms with the appropriate definition.

2. unconscious	____ a. energy that comes from the sexual instinct
3. superego	____ b. mediator between reality, the superego, and the id
4. id	____ c. unconscious urges seeking expression
5. ego	____ d. ideas and feelings of which we are normally not aware
6. libido	____ e. moral guardian of the ego

Match the following of Jung's terms with the appropriate definition.

7. persona	____ a. typical mental image or mythical representation
8. collective unconscious	____ b. memories and behavior patterns inherited from past generations
9. archetype	____ c. aspect of the personality by which one is known to other people

Match the following of Adler's terms with the appropriate definition.

10. inferiority complex	____ a. fixation on or belief in a negative characteristic
11. compensation	____ b. individual's effort to overcome weaknesses

12. Horney believed that ____ is a stronger source of emotional disturbance than sexual urges.

13. Erikson held a ____ oriented view of personality development.

Answers: 1. time, situations. 2. d. 3. e. 4. c. 5. b. 6. a. 7. c. 8. b. 9. a. 10. a. 11. b. 12. anxiety, 13. socially.

Carl Rogers believed that the goal of life is to fulfill our innate potential, which ideally comes to be reflected in the image we have of ourselves. This young woman's work painting houses for the poor suggests that she sees herself as kind and caring and is striving to reflect that image in her actions. In Rogers's view she may be on the way to becoming a self-actualized person.

Humanistic personality theory
Any personality theory that asserts the fundamental goodness of people and their striving toward higher levels of functioning.

Actualizing tendency
According to Rogers, the drive of every organism to fulfill its biological potential and become what it is inherently capable of becoming.

Self-actualizing tendency
According to Rogers, the drive of human beings to fulfill their self-concepts, or the images they have of themselves.

Fully functioning person
According to Rogers, an individual whose self-concept closely resembles his or her inborn capacities or potentials.

Humanistic Personality Theories

What are the major ways that humanistic personality theory differs in emphasis from psychodynamic theories?

Freud believed that personality grows out of the resolution of unconscious conflicts and developmental crises. Many of his followers—including some who modified his theory and others who broke away from his circle—also embraced this basic point of view. But in the theory of Alfred Adler, we glimpsed a very different view of human nature. Because Adler wrote about forces that contribute to positive growth and a move toward personal perfection, he is sometimes called the first *humanistic* personality theorist.

Humanistic personality theory emphasizes that we are positively motivated and progress toward higher levels of functioning—in other words, that there is more to human existence than dealing with hidden conflicts. Humanists stress people's potential for growth and change—as well as the ways in which they subjectively experience their lives right now—rather than dwelling on how they felt or acted in the past. As a result, this approach holds all of us personally responsible for our lives and their outcome. Finally, humanists also believe that given reasonable life conditions, people will develop in desirable directions (Cloninger, 1993). Adler's concept of striving for perfection laid the groundwork for later humanistic personality theorists such as Abraham Maslow and Carl Rogers. We discussed Maslow's theory of the hierarchy of needs leading to self-actualization in Chapter 8, Motivation and Emotion. We now turn to Rogers's theory of self-actualization.

Carl Rogers

What important capacities did Carl Rogers believe we are born with?

Humanistic psychologists believe that life is a process of striving to achieve our potential, of opening ourselves to the world around us and experiencing joy in living. Carl Rogers, who died in 1987, was one of the most prominent humanistic theorists who contended that men and women develop their personalities in the service of positive goals. According to Rogers, every organism is born with certain innate capacities, capabilities, or potentials—"a sort of genetic blueprint, to which substance is added as life progresses" (Maddi, 1989, p. 102). The goal of life, Rogers believed, is to fulfill this genetic blueprint, to become the best of whatever each of us is inherently capable of becoming. Rogers called this biological push toward fulfillment the **actualizing tendency.** While Rogers maintained that the actualizing tendency characterizes all organisms—plants, animals, and humans—he noted that human beings also form images of themselves, or *self-concepts.* Just as we try to fulfill our inborn biological potential, so, too, we attempt to fulfill our self-concept, our conscious sense of who we are and what we want to do with our lives. Rogers called this striving the **self-actualizing tendency.** If you think of yourself as "intelligent" and "athletic," for example, you will strive to live up to those images of yourself.

When our self-concept is closely matched with our inborn capacities, we are likely to become what Rogers called a **fully functioning person.** Such people are self-directed: They decide for themselves what it is they wish to do and to become, even though their choices may not always be sound ones. They are not unduly swayed by other people's expectations for them. Fully functioning people are also open to experience—to their own feelings as well as to the world and other people around them—and thus find themselves "increasingly willing to be, with greater accuracy and depth, that self which [they] most truly [are]" (C. R. Rogers, 1961, pp. 175–76).

According to Rogers, when people are brought up with **unconditional positive regard**—or the experience of being treated with warmth, respect, acceptance, and love, regardless of their own feelings, attitudes, and behaviors—they are fully functioning, having developed self-concepts that are consistent with their unique genetic blueprints. When people lose sight of their inborn potential, they feel threatened, anxious, and uncomfortable and become constricted, rigid, and defensive. Because their lives are directed toward what other people want, they are unlikely to experience much real satisfaction. At some point they may realize that they don't really know who they are or what they want.

A Humanistic View of Jaylene Smith

How would humanistic theorists view the development of Jaylene Smith's personality?

Humanistic personality theory would focus on the discrepancy between Jay's self-concept and her inborn capacities. Rogers would point out that Jay is intelligent and achievement-oriented but nevertheless feels that she doesn't deserve to be a doctor, worries about whether she will ever be truly happy, and remembers that when she was 13 she never was able to be herself and to really express her feelings, even with a good friend. Her unhappiness, fearfulness, loneliness, insecurity, and other dissatisfactions similarly stem from Jay's inability to become what she "most truly is." Rogers would suspect that in Jay's life, acceptance and love were conditioned on her living up to other people's ideas of what she should become. We know that for most of her life Jay's father was her primary source of positive regard. We don't know with certainty that Dr. Smith's love for Jay was conditional on her living up to his goals for her, but it seems very possible that it was.

Evaluating Humanistic Theories

What are the major criticisms of humanistic theories?

A major criticism of most humanistic personality theories is that their central tenet—that the overriding purpose of the human condition is to realize one's potential—is difficult if not impossible to verify scientifically. In addition, some critics claim that these theories fail to take into account the evil in human nature. Others contend that the humanistic view fosters self-centeredness and narcissism and reflects Western values of individual achievement rather than universal human potential.

Nevertheless, Maslow and especially Rogers did attempt to test some aspects of their theories scientifically. For example, Rogers studied the discrepancy between the way people perceive themselves and the way they ideally want to be. He presented participants with statements such as "I often feel resentful" and "I feel relaxed and nothing really bothers me." First his participants were asked to sort the statements into several piles indicating how well the statements described their real selves. Then they were asked to sort them again, this time according to how well they described their ideal selves. In this way, Rogers discovered that people whose real selves were considerably different from their ideal selves were more likely to be unhappy and dissatisfied. A subsequent study showed that Rogers's client-centered approach to therapy does help to close the gap between a person's real and ideal selves, leading to greater self-acceptance and an ideal self that includes qualities that the person already possesses (Butler & Haigh, 1954).

Unconditional positive regard
In Rogers's theory the full acceptance and love of another person regardless of that person's behavior.

REVIEW QUESTIONS

1. Humanistic personality theory emphasizes that we are ____ ____, whereas psychodynamic personality theory emphasizes ____ ____.
2. Rogers believed that a person strives to live up to and fulfill a self-image; he called this a person's ____-____ tendency.
3. When children feel they are loved regardless of their behaviors, Rogers would say they are receiving ____ ____ ____ from others.

Indicate whether the following are true (T) or false (F).

4. The goal of life, Rogers believed, is to become the best of whatever each of us is inherently capable of becoming. ____
5. Our self-concept is our inborn biological potential. ____
6. When people lose sight of their inborn potential, they are unlikely to experience much satisfaction. ____

Answers: 1. positively motivated, hidden conflicts. 2. self-actualizing. 3. unconditional positive regard. 4. T. 5. F. 6. T.

Trait Theories

What is the key focus of trait theories?

The personality theories we have examined all emphasize early childhood experiences and all attempt to explain the varieties of human personality. Other personality theorists focus on the present, describing the ways in which already developed adult personalities differ from one another. These *trait theorists* assert that people differ according to the degree to which they possess certain **personality traits,** such as dependency, anxiety, aggressiveness, and sociability. Although traits cannot be observed directly, we can infer a trait from how a person behaves. If, for example, someone consistently throws parties and regularly participates in groups, we might conclude that the person possesses a high degree of sociability.

Psychologist Gordon Allport believed that traits—or "dispositions," as he called them—are literally encoded in the nervous system as structures that guide consistent behavior across a wide variety of situations. Allport also believed that while traits describe behaviors that are common to many people, each individual personality consists of a unique group of traits (Allport & Odbert, 1936). Raymond Cattell (1965), using a statistical technique called **factor analysis,** has demonstrated that various traits tend to cluster in groups. For example, a person who is described as persevering or determined is also likely to be thought of as responsible, ordered, attentive, and stable and probably would not be described as frivolous, neglectful, and changeable (Cattell & Kline, 1977). According to Cattell, each individual personality consists of a relatively unique constellation of basic traits.

Other theorists thought that Cattell used too many traits to describe personality. Eysenck (1976) argued that personality could be reduced to three basic dimensions: *emotional stability, introversion–extroversion*, and *psychoticism*. According to Eysenck, emotional *stability* refers to how well a person controls emotions. On a continuum, individuals at one end of this trait would be seen as poised, calm, and composed, while people at the other end might be described as anxious, nervous, and excitable. *Introversion–extroversion* refers to the degree to which a person is inwardly or outwardly oriented. At one end of this dimension would be the socially outgoing, talkative, and affectionate people, known as extroverts. *Introverts*—generally described as reserved, silent, shy, and socially withdrawn—would be at the other extreme. Eysenck used the term *psychoticism* to describe people characterized by insensitivity and uncooperativeness at one end and warmth, tenderness, and helpfulness at the other end.

Personality traits
Dimensions or characteristics on which people differ in distinctive ways.

Factor analysis
A statistical technique that identifies groups of related objects; used by Cattell to identify trait clusters.

TABLE 10-1	THE "BIG FIVE" DIMENSIONS OF PERSONALITY
Extroversion	High scorers: enthusiastic, gregarious, playful, expressive, happy-go-lucky, impetuous, energetic, talkative, assertive, demonstrative, daring, confident, frank, witty, enterprising, optimistic
	Low scorers: unsociable, untalkative, detached, timid, restrained, unadventurous, submissive, lethargic, moody
Agreeableness	High scorers: accommodating, genial, understanding, lenient, courteous, generous, flexible, unassuming, principled, affectionate, down-to-earth, natural
	Low scorers: antagonistic, unsympathetic, demanding, impolite, cruel, condescending, irritable, conceited, stubborn, distrustful, selfish, insensitive, surly, devious, prejudiced, unfriendly, volatile, stingy, deceitful, thoughtless
Conscientiousness/ Dependability	High scorers: organized, efficient, reliable, meticulous, persistent, cautious, punctual, decisive, dignified, consistent, thrifty, conventional, analytical
	Low scorers: disorganized, careless, inconsistent, forgetful, rash, aimless, lazy, indecisive, impractical, nonconforming
Emotional Stability	High scorers: unexcitable, unemotional, autonomous, individualistic
	Low scorers: insecure, anxious, touchy, emotional, envious, gullible, meddlesome
Culture/Intellect/ Openness	High scorers: introspective, deep, insightful, intelligent, creative, curious, sophisticated
	Low scorers: shallow, unimaginative, unobservant, ignorant

The Big Five

What five basic traits describe most differences in personality?

Although trait theorists have disagreed about the number of traits needed to describe personality, an early study by Tupes and Christal (1961) demonstrated that personality traits can be reduced to 5 basic dimensions—*extroversion, agreeableness, conscientiousness, emotional stability,* and *culture*—a finding confirmed repeatedly in subsequent research (Borgatta, 1964; Botwin & Buss, 1989; Goldberg, 1981, 1982, 1993; Norman, 1963; Wiggins, 1996). There is some disagreement about whether the fifth dimension should be called *culture* or *openness to experience* or *intellect.* Nevertheless, there is a growing consensus that the **"Big Five"** personality dimensions (see Table 10–1), also known as the *five-factor model,* do capture the most salient dimensions of human personality (Funder, 1991; John, 1988; McCrae & Costa, 1996; Wiggins, 1996). Furthermore, cross-cultural studies indicate that the Big-Five model generally applies across a wide variety of Western and non-Western cultures, suggesting that these traits may represent universal dimensions of personality (see *Highlights*).

Evidence that basic personality traits may be universal is also derived from studies showing that at least some traits may in part have a genetic basis (Zuckerman, 1995; see also Mayer & Sutton, 1996). Some early theorists (Eysenck, 1947) thought that biological factors influenced basic personality traits, but only recently has solid evidence from twin studies begun to support this idea (Eaves et al., 1994; Heath, Cloninger, & Martin, 1994; Plomin, 1994). Although the precise role that genes play in personality is not completely understood, most contemporary psychologists agree that biological and environmental factors contribute to the development of personality.

The Big-Five dimensions of personality may have some important real-world applications—particularly as they relate to employment decisions (Hogan, Hogan, & Roberts, 1996). In one study (Ones, Viswesvaran, & Schmidt, 1993), for example, two of the Big Five dimensions—conscientiousness and emotional stability—were found to be reliable predictors of job performance in a wide

PETER WAS A BORN WORRIER ...

Source: Drawing by Chas Addams © 1984 *The New Yorker* Magazine, Inc.

Big Five
Five traits or basic dimensions currently thought to be of central importance in describing personality.

HIGHLIGHTS

Are the Big Five Personality Traits Universal?

In Chapter 1 we pointed out that "appreciating the rich diversity in behavior and mental processes that exists within our human species" is important to reaching a fuller understanding of human psychology. And indeed every chapter of this book has echoed the theme of human diversity. But respect for diversity does not mean that we should ignore commonalities and universals that seem to cut across different cultures and societies.

As a case in point, in this chapter we have seen that the Big Five personality dimensions are increasingly being accepted as the most salient dimensions of human personality. Most studies of the Big Five, however, have been conducted in the United States. Would the same five personality dimensions be evident in other cultures? The answer appears to be yes.

Costa and McCrae (1992) developed a questionnaire to measure the Big Five personality dimensions that has since been translated into numerous languages including German, Portuguese, Hebrew, Chinese, Korean, and Japanese. McCrae and Costa (1997) then compared the results from the various questionnaires in an effort to determine whether the same Big

Five personality dimensions would emerge regardless of the language in which the questionnaires were written. The results from the 6 foreign cultures were virtually identical to the data from American samples: The Big Five personality dimensions were clearly evident. As the authors noted, "The structure found in American volunteers was replicated in Japanese undergraduates and Israeli job applicants. A model of personality

---

Would the same five personality dimensions be evident in other cultures?

---

rooted in English-language trait adjectives could be meaningfully applied not only in a closely related language like German but also in such utterly distinct languages as Chinese and Korean" (p. 514).

The fact that other researchers have found much the same thing using quite different techniques (deRaad & Szirmak, 1994; Narayanan, Menon, & Levin, 1995; Noller, Law, & Comrey,

1987) raises some intriguing questions for personality researchers. Is there perhaps a common genetic basis for the Big Five personality traits? Do these traits perhaps have some evolutionary significance? Or are they shaped by common child-rearing practices and values that cut across different cultures? We don't yet know the answers to these questions, though they are actively being explored.

Applying critical-thinking skills to the results of these studies, can we conclude that the Big Five are in fact universal personality traits? Not necessarily. Thus far only a few cultures have been studied; preliterate societies and sub-Saharan African languages are missing entirely. Moreover, we can't conclude that the Big Five traits are the most important personality traits in the cultures that have been studied. There may be other important personality traits not measured by the questionnaires that are unique to the various cultures. The best we can say at this point is that the Big Five personality traits are at least recognized by people in a number of quite diverse cultures. To go farther than that we must await the results of further research.

---

variety of occupational settings. In another (McDaniel & Frei, 1994), agreeableness and emotional stability were good predictors of performance for employees in customer-service positions. The Big Five may turn out to be reliable predictors of job performance when other criteria such as technical skills and experience are also considered (Hogan et al., 1996).

A Trait View of Jaylene Smith

How would trait theorists describe Jaylene Smith's personality?

A psychologist working from the trait perspective would infer certain traits from Jay's behavior. When we observe that Jay decided at an early age to become a doctor, did well academically year after year, and graduated first in her medical-school class, it seems reasonable to infer a trait of determination or persistence to account for her behavior. A trait theorist would also identify sincerity, motivation, and intelligence, as well as insecurity, introversion, shyness, and anxiety.

These relatively few traits account for a great deal of Jay's behavior, and they also provide a thumbnail sketch of "what Jay is like."

Evaluating Trait Theories

What are the major criticisms of trait theory?

Traits are the language that we commonly use when we describe people as shy, insecure, or arrogant. Thus the trait view of personality has considerable commonsense appeal. Moreover, although psychologists disagree as to the exact number of traits, it is easier to study personality traits scientifically than to study such things as "self-actualization" and "unconscious motives." But trait theories have several shortcomings (Eysenck, 1993; Kroger & Wood, 1993).

First, they primarily are descriptive: They seek to describe the basic dimensions of personality but generally do not try to explain causes (Funder, 1991). Some critics argue that the dangers in reducing the diversity and complexity of human nature to just a few traits are greater than the usefulness that traits offer in terms of description and classification (Mischel, 1984; Mischel & Shoda, 1995). Moreover, psychologists disagree about whether 35 traits, 5 traits, 20 traits, or even 100 traits are sufficient to capture the complexity of human personality (Almagor, Tellegen, & Waller, 1995; Eysenck, 1992; Funder, 1991; Mershon & Gorsuch, 1988).

Finally, some psychologists question whether traits are in fact useful even as descriptors and predictors of behavior. If you label a friend "agreeable," does this mean that he or she is agreeable in different situations and all the time? Of course not. But if not, then how useful is the trait designation to begin with? This last question raises the issue of consistency in human behavior. We have been assuming that behavior is generally consistent across both situations and time, but some theorists question this assumption. For example, a marine sergeant who is aggressive toward his recruits may be quite submissive toward a captain, and he may act much more aggressively one day than the next. A given situation, moreover, may elicit similar behavior from a wide variety of people whatever their personality traits. If much human behavior is actually quite inconsistent across situations and over time, then why does behavior usually *appear* to be far more consistent than it actually is? And how can personality theories account for inconsistency in behavior? A fully satisfactory theory of personality must account for both consistencies and inconsistencies in behavior. The cognitive–social learning approach to personality does consider both personal and situational determinants of behavior, as we shall see in the next section (Bowers, 1973; Funder, 1991).

REVIEW QUESTIONS

1. Trait theorists assert that people differ according to the degree to which they possess certain _____ _____.
2. Eysenck stated that personality could be reduced to three basic dimensions: _____ _____, _____-_____, and _____.
3. What are the Big Five traits?

Answers: 1. personality traits. 2. emotional stability, introversion–extroversion, psychoticism. 3. extroversion, agreeableness, conscientiousness, emotional stability, and culture/intellect.

Cognitive–Social Learning Theories

How do our internal expectancies affect our behavior?

Cognitive–social learning theorists believe that people internally organize their expectancies and values to guide their behavior. This set of personal standards is unique to each one of us, growing out of our life history. Our behavior is

Cognitive–social learning theories
Personality theories that view behavior as the product of the interaction of cognitions, learning and past experiences, and the immediate environment.

the product of the interaction of *cognitions* (how people think about a situation and how they view their behavior in that situation), *learning and past experiences* (including re-inforcement, punishment, and modeling), and the immediate *environment*. For example, Albert Bandura (1977, 1986) asserts that people evaluate a situation according to certain internal **expectancies,** such as personal preferences, and that this evaluation affects their behavior. Environmental feedback that follows the actual behavior, in turn, influences future expectancies. In this way, expectancies guide behavior in a given situation, and the results of the behavior in that situation shape expectancies in future situations. For example, two young women trying a video game for the first time may experience the situation quite differently, even if their scores are similarly low. One woman may find the experience fun and be eager to gain the skills necessary to go on to the next level of games, while the other may be disheartened by getting a low score, assume she will never be any good at video games, and never play again. Similarly, a person who interprets math problems as a challenge will approach math aptitude tests with a different expectancy than someone who sees math problems as opportunities to fail.

To Rotter (1954), **locus of control** is a prevalent expectancy, or cognitive strategy, by which we evaluate situations. People with an *internal locus* of control are convinced that they can control their own fate. They believe that through hard work, skill, and training, they can find reinforcements and avoid punishments. People with an *external locus* of control are convinced that chance, luck, and the behavior of others determine their destiny and that they are helpless to change the course of their lives (Strickland, 1989). There is some evidence that drug use, inactivity among people suffering from depression, and school truancy are linked to an external locus of control (Lefcourt, 1992). In all these cases people think that being active or productive will not have any positive consequences.

Both Bandura and Rotter have tried to combine personal variables (such as expectancies) with situational variables in an effort to understand the complexities of human behavior. Both theorists believe that expectancies become part of a person's *explanatory style*, which in turn greatly influences behavior. Explanatory style separates optimists from pessimists. It is what causes two beginners who get the same score on a video game to respond so differently.

General expectancies or explanatory styles such as optimism or pessimism can have a significant effect on behavior. In one study (Peterson, Vaillant, & Seligman, 1988) researchers tracked 99 World War II veterans from the Harvard graduation classes of 1939 to 1944 and found that explanatory style predicted the state of an individual's health decades later. Men who were optimists at age 25 tended to be healthier at age 65, while the health of the pessimists had begun to deteriorate at about age 45. Although the reasons for these findings are not clear, Peterson found that pessimists were less careful about their health than were optimists. In some studies, children as young as 8 years old demonstrate a habitual explanatory style. Those with a more pessimistic style are more prone to depression and do worse on achievement tests (Nolen-Hoeksema, Girgus, & Seligman, 1986).

Explanatory style dovetails with what Albert Bandura describes as **self-efficacy,** or the degree to which we feel we can meet our goals. Suppose that a math professor has a son whose mathematical aptitude is low and a daughter who is especially gifted in this area. Imagine further that both children develop a **performance standard** that calls for high achievement in mathematics. The son will most likely feel incapable of meeting his standard, while the daughter will almost certainly feel capable of meeting hers. In Bandura's terms the son will probably develop a

People with an internal locus of control are convinced they can control their own fate. This student believes that by studying he can be successful in school.

Expectancies
In Bandura's view what a person anticipates in a situation or as a result of behaving in certain ways.

Locus of control
According to Rotter, an expectancy about whether reinforcement is under internal or external control.

Self-efficacy
According to Bandura, the expectancy that one's efforts will be successful.

Performance standard
In Bandura's theory a standard that people develop to rate the adequacy of their own behavior in a variety of situations.

low sense of self-efficacy and thus feel generally incapable of meeting his life goals, while the daughter will likely develop a strong sense of self-efficacy. In turn these explanatory styles will have a profound effect on their behavior.

In distinguishing between self-efficacy and locus of control, remember that while self-efficacy expectancies are concerned with whether a person *thinks* that he or she can actually perform a given act, locus of control expectancies are concerned with whether a person thinks that his or her actions are linked to reinforcements and punishments.

If all this sounds pessimistic and deterministic, we must point out that Bandura also emphasizes that people have the power of self-determination (1986). For example, the frustrated son in the preceding example might modify his behavior and try to excel in other areas. In this way performance standards may be modified by experience, affecting future behavior. Bandura calls such interactions between personalities and their environment **reciprocal determinism.** Personality variables, situational variables, and actual behaviors constantly interact. You may be prone to display aggressive behavior, for example, but whether you actually behave aggressively is determined by your perception of a given situation. Are you prepared to cope with aggressive behavior in return? Furthermore, the consequences of behaving aggressively will affect your behavior in similar situations in the future. In short, you learn where and when it is rewarding to be aggressive. For Bandura, human personality develops out of this ongoing interaction among personal standards (learned by observation and reinforcement), situations, and behavioral consequences.

A Cognitive–Social Learning View of Jaylene Smith

How would cognitive–social learning theorists describe the factors that shaped Jaylene Smith's personality?

Jaylene may have *learned* to be shy and introverted because she was rewarded for spending much time by herself studying. Her father probably encouraged her devotion to her studies; certainly she earned the respect of her teachers. Moreover, long hours of studying helped her to avoid the discomfort she felt being around other people for long periods. Reinforcement may also have shaped Jay's self-discipline and her need to achieve academically.

In addition, at least some aspects of Jaylene's personality were formed by watching her parents and brothers and learning subtle lessons from these family interactions. Her aggressive behavior with boyfriends, for example, may have grown out of seeing her parents fight. As a young child, she may have observed that some people deal with conflict by means of outbursts. Moreover, as Bandura's concept of self-efficacy would predict, Jay surely noticed that her father, a successful medical researcher, enjoyed and prospered in both his career and his family life, while her mother's two jobs as homemaker and store manager left her frustrated and tired. This contrast may have contributed to Jay's interest in medicine and to mixed feelings about establishing a close relationship that might lead to marriage.

Evaluating Cognitive–Social Learning Theories

What are the major criticisms of cognitive–social learning theories of personality?

Cognitive–social learning theories of personality seem to have great potential. They put mental processes back at the center of personality. The key concepts of these theories, such as self-efficacy and locus of control, can be defined and studied scientifically, which is not true of the key concepts of psychodynamic and humanistic theories. Moreover, cognitive–social learning theories help to

Reciprocal determinism
In Bandura's personality model the concept that the person influences the environment and is in turn influenced by the environment.

explain why people behave inconsistently, an area where trait approaches fall short. Cognitive–social learning theories of personality have also spawned useful therapies that help people to recognize and change a negative sense of self-efficacy or explanatory style. As we will see in Chapter 13, these therapies have been particularly useful in helping people overcome depression. It is still too early, however, to say how well cognitive–social learning theories account for the complexity of human personality. Some critics point out that with the benefit of hindsight, any behavior can be explained as the product of certain cognitions, but that doesn't mean those cognitions were the causes—or at least the sole causes—of the behavior.

Just as there is great diversity in the way psychologists view personality, psychologists also disagree on the best way to measure or assess personality, the topic we turn to next.

REVIEW QUESTIONS

1. Cognitive–social learning theorists believe that people internally organize their ____ and ____ to guide their behavior.
2. In Bandura's view, what a person anticipates in a situation or as a result of behaving in certain ways is known as ____.
3. Cognitive–social learning theorists believe that locus of control is a cognitive strategy by which people ____ situations.

Match the following terms with the appropriate definition.

4. internal locus of control   ____ a. separates optimists from pessimists
5. external locus of control   ____ b. degree to which we believe we can meet our goals
6. explanatory style   ____ c. belief that luck controls destiny
7. self-efficacy   ____ d. belief that people control their own fate

Answers: 1. expectancies, values. 2. expectancies. 3. evaluate. 4. d. 5. c. 6. a. 7. b.

Personality Assessment

Can personality be effectively measured?

In some ways, testing personality resembles testing intelligence (see Chapter 7). Both try to measure something intangible and invisible. And in both cases the best kind of test is *reliable* and *valid:* It gives dependable and consistent results, and it measures what it claims to measure. Because personality reflects *characteristic* behavior—how people usually react to their environment—we are not interested in someone's *best* behavior. We want to learn how a person typically behaves in ordinary situations. Further complicating the measurement process, such factors as fatigue or anxiety, the desire to impress the examiner, and the fear of being tested can profoundly affect a person's behavior in a personality-assessment situation. In the intricate task of measuring personality, psychologists use four basic tools: (1) the personal interview; (2) direct observation of behavior; (3) objective tests; and (4) projective tests. We look at each in turn.

The Personal Interview

What are the advantages and disadvantages of structured or unstructured interviews?

An interview is a conversation with a purpose: The interviewer seeks information from the person being interviewed. In clinical settings, interviewers want to learn why someone is seeking treatment and how the client's problem can be diagnosed. Such interviews are generally *unstructured*—that is, the interviewer asks the client questions about any material that comes up and asks follow-up questions whenever appropriate. The most effective interviewers are warm, interested in what the respondent has to say, calm, relaxed, and confident (Feshbach & Weiner, 1982; Saccuzzo, 1975). Ideally, the interviewer directs the conversation over a wide range of subjects and encourages the person to discuss his or her experiences, feelings, and attitudes freely. The interviewer also pays attention to the person's behavior—manner of speaking, poise, or tenseness when it comes to certain topics. Because the behavior of the interviewer may color the outcome of unstructured interviews, such interviews are often used in combination with more objective tests of personality.

When conducting systematic research on personality, investigators more often rely on the *structured* interview. Here the order and content of the questions are fixed ahead of time, and the interviewer adheres to the set format. While less personal, this kind of interview allows the interviewer to obtain comparable information from everyone interviewed. Generally speaking, structured interviews draw out information about sensitive topics that might not come up in an unstructured interview.

Observation

Why might an observer misinterpret someone's behavior?

One way to find out how a person usually behaves is to *observe* that person in ordinary situations over a long period of time. Behaviorists and social-learning theorists prefer this method of assessing personality because it allows them to see firsthand how situation and environment influence behavior as they note the range of behaviors the person is capable of exhibiting.

In *direct observation*, however, an observer runs the risk of misinterpreting the true meaning of an act. For example, the observer may think that a child is being hostile or aggressive when he is merely protecting himself from the class bully. An expensive and time-consuming method of research, direct observation may also yield faulty results if the presence of the observer affects the subject's behavior.

Objective Tests

In what ways are objective tests designed to eliminate some of the problems of personality assessment?

Seeking to measure personality without depending on the skills of an interviewer or on the interpretive abilities of an observer, psychologists developed **objective tests,** or personality inventories. Generally these are written tests administered and scored according to a standard procedure. Usually, the person simply marks "yes" or "no" or selects one answer among many choices. These tests may be used for a wide variety of purposes, including studying the relationship between personality and success in academic and career settings.

Objective tests are the most widely used tools for assessing personality, but before we describe several of them, we must note that they have two serious drawbacks. First, they rely entirely on *self-report*, so they have limited usefulness with people who do not know themselves well, cannot be entirely objective about themselves, or who want to present themselves in a particular way (Funder, 1991). In fact, peers who know you well often do a better job of characterizing you than you do yourself (Funder, 1995, 1987, 1989). Second, if subjects have taken other personality questionnaires, their familiarity with the test format may affect their responses to the present questionnaire. This is a particular problem on college campuses, where students are likely to

Objective tests
Personality tests that are administered and scored in a standard way.

participate in multiple research studies, many of which rely on some kind of personality inventory (Council, 1993).

Because of their interest in accurately measuring personality traits, trait theorists favor objective tests. Cattell, for example, developed a 374-question personality test called the **Sixteen Personality Factor Questionnaire (16PF)**, which provides scores on each of the 16 traits he identified. More recently, objective tests have been developed to assess the Big Five personality traits described earlier in this chapter (Costa & McCrae, 1995; Goldberg, 1993).

The most widely used and thoroughly researched objective personality test is the **Minnesota Multiphasic Personality Inventory (MMPI)** (Butcher & Rouse, 1996; Hathaway & McKinley, 1942; Lubin et al., 1985). The person taking the test is asked to answer "true," "false," or "cannot say" to such statements as "Once in a while I put off until tomorrow what I ought to do today," "At times I feel like swearing," and "There are persons who are trying to steal my thoughts and ideas." Some of the items repeat very similar thoughts in different words, and this redundancy contributes to ease of scoring and provides a check on the possibility of false or inconsistent answers.

Researchers have devised several personality scales from this test, including ratings for masculinity–femininity, depression, and hypochondriasis. These elements of the MMPI are highly regarded as useful tools for differentiating among psychiatric populations (Anastasi, 1982; Anastasi & Urbina, 1997; J. R. Graham & Lilly, 1984). The MMPI is also used to differentiate among more normal personality dimensions, such as extroversion–introversion and assertiveness, but with less success. To accommodate social changes over the past 50 years, the MMPI was revised and updated in the 1980s, and there are now two versions of the test: the full-length adult form and the shorter adolescent form.

Projective Tests

What do projective tests try to measure?

Psychodynamic theorists, who believe that people are often unaware of the determinants of their behavior, put very little faith in objective personality tests that rely on self-reports. Instead they prefer to use **projective tests** of personality. Most projective tests consist of simple, ambiguous stimuli that can elicit an unlimited number of responses. People may be shown some essentially meaningless material or a vague picture and be asked to explain what the material means to them. Or they may be given a sentence fragment such as "When I see myself in the mirror, I . . ." or "My brother is . . ." and be asked to complete the statement. No clues suggest the "best way" to interpret the material or complete the sentence. Some psychologists believe that in devising their own answers, people "project" their personality into the test materials, revealing unconscious thoughts and fantasies, such as latent sexual or family problems.

Projective tests have several advantages for testing personality. Because these tests are flexible and can be treated as games or puzzles, they can be given in a relaxed atmosphere, without the tension and self-consciousness that sometimes accompany objective tests. Often the true purpose of the test can be hidden from the person being examined, so responses are less likely to be faked. The accuracy and usefulness of projective tests, however, depend on the skill of the examiner.

The best-known and one of the most frequently used projective personality tests (Ball, Archer, & Imhof, 1994; Watkins et al., 1995) is the **Rorschach test.** The test is named for Hermann Rorschach, a Swiss psychiatrist who in 1921 published the results of his research on interpreting inkblots as a key to assessing personality (see Figure 10–4). Each inkblot design is printed on a separate card and is unique in form, color, shading, and white space. Subjects are asked what they see in each blot. Very few instructions are given, so that responses will be

Sixteen Personality Factor Questionnaire (16PF)
Objective personality test created by Cattell that provides scores on the 16 traits he identified.

Minnesota Multiphasic Personality Inventory (MMPI)
The most widely used objective personality test, originally intended for psychiatric diagnosis.

Projective tests
Personality tests, such as the Rorschach inkblot test, consisting of ambiguous or unstructured material.

Rorschach test
A projective test composed of ambiguous inkblots; the way people interpret the blots is thought to reveal aspects of their personality.

FIGURE 10–4
Inkblots used in the Rorschach projective test.

completely personal. After interpreting all the blots, the person explains which part of each blot prompted each response.

Somewhat more demanding is the **Thematic Apperception Test (TAT),** a series of 20 cards depicting human figures in deliberately ambiguous situations (see Figure 10–5). The examiner shows the cards one by one and asks the person to write a complete story about each picture, including what led up to the scene, what the characters are doing at that moment, what their thoughts and feelings are, and what the outcome will be.

Various scoring systems have been devised for the TAT, but examiners usually interpret the stories in light of their personal knowledge of the participants. One key in evaluating the TAT is whether the participant identifies with the hero or heroine of the story or with one of the minor characters. Then the examiner determines what the attitudes and feelings of the character reveal about the storyteller. The examiner also assesses each story for content, language, originality, organization, and consistency. Certain themes—such as the need for affection, repeated failure, or parental domination—may recur in several plots.

Both the Rorschach and the TAT may open up a conversation between a clinician and a person who is reluctant or unable to talk about personal problems. Both may also reveal motives, events, or feelings of which the person is unaware (Stricker & Healy, 1990). Because projective tests are often not administered in a standard way, they may lack validity and reliability (Dawes, 1994; Wierzbicki, 1993). As a result their use has declined since the 1970s. Still, when interpreted by a skilled examiner, these tests can offer insights into a person's attitudes and feelings.

FIGURE 10–5
Revealing stories. A person taking the Thematic Apperception Test is asked to make up a story to explain the scene depicted in the picture. The examiner must then interpret and evaluate the participant's story.

REVIEW QUESTIONS

1. ____ tests require people to fill out questionnaires, which are then scored according to a standardized procedure.

2. In ____ tests of personality, people are shown ambiguous stimuli and asked to describe them or to make up a story about them.

Match the following tests with the appropriate description.

3. objective tests ____ a. most widely used and researched personality test
4. MMPI ____ b. pictures of people in ambiguous situations
5. Rorschach ____ c. projective test using pictures of inkblots
6. TAT ____ d. designed to eliminate researcher bias

Answers: 1. objective. 2. projective. 3. d. 4. a. 5. c. 6. b.

Thematic Apperception Test (TAT)
A projective test composed of ambiguous pictures about which a person is asked to write a complete story.

KEY TERMS

personality, p. 362

Psychodynamic theories

psychodynamic theories, p. 363

unconscious, p. 363

psychoanalysis, p. 363

id, p. 364

pleasure principle, p. 364

ego, p. 364

reality principle, p. 364

superego, p. 365

ego ideal, p. 365

libido, p. 366

fixation, p. 366

oral stage, p. 366

anal stage, p. 366

phallic stage, p. 366

Oedipus complex, p. 366

Electra complex, p. 366

latency period, p. 367

genital stage, p. 367

personal unconscious, p. 368

collective unconscious, p. 368

archetypes, p. 368

persona, p. 368

anima, p. 368

animus, p. 368

compensation, p. 368

inferiority complex, p. 369

neurotic trends, p. 369

Humanistic personality theories

humanistic personality theory, p. 374

actualizing tendency, p. 374

self-actualizing tendency, p. 374

fully functioning person, p. 374

unconditional positive regard, p. 375

Trait theories

personality traits, p. 376

factor analysis, p. 376

Big Five, p. 377

Cognitive–social learning theories

cognitive–social learning theories, p. 379

expectancies, p. 380

locus of control, p. 380

self-efficacy, p. 380

performance standard, p. 380

reciprocal determinism, p. 381

Personality assessment

objective tests, p. 383

Sixteen Personality Factor Questionnaire (16PF), p. 384

Minnesota Multiphasic Personality Inventory (MMPI), p. 384

projective tests, p. 384

Rorschach test, p. 384

Thematic Apperception Test (TAT), p. 385

CHAPTER REVIEW

☐ **How do psychologists define personality?**

Ever since the discipline of psychology began, psychologists have been attempting to define those characteristic thoughts, feelings, and behaviors that persist over time and that distinguish one person from another. **Personality** is a person's unique psychological signature; it colors all the person's actions and marks the person's passage through time.

☐ **According to psychodynamic theorists, how is personality determined?**

Psychodynamic theories of personality consider behavior to be the result of psychological dynamics within the individual. Often these dynamics are **unconscious** processes.

☐ **When Freud stated that the sexual instinct is the basis of behavior, how was he defining sexual instinct?**

Freud used the term *sexual instinct* to refer to the desire for virtually any form of pleasure. Freud called energy generated by the sexual instinct **libido.** As infants mature, their libido becomes focused on different sensitive parts of the body. A **fixation** occurs if a child is deprived of or receives too much pleasure from the part of the body that dominates one of the five developmental stages—**oral, anal, phallic, latency,** and **genital**—and some sexual energy may lodge in that part of the body. Strong attachment to the parent of the opposite sex and jealousy of the parent of the same sex—

which develops during the phallic stage—is termed the **Oedipus complex** in boys and the **Electra complex** in girls. At the end of the phallic stage, the child enters the latency period, characterized by a loss of interest in sexual behavior. Finally, at puberty, the individual enters the genital stage of mature sexuality.

☐ **How did Carl Jung's view of the unconscious differ from Freud's?**

Freud saw the **id** as a "seething cauldron" of excitations, but Jung viewed the unconscious as the **ego's** source of strength. He believed that the unconscious consisted of two distinct components: the **personal unconscious,** encompassing an individual's repressed thoughts, forgotten experiences, and undeveloped ideas; and the **collective unconscious,** a subterranean river of memories and behavior patterns flowing to us from previous generations. Over the millennia the human mind has developed certain thought forms, called **archetypes,** which give rise to mental images or mythological representations.

☐ **What did Alfred Adler believe was the major determinant of personality?**

Adler believed that people possess innate positive motives and strive toward personal and social perfection. He originally proposed that the principal determinant of personality was the individual's attempt to **compensate** for actual physical weakness, but he later modified his theory to stress the importance of *feelings* of **inferiority,** whether or not those feelings are justified. Adler concluded that strivings for superiority and perfection, both in one's own life and in the society in which one lives, are crucial to personality development.

☐ Freud's theory emphasized unconscious conflicts. What external factors did Horney add to this theory?

For Horney, *anxiety*—a person's reaction to real or imagined dangers or threats—is a stronger motivating force than the sexual drive, or libido. By emphasizing that culture and not anatomy determines many of the personality traits that differentiate women from men, Horney also challenged the prevailing notion of her time that biological imperatives underlie the personality characteristics of men and women.

☐ Erikson's theory focused less on unconscious conflict and more on what factors?

Erikson argued that the quality of the parent–child relationship affects the development of personality because out of this interaction the child either feels competent and valuable and is able to form a secure sense of identity or feels incompetent and worthless and fails to build a secure identity.

☐ Psychodynamic theorists would consider Jaylene Smith's personality the result of what unresolved issues?

Freud would probably conclude that Jay had not successfully resolved her Electra complex. Erikson might suggest that Jay has problems achieving intimacy (Stage 6) because she had failed to develop satisfactory relations with other people earlier in her life.

☐ What are the major criticisms of psychodynamic theories?

Psychodynamic theories have had a profound impact on the way we view ourselves and others, but some of Freud's theories have been criticized as unscientific and culture-bound, based on the anecdotal accounts of individuals who felt troubled enough to seek treatment. Further, research does not show a clear link between unconscious processes and personality. As a therapy, psychoanalysis has been shown to be beneficial in some cases but no more so than other therapies.

☐ What are the major ways in which humanistic personality theory differs in emphasis from psychodynamic theories?

Freud and many of his followers believed that personality grows out of the resolution of unconscious conflicts and developmental crises from the past. **Humanistic personality theory** emphasizes that we are positively motivated and progress toward higher levels of functioning,

and it stresses people's potential for growth and change in the present.

☐ What important capacities did Carl Rogers believe we are born with?

Rogers contended that every person is born with certain innate potentials and the **actualizing tendency** to realize our biological potential as well as our conscious sense of who we are.

☐ How would humanistic theorists view the development of Jaylene Smith's personality?

Humanistic theorists would focus on the difference between Jay's self-concept and her actual capacities. Her inability to become what she "most truly is" would account for her anxiety, loneliness, and general dissatisfaction. Rogers would suspect that throughout Jay's life acceptance and love came from satisfying other people's ideas of what she should become.

☐ What are the major criticisms of humanistic theories?

There is a lack of scientifically derived evidence for humanistic theories of personality. In addition, these theories are criticized for taking too rosy a view of human nature and for fostering self-centeredness. Research on humanist therapies, however, particularly Rogers's client-centered therapy, has shown that humanistic theorists do promote self-acceptance.

☐ What is the key focus of trait theories?

Trait theorists reject the notion that there are just a few distinct personality types. Instead they insist that each person possesses a unique constellation of fundamental **personality traits,** which can be inferred from how the person behaves.

☐ What five basic traits describe most differences in personality?

Psychologists disagree about how many different personality traits there are, but recent research suggests that there may be just five universal personality traits: extroversion, agreeableness, conscientiousness, emotional stability, and culture or intellect.

☐ How would trait theorists describe Jaylene Smith's personality?

Trait theorists would probably ascribe Jaylene's high achievements to the traits of determination or persistence. Sincerity, motivation, intelligence, anxiety, and introversion would also describe Jay.

☐ What are the major criticisms of trait theory?

Trait theories are primarily descriptive and provide a way of classifying personalities, but they do not explain why someone's personality developed as it did. Unlike psychodynamic and humanistic theories, however, trait theories are relatively easy to test experimentally, and research confirms the value of the five-factor model, referred to as the **"Big Five,"** in pinpointing personality. Also, although most personality theories assume that behavior is consistent across situations and over a lifetime, a number of psychologists believe that situational variables have a greater effect on behavior than do personality traits.

☐ How do our internal expectancies affect our behavior?

Cognitive–social learning theories of personality view behavior as the product of the interaction of cognitions, learning and past experiences, and the immediate environment. Albert Bandura maintains that certain internal **expectancies** determine how a person evaluates a situation and that this evaluation has an effect on the person's behavior. People with an internal **locus of control**—one expectancy—believe they can control their own fate through their actions. Expectancies prompt people to conduct themselves according to unique performance standards, individually determined measures of excellence by which they judge their behavior. Those who succeed in meeting their own internal performance standards develop an attitude that Bandura calls **self-efficacy.**

☐ How would cognitive–social learning theorists describe the factors that shaped Jaylene Smith's personality?

These theorists would assert that Jaylene *learned* to be shy because she was rewarded for the many hours she spent alone studying. Reinforcement would also have shaped her self-discipline and high need to achieve. By watching her parents, Jay could have learned to respond to conflicts with aggressive outbursts.

☐ What are the major criticisms of cognitive–social learning theories of personality?

Cognitive–social learning theories avoid the narrowness of trait and behavioral theories, as well as the reliance on case studies and anecdotal evidence that weakens psychodynamic and humanistic theories. Expectancies and locus of control can be tested scientifically, and they have proved to be useful concepts for predicting health and depression. Correlations such as these, however, do not provide evidence for causes of behavior.

☐ Can personality be effectively measured?

Psychologists use four different methods to assess personality: the personal interview, direct observation of behavior, **objective tests,** and projective tests. Factors such as the desire to impress the examiner, fatigue, and fear of being tested can profoundly affect the reliability and validity of such tests, though researchers are attempting to eliminate potential errors from such sources.

☐ What are the advantages and disadvantages of structured or unstructured interviews?

During an unstructured interview, the interviewer asks questions about any material that comes up during the conversation as well as follow-up questions where appropriate, but the behavior of the interviewer may affect the results. In a structured interview the order and the content of the questions are fixed and the interviewer does not deviate from the format, so it may not address some of the issues that come up in an unstructured interview. Structured interviews are more likely to be used for systematic research on personality because they solicit comparable information from all interviewees.

☐ Why might an observer misinterpret someone's behavior?

Direct observation of a person over a period of time to determine the environmental influence on that person's behavior has the advantage of not relying on people's self-reports of their behavior. The subject's behavior may be affected by the observer's presence in ways that can be misinterpreted, however—for example, a child who is being self-protective may seem to be hostile.

☐ In what ways are objective tests designed to eliminate some of the problems of personality assessment?

Because scores are obtained through self-report, "truth" questions built into objective tests such as the **Minnesota Multiphasic Personality Inventory (MMPI)** help to determine the accuracy of a subject's answers throughout.

☐ What do projective tests try to measure?

Psychodynamic theorists, who believe that much behavior is determined by unconscious processes, tend to discount tests that rely on self-reports. They are more likely to use **projective tests,** which consist of ambiguous stimuli that can draw out an unlimited number of interpretations based on these unconscious processes.

CRITICAL THINKING AND APPLICATIONS

1. Explain how Jung, Adler, Horney, and Erikson modified Freud's psychodynamic theory of personality.
2. Twelve-step programs such as Alcoholics Anonymous welcome people back into the program without judging them, no matter how many times they have "gone out again." This is consistent with which concept in Carl Rogers's theory? Why?
3. One of the key issues addressed by personality theorists is consistency: Does a person behave the same way across different situations, or does behavior vary with circumstances?
4. Look back at the case study of Jaylene Smith. Which theory or theories do you think best explains her behavior? Why do you feel this way?
5. What are the major forms of personality assessment? Which do you consider the most valuable? the least valuable? Why?

On the Web...

Visit these online resources at our Companion Website www.prenhall.com/morris

The Psychology Place
Learning Activity　　1. Investigating graphology: Is the writing on the wall?, p. 385

Readings
1. Sigmund Freud, p. 364
2. The Rorschach Chronicles, p. 384

Games
1. The Sea of Traits, p. 376

Web Links
1. **http://www.learner.org/exhibits/personality/**, p. 361
   Personality: What makes us who we are? Descriptions and exhibits of personality as it relates to reputation, behavior, thoughts and feelings, the unconscious, genes, society, and human nature.
2. **http://galton.psych.nwu.edu/GreatIdeas.html**, p. 361
   Great ideas in personality: General links, professional links, and links to research programs (attachment theory, basic emotions, behavior genetics, behaviorism, cognitive–social theories, five-factor model, intelligence, interpersonal theory, PEN model, personality disorders, psychoanalysis, and sociobiology).
3. **http://ksi.cpsc.ucalgary.ca/PCP/PCP.html**, p. 362
   Personal construct psychology: Related Web sites, journals, and conferences.
4. **http://www.canisius.edu/~gallaghr/pi.html**, p. 363
   Concepts of person, self, personal identity: Bibliographies and texts.
5. **http://plaza.interport.net/nypsan/freudarc.html**, p. 363
   Sigmund Freud and the Freud Archives: Links to related Internet resources, Freud's works, and writings on Freud.
6. **http://cweb.loc.gov/exhibits/freud/preview.html**, p. 364
   Sigmund Freud: Conflict and culture (online exhibit).
7. **http://www.wynja.com/personality/top.html**, p. 367
   Personality and consciousness.
8. **http://www.cgjung.com/cgjung/**, p. 367
   The C.G. Jung page: Resources, articles, online events, and Web sites of C.G. Jung, analytical psychology, and culture.
9. **http://maple.lemoyne.edu/~hevern/psychref4-11.html**, p. 382
   Psychological testing, assessment, and psychometrics: Intelligence. Contains links to related Web sites.

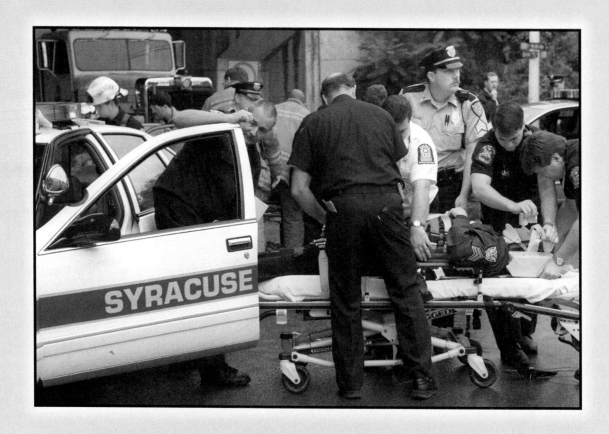

STRESS AND HEALTH PSYCHOLOGY

I N 1979 IRANIAN MILITANTS STORMED THE U.S. EMBASSY IN TEHRAN and took more than 50 Americans hostage. For 444 days the hostages were threatened with death and endured the humiliations of captivity. To feel less like a prisoner and more like a person in charge of his life, one hostage saved food from meals brought to him by his captors and then played gracious host by offering the food to other hostages who visited him in his cell. A diary kept by one prisoner records some other prisoners' strategies: "Al's working on his painting.... Dick's walking his daily three miles back and forth across the room, and Jerry's lying on his mattress reading."

- When Eric de Wilde, an orphan, found a bag of jewels worth $350,000 on a Florida railroad track, he thought it was a fairy tale come true. But reporters hounded him, and schoolmates and others kept calling him up with demands and threats. "Life is very difficult for the young man—a lot of things have happened to him in a hurry," said the lawyer whom de Wilde was forced to retain. But when the boy arrived in New York to sell his jewels at a public auction, he conducted himself with dignified restraint, maintaining his privacy and self-possession.

- When Janet Garcia had her first baby at age 34, she was joyous, but also exhausted by the constant demands of caring for a newborn. Her husband, Michael, resented her constant fatigue and felt displaced by the baby in his wife's affections. Janet and Michael decided to draw on their savings to pay for household help, and Michael became more involved in caring for the baby. These measures relieved some of Janet's burden, leaving her with more time and energy for her other responsibilities and for her life with Michael.

These three stories are quite different, but they share some important things of interest to psychologists. First, all involve some degree of *stress*—that is, the people in the stories were faced with significant new demands from their environment that gave rise to a state of tension or threat. Second, the people under stress had to find ways to *cope* with these new events. Finally, in all three situations the people found ways to *adjust* to their circumstances.

All of us must adjust to a life that is less than perfect, a life in which bad things happen and even pleasures come with built-in complications. Stress comes, too, in the form of everyday minor demands.

Every **adjustment** is an attempt—successful or not—to balance our desires against the demands of the environment, to weigh our needs against realistic possibilities, and to cope as well as we can within the limits of our situation. The student who fails to get the lead in the school play may quit the production in a huff, accept a smaller role, serve as theater critic for the school paper, or join the debating team. Each response is an adjustment to failure, and some will be more constructive than others.

How we adjust to the stresses—both major and minor—that we encounter is crucial to our health and the quality of our lives. As we shall see in this chapter and the following one on psychological disorders, stress can contribute both to psychological and physical illness. In fact, researchers have found that all physical ailments, from colds to ulcers to cancer, have a psychological as well as a physical component. For this reason, stress and its effects on people's lives is a key focus of **health psychology,** a subfield of psychology (see Table 1–1, p. 4) concerned with the relationship between psychological factors and physical health and illness. Health psychologists seek to understand why some people manage stress well enough to remain healthy while others become ill, whether certain character traits help people recover from serious illness, and how we can promote healthy behaviors.

In this chapter we examine the characteristics of stressful events and how people cope with stress. We look closely at how the body deals with stress and which coping methods seem to lessen its harmful effects.

Some major events, such as earthquakes, are inherently stressful.

Sources of Stress

What is stress?

Stress refers to any environmental demand that creates a state of tension or threat and requires change or adaptation. Many situations prompt us to change our behavior in some way: We stop when a traffic light turns red; we switch television channels to avoid a boring program; we go inside when it starts to rain. Under normal circumstances these situations are not stressful, because they are not accompanied by tension or threat. Now imagine that when the light turns red you are rushing to an important appointment, or that the person watching television with you does not want to switch the channel, or that you are about to host a large outdoor party when it starts to rain. Now the same events can be quite stressful.

Some events, such as wars and natural disasters, are inherently stressful. Danger is real, lives are threatened, and often there is little or nothing people can do to save themselves. But even in inherently stressful situations the time of greatest stress is not when danger is actually present. *Anticipating* the danger is actually the time of greatest stress. Parachutists, for example, are most afraid as the time for the jump approaches. Once in line, unable to turn back, they calm down. During the most dangerous part of the jump—in free fall, waiting for their chutes to open—they are much less frightened (Epstein, 1982).

Stress is not limited to dangerous situations or even to unpleasant situations. Good things can also cause stress, because they "require change or adaptation if an individual is to meet his or her needs" (Morris, 1990, p. 72). A wedding is a stressful as well as an exciting event. A promotion at work is gratifying, but it demands that we relate to new people in new ways, learn to carry more responsibility, and perhaps work longer hours.

Change

Why is change so stressful for most people?

All the stressful events we've discussed so far involve change. Most people have a strong preference for order, continuity, and predictability in their lives. Therefore, anything—good or bad—that requires change will be experienced as stressful. The more change required, the more stressful the situation. In fact, some questionnaires measure stress in a person's life by calculating "life changes" over a specified period of time. For example, the Social Readjustment Rating Scale (SRRS) devised by T. H. Holmes and R. H. Rahe (1967) assigns a point value to several dozen events, depending on the amount of change each requires (see Table 11–1). Notice that the stress ratings of events on the SRRS are not related to whether the events are desirable or undesirable. For example, "Change in responsibilities at work" carries 29 "life-change units" whether it is due to a promotion to more interesting and rewarding work or to being assigned a much larger volume of boring work.

Using the SRRS, one simply adds up the stress ratings of all the events that a person has lived through in the past year to determine the amount of stress that he or she has experienced. In general a score of 150 or less is considered normal; 150–199 corresponds to mild stress; 200–299 suggests a moderate crisis; and 300 or higher indicates a major life crisis. According to Holmes and Rahe, the likelihood that a person will experience a "stress-induced illness" increases sharply for scores above 300.

Although this approach is intuitively appealing, studies have often failed to confirm a relationship between a person's SRRS score and health (see Krantz, Grunberg, & Baum, 1985). Indeed, many people with very high scores on the

Adjustment
Any effort to cope with stress.

Health psychology
A subfield of psychology concerned with the relationship between psychological factors and physical health and illness.

Stress
Any environmental demand that creates a state of tension or threat and requires change or adaptation.

TABLE 11-1	SOCIAL READJUSTMENT RATING SCALE*

Life Event	Life-Change Units
Death of one's spouse	100
Divorce	73
Personal injury or illness	53
Marriage	50
Being fired at work	47
Retirement	45
Pregnancy	40
Gain of a new family member	39
Change in one's financial state	38
Death of a close friend	37
Change to a different line of work	36
Foreclosure of a mortgage or a loan	30
Change in responsibilities at work	29
Son or daughter leaving home	29
Outstanding personal achievement	28
Beginning or ending school	26
Change in living conditions	25
Trouble with one's boss	23
Change in residence	20
Change in schools	20
Change in social activities	18
Change in sleeping habits	16
Change in eating habits	15
Vacation	13

*The SRRS assigns "life-change units" to several dozen stressful events. Holmes and Rahe linked the number of units to risk for medical problems, based on the premise that stress undermines health.

Source: From "The social readjustment rating scale," by T. H. Holmes and R. H. Rahe, *Journal of Psychosomatic Research, 11,* 1967. Copyright © 1967, Pergamon Press. Reprinted with permission.

GAMES
G

SRRS do not experience stress-induced illnesses. Another drawback of the SRRS is that it applies the same number of points to a given stressor or life event regardless of the circumstances surrounding the event. For instance, the SRRS would assign the same score to an accidental pregnancy as it would a planned one, even though in real life one might be far more stressful than the other. Nevertheless, the SRRS is still widely used.

Hassles

Can everyday hassles contribute to stress?

Holmes and Rahe's SRRS emphasizes the kind of stress that arises from fairly dramatic, infrequent life events. But as other psychologists (Lazarus et al., 1985; Lazarus & De Longis, 1983; Ruffin, 1993; Whisman & Kwon, 1993) have pointed out, much stress is generated by "chronic or repeated conditions of living—boredom, continuing tension in a family relationship, lack of occupational progress, isolation and loneliness, absence of meaning and commitment" (Lazarus, 1981, p. 60).

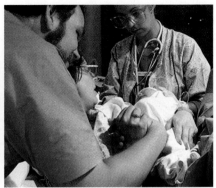

All major life changes—whether positive or negative—involve a certain amount of stress. This is partly because major life changes typically bring strong emotion, and even joy and elation can arouse the body and begin to take a toll on its resources. Major life events can also be stressful because any new experience requires some adjustment.

Lazarus pays particular attention to "hassles," which he defines as petty annoyances, irritations, and frustrations. He contends that such seemingly minor matters as being stuck in traffic, misplacing keys, and getting into a trivial argument may be as stressful as the major life events listed on the Holmes–Rahe scale. Lazarus believes that big events matter so much not because they directly create stress but because they trigger the little hassles that eventually overwhelm us with stress. Research has shown, for example, that people who have recently experienced a major traumatic event are more likely to be plagued by minor stressors than those who have not had a recent shock (Pillow, Zautra, & Sandler, 1996). "In sum," Lazarus says, "it is not the large dramatic events that make the difference, but what happens day in and day out, whether provoked by major events or not" (1981, p. 62).

We have been looking at external events and situations, both major and minor, as sources of stress. These events are stressful because they give rise to feelings of pressure, frustration, conflict, and anxiety. Let's see how each of these emotional experiences contributes to our overall feeling of stress before we consider the different ways in which people perceive and adjust to stress.

Pressure

What are internal and external sources of pressure?

Pressure, another common source of stress, occurs when we feel forced to speed up, intensify, or shift direction in our behavior, or when we feel compelled to meet a higher standard of performance (Morris, 1990). Pressure may come from within, as when we push ourselves to reach personal standards of excellence. This internal pressure may be either constructive or destructive. For instance, it may drive us to learn how to play a musical instrument, which may ultimately bring us great pleasure, or it may erode our self-esteem if we set standards for ourselves that are impossible to achieve. Outside demands also give us pressure: We compete for grades, for popularity, for sexual and marital partners, and for jobs. In addition, we're pressured to live up to the expectations of our family and close friends.

Frustration

What are the major sources of frustration?

Frustration also contributes to stress; it occurs when something or someone prevents us from reaching a goal. Morris (1990) identifies 5 common sources of frustration in American life. *Delays* are annoying because our culture puts great stock in the value of time. *Lack of resources* is especially frustrating to low-income Americans, who cannot afford the luxuries that the mass media tout as symbols of success. *Losses*, such as the end of a marriage, a romance, or a cherished friendship, cause frustration because they can make us feel helpless, unimportant, or worthless. *Failure* generates intense frustration—and accompanying guilt—in our competitive society. As we imagine that if we had done things differently we might have succeeded, so we feel responsible for our own or someone else's pain and disappointment. *Discrimination* also makes for frustration: Being denied opportunities or recognition because of one's race, sex, age, religion, or ethnic group is immensely frustrating.

Conflict

What leads to conflict in our lives?

Of all life's troubles, conflict is probably the most common. A student finds that she needs more time to study, but she needs to work to pay her tuition. We agree with the foreign policy views of one political candidate, but we prefer the domestic programs proposed by the opponent. A child does not want to do his homework, but neither does he want to get low grades.

Conflict arises when we face two or more incompatible demands, opportunities, needs, or goals. We can never resolve conflict completely. In trying, we must give up some of our goals, modify others, delay our pursuit of some, or resign ourselves to not attaining all of them. Whatever we do, we are bound to experience some frustration, which adds to the stressfulness of conflicts.

Conflict has been described in terms of two opposite tendencies: approach and avoidance. When something attracts us, we want to approach it; when something frightens us, we try to avoid it. Different combinations of these tendencies create three basic types of conflict: *approach/approach conflict*, *avoidance/avoidance conflict*, and *approach/avoidance conflict* (Lewin, 1935).

Approach/approach conflict occurs when we are simultaneously attracted to two appealing goals. For example, a student who has been accepted at two equally desirable colleges, neither of which has any significant drawbacks, will experience an approach/approach conflict in choosing between two desirable options.

Much of the stress we experience in our lives arises not from major traumas but rather from small everyday hassles such as traffic jams, petty arguments, and equipment that doesn't work right.

SUMMARY TABLE

Types of Conflict

Type of Conflict	Nature of Conflict
Approach/Approach	You are attracted to two incompatible goals at the same time.
Avoidance/Avoidance	Repelled by two undesirable alternatives at the same time, you are inclined to escape, but other factors often prevent such an escape.
Approach/Avoidance	You are both repelled by, and attracted to, the same goal.

Approach/approach conflict
According to Lewin, the result of simultaneous attraction to two appealing possibilities, neither of which has any negative qualities.

The reverse is **avoidance/avoidance conflict,** in which we confront two undesirable or threatening possibilities, neither of which has any positive attributes. When faced with an avoidance/avoidance conflict, people usually try to escape the situation altogether. If escape is impossible, their coping method depends on how threatening each alternative is. Most often they vacillate between choosing one threat or the other, like a baseball player caught in a rundown between first and second base. In no-exit situations people sometimes simply wait for events to resolve their conflict for them.

An **approach/avoidance conflict,** in which a person is both attracted to and repelled by the same goal, is the most common form of conflict. The closer we come to a goal with good and bad features, the stronger grow our desires both to approach and to avoid, but the tendency to avoid increases more rapidly than the tendency to approach. In an approach/avoidance conflict, therefore, we approach the goal until we reach the point at which the tendency to approach equals the tendency to avoid the goal. Afraid to go any closer, we stop and vacillate, making no choice at all, until the situation changes.

Self-Imposed Stress

How do we create stress?

So far we have considered sources of stress outside the individual. Sometimes, however, people create problems for themselves quite apart from stressful events in their environment. Some psychologists argue that many people carry around a set of irrational, self-defeating beliefs that add unnecessarily to the normal stresses of living (Ellis & Harper, 1975). For example, some people believe that "It is essential to be loved or approved by almost everyone for everything I do." For such people any sign of disapproval will be a source of considerable stress. Others believe that "I must be competent, adequate, and successful at everything I do." For them, the slightest sign of failure or inadequacy means they are worthless human beings. Still other people believe that "It is disastrous if everything doesn't go the way I would like." These people feel upset, miserable, and unhappy when things don't go perfectly. As we will see in the next chapter, self-defeating thoughts like these can contribute to depression (Beck, 1976, 1984).

Stress and Individual Differences

Do people who are resistant to stress share certain traits?

Some people cope well with major life stresses, whereas others are thrown by even minor problems. What accounts for these differences? The answer seems to lie in individual differences in perceiving and reacting to potentially stressful events.

An obstacle that seems insurmountable to one person is simply challenging to another. An experienced construction worker happily eats his lunch perched on a girder hundreds of feet above the ground, but just watching him may make a passerby anxious. The person who gets fired from a job and the soldier who gets caught behind enemy lines may feel equally threatened. In short, how much stress we experience depends partly on the way we interpret the situation. Self-confident people who feel capable of coping with life will feel less stress in a given situation than will the person who lacks self-assurance (Kessler, Price, & Wortman, 1985). For example, students who know they can study when they have to and have done well on exams in the past tend to be calmer the night before an important test than students who have done poorly on previous exams. People who have handled job changes well in the past are likely to find new change less stressful than those who have had great difficulty adjusting to previous job changes.

Avoidance/avoidance conflict
According to Lewin, the result of facing a choice between two undesirable possibilities, neither of which has any positive qualities.

Approach/avoidance conflict
According to Lewin, the result of being simultaneously attracted to and repelled by the same goal.

Suzanne Kobasa (1979) studied a group of people who either tolerated stress exceptionally well or actually thrived on it. What these stress-resistant people had in common was a trait that Kobasa called *hardiness:* They felt very much in control of their lives, were deeply committed to their work and their own values, and experienced difficult demands from the environment as challenging rather than intimidating. Kobasa's study suggests that people's response to stress depends partly on whether they believe they have some control over events or feel helpless. Conversely, you may recall from our discussion of *learned helplessness* in Chapter 5, Learning, that when people are placed in seemingly hopeless situations long enough, they sometimes develop feelings of powerlessness and apathy (Peterson, Maier, & Seligman, 1993). In fact, even when the situation changes, such people often fail. Research cited by M. E. P. Seligman (1975) shows that some people in seemingly hopeless situations not only become apathetic but, when the situation changes, fail to recognize that it is now possible to cope more effectively. They remain passive even when there are opportunities for improving the situation.

Behavior under stress also reflects individual differences. In natural disasters, for example, some people immediately mobilize to save themselves. Others fall apart, and still others are shaken but regain their composure—and ability to respond—almost instantly. And then there are those who refuse to admit that there is any danger. In the next section we look at the ways in which people respond to stress.

REVIEW QUESTIONS

1. _____ is any environment demand that creates a state of tension or threat and requires change or adaptation.

2. _____ is an attempt—successful or not—to balance our desires against the demands of the environment, to weigh our needs against realistic possibilities, and to cope as well as we can within the limits of our situation.

3. _____ is usually the most stressful life event we face.

Indicate whether the following are true (T) or false (F).

4. Stress is always a response to negative events in our life. ____

5. Stressful events almost always involve changes in our lives. ____

6. Big events in life are always much more stressful than everyday hassles. ____

Match each type of conflict with the appropriate definition.

7. approach/approach ____   a. choosing between two undesired yet unavoidable alternatives

8. avoidance/avoidance ____   b. attracted to and repelled by the same goal

9. approach/avoidance ____   c. attracted to two goals at once

Answers: 1. stress. 2. adjustment. 3. the death of one's spouse. 4. F. 5. T. 6. F. 7. c. 8. a. 9. b.

How People Cope With Stress

What is the difference between direct coping and defensive coping?

Whatever its source, stress calls for adjustment. Psychologists distinguish between two general types of adjustment: direct coping and defensive coping. *Direct coping* refers to any action we take to change an uncomfortable situation. When our needs or desires are frustrated, for example, we attempt to remove the obstacles between ourselves and our goal or we give up. Similarly, when we are threatened, we try to eliminate the source of the threat, either by attacking it or by escaping from it.

Defensive coping refers to the different ways in which people convince themselves that they are not really threatened or that they do not really want something they cannot get. A form of self-deception, defensive coping is characteristic of internal, often unconscious conflicts when we are emotionally unable to bring a problem to the surface of consciousness and deal with it directly, because it is too threatening. We decide to avoid it out of self-defense.

Direct Coping

What are three strategies that deal directly with stress?

When we are threatened, frustrated, or in conflict we have three basic choices for coping directly: *confrontation, compromise,* or *withdrawal.* We can meet a situation head-on and intensify our efforts to get what we want (confrontation). We can give up some of what we want and perhaps persuade others to give up part of what they want (compromise). Or we can admit defeat and stop fighting (withdrawal). (See *Applying Psychology* for a discussion of coping with stress at college.)

Take the case of a woman who has worked hard at her job for years but is not promoted. She learns that the reason is her stated unwillingness to move temporarily from the company's main office to a branch office in another part of the country to acquire more experience. Her unwillingness to move stands between her and her goal of advancing in her career. She has several choices, which we explore.

Confrontation   Facing a stressful situation forthrightly, acknowledging to oneself that there is a problem for which a solution must be found, attacking the problem head-on, and pushing resolutely toward one's goal is called **confrontation.** The hallmark of the "confrontational style" (Morris, 1990) is making intense efforts to cope with stress and to accomplish one's aims. This may involve learning skills, enlisting other people's help, or just trying harder. Or it may require steps to change either oneself or the situation. The woman who wants to advance her career might gather more information about the options open to her and their effect on her career. Or she might challenge the assumption that working at the branch office would give her the kind of experience her supervisor thinks she needs. She might try to persuade her boss that even though she has never worked in a branch office, she nevertheless has acquired enough experience to handle a better job in the main office. Or she might remind her supervisor of the company's stated goal of promoting more women to top-level positions.

Confrontation may also include expressions of anger. Anger may be effective, especially if we really have been treated unfairly and if we express our anger with restraint instead of exploding in rage. A national magazine once reported an amusing, and effective, example of controlled anger in response to an annoying little hassle. As a motorist came to an intersection, he had to stop for a frail elderly woman crossing the street. The driver of the car behind his honked his horn impatiently, whereupon the first driver shut off his ignition, removed the key, walked back to the other car, and handed the key to the second driver. "Here," he said, "you run over her. I can't do it. She reminds me of my grandmother."

Compromise   Compromise is one of the most common and effective ways of coping directly with conflict or frustration. We often recognize that we cannot have everything we want and that we cannot expect others to do just what we would like them to do. In such cases we may decide to settle for less than we originally sought. A young person who has loved animals all his life and has long cherished the desire to become a veterinarian may discover in college that he has

Confrontation
Acknowledging a stressful situation directly and attempting to find a solution to the problem or attain the difficult goal.

Compromise
Deciding on a more realistic solution or goal when an ideal solution or goal is not practical.

APPLYING PSYCHOLOGY

Coping with Stress at College

It is 2 weeks before finals, and you have 2 papers to write and 4 exams to study for. You are very worried. You are not alone. To help students cope with the pressures of finals week and, indeed, the stress that many students feel throughout the semester, many colleges and universities offer stress-reduction workshops, aerobics classes, and counseling. At the University of California at Los Angeles students are taught to visualize themselves calmly answering difficult test questions. Even if you do not attend a special program for reducing stress, there are many techniques you can teach yourself to help cope with the pressures of college life.

1. Plan ahead, do not procrastinate, get things done well before deadlines. Start work on large projects well in advance.

2. Exercise; do whatever activity you enjoy.

3. Listen to your favorite music, watch a television show, or go to a movie as a study break.

4. Talk to other people.

5. Meditate or use other relaxation techniques. See the paperback *The Relaxation Response*.

One very effective technique is to make a list of *everything* you have to do, right down to doing the laundry, getting birthday cards for family and friends, and so on. Then star the highest-priority tasks—the ones that *really* have to be done first or those that will take a long time. Use all available time to work on *only* those tasks. Free up time by not doing things that are not on the highest-priority list. Cross off high-priority tasks as they are done, add new tasks as they arrive, and continually adjust the priorities so the most critical tasks are always starred.

This technique serves various purposes. It removes the fear that you'll forget something important, because everything you can think of is on a single sheet of paper. It helps you realize that things are not as overwhelming as they might otherwise

seem (the list is finite, and there are probably only a few things that truly are high-priority tasks). It lets you focus your energy on the most important tasks and makes it easy to avoid spending time on less important things that might drift into your attention. Finally, it assures you that you are doing everything possible to do the most important things in your life, and if you don't manage to do them all, you can truly say, "There's no way I could have done any better; it simply wasn't possible in the time available." Actually, that will seldom be the case. Usually the highest-priority tasks get done and the lower-priority tasks simply wait, often for weeks or months, after which you wonder how important they really are if they always come out on the bottom of the totem pole.

To learn more about relaxation techniques and study skills, visit our Web site at **www.prenhall.com/morris.**

---

less aptitude for biology than he thought and that he finds dissecting lab specimens so distasteful that he could never bring himself to operate on animals. He may decide to compromise by becoming an animal technician, a person who assists veterinarians. The woman who does not want to relocate could propose alternatives such as spending several weeks of intensive training at the branch office or a special assignment at the home office that would give her equivalent experience. Or she might agree to the temporary move in return for a guaranteed promotion or a significant salary increase upon her return.

Withdrawal   In some circumstances the most effective way of coping with stress is to withdraw from the situation. A person at an amusement park who is overcome by anxiety just looking at a roller coaster may simply move on to a less threatening ride or may even leave the park entirely. The woman whose promotion depends on temporarily relocating might just quit her job and join another company.

When we realize that our adversary is more powerful than we are, that there is no way we can effectively modify ourselves or the situation, that there is no possible compromise, and that any form of aggression would be self-destructive, **withdrawal** is a positive and realistic response. In seemingly hopeless situations,

Withdrawal
Avoiding a situation when other forms of coping are not practical.

such as submarine and mining disasters, few people panic (Mintz, 1951). Believing there is nothing they can do to save themselves, they give up. If in fact a situation is hopeless, resignation may be the most effective way of coping with it.

Perhaps the greatest danger of coping by withdrawal is that the person will come to avoid all similar situations. The person who grew extremely anxious looking at the roller coaster may refuse to go to an amusement park or carnival again. The woman who did not want to take a job at her company's branch office may not only quit her present job but leave the workforce entirely. In such cases coping by withdrawal can become maladaptive avoidance. Moreover, people who have given up on a situation are in a poor position to take advantage of an effective solution if one should come along. For example, one group of fifth-grade students was given unsolvable problems by one teacher and solvable problems by another. When the teacher who had handed out the "unsolvable" problems later presented the students with problems that could be solved, the students were unable to solve them, even though they had solved nearly identical problems given out by the other teacher (Dweck & Reppucci, 1973).

Withdrawal, in whatever form, is a mixed blessing. Although it can be an effective method of coping, it has built-in dangers. The same tends to be true of defensive coping, to which we now turn.

Defensive Coping

What are the major ways of coping defensively?

Thus far we have been speaking of coping with stress that arises from recognizable sources. But there are times when we either cannot identify or cannot deal directly with the source of our stress. For example, you return to a parking lot to discover that your car has been damaged. In other cases a problem is so emotionally threatening that it cannot be faced directly: Someone close to you is terminally ill, or after 4 years of hard work you have failed to gain admission to medical school and may have to abandon your lifelong ambition to become a doctor.

In all of these cases you are under stress, and there is little or nothing you can do to cope with the stress directly. In such situations people may turn to **defense mechanisms** as a way of coping. Defense mechanisms are techniques for *deceiving* oneself about the causes of a stressful situation to reduce pressure, frustration, conflict, and anxiety. The self-deceptive nature of such adjustments led Freud to conclude that they are entirely unconscious, but not all psychologists agree that they always spring from unconscious conflicts over which we have little or no control. Often we realize that we are pushing something out of our memory or otherwise deceiving ourselves. For example, all of us have blown up at someone when we *knew* we were really angry at someone else. Whether defense mechanisms operate consciously or unconsciously, they provide a means of coping with stress that might otherwise be unbearable.

Denial   **Denial** is the refusal to acknowledge a painful or threatening reality. Lazarus (1969) cites the example of a woman who was near death from severe burns. At first she was depressed and frightened, but after a few days she felt sure she would soon be able to return home and care for her children, even though all medical indications were to the contrary. By denying the extent of her injuries, this woman was able to stay calm and cheerful. She was not merely putting on an act for her relatives and friends: She *believed* that she would recover.

Denial is not always a positive way of coping. Students who deny their need to study may fail their exams. Similarly, frequent drug users who insist that they merely are experimenting with drugs are also deluding themselves.

Defense mechanisms
Self-deceptive techniques for reducing stress, including denial, repression, projection, identification, regression, intellectualization, reaction formation, displacement, and sublimation.

Denial
Refusal to acknowledge a painful or threatening reality.

Repression   The most common mechanism for blocking out painful feelings and memories is **repression,** a form of forgetting that excludes painful thoughts from consciousness. Soldiers who break down in the field often block out the memory of the experiences that led to their collapse (Grinker & Spiegel, 1945). Many psychologists believe that repression is a symptom that the person is struggling against impulses (such as aggression) that conflict with conscious values. For example, most of us were taught in childhood that violence and aggression are wrong. This conflict between our feelings and our values can create stress, and one way of coping defensively with that stress is to repress our feelings—to block out completely any awareness of our underlying anger and hostility.

Denial and repression are the most basic defense mechanisms. In denial we block out situations we can't cope with; in repression we block out unacceptable impulses or thoughts. These psychic strategies form the bases for other defensive ways of coping, which we examine now.

Projection   If a problem cannot be denied or completely repressed, we may be able to distort its nature so that we can handle it more easily through **projection,** the attribution of one's repressed motives, ideas, or feelings to others. We ascribe feelings to someone else that we do not want to acknowledge as our own, thus locating the source of our conflict outside ourselves. A corporate executive who feels guilty about the way he rose to power may project his own ruthless ambition onto his colleagues. He simply is doing his job, he believes, while his associates are all crassly ambitious and consumed with power.

Through identification with an admired person we vicariously take on that other person's highly regarded characteristics. In this way we counteract painful perceptions about our own shortcomings. Parents who themselves have never been stars at anything may identify with their child's outstanding achievements, taking pride in these achievements as if they were their own.

Identification   The reverse of projection is **identification.** Through projection we *rid* ourselves of undesirable characteristics that we have repressed by attributing them to someone else. Through identification we *take on* the characteristics of someone else so that we can vicariously share in that person's triumphs and overcome feeling inadequate. The admired person's actions, that is, become a substitute for our own. A mother with unfulfilled career ambitions may share emotionally in a daughter's professional success. When the daughter is promoted, the mother may feel as if *she* has triumphed. Identification is often used as a form of self-defense in situations where a person feels utterly helpless, including being taken as a hostage or being a prisoner in a Nazi concentration camp. Some prisoners gradually come to identify with their guards as a way of defensively coping with unbearable and inescapable stress.

Regression   People under stress may revert to childlike behavior through a process called **regression.** Why do people regress? Some psychologists say that it is because an adult cannot stand feeling helpless. Children, on the other hand, feel helpless and dependent every day, so becoming more childlike can make total dependency or helplessness more bearable.

Regression is sometimes used as a manipulative strategy, too, albeit an immature and inappropriate one. Adults who cry or throw temper tantrums when their arguments fail may expect those around them to react sympathetically, as their parents did when they were children.

Repression
Excluding uncomfortable thoughts, feelings, and desires from consciousness.

Projection
Attributing one's repressed motives, feelings, or wishes to others.

Identification
Taking on the characteristics of someone else to avoid feeling incompetent.

Regression
Reverting to childlike behavior and defenses.

Intellectualization The defense mechanism known as **intellectualization** is a subtle form of denial in which we detach ourselves from our feelings about our problems by analyzing them intellectually and thinking of them almost as if they concerned other people. Parents who start out intending to discuss their child's difficulties in a new school and then find themselves engaged in a sophisticated discussion of educational philosophy may be intellectualizing a very upsetting situation. They appear to be dealing with their problems, but in fact they are not, because they have cut themselves off from their emotions.

Reaction Formation The term **reaction formation** refers to a behavioral form of denial in which people express, with exaggerated intensity, ideas and emotions that are the opposite of their own. *Exaggeration* is the clue to this behavior. The woman who extravagantly praises a rival may be covering up jealousy over her opponent's success. Reaction formation may also be a way of convincing oneself that one's motives are pure. The man who feels ambivalent about being a father may devote a disproportionate amount of time to his children in an attempt to prove to *himself* that he is a good father.

Displacement **Displacement** involves the redirection of repressed motives and emotions from their original objects to substitute objects. The man who has always wanted to be a father may feel inadequate when he learns that he cannot have children. As a result, he may become extremely attached to a pet or to a niece or nephew. In another example of displacement, the woman who must smile and agree with her boss all day may come home and yell at her husband or children.

Sublimation **Sublimation** refers to transforming repressed motives or feelings into more socially acceptable forms. Aggressiveness, for instance, might be channeled into competitiveness in business or sports. A strong and persistent desire for attention might be transformed into an interest in acting or politics.

From the Freudian perspective, sublimation is not only necessary but also desirable. People who can transform their sexual and aggressive drives into more socially acceptable forms are clearly better off, for they are able to at least partially gratify instinctual drives with relatively little anxiety and guilt. Moreover, society benefits from the energy and effort such people channel into the arts, literature, science, and other socially useful activities.

We have seen that there are many different ways of coping defensively with stress. Is defensive coping a sure sign that a person is immature, unstable, on the edge of a "breakdown"? Not at all. The effects of prolonged stress may be so severe, as we will see in the next section, that in some cases defensive coping not only contributes to our overall ability to adapt and adjust but even becomes essential to survival. And in less extreme situations, people may rely on defense mechanisms to cope with everyday problems and stress.

Socioeconomic and Gender Differences in Coping with Stress

Who experiences the most stress?

People use the various coping strategies we have been discussing in different combinations and in different ways to deal with stressful events. In particular, economic and social factors figure not only in the amount of stress that people encounter but also in their ability to cope with that stress. Poor people frequently have to deal with more stress than people who are better off (N. Adler et al., 1994; S. Cohen & Williamson, 1988; Kessler, 1979). They often live in substandard housing in neighborhoods with high rates of crime and violence. They are more likely than others to experience long-term joblessness, and they face greater obsta-

Intellectualization
Thinking abstractly about stressful problems as a way of detaching oneself from them.

Reaction formation
Expression of exaggerated ideas and emotions that are the opposite of one's repressed beliefs or feelings.

Displacement
Shifting repressed motives and emotions from an original object to a substitute object.

Sublimation
Redirecting repressed motives and feelings into more socially acceptable channels.

SUMMARY TABLE

Defense Mechanisms

Denial	Refusing to acknowledge a painful or threatening reality: Ray, whose best friend has just been killed in a car accident, insists that it is a case of mistaken identity and that his friend is still alive.
Repression	Excluding uncomfortable thoughts from consciousness: Lisa, whose grandmother died of breast cancer, is at higher-than-average risk for developing breast cancer herself; still she routinely forgets to get a mammogram.
Projection	Attributing one's repressed motives, feelings, or wishes to others: Marilyn is unfairly passed over for a promotion; she denies that she is angry about this but is certain that her supervisor is angry with her.
Identification	Taking on the characteristics of someone else to avoid feeling inadequate: Anthony, uncertain of his own attractiveness, takes on the dress and mannerisms of a popular teacher.
Regression	Reverting to childlike behavior and defenses: Furious because his plan to reorganize his division has been rejected, Bob throws a tantrum.
Intellectualization	Thinking abstractly about stressful problems as a way of detaching oneself from them: After learning that she has not been asked to a classmate's costume party, Tina coolly discusses the ways in which social cliques form and how they serve to regulate and control school life.
Reaction formation	Expression of exaggerated ideas and emotions that are the opposite of one's repressed beliefs or feelings: At work Michael loudly professes that he would never take advantage of a rival employee, though his harassing behavior indicates quite the opposite.
Displacement	Shifting repressed motives from an original object to a substitute object: Infuriated at his instructor's unreasonable request that he rewrite his term paper, but afraid to say anything for fear he will make the instructor angry, Nelson comes home and yells at his housemates for telling him what to do.
Sublimation	Redirecting repressed motives and feelings into more socially acceptable channels: The child of parents who never paid attention to him, Bill is running for public office.

cles in addressing such basic needs as feeding their children adequately, maintaining good health and securing high-quality medical care, and providing a home.

Moreover, some data indicate that people in low-income groups cope less effectively with stress and that, as a result, stressful events have a harsher impact on their emotional lives (Kessler, 1979; Wills & Langer, 1980). Psychologists have offered several possible explanations for these data. People in lower socio-economic classes often have fewer means for coping with hardship and stress (Pearlin & Schooler, 1978). Low-income people also have fewer people to turn to and fewer community resources to draw on for support during stressful times (Liem & Liem, 1978). In addition, people living in poverty may believe to a greater extent than other people that external factors are responsible for what happens to them and that they have

These children in a low-income neighborhood of Chicago probably experience more stress in their lives than their middle- and upper-class peers. They inhabit a world with high rates of crime and violence, and their families are often struggling just to meet basic needs. Such stresses can take a harsh toll on the poor when they have few means of coping with them effectively.

little personal control over their lives. Finally, there is some evidence that members of low-income groups are more likely to have low self-esteem and to doubt their ability to master difficult situations. All of these factors help to explain why stress often takes a greater toll on people in lower socio-economic classes.

Researchers have also studied gender differences in relation to stress and coping. One study of victims of Hurricane Andrew found that although women reported experiencing more stress than men, men and women turned out to be affected equally when stress was measured physiologically (Adler, 1993b). In another study of 300 dual-earner couples, women and men felt equally stressed by the state of their marriage, their jobs, and how well their children were doing. The women in this study, however, experienced greater stress than men when problems developed in long-term relationships, largely because they were more committed to their personal and professional relationships than the men were (Barnett, Brennan, & Marshall, 1994). Moreover, while earlier research suggested that men and women often use different strategies to cope with stress (Ptacek, Smith, & Dodge, 1994), a more recent investigation found that when faced with equally stressful situations, the coping strategies used by men and women are generally quite similar (Porter & Stone, 1995).

REVIEW QUESTIONS

1. There are two general types of coping: _____ and _____.
2. Confronting problems, compromising, or withdrawing from the situation entirely are all forms of _____ coping.
3. _____ coping is a means of dealing with situations that people feel unable to resolve.

Match the following defense mechanisms with the appropriate definition.

4. ____ denial
5. ____ repression
6. ____ projection
7. ____ identification
8. ____ regression
9. ____ intellectualization
10. ____ reaction formation
11. ____ displacement
12. ____ sublimation

a. a form of forgetting
b. detachment from problems through rational analysis
c. reversion to less mature, even childlike behavior
d. exaggerated expression of emotions or ideas that are the opposite of what we really feel or believe
e. redirection of motives or emotions to other objects
f. refusal to acknowledge that a painful or threatening situation exists
g. attributing one's motives and feelings to others
h. redirection of motives or emotions into more socially acceptable forms
i. taking on the characteristics of someone else to share that person's successes and avoid feelings of personal inadequacy

Answers: 1. direct, defensive. 2. direct. 3. defensive. 4. f. 5. a. 6. g. 7. i. 8. c. 9. b. 10. d. 11. e. 12. h.

How Stress Affects Health

What long-lasting effects of stress do we need to be concerned with?

To understand how our body responds to stress, we must first examine how we react to danger. Suppose you are walking alone down an unfamiliar street late at night when you notice a suspicious stranger is following you. Suddenly your heart begins to pound, your respiration increases, and you develop a queasy feeling in your stomach. What is happening to you? The hypothalamus, a center

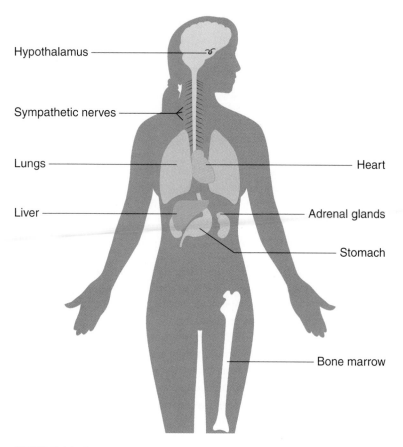

Hypothalamus

Sympathetic nerves

Lungs

Heart

Liver

Adrenal glands

Stomach

Bone marrow

FIGURE 11–1

The physiological response to stress. When the body is confronted with a stressful situation, the hypothalamus stimulates the sympathetic nervous system and the adrenal glands to release stress hormones. Other organs, including the stomach and liver, are also affected.

deep in your brain, is reacting to your perception of danger by organizing a generalized response that affects several organs throughout your body (see Figure 11–1). Almost immediately the hypothalamus stimulates the sympathetic branch of the autonomic nervous system and the adrenal glands to release stress hormones such as *adrenaline* and *norepinephrine* into the blood. This in turn leads to increases in heart rate, blood pressure, respiration, and perspiration. Other organs also respond; for example, the liver increases the available sugar in the blood for extra energy, and the bone marrow increases the white blood cell count to combat infection. Conversely, the rate of some bodily functions decreases; for example, the rate of digestion slows down, which accounts for the queasy feeling in the stomach.

The noted physiologist Walter Cannon (1929) first described the basic elements of this sequence of events as a *fight-or-flight* response, because it appeared that its primary purpose was to prepare an animal to respond to external threats by either attacking or fleeing from them. Cannon also observed that this physiological mobilization occurred uniformly regardless of the nature of the threat. For instance, the fight-or-flight response can be triggered by physical trauma, fear, emotional arousal, or simply by having a *really* bad incident happen at work or school. The adaptive significance of the fight-or-flight response in people was obvious to Cannon, in that it assured the survival of early humans when faced with danger.

Extending Cannon's theory of the fight-or-flight response, the Canadian physiologist Hans Selye (1907–82) contended that we react to physical and psychological stress in three stages he collectively called the **general adaptation syndrome (GAS)** (Selye, 1956, 1976). These three stages are alarm reaction, resistance, and exhaustion.

Stage 1, *alarm reaction*, is the first response to stress. It begins when the body recognizes that it must fend off some physical or psychological danger. Emotions run high. Activity of the sympathetic nervous system is increased, resulting in the release of hormones from the adrenal gland. We become more sensitive and alert, our respiration and heartbeat quicken, our muscles tense, and we experience other physiological changes as well. All of these changes help us to mobilize our coping resources in order to regain self-control. At the alarm stage we might use either direct or defensive coping strategies. If neither of these approaches reduces the stress, we eventually enter the second stage of adaptation.

During Stage 2, *resistance*, physical symptoms and other signs of strain appear as we struggle against increasing psychological disorganization. We intensify our use of both direct and defensive coping techniques. If we succeed in reducing the stress, we return to a more normal state. But if the stress is extreme or prolonged, we may turn in desperation to inappropriate coping techniques and cling to them rigidly, despite the evidence that they are not working. When that happens, physical and emotional resources are further depleted, and signs of psychic and physical wear and tear become even more apparent.

In the third stage, *exhaustion*, we draw on increasingly ineffective defense mechanisms in a desperate attempt to bring the stress under control. Some people lose touch with reality and show signs of emotional disorder or mental illness at this stage. Others show signs of "burnout," including the inability to concentrate, irritability, procrastination, and a cynical belief that nothing is worthwhile (Freudenberger, 1983; Freudenberger & Richelson, 1980; Maslach & Leiter, 1982, 1997). Physical symptoms such as skin or stomach problems may erupt, and some victims of burnout turn to alcohol or drugs to cope with the stress-induced exhaustion. If the stress continues, the person may suffer irreparable physical or psychological damage or even death.

One of the most startling implications of Selye's theory is the possibility that prolonged psychological stress can make us sick. How can psychological stress lead to or influence physical illness? There are at least two routes. First, when a person experiences stress, his heart, lungs, nervous system, and other physiological systems are forced to work harder. The human body is not designed to be exposed for long periods to the powerful biological changes that accompany alarm and mobilization, so when stress is prolonged, people are more likely to experience some kind of physical disorder. Second, stress has a powerful negative effect on the body's immune system, and prolonged stress can destroy the body's ability to defend itself from disease.

Stress and Heart Disease

How is Type A behavior related to heart disease?

Stress is a major contributing factor in the development of coronary heart disease (CHD), the leading cause of death and disability in the United States (McGinnis, 1994). Heredity also affects the likelihood of developing CHD, but even among identical twins the incidence of CHD is closely linked to attitudes toward work, problems in the home, and the amount of leisure time available (Kringlen, 1981). Generally life stress and social isolation are significant predictors of mortality among those who have suffered heart attacks for whatever reason (Ruberman et al., 1984).

General adaptation syndrome (GAS) According to Selye, the three stages the body passes through as it adapts to stress: alarm reaction, resistance, and exhaustion.

Mental stress on the job is linked to CHD, as is individual personality. A great deal of research has been done, for example, on people who exhibit the *Type A behavior pattern*—that is, who respond to life events with impatience, hostility, competitiveness, urgency, and constant striving (M. Friedman & Rosenman, 1959). Type A people are distinguished from more easygoing *Type B* people. The two cardiologists who first identified the characteristics of Type A's were convinced that this behavior pattern was most likely to surface in stressful situations.

A number of studies have shown that Type A behavior predicts CHD (Booth-Kewley & Friedman, 1987). For example, when Type A personalities were being evaluated, subjected to harassment or criticism, or playing video games, their heart rate and blood pressure were much higher than those of Type B personalities under the same circumstances (Lyness, 1993). Both high heart rate and high blood pressure are known to contribute to CHD.

Other studies maintain that the link between Type A behavior and CHD is less direct—that the tendency toward Type A behavior may influence people to engage in behaviors, such as smoking or overeating, that directly contribute to heart disease (K. A. Matthews, 1988). Based on the preponderance of evidence, however, it seems clear that *chronic anger* and *hostility* (both components of Type A behavior) do indeed predict heart disease (C. D. Jenkins, 1988; Miller et al., 1996). Counseling designed to diminish the intensity of time urgency and hostility in patients with Type A behavior has been moderately successful in reducing the incidence of CHD (Friedman et al., 1996).

Because long-term stress increases the likelihood of developing CHD, reducing stress has become part of the treatment used to slow the progress of *atherosclerosis*, or blockage of the arteries, which can lead to a heart attack. Both a very low-fat diet and stress-management techniques, such as yoga and deep relaxation, have been effective in treating this disease (Ornish, 1990).

Evidence appears to show that the chronic anger and hostility associated with Type A behavior can predict heart disease.

Stress and the Immune System

Why do so many students get sick during finals?

So many people develop colds or flu after a stressful period in their lives that scientists have long suspected that the immune system is affected by stress. Because the immune system responds to hormones and signals from the brain, the nervous and endocrine systems are involved in the interactions between stress and the immune system, the focus of the relatively new field of **psychoneuroimmunology** (Ader & Cohen, 1993; Maier, Watkins, & Fleshner, 1994). Research now confirms that to the extent that stress—including stress associated with college exams and with depression—disrupts the functioning of the immune system, it can impair health. Further, chronic stress, such as caring for an elderly parent or living in poverty, also compromises the body's defenses (Cohen & Herbert, 1996; O'Leary, 1990; Oltmanns & Emery, 1994).

Increased stress may make us more susceptible to upper respiratory infections, such as the common cold (Cohen, 1996). For example, volunteers who reported being under severe stress and who had experienced two or more major stressful events during the previous year were more likely to develop a cold when they were exposed to a cold virus (Cohen, Tyrrell, & Smith, 1991). A control group of volunteers who reported lower levels of stress were less likely to develop cold symptoms even though they were equally exposed to the virus.

Prolonged stress has also been shown to increase vulnerability to cancer. Stress does not *cause* cancer, but it apparently impairs the immune system so that

Psychoneuroimmunology
A new field that studies the interaction between stress on the one hand and immune, endocrine, and nervous system activity on the other.

The Benefits of Group Therapy for Breast Cancer Patients

Faced with the diagnosis of late-stage breast cancer, women understandably experience extraordinarily high levels of depression and mental stress. To make matters worse, the stress and depression often undermine their compliance with vitally important medical treatments (Anderson, Kiecolt-Glaser, & Glaser, 1994). Many physicians now routinely recommend that their breast cancer patients attend group therapy sessions, which seem to be effective in reducing depression and mental stress (Kissane et al., 1997; Spiegel, 1995).

Interestingly, intensive group therapy may do more than simply help terminally ill breast cancer patients cope with psychological stress—*it may actually increase their survival rate* (Spiegel & Moore, 1997). In a study of 86 women with late-stage breast cancer,

women who had received intensive group therapy survived, on average, a year and a half longer than those who did not receive therapy. But was this outcome due to greater compliance with medical services on the part of

---

Intensive group therapy may increase terminally ill patients' survival rate.

---

the women who attended group therapy as compared with those who did not? A follow-up study (Kogon et al., 1997) ruled out that possibility. "Whatever it was," according to psychiatrist David Spiegel, "it wasn't sim-

ply that they used their health-care services differently. It must have been something else . . . that occurred as a result of the therapy that allowed these women to live longer" (NPR, 1997).

Because stress affects both the immune and endocrine systems, subsequent studies (van der Pompe et al., 1997) have already begun to explore the effect that psychosocial intervention may have on these systems. According to Dr. Robert Carlson, a colleague of Dr. Spiegel, "We know that the immune system has some impact on how individuals handle their cancer. And one of the things we're doing [in our current research] is seeing whether the immune responses are different in the women who are in the psychosocial intervention group compared with those women who are not" (NPR, 1997).

---

cancerous cells are better able to establish themselves and spread throughout the body. Animal research has demonstrated this connection between stress and cancer. In one study a group of mice known to be vulnerable to cancer was kept for 400 days in crowded conditions in which they heard noise made by people and other animals. By the end of this period 92 percent of the mice had developed cancer. By contrast, only 7 percent of a comparable group of mice kept in quiet, low-stress conditions developed cancer.

Studies of humans also show a link between life stress and incidence of cancer. For example, researchers have found that people who developed cancer generally had experienced a number of stressful life events in the year before diagnosis (O'Leary, 1990). They were also likely to be fatigued and to feel helpless. Interestingly, these people reported less distress and were less likely to express negative emotions, such as anger, than others who had the same number of stressful life events, which suggests that suppressing negative emotions may be more stressful (and less healthful) than expressing them. Some studies indicate that relaxation techniques improve immune functioning and thus increase survival rates among cancer patients (Andersen et al., 1994). For that reason cancer therapy now often includes stress-reduction components such as group therapy (see *Highlights*).

Social Support and Health

What is the relationship between social support and health?

Having a strong network of friends and family who provide *social support* is linked to good health (see Uchino, Cacioppo, & Kiecolt-Glaser, 1996). Indeed, one review of the literature concluded that the relationship between social support and health is comparable to other, more well-established health-risk factors, such as physical activity, smoking, and blood pressure (House, Landis, & Umberson, 1988). Similarly, people who attend religious services regularly enjoy better health and have markedly lower rates of depression than those who do not (Koenig, 1997).

Exactly *why* a strong social support system is related to health is not fully understood. Clearly, friends and relatives can provide strength and encouragement when we are faced with stressful situations (Williams et al., 1992). Discussing problems in a supportive and sensitive environment allows us to reassess them, leading to new ways of reducing the perceived stress. Social support may directly affect our response to stress and health by producing physiological changes in endocrine, cardiac, and immune functioning (Uchino et al., 1996).

REVIEW QUESTIONS

Match the following terms with the appropriate definition.

1. ____ alarm reaction   a. signs of psychic and physical wear and tear begin to show

2. ____ resistance   b. body recognizes that it must fend off danger

3. ____ exhaustion   c. some people show signs of "burnout"

4. ____ is the term given to the set of characteristics, such as hostility and a sense of urgency, that many people believe make a person more susceptible to coronary heart disease.

Indicate whether the following are true (T) or false (F).

5. Research so far has been unable to find a relationship between stress and the strength of the body's immune system. ____

6. Prolonged psychological stress can make certain diseases worse. ____

7. Increased stress may make us more susceptible to the common cold. ____

8. Prolonged stress has been shown to increase vulnerability to cancer. ____

9. People who attend religious services regularly do not enjoy better health than those who do not attend regularly. ____

Answers: 1. b. 2. a. 3. c. 4. Type A behavior pattern. 5. F. 6. T. 7. T. 8. T. 9. F.

Sources of Extreme Stress

What are some sources of extreme stress, and what impact do they have?

Major stress can be caused by anything from unemployment to wartime combat, from violent natural disaster to rape. In this section we look briefly at some major stressors, their effects, and the coping mechanisms people use to deal with them.

Unemployment   Joblessness is a major source of stress. In fact, when the jobless rate rises, so do first admissions to psychiatric hospitals, infant mortality, deaths from heart disease, alcohol-related diseases, and suicide (Brenner, 1973, 1979; Rayman & Bluestone, 1982). In a study of aircraft workers who lost their jobs, many of the workers reported suffering from high blood pressure, alcoholism, heavy smoking, and anxiety. Other studies have found that family strain increases. "Things just fell apart," one worker said after both he and his wife suddenly found themselves unemployed.

Finally, two studies have shown that death rates go up and psychiatric symptoms worsen not just during periods of unemployment but also during short,

A scene from an unemployment office. As unemployment rates rise, so do first admissions to psychiatric hospitals, deaths from heart disease, and suicides.

rapid upturns in the economy (Brenner, 1979; Eyer, 1977). This finding lends support to the view that change, whether good or bad, causes stress.

Divorce and Separation   "The deterioration or ending of an intimate relationship is one of the more potent of stressors and one of the more frequent reasons why people seek psychotherapy" (Coleman et al., 1988, p. 155). After a breakup both partners often feel they have failed at one of life's most important endeavors, but strong emotional ties continue to bind the pair. If only one spouse wants to end the marriage, the one initiating the divorce may feel sadness and guilt at hurting his or her partner; the rejected spouse may feel anger, humiliation, and guilt over his or her role in the failure. Even if the decision to separate was mutually agreed on, ambivalent feelings of love and hate can make life turbulent. People commonly use defensive coping techniques, particularly denial and projection, to cushion the impact of divorce or separation.

Bereavement   Following the death of a loved one, people generally experience the strong feelings of grief and loss known as *bereavement*. Most people emerge from this experience without suffering permanent psychological harm, but usually not before they pass through a long process that Freud called the "work of mourning." Normal grief begins with numbness and progresses through months of distress in which anger, despair, intense grief and yearning, depression, and apathy may all come to the fore (Janis et al., 1969). During this phase people in mourning tend to cope defensively with an inescapable and extremely painful reality. In most cases denial, displacement, and other defense mechanisms allow the survivor to gather strength for the more direct coping efforts that will be necessary later on—such as, in the case of a spouse's death, selling belongings and perhaps moving to a different home.

Catastrophes   Catastrophes, natural and otherwise—including floods, earthquakes, violent storms, fires, and plane crashes—produce certain psychological reactions common to all stressful events. At first, in the *shock stage*, "the victim is stunned, dazed, and apathetic" and sometimes even "stuporous, disoriented, and amnesic for the traumatic event." Then, in the *suggestible stage*, victims are passive and quite ready to do whatever rescuers tell them to do. In the third phase, the *recovery stage*, emotional balance is regained, but anxiety often persists, and victims may need to recount their experiences over and over again (Morris, 1990). In later stages survivors may feel irrationally guilty because they lived while others died.

Combat and Other Threatening Personal Attacks   Wartime experiences often cause soldiers intense and disabling combat stress. Similar reactions—including bursting into rage over harmless remarks, sleep disturbances, cringing at sudden loud noises, psychological confusion, uncontrollable crying, and silently staring into space for long periods—are also frequently seen in survivors of serious accidents and violent crimes, such as rapes and muggings.

Posttraumatic Stress Disorder

What experiences can lead to posttraumatic stress disorder?

In extreme cases severely stressful events can cause a psychological disorder known as **posttraumatic stress disorder (PTSD).** Dramatic nightmares in

---

Posttraumatic stress disorder (PTSD) Psychological disorder characterized by episodes of anxiety, sleeplessness, and nightmares resulting from some disturbing past event.

which the victim re-experiences the terrifying event exactly as it happened are common. So are daytime *flashbacks*, in which the victim relives the trauma. Often victims of PTSD cannot function well in their day-to-day existence and may withdraw from social life and from job and family responsibilities.

Posttraumatic stress disorders may occur right after a traumatic event, but in some cases months or years may go by in which the victim seems to have recovered from the experience, and then, without warning, psychological symptoms appear. The symptoms may disappear quickly, although they may recur repeatedly or continue unabated for weeks, months, or even years (Kessler et al., 1995). Exposure to events reminiscent of the original trauma may cause the symptoms of PTSD to worsen. For example, following the bombing of the Federal Building in Oklahoma City in 1995, some veterans of World War II, the Korean War, and the Vietnam War experienced an increase in PTSD symptoms, including images of combat and sleep disturbances (Moyers, 1996).

Combat veterans appear to be especially vulnerable to PTSD. More than one-third of the men who took part in heavy combat in Vietnam showed signs of serious PTSD. Veterans of World War II also experienced PTSD; after more than half a century, many still have nightmares from which they awake sweating and shaking (Gelman, 1994).

Yet not everyone who is exposed to severely stressful events such as heavy combat or childhood sexual abuse develops PTSD. Individual characteristics—including gender (Curle & Williams, 1996), personality, a family history of mental disorders (Friedman, Schnurr, & McDonagh-Coyle, 1994), substance abuse among relatives (Gurvits, 1997), and even pre-existing neurological disorders—appear to predispose some people to PTSD more than others. Both men and women who have a history of emotional problems are more likely to experience severe trauma and to develop PTSD as a consequence of trauma (Breslau, Davis, & Andreski, 1995).

Recovery from posttraumatic stress disorder depends a great deal on the amount of emotional support that survivors receive from family, friends, and the community. Treatment consists of helping those who have experienced severe trauma to come to terms with their terrifying memories. Immediate treatment near the site of the trauma coupled with the expectation that the individual will return to everyday life are often effective. Reliving the traumatic event in a safe setting is also crucial to successful treatment. This helps desensitize people to the traumatic memories haunting them (Oltmanns & Emery, 1995).

A devastating trauma like the bombing of the federal building in Oklahoma City in April 1995 can trigger posttraumatic stress disorders in its victims. Survivors may suffer terrifying nightmares and vivid daytime flashbacks. Even for trained rescue workers, exposure to the horrors of the trauma can sometimes prompt strong emotional reactions that endure for weeks or even months.

REVIEW QUESTIONS

List two consequences of each of the following extreme sources of stress.

1. Unemployment: ____ and ____.

2. Divorce: ____ and ____.

3. Bereavement: ____ and ____.

4. Catastrophes: ____ and ____.

5. Combat or personal attacks: ____ and ____.

6. The three stages of reactions to catastrophes and other extremely traumatic events are the ____ stage, the ____ stage, and the ____ stage.

7. In extreme cases severely stressful events can cause a psychological disorder known as ____ ____ ____.

Indicate whether the following are true (T) or false (F).

8. People commonly use defensive coping techniques, particularly denial and projection, to cushion the impact of divorce or separation. ____

9. Catastrophes, natural and otherwise—including floods, earthquakes, violent storms, fires, and plane crashes—produce different psychological reactions than do other kinds of stressful events. ____

10. Posttraumatic stress disorder always becomes evident immediately. ____

11. Combat veterans appear to be especially vulnerable to PTSD. ____

Answers: 1. psychiatric problems, heart disease, suicide. 2. feelings of failure, sadness, guilt, rejection. 3. numbness, despair, anger, yearning, depression, apathy. 4. shock, suggestibility, irrational guilt. 5. rage, sleep disturbance, confusion, crying. 6. shock, suggestibility, recovery. 7. posttraumatic stress disorder. 8. T. 9. T. 10. F. 11. T.

The Well-Adjusted Person

What qualities describe a well-adjusted person?

We noted at the beginning of the chapter that adjustment is any effort to cope with stress. (For a discussion of successful adjustment, see *Highlights*.) Psychologists disagree, however, about what constitutes *good* adjustment. Some think it is the ability to live according to social norms. Thus a woman who grows up in a small town, attends college, teaches for a year or two, and then settles down to a peaceful family life might be considered well adjusted because she is living by the predominant values of her community.

Other psychologists disagree strongly with this view. They argue that society is not always right. Thus if we accept its standards blindly, we renounce the right to make individual judgments. Barron (1963) argues that well-adjusted people enjoy the difficulties and ambiguities of life, treating them as challenges to be overcome. Such people are aware of their strengths and weaknesses; this enables them to live in harmony with their inner selves.

We may also evaluate adjustment by using specific criteria, such as the following (Morris, 1990), to judge an action:

1. Does the action realistically meet the demands of the situation, or does it simply postpone resolving the problem?

2. Does the action meet the individual's needs?

3. Is the action compatible with the well-being of others?

Abraham Maslow, whose hierarchy of needs was discussed in Chapter 8, believes that well-adjusted people attempt to "actualize" themselves. That is, they live in a way that enhances their own growth and fulfillment, regardless of what others might think. According to Maslow, well-adjusted people are unconventional and creative thinkers, perceive people and events realistically, and set goals for themselves. They also tend to form deep, close relationships with a few chosen individuals.

As we have seen, there are many standards for judging whether an individual is well adjusted. A person deemed well adjusted by one standard might not be considered well adjusted by other standards. The same holds true when we try to specify what behaviors are "abnormal"—the topic of the next chapter.

REVIEW QUESTIONS

1. The well-adjusted person has learned to balance (check one):

____ a. conformity and nonconformity

____ b. self-control and spontaneity

____ c. flexibility and structure

____ d. all of the above

2. Well-adjusted people know their _____ and _____.

Answers: 1. d. 2. strengths, weaknesses.

HIGHLIGHTS

Why Are Some People Happier than Others?

Psychologists study stress and health so that they can help people live happy and fulfilled lives. They are therefore curious about the nature of happiness. For psychologists, happiness is just one aspect of *subjective well-being* (SWB). In addition to happiness, SWB includes having more positive than negative emotions and having feelings of overall life satisfaction.

To understand the roots of happiness and feelings of well-being, researchers looked first at external events and the demographic characteristics of happy people. But after decades of research, and despite what "common sense" might suggest, they found that external events and demographic characteristics have very little influence on SWB (DeNeve & Cooper, 1998; Diener, Suh, Lucas, & Smith, 1999). More specifically, they found no correlation between age, gender, or intelligence and happiness (DeNeve & Cooper, 1998; Diener & Suh, 1998; Diener et al., 1999). They did find that people who are married, wealthy, well educated, and in good health tend to be happier than others, but the difference is often a small one (Breetvelt & Van Dam, 1991; Brickman, Coates, & Janoff-Bulman, 1978; Diener et al., 1999).

If these variables don't have a major effect on happiness, then what *does* account for SWB? Increasingly,

researchers are coming to believe that the keys to happiness are the goals people have, their ability to adapt to conditions around them, and their personalities. Consistent with this view is the fact that personality is a strong and consistent predictor of well-being over a period of years (DeNeve & Cooper, 1998; Diener et al., 1999). Also, people who are happy in one area of their lives (such as at work) tend to be happy in other areas

---

Personality is a strong and consistent predictor of well-being over a period of years.

---

as well. Thus researchers believe that stable personality factors predispose people to feel happy or unhappy in a wide range of situations, though current life events significantly influence happiness at any given moment.

Using the Big Five trait model described in the previous chapter, DeNeve and Cooper (1998) found that happy people and those reporting more positive than negative emotions tend to be high on extraversion and low on neuroticism. They also found

that people who are satisfied with their lives tend to be high on conscientiousness and low on neuroticism. To a lesser extent, people high in agreeableness also tend to be more satisfied with their lives.

Why personality should predict SWB so well is not yet known. There is some evidence that to a great extent people may be genetically predisposed to be happy or unhappy (Lykken & Tellegen, 1996). Exactly how genes might affect SWB is currently being explored.

Techniques for adapting and coping also seem to contribute to SWB. Many people who suffer severe injuries or who are imprisoned for long periods of time report that within a relatively short time they have regained their normal levels of happiness. Most people who lose life partners take longer to return to normal, but many do so eventually (Loewenstein & Frederick, in press). We don't yet know exactly how adaptation contributes to SWB. It may be that most people simply "get used to" unpleasant situations, it may be that they change the way they *perceive* the new situation, it may be that they restructure their lives to fit the changed conditions, or the explanation may lie elsewhere entirely. But adaptive techniques could help to explain the relative stability of happiness and feelings of well-being over time.

KEY TERMS

CHAPTER REVIEW

◻ What is stress?

We experience **stress** when we are faced with a tense or threatening situation that requires us to change or adapt our behavior. Some life-and-death situations, like war and natural disasters, are inherently stressful. Even events that are usually viewed as positive, like a wedding or a job promotion, can be stressful, because they require change or adaptation. How we adjust to the stresses in our lives affects our health; prolonged or severe stress can contribute to physical and psychological disorders.

◻ Why is change so stressful for most people?

Because most people have a strong desire to maintain order in their lives, any event that involves change will be experienced as stressful.

◻ Can everyday hassles contribute to stress?

Many psychologists believe day-to-day petty annoyances and irritations—such as being stuck in traffic, misplacing car keys, and getting into trivial arguments—to be as stressful as major life events because, although seemingly minor, these incidents give rise to feelings of pressure, frustration, conflict, and anxiety.

◻ What are internal and external sources of pressure?

When we experience **pressure** from either internal or external forces, we feel forced to intensify our efforts or to perform at higher levels. Internal forces include meeting our personal standards; external forces include competition or imposed standards in jobs, grades, and parental demands.

◻ What are the major sources of frustration?

We feel frustrated when someone or something stands between us and our goal. Five basic sources of **frustration** are delays, lack of resources, losses, failure, and discrimination.

◻ What leads to conflict in our lives?

Conflict arises when we are faced with two or more incompatible demands, opportunities, needs, or goals. Someone who is simultaneously attracted to two incompatible goals experiences an **approach/approach conflict,** in which the person must either make a choice between the two goals or opportunities or modify them so as to take some advantage of both goals. The reverse of this problem is **avoidance/avoidance conflict,** in which a person confronts two undesirable or threatening possibilities. People usually try to escape this kind of conflict, but if escape is impossible, they cope in one of several ways, often by vacillating between the two possibilities. Also difficult to resolve is an **approach/avoidance conflict,** in which a person is both attracted to and repelled by the same goal or opportunity. Because both the desire to approach and the desire to avoid the goal grow stronger as the person in this dilemma nears the goal, the situation eventually reaches a point at which the tendency to approach equals the tendency to avoid. The person then vacillates until he or she finally makes a decision or until the situation changes.

◻ How do we create stress?

Sometimes we subject ourselves to stress by internalizing a set of irrational, self-defeating beliefs that add unnecessarily to the normal stresses of living and that are independent of outside forces.

◻ Do people who are resistant to stress share certain traits?

Suzanne Kobasa suggests that stress-resistant people share a trait called *hardiness*—a tendency to experience difficult demands as challenging rather than threatening. She also found that people who feel that they have some control over an event are far less susceptible to stress than are those who feel powerless in the same situation.

◻ What is the difference between direct coping and defensive coping?

People generally adjust to stress in one of two ways: *Direct coping* describes any action people take to change an uncomfortable situation, while *defensive coping* denotes the various ways people convince themselves—through a form of self-deception—that they are not really threatened or do not really want something they cannot get.

◻ What are three strategies that deal directly with stress?

When we cope directly with a particular threat or conflict we do it in one of three ways: **confrontation, compromise,** or **withdrawal.** When we confront a stressful situation and admit to ourselves that there is a problem that needs to be solved we may learn new skills, enlist other people's aid, or try harder to reach our goal. Confrontation may also include expressions of anger. Compromise usually requires adjusting expectations or desires; the conflict is resolved by settling for less than what was originally sought. Sometimes the most effective way of coping with a stressful situation is to distance oneself from it. The danger of withdrawal, however, is that it may become a maladaptive habit.

◻ What are the major ways of coping defensively?

When a stressful situation arises and there is little that can be done to deal with it directly, people often turn to

defense mechanisms as a way of coping. Defense mechanisms are ways of deceiving ourselves about the causes of stressful events, thus reducing conflict, frustration, pressure, and anxiety. **Denial** is the refusal to acknowledge a painful or threatening reality. **Repression** is the blocking out of unacceptable thoughts or impulses from consciousness. When we cannot deny or repress a particular problem, we might resort to **projection**—attributing our repressed motives or feelings to others, thereby locating the source of our conflict outside of ourselves. **Identification** is another form of defensive coping and may occur in situations in which people feel completely powerless. People who adopt this technique take on the characteristics of a powerful person in order to gain a sense of control. People under severe stress sometimes revert to childlike behavior, called **regression**. Because adults can't stand feeling helpless, becoming more childlike can make total dependency or helplessness more tolerable. Sometimes people **intellectualize** their problems in order to emotionally distance themselves from a particularly disturbing situation. **Reaction formation** refers to a behavioral form of denial in which people express with exaggerated intensity ideas and emotions that are the opposite of their own. Through **displacement**, repressed motives and feelings are redirected from their original objects to substitute objects. **Sublimation** involves transforming repressed emotions into more socially accepted forms.

Who experiences the most stress?

People living in poverty tend to experience greater stress than other people, primarily because the environments in which they live are generally more threatening. In addition, they have fewer resources to help them cope with that stress. As a result they experience more health problems than do people in better financial circumstances. Contrary to popular belief, women and men seem to be equally affected by stress, although women are more likely than men to experience stress when their marriage or other long-term relationships are deeply troubled. This appears to be a sign of greater commitment to the relationship rather than an indication of greater vulnerability to stress.

What long-lasting effects of stress do we need to be concerned with?

Physiologist Hans Selye contends that people react to physical and psychological stress in three stages that he called the **general adaptation syndrome (GAS)**. In Stage 1, *alarm reaction*, the body recognizes that it must fight off some physical or psychological danger. This recognition results in quickened respiration and heart rate, increased sensitivity and alertness, and a highly charged emotional state—a physical adaptation that augments our coping resources and helps us to regain self-control. If neither direct nor defensive coping mechanisms succeed in reducing the stress, we move on to Selye's second stage of adaptation. During this *resistance stage* physical symptoms of strain appear as we intensify our efforts to cope both directly and defensively. If these attempts to regain psychological equilibrium fail, psychological disorganization rages out of control until we reach *exhaustion*, Selye's third stage. In this phase we use increasingly ineffective defense mechanisms to bring the stress under control. At this point some people lose touch with reality, while others show signs of "burnout," such as shorter attention spans, irritability, procrastination, and general apathy.

How is Type A behavior related to heart disease?

Stress is known to be an important factor in the development of coronary heart disease. Type A behavior pattern—a set of stressful characteristics that includes hostility, urgency, competitiveness, and striving—has been linked to a greater likelihood of coronary heart disease.

Why do so many students get sick during finals?

Stress—such as that experienced by students during examination periods—can suppress the functioning of the immune system, the focus of the relatively new field of **psychoneuroimmunology**. Stress can also increase one's susceptibility to the common cold.

What is the relationship between social support and health?

People with strong social-support systems enjoy better health and in some cases increased longevity. Some evidence suggests that social support may directly affect immune-system functioning. Other studies suggest that the link between social support and health may occur because people with high levels of social support more frequently engage in healthier behaviors such as better diets and more physical exercise.

What are some sources of extreme stress, and what impact do they have?

Stress derives from a number of sources, including unemployment, divorce and separation, bereavement, combat, and catastrophes. People try to cope with these intense life-altering events in various ways; most resort to defense mechanisms at one or more stages to allow themselves time to gather their energies for more direct coping efforts later on.

What experiences can lead to posttraumatic stress disorder?

Extreme traumas may result in **posttraumatic stress disorder (PTSD)**, a disabling emotional disorder whose symptoms include anxiety, sleeplessness, and nightmares. Combat veterans and people with a history of emotional problems are especially vulnerable to PTSD.

■ **What qualities describe a well-adjusted person?**

Psychologists are of several minds on what constitutes good adjustment. Some believe that well-adjusted people live according to social norms, having learned to control socially forbidden impulses and to limit their goals to those that society allows. Others vehemently disagree; Barron, for example, argues that the refusal to adjust to social norms is the mark of a healthy character. He suggests that well-adjusted people enjoy the difficulties and ambiguities of life; they accept challenges and are willing to experience pain and confusion because they are confident of their ability to deal with problems in a realistic and mature way. Still other psychologists believe that well-adjusted people are those who have learned to balance conformity and nonconformity, self-control and spontaneity. They can change themselves when society so dictates, but they try to change society when this seems the better course. Flexibility of this sort is considered a sign of being able to judge realistically both the world and one's own needs. It also signifies that one has chosen to live in harmony with one's inner self. Finally, some psychologists use specific criteria to evaluate a person's ability to adjust, such as how well the adjustment solves the problem and satisfies both personal needs and the needs of others.

CRITICAL THINKING AND APPLICATIONS

1. Because conflict is considered a major source of stress, what strategies could help reduce conflict?
2. Are defense mechanisms bad for you, or do they foster good health? Give an example of defensive coping.
3. What psychological or physical wear and tear do you show when you experience stress, such as during final exams?
4. How would you help children who live in a violent community?
5. In what areas of your life are you well adjusted, and in what areas could you improve?

Visit these online resources at our Companion Website www.prenhall.com/morris

The Psychology Place

Research News
1. Social Control: Good and Bad for Your Health, p. 394
2. Procrastination May Be Dangerous to Your Health and Performance, p. 399
3. Rethinking the Power of Positive Thinking, p. 409

Readings

1. The Mind-Body Interaction in Disease, p. 404
2. Long-Term Litany of Tension Can Batter the Brain, p. 406
3. The Grief Brigade, p. 410
4. Witnesses to Violence Struggle to Overcome Long-Term Effects, p. 411

Games

1. Life Events, p. 393
2. Defense Mechanisms, p. 400

Web Links

1. **http://www.pitt.edu/~tawst14/hthpsych/body.htm**, p. 391
   Health Psychology Body File
2. **http://www.teachhealth.com**, p. 391
   Health Education: Stress, Depression, Anxiety, Drug Use. The basis of stress, depression, anxiety, sleep problems, and drug use explained in simple terms.
3. **http://maple.lemoyne.edu/~hevern/psychref4-7.html**, p. 397
   PsychREF: Clinical and Behavioral Medicine – Health Psychology. Links to Web sites related to general medicine and health/well-being, AIDS, dieting – obesity – weight control, sleep and sleeping disorders/dreaming, sport and exercise psychology, and stress and relaxation.
4. **http://www.ncptsd.org/**, p. 411
   National Center for PTSD. Offers links to Web sites about the research and education on post-traumatic stress disorder.
5. **http://www.imt.net/~randolfi/StressPage.html**, p. 412
   The Web's Stress Management and Emotional Wellness Page. Includes comprehensive list of links, discussion forum, and stress and emotional wellness quotes about managing stress, maximizing performance, and enhancing emotional health.

12

PSYCHOLOGICAL DISORDERS

WHEN IS BEHAVIOR ABNORMAL? THE ANSWER TO THIS QUESTION IS more complicated than it may seem. There is no doubt that the man on the street corner claiming to be Jesus Christ or the woman insisting that aliens from outer space are trying to kill her is behaving abnormally. But what about the members of a religious cult who follow through on a suicide pact? A business executive who drinks three martinis every day for lunch? A young woman who feels depressed much of the time but still functions effectively at her job?

Impartial laboratory tests can detect many physical diseases, but the presence or absence of mental illness cannot be determined so objectively. Whether an individual suffers from an emotional disorder is partly a matter of judgment—and judgments can differ, depending on perspective.

Perspectives on Psychological Disorders

How does a mental-health professional define a psychological disorder?

Society, the individual, and mental-health professionals all use different standards to distinguish normal behavior from psychological disorders (see Table 12–1). Society's main standard is whether behavior conforms to the existing social order. The individual's primary criterion is his or her own sense of well-being. The mental health professional looks chiefly at *personality characteristics*, *personal discomfort* (the experience of inner distress), and *life functioning* (success in meeting society's expectations for performance in work, school, or social relationships). Serious personal discomfort and inadequate life functioning often go together, complicating the definition of psychological disorder. Consider the imbalance between personal discomfort and life functioning in each of the following examples:

- A young executive is in a state of profound euphoria. He feels exhilarated, invulnerable, and all-powerful. He suddenly decides he's been caught up in a "rat race," quits his job, withdraws his life savings from the bank, and hands it out on the street corner, telling startled passersby that "it's only paper."

- A 40-year-old successful computer programmer who lives alone feels insecure when relating to others. She makes little eye contact, rarely initiates a conversation, and almost always acts "jittery." Inwardly she feels so tense and restless that she avoids being around people. Often she finds it difficult to sleep at night.

- A 14-year-old boy has been uncontrollable at home and disruptive in school since early childhood. He abuses alcohol and other drugs and frequently steals from stores. As part of his initiation into a gang, he fires a semi-automatic pistol into the air while driving through the territory of a rival gang.

Is each of these brief vignettes an example of a psychological disorder? The answer depends, in part, on whose perspective you adopt. The euphoric young executive certainly feels happy, and the adolescent gang member does not think he has a psychological problem. Although society would label their actions disordered, from their own perspectives neither suffers from the sort of personal discomfort that can define psychological disorder. The opposite is true of the computer programmer. Society might judge her behavior as eccentric, because it does not violate any essential social rules and because she is functioning adequately. Nevertheless, she is experiencing much discomfort, and *from her own perspective* something is seriously wrong.

TABLE 12-1	PERSPECTIVES ON PSYCHOLOGICAL DISORDERS	
	Standards/Values	**Measures**
Society	Orderly world in which people assume responsibility for their assigned social roles (e.g., breadwinner, parent), conform to prevailing mores, and meet situational requirements.	Observations of behavior, extent to which a person fulfills society's expectations and measures up to prevailing standards.
Individual	Happiness, gratification of needs.	Subjective perceptions of self-esteem, acceptance, and well-being.
Mental health professional	Sound personality structure characterized by growth, development, autonomy, environmental mastery, ability to cope with stress, adaptation.	Clinical judgment, aided by behavioral observations and psychological tests of such variables as self-concept; sense of identity; balance of psychic forces; unified outlook on life; resistance to stress; self-regulation; the ability to cope with reality; the absence of mental and behavioral symptoms; adequacy in love, work, and play; adequacy in interpersonal relationships.

Source: H. H. Strupp and S. W. Hadley (1977). " A tripartite model of mental health and therapeutic outcomes with special reference to negative effects on psychotherapy," in *American Psychologist*, 32, 187–96. Copyright © 1977 by the American Psychological Association. Adapted by permission of the authors.

Although the individual's perspective and society's view conflict in these cases, mental health professionals would assert that all three people are displaying psychological disorders. For clinicians, a psychological disorder exists when behavior is *either* maladaptive for life functioning *or* when it causes serious personal discomfort *or both*. But now imagine that the cases are slightly different. What if the young executive takes a trip around the world or gives his savings to a worthy charity instead of handing out money on the street? What if the programmer is not very anxious and honestly prefers being a "loner"? What if the teenager had been basically a "good kid" until he got involved with the gang members, who pressure him to do things he knows are wrong?

These questions bring us to a second, essential point about the definition of psychological disorders. Normal and abnormal behavior often differ only in degree. It is tempting to divide mental health and mental illness into categories that are *qualitatively different* from each other—like apples and oranges. It is often more accurate, however, to think of mental illness as being *quantitatively different* (that is, different in degree) from normal behavior.

To understand the distinction between these two approaches to classification, think about how we classify people's weight. There are no absolute dividing lines between normal and abnormal weight—between someone who is underweight or overweight and someone of normal weight. Because the distinction between normal and abnormal weight is a matter of degree, the dividing line between "normal" and "abnormal" is somewhat arbitrary. Still, it is often useful to divide the dimension of weight into categories such as "obese," "overweight," "normal," "thin," and "skinny." In the same way abnormal behavior differs only *quantitatively* from normal behavior, but it is often useful to divide the dimension "normal–abnormal" into discrete categories. Nevertheless, it is important to remember that the line separating normal from abnormal behavior is somewhat arbitrary and that cases are always much easier to judge when they fall at the extreme end of a dimension than when they fall near the "dividing line." Remember, too, that individuals, society, and mental health professionals do not always view abnormality from the same viewpoint.

Does this behavior strike you as being abnormal? Psychologists would say no, as long as the behavior does not lead to personal discomfort or inadequate life functioning.

Historical Views of Psychological Disorders

How has the view of psychological disorders changed over time?

We can only speculate about what was considered an emotional disorder thousands of years ago. Mysterious behaviors were probably attributed to supernatural powers, and madness was a sign that spirits had possessed a person. Sometimes "possessed" people were seen as sacred; their visions were considered messages from the gods. At other times their behavior indicated possession by evil spirits, signaling danger to the community. It is likely that this *supernatural view* of psychological disorders dominated all early societies.

The roots of a more *naturalistic view* can be traced to ancient Greece. The Greek physician Hippocrates (ca. 450–ca. 377 B.C.), for example, maintained that madness was like any other sickness—a natural event arising from natural causes. Hippocrates's theories encouraged a systematic search for the causes of mental illness and implied that disturbed people should be treated with the same care and sympathy that is given to people suffering from physical ailments.

During the Middle Ages, Europeans reverted to the supernatural view (although more naturalistic accounts were kept alive in Arab cultures). The emotionally disturbed person was thought to be a witch or possessed by the devil. Exorcisms, ranging from the mild to the hair-raising, were performed, and many people endured horrifying tortures. Some people were even burned at the stake.

The systematic, naturalistic approach to mental illness would not resurface until the eighteenth century, but by the late Middle Ages there was a move away from viewing the mentally ill as witches and demon-possessed, and they were increasingly confined to public and private asylums. Although these institutions were founded with good intentions, most were little more than prisons. In the worst cases, inmates were chained down and deprived of food, light, or air to "cure" them.

Little was done to ensure humane standards in mental institutions until 1793, when Philippe Pinel became director of the Bicêtre Hospital in Paris. Under his direction the hospital was drastically reorganized: Patients were released from their chains and allowed to move about the hospital grounds, rooms were made more comfortable and sanitary, and dubious and violent medical treatments were abandoned. Pinel's reforms were soon followed by similar efforts in England and, somewhat later, in the United States.

The most notable American reformer was Dorothea Dix (1802–87), a schoolteacher from Boston who led a nationwide campaign for humane treatment of mentally ill people. Under her influence the few existing asylums in the United States were gradually turned into hospitals, but these hospitals often failed to provide the compassionate care that Dix had envisioned.

The basic reason for the failed—and sometimes abusive—treatment of mentally disturbed people throughout history has been the lack of understanding of the nature and causes of psychological disorders. Although our knowledge is still inadequate, important advances in understanding abnormal behavior can be traced to the late nineteenth and early twentieth centuries, when three influential but conflicting models of abnormal behavior emerged: the biological model, the psychoanalytic model, and the cognitive–behavioral model.

Dorothea Dix was a nineteenth-century reformer who led a nationwide campaign for the humane treatment of mentally ill people.

The Biological Model

How can biology influence the development of psychological disorders?

The **biological model** holds that psychological disorders are caused by physiological disorders—for example, of the nervous system or the endocrine glands.

Biological model
View that psychological disorders have a biochemical or physiological basis.

In this model the physical problems often stem from hereditary factors. There is growing evidence that genetic factors are involved in mental disorders as diverse as schizophrenia, depression, and anxiety and that the biochemistry of the nervous system is linked to some cases of depression and schizophrenia. Few contemporary theorists believe, however, that biology alone accounts for all forms of mental illness.

The Psychoanalytic Model

What did Freud and his followers believe was the underlying cause of psychological disorders?

Freud and his followers developed the **psychoanalytic model** at the end of the nineteenth and during the first half of the twentieth century (see Chapter 10). According to this model, behavior disorders are symbolic expressions of unconscious conflicts, which can usually be traced to childhood. For example, a man who behaves toward women in a violent way may be unconsciously expressing rage at his mother for being unaffectionate toward him during his childhood. The psychoanalytic model argues that in order to resolve their problems effectively, people must become aware that the source of their problems lies in their childhood and infancy.

The psychoanalytic model is rich in theory. Freud was a brilliant thinker who called attention to the complexity of personality development, including competing human needs (represented by the id, ego, and superego), unconscious cognitive and emotional processes (the unconscious mind), distortions in interpretation and memory (defense mechanisms), and the importance of child development (psychosexual stages). Although Freud and his followers profoundly influenced both the mental health disciplines and Western culture, only weak and scattered scientific evidence supports their psychoanalytic theories about the causes and effective treatment of mental disorders.

The Cognitive–Behavioral Model

According to the cognitive–behavioral model, what causes abnormal behavior?

A third model of abnormal behavior grew out of twentieth-century research on learning and cognition. The **cognitive–behavioral model** suggests that psychological disorders, like all behavior, result from learning. From this perspective, fear, anxiety, sexual deviations, and other maladaptive behaviors are learned—and they can be unlearned.

As we saw in Chapter 5, cognitive psychologists now highlight the importance of internal processes, such as expectations, for learning. The cognitive–behavioral model stresses both internal and external learning processes in the development and treatment of psychological disorders. For example, a bright student who believes that he is academically inferior to his classmates and can't perform well on a test may not put much effort into studying. Naturally, he performs poorly, and his poor test score both punishes his minimal efforts and confirms his belief that he is academically inferior. This student is caught up in a vicious cycle (Turk & Salovey, 1985). A cognitive–behavior therapist might try to modify both the young man's dysfunctional studying behavior and his inaccurate and maladaptive cognitive processes.

The cognitive–behavioral model has led to innovations in the treatment of psychological disorders, but the model has been criticized for its limited perspective, especially its emphasis on environmental causes and treatments.

Psychoanalytic model
View that psychological disorders result from unconscious internal conflicts.

Cognitive–behavioral model
View that psychological disorders result from learning maladaptive ways of thinking and behaving.

The Diathesis–Stress Model and Systems Theory

Why do some people with a family history of a psychological disorder develop the disorder while other family members do not?

Each of the three major competing theories continues to clarify the origins of certain types of disorders. The most exciting recent developments, however, emphasize integration of the various theoretical models to discover specific causes and specific treatments for different mental disorders.

The **diathesis–stress model** is one promising approach to integration. This model suggests that a biological predisposition called a **diathesis** must combine with some kind of stressful circumstance before the predisposition to a mental disorder shows up as behavior (D. Rosenthal, 1970). According to this model, some people are biologically prone to developing a particular disorder under stress while others are not.

The **systems approach** examines how biological, psychological, and social risk factors combine to produce psychological disorders. It is also known as the *biopsychosocial model*. According to this model, emotional problems are "lifestyle diseases" that, much like heart disease and many other physical illnesses, result from a combination of biological risks, psychological stresses, and social pressures and expectations. Just as heart disease can result from a combination of genetic predisposition, personality styles, poor health habits (such as smoking) and stress, psychological problems, in the systems approach, result from several risk factors that influence one another. In this chapter we follow the systems approach in examining the causes and treatments of abnormal behavior.

Classifying Abnormal Behavior

Why is it useful to have a manual of psychological disorders?

For nearly 40 years the American Psychiatric Association (APA) has issued an official manual describing and classifying the various kinds of abnormal behavior, called the *Diagnostic and Statistical Manual of Mental Disorders*, with the fourth edition, the DSM-IV, published in 1994. The DSM attempts to provide a complete list of mental disorders, with descriptions of significant behavior patterns for each disorder. That way diagnoses based on the manual will be reliable from doctor to doctor. Warning: As you read this chapter you may occasionally feel an uncomfortable twinge of recognition. Do not worry. Many psychological disorders are normal behavior greatly exaggerated or displayed in inappropriate situations.

REVIEW QUESTIONS

1. The individual's primary criterion for mental health is his or her own ____ ____ ____.

2. For mental health professionals, behavior that interferes with a person's ability to ____ *or* that causes serious ____ or both is considered a symptom of a psychological disorder.

3. It is likely that people in early societies believed that ____ forces caused abnormal behavior.

4. The basic reason for the failed and sometimes abusive treatment of mentally disturbed people throughout history has been the lack of understanding of the ____ and ____ of abnormal behavior.

5. There is growing evidence that ____ factors are involved in mental disorders as diverse as schizophrenia, depression, and anxiety.

Diathesis–stress model
View that people biologically predisposed to a mental disorder (those with a certain diathesis) will tend to exhibit that disorder when particularly affected by stress.

Diathesis
Biological predisposition.

Systems approach
View that biological, psychological, and social risk factors combine to produce psychological disorders. Also known as the biopsychosocial model of psychological disorders.

Match the following model of abnormal behavior with the appropriate description.

6. biological model____   a. abnormal behaviors result from unconscious internal conflicts

7. psychoanalytic model ____   b. abnormal behavior is the product of biological, psychological, and social-risk factors

8. biopsychosocial model ____   c. abnormal behavior is the result of learning and can be unlearned

9. the cognitive–behavioral model ____   d. abnormal behavior is caused by heredity, the malfunctioning of the nervous system, or endocrine dysfunction

10. Two models that attempt to integrate the various other theoretical models to explain specific causes and specific treatments for different mental disorders are the ____-____ model and the ____ model.

Indicate whether the following are true (T) or false (F).

11. Many mental illnesses can be detected by objective, impartial laboratory tests. ____

12. The line separating normal from abnormal behavior is somewhat arbitrary.____

13. The psychoanalytic model has generated strong scientific evidence to support its theories about the causes and effective treatment of mental disorders. ____

Answers: 1. sense of well-being. 2. function, personal discomfort. 3. supernatural. 4. nature, causes. 5. genetic. 6. d. 7. a. 8. b. 9. c. 10. diathesis–stress, systems. 11. F. 12. T. 13. F.

Television news reporter Mike Wallace was once hospitalized for depression. The willingness of Wallace and other celebrities to discuss their struggle with this disorder might encourage other afflicted people to seek assistance.

Mood disorders
Disturbances in mood or prolonged emotional state.

Depression
A mood disorder characterized by overwhelming feelings of sadness, lack of interest in activities, and perhaps excessive guilt or feelings of worthlessness.

Mood Disorders

How do mood disorders differ from ordinary mood changes?

Mood disorders are characterized by disturbances in mood or prolonged emotional state, sometimes referred to as *affect*. Most people have a wide emotional range; they can be happy or sad, animated or quiet, cheerful or discouraged, overjoyed or miserable, depending on the circumstances. In some people with mood disorders, this range is greatly restricted. They seem stuck at one or the other end of the emotional spectrum—either consistently excited and euphoric or consistently sad—regardless of the circumstances of their lives. Other people with a mood disorder alternate between the extremes of euphoria and sadness.

Depression

How does clinical depression differ from ordinary sadness?

The most common mood disorder is **depression,** a state in which a person feels overwhelmed with sadness. Depressed people lose interest in the things they normally enjoy. Intense feelings of worthlessness and guilt leave them unable to feel pleasure. They are tired and apathetic, sometimes to the point of being unable to make the simplest decisions. Many depressed people feel as if they have failed utterly in life, and they tend to blame themselves for their problems. Seriously depressed people often have insomnia and lose interest in food and sex. They may have trouble thinking or concentrating—even to the extent of finding it difficult to read a newspaper. In very serious cases depressed people may be plagued by suicidal thoughts or even attempt suicide (see *Highlights*).

We want to point out that clinical depression is different from the "normal" kind of depression that all people experience from time to time. It is entirely normal to become sad when a loved one has died, when romantic relationships end, when you have problems on the job or at school—even when the weather's bad or you don't have a date for Saturday night. Most psychologically healthy people also get "the blues" occasionally for no apparent reason. But in all of

HIGHLIGHTS

Suicide

More than 30,000 people in the United States commit suicide annually (Moscicki, 1995). More women than men attempt suicide, but more men succeed, partly because men tend to choose violent and lethal means, such as guns.

Although the largest number of suicides occurs among older white males, since the 1960s the rates of suicide attempts have been rising among adolescents and young adults (see Figure 12–1). In fact, adolescents account for 12 percent of all suicide attempts in the United States, and suicide is the third leading cause of death in that age group (Centers for Disease Control and Prevention, 1999; Hoyert et al., 1999). We cannot as yet explain the increase, though the stresses of leaving home, meeting the demands of college or career, and surviving loneliness or broken romantic attachments seem to be particularly great at this stage of life. Although external problems such as unemployment and financial strain may also contribute to personal problems, suicidal behavior is most common among adolescents with psychological problems. Several myths concerning suicide can be quite dangerous:

Myth: Someone who talks about committing suicide will never do it.

Fact: Most people who kill themselves have talked about it. Such comments should always be taken seriously.

Myth: Someone who has tried suicide and failed is not serious about it.

Fact: Any suicide attempt means that the person is deeply troubled and needs help immediately. A suicidal person will try again, picking a more deadly method the second or third time around.

Myth: Only people who are life's losers—those who have failed in their careers and in their personal lives—commit suicide.

Most suicidal people do want help.

Fact: Many people who kill themselves have prestigious jobs, conventional families, and a good income. Physicians, for example, have a suicide rate several times higher than that for the general population; in this case the tendency to suicide may be related to their work stresses.

People considering suicide are overwhelmed with hopelessness. They feel that things cannot get better and see no way out of their difficulties. This is depression in the extreme, and it is not a state of mind that someone can easily be talked out of. Telling a suicidal person that things aren't really so bad does no good; in fact, the person may only take this as further evidence that no one understands his or her suffering. But most suicidal people do want help, however much they may despair of obtaining it. If a friend or family member seems at all suicidal, getting professional help is urgent. A community mental health center is a good starting place, as are the national suicide hotlines (see the telephone numbers in Chapter 13).

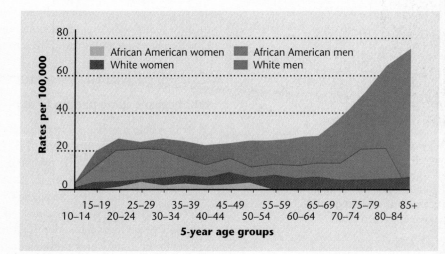

FIGURE 12–1

Gender and race differences in the suicide rate across the life span. The suicide rate for white males, who commit the largest number of suicides at all ages, shows a sharp rise beyond the age of 65. In contrast, the suicide rate for African American females, which is the lowest for any group, remains relatively stable throughout the life span.

Source: Moscicki (1995).

these instances the mood disturbance either is a normal reaction to a "real world" problem (for example, grief), or it passes quickly. Only when depression is long-lasting and goes well beyond the typical reaction to a stressful life event is it classified as a mood disorder (APA, 1994).

DSM-IV distinguishes between two forms of depression: *Major depressive disorder* is an episode of intense sadness that may last for several months; in contrast, *dysthymia* involves less intense sadness (and related symptoms) but persists with little relief for a period of 2 years or more. Depression is 2 to 3 times more prevalent in women than in men (Simpson, Nee, & Endicott, 1997; Weissman & Olfson, 1995).

Mania and Bipolar Disorder

Why does mania, which is generally characterized by a high level of activity, produce very few constructive outcomes? What is bipolar disorder?

Another mood disorder, which is less common than depression, is **mania,** a state in which the person becomes euphoric or "high," extremely active, excessively talkative, and easily distracted. People suffering from mania may become grandiose—that is, their self-esteem is greatly inflated. They typically have unlimited hopes and schemes but little interest in realistically carrying them out. People in a manic state sometimes become aggressive and hostile toward others as their self-confidence grows more and more exaggerated. At the extreme, people going through a manic episode may become wild, incomprehensible, or violent until they collapse from exhaustion.

The mood disorder in which both mania and depression are present is known as **bipolar disorder.** In people with bipolar disorder, periods of mania and depression alternate (each lasting from a few days to a few months), sometimes with periods of normal mood intervening. Occasionally bipolar disorder occurs in a mild form, with moods of unrealistically high spirits followed by moderate depression. Research suggests that bipolar disorder is much less common than depression and, unlike depression, occurs equally in men and women. Bipolar disorder also seems to have a stronger biological component than depression: It is more strongly linked to heredity and is most often treated with drugs (Gershon, 1990).

Causes of Mood Disorders

What causes some people to experience extreme mood changes?

Most psychologists believe that mood disorders result from a combination of risk factors. Biological factors seem to be most important in some cases—for example, bipolar disorder—while psychological factors appear to be chiefly responsible in other cases—for example, depression following the experience of a loss (Katz & McGuffin, 1993). Social factors seem to be most important in still other cases—for example, some instances of depression among women. Nevertheless, although researchers have identified many of the causative factors, they still do not yet know exactly how these elements interact to cause a mood disorder.

Biological Factors   Genetic factors can play an important role in the development of depression, particularly in bipolar disorder (Andreasen et al., 1987; Katz & McGuffin, 1993). The strongest evidence comes from studies of twins (Chapter 2, The Biological Basis of Behavior). If one identical twin is clinically depressed, the other twin (with identical genes) is likely to become clinically depressed also. Among fraternal twins (who share only about half their genes), if one twin is clinically depressed, the risk for the second twin is much lower (McGuffin et al., 1996).

Mania
A mood disorder characterized by euphoric states, extreme physical activity, excessive talkativeness, distractedness, and sometimes grandiosity.

Bipolar disorder
A mood disorder in which periods of mania and depression alternate, sometimes with periods of normal mood intervening.

Just what is it that genetically predisposes some people to a mood disorder? Research has linked mood disorders to chemical imbalances in the brain, principally to high and low levels of certain neurotransmitters. These chemicals influence the transmission of nerve impulses from one cell to another (see Chapter 2), and when their levels are altered with medication, mood disorders can be greatly alleviated (Delgado, Price, Heninger, & Charney, 1992). Depression has also been linked to the release of high levels of hormones by the endocrine system (Friedman, Clark, & Gershon, 1992).

Despite the links between biology and mood disorders, high or low levels of neurotransmitters may not indicate a genetic risk for mood disorders. In fact, the chemical imbalance in the brain associated with depression could be caused by stressful life events: Just as biology affects psychological experience, psychological experience can alter our biological functioning.

Psychological Factors Can the way that we think about ourselves and our experiences actually cause us to become depressed? That is the question that Aaron Beck has been studying for the past couple of decades, and his answer is that it can (Beck, 1967, 1976, 1984). Many depressed people, says Beck, view their experiences in a distorted way, so that they always feel inadequate, at fault, or guilty. This pattern of illogical thinking, which he calls **cognitive distortions,** can contribute to feelings of depression.

Beck describes several kinds of illogical thinking that can be linked to depression. For example, a man who is scheduled to make an important presentation at work is having car trouble. He makes the sweeping—and wrong—conclusion that he is professionally incompetent. Or an athlete blames herself for her team's loss, even though the team as a whole played badly. A high school senior fails a quiz that she didn't study for and feels that she does not deserve admission to a good college. A man who hasn't had a driving accident in 20 years ignores his record for safety and focuses on a dent he put in a fender while getting out of a tight parking space.

Through his work with depressed people, Beck has traced this kind of distorted thinking back to childhood experiences and feelings. Children who frequently are humiliated or criticized by adults often develop a negative self-image, feeling unworthy, inadequate, or bad. They carry this self-concept into adulthood, criticizing themselves unfairly, just as their parents did. A new situation that resembles earlier situations when they were unfairly criticized can be misinterpreted, shifting blame onto themselves, regardless of the facts.

Social Factors Considerable research links depression with troubled close relationships (Monroe & Simons, 1991). Some theorists believe that this explains the higher rates of depression among women, who, in our society, tend to be more relationship-oriented than men (Gilligan, 1982). Of course, not everyone who experiences a troubled relationship becomes depressed. The systems approach would predict that a genetic predisposition or cognitive distortion is necessary before significant stress—from a difficult relationship or some other life event—results in depression.

One final but important point: People with a genetic predisposition to depression, or those whose thinking is distorted, may actually have more stress in their lives than other people, because their personalities can lead others to react negatively to them. Depressed people tend to evoke anxiety and even hostility in others, partly because they require more emotional support than most people feel comfortable giving (Coyne, 1976, 1982). Others may also avoid depressed people, leading to even deeper depression (Lewinsohn & Arconad, 1981). In short, depression-prone people may become trapped in a vicious cycle that is at least partly of their own making.

Cognitive distortions
An illogical and maladaptive response to early negative life events that leads to feelings of incompetence and unworthiness that are re-activated whenever a new situation arises that resembles the original events.

REVIEW QUESTIONS

1. Mood disorders are characterized by
   a. anger and sadness
   b. mania and depression
   c. psychosis and neurosis
   d. fear and rage

2. The most common mood disorder is ____.

3. ____ is a mood disorder in which the person becomes euphoric or "high," extremely active, excessively talkative, and easily distracted.

4. The mood disorder in which both mania and depression alternate is known as ____ ____.

5. Biological research indicates that mood disorders may be linked to a ____ ____ in the brain.

6. According to Beck, excessive criticism during childhood and adolescence may lead to a negative self-concept and the ____ ____ typical of depression.

Indicate whether the following are true (T) or false (F).

7. People with a mood disorder always alternate between the extremes of euphoria and sadness. ____

8. People going through a manic episode are quite unlikely to become violent. ____

9. Most psychologists now believe that mood disorders result from a combination of risk factors. ____

10. Diathesis–stress theory would predict that a genetic predisposition or cognitive distortion is necessary before a significant life stressor results in a mood disorder. ____

Answers: 1. b. 2. depression. 3. mania. 4. bipolar disorder. 5. chemical imbalance. 6. cognitive distortions. 7. F. 8. F. 9. T. 10. T.

Anxiety Disorders

How does an anxiety disorder differ from ordinary anxiety?

All of us are afraid from time to time, but we usually know why we are fearful. Our fear is caused by something appropriate and identifiable, and it passes with time. In the case of **anxiety disorders,** however, either the person does not know why he or she is afraid or the anxiety is inappropriate to the circumstances. In either case the person's fear and anxiety just don't seem to make sense.

Until the publication of DSM-III in 1980, anxiety disorders were part of the broader diagnostic category of *neurosis*, which also included mood disorders and several other very different problems that we discuss shortly. Although the term *neurotic* has passed into everyday language ("I cleaned my room three times this week—I guess that's pretty neurotic!"), psychologists and psychiatrists cannot agree on precisely what neurosis means. Therefore DSM has dropped the term in favor of more specific diagnostic categories.

Specific Phobias

How does a phobia differ from fear?

One recent national survey found that anxiety disorders are more common than any other form of mental disorder (Kessler et al., 1994). Anxiety disorders can be subdivided into several diagnostic categories, such as the **specific phobias.** A specific phobia is an intense, paralyzing fear of something that perhaps should be feared, but the fear is excessive and unreasonable. In fact, the fear in a specific

Anxiety disorders
Disorders in which anxiety is a characteristic feature or the avoidance of anxiety seems to motivate abnormal behavior.

Specific phobia
Anxiety disorder characterized by an intense, paralyzing fear of something.

phobia is so great that it leads the person to avoid routine or adaptive activities and thus interferes with life functioning. For example, it is appropriate to be a bit fearful as an airplane takes off or lands, but people with a phobia about flying refuse to get on or even go near an airplane. Other common phobias focus on animals, heights, closed places, blood, needles, and injury. About 10 percent of people in the United States suffer from at least one specific phobia.

Most people feel some mild fear or uncertainty in many social situations, but when these fears interfere significantly with life functioning, they are considered to be **social phobias.** Intense fear of public speaking is a common form of social phobia. In other cases simply talking with people or eating in public causes such severe anxiety that the phobic person will go to great lengths to avoid these situations.

Agoraphobia is much more debilitating than social phobia. The term comes from Greek and Latin words that literally mean "fear of the marketplace," but the disorder typically involves multiple, intense fears, such as the fear of being alone, of being in public places from which escape might be difficult, of being in crowds, of traveling in an automobile, or of going through tunnels or over bridges. The common element in all of these situations seems to be a great dread of being separated from sources of security, such as the home or a loved one with whom the person feels safe.

Agoraphobia can greatly interfere with life functioning: Some sufferers are so fearful that they will venture only a few miles from home, while others will not leave their homes at all. Although agoraphobia is less common than social phobia (it affects about 3 percent of the population), because of the severity of its effects it is more likely to cause the sufferer to seek treatment (Robins & Regier, 1991).

Fear of heights is an example of a specific phobia. In this photo people are learning to overcome this phobia through desensitization therapy.

Panic Disorder

How does a panic attack differ from fear?

Another type of anxiety disorder is **panic disorder,** characterized by recurring episodes of a sudden, unpredictable, and overwhelming fear or terror. Panic attacks occur without any reasonable cause and are accompanied by feelings of impending doom, chest pain, dizziness or fainting, sweating, difficulty breathing, and a fear of losing control or dying. Panic attacks usually last only a few minutes, but they may recur for no apparent reason. For example:

> A 31-year-old stewardess . . . had suddenly begun to feel panicky, dizzy, had trouble breathing, started to sweat, and trembled uncontrollably. She excused herself and sat in the back of the plane and within ten minutes the symptoms had subsided. Two similar episodes had occurred in the past: the first, four years previously, when the plane had encountered mild turbulence; the second, two years earlier, during an otherwise uneventful flight, as in this episode. (Spitzer et al., 1981, p. 219)

Panic attacks not only cause tremendous fear while they are happening but also leave a dread of having another panic attack that can persist for days or even weeks after the original episode. In some cases this dread is so overwhelming that it can lead to the development of agoraphobia: To prevent a recurrence, people may avoid any circumstance that might cause anxiety, clinging to people or situations that help keep them calm.

Other Anxiety Disorders

What is the difference between specific phobias and generalized anxiety disorder?

In the various phobias and in panic attacks, there is a specific source of anxiety, such as fear of heights, fear of social situations, or fear of being in crowds. In contrast, **generalized anxiety disorder** is defined by prolonged vague but

Social phobia
An anxiety disorder characterized by excessive, inappropriate fears connected with social situations or performances in front of other people.

Agoraphobia
An anxiety disorder that involves multiple, intense fears of crowds, public places, and other situations that require separation from a source of security such as the home.

Panic disorder
An anxiety disorder characterized by recurrent panic attacks in which the person suddenly experiences intense fear or terror without any reasonable cause.

Generalized anxiety disorder
An anxiety disorder characterized by prolonged vague but intense fears that are not attached to any particular object or circumstance.

intense fears that are not attached to any particular object or circumstance. Generalized anxiety disorder perhaps comes closest to the everyday meaning attached to the term *neurotic*. Its symptoms include the inability to relax, muscle tension, rapid heartbeat or pounding heart, apprehensiveness about the future, constant alertness to potential threats, and sleeping difficulties.

A very different form of anxiety disorder is **obsessive–compulsive disorder.** *Obsessions* are involuntary thoughts or ideas that keep recurring despite the person's attempts to stop them, while *compulsions* are repetitive, ritualistic behaviors that a person feels compelled to perform (Patrick, 1994). The thoughts are often horrible and frightening. One patient, for example, reported that "when she thought of her boyfriend, she wished he were dead"; when her mother went down the stairs, she "wished she'd fall and break her neck"; when her sister spoke of going to the beach with her infant daughter she "hoped that they would both drown" (Carson & Butcher, 1992, p. 190). Truly compulsive behaviors may be equally dismaying to the person who feels driven to perform them. They often take the form of washing or cleaning, as if the compulsive behavior were the person's attempt to "wash away" the contaminating thoughts. One patient reported that her efforts to keep her clothes and body clean eventually took up 6 hours of her day, and even then, "washing my hands wasn't enough, and I started to use rubbing alcohol" (Spitzer et al., 1981, p. 137).

Another common type of compulsion is checking: repeatedly performing some kind of behavior to make sure that something was or was not done. For example, a person might feel compelled to check dozens of times whether the doors are locked before going to bed.

People who experience obsessions and compulsions often do not seem particularly anxious, so why is this disorder considered an anxiety disorder? The answer is that if such people try to *stop* their irrational behavior—or if someone else tries to stop them—they experience severe anxiety. In other words, the obsessive–compulsive behavior seems to have developed to keep anxiety under control.

Extreme stress can cause acute stress disorder. The soldier at left has just learned that his close friend was killed by friendly fire during the Gulf War.

Finally, two types of anxiety disorder are clearly caused by some specific highly stressful event. Some people who have lived through fires, floods, tornadoes, or disasters like an airplane crash experience repeated episodes of fear and terror after the event itself is over. If the anxious reaction occurs soon after the event, the diagnosis is *acute stress disorder*. If it takes place long after the event is over, the diagnosis is likely to be *posttraumatic stress disorder*, discussed in Chapter 11 (Oltmanns & Emery, 1998). Posttraumatic stress disorder is characterized by hyperarousal, avoidance of situations that recall the trauma, and "re-experiencing"—reliving the traumatic event in detail. Two kinds of traumatic experience are particularly likely to lead to acute or posttraumatic stress disorder: military combat and rape.

Causes of Anxiety Disorders

What can the cognitive perspective and the biological perspective tell us about the causes of anxiety?

Obsessive–compulsive disorder
An anxiety disorder in which a person feels driven to think disturbing thoughts or to perform senseless rituals.

Recall from Chapter 5, Learning, that phobias are often learned after only one fearful event; they are extremely hard to shed, and there is a limited and predictable range of phobic objects. People are more likely to be injured in an auto-

mobile accident than by a snake or spider bite, yet snake and spider phobias are far more common than car phobias. It may be that phobias are *prepared responses*. That is, through evolution we may have become biologically predisposed to associate certain stimuli with intense fears (Marks & Nesse, 1994; Öhman, 1996). Consider a young boy who is savagely attacked by a large dog. Because of this experience, he is now terribly afraid of all dogs. Other children who witnessed the attack or only heard about it may also come to fear dogs. In that way a realistic fear can be transformed into a phobia.

From a more cognitive perspective, people who feel they are not in control of stressful events in their lives are more likely to experience anxiety than those who believe they have control over such events. For example, African Americans who live in high-crime areas have a higher incidence of anxiety disorders than other Americans (Neal & Turner, 1991). In the same situation, though, some people develop unrealistic fears while others do not. Why? Psychologists working from the biological perspective point to heredity. We know that (1) the autonomic nervous system is involved in all kinds of fear and (2) autonomic responsiveness is genetically influenced. It is possible, then, that we can inherit a predisposition to anxiety disorders (Eysenck, 1970; Sarason & Sarason, 1987). In fact, anxiety disorders tend to run in families (Kendler et al., 1992; Torgersen, 1983; Weissman, 1993), although the evidence linking specific kinds of anxiety disorders to genetic factors is less clear (Oltmanns & Emery, 1998). Some people with obsessions and compulsions show brain abnormalities and respond positively to treatment with drugs (de-Veaugh-Geiss, 1993).

Finally, we need to consider the vital role that internal psychological conflicts play in producing feelings of anxiety. From the Freudian perspective, defense mechanisms protect us from unacceptable impulses or thoughts (usually sexual or aggressive in nature), but at a cost in anxiety. For example, psychoanalytic theorists view phobias as the result of *displacement* in which people redirect strong feelings from whatever originally aroused them toward something else (see Chapter 11). Thus a woman who is afraid of her spouse but represses these feelings might redirect her fear toward elevators or spiders. Although we may doubt the validity of specific psychoanalytic interpretations of phobias, inner conflicts—as well as defenses and other internal distortions of these conflicts—certainly seem to play a role in the development of anxiety and its associated disorders.

REVIEW QUESTIONS

Match the following terms with the appropriate description.

1. specific phobia _____	a. great dread of being separated from sources of security
2. social phobia _____	b. an unreasonable, paralyzing fear of something
3. agoraphobia _____	c. a sudden, unpredictable, and overwhelming experience of intense fear or terror without any reasonable cause
4. panic attack _____	d. feeling driven to think disturbing thoughts or to perform meaningless rituals
5. generalized anxiety disorder _____	e. excessive inappropriate fears connected with social situations or performances in front of other people
6. obsessive–compulsive disorder _____	f. prolonged vague but intense fears not attached to any particular object or circumstance

Indicate whether the following are true (T) or false (F).

7. The fear in a specific phobia often interferes with life functioning. ____

8. People who experience obsessions and compulsions appear highly anxious. ____

9. Research indicates that people who feel that they are not in control of stressful events in their lives are more likely to experience ____ than those who believe they have control over such events.

10. Research suggests a link between the functioning of the autonomic nervous system and ____ disorder.

11. According to the psychoanalytic view, anxiety results from ____ ____.

Answers: 1. b, 2. e, 3. a, 4. c, 5. f, 6. d, 7. T, 8. F, 9. anxiety, 10. panic, 11. unconscious conflicts.

Psychosomatic and Somatoform Disorders

What is the difference between psychosomatic and somatoform disorders?

The term *psychosomatic* perfectly captures the interplay of *psyche* (mind) and *soma* (body), which characterizes these disorders. A **psychosomatic disorder** is a physical disorder with a valid physical basis. In a psychosomatic disorder, physical damage to the body can be proved with testing.

Scientists used to believe that psychological factors contributed to the development of some physical illnesses—principally ulcers, headaches, allergies, asthma, and high blood pressure—but not others, such as infectious diseases. Modern medicine leans toward the idea that *all* physical ailments are to some extent "psychosomatic," in the sense that stress, anxiety, and various states of emotional arousal alter body chemistry, the functioning of bodily organs, and the body's immune system (which is vital to fighting infections). As we saw in Chapter 11, stress and psychological strains can also alter health behavior, which includes positive actions such as eating a balanced diet and exercising as well as negative activities like cigarette smoking and excessive alcohol consumption. Both physical and mental illnesses are now viewed as "lifestyle diseases" that are caused by a combination of biological, psychological, and social factors.

Because virtually every physical disease can be linked to psychological stress, DSM-IV does not contain a separate list of psychosomatic disorders. Rather, the manual includes physical illnesses only if they are related to a diagnosed mental disorder. For example, a child's asthma may be included in a DSM-IV diagnosis if it contributes to the symptoms of *separation anxiety disorder*, which comprises various fears of being away from a parent.

Psychosomatic disorders involve genuine physical illnesses, but in **somatoform disorders** physical symptoms occur without any identifiable physical cause. Common complaints are back pain, dizziness, abdominal pain, and sometimes anxiety and depression. People suffering from somatoform disorders believe they are physically ill and describe symptoms that sound like physical illnesses, but medical examinations reveal no organic problems. Nevertheless, people who suffer from these disorders are not consciously seeking to mislead others about their physical condition. The symptoms are real to them and are not under voluntary control (APA, 1994).

One form of somatoform disorder involves complaints of paralysis, blindness, deafness, seizures, loss of feeling, or pregnancy. In these **conversion disorders** no physical causes appear, yet the symptoms are very real.

Yet another somatoform disorder is **hypochondriasis.** Here the person interprets some small symptom—perhaps a cough, bruise, or perspiration—as a sign of a serious disease. Although the symptom may actually exist, there is no evidence that the serious illness does. Repeated assurances have little effect, and the

Psychosomatic disorders
Disorders in which there is real physical illness that is largely caused by psychological factors such as stress and anxiety.

Somatoform disorders
Disorders in which there is an apparent physical illness for which there is no organic basis.

Conversion disorders
Somatoform disorders in which a dramatic specific disability has no physical cause but instead seems related to psychological problems.

Hypochondriasis
A somatoform disorder in which a person interprets insignificant symptoms as signs of serious illness in the absence of any organic evidence of such illness.

person is likely to visit one doctor after another, searching for a medical authority who will share his or her conviction.

Body dysmorphic disorder, or imagined ugliness, is a recently diagnosed and poorly understood type of somatoform disorder. Cases of body dysmorphic disorder can be very striking. One man, for example, felt that people stared at his "pointed ears" and "large nostrils" so much that he eventually could not face going to work, so he quit his job. Clearly, people who become that preoccupied with their appearance cannot lead a normal life. Ironically, most people who suffer body dysmorphic disorder are not ugly. They may be average looking or even attractive, but they are unable to evaluate their looks realistically. Many people with this disorder seek physical treatment (such as plastic surgery) rather than psychotherapy.

Somatoform disorders (especially conversion disorders) present a challenge for psychological theorists because they seem to involve some kind of unconscious processes. Freud concluded that the physical symptoms were often related to traumatic experiences buried in a patient's past. Cognitive–behavioral theorists focus on Freud's idea of secondary gain—that is, they look for ways in which the symptomatic behavior is being rewarded.

From the biological perspective, research has shown that at least some diagnosed somatoform disorders actually were real physical illnesses that were overlooked or misdiagnosed. For example, some cases of "conversion disorder" eventually proved to be neurological problems such as epilepsy or multiple sclerosis (Shalev & Munitz, 1986). Nevertheless, most cases of conversion disorder cannot be explained by current medical science. These cases pose as much of a theoretical challenge today as they did when conversion disorders captured Freud's attention more than a century ago.

REVIEW QUESTIONS

Match the following terms with the appropriate description.

1. somatoform disorder _____
2. body dysmorphic disorder _____
3. conversion disorders _____
4. hypochondriasis _____

a. the person interprets some small symptom as a sign of a serious disease
b. recurring physical symptoms for which no organic cause is found
c. imagined ugliness
d. sufferers have healthy muscles and nerves, yet their symptoms of paralysis, blindness, deafness, seizures, loss of feeling, or pregnancy are real

Indicate whether the following are true (T) or false (F).

5. Modern medicine leans toward the idea that *all* physical ailments are to some extent "psychosomatic." _____
6. People who suffer from somatoform disorders do not consciously seek to mislead others about their physical condition. _____
7. Research has shown that at least some diagnosed somatoform disorders actually were real physical illnesses that were overlooked or misdiagnosed. _____
8. Most cases of conversion disorder can be explained by current medical science. _____

Answers: 1. b. 2. c. 3. d. 4. a. 5. T. 6. T. 7. T. 8. F.

Dissociative Disorders

What do dissociative disorders have in common?

Dissociative disorders are among the most puzzling forms of mental disorders, both to the observer and to the sufferer. In *dissociation* part of an individual's personality appears to be separated from the rest. The disorder usually involves

Body dysmorphic disorder
A somatoform disorder in which a person becomes so preoccupied with his or her imagined ugliness that normal life is impossible.

Dissociative disorders
Disorders in which some aspect of the personality seems separated from the rest.

When she was found by a Florida park ranger, Jane Doe was suffering from amnesia. She could not recall her name, her past, or how to read and write. She never regained her memory of the past.

memory loss and a complete, though generally temporary, change in identity. More rarely, several distinct personalities appear in one person.

Loss of memory without an organic cause can occur as a reaction to an extremely stressful event or period. During World War II, for example, some hospitalized soldiers could not recall their names, where they lived, where they were born, or how they came to be in battle. But war and its horrors are not the only causes of *dissociative amnesia*. The person who betrays a friend in a business deal or the victim of rape may also forget, selectively, what has happened. Sometimes an amnesia victim leaves home and assumes an entirely new identity, although this phenomenon, known as *dissociative fugue*, is very unusual.

In *dissociative identity disorder*, commonly known as *multiple personality disorder*, several distinct personalities emerge at different times. Although this dramatic disorder has been the subject of popular fiction and films, most psychologists believe it to be extremely rare. In the true multiple personality the various personalities are distinct people with their own names, identities, memories, mannerisms, speaking voices, and even IQs. Sometimes the personalities are so separate that they don't know they inhabit a body with other "people." At other times the personalities do know of the existence of other "people" and even make disparaging remarks about them. Typically the personalities contrast sharply with one another, as if each one represents different aspects of the same person—one the more socially acceptable, "nice" side of the person and the other the darker, more uninhibited or "evil" side.

The origins of dissociative identity disorder are still not understood. One theory suggests that it develops as a response to childhood abuse. The child learns to cope with abuse by a process of dissociation—by having the abuse, in effect, happen to "someone else"; that is, to a personality who is not conscious most of the time (Putnam et al., 1986). The fact that one or more of the multiple personalities in almost every case is a child (even when the patient is an adult) seems to support this idea, and clinicians report a history of child abuse in more than three-quarters of their cases of dissociative identity disorder (Ross, Norton, & Wozney, 1989).

Other clinicians suggest that dissociative identity disorder is not a real disorder at all but an elaborate kind of role playing—feigned in the beginning and then perhaps genuinely believed in by the patient (Mersky, 1992). Some intriguing biological data show that in at least some patients, however, the various personalities have different blood pressure readings, different responses to medication, different allergies, different vision problems (necessitating a different pair of glasses for each personality), and different handedness—all of which would be difficult to feign. Each personality may also exhibit distinctly different brain-wave patterns (Putnam, 1984).

A far less dramatic (and much more common) dissociative disorder is **depersonalization disorder,** in which the person suddenly feels changed or different in a strange way. Some people feel they have left their bodies, while others find that their actions have suddenly become mechanical or dreamlike. This kind of feeling is especially common during adolescence and young adulthood, when our sense of ourselves and our interactions with others change rapidly. Only when the sense of depersonalization becomes a long-term or chronic problem or when the alienation impairs normal social functioning can this be classified a dissociative disorder (APA, 1994).

Dissociative disorders, like conversion disorders, seem to involve some kind of unconscious processes. Trauma is one important psychological factor in the onset of amnesia and fugue and appears to play a role in the development of dissociative identity disorder (Oltmanns & Emery, 1998). The loss of memory is real in amnesia, fugue, and in many cases of multiple personality disorder. Patients often lack awareness of their own memory loss and cannot overcome memory impairments despite their desire and effort to do so. Biological factors may also play a role. Dissociation and amnesia are commonly associated with aging and disorders

Depersonalization disorder
A dissociative disorder whose essential feature is that the person suddenly feels changed or different in a strange way.

such as Alzheimer's disease, and dissociative experiences are a common consequence of the ingestion of drugs such as LSD. Nevertheless, all of these observations are only leads in the mystery of what causes dissociative disorders.

REVIEW QUESTIONS

1. ____ ____ usually involve memory loss and a complete—though generally temporary—change in identity.

Match the following terms with the appropriate description.

2. dissociative amnesia ____

3. dissociative fugue ____

4. depersonalization disorder ____

a. loss of memory without an organic cause, possibly in reaction to intolerable experiences

b. the person suddenly feels changed or different in a strange way that becomes a long-term or chronic problem

c. a highly unusual amnesia during which the victim leaves home and assumes an entirely new identity

____ 5. "Clinicians report a history of child abuse in over three-quarters of their cases of dissociative identity disorder." True or false.

____ 6. "Biological factors may play a role in some cases of dissociation and amnesia." True or false.

Answers: 1. dissociative disorders. 2. a. 3. c. 4. b. 5. T. 6. T.

Sexual and Gender-Identity Disorders

What are the three main types of sexual disorders?

Ideas about what is normal and abnormal in sex vary with the times—and the individual. Alfred Kinsey and his associates showed years ago that many Americans enjoy a variety of sexual activities, some of which are forbidden by law (1948, 1953). As psychologists became more aware of the diversity of "normal" sexual behaviors, they increasingly narrowed their definition of abnormal sexual behavior. Today the DSM-IV recognizes only three main types of sexual disorders: sexual dysfunction, paraphilias, and gender-identity disorders.

Sexual dysfunction is the loss or impairment of the ordinary physical responses of sexual function. In men this usually takes the form of *erectile disorder*, the inability to achieve or maintain an erection. In women it often takes the form of *female sexual arousal disorder*, the inability to become sexually excited or to reach orgasm. (These conditions were once called "impotence" and "frigidity," respectively, but professionals in the field have rejected these terms as too negative and judgmental.) Occasional problems with achieving or maintaining an erection in men or with lubrication or reaching orgasm in women are common. Only when the condition is frequent or constant and when enjoyment of sexual relationships becomes impaired should it be considered a problem.

A second group of sexual disorders, known as **paraphilias,** involves the use of unconventional sex objects or situations to obtain sexual arousal. Most people have unusual sexual fantasies at some time, and this kind of fantasizing can be a healthy stimulant of normal sexual enjoyment. **Fetishism**—the repeated use of a nonhuman object such as a shoe or underwear as the preferred or exclusive method of achieving sexual excitement—is considered a sexual disorder, however. Fetishes are typically articles of women's clothing or items made out of rubber or leather (Junginger, 1997; Mason, 1997). Most people who practice fetishism are male, and the fetish frequently begins during adolescence. At least one theorist has suggested that fetishes derive from unusual learning experiences: As their sexual drive develops during adolescence, some boys learn to associate arousal

Sexual dysfunction
Loss or impairment of the ordinary physical responses of sexual function.

Paraphilias
Sexual disorders in which unconventional objects or situations cause sexual arousal.

Fetishism
A paraphilia in which a nonhuman object is the preferred or exclusive method of achieving sexual excitement.

with inanimate objects, perhaps as a result of early sexual exploration while masturbating or because of difficulties in social relationships (Wilson, 1987).

One of the most serious paraphilias is **pedophilia,** which is technically defined as "recurrent, intense sexually arousing fantasies, sexual urges, or behaviors involving sexual activity with a prepubescent child" (APA, 1994, p. 528). Child sexual abuse is shockingly common in the United States, and the abuser usually is someone close to the child, not a stranger.

Pedophiles are almost invariably men under age 40 (Barbaree & Seto, 1997). Although there is no single cause of pedophilia, some of the most common explanations are that pedophiles cannot adjust to the adult sexual role and have been interested exclusively in children as sex objects since adolescence; they turn to children as sexual objects in response to stress in adult relationships in which they feel inadequate; or they have records of unstable social adjustment and generally commit sexual offenses against children in response to a temporary aggressive mood. Studies also indicate that the majority of pedophiles have histories of sexual frustration and failure, tend to perceive themselves as immature, and are rather dependent, unassertive, lonely, and insecure.

Gender-identity disorders involve the desire to become—or the insistence that one really is—a member of the other sex. Some little boys, for example, want to be girls instead. They may reject boys' clothing, desire to wear their sister's clothes, and play only with girls and with toys that are considered "girls' toys." Similarly, some girls wear boys' clothing and play only with boys and "boys' toys." When such children are uncomfortable being a male or a female and are unwilling to accept themselves as such, the diagnosis is **gender-identity disorder in children.**

The causes of gender-identity disorders are not known. Both animal research and the fact that these disorders are often apparent from early childhood suggest that biological factors, such as prenatal hormonal imbalances, are major contributors. Family dynamics and learning experiences, however, may also be contributing factors.

REVIEW QUESTIONS

1. ____ ____ is the loss or impairment of the ordinary physical responses of sexual function.
2. In men ____ ____ is the inability to achieve or maintain an erection.
3. In women ____ ____ ____ ____ is the inability to become sexually excited or to reach orgasm.
4. ____ involve the use of unconventional sex objects or situations to obtain sexual arousal.
5. The repeated use of a nonhuman object as the preferred or exclusive method of achieving sexual excitement is known as ____.
6. ____ is recurrent, intense sexually arousing fantasies, sexual urges, or behaviors involving sexual activity with a prepubescent child.
7. ____ ____ ____ involve the desire to become—or the insistence that one really is— a member of the other biological sex.

Answers: 1. sexual dysfunction. 2. erectile disorder. 3. female sexual arousal disorder. 4. paraphilias. 5. fetishism. 6. pedophilia. 7. gender-identity disorders.

Pedophilia
Desire to have sexual relations with children as the preferred or exclusive method of achieving sexual excitement.

Gender-identity disorders
Disorders that involve the desire to become, or the insistence that one really is, a member of the other biological sex.

Gender-identity disorder in children
Rejection of one's biological gender in childhood, along with the clothing and behavior that society considers appropriate to that gender.

Personality Disorders

Which personality disorder creates the most significant problems for society?

In Chapter 10 we saw that personality is the individual's unique and enduring pattern of thoughts, feelings, and behavior. We also saw that despite having certain characteristic views of the world and ways of doing things, people normally can adjust their behavior to fit different situations. But some people, starting at some point early in life, develop inflexible and maladaptive ways of thinking and behaving that are so exaggerated and rigid that they cause serious distress to themselves or problems to others. People with such **personality disorders** range from harmless eccentrics to cold-blooded killers. A personality disorder may also coexist with one of the other problems already discussed in this chapter; that is, someone with a personality disorder may also become depressed, develop sexual problems, and so on.

One group of personality disorders is characterized by odd or eccentric behavior. For example, people who exhibit **schizoid personality disorder** lack the ability or desire to form social relationships and have no warm or tender feelings for others. Such loners cannot express their feelings and appear cold, distant, and unfeeling. Moreover, they often seem vague, absentminded, indecisive, or "in a fog." Because their withdrawal is so complete, persons with schizoid personality disorder seldom marry and may have trouble holding jobs that require them to work with or relate to others (APA, 1994).

People with **paranoid personality disorder** also appear to be odd. Although they often see themselves as rational and objective, they are guarded, secretive, devious, scheming, and argumentative. They are suspicious and mistrustful even when there is no reason to be; they are hypersensitive to any possible threat or trick; and they refuse to accept blame or criticism even when it is deserved.

A cluster of personality disorders characterized by anxious or fearful behavior includes dependent personality disorder and avoidant personality disorder. People with **dependent personality disorder** are unable to make decisions on their own or to do things independently. Rather, they rely on parents, a spouse, friends, or others to make the major choices in their lives and usually are extremely unhappy being alone. Their underlying fear seems to be that they will be rejected or abandoned by important people in their lives. In **avoidant personality disorder** the person is timid, anxious, and fearful of rejection. Not surprisingly, this social anxiety leads to isolation, but unlike the schizoid type, the person with avoidant personality disorder *wants* to have close relationships with others.

Another cluster of personality disorders is characterized by dramatic, emotional, or erratic behavior. People with **narcissistic personality disorder,** for example, display a grandiose sense of self-importance and a preoccupation with fantasies of unlimited success. Such people believe they are extraordinary, need constant attention and admiration, display a sense of entitlement, and tend to exploit others. They are given to envy and arrogance and lack the ability to really care for anyone else (APA, 1994).

Many psychologists believe that narcissism begins early in life. All infants tend to be narcissistic but most outgrow this attitude in childhood. For reasons we still do not understand, however, the narcissistic person never makes the transition.

Borderline personality disorder is characterized by marked instability in self-image, mood, and interpersonal relationships. People with this personality disorder tend to act impulsively and often in self-destructive ways. They feel uncomfortable being alone and often manipulate self-destructive impulses in an effort to control or solidify their personal relationships.

Borderline personality disorder is both common and serious. The available evidence indicates that although it runs in families, genetics does not seem to play an important role in its development (Oltmanns & Emery, 1998). Instead studies point to the influence of dysfunctional relationships with parents, including a marked lack of supervision, frequent exposure to domestic violence, and physical and sexual abuse (Guzder et al., 1996).

One of the most widely studied personality disorders is **antisocial personality disorder.** People who exhibit this disorder lie, steal, cheat, and show little or no sense of responsibility, although they often seem intelligent and charming at

GAMES
G

Personality disorders
Disorders in which inflexible and maladaptive ways of thinking and behaving learned early in life cause distress to the person or conflicts with others.

Schizoid personality disorder
Personality disorder in which a person is withdrawn and lacks feelings for others.

Paranoid personality disorder
Personality disorder in which the person is inappropriately suspicious and mistrustful of others.

Dependent personality disorder
Personality disorder in which the person is unable to make choices and decisions independently and cannot tolerate being alone.

Avoidant personality disorder
Personality disorder in which the person's fears of rejection by others lead to social isolation.

Narcissistic personality disorder
Personality disorder in which the person has an exaggerated sense of self-importance and needs constant admiration.

Borderline personality disorder
Personality disorder characterized by marked instability in self-image, mood, and interpersonal relationships.

Antisocial personality disorder
Personality disorder that involves a pattern of violent, criminal, or unethical and exploitative behavior and an inability to feel affection for others.

People with antisocial personality disorder will lie, cheat, or kill without regret. Ted Bundy, shown here, was a serial killer who expressed no remorse for murdering as many as 50 women.

first. The "con man" exemplifies many of the features of the antisocial personality, as does the person who compulsively cheats business partners because he or she knows their weak points. Antisocial personalities rarely show any anxiety or guilt about their behavior. Indeed, they are likely to blame society or their victims for the antisocial actions that they themselves commit.

People with antisocial personality disorder, like this man, are responsible for a good deal of crime and violence:

> Although intelligent, [G.] was a poor student and was frequently accused of stealing from his schoolmates. At the age of 14, he stole a car, and at the age of 20, he was imprisoned for burglary. After he was released, he spent another two years in prison for drunk driving and then eleven years for a series of armed robberies.
>
> Released from prison yet one more time in 1976, he tried to hold down several jobs but succeeded at none of them. He moved in with a woman whom he had met one day earlier, but he drank heavily (a habit that he had picked up at age 10) and struck her children until she ordered him out of the house at gunpoint. "It seems like things have always gone bad for me," he later said. "It seems like I've always done dumb things that just caused trouble for me." (Spitzer et al., 1983, p. 68)

On psychiatric evaluation, this man was found to have a superior IQ of 129 and considerable general knowledge. He slept and ate well and showed no significant changes of mood. He admitted to having "made a mess of life" but added that "I never stew about the things I have done." This person, Gary Gilmore, was executed for murder in 1977.

Approximately 3 percent of American men and less than 1 percent of American women suffer from antisocial personality disorder. Not surprisingly, prison inmates show high rates of personality disorder: One study identified it in 50 percent of the populations of two prisons (Hare, 1983). Not all people with antisocial personality disorder are convicted criminals, however. Many manipulate others for their own gain while avoiding the criminal justice system.

Antisocial personality disorder seems to result from a combination of biological predisposition, difficult life experiences, and an unhealthy social environment (Moffitt, 1993). Some findings suggest that heredity is a risk factor for the later development of antisocial behavior (Lyons et al., 1995). Impulsive violence and aggression have also been linked with abnormal levels of certain neurotransmitters (Virkkunen, 1983). Although none of this research is definitive, the weight of evidence suggests that some people with antisocial personalities are less responsive to stress and thus are more likely to engage in thrill-seeking behaviors that may be harmful to themselves or others (Patrick, 1994). And, because they respond less emotionally to stress, punishment does not affect them as it does other people (Hare, 1993).

Some psychologists feel that emotional deprivation in early childhood predisposes people to antisocial personality disorder. The child for whom no one cares, say psychologists, cares for no one. The child whose problems no one identifies with can identify with no one else's problems. Respect for others is the basis of our social code, but when you cannot see things from another person's perspective, behavior "rules" seem like nothing more than an assertion of adult power to be defied.

Family influences may also prevent the normal learning of rules of conduct in the preschool and school years. A child who has been rejected by one or both parents is not likely to develop adequate social skills or appropriate social behavior. Further, the high incidence of antisocial behavior in people with an antisocial parent suggests that antisocial behavior may be partly learned and partly inherited. Once serious misbehavior begins in childhood, there is an almost predictable progression: The child's conduct leads to rejection by peers and failure in school, followed by affiliation with other children who have behavior problems. By late childhood or adolescence the deviant patterns that will later show up as a full-blown antisocial personality disorder are well established (Patterson, DeBaryshe, & Ramsey, 1989).

Cognitive theorists emphasize that in addition to the failure to learn rules and develop self-control, moral development may be arrested among children who are emotionally rejected and inadequately disciplined. For example, between the ages of about 7 and 11, all children are apt to respond to unjust treatment by behaving unjustly toward someone else who is vulnerable. At about age 13, when they are better able to reason in abstract terms, most children begin to think more in terms of fairness than vindictiveness, especially if new cognitive skills and moral concepts are reinforced by parents and peers (M. W. Berkowitz & Gibbs, 1983).

REVIEW QUESTIONS

1. Lifelong patterns of relatively "normal" but rigid and maladaptive behaviors are called
   ____ a. schizophrenia
   ____ b. personality disorders
   ____ c. anxiety disorders

Match the following personality disorders with the appropriate description.

2. schizoid personality disorder ____
3. paranoid personality disorder ____
4. dependent personality disorder ____
5. avoidant personality disorder ____
6. narcissistic personality disorder ____
7. borderline personality disorder ____
8. antisocial personality disorder ____

a. instability in self-image, mood, and relationships
b. fearful and timid
c. mistrustful even when there is no reason
d. shows little sense of responsibility
e. exhibits extreme dramatic behavior and self-centeredness
f. lacks the ability to form social relationships
g. unable to make own decisions

Answers: 1. b. 2. f. 3. c. 4. g. 5. b. 6. e. 7. a. 8. d.

Schizophrenic Disorders

How is schizophrenia different from multiple-personality disorder?

A common misconception is that *schizophrenia* means "split personality." But, as we have seen, split personality (or multiple personality) is actually a dissociative identity disorder. The misunderstanding comes from the fact that the root *schizo* derives from the Greek verb meaning "to split." What is split in schizophrenia is not so much personality as the connections among thoughts.

Schizophrenic disorders are severe conditions marked by disordered thoughts and communications, inappropriate emotions, and bizarre behavior that lasts for months or even years. People with schizophrenia are out of touch with reality, or psychotic. *Psychosis* is sometimes confused with *insanity*, but the terms are not synonymous. **Insanity** is the legal term for people who are found not to be responsible for their criminal actions (see *Highlights*).

People with schizophrenia often suffer from **hallucinations**, false sensory perceptions that usually take the form of hearing voices that are not really there (visual, tactile, or olfactory hallucinations are more likely to indicate substance abuse or organic brain damage). They also frequently have **delusions**—false beliefs

Schizophrenic disorders
Severe disorders in which there are disturbances of thoughts, communications, and emotions, including delusions and hallucinations.

Insanity
Legal term for mentally disturbed people who are not considered responsible for their criminal actions.

Hallucinations
Sensory experiences in the absence of external stimulation.

Delusions
False beliefs about reality that have no basis in fact.

HIGHLIGHTS

The Insanity Defense

Many people attribute particularly horrifying crimes—assassinations of public figures, mass murders, and serial murders, for instance—to mental disturbance, because it seems that anyone who could commit such crimes must be crazy. But if a person is truly "crazy," is the legal system justified in holding him or her responsible for criminal acts? The legal answer to this question is a qualified *yes*. A mentally ill person is responsible for his or her crimes unless he or she is determined to be *insane*. What's the difference between being "mentally ill" and being "insane"? *Insanity* is a legal term, not a psychological one. It is typically applied to defendants who, when they committed the offense with which they are charged, were so mentally disturbed that they either could not distinguish right from wrong or could not control the act—it was an "irresistible impulse."

When a defendant is suspected of being mentally disturbed, another important question must be answered before that person is brought to trial: Can he or she understand the charges and participate in a defense in court? The issue of competency to stand trial is determined by a court-appointed expert. The person found to be incompetent is sent to a psychiatric institution, often for an indefinite period. The person judged to be competent is required to stand trial. At this point the defendant may plead not guilty by reason of insanity, an assertion that at the time of the crime the defendant lacked substantial capacity to appreciate the criminality of his or her action (know right from wrong) or to conform to the requirements of the law (control his or her behavior).

Was the defendant unable to distinguish right from wrong?

When a defendant enters an insanity plea, the court system relies heavily on the testimony of forensic psychologists and psychiatrists to determine the mental state of the defendant at the time of the crime. Because most such trials feature experts testifying both for the defense and for the prosecution, the jury is often conflicted about which side to believe. Further-

Theodore J. Kaczynski, the serial terrorist known as the Unabomber, was sought by the FBI for 17 years. Kaczynski pleaded guilty to three killings to avoid a trial in which his lawyers had planned to argue that he was legally insane.

more, many people are cynical about professionals who receive large fees to appear in court and argue that a defendant is or is not sane. The public, skeptical about professional jargon, often feels that psychological testimony allows dangerous criminals to "get off." Actually, those who successfully plead insanity often are confined longer in mental hospitals than they would have been in prison if convicted of their crimes. Therefore the insanity plea is not an easy way out of responsibility for a crime.

about reality with no factual basis—that distort their relationships with their surroundings and with other people. Typically these delusions are *paranoid*: People with schizophrenia believe that someone is out to harm them. They may think that a doctor wishes to kill them or that they are receiving radio messages from aliens invading from outer space. They often regard their own bodies—as well as the outside world—as hostile and alien. Because their world is utterly different from the one most of us live in, people with schizophrenia usually cannot live anything like a normal life unless they are successfully treated with medication (see Chapter 13). Often they are unable to communicate with others, for when they speak, their words are incoherent. The following case illustrates some of the major characteristics of schizophrenia:

> For many years [a 35-year-old widow] has heard voices, which insult her and cast suspicion on her chastity. . . . The voices are very distinct, and in her opinion, they must be carried by telescope or a machine from her home. Her thoughts are

dictated to her; she is obliged to think them, and hears them repeated after her. She . . . has all kinds of uncomfortable sensations in her body, to which something is "done." In particular, her "mother parts" are turned inside out, and people send a pain through her back, lay ice water on her heart, squeeze her neck, injure her spine, and violate her. There are also hallucinations of sight—black figures and the altered appearance of people—but these are far less frequent. (Spitzer et al., 1981, pp. 308–309)

There are actually several kinds of schizophrenic disorders, which have different characteristic symptoms.

Disorganized schizophrenia includes some of the more bizarre symptoms of schizophrenia, such as giggling, grimacing, and frantic gesturing. People suffering from disorganized schizophrenia show a childish disregard for social conventions and may urinate or defecate at inappropriate times. They are active but aimless, and they are often given to incoherent conversations.

In **catatonic schizophrenia** motor activity is severely disturbed. People in this state may remain immobile, mute, and impassive. They may behave in a robotlike fashion when ordered to move, and they may even let doctors put their arms and legs into uncomfortable positions that they maintain for hours. At the opposite extreme, they may become excessively excited, talking and shouting continuously.

Paranoid schizophrenia is marked by extreme suspiciousness and complex delusions. People with paranoid schizophrenia may believe themselves to be Napoleon or the Virgin Mary, or they may insist that Russian spies with laser guns are constantly on their trail because they have learned some great secret. Because they are less likely to be incoherent or to look or act "crazy," these people can appear more "normal" than people with other schizophrenic disorders if their delusions are compatible with everyday life. They may, however, become hostile or aggressive toward anyone who questions their thinking or delusions. Note that this disorder is far more severe than paranoid personality disorder, which does not involve bizarre delusions or loss of touch with reality.

Finally, **undifferentiated schizophrenia** is the classification developed for people who have several of the characteristic symptoms of schizophrenia—such as delusions, hallucinations, or incoherence—yet do not show the typical symptoms of any other subtype of the disorder.

Because schizophrenia is a very serious disorder, considerable research has been directed at trying to discover its causes. Many studies indicate that schizophrenia has a genetic component (Gottesman, 1991). People with schizophrenia are more likely than other people to have children with schizophrenia, even when those children have lived with adoptive parents since early in life. And if one identical twin suffers from schizophrenia, the chances are almost 50 percent that the other twin will also develop this disorder. In fraternal twins, if one twin has schizophrenia, the chances are only about 17 percent that the other twin will develop it as well. As shown in Figure 12–2, the average risk of schizophrenia steadily increases in direct relation to the closeness of one's biological relationship to an individual with the disorder.

Recent research suggests that the biological predisposition to schizophrenia may be related to excessive amounts of the neurotransmitter *dopamine* in the central nervous system. Drugs that relieve schizophrenic symptoms decrease the amount of dopamine in the brain and block dopamine receptors. Some research also indicates that pathology in various structures of the brain may influence the onset of schizophrenia (Weinberger, 1997). Other studies link schizophrenia to some form of early prenatal disturbance (Wolf & Weinberger, 1996). Nevertheless, scientists have found only average differences in brain structure and chemistry between schizophrenic and healthy people (Noga et al., 1996). As yet, no

Disorganized schizophrenia
Schizophrenic disorder in which bizarre and childlike behaviors are common.

Catatonic schizophrenia
Schizophrenic disorder in which disturbed motor behavior is prominent.

Paranoid schizophrenia
Schizophrenic disorder marked by extreme suspiciousness and complex, bizarre delusions.

Undifferentiated schizophrenia
Schizophrenic disorder in which there are clear schizophrenic symptoms that don't meet the criteria for another subtype of the disorder.

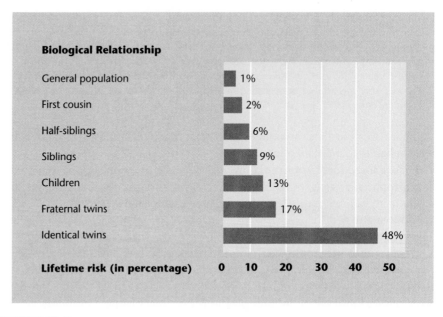

FIGURE 12–2

Average risk of schizophrenia among biological relatives of people with schizophrenia.
Source: Adapted from Gottesman (1991, p. 96).

laboratory tests can diagnose schizophrenia based on brain abnormalities. In fact, studies of identical twins in which only one suffers from schizophrenia have sometimes found more evidence of brain abnormalities in the *well* twin than in the sick twin.

Studies of identical twins have also been used to identify the importance of environment in causing schizophrenia. Because identical twins are genetically identical and because half of the identical twins of people with schizophrenia do not develop schizophrenia themselves, this severe and puzzling disorder cannot be caused by genetic factors alone. Environmental factors—ranging from disturbed family relations to taking drugs to biological damage that may occur at any age, even before birth—must also figure in determining whether a person will develop schizophrenia. Recall that the systems model would predict that environment and experience can increase or decrease the effects of any inherited tendency. Consequently, identical twins (or triplets) afflicted with psychological disorders will show different degrees of functioning.

Finally, although quite different in emphasis, the various explanations for schizophrenic disorders are not mutually exclusive. Genetic factors are universally acknowledged, but many theorists believe that only a combination of biological, psychological, and social factors produces schizophrenia (Gottesman, 1991). According to the systems model, genetic factors predispose some people to schizophrenia, and family interaction and life stress activate the predisposition.

REVIEW QUESTIONS

1. Schizophrenic disorders are characterized by ____ symptoms, or loss of contact with reality.

2. ____ is the legal term for mentally disturbed people who are found not to be responsible for their criminal actions.

3. People with schizophrenia often suffer from ____ , false sensory perceptions that usually take the form of hearing voices that are not really there.

Match the following terms with the appropriate description.

4. disorganized schizophrenia ____   a. marked by extreme suspiciousness and complex delusions

5. catatonic schizophrenia ____

    b. bizarre symptoms may include giggling, grimacing, frantic gesturing, and a childish disregard for social conventions

6. paranoid schizophrenia ____

    c. a severe disturbance of motor activity

7. undifferentiated schizophrenia ____

    d. people who have several characteristic symptoms of schizophrenia but do not show the typical symptoms of any other subtype

8. Which of the following has *not* been related to the onset of schizophrenia?

    a. genetic predisposition

    b. excessive amounts of the neurotransmitter dopamine in the central nervous system

    c. an overactive thyroid gland

    d. pathology in various structures of the brain

Indicate whether the following are true (T) or false (F).

9. *Schizophrenia* means "split personality." ____

10. People with schizophrenia may think that a doctor wishes to kill them. ____

11. Studies indicate that a biological predisposition to schizophrenia may be inherited. ____

12. Laboratory tests can be used to diagnose schizophrenia based on brain abnormalities. ____

Answers: 1. psychotic. 2. insanity. 3. hallucinations. 4. b. 5. c. 6. a. 7. d. 8. c. 9. F. 10. T. 11. T. 12. F.

Childhood Disorders

Why do stimulants appear to slow down hyperactive children and adults?

Children may suffer from conditions already discussed in this chapter—for example, depression and anxiety disorders. But other disorders are either characteristic of children or are first evident in childhood. The DSM-IV contains a long list of "disorders usually first diagnosed in infancy, childhood, or adolescence." Two of these disorders are attention-deficit/hyperactivity disorder and autistic disorder.

Attention-deficit/hyperactivity disorder (ADHD) was once known simply as *hyperactivity*. The new name reflects the fact that children with the disorder typically have trouble focusing their attention in the sustained way that other children do. Instead they are easily distracted, often fidgety and impulsive, and almost constantly in motion. Many theorists believe that this disorder—which affects nearly 5 percent of all school-age children and is much more common in boys than girls—is present at birth but becomes a serious problem only after the child starts school. The class setting demands that children sit quietly, pay attention as instructed, follow directions, and inhibit urges to yell and run around. The child with ADHD simply cannot conform to these demands.

We do not yet know what causes ADHD, but most theorists assume that biological factors are very influential. Family interaction and other social experiences may be more important in preventing the disorder than in causing it. That is, some exceptionally competent parents and patient, tolerant teachers may be able to teach "difficult" children to conform to the demands of schooling. While some psychologists train the parents of children with ADHD in these management skills, the most frequent treatment for these children is a type of drug known as a *psychostimulant*. Psychostimulants do not work by "slowing down" hyperactive

WEB LINKS

Attention-deficit/hyperactivity disorder (ADHD)
A childhood disorder characterized by inattention, impulsiveness, and hyperactivity.

Temple Grandin is an autistic woman who has earned a Ph.D. in animal science. Few people with autism can ever function on this level.

children; rather, they appear to increase the children's ability to focus their attention so they can attend to the task at hand, which decreases their hyperactivity (Barkley, 1990). Unfortunately, psychostimulants often produce only short-term benefits.

A very different and profoundly serious disorder that usually becomes evident in the first few years of life is **autistic disorder.** Autistic children fail to form normal attachments to parents, remaining distant and withdrawn into their own separate worlds. As infants, they may even show distress at being picked up or held. As they grow older, they typically do not speak, or they develop a peculiar speech pattern called *echolalia*, in which they repeat the words said to them. Autistic children typically show strange motor behavior, such as repeating body movements endlessly or walking constantly on tiptoe. They don't play as normal children do; they are not at all social and may use toys in odd ways, constantly spinning the wheels on a toy truck or tearing paper into strips. Autistic children often display the symptoms of retardation, but it is hard to test their mental ability because they generally don't talk. The disorder lasts into adulthood in the great majority of cases (recall the character Raymond in the movie *Rain Man*).

We don't know what causes autism, although most theorists believe that it results almost entirely from biological conditions. Some causes of mental retardation, such as fragile X syndrome (see Chapter 7), also seem to increase the risk of autistic disorder. Recent evidence suggests that genetics also plays a strong role in causing the disorder (Bailey et al., 1995).

REVIEW QUESTIONS

1. Children with _____ typically lack the ability to focus their attention in the sustained way that other children do.
2. The most frequent treatment for ADHD is a type of drug known as a ___.
3. Which of the following is not a characteristic of children with autistic disorder?
   a. They fail to form normal attachments to parents.
   b. They often have exceptionally high IQs.
   c. They typically show strange motor behavior, such as repeating body movements endlessly.
   d. As they grow older, they often do not develop speech.

Indicate whether the following are true (T) or false (F).

4. ADHD is much more common in boys than in girls. _____
5. Psychostimulants work by "slowing down" hyperactive children. _____
6. Most theorists believe that autistic disorder results almost entirely from biological conditions. _____

Answers: 1. attention-deficit/hyperactivity disorder (ADHD). **2.** psychostimulant. **3.** b. **4.** T. **5.** F. **6.** T.

Gender Differences in Abnormal Behavior

What complex factors contribute to different rates of abnormal behavior in men and women?

Throughout this chapter we have rarely examined the differences between men and women despite the oversimplified conclusion of many studies that women have a higher rate of psychological disorders than men do. Prevalence rates of mental disorders vary by a number of factors: gender, age, race, ethnicity, marital status, income, and type of disorder (see *Highlights*). Furthermore, how do we determine the "rate of psychological disorders"? Do we

Autistic disorder
A childhood disorder characterized by lack of social instincts and strange motor behavior.

HIGHLIGHTS

The Prevalence of Psychological Disorders

How common are psychological disorders in the United States? Are they increasing or decreasing over time? Are some population groups more prone to these disorders than other groups? These questions are of interest to psychologists and public health experts who are concerned with both the prevalence and the incidence of mental health problems. If, for example, there were 100 cases of depression in a population of 1,000, the *prevalence*—the frequency with which a given disorder occurs at a given time—would be 10 percent. The *incidence* of a disorder is the number of new cases in a given period. In a population of 1,000, if there were 10 new cases of depression in a year, the incidence rate would be 1 percent per year.

A very large study conducted in the United States suggests that mental disorders affect a far larger proportion of the population than was once thought. Starting in 1980, the National Institute of Mental Health interviewed nearly 20,000 people in an ambitious and wide-ranging study of the prevalence of psychological disorders (see table). Among the study's surprising findings were that 32.2 percent of Americans suffer from one or more serious mental disorders during

---

Abuse of alcohol is more prevalent than abuse of all other drugs combined.

---

their lifetime (Robins & Reiger, 1991) and that at any given time more than 15 percent of the population is experiencing a mental disorder. The most common problem is drug abuse, with abuse of alcohol being more prevalent than abuse of all other drugs combined. More than 13 percent of adults over 18 experience alcoholism at some point in their lives. Anxiety disorders are the next most common psychological disorder. Mood disorders—principally depression—are a problem for almost 8 percent of the population at some point in their lives. In contrast, schizophrenia afflicts only 1.5 percent of the population (but note that this percentage represents more than 3 million people).

Every culture acknowledges some types of mental disorders, although the labels and symptoms may differ. Schizophrenia and depression, for example, are recognized even in most cultures that do not practice psychology as a scientific discipline. A pattern of behavior involving bizarre physical activity, distorted communications, hallucinations, and delusions is understood as "crazy" in cultures as diverse as the Yoruba of West Africa and the Baffin Island Eskimos (Murphy, 1976). Perhaps in future years *epidemiologists*—scientists who study the distribution of health problems—will determine whether our 15 percent prevalence figure for mental disorders is typical of the rest of the world.

THE PREVALENCE OF PSYCHOLOGICAL DISORDERS IN THE UNITED STATES

	Ethnicity			Sex		
	White	*Black*	*Hispanic*	*Men*	*Women*	*Total*
Alcohol abuse or dependence	13.6	13.8	16.7	23.8	4.6	13.8
Generalized anxiety	3.4	6.1	3.7	2.4	5.0	3.8
Phobic disorder	9.7	23.4	12.2	10.4	17.7	14.3
Obsessive–compulsive disorder	2.6	2.3	1.8	2.0	3.0	2.6
Mood disorder	8.0	6.3	7.8	5.2	10.2	7.8
Schizophrenic disorders	1.4	2.1	0.8	1.2	1.7	1.5
Antisocial personality	2.6	2.3	3.4	4.5	0.8	2.6

Source: From *Psychiatric Disorders in America,* by Lee N. Robins and Darrel A. Regier, Free Press, 1991.
Copyright © 1991 by Lee N. Robins and Darrel A. Regier. Reprinted with permission of the Free Press, a Division of Macmillan, Inc.

count only people admitted to mental hospitals? those who receive a formal diagnosis in an outpatient-treatment setting? Or do we count all those persons in the general population who are judged to suffer from mental disorders even if they have not sought treatment or received a formal diagnosis? These questions illustrate how hard it is to make a firm generalization about differences between the sexes.

We do know that more women than men are *treated* for mental disorders. Indeed, as one expert observed, "Women have always been the main consumers of psychotherapy from Freud's era onward" (Williams, 1987, p. 465). But this observation does not mean that more women than men *have* mental disorders, for in our society it is much more acceptable for women to discuss their emotional difficulties and to seek professional help. Perhaps mental disorders are equally common among men—or even more common—but men do not typically go to therapists and therefore are not counted in the studies.

All of the disorders listed in the DSM-IV (with the exception of a few sexual disorders) affect both men and women. Indeed, those mental disorders for which there seems to be a strong biological component, such as bipolar disorder and schizophrenia, are distributed fairly equally between the sexes. Differences tend to be found for those disorders *without* a strong biological component—that is, disorders in which learning and experience play a more important role. For example, men are more likely than women to suffer from substance abuse and antisocial personality disorder. Women, in contrast, are more likely to suffer from depression, agoraphobia, simple phobia, obsessive–compulsive disorder, and somatization disorder (Basow, 1986; Douglas et al., 1995; Russo, 1990). These tendencies suggest that socialization plays a part in developing a disorder: When men display abnormal behavior, they are more likely to drink too much or act aggressively; when women display abnormal behavior, they are more likely to become fearful, passive, hopeless, and "sick" (Basow, 1986).

We saw in Chapter 11 that the effects of stress are greater to the extent that a person feels alienated, powerless, and helpless—situations more frequent among women than men. These factors are especially common among minority women, and, not surprisingly, psychological disorders are more prevalent among these women than among other women (Russo & Sobel, 1981).

Once past puberty, women seem to have higher rates of anxiety disorders and depression than men do, and they are more likely than men to seek professional help for their problems. Greater stress—partly owing to socialization and lower status rather than psychological "weakness"—apparently accounts for this statistic, however. Marriage and family life, associated with lower rates of mental disorders among men, introduce additional stress into the lives of women, particularly young women (25–45), and in some instances this added stress translates into a psychological disorder.

REVIEW QUESTIONS

1. Prevalence rates of mental disorders vary by
   - a. age
   - b. race
   - c. ethnicity
   - d. marital status
   - e. income
   - f. type of disorder
   - g. all of the above
   - h. a and f only
   - i. a, c, and f only

2. Mental disorders for which there seems to be a strong ____ component are distributed fairly equally between the sexes.

3. Men are more likely than women to suffer from ____ and ____.

4. Women are more likely than men to suffer from ____, ____, ____, ____, and ____.

Indicate whether the following are true (T) or false (F).

5. More women than men are treated for mental disorders. ____

6. The prevalence of psychological disorders is greatest among minority women. ____

7. Marriage and family life are associated with higher rates of mental disorders among men. ____

Answers: 1. g. 2. biological. 3. substance abuse, antisocial personality disorder. 4. depression, agoraphobia, simple phobia, obsessive–compulsive disorder, somatization disorder. 5. T. 6. T. 7. F.

KEY TERMS

Perspectives on psychological disorders
biological model, p. 421
psychoanalytic model, p. 422
cognitive–behavioral model, p. 422
diathesis-stress model, p. 423
diathesis, p. 423
systems approach, p. 423

Mood disorders
mood disorders, p. 424
depression, p. 424
mania, p. 426
bipolar disorder, p. 426
cognitive distortions, p. 427

Anxiety disorders
anxiety disorders, p. 428
specific phobia, p. 428
social phobia, p. 429
agoraphobia, p. 429
panic disorder, p. 429

generalized anxiety disorder, p. 429
obsessive–compulsive disorder, p. 430

Psychosomatic and somatoform disorders
psychosomatic disorders, p. 432
somatoform disorders, p. 432
conversion disorders, p. 432
hypochondriasis, p. 432
body dysmorphic disorder, p. 432

Dissociative disorders
dissociative disorders, p. 433
depersonalization disorder, p. 434

Sexual and gender-identity disorders
sexual dysfunction, p. 435
paraphilias, p. 435

fetishism, p. 435
pedophilia, p. 436
gender-identity disorders, p. 436
gender-identity disorders in children, p. 436

Personality disorders
personality disorders, p. 437
schizoid personality disorder, p. 437
paranoid personality disorder, p. 437
dependent personality disorder, p. 437
avoidant personality disorder, p. 437
narcissistic personality disorder, p. 437
borderline personality disorder, p. 437
antisocial personality disorder, p. 437

Schizophrenic disorders
schizophrenic disorders, p. 439
insanity, p. 439
hallucinations, p. 439
delusions, p. 439
disorganized schizophrenia, p. 441
catatonic schizophrenia, p. 441
paranoid schizophrenia, p. 441
undifferentiated schizophrenia, p. 441

Childhood disorders
attention-deficit/hyperactivity disorder (ADHD), p. 443
autistic disorder, p. 444

CHAPTER REVIEW

☐ How does a mental health professional define a psychological disorder?

Mental health professionals define a psychological disorder as a condition that either seriously impairs a person's ability to function in life or creates a high level of inner distress (or sometimes both). This does not mean that the category "disordered" is always easy to distinguish from the category "normal." In fact, it may be more accurate to view abnormal behavior as merely quantitatively different from normal behavior.

☐ How has the view of psychological disorders changed over time?

In early societies abnormal behavior was often attributed to supernatural powers. The roots of a more naturalistic view can be traced to Hippocrates, who maintained that

madness was like any other sickness, arising from natural causes. This approach fell into disfavor in the Middle Ages, when possession by devils became the predominant explanation of psychological disorders. A naturalistic view didn't resurface until the eighteenth century. In modern times three approaches have helped to advance our understanding of abnormal behavior: the biological, the psychoanalytic, and the cognitive–behavioral.

☐ How can biology influence the development of psychological disorders?

The **biological model** holds that abnormal behavior is caused by some physiological malfunction, especially of the brain. It is assumed that these malfunctions are often hereditary in origin. Although there is evidence that genetic/biochemical factors are indeed involved in some psychological disorders, biology alone cannot account for most mental illnesses.

☐ What did Freud and his followers believe was the underlying cause of psychological disorders?

The **psychoanalytic model** originating with Freud holds that abnormal behavior is a symbolic expression of unconscious conflicts that generally can be traced to childhood. Little scientific evidence supports this theory, however, even though it has been widely influential.

☐ According to the cognitive–behavioral model, what causes abnormal behavior?

The **cognitive–behavior model** states that psychological disorders arise when people learn maladaptive ways of thinking and acting. What has been learned can be unlearned, however. Cognitive–behavior therapists therefore strive to modify their patients' dysfunctional behaviors and distorted, self-defeating processes of thought.

☐ Why do some people with a family background of a psychological disorder develop the disorder while other family members do not?

The **diathesis–stress model** is one promising approach to answering this question. As an attempt to integrate the biological perspective with environmentally based ones, it holds that psychological disorders develop when a **diathesis** (or biological predisposition) is set off by stressful circumstances. Another attempt at integrating causes is the **systems approach.** It contends that psychological disorders are "lifestyle diseases" that arise from a combination of biological risk factors, psychological stresses, and societal pressures on people. This approach, too, can help to explain why a family background of a disorder doesn't always mean that the disorder will develop.

☐ Why is it useful to have a manual of psychological disorders?

For nearly 40 years the American Psychiatric Association has published the *Diagnostic and Statistical Manual of Mental Disorders (DSM).* The current fourth edition, known as DSM-IV, provides careful descriptions of the symptoms of different disorders so that diagnoses based on them will be reliable from one mental health professional to another. One criticism of DSM-IV is that it includes little on causes and treatments.

☐ How do mood disorders differ from ordinary mood changes?

Most people have a wide emotional range, but in some people with **mood disorders** this range is greatly restricted. They seem stuck at one or the other end of the emotional spectrum. The most common mood disorder is **depression,** a state in which a person feels overwhelmed with sadness,

loses interest in activities, and displays other symptoms, such as excessive guilt or feelings of worthlessness.

☐ How does clinical depression differ from ordinary sadness?

The DSM-IV distinguishes between two forms of clinical depression. *Major depressive disorder* is an episode of intense sadness that may last for several months; in contrast, *dysthymia* involves less intense sadness but persists with little relief for a period of 2 years or more.

☐ Why does mania, which is generally characterized by a high level of activity, produce very few constructive outcomes? What is bipolar disorder?

People suffering from **mania** become euphoric ("high"), extremely active, excessively talkative, and easily distractible. They typically have unlimited hopes and schemes but little interest in realistically carrying them out. At the extreme, they may collapse from exhaustion. Manic episodes rarely appear by themselves; rather, they usually alternate with depression. Such a mood disorder, in which both mania and depression are alternately present, sometimes interrupted by periods of normal mood, is known as **bipolar disorder.**

☐ What causes some people to experience extreme mood changes?

Mood disorders can result from a combination of biological, psychological, and social factors. Biological factors—including genetics and chemical imbalances in the brain—seem to play an important role in the development of depression and especially bipolar disorder. The psychological factor of **cognitive distortions** (unrealistically negative views about the self) occurs in many depressed people, although it is uncertain whether these distortions cause the depression or are caused by it. Finally, social factors, such as troubled relationships, have also been linked with mood disorders.

☐ How does an anxiety disorder differ from ordinary anxiety?

Normal fear is caused by something identifiable, and the fear subsides with time. In the case of **anxiety disorder,** however, either the person doesn't know why he or she is afraid or the anxiety is inappropriate to the circumstances.

☐ How does a phobia differ from fear?

A **specific phobia** is an intense, paralyzing fear of something that it is unreasonable to fear so excessively. A **social phobia** is excessive, inappropriate fear connected with social situations or performances in front of other people. **Agoraphobia** is a less common and much more debilitating type of anxiety disorder that involves multiple, intense fears such as the fear of being alone or of being in public places or other situations that require separation from a source of security.

☐ How does a panic attack differ from fear?

Panic disorder is characterized by recurrent panic attacks, which are sudden, unpredictable, and overwhelming experiences of intense fear or terror without any reasonable cause.

☐ What is the difference between specific phobias and generalized anxiety disorder?

Generalized anxiety disorder is defined by prolonged vague but intense fears that, unlike phobias, are not attached to any particular object or circumstance. In contrast, **obsessive–compulsive disorder** involves either involuntary thoughts that recur despite the person's attempt to stop them or compulsive rituals that a person feels compelled to perform. Two other types of anxiety disorder are caused by highly stressful events. If the anxious reaction occurs soon after the event, the diagnosis is *acute stress disorder*; if it occurs long after the event is over, the diagnosis is *posttraumatic stress disorder*.

☐ What can the cognitive perspective and the biological perspective tell us about the causes of anxiety?

Psychologists with a biological perspective propose that a predisposition to anxiety disorders may be inherited because these types of disorders tend to run in families. Cognitive psychologists suggest that people who believe they have no control over stressful events in their lives are more likely to suffer from anxiety disorders than other people are. There are also views of anxiety disorders based on evolutionary and psychoanalytic perspectives. Evolutionary psychologists hold that we are predisposed by evolution to associate certain stimuli with intense fears and that this is the origin of many phobias. Psychoanalytic thinkers focus on inner psychological conflicts and the defense mechanisms they trigger as the sources of anxiety disorders.

☐ What is the difference between psychosomatic and somatoform disorders?

Psychosomatic disorders are illnesses that have a valid physical basis but are largely caused by psychological factors such as excessive stress and anxiety. In contrast, **somatoform disorders** are characterized by physical symptoms without any identifiable physical cause. Examples are **conversion disorder** (a dramatic specific disability without organic cause), **hypochondriasis** (insistence that minor symptoms mean serious illness), and **body dysmorphic disorder** (imagined ugliness in some part of the body).

☐ What do dissociative disorders have in common?

In **dissociative disorders** some part of a person's personality or memory is separated from the rest. Dissociative amnesia involves the loss of at least some significant aspects of memory. When an amnesia victim leaves home and assumes an entirely new identity the disorder is known as dissociative fugue. In dissociative identity disorder, commonly known as multiple personality, a person has several distinct personalities that emerge at different times. In **depersonalization disorder** the person suddenly feels changed or different in a strange way.

☐ What are the three main types of sexual disorders?

DSM-IV recognizes three main types of sexual disorders. One is **sexual dysfunction**—loss or impairment of the ability to function effectively during sex. In men this may take the form of erectile disorder (inability to achieve or keep an erection), and in women it often occurs as female sexual arousal disorder (inability to become sexually excited or to reach orgasm). Another main class of sexual disorders consists of the **paraphilias**, in which the person has sexual interest in unconventional objects or situations. One example is **fetishism**, or repeated use of a nonhuman object to achieve sexual excitement. Another is **pedophilia**, or sexual arousal that involves a prepubescent child. **Gender-identity disorders** make up the third main type of sexual disorders. These involve the desire to become, or the insistence that one really is, a member of the other sex.

☐ Which personality disorder creates the most significant problems for society?

Personality disorders are enduring, inflexible, and maladaptive ways of thinking and behaving that are so exaggerated and rigid that they cause serious inner distress or conflicts with others. One group of personality disorders is characterized by odd or eccentric behavior. For example, people who exhibit **schizoid personality disorder** lack the ability or desire to form social relationships and have no warm feelings for other people; those with **paranoid personality disorder** are inappropriately suspicious of others. Another cluster of personality disorders is characterized by anxious or fearful behavior. Examples are **dependent personality disorder** (the inability to think or act independently) and **avoidant personality disorder** (social anxiety leading to isolation). A third group of personality disorders is characterized by dramatic, emotional, or erratic behavior. For instance, people with **narcissistic personality disorder** have a highly overblown sense of self-importance, while those with **borderline personality disorder** show much instability in self-image, mood, and interpersonal relationships. Finally, people with **antisocial personality disorder** chronically lie, steal, and cheat with little or no remorse. Because this disorder is responsible for a good deal of crime and violence, it creates the greatest problems for society.

☐ **How is schizophrenia different from multiple-personality disorder?**

In multiple-personality disorder consciousness is split into two or more distinctive personalities, each of which is coherent and intact. This condition is different from **schizophrenic disorders,** which involve dramatic disruptions in thought and communication, inappropriate emotions, and bizarre behavior that lasts for years. People with schizophrenia are out of touch with reality and usually cannot live anything like a normal life unless successfully treated with medication. They often suffer from **hallucinations** (false sensory perceptions) and **delusions** (false beliefs about reality). Subtypes of schizophrenic disorders include **disorganized schizophrenia** (childish disregard for social conventions), **catatonic schizophrenia** (mute immobility or excessive excitement), **paranoid schizophrenia** (extreme suspiciousness related to complex delusions), and **undifferentiated schizophrenia** (characterized by a diversity of symptoms).

☐ **Why do stimulants appear to slow down hyperactive children and adults?**

DSM-IV contains a long list of disorders usually first diagnosed in infancy, childhood, or adolescence. Two of them discussed in this chapter are **attention-deficit/ hyperactivity disorder (ADHD)** and **autistic disorder.** Children with ADHD are highly distractible, often fidgety and impulsive, and almost constantly in motion. The psychostimulants frequently prescribed for ADHD appear to slow such children down because they increase the ability to focus attention on routine tasks. Autistic disorder is a profound problem identified in the first few years of life. It is characterized by a failure to form normal social attachments, severe speech impairment, and strange motor behaviors.

☐ **What complex factors contribute to different rates of abnormal behavior in men and women?**

Studies show that women have a higher rate of psychological disorders than men do, especially for the mood and anxiety disorders. There is controversy over what accounts for these differences, but it seems that both socialization and biology play important roles.

CRITICAL THINKING AND APPLICATIONS

1. Imagine that a halfway house for the mentally ill is proposed to be built in a residential neighborhood, but many of the residents are frightened by the prospect of living near recovering mentally ill people. Should they be able to prevent the house from being built? Why or why not?

2. Do feelings of depression and anxiety indicate that a person is suffering from a mood disorder?

3. How do you feel about the rehabilitation of prisoners, given the fact that antisocial personality disorder may occur in 50 percent of prison populations?

On the Web...

Visit these online resources at our Companion Website www.prenhall.com/morris

The Psychology Place

Learning Activities
1. DSM-IV: How Many Entries for The Book of Names?, p. 423
2. Recognizing Mood Disorders, p. 424

Scientific American Connection
3. Teen Suicide—Symptom of a Changing World or Exaggerated Suggestibility in Adolescence?, p. 426
4. Depression's Double Standard, p. 426

Research News
5. Manic-Depressive Illness and Creativity, p. 426
6. The Manic-depressive Brain, p. 427
7. Beyond Shyness: Diagnosing and Treating Social Phobia, p. 429
8. Schizophrenic Disorder: When People Hear Voices, Who's Talking?, p. 439
9. The Insanity Defense and the Unabomber Trial p. 440
10. Editor's Note: Unabomber Update, p. 440
11. Understanding Schizophrenia: Where and When You Were Born Makes a Difference, p. 441
12. Investigating Sex Differences in Depression, p. 446

Games
1. Sexual Disorders, p. 435
2. Personality Disorders, p. 437

Web Links
1. **http://www.mhnet.org/disorders/**, p. 419
   Mental Health Net–Mental Disorders Index: Comprehensive descriptions of the symptoms and treatment of mental disorders, including adult disorders, child disorders, and personality disorders.
2. **http://www.save.org/**, p. 426
   SAVE – Suicide Awareness/Voices of Education. Provides education and links about symptoms, misconceptions, and prevention of suicide
3. **http://www.psycom.net/depression.central.html**, p. 427
   Dr. Ivan's Depression Central. Includes comprehensive list of links related to depression and other mood disorders.
4. **http://www.algy.com/anxiety.index.shtml**, p. 428
   The Anxiety Panic Internet Resource. Shares information about anxiety and its treatments and offers links to anxiety resources.
5. **http://www.sonic.net/~fredd/phobia1.html**, p. 429
   The Phobia List. Includes questions and answers about phobias, treatments, and a complete list of the names and definitions of all types of phobias.
6. **http://text.hlm.hih.gov/nih.cdc/www/85txt.html**, p. 429
   Treatment of Panic Disorder. National Institutes of Health Consensus Development Conference Statement.
7. **http://www.ocfoundation.org/indright.htm**, p. 430
   Obsessive-Compulsive Foundation: Home Page. Explains symptomology of OCD, effective treatments, and supportive resources.
8. **http://www.trauma-pages.com/index.phtml**, p. 430
   David Baldwin's Trauma Information Pages. Links to descriptions of trauma, trauma articles, general support, and disaster handouts and links.
9. **http://odp.od.nih.gov/consensus/cons/110.110_statement.htm**, p. 443
   NIH Consensus Statements: Diagnosis and Treatment of Attention Deficit Hyperactivity Disorder. Provides definition of ADHD, effective treatments, and barriers to appropriate identification, evaluation, and research.

13

THERAPIES

I N Chapter 1 we introduced the concept of **PSYCHOTHERAPY,** techniques to treat personality and behavior disorders. To many people, psychotherapy still evokes an image of an analyst sitting silently in a chair while a client, reclining on a nearby couch, recounts traumatic childhood events. As the anxious client reveals dreams, fantasies, fears, and obsessions, the therapist nods, scribbles in a notebook, and perhaps asks a question or two. The therapist rarely offers the client advice and never reveals details of his or her own personal experiences.

This cliché of psychotherapy has some truth to it: Scenes like this do occur, but there are many other forms of psychotherapy. Literally hundreds of variations are practiced by several different types of mental health professionals. In some forms of psychotherapy, therapists are very directive, even confrontational, in exploring their clients' thoughts and feelings. Some types of psychotherapy occur outside the therapist's office, as clients confront their fears in real life. Other psychotherapies treat couples or entire families, and still others treat groups of people with similar problems or goals. Despite the popular image of the clinical, detached analyst, most psychotherapists are warm, understanding, and willing to offer at least some direct information and advice.

In addition to holding inaccurate views of therapists, many people are confused about the effectiveness of psychotherapy. Some who have gone through therapy claim that it changed their lives; others complain that it made little difference. The public's perception of the effectiveness of psychotherapy is particularly important now that health care costs have escalated and treatments of psychological disorders are being monitored more closely in terms of their costs and outcomes. The future of psychotherapy rests in demonstrating its effectiveness.

In this chapter we survey the major types of therapies, including individual therapies and group therapies. We discuss these in the order in which they were developed: insight therapies, which began in the early twentieth century; behavior therapies, which became popular in the 1960s and 1970s; and the even more recent cognitive therapies. We also examine research comparing the effectiveness of different approaches, and we explore the role of medication and other biological treatments. Finally, we discuss the important issues of caring for the seriously disturbed, and we consider the factor of human diversity when providing treatments.

Insight Therapies

What do insight therapies have in common?

Several of the individual psychotherapies used in both private practice and institutions fall under the heading of **insight therapies.** Although the various insight therapies differ in their details, their common goal is to give people a better awareness and understanding of their feelings, motivations, and actions in the hope that this will lead to better adjustment. In this section we consider three major insight therapies: psychoanalysis, client-centered therapy, and Gestalt therapy.

Psychoanalysis

How does "free association" in psychoanalysis help a person to become aware of hidden feelings?

Psychoanalysis, the approach to psychotherapy developed by Sigmund Freud, is based on the belief that anxiety and other problems are symptoms of inner conflicts dating back to childhood. Usually these problems concern aggressive or sexual drives whose expression was dangerous or forbidden to the child. According to Freud, the

The consulting room where Freud met his clients. Note the position of Freud's chair at the head of the couch. In order to encourage free association, the psychoanalyst has to function as a blank screen onto which the client can project his or her feelings. To accomplish this, Freud believed, the psychoanalyst has to stay out of sight of the patient.

WEB LINKS
Ⓦ

Psychotherapy
The use of psychological techniques to treat personality and behavior disorders.

Insight therapies
A variety of individual psychotherapies designed to give people a better awareness and understanding of their feelings, motivations, and actions in the hope that this will help them to adjust.

Psychoanalysis
The theory of personality Freud developed as well as the form of therapy he invented.

Free association
A psychoanalytic technique that encourages the patient to talk without inhibition about whatever thoughts or fantasies come to mind.

Transference
The patient's carrying over to the analyst feelings held toward childhood authority figures.

Insight
Awareness of previously unconscious feelings and memories and how they influence present feelings and behavior.

impulses that the child repressed lurk in the adult's unconscious mind, where they can give rise to various psychological disorders. Psychoanalysis is designed to bring these hidden feelings to conscious awareness so that the person can deal with them more effectively.

In Freudian psychoanalysis the patient is instructed to talk about whatever comes to mind, with as little editing as possible and without inhibiting or controlling thoughts and fantasies. This process is called **free association.** Freud believed that the resulting "stream of consciousness" would provide insight into the patient's unconscious mind. During the early stages of psychoanalysis, the analyst remains impassive, mostly silent, and out of the patient's sight. In classical psychoanalysis the patient lies on a couch while the neutral analyst sits behind him or her. The analyst's silence is a kind of "blank screen" onto which the patient eventually projects unconscious thoughts and feelings.

Eventually patients may test their analyst by talking about forbidden desires and fantasies they have never revealed to anyone else. But the analyst maintains neutrality throughout, showing little of his or her own feelings and personality. When patients discover that their analyst is not shocked or disgusted by their revelations, they are reassured and transfer to their analyst feelings they have toward authority figures from their childhood. This process is known as **transference.** It is said to be *positive transference* when the patient feels good about the analyst.

As patients continue to expose their innermost feelings, they begin to feel increasingly vulnerable. They want reassurance and affection, but their analyst remains silent. Their anxiety builds. Threatened by their analyst's silence and by their own thoughts, patients may feel cheated and perhaps accuse their analyst of being a money-grabber. Or they may suspect that their analyst is really disgusted by their disclosures or is laughing about them behind their backs. This *negative transference* is thought to be a crucial step in psychoanalysis, for it presumably reveals negative feelings toward authority figures and resistance to uncovering repressed emotions.

As therapy progresses the analyst takes a more active role and begins to *interpret* or suggest alternative meanings for patients' feelings, memories, and actions. The goal of interpretation is to help patients to gain **insight**—to become aware of what was formerly outside of their awareness. As what was unconscious becomes conscious, patients may come to see how their childhood experiences have determined how they currently feel and act. Analysts encourage patients to confront childhood events and recall them fully. As patients relive their childhood traumas, they become able to resolve conflicts they could not resolve in the past. *Working through* old conflicts is thought to provide people with the chance to review and revise the feelings and beliefs that underlie their problems. In the following therapy session, the analyst helps a woman gain insight into why she tends to suppress emotions and to often act ill. The woman discovers a link between these behaviors and childhood fears regarding her mother, which she has transferred to the analyst.

> *Therapist: (summarizing and restating)* It sounds as if you would like to let loose with me, but you are afraid of what my response would be.
>
> *Patient:* I get so excited by what is happening here. I feel I'm being held back by needing to be nice. I'd like to blast loose sometimes, but I don't dare.
>
> *Therapist:* Because you fear my reaction?
>
> *Patient:* The worst thing would be that you wouldn't like me. You wouldn't speak to me friendly; you wouldn't smile; you'd feel you can't treat me and discharge me from treatment. But I know this isn't so; I know it.
>
> *Therapist:* Where do you think these attitudes come from?
>
> *Patient:* When I was 9 years old, I read a lot about great men in history. I'd quote them and be dramatic, I'd want a sword at my side; I'd dress like an Indian. Mother would scold me: Don't frown; don't talk so much. Sit on your hands, over and over again. I did all kinds of things. I was a naughty child. She told me I'd be hurt. Then, at 14, I fell off a horse and broke my back. I had to be in bed. Mother told me on the day I went riding not to, I'd get hurt because the ground was frozen. I was a stubborn, self-willed child. Then I went against her will and suffered an accident that changed my life, a fractured back. Her attitude was, "I told you so." I was put in a cast and kept in bed for months.
>
> *Therapist:* You were punished, so to speak, by this accident.
>
> *Patient:* But I gained attention and love from Mother for the first time. I felt so good. I'm ashamed to tell you this: Before I healed, I opened the cast and tried to walk, to make myself sick again so I could stay in bed longer.
>
> *Therapist:* How does that connect up with your impulse to be sick now and stay in bed so much?
>
> *Patient:* Oh. . . . *(pause)*
>
> *Therapist:* What do you think?
>
> *Patient:* Oh, my God, how infantile, how ungrownup *(pause)*. It must be so. I want people to love me and be sorry for me. Oh, my God. How completely childish. It is, *is* that. My mother must have ignored me when I was little, and I wanted so to be loved.
>
> *Therapist:* So that it may have been threatening to go back to being self-willed and unloved after you got out of the cast *(interpretation)*.
>
> *Patient:* It did. My life changed. I became meek and controlled. I couldn't get angry or stubborn afterward.
>
> *Therapist:* Perhaps if you go back to being stubborn with me, you would be returning to how you were before, that is, active, stubborn, but unloved.
>
> *Patient: (excitedly)* And, therefore, losing your love. I need you, but after all, you aren't going to reject me. But the pattern is so established now that the threat of the loss of love is too overwhelming with everybody, and I've got to keep myself from acting selfish or angry. (Wolberg, 1977, pp. 560–61)

Only a handful of people who seek therapy go into traditional psychoanalysis, as this woman did. As Freud himself recognized, analysis requires great motivation to change and an ability to deal rationally with whatever the analysis uncovers. Moreover, traditional analysis may take 5 years or longer, with 3, sometimes 5, sessions a week. Few people can afford this kind of treatment. And many want more immediate help for their problems. Moreover, for those with severe disorders, psychoanalysis is not effective.

Many therapists today believe that traditional psychoanalysis has become outdated. Since Freud invented psychoanalysis around the turn of the century,

"I really don't see how giving you a six-letter word for a sixteenth-century crested metal helmet helps my problem." (c)The New Yorker Collection 1999 J.C. Duffy from cartoonbank.com. All rights Reserved.

psychodynamic personality theory has changed significantly, as we saw in Chapter 10, Personality. Many of these changes have led to modified psychoanalytic techniques as well as to different approaches to therapy. For example, although Freud felt that to understand the present, one must understand the past, most neo-Freudians encourage their patients to cope directly with current problems in addition to, or as a way of, addressing unresolved conflicts from the past. Neo-Freudians also favor face-to-face discussions with their patients, and most take an active role in analysis from the start by interpreting patients' statements freely and suggesting topics for discussion.

Client-Centered Therapy

Why did Carl Rogers call his approach to therapy "client-centered"?

Carl Rogers, the founder of **client-centered** (or **person-centered) therapy**, took bits and pieces of the neo-Freudians' views and revised and rearranged them into a radically different approach to therapy. According to Rogers, the goal of therapy is to help people to become fully functioning, to open them up to all of their experiences and to all of themselves. Such inner awareness is a form of insight, but for Rogers, insight into current feelings was more important than insight into unconscious wishes with roots in the distant past. Rogers called his approach to therapy *client-centered* because he placed the responsibility for change on the person with the problem. The image of a patient seeking advice from an expert, the doctor, contradicted Rogers's view of therapeutic change. He intentionally used the term *client* rather than *patient* to highlight the more active and equal role he assigned to the person who sought therapy.

Rogers's ideas about therapy are quite specific. He believed that people's defensiveness, rigidity, anxiety, and other signs of discomfort stem from their experiences of conditional positive regard. They have learned that love and acceptance are contingent on conforming to what other people want them to be. The cardinal rule in person-centered therapy is for the therapist to express *un-*

Client-centered (or person-centered) therapy
Nondirectional form of therapy developed by Carl Rogers that calls for unconditional positive regard of the client by the therapist with the goal of helping the client become fully functioning.

Carl Rogers (far right) leading a group therapy session. Rogers was the founder of client-centered therapy.

conditional positive regard—that is, to show true acceptance of clients no matter what they may say or do. Rogers felt that this was a crucial first step toward getting clients to accept themselves.

Rather than taking an objective approach, Rogerian therapists try to understand things from the clients' point of view. They are also emphatically *nondirective*. They do not suggest reasons why clients feel as they do or how they might better handle a difficult situation. Instead, they try to reflect clients' statements, sometimes asking questions and sometimes hinting at feelings that clients have not put into words. Rogers felt that when therapists provide an atmosphere of openness and genuine respect, clients can find themselves, as the man in this session starts to do as he explores his debilitating lack of confidence.

> *Client:* I guess I do have problems at school. . . . You see, I'm chairman of the Science Department, so you can imagine what kind of a department it is.
>
> *Therapist:* You sort of feel that if you're in something that it can't be too good. Is that . . .
>
> *Client:* Well, it's not that I . . . It's just that I'm . . . I don't think that I could run it.
>
> *Therapist:* You don't have any confidence in yourself?
>
> *Client:* No confidence, no confidence in myself. I never had any confidence in myself. I—like I told you—like when even when I was a kid I didn't feel I was capable and I always wanted to get back with the intellectual group.
>
> *Therapist:* This has been a long-term thing, then. It's gone on a long time.
>
> *Client:* Yeah, the *feeling* is—even though I know it isn't, it's the feeling that I have that—that I haven't got it, that—that—that—people will find out that I'm dumb or—or . . .
>
> *Therapist:* Masquerade.
>
> *Client:* Superficial, I'm just superficial. There's nothing below the surface. Just superficial generalities, that . . .
>
> *Therapist:* There's nothing really deep and meaningful to you.
>
> *Client:* No—they don't know it, and . . .
>
> *Therapist:* And you're terrified they're going to find out.
>
> *Client:* My wife has a friend, and—and she and the friend got together so we could go out together with her and my wife and her husband. . . . And the guy, he's an engineer and he's you know—he's got it, you know; and I don't want to go, I

don't want to go because—because if—if we get together he's liable to start to—to talk about something I don't know, and I'll—I won't know about that.

Therapist: You'll show up very poorly in this kind of situation.

Client: That I—I'll show up poorly, that I'll—that I'll just clam up, that I . . .

Therapist: You're terribly frightened in this sort of thing.

Client: I—I'm afraid to be around people who—who I feel are my peers. Even in pool—now I—I play pool very well and—if I'm playing with some guy that I—I know I can beat, *psychologically*, I can run 50, but—but if I start playing with somebody that's my level, I'm done. I'm done. I—I—I'll miss a ball every time.

Therapist: So the . . . the fear of what's going on just immobilizes you, keeps you from doing a good job. (Hersher, 1970, pp. 29–32).

Rogers was not interested in comparing his therapy to others, nor was he concerned simply with statistics on outcomes (such as the percentage of clients who experienced emotional improvements). Rather, he wanted to discover those processes in client-centered therapy that were associated with positive results. Rogers's interest in the *process* of therapy resulted in important and lasting contributions to the field. For example, research has shown that a therapist's warmth and understanding increase success, no matter what therapeutic approach is used (Frank & Frank, 1991).

Gestalt Therapy

How is Gestalt therapy different from psychoanalysis?

Gestalt therapy is largely an outgrowth of the work of Frederick (Fritz) Perls at the Esalen Institute in California. Perls began his career as a psychoanalyst but later turned vehemently against Freud and psychoanalytic techniques. He felt that "Freud invented the couch because he could not look people in the eye" (Perls, 1969, p. 118). Gestalt therapy emphasizes the here and now and encourages face-to-face confrontations.

Gestalt therapy is designed to help people become more genuine or "real" in their day-to-day interactions. It may be conducted with individuals or with groups ("encounter groups"). The therapist is active and directive, and the emphasis is on the *whole* person (the term *Gestalt* means "whole"). The therapist's role is to "fill in the holes in the personality to make the person whole and complete again" (Perls, 1969, p. 2).

Gestalt therapists try to make people aware of their feelings using a variety of techniques. For example, they tell people to "own their feelings" by talking in an active rather than a passive way ("I feel angry when he's around" instead of "He makes me feel angry when he's around"). They also ask people to speak to a part of themselves they imagine to be sitting next to them in an empty chair. This *empty-chair technique* and others are illustrated in the following excerpt.

Therapist: Try to describe just what you are aware of at each moment as fully as possible. For instance, what are you aware of now?

Client: I'm aware of wanting to tell you about my problem, and also a sense of shame—yes, I feel very ashamed right now.

Therapist: Okay. I would like you to develop a dialogue with your feeling of shame. Put your shame in the empty chair over here *(indicates chair)*, and talk to it.

Client: Are you serious? I haven't even told you about my problem yet.

Therapist: That can wait—I'm perfectly serious, and I want to know what you have to say to your shame.

Client: (awkward and hesitant at first, but then becoming looser and more involved) Shame, I hate you. I wish you would leave me—you drive me crazy, always reminding me that I have a problem, that I'm perverse, different, shameful—even ugly. Why don't you leave me alone?

Therapist: Okay, now go to the empty chair, take the role of shame, and answer yourself back.

Gestalt therapy
An insight therapy that emphasizes the wholeness of the personality and attempts to reawaken people to their emotions and sensations in the here and now.

Client: (moves to the empty chair) I am your constant companion—and I don't *want* to leave you. I would feel lonely without you, and I don't hate you. I pity you, and I pity your attempts to shake me loose, because you are doomed to failure.

Therapist: Okay, now go back to your original chair and answer back.

Client: (once again as himself) How do you know I'm doomed to failure? *(Spontaneously shifts chairs now, no longer needing direction from the therapist; answers himself back, once again in the role of shame.)* I know that you're doomed to failure because *I* want you to fail and because I control your life. You can't make a single move without me. For all you know, you were *born* with me. You can hardly remember a single moment when you were without me, totally unafraid that I would spring up and suddenly remind you of your loathsomeness. *(Client again speaking as himself.)* You're right; so far you *have* controlled my life—I feel constantly embarrassed and awkward. *(His voice grows stronger.)* But that doesn't mean that you'll continue to control my life. That's why I've come here—to find some way of destroying you. *(Shifts to the "shame" chair.)* Do you think *he* can help you? *(As shame, points to the therapist.)* What can he do? He hardly knows you as I know you. Besides, he's only going to see you once or twice each week. I am with you every single moment of every day!

Therapist: Bill, look how one hand keeps rubbing the other when you speak for shame. Could you exaggerate that motion? Who does that remind you of?

Client: (rubbing his hands together harder and harder) My mother would do this— yes, whenever she was nervous she would rub her hands harder and harder.

Therapist: Okay, now speak for your mother. (Shaffer, 1978, pp. 92–93)

In this way the client becomes more aware of conflicting inner feelings and, with insight, can become more genuine.

Recent Developments

What are some recent developments in insight therapies?

Although Freud, Rogers, and Perls originated the three major forms of insight therapy, others have developed hundreds of variations on this theme. Most involve a therapist who is far more active and emotionally engaged with clients than traditional psychoanalysts thought fit. These therapists give clients direct guidance and feedback, commenting on what they are told rather than just listening to their clients in a neutral manner. Most of these newer therapies are also much shorter-term than traditional psychoanalysis. Insight remains the goal of so-called **short-term psychodynamic therapy,** but the treatment is usually time-limited—for example, to 25 sessions. This trend is based on research showing that most people (75 percent) experience improvement in this time frame (Howard et al., 1986), even though longer therapy may often be even more beneficial (Seligman, 1995). Finally, with the trend to a time-limited framework, insight therapies have become more symptom-oriented, trying to help clients correct the *immediate* problems in their lives. They see people as less at the mercy of early childhood events than Freud did. Although they do not discount childhood experiences, they focus on the client's current life situation and relationships.

REVIEW QUESTIONS

1. Which of the following is the major goal of working through problems in psychoanalysis?
   a. free association
   b. positive transference
   c. countertransference
   d. insight

2. Insight therapies focus on giving people
   a. skills to change their behavior.
   b. clearer understanding of their feelings, motives, and actions.
   c. an understanding of perceptual processes.
   d. an understanding of biological influences on behavior.

Short-term psychodynamic therapy
Insight therapy that is time-limited and focused on trying to help clients correct the immediate problems in their lives.

3. Which of the following is *not* a type of insight therapy?
   a. client-centered therapy
   b. psychoanalysis
   c. Gestalt therapy
   d. Beck's cognitive therapy
4. ____ ____ is a technique in psychoanalysis whereby the patient lets thoughts flow without interruption or inhibition.
5. The process called ____ involves clients projecting their feelings toward authority figures onto their therapist.
6. Rogerian therapists show that they value and accept their clients by providing them with ____ ____ regard.

   Indicate whether the following are true (T) or false (F).

7. Psychoanalysis is based on the belief that problems are symptoms of inner conflicts dating back to childhood. ____
8. Rogers's interest in the process of therapy was one avenue of exploration that did not prove very fruitful. ____
9. In Gestalt therapy the therapist is active and directive. ____
10. Gestalt therapy emphasizes the client's problems in the here and now. ____

Answers: 1. d. 2. b. 3. d. 4. free association. 5. transference. 6. unconditional positive. 7. T. 8. F. 9. T. 10. T

Behavior Therapies

What do behaviorists believe should be the focus of psychotherapy?

Behavior therapies sharply contrast with insight-oriented approaches. They concentrate on changing people's *behavior* rather than on discovering insights into their thoughts and feelings. Behavior therapies are based on the belief that all behavior, both normal and abnormal, is learned. Hypochondriacs *learn* that they get attention when they are sick; paranoid personalities *learn* to be suspicious of others. It is also assumed that maladaptive behaviors *are* the problem, not symptoms of deeper underlying causes. If behavior therapists can teach people to behave in more appropriate ways, they believe they have cured the problem. The therapist does not need to know exactly how or why people learned to behave abnormally in the first place. The job of the therapist is simply to teach people new, more satisfying ways of behaving based on scientifically studied principles of learning, such as classical conditioning, operant conditioning, and modeling.

Therapies Based on Classical Conditioning

How can classical conditioning be used as the basis of treatment?

As you saw in Chapter 5, Learning, *classical conditioning* involves the repeated pairing of a neutral stimulus with one that evokes a certain reflex response. Eventually the formerly neutral stimulus alone comes to elicit the same response. The approach is one of learned stimulus-response associations. Several variations on classical conditioning have been used to treat psychological problems.

Desensitization, Extinction, and Flooding   **Systematic desensitization,** a method for gradually reducing fear and anxiety, is one of the oldest behavior therapy techniques (Wolpe, 1990). The method works by gradually associating a new response (relaxation) with stimuli that have been causing anxiety. For example, an aspiring politician might seek therapy because he is very anxious about speaking to crowds. The therapist explores the kinds of crowds that are most threatening: Is an audience of 500 worse than one of 50? Is it

Behavior therapies
Therapeutic approaches that are based on the belief that all behavior, normal and abnormal, is learned, and that the objective of therapy is to teach people new, more satisfying ways of behaving.

Systematic desensitization
A behavioral technique for reducing a person's fear and anxiety by gradually associating a new response (relaxation) with stimuli that have been causing the fear and anxiety.

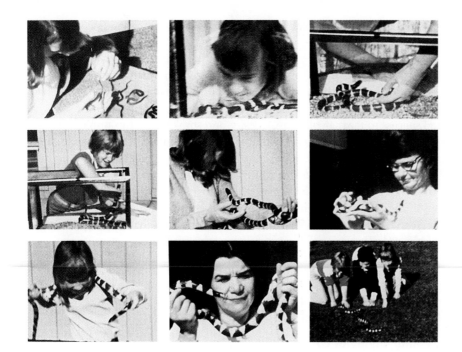

The clients in these photographs are overcoming a simple phobia: fear of snakes. After practicing a technique of deep relaxation, clients in desensitization therapy work from the bottom of their hierarchy of fears up to the situation that provokes the greatest fear or anxiety. Here, clients progress from handling rubber snakes (top left) to viewing live snakes through a window (top center) and finally to handling live snakes. This procedure can also be conducted vicariously in the therapist's office, where clients combine relaxation techniques with imagining anxiety-provoking scenes.

harder to speak to men than it is to women? Is there more anxiety facing strangers than a roomful of friends? From this information the therapist develops a *hierarchy of fears*—a list of situations from the least to the most anxiety-provoking. The therapist then teaches the client how to relax, including both mental and physical techniques of relaxation. Once the client has mastered deep relaxation, he or she begins work at the bottom of the hierarchy of fears. The client is told to relax while imagining the least threatening situation on the list, then the next most threatening, and so on, until the most fear-arousing one is reached and the client can still remain calm.

Numerous studies show that systematic desensitization helps many people overcome their fears and phobias (Wolpe, 1990). The key to its success may not be the learning of a new conditioned relaxation response but rather the *extinction* of the old fear response through mere exposure. Recall from Chapter 5 that in classical conditioning extinction occurs when the learned, conditioned stimulus is repeatedly presented without the unconditioned stimulus following. Thus if a person repeatedly imagines a frightening situation without actually encountering danger, the fear associated with that situation should gradually decline.

Desensitization is most effective when clients gradually confront their fears in the real world rather than merely in their imaginations. People who are deathly afraid of flying, for example, might first simply drive to an airport. When they are able to do this without anxiety, they may move on to walking near a plane on the ground. When they can do that calmly, they may go inside a stationary plane. Eventually they may take a short flight. This commonsense approach of working step by step through a hierarchy of fears in real life is probably familiar to you. For example, folk wisdom says that if you fall off a horse, the best way to get over your fear of riding is to get right back on the horse and continue to ride until the fear is gone. That's an example of desensitization in the real world.

The technique of *flooding* is a less familiar and more frightening method of desensitization. It involves full-intensity exposure to a feared stimulus for a prolonged period of time (O'Leary & Wilson, 1987; Wolpe, 1990). For example, someone with a powerful fear of snakes might be forced to handle dozens of snakes, or someone with an overwhelming fear of spiders might be forced to stroke a tarantula and allow it to crawl up an arm. If you think that flooding is an unnecessarily harsh method, keep in mind how debilitating many untreated anxiety disorders can be (see Chapter 12).

Aversive Conditioning   Another classical conditioning technique is **aversive conditioning**, in which pain and discomfort are associated with the behavior that the client wants to unlearn. Aversive conditioning has been used with limited success to treat alcoholism, obesity, and smoking. For example, the taste and smell of alcohol are sometimes paired with drug-induced nausea and vomiting. Before long, patients feel sick just seeing a bottle of liquor. A follow-up study of nearly 800 patients who completed alcohol-aversion treatment found that 63 percent had maintained continuous abstinence for at least 12 months (Wiens & Menustik, 1983). Still, the use of aversive conditioning has declined in recent years partly because its long-term effectiveness has been questioned. When the punishment no longer follows, the undesired behavior may reemerge. In addition, aversive conditioning is a controversial technique because of its unpleasant nature.

Therapies Based on Operant Conditioning

How could "behavior contracting" improve your study habits?

In *operant conditioning* a person learns to behave in a certain way because that behavior is reinforced, or rewarded. One therapy based on the principle of reinforcement is called **behavior contracting**. The therapist and the client agree on behavioral goals and on the reinforcement that the client will receive when he or she reaches those goals. These goals and reinforcements are often written in a contract that binds both the client and the therapist, as if by legal agreement. For instance, a contract to help a person stop smoking might read: "For each day that I smoke fewer than 20 cigarettes, I will earn 30 minutes of time to go bowling. For each day that I exceed the goal, I will lose 30 minutes from the time that I have accumulated."

Another therapy based on operant conditioning is called the **token economy**. Token economies are usually used in schools and hospitals, where controlled conditions are most feasible (O'Leary & Wilson, 1987). People are rewarded with tokens or points for behaviors that are considered appropriate and adaptive. The tokens or points can be exchanged for desired items and privileges. On the ward of a mental hospital, for example, improved grooming habits might earn points that can be used to purchase special foods or weekend passes. Token economies have proved effective in modifying the behavior of patients, such as people with chronic schizophrenia, who are resistant to other forms of treatment (Paul, 1982; Paul & Lentz, 1977). The positive changes in behavior, however, do not always generalize to everyday life outside the hospital or clinic, where adaptive behavior is not always reinforced and maladaptive behavior punished.

Therapies Based on Modeling

What are some therapeutic uses of modeling?

Modeling—the process of learning a behavior by watching someone else perform it—can also be used to treat problem behaviors. For instance, one group of researchers helped people to overcome a snake phobia by showing films in which models confronted snakes and gradually moved closer and closer to them (Bandura, Blanchard, & Ritter, 1969). Similar techniques have succeeded in reducing such common phobias as fear of dental work (Melamed et al., 1975). Moreover, a combination of modeling and positive reinforcement was successful in helping schizophrenic patients learn and use appropri-

---

Aversive conditioning
Behavioral therapy techniques aimed at eliminating undesirable behavior patterns by teaching the person to associate them with pain and discomfort.

Behavior contracting
Form of operant conditioning therapy in which the client and therapist set behavioral goals and agree on reinforcements that the client will receive on reaching those goals.

Token economy
An operant conditioning therapy in which patients earn tokens (reinforcers) for desired behaviors and exchange them for desired items or privileges.

Modeling
A behavior therapy in which the person learns desired behaviors by watching others perform those behaviors.

ate behavior both inside and outside the hospital (Bellack, Hersen, & Turner, 1976). Modeling has also been used to teach people with mental retardation job skills and appropriate responses to problems encountered at work (La-Greca, Stone, & Bell, 1983).

REVIEW QUESTIONS

1. In contrast to ____ therapies, which seek to increase clients' self-awareness, ____therapies teach people more appropriate ways of acting.
2. The behavioral technique of ____ ____ trains people to remain relaxed and calm in the presence of a formerly feared stimulus.
3. The behavior therapy known as ____ conditioning discourages undesirable behaviors by associating them with discomfort.
4. The therapeutic use of rewards to encourage desired behavior is based on a form of learning called ____ ____.
5. When client and therapist agree on a written set of behavioral goals and a specific schedule of reinforcement when each goal is met, they are using a technique called ____ ____.
6. "Therapy based on classical conditioning involves learning desired behaviors by watching others perform those actions." True or false.
7. A ____ ____ is an operant conditioning technique in which people earn some tangible item for desired behavior, which can then be exchanged for more basic rewards and privileges.
8. "Extinction occurs when a conditioned stimulus is repeatedly presented without the unconditioned stimulus being present." True or false.
9. The technique of ____ involves intense and prolonged exposure to something feared.

Answers: 1. insight, behavior. 2. systematic desensitization. 3. aversive. 4. operant conditioning. 5. behavior contracting. 6. F. 7. token economy. 8. T. 9. flooding.

Cognitive Therapies

How do cognitive therapies differ from behavior therapies?

Cognitive therapies are based on the belief that if people can change their distorted ideas about themselves and the world, they can also change their problem behaviors and make their lives more enjoyable. The task facing cognitive therapists is to identify such erroneous ways of thinking and to correct them. This focus on learning new ways of thinking shares many similarities with behavior therapies, which also focus on learning. In fact, many professionals consider themselves to be *cognitive behavior therapists*—therapists who combine both cognitive and behavior therapies (Brewin, 1996). Three popular forms of cognitive therapy are stress inoculation, rational-emotive therapy, and Aaron Beck's cognitive approach.

Stress-Inoculation Therapy

How can self-talk help us deal with difficult situations?

As we go about our lives we talk to ourselves constantly—proposing courses of action, commenting on our performance, expressing wishes, and so on. **Stress-inoculation therapy** makes use of this self-talk to help clients cope with stressful situations (Meichenbaum & Cameron, 1982). The client is taught to suppress any negative, anxiety-evoking thoughts and to replace them with positive, "coping" thoughts. Take a student with exam anxiety who faces every test telling herself, "Oh no, another test. I'm so nervous. I'm sure I won't think

Cognitive therapies
Psychotherapies that emphasize changing clients' perceptions of their life situation as a way of modifying their behavior.

Stress-inoculation therapy
A type of cognitive therapy that trains clients to cope with stressful situations by learning a more useful pattern of self-talk.

calmly enough to remember the answers. If only I'd studied more. If I don't get through this course, I'll never graduate!" This pattern of thought is highly dysfunctional because it only makes anxiety worse. With the help of a cognitive therapist, the student learns a new pattern of self-talk: "I studied hard for this exam, and I know the material well. I looked at the textbook last night and reviewed my notes. I should be able to do well. If some questions are hard, they won't all be, and even if it's tough, my whole grade doesn't depend on just one test." Then the client tries out the new strategy in a real situation, ideally one of only moderate stress (like a short quiz). Finally, the person is ready to use the strategy in a more stressful situation (like a final exam). Stress-inoculation therapy works by turning the client's thought patterns into a kind of vaccine against stress-induced anxiety.

Rational-Emotive Therapy

What irrational beliefs do many people hold?

Another type of cognitive therapy, **rational-emotive therapy (RET)**, developed by Albert Ellis (1973), is based on the view that most people in need of therapy hold a set of irrational and self-defeating beliefs. They believe they should be competent at *everything*, liked by *everyone*, *always* treated fairly, quick to find solutions to *every* problem, and so forth. Such beliefs involve absolutes—"musts" and "shoulds"—that allow for no exceptions, no room for making mistakes. When people with such irrational beliefs come up against real-life struggles, they often experience excessive psychological distress. For example, when a college student who believes he must be liked by everyone isn't invited to join a certain fraternity, he may view the rejection as a catastrophe and become deeply depressed rather than just feeling disappointed.

Rational-emotive therapists confront such dysfunctional beliefs vigorously, using a variety of techniques, including persuasion, challenge, commands, and theoretical arguments. Studies have shown that RET often does enable people to reinterpret their negative beliefs and experiences in a more positive light, decreasing the likelihood of becoming depressed (Blatt et al., 1996; Bruder et al., 1997). Consider the following excerpt from a rational-emotive therapy session in which a person is concerned about being a bad teacher.

> *Therapist:* Don't you think there are lots of teachers in the school system who are not very good teachers?
> *Client:* Yes, I know there are a lot of them, and I don't respect them. I don't feel they should be teachers if they aren't qualified.
> *Therapist:* So you're saying that you don't respect yourself, if you act ineffectively as a teacher. Right?
> *Client:* Yes, I wouldn't respect myself.
> *Therapist:* Why not?
> *Client:* Because if . . . well, it wouldn't be right to say that I'm teaching when . . . if I haven't got the qualifications, if I'm not capable to do the job.
> *Therapist:* Let's assume you're a lousy teacher. . . . You are a lousy teacher and may always be a lousy teacher. Why are you tying that aspect of you up with your total self? I am a slob because my teaching is slobbish. Do you see any inconsistency with that conclusion?
> *Client:* No, but I agree that I would be . . . it would be a terrible thing if I were to teach and it wouldn't . . . and I wouldn't be capable. That it wouldn't be right. That would be like I was a fraud.
> *Therapist:* Well, yeah. What's terrible about that?
> *Client:* Well, it's terrible.
> *Therapist:* But according to you, about half or more of the teachers in the school system are not-so-hot teachers. Right?
> *Client:* Yes, and if I were the administrator, I would have to do something about that.

Rational-emotive therapy (RET)
A directive cognitive therapy based on the idea that clients' psychological distress is caused by irrational and self-defeating beliefs and that the therapist's job is to challenge such dysfunctional beliefs.

Therapist: Meaning fire them?
Client: Fire them.
Therapist: And then who would teach the kids?
Client: You mean, if I was the administrator I'd have to . . .
Therapist: Tolerate.
Client: To tolerate it. (Hersher, 1970, pp. 64–66)

Beck's Cognitive Therapy

How can cognitive therapy be used to combat depression?

One of the most important and promising forms of cognitive therapy was developed by Aaron Beck (1967) for the treatment of depression. It is usually known simply as **cognitive therapy** but is sometimes referred to as "Beck's cognitive therapy" to avoid confusion with the broader category of cognitive therapies.

Beck believes that depression results from inappropriately self-critical patterns of thought about the self. Such people have unrealistic expectations, magnify their failures, make sweeping negative generalizations about themselves from little evidence, notice only negative feedback from the outside world, and interpret anything less than total success as failure. This negative chain of thinking may often spiral downward from small setbacks, until the person concludes that he or she is worthless. According to Beck, this downward spiral of negative, distorted thoughts is at the heart of depression.

Beck's assumptions about the cause of depression are very similar to those underlying RET, but the style of treatment differs considerably. Cognitive therapists are much less challenging and confrontational than rational-emotive therapists. Instead they try to help clients examine each dysfunctional thought in a supportive but objectively scientific manner ("Are you *sure* your whole life will be totally ruined if you break up with Frank? What is your evidence for that? Didn't you once tell me how happy you were *before* you met him?"). Like RET, Beck's cognitive therapy tries to lead the client to more realistic and flexible ways of thinking.

REVIEW QUESTIONS

1. Developing new ways of thinking that lead to more adaptive behavior lies at the heart of all _____ therapies.

2. A therapist believes that her client suffers from self-defeating beliefs about himself based on unrealistic expectations. The focus of therapy is to change these beliefs to more rational ones. The therapist is probably using _____-_____ therapy techniques.

3. _____-_____ therapy trains clients to cope with stressful situations by learning a more positive pattern of self-talk.

4. Rational-emotive therapy, founded by Albert _____, assumes that most people in need of therapy hold a set of irrational and self-defeating beliefs.

5. An important form of cognitive therapy used to combat depression was developed by Aaron _____.

6. "The immediate focus in cognitive therapies is to help clients change their behaviors." True or false.

7. Which of the following statements is an irrational belief, according to rational-emotive therapy?

   a. I must be good at whatever I do.

   b. Everyone should like me.

   c. If this person leaves me, it will be the worst thing that ever happened to me.

   d. all of the above

Answers: 1. cognitive. 2. rational-emotive. 3. stress-inoculation. 4. Ellis. 5. Beck. 6. F. 7. d.

Cognitive therapy
Therapy that depends on identifying and changing inappropriately negative and self-critical patterns of thought.

Group Therapies

What are some advantages of group therapies?

Some therapists believe that treating several clients simultaneously is preferable to treating each alone. Such **group therapy** allows both client and therapist to see how the client acts around other people. If a client is painfully anxious and tongue-tied, chronically self-critical, or hostile and aggressive, these tendencies will show up quickly in a group.

Group therapies have other advantages, too. A good group offers social support, a feeling that one is not the only person in the world with problems. Group members can also help one another learn useful new behaviors (how to express feelings, how to disagree without antagonizing others). Interactions in a group can lead people toward insights into their own behavior, such as why they are so defensive or feel compelled to constantly complain. Finally, because group therapy consists of several clients "sharing" a therapist, it is less expensive for each participant than individual therapy is (Yalom, 1995).

There are many kinds of group therapy. Some groups follow the general outlines of the therapies we've already mentioned. Others are oriented toward a very specific goal, such as stopping smoking, drinking, or overeating. And some have a single but more open-ended goal—for example, a happier marriage. The *self-help group* is a particularly popular form of group therapy today. A list of some self-help organizations is included in the *Applying Psychology* box on page 468.

Self-Help Groups

Why are self-help groups so popular?

Because an estimated 40–45 million Americans suffer some kind of psychological problem, and because the cost of individual treatment can be so high, more and more people faced with life crises are turning to low-cost self-help groups. Most such groups are small, local gatherings of people who share a common problem or predicament and who provide mutual assistance. Alcoholics Anonymous is perhaps the best-known self-help group, but similar types of groups exist for people suffering from anorexia, arthritis, cancer, divorce, and drug abuse; for parents whose children have died or are chronically ill or handicapped; and for adolescents, retirees, overeaters, compulsive gamblers, AIDS victims, former mental patients, and people suffering from depression or anxiety. In short, there are self-help groups for virtually every conceivable life problem.

Do these self-help groups work? In many cases they apparently do. Alcoholics Anonymous has developed an enviable reputation for helping people cope with alcoholism. Research confirms that most group members express strong support for their groups (Riordan & Beggs, 1987), and studies that have directly measured the success of self-help groups have demonstrated that they can indeed be effective (Galanter, 1984; Pisani et al., 1993). Such groups also help to prevent more serious psychological disorders by reaching out to people who are near the limits of their ability to cope with stress. The social support they offer is particularly important in an age when divorce, geographic mobility, and other factors have reduced the ability of the family to comfort people.

Family Therapy

Who is the client in family therapy?

Family therapy is another form of group therapy (Lebow & Gurman, 1995; Molineux, 1985). Family therapists believe that it is a mistake to treat a client in a vacuum, making no attempt to meet the client's parents, spouse, and children, for if one person in the family is having problems it is often a signal that the en-

Group therapy can help to identify problems that a client has interacting with other people. The group also offers social support, helping clients to feel less alone with their problems.

Group therapy
Type of psychotherapy in which clients meet regularly to interact and help one another achieve insight into their feelings and behavior.

Family therapy
A form of group therapy that sees the family as at least partly responsible for the individual's problems and that seeks to change all family members' behaviors to the benefit of the family unit as well as the troubled individual.

tire family needs assistance. Family therapists do not try to reshape the personalities of family members (Gurman & Kniskern, 1990). Instead the primary goals of family therapy are improving family communication, encouraging family members to become more empathetic, getting them to share responsibilities, and reducing conflict within the family. To achieve these goals, all family members must believe that they will benefit from changes in their behavior.

Although family therapy is especially appropriate when there are problems between husband and wife or parents and children, it is increasingly being used when only one family member has a clear psychological disorder, such as schizophrenia, agoraphobia, or in some cases depression (Lebow & Gurman, 1996). The goal of treatment in these circumstances is to help the mentally healthy members of the family cope more effectively with the impact of the disorder on the family unit. The improved coping of the well-adjusted family members may in turn help the troubled person. Family therapy is also called for when a person's progress in individual therapy is slowed by the family for some reason (often because other family members have trouble adjusting to a client's improvement).

Unfortunately, not all families benefit from family therapy. Sometimes the problems are too entrenched. In the other cases important family members may be absent or unwilling to cooperate. In still others one family member monopolizes sessions, making it hard for anyone else's views to be heard. In all these cases a different therapeutic approach is needed.

Family therapy is often valuable even when only one family member has a clear psychological disorder.

Couple Therapy

What are some techniques used in couple therapy?

A third form of group therapy is **couple therapy,** which is designed to assist partners who are having difficulties with their relationship. In the past this therapy was generally called *marital therapy*, but the term "couple therapy" is considered more appropriate today because it captures the broad range of partners who may seek help (Oltmanns & Emery, 1998).

Most couple therapists concentrate on improving patterns of communication and mutual expectations. In *empathy training*, for example, each member of the couple is taught to share inner feelings and to listen to and understand the partner's feelings before responding to them. This technique requires that people spend more time listening, trying to grasp what is really being said, and less time in self-defensive rebuttal. Other couple therapists use behavioral techniques. For example, a couple might be helped to develop a schedule for exchanging specific caring actions, such as doing favors for each other or saying kind, supportive things. This approach may not sound very romantic, but proponents of it say it can break a cycle of dissatisfaction and hostility in a relationship and so is an important step in the right direction (Margolin, 1987).

Couple therapy for both partners is generally more effective than therapy for only one of them (Dunn & Schwebel, 1995). For instance, one study found that when two married partners underwent therapy together, 56 percent were still married 5 years later, as opposed to only 29 percent who underwent therapy separately (Cookerly, 1980).

REVIEW QUESTIONS

1. Which of the following is an advantage of group therapy?
   a. The client has the experience of interacting with other people in a therapeutic setting.
   b. It often reveals a client's problems more quickly than individual therapy.
   c. It can be cheaper than individual therapy.
   d. all of the above

Couple therapy
A form of group therapy intended to help troubled partners improve their problems of communication and interaction.

APPLYING PSYCHOLOGY

How to Find Help

The idea that seeking help for psychological problems is a sign that you are "crazy" or "not strong enough" to help yourself is very common in our society. But the fact is that tens of thousands of people are helped by psychological counseling and therapy every year. These people include business executives, artists, sports heroes, celebrities—and students. Therapy is a common, useful aid in coping with daily life.

College is a time of stress and anxiety for many people. The pressure of work, the competition for grades, the exposure to many different kinds of people with unfamiliar views, the tension of relating to peers—all these factors take a psychological toll, especially for students away from home for the first time. Most colleges and universities have their own counseling services, and many of them are as sophisticated as the best clinics in the country. Most communities also have mental health programs. As an aid to a potential search for the right counseling service, we include here a list of

some of the other available resources for people who would like the advice of a mental health professional. Many of these services have national offices that will provide you with local branches and the appropriate people to contact in your area.

For Alcohol and Drug Abuse

National Clearinghouse for Alcohol and Drug Information
P.O. Box 2345
Rockville, MD 20847-2345
(301) 468-2600

General Service Board Alcoholics Anonymous, Inc.
P.O. Box 459, Grand Central Station
New York, NY 10163
(212) 870-3400

For Those with a Friend or Relative Who Has an Alcohol Problem

Al-Anon Family Groups
1600 Corporate Landing Parkway
Virginia Beach, VA 23454
(888) 4alanon (meeting information)

(757) 563-1600 (personal assistance)
Web site: www.alanon.alateen.org

National Association for Children of Alcoholics
11426 Rockville Pike
Rockville, MD 20852
(301) 468-0985

For Eating Abuses

Overeaters Anonymous
(323) 460-2459

For Depression and Suicide

Mental Health Counseling Hotline
33 East End Avenue
New York, NY 10028
(212) 734-5876

International Association for Suicide Prevention Suicide Prevention Center
(213) 381-5111

Heartbeat (for survivors of suicides)
2015 Devon Street
Colorado Springs, CO 80909
(719) 596-2575

2. A form of therapy that sees an individual's problems as related to relationships within the family system is called ____ therapy.
3. Marital therapy is now called ____ therapy to include a broader range of partners who may seek help together.
4. "Group therapy is always the preferred type of therapy." True or false.
5. A widely popular form of group therapy today is the ____-____ group.

Answers: 1. d. 2. family. 3. couple. 4. F. 5. self-help.

Effectiveness of Psychotherapy

How much better off is a person who receives psychotherapy than one who gets no treatment at all?

We have already mentioned that certain psychotherapies are generally effective. But how much better are they than no treatment at all? The British psychologist Hans Eysenck (1952) was one of the first investigators to raise questions about the effectiveness of psychotherapy. After surveying 19 published reports covering more than 7,000 cases, Eysenck concluded that therapy significantly helped about

For Sexual and Sex-Related Problems

Sex Information and Education Council of the United States (SIECUS)
130 W. 42nd Street, Suite 350
New York, NY 10036-7802
(212) 819-9770

National Organization for Women
Legislative Office
1000 16th Street, N.W.
Washington, DC 20036
(202) 331-0066

National Clearinghouse on Marital and Date Rape
2325 Oak Street
Berkeley, CA 94708
(510) 524-1582 (fee required)

People against Rape
P.O. Box 5876
Naperville, IL 60567-5876
(630) 717-0310

For Physical Abuse

Child Abuse Listening and Mediation (CALM)

P.O. Box 90754
Santa Barbara, CA 93190-0754
(805) 965-2376
(805) 692-4011 (hotline)

For Stress

Anxiety Disorders Association of America
6000 Executive Boulevard, Suite 513
Rockville, MD 20852
(301) 231-8368

For Help in Selecting a Therapist

Depressives Anonymous: Recovery from Depression
(212) 689-2600

National Mental Health Consumer Self-Help Clearinghouse
(215) 751-1810

Mental Health Help Line
(212) 222-7666

For General Information on Mental Health and Counseling

The National Alliance for the Mentally Ill
200 N. Glebe Road, Suite 1015

Arlington, VA 22203
(703) 524-7600

The National Mental Health Association
1021 Prince Street
Alexandria, VA 22314
(703) 684-7722

The American Psychiatric Association
1400 K Street. N.W.
Washington, DC 20005
(202) 682-6000

The American Psychological Association
750 1st Street, N.E.
Washington, DC 20002
(202) 336-5500

The National Institute of Mental Health
5600 Fishers Lane
Rockville, MD 20857
(301) 443-4513

To learn more about finding help, visit our Web site at **www. pren-hall.com/morris.**

---

2 out of 3 people. Yet he also calculated that roughly the same proportion of neurotic patients improve to a marked extent within about 2 years even without any treatment. This second conclusion caused a storm of controversy and stimulated much research. Many questioned the high "spontaneous recovery" rate of the no-therapy control subjects in the studies Eysenck surveyed (Bergin & Lambert, 1978). They concluded that only about 1 out of every 3 people improves without treatment (not the 2 out of 3 Eysenck cited). Because twice as many people improve with formal therapy, therapy is indeed more effective than no treatment at all (Borkovec & Costello, 1993; Lambert, Shapiro, & Bergin, 1986). Furthermore, many people who do not receive formal therapy get therapeutic help from friends, clergy, physicians, and teachers. So the recovery rate for people who receive *no* therapeutic help at all is quite possibly even less than one-third.

Other attempts to study the effectiveness of psychotherapy have generally agreed that psychotherapy is effective (Lipsey & Wilson, 1993; Shapiro & Shapiro, 1982; Wampold et al., 1997), although its value appears to be related to a number of other factors. For instance, psychotherapy works best for relatively mild psychological problems (Kopta et al., 1994) and seems to provide the greatest benefits to people who really *want* to change (Orlinsky & Howard, 1994). There also seems to be greater improvement among people who have undergone

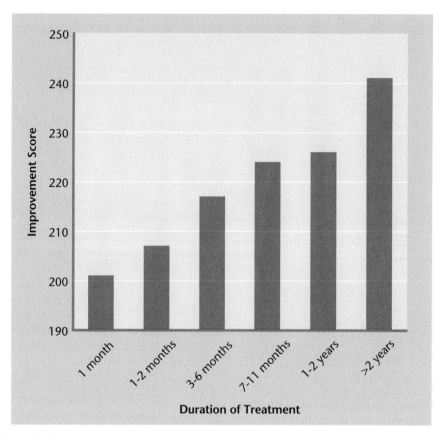

FIGURE 13–1

Duration of treatment and improvement.   One of the most dramatic results of a *Consumer Reports* (1995) study on the effectiveness of psychotherapy was the strong relationship between reported improvement and the duration of therapy.
Source: Adapted from Seligman (1995).

long-term therapy than among those who have received short-term treatments (Seligman, 1995). This last finding is illustrated in Figure 13–1.

Another important question is whether some forms of psychotherapy are more effective than others. Is behavior therapy, for example, more effective than insight therapy? In general, the answer seems to be "not much" (Garfield, 1983; Michelson, 1985; Smith, Glass, & Miller, 1980; Wampold et al., 1997). Most of the benefits of treatment seem to come from being in *some* kind of therapy, regardless of the particular type.

As we have seen, the various forms of psychotherapy are based on very different views about what causes mental disorders and, at least on the surface, approach the treatment of mental disorders in different ways. Why, then, is there no difference in their effectiveness? To answer this question some psychologists have focused their attention on what the various forms of psychotherapy have in common rather than emphasizing their differences (Barker, Funk, & Houston, 1988; Roberts et al., 1993). First, all forms of psychotherapy provide patients with an *explanation for their problems*. Along with this explanation often comes a new perspective providing patients with specific actions to help them cope more effectively. Second, most forms of psychotherapy offer patients *hope*. Because most people who seek therapy have low self-esteem and feel demoralized and depressed, hope and the expectation for improvement increase their feelings of self-worth. And third, all major types of psychotherapy engage the patient in a *therapeutic alliance* with a therapist. Although their therapeutic approaches may differ, effective therapists are warm, empathetic, and caring people who understand the importance of establishing a strong emotional bond with their patients built on mutual respect and understanding (Blatt et al., 1996). Together, these *nonspecific factors* common to all forms of psychotherapy appear, at least in part, to explain why most patients who receive any form of therapy show some benefits as compared with those who receive no therapeutic help at all.

Still, some kinds of psychotherapy seem to be particularly appropriate for certain people and problems. Insight therapy, for example, seems to be best suited to people seeking profound self-understanding, relief of inner conflict and anxiety, or better relationships with others. Behavior therapy is apparently most appropriate for treating specific anxieties or other well-defined behavioral problems, such as sexual dysfunctions. Cognitive therapies have been shown to be effective treatments for depression (Elkin et al., 1989; Robinson, Berman, & Neimeyer, 1990) and seem to be promising treatments for anxiety disorders as well. The trend in psychotherapy is toward **eclecticism**—that is, toward a recognition of the value of a broad treatment package rather than commitment to a single form of therapy (Norcross, Alford, & DeMichele, 1994).

REVIEW QUESTIONS

Indicate whether the following are true (T) or false (F).

1. In studies of the effectiveness of psychotherapy "no treatment" control groups can sometimes inadvertently include people who have had some form of help with their problem. ____

2. The consensus among studies of the effectiveness of psychotherapy is that psychotherapy is effective. ____

3. Behavior therapies have been shown to be effective for treating phobias and specific anxieties, while cognitive therapies have been shown to be effective for treating depression. ____

4. There is a trend among psychotherapists to combine treatment techniques in what is called ____.

5. Most researchers agree that psychotherapy helps about ____ ____ of the people treated.

6. Psychotherapy works best for relatively ____ disorders, as compared with ____ ones.

Answers: 1. T. 2. T. 3. T. 4. eclecticism. 5. two-thirds. 6. mild, severe.

Biological Treatments

What are biological treatments, and who can provide them?

Biological treatments—a group of approaches including medication, electroconvulsive therapy, and psychosurgery—may be used to treat psychological disorders in addition to, or instead of, psychotherapy. Patients or therapists select biological treatments for several reasons. First, some patients are too agitated, disoriented, or unresponsive to be helped by psychotherapies. In these cases therapists may use some kind of biological treatment to change clients' behavior so that they can benefit from psychotherapy. Second, biological treatment is virtually always used for disorders that have a strong biological component. Schizophrenia and bipolar disorder, for example, cannot be effectively treated with psychotherapy but often respond to medication. For other disorders, like depression, psychotherapy can be effective, but patients may prefer to take medication because it costs less, is more convenient, and allows them to avoid the stigma of seeing a psychotherapist. Third, biological treatment is often used for

Eclecticism
Psychotherapeutic approach that recognizes the value of a broad treatment package over a rigid commitment to one particular form of therapy.

Biological treatments
A group of approaches, including medication, electroconvulsive therapy, and psychosurgery, that are sometimes used to treat psychological disorders in conjunction with, or instead of, psychotherapy.

clients who are dangerous to themselves and to others, especially if they are residing in institutions where only a few therapists care for many patients. The only mental health professionals licensed to offer biological treatments are psychiatrists, who are physicians.

Drug Therapies

What are some of the drugs used to treat psychological disorders?

Medication is frequently and effectively used to treat a number of different psychological problems (see Table 13–1). In fact, Prozac, a drug used to treat depression, is today the best selling of all prescribed medications—including all drugs used to treat *physical* disorders (like antibiotics). Two major reasons for the widespread use of drug therapies today are the development of several very effective psychoactive medications and the fact that drug therapies cost less than psychotherapy. Another reason, critics charge, is our society's "pill mentality" (take a medicine to fix any problem). The medications used to treat psychological disorders are prescribed not only by psychiatrists but even more commonly by primary-care physicians such as family practitioners, pediatricians, and gynecologists.

Antipsychotic Drugs   Before the mid-1950s, drugs were not widely used to treat psychological disorders, because the only available sedatives induced sleep as well as calm. Then the major tranquilizers *reserpine* and the *phenothiazines* were introduced. In addition to alleviating anxiety and aggression, both drugs reduce psychotic symptoms, such as hallucinations and delusions, which is why they are called **antipsychotic drugs.** Antipsychotic drugs are prescribed primarily for very severe psychological disorders, particularly schizophrenia. They are very effective for treating schizophrenia's "positive symptoms," like hallucinations, but less effective for the "negative symptoms," like social withdrawal. Antipsychotic drugs work by blocking the brain's receptors for dopamine, a major neurotransmitter. The better a drug blocks these receptors, the more effective it is (Oltmanns & Emery, 1998).

Antipsychotics can sometimes have dramatic effects (Grinspoon, Ewalt, & Schader, 1972). People who take them can go from being perpetually fright-

TABLE 13-1	MAJOR TYPES OF PSYCHOACTIVE MEDICATIONS	
Therapeutic Use	**Chemical Structure***	**Trade Name***
Antipsychotics	Phenothiazines	Thorazine
Antidepressants	Tricyclics	Elavil
	MAO inhibitors	Nardil
	SSRIs	Prozac
Psychostimulants	Amphetamines	Dexedrine
	Other	Ritalin
Antimanic	(n.a.)	Tegretol
Anti-anxiety	Benzodiazepines	Valium
Sedatives	Barbiturates	
Antipanic	Tricyclics	Tofranil
Anti-obsessional	Tricyclics	Anafranil

*The chemical structures and especially the trade names listed in this table are often just one example of the many kinds of medications available for the specific therapeutic use.

Source: Klerman et al., 1994.

Antipsychotic drugs
Drugs used to treat very severe psychological disorders, particularly schizophrenia.

ened, angry, confused, and plagued by auditory and visual hallucinations to being totally free of such symptoms. But antipsychotic drugs can also have a number of undesirable side effects (Kane & Lieberman, 1992). Blurred vision and constipation are among the common complaints, as are temporary neurological impairments such as muscular rigidity or tremors. A very serious potential side effect is *tardive dyskinesia*, a permanent disturbance of motor control, particularly of the face (uncontrollable smacking of the lips, for instance), which can be only partially alleviated with other drugs (Diaz, 1997). The risk of tardive dyskinesia increases with the length of time antipsychotics are taken, which leads to another important point. Antipsychotic drugs do not cure schizophrenia; they only alleviate the symptoms while the patient is taking the drug. This means that most patients with schizophrenia must take antipsychotics for years—perhaps for the rest of their lives (Mueser & Glynn, 1995; Oltmanns & Emery, 1998).

Another problem is that antipsychotics are of little value in treating the problems of social adjustment that schizophrenic patients face outside an institutional setting. And because many discharged patients fail to take their medications, relapse is common. The relapse rate can be reduced if drug therapy is effectively combined with psychotherapy.

Antidepressant Drugs   A second group of drugs, known as *antidepressants*, are used to combat depression. Until the end of the 1980s there were only two main types of antidepressant drugs: *monoamine oxidase inhibitors (MAO inhibitors)* and *tricyclics* (named for their chemical properties). Both drugs work by increasing the concentration of the neurotransmitters serotonin and norepinephrine in the brain (McKim, 1997). Both are effective for most patients with serious depression, but both produce a number of serious and troublesome side effects. The MAO inhibitors require careful dietary restriction, as they can be lethal in combination with some foods. The tricyclics often cause blurred vision, dry mouth, dizziness, low blood pressure, constipation, and other problems. Because of the seriousness of these side effects, the search has continued for better antidepressant drugs.

In 1988 Prozac came onto the market. This drug works by reducing the uptake of serotonin in the nervous system, thus increasing the amount of serotonin active in the brain at any given moment. Prozac has fewer side effects than MAO inhibitors or tricyclics and has been heralded in the popular media as a "wonder drug" for the treatment of depression. Its widespread use is considered testimony to its effectiveness. We must be cautious in jumping to such conclusions, however. Prozac undoubtedly has helped many depressed people, but often because of its placebo effect—that is, Prozac frequently works because people believe it will work. This fact underscores the very important point that the success of an antidepressant medication does not mean that depression is caused by a "chemical imbalance in the brain." Aspirin relieves headaches, but this does not mean that a lack of aspirin is the cause of headaches. Although antidepressants clearly play an important role in the treatment of depression, some therapists are concerned that too many people are trying to solve their emotional problems with a pill rather than through their own efforts to cope with life more effectively.

Lithium   Bipolar disorder, or manic-depressive illness, is frequently treated with lithium carbonate. Lithium is not a drug but a naturally occurring salt that helps level out the wild and unpredictable mood swings of manic depression. Although it is effective in approximately 75 percent of cases, lithium is often prescribed along with antidepressants because it is slow to take effect (Solomon et al., 1995). We do not know exactly how lithium works, but it appears to affect the levels of serotonin and epinephrine in the brain (Oltmanns & Emery, 1998).

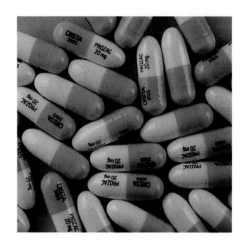

The antidepressant drug Prozac is now the best-selling medication in the United States.

Other Medications   Several other medications can be used to alleviate the symptoms of various psychological problems (see Table 13–1). *Psychostimulants*, for example, heighten alertness and arousal. They are also commonly used to treat children with attention-deficit/hyperactivity disorder. In these cases they have a calming rather than a stimulating effect. As with the antidepressants, some professionals worry that psychostimulants are being overused. *Anti-anxiety medications*, such as Valium, are commonly prescribed as well. Quickly producing a sense of calm and mild euphoria, they are often used to reduce general tension and stress. Because they are potentially addictive, however, they must be used with caution. Another class of drugs, the *sedatives*, produce both calm and drowsiness, and they are used to treat agitation or to induce sleep. These drugs, too, can become addictive. Finally, for reducing episodes of panic and alleviating obsessive-compulsive symptoms, certain types of *antidepressant medications* are effective (Klerman et al., 1994).

Electroconvulsive Therapy

How is the electroconvulsive therapy of today different from that of the past?

Electroconvulsive therapy (ECT) is most often used for cases of prolonged and severe depression that do not respond to other forms of treatment. The technique of ECT remained largely unchanged for many years. One electrode was placed on each side of the patient's head, and a mild current was turned on for a very short time (about 1.5 seconds). The electrical current passed from one side of the patient's brain to the other, producing a brief convulsion, followed by a temporary loss of consciousness. Muscle relaxants administered in advance prevented dangerously violent contractions. When patients awoke several minutes later, they normally had amnesia for the period immediately before the procedure and remained confused for the next hour or so. With repeated treatments, people often became disoriented, but this condition usually cleared after treatment concluded. Treatment normally consisted of 10 or fewer sessions of ECT.

Recently an important modification was made to traditional ECT. In this new procedure, called *unilateral ECT*, the electrical current is passed through only one side of the brain. Unilateral ECT produces fewer side effects, such as memory impairment and confusion, and is only slightly less effective than the traditional method (Diaz, 1997; Khan, 1993). Another modification uses less powerful electric currents for shorter durations (only 0.04 of a second), which also seems to lessen the severity of side effects.

No one knows exactly why ECT works, but evidence clearly demonstrates its effectiveness. In addition, the fatality rate for ECT is markedly lower than for patients taking antidepressant drugs (Henry, Alexander, & Sener, 1995). Still, ECT has many critics, and its use remains controversial. The procedure often produces memory loss, and it is certainly capable of damaging the brain. For these reasons, ECT is best considered a "last resort" treatment when all other methods have failed.

Psychosurgery

What is psychosurgery, and how is it used today?

Psychosurgery refers to brain surgery performed to change a person's behavior and emotional state. This is a drastic step, especially because the effects of psychosurgery are difficult to predict. In a *prefrontal lobotomy* the frontal lobes of the brain are severed from the deeper centers beneath them. The assumption is that in extremely disturbed patients the frontal lobes intensify emotional impulses from the lower brain centers (chiefly the thalamus and hypothalamus). Unfortunately, lobotomies can work with one person and fail completely with another—

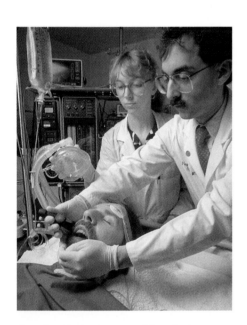

A patient being prepared for electroconvulsive therapy (ECT). Although no one knows precisely why ECT works, it has been successful in treating cases of severe, prolonged depression.

Electroconvulsive therapy (ECT)
Biological therapy in which a mild electrical current is passed through the brain for a short period, often producing convulsions and temporary coma; used to treat severe, prolonged depression.

Psychosurgery
Brain surgery performed to change a person's behavior and emotional state; a biological therapy rarely used today.

possibly producing permanent, undesirable side effects, such as the inability to inhibit impulses or a near-total absence of feeling.

Prefrontal lobotomies are rarely performed today. In fact, very few psychosurgical procedures are done nowadays except as desperate measures to control such conditions as intractable psychoses, epilepsy that does not respond to other treatments, severe obsessive-compulsive disorders (Baer et al., 1995), and pain in a terminal illness.

REVIEW QUESTIONS

1. The only mental health professionals licensed to provide drug therapy are ____.
2. All of the following are biological therapies *except*
   a. RET.
   b. ECT.
   c. drug therapy.
   d. psychosurgery.
3. Prozac, tricyclics, and monoamine oxidase inhibitors are all medications used for treating ____.
4. "One reason for the widespread use of drug therapy is that it costs less than psychotherapy." True or false.
5. Most antipsychotic drugs work by
   a. increasing acetylcholine in the brain.
   b. increasing serotonin in the brain.
   c. inhibiting the function of the hypothalamus.
   d. blocking dopamine receptors in the brain.
6. Which of the following is true of psychosurgery?
   a. It never produces undesirable side effects.
   b. It is useless in controlling pain.
   c. It is widely used today.
   d. Its effects are hard to predict.
7. Electroconvulsive therapy is considered ____ effective in treating cases of severe depression.
   a. hardly ever
   b. mildly
   c. highly
8. Match the following medications with the neurotransmitter(s) each is believed to influence.

   ____ monoamine oxidase inhibitors   a. norepinephrine

   ____ tricyclics   b. serotonin

   ____ Prozac   c. epinephrine

   ____ lithium
9. "Because of its potential negative side effects, ECT is considered a treatment of last resort." True or false.
10. Bipolar disorder (also called manic-depressive illness) is often treated with ____.

Answers: 1. psychiatrists. 2. a. 3. depression. 4. T. 5. d. 6. d. 7. c. 8. monoamine oxidase inhibitors: a and b; tricyclics: a and b; Prozac: b; lithium: b and c. 9. T. 10. lithium.

Caring for the Seriously Disturbed

How were people with severe psychological disorders cared for in the past?

For the severely mentally ill, hospitalization has been the treatment of choice in the United States for the past 150 years. Several different kinds of hospitals offer care to the mentally ill. General hospitals admit many people suffering from mental disorders, usually for short-term stays until they can be released to their families or to other institutional care. Private hospitals—some nonprofit and some for-profit—offer services to patients with adequate insurance. And for veterans with psychological disorders there are Veterans Administration hospitals.

When most people think of "mental hospitals," however, large, state-run institutions come to mind. These public hospitals, many with beds for thousands of patients, were often built in rural areas in the nineteenth century, the idea being that a country setting would calm patients and help to restore their mental health. Whatever the good intentions behind the establishment of these hospitals, for most of their history they have not provided adequate care or therapy for their residents. Perpetually underfunded and understaffed, state hospitals have often been little more than warehouses for victims of serious mental illness who were unwanted by their families. Except for new arrivals, who were often intensively treated in the hope of quickly discharging them, patients received little therapy besides drugs, and most spent their days watching television or staring into space. Under these conditions many patients became completely apathetic and accepted a permanent "sick role."

The development of effective drug therapies starting in the 1950s led to a number of changes in state hospitals. For one thing, patients who were agitated (engaging in violent behavior, for example) could now be sedated with drugs. Although the drugs often produced lethargy, this was considered an improvement over the use of physical restraints. The second major, and more lasting, result of the new drug therapies was the widespread release of patients with severe psychological disorders back into the community—a policy called **deinstitutionalization.** As you will see, this movement toward deinstitutionalization created new problems, both for patients and for society.

Deinstitutionalization

What problems have resulted from deinstitutionalization?

The advent of antipsychotic drugs in the 1950s created a favorable climate for deinstitutionalization, which was then strengthened in 1963, when Congress passed legislation establishing a network of community mental health centers around the nation. The practice of placing patients in smaller, more humane facilities or returning them under medication to care within the community intensified during the 1960s and 1970s. By 1975 there were 600 regional mental health centers accounting for 1.6 million cases of outpatient care.

In recent years, however, deinstitutionalization has created serious problems. Discharged patients often find poorly funded community mental health centers—or none at all. Many of these former patients are not prepared to live in the community, and they receive little guidance in coping with the mechanics of daily life. Those who return home can become a burden to their families, especially when they don't get adequate follow-up care. Residential centers, such as halfway houses, vary in quality, but many provide poor care and minimal contact with the outside world. Insufficient sheltered housing forces many former patients into nonpsychiatric facilities—often rooming houses located in dirty, unsafe, isolated neighborhoods. The patients are further burdened by the social stigma of mental illness, which may be the largest single obstacle to their rehabilitation. Moreover, although outpatient care is presumed to be a well-established national policy objective in mental health, Medicare, Medicaid, Blue Cross–Blue Shield, and other large insurers typically do not cover it completely (or nearly so) and limit the number of treatment visits.

The full effects of deinstitutionalization are not yet known. Few follow-up studies have been done on discharged patients, who are difficult to keep track of for long periods. But it is obvious that deinstitutionalization, though a worthy

Deinstitutionalization
Policy of treating people with severe psychological disorders in the larger community, or in small residential centers such as halfway houses, rather than in large public hospitals.

ideal, has had dire effects on patients and society. Many patients who were released were unable to obtain follow-up care or find housing and were incapable of looking after their own needs. Consequently many have ended up on the streets. Without supervision, they have stopped taking the drugs that made their release possible in the first place and have again become psychotic. Every major U.S. city now has a population of homeless mentally ill men and women living in makeshift shelters or sleeping in doorways, bus stations, parks, and other public spaces. Estimates of the percentage of homeless people who are mentally ill run from 10 percent to 47 percent of the total homeless population, which is gauged to be about 600,000 on any given night (Levine & Rog, 1990). This situation is not only tragic for the mentally ill homeless, who, often incoherent, are easy prey for criminals. It is also contributing to the coarsening of our society, as the public, finding the constant presence of "crazies" among them unpleasant, has begun to lose compassion for both the homeless and the mentally ill and to pressure public officials to "get them off the street." Most mental health professionals now agree that many chronically ill patients should not be released to live "in the community" without better planning, more funding, more community support, and readily available short-term rehospitalization for those who require it.

Alternative Forms of Treatment

Are there any alternatives to deinstitutionalization other than rehospitalizing patients?

For the past two decades Charles Kiesler has argued for a shift from the focus on institutionalization to forms of treatment that avoid hospitalization altogether (Kiesler & Simpkins, 1993). Kiesler (1982) examined 10 controlled studies in which seriously disturbed patients were randomly assigned either to hospitals or to an alternative program. The alternative programs took many forms: training patients living at home to cope with daily activities; assignment to a small, homelike facility in which staff and residents shared responsibility for residential life; placement in a hostel offering therapy and crisis intervention; providing family-crisis therapy and day-care treatment; providing visits from public-health nurses, combined with medication; and offering intensive outpatient counseling combined with medication. All of these alternatives involved daily professional contact and skillful preparation of the community to receive the patients. Even though the hospitals to which some people in these studies were assigned provided very good patient care—probably substantially above average for institutions in the United States—9 out of the 10 studies found that the outcome was more positive for alternative treatments than for the more expensive hospitalization. Moreover, the patients who received alternative care were less likely to undergo hospitalization later, which suggests that hospitalizing mental patients is a self-perpetuating process. Many such people "could be treated in alternative settings more effectively and less expensively," Kiesler concludes (1982, p. 358).

Prevention

What is the difference between primary, secondary, and tertiary prevention?

Yet another approach to serious mental illness is trying to prevent it in the first place. Such *prevention* requires finding and eliminating the conditions that cause or contribute to mental disorders and substituting conditions that foster well-being. Prevention takes three forms: primary, secondary, and tertiary.

Primary prevention refers to efforts to improve the overall environment so that new cases of mental disorders do not develop. Family planning and genetic counseling are two examples of primary prevention programs. They assist prospective

Lacking adequate funding and staff, mental hospitals frequently failed to provide adequate treatment to their residents. Beginning in the 1950s and 1960s, the policy of deinstitutionalization led to the release of many individuals, who, without proper follow-up care, ended up living on the streets. Although not all homeless people are mentally ill, estimates suggest that between 10 and 47 percent of homeless persons suffer from some type of mental disorder.

Primary prevention
Techniques and programs to improve the social environment so that new cases of mental disorders do not develop.

Suicide hotlines and other crisis intervention programs are secondary prevention measures designed to serve individuals and groups at high risk for mental disorders.

parents to think through such questions as how many children to have and when. They also provide testing to diagnose genetic defects in embyros, and they direct parents to treatments, including fetal surgery, that may be able to alleviate those defects before the baby is born. Other primary prevention programs aim at increasing personal and social competencies in a wide variety of groups. For example, there are programs designed to help mothers encourage problem-solving skills in their children and programs to enhance competence and adjustment among the elderly. Current campaigns to educate young people about drugs, violence, and date rape are other examples of primary prevention (Avery-Leaf et al., 1995).

Secondary prevention involves identifying groups at high risk for mental disorders—for example, abused children, people who have recently divorced, and those who have been laid off from their jobs. The main thrust of secondary prevention is *intervention* with such high-risk groups—that is, detecting maladaptive behavior early and treating it promptly. One form of intervention is *crisis intervention*, which includes such programs as suicide hotlines. Another is the establishment of short-term crisis facilities at which a therapist can provide face-to-face counseling and support.

The main objective of **tertiary prevention** is to help people adjust to community life after release from a mental hospital. For example, hospitals often grant passes to encourage patients to leave the institution for short periods of time prior to their release. Other tertiary prevention measures are halfway houses, where patients find support and skills training during the period of transition between hospitalization and full integration into the community, and nighttime and outpatient programs that provide supportive therapy while patients live at home and hold down a full-time job. Tertiary prevention also includes efforts to educate the community that the patient will re-enter.

Preventing behavior disorders has been the ideal of the mental health community since at least 1970, when the final report of the Joint Commission on Mental Health of Children called for a new focus on prevention in mental health work. Ironically, because preventive programs are usually long-range and indirect, they are often the first mental health programs to be eliminated in times of economic hardship. Such cuts, predicated on cost effectiveness, exemplify the old adage about being penny-wise and pound-foolish.

REVIEW QUESTIONS

1. The practice of treating severely mentally ill people in large, state-run facilities is known as ____.

2. "Many patients released from mental hospitals have ended up homeless and on the streets." True or false.

3. Which of the following were factors that helped promote deinstitutionalization?
   a. the development of effective antipsychotic drugs
   b. the establishment of a network of community mental health centers
   c. federal budget cuts in the 1960s
   d. all of the above

4. "Alternative treatments to hospitalizing people with severe mental disorders are less effective than hospitalization but have the benefit of costing less." True or false.

5. Match the following with the appropriate form of prevention.

   ____ halfway houses   a. primary prevention
   ____ educational TV commercials   b. secondary prevention
   ____ hotlines   c. tertiary prevention
   ____ crisis intervention
   ____ genetic counseling

Secondary prevention
Programs to identify groups that are at high risk for mental disorders and to detect maladaptive behavior in these groups and treat it promptly.

Tertiary prevention
Programs to help people adjust to community life after release from a mental hospital.

Answers: 1. institutionalization. 2. T. 3. a and b. 4. F. 5. halfway houses: c; TV commercials: a; hotlines: b; crisis intervention: b; genetic counseling: a.

Client Diversity and Treatment

Are there particular groups of people who may require special approaches in the treatment of psychological problems?

A major theme of this book is human diversity, the wide range of differences that exist in human beings. Although we all share certain basic human characteristics, as individuals and as groups we also have our own distinctive traits, our own distinctive ways of responding to the world. Do such human differences affect the treatment of psychological problems? Two areas that researchers have explored to answer this question are gender differences and cultural differences.

Gender Differences in Treatment

How can gender stereotypes be avoided in treatment?

In Chapter 12 we saw that there are some significant gender differences in the prevalence of many psychological disorders. Women are more likely than men to be in psychotherapy. One national survey found that 60 percent of those seeing psychologists and psychiatrists were women (Williams, 1987). In part, this is because women are more willing than men to admit that they have psychological problems and need help to solve them. Moreover, psychotherapy is more socially accepted for women than for men (Williams, 1987).

If there are gender differences in the prevalence of psychological disorders, are there gender differences in their treatment as well? In most respects the treatment given women is the same as that given men, a fact that has become somewhat controversial in recent years (Enns, 1993). Because most therapists are male and most vocational and rehabilitation programs are male-oriented, some critics of "equal treatment" have claimed that women in therapy are often encouraged to adopt traditional, male-oriented views of what is "normal" or "appropriate." For instance, male therapists tend to urge women to adapt or conform to their surroundings passively. They also tend to be insufficiently sensitive to the fact that much of the stress women experience comes from trying to cope with a world in which they are *not* treated equally (Brown & Ballou, 1992). For all these reasons there has been an increase recently in the number of "feminist therapists." These therapists help their female clients to become aware of the extent to which their problems derive from external controls and inappropriate sex roles, to become more conscious of and attentive to their own needs and goals, and to develop a sense of pride in their womanhood rather than passively accepting or identifying with the status quo.

Because most traditional therapeutic programs are male-oriented, many female clients seek out female therapists who are more sensitive to their situation.

Although in *most* respects women receive the same kinds of treatment men receive, there is one very important difference: Women receive a disproportionate share of the drugs prescribed for psychological disorders. Overall, more than 70 percent of all prescriptions written by psychiatrists are for women, although women account for only 58 percent of their office visits (Basow, 1986; Russo, 1985). Similarly, women receive 70 to 80 percent of all antidepressant medications, even though they make up only two-thirds of all cases of depressive disorders. We don't yet know the reasons for this sex bias in drug prescriptions, but it has become a source of considerable concern. Professionals' willingness to prescribe drugs to women may encourage women to see their problems as having physical causes. Moreover, the readiness to prescribe drugs for women at least partly accounts for women's tendency to abuse prescription drugs more often than men do (Russo, 1985).

As researchers continue to explore these various issues, the American Psychological Association has established a set of guidelines regarding treatment of women in psychotherapy:

1. The conduct of therapy should be free of constrictions based on gender-defined roles, and the options explored between client and practitioner should be free of sex-role stereotypes.

2. Psychologists should recognize the reality, variety, and implications of sex-discriminatory practices in society and should facilitate client examination of options in dealing with such practices.

3. The therapist should be knowledgeable about current empirical findings on sex roles, sexism, and individual differences resulting from the client's gender-defined identity.

4. The theoretical concepts used by the therapist should be free of sex bias and sex-role stereotypes.

5. The psychologist should demonstrate acceptance of women as equal to men by using language free of derogatory labels.

6. The psychologist should avoid establishing the source of personal problems within the client when they are more properly attributable to situational or cultural factors.

7. The psychologist and a fully informed client mutually should agree on aspects of the therapy relationship such as treatment modality, time factors, and fee arrangements.

8. While the importance of the availability of accurate information to a client's family is recognized, the privilege of communication about diagnosis, prognosis, and progress ultimately resides with the client, not with the therapist.

9. If authoritarian processes are used as a technique, the therapy should not have the effect of maintaining or reinforcing the stereotypic dependency of women.

10. The client's assertive behaviors should be respected.

11. The psychologist whose female client is subjected to violence in the form of physical abuse or rape should recognize and acknowledge that the client is the victim of a crime.

12. The psychologist should recognize and encourage exploration of a woman client's sexuality and should recognize her right to define her own sexual preferences.

13. The psychologist should not have sexual relations with a woman client nor treat her as a sex object. (APA, 1978)

Cultural Differences in Treatment

How can a therapist interact appropriately with clients from different cultures?

Imagine the following scenario: As a Native American client is interviewed by a psychologist, he stares at the floor. He answers questions politely, but during the entire consultation he looks away continually, never meeting the doctor's eye. This body language might lead the psychologist to suppose that the man is depressed or has low self-esteem. Unless, that is, the psychologist knows that in the client's culture not making eye contact is a sign of respect.

This example shows that our ideas of what constitutes normal behavior are culture-bound. When psychotherapist and client come from very different cultures, misunderstandings of speech, body language, and customs are almost inevitable. Even when client and therapist are of the same nationality and speak the same language, there can be striking differences if they belong to different racial and ethnic groups (Casas, 1995). Some black clients, for example, are wary of confiding in a white therapist—so much so that their wariness is sometimes mistaken for paranoia. For this reason many black clients seek out a black therapist, a tendency that is becoming more common as larger numbers of black middle-class people enter therapy (Williams, 1989).

One of the challenges for U.S. therapists in recent years has been to treat refugees from foreign countries, many of whom have fled such horrifying circumstances at home that they arrive in the United States exhibiting posttraumatic stress disorder. These refugees must overcome not only the effects of past trauma but also the new stresses of settling in a strange country, which often include separation from their families, ignorance of the English language, and inability to practice their traditional occupations. Therapists in such circumstances must learn something of their clients' culture. Often they have to conduct interviews through an interpreter—hardly an ideal circumstance for therapy.

Therapists need to recognize that some disorders that afflict people from other cultures may not exist in Western culture at all. For example, *Taijin Kyofusho* (roughly translated as "fear of people") involves a morbid fear that one's body or actions may be offensive to others. Because this disorder is rarely seen outside of Japan, American therapists require specialized training to identify it.

In August 1990 the American Psychological Association approved a document titled "Guidelines for Psychological Practice with Ethnic and Culturally Diverse Populations." In it the APA reminds practitioners that different groups may perform differently on psychological tests, express symptoms in different ways, and relate differently to family members and outsiders than members of the dominant population (Moses, 1990). In 1991, following practitioners' observations that in other countries the "standard" dosages of medication are quite different than in the United States, the National Institutes of Health began a study to measure the responses of different ethnic groups to several psychiatric medications (DeAngelis, 1991b).

Ultimately, however, the best solution to the difficulties of serving a multicultural population is to train therapists of many different backgrounds so that members of ethnic, cultural, and racial minorities can choose therapists of their own group if they wish to do so (Bernal & Castro, 1994). Research has shown that psychotherapy is more likely to be effective when the client and the therapist share a similar cultural background (Sue et al., 1994).

Many African American clients are more comfortable dealing with a therapist of the same racial background.

REVIEW QUESTIONS

Indicate whether the following are true (T) or false (F).

1. Men are more likely to be in psychotherapy than women. ____
2. Women receive a disproportionate share of the drugs prescribed for psychological problems. ____
3. An important point in the APA guidelines regarding the treatment of women in psychotherapy is that the therapy be free of constrictions based on gender roles and stereotypes. ____
4. Our ideas about what constitutes normal behavior are culture-bound. ____
5. Trained mental health professionals rarely misinterpret the body language of a client from another culture. ____
6. Research has shown that psychotherapy is more likely to be effective when the client and therapist share similar cultural backgrounds.

Answers: 1. F. 2. T. 3. T. 4. T. 5. F. 6. T.

KEY TERMS

psychotherapy, p. 454

Insight therapies
insight therapies, p. 454
psychoanalysis, p. 454
free association, p. 454
transference, p. 454
insight, p. 454
client-centered (or person-
centered) therapy, p. 456
Gestalt therapy, p. 458
short-term psychodynamic
therapy, p. 459

Behavior therapies
behavior therapies, p. 460
systematic desensitization,
p. 460
aversive conditioning
p. 462
behavior contracting,
p. 462
token economy, p. 462
modeling, p. 462

Cognitive therapies
cognitive therapies, p. 463

stress-inoculation therapy,
p. 463
rational-emotive therapy
(RET), p. 464
cognitive therapy, p. 465

Group therapies
group therapy, p. 466
family therapy, p. 466
couple therapy, p. 467

**Effectiveness of
psychotherapy**
eclecticism, p. 471

Biological treatments
biological treatments, p. 471
antipsychotic drugs, p. 472
electroconvulsive therapy
(ECT), p. 474
psychosurgery, p. 474

**Caring for the seriously
disturbed**
deinstitutionalization, p. 476
primary prevention, p. 477
secondary prevention, p. 478
tertiary prevention, p. 478

CHAPTER REVIEW

☐ **What do insight therapies have in common?**

Insight therapy is a major category of treatment for psychological problems. Insight therapies have in common the goal of providing people with better awareness and understanding of their feelings, motivations, and actions in the hope that this will lead to better adjustment. Three examples of insight therapies are psychoanalysis, client-centered therapy, and Gestalt therapy.

☐ **How does "free association" in psychoanalysis help a person to become aware of hidden feelings?**

Psychoanalysis is based on the belief that psychological problems stem from feelings and conflicts repressed during childhood. One way of uncovering what has been repressed is through the process of **free association,** in which the client discloses whatever thoughts or fantasies come to mind without editing or otherwise inhibiting them. As therapy progresses, the analyst takes a more active role and begins to interpret or suggest meanings for patients' feelings, memories, and actions.

☐ **Why did Carl Rogers call his approach to therapy "client-centered"?**

The insight therapy founded by Carl Rogers is built on the idea that treatment for psychological problems should be based on the client's view of the world rather than on the therapist's. This is why it is called **client-centered** or **person-centered therapy.** The therapist's most important task is to provide unconditional positive regard for clients so that they will learn to accept themselves.

☐ **How is Gestalt therapy different from psychoanalysis?**

Gestalt therapy grew out of the work of Fritz Perls and is designed to help people become more aware of their feelings and thus more genuine. Unlike Freud, who sat quietly out of sight while his clients free-associated to dredge up memories from the past, Perls believed that therapy should emphasize the here and now and face-to-face confrontations. The Gestalt therapist is much more active and directive than the psychoanalyst, and the focus is on the *whole* person.

☐ **What are some recent developments in insight therapies?**

Contemporary insight therapists are more active than traditional psychoanalysts, giving clients direct guidance and feedback. They are also more focused on clients' immediate problems than on their childhood traumas. An especially significant development is the trend to **short-term psychodynamic therapy,** which recognizes that most people can be successfully treated within a limited time frame.

☐ **What do behaviorists believe should be the focus of psychotherapy?**

Behavior therapies are based on the belief that all behavior, normal and abnormal, is learned and that the goal of therapy is to teach people more satisfying ways of behaving. To behaviorists the focus of psychotherapy should be the problem behaviors themselves, not some deeper, underlying conflicts that are presumably causing those behaviors.

☐ **How can classical conditioning be used as the basis of treatment?**

When therapies attempt to evoke new conditioned responses to old stimuli, they are using classical conditioning as a basis for treatment. One example is a technique called **systematic desensitization,** in which people learn to remain in a deeply relaxed state while confronting situations that they fear. *Flooding,* which exposes phobic people to feared situations at full intensity for a prolonged period, is a harsh but effective method of desensitization. In **aversive conditioning** the goal is to eliminate undesirable behavior by associating it with pain and discomfort.

☐ How could "behavior contracting" improve your study habits?

Therapies based on operant conditioning encourage or discourage behaviors by reinforcing or punishing them. In the technique called **behavior contracting,** client and therapist agree on certain behavioral goals and on the reinforcement that the client will receive on reaching them. To improve your study habits using behavioral contracting, you might reward yourself with pizza or a movie for a certain number of hours spent reading and taking careful notes. In another technique, called the **token economy,** tokens that can be exchanged for rewards are used for positive reinforcement.

☐ What are some therapeutic uses of modeling?

In **modeling** a person learns new behaviors by watching others perform them. Modeling has been used to teach fearless behaviors to phobic people, job skills to mentally retarded people, and more appropriate ways of responding to schizophrenic patients.

☐ How do cognitive therapies differ from behavior therapies?

Cognitive therapies focus not so much on maladaptive behaviors as on maladaptive ways of thinking. By changing people's distorted, self-defeating ideas about themselves and the world, cognitive therapies hope to encourage better coping skills and adjustment.

☐ How can self-talk help us to deal with difficult situations?

The things we say to ourselves as we go about our daily lives can encourage either success or failure, a self-confident outlook or acute anxiety. **Stress-inoculation therapy** takes advantage of this fact by teaching clients how to use self-talk to "coach" themselves through stressful situations.

☐ What irrational beliefs do many people hold?

Rational-emotive therapy (RET) is based on the idea that people's emotional problems derive from a set of irrational and self-defeating beliefs that they hold about themselves and the world. They think in terms of absolutes—they must be liked by *everyone*, competent at *everything*, *always* treated fairly, *never* stymied by a problem. The therapist vigorously challenges these beliefs until the client comes to see just how irrational and dysfunctional these beliefs are.

☐ How can cognitive therapy be used to combat depression?

Aaron Beck believes that depression results from negative patterns of thought—patterns that are strongly and inappro-priately self-critical. The depression-prone person magnifies failures and makes sweeping negative generalizations about the self based on little evidence. Beck's **cognitive therapy** tries to help such people think more objectively and positively about themselves and their life situations.

☐ What are some advantages of group therapies?

Group therapies are based on the idea that psychological problems are at least partly interpersonal and are therefore best approached in a group. Group therapies offer a circle of support for clients, shared insights into problems, and the opportunity to obtain psychotherapy at a lower cost. Among the many different kinds of group therapy are self-help groups, family therapy, and couple therapy.

☐ Why are self-help groups so popular?

As the cost of private psychotherapy has risen, self-help groups have become increasingly popular because of their low cost. In such groups, people share their concerns and feelings with others who are experiencing similar problems. Alcoholics Anonymous is a very effective self-help group.

☐ Who is the client in family therapy?

Family therapy is based on the idea that a person's psychological problems are to some extent family problems also. Therefore, the therapist treats the entire family rather than just the individual reportedly having difficulties. The major goals are to improve communication and empathy and to reduce conflict within the family.

☐ What are some techniques used in couple therapy?

Couple therapy concentrates on improving patterns of communication and interaction between couples. Like family therapy, it attempts to change relationships, not just individuals. Empathy training and scheduled exchanges of rewards are two of the techniques used to turn a hostile, unsatisfying relationship around.

☐ How much better off is a person who receives psychotherapy than one who gets no treatment at all?

Most researchers agree that psychotherapy helps about two-thirds of the people treated. Although there is some debate over how many untreated people also recover, the consensus is that those who get therapy are generally better off than those who don't. Each kind of therapy, however, works better for some problems than for others. The general trend in psychotherapy is toward **eclecticism,** the use of whatever treatment works best for a particular problem.

☐ What are biological treatments, and who can provide them?

Biological treatments—including medication, electroconvulsive therapy, and psychosurgery—are sometimes used when psychotherapy does not work or when a client has a disorder for which biological treatment is known to be safe and effective. Medication, especially, is very often used in conjunction with psychotherapy. Psychiatrists (who are also physicians) are the only mental health professionals licensed to offer biological treatments.

What are some of the drugs used to treat psychological disorders?

Drugs are the most common form of biological therapy. **Antipsychotic drugs** are valuable in treating schizophrenia. They do not cure the disorder, but they reduce its symptoms, although side effects can be severe. Antidepressant drugs alleviate depression, though some also have serious side effects. Many other types of medications are used to treat psychological disorders, including antimanic and antianxiety drugs, sedatives, and psychostimulants for children with attention-deficit/hyperactivity disorder.

How is the electroconvulsive therapy of today different from that of the past?

Electroconvulsive therapy (ECT) is used for cases of severe depression that do not respond to other treatments. An electric current briefly passed through the brain of the patient produces convulsions and temporary loss of consciousness, but afterward depression often lifts. Newer forms of ECT are given to only one side of the brain, use less powerful currents, and are applied for a shorter time.

What is psychosurgery, and how is it used today?

Psychosurgery is brain surgery performed to change a person's behavior and emotional state. It is rarely used today, and then only as a last, desperate measure on patients who have severe and intractable problems and don't respond to any other form of treatment.

How were people with severe psychological disorders cared for in the past?

In the past, institutionalization in large mental hospitals was the most common approach to caring for people with serious mental disorders. Patients were given shelter and some degree of treatment, but a great many were never able to be released. Then, with the advent of antipsychotic drugs, a trend began toward **deinstitutionalization**, or integrating patients with serious mental disorders back into the community.

What problems have resulted from deinstitutionalization?

The idea behind deinstitutionalization was that patients would be cared for in a community setting, but community mental health centers and other support services proved inadequate to the task. As a result, many former patients stopped taking their medication, became homeless, and ended up suffering from psychosis and living on the streets. Thus, although deinstitutionalization may have been a good idea in principle, in practice it has not worked out well for many patients or for society.

Are there any alternatives to deinstitutionalization other than rehospitalizing patients?

Alternatives to hospitalization include living in the family with adequate supports provided to all family members; living in small, homelike facilities in which residents and staff share responsibilities; and providing intensive outpatient counseling or frequent visits from public health nurses. Most alternative treatments involve some medication and skillful preparation of the family and community. Most studies have found more positive outcomes for alternative treatments than for hospitalization.

What is the difference between primary, secondary, and tertiary prevention?

Prevention refers to efforts to reduce the incidence of mental illness before it arises. **Primary prevention** consists of improving the social environment through assistance to parents, education, and family planning. **Secondary prevention** involves identifying high-risk groups and directing service to them. **Tertiary prevention** involves helping hospitalized patients return to the community.

Are there particular groups of people who may require special approaches in the treatment of psychological problems?

Given that human beings differ as much as they do, it isn't surprising that a one-size-fits-all concept isn't always appropriate in the treatment of psychological problems. In recent years the special needs of women and people from other cultures have particularly occupied the attention of mental health professionals.

How can gender stereotypes be avoided in treatment?

Women are more likely than men to be in psychotherapy, and they are more likely to be given psychoactive medication. Because, in traditional therapy, women are often expected to conform to gender stereotypes in order to be pronounced "well," many women have turned to "feminist therapists." The American Psychological Association has issued guidelines to ensure that women receive treatment that is not tied to traditional ideas about appropriate behavior for the sexes.

How can a therapist interact appropriately with clients from different cultures?

When client and therapist come from different cultural backgrounds or belong to different racial or ethnic groups, misunderstandings can arise in therapy. The APA has issued guidelines to help psychologists deal more effectively with our ethnically and culturally diverse population. Following these guidelines is an important step toward avoiding cultural misunderstandings.

CRITICAL THINKING AND APPLICATIONS

1. How do you think free association leads to insights in traditional psychoanalysis?

2. What are some of the major differences between insight therapies and behavior therapies in the treatment of psychological disorders? Do you agree with the behavioral view that undesirable behaviors *are* the problem, not symptoms of some underlying cause? Why or why not?

3. In what ways does cognitive therapy build on behavior therapy?

4. Do you think that deinstitutionalization of people with serious mental disorders was a good idea? Why or why not?

5. Does drug therapy encourage better results from psychotherapy, or does it interfere with psychotherapy because it takes away the discomfort that motivated the person to seek help? Discuss the reasons for your answer.

On the Web...

Visit these online resources at our Companion Website www.prenhall.com/morris

The Psychology Place

Research News
1. Beyond Shyness: Diagnosing and Treating Social Phobia, p. 472
2. Childhood and Adolescent Depression – To Medicate or Not?, p. 473
3. Mental Illness: Dangers, Treatment, and Civil Liberties, p. 476

Readings
1. Concern Over On-line Counseling, p. 469
2. How Much Therapy is Enough?, p. 469
3. Music is Good Medicine, p. 471
4. "Two-Plus-One" Therapy Works for Mild Depression, Study Shows, p. 471
5. The Age of Ritalin, p. 474
6. Federal Report Praising Electroshock Stirs Uproar, p. 474

Games
1. Goals of Therapy, p. 453

Web Links

1. **http://maple.lemoyne.edu/~hevern/psychref4-1.html**, p. 453
   PsychREF: Clinical Psychology and Psychiatry; Self-Help; Therapeutics. Offers links to general resources and links related to counseling and psychotherapy, psychoanalysis and psychodynamic psychotherapy, creative arts therapies, forensic psychology/psychiatry, and law/criminal justice.

2. **http://www.shef.ac.uk/~psysc/psastud/index.html**, p. 454
   Psychoanalytic Studies. Electronic and print journal from the Centre for Psychotherapeutic Studies, University of Sheffield.

3. **http://www.enabling.org/ia/gestalt/gerhards/archive.html**, p. 458
   Gestalt Archive–The International Society for Gestalt Theory and Its Applications.

4. **http://www.yalom.com**, p. 466
   Irwin Yalom – Group Therapy. Offers information about Yalom and directions for getting a better understanding of group therapy.

5. **http://maple.lemoyne.edu/~hevern/psychref4-2.html**, p. 472
   PsychREF: Psychopharmacology and Psychotherapy (Medications).

SOCIAL PSYCHOLOGY

OVERVIEW

Social Cognition
☐ Impression Formation
☐ Attribution
☐ Interpersonal Attraction

Attitudes
☐ The Nature of Attitudes
☐ Prejudice and Discrimination
☐ Attitude Change

Social Influence
☐ Cultural Influences
☐ Conformity
☐ Compliance
☐ Obedience

Social Action
☐ Deindividuation
☐ Helping Behavior
☐ Group Dynamics
☐ Organizational Behavior

I N 1939, WHEN THE GERMANS OCCUPIED WARSAW, POLAND, THE NAZI army segregated the city's Jews into a ghetto surrounded by barbed wire. Deeply concerned about the fate of her Jewish friends, a 16-year-old Catholic girl named Stefania Podgórska made secret expeditions into the ghetto with gifts of food, clothing, and medicine. When the Jewish son of her former landlord made a desperate flight from the ghetto to avoid being deported to a concentration camp, Stefania agreed to hide him in her apartment. At one point, Stefania and her sister sheltered 13 Jews in their attic at the same time that two German soldiers were bivouacked in their small apartment.

In May of 1991 the "hidden children" of the Holocaust gathered with their friends and relatives to pay tribute to 22 Christian rescuers who literally saved their lives during World War II.

- Gustave Collet, one of the people honored, was a Belgian soldier during World War II who helped hundreds of Jewish children by hiding them in the sanctuary of a Catholic church. According to Gustave, "We all are the sons of the same Father, and there is no reason there should be differences."
- Gisela Sohnlein, a student during World War II and a member of the Dutch underground, helped save thousands of Jewish children. In 1943 she was arrested by Nazi soldiers and spent 1½ years in a concentration camp. According to Gisela, "We didn't feel like rescuers at all. We were just ordinary students doing what we had to do."
- Wanda Kwiatkowska-Biernacka was 20 when she falsely claimed that a 1-month-old Jewish baby was her illegitimate child. (Lipman, 1991)

Are these people heroes or, as Gisela Sohnlein stated, were they simply doing what had to be done? Why did they do what so many millions of other people failed to do? What caused many people to acquiesce in the murder of millions of innocent people? Were they following orders? What brought about such hatred?

Social psychologists address questions like these. **Social psychology** is the scientific study of how a person's thoughts, feelings, and behaviors are influenced by the behavior and characteristics of other people, whether real, imagined, or inferred. All the topics in this chapter—from attitude change to group decision making, from conformity to mob action—involve the influence of one or more persons on other people. We begin this chapter by exploring the social forces that are at work when people form impressions of and make judgments about one another, in addition to examining the factors that influence interpersonal attraction.

Social Cognition

What do forming impressions, explaining others' behavior, and experiencing interpersonal attraction have in common?

Part of the process of being influenced by other people involves organizing and interpreting information about them so as to form first impressions, to try to understand their behavior, and to determine to what extent we are attracted to them. This taking in and assessing of information about other people is called **social cognition.** Social cognition is a major area of interest to social psychologists.

If you were to hail this taxi in New York City, based on your assumptions about cab drivers, and about immigrants, you might never guess that this man from the Middle East holds an advanced degree in biology and is looking for a job at a university. Schemata can be useful, but they can also keep us from finding out what lies beneath the surface.

Social psychology
The scientific study of the ways in which the thoughts, feelings, and behaviors of one individual are influenced by the real, imagined, or inferred behavior or characteristics of other people.

Social cognition
Knowledge and understanding concerning the social world and the people in it (including oneself).

Schema
A set of beliefs or expectations about something that is based on past experience.

Primacy effect
The fact that early information about someone weighs more heavily than later information in influencing one's impression of that person.

Impression Formation

How do we form first impressions of people?

Forming first impressions of people is more complex than you may think. You must direct your attention to various aspects of the person's appearance and behavior and make a rapid assessment of what those characteristics mean. How do you do this? What cues do you focus on? And how accurate are the impressions you form? The concept of *schemata* helps to answer these questions.

Schemata   When we meet someone for the first time, we notice a number of things about that person—clothes, gestures, manner of speaking, body build, facial features. We then draw on these cues to fit the person into a category. No matter how little information we have or how contradictory it is, no matter how many times in the past our initial impressions have been wrong, we still categorize people after meeting them only briefly. Associated with each category is a **schema**—a set of beliefs and expectations based on past experience that is presumed to apply to all members of that category (Fiske & Taylor, 1991). Schemata (the plural of schema) flesh out our impressions after we have pegged people into categories. For example, if a woman is wearing a white coat and has a stethoscope around her neck, you could reasonably categorize her as a doctor. Associated with this category is a schema of various beliefs and expectations: highly trained professional, knowledgeable about diseases and their cures, qualified to prescribe medication, and so on. By applying this schema, you expect that this particular woman has these traits.

But schemata can also lead us astray. They can lure us into "seeing" things about a person that we don't actually observe. For instance, most of us associate the traits of shyness, quietness, and the preoccupation of one's own thoughts with the schema *introvert*. If we notice that Melissa is shy, we are likely to categorize her as an introvert. Later we may "remember" that she also seemed preoccupied with her own thoughts. In other words, thinking of Melissa as an introvert saves us the trouble of taking into account all the subtle shadings of her personality. But this kind of thinking can easily lead to errors if we attribute to Melissa qualities that belong to the schema but not to her.

Over time, as we continue to interact with people, we add new information about them to our mental files. Our later experiences, however, generally do not influence us nearly so much as our earliest impressions. This phenomenon is called the **primacy effect.** Solomon Asch (1946) was the first to conduct research on the primacy effect. He gave people one of two lists describing a target person's traits. One list began with positive traits (for example, "industrious") and ended with negative descriptors (for instance, "stubborn"). The other list presented the same traits in reverse order. People who read the positive-to-negative sequence formed more favorable impressions of the people described than did those who read the same list in negative-to-positive sequence. Asch concluded that early impressions create the context for evaluating later information. Thus if you already like a new acquaintance, you may excuse a flaw you discover later. Conversely, if someone has made an early bad impression on you, you may refuse to believe subsequent evidence of that person's good qualities.

The primacy effect reflects a desire to lessen our mental effort. We humans have been called "cognitive misers" (Fiske & Taylor, 1991). Instead of exerting ourselves to interpret every detail we learn about a person, we are stingy with our mental efforts. Once we have formed an impression about someone, we keep it, even if that impression was formed by jumping to conclusions.

If people are specifically warned to beware of first impressions, or if they are encouraged to interpret information about others slowly and carefully, the primacy effect can be weakened or even eliminated (Luchins, 1957; Stewart, 1965).

Generally speaking, however, the first impression is the lasting impression, and it can affect our behavior even when it is inaccurate. In one study, pairs of participants played a competitive game (Snyder & Swann, 1978). The researchers told one member of each pair that his or her partner was either hostile or friendly. Players who were led to believe that their partner was hostile behaved differently toward the partner than players led to believe that their partner was friendly. In turn, those treated as hostile actually began to display hostility. In fact, these people continued to show hostility later on, when they were paired with new players who had no expectations about them at all. The expectation of hostility, it seems, produced actual aggressiveness, and this behavior persisted. When we bring about expected behavior in another person in this way, our impression becomes a **self-fulfilling prophecy.**

Considerable scientific research has shown how teacher expectations can take the form of a self-fulfilling prophecy and influence student performance in the classroom (Cooper, 1993; Harris & Rosenthal, 1985; Weinstein, Madison, & Kuklinski, 1995). This finding has been named the *Pygmalion effect* after the mythical sculptor who created the statue of a woman and then brought it to life. Although the research does not suggest that high teacher expectations can turn an "F" student into an "A" student, it does show that both high and low expectations can exert a powerful influence on student achievement. One study, for example, compared the performance of "at risk" ninth-grade students who had been assigned to regular classrooms with that of students assigned to experimental classrooms that received a year-long intervention aimed at increasing teachers' expectations. After 1 year, the students in the experimental classrooms had higher grades in English and history than the students who were not in the intervention classrooms. Two years later, the experimental students were less likely to drop out of high school (Weinstein et al., 1991).

Stereotypes   Just as schemata shape our impressions of others, so do stereotypes. A **stereotype** is a set of characteristics presumed to be shared by all members of a social category. A stereotype is actually a special kind of schema, one that is simplistic but very strongly held, and not necessarily based on much first-hand experience. A stereotype can involve almost any distinguishing feature of a person—age, sex, race, occupation, place of residence, or membership in a certain group (Hilton & Von Hipple, 1996).

When our first impression of a person is governed by a stereotype, we tend to infer things about that person solely on the basis of some key distinguishing feature and to ignore facts that are inconsistent with the stereotype, no matter how apparent they are. As a result we may perceive things about the person selectively or inaccurately, thereby perpetuating our initial stereotype. For example, once you have categorized someone as male or female, you may rely more on your stereotype of that gender than on your own observations of how the person acts. Because women are traditionally stereotyped as more emotional and submissive, and men as more rational and assertive (Deaux & Kite, 1993; Williams & Best, 1990), you may come to see these traits in men and women more than they really exist.

Attribution

How do we decide why people act as they do?

Suppose you run into a friend at the supermarket. You greet him warmly, but he barely acknowledges you, mumbles "Hi," and walks away. You feel snubbed and try to figure out why he acted like that. Did he behave that way because of something in the situation? Did you say something to offend him? Was he somehow embarrassed by meeting you at the particular time and place? Or is his behavior

---

Self-fulfilling prophecy
The process in which a person's expectation about another elicits behavior from the second person that confirms the expectation.

Stereotype
A set of characteristics presumed to be shared by all members of a social category.

more correctly attributed to something within him—to some personal trait such as moodiness or arrogance?

Explaining Behavior   Social interaction is filled with occasions such as this—occasions that invite us to make judgments about the causes of behavior. Especially when something unexpected or unpleasant occurs, we wonder about it and try to understand it. Social psychologists' observations about how we go about attributing causes to behavior form the basis of **attribution theory.**

An early attribution theorist, Fritz Heider (1958), argued that we attribute behavior to either internal or external causes, but not both. Thus you might conclude that a classmate's lateness was caused by his laziness (a personal factor or internal attribution) *or* by traffic congestion (a situational factor or external attribution).

How do we decide whether to attribute a given behavior to causes inside or outside a person? According to another influential attribution theorist, Harold Kelley (1967), we rely on three kinds of information about the behavior: distinctiveness, consistency, and consensus. For example, if your instructor asks you to stay briefly after class so that she can talk with you, you will probably try to figure out what lies behind her request by asking yourself three questions.

First, how *distinctive* is the instructor's request? Does she often ask students to stay and talk (low distinctiveness), or is such a request unusual (high distinctiveness)? If she often asks students to speak with her, you will probably conclude that she has personal reasons for talking with you. But if her request is highly distinctive, you will probably conclude that something about you, not her, underlies her request.

Second, how *consistent* is the instructor's behavior? Does she regularly ask you to stay and talk (high consistency), or is this a first for you (low consistency)? If she has consistently made this request of you before, you will probably guess that this occasion is like those others. But if her request is inconsistent with past behavior, you will probably wonder whether some particular event—perhaps something you said in class—motivated her to request a private conference.

Finally, what degree of *consensus* among teachers exists regarding this behavior? Do your other instructors ask you to stay and talk with them (high consensus), or is this instructor unique in making such a request (low consensus)? If it is common for your instructors to ask to speak with you, this instructor's request is probably due to some external factor. But if she is the only instructor ever to ask to speak privately with you, it must be something about this particular person—an internal motive or concern—that accounts for her behavior (Iacobucci & McGill, 1990).

If you conclude that the instructor has her own reasons for wanting to speak with you, you may feel mildly curious for the remainder of class until you can find out what she wants. But if you think external factors—like your own actions—have prompted her request, you may worry about whether you are in trouble and nervously wait for the end of class.

Biases   Unfortunately, the causal attributions we make are often vulnerable to *biases*. For instance, imagine that you are at a party and you see an acquaintance, Ted, walk across the room carrying several plates of food and a drink. As he approaches his chair, Ted spills food on himself. You may attribute the spill to Ted's personal characteristics—he is clumsy. Ted, however, is likely to make a very different attribution. He will likely attribute the spill to an external factor—he was carrying too many other things. Your explanation for this behavior reflects the **fundamental attribution error**—the tendency to attribute the behavior of others to causes within themselves (Ross, 1977; Ross & Nisbett, 1991).

The fundamental attribution error is part of the *actor–observer bias*—the tendency to explain the behavior of others as caused by internal factors, while attributing *one's own* behavior to *external* forces (Fiske & Taylor, 1991). Thus

Attribution theory
The theory that addresses the question of how people make judgments about the causes of behavior.

Fundamental attribution error
The tendency of people to overemphasize personal causes for other people's behavior and to underemphasize personal causes for their own behavior.

Ted, the actor, attributed his own behavior to an external source while you, the observer, attributed the behavior to an internal one. Recall the examples used to introduce this chapter—those who risked their own safety to help others in Nazi-occupied Europe. From the perspective of an observer, we tend to attribute this behavior to personal qualities. Indeed, Robert Goodkind, chairman of the foundation that honored the rescuers, called for parents to "inculcate in our children the values of altruism and moral courage as exemplified by the rescuers." Clearly Goodkind was making an internal attribution for the heroic behavior. The rescuers themselves, however, attribute their actions to external factors: "We were only ordinary students who did what we had to do."

A related class of biases is called **defensive attribution.** These types of attributions occur when we are motivated to present ourselves well, either to impress others or to feel good about ourselves (Agostinelli, Sherman, Presson, & Chassin, 1992). One example of a defensive attribution is the *self-serving bias*, which is a tendency to attribute our successes to our personal attributes while chalking up our failures to external forces beyond our control (Schlenker, Weigold, & Hallam, 1990; Schlenker & Weingold, 1992). Students do this all the time. They tend to regard exams on which they do well as good indicators of their abilities and exams on which they do poorly as bad indicators (Davis & Stephan, 1980). Similarly, teachers are more likely to assume responsibility for students' successes than for their failures (Arkin, Cooper, & Kolditz, 1980).

A second type of defensive attribution comes from thinking that people get what they deserve: Bad things happen to bad people, and good things happen to good people. This is called the **just-world hypothesis** (Lerner, 1980). When misfortune strikes someone, we often jump to the conclusion that the person deserved it, rather than giving full weight to situational factors that may have been responsible. Why do we do this? One reason is that it gives us the comforting illusion that such a thing could never happen to us. By reassigning the blame for a terrible misfortune from a chance event (something that could happen to us) to the victim's own negligence (a trait that *we*, of course, do not share), we delude ourselves into believing that we could never suffer such a fate (Chaiken & Darley, 1973). For instance, rape victims are perceived as having "asked for it" by wearing revealing clothes, and some AIDS victims are thought to have acquired the disease because of immoral behavior (Bell, Kuriloff, & Lottes, 1994; Kristiansen & Giulietti, 1990).

Attribution across Cultures Historically, most of the research on attribution theory has been conducted in Western cultures. Do the basic principles of attribution theory apply to people in other cultures as well? The answer is no. For example, in one study Japanese students studying in the United States usually explained failure as a lack of effort (an internal attribution) and attributed their successes to the assistance they received from others (an external attribution) (Tashina & Triandis, 1986). This is the reverse of the self-serving bias. Similarly, the fundamental attribution error may not be universal. In some other cultures people are much less likely to attribute behavior to internal personal characteristics; they place more emphasis on the role of external, situational factors in explaining both their own behavior and that of others (Cousins, 1989; Markus & Kitayama, 1991). For example, a study comparing the descriptions of others given by Indian and American college students found that the Americans used three times as many trait descriptions (internal attributions) and the Indians used twice as many context-related explanations (J. Miller, 1984). This suggests that the Indian students were more accurate in assessing the role of external forces in explaining others' behavior.

Defensive attribution
The tendency to attribute our successes to our own efforts or qualities and our failures to external factors.

Just-world hypothesis
Attribution error based on the assumption that bad things happen to bad people and good things happen to good people.

Interpersonal Attraction

Do "birds of a feather flock together" or do "opposites attract"?

A third aspect of social cognition has to do with interpersonal attraction. When people meet, what determines if they will like each other? This is the subject of much speculation and even mystification, with popular explanations running the gamut from fate to compatible astrological signs. Romantics believe that irresistible forces propel them toward an inevitable meeting with their beloved, but social psychologists take a more hardheaded view. They have found that attraction and the tendency to like someone else are closely linked to such factors as *proximity*, *physical attractiveness*, *similarity*, *exchange*, and *intimacy*.

Proximity   **Proximity** is usually the most important factor in determining attraction. The closer two people live to each other, the more likely they are to interact; the more frequent their interaction, the more they will tend to like each other. Conversely, two people separated by considerable geographic distance are not likely to run into each other and thus have little chance to develop a mutual attraction. The proximity effect has less to do with simple convenience than with the security and comfort we feel with people and things that have become familiar. Familiar people are predictable and safe—thus more likable (Bornstein, 1989).

Physical Attractiveness   Physical attractiveness can powerfully influence the conclusions that we reach about a person's character. We actually give attractive people credit for more than their beauty. We presume them to be more intelligent, interesting, happy, kind, sensitive, moral, and successful than people who are not perceived as attractive. They are also thought to make better spouses and to be more sexually responsive (Dion, 1972; Feingold, 1992; Zuckerman, Miyake, & Elkin, 1995).

Not only do we tend to credit physically attractive people with a wealth of positive qualities, we also tend to like them more than we do less attractive people. One reason is that physical attractiveness itself is generally considered a positive attribute (Baron & Byrne, 1991). We often perceive beauty as a valuable asset that can be exchanged for other things in social interactions. We may also believe that beauty has a "radiating effect"—that the glow of a companion's good looks enhances our own public image (Kernis & Wheeler, 1981).

Whatever its origins, our preoccupation with physical attractiveness has material consequences. Attractive people tend to be happier, make more money, and are more likely to be treated leniently by teachers (McCall, 1997). In addition, research has found that mothers of more attractive infants tend to show their children more affection and play with them more often than mothers of unattractive infants (Langlois, Ritter, Casey, & Sawin, 1995). In general we tend to give good-looking people the benefit of the doubt: If they don't live up to our expectations during the first encounter, we give them a second chance, ask for or accept a second date, or seek further opportunities for interaction. These reactions can give attractive people substantial advantages in life and lead to self-fulfilling prophecies. Physically attractive people may come to think of themselves as good or lovable because they are continually treated as if they are. Conversely, unattractive people may begin to see themselves as bad or unlovable because they have always been regarded that way—even as children.

Similarity   Similarity of attitudes, interests, values, backgrounds, and beliefs underlies much interpersonal attraction (P. M. Buss, 1985; Tan & Singh, 1995). When we know that someone shares our attitudes and interests, we tend to have more positive feelings toward that person (Byrne, 1961). The higher the proportion of attitudes that two people share, the stronger the attraction between

Proximity
How close two people live to each other.

them (Byrne & Nelson, 1965). We value similarity because it is important to us to have others agree with our choices and beliefs. By comparing our opinions with those of other people, we clarify our understanding of and reduce our uncertainty about social situations. Finding that others agree with us strengthens our convictions and boosts our self-esteem (Suls & Fletcher, 1983).

If similarity is such a critical determinant of attraction, what about the notion that opposites attract? Aren't people sometimes attracted to others who are completely different from them? Extensive research has failed to confirm this notion. In long-term relationships, where attraction plays an especially important role, people overwhelmingly prefer to associate with people who are similar to themselves (D. M. Buss, 1985).

In some cases in which people's attraction seems to be founded on their "differentness," their critical qualities are not opposites but complements. Complementary traits are needs or skills that complete or balance each other (Dryer & Horowitz, 1997; Hendrick & Hendrick, 1992). For example, a person who likes to care for and fuss over others will be most compatible with a mate who enjoys receiving such attention. These people are not really opposites, but their abilities and desires complement each other to their mutual satisfaction. Complementarity almost always occurs between people who share similar goals and values and are willing to adapt to each other. True opposites are unlikely even to meet each other, much less interact long enough to achieve such compatibility.

Exchange According to the *reward theory of attraction*, we tend to like people who make us feel rewarded and appreciated. But the relationship between attraction and rewards is subtle and complex. For example, Aronson's gain–loss theory of attraction (1994) suggests that *increases* in rewarding behavior influence attractiveness more than constant rewarding behavior does. Say you were to meet and talk with someone at three successive parties, and during these conversations that person's behavior toward you changed from polite indifference to overt flattery. You would be inclined to like this person more than if he or she had immediately started to praise you during the first conversation and kept up the stream of praise each time you met. The reverse also holds true: We tend to dislike people whose opinion of us changes from good to bad even more than we dislike those who consistently display a low opinion of us.

The reward theory of attraction is based on the concept of **exchange.** In social interactions people make exchanges. For example, you may agree to help a friend paint his apartment in exchange for his preparing dinner for you. Every exchange involves both rewards (you get a free dinner; he gets his apartment painted) and costs (you have to paint first; he then has to cook you dinner). As long as both parties find their interactions more rewarding than costly, their exchanges will continue (Clore & Byrne, 1974; Lott & Lott, 1974). People seem to "keep score" in their interactions, especially in the early stages of relationships (M. S. Clark & Mills, 1979).

Exchanges work only insofar as they are fair or equitable. A relationship is based on **equity** when what one person "gets out of it" is equal to what the other gets (Walster, Walster, & Berscheid, 1978; van Yperen & Buunk, 1990). When exchanges are consistently unfair, the one who reaps fewer rewards feels cheated, and the one who gains is apt to feel guilty. This may undermine the attraction that once drew the two people together.

Intimacy When does liking someone become something more? Social psychologists have found that love depends on several critical processes beyond interpersonal attraction. One is *intimacy*, the quality of genuine closeness and trust achieved in communication with another person. When people communicate, they do more than just interact—they share deep-rooted feelings and ideas. When you are first

Attraction and liking are closely linked to such factors as proximity, similar interests and attitudes, and rewarding behavior.

Exchange
The concept that relationships are based on trading rewards among partners.

Equity
Fairness of exchange achieved when each partner in the relationship receives the same proportion of outcomes to investments.

getting to know someone, you communicate about "safe," superficial topics like the weather, sports, or shared activities. As you get to know each other better over time, your conversation progresses to more personal subjects: your personal experiences, memories, hopes and fears, goals and failures (Altman & Taylor, 1973).

Intimate communication is based on the process of *self-disclosure* (Prager, 1995). As you talk with friends, you disclose or reveal personal experiences and opinions that you might conceal from strangers. Because self-disclosure is possible only when you trust the listener, you will seek—and usually receive—a reciprocal disclosure to keep the conversation balanced. For example, after telling your roommate about something that embarrassed you, you may expect him or her to reveal a similar episode; you might even ask directly, "Has anything like that ever happened to you?" Such reciprocal intimacy keeps you "even" and makes your relationship more emotionally satisfying (Collins & Miller, 1994). The pacing of disclosure is important. If you "jump levels" by revealing too much too soon—or to someone who is not ready to make a reciprocal personal response—the other person will retreat, and communication will go no further.

REVIEW QUESTIONS

1. The scientific study of how a person's thoughts, feelings, and behaviors are influenced by the behavior and characteristics of other people, whether real, imagined, or inferred, is called ____ ____.

2. ____ ____ refers to the process of taking in and assessing information about other people.

3. Associated with the many categories into which we "peg" people are sets of beliefs and expectations called ____ that are assumed to apply to all members of a category. When these are quite simplistic but deeply held, they are often referred to as ____.

4. When the first information we receive about a person weighs more heavily in forming an impression than later information does, we are experiencing the ____ effect.

5. Understanding how we make inferences about why people act as they do is part of ____ theory.

6. According to Fritz Heider, we usually attribute someone's behavior to

   a. internal and external causes both at the same time.

   b. either internal or external causes, but not both at the same time.

   c. external causes only.

   d. internal causes only.

7. Match the following biases in attributing causes to behavior with the appropriate definition.

   ____ fundamental attribution error

   ____ actor–observer bias

   ____ self-serving bias

   ____ just-world hypothesis

   a. attributing the behavior of others to internal causes and one's own behavior to external causes

   b. attributing our success to ourselves and our failures to factors beyond our control

   c. assuming that people must deserve the bad things that happen to them

   d. the tendency to attribute the behavior of others to personal characteristics

8. Which of the following is a basis for interpersonal attraction? (There can be more than one correct answer.)

   a. proximity

   b. similarity

   c. exchange

   d. attraction of true opposites

   e. all of the above

Answers: 1. social psychology. **2.** Social cognition. **3.** schemata, stereotypes. **4.** primacy. **5.** attribution. **6. b. 7.** fundamental attribution error: d; actor–observer bias: a; self-serving bias: b; just-world hypothesis: c. **8.** a, b, and c.

Attitudes

Why are attitudes important?

The phrase "I don't like his attitude" is a telling one. People are often told to "change your attitude" or make an "attitude adjustment." An **attitude** is a relatively stable organization of beliefs, feelings, and tendencies toward something or someone—called an attitude object. Attitudes are important mainly because they often influence our behavior. Discrimination, for example, is often caused by prejudiced attitudes. Psychologists wonder how attitudes are formed and how they can be changed.

The Nature of Attitudes

What are the three major components of attitudes?

An attitude has three major components: *evaluative beliefs* about the object, *feelings* about the object, and *behavior tendencies* toward the object. Beliefs include facts, opinions, and our general knowledge. Feelings encompass love, hate, like, dislike, and similar sentiments. Behavior tendencies refer to our inclinations to act in certain ways toward the object—to approach it, avoid it, and so on. For example, our attitude toward a political candidate includes our beliefs about the candidate's qualifications and positions on crucial issues and our expectations about how the candidate will vote on those issues. We also have feelings about the candidate—like or dislike, trust or mistrust. And because of these beliefs and feelings, we are inclined to behave in certain ways toward the candidate—to vote for or against the candidate, to contribute time or money to the candidate's campaign, to make a point of attending or staying away from rallies for the candidate, and so forth.

As we will see shortly, these three aspects of an attitude are very often consistent with one another. For example, if we have positive feelings toward something, we tend to have positive beliefs about it and to behave positively toward it. This does not mean, however, that our every action will accurately reflect our attitudes. For example, our feelings about going to dentists are often negative, yet most of us make an annual visit anyway. Let's look more closely at the relationship between attitudes and behavior.

Attitudes and Behavior   The relationship between attitudes and behavior is not always straightforward. In a classic study, LaPiere (1934) traveled through the United States with a Chinese couple in the early 1930s—a time when prejudice against the Chinese was running high. They were refused service at only 1 of the 250 hotels and restaurants they visited. Yet 6 months later, when LaPiere sent a questionnaire to each of these establishments and asked if they would serve Chinese people, most said they would not. LaPiere therefore concluded that attitudes are not reliable predictors of behavior.

Subsequent research, however, suggests that attitudes *can* predict behavior—at least in some situations (Eagly, 1992; Kraus, 1995). Variables like the strength of the attitude, how easily it comes to mind, how salient a particular attitude is in a given situation, and how relevant the attitude is to the particular behavior in question help to determine whether a person will act in accordance with an attitude (Eagly & Chaiken, 1994). For example, had LaPiere asked about attitudes toward the particular well-dressed, middle-class Chinese who traveled with him rather than about Chinese people in general, the correlation between attitudes and behavior probably would have been higher.

Personality traits are also important. Some people consistently match their actions to their attitudes (R. Norman, 1975). Others have a tendency to override

Our attitude toward a political candidate includes our beliefs about the candidate's qualifications and positions, our feelings about the candidate, and our behaviors toward the candidate. Beliefs, feelings, and behavioral tendencies are frequently—but not always—consistent with one another.

Attitude
Relatively stable organization of beliefs, feelings, and behavior tendencies directed toward something or someone—the attitude object.

their own attitudes in order to behave properly in a given situation. As a result, attitudes predict behavior better for some people than for others (M. Snyder & Tanke, 1976). People who rate highly on **self-monitoring** are especially likely to override their attitudes to behave in accordance with others' expectations. Before speaking or acting, high self-monitors observe the situation for clues about how they should react. Then they try to meet those "demands" rather than behave according to their own beliefs or sentiments. In contrast, low self-monitors express and act on their attitudes with great consistency, showing little regard for situational clues or constraints. Thus a high self-monitor who disagrees with the politics of a fellow dinner guest may keep his thoughts to himself in an effort to be polite and agreeable, while a low self-monitor who disagrees might dispute the speaker openly, even though doing so might disrupt the social occasion (Snyder, 1987).

Attitude Development   How do we acquire our attitudes? Where do they come from? Many of our most basic attitudes derive from early, direct personal experience. Children are rewarded with smiles and encouragement when they please their parents, and they are punished through disapproval when they displease them. These early experiences give children enduring attitudes (Oskamp, 1991). Attitudes are also formed by imitation. Children mimic the behavior of their parents and peers, acquiring attitudes even when no one is deliberately trying to shape them.

But parents are not the only source of attitudes. Teachers, friends, and even famous people are also important in shaping our attitudes. New fraternity or sorority members, for example, may model their behavior and attitudes on upper-class members. A student who idolizes a teacher may adopt many of the teacher's attitudes toward controversial subjects, even if they run counter to attitudes of parents or friends.

The mass media, particularly television, also have a great impact on attitude formation. Television bombards us with messages—not merely through its news and entertainment but also through commercials: Violence is commonplace in life. . . . Women are dependent on men. . . . Having possessions is important in life, and so on. Without experience of their own against which to measure the merit of these messages, children are particularly susceptible to the influence of television on their attitudes. One study found that white children in England who had little contact with nonwhites tended to associate race relations with conflicts and hostility more often than white children who lived in integrated neighborhoods (Hartmann & Husband, 1971). The only source of information for the first group of children was television news reports that focused on the problems caused by integration.

Prejudice and Discrimination

How does a person develop a prejudice toward someone else?

Although the terms *prejudice* and *discrimination* are often used interchangeably, they actually refer to different concepts. **Prejudice**—an attitude—is an unfair, intolerant, or unfavorable view of a group of people. **Discrimination**—a behavior—is an unfair act or a series of acts directed against an entire group of people or individual members of that group. To discriminate is to treat an entire class of people in an unfair way.

Prejudice and discrimination do not always occur together. It is possible to be prejudiced against a particular group without openly behaving in a hostile or discriminatory manner toward its members. A racist store owner may smile at a black customer, for example, to disguise opinions that could hurt his business. Likewise, many institutional practices can be discriminatory even though they

Self-monitoring
The tendency for an individual to observe the situation for cues about how to react.

Prejudice
An unfair, intolerant, or unfavorable attitude toward a group of people.

Discrimination
An unfair act or series of acts taken toward an entire group of people or individual members of that group.

Scenes like this were common in the South before the civil rights movement.

are not based on prejudice. For example, regulations establishing a minimum height requirement for police officers may discriminate against women and certain ethnic groups whose average height falls below the arbitrary standard, even though the regulations do not stem from sexist or racist attitudes.

Prejudice   Like attitudes in general, prejudice has three components: beliefs, feelings, and behavioral tendencies. Prejudicial beliefs are virtually always stereotypes, and as mentioned earlier, reliance on stereotypes can lead to erroneous thinking about other people. When a prejudiced white employer interviews an African American, for example, the employer may attribute to the job candidate all the traits associated with the African-American stereotype. Qualities of the candidate that do not match the stereotype are likely to be ignored or quickly forgotten (Allport, 1954). For example, the employer whose stereotype includes the belief that African Americans are lazy may belittle the candidate's hard-earned college degree by thinking, "I never heard of that college. It must be an easy school."

This thinking, which is similar to the fundamental attribution error, is known as the *ultimate attribution error*. This error refers to the tendency for a person with stereotyped beliefs about a particular group of people to make internal attributions for their shortcomings and external attributions for their successes. In the example above the employer is making an external attribution (an easy school) for the college success of the African American job seeker. The other side of the ultimate attribution error is to make internal attributions for the failures of people who belong to groups we dislike. For instance, many white Americans believe that lower average incomes among black Americans than whites is due to lack of ability or low motivation (Kluegel, 1990).

Along with stereotyped beliefs, prejudiced attitudes are usually marked by strong emotions, such as dislike, fear, hatred, or loathing. Understandably, such feelings are likely to lead to discrimination against the disliked group.

Sources of Prejudice   Many theories attempt to sort out the causes and sources of prejudice. According to the **frustration–aggression theory,** prejudice is the result of people's frustrations (Allport, 1954). As you saw in Chapter 8, Motivation and Emotion, under some circumstances frustration can spill over into anger and hostility. People who feel exploited and oppressed often cannot vent their anger against an identifiable or proper target, so they displace their

Frustration–aggression theory
The theory that under certain circumstances people who are frustrated in their goals turn their anger away from the proper, powerful target and toward another, less powerful target that is safer to attack.

hostility onto those even "lower" on the social scale than themselves. The result is prejudice and discrimination. The people who are the victims of this displaced aggression become *scapegoats* and are blamed for the problems of the times.

Historical research lends some support to the frustration–aggression theory. Violence against the Jews has often followed periods of economic unrest or natural catastrophe, when frustration would be high. Research on violence against African Americans in the South between 1882 and 1930 shows a strong relationship between the level of economic prosperity and the number of lynchings (Hepworth & West, 1988; Hovland & Sears, 1940). When cotton prices were low, there were more lynchings than when cotton prices were high. Similarly, African Americans have been scapegoats for the economic frustrations of some lower-income whites who feel powerless to improve their own condition. Latinos, Asian Americans, and women are also scapegoated—at times by African Americans. Like kindness, greed, and all other human qualities, prejudice is not restricted to a particular race or ethnic group.

Another theory locates the source of prejudice in a bigoted or **authoritarian personality** (Adorno et al., 1950). Authoritarian people tend to be rigidly conventional. They favor following the rules and abiding by tradition and are hostile to those who defy social norms (Stone, Lederer, & Christie, 1993). They respect and submit to authority and are preoccupied with power and toughness. Looking at the world through a lens of rigid categories, they are cynical about human nature, fearing, suspecting, and rejecting all groups other than those to which they belong. Prejudice is only one expression of their suspicious, mistrusting views.

There are also cognitive sources of prejudice. As we saw earlier, people are "cognitive misers" who try to simplify and organize their social thinking as much as possible. Too much simplification—*oversimplification*—leads to erroneous thinking, stereotypes, prejudice, and discrimination. For example, a stereotyped view of women as indecisive or weak will prejudice an employer against hiring a qualified woman as a manager. Belief in a just world—where people get what they deserve and deserve what they get—also oversimplifies one's view of the victims of prejudice as somehow "deserving" their plight (Fiske & Neubers, 1990).

In addition, prejudice and discrimination may have their roots in people's attempts to conform. If we associate with people who express prejudices, we are more likely to go along with their ideas than to resist them. During the 1960s in the South, for example, many restaurant owners maintained that they themselves would not mind serving African American patrons but claimed that their white customers would not tolerate it (Deaux & Wrightsman, 1984). The pressures of social conformity help to explain why children quickly absorb the prejudices of their parents and playmates long before they have formed their own beliefs and opinions on the basis of experience. Peer pressure often makes it "cool" or acceptable to express certain biases rather than to behave tolerantly toward members of other social groups.

Racism is prejudice and discrimination directed at a particular racial group. The prevalence and social importance of racism in the United States have made it one of the most studied topics in social psychology. The most blatant form of racism, based on beliefs in white racial superiority and segregation, has, fortunately, been declining in the last several decades. Most Americans today believe in the importance of racial integration, equality, and equal opportunity. For instance, in 1994, 87 percent of a national survey approved of the Supreme Court's 1954 ruling to desegregate schools, a very controversial decision at the time (McAnaney & Saad, 1994).

Based on statistics such as these, many students today believe that racial prejudice is a thing of the past. But the truth is that *modern racism* is a subtle and less

Authoritarian personality
A personality pattern characterized by rigid conventionality, exaggerated respect for authority, and hostility toward those who defy society's norms.

Racism
Prejudice and discrimination directed at a particular racial group.

extreme form of prejudice. It is reflected in agreement with statements that civil rights groups are too extreme or that black Americans receive more respect and benefits than they deserve. A 1993 national survey found that 70 percent of whites but only 30 percent of blacks agreed that blacks had as good a chance as whites in their community to get a job for which they were qualified (Wheeler, 1993). Studies show that even whites who profess to be without racial prejudice are quicker to associate positive traits with the word "white" than with "black" (Dovidio, Evans, & Tyler, 1986; Gaertner & McLaughlin, 1983).

Many ethnic minorities continue to be disadvantaged today, not so much because of individual beliefs or actions but owing to the overall effect of institutions and policies, sometimes called *institutional racism*. For instance, in 1997 the average yearly income for white, non-Hispanic families in the United States was $40,577, whereas for black families it was $25,050. On average, 9 percent of white Americans were living in poverty, as compared with 27 percent of black Americans (Dalaker & Naifeh, 1998; U.S. Bureau of the Census, 1998). Nearly 1 in 4 white Americans has attended 4 or more years of college, while only 1 in 9 black Americans has. These differences are not due just to individual beliefs or actions; they also reflect the overall effect of institutional racism (Campbell, 1995).

Thus although traditional racism has declined in American society, modern and institutional racism continue to disadvantage ethnic minorities. This leads to an important application of social psychology. How can we use our knowledge of prejudice, stereotypes, and discrimination to reduce prejudice and its expression? Three strategies appear promising: recategorization, controlled processing, and improving contact between groups (see *Highlights* on p. 501 for a discussion of how these strategies can be used to reduce ethnic conflict).

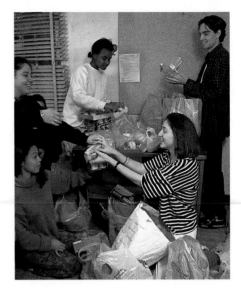

Prejudice and discrimination can be reduced when members of different groups are brought together in a cooperative effort. This diverse group of teenagers is collecting food for needy people.

- When we *recategorize*, we try to expand our schema of a particular group—say, by viewing people from different races or genders as sharing similar qualities. These more inclusive schemata become *superordinate categories*. For instance, Catholics and Protestants in the United States tend to view themselves both as Christians rather than as separate competing groups (as in Northern Ireland). If people can create such superordinate categories, they can often reduce stereotypes and prejudice (Dovidio, Gaertner, Isen, & Lowrance, 1995; Hewstone et al., 1993).

- It is also possible to train ourselves to be more "mindful" of people who differ from us. For example, a group of sixth-graders were taught to be more understanding of the handicapped by having them view slides of handicapped people and think about their situations, answering such questions as "How might a handicapped person drive a car?" The group showed far less prejudice toward the handicapped after this procedure (Langer et al., 1985). Apparently, tolerance can be taught. Some researchers (Devine et al., 1989, 1991) believe that we all learn the stereotypes in our culture, so the primary difference between someone who is prejudiced and someone who is not is the ability to suppress prejudiced beliefs through *controlled processing*.

- Finally, we can reduce prejudice and tensions between groups by bringing them together. This was one of the intentions of the famous 1954 U.S. Supreme Court's decision in *Brown* v. *Board of Education of Topeka, Kansas*, which mandated that public schools become racially integrated. Intergroup contact alone is not enough, however (Taylor & Moghaddam, 1994). It *can* work to undermine prejudicial attitudes if certain conditions are met:

1. *Group members must have equal status.* When blacks and whites were first integrated in the army and in public housing, they had relatively equal status, so prejudice between them was greatly reduced (Pettigrew, 1969). School desegregation has been less than successful because the structure of our school system

tends to reward the economic and academic advantages of white children, giving them an edge over black schoolchildren (E. G. Cohen, 1984).

2. *People need to have one-on-one contact with members of the other group.* Simply putting black and white students together in a classroom does not change attitudes. Personal contact such as that which occurs among friends at lunch and after school needs to be encouraged.

3. *Members of the two groups must cooperate rather than compete.* Perhaps because it provides the kind of personal contact just mentioned, as well as common ground and equal status, working together to achieve a goal helps to break down prejudice. Integrated sports teams are one example. Cooperative learning techniques have also proved to be effective in overcoming prejudice in schools (D. W. Johnson, Johnson, & Maruyama, 1984; Slavin & Madden, 1994).

4. *Social norms should encourage intergroup contact.* In many cases school desegregation took place in a highly charged atmosphere. Busloads of black children arrived at their new schools only to face the protests of angry white parents. These conditions did not promote genuine intergroup contact. In situations where contact is encouraged by social norms, prejudiced attitudes are less likely.

In all of these suggestions, the primary focus is on changing behavior, not on changing attitudes directly. But changing behavior is often a first step toward changing attitudes. This is not to say that attitude change follows automatically. Attitudes can be difficult to budge because they are often so deeply rooted. Completely eliminating deeply held attitudes, then, can be very difficult. That is why social psychologists have concentrated so much effort on techniques that encourage attitude change. The following section examines some of the major findings in the psychological research on attitude change.

Attitude Change

What factors encourage someone to change an attitude?

A man watching television on Sunday afternoon ignores scores of beer commercials but listens to a friend who recommends a particular brand. A political speech convinces one woman to change her vote in favor of the candidate but leaves her next-door neighbor determined to vote against him. Why would a personal recommendation have greater persuasive power than an expensively produced television commercial? How can two people with similar initial views derive completely different messages from the same speech? What makes one attempt to change attitudes fail and another succeed? Are some people more resistant to attitude change than others? We begin answering these questions by looking at the process of persuasion.

The Process of Persuasion   To be persuaded, you must first pay attention to the message; then you must comprehend it; finally, you must accept it as convincing. Consider how advertising accomplishes the first step of grabbing your attention.

An ad must catch your attention or you will "filter it out" along with all of the other stimuli you ignore every hour of the day (Conen & Chakravarti, 1994). As the competition has stiffened, advertisers have become increasingly creative in seizing your attention. For example, ads that arouse emotions, especially feelings you want to act on, can be memorable and thus persuasive (Engel, Black, & Miniard, 1986). Humor, too, is an effective way to keep you watching or reading an ad you would otherwise ignore (Scott, Klein, & Bryant, 1990).

HIGHLIGHTS

Ethnic Conflict and Violence

With the end of the Cold War, interethnic conflict has become the dominant form of war (Mays et al., 1998; Rouhana & Bar-Tal, 1998). Bosnia, Croatia, East Timor, Russia, Turkey, Iraq, Ireland, Israel, Sri Lanka . . . the list of countries torn by ethnic conflict goes on and on, and civilian deaths continue to increase by the thousands. Why does such conflict arise, and why is it so difficult to resolve?

Ethnic conflict has no single cause. In part, ethnic conflict "is often rooted in histories of colonialism, enthnocentrism, racism, political oppression, human rights abuses, social injustice, poverty, and environmental degradation" (Mays et al., 1998, p. 737). But these structural problems are only part of the story, determining primarily who fights whom. The rest of the story is to be found in psychological processes such as intense group loyalty, personal and social identity, shared memories, polarization and deep-rooted prejudice, and societal beliefs (Cairns & Darby, 1998; Mays et al., 1998; Rouhana & Bar-Tal, 1998). In other words, structural problems don't have the same effect if people are not prepared to hate and fear others. This hate and fear largely determine the extent to which ethnic conflict becomes violent (Des Forges, 1995; Ross, 1993; Smith, 1998).

Looking more closely at some of the psychological forces at work, *propaganda* often plays a significant role by portraying opponents in the most negative fashion possible, thus perpetuating racism, prejudice, and stereotypes. In Rwanda, for example, Tutsis (who were almost exterminated by the resulting violence with Hutus) for years were accused in the mass media of having committed horrible crimes and of plotting the mass murder of

Hutus, none of which was true (Smith, 1998). When ethnic violence is protracted, *shared collective memories* become filled with instances of violence, hostility, and victimization. Prejudices are thus reinforced, and people increasingly come to view the conflict as inevitable and their differences as irreconcilable (Rouhana & Bar-Tal, 1998).

Personal and social identity can also contribute to ethnic conflict. Because group memberships contribute to self-image, if the groups to which you belong are maligned or threatened, then to some extent you are personally maligned and threatened. If you are unable to leave those groups, then

---

Structural problems don't have the same effect if people are not prepared to hate and fear others.

---

you are pressured to defend them in order to enhance your own feelings of self-esteem (Cairns & Darby, 1998). In this way, what starts out as ethnic conflict quickly becomes a highly personal threat.

Finally, widespread *societal beliefs* about the conflict and the parties to the conflict also play a role in prolonged ethnic conflicts. Four especially important societal beliefs are "Our goals are just," "The opponent has no legitimacy," "We can do no wrong," and "We are the victims" (Rouhana & Bar-Tal, 1998). These societal beliefs "provide a common social prism through which society members view the conflict. Once formed, they become incorporated into an ethos and are reflected

in the group's language, stereotypes, images, myths, and collective memories" (Rouhana & Bar-Tal, 1998, p. 765). The result is a form of "cognitive freezing" in which people selectively seek out and process information in a way that perpetuates the societal beliefs. This cognitive freezing heightens fear, anger, and hatred—the emotions that are the basis of ethnic violence.

It follows that attempts to build peace cannot address only structural problems. Attempts to redistribute resources more equitably, to reduce oppression and victimization, and to increase social justice are essential, but they will succeed only if attention is also given to important psychological processes. Concerted efforts must be made to increase tolerance and improve intergroup relations while also developing new, nonviolent means for resolving conflicts (Mays et al., 1998; Smith, 1998). The strategies of recategorization, controlled processing, and contact between groups (see p. 499) have helped reduce the level of ethnic conflict in some countries (Smith, 1998). But cognitive changes must also be made: Societal beliefs must be changed, and new beliefs must be developed that are more consistent with conflict resolution and peaceful relationships. In addition, multidisciplinary techniques will need to be developed if programs are to be fully effective in addressing conflicts in different cultures. As one group of experts put it, "It is both risky and ethnocentric to assume that methods developed in Western contexts can be applied directly in different cultures and contexts. Research on different cultural beliefs and practices and their implications for ethnopolitical conflict analysis and prevention is essential if the field of psychology is going to be successful in its contributions" (Mays et al., 1998, p. 739).

For an ad to affect our behavior, it must first attract our attention.

Other ads "hook" the audience by involving them in a narrative. A commercial might open with a dramatic scene or situation—for example, two people seemingly "meant" for each other but not yet making eye contact—and the viewer stays tuned to find out what happens. Some commercials even feature recurring characters and story lines so that each new commercial in the series is really the latest installment in a soap opera. Even ads that are annoying can still be effective in capturing attention, because people tend to notice them when they appear (Aaker & Bruzzone, 1985).

With so many clever strategies focused on seizing and holding your attention, how can you shield yourself from unwanted influences and resist persuasive appeals? One strategy for resisting persuasion is to analyze ads to identify which attention-getting strategies are at work. Make a game of deciphering the advertisers' "code" instead of falling for the ad's appeal. And raise your standards for the kinds of messages that are worthy of your attention and commitment.

The Communication Model   The second and third steps in persuasion—comprehending and then accepting the message—are influenced by both the message itself and the way in which it is presented. The *communication model* of persuasion spotlights four key elements to achieve these goals: the source, the message itself, the medium of communication, and characteristics of the audience. Persuaders manipulate each of these factors in the hopes of changing your attitudes.

The effectiveness of a persuasive message first depends on its *source*, the author or communicator who appeals to the audience to accept the message. Here credibility makes a big difference (McGuire, 1985). For example, we are less likely to change our attitude about the oil industry's antipollution efforts if the president of a major refining company tells us about them than if we hear the same information from an impartial commission appointed to study the situation.

The credibility of the source is most important when we are not inclined to pay attention to the message (Cooper & Croyle, 1984; Petty & Cacioppo, 1981, 1986a). In cases where we have some interest in the message, the message itself plays the greater role in determining whether we change our attitudes (Petty & Cacioppo, 1986b). The more arguments a message makes in support of a position, the more effective that message is (Calder, Insko, & Yandell, 1974). Novel arguments are more persuasive than rehashes of old standbys, heard many times before. *Fear* sometimes works well, too, especially in convincing people to get tetanus shots (Dabbs & Leventhal, 1966), to drive safely (Leventhal & Niles, 1965), and to take care of their teeth (Evans et al., 1970). But if a message generates too much fear, it will turn off the audience and be ignored (Worchel, Cooper, & Goethals, 1991). In addition, messages designed to persuade are more successful when they present both sides of an argument. A two-sided presentation generally makes the speaker seem less biased and thus enhances his or her credibility. We have greater respect and trust for a communicator who acknowledges that there is another side to a controversial issue.

When it comes to choosing an effective *medium* of persuasion, writing is best suited to making people understand complex arguments, while videotaped or live presentations are more effective with an audience that already grasps the gist of an argument (Chaiken & Eagly, 1976). Most effective, however, are face-to-face appeals or the lessons of our own experience. Salespeople who sell products door-to-door rely on the power of personal contact.

The most critical factors in changing attitudes—and the most difficult to control—have to do with the *audience*. Attitudes are most resistant to change if (1) the audience has a strong commitment to its present attitudes, (2) those attitudes are shared by others, and (3) the attitudes were instilled during early childhood by such pivotal groups as the family. The *discrepancy* between the content of the message and the present attitudes of the audience also affects how well the message will be received. Up to a point, the greater the difference between the two, the greater the likelihood of attitude change, as long as the person delivering the message is considered an expert on the topic. If the discrepancy is *too* great, however, the audience may reject the new information altogether, even though it comes from an expert. Finally, certain personal characteristics make some people more susceptible to attitude change than others. People with low self-esteem are more easily influenced, especially when the message is complex and hard to understand. Highly intelligent people tend to resist persuasion because they can think of counterarguments more easily.

Attitudes, then, are open to change, but it isn't easy to change them. Fortunately for advertisers, politicians, and others, attitude change is often less crucial than a shift in behavior—buying brand X, voting for Jane Smith. In fact, in many cases it is possible to first change behavior and *then* to obtain attitude change as a result. This is one of the central findings from research on cognitive dissonance.

Cognitive Dissonance Theory   One of the more fascinating approaches to understanding the process of attitude change is the theory of **cognitive dissonance,** developed by Leon Festinger (1957). Cognitive dissonance exists whenever a person has two contradictory cognitions, or beliefs, at the same time. "I am a considerate and loyal friend" is one cognition; so is "Yesterday I repeated some juicy gossip I heard about my friend Chris." These two cognitions are dissonant—each one implies the opposite of the other. According to Festinger, cognitive dissonance creates unpleasant psychological tension, which motivates us to try to resolve the dissonance in some way.

Sometimes changing one's attitude is the easiest way to reduce the discomfort of dissonance. I cannot easily change the fact that I have repeated gossip about a friend. Therefore it is easier to change my attitude toward my friend. If I conclude that Chris is not really a friend but simply an acquaintance, then my new attitude now fits my behavior—spreading gossip about someone who is *not* a friend does not contradict the fact that I am loyal and considerate to those who *are* my friends.

Discrepant behavior that contradicts an attitude does not necessarily bring about attitude change, however, because there are other ways a person can reduce cognitive dissonance. One alternative is to *increase the number of consonant elements*—that is, the thoughts that are consistent with one another. For example, I might recall the many times I defended Chris when others were critical of him. Now my repeating a little bit of gossip seems less at odds with my attitude toward Chris as a friend. Another option is to reduce the importance of one or both dissonant cognitions. For instance, I could tell myself, "The person I repeated the gossip to was Terry, who doesn't really know Chris very well. Terry doesn't care and won't repeat it. It was no big deal, and Chris shouldn't be upset about it." By reducing the significance of my disloyal action, I reduce the dissonance that I experience and so make it less necessary to change my attitude toward Chris.

But why would someone engage in behavior that goes against an attitude in the first place? One answer is that cognitive dissonance is a natural part of everyday life. Simply choosing between two or more desirable alternatives leads inevitably to dissonance. Suppose you are in the market for a computer but can't decide between an IBM and a Macintosh. If you choose the IBM, all of its bad features and all the good aspects of the Macintosh contribute to dissonance. After you have bought the IBM, you can reduce the dissonance by changing your attitude: You might decide that the Macintosh keyboard wasn't "quite right" and that some of the "bad" features of the IBM aren't so bad after all.

You may also engage in behavior at odds with an attitude because you are enticed to do so. Perhaps someone offers you a small bribe or reward: "I will pay you 25 cents just to try my product." Curiously, the larger the reward, the

Cognitive dissonance
Perceived inconsistency between two cognitions.

smaller the change in attitude that is likely to result. When rewards are large, dissonance is at a minimum and attitude change is small, if it happens at all. Apparently, when people are convinced that there is a good reason to do something that goes against their beliefs ("I'll try almost anything in exchange for a large cash incentive"), they experience little dissonance and their attitudes are not likely to shift, even though their behavior may change for a time. If the reward is small, however—just barely enough to induce behavior that conflicts with one's attitude—dissonance will be great, maximizing the chances of attitude change: "I only got 25 cents to try this product, so it couldn't have been the money that attracted me. I must really *like* this product after all." The trick is to induce the behavior that goes against an attitude while leaving people feeling personally responsible for the dissonant act. That way they are more likely to change their attitudes than if they feel they were blatantly induced to act in a way that contradicted their attitudes (J. Cooper, 1971; Kelman, 1974).

REVIEW QUESTIONS

1. A(n) _____ is a fairly stable organization of beliefs, feelings, and behavioral tendencies directed toward some object, such as a person or group.

2. "The best way to predict behavior is to measure attitudes." True or false.

3. Prejudice is to _____ as discrimination is to _____.
   a. an unfavorable attitude; an unfair act
   b. tolerance; oppression
   c. an unfair act; an unfavorable attitude
   d. oppression; tolerance

4. Which of the following can be an effective way to reduce prejudice (there can be more than one correct answer)?
   a. equal status contact
   b. one-on-one contact
   c. cooperative group projects
   d. social norms that encourage contact
   e. all of the above

5. The message that *most* likely will result in a change in attitude is one with
   a. high fear from a highly credible source.
   b. high fear from a moderately credible source.
   c. moderate fear from a highly credible source.
   d. moderate fear from a moderately credible source.

6. When trying to change someone's opinion, it is generally better to
   a. present only your side of an argument.
   b. present only criticisms of the opposing viewpoint.
   c. present both sides of an argument.

7. _____ _____ exists whenever a person has two contradictory beliefs at the same time. The cognitive conflict is often resolved through attitude change.

Answers: 1. attitude. 2. F. 3. a. 4. e. 5. c. 6. c. 7. Cognitive dissonance.

Social Influence

What are some areas in which the power of social influence is highly apparent?

Social influence
The process by which others individually or collectively affect one's perceptions, attitudes, and actions.

In a sense all social psychology is the study of **social influence**—of how people's thoughts, feelings, and actions are affected by the behavior and characteristics of others. In some areas that social psychologists study, however, the power of social influence is even more apparent than usual. Among these are the study of cultural influences and of conformity, compliance, and obedience.

Cultural Influences

How does your culture influence how you dress or what you eat?

Culture exerts an enormous influence on our attitudes and behavior, and culture is itself a creation of people. As such, culture is a major form of social influence. Consider for a moment the many aspects of day-to-day living that are derived from culture:

- Your culture dictates how you dress. A Saudi woman covers her face before venturing outside her home; a North American woman freely displays her face, arms, and legs; and women in some other societies go about completely naked (Myers, 1992).

- Culture specifies what you eat—and what you do *not* eat. Americans do not eat dog or reptile meat, the Chinese eat no cheese, and the Hindus refuse to eat beef. Culture further guides *how* you eat: with a fork, chopsticks, or your bare hands.

- People from different cultures seek different amounts of personal space. Latin Americans, French people, and Arabs get closer to one another in most face-to-face interactions than do Americans, English people, or Swedes. (E. T. Hall, 1966)

To some extent, culture influences us through formal instruction. For example, your parents might have reminded you from time to time that certain actions are considered "normal" or the "right way" to behave. But more often we learn cultural lessons through modeling and imitation, with reinforcement also involved. We are rewarded (reinforced) for doing as our companions and fellow citizens do in most situations—for going along with the crowd. This social learning process is one of the chief mechanisms by which a culture transmits its central lessons and values. In the course of comparing and adapting our own behavior to that of others, we learn the norms of our culture. A **norm** is a shared idea or expectation about how to behave. Norms are often steeped in tradition and strengthened by habit. For example, it is "normal" in the United States for women to become nurses and teachers, but not to become construction workers. When visiting a friend in the hospital, you may be surprised and uncomfortable if the nurse in attendance turns out to be a man. Lawmakers and politicians are likewise uncomfortable with images of women flying combat missions into enemy territory.

Cultures seem strange to us if their norms are very different from our own. It is tempting to conclude that *different* means "wrong," simply because unfamiliar patterns of behavior can make us feel uncomfortable. To transcend our differences and get along better with people from other cultures, we must find ways to overcome such discomfort. Because cultural norms are learned—not inherited—it is possible to *relearn* or otherwise modify our responses to unfamiliar cultures. For example, if you know that the hand gesture that signifies "OK" in our culture (putting the thumb and forefinger together to form a circle) means something offensive or obscene in another person's culture, you can avoid insulting that person simply by refraining from making that gesture.

One technique for understanding other cultures is the *cultural assimilator*, a strategy for perceiving the norms and values of another group (Baron & Graziano, 1991; Brislin et al., 1986). This technique teaches by example, asking students to explain why a member of another culture has behaved in a particular way. For example, why do the members of a Japanese grade school class silently follow their teacher single file through a park on a lovely spring day? Are they

Culture can dictate how you dress. These Saudi women wear veils when in public, in contrast to American women.

Norm
A shared idea or expectation about how to behave.

afraid of being punished for disorderly conduct if they do otherwise? Are they naturally placid and compliant? Once you understand that Japanese children are raised to value the needs and feelings of others over their own selfish concerns, their orderly, obedient behavior seems much less perplexing. Cultural assimilators encourage us to remain open-minded about others' norms and values by challenging such cultural truisms as "Our way is the right way."

Conformity

What increases the likelihood that someone will conform?

Accepting the norms of one's culture should not be confused with conformity. For instance, millions of Americans drink coffee in the morning, but they do not do so because they are conforming. They drink coffee because through cultural experience they have learned to like and desire it. **Conformity,** in contrast, implies a conflict between an individual and group—a conflict that is resolved when the individual yields his or her own preferences or beliefs to the norms or expectations of the larger group.

Since the early 1950s, when Solomon Asch conducted the first systematic study of the subject, conformity has been a major topic of research in social psychology. Asch demonstrated in a series of experiments that under some circumstances people will conform to group pressures even if this forces them to deny obvious physical evidence. His studies ostensibly tested visual judgment by asking people to choose from a card with several lines of differing lengths the line most similar to the line on a comparison card (see Figure 14–1). The lines were deliberately drawn so that the comparison was obvious and the correct choice was clear. All but one of the participants were confederates of the experimenter. On certain trials these confederates deliberately gave the same wrong answer. This put the lone dissenter on the spot: Should he conform to what he knew to be a wrong decision and agree with the group, thereby denying the evidence of his own eyes, or should he disagree with the group, thereby risking the social consequences of nonconformity?

Overall, participants conformed on about 35 percent of the trials. There were large individual differences, however, and in subsequent research, experimenters discovered that two sets of factors influence the likelihood that a person will conform: characteristics of the situation and characteristics of the person.

The *size* of the group is one situational factor that has been studied extensively. Asch (1951) found that the likelihood of conformity increased with group size until 4 confederates were present. After that point, the number of others made no difference to the frequency of conformity.

Another important situational factor is the degree of *unanimity* in the group. If just one confederate broke the perfect agreement of the majority by giving the correct answer, conformity among participants in the Asch experiments fell from an average of 35 percent to about 25 percent (Asch, 1956). Apparently, having just one "ally" eases the pressure to conform. The ally does not even have to share the person's viewpoint—just breaking the unanimity of the majority is enough to reduce conformity (Allen & Levine, 1971).

The *nature of the task* is still another situational variable that affects conformity. For instance, conformity has been shown to vary with the difficulty and ambiguity of a task. When the task is difficult or poorly defined, conformity tends to be higher (Blake, Helson, & Mouton, 1956). In an ambiguous situation, people are less sure of their own opinion and more willing to conform to the majority view.

Personal characteristics also influence conforming behavior. The more a person is attracted to the group, expects to interact with its members in the future, holds a position of relatively low status, and does not feel completely accepted

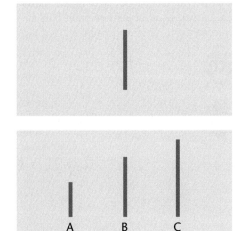

FIGURE 14–1

Asch's experiment on conformity. In Asch's experiment on *conformity,* participants were shown a comparison card like the top one and asked to indicate which of the three lines on the bottom card was the most similar. Participants frequently chose the wrong line in order to conform to the group choice.

Conformity
Voluntarily yielding to social norms, even at the expense of one's preferences.

APPLYING PSYCHOLOGY

Changing Beliefs about Binge Drinking

Her friends believe that Leslie Baltz, a senior honors student at the University of Virginia, was following a school tradition of the "fourth-year fifth"—drinking a fifth of liquor to celebrate the last home football game. When friends found her that evening unconscious, they rushed her to the hospital. But it was too late. She died the next day, another victim of alcohol poisoning through binge drinking (Winerip, 1998).

Binge drinking, defined as taking five or more alcoholic drinks in a row, has been identified as the number one health hazard for college students (Wechsler, Fulop, Padilla, Lee, & Patrick, 1997). Not only do binge drinkers risk their lives, but their drinking has been linked to higher rates of drunk driving, unplanned and unsafe sexual activity, physical and sexual assault, unintentional injuries, interpersonal problems, physical or cognitive impairment, and poor academic performance (Wechsler, Davenport, Dowdall, Moeykens, & Castillo, 1994).

So alarming are the consequences of alcohol abuse that the creation of alcohol task forces and education programs has become a growth industry on college campuses. Yet attempts to reduce binge drinking by teaching social skills, increasing awareness of support systems, improving coping skills, and raising self-esteem have met with relatively little success. What more can be done?

It may be as simple as making students aware that most of their peers do *not* indulge in binge drinking and relying on their tendency to conform to social norms. However serious the problem may be, binge drinking is not as prevalent as many students believe it to be. In some surveys, students estimate that as many as 70 percent of their classmates binge drink (Gose, 1997). Yet a national survey indicates that the actual figure may be closer to 38 percent (Winerip, 1998). When students realize that binge drinking is less common than they think, they are considerably less likely to try it themselves (Donaldson et al., 1994; Gose, 1997; Haines & Spears, 1996; Hansen, 1993; Hansen & Graham, 1991).

To learn more about problems related to alcohol, visit our Web site at **www.prenhall.com/morris**.

by the group, the more that person tends to conform. The fear of rejection apparently motivates conformity when a person scores high on one or more of these factors.

Sometimes we can be misled by what we *think* are group norms and conform to what is not, in fact, a norm. Perception, more than reality, for example, could be influencing the dangerous practice of "binge drinking," discussed in the *Applying Psychology* box.

Conformity across Cultures   A Chinese proverb states that "if one finger is sore, the whole hand will hurt." In a collectivist culture such as China, community and harmony are very important. Although members of all societies show a tendency to conform, you might suspect that members of collectivist cultures conform more frequently to the will of a group than do members of noncollectivist cultures. Psychologists who have studied this question have used tests similar to those Asch used in his experiments. They have found that levels of conformity in collectivist cultures are in fact frequently higher than those found by Asch. In collectivist societies as diverse as Fiji, Zaire, Hong Kong, Lebanon, Zimbabwe, Kuwait, Japan, and Brazil, conformity rates ranged from 25 percent to 51 percent (P. B. Smith & Bond, 1994). The rate is typically higher in farming societies (where members are more dependent on one another for long-term group survival) than in hunting and gathering societies (where people must exercise a good deal of independence to survive) (Berry, 1967).

GAMES
G

So what conclusions can we draw about conformity? The fact that rates of conformity in the Asch situation are relatively high across a variety of cultures suggests that a universal tendency to conform may exist. But conformity is often greater in collectivist societies, implying that culture can heighten (or lessen) any tendency toward it. There are also situational factors that can make conformity more or less likely, and these, too, can vary depending on a person's culture. Japanese people, for example, often deliberately oppose a majority opinion (even a correct one) when the other members of a group are strangers—something they are much less apt to do when the group is made up of friends (Frager, 1970; Williams & Sogon, 1984). As psychologists learn more about the differences between cultures, they will better understand what is universal about human behavior and what is culturally determined.

Compliance

How could a salesperson increase a customer's compliance in buying a product?

Conformity is a response to pressure exerted by norms that are generally left unstated. In contrast, **compliance** is a change of behavior in response to an explicitly stated request. One technique for inducing compliance is the so-called *foot-in-the-door effect*. Every salesperson knows that the moment a prospect allows the sales pitch to begin, the chances of making a sale improve greatly. The same effect operates in other areas of life: Once people have granted a small request, they are more likely to comply with a larger one.

In the most famous study of this phenomenon, Freedman and Fraser (1966) approached certain residents of Palo Alto, California, posing as members of a committee for safe driving. They asked residents to place a large ugly sign reading "Drive Carefully" in their front yards. Only 17 percent agreed to do so. Then other residents were asked to sign a petition calling for more safe-driving laws. When these same people were later asked to place the ugly "Drive Carefully" sign in their yards, an amazing 55 percent agreed. Compliance with the first small request more than tripled the rate of compliance with the larger request.

Why does the foot-in-the-door technique work so well? One possible explanation is that agreeing to the token act (signing the petition) realigns the subject's self-perception to that of someone who more strongly favors the cause. When presented with the larger request, the subject then feels obligated to comply (Snyder & Cunningham, 1975).

Another strategy commonly used by salespeople is the *lowball procedure* (Cialdini et al., 1978). The first step is to induce a person to agree to do something. The second step is to raise the cost of compliance. Among new-car dealers, lowballing works like this: The dealer persuades the customer to buy a new car by reducing the price well below that offered by competitors. Once the customer has agreed to buy the car, however, the terms of the sale shift abruptly (for example, the trade-in value promised by the used-car manager is cut) so that in the end the car is *more* costly than it would be at other dealerships. Despite the added costs, many customers follow through on their commitment to buy. Although the original inducement was the low price (the "lowball" the salesperson originally pitched), once committed, the buyer remains committed to the now pricier car.

Under certain circumstances, a person who has refused to comply with one request may be more likely to comply with a second. For example, if saying no to the first request made you feel guilty, you may say yes to something else. This phenomenon has been dubbed the *door-in-the-face effect* (Cialdini et al., 1975). In one study, researchers approached students and asked them to make an unreasonably large commitment: Would they counsel delinquent youths at a detention center for 2 years? Nearly everyone declined, thus effectively "slamming the door" in the researcher's face. But when later asked to make a much smaller commitment—supervising children during a trip to the zoo—many of the same

Compliance
Change of behavior in response to an explicit request from another person or group.

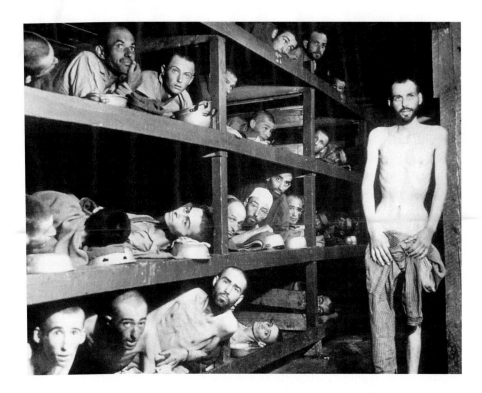

The Nazi concentration camps are a dramatic illustration of the extremes to which some people will go to obey orders. How do you explain the behaviors of the people who ran these camps?

students quickly agreed. The door-in-the-face effect may work because people interpret the smaller request as a concession and feel pressured to comply.

Obedience

How does the "power of the situation" affect obedience?

Compliance is agreement to change behavior in response to a request. **Obedience** is compliance with a command. Like compliance, it is a response to an explicit message; in this case, however, the message is a direct order, generally from a person in authority, such as a police officer, principal, or parent, who can back up the command with some sort of force if necessary. Obedience embodies social influence in its most direct and powerful form.

Several studies by Stanley Milgram, mentioned in Chapter 1, The Science of Psychology, showed how far many people will go to obey someone in authority (Milgram, 1963). People who agreed to participate in what they believed was a learning experiment administered what they thought were severe electrical shocks to the "learners." What factors influence the degree to which people will do what they are told? Studies in which people were asked to put a dime in a parking meter by people wearing uniforms show that one important factor is the amount of *power* vested in the person giving the orders. People obeyed a guard whose uniform looked like that of a police officer more often than they obeyed a man dressed either as a milkman or as a civilian. Another factor is *surveillance*. If we are ordered to do something and then left alone, we are less likely to obey than if we are being watched, especially if the act seems unethical to us. Milgram, for instance, found that his "teachers" were less willing to give severe shocks when the experimenter was out of the room.

Milgram's experiments revealed other factors that influence a person's willingness to follow orders. When the victim was in the same room as the "teacher," obedience dropped sharply. When another "teacher" was present, who refused to give shocks, obedience also dropped. But when responsibility for an act was shared, so that the person was only one of many doing it, the degree of obedience was much greater.

Obedience
Change of behavior in response to a command from another person, typically an authority figure.

Why do people willingly obey an authority figure, even if it means violating their own principles? Milgram (1974) thought that people feel obligated to those in power, first, because they respect their credentials and assume that they know what they are doing and, second, because they often have established trust with those authority figures by agreeing to do whatever they ask. Once this happens, participants may feel conflicted over what they are doing, but they manage through rationalization to push the conflict aside. The essence of obedience, says Milgram, is that people come to see themselves as the agents of *another* person's wishes and therefore not responsible for the obedient actions or their consequences. Once this shift in self-perception has occurred, obedience follows, because in their own minds, they have relinquished control of their actions.

Milgram's analysis emphasizes the *power of the situation:* Once people volunteered to take part in the study, they became caught up in the bizarre circumstances of it and felt compelled to respond to external forces (the experimenter's commands) rather than internal ones (their own moral opposition to harming others). An alternative explanation is also possible, however. Perhaps obedient participants do not succumb to situational forces but rather fail to *perceive* the situation correctly (Nissani, 1990). Thus in Milgram's study, the participants began with the belief that the experiment would be safe and the experimenter would be trustworthy. When these assumptions proved false—when the experiment turned out to be dangerous and the experimenter disregarded the victim's obvious suffering—the participants' assumptions were invalidated. But it is hard—sometimes impossible—to change one's beliefs and assumptions quickly, despite irrefutable evidence. The real emotional struggle for the obedient participants, then, may not have been in deciding whether to obey malevolent orders but in recognizing that a trusted authority figure proved to be treacherous.

REVIEW QUESTIONS

1. Match the following terms with the appropriate definition.

   social influence _____

       a. voluntarily yielding to social norms, even at the expense of one's own preferences

   compliance _____

       b. a change of behavior in response to a command from another person

   obedience _____

       c. a change of behavior in response to an explicit request from another person or from a group

   conformity _____

       d. any actions performed by one or more persons to change the attitudes, behavior, or feelings of others

2. A _____ is a shared idea or expectation about how to behave.

3. Solomon Asch found that the likelihood of a person conforming [increased/decreased] as the group size expanded to 4.

4. Which of the following are factors that influence the likelihood that a person will conform?

   a. the degree of unanimity in the group

   b. the difficulty or ambiguity of the task the group faces

   c. strong attachment to the group

   d. the group's gender makeup

5. "Research shows that compliance is often higher in collectivist cultures than in noncollectivist ones." True or false.

6. Once people have granted a small request, they are more likely to comply with a larger one. This is called the _____-_____-_____-_____ effect.

7. "Many people are willing to obey an authority figure, even if it means violating their own principles." True or false.

Answers: 1. social influence: d; compliance: c; obedience: b; conformity: a. **2.** norm. **3.** increased. **4.** a, b, and c. **5.** T. **6.** foot-in-the-door. **7.** T.

Social Action

Do we behave differently when other people are present?

The various kinds of social influence we have just discussed may take place even when no one else is physically present. We refrain from playing our stereo at full volume when our neighbors are sleeping, comply with jury notices that we received in the mail, and obey traffic signals even when no one is on the road to enforce them. We now turn to processes that *do* depend on the presence of others. Specifically, we examine processes that occur when people interact one on one and in groups. One of these social actions is called *deindividuation*.

Deindividuation

What negative outcomes can result from deindividuation?

We have seen several cases of social influence in which people act differently in the presence of others from the way they would if they were alone. The most striking and frightening instance of this phenomenon is *mob behavior*. Some well-known violent examples of mob behavior are the beatings and lynchings of African Americans, the looting that sometimes accompanies urban rioting, and the wanton destruction of property that mars otherwise peaceful protests and demonstrations. After a power outage in New York City in 1977, during which considerable looting took place, some of the looters were interviewed. Strangely, many said they would never have thought of looting had they been alone, and others were later shocked by their own behavior.

One reason for such behavior is that people lose their personal sense of responsibility in a group, especially in a group subjected to intense pressures and anxiety. This process is called **deindividuation,** because people respond not as individuals but as anonymous parts of a larger group. In general the more anonymous people feel in a group, the less responsible they feel as individuals.

But deindividuation only partly explains mob behavior. Another contributing factor is that, in a group, one dominant and persuasive person can convince people to act through a *snowball effect:* If the persuader convinces just a few people, those few will convince others, who will convince still others, and the group becomes an unthinking mob. Moreover, large groups provide *protection*. Anonymity makes it difficult to press charges. If 2, or even 10, people start smashing windows, they will probably be arrested. If a thousand people do it, very few of them will be caught or punished.

In the process called *deindividuation,* members of a group lose their personal sense of responsibility and behave in ways they would not act if they were alone. These people are looting a hardware truck following a rock concert.

Helping Behavior

What factors make us more inclined to help a person in need?

Research on deindividuation seems to support the unfortunate—and inaccurate—notion that when people get together they become more destructive and irresponsible than they would be individually. But human society depends on people's willingness to work together and help one another. In fact, instances of cooperation and mutual assistance are just as abundant as examples of human conflict and hostility. If, as we saw in the chapter on motivation and emotion, our willingness to harm others is influenced by social forces, so is our willingness to help others.

What are some of the social forces that can promote helping behavior? One is perceived self-interest. We offer our boss a ride home from the office because we know that our next promotion depends on how much he or she likes us. We volunteer to feed a neighbor's cat while he is away because we want him to do the same for us. But when helpful actions are not linked to such personal gain,

Deindividuation
A loss of personal sense of responsibility in a group.

they are considered **altruistic behavior.** A person who acts in an altruistic way does not expect any recognition or reward in return, except perhaps the good feeling that comes from helping someone in need. Many people direct altruistic acts, including many charitable contributions, at strangers and make them anonymously (M. L. Hoffman, 1977). (See the *Highlights* box to gain additional insight into the factors that influenced Gentiles to help Jewish victims of the Holocaust.)

Under what conditions is helping behavior most likely to occur? Like other things that social psychologists study, helping is influenced by two sets of factors: those in the situation and those in the individual.

The most important situational variable is the *presence of other people*. In a phenomenon called the **bystander effect,** the likelihood that a person will help someone else in trouble *decreases* as the number of bystanders present increases. In one experiment, people filling out a questionnaire heard a taped "emergency" in the next room, complete with a crash and screams. Of those who were alone, 70 percent offered help to the unseen female victim, but of those who waited with a companion—a stranger who did nothing to help—only 7 percent offered help (Latane & Rodin, 1969).

Another key aspect of the situation is its *ambiguity*. Any factors that make it harder for others to recognize a genuine emergency reduce the probability of altruistic actions. One experiment had a "workman" carry a ladder and a venetian blind past a waiting room in which participants were sitting (Clark & Word, 1974). What followed was a loud crash. In this ambiguous situation, especially when a sizable number of bystanders were present, many people failed to offer help. But when the workman clarified matters by calling out that he was hurt, all participants without exception rushed to his aid.

The *personal characteristics* of bystanders also affect helping behavior. Not all bystanders are equally likely to help a stranger. Increasing the amount of personal responsibility that one person feels for another boosts the likelihood that help will be extended. In one experiment, subjects were more likely to try to stop the theft of a stranger's property if they had promised to watch the property while the stranger was away than if they had had no contact with the stranger (Moriarty, 1975). The amount of *empathy* that we feel toward another person affects our willingness to help, too. When participants in a study felt that their values and personalities were similar to a victim's, they were more likely to offer help, even if that meant jeopardizing their own safety (Krebs, 1975). *Mood* also makes a difference. A person in a good mood is more likely to help another in need than is someone who is in a neutral or bad mood. Researchers demonstrated this by leaving a dime in the scoop of a pay phone to put the finder in a good mood (Isen & Levin, 1972). People finding the dime were much more likely than other people to help a confederate who dropped a folderful of papers on the sidewalk near the phone booth. In addition, helping behavior is increased when people don't *fear embarrassment* by offering assistance that isn't really needed (McGovern, 1976). Finally, when others are watching, people who score high on the need for approval are more likely to help than are low scorers (Satow, 1975).

Helping Behavior across Cultures   People often assume that there is a "helping personality" or a set of traits that determines who is helpful and who is not. This is unlikely. Several conditions, both individual and situational, combine to determine when help will be offered. Similarly, it's doubtful that there is such a thing as a "helpful culture"—that is, a society, nation, or group whose members are invariably "more helpful" than those of other groups. Psychologists have instead focused on the cultural factors that make helping more or less likely to take place.

Altruistic behavior
Helping behavior that is not linked to personal gain.

Bystander effect
The tendency for an individual's helpfulness in an emergency to decrease as the number of passive bystanders increases.

HIGHLIGHTS

Altruism and the Holocaust

This chapter began with the story of a 16-year-old Catholic girl and others who hid Jewish children from the Nazis throughout Nazi-occupied Europe. Only a few thousand non-Jews risked their lives to rescue Jews from persecution, deportation, and death. Why did they do what so many millions of others failed to do? What qualities enabled them to behave so altruistically and bravely?

In 1981 several researchers set out to find answers to questions like these and combined their efforts 2 years later in the Altruistic Personality Project. By 1985 the project had published findings based on interviews with 25 rescuers and 50 survivors, as well as historical documents about the activities of others (Fogelman & Wiener, 1985). The people with whom the researchers spoke came from several countries and differed widely in education and vocation. The rescuers did, however, share some characteristics. For one thing, most had an uncommon capacity for perseverance and a strong belief in their own competence to risk and

survive danger. For another, they preferred not to see themselves as heroes but instead considered their behavior to be natural.

Although no single personality characteristic emerged, researchers could identify some common threads. For example, rescuers tended to fall into one of two groups: those who were motivated by deeply rooted

---

Most had a strong belief in their own competence to risk and survive danger.

---

moral values and felt ethically bound to rescue victims, and those who were attached personally to the victims and sometimes identified with them emotionally. These findings support the contention of social psychologist Carol Gilligan (1982) that there are fundamentally two forms of moral reasoning: one based on a sense of

justice and the other based on a sense of responsibility and caring.

Morally motivated rescuers often harbored intense anti-Nazi attitudes. For some, religious belief played a paramount role in their lives. These rescuers also tended to help victims regardless of whether they liked or disliked them. Many of them belonged to families with traditions of concern for others outside the family, and many stated that their behavior was strongly guided by their parents' values. Stefania cited her parents' belief in religious tolerance.

In contrast, emotionally motivated rescuers frequently had strong personal attachments to the people whom they helped—neighbors, for instance. Some helped people whom they scarcely knew but with whom they identified. In certain cases the empathy sprang from the rescuer's belief that he or she was also vulnerable to persecution. "It is easy to understand what the Jews felt," explained one Ukrainian rescuer, "because Jews and the Ukrainians were in similar positions everywhere" (Fogelman & Wiener, 1985, p. 63).

Individualism/collectivism is an important dimension in this area: It seems plausible that members of individualist cultures feel less obligated to help other people than do members of collectivist cultures. A study using Indian and American subjects investigated this possibility (Miller, Bersoff, & Harwood, 1990). Participants were presented with helping scenarios involving either a stranger, a friend, or a close relative whose need was either minor, moderate, or extreme. There were no cultural differences in cases of extreme need; members of both cultures reported being equally willing to help. But the two groups differed in cases of minor needs. Almost three times as many Indians (from a collectivist culture) as Americans (from an individualist culture) felt obligated to help in a scenario involving a close friend or a stranger asking for minor assistance. Even within collectivist cultures, however, the prediction of when help will be offered can be problematic (Triandis, 1994). Some members of collectivist societies are reluctant to offer help to anyone outside of their in-group. They are therefore less likely to help strangers. Other cultures treat a stranger as a member of their group until that person's exact status can be determined.

Group Dynamics

How is making a decision in a group different from making a decision on your own?

There is a tendency in our society to turn important decisions over to groups. In the business world key decisions are often made around a conference table rather than behind one person's desk. In politics major policy decisions are seldom vested in just one person. Groups of advisers, cabinet officers, committee members, or aids meet to deliberate and forge a course of action. In the courts, a defendant may request a trial by jury, and for some serious crimes, jury trial is required by law. The 9-member U.S. Supreme Court renders group decisions on legal issues affecting the entire nation.

Many people trust these group decisions more than decisions made by individuals. And yet the dynamics of social interaction within groups sometimes conspire to make group decisions *less* sound than those made by someone acting alone. Social psychologists are intrigued by how this happens.

Polarization in Group Decision Making   People often assume that an individual acting alone is more likely to take risks than a group considering the same issue. This assumption remained unchallenged until the early 1960s. At that time, James Stoner (1961) designed an experiment to test the idea. He asked participants individually to counsel imaginary people who had to choose between a risky but potentially rewarding course of action and a conservative but less rewarding alternative. Next the participants met in small groups to discuss each decision until they reached unanimous agreement. Surprisingly, the groups consistently recommended a riskier course of action than the people working alone did. This phenomenon is known as the **risky shift**.

The risky shift is simply one aspect of a more general group phenomenon called **polarization**—the tendency for people to become more extreme in their attitudes as a result of group discussion. Polarization begins when group members discover during discussion that they share views to a greater degree than they realized. Then, in an effort to be seen in a positive light by the others, at least some group members become strong advocates for what is shaping up to be the dominant sentiment in the group. Arguments leaning toward one extreme or the other not only reassure people that their initial attitudes are correct but also intensify those attitudes so that the group as a whole becomes more extreme in its position. So if you want a group decision to be made in a cautious, conservative direction, you should make sure that the members of the group hold cautious and conservative views in the first place. Otherwise the group decision may polarize in the opposite direction.

The Effectiveness of Groups   The adage "Two heads are better than one" reflects the common assumption that members of a group will pool their abilities and arrive at a better decision than will individuals working alone. In fact, groups are more effective than individuals only under certain circumstances. For one thing, it depends on the task they are faced with. If the requirements of the task match the skills of the group members, the group is likely to be more effective than any single individual.

Even if task and personnel are perfectly matched, however, the ways in which group members *interact* may reduce the group's efficiency. For example, high-status individuals tend to exert more influence in groups, so if they do not possess the best problem-solving skills, group decisions may suffer (Torrance, 1954). Another factor affecting group interaction and effectiveness is group *size*. The larger the group, the more likely it is to include someone who has the skills needed to solve a difficult problem. On the other hand, it is much harder

Risky shift
Greater willingness of a group than an individual to take substantial risks.

Polarization
Shift in attitudes by members of a group toward more extreme positions than the ones held before group discussion.

to coordinate the activities of a large group. In addition, large groups may be more likely to encourage *social loafing*, the tendency of group members to exert less effort on the assumption that others in the group will do the work. Finally, the quality of group decision making also depends on the *cohesiveness* of a group. When the people in a group like one another and feel committed to the goals of the group, cohesiveness is high. Under these conditions, members may work hard for the group, spurred on by high morale. But cohesiveness can undermine the quality of group decision making. If the group succumbs to *groupthink*, according to Irvine Janis (1982), strong pressure to conform prevents its members from criticizing the emerging group consensus. In such a group, amiability and morale supersede judgment. Members with doubts may hesitate to express them. The result may be disastrous decisions—such as the Bay of Pigs invasion, the Watergate cover-up, or the go-ahead for the *Challenger* space flight (Kruglanski, 1986).

Group Leadership Every group has a leader, but how do group leaders come to the fore? For many years the predominant answer was the **great person theory,** which states that leaders are extraordinary people who assume positions of influence and then shape events around them. In this view, people like George Washington, Winston Churchill, and Nelson Mandela were "born leaders"—who would have led any nation at any time in history.

Most historians and psychologists now regard this theory as naïve, because it ignores social and economic factors. An alternative theory holds that leadership emerges when the right person is in the right place at the right time. For instance, in the later 1950s and early 1960s Dr. Martin Luther King, Jr., rose to lead the black civil rights movement. Dr. King was clearly a "great person"—intelligent, dynamic, eloquent, and highly motivated. Yet had the times not been right (for instance, had he lived 30 years earlier) it is doubtful that he would have been as successful as he was.

And there is probably even more to becoming a leader than either the great person theory or the right-place-at-the-right-time perspective implies. According to what is called the *transactional view*, a sizable number of factors interact to determine who emerges as a leader. The leader's traits, certain aspects of the situation in which the group finds itself, and the response of the group and the leader to each other are all important considerations.

These same considerations are also important in determining how effective a leader turns out to be. Personal characteristics, for example, such as leadership style, are significant only in relation to other aspects of the group and its situation. This point is stressed in Fred Fiedler's *contingency model* of leader effectiveness. According to Fiedler (1978, 1993), some leaders are *task-oriented*—that is, concerned mainly with getting the group's goals accomplished—while others are *relationship-oriented*—concerned mainly with fostering group cohesiveness and harmony. Which style is more effective depends on the particular situation, such as the clarity of the tasks to be accomplished, the quality of leader–member relations, and the amount of power the leader exercises. When the situation is very favorable for the leader (clear tasks, good relations with members, much power held) a task-oriented style is usually more effective. This is also true when conditions are very *un*favorable (when tasks are vague, relations with members are poor, and little power is exercised). It is when conditions for the leader are somewhere between these two extremes that a relationship-oriented leader becomes most successful, according to Fiedler's research. In Fiedler's view there is no such thing as an ideal leader for all situations. "It is simply not meaningful to speak of an effective or ineffective leader," he writes. "We can only speak of a leader who tends to be effective in one situation and ineffective in another" (Fiedler, 1967, p. 261).

One theory of leadership holds that the particularly effective leader is the right person in the right place at the right time. For the American civil rights movement, Martin Luther King, Jr., was such a leader.

Great person theory
The theory that leadership is a result of personal qualities and traits that qualify one to lead others.

Leadership across Cultures   The distinction between task-oriented and relationship-oriented leaders seems to be a main operating principle in most work groups in the United States. Someone explicitly appointed manager or crew chief is charged with making sure that the job gets done, while someone else usually emerges informally to act as the relationship-oriented specialist who tells jokes, remembers everyone's birthday, smooths disputes, and generally maintains morale (Bales, 1951). In the Western world this division of leadership often operates in informal social groups as well. Yet it is not the only approach to leadership. Consider a collectivist culture that values cooperation and interdependence among group members. In such an environment it is unlikely that individuals would emerge to serve specific functions within a group. Although one member may be named "the manager," there is less need for individuals to have clearly defined roles as "this type of leader" or "that type of leader." All members see themselves as working together to accomplish the group's goals.

Leadership in American businesses is currently being transformed through the introduction of a management style that has proved successful in Japan and other Eastern collectivist cultures (J. W. Dean & Evans, 1994; McFarland, Senn, & Childress, 1993). This approach emphasizes decision-making input from all group members, small work teams that promote close cooperation, and a style of leadership in which managers receive much the same treatment as any other employee. In the West it is not uncommon for executives to have their own parking spaces, dining facilities, fitness and social clubs, as well as separate offices and independent schedules. Most Japanese executives consider this privileged style of management very strange. In many Eastern cultures, managers and executives share the same facilities as their workers, hunt for parking spaces like everyone else, and eat and work side by side with their employees. Interestingly, the Japanese model has effectively combined the two leadership approaches—task-oriented and relationship-oriented—into a single overall style. By being a part of the group, the leader can simultaneously work toward and direct the group's goals, while also contributing to the group's morale and social climate. Combining these roles is an effective strategy for Japanese leaders in such diverse workplaces as banks, bus companies, shipyards, coal mines, and government offices (Misumi, 1985).

Organizational Behavior

Can psychology help to increase worker output and satisfaction?

The places where we work and the various organizations to which we belong shape much of our behavior. **Industrial organizational (I/O) psychology** spotlights the influence on human interaction of large, complex organizational settings, with special emphasis on behavior in the workplace.

Productivity   I/O psychologists focus on practical problems, such as how to reduce employee turnover, improve worker morale, and increase productivity. One of the first studies of the relationship between productivity and working conditions was conducted in the late 1920s by Elton Mayo and his colleagues, who gradually increased the lighting in the Western Electric Hawthorne plant in Cicero, Illinois. The researchers were testing the hypothesis that better lighting would boost worker output. But their results showed something else entirely: Productivity increased with better lighting, too much lighting, and too little lighting. In what has become known as the **Hawthorne effect,** the workers' efficiency rose no matter what was done to their conditions, simply because of the attention that the researchers were giving to them.

The methods of Mayo's team have since come under criticism (Parsons, 1974), but their study was one of the first to highlight the importance of psycho-

Industrial/organizational (I/O) psychology
The area of psychology concerned with the application of psychological principles to the problems of human organizations, especially work organizations.

Hawthorne effect
The principle that people will alter their behavior because of researchers' attention and not necessarily because of any specific treatment condition.

logical and social factors on behavior in the workplace. Since the 1930s, I/O psychologists have attempted to analyze that relationship in more specific terms. For example, workers whose jobs call for a greater variety of skills are more likely to think of their work as meaningful and to exhibit increased motivation and satisfaction, and workers whose jobs entail more autonomy generally produce work of a higher quality (Melamed et al., 1995). Thus motivation, satisfaction, and productivity in the workplace can all be improved by making the right changes in job components.

Research by I/O psychologists has also found that small, cohesive work groups are more productive than large, impersonal ones. Putting this idea into practice, managers of assembly-line workers have developed the *autonomous work group*, replacing the massive assembly line with small groups of workers who produce an entire unit (a whole car, for instance) and periodically alternate their tasks. Additional benefits derived from this approach include greater worker satisfaction, higher-quality output, and decreased absenteeism and turnover (Pearson, 1992).

Communication and Responsibility

The way in which communications are handled within an organization also has an impact on organizational efficiency and the attitudes of its members. A system in which members communicate with just one person in authority—a centralized system—typically works well in solving simple problems. Complex problems, in contrast, are better handled in a decentralized way, with group members freely communicating with one another (Porter & Roberts, 1976).

I/O psychologists have also examined the issue of assigning responsibility for key decisions to work groups. While some groups make better decisions than others, group decision making in general enhances member satisfaction (Cotton, 1993). If people believe that they had an input into a decision, they are more satisfied with the outcome and their membership in the group. Increasing the number of people who participate in the decision-making process does *not*, however, lead to increased productivity.

REVIEW QUESTIONS

1. ____ is a process by which people feel anonymous in a large group.

2. In a mob one dominant person can often convince other people to engage in an action they wouldn't otherwise do as a result of the ____ effect.

3. ____ behavior is helping other people with no expectation of personal gain.

4. "According to the bystander effect, the likelihood that someone will help another person in trouble increases with the number of passive bystanders present." True or false.

5. If group members are inclined to take risks, their group decision is likely to be riskier than decisions arrived at by each individual acting alone. This phenomenon is known as the ____ ____.

6. A shift in attitudes by the members of a group toward more extreme positions than those they held before group discussion is called group ____.

7. The poor decisions made in the Watergate cover-up, the *Challenger* space flight, and the Bay of Pigs invasion were due primarily to a process called ____.

8. Which is most important in determining who will lead a group?
   a. the personal characteristics of potential leaders
   b. the situation in which the group finds itself
   c. both personal traits and situational factors interacting with each other

9. "Motivation, satisfaction, and productivity in the workplace can all be increased by making the right changes in how jobs are structured." True or false.

Answers: 1. Deindividuation. 2. snowball. 3. Altruistic. 4. F. 5. risky shift. 6. polarization. 7. groupthink. 8. c. 9. T.

KEY TERMS

social psychology, p. 488

Social cognition
social cognition, p. 488
schema, p. 488
primacy effect, p. 488
self-fulfilling prophecy, p. 489
stereotype, p. 489
attribution theory, p. 490
fundamental attribution
  error, p. 490
defensive attribution, p. 491

just-world hypothesis, p. 491
proximity, p. 492
exchange, p. 493
equity, p. 493

Attitudes
attitude, p. 495
self-monitoring, p. 496
prejudice, p. 496
discrimination, p. 496
frustration-aggression
  theory, p. 497

authoritarian personality,
  p. 498
racism, p. 498
cognitive dissonance, p. 503

Social influence
social influence, p. 504
norm, p. 505
conformity, p. 506
compliance, p. 508
obedience, p. 509

Social action
deindividuation, p. 511
altruistic behavior, p. 512
bystander effect, p. 512
risky shift, p. 514
polarization, p. 514
great person theory, p. 515
industrial organizational
  (I/O) psychology, p. 516
Hawthorne effect, p. 516

CHAPTER REVIEW

□ **What do forming impressions, explaining others' behavior, and experiencing interpersonal attraction have in common?**

Forming impressions, explaining others' behavior, and experiencing interpersonal attraction are all examples of social cognition. **Social cognition** is the process of taking in and assessing information about other people. It is one way in which we are influenced by the thoughts, feelings, and behaviors of others.

□ **How do we form first impressions of people?**

When forming impressions of others, we rely on schemata, or sets of expectations and beliefs about categories of people. Impressions are also affected by the order in which information is acquired. First impressions are the strongest (the **primacy effect**), probably because we prefer not to expend a great deal of cognitive effort analyzing large amounts of subsequent data. This same preference also encourages us to form impressions using simplistic but strongly held schemata called **stereotypes.**

□ **How do we decide why people act as they do?**

Attribution theory holds that people seek to understand human behavior by attributing it either to causes within the person or causes in the situation. Biases in perception can lead to the **fundamental attribution error,** in which we overemphasize personal traits in attributing causes to others' behavior. **Defensive attribution** motivates us to explain our own actions in ways that protect our self-esteem. We tend to attribute our successes to internal factors and our failures to external ones. The **just-world hypothesis** may lead us to blame the victim when bad things happen to other people.

□ **Do "birds of a feather flock together," or do "opposites attract"?**

When it comes to interpersonal attraction, the adage "Birds of a feather flock together" has more validity than "Opposites attract." People who are similar in attitudes, interests, backgrounds, and values tend to like one another. **Proximity** is another factor that promotes liking. The more we are in contact with certain people, the more we tend to like them. We also tend to like people who make us feel appreciated and rewarded, an idea based on the concept of **exchange.**

□ **Why are attitudes important?**

An **attitude** is a relatively stable organization of beliefs, feelings, and tendencies toward something or someone—called an attitude object. Attitudes are important because they often influence behavior. We cannot always tell people's attitudes from their actions, however.

□ **What are the three major components of attitudes?**

The three major components of attitudes are (1) evaluative beliefs about the attitude object, (2) feelings about that object, and (3) behavioral tendencies toward it. These three components are very often (but not always) consistent with one another.

□ **How does a person develop a prejudice toward someone else?**

Prejudice is an unfair negative attitude directed toward a group and its members, while **discrimination** is behavior based on prejudice. One explanation of prejudice is the **frustration–aggression theory,** which states that people who feel exploited and oppressed displace their hostility toward the powerful onto people who are "lower" on the social scale than they are. Another theory links prejudice to the **authoritarian personality,** a rigidly conformist and bigoted personality type marked by exaggerated respect for authority and hostility toward those who defy society's norms. A third theory proposes a cognitive source of prejudice—oversimplified or stereotyped thinking about categories of people. Finally, conformity to the prejudices of one's social group can help to explain prejudice.

◻ What factors encourage someone to change an attitude?

Attitudes can change in response to new experiences, including efforts at persuasion. The first step in persuasion is to get the audience's attention. Then the task is to get the audience to comprehend and accept the message. According to the communication model, persuasion is a function of the source, the message itself, the medium of communication, and the characteristics of the audience. Attitudes may also be changed when new actions, beliefs, or perceptions contradict pre-existing attitudes, called **cognitive dissonance.**

◻ What are some areas in which the power of social influence is highly apparent?

Social influence is the process by which people's thoughts, feelings, and actions are affected by the behavior and characteristics of other people. In some topics that social psychologists study, the power of social influence is even more apparent than usual. Among these are the study of cultural influences and of conformity, compliance, and obedience.

◻ How does your culture influence how you dress or what you eat?

The culture in which you are immersed has an enormous influence on your thoughts and actions. Culture dictates differences in diet, dress, and personal space. The fact that you eat pizza and shun rattlesnake meat, dress in jeans and a T-shirt instead of a loincloth or sari, and feel uncomfortable when others stand very close to you when they speak are all results of culture. In the course of adapting our behavior to that of others, we learn the **norms** of our culture, as well as its beliefs and values.

◻ What increases the likelihood that someone will conform?

Voluntarily yielding one's preferences, beliefs, or judgments to those of a larger group is called **conformity.** Research by Solomon Asch and others has shown that characteristics of both the situation and the person influence the likelihood of conforming. There are also cultural influences on the tendency to conform, with people in collectivist cultures often being more prone to conformity than those in noncollectivist ones.

◻ How could a salesperson increase a customer's compliance in buying a product?

Compliance is a change in behavior in response to an explicit request from someone else. One technique to encourage compliance is the foot-in-the-door approach, or getting people to go along with a small request in order to make them more likely to comply with a larger one. For instance, a salesperson might get you to agree to try a product "free" for 30 days in order to make you more apt to buy the product later. Another technique is the lowball procedure: initially offering a low price to win commitment, and then gradually escalating the cost. Also effective is the door-in-the-face tactic, or initially making an unreasonable request, which is bound to be turned down but will perhaps generate enough guilt to make compliance with another request more likely.

◻ How does the "power of the situation" affect obedience?

Classic work by Stanley Milgram showed that many people were willing to obey orders to administer harmful shocks to other people. This **obedience** to an authority figure was more likely when certain situational factors were present. For example, people found it harder to disobey when the authority figure issuing the order was nearby. They were also more apt to obey the command when the person being given the shock was some distance from them. According to Milgram, obedience is brought on by the constraints of the situation.

◻ Do we behave differently when other people are present?

Conformity, compliance, and obedience may take place even when no one else is physically present, but other processes of social influence depend on the presence of others. Among these are deindividuation, the bystander effect, group decision making, and organizational behavior.

◻ What negative outcomes can result from deindividuation?

Immersion in a large, anonymous group may lead to **deindividuation,** the loss of a sense of personal responsibility for one's actions. Deindividuation can sometimes lead to violence or other forms of irresponsible behavior. The greater the sense of anonymity, the more this effect occurs.

◻ What factors make us more inclined to help a person in need?

Helping someone in need without expectation of a reward is called **altruistic behavior.** Altruism is influenced by situational factors such as the presence of other people. According to the **bystander effect,** a person is less apt to offer assistance when other potential helpers are present. Conversely, being the only person to spot someone in trouble tends to encourage helping. Also encouraging helping are an unambiguous emergency situation and certain personal characteristics, such as empathy for the victim and being in a good mood.

☐ **How is making a decision in a group different from making a decision on your own?**

Research on the **risky shift** and the broader phenomenon of group **polarization** shows that group decision making actually increases tendencies toward extreme solutions, encouraging members to lean toward either greater risk or greater caution. People deliberating in groups may also display social loafing, or a tendency to exert less effort on the assumption that others will do most of the work. And in very cohesive groups there is a tendency toward groupthink, or an unwillingness to criticize the emerging group consensus even when it seems misguided.

☐ **Can psychology help to increase worker output and satisfaction?**

Industrial/organizational (I/O) psychology studies behavior in organizational settings such as the workplace. Research in this field shows that worker output and satisfaction can be raised by a variety of situational changes. For instance, worker output often increases simply because of attention from others, a phenomenon called the **Hawthorne effect.** I/O findings have led organizations to establish autonomous work groups to replace less efficient assembly-line arrangements. Productivity and morale may also be improved by increasing worker responsibility and facilitating communication in the workplace.

CRITICAL THINKING AND APPLICATIONS

1. What is a self-fulfilling prophecy? How does this concept apply to human relationships? Can you think of instances from your own experience when self-fulfilling prophecies seemed to be at work?

2. Think of an advertisement that influenced your decision to buy something. What kind of message did the ad convey? How was this message communicated? Why did you respond to it? Were you aware at the time that the ad was designed to elicit this response? Is advertising inherently dishonest and manipulative, or does it sometimes serve a useful purpose?

On the Web...

Visit these online resources at our Companion Website www.prenhall.com/morris

The Psychology Place

Learning Activities	1. Predicting Our Own Social Behavior, p. 487
Research News	2. Another Explanation for Differences in Intellectual Performance: Stereotype Threat, p. 489
	3. How Stereotypes Affect Test Performance, p. 489
	4. Investigating Social Judgments, p. 490
	5. The Shape of Beauty: In the Eye of the Beholder?, p. 492
	6. The Mathematics of Beauty, p. 492
	7. Racism Requires Racial Categorization, p. 498
	8. The Social Consequences of Affirmative Action, p. 499
Op-Ed Forum	9. Are We Sugarcoating Culture? Thinking Critically About the Study of Diversity, p. 500
	10. Social Control: Good and Bad for Your Health, p. 504
	11. What Makes a Good Leader?, p. 505

Games	1. Define Concepts, p. 487
	2. Social Situations, p. 505
	3. Individualism vs. Collectivism, p. 507

Web Links:

1. **http://www.socialpsychology.org/**, p. 487
   Social Psychology Network.
2. **http://www.socialpsychology.org/social.htm**, p. 496
   Social Psychology Links by Subtopic: Comprehensive list of links to key components of social psychology, including such topics as prejudice and discrimination, gender, culture, social influence, interpersonal relations, group behavior, and aggression.
3. **http://server.bmod.athabascau.ca/html/aupr/social.htm**, p. 505
   Psychology Centre: Social and Cultural Psychology.
4. **http://miavx1.muohio.edu/~shermarc/p324tuta.htmlx**, p. 511
   Web Tutorials in Social Psychology: Living in a Social World.
5. **http://maple.lemoyne.edu/~hevern/psychref4-6a.html**, p. 516
   PsychREF: Industrial/Organizational Psychology: Psychology in Business and Advertising.

APPENDIX

Measurement and Statistical Methods

Most of the experiments described in this book involve measuring one or more variables and then analyzing the data statistically. The design and scoring of all the tests we have discussed are also based on statistical methods. **Statistics** is a branch of mathematics. It provides techniques for sorting out quantitative facts and ways of drawing conclusions from them. Statistics let us organize and describe data quickly; they guide the conclusions we draw and help us to make inferences.

Statistical analysis is essential to conducting an experiment or designing a test, but statistics can only handle numbers—groups of them. To use statistics, the psychologist first must measure things—count and express them in quantities.

Scales of Measurement

No matter what we are measuring—height, noise, intelligence, attitudes—we have to use a scale. The data we want to collect determine the scale we use, and, in turn, the scale we use helps to determine the conclusions we can draw from our data.

Nominal Scales   A nominal scale is a set of arbitrarily named or numbered categories. If we decide to classify a group of people by the color of their eyes, we are using a **nominal scale.** We can count how many people have blue eyes, how many have green eyes, how many have brown eyes, and so on, but we cannot say that one group has more or less eye color than the other. The colors are simply different. Because a nominal scale is more of a way of classifying than of measuring, it is the least informative kind of scale. If we want to compare our data more precisely, we will have to use a scale that tells us more.

Ordinal Scales   If we list horses in the order in which they finish a race, we are using an **ordinal scale.** On an ordinal scale, data are ranked from first to last according to some criterion. An ordinal scale tells the order, but nothing about the distances between what is ranked first and second or ninth and tenth. It does not tell us how much faster the winning horse ran than the

---

Statistics
A branch of mathematics that psychologists use to organize and analyze data.

Nominal scale
A set of categories for classifying objects.

Ordinal scale
Scale indicating order or relative position of items according to some criterion.

523

horses that placed or showed. If a person ranks her preferences for various kinds of soup—pea soup first, then tomato, then onion, and so on—we know what soup she likes most and what soup she likes least, but we have no idea how much better she likes tomato than onion, or if pea soup is far more favored than either one of them. Because we do not know the distances between the items ranked on an ordinal scale, we cannot add or subtract ordinal data. If mathematical operations are necessary, we need a still more informative scale.

Interval Scales   An **interval scale** is often compared to a ruler that has been broken off at the bottom—it only goes from, say, 5½ to 12. The intervals between 6 and 7, 7 and 8, 8 and 9, and so forth are equal, but there is no zero. A thermometer is an interval scale—even though a certain degree registered on a Fahrenheit or Centigrade thermometer specifies a certain state of cold or heat, there is no such thing as no temperature at all. One day is never twice as hot as another; it is only so many equal degrees hotter.

An interval scale tells us how many equal-size units that one thing lies above or below another thing of the same kind, but it does not tell us how many times bigger, smaller, taller, or fatter one thing is than another. An intelligence test cannot tell us that one person is three times as intelligent as another, only that he or she scored so many points above or below someone else.

Ratio Scales   We can only say that a measurement is two times as long as another or three times as high when we use a **ratio scale,** one that has a true zero. For instance, if we measure the snowfall in a certain area over several winters, we can say that six times as much snow fell during the winter in which we measured a total of 12 feet as during a winter in which only 2 feet fell. This scale has a zero—there may be no snow.

Measurements of Central Tendency

Usually, when we measure a number of instances of anything—from the popularity of television shows to the weights of 8-year-old boys to the number of times a person's optic nerve fires in response to electrical stimulation—we get a distribution of measurements that range from smallest to largest or lowest to highest. The measurements will usually cluster around some value near the middle. This value is the **central tendency** of the distribution of the measurements.

Suppose, for example, that you want to keep 10 children busy tossing rings around a bottle. You give them three rings to toss each turn, the game has 6 rounds, and each player scores 1 point every time he or she gets the ring around the neck of the bottle. The highest possible score is 18. The distribution of scores might end up like this: 11, 8, 13, 6, 12, 10, 16, 9, 12, 3.

What could you quickly say about the ring-tossing talent of the group? First, you could arrange the scores from lowest to highest: 3, 6, 8, 9, 10, 11, 12, 12, 13, 16. In this order, the central tendency of the distribution of scores becomes clear. Many of the scores cluster around the values between 8 and 12. There are three ways to describe the central tendency of a distribution. We usually refer to all three as the *average*.

The arithmetical average is called the **mean**—the sum of all of the scores in the group divided by the number of scores. If you add up all the scores and divide by 10, the total number of scores in this group of ring tossers, you find that the mean for the group is 10.

Interval scale
Scale with equal distances between the points or values, but without a true zero.

Ratio scale
Scale with equal distances between the points or values and with a true zero.

Central tendency
Tendency of scores to congregate around some middle value.

Mean
Arithmetical average calculated by dividing a sum of values by the total number of cases.

The **median** is the point that divides a distribution in half—50 percent of the scores fall above the median, and 50 percent fall below. In the ring-tossing scores, 5 scores fall at 10 or below, 5 at 11 or above. The median is thus halfway between 10 and 11—10.5.

The point at which the largest number of scores occurs is called the **mode**. In our example, the mode is 12. More people scored 12 than any other number.

Differences between the Mean, Median, and Mode

If we take many measurements of anything, we are likely to get a distribution of scores in which the mean, median, and mode are all about the same—the score that occurs most often (the mode) will also be the point that half the scores are below and half above (the median). And the same point will be the arithmetical average (the mean). This is not always true, of course, and small samples rarely come out so symmetrically. In these cases, we often have to decide which of the three measures of central tendency—the mean, the median, or the mode—will tell us what we want to know.

For example, a shopkeeper wants to know the general incomes of passersby so that he can stock the right merchandise. He might conduct a rough survey by standing outside his store for a few days from 12:00 to 2:00 and asking every tenth person who walks by to check a card showing the general range of his or her income. Suppose most of the people checked the ranges between $15,000 and $25,000 a year. A couple of the people, however, made a lot of money—one checked $100,000–$150,000 and the other checked the $200,000-or-above box. The mean for the set of income figures would be pushed higher by those two large figures and would not really tell the shopkeeper what he wants to know about his potential customers. In this case he would be wiser to use the median or the mode.

Suppose that instead of meeting two people whose incomes were so great, he noticed that people from two distinct income groups walked by his store—several people checked the box for $15,000–$17,000, and several others checked $23,000–$25,000. The shopkeeper would find that his distribution was bimodal. It has two modes—$16,000 and $24,000. This might be more useful to him than the mean, which could lead him to think his customers were a unit with an average income of about $20,000.

Another way of approaching a set of scores is to arrange them into a **frequency distribution**—that is, to select a set of intervals and count how many scores fall into each interval. A frequency distribution is useful for large groups of numbers; it puts the number of individual scores into more manageable groups.

Suppose that a psychologist tests memory. She asks 50 college students to learn 18 nonsense syllables, then records how many syllables each student can recall 2 hours later. She arranges her raw scores from lowest to highest in a rank distribution:

2	6	8	10	11	14
3	7	9	10	12	14
4	7	9	10	12	15
4	7	9	10	12	16
5	7	9	10	13	17
5	7	9	11	13	
6	8	9	11	13	
6	8	9	11	13	
6	8	10	11	13	

Median
Point that divides a set of scores in half.

Mode
Point at which the largest number of scores occurs.

Frequency distribution
A count of the number of scores that fall within each of a series of intervals.

The scores range from 2 to 17, but 50 individual scores are too cumbersome to work with. So the psychologist chooses a set of 2-point intervals and tallies the number of scores in each interval:

Interval	Tally	Frequency
1–2	|	1
3–4	|||	3
5–6	|||| |	6
7–8	|||| ||||	9
9–10	|||| |||| |||	13
11–12	|||| |||	8
13–14	|||| ||	7
15–16	||	2
17–18	|	1

Now the psychologist can tell at a glance what the results of her experiment were. Most of the students had scores near the middle of the range, and very few had scores in the high or low intervals. She can see these results even better if she uses the frequency distribution to construct a bar graph—a **frequency histogram.** Marking the intervals along the horizontal axis and the frequencies along the vertical axis would give her the graph shown in Figure A–1. Another way is to construct a **frequency polygon,** a line graph. A frequency polygon drawn from the same set of data is shown in Figure A–2. Note that the figure is not a smooth curve, as the points are connected by straight lines. With many scores, however, and with small intervals, the angles would smooth out, and the figure would resemble a rounded curve.

FIGURE A–1

A frequency histogram for a memory experiment. The bars indicate the frequency of scores within each interval.

Frequency histogram
Type of bar graph that shows frequency distributions.

Frequency polygon
Type of line graph that shows frequency distributions.

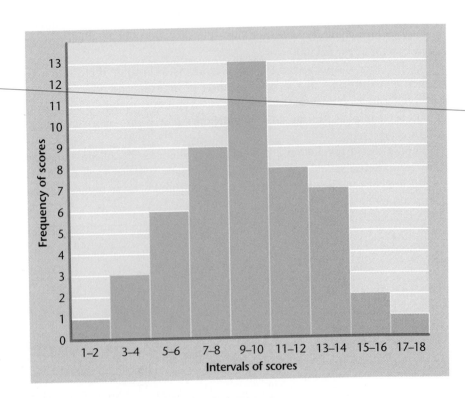

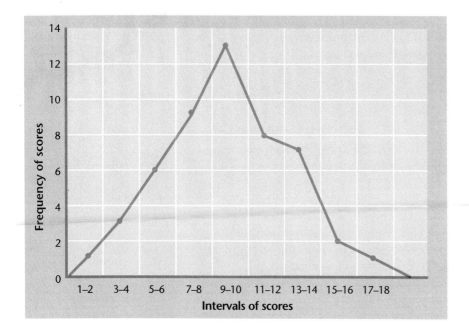

FIGURE A–2
A frequency polygon drawn from data used in Figure A–1. The dots, representing the frequency of scores in each interval, are connected by straight lines.

The Normal Curve

Ordinarily, if we take enough measurements of almost anything, we get a *normal distribution.* Tossing coins is a favorite example of statisticians. If you tossed 10 coins into the air 1,000 times and recorded the heads and tails on each toss, your tabulations would reveal a normal distribution. Five heads and 5 tails would occur most often, 6 heads/4 tails and 4 heads/6 tails would be the next most frequent, and so on down to the rare all heads or all tails.

Plotting a normal distribution on a graph yields a particular kind of frequency polygon, called a **normal curve.** Figure A–3 shows data on the heights of 1,000 men. Superimposed over the gray bars that reflect the actual data is an "ideal" normal curve for the same data. Note that the curve is absolutely symmetrical—the left slope parallels the right slope exactly. Moreover, the mean, median, and mode all fall on the highest point on the curve.

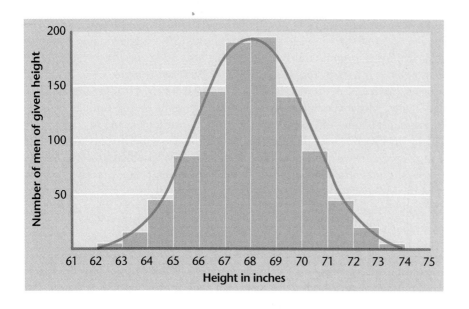

FIGURE A–3
A normal curve, based on measurements of the heights of 1,000 adult males.
Source: From Hill, 1966.

Normal curve
Hypothetical bell-shaped distribution curve that occurs when a normal distribution is plotted as a frequency polygon.

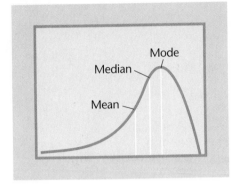

FIGURE A–4

A skewed distribution. Most of the scores are gathered at the high end of the distribution, causing the hump to shift to the right. Because the tail on the left is longer, we say that the curve is skewed to the left. Note that the *mean, median,* and *mode* are different.

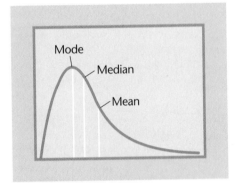

FIGURE A–5

In this distribution most of the scores are gathered at the low end, so the curve is skewed to the right. The *mean, median,* and *mode* do not coincide.

Range
Difference between the largest and smallest measurements in a distribution.

Standard deviation
Statistical measure of variability in a group of scores or other values.

The normal curve is a hypothetical entity. No set of real measurements shows such a smooth gradation from one interval to the next, or so purely symmetrical a shape. But because so many things do approximate the normal curve so closely, the curve is a useful model for much that we measure.

Skewed Distributions

If a frequency distribution is asymmetrical—if most of the scores are gathered at either the high end or the low end—the frequency polygon will be *skewed*. The hump will sit to one side or the other, and one of the curve's tails will be disproportionately long.

If a high school mathematics instructor, for example, gives her students a sixth-grade arithmetic test, we would expect nearly all the scores to be quite high. The frequency polygon would probably look like the one in Figure A–4. But if a sixth-grade class is asked to do advanced algebra, the scores would probably be quite low. The frequency polygon would be very similar to the one shown in Figure A–5.

Note, too, that the mean, median, and mode fall at different points in a skewed distribution, unlike in the normal curve, where they coincide. Usually, if you know that the mean is greater than the median of a distribution, you can predict that the frequency polygon will be skewed to the right. If the median is greater than the mean, the curve will be skewed to the left.

Measures of Variation

Sometimes it is not enough to know the distribution of a set of data and what their mean, median, and mode are. Suppose an automotive safety expert feels that too much damage occurs in tail-end accidents because automobile bumpers are not all the same height. It is not enough to know what the average height of an automobile bumper is. The safety expert also wants to know about the variation in bumper heights: How much higher is the highest bumper than the mean? How do bumpers of all cars vary from the mean? Are the latest bumpers closer to the same height?

Range

The simplest measure of variation is the **range**—the difference between the largest and smallest measurements. Perhaps the safety expert measured the bumpers of 1,000 cars 2 years ago and found that the highest bumper was 18 inches from the ground, and the lowest was only 12 inches from the ground. The range was thus 6 inches—18 minus 12. This year the highest bumper is still 18 inches high, and the lowest is still 12 inches from the ground. The range is still 6 inches. Moreover, our safety expert finds that the means of the two distributions are the same—15 inches off the ground. But look at the two frequency polygons in Figure A–6—there is still something the expert needs to know, as the measurements cluster around the mean in drastically different ways. To find out how the measurements are distributed around the mean, our safety expert has to turn to a slightly more complicated measure of variation—the standard deviation.

The Standard Deviation

The **standard deviation,** in a single number, tells us much about how the scores in any frequency distribution are dispersed around the mean. Calculating the standard deviation is one of the most useful and widely employed statistical tools.

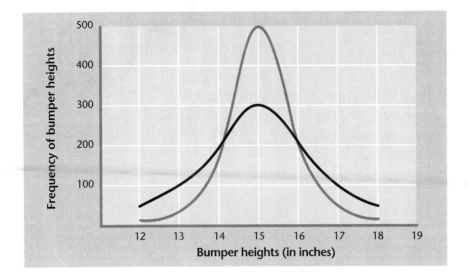

FIGURE A–6

Frequency polygons for two sets of measurements of automobile bumper heights. Both are normal curves, and in each distribution the *mean, median,* and *mode* are 15. But the variation from the mean is different, causing one curve to be flattened and the other to be much more sharply peaked.

To find the standard deviation of a set of scores, we first find the mean. Then we take the first score in the distribution, subtract it from the mean, square the difference, and jot it down in a column to be added up later. We do the same for all the scores in the distribution. Then we add up the column of squared differences, divide the total by the number of scores in the distribution, and find the square root of that number. Figure A–7 shows the calculation of the standard deviation for a small distribution of scores.

In a normal distribution, however peaked or flattened the curve, about 68 percent of the scores fall between 1 standard deviation above the mean and 1 standard deviation below the mean (see Figure A–8). Another 27 percent fall between 1 standard deviation and 2 standard deviations on either side of the mean, and 4 percent more between the second and third standard deviations on either side. Overall, then, more than 99 percent of the scores fall between 3 standard deviations above and 3 standard deviations below the mean. This makes the standard deviation useful for comparing two different normal distributions.

Number of scores = 10		Mean = 7
Scores	Difference from mean	Difference squared
4	$7 - 4 = 3$	$3^2 = 9$
5	$7 - 5 = 2$	$2^2 = 4$
6	$7 - 6 = 1$	$1^2 = 1$
6	$7 - 6 = 1$	$1^2 = 1$
7	$7 - 7 = 0$	$0^2 = 0$
7	$7 - 7 = 0$	$0^2 = 0$
8	$7 - 8 = -1$	$-1^2 = 1$
8	$7 - 8 = -1$	$-1^2 = 1$
9	$7 - 9 = -2$	$-2^2 = 4$
10	$7 - 10 = -3$	$-3^2 = 9$

Sum of squares = 30
÷
Number of scores = 10
Variance = 3
Standard deviation = $\sqrt{3} = 1.73$

FIGURE A–7

Step-by-step calculation of the *standard deviation* for a group of 10 scores with a mean of 7.

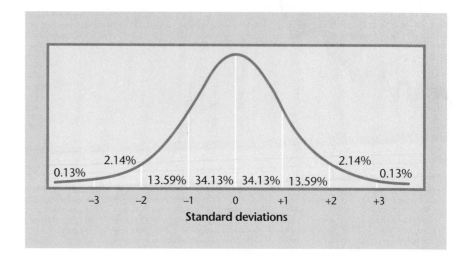

FIGURE A–8

A normal curve, divided to show the percentage of scores that fall within each *standard deviation* from the *mean.*

Now let us see what the standard deviation can tell our automotive safety expert about the variations from the mean in the two sets of data. The standard deviation for the cars measured 2 years ago is about 1.4. A car with a bumper height of 16.4 is 1 standard deviation above the mean of 15; one with a bumper height of 13.6 is 1 standard deviation below the mean. Because the engineer knows that the data fall into a normal distribution, he or she can figure that about 68 percent of the 1,000 cars he or she measured will fall somewhere between these two heights: 680 cars will have bumpers between 13.6 and 16.4 inches high. For the more recent set of data, the standard deviation is just slightly less than 1. A car with a bumper height of about 14 inches is 1 standard deviation below the mean; a car with a bumper height of about 16 is 1 standard deviation above the mean. Thus, in this distribution, 680 cars have bumpers between 14 and 16 inches high. This tells the safety expert that car bumpers are becoming more similar, although the range of heights is still the same (6 inches), and the mean height of bumpers is still 15.

Measures of Correlation

Measures of central tendency and measures of variation can be used to describe a single set of measurements—like the children's ring-tossing scores—or to compare two or more sets of measurements—like the two sets of bumper heights. Sometimes, however, we need to know if two sets of measurements are in any way associated with each other—if they are *correlated.* Is parental IQ related to children's IQ? Does the need for achievement relate to the need for power? Is watching violence on television related to aggressive behavior?

One fast way to determine if two variables are correlated is to draw a **scatter plot.** We assign one variable (X) to the horizontal axis of a graph, the other variable (Y) to the vertical axis. Then we plot a person's score on one characteristic along the horizontal axis and his or her score on the second characteristic along the vertical axis. Where the two scores intersect, we draw a dot. When several scores have been plotted in this way, the pattern of dots tells if the two characteristics are in any way correlated with each other.

If the dots on a scatter plot form a straight line running between the lower left-hand corner and the upper right-hand corner, as they do in Figure A–9a, we have a perfect positive correlation—a high score on one of the characteristics is always associated with a high score on the other. A straight line running between

Scatter plot
Diagram showing the association between scores on two variables.

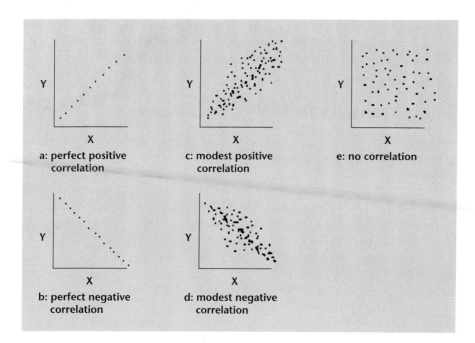

the upper-left-hand corner and the lower-right-hand corner, as in Figure A–9b, is the sign of a perfect negative correlation—a high score on one of the characteristics is always associated with a low score on the other. If the pattern formed by the dots is cigar shaped in either of these directions, as in Figure A–9c and d, we have a modest correlation—the two characteristics are related but not highly correlated. If the dots spread out over the whole graph, forming a circle or a random pattern, as they do in Figure A–9e, there is no correlation between the two characteristics.

A scatter plot can give us a general idea if a correlation exists and how strong it is. To describe the relation between two variables more precisely, we need a **correlation coefficient**—a statistical measure of the degree to which two variables are associated. The correlation coefficient tells us the degree of association between two sets of matched scores—that is, to what extent high or low scores on one variable tend to be associated with high or low scores on another. It also provides an estimate of how well we can predict from a person's score on one characteristic how high he or she will score on another. If we know, for example, that a test of mechanical ability is highly correlated with success in engineering courses, we could predict that success on the test would also mean success as an engineering major.

Correlation coefficients can run from +1.0 to –1.0. The highest possible value (+1.0) indicates a perfect positive correlation—high scores on one variable are always and systematically related to high scores on a second variable. The lowest possible value (–1.0) means a perfect negative correlation—high scores on one variable are always and regularly related to low scores on the second variable. In life, most things are far from perfect, so most correlation coefficients fall somewhere between +1.0 and –1.0. A correlation smaller than ±0.20 is considered very low, from ±0.20 to ±0.40 is low, from ±0.40 to ±0.60 is moderate, from ±0.60 to ±0.80 is high, and from ±0.80 to ±1.0 is very high. A correlation of zero indicates that there is no correlation between two sets of scores—no regular relation between them at all.

Correlation tells us nothing about causality. If we found a high positive correlation between participation in elections and income levels, for example, we still could not say that being wealthy made people vote or that voting made people

Correlation coefficient
Statistical measure of the strength of association between two variables.

wealthy. We would still not know which came first, or if some third variable explained both income levels and voting behavior. Correlation only tells us that we have found some association between scores on two specified characteristics.

Using Statistics to Make Predictions

Behind the use of statistics is the hope that we can generalize from our results and use them to predict behavior. We hope, for example, that we can use the record of how well a group of rats run through a maze today to predict how another group of rats will do tomorrow, that we can use a person's scores on a sales aptitude test to predict how well he or she will sell life insurance, that we can measure the attitudes of a relatively small group of people about pollution control to indicate what the attitudes of the whole country are.

First we have to determine if our measurements are representative and if we can have confidence in them. In Chapter 1 we discussed this problem when we considered the problem of proper sampling.

Probability

Errors based on inadequate sampling procedures are somebody's fault. Other kinds of errors occur randomly. In the simplest kind of experiment, a psychologist will gather a representative sample, split it randomly into two groups, and then apply some experimental manipulation to one of the groups. Afterward the psychologist will measure both groups and determine if the experimental group's score is now different from the score of the control group. But even if there is a large difference between the scores of the two groups, it may still be wrong to attribute the difference to the manipulation. Random effects might influence the results and introduce error.

Statistics give the psychologist many ways to determine precisely if the difference between the two groups is really significant, if something other than chance produced the results, and if the same results would be obtained with different subjects. These probabilities are expressed as measures of **significance.** If the psychologist computes the significance level for the results as 0.05, he or she knows that there are 19 chances out of 20 that the results are not due to chance. But there is still 1 chance in 20—or a 0.05 likelihood—that the results are due to chance. A 0.01 significance level would mean that there is only 1 chance in 100 that the results are due to chance.

Significance
Probability that results obtained were due to chance.

GLOSSARY

Absolute refractory period   A period after firing when a neuron will not fire again no matter how strong the incoming messages may be.

Absolute threshold   The least amount of energy that can be detected as a stimulation 50 percent of the time.

Achievement motive   The need to excel, to overcome obstacles; a social motive.

Actualizing tendency   According to Rogers, the drive of every organism to fulfill its biological potential and become what it is inherently capable of becoming.

Adaptation   An adjustment of the senses to the level of stimulation they are receiving.

Additive color mixing   The process of mixing lights of different wavelengths to create new hues.

Adjustment   Any effort to cope with stress.

Adoption studies   Research carried out on children, adopted at birth by parents not related to them, to determine the relative influence of heredity and environment on human behavior.

Adrenal glands   Two endocrine glands located just above the kidneys.

Aerial perspective   Monocular cue to distance and depth based on the fact that more distant objects are likely to appear hazy and blurred.

Afferent neurons   Neurons that carry messages from sense organs to the spinal cord or brain.

Affiliation motive   The need to be with others; a social motive.

Afterimage   Sense experience that occurs after a visual stimulus has been removed.

Agoraphobia   An anxiety disorder that involves multiple, intense fears of crowds, public places, and other situations that require separation from a source of security such as the home.

Algorithm   A step-by-step method of problem solving that guarantees a correct solution.

All-or-none law   Principle that the action potential in a neuron does not vary in strength; the neuron either fires at full strength or it does not fire at all.

Altered states of consciousness (ASC)   Mental states that differ noticeably from normal waking consciousness.

Altruistic behavior   Helping behavior that is not linked to personal gain.

Alzheimer's disease   A disorder of late adulthood that is characterized by progressive losses in memory and cognition and changes in personality that is believed to be caused by a deterioration of the brain's structure and function.

Amphetamines   Stimulant drugs that initially produce "rushes" of euphoria often followed by sudden "crashes" and, sometimes, severe depression.

Amplitude   The magnitude of a wave; in sound, the primary determinant of loudness.

Anal stage   Second stage in Freud's theory of personality development, in which a child's erotic feelings center on the anus and on elimination.

Anima   According to Jung, the female archetype as it is expressed in the male personality.

Animus   According to Jung, the male archetype as it is expressed in the female personality.

Anorexia nervosa   A serious eating disorder that is associated with an intense fear of weight gain and a distorted body image.

Antipsychotic drugs   Drugs used to treat very severe psychological disorders, particularly schizophrenia.

Antisocial personality disorder   Personality disorder that involves a pattern of violent, criminal, or unethical and exploitative behavior and an inability to feel affection for others.

Anxiety disorders   Disorders in which anxiety is a characteristic feature or the avoidance of anxiety seems to motivate abnormal behavior.

Apnea   Sleep disorder characterized by breathing difficulty during the night and feelings of exhaustion during the day.

Approach/approach conflict   According to Lewin, the result of simultaneous attraction to two appealing possibilities, neither of which has any negative qualities.

Approach/avoidance conflict   According to Lewin, the result of being simultaneously attracted to and repelled by the same goal.

Archetypes   In Jung's theory of personality thought forms common to all human beings, stored in the collective unconscious.

Association areas   Areas of the cerebral cortex that integrate information from diverse parts of the cortex and are involved in mental processes such as learning, thinking, and remembering.

Attachment   Emotional bond that develops in the first year of life that makes human babies cling to their caregivers for safety and comfort.

Attention   The selection of some incoming information for further processing.

Attention-deficit/hyperactivity disorder (ADHD)   A childhood disorder characterized by inattention, impulsiveness, and hyperactivity.

Attitude   Relatively stable organization of beliefs, feelings, and behavior tendencies directed toward something or someone—the attitude object.

Attribution theory   The theory that addresses the question of how people make judgments about the causes of behavior.

Auditory nerve   The bundle of axons that carries signals from each ear to the brain.

Authoritarian personality   A personality pattern characterized by rigid conventionality, exaggerated respect for authority, and hostility toward those who defy society's norms.

Autistic disorder   A childhood disorder characterized by lack of social instincts and strange motor behavior.

Autokinetic illusion   The perception that a stationary object is actually moving.

Autonomic nervous system   The part of the peripheral nervous system that carries messages between the central nervous system and the internal organs.

Autonomy   Sense of independence; a desire not to be controlled by others.

Availability heuristic   A heuristic by which a judgment or decision is based on information that is most easily retrieved from memory.

Aversive conditioning   Behavioral therapy techniques aimed at eliminating undesirable behavior patterns by teaching the person to associate them with pain and discomfort.

Avoidance training   Learning a desirable behavior to prevent the occurrence of something unpleasant such as punishment.

Avoidance/avoidance conflict   According to Lewin, the result of facing a choice between two undesirable possibilities, neither of which has any positive qualities.

Avoidant personality disorder   Personality disorder in which the person's fears of rejection by others lead to social isolation.

Axon   Single long fiber extending from the cell body; it carries outgoing messages.

Barbiturates   Potentially deadly depressants, first used for their sedative and anticonvulsant properties, now used only to treat such conditions as epilepsy and arthritis.

Basilar membrane   Vibrating membrane in the cochlea of the inner ear; it contains sense receptors for sound.

Behavior contracting   Form of operant conditioning therapy in which the client and therapist set behavioral goals and agree on reinforcements that the client will receive on reaching those goals.

Behavior genetics   Study of the relationship between heredity and behavior.

Behavior therapies Therapeutic approaches that are based on the belief that all behavior, normal and abnormal, is learned, and that the objective of therapy is to teach people new, more satisfying ways of behaving.

Behaviorism School of psychology that studies only observable and measurable behavior.

Big Five Five traits or basic dimensions currently thought to be of central importance in describing personality.

Binaural cue Cue to sound location that involves both ears working together.

Binocular cues Visual cues requiring the use of both eyes.

Biofeedback A technique that uses monitoring devices to provide precise information about internal physiological processes, such as heart rate or blood pressure, to teach people to gain voluntary control over these functions.

Biographical (or retrospective) study A method of studying developmental changes by reconstructing subjects' past through interviews and investigating the effects of past events on current behaviors.

Biological model View that psychological disorders have a biochemical or physiological basis.

Biological treatments A group of approaches, including medication, electroconvulsive therapy, and psychosurgery, that are sometimes used to treat psychological disorders in conjunction with, or instead of, psychotherapy.

Bipolar cells Neurons that have only one axon and one dendrite; in the eye, these neurons connect the receptors on the retina to the ganglion cells.

Bipolar disorder A mood disorder in which periods of mania and depression alternate, sometimes with periods of normal mood intervening.

Blind spot The place on the retina where the axons of all the ganglion cells leave the eye and where there are no receptors.

Blocking A process whereby prior conditioning prevents conditioning to a second stimulus even when the two stimuli are presented simultaneously.

Body dysmorphic disorder A somatoform disorder in which a person becomes so preoccupied with his or her imagined ugliness that normal life is impossible.

Borderline personality disorder Personality disorder characterized by marked instability in self-image, mood, and interpersonal relationships.

Brain stem The top of the spinal column; it widens out to form the hindbrain and midbrain.

Brainstorming A problem-solving strategy in which an individual or a group produces numerous ideas and evaluates them only after all ideas have been collected.

Brightness constancy The perception of brightness as the same, even though the amount of light reaching the retina changes.

Brightness The nearness of a color to white as opposed to black.

Bulimia An eating disorder characterized by binges of eating followed by self-induced vomiting.

Bystander effect The tendency for an individual's helpfulness in an emergency to decrease as the number of passive bystanders increases.

Cannon–Bard theory States that the experience of emotion occurs simultaneously with biological changes.

Case study Intensive description and analysis of a single individual or just a few individuals.

Catatonic schizophrenia Schizophrenic disorder in which disturbed motor behavior is prominent.

Central nervous system (CNS) Division of the nervous system that consists of the brain and spinal cord.

Cerebellum Structure in the hindbrain that controls certain reflexes and coordinates the body's movements.

Cerebral cortex The outer surface of the two cerebral hemispheres that regulate most complex behavior.

Cerebral hemispheres The largest part of the brain, developed more in humans than in any other animal.

Chromosomes Pairs of threadlike bodies within the cell nucleus that contain the genes.

Chunking The grouping of information into meaningful units for easier handling by short-term memory.

Classical (or Pavlovian) conditioning The type of learning in which a response naturally elicited by one stimulus comes to be elicited by a different, formerly neutral stimulus.

Client-centered (or person-centered) therapy Nondirectional form of therapy developed by Carl Rogers that calls for unconditional positive regard of the client by the therapist with the goal of helping the client become fully functioning.

Cliques Groups of adolescents with similar interests and strong mutual attachment.

Cocaine Drug derived from the coca plant that, while producing a sense of euphoria by stimulating the sympathetic nervous system, also leads to anxiety, depression, and addictive cravings.

Cochlea Part of the inner ear containing fluid that vibrates, which in turn causes the basilar membrane to vibrate.

Cognition The processes whereby we acquire and use knowledge.

Cognitive therapies Psychotherapies that emphasize changing clients' perceptions of their life situation as a way of modifying their behavior.

Cognitive dissonance Perceived inconsistency between two cognitions.

Cognitive distortions An illogical and maladaptive response to early negative life events that leads to feelings of incompetence and unworthiness that are re-activated whenever a new situation arises that resembles the original events.

Cognitive learning Learning that depends on mental processes that are not directly observable.

Cognitive map A learned mental image of a spatial environment that may be called on to solve problems when stimuli in the environment change.

Cognitive psychology School of psychology devoted to the study of mental processes in the broadest sense.

Cognitive theory States that emotional experience depends on one's perception or judgment of the situation one is in.

Cognitive therapy Therapy that depends on identifying and changing inappropriately negative and self-critical patterns of thought.

Cognitive–behavioral model View that psychological disorders result from learning maladaptive ways of thinking and behaving.

Cognitive–social learning theories Personality theories that view behavior as the product of the interaction of cognitions, learning and past experiences, and the immediate environment.

Cohort A group of people born during the same period in historical time.

Collective unconscious In Jung's theory of personality the level of the unconscious that is inherited and common to all members of a species.

Color constancy An inclination to perceive familiar objects as retaining their color despite changes in sensory information.

Colorblindness Partial or total inability to perceive hues.

Compensation According to Adler, the person's effort to overcome imagined or real personal weaknesses.

Compensatory model A rational decision-making model in which choices are systematically evaluated on various criteria.

Compliance Change of behavior in response to an explicit request from another person or group.

Componential intelligence According to Sternberg, the ability to acquire new knowledge, to solve problems effectively.

Compromise Deciding on a more realistic solution or goal when an ideal solution or goal is not practical.

Concept A mental category for classifying objects, people, or experiences.

Concrete-operational stage In Piaget's theory, the stage of cognitive development between 7 and 11 years of age in which the individual can attend to more than one thing at a time and understand someone else's point of view, though thinking is limited to concrete matters.

Conditioned response (CR) After conditioning, the response an organism produces when a conditioned stimulus is presented.

Conditioned stimulus (CS) An originally neutral stimulus that is paired with an unconditioned stimulus and eventually produces the desired response in an organism when presented alone.

Conditioned taste aversion Conditioned avoidance of certain foods even if there is only one pairing of conditioned and unconditioned stimuli.

Cones Receptor cells in the retina responsible for color vision.

Confirmation bias The tendency to look for evidence in support of a belief and to ignore evidence that would disprove a belief.

Conformity Voluntarily yielding to social norms, even at the expense of one's preferences.

Confrontation Acknowledging a stressful situation directly and attempting to find a solution to the problem or attain the difficult goal.

Consciousness Our awareness of various cognitive processes, such as sleeping, dreaming, concentrating, and making decisions.

Content validity Refers to a test's having an adequate sample of questions measuring the skills or knowledge it is supposed to measure.

Contextual intelligence According to Sternberg, the ability to select contexts in which you can excel, to shape the environment to fit your strengths.

Contingency A reliable "if–then" relationship between two events such as a CS and a US.

Control group In a controlled experiment, the group not subjected to a change in the independent variable; used for comparison with the experimental group.

Convergence A visual depth cue that comes from muscles controlling eye movement as the eyes turn inward to view a nearby stimulus.

Convergent thinking Thinking that is directed toward one correct solution to a problem.

Conversion disorders Somatoform disorders in which a dramatic specific disability has no physical cause but instead seems related to psychological problems.

Cornea The transparent protective coating over the front part of the eye.

Corpus callosum A thick band of nerve fibers connecting the left and right cerebral cortex.

Correlational research Research technique based on the naturally occurring relationship between two or more variables.

Couple therapy A form of group therapy intended to help troubled partners improve their problems of communication and interaction.

Creativity The ability to produce novel and socially valued ideas or objects.

Criterion-related validity Validity of a test as measured by a comparison of the test score and independent measures of what the test is designed to measure.

Critical period Time when certain internal and external influences have a major effect on development; at other periods the same influences will have little or no effect.

Cross-sectional study A method of studying developmental changes by examining groups of subjects who are of different ages.

Culture The tangible goods and the values, attitudes, behaviors, and beliefs that are passed from one generation to another.

Culture-fair tests Intelligence tests designed to eliminate cultural bias by minimizing skills and values that vary from one culture to another.

Dark adaptation Increased sensitivity of rods and cones in darkness.

Decay theory The theory that the passage of time causes forgetting.

Decibel Unit of measurement for the loudness of sounds.

Deep structure The underlying meaning of a sentence.

Defense mechanisms Self-deceptive techniques for reducing stress, including denial, repression, projection, identification, regression, intellectualization, reaction formation, displacement, and sublimation.

Defensive attribution The tendency to attribute our successes to our own efforts or qualities and our failures to external factors.

Deindividuation A loss of personal sense of responsibility in a group.

Deinstitutionalization Policy of treating people with severe psychological disorders in the larger community, or in small residential centers such as halfway houses, rather than in large public hospitals.

Delusions False beliefs about reality that have no basis in fact.

Dendrites Short fibers that branch out from the cell body and pick up incoming messages.

Denial Refusal to acknowledge a painful or threatening reality.

Deoxyribonucleic acid (DNA) Complex molecule in a double-helix configuration that is the main ingredient of chromosomes and genes and forms the code for all genetic information.

Dependent personality disorder Personality disorder in which the person is unable to make choices and decisions independently and cannot tolerate being alone.

Dependent variable In an experiment, the variable that is measured to see how it is changed by manipulations in the independent variable.

Depersonalization disorder A dissociative disorder whose essential feature is that the person suddenly feels changed or different in a strange way.

Depressants Chemicals that slow down behavior or cognitive processes.

Depression A mood disorder characterized by overwhelming feelings of sadness, lack of interest in activities, and perhaps excessive guilt or feelings of worthlessness.

Desensitization therapy A conditioning technique designed to gradually reduce anxiety about a particular object or situation.

Developmental psychology The study of the changes that occur in people from birth through old age.

Diathesis Biological predisposition.

Diathesis–stress model View that people biologically predisposed to a mental disorder (those with a certain diathesis) will tend to exhibit that disorder when particularly affected by stress.

Dichromats Organisms that are blind to either red-green or yellow-blue.

Difference threshold or just noticeable difference (jnd) The smallest change in stimulation that can be detected 50 percent of the time.

Discrimination An unfair act or series of acts taken toward an entire group of people or individual members of that group.

Disorganized schizophrenia Schizophrenic disorder in which bizarre and childlike behaviors are common.

Displacement Shifting repressed motives and emotions from an original object to a substitute object.

Display rules Culture-specific rules that govern how, when, and why facial expressions of emotion are displayed.

Dissociative disorders Disorders in which some aspect of the personality seems separated from the rest.

Divergent thinking Thinking that meets the criteria of originality, inventiveness, and flexibility.

Dominant gene Member of a gene pair that controls the appearance of a certain trait.

Double-blind procedure Experimental design, useful in studies of the effects of drugs, in which neither the subject nor the researcher knows at the time of administration which subjects are receiving an active drug and which are receiving an inactive substitute.

Drive State of tension or arousal brought on by biological needs.

Drive-reduction theory Theory that motivated behavior is aimed at reducing a state of bodily tension or arousal and returning the organism to homeostasis.

Eclecticism Psychotherapeutic approach that recognizes the value of a broad treatment package over a rigid commitment to one particular form of therapy.

Efferent neurons Neurons that carry messages from the spinal cord or brain to the muscles and glands.

Ego Freud's term for the part of the personality that mediates between environmental demands (reality), conscience (superego), and instinctual needs (id); now often used as a synonym for "self."

Ego ideal The part of the superego that consists of standards of what one would like to be.

Egocentric Unable to see things from another's point of view.

Elaborative rehearsal The linking of new information in short-term memory to familiar material stored in long-term memory.

Electroconvulsive therapy (ECT) Biological therapy in which a mild electrical current is passed through the brain for a short period, often producing convulsions and temporary coma; used to treat severe, prolonged depression.

Elevation   Monocular cue to distance and depth based on the fact that the higher on the horizontal plane an object is, the farther away it appears.

Emotion   Feeling, such as fear, joy, or surprise, that underlies behavior.

Emotional intelligence   According to Goleman, a form of intelligence that refers to how effectively people perceive and understand their own emotions and the emotions of others and can regulate and manage their emotional behavior.

Endocrine glands   Glands of the endocrine system that release hormones into the bloodstream.

Episodic memory   The portion of long-term memory that stores more specific information that has personal meaning.

Equity   Fairness of exchange achieved when each partner in the relationship receives the same proportion of outcomes to investments.

Ethnicity   A common cultural heritage—including religion, language, or ancestry—that is shared by a group of individuals.

Evolutionary psychology   A subfield of psychology concerned with the origins of behaviors and mental processes, their adaptive value, and the purposes they continue to serve.

Evolutionary psychology   An approach to, and subfield of, psychology that is concerned with the evolutionary origins of behaviors and mental process, their adaptive value, and the purposes they continue to serve.

Exchange   The concept that relationships are based on trading rewards among partners.

Existential psychology   School of psychology that focuses on the meaninglessness and alienation of modern life, and how these factors lead to apathy and psychological problems.

Expectancies   In Bandura's view what a person anticipates in a situation or as a result of behaving in certain ways.

Experiential intelligence   Sternberg's term for the ability to adapt creatively in new situations, to use insight.

Experimental group   In a controlled experiment, the group subjected to a change in the independent variable.

Experimental method   Research technique in which an investigator deliberately manipulates selected events or circumstances and then measures the effects of those manipulations on subsequent behavior.

Experimenter bias   Expectations by the experimenter that might influence the results of an experiment or its interpretation.

Explicit memory   Memory for information that was intentionally committed to memory or intentionally retrieved from memory.

Extinction   A decrease in the strength or frequency of a learned response because of failure to continue pairing the US and CS (classical conditioning) or withholding of reinforcement (operant conditioning).

Extrinsic motivation   A desire to perform a behavior to obtain an external reward or to avoid punishment.

Factor analysis   A statistical technique that identifies groups of related objects; used by Cattell to identify trait clusters.

Family studies   Studies of heritability in humans based on the assumption that if genes influence a certain trait, close relatives should be more similar on that trait than distant relatives.

Family therapy   A form of group therapy that sees the family as at least partly responsible for the individual's problems and that seeks to change all family members' behaviors to the benefit of the family unit as well as the troubled individual.

Feminist theory   Feminist theories offer a wide variety of views on the social roles of women and men, the problems and rewards of those roles, and prescriptions for changing those roles.

Fetishism   A paraphilia in which a nonhuman object is the preferred or exclusive method of achieving sexual excitement.

Fetus   A developing human between 3 months after conception and birth.

Fixation   According to Freud, a partial or complete halt at some point in the individual's psychosexual development.

Fixed-interval schedule   A reinforcement schedule in which the correct response is reinforced after a fixed length of time since the last reinforcement.

Fixed-ratio schedule   A reinforcement schedule in which the correct response is reinforced after a fixed number of correct responses.

Flashbulb memory   A vivid memory of a certain event and the incidents surrounding it even after a long time has passed.

Formal-operational stage   In Piaget's theory, the stage of cognitive development beginning at about age 11, in which the individual becomes capable of abstract thought.

Fovea   The area of the retina that is the center of the visual field.

Fraternal twins   Twins developed from two separate fertilized ova and therefore different in genetic makeup.

Free association   A psychoanalytic technique that encourages the patient to talk without inhibition about whatever thoughts or fantasies come to mind.

Frequency   The number of cycles per second in a wave; in sound, the primary determinant of pitch.

Frequency theory   Theory that pitch is determined by the frequency with which hair cells in the cochlea fire.

Frontal lobes   Part of the cerebral cortex that is responsible for voluntary movement; it is also important for attention, goal-directed behavior, and appropriate emotional experiences.

Frustration–aggression theory   The theory that under certain circumstances people who are frustrated in their goals turn their anger away from the proper, powerful target and toward another, less powerful target that is safer to attack.

Fully functioning person   According to Rogers, an individual whose self-concept closely resembles his or her inborn capacities or potentials.

Functional fixedness   The tendency to perceive only a limited number of uses for an object, thus interfering with the process of problem solving.

Functionalism   Theory of mental life and behavior that is concerned with how an organism uses its perceptual abilities to function in its environment.

Fundamental attribution error   The tendency of people to overemphasize personal causes for other people's behavior and to underemphasize personal causes for their own behavior.

Ganglion cells   Neurons that connect the bipolar cells in the eyes to the brain.

Gate control theory   The theory that a "neurological gate" in the spinal cord controls the transmission of pain messages to the brain.

Gender constancy   The realization by a child that gender cannot be changed.

Gender identity   A little girl's knowledge that she is a girl, and a little boy's knowledge that he is a boy.

Gender stereotypes   General beliefs about characteristics that men and women are presumed to have.

Gender   The psychological and social meanings attached to being biologically male or female.

Gender-identity disorder in children   Rejection of one's biological gender in childhood, along with the clothing and behavior that society considers appropriate to that gender.

Gender-identity disorders   Disorders that involve the desire to become, or the insistence that one really is, a member of the other biological sex.

Gender-role awareness   Knowledge of what behavior is appropriate for each gender.

General adaptation syndrome (GAS)   According to Selye, the three stages the body passes through as it adapts to stress: alarm reaction, resistance, and exhaustion.

Generalized anxiety disorder   An anxiety disorder characterized by prolonged vague but intense fears that are not attached to any particular object or circumstance.

Genes   Elements that control the transmission of traits; they are found on the chromosomes.

Genetics   Study of how traits are transmitted from one generation to the next.

Genital stage   In Freud's theory of personality development the final stage of normal adult sexual development, which is usually marked by mature sexuality.

Gestalt psychology   School of psychology that studies how people perceive and experience objects as whole patterns.

Gestalt therapy   An insight therapy that emphasizes the wholeness of the personality and attempts to reawaken people to their emotions and sensations in the here and now.

Giftedness   Refers to superior IQ combined with demonstrated or potential ability in such areas as academic aptitude, creativity, and leadership.

Glial cells or glia   Cells that insulate and support neurons by holding them together, removing waste products, and preventing harmful substances from passing from the bloodstream into the brain.

Golgi tendon organs   Receptors that sense movement of the tendons, which connect muscle to bone.

Gonads   The reproductive glands—testes in males and ovaries in females.

Graded potentials   A shift in the electrical charge in a tiny area of a neuron.

Grammar   The language rules that determine how sounds and words can be combined and used to communicate meaning within a language.

Great person theory   The theory that leadership is a result of personal qualities and traits that qualify one to lead others.

Group tests   Written intelligence tests administered by one examiner to many people at one time.

Group therapy   Type of psychotherapy in which clients meet regularly to interact and help one another achieve insight into their feelings and behavior.

Hallucinations   Sensory experiences in the absence of external stimulation.

Hallucinogens   Any of a number of drugs, such as LSD and mescaline, that distort visual and auditory perception.

Hawthorne effect   The principle that people will alter their behavior because of researchers' attention and not necessarily because of any specific treatment condition.

Health psychology   A subfield of psychology concerned with the relationship between psychological factors and physical health and illness.

Heredity   The transmission of traits from one generation to the next.

Heritability   The extent to which variations in a trait can be attributed to genetic factors.

Hertz (Hz)   Cycles per second; unit of measurement for the frequency of sound waves.

Heuristics   Rules of thumb that help in simplifying and solving problems, although they do not guarantee a correct solution.

Higher-order conditioning   Conditioning based on previous learning; the conditioned stimulus serves as an unconditioned stimulus for further training.

Hill climbing   A heuristic problem-solving strategy in which each step moves you progressively closer to the final goal.

Homeostasis   State of balance and stability in which the organism functions effectively.

Hormones   Chemical substances released by the endocrine glands; they help regulate bodily activities.

Hue   The aspect of color that corresponds to names such as red, green, and blue.

Human genome   The full complement of genes within a human cell.

Humanistic personality theory   Any personality theory that asserts the fundamental goodness of people and their striving toward higher levels of functioning.

Humanistic psychology   School of psychology that emphasizes nonverbal experience and altered states of consciousness as a means of realizing one's full human potential.

Hypnosis   Trancelike state in which a person responds readily to suggestions.

Hypochondriasis   A somatoform disorder in which a person interprets insignificant symptoms as signs of serious illness in the absence of any organic evidence of such illness.

Hypothalamus   Forebrain region that governs motivation and emotional responses.

Hypotheses   Specific, testable predictions derived from a theory.

Id   In Freud's theory of personality, the collection of unconscious urges and desires that continually seek expression.

Identical twins   Twins developed from a single fertilized ovum and therefore identical in genetic makeup at the time of conception.

Identification   Taking on the characteristics of someone else to avoid feeling incompetent.

Identity crisis   Period of intense self-examination and decision making; part of the process of identity formation.

Identity formation   Erikson's term for the development of a stable sense of self necessary to make the transition from dependence on others to dependence on oneself.

Image   A mental representation of a sensory experience.

Implicit memory   Memory for information that was either unintentionally committed to memory or unintentionally retrieved from memory.

Imprinting   A form of primitive bonding seen in some species of animals; the newborn animal has a tendency to follow the first moving thing (usually its mother) it sees after it is born or hatched.

Incentives   External stimuli that prompt goal-directed behavior.

Independent variable   In an experiment, the variable that is manipulated to test its effects on the other, dependent variables.

Industrial/organizational (I/O) psychology   The area of psychology concerned with the application of psychological principles to the problems of human organizations, especially work organizations.

Inferiority complex   In Adler's theory the fixation on feelings of personal inferiority that results in emotional and social paralysis.

Information-processing model   A computerlike model used to describe the way humans encode, store, and retrieve information.

Insanity   Legal term for mentally disturbed people who are not considered responsible for their criminal actions.

Insight   Awareness of previously unconscious feelings and memories and how they influence present feelings and behavior.

Insight   Learning that occurs rapidly as a result of understanding all the elements of a problem.

Insight therapies   A variety of individual psychotherapies designed to give people a better awareness and understanding of their feelings, motivations, and actions in the hope that this will help them to adjust.

Insomnia   Sleep disorder characterized by difficulty in falling asleep or remaining asleep throughout the night.

Instincts   Inborn, inflexible, goal-directed behavior that is characteristic of an entire species.

Intellectualization   Thinking abstractly about stressful problems as a way of detaching oneself from them.

Intelligence   A general term referring to the ability or abilities involved in learning and adaptive behavior.

Intelligence quotient (IQ)   A numerical value given to intelligence that is determined from the scores on an intelligence test; based on a score of 100 for average intelligence.

Interference theory   The theory that interference from other information causes forgetting.

Intermittent pairing   Pairing the conditioned stimulus and the unconditioned stimulus on only a portion of the learning trials.

Intrinsic motivation   A desire to perform a behavior that originates within the individual.

Ions   Electrically charged particles found both inside and outside the neuron.

Iris   The colored part of the eye.

James–Lange theory   States that stimuli cause physiological changes in our bodies, and emotions result from those physiological changes.

Just-world hypothesis   Attribution error based on the assumption that bad things happen to bad people and good things happen to good people.

Kinesthetic senses   Senses of muscle movement, posture, and strain on muscles and joints.

Language acquisition device   An internal mechanism for processing speech that is "wired into" all humans.

Latency period   In Freud's theory of personality development a period in which the child appears to have no interest in the other sex; occurs after the phallic stage.

Latent Learning   Learning that is not immediately reflected in a behavior change.

Law of effect (principle of reinforcement)   Thorndike's theory that behavior consistently rewarded will be "stamped in" as learned behavior, and behavior that brings about discomfort will be "stamped out" (also known as the principle of reinforcement).

Learned helplessness   Failure to take steps to avoid or escape from an unpleasant or aversive stimulus that occurs as a result of previous exposure to unavoidable painful stimuli.

Learning set   The ability to become increasingly more effective in solving problems as more problems are solved.

Learning   The process by which experience or practice results in a relatively permanent change in behavior or potential behavior.

Lens   The transparent part of the eye inside the pupil that focuses light onto the retina.

Libido   According to Freud, the energy generated by the sexual instinct.

Light adaptation   Decreased sensitivity of rods and cones in bright light.

Limbic system   Ring of structures that plays a role in learning and emotional behavior.

Linear perspective   Monocular cue to distance and depth based on the fact that two parallel lines seem to come together at the horizon.

Linguistic relativity hypothesis   Whorf's idea that patterns of thinking are determined by the specific language one speaks.

Locus of control   According to Rotter, an expectancy about whether reinforcement is under internal or external control.

Long-term memory (LTM)   The portion of memory that is more or less permanent, corresponding to everything we "know."

Longitudinal study   A method of studying developmental changes by examining the same group of subjects two or more times as they grow older.

Lysergic acid diethylamide (LSD)   Hallucinogenic or "psychedelic" drug that produces hallucinations and delusions similar to those occurring in a psychotic state.

Mania   A mood disorder characterized by euphoric states, extreme physical activity, excessive talkativeness, distractedness, and sometimes grandiosity.

Marijuana   A mild hallucinogen that produces a "high" often characterized by feelings of euphoria, a sense of well-being, and swings in mood from gaiety to relaxation; may also cause feelings of anxiety and paranoia.

Maturation   An automatic biological unfolding of development in an organism as a function of the passage of time.

Means-end analysis   A heuristic strategy that aims to reduce the discrepancy between the current situation and the desired goal at a number of intermediate points.

Meditation   Any of the various methods of concentration, reflection, or focusing of thoughts undertaken to suppress the activity of the sympathetic nervous system.

Medulla   Part of the hindbrain that controls such functions as breathing, heart rate, and blood pressure.

Menarche   First menstrual period.

Menopause   The time in a woman's life when menstruation ceases.

Mental representation   Mental images or symbols (such as words) used to think about or remember an object, a person, or an event.

Mental retardation   Condition of significantly subaverage intelligence combined with deficiencies in adaptive behavior.

Midbrain   Region between the hindbrain and the forebrain; it is important for hearing and sight, and it is one of several places in the brain where pain is registered.

Midlife crisis   A time when adults discover that they no longer feel fulfilled in their jobs or personal lives and attempt to make a decisive shift in career or lifestyle.

Midlife transition   According to Levinson, a process whereby adults assess the past and formulate new goals for the future.

Minnesota Multiphasic Personality Inventory (MMPI)   The most widely used objective personality test, originally intended for psychiatric diagnosis.

Mnemonics   Techniques that make material easier to remember.

Modeling   A behavior therapy in which the person learns desired behaviors by watching others perform those behaviors.

Monaural cue   Cue to sound location that requires just one ear.

Monochromats   Organisms that are totally colorblind.

Monocular cues   Visual cues requiring the use of one eye.

Mood disorders   Disturbances in mood or prolonged emotional state.

Morphemes   The smallest meaningful units of speech, such as simple words, prefixes, and suffixes.

Motion parallax   Monocular distance cue in which objects closer than the point of visual focus seem to move in the direction opposite to the viewer's moving head, and objects beyond the focus point appear to move in the same direction as the viewer's head.

Motive   Specific need, desire, or want, such as hunger, thirst, or achievement, that prompts goal-oriented behavior.

Myelin sheath   White fatty covering found on some axons.

Narcissistic personality disorder   Personality disorder in which the person has an exaggerated sense of self-importance and needs constant admiration.

Narcolepsy   Hereditary sleep disorder characterized by sudden nodding off during the day and sudden loss of muscle tone following moments of emotional excitement.

Natural selection   The mechanism proposed by Charles Darwin in his theory of evolution, which states that organisms best adapted to their environment tend to survive, transmitting their genetic characteristics to succeeding generations, whereas organisms with less adaptive characteristics tend to vanish from the earth.

Naturalistic observation   Research method involving the systematic study of animal or human behavior in natural settings rather than in the laboratory.

Nature versus nurture debate   A debate surrounding the relative importance of heredity (nature) and environment (nurture) in determining behavior.

Negative reinforcer   Any event whose reduction or termination increases the likelihood that ongoing behavior will recur.

Neonate   Newborn baby.

Nerve or tract   Group of axons bundled together.

Neural impulse or action potential   The firing of a nerve cell.

Neurogenesis   The growth of new neurons.

Neuron   Individual cell that is the smallest unit of the nervous system.

Neurotic trends   Horney's term for irrational strategies for coping with emotional problems and minimizing anxiety.

Neurotransmitters   Chemicals released by the synaptic vesicles that travel across the synaptic space and affect adjacent neurons.

Non-REM (NREM) sleep   Non-rapid-eye-movement stages of sleep that alternate with REM stages during the sleep cycle.

Noncompensatory model   A decision-making model in which weaknesses in one or more criteria are not offset by strengths in other criteria.

Norm   A shared idea or expectation about how to behave.

Obedience   Change of behavior in response to a command from another person, typically an authority figure.

Object permanence   The concept that things continue to exist even when they are out of sight.

Objective tests   Personality tests that are administered and scored in a standard way.

Observational (or vicarious) learning   Learning by observing other people's behavior.

Observer bias   Expectations or biases of the observer that might distort or influence his or her interpretation of what was actually observed.

Obsessive–compulsive disorder   An anxiety disorder in which a person feels driven to think disturbing thoughts or to perform senseless rituals.

Occipital lobes   Part of each cerebral hemisphere that receives and interprets visual information.

Oedipus complex and Electra complex   According to Freud, a child's sexual attachment to the parent of the opposite sex and jealousy toward the parent of the same sex; generally occurs in the phallic stage.

Olfactory bulb   The smell center in the brain.

Operant (or instrumental) conditioning   The type of learning in which behaviors are emitted (in the presence of specific stimuli) to earn rewards or avoid punishments.

Operant behavior   Behavior designed to operate on the environment in a way that will gain something desired or avoid something unpleasant.

Opiates   Drugs, such as opium and heroin, derived from the opium poppy, that dull the senses and induce feelings of euphoria, well-being, and relaxation. Synthetic drugs resembling opium derivatives are also classified as opiates.

Opponent-process theory   Theory of color vision that holds that three sets of color receptors (yellow-blue, red-green, black-white) respond to determine the color you experience.

Optic chiasm   The point near the base of the brain where some fibers in the optic nerve from each eye cross to the other side of the brain.

Optic nerve   The bundle of axons of ganglion cells that carries neural messages from each eye to the brain.

Oral stage   First stage in Freud's theory of personality development, in which the infant's erotic feelings center on the mouth, lips, and tongue.

Oval window   Membrane across the opening between the middle ear and inner ear that conducts vibrations to the cochlea.

Overtones   Tones that result from sound waves that are multiples of the basic tone; primary determinant of timbre.

Pancreas   Organ lying between the stomach and small intestine; it secretes insulin and glucagon to regulate blood-sugar levels.

Panic disorder   An anxiety disorder characterized by recurrent panic attacks in which the person suddenly experiences intense fear or terror without any reasonable cause.

Paranoid personality disorder   Personality disorder in which the person is inappropriately suspicious and mistrustful of others.

Paranoid schizophrenia   Schizophrenic disorder marked by extreme suspiciousness and complex, bizarre delusions.

Paraphilias   Sexual disorders in which unconventional objects or situations cause sexual arousal.

Parasympathetic division   Branch of the autonomic nervous system; it calms and relaxes the body.

Parathyroids   Four tiny glands embedded in the thyroid; they secrete parathormone.

Parietal lobes   Part of the cerebral cortex that receives sensory information from throughout the body.

Pedophilia   Desire to have sexual relations with children as the preferred or exclusive method of achieving sexual excitement.

Peer group   A network of same-aged friends and acquaintances who give one another emotional and social support.

Perception   The process of creating meaningful patterns from raw sensory information.

Perceptual constancy   A tendency to perceive objects as stable and unchanging despite changes in sensory stimulation.

Performance standard   In Bandura's theory a standard that people develop to rate the adequacy of their own behavior in a variety of situations.

Performance tests   Intelligence tests that minimize the use of language.

Peripheral nervous system (PNS)   Division of the nervous system that connects the central nervous system to the rest of the body.

Persona   According to Jung, our public self, the mask we put on to represent ourselves to others.

Personal unconscious   In Jung's theory of personality one of the two levels of the unconscious; it contains the individual's repressed thoughts, forgotten experiences, and undeveloped ideas.

Personality   An individual's unique pattern of thoughts, feelings, and behaviors that persists over time and across situations.

Personality disorders   Disorders in which inflexible and maladaptive ways of thinking and behaving learned early in life cause distress to the person or conflicts with others.

Personality traits   Dimensions or characteristics on which people differ in distinctive ways.

Phallic stage   Third stage in Freud's theory of personality development, in which erotic feelings center on the genitals.

Pheromone   Chemical that communicates information to other organisms through smell.

Phi phenomenon   Apparent movement caused by flashing lights in sequence, as on theater marquees.

Phonemes   The basic sounds that make up any language.

Pineal gland   A gland located roughly in the center of the brain that appears to regulate activity levels over the course of a day.

Pitch   Auditory experience corresponding primarily to frequency of sound vibrations, resulting in a higher or lower tone.

Pituitary gland   Gland located on the underside of the brain; it regulates the largest number of behaviors and affects the output of the other endocrine glands.

Place theory   Theory that pitch is determined by the location of greatest vibration on the basilar membrane.

Placebo   Chemically inactive substance used for comparison with active drugs in experiments on the effects of drugs.

Plasticity   The ability of the brain to change its structure and function in response to the environment.

Plasticity   The ability of the brain to change its structure and function in response to the environment.

Pleasure principle   According to Freud, the way in which the id seeks immediate gratification of an instinct.

Polarization   Shift in attitudes by members of a group toward more extreme positions than the ones held before group discussion.

Polarized   The condition of a neuron when the inside is negatively charged relative to the outside; for example, when the neuron is at rest.

Polygenic inheritance   Process by which several genes interact to produce a certain trait; responsible for our most important traits.

Pons   Part of the hindbrain that connects the cerebral cortex at the top of the brain to the cerebellum.

Positive reinforcer   Any event whose presence increases the likelihood that ongoing behavior will recur.

Posttraumatic stress disorder (PTSD)   Psychological disorder characterized by episodes of anxiety, sleeplessness, and nightmares resulting from some disturbing past event.

Power motive   The need to win recognition or to influence or control individuals or groups; a social motive.

Prejudice   An unfair, intolerant, or unfavorable attitude toward a group of people.

Prenatal development   Development from conception to birth.

Preoperational stage   In Piaget's theory, the stage of cognitive development between 2 and 7 years of age in which the individual becomes able to use mental representations and language to describe, remember, and reason about the world, though only in an egocentric fashion.

Preparedness   A biological readiness to learn certain associations because of their survival advantages.

Primacy effect   The fact that early information about someone weighs more heavily than later information in influencing one's impression of that person.

Primary drive   Physiologically based unlearned motive, such as hunger.

Primary prevention   Techniques and programs to improve the social environment so that new cases of mental disorders do not develop.

Primary reinforcer   A reinforcer that is rewarding in itself, such as food, water, and sex.

Principles of conservation   The concept that basic amounts remain constant despite superficial changes in appearance, such as the idea that the volume of a liquid stays the same regardless of the size and shape of the container into which it is poured.

Proactive interference   The process by which old material already in memory interferes with new information.

Problem representation   The first step in solving a problem; it involves interpreting or defining the problem.

Procedural memory   The portion of long-term memory that stores information relating to skills, habits, and other complex perceptual-motor tasks.

Projection Attributing one's repressed motives, feelings, or wishes to others.

Projective tests Personality tests, such as the Rorschach inkblot test, consisting of ambiguous or unstructured material.

Prototype According to Rosch, a mental model containing the most typical features of a concept.

Proximity How close two people live to each other.

Psychoactive drugs Chemical substances that change moods and perceptions.

Psychoanalysis The theory of personality Freud developed as well as the form of therapy he invented.

Psychoanalysis The theory of personality that Freud developed as well as the form of therapy he invented.

Psychoanalytic model View that psychological disorders result from unconscious internal conflicts.

Psychobiology The area of psychology that focuses on the biological foundations of behavior and mental processes.

Psychodynamic theories Personality theories contending that behavior results from psychological dynamics that interact within the individual, often outside conscious awareness.

Psychodynamic theories Personality theories contending that behavior results from psychological factors that interact within the individual, often outside conscious awareness.

Psychology The scientific study of behavior and mental processes.

Psychoneuroimmunology A new field that studies the interaction between stress on the one hand and immune, endocrine, and nervous system activity on the other.

Psychosomatic disorders Disorders in which there is real physical illness that is largely caused by psychological factors such as stress and anxiety.

Psychosurgery Brain surgery performed to change a person's behavior and emotional state; a biological therapy rarely used today.

Psychotherapy The use of psychological techniques to treat personality and behavior disorders.

Puberty The onset of sexual maturation, with accompanying physical development.

Punisher A stimulus that follows a behavior and decreases the likelihood that the behavior will be repeated.

Punishment Any event whose presence decreases the likelihood that ongoing behavior will recur.

Pupil A small opening in the iris through which light enters the eye.

Race A subpopulation of a species, defined according to an identifiable characteristic (that is, geographic location, skin color, hair texture, genes, facial features, and so forth).

Racism Prejudice and discrimination directed at a particular racial group.

Random sample Sample in which each potential participant has an equal chance of being selected.

Rational-emotive therapy (RET) A directive cognitive therapy based on the idea that clients' psychological distress is caused by irrational and self-defeating beliefs and that the therapist's job is to challenge such dysfunctional beliefs.

Reaction formation Expression of exaggerated ideas and emotions that are the opposite of one's repressed beliefs or feelings.

Reality principle According to Freud, the way in which the ego seeks to satisfy instinctual demands safely and effectively in the real world.

Receptor cell A specialized cell that responds to a particular type of energy.

Receptor site A location on a receptor neuron into which a specific neurotransmitter fits like a key into a lock.

Recessive gene Member of a gene pair that can control the appearance of a certain trait only if it is paired with another recessive gene.

Reciprocal determinism In Bandura's personality model the concept that the person influences the environment and is in turn influenced by the environment.

Regression Reverting to childlike behavior and defenses.

Reinforcer A stimulus that follows a behavior and increases the likelihood that the behavior will be repeated.

Relative refractory period A period after firing when a neuron is returning to its normal polarized state and will fire again only if the incoming message is much stronger than usual.

Reliability Ability of a test to produce consistent and stable scores.

REM (paradoxical) sleep Sleep stage characterized by rapid eye movement and increased dreaming.

Representative sample Sample carefully chosen so that the characteristics of the participants correspond closely to the characteristics of the larger population.

Representativeness heuristic A heuristic by which a new situation is judged on the basis of its resemblance to a stereotypical model.

Repression Excluding uncomfortable thoughts, feelings, and desires from consciousness.

Response generalization Giving a response that is somewhat different from the response originally learned to that stimulus.

Resting potential Electrical charge across a neuron membrane owing to excess positive ions concentrated on the outside and excess negative ions on the inside.

Reticular formation Network of neurons in the hindbrain, midbrain, and part of the forebrain, the primary function of which is to alert and arouse the higher parts of the brain.

Retina The lining of the eye containing receptor cells that are sensitive to light.

Retinal disparity Binocular distance cue based on the difference between the images cast on the two retinas when both eyes are focused on the same object.

Retroactive interference The process by which new information interferes with old information already in memory.

Retrograde amnesia The inability to recall events immediately preceding an accident or injury, but without loss of earlier memory.

Risky shift Greater willingness of a group than an individual to take substantial risks.

Rods Receptor cells in the retina responsible for night vision and perception of brightness.

Rorschach test A projective test composed of ambiguous inkblots; the way people interpret the blots is thought to reveal aspects of their personality.

Rote rehearsal Retaining information in STM simply by repeating it over and over.

Saturation The vividness or richness of a hue.

Schedule of reinforcement In operant conditioning, the rule for determining when and how often reinforcers will be delivered.

Schema A set of beliefs or expectations about something that is based on past experience.

Schizoid personality disorder Personality disorder in which a person is withdrawn and lacks feelings for others.

Schizophrenic disorders Severe disorders in which there are disturbances of thoughts, communications, and emotions, including delusions and hallucinations.

Scientific method An approach to knowledge that relies on collecting data, generating a theory to explain the data, producing testable hypotheses based on the theory, and testing those hypotheses empirically.

Secondary prevention Programs to identify groups that are at high risk for mental disorders and to detect maladaptive behavior in these groups and treat it promptly.

Secondary reinforcer A reinforcer whose value is acquired through association with other primary or secondary reinforcers.

Self-actualizing tendency According to Rogers, the drive of human beings to fulfill their self-concepts, or the images they have of themselves.

Self-efficacy According to Bandura, the expectancy that one's efforts will be successful.

Self-fulfilling prophecy The process in which a person's expectation about another elicits behavior from the second person that confirms the expectation.

Self-monitoring The tendency for an individual to observe the situation for cues about how to react.

Semantic memory   The portion of long-term memory that stores general facts and information.

Sensation   The experience of sensory stimulation.

Sensory deprivation   Extreme reduction of sensory stimuli.

Sensory registers   Entry points for raw information from the senses.

Sensory-motor stage   In Piaget's theory, the stage of cognitive development between birth and 2 years of age in which the individual develops object permanence and acquires the ability to form mental representations.

Set point   A homeostatic mechanism in the body that regulates metabolism, fat storage, and food intake so as to maintain a preprogrammed weight.

Set   The tendency to perceive and to approach problems in certain ways.

Sex-typed behavior   Socially prescribed ways of behaving that differ for boys and girls.

Sexual dysfunction   Loss or impairment of the ordinary physical responses of sexual function.

Shadowing   Monocular cue to distance and depth based on the fact that shadows often appear on the parts of objects that are more distant.

Shape constancy   A tendency to see an object as the same shape no matter what angle it is viewed from.

Shaping   Reinforcing successive approximations to a desired behavior.

Short-term memory (STM)   Working memory; briefly stores and processes selected information from the sensory registers.

Short-term psychodynamic therapy   Insight therapy that is time-limited and focused on trying to help clients correct the immediate problems in their lives.

Sixteen Personality Factor Questionnaire (16PF)   Objective personality test created by Cattell that provides scores on the 16 traits he identified.

Size constancy   The perception of an object as the same size regardless of the distance from which it is viewed.

Skinner box   A box often used in operant conditioning of animals; it limits the available response and thus increases the likelihood that the desired response will occur.

Social cognition   Knowledge and understanding concerning the social world and the people in it (including oneself).

Social influence   The process by which others individually or collectively affect one's perceptions, attitudes, and actions.

Social learning theorists   Psychologists whose view of learning emphasizes the ability to learn by observing a model or receiving instructions, without firsthand experience by the learner.

Social phobia   An anxiety disorder characterized by excessive, inappropriate fears connected with social situations or performances in front of other people.

Social psychology   The scientific study of the ways in which the thoughts, feelings, and behaviors of one individual are influenced by the real, imagined, or inferred behavior or characteristics of other people.

Socialization   Process by which children learn the behaviors and attitudes appropriate to their family and culture.

Somatic nervous system   The part of the peripheral nervous system that carries messages from the senses to the central nervous system and between the central nervous system and the skeletal muscles.

Somatoform disorders   Disorders in which there is an apparent physical illness for which there is no organic basis.

Specific phobia   Anxiety disorder characterized by an intense, paralyzing fear of something.

Spinal cord   Complex cable of neurons that runs down the spine, connecting the brain to most of the rest of the body.

Split-half reliability   A method of determining test reliability by dividing the test into two parts and checking the agreement of scores on both parts.

Spontaneous recovery   The reappearance of an extinguished response after the passage of time, without further training.

Stereoscopic vision   Combination of two retinal images to give a three-dimensional perceptual experience.

Stereotype   A set of characteristics presumed to be shared by all members of a social category.

Stimulants   Drugs, including amphetamines and cocaine, that stimulate the sympathetic nervous system and produce feelings of optimism and boundless energy.

Stimulus control   Control of conditioned responses by cues or stimuli in the environment.

Stimulus discrimination   Learning to respond to only one stimulus and to inhibit the response to all other stimuli.

Stimulus generalization   The transfer of a learned response to different but similar stimuli.

Stimulus motives   Unlearned motives, such as curiosity or contact, that prompt us to explore or change our world.

Stress   Any environmental demand that creates a state of tension or threat and requires change or adaptation.

Stress-inoculation therapy   A type of cognitive therapy that trains clients to cope with stressful situations by learning a more useful pattern of self-talk.

Stretch receptors   Receptors that sense muscle stretch and contraction.

Stroboscopic motion   Apparent movement that results from flashing a series of still pictures in rapid succession, as in a motion picture.

Structuralism   School of psychology that stresses the basic units of experience and the combinations in which they occur.

Subgoals   Intermediate, more manageable goals used in one heuristic strategy to make it easier to reach the final goal.

Subjects or participants   Individuals whose reactions or responses are observed in an experiment.

Sublimation   Redirecting repressed motives and feelings into more socially acceptable channels.

Substance abuse   A pattern of drug use that diminishes the ability to fulfill responsibilities at home or at work or school, that results in repeated use of a drug in dangerous situations, or that leads to legal difficulties related to drug use.

Substance dependence   A pattern of compulsive drug taking that results in tolerance, withdrawal symptoms, or other specific symptoms for at least a year.

Subtractive color mixing   The process of mixing pigments, each of which absorbs some wavelengths of light and reflects others.

Superego   According to Freud, the social and parental standards that the individual has internalized; the conscience and the ego ideal.

Superposition   Monocular distance cue in which one object, by partly blocking a second object, is perceived as being closer.

Surface structure   The particular words and phrases used to make up a sentence.

Survey research   Research technique in which questionnaires or interviews are administered to a selected group of people.

Sympathetic division   Branch of the autonomic nervous system; it prepares the body for quick action in an emergency.

Synapse   Area composed of the terminal button of one neuron, the synaptic space, and the dendrite or cell body of the next neuron.

Synaptic space or synaptic cleft   Tiny gap between the axon terminal of one neuron and the dendrites or cell body of the next neuron.

Synaptic vesicles   Tiny sacs in a terminal button that release chemicals into the synapse.

Systematic desensitization   A behavioral technique for reducing a person's fear and anxiety by gradually associating a new response (relaxation) with stimuli that have been causing the fear and anxiety.

Systems approach   View that biological, psychological, and social risk factors combine to produce psychological disorders. Also known as the biopsychosocial model of psychological disorders.

Taste buds   Structures on the tongue that contain the receptor cells for taste.

Temperament   Term used by psychologists to describe the physical/emotional characteristics of the newborn child and young infant; also referred to as personality.

Temporal lobes   Part of each cerebral hemisphere that helps to regulate hearing, balance and equilibrium and certain emotions and motivations.

Terminal button or axon terminal   Structure at the end of an axon terminal branch.

Tertiary prevention   Programs to help people adjust to community life after release from a mental hospital.

Texture gradient   Monocular cue to distance and depth based on the fact that objects seen at greater distances appear to be smoother and less textured.

Thalamus   Forebrain region that relays and translates incoming messages from the sense receptors, except those for smell.

Thematic Apperception Test (TAT)   A projective test composed of ambiguous pictures about which a person is asked to write a complete story.

Theory   Systematic explanation of a phenomenon; it organizes known facts, allows us to predict new facts, and permits us to exercise a degree of control over the phenomenon.

Threshold of excitation   The level that graded potentials must reach to cause a neuron to fire.

Thyroid gland   Endocrine gland located below the voice box; it produces the hormone thyroxin.

Timbre   The quality of texture of sound; caused by overtones.

Token economy   An operant conditioning therapy in which patients earn tokens (reinforcers) for desired behaviors and exchange them for desired items or privileges.

Traits   Characteristics on which organisms differ.

Transference   The patient's carrying over to the analyst feelings held toward childhood authority figures.

Trichromatic theory   The theory of color vision that holds that all color perception derives from three different color receptors in the retina (usually red, green, and blue receptors).

Trichromats   Organisms that have normal color vision.

Twin studies   Studies of identical and fraternal twins to determine the relative influence of heredity and environment on human behavior.

Unconditional positive regard   In Rogers's theory the full acceptance and love of another person regardless of that person's behavior.

Unconditioned response (UR)   A response that takes place in an organism whenever an unconditioned stimulus occurs.

Unconditioned stimulus (US)   A stimulus that invariably causes an organism to respond in a specific way.

Unconscious   In Freud's theory all the ideas, thoughts, and feelings of which we are not and normally cannot become aware.

Undifferentiated schizophrenia   Schizophrenic disorder in which there are clear schizophrenic symptoms that don't meet the criteria for another subtype of the disorder.

Validity   Ability of a test to measure what it has been designed to measure.

Variable-interval schedule   A reinforcement schedule in which the correct response is reinforced after varying lengths of time following the last reinforcement.

Variable-ratio schedule   A reinforcement schedule in which a varying number of correct responses must occur before reinforcement is presented.

Vestibular senses   The senses of equilibrium and body position in space.

Vicarious reinforcement or vicarious punishment   Reinforcement or punishment experienced by models that affects the willingness of others to perform the behaviors they learned by observing those models.

Visual acuity   The ability to distinguish fine details visually.

Volley principle   Refinement of frequency theory; it suggests that receptors in the ear fire in sequence, with one group responding, then a second, then a third, and so on, so that the complete pattern of firing corresponds to the frequency of the sound wave.

Waking consciousness   Mental state that encompasses the thoughts, feelings, and perceptions that occur when we are awake and reasonably alert.

Wavelengths   The different energies represented in the electromagnetic spectrum.

Weber's law   The principle that the jnd for any given sense is a constant fraction or proportion of the stimulation being judged.

Wechsler Adult Intelligence Scale-Third Edition (WAIS–III)   An individual intelligence test developed especially for adults; measures both verbal and performance abilities.

Wechsler Intelligence Scale for Children-Third Edition (WISC–III)   An individual intelligence test developed especially for school-aged children; measures verbal and performance abilities and also yields an overall IQ score.

Withdrawal   Avoiding a situation when other forms of coping are not practical.

Working backward   A heuristic strategy in which one works backward from the desired goal to the given conditions.

Yerkes–Dodson law   States that there is an optimal level of arousal for the best performance of any task; the more complex the task, the lower the level of arousal that can be tolerated before performance deteriorates.

REFERENCES

aker, D.A., & Bruzzone, D.E. (1985). Causes of irritation in advertising. *Journal of Marketing, 49,* 47–57.

Aaronson, D., & Scarborough, H.S. (1976). Performance theories for sentence coding: Some quantitative evidence. *Journal of Experimental Psychology: Human Perception and Performance, 2,* 56–70.

Aaronson, D., & Scarborough, H.S. (1977). Performance theories for sentence coding: Some quantitative models. *Journal of Verbal Learning and Verbal Behavior, 16,* 277–304.

Abramov, I., & Gordon, J. (1994). Color appearance: On seeing red or yellow, or green, or blue. *Annual Review of Psychology, 45,* 451–485.

Acredolo, L.P., & Hake, J.L. (1982). Infant perception. In B.B. Wolman (ed.), *Handbook of developmental psychology* (pp. 244–283). Englewood Cliffs, NJ: Prentice Hall.

Adams, D.B., Gold, A.R., & Burt, A.D. (1978). Rise in female-initiated sexual activity at ovulation and its suppression by oral contraceptives. *New England Journal of Medicine, 299,* 1145–1150.

Adams, G.R., & Gullota, T. (1983). *Adolescent life experiences.* Monterey, CA: Brooks/Cole.

Adams, J.L. (1980*). Conceptual blockbusting: A guide to better ideas* (2nd ed.). New York: Norton.

Adams, K., & Johnson-Greene, D. (1995). *PET and neuropsychological performance among chronic alcoholics.* Paper presented at the annual meeting of the American Psychological Association, New York.

Adelmann, P.K., & Zajonc, R.B. (1989). Facial efference and the experience of emotion. *Annual Review of Psychology, 40,* 249–280.

Ader, R., & Cohen, N. (1993). Ps. of Psychology, *44,* 53–85.

Adler, N., Boyce, T., Chesney, M.A., Cohen, S., Folkman, S., Kahn, R.I., & Syme, S.L. (1994). Socioeconomic status and health. The challenge of the gradient. *American Psychologist, 49,* 15–24.

Adler, T. (1990, January). PMS diagnosis draws fire from researchers. *APA Monitor,* p. 12.

Adler, T. (1993a, May). Raising the cigarette tax can lower smoking rates. *APA Monitor,* p. 15.

Adler, T. (1993b, July). Men and women affected by stress, but differently. *APA Monitor,* pp. 8–9.

Adorno, T.W., Frenkel-Brunswick, E., Levinson, D.J., & Sanford, R.N. (1950). *The authoritarian personality.* New York: Harper & Row.

Agostinelli, G., Sherman, S.J., Presson, C.C., & Chassin, L. (1992). Self-protection and self-enhancement biases in estimates of population prevalence. *Personality and Social Psychology Bulletin, 18*(5), 631–642.

Aiken, L.R. (1988). *Psychological testing and assessment* (6th ed.). Boston: Allyn & Bacon.

Ainsworth, M.D., Blehar, M.C., Waters, E., & Wall, S. (1978). *Patterns of attachment.* New York: Halstead Press.

Ainsworth, M.D.S. (1977). Attachment theory and its utility in cross-cultural research. In P.H. Leiderman, S.R. Tulkin, & A. Rosenfields (eds.), *Culture and infancy: Variation in the human experience.* New York: Academic Press.

Alan Guttmacher Institute. (1990). *Adolescent sexuality.* New York: Alan Guttmacher Institute.

Albert, D.J., Walsh, M.L., & Jonik, R.H. (1993). Aggression in humans: What is its biological foundation? *Neuroscience Biobehavior Review, 17*(4), 405–425.

Albus, M. (1989). Cholecystokinin. *Progress in Neuro-Psychoparmacology and Biological Psychiatry, 12*(Suppl.), 5–21.

Allen, L.S., & Gorski, R.A. (1992). Sexual orientation and size of the anterior commissure in the human brain. *Proceedings of the National Academy of Sciences, 89,* 7199–7202.

Allen, V.L., & Levine, J.M. (1971). Social support and conformity: The role of independent assessment of reality. *Journal of Experimental Social Psychology, 7,* 48–58.

Allport, G.W. (1954). *The nature of prejudice.* New York: Anchor.

Allport, G.W., & Odbert, H.S. (1936). Trait-names: A psycholexical study. *Psychological Monographs, 47*(1, Whole No. 211).

Almagor, M., Tellegen, A., & Waller, N.G. (1995). The big seven model: A cross-cultural replication and further explorations of the basic dimensions of natural language descriptors. *Journal of Personality and Social Psychology, 69,* 300–307.

Altabe, M.N., & Thompson, J.K. (1994). Body image. In *Encyclopedia of human behavior* (Vol. 1, pp. 407–414). San Diego, CA: Academic Press.

Altman, I., & Taylor, D.A. (1973). *Social penetration: The development of interpersonal relationships.* New York: Holt, Rinehart & Winston.

Altman, L.K. (1995, April 18). Research dispels myth that brain in adults is unable to renew itself. *New York Times,* p. B9.

Amabile, T.M. (1983a). The social psychology of creativity: A comparative conceptualization. *Journal of Personality and Social Psychology, 45,* 357–376.

Amabile, T.M., (1983b). *The social psychology of creativity.* New York: Springer-Verlag.

Amabile, T.M., Hennessey, B.A., & Grossman, B.S. (1986). Social influences on creativity: The effects of contracted-for reward. *Journal of Personality and Social Psychology, 50,* 14–23.

Amen, D.G., Stubblefield, M., Carmichael, B., & Thisted R. (1996). Brain SPECT findings and aggressiveness. *Annals of clinical psychiatry, 8*(3), 129–137.

American Psychological Association (APA). (1953*). Ethical standards of psychologists.* Washington, DC: American Psychological Association.

American Psychological Association (APA). (1992). *Big world, small screen.* Washington, DC: American Psychological Association.

American Psychological Association (APA). (1993). *Violence and youth.* Washington, DC: American Psychological Association.

American Psychiatric Association (APA). (1994*). Diagnostic and statistical manual of mental disorders* (4th ed.). Washington, DC: American Psychiatric Press.

Anastasi, A., & Urbina, S. (1997). *Psychological testing* (7th ed.). Upper Saddle River, NJ: Prentice Hall.

Anch, A.M., Browman, C.P., Mitler, M.M., & Walsh, J.K. (1988). *Sleep: A scientific perspective.* Englewood Cliffs, NJ: Prentice Hall.

Anderson, B.L., Kiecolt-Glaser, J.K., & Glaser, R. (1994). A biobehavioral model of cancer stress and disease course. *American Psychologist, 49*(5), 389–404.

Anderson, R.C., & Pichert, J.W. (1978). Recall of previously unrecallable information following a shift in perspective. *Journal of Verbal Learning and Verbal Behavior, 17,* 1–12.

Andreasen, N.C., Rice, J., Endicott, J., Coyell, W., Grove, W.M., & Reich, T. (1987). Familial rates of affective disorder. *Archives of General Psychiatry, 44,* 451–469.

Andrews, J.A., & Lewinsohn, P.M. (1992). Suicidal attempts among older adolescents: Prevalence and co-occurrence with psychiatric disorders. *Journal of the American Academy of Child and Adolescent Psychiatry, 31,* 655–662.

Angier, N. (1992, May 20). Is there a male menopause? Jury is still out. *New York Times,* p. A1.

Anthony, J.C., & Aboraya, A. (1992). The epidemiology of selected mental disorders in later life. In J.E. Birren, R.B. Sloane, & G.D. Choen (eds.), *Handbook of mental health and aging* (2nd ed., pp. 3–143). San Diego, CA: Academic Press.

Aranya, N., Kushnir, T., & Valency, A. (1986). Organizational commitment in a male dominated profession. *Human Relations, 39,* 433–438.

Archer, J. (1996). Sex differences in social behavior: Are the social role and evolutionary explanations compatible? *American Psychologist, 51*(9), 909–917.

Arias, C., Curet, C.A., Moyano, H.F., Joekes, S., & Blanch, N. (1993). Echolocation: A study of auditory functioning in blind and sighted subjects. *Journal of Visual Impairment and Blindness, 87,* 73–77.

Arkin, R.M., Cooper, H., & Kolditz, T. (1980). A statistical review of literature concerning the self-serving attribution bias in interpersonal influence situations. *Journal of Personality, 48,* 435–448.

Arnett, J. (1991, April). *Sensation seeking and egocentrism as factors in reckless behaviors among a college-age sample.* Paper presented at the meeting of the Society for Research in Child Development, Seattle, WA.

Arnett, J. (1995). The young and the reckless: Adolescent reckless behavior. *American Psychological Society, 4*(3), 67–71.

Aronoff, G.M. (ed.). (1993). *Evaluation and treatment of chronic pain* (2nd ed.). Baltimore, MD: Williams & Wilkins.

Aronson, E. (1994). *The social animal* (7th ed.). New York: Freeman.

Ary, D.V., Duncan, T.E., Duncan, S.C., & Hops, H. (1999). Adolescent problem behavior: The influence of parents and peers. *Behaviour Research and Therapy, 37,* 217–230.

Asch, S.E. (1946). Forming impressions of personality. *Journal of Abnormal and Social Psychology, 41,* 258–290.

Asch, S.E. (1951). Effects of group pressure upon the modification and distortion of judgments. In H. Guetzkow (ed.), *Groups, leadership, and men.* Pittsburgh: Carnegie Press.

Asch, S.E. (1956). Studies of independence and conformity: I. A minority of one against a unanimous majority. *Psychological Monographs, 70*(9, Whole No. 416).

Aslin, R.N., & Smith, L.B. (1988). Perceptual development. *Annual Review of Psychology, 39,* 435–473.

Aston, R. (1972). Barbiturates, alcohol and tranquilizers. In S.J. Mule & H. Brill (eds.), *The chemical and biological aspects of drug dependence.* Cleveland, OH: CRC Press.

Atchley, R.C. (1982). Retirement as a social institution. *Annual Review of Sociology, 8,* 263–287.

Aved, B.M., Irwin, M.M., Cummings, L.S., & Findeisen, N. (1993). Barriers to prenatal care for low-income women. *Western Journal of Medicine, 158*(5), 493–498.

Avery-Leaf, S., Cano, A., Cascardi, M., & O'Leary, K.D. (1995). *Evaluation of a dating violence prevention program.* Paper presented at the International Family Violence Research Conference, Durham, NH.

Azar, B. (1998). Why can't this man feel whether or not he's standing up? *APA Monitor,* June, pp. 18, 20.

Azar, B. (1998, February). APA launches "Decade of Behavior." *APA Monitor* [online]. **http://www.apa.org/monitor/feb98/behave.html.**

Azar, B. (1998, November). Plans accelerate for "Decade of Behavior" project. *APA Monitor* [online]. **http://www.apa.org/monitor/nov98/decade.html.**

Bachtold, L.M., & Werner, E.E. (1973). Personality characteristics of creative women. *Perception and Motor Skills, 36,* 311–319.

Baddeley, A.D. (1986). *Working memory.* Oxford: Clarendon Press.

Baddeley, A.D. (1987). Amnesia. In R.L. Gregory (ed.), *The Oxford companion to the mind* (pp. 20–22). Oxford: Oxford University Press.

Baddeley, A.D. (1994). The magical number seven: Still magic after all these years? *Psychological Review, 101,* 353–356.

Baddeley, A.D., & Hitch, G.J. (1994). Developments in the concept of working memory. *Neuropsychology, 6,* 485–493.

Baer, L., Rauch, S.L., & Ballantine, T. (1995). Cingulotomy for intractable obsessive-compulsive disorder: Prospective long-term follow-up of 18 patients. *Archives of General Psychiatry, 52,* 384–392.

Bahrick, H.P., Bahrick, P.O., & Wittlinger, R.P. (1974, December). Those unforgettable high school days. *Psychology Today,* pp. 50–56.

Bailey, A., LeCouteur, A., Gottesman, I., Bolton, P., Simonoff, E., Yuzda, E., & Rutter, M. (1995). Autism as a strongly genetic disorder: Evidence from a British twin study. *Psychological Medicine, 25*(1), 63–77.

Bailey, J.M., & Bell, A.P. (1993). Familiality of female and male homosexuality. *Behavior Genetics, 23,* 313–322.

Bailey, J.M., & Benishay, D.S. (1993). Familial aggregation of female sexual orientation. *American Journal of Psychiatry, 150,* 272–277.

Baillargeon, R. (1994). How do infants learn about the physical world? *American Psychological Society, 3*(5), 133–140.

Balaguer, A., & Markman, H. (1994). Mate selection. In *Encyclopedia of human behavior* (Vol. 3, pp. 127–135).

Balch, W.R., & Lewis, B.S. (1996). Music-dependent memory: The roles of tempo change and mood mediation. *Journal of Experimental Psychology: Learning, Memory and Cognition, 22,* 1354–1363.

Baldwin, A.Y. (1985). Programs for the gifted and talented: Issues concerning minority populations. In F.D. Horowitz & M. O'Brien (eds.), *The gifted and talented: Developmental perspectives.* Washington, DC: American Psychological Association.

Bales, R.F. (1951). *Interaction Process Analysis: A method for the study of small groups.* Reading, MA: Addison-Wesley.

Ball, J.D., Archer, R.P., & Imhof, E.A. (1994). Time requirements of psychological testing: A survey of practitioners. *Journal of Personality Assessment, 63,* 239–249.

Bandura, A. (1962). Social learning through imitation. In M.R. Jones (ed.), *Nebraska Symposium on Motivation.* Lincoln: University of Nebraska Press.

Bandura, A. (1965). Influence of models' reinforcement contingencies on the acquisition of imitative responses. *Journal of Personality and Social Psychology, 1*, 589–595.

Bandura, A. (1973). *Aggression: A social learning analysis.* Englewood Cliffs, NJ: Prentice Hall.

Bandura, A. (1977). *Social learning theory.* Englewood Cliffs, NJ: Prentice Hall.

Bandura, A. (1986). *Social foundations of thought and action: A social cognitive theory.* Englewood Cliffs, NJ: Prentice Hall.

Bandura, A., Blanchard, E.B., & Ritter, B. (1969). Relative efficacy of desensitization and modeling approaches for inducing behavioral, affective, and attitudinal changes. *Journal of Personality and Social Psychology, 13*, 173–199.

Banyai, E.I., & Hilgard, E.R. (1976). A comparison of active-alert hypnotic induction with traditional relaxation induction. *Journal of Abnormal Psychology, 85*, 218–224.

Barbaree, H.E., & Marshall, W.L. (1991). The role of male sexual arousal in rape: Six models. *Journal of Consulting and Clinical Psychology, 59*, 621–630.

Barbaree, H.E., & Seto, M.C. (1997). Pedophilia: Assessment and treatment. In D.R. Laws & W.T. O'Donohue (eds.), *Handbook of sexual deviance: Theory and application.* New York: Guilford.

Barber, B.L., & Eccles, J.E. (1992). Long-term influence of divorce and single parenting on adolescent family- and work-related values, behaviors and aspirations. *Psychological Bulletin, 111*, 108–126.

Barber, T.X. (1969). An empirically-based formulation of hypnotism. *American Journal of Clinical Hypnotism, 12*(2), 100–130.

Barbur, J.L., Harlow, A.J., & Weiskrantz, L. (1994). Spatial and temporal response properties of residual vision in a case of hemianopia. *Philosophical Transactions of the Royal Society of London, B, 43*, 157–160.

Barglow, P., Vaughn, B.E., & Molitor, N. (1987). Effects of maternal absence due to employment on the quality of infant-mother attachment in a low-risk sample. *Child Development, 58*, 945–954.

Barker, S.L., Funk, S.C., & Houston, B.K. (1988). Psychological treatment versus nonspecific factors: A meta-analysis of conditions that engender comparable expectations for improvement. *Clinical Psychology Review, 8*, 579–594.

Barkley, R.A. (1990). *Hyperactive children: A handbook for diagnosis and treatment* (2nd ed.). New York: Guilford.

Barnett, R.C., Brennan, R.T., & Marshall, N.L. (1994). Gender and the relationship between parent role quality and psychological distress: A study of men and women in dual-earner couples. *Journal of Family Issues, 15*(2), 229–252.

Barnouw, D. (1985). *Culture and personality.* Chicago: Dorsey Press.

Baron, R.A., & Byrne, D. (1991). *Social psychology: Understanding human interaction* (6th ed.). Boston: Allyn & Bacon.

Baron, R.M., Graziano, W.G., & Stangor, C. (1991). *Social psychology.* Fort Worth: Holt, Rinehart & Winston.

Barnett, R.C., Brennan, R.T., & Marshall, N.L. (1994). Gender and relationship between parent role quality and psychological distress. A study of men and women in dual-earner couples. *Journal of Family Issues, 15*, 229–252.

Barrett-Connor, E., & Bush, T.L. (1991). Estrogen and coronary heart disease in women. *AMA, Journal of the American Medical Association, 265*(14), 1861–1867.

Barron, F. (1963). *Creativity and psychological health.* Princeton, NJ: Van Nostrand.

Barron, F., & Harrington, D.M. (1981). Creativity, intelligence, and personality. *Annual Review of Psychology, 32*, 439–476.

Bartlett, F.C. (1932). *Remembering: A study in experimental and social psychology.* New York: Macmillan.

Bartoshuk, L.M., & Beauchamp, G.K. (1994). Chemical senses. *Annual Review of Psychology, 45*, 419–449.

Baruch, F., & Barnett, R. (1986). Role quality, multiple role involvement, and psychological well-being in mid-life women. *Journal of Personality and Social Psychology, 51*, 578–585.

Basow, S.A. (1986). *Gender stereotypes: Traditions and alternatives* (2nd ed.). Pacific Grove, CA: Brooks/Cole.

Bates, M.S., & Rankin-Hill, L. (1994). Control, culture, and chronic pain. *Social Science and Medicine, 39*, 629–645.

Bauer, P.J. (1996). What do infants recall of their lives? Memory for specific events by one- to two-year-olds. *American Psychologist, 51*(1), 29–41.

Baumrind, D. (1972). Socialization and instrumental competence in young children. In W.W. Hartup (ed.), *The young child: Reviews of research* (Vol. 2). Washington, DC: National Association for the Education of Young Children.

Baumrind, D. (1985). Research using intentional deception. *American Psychologist, 40*, 165–174.

Baxter, D.W., & Olszewski, J. (1960). Congenital insensitivity to pain. *Brain, 83*, 381.

Bayley, N. (1956). Individual patterns of development. *Child Development, 27*, 45–74.

Beatty, S.E., & Hawkins, D.I. (1989). Subliminal stimulation: Some new data and interpretation. *Journal of Advertising, 18*, 4–8.

Bechara, A., et al. (1997). Deciding advantageously before knowing the advantageous strategy. *Science, 275*, 1293–1295.

Beck, A.T. (1967). *Depression: Clinical, experimental and theoretical aspects.* New York: Harper (Hoeber).

Beck, A.T. (1976). *Cognitive therapy and emotional disorders.* New York: International Universities Press.

Beck, A.T. (1984). Cognition and therapy. *Archives of General Psychiatry, 41*, 1112–1114.

Beck, R. (1983). *Motivation: Theories and principles* (2nd ed.). Englewood Cliffs, NJ: Prentice Hall.

Beecher, H.K. (1972). The placebo effect as a nonspecific force surrounding disease and the treatment of disease. In R. Jansen, W.D. Kerdel, A. Herz, C. Steichele, J.P. Payne, &R.A.P. Burt (eds.), *Pain, basic principles, pharmacology, and therapy.* Stuttgart: Thieme.

Begley, S. (May 3, 1999). Why the young kill. *Newsweek*, pp. 32–35.

Beirne-Smith, M., Patton, J., & Ittenbach, R. (1994). *Mental retardation* (4th ed.). New York: Macmillan.

Bell, S.T., Kuriloff, P.J., & Lottes, I. (1994). Understanding attributions of blame in stranger rape and date rape situations: An examination of gender, race, identification, and students' social perceptions of rape victims. *Journal of Applied Social Psychology, 24*(19), 1719–1734.

Bellack, A.S., Hersen, M., & Turner, S.M. (1976). Generalization effects of social skills training in chronic schizophrenics: An experimental analysis. *Behavior Research and Therapy, 14*, 391–398.

Belsky, J., & Rovine, M. (1988). Nonmaternal care in the first year of life and infant parent attachment security. *Child Development, 59*, 157–167.

Belsky, J., Lang, M.E., & Rovine, M. (1985). Stability and change in marriage across the transition to parenthood: A second study. *Journal of Marriage and the Family, 97*, 855–865.

Belsky, J., Spritz, B., & Crnic, K. (1996). Infant attachment security and affective-cognitive information processing at age 3. *American Psychological Society, 7*(2), 111–114.

Bem, D.J., & Honorton, C. (1994). Does psi exist? Replicable evidence for an anomalous information transfer. *Psychological Bulletin, 115*, 4–18.

Bem, S.L. (1989). Genital knowledge and gender constancy in preschool children. *Child Development, 60*, 649–662.

Benin, M.H., & Agostinelli, J. (1988). Husbands' and wives' satisfaction with the division of labor. *Journal of Marriage and the Family, 50*, 349–361.

Bennett, D.A., & Knopman, D.S. (1994). Alzheimer's disease: A comprehensive approach to patient management. *Geriatrics, 49*(8), 20–26.

Bennett, W., & Gurin, J. (1982). *The dieter's dilemma: Eating less and weighing more.* New York: Basic Books.

Benson, H. (1975). *The relaxation response.* New York: William Morrow.

Benson, H., Alexander, S., & Feldman, E.L. (1975). Decreased premature ventricular contractions through use of the relaxation response in patients with stable ischemic heart disease. *Lancet, 2*, 380–382.

Benson, H., Kotch, J.B., Crassweller, K.D., & Greenwood, M.M. (1979). The relaxation response. In D. Goleman & R. Davidson (eds.), *Consciousness: Brain, states of awareness and mysticism.* New York: Harper & Row.

Benton, D., & Roberts, G. (1988). Effect of vitamin and mineral supplementation on intelligence of a sample of schoolchildren. *Lancet, 1*, 14–144.

Berenbaum, S.A., & Snyder, E. (1995). Early hormonal influences on childhood sex-typed activity and playmate preferences: Implications for the development of sexual orientation. [Special issue: Sexual orientation and human development.] *Developmental Psychology, 31*(1), 31–42.

Berger, R.J. (1969). The sleep and dream cycle. In A. Kales (ed.), *Sleep: Physiology and pathology.* Philadelphia: Lippincott.

Bergin, A.E., & Lambert, M.J. (1978). The evaluation of therapeutic outcomes. In S.L. Garfield & A.E. Bergin (eds.), *Handbook of psychotherapy and behavior change: An empirical analysis.* New York: Wiley.

Berkowitz, L. (1983). Aversively stimulated aggression. *American Psychologist, 38*, 1135–1144.

Berkowitz, M.W., & Gibbs, J.C. (1983). Measuring the developmental features of moral discussion. *Merrill-Palmer Quarterly, 29*, 399–410.

Berlin, B., & Kay, P. (1969). *Basic color terms: Their universality and evolution.* Berkeley: University of California Press.

Berliner, L., & Williams, L.M. (1994). Memories of child sexual abuse: A response to Lindsay and Read. [Special issue: Recovery of memories of childhood sexual abuse.] *Applied Cognitive Psychology, 8*(4), 379–387.

Bernal, M.E., & Castro, F.G. (1994). Are clinical psychologists prepared for service and research with ethnic minorities? *American Psychologist, 49*(9), 797–805.

Berry, B.D., & Pollard, R. (1998). Homeostasis, stress, trauma, and adaptation: A neurodevelopmental view of childhood trauma. *Child and adolescent psychiatric clinics of North America, 7*, 33–51.

Berry, J.W. (1967). Independence and conformity in subsistence level societies. *Journal of Personality and Social Psychology, 7*, 415–518.

Bertenthal, B.I., Campos, J.J., & Kermoian, R. (1994). An epigenetic perspective on the development of self-produced locomotion and its consequences. *American Psychological Society, 3*(5), 140–145.

Bertrand, S., & Masling, J. (1969). Oral imagery and alcoholism. *Journal of Abnormal Psychology, 74*, 50–53.

Betancourt, H., & López, S.R. (1993). The study of culture, ethnicity, and race in American psychology. *American Psychologist, 48*, 629–637.

Bettencourt, B.A., & Miller, N. (1996). Gender differences in aggression as a function of provocation: A meta-analysis. *Psychological Bulletin, 119*(3), 422–427.

Birchler, G.R., & Fals-Stewart, W.S. (1994). Marital dysfunction. In *Encyclopedia of human behavior* (Vol. 3, pp. 103–113). San Diego, CA: Academic Press.

Birren, J.E. (1983). Aging in America: Role for psychology. *American Psychologist, 38*, 298–299.

Birren, J.E., & Fisher, L.M. (1995). Aging and speed of behavior: Possible consequences for psychological functioning. *Annual Review of Psychology, 46*, 329–353.

Bjorklund, D.F. (1989). *Children's thinking, developmental function and individual differences.* Pacific Grove, CA: Brooks/Cole.

Blake, R.R., Helson, H., & Mouton, J. (1956). The generality of conformity behavior as a function of factual anchorage, difficulty of task and amount of social pressure. *Journal of Personality, 25*, 294–305.

Blakeslee, S. (1994, October 5). Yes, people are right. Caffeine is addictive. *New York Times.*

Blanck, D.C., Bellack, A.S., Rosnow, R.L., Rotheram-Borus, M.J., & Schooler, N.R. (1992). Scientific rewards and conflicts of ethical choices in human subjects research. *American Psychologist, 47*, 959–965.

Blatt, S.J., Zuroff, D.C., Quinlan, D.M., & Pilkonis, P. (1996). Interpersonal factors in brief treatment of depression: Further analysis of the NIMH Treatment of Depression Collaborative Research Program. *Journal of Consulting and Clinical Psychology, 64*, 162–171.

Bliss, T.V., & Collingridge, G.L. (1993). A synaptic model of memory: Long-term potentiation in the hippocampus. *Nature, 361*: 31–39.

Bliwise, D.L. (1996). Chronologic age, physiologic age and mortality in sleep apnea. *Sleep, 19*, 277–282.

Block, J. (1971). *Lives through time.* Berkeley, CA: Bancroft.

Block, J., & Robbins, R.W. (1993). A longitudinal study of consistency and change in self-esteem from early adolescence to early adulthood. *Child Development, 64*, 902–923.

Block, R.I. (1996). Does heavy marijuana use impair human cognition and brain function? *Journal of the American Medical Association, 275*, 521–527.

Bloom, L. (1970). *Language development: Form and function in emerging grammar.* Cambridge, MA: MIT Press.

Blum, J.M. (1979). *Pseudoscience and mental ability: The origins and fallacies of the IQ controversy.* New York: Monthly Review Press.

Blumenthal, S.J. (1990). Youth suicide: The physician's role in suicide prevention. *JAMA, Journal of the American Medical Association, 264*(24), 3194–3196.

Blundell, J.E., & Halford, J.C.G. (1998). Serotonin and appetite regulation: Implications for the pharmacological treatment of obesity. *CNS Drugs, 9*, 473–495.

Boivin, D.B., Czeisler, C.A., Kijk, D.J., Duffy, J.F., Folkard, S., Minors, D.S., Totterdell, P., & Waterhouse, J.M. (1997). Complex interaction of the sleep-wake cycle and circadian phase modulates mood in healthy subjects. *Archives of General Psychiatry, 54*, 145–152.

Bok, S. (1999). *Mayhem: Violence as public entertainment.* Cambridge, MA: Perseus Books.

Bokert, E. (1970). *The effects of thirst and related auditory stimulation on dream reports.* Paper presented to the Association for the Physiological Study of Sleep, Washington, DC.

Bolles, R.C. (1972). Reinforcement, expectancy, and learning. *Psychological Review, 79,* 394–409.

Bolos, A.M., Dean, M., Lucas-Derse, S., Ramsburg, M., Brown, G.L., & Goldman, D. (1990). Population and pedigree studies reveal a lack of association between the dopamine D2 receptor gene and alcoholism. *JAMA, Journal of the American Medical Association, 264,* 3156–3160.

Boomsma, D.I., Koopmans, J.R., Van Doornen, L.J.P., & Orlebeke, J.M. (1994). Genetic and social influences on starting to smoke: A study of Dutch adolescent twins and their parents. *Addiction, 89,* 219–226.

Booth-Kewley, S., & Friedman, H.S. (1987). Psychological predictors of heart disease: A quantitative review. *Psychological Bulletin, 101,* 343–362.

Borbely, A. (1986). *Secrets of sleep.* New York: Basic Books.

Borkovec, T.D., & Costello, E. (1993). Efficacy of applied relaxation and cognitive-behavioral therapy in the treatment of generalized anxiety disorder. *Journal of Consulting and Clinical Psychology, 61,* 611–619.

Bornstein, R.F. (1989). Exposure and affect: Overview and meta-analysis of research, 1968–1987. *Psychological Reports, 106,* 265–289.

Botwin, M.D., & Buss, D.M. (1989). The structure of act report data: Is the five factor model of personality recaptured? *Journal of Personality and Social Psychology, 56,* 988–1001.

Bouchard, C., Tremblay, A., Despres, J.P., Nadeau, A., Lupien, P.J., Theriault, G., Dussault, J., Moorjani, S., Pinault, S., & Fournier, G. (1990). The response to long-term overfeeding in identical twins. *New England Journal of Medicine, 322,* 1477–1482.

Bouchard, T.J., Jr., Lykken, D.T., McGue, M., Segal, N.L., & Tellegren, A. (1990). Sources of human psychological differences: The Minnesota study of twins reared apart. *Science, 250,* 223–228.

Bourne, L.E., Dominowski, R.L., Loftus, E.F., & Healy, A.F. (1986). *Cognitive process* (2nd ed.). Englewood Cliffs, NJ: Prentice Hall.

Bouton, M.E. (1993). Context, time and memory retrieval in the interference paradigms of Pavlovian conditioning. *Psychological Bulletin, 114,* 80–99.

Bouton, M.E. (1994). Context, ambiguity and classical conditioning. *Current Directions in Psychological Science, 3,* 49–52.

Bowden, S.C. (1990). Separating cognitive impairment in neurologically asymptomatic alcoholism from Wernicke-Korsakoff's syndrome: Is the neuropsychological distinction justified? *Psychological Bulletin, 107,* 355–366.

Bower, G.H., & Mann, T. (1992). Improving recall by recoding interfering material at the time of recall. *Journal of Experimental Psychology: Learning, Memory, and Cognition, 18,* 1310–1320.

Bowers, K.S. (1973). Situationism in psychology: An analysis and a critique. *Psychological Review, 80*(5), 307–336.

Bowlby, J. (1982). *Attachment and loss* (2nd ed.). New York: Basic Books. (Original work published in 1969.)

Brainerd, C.J. (1978). The stage question in cognitive-developmental theory. *Behavioral and Brain Sciences, 2,* 172–213.

Brainerd, C.J. (1996). Piaget: A centennial celebration. *American Psychological Society, 7*(4), 191–225.

Brainerd, C.J., Reyna, V.F., & Brandse, E. (1995). Are children's false memories more persistent than their true memories? *Psychological Science, 6*(6), 359–364.

Brandon, T.H. (1994). Negative affect as motivation to smoke. *Current Directions in Psychological Science, 3,* 33–37.

Bredemeier, B., & Shields, D. (1985, October). Values and violence in sports today. *Psychology Today,* pp. 23–32.

Breetvelt, I.S., & Van Dam, F.S.A.M. (1991). Underreporting by cancer patients: The case of response-shift. *Social Science and Medicine, 32,* 981–987.

Brenner, M.H. (1973). *Mental illness and the economy.* Cambridge, MA: Harvard University Press.

Brenner, M.H. (1979). Influence of the social environment on psychopathology: The historic perspective. In J.E. Barrett (ed.), *Stress and mental disorder.* New York: Raven Press.

Breslau, N., Davis, G.C., & Andreski, P. (1995). Risk factors for PTSD-related traumatic events: A prospective analysis. *American Journal of Psychiatry, 152,* 529–535.

Brewer, W.F., & Nakamura, G.V. (1984). The nature and function of schemas. In R.S. Wyer & T.K. Srull (eds.), *Handbook of social cognition.* Hillsdale, NJ: Erlbaum.

Brewin, C.R. (1996). Theoretical foundations of cognitive-behavior therapy for anxiety and depression. *Annual Review of Psychology, 47,* 33–57.

Brickman, P., Coates, D., & Janoff-Bulman, R. (1978). Lottery winners and accident victims: Is happiness relative? *Journal of Personality and Social Psychology, 36,* 917–927.

Brislin, R.W., Cushner, K., Cherries, C., & Yong, M. (1986). *Intercultural interactions: A practical guide.* Beverly Hills, CA: Sage.

Broadbent, D.E. (1958). *Perception and communication.* New York: Pergamon.

Brody, J.E. (1990, May 10). Personal health: On menopause and the toll that loss of estrogens can take on a woman's sexuality. *New York Times,* Sec. B.

Brody, L. (1985). Gender differences in emotional development: A review of theories and research. In A.J. Stewart & M.B. Lykes (eds.), *Gender and personality: Current perspectives on theory and research* (pp. 14–61). Durham, NC: Duke University Press.

Broida, J., Tingley, L., Kimball, R., & Miele, J. (1993). Personality differences between pro- and anti-vivisectionists. *Society and Animals, 1,* 129–144.

Brooks-Gunn, J. (1993). *Adolescence.* Paper presented at the meeting of the Society for Research in Child Development, Kansas City, MO.

Brooks-Gunn, J., & Lewis, M. (1984). The development of early visual self-recognition. *Developmental Review, 4,* 215–239.

Brown, A.S. (1991). A review of the tip-of-the-tongue experience. *Psychological Bulletin, 109*(2), 204–223.

Brown, B., & Grotberg, J.J. (1981). Head Start: A successful experiment. *Courrier.* Paris: International Children's Centre.

Brown, L.S., & Ballou, M. (1992). *Personality and psychopathology: Feminists reappraisals.* New York: Guilford.

Brown, R. (1958). *Words and things.* New York: Free Press/Macmillan.

Brown, R., & Kulik, J. (1977). Flashbulb memories. *Cognition, 5,* 73–99.

Brown, R., & McNeill, D. (1966). The "tip of the tongue phenomenon." *Journal of Verbal Learning and Verbal Behavior, 8,* 325–337.

Brown, R.W., & Lenneberg, E.H. (1954). A study in language and cognition. *Journal of Abnormal and Social Psychology, 49,* 454–462.

Browne, A. (1993). Violence against women by male partners: Prevalence, outcomes and policy implications. *American Psychologist, 48,* 1077–1087.

Bruch, H. (1980). *The golden cage: The enigma of anorexia nervosa.* New York: Random House.

Bruder, G.E., Stewart, M.W., Mercier, M.A., Agosti, V., Leite, P., Donovan, S., & Quitkin, F.M. (1997). Outcome of cognitive-behavioral therapy for depression: Relation to hemispheric dominance for verbal processing. *Journal of Abnormal Psychology, 106,* 138–144.

Brumberg, J.J. (1988). *Fasting girls: The emergence of anorexia nervosa as a modern disease.* Cambridge, MA: Harvard University Press.

Brunner, H.G., Nelen, M., Breakefield, X.O., Ropers, H.H., & Van Oost, B.A. (1993a). Abnormal behavior associated with a point mutation in the structural gene for monoamine oxidase A. *Science, 262,* 578–580.

Brunner, H.G., Nelen, M., Breakfield, X.O., & Ropers, H.H. (1993b). Abnormal structures associated with a point mutation in the structural gene for monoamine oxidase A. *Science, 263,* 578–580.

Budzynski, T., Stoyva, J., & Adler, C. (1970). Feedback-induced muscle relaxation: Application to tension headache. *Journal of Behavior Therapy and Experimental Psychiatry, 1,* 205–211.

Burke, D.M., McKay, D.G., Worthley, J.S., & Wade, E. (1991). On the tip of the tongue: What causes word finding failures in young and older adults? *Journal of Memory and Language, 30,* 542–579.

Bushman, B.J. (1993). Human aggression while under the influence of alcohol and other drugs: An integrative research review. *Current Directions in Psychological Science, 2,* 148–152.

Bushman, B.J., & Baumeister, R.F. (1998). Threatened egotism, narcissism, self-esteem, and direct and displaced aggression: Does self-love or self-hate lead to violence? *Journal of Personality & Social Psychology, 75,* 219–229.

Bushman, B.J., & Cooper, H.M. (1990). Effects of alcohol on human aggression: An integrative research review. *Psychological Bulletin, 107,* 341–354.

Buss, D.M. (1985). Human mate selection. *American Scientist, 73,* 47–51.

Buss, D.M. (1989). Sex differences in human mate preferences: Evolutionary hypotheses tested in 37 cultures. *Behavioral and Brain Sciences, 12,* 1–49.

Buss, D.M. (1992). Do women have evolved preferences for men with resources? *Ethology and Sociobiology, 12,* 401–408.

Butcher, J.N., & Rouse, S.V. (1996). Personality: Individual differences and clinical assessment. *Annual Review of Psychology, 47,* 87–111.

Butler, R.N. (1963). The life review: An interpretation of reminiscence in the aged. *Psychiatry, 26,* 63–76.

Butler, R.N., & Lewis, M.I. (1982). *Aging and mental health: Positive psychological and biomedical approaches.* St. Louis, MO: Mosby.

Byne, W., & Parsons, B. (1994). Biology and human sexual orientation. *Harvard Mental Health Letter, 10,* 5–7.

Byrd, K.R. (1994). The narrative reconstructions of incest survivors. *American Psychologist, 49,* 439–440.

Byrne, D. (1961). Interpersonal attraction and attitude similarity. *Journal of Abnormal and Social Psychology, 62,* 713–715.

Byrne, D., & Nelson, D. (1965). Attraction as a linear function of properties of positive reinforcements. *Journal of Personality and Social Psychology, 1,* 659–663.

Cain, W.S. (1981, July). Educating your nose. *Psychology Today,* pp. 48–56.

Cairns, E., & Darby, J. (1998). The conflict in Northern Ireland: Causes, consequences, and controls. *American Psychologist, 53,* 754–760.

Calder, B.J., Insko, C.A., & Yandell, B. (1974). The relation of cognitive and memorial processes to persuasion in simulated jury trial. *Journal of Applied Social Psychology, 4,* 62–92.

Calvert, S., & Cocking, R. (1992). Health promotion through mass media. *Journal of Applied Developmental Psychology, 13,* 143–149.

Campbell, C.P. (1995). *Race, myth and the news.* Thousand Oaks, CA: Sage.

Campos, J.L., Langer, A., & Krowitz, A. (1970). Cardiac responses on the visual cliff in prelocomotor human infants. *Science, 170,* 196–197.

Cannon, W.B. (1929). *Bodily changes in pain, hunger, fear, and rage,* rev. ed. New York: Appleton-Century.

Capron, C., & Duyme, M. (1989). Assessment of effects of socio-economic status on IQ in a full cross-fostering study. *Nature (London), 340,* 552–554.

Carlson, N.R. (1998). *Physiology of behavior.* Boston: Allyn & Bacon.

Carlson, V. (1994). Child abuse. In *Encyclopedia of human behavior* (Vol. 1, pp. 561–578). San Diego, CA: Academic Press.

Carr, M., Borkowski, J.G., & Maxwell, S.E. (1991). Motivational components of underachievement. *Developmental Psychology, 27,* 108–118.

Carroll, J.B., & Horn, J.L. (1981). On the scientific basis of ability testing. *American Psychologist, 36,* 1012–1020.

Carroll, J.M., Thomas, J.C., & Malhotra, A. (1980). Presentation and representation in design problem solving. *British Journal of Psychology, 71,* 143–153.

Carson, R.C., & Butcher, J.N. (1992). *Abnormal psychology and modern life.* New York: HarperCollins.

Carstensen, L. (1995). Evidence for a life-span theory of socio-emotional selectivity. *American Psychological Society, 4*(5), 151–156.

Carter, B. (1996, February 7). New report becomes a weapon in the debate over TV violence. *New York Times.*

Casas, J.M. (1995). Counseling and psychotherapy with racial/ethnic minority groups in theory and practice. In B. Bongar & L.E. Beutler (eds.), *Comprehensive handbook of psychotherapy* (pp. 311–335). New York: Oxford University Press.

Caspi, A., & Elder, G.H., Jr. (1986). Life satisfaction in old age: Linking social psychology and history. *Journal of Psychology and Aging, 1,* 18–26.

Cattell, R.B. (1965). *The scientific analysis of personality.* Baltimore: Penguin.

Cattell, R.B. (1971). *Abilities: Their structure, growth, and action.* Boston: Houghton Mifflin.

Cattell, R.B., & Kline, P. (1977). *The specific analysis of personality and motivation.* New York: Academic Press.

Cavanaugh, J.C. (1990). *Adult development and aging.* Belmont, CA: Wadsworth.

Celis, W. (1994, June 8). More college women drinking to get drunk. *New York Times,* p. B8.

Centers for Disease Control. (1991). Attempted suicide among high school students—United States, 1990. *JAMA, Journal of the American Medical Association, 266*(14), 1911.

Centers for Disease Control and Prevention. (1999). Suicide deaths and rates per 100,000 [On-line]. Available: **http://www.cdc.gov/ncipc/data/us9794/suic.htm**

Chaiken, S., & Eagly, A. H. (1976). Communication modality as a determinant of message persuasiveness and message comprehensibility. *Journal of Personality and Social Psychology, 34,* 605–614.

Chaikin, A. L., & Darley, J. M. (1973). Victim or perpetrator? Defensive attribution of responsibility and the need for order and justice. *Journal of Personality and Social Psychology, 25,* 268–275.

Chait, L. D., & Pierri, J. (1992). Effects of smoked marijuana on human performance: A critical review. In L. Murphy & A. Bartke (eds.), *Marijuana/cannabinoids: Neurobiology and neurophysiology* (pp. 387–424). Boca Raton, FL: CRC Press.

Cherry, C. (1966). *On human communication: A review, a survey, and a criticism* (2nd ed.). Cambridge, MA: MIT Press.

Chipman, S. F., Krantz, D. H., & Silver, R. (1992). Mathematics anxiety and science careers among able bodied college women. *Psychological Science, 5,* 292–295.

Chomsky, N. (1957). *Syntactic structures.* The Hague: Mouton.

Chomsky, N. (1965). *Aspects of the theory of syntax.* Cambridge, MA: MIT Press.

Christensen, F. (1986). *Pornography: The other side.* Unpublished paper, University of Alberta.

Chua, S. C., Chung, W. K., Wu-Peng, X. S., Zhang, Y., Liu, S. M., Tartaglia, L., & Leibel, R. L. (1996). Phenotypes of mouse diabetes and rat fatty due to mutations in OB (leptin) receptor. *Science, 271,* 994–996.

Chwalisz, K., Diener, E., & Gallagher, D. (1988). Autonomic arousal feedback and emotional experience: Evidence from the spinal cord injured. *Journal of Personality and Social Psychology, 54,* 820–828.

Cialdini, R. B., Cacioppo, J. T., Bassett, R., & Miller, J. A. (1978). Lowball procedure for producing compliance: Commitment then cost. *Journal of Personality and Social Psychology, 36,* 463–476.

Cialdini, R. B., Vincent, J. E., Lewis, S. K., Catalan, J., Wheeler, D., & Darby, B. L. (1975). A reciprocal concessions procedure for inducing compliance: The door-in-the-face technique. *Journal of Personality and Social Psychology, 21,* 206–215.

Clark, J. E. (1994). Motor development. In *Encyclopedia of human behavior* (Vol. 3, pp. 245–55). San Diego, CA: Academic Press.

Clark, M. S., & Mills, J. (1979). Interpersonal attraction in exchange and communal relationships. *Journal of Personality and Social Psychology, 37,* 12–24.

Clark, R. D., & Word, L. E. (1974). Where is the apathetic bystander? Situational characteristics of the emergency. *Journal of Personality and Social Psychology, 29,* 279–287.

Clausen, J. A. (1975). The social meaning of differential physical and sexual maturation. In S. E. Dragastin & G. H. Elder, Jr. (eds.), *Adolescence in the life cycle: Psychological change and social context* (pp. 25–47). New York: Wiley.

Cloninger, S. C. (1993). *Theories of personality. Understanding persons.* Englewood Cliffs, NJ: Prentice Hall.

Clore, G. L., & Byrne, D. (1974). A reinforcement-affect model of attraction. In T. L. Huston (ed.), *Foundations of interpersonal attraction* (pp. 143–170). New York: Academic Press.

Cloud, J. (July 6, 1998). Of arms and the boy. *Time,* pp. 58–62.

Cohen, A., & Raffal, R. D. (1991). Attention and feature integration: Illusory conjunctions in a patient with a parietal lobe lesion. *Psychological Science, 2,* 106–110.

Cohen, A. G., & Gutek, B. A. (1991). Differences in the career experiences of members of two APA divisions. *American Psychologist, 46,* 1292–1298.

Cohen, D. B. (1974, May). Repression is not the demon who conceals and hoards our forgotten dreams. *Psychology Today,* pp. 50–54.

Cohen, E. G. (1984). The desegregated school: Problems in status, power and interethnic climate. In N. Miller & M. B. Brewer (eds.), *Groups in contact: The psychology of desegregation* (pp. 77–96). New York: Academic Press.

Cohen, S. (1996). Psychological stress, immunity, and upper respiratory infections. *Current Directions in Psychological Science, 5*(3), 86–88.

Cohen, S., & Herbert, T. B. (1996). Health psychology: Psychological factors and physical disease from the perspective of human psychoneuroimmunology. *Annual Review of Psychology, 47,* 113–142.

Cohen, S., & Williamson, G. M. (1988). Stress and infectious disease in humans. *Psychological Bulletin, 109,* 5–24.

Colegrove, F. W. (1982). Individual memories. *American Journal of Psychology, 10,* 228–55. (Original work published in 1899.) (Reprinted in V. Neisser (ed.), *Memory observed: Remembering in natural contexts.* San Francisco: Freeman.)

Collaer, M. L., & Hines, M. (1995). Human behavioral sex differences: A role for gonadal hormones during early development? *American Psychological Associations, 118*(1), 55–107.

Collins, N. L., & Miller, L. C. (1994). Self-disclosure and liking: A meta-analytic review. *Psychological Bulletin, 116,* 457–475.

Collins, R. C. (1993). Head Start: Steps toward a two-generation program strategy. *Young Children, 48*(2), 25–73.

Compas, B. E., Hinden, B. R., & Gerhardt, C. A. (1995). Adolescent development: Pathways and processes of risk and resilience. *Annual Review of Psychology, 46,* 265–293.

Conger, J. J., & Petersen, A. C. (1991). *Adolescence and youth* (4th ed.). New York: HarperCollins.

Connelly, B., Johnston, D., Brown, I. D., Mackay, S., & Blackstock, E. G. (1993). The prevalence of depression in a high school population. *Adolescence, 28*(109), 149–158.

Conrad, R. (1972). Short-term memory in the deaf: A test for speech coding. *British Journal of Psychology, 63,* 173–180.

Conroy, J. W. (1996). The small ICF/MR program: Dimensions of quality and cost. *Mental Retardation, 34,* 13–26.

Contreras, D., Destexhe, A., Sejnowski, T. J., & Steriade, M. (1996). Control of spatiotemporal coherence of a thalamic oscillation by corticothalamic feedback. *Science, 274*(5288), 771–774.

Conway, M. A. (1996). Failures of autobiographical remembering. In D. Hermann, C. McEvoy, C. Hertzog, P. Hertel, & M. K. Johnson (eds.), *Basic and applied memory research: Theory in context.* Nahwah, NJ: Erlbaum.

Cookerly, J. R. (1980). Does marital therapy do any lasting good? *Journal of Marital and Family Therapy, 6,* 393–397.

Cooper, H. (1993). In search of a social fact. A commentary on the study of interpersonal expectations. In P. Blanck (ed.), *Interpersonal expectations: Theory, research, and application* (pp. 218–226). Paris; Cambridge University Press.

Cooper, J. (1971). Personal responsibility and dissonance. *Journal of Personality and Social Psychology, 18,* 354–363.

Cooper, J., & Croyle, R. T. (1984). Attitudes and attitude change. *Annual Review of Psychology, 35,* 395–3426.

Corder, B., Saunders, A. M., Strittmatter, W. J., Schmechel, D. E., Gaskell, P. C., & Small, D. E. (1993). Gene dose of apolipoprotein E type 4 allele and the risk of Alzheimer's disease in late onset families. *Science, 261,* 921–923.

Coren, S., Porac, C., & Ward, L.M. (1984). *Sensation and perception* (2nd ed.). Orlando, FL: Academic Press.

Cornelius, R.R. (1996). *The science of emotion: Research and tradition in the psychology of emotions.* Upper Saddle River, NJ: Prentice Hall.

Costa, P.T., Jr., & McCrae, R.R. (1992). *Revised NEO Personality Inventory (NEO-PI-R) and NEO Five-Factor Inventory (NEO-FFI) professional manual.* Odessa, FL: Psychological Assessment Resources, Inc.

Costa, P.T., & McCrae, R.R. (1995). Domains and facets: Hierarchical personality assessment using the Revised NEO Personality Inventory. *Journal of Personality Assessment, 64,* 21–50.

Cotton, J.L. (1993). *Employee involvement: Methods for improving performance and work attitudes.* Newbury Park, CA: Sage.

Council, J.R. (1993). Context effects in personality research. *Current Directions, 2,* 31–34.

Cousins, S. (1989). Culture and self-perception in Japan and in the United States. *Journal of Personality and Social Psychology, 56,* 124–131.

Cowan, N. (1988). Evolving conceptions of memory storage, selective attention, and their mutual constraints within the human information-processing system. *Psychological Bulletin, 104,* 163–191.

Cox, D.J., Sutphen, J., Borowitz, S., & Dickens, M.N. (1994). Simple electromyographic biofeedback treatment for chronic pediatric constipation/encopresis: Preliminary report. *Biofeedback & Self Regulation, 19*(1), 41–50.

Coyle, J.T. (1987). Alzheimer's disease. In G. Adelman (ed.), *Encyclopedia of neuroscience* (pp. 29–31). Boston: Birkhauser.

Craig, A.D., & Bushnell, M.C. (1994). The thermal grill illusion: Unmasking the burn of cold pain. *Science, 265,* 252–255.

Craighead, L. (1990). Supervised exercise in behavioral treatment for moderate obesity. *Behavior Therapy, 20,* 49–59.

Craik, F.I.M., & Lockhart, R.S. (1972). Levels of processing: A framework for memory research. *Journal of Verbal Learning and Verbal Behavior, 11,* 671–684.

Craik, F.I.M., & Watkins, M.J. (1973). The role of rehearsal in short-term memory. *Journal of Verbal Learning and Verbal Behavior, 12,* 599–607.

Crandall, C.S. (1994). Prejudice against fat people: Ideology and self-interest. *Journal of Personality and Social Psychology, 66,* 882–894.

Crick, F., & Mitchison, G. (1983). The function of dreamsleep. *Nature (London), 304*(5922), 111–114.

Cronan, T.A., Walen, H.R., & Cruz, S.G. (1994). The effects of community-based literacy training on Head Start parents. *Journal of Community Psychology, 22,* 248–258.

Cronbach, L.J. (1990). *Essentials of psychological testing* (5th ed.). New York: HarperCollins.

Crovitz, H.F., & Schiffman, H. (1974). Frequency of episodic memories as a function of their age. *Bulletin of the Psychonomic Society, 4,* 517–518.

Crutchfield, R.A. (1955). Conformity and character. *American Psychologist, 10,* 191–198.

Crystal, D.S., et al. (1994). Psychological maladjustments and academic achievement: A cross-cultural study of Japanese, Chinese, and American high school students. *Child Development, 65,* 738–753.

Csikszentmihalyi, M., Rathunde, K., & Whalen, S. (1993). *Talented teenagers: The roots of success and failure.* New York: Cambridge University Press.

Cumming, E., & Henry, W.E. (1961). *Growing old: The process of disengagement.* New York: Basic Books.

Curle, C.E., & Williams, C. (1996). Post-traumatic stress reactions in children: Gender differences in the incidence of trauma reactions at two years and examination of factors influencing adjustment. *British Journal of Clinical Psychology, 35,* 297–309.

Dabbs, J.M., & Leventhal, H. (1966). Effects of varying the recommendations in a fear-arousing communication. *Journal of Personality and Social Psychology, 4,* 525–531.

Daehler, M.W. (1994). Cognitive development. In *Encyclopedia of human behavior* (Vol. 1, pp. 627–637).

Dadona, L., Hendrickson, A., & Quigley, H.A. (1991). Selective effects of experimental glaucoma on axonal transport by retinal ganglion cells to the dorsal lateral geniculate nucleus. *Investigations in Ophthalmology & Visual Science, 32,* 1593–1599.

Dahlström, W.G. (1993). Tests: Small samples, large consequences. *American Psychologist, 48,* 393–399.

Dalaker, J., & Naifeh, M. (1998). U.S. Bureau of the Census, Current Population Reports, Series P60-201, Poverty in the United States: 1997. Washington, DC: U.S. Government Printing Office.

Daley, S. (1991, January 9). Girls' self-esteem is lost on way to adolescence, new study finds. *New York Times,* Sec. B.

Daly, M., & Wilson, M. (1988). Evolutionary social psychology and family homicide. *Science, 242*(4878), 519–524.

Daly, M., & Wilson, M.I. (1996). Violence against stepchildren. *American Psychological Society, 5*(3), 77–81.

Damasio, A.R., Tranel, D., & Damasio, H. (1990b). Individuals with sociopathic behavior caused by frontal damage fail to respond autonomically to social stimuli. *Behavioral Brain Research, 41,* 81–94.

Darwin, C.R. (1859). *Origin of species.* London.

Darwin, C.R. (1871). *The decent of man.* London.

Daunton, N.G. (1990). Animal models in motion sickness research. In G.H. Crampton (ed.), *Motion and space sickness* (pp. 87–104). Boca Raton, FL: CRC Press.

Davidson, E.S., & Schenk, S. (1994). Variability in subjective responses to marijuana: Initial experiences of college students. *Addictive Behaviors, 19,* 531–538.

Davidson, R.J. (1992). Emotion and affective style: Hemispheric substrates. *Psychological Science, 3,* 39–43.

Davies, M., Stankov, L. & Roberts, R.D. (1998). Emotional intelligence: In search of an elusive construct. *Journal of Personality and Social Psychology, 75,* 989–1015.

Davies, P.T., & Cummings, E.M. (1994). Marital conflict and child adjustment: An emotional security hypothesis. *Psychological Bulletin, 166*(3), 387–411.

Davis, J.R., et al. (1988). Space motion sickness during 24 flights of the space shuttle. *Aviation, Space, and Environmental Medicine, 59,* 1185–1189.

Davis, M.H., & Stephan, W.G. (1980). Attributions for exam performance. *Journal of Applied Social Psychology, 10,* 235–248.

Dawes, R.M. (1994). *House of cards: The collapse of modern psychotherapy.* New York: Free Press.

Dawkins, M.P. (1997). Drug use and violent crime among adolescents. *Adolescence, 32*(126), 395–405.

de Raad, B., & Szirmak, Z. (1994). The search for the "Big Five" in a non–Indo-European language: The Hungarian trait structure and its relationship to the EQP and the PTS. *Revue Européenne de Psychologie Appliqué, 44,* 17–24.

Dean, J.W., Jr., & Evans, J.R. (1994). *Total quality: Management, organization, and strategy.* St. Paul, MN: West.

Dean, S.R. (1970). Is there an ultraconscious? *Canadian Psychiatric Association Journal, 15,* 57–61.

DeAngelis, T. (1991a, June). Hearing pinpoints gaps in research on women. *APA Monitor,* p. 8.

DeAngelis, T. (1991b, August). Ethnic groups respond differently to medication. *APA Monitor,* p. 28.

Deaux, K., & Kite, M. (1993). Gender stereotypes. In F.L. Denmark & M.A. Paludi (eds.), *Psychology of women: A handbook of issues and theories* (pp. 107–139). Westport, CT: Greenwood.

Deaux, K., & Wrightsman, L. (1984). *Social psychology in the 80s* (4th ed.). Monterey, CA: Brooks/Cole.

DeCasper, A.J., & Spence, M.J. (1986). Prenatal maternal speech influences newborns' perception of speech sounds. *Infant Behavior and Development, 9,* 133–150.

Deikman, A.J. (1973). Deautomatization and the mystic experience. In R.W. Ornstein (ed.), *The nature of human consciousness.* San Francisco: Freeman.

DeKay, W.T., & Buss, D.M. (1992). Human nature, individual differences and the importance of context: Perspectives from evolutionary psychology. *Current Directions in Psychological Science, 1,* 184–189.

DeMaris, A., & Rao, K.V. (1992). Premarital cohabitation and subsequent marital stability in the United States: A reassessment. *Journal of Marriage and the Family, 54,* 178–190.

Dement, W.C. (1965). An essay on dreams: The role of physiology in understanding their nature. In F. Barron (ed.), *New directions in psychology* (Vol. 2). New York: Holt, Rinehart & Winston.

Dement, W.C. (1974). *Some must watch while some must sleep.* San Francisco: Freeman.

DeNeve, K.M., & Cooper, H. (1998). The happy personality: A meta-analysis of 137 personality traits and subjective well-being. *Psychological Bulletin, 124,* 197–229.

Denmark, F.L. (1994). Engendering psychology. *American Psychologist, 49*(4), 329–334.

Dennerstein, L., & Burrows, G.D. (1982). Hormone replacement therapy and sexuality in women. *Clinics in Endocrinology and Metabolism, 11,* 661–679.

Denney, N.W. (1984). A model of cognitive development across the life span. *Developmental Review 4,* 171–191.

Des Forges, A.L. (1995). The ideology of genocide. *Issue, 23*(2), 44–47.

Devane, W.A., Hanus, L., Breuer, A., Pertwee, R.G., Stevenson, L.A., Griffin, G., Gibson, D., Mandelbaum, A., Etinger, A., & Mechoulam, R. (1992). Isolation and structure of a brain constituent that binds to the cannabinoid receptor. *Science, 258,* 1946–1949.

deVeaugh-Geiss, J. (1993). Diagnosis and treatment of obsessive-compulsive disorder. *Annual Review of Medicine, 44,* 53–61.

Diamond, J. (1994). Race without color. *Discover, 15,* 82–92.

Diaz, J. (1997). *How drugs influence behavior: Neuro-behavioral approach.* Upper Saddle River, NJ: Prentice Hall.

Diener, E., Suh, E.M., Lucas, R.E., & Smith, H.L. (1999). Subjective well-being: Three decades of progress. *Psychological Bulletin, 125,* 276–302.

Diener, E., & Suh, E. (1998). Age and subjective well-being: An international analysis. *Annual Review of Gerontology and Geriatrics, 17,* 304–324.

DiFranza, J.R., & Lew, R.A. (1995). Effect of maternal cigarette smoking on pregnancy complications and sudden infant death syndrome. *Journal of Family Practice, 40*(4), 385–394.

DiGiovanna, A.G. (1994). *Human aging: Biological perspectives.* New York: McGraw-Hill.

Dill, S. (1994, January 16). Babies' grunts may have meaning. *Associated Press.*

Dillon, S. (1994, October 21). Bilingual education effort is flawed, study indicates. *New York Times,* p. A20.

DiMatteo, M.R., & Friedman, H.S. (1982). *Social psychology and medicine.* Cambridge, MA: Oelgeschlager, Gunn, & Hain.

Dion, K.K. (1972). Physical attractiveness and evaluations of children's transgressions. *Journal of Personality and Social Psychology, 24,* 285–290.

Doherty, W.J., & Jacobson, N.S. (1982). Marriage and the family. In B.B. Wolman (ed.), *Handbook of developmental psychology* (pp. 667–80). Englewood Cliffs, NJ: Prentice Hall.

Dole, A.A. (1995). Why not drop race as a term? *American Psychologist, 50,* 40.

Domhoff, G.W. (1996). *Finding meaning in dreams: A quantitative approach.* New York: Plenum Press.

Domjan, M. (1987). Animal learning comes of age. *American Psychologist, 42,* 556–564.

Domjan, M., & Purdy, J.E. (in press). Animal research in psychology: More than meets the eye of the general psychology student. *American Psychologist.*

Donatelle, R.J., & Davis, L.G. (1993). *Access to health* (2nd ed.). Englewood Cliffs, NJ: Prentice Hall.

Douglas, H.M., Moffitt, T.E., Dar, R., McGee, R., & Silva, P. (1995). Obsessive-compulsive disorder in a birth cohort of 18-year-olds: Prevalence and predictors. *Journal of the American Academy of Child and Adolescent Psychiatry, 34,* 1424–1429.

Dovidio, J.F., Evans, N., & Tyler, R.B. (1986). Racial stereotypes: The contents of their cognitive representations. *Journal of Experimental Social Psychology, 22,* 22–37.

Dovidio, J.F., Gaertner, S.L., Isen, A.M., & Lawrence, R. (1995). Group representations and intergroup bias: Positive affect, similarity, and group size. *Personality and Social Psychology Bulletin, 21,* 856–865.

Downs, H. (1994, August 21). Must we age? *Parade Magazine,* pp. 3, 5, 7.

Druckman, D., & Bjork, R.A. (eds.). (1991). *In the mind's eye: Enhancing human performance.* Washington, DC: National Academy Press.

Dryer, D.C., & Horowitz, L.M. (1997). When do opposites attract? Interpersonal complementarity versus similarity. *Journal of Personality and Social Psychology, 72*(3), 592–603.

Dunkle, T. (1982, April). The sound of silence. *Science,* pp. 30–33.

Dunn, R.L., & Schwebel, A.I. (1995). Meta-analytic review of marital therapy outcome research. *Journal of Family Psychology, 9,* 58–68.

Dyk, P.K. (1993). Anatomy, physiology and gender issues in adolescence. In T.P. Gullota, G.R. Adams, & R. Montemayor (eds.), *Adolescent sexuality: Advances in adolescent development* (pp. 35–36). Newbury Park, CA: Sage.

Eagly, A.H. (1992). Uneven progress: Social psychology and the study of attitudes. *Journal of Personality and Social Psychology, 63*(5), 693–710.

Eagly, A.H. (1995). The science and politics of comparing women and men. *American Psychologist, 50*(3), 145–158.

Eagly, A.H., & Carli, L.L. (1981). Sex of researchers and sex-typed communications as determinants of sex differences in influenceability: A meta-analysis of social influence studies. *Psychological Bulletin, 90,* 1–20.

Eagly, A.H., & Steffen, V.J. (1986). Gender and aggressive behavior: A meta-analytic review of the social psychological literature. *Psychological Bulletin, 100,* 309–330.

East, P., & Felice, M.E. (1992). Pregnancy risk among the younger sisters of pregnant and childbearing adolescents. *Developmental and Behavioral Pediatrics, 13,* 128–136.

Eccles, J., et al. (1993). Development during adolescence: The impact of stage-environment fit on young adolescents' experiences in school and families. *American Psychologist, 2,* 90–101.

Eckerman, C.O., Davis, C.C., & Didow, S.M. (1989). Toddlers' emerging ways of achieving social coordinations with a peer. *Child Development, 60,* 440–453.

Eibl-Eibesfeldt, I. (1972). *Love and hate.* New York: Holt, Rinehart & Winston.

Eich, E. (1989). Theoretical issues in state dependent memory. In H.L. Roediger & F. Craik (eds.), *Varieties of memory and consciousness.* Hillsdale, NJ: Lawrence Erlbaum Associates.

Eich, J.E., Weingartner, H., Stillman, R.C., & Gillin, J.C. (1975). State dependent accessibility of retrieval cues in the retention of a categorized list. *Journal of Verbal Learning and Verbal Behavior, 14,* 408–417.

Eimas, P.D., & Tartter, V.C. (1979). The development of speech perception. In H.W. Reese & L.P. Lipsitt (eds.), *Advances in child development and behavior* (Vol. 13). New York: Academic Press.

Eisenberg, N., & Lennon, R. (1983). Sex differences in empathy and related capacities. *Psychological Bulletin, 94,* 100–131.

Eisenberger, R., & Cameron, J. (1996). Detrimental effects of reward. *American Psychologist, 51,* 1153–1166.

Eisenman, R. (1994). Birth order, effect on personality and behavior. In *Encyclopedia of human behavior* (Vol. 1, pp. 401–405).

Ekman, P., Sorenson, E.R., & Friesen, W.V. (1969). Pancultural elements in facial displays of emotion. *Science, 164,* 86–88.

Ekman, P. (1993). Facial expression and emotion. *American Psychologist, 48*(4), 384–392.

Ekman, P. (1994). Strong evidence for universals in facial expressions: A reply to Russell's mistaken critique. *Psychological Bulletin, 115*(2), 268–287.

Ekman, P., & Davidson, R.J. (1993). Voluntary smiling changes regional brain activity. *Psychological Science, 4,* 342–345.

Ekman, P., & Friesen, W.V. (1971). Constants across cultures in the face and emotion. *Journal of Personality and Social Psychology, 17,* 124–129.

Ekman, P., & Friesen, W.V. (1975). *Unmasking the face.* Englewood Cliffs, NJ: Prentice Hall.

Ekman, P., & Friesen, W.V. (1986). A new pan-cultural facial expression of emotion. *Motivation and Emotion, 10,* 159–168.

Ekman, P., Freisen, W.V., & Ancoli, S. (1980). Facial signs of emotional experience. *Journal of Personality & Social Psychology, 39*(1-6), 1125–1134.

Ekman, P., Friesen, W.V., & Ellsworth, P. (1972). *Emotion in the human face.* Elmsford, NY: Pergamon.

Ekman, P., Friesen, W.V., O'Sullivan, M., Chan, A., Diacoyanni-Tarlatzis, I., Heider, K., Krause, R., LeCompte, W.A., Pitcairn, T., Ricci-Bitti, P.E., Scherer, K., Tomita, M., & Tzavaras, A. (1987). Universals and cultural differences in the judgments of facial expressions of emotion. *Journal of Personality and Social Psychology, 53,* 712–717.

Elbert, T., Pantev, C., Wienbruch, C., Rockstroh, B., & Taub, E. (1995). Increased cortical representation of the fingers of the left hand in string players. *Science, 270,* 305–307.

Elkin, I., Shea, T., Watkins, J.T., Imber, S.D., Sotsky, S.M., Collins, J.F., Glass, D.R., Pikonis, P.A., Leber, W.R., Docherty, J.P., Fiester, S.J., & Parloff, M.B. (1989). National Institute of Mental Health treatment of depression collaborative research program: General effectiveness of treatments. *Archives of General Psychiatry, 46,* 971–982.

Elkind, D. (1968). Cognitive development in adolescence. In J.F. Adams (ed.), *Understanding adolescence.* Boston: Allyn & Bacon.

Elkind, D. (1969). Egocentrism in adolescence. In R.W. Grinder (ed.), *Studies in adolescence* (2nd ed.). New York: Macmillan.

Elliott, D.S., Hamburg, B.A., & Williams, K.R. (eds) (1998). *Violence in American schools: A new perspective.* NY: Cambridge University Press.

Ellis, A. (1973). *Humanistic psychotherapy: The rational emotive approach.* New York: Julian Press.

Ellis, A., & Harper, R.A. (1975). *A new guide to rational living.* North Hollywood, CA: Wilshire Book Co.

Ellis, L., & Coontz, P.D. (1990). Androgens, brain functioning, and criminality: The neurohormonal foundations of antisociality. In L. Ellis & H. Hoffman (eds.), *Crime in biological, social, and moral contexts* (pp. 36–49). New York: Praeger Press.

Emmorey, K. (1994). Sign language. In *Encyclopedia of human behavior* (Vol. 4, pp. 193–204). San Diego, CA: Academic Press.

Engel, J.F., Black, R.D., & Miniard, P.C. (1986). *Consumer behavior.* Chicago: Dryden Press.

Enns, C.Z. (1993). Twenty years of feminist counseling and therapy: From naming biases to implementing multifaceted practice. *Counseling Psychologist, 21,* 3–87.

Eppley, K.R., Abrams, A.I., & Shear, J. (1989). Differential effects of relaxation techniques on trait anxiety: A meta-analysis. *Journal of Clinical Psychology, 45,* 957–974.

Epstein, N., Evans, L. & Evans, J. (1994). Marriage. *Encyclopedia of human behavior* (Vol. 3, pp. 115–125). San Diego, CA: Academic Press.

Epstein, R., Kirshnit, C.E., Lanza, R.P., & Rubin, L.C. (1984). "Insight" in the pigeon: Antecedents and determinants of an intelligent performance. *Nature (London), 308,* 61–62.

Epstein, S. (1962). The measurement of drive and conflict in humans: Theory and experiment. In M.R. Jones (ed.), *Nebraska Symposium on Motivation.* Lincoln: University of Nebraska Press.

Erdley, C.A., & D'Agostino, P.R. (1988). Cognitive and affective components of automatic priming effects. *Journal of Personality and Social Psychology, 54,* 741–747.

Erikson, E.H. (1963). *Childhood and society* (2nd ed.). New York: Norton.

Erikson, E.H. (1968). *Identity: Youth in crisis.* New York: Norton.

Eriksson, P.S., Perfilieva, E., Björk-Eriksson, T., Alborn, A.M., Nordborg, C., Peterson, D.A., & Gage, F.H. (1998). Neurogenesis in the adult human hippocampus. *Nature Medicine, 4,* 1313–1317.

Eron, L.D. (1982). Parent–child interaction, television violence, and aggression of children. *American Psychologist, 37,* 197–211.

Evans, L.I., Rozelle, R.M., Lasater, T.M., Dembroski, R.M., & Allen, B.P. (1970). Fear arousal, persuasion and actual vs. implied behavioral change: New perspective utilizing a real-life dental hygiene program. *Journal of Personality and Social Psychology, 16,* 220–227.

Eyer, J. (1977). Prosperity as a cause of death. *International Journal of Health Services, 7,* 125–150.

Eysenck, H.J. (1947). *Dimensions of personality.* London: Routledge & Kegan Paul.

Eysenck, H.J. (1952). The effects of psychotherapy: An evaluation. *Journal of Consulting and Clinical Psychology, 16,* 319–324.

Eysenck, H.J. (1970). *The structure of human personality* (3rd ed.). London: Methuen.

Eysenck, H. J. (1976). *The measurement of personality.* Baltimore, MD: University Park Press.

Eysenck, H. J. (1992). Four ways five factors are *not* basic. *Personality and Individual Differences, 13,* 667–673.

Eysenck, H. J. (1993). Commentary on Goldberg. *American Psychologist, 48,* 1299–1300.

Fagot, B. I. (1994). Parenting. In *Encyclopedia of human behavior* (Vol. 3, pp. 411–419). San Diego, CA: Academic Press.

Fairburn, C. G., & Wilson, G. T. (eds.). (1993). *Binge eating: Nature, assessment and treatment.* New York: Guilford Press.

Fallon, A., & Rozin, P. (1985). Sex differences in perceptions of desirable body states. *Journal of Abnormal Psychology, 84,* 102–105.

Fantz, R. L., Fagan, J. F., & Miranda, S. B. (1975). Early visual selectivity. In L. B. Cohen & P. Salapatek (eds.), *Infant perception: From sensation to cognition* (Vol. 1). New York: Academic Press.

Farthing, C. W. (1992). *The psychology of consciousness.* Englewood Cliffs, NJ: Prentice Hall.

Feingold, A. (1992). Good-looking oeioke are not what we think. *Psychological Bulletin, 111,* 304–341.

Feinson, M. C. (1986). Aging widows and widowers: Are there mental health differences? *International Journal of Aging and Human Development, 23,* 244–255.

Feldhusen, J. F., & Goh, B. E. (1995). Assessing and accessing creativity: An integrative review of theory, research, and development. *Creativity Research Journal, 8,* 231–247.

Feldman, R. S., Salzinger, S., Rosario, M., Alvarado, L., Caraballo, L., & Hammer, M. (1995). Parent, teacher, and peer ratings of physically abused and nonmaltreated children's behavior. *Journal of Abnormal Child Psychology, 23*(3), 317–334.

Feldman-Summers, S., & Pope, K. S. (1994). The experience of "forgetting" childhood abuse: A national survey of psychologists. *Journal of Consulting and Clinical Psychology, 62,* 636–639.

Ferguson, C. A., & Macken, M. A. (1983). The role of play in phonological development. In K. E. Nelson (ed.), *Children's language* (Vol. 4). Hillsdale, NJ: Erlbaum.

Feshbach, S., & Weiner, B. (1982). *Personality.* Lexington, MA: D. C. Heath.

Festinger, L. (1957). *A theory of cognitive dissonance.* Evanston, IL: Row, Peterson.

Fiedler, F. E. (1967). *A theory of leadership effectiveness.* New York: McGraw-Hill.

Fiedler, F. E. (1978). The contingency model and the dynamics of the leadership process. In L. Berkowitz (ed.), *Advances in experimental social psychology* (Vol. 11, pp. 59–112). New York: Academic Press.

Fiedler, F. E. (1993). The leadership situation and the black box contingency theories. In M. Chemers & R. Ayman (eds.), *Leadership theory and research: Perspective and directions* (pp. 1–28). San Diego, CA: Academic Press.

Field, T. M. (1986). Interventions for premature infants. *Journal of Pediatrics, 109,* 183–191.

Fischer, K. W., & Henke, R. W. (1996). Infants' construction of actions in context: Piaget's contribution to research on early development. *Psychological Science, 7*(4), 204–210.

Fischman, J. (1985, September). Mapping the mind. *Psychology Today,* pp. 18–19.

Fisher, S., & Greenberg, R. P. (1985). *The scientific credibility of Freud's theories and therapy.* New York: Columbia University Press.

Fiske, S. T., & Neuberg, S. L. (1990). A continuum of impression formation, from category-based to individuating processes: In-fluence of information and motivation on attention and interpretation. In M. P. Zanna (ed.), *Advances in experimental social psychology* (Vol. 23, pp. 399–427). New York: Academic Press.

Fiske, S. T., & Taylor, S. E. (1991). *Social cognition* (2nd ed.). New York: McGraw-Hill.

Fitzgerald, L. F. (1993). Sexual harassment. Violence against women in the workplace. *American Psychologist, 48,* 1070–1076.

Flavell, J. F. (1986). The development of children's knowledge about the appearance–reality distinction. *American Psychologist, 41,* 418–425.

Flavell, J. H. (1996). Piaget's legacy. *Psychological Science, 7*(4), 200–204.

Flexser, A. J., & Tulving, E. (1978). Retrieval independence in recognition and recall. *Psychological Review, 85,* 153–171.

Flier, J. S., & Maratos-Flier, E. (1998). Obesity and the hypothalamus: Novel peptides for new pathways. *Cell, 92,* 437–440.

Flynn, J. R. (1987). Massive IQ gains in 14 nations: What IQ tests really measure. *Psychological Bulletin, 101,* 171–191.

Fogelman, E., & Wiener, V. L. (1985, August). The few, the brave, the noble. *Psychology Today,* pp. 60–65.

Frager, R. (1970). Conformity and anticonformity in Japan. *Journal of Personality and Social Psychology, 15,* 203–210.

Frank, J. D., & Frank, J. B. (1991). *Persuasion and healing* (3rd ed.). Baltimore: Johns Hopkins University Press.

Freedman, J. L., & Fraser, S. C. (1966). Compliance without pressure: The foot-in-the-door technique. *Journal of Personality and Social Psychology, 4,* 195–202.

Freud, S. (1900). The interpretation of dreams. In J. Strachey (ed.), *The standard edition of the complete psychological works of Sigmund Freud* (Vol. 5). London: Hogarth Press.

Freud, S. (1909). Analysis of a phobia in a five-year-old boy. In J. Strachey (ed.), *The standard edition of the complete psychological works of Sigmund Freud* (Vol. 10). London: Hogarth Press.

Freudenheim, M. (1988, December 12). Workers' substance abuse is increasing, survey says. *New York Times,* Business Sec.

Freyd, J. J. (1996). *Betrayal trauma theory: The logic of forgetting abuse.* Cambridge, MA: Harvard University Press.

Frezza, M., di Padova, C., Pozzato, G., Terpin, M., Baraona, E., & Lieber, C. S. (1990). High blood alcohol levels in women: The role of decreased gastric alcohol dehydrogenase activity and first-pass metabolism. *New England Journal of Medicine, 322,* 95–99.

Friedman, E. S., Clark, D. B., & Gershon, S. (1992). Stress, anxiety, and depression: Review of biological, diagnostic, and nosologic issues. *Journal of Anxiety Disorders, 6,* 337–363.

Friedman, M., & Rosenman, R. H. (1959). Association of specific overt behavior patterns with blood and cardiovascular findings: Blood cholesterol level, blood clotting time, incidence of arcus senilis and clinical coronary artery disease. *JAMA, Journal of the American Medical Association, 169,* 1286–1296.

Friedman, M., Breall, W. S., Goodwin, M. L., Sparagon, B. J., Ghandour, G., & Fleischmann, N. (1996). Effect of Type A behavioral counseling on frequency of episodes of silent myocardial ischemia in coronary patients. *American Heart Journal, 132*(5), 933–937.

Friedman, M. J., Schnurr, P. P., & McDonagh-Coyle, A. (1994). Post-traumatic stress disorder in the military veteran. *Psychiatric Clinic of North America, 17*(2), 265–277.

Friedman, S., Paradis, C. M., & Hatch, M. (1994). Characteristics of African-American and white patients with panic disorder and agoraphobia. *Hospital and Community Psychiatry, 45,* 798–803.

Friman, P.C., Allen, K.D., Kerwin, M.L.E., & Larzelere, R. (1993). Changes in modern psychology. *American Psychology, 48,* 658–664.

Frumkin, B., & Ainsfield, M. (1977). Semantic and surface codes in the memory of deaf children. *Cognitive Psychology, 9,* 475–493.

Funder, D.C. (1991). Global traits: A neo-Allportian approach to personality. *Psychological Science, 2,* 31–39.

Funder, D.C. (1995). On the accuracy of personality judgment: A realistic approach. *Psychological Review, 102*(4), 652–670.

Furstenberg, F.F., Jr., Brooks-Gunn, J., & Chase-Lansdale, L. (1989). Teenaged pregnancy and childbearing. *American Psychologist, 44,* 313–320.

Gabrieli, J.D., Desmond, J.E., Bemb, J.B., Wagner, A.D., Stone, M.V., Vaidya, C.J. & Glover, G.H. (1996). Functional magnetic resonance imaging of semantic memory processes in the frontal lobes. *Psychological Science, 7,* 278–283.

Gaertner, S.L., & McLaughlin, J.P. (1983). Racial stereotypes: Associations and ascriptions of positive and negative characteristics. *Social Psychology Quarterly, 46,* 23–30.

Gage, F.H. (1998). Stem cells of the central nervous system. *Current Opinions in Neurobiology, 8,* 671–676.

Gagnon, J.H., et al. (1994*). Sex in America: A definitive study.* Boston: Little, Brown.

Galanter, M. (1984). Self-help large-group therapy for alcoholism: A controlled study. *Alcoholism, Clinical and Experimental Research, 8*(1), 16–23.

Gallistel, C.R. (1981). Bell, Magendie, and the proposals to restrict the use of animals in neurobehavioral research. *American Psychologist, 36,* 357–360.

Gannon, L., et al. (1992). Sex bias in psychological research. *American Psychologist, 47,* 389–396.

Garbarino, J. (1999). *Lost boys: Why our sons turn violent and how we can save them.* NY: Free Press.

Garber, H., & Heber, R. (1982). Modification of predicted cognitive development in high risk children through early intervention. In D.K. Detterman & R.J. Sternberg (eds.), *How and how much can intelligence be increased?* (pp. 121–137). Norwood, NJ: Ablex.

Gardner, H. (1982). *Developmental psychology* (2nd ed.). Boston: Little, Brown.

Gardner, H. (1983a). *Frames of mind: The theory of multiple intelligences.* New York: Basic Books.

Gardner, H. (1983b, May). Prodigies' progress. *Psychology Today,* pp. 75–79.

Gardner, H. (1990). *The Chinese experience.* [Videocassette.] Middlesex Community College Professional Development Day.

Gardner, H. (1993). *Multiple intelligences: The theory in practice.* New York: Basic Books.

Garfield, S.L. (ed.). (1983). Special section: Meta-analysis and psychotherapy. *Journal of Consulting and Clinical Psychology, 51,* 3–75.

Garfinkel, P.E., & Garner, D.M. (1982*). Anorexia nervosa: A multidimensional perspective.* New York: Brunner/Mazel.

Garland, A.F., & Zigler, E. (1993). Adolescent suicide prevention. *American Psychologist, 48,* 169–182.

Garry, M., Loftus, E.F., & Brown, S.W. (1994). Memory: A river runs through it. [Special issue: The recovered memory/false memory debate.] *Consciousness & Cognition: An International Journal, 3*(3–4), 438–451.

Geldard, F.A. (1972). *The human senses* (2nd ed.). New York: Wiley.

Gelman, D. (1990, October 29). A fresh take on Freud. *Newsweek,* pp. 84–86.

Gelman, D. (1994, June 13). Reliving the painful past. *Newsweek,* pp. 20–22.

Gergen, K.J. (1973). The codification of research ethics—views of a Doubting Thomas. *American Psychologist, 28,* 907–912.

Gershon, E.S. (1990). Genetics. In F.K. Goodwin & K.R. Jamison (eds.), *Manic depressive illness* (pp. 373–401). New York: Oxford University Press.

Getzels, J.W. (1975). Problem finding and the inventiveness of solutions. *Journal of Creative Behavior, 9,* 12–18.

Getzels, J.W., & Jackson, P. (1962). *Creativity and intelligence.* New York: Wiley.

Giambra, L. (1974, December). Daydreams: The backburner of the mind. *Psychology Today,* pp. 66–68.

Gibbs, R. (1986). On the psycholinguistics of sarcasm. *Journal of Experimental Psychology: General, 115,* 3–15.

Gift of sight came with burdens. (1999, February 1). *News-Press,* p. 10A.

Gilbert, E.H., & DeBlassie, R.R. (1984). Anorexia nervosa: Adolescent starvation by choice. *Adolescence, 19,* 839–853.

Gilbert, L.A. (1994). Current perspectives on dual-career families. *Current Directions in Psychological Science, 3,* 101–105.

Gilligan, C. (1982). *In a different voice: Psychological theory and women's development.* Cambridge, MA: Harvard University Press.

Gilligan, C. (1992). *Joining the resistance: Girls' development in adolescence.* Paper presented at the meeting of the American Psychological Association, Montreal.

Gilovich, T. (1991). *How we know what isn't so: The fallibility of human reason in everyday life.* New York: Free Press.

Ginsberg, H. (1972). *The myth of the deprived child.* Englewood Cliffs, NJ: Prentice Hall.

Glassman, A.H., & Koob, G.F. (1996). Neuropharmacology. Psychoactive smoke. *Nature, 379,* 677–678.

Glenberg, A., Smith, S.M., & Green, C. (1977). Type I rehearsal: Maintenance and more. *Journal of Verbal Learning and Verbal Behavior, 16,* 339–352.

Glenner, G.G. (1994). Alzheimer's disease. In *Encyclopedia of human behavior* (Vol. 1, pp. 103–111). San Diego, CA: Academic Press.

Gluck, M.A., & Myers, C.E. (1997). Psychobiological models of hippocampal function in learning and memory. *Annual Review of Psychology, 8,* 481–514.

Godden, D.R., & Baddeley, A.D. (1975). Context-dependent memory in two natural environments: On land and underwater. *British Journal of Psychology, 66,* 325–331.

Goldberg, L.R. (1993). The structure of phenotypic personality traits. *American Psychologist, 48,* 26–34.

Goldman, S.A., & Nottebohm F. (1983). Neuronal production, migration, and differentiation in a vocal control nucleus of the adult female canary brain. *Proceedings of the National Academy of Sciences of the U.S.A., 80,* 2390–2394.

Goldsmith, H.H., & Harman, C. (1994). Temperament and attachment: Individuals and relationships. *Current Directions in Psychological Sciences, 3*(2), 53–57.

Goldstein, A.P., & Segall, M.H. (1983). *Aggression in global perspective.* New York: Pergamon.

Goleman, D. (1996, February 26). Studies suggest older minds are stronger than expected. *New York Times.*

Goleman, D. (1997). *Emotional Intelligence.* New York: Bantam Books.

Golomb, J., Kluger, A., de Leon, M.J., Ferris, S.H., Convit, A., Mittelman, M.S., Cohen, J., Rusinek, H., DeSanti, S., & George, A.E. (1994). Hippocampal formation size in normal human aging: A correlate of delayed secondary memory performance. *Learning & Memory, 1,* 45–54.

Goodall, J. (1971). *In the shadow of man.* New York: Dell.

Gopnik, A. (1996). The post-Piaget era. *Psychological Science, 7*(4), 221–225.

Gordis, E. (1996). Alcohol research: At the cutting edge. *Archives of General psychiatry, 53,* 199–201.

Gose, B. (1997, October 24). Colleges try to curb excessive drinking by saying moderation is okay. *Chronicle of Higher Education,* pp. A61–A62.

Gottesman, I.I. (1991). *Schizophrenia genesis: The origins of madness.* New York: Freeman.

Grady, D. (1997, March 21). Importance of a sleep disorder is played down in a British study. *New York Times,* p. A15.

Graf, P., & Schacter, D.L. (1985). Implicit and explicit memory for new associations in normal and amnesic subjects. *Journal of Experimental Psychology: Learning, Memory, and Cognition, 11*(3), 501–518.

Graf, P., Squire, L.R., & Mandler, G. (1984). The information that amnesic patients do not forget. *Journal of Experimental Psychology: Learning, Memory and Cognition, 10,* 164–178.

Graham, J.R., & Lilly, R.S. (1984). *Psychological testing.* Englewood Cliffs, NJ: Prentice Hall.

Graham, K. (1997). *Personal history.* New York: Knopf.

Graham, S. (1992). Most of the subjects were white and middle class. *American Psychologist, 47,* 629–639.

Greaves, G.B. (1980). Psychosocial aspects of amphetamine and related substance abuse. In J. Caldwell (ed.), *Amphetamines and related stimulants: Chemical, biological, clinical and sociological aspects.* Boca Raton, FL: CRC Press.

Greene, R.L. (1987). Effects of maintenance rehearsal on human memory. *Psychological Bulletin, 102,* 403–413.

Greenfield, P.M., & Smith, J.H. (1976). *The structure of communication in early language development.* New York: Academic Press.

Greenwald, A.G. (1992). New Look 3: Unconscious cognition reclaimed. *American Psychologist, 47,* 766–779.

Greenwald, A.G., Spangenberg, E.R., Pratkanis, A.R., & Eskenazi, J. (1991). Double-blind tests of subliminal self-help audiotapes. *Psychological Science, 2,* 119–122.

Grinker, R.R., & Spiegel, J.P. (1945). *War neurosis.* Philadelphia: Blakiston.

Grinspoon, L., Ewalt, J.R., & Shader, R.I. (1972). *Schizophrenia: Pharmacotherapy and psychotherapy.* Baltimore: Williams & Wilkins.

Gruber, J.E., & Bjorn, L. (1986). Women's responses to sexual harassment: An analysis of sociocultural, organizational, and personal resource models. *Social Science Quarterly, 67,* 814–826.

Gruetzner, H. (1988). *Alzheimer's: A caregiver's guide and sourcebook.* New York: Wiley.

Guérin, D. (1994). *Fussy infants at risk.* Paper presented at the meeting of the American Psychological Association, Los Angeles.

Guilford, J.P. (1967). *The nature of human intelligence.* New York: McGraw-Hill.

Gunne, L.M., & Anggard, E. (1972). *Pharmical kinetic studies with amphetamines—relationship to neuropsychiatric disorders.* International Symposium on Pharmical Kinetics, Washington, DC.

Gurvits, T.V., Gilbertson, M.W., Lasko, N.B., Orr, S.P., & Pitman, R.K. (1997). Neurological status of combat veterans and adult survivors of sexual abuse PTSD. *Annals of the New York Academy of Sciences, 821,* 468–471.

Guzder, J., Paris, J., Zelkowitz, P., & Marchessault, K. (1996). Risk factors for borderline personality in children. *Journal of the American Academy of Child and Adolescent Psychiatry, 35,* 26–33.

Gwirtsman, H.E. (1984). Bulimia in men: Report of three cases with neuro-endocrine findings. *Journal of Clinical Psychiatry, 45,* 78–81.

Haberlandt, K. (1997). *Cognitive psychology.* Boston: Allyn & Bacon.

Hack, M., Breslau, N., Weissman, B., Aram, D., Klein, N., & Borawski, E. (1991). Effect of very low birth weight and subnormal head size on cognitive abilities at school age. *New England Journal of Medicine, 325,* 231–237.

Haefele, J.W. (1962). *Creativity and innovation.* New York: Reinhold.

Haines, M., & Spear, S.F. (1996). Changing the perception of the norm: A strategy to decrease binge drinking among college students. *Journal of American College Health, 45,* 134–140.

Hall, C., & Van de Castle, R. (1966). *The content analysis of dreams.* New York: Appleton-Century-Crofts.

Hall, E.T. (1966). *The hidden dimension.* New York: Doubleday.

Hall, G.S. (1904). *Adolescence: Its psychology and its relations to physiology, anthropology, sex, crime, religion and education* (Vol. 1). New York: Appleton-Century-Crofts.

Hall, J.A. (1984). *Nonverbal sex differences: Communication accuracy and expressive style.* Baltimore: Johns Hopkins University Press.

Halpern, D.F. (1992). *Sex differences in cognitive abilities* (2nd ed.). Hillsdale, NJ: Erlbaum.

Hamilton, J.A., Haier, R.J., & Buchsbaum, M.S. (1984). Intrinsic enjoyment and boredom coping scales: Validation with personality evoked potential and attentional measures. *Personality and Individual Differences, 5*(2), 183–193.

Hampson, E., & Kimura, D. (1992). Sexual differentiation and hormonal influences on cognitive function in humans. In J.B. Becker, S.M. Breedlove, & D. Crews (eds.), *Behavioral endocrinology.* Cambridge, MA: MIT Press.

Hampson, J., & Nelson, K. (1993). The relation of maternal language to variation in rate and style of language acquisition. *Journal of Child Language, 20,* 313–342.

Hansel, C.E. (1969). ESP: Deficiencies of experimental method. *Nature, 221,* 1171–1172.

Hansen, W.B. (1993). School-based alcohol prevention programs. *Alcohol, Health and Research World, 17,* 54–60.

Hansen, W.B., & Graham, J.W. (1991). Preventing alcohol, marijuana, and cigarette use among adolescents: Peer pressure resistance training versus establishing conservative norms. *Preventive Medicine, 20,* 414–430.

Harburg, E., DiFranceisco, W., Webster, D.W., Gleiberman, L., & Schork, A. (1990a). Familial transmission of alcohol use: II. Imitation of and aversion to parent drinking (1960) by adult offspring (1977)—Tecumseh, Michigan. *Journal of Studies on Alcohol, 51,* 245–256.

Harburg, E., Gleiberman, L., DiFranceisco, W., Schork, A. & Weissfeld, L.A. (1990b). Familial transmission of alcohol use: III. Impact of imitation/non-imitation of parent alcohol use (1960) on the sensible/problem drinking of their offspring (1977). *British Journal of Addiction, 85,* 1141–1155.

Hare, R.D. (1983). Diagnosis of antisocial personality disorder in two prison populations. *American Journal of Psychiatry, 140,* 887–890.

Hare, R.D. (1993). *Without conscience: The disturbing world of the psychopaths among us.* New York: Pocket Books.

Harlow, H.F. (1949). The formation of learning sets. *Psychological Review, 56,* 51–65.

Harlow, H.F. (1958). The nature of love. *American Psychologist, 13,* 673–685.

Harlow, H.F., & Zimmerman, R.R. (1959). Affectional responses in the infant monkey. *Science, 130,* 421–432.

Harrell, R.F., Woodyard, E., & Gates, A.I. (1955). *The effect of mother's diet on the intelligence of the offspring.* New York: Teacher's College, Columbia Bureau of Publications.

Harrington, D.M., Block, J.H., & Block, J. (1987). Testing aspects of Carl Rogers's theory of creative environments: Child-rearing antecedents of creative potential in young adolescents. *Journal of Personality and Social Psychology, 52,* 851–856.

Harris, J.R. (1998). *The nurture assumption: Why children turn out the way they do.* New York: Free Press.

Harris, J.R., & Liebert, R.M. (1991). *The child: A contemporary view of development* (3rd ed.). Englewood Cliffs, NJ: Prentice Hall.

Harris, M., & Rosenthal, R. (1985). Mediation of the interpersonal expectancy effect: A taxonomy of expectancy situations. In P. Blanck (ed.), *Interpersonal expectations: Theory, research, and application* (pp. 350–378). Paris: Cambridge University Press.

Hart, B., & Risley, T.R. (1995). *Meaningful differences in the everyday experience of young American children.* Baltimore: Brookes.

Hartmann, P., & Husband, C. (1971). The mass media and racial conflict. *Race, 12,* 267–282.

Hathaway, S.R., & McKinley, J.C. (1942). A multiphasic personality schedule (Minnesota): III. The measurement of symptomatic depression. *Journal of Psychology, 14,* 73–84.

Hauri, P. (1970). Evening activity, sleep mentation, and subjective sleep quality. *Journal of Abnormal Psychology, 76,* 270–275.

Hauri, P. (1982). *Sleep disorders.* Kalamazoo, MI: Upjohn.

Hazan, C., & Shaver, P. (1987). Romantic love conceptualized as attachment process. *Journal of Personality and Social Psychology, 52,* 511–524.

He, L. (1987). Involvement of endogenous opioid peptides in acupuncture analgesia. *Pain, 31,* 99–122.

Hearst, E. (1975). The classical-instrumental distinction: Reflexes, voluntary behavior, and categories of associative learning. In W.K. Estes (ed.), *Handbook of learning and cognitive processes: Vol. 2. Conditioning and behavior theory.* Hillsdale, NJ: Erlbaum.

Heath, A.C., & Martin, N.G. (1993). Genetic models for the natural history of smoking: Evidence for a genetic influence on smoking persistence. *Addictive Behavior, 18,* 19–34.

Heath, A.C., Cloninger, C.R., & Martin, N.G. (1994). Testing a model for the genetic structure of personality: A comparison of the personality systems of Cloninger and Eysenck. *Journal of Personality and Social Psychology, 66,* 762–775.

Heath, A.C., Madden, P.A.F., Bucholz, K.K., Dinwiddie, S.H., & Slutske, W.S. (1994). Genetic contribution to alcoholism risk in women. *Alcohol: Clinical and Experimental Research, 18,* 448. [Abstract.]

Heath, R.C. (1972). Pleasure and brain activity in man. *Journal of Nervous and Mental Disease, 154,* 3–18.

Heatherton, T.F., & Baumeister, R.F. (1991). Binge eating as escape from self-awareness. *Psychological Bulletin, 110,* 86–108.

Heber, R., Garber, H., Harrington, S., & Hoffman, C. (1972). *Rehabilitation of families at risk for mental retardation.* Madison: University of Wisconsin, Rehabilitation Research and Training Center in Mental Retardation.

Hechtman, L. (1989). Teenage mothers and their children: Risks and problems: A review. *Canadian Journal of Psychology, 34,* 569–575.

Hedges, L.V., & Nowell, A. (1995). Sex differences in mental test scores, variability, and numbers of high-scoring individuals. *Science, 269,* 41–45.

Heider, E.R. (1972). Universals in color naming and memory. *Journal of Experimental Psychology, 93,* 10–20.

Heider, E.R., & Oliver, D.C. (1972). The structure of the color space in naming and memory in two languages. *Cognitive Psychology, 3,* 337–354.

Heider, F. (1958). *The psychology of interpersonal relations.* New York: Wiley.

Hellige, J.B. (1990). Hemispheric asymmetry. *Annual Review of Psychology, 41,* 55–80.

Hellige, J.B. (1993). *Hemispheric asymmetry: What's right and what's left.* Cambridge, MA: Harvard University Press.

Helmreich, R., & Spence, J. (1978). The Work and Family Orientation Questionnaire: An objective instrument to assess components of achievement motivation and scientific attainment. *Personality and Social Psychology Bulletin, 4,* 222–226.

Hendrick, S., & Hendrick, C. (1992). *Liking, loving and relating* (2nd ed.). Pacific Grove, CA: Brooks/Cole.

Henriques, J.B., & Davidson, R.J. (1990). Regional brain electrical asymmetries discriminate between previously depressed and healthy control subjects. *Journal of Abnormal Psychology, 99,* 22–31.

Henry, J.A., Alexander, C.A., & Sener, E.K. (1995). Relative mortality from overdose of antidepressants. *British Medical Journal, 310,* 221–224.

Henry, S. (1996, March 7). Keep your brain fit for life. *Parade Magazine,* pp. 8–11.

Herkenham, M., et al. (1990). Cannabinoid receptor localization in brain. *Proceedings of the National Academy of Sciences of the U.S.A., 87,* 1932–1936.

Heron, W. (1957). The pathology of boredom. *Scientific American, 199,* 52–56.

Herrnstein, R.J., & Murray, C. (1994). *The bell curve.* New York: Free Press.

Hersher, L. (ed.). (1970). *Four psychotherapies.* New York: Appleton-Century-Crofts.

Herz, R.S. (1997). The effects of cue distinctiveness on odor-based context-dependent memory. *Memory & Cognition, 35,* 375–380.

Herzog, H.A. (1995). Has public interest in animal rights peaked? *American Psychologist, 50,* 945–947.

Hewstone, M., Islam, M.R., & Judd, C.M. (1993). Models of cross categorization and intergroup relations. *Journal of Personality and Social psychology, 64,* 779–793.

Hilgard, E.R. (1965). *Hypnotic susceptibility.* New York: Harcourt Brace Jovanovich.

Hilgard, E.R., Hilgard, J.R., & Kaufmann, W. (1983). *Hypnosis in the relief of pain* (2nd ed.). Los Altos, CA: Kaufmann.

Hillier, L., Hewitt, K.L., & Morrongiello, B.A. (1992). Infants' perception of illusions in sound locations: Responding to sounds in the dark. *Journal of Experimental Child Psychology, 53,* 159–179.

Hilton, J., & von Hipple, W. (1996). Stereotypes. *Annual Review of Psychology, 47,* 237–271.

Hobson, J.A. (1994). *The chemistry of conscious states: How the brain changes its mind.* Boston: Little, Brown.

Hobson, J.A., & McCarley, R. (1977). The brain as a dream state generator: An activation–synthesis hypothesis of the dream process. *American Journal of Psychiatry, 134,* 1335–1348.

Hochberg, J. (1978). *Perception* (2nd ed.). Englewood Cliffs, NJ: Prentice Hall.

Hofferth, S.L., Brayfield, A., Beich, S., & Holcomb, P. (1990). *National Child Care Survey.* Washington, DC: Urban Institute.

Hoffman, H.S., & DePaulo, P. (1977). Behavioral control by an imprinting stimulus. *American Scientist, 65,* 58–66.

Hoffman, L. (1989). Effects of maternal employment in the two-parent family. *American Psychologist, 44,* 283–292.

Hoffman, M. (1991). Unraveling the genetics of fragile X syndrome. *Science, 252,* 1070.

Hoffman, M.L. (1977). Personality and social development. *Annual Review of Psychology, 28,* 295–321.

Hogan, R., Hogan, J., & Roberts, B.W. (1996). Personality measurement and employment decisions: Questions and answers. *American Psychologist, 51*(5), 469–477.

Holland, C.A., & Rabbitt, P.M.A. (1990). Aging memory: Use versus impairment. *British Journal of Psychology, 82,* 29–38.

Hollister, L.E. (1986). Health aspects of cannibis. *Pharmacological Reviews, 38,* 1–20.

Holmbeck, G.N. (1994). Adolescence. In *Encyclopedia of human behavior* (Vol. 1, pp. 17–28). San Diego, CA: Academic Press.

Holmes, D.S. (1976). Debriefing after psychological experiments. II. Effectiveness of spot experimental desensitizing. *American Psychologist, 31*(12), 868–875.

Holmes, D.S. (1984). Meditation and somatic arousal reduction: A review of the experimental evidence. *American Psychologist, 39,* 1–12.

Holmes, T.H., & Rahe, R.H. (1967). The social readjustment rating scale. *Journal of Psychosomatic Research, 11,* 213.

Hopkins, B., & Westra, T. (1989). Maternal expectations of their infants' development: Some cultural differences. *Developmental Medicine and Child Neurology, 31*(3), 384–390.

Hopkins, B., & Westra, T. (1990). Motor development, maternal expectation, and the role of handling. *Infants Behavior and Development, 13,* 117–122.

Hoptman, M.J., & Davidson, R.J. (1994). How and why do the two cerebral hemispheres interact? *Psychological Bulletin, 116,* 195–219.

Horn, J. (1983). The Texas Adoption Project: Adopted children and their intellectual resemblance to biological and adoptive parents. *Child Development, 54,* 268–275.

Horney, K. (1937). *The neurotic personality of our time.* New York: Norton.

Horowitz, F.D., & O'Brien, M. (1986). Gifted and talented children: State of knowledge and directions for research. *American Psychologist, 41,* 1147–1152.

Horvath, F.S. (1977). The effect of selected variables on interpretation of polygraph records. *Journal of Applied Psychology, 62,* 127–136.

House, J.S., Landis, K.R., & Umberson, D. (1988). Social relationships and health. *Science, 241,* 540–545.

Hovland, C.I., & Sears, R.R. (1940). Minor studies in aggression: VI. Correlation of lynchings with economic indices. *Journal of Abnormal and Social Psychology, 9,* 301–310.

Howard, K.I., Kopta, S.M., Krause, M.S., & Orlinsky, D.E. (1986). The dose-effect relationship in psychotherapy. *American Psychologist, 41,* 159–164.

Howlett, A.C., Evans, D.M., & Houston, D.B. (1992). The cannabinoid receptor. In L. Murphy & A. Bartke (eds.), *Marijuana/cannabinoids: Neurobiology and neurophysiology* (pp. 35–72). Boca Raton, FL: CRC Press.

Hoyert, D.L., Kochanek, K.D., & Murphy, S.L. (1999). Deaths: Final data for 1997. *National Vital Statistics Reports, 47*(9). Hyattsville, MD: National Center for Health Statistics.

Hoyt, S., & Scherer, D.G. (1998). Female juvenile delinquency: Misunderstood by the juvenile justice system, neglected by social science. *Law and Human Behavior, 22*(1), 81–107.

Hsu, L.K. (1996). Epidemiology of the eating disorder. *Psychiatric Clinics of North America, 19*(4), 681–700.

Hudspeth, A.J. (1983). The hair cells of the inner ear. *Scientific American, 248,* 54–64.

Huebner, A.M., Garrod, A., & Snarey, J. (1990). *Moral development in Tibetan Buddhist monks: A cross-cultural study of adolescents and young adults in Nepal.* Paper presented at the meeting of the Society for Research in Adolescence, Atlanta, GA.

Hunt, E., Streissguth, A.P., Kerr, B., & Olson, H.C. (1995). Mothers' alcohol consumption during pregnancy: Effects on spatial-visual reasoning in 14-year-old children. *Psychological Science, 6*(6), 339–342.

Huston, A.C., Watkins, B.A., & Kunkel, D. (1989). Public policy and children's television. *American Psychologist, 44,* 424–433.

Hyde, J.S. (1982). *Understanding human sexuality* (2nd ed.). New York: McGraw-Hill.

Hyde, J.S., & Linn, M.C. (1988). Gender differences in verbal ability: A meta-analysis. *Psychological Bulletin, 104,* 53–69.

Hyde, J.S., Fennema, E., & Lamon, S.J. (1990). Gender differences in mathematics performance: A meta-analysis. *Psychological Bulletin, 107,* 139–155.

Hyman, I.E., Jr., & Pentland, J. (1996). The role of mental imagery in the creation of false childhood memories. *Journal of Memory and Language, 35,* 101–117.

Iacobucci, D., & McGill, A.L. (1990). Analysis of attribution data: Theory testing and effects estimation. *Journal of Personality and Social Psychology, 59*(3), 426–441.

Irwin, R.J., & Whitehead, P.R. (1991). Towards an objective psychophysics of pain. *Psychological Science, 2,* 230–235.

Isaksen, S.G., Murdock, M., Firestien, R.L., & Treffinger, D.J. (eds.). (1993). *Understanding and recognizing creativity: The emergence of a discipline.* Norwood, NJ: Ablex.

Isen, A.M., & Levin, P.F. (1972). The effect of feeling good on helping: Cookies and kindness. *Journal of Personality and Social Psychology, 21,* 384–388.

Ito, T.A., Miller, N., & Pollock, V. (1996). Alcohol and aggression: A meta-analysis on the moderating effects of inhibitory cues, triggering events, and self-focused attention. *Psychological Bulletin, 120,* 60–82.

Izard, C.E. (1971). *The face of emotion.* New York: Appleton-Century-Crofts.

Izard, C.E. (1980). Cross-cultural perspectives on emotion and emotion communication. In H.C. Triandis & W.J. Lonner (eds.), *Handbook of cross-cultural psychology* (Vol. 3). Boston: Allyn & Bacon.

Izard, C.E. (1994). Innate and universal facial expressions: Evidence from developmental and cross-cultural research. *Psychological Bulletin, 115*(2), 288–299.

Jacobs, G.H. (1993). The distribution and nature of color vision among the mammals. *Biological Review of the Cambridge Philosophical Society, 68,* 413–471.

Jacobsen, P.B., Bovbjerg, D.H., Schwartz, M.D., & Andrykowski, M.A. (1994). Formation of food aversions in patients receiving repeated infusions of chemotherapy. *Behaviour Research & Therapy, 38,* 739–748.

James, W. (1890). *The principles of psychology.* New York: Holt.

Jamison, K.R. (1989). Mood disorders and patterns of creativity in British writers and artists. *Psychiatry, 52,* 125–134.

Janis, I. (1982). *Groupthink: Psychological studies of policy decisions and fiascoes* (2nd ed.). Boston: Houghton Mifflin.

Janis, I.L., Mahl, G.G., & Holt, R.R. (1969). *Personality: Dynamics, development and assessment.* New York: Harcourt Brace Jovanovich.

Janofsky, M. (1994, December 13). Survey reports more drug use by teenagers. *New York Times,* p. A1.

Jaynes, J.H., & Wlodkowski, R.J. (1990). *Eager to learn: Helping children become motivated and love learning.* San Francisco: Jossey-Bass.

Jensen, A. R. (1969). How much can we boost IQ and scholastic achievement? *Harvard Educational Review, 39,* 1–123.

Johansson, C.B., et al. (1999). Identification of a neural stem cell in the adult mammalian central nervous system. *Cell, 96,* 25–34.

Johnson, C., Lewis, C., Love, S., & Stuckey, M. (1984). Incidence and correlates of bulimic behavior in a female high school population. *Journal of Youth and Adolescence, 13,* 15–26.

Johnson, D. (1990). Can psychology ever be the same again after the human genome is mapped? *Psychological Science, 1,* 331–332.

Johnson, D.W., Johnson, R.T., & Maruyama, G. (1984). Effects of cooperative learning: A meta-analysis. In N. Miller & M.B. Brewer (eds.), *Groups in contact: The psychology of desegregation* (pp. 187–212). New York: Academic Press.

Johnson, H.G., Ekman, P., & Friesen, W.V. (1975). Communicative body movements: American emblems. *Semiotica, 15,* 335–353.

Johnson, M.K., & Raye, C.L. (1981). Reality monitoring. *Psychological Review, 88,* 67–85.

Johnson-Greene, D., Adams, K.M., Gilman, S., Kluin, K.J., Junck, L., Martorello, S., & Heumann, M. (1997). Impaired upper limb coordination in alcoholic cerebellar degeneration. *Archives of Neurology, 54,* 436–439.

Jones, C.P., & Adamson, L.B. (1987). Language use and mother-child-sibling interactions. *Child Development, 58,* 356–366.

Jones, F.D., & Koshes, R.J. (1995). Homosexuality and the military. *American Journal of Psychiatry, 152,* 16–21.

Jones, M.A., & Krisberg, B. (1994) *Images and reality: Juvenile crime, youth violence, and public policy.* San Francisco, CA: National Council on Crime and Delinquency.

Jones, M.C. (1924). Elimination of children's fears. *Journal of Experimental Psychology, 7,* 381–390.

Joseph, R. (1999). Environmental influences on neural plasticity, the limbic system, emotional development and attachment: A review. *Child Psychiatry and Human Development, 29,* 189–208.

Junginger, J. (1997). Fetishism. In D.R. Laws & W.T. O'Donohue (eds.), *Handbook of sexual deviance: Theory and application.* New York: Guilford.

Kagan, J. (1989). Temperamental contributions to social behavior. *American Psychologist, 44*(4), 668–674.

Kagan, J. (1994, October 5). The realistic view of biology and behavior. *Chronicle of Higher Education.*

Kagan, J., & Snidman, N. (1991). Infant predictors of inhibited and uninhibited profiles. *Psychological Science, 2*(1), 40–44.

Kagan, J., Arcus, D., & Snidman, N. (1993). The idea of temperament: Where do we go from here? In R. Plomin & G.E. McClearn (eds.), *Nature, nurture, and psychology.* Washington, DC: American Psychological Association.

Kagan, J., Reznick, J.S., Snidman, N., Gibbons, J., & Johnson, M.O. (1988). Childhood derivatives of inhibition and lack of inhibition to the unfamiliar. *Child Development, 59,* 1580–1589.

Kahneman, D., & Tversky, A. (1996). On the reality of cognitive illusions. *Psychological Review, 103*(3), 582–591.

Kalat, J.W. (1988). *Biological psychology* (3rd ed.). Belmont, CA: Wadsworth.

Kalderon, N., & Fuks, Z. (1996). Structural recovery in lesioned adult mammalian spinal cord by x-irradiation of the lesion site. *Proceedings of the National Academy of Sciences of the U.S.A., 93,* 11179.

Kales, J.D., Kales, A., Soldatos, C.R., Caldwell, A.B., Charney, D.S., & Martin, E.D. (1980). Night terrors: Clinical characteristics and personality patterns. *Archives of General Psychiatry, 137,* 1413–1417.

Kamin, L.J. (1969). Selective association and conditioning. In N.J. Mackintosh & W.K. Honig (eds.), *Fundamental issues in associative learning.* Halifax: Dalhousie University Press.

Kane, J., & Lieberman, J. (1992). *Adverse effects of psychotropic drugs.* New York: Guilford Press.

Kantrowitz, B., Rosenberg, D., Rogers, P., Beachy, L., & Holmes, S. (1993, November 1). Heroin makes an ominous comeback. *Newsweek.*

Kaplan, C.A., & Simon, H.A. (1990). In search of insight. *Cognitive Psychology, 22,* 374–419.

Kassebaum, N.L. (1994). Head Start: Only the best for America's children. *American Psychologist, 49,* 123–126.

Katz, R., & McGuffin, P. (1993). The genetics of affective disorders. In D. Fowles (ed.), *Progress in experimental personality and psychopathology research.* New York: Springer.

Kaufman, L. (1979). *Perception: The world transformed.* New York: Oxford University Press.

Keck, J.O., Staniunas, R.J., Coller, J.A., Barrett, R.C., & Oster, M.E. (1994). Biofeedback training is useful in fecal incontinence but disappointing in constipation. *Disorders of the Colon and Rectum, 37,* 1271–1276.

Kelley, H.H. (1967). Attribution theory in social psychology. In D. Levine (ed.), *Nebraska Symposium on Motivation.* Lincoln: University of Nebraska Press.

Kelly, I.W., & Saklofske, D.H. (1994). Psychology pseudoscience. *Encyclopedia of human behavior* (Vol. 3, pp. 611–618). San Diego, CA: Academic Press.

Kelly, J.B. (1982). Divorce: The adult perspective. In B.B. Wolman (ed.), *Handbook of developmental psychology* (pp. 734–750). Englewood Cliffs, NJ: Prentice Hall.

Kelly, K., & Dawson, L. (1994). Sexual orientation. *Encyclopedia of human behavior* (Vol. 4, pp. 183–192). San Diego, CA: Academic Press.

Kelman, H.C. (1974). Attitudes are alive and well and gainfully employed in the sphere of action. *American Psychologist, 230,* 310–324.

Kendler, K.S., Neale, M.C., Kessler, R.C., Heath, A.C., & Eaves, L.J. (1992). Generalized anxiety disorder in women: A population-based twin study. *Archives of General Psychiatry, 49,* 267–272.

Kernis, M.H., & Wheeler, L. (1981). Beautiful friends and ugly strangers: Radiation and contrast effects in perception of same-sex pairs. *Personality and Social Psychology Bulletin, 7,* 617–620.

Kessler, R.C. (1979). Stress, social status, and psychological distress. *Journal of Health and Social Behavior, 20,* 259–272.

Kessler, R.C., McGonagle, K.A., Zhao, S., Nelson, C.R., Highes, M., Eshleman, S., Wittchen, H., & Kendler, K.S. (1994). Lifetime and 12-month prevalence of DSM-III-R psychiatric disorders in the United States: Results from the National Comorbidity Survey. *Archives of General Psychiatry, 51,* 8–19.

Kessler, R.C., Price, R.H., & Wortman, C.B. (1985). Social factors in psychopathology: Stress, social support, and coping processes. *Annual Review of Psychology, 36,* 531–572.

Kessler, R.C., Sonnega, A., Bromet, E., Hughes, M., & Nelson, C.B. (1995). Post-traumatic stress disorder in the national Comorbidity Survey. *Archives of General Psychiatry, 52,* 1057.

Khan, A. (1993). Electroconvulsive therapy: Second edition. *Journal of Nervous and Mental Disease, 181*(9), n.p.

Khantzian, E.J. (1990). Self-regulation and self-medication factors in alcoholism and the addictions: Similarities and differences. *Recent Developments in Alcoholism, 8,* 255–271.

Kiesler, C.A. (1982a). Mental hospitals and alternative care: Non-institutionalization as a potential public policy for mental patients. *American Psychologist, 37,* 349–360.

Kiesler, C.A. (1982b). Public and professional myths about mental hospitalization: An empirical reassessment of policy-related beliefs. *American Psychologist, 37*(12), 1323–1339.

Kiesler, C.A., & Simpkins, C.G. (1993). *The unnoticed majority in psychiatric inpatient care.* New York: Plenum.

Kihlström, J.F., & Harackiewicz, J.M. (1982). The earliest recollection: A new survey. *Journal of Personality, 50,* 134–148.

Kihlström, J.F., & McConkey, K.M. (1990). William James and hypnosis: A centennial reflection. *Psychological Science, 1,* 174–178.

Kim, D.O. (1985). Functional roles of the inner and outer-haircell subsystems in the cochlea and brain stem. In C.J. Berlin (ed.), *Hearing science: Recent advances.* San Diego, CA: College Hill.

Kimmel, D.C. (1974). *Adulthood and aging.* New York: Wiley.

Kimura, D., & Hampson, E. (1994). Cognitive pattern in men and women is influenced by fluctuations in sex hormones. *Current Directions in Psychological Science, 3* (2), 57–61.

King, M., & McDonald, E. (1992). Homosexuals who are twins. *British Journal of Psychiatry, 160,* 407–409.

Kingstone, A., Enns, J.T., Mangun, G.R., & Gazzaniga, M.S. (1995). Right-hemisphere memory superiority: Studies of a split-brain patient. *Psychological Science, 6,* 118–121.

Kinsey, A.C., Pomeroy, W.B., & Martin, C.E. (1948*). Sexual behavior in the human male.* Philadelphia: Saunders.

Kinsey, A.C., Pomeroy, W.B., Martin, C.E., & Gebhard, P.H. (1953). *Sexual behavior in the human female.* Philadelphia: Saunders.

Kirchner, W.H., & Towne, W.F. (1994). The sensory basis of the honeybee's dance language. *Scientific American, 270,* 74–80.

Kirsch, I., Montgomery, G., & Saperstein, G. (1995). Hypnosis as an adjunct to cognitive behavioral psychotherapy: A meta analysis. *Journal of Consulting and Clinical Psychology, 63,* 214–220.

Kissane, D.W., Bloch, S., Miach, P., Smith, G.C., Seddon, A., & Keks, N. (1997). Cognitive-existential group therapy for patients with primary breast cancer–techniques and themes. *Psychooncology, 6*(1), 25–33.

Klatzky, R.L. (1980). *Human memory: Structures and processes* (2nd ed.). San Francisco: Freeman.

Klein, G.S. (1951). The personal world through perception. In R.R. Blake & G.V. Ramsey (eds.), *Perception: An approach to personality.* New York: Ronald Press.

Klerman, G.L., Weissman, M.M., Markowitz, J.C., Glick, I., Wilner, P.J., Mason, B., & Shear, M.K. (1994). Medication and psychotherapy. In A.E. Bergin & S.L. Garfield (eds.), *Handbook of psychotherapy and behavior change* (4th ed., pp. 734–782). New York: Wiley.

Klingenspor, B. (1994). Gender identity and bulimic eating behavior. *Sex Roles, 31,* 407–432.

Klinger, E. (1990). *Daydreaming: Using waking fantasy and imagery for self-knowledge and creativity.* New York: J.P. Tarcher.

Kluegel, J.R. (1990). Trends in white's explanations of the black–white gap in socioeconomic status, 1977–89. *American Sociological Review, 55,* 512–525.

Knight, G.P., Fabes, R.A., & Higgins, D.A. (1996). Concerns about drawing causal inferences from meta-analyses: An example in the study of gender differences in aggression. *Psychological Bulletin, 119*(3), 410–421.

Knutson, J.R. (1995). Psychological characteristics of maltreated children: Putative risk factors and consequences. *Annual Review of Psychology, 46,* 401–431.

Kobasa, S.C. (1979). Stressful life events, personality, and health: An inquiry into hardiness. *Journal of Personality and Social Psychology, 37,* 1–11.

Koenig, H.G. (1997). *Is religion good for your health? The effects of religion on physical and mental health.* Binghamton, NY: Haworth Press.

Kogon, M.M., Biswas, A., Pearl, D., Carlson, R.W., & Spiegel, D. (1997). The effects of medical and psychotherapeutic treatment on the survival of women with metastatic breast carcinoma. *Cancer, 80*(2), 225–230.

Kohlberg, L. (1969). Stage and sequence: The cognitive–developmental approach to socialization. In D.A. Goslin (ed.), *Handbook of socialization theory and research.* Chicago: Rand McNally.

Kohlberg, L. (1979). *The meaning and measurement of moral development* (Clark Lectures). Worcester, MA: Clark University.

Kohlberg, L. (1981). *The philosophy of moral development* (Vol. 1). San Francisco: Harper & Row.

Kohn, A. (1993). *Punished by rewards.* Boston: Houghton Mifflin.

Kokmen, E. (1991). The EURODEM collaborative re-analysis of case-control studies of Alzheimer's disease: Implications for clinical research and practice. *International Journal of Epidemiology, 20*(Suppl. 2), S65–S67.

Kolata, G. (1992, November 16). New views on life spans alter forecast on elderly. *New York Times,* p. A1.

Kolb, B. & Whishaw, I.Q. (1999). Brain plasticity and behavior. *Annual Review of Psychology, 49,* 43–64.

Kolbert, E. (1991, October 11). Sexual harassment at work is pervasive, survey suggests. *New York Times,* Sec. A.

Komatsu, L.K. (1992). Recent views of conceptual structure. *Psychological Bulletin, 112,* 500–526.

Kopta, S.M., Howard, K.I., Lowry, J.L., & Beutler, L.E. (1994). Patterns of symptomatic recovery in psychotherapy. *Journal of Consulting and Clinical Psychology, 62,* 1009–1016.

Koulack, D., & Goodenough, D.R. (1976). Dream recall and dream recall failure: An arousal-retrieval model. *Psychological Bulletin, 83,* 975–984.

Krantz, D.S., Grunberg, N.D., & Baum, A. (1985). Health psychology. *Annual Review of Psychology, 36,* 349–383.

Krasne, F.B., & Glanzman, D.L. (1995). What we can learn from invertebrate learning. *Annual Review of Psychology, 46,* 585–624.

Kraut, R., Patterson, M., Lundmark, V., Kiesler, S., Mukopadhyay, T., & Scherlis, W. (1998). Internet paradox: A social technology that reduces social involvement and psychological well-being? *American Psychologist, 53,* 1017–1031.

Krebs, D. (1975). Empathy and altruism. *Journal of Personality and Social Psychology, 32,* 1134–1140.

Kringlen, E. (1981). *Stress and coronary heart disease. Twin research 3: Epidemiological and clinical studies.* New York: Alan R. Liss.

Kristiansen, C.M., & Giulietti, R. (1990). Perceptions of wife abuse: Effects of gender, attitudes towards women, and just-world beliefs among college students. *Psychology of Women Quarterly, 14,* 177–189.

Kroger, R.O., & Wood, L.A. (1993). Reification, "faking" and the Big Five. *American Psychologist, 48,* 1297–1298.

Kruglanski, A.W. (1986, August). Freeze-think and the Challenger. *Psychology Today,* pp. 48–49.

Kübler-Ross, E. (1969). *On death and dying.* New York: Macmillan.

Kübler-Ross, E. (1975). *Death: The final stage of growth.* Englewood Cliffs, NJ: Prentice Hall.

Kuebli, J. (1999). Young children's understanding of everyday emotions. In L.E. Berk (ed.), *Landscapes of development* (pp. 123–136). Belmont, CA: Wadsworth.

Kuhl, P.K., Williams, K.A., & Lacerda, F. (1992). Linguistic experience alters phonetic perception in infants by 6 months of age. *Science, 255,* 606–608.

Kupfermann, I. (1991). Hypothalamus and limbic system motivation. In E.R. Kandel, J.H. Schwartz, & T.M. Jessel (eds.), *Principles of neural science* (3rd ed., pp. 750–760). New York: Elsevier.

Kurdek, L.A. (1991). Correlates of relationship satisfaction in cohabiting gay and lesbian couples: Integration of contextual, investment, and problem-solving models. *Journal of Personality & Social Psychology, 61*(6), 910–922.

Kurdek, L.A. (1992). Assumptions versus standards: The validity of two relationship cognitions in heterosexual and homosexual couples. *Journal of Family Psychology, 6*(2), 164–170.

Laan, E., Everaerd, W., van Berlo, R., & Rijs, L. (1995). Mood and sexual arousal in women. *Behavior Research Therapy, 33*(4), 441–443.

Labouvie-Vief, G. (1986). Modes of knowledge and the organization of development. In M.L. Commons, L. Kohlberg, F.A. Richards, & J. Sinott (eds.), *Beyond formal operations: 3. Models and methods in the study of adult and adolescent thoughts.* New York: Praeger.

Lacayo, R. (April 6, 1998). Toward the root. *Time,* pp. 38–39.

Lachman, S.J. (1984). *Processes in visual misperception: Illusions for highly structured stimulus material.* Paper presented at the 92nd annual convention of the American Psychological Association, Toronto, Canada.

Lachman, S.J. (1996). Processes in perception: Psychological transformations of highly structured stimulus material. *Perceptual and Motor Skills, 83,* 411–418.

LaGreca, A.M., Stone, W.L., & Bell, C.R., III. (1983). Facilitating the vocational-interpersonal skills of mentally retarded individuals. *American Journal of Mental Deficiency, 88,* 270–278.

Lambert, M.J., Shapiro, D.A., & Bergin, A.E. (1986). The effectiveness of psychotherapy. In S.L. Garfield & A.E. Bergin (eds.), *Handbook of psychotherapy and behavior change* (3rd ed., pp. 157–212). New York: Wiley.

Lambert, W.W., Solomon, R.L., & Watson, P.D. (1949). Reinforcement and extinction as factors in size estimation. *Journal of Experimental Psychology, 39,* 637–641.

Lampl, M., Veidhuis, J.D., & Johnson, M.L. (1992). Saltation and stasis: A model of human growth. *Science, 258,* 801–803.

Lande, R. (1993). The video violence debate. *Hospital and Community Psychiatry, 44,* 347–351.

Landesman, S., & Butterfield, E.C. (1987). Normalization and deinstitution of mentally retarded individuals: Controversy and facts. *American Psychologist, 42,* 809–816.

Langer, E.J., Bashner, R.S., & Chanowitz, B. (1985). Decreasing prejudice by increasing discrimination. *Journal of Personality and Social Psychology, 49,* 113–120.

Langlois, J.H., Ritter, J.M., Casey, R.J., & Sawin, D.B. (1995). Infant attractiveness predicts maternal behaviors and attitudes. *Developmental Psychology, 31,* 464–472.

LaPiere, R.T. (1934). Attitudes versus actions. *Social Forces, 13,* 230–237.

LaRue, A., & Jarvik, L. (1982). Old age and biobehavioral changes. In B.B. Wolman (ed.), *Handbook of developmental psychology* (pp. 791–806). Englewood Cliffs, NJ: Prentice Hall.

Latané, B., & Rodin, J. (1969). A lady in distress: Inhibiting effects of friends and strangers on bystander intervention. *Journal of Experimental Social Psychology, 5,* 189–202.

Laumann, E.O., Gagnon, J.H., Michael, R.T., & Michaels, S. (1994). *The social organization of sexuality: Sexual practices in the United States.* Chicago: University of Chicago Press.

Lazarus, R.S. (1969). *Patterns of adjustment and human effectiveness.* New York: McGraw-Hill.

Lazarus, R.S. (1981, July). Little hassles can be hazardous to health. *Psychology Today,* pp. 58–62.

Lazarus, R.S. (1982). Thoughts on the relations between emotion and cognition. *American Psychologist, 37,* 1019–1024.

Lazarus, R.S. (1991a). Cognition and motivation in emotion. *American Psychologist, 46,* 352–367.

Lazarus, R.S. (1991b). Progress on a cognitive-motivational-relational theory of emotion. *American Psychologist, 46,* 819–834.

Lazarus, R.S. (1991c). *Emotion and adaptation.* New York: Oxford University Press.

Lazarus, R.S., De Longis, A., Folkman, S., & Gruen, R. (1985). Stress and adaptional outcomes. *American Psychologist, 40,* 770–779.

Leary, W.E. (1990, January 25). Risk of hearing loss is growing, panel says. *New York Times,* Sec. B.

Leary, W.E. (1995, April 21). Young who try suicide may succeed more often. *New York Times.*

Lebow, J.L., & Gurman, A.S. (1995). Research assessing couple and family therapy. *Annual Review of Psychology, 46,* 27–57.

Leccese, A.P. (1991). *Drugs and society.* Englewood Cliffs, NJ: Prentice Hall.

Lee, G.P., Loring, D.W., Dahl, J.I., & Meador, K.J. (1993). Hemispheric specialization for emotional expression. *Neuropsychiatry, Neuropsychology, & Behavioral Neurology, 6*(3), 143–148.

Lefcourt, H.M. (1992). Durability and impact of the locus of control construct. *Psychological Bulletin, 112,* 411–414.

Lehman, D.R., Lempert, R.O., Nisbett, R.E. (1988). The effects of graduate training on reasoning: Formal discipline and thinking about everyday-life events. *American Psychologist, 43,* 431–442.

Leibowitz, H.W., & Owens, D.A. (1977). Nighttime driving accidents and selective visual degradation. *Science, 197,* 422–423.

Leigh, R.J. (1994). Human vestibular cortex. *Annals of Neurology, 35,* 383–384.

Leigenberg, H., & Henning, K. (1995). Sexual fantasy. *Psychological Bulletin, 117*(3), 469–496.

Lemish, D., & Rice, M.L. (1986, June). Television as a talking picture book: A prop for language acquisition. *Journal of Child Language, 13,* 251–274.

Leonard, J.M., & Whitten, W.B. (1983). Information stored when expecting recall or recognition. *Journal of Experimental Psychology: Learning, Memory, and Cognition, 9,* 440–455.

Lerner, M.J. (1980). *The belief in a just world: A fundamental delusion.* New York: Plenum.

Leroy, P., Dessolin, S., Villageois, P., Moon, B.C., Friedman, J.M., Ailhaud, G., & Dani, C. (1996). Expression of ob gene in adipose cells. Regulation by insulin. *Journal of Biological Chemistry, 271*(5), 2365–2368.

Leshner, A.I. (1996). Understanding drug addiction: Implications for treatment. *Hospital Practice, 31,* 7–54.

Lev, M. (1991, May). No hidden meaning here: Survey sees subliminal ads. *New York Times,* Sec. C.

LeVay, S. (1991). A difference in hypothalamic structure between heterosexual and homosexual men. *Science, 253,* 1034–1038.

LeVay, S. (1993). *The sexual brain.* Cambridge, MA: MIT Press.

LeVay, S., & Hamer, D.H. (1994, May). Evidence for a biological influence in male homosexuality. *Scientific American,* pp. 44–49.

Levenson, M.R., & Aldwin, C.M. (1994). Aging, personality, and adaptation. In *Encyclopedia of human behavior* (Vol. 1, pp. 47–55). San Diego, CA: Academic Press.

Levenson, R.W. (1992). Autonomic nervous system differences among emotions. *Psychological Science, 3,* 23–27.

Leventhal, H., & Niles, P. (1965). Persistence of influence for varying duration of exposure to threat stimuli. *Psychological Reports, 16,* 223–233.

Levine, I.S., & Rog, D.J. (1990). Mental health services for homeless mentally ill person: Federal initiatives and current service trends. *American Psychologist, 45,* 963–968.

Levine, S., Johnson, D.F., & Gonzales, C.A. (1985). Behavioral and hormonal responses to separation in infant rhesus monkeys and mothers. *Behavioral Neuroscience, 99,* 399–410.

Levinson, D.J. (1978). *The seasons of a man's life.* New York: Knopf.

Levinson, D.J. (1986). A conception of adult development. *American Psychologist, 41,* 3–13.

Levinson, D.J. (1987). *The seasons of a woman's life.* New York: Knopf.

Lewin, K.A. (1935). *A dynamic theory of personality* (K.E. Zener & D.K. Adams, trans.). New York: McGraw-Hill.

Lewin, T. (1994a, May 18). Boys are more comfortable with sex than girls are, survey finds. *New York Times,* p. A10.

Lewin, T. (1994b, October 7). Sex in America: Faithfulness thrives after all. *New York Times,* p. A1.

Lewin, T. (1995, May 30). The decay of families is global study says. *New York Times,* p. A5.

Lewin, T. (1996, March 27). Americans are firmly attached to traditional roles for sexes, poll finds. *New York Times,* p. A12.

Lewis, M., & Bendersky, M. (1995). *Mothers, babies, and cocaine: The role of toxins in development.* Hillsdale, NJ: Erlbaum.

Liem, R., & Liem, J.V. (1978). Social class and mental illness reconsidered: The role of economic stress and social support. *Journal of Health and Social Behavior, 19,* 139–156.

Limber, J. (1977). Language in child and chimp. *American Psychologist, 32,* 280–295.

Lin, L., Umahara, M., York, D.A., & Bray, G.A. (1998). Beta-casomophins stimulate and enterostatin inhibits the intake of dietary fat in rats. *Peptids, 19,* 325–331.

Lindsay, D.S. (1993). Eyewitness suggestibility. *Current Directions in Psychological Science, 2,* 86–89.

Lindsay, D.S., & Johnson, M.K. (1989). The eyewitness suggestibility effect and memory for source. *Memory & Cognition, 17,* 349–358.

Linn, R.L. (1982). Admissions testing on trial. *American Psychologist, 37,* 279–291.

Lipman, S. (1991). *Laughter in Hell: The use of humor during the Holocaust.* Northvale, NJ: J. Aronson.

Lipsey, M., & Wilson, D. (1993). The efficacy of psychological, educational, and behavioral treatment: Confirmation from meta-analysis. *American Psychologist, 48,* 1181–1209.

Lipsky, D.K., & Gartner, A. (1996). Inclusive education and school restructuring. In W. Stainback & S. Stainback (eds.), *Controversial issues confronting special education: Divergent perspectives* (pp. 3–15). Baltimore: Brookes.

Llinás, R. (1996). *The mind-brain continuum.* Proceedings of a meeting held in Madrid, 1995. Cambridge, MA: MIT Press.

Loehlin, J.C., Horn, J.M., & Willerman, L. (1997). Heredity, environment, and IQ in the Texas adoption study. In R.J. Sternberg & E. Grigorenko (eds.), *Intelligence: Heredity and environment.* New York: Cambridge University Press.

Loehlin, J.C., Willerman, L., & Horn, J.M. (1988). Human behavior genetics. *Annual Review of Psychology, 39,* 101–133.

Loewenstein, G. (1994). The psychology of curiosity: A review and reinterpretation. *Psychological Bulletin, 116,* 75–98.

Loewenstein, G., & Frederick, S. (in press). Hedonic adaptation: From the bright side to the dark side. In D. Kahneman, E. Diener, & N. Schwarz (eds.) *Well-being: The foundations of hedonic psychology.* New York: Russell Sage Foundation.

Loftus, E.F. (1983). Silence is not golden. *American Psychologist, 38,* 564–572.

Loftus, E.F. (1993a). The reality of repressed memories. *American Psychologist, 48,* 518–537.

Loftus, E.F. (1993b). Psychologists in the eyewitness world. *American Psychologist, 48,* 550–552.

Loftus, E.F. (1996). Memory distortion and false memory creation. *Bulletin of the American Academy of Psychiatry & The Law, 24*(3), 281–295.

Loftus, E.F. (1997). Repressed memory accusations: Devastated families and devastated patients. *Applied Cognitive Psychology, 11*(1), 25–30.

Loftus, E.F., & Hoffman, H.G. (1989). Misinformation and memory: The creation of new memories. *Journal of Experimental Psychology: General, 118,* 100–114.

Loftus, E.F., & Palmer, J.C. (1974). Reconstruction of automobile destruction: An example of the interaction between language and memory. *Journal of Verbal Learning and Verbal Behavior, 13,* 585–589.

Loftus, E.F., & Pickrell, J.E. (1995). The formation of false memories. *Psychiatric Annals, 25,* 720–725.

Loftus, E.F., Milo, E., & Paddock, J. (1995). The accidental executioner: Why psychotherapy must be informed by science. *Counseling Psychologist, 23,* 300–309.

Logan, C.G., & Grafton, S.T. (1995). Functional anatomy of human eyeblink conditioning determined with regional cerebral glucose metabolism and positron emission tomography. *Proceedings of the National Academy of Science, U.S.A., 92,* 7500–7504.

Logue, A.W., Ophir, I., & Strauss, K.E. (1981). The acquisition of taste aversions in humans. *Behavior Research and Therapy, 19,* 319–333.

Lois, C., & Alvarez-Buylla, A. (1994). Long-distance neuronal migration in the adult mammalian brain. *Science, 264,* 1145–1148.

Lorenz, K. (1935). Der Kumpan inder Umwelt des Vogels. *Journal of Ornithology, 83,* 137–213, 289–413.

Lott, A.J., & Lott, B.E. (1974). The role of reward in the formation of positive interpersonal attitudes. In T.L. Huston (Ed.), *Foundations of interpersonal attraction* (pp. 171–192). New York: Academic Press.

Luchins, A. (1957). Primacy-recency in impression formation. In C. Hovland, W. Mandell, E. Campbell, T. Brock, A. Luchins, A. Cohen, W. McGuire, I. Janis, R. Feierbend, & N. Anderson (eds.), *The order of presentation in persuasion.* New Haven, CT: Yale University Press.

Lykken, D.T. (1975, March). Guilty knowledge test: The right way to use a lie detector. *Psychology Today,* pp. 56–60.

Lykken, D., & Tellegen, A. (1996). Happiness is a stochastic phenomenon. *Psychological Science, 7,* 186–189.

Lyness, S.A. (1993). Predictors of differences between Type A and B individuals in heart rate and blood pressure reactivity. *Psychological Bulletin, 114,* 266–295.

Lynn, S.J., & Rhue, J.W. (1988). Fantasy proneness, hypnosis, developmental antecedents, and psychopathology. *American Psychologist, 43,* 35–44.

Lyons, M.J., True, W.R., Eisen, S.A., Goldberg, J., Meyer, J.M., Faraone, S.V., Eaves, L.J., & Tsuang, M.T. (1995). Differential heritability of adult and juvenile antisocial traits. *Archives of General Psychiatry, 52,* 906–915.

Lytton, H., & Romeny, D.M. (1991). Parents' differential socialization of boys and girls: A meta-analysis. *Psychological Bulletin, 109*(2), 267–296.

Maas, J. (1998). *Power sleep: The revolutionary program that prepares your mind for peak performance.* New York: Villard.

Maccoby, E.E. (1990). Gender and relationships: A developmental account. *American Psychologist, 45,* 513–520.

Macionis, J.J. (1993). *Sociology* (4th ed.). Englewood Cliffs, NJ: Prentice Hall.

Mackavey, W.R., Malley, J.E., & Stewart, A.J. (1991). Remembering autobiographically consequential experiences: Content analysis of psychologists' accounts of their lives. *Psychology and Aging, 6,* 50–59.

Mackworth, N. (1965). Originality. *American Psychologist, 20,* 51–66.

MacLean, P.D. (1970). The limbic brain in relation to the psychoses. In P. Black (ed.), *Physiological correlates of emotion* (pp. 129–146). New York: Academic Press.

MacLeod, D.I.A. (1978). Visual sensitivity. *Annual Review of Psychology, 29,* 613–645.

Maddi, S.R. (1989). *Personality theories: A comparative approach* (5th ed.). Homewood, IL: Dorsey.

Maier, S.F., Watkins, L.R., & Fleshner, M. (1994). Psychoneuroimmunology: The interface between behavior, brain and immunity. *American Psychologist, 49*(12), 1004–1017.

Maisto, A.A., & Hughes, E. (1995). Adaptation to group home living for adults with mental retardation as a function of previous residential placement. *Journal of Intellectual Disability Research, 39,* 15–18.

Manfredi, M., Bini, G., Cruccu, G., Accornero, N., Beradelli, A., & Medolago, L. (1981). Congenital absence of pain. *Archives of Neurology (Chicago), 38,* 507–511.

Marano, H.E. (1997, July 1). Puberty may start at 6 as hormones surge. *New York Times.*

Marcia, J.E. (1980). Identity in adolescence. In J. Adelson (ed.), *Handbook of adolescent psychology.* New York: Wiley.

Marcus, G.F. (1996). Why do children say "breaked"? *American Psychological Society, 5*(3), 81–85.

Margolin, G. (1987). Marital therapy: A cognitive-behavioral-affective approach. In N.S. Jacobson (ed.), *Psychotherapists in clinical practice* (pp. 232–285). New York: Guilford.

Marks, I.M., & Nesse, R.M. (1994). Fear and fitness: An evolutionary analysis of anxiety disorders. *Ethology and Sociobiology, 15,* 247–261.

Markus, H.R., & Kitayama, S. (1991). Culture and self: Implications for cognition, emotion, and motivation. *Psychological Review, 98,* 224–253.

Martinez, J.L., Barea-Rodriguez, E.J., & Derrick, B.E. (1998). Long-term potentiation, long-term depression, and learning. In *Neurobiology of learning and memory,* ed. J.L. Martinez & R.P. Kesner, pp. 211–246. San Diego, CA, Academic Press.

Martinez, J.L., & Derrick, B.E. (1996). Long-term potentiation and learning. *Annual Review of Psychology, 47,* 173–203.

Martino, A. (1995, February 5). Mid-life usually brings positive change, not crisis. *Ann Arbor News.*

Maslach, C., & Leiter, M.P. (1997). *The truth about burnout.* San Francisco: Jossey-Bass.

Masling, J., Rabie, L., & Blondheim, S.H. (1967). Obesity, level of aspiration, and Rorschach and TAT measures of oral dependence. *Journal of Consulting Psychology, 31,* 233–239.

Maslow, A.H. (1954). *Motivation and personality.* New York: Harper & Row.

Mason, F.L. (1997). Fetishism: Psychopathology and theory. In D.R. Laws & W.T. O'Donohue (eds.), *Handbook of sexual deviance: Theory and application.* New York: Guilford.

Massaro, D.W., & Cowan, N. (1993). Information processing models: Microscopes of the mind. *Annual Review of Psychology, 44,* 383–425.

Massimini, F., Czikszentmihalyi, M., & Della Fave, A. (1988). Flow and biocultural evolution. In M. Czikszentmihalyi & I.S. Czikszentmihalyi (eds.), *Optimal experience: Studies of flow in consciousness* (pp. 60–81). New York: Cambridge University Press.

Masters, W.H., & Johnson, V.E. (1966). *Human sexual response.* Boston: Little Brown & Co.

Masters, W.H., Johnson, V.E., & Kolodny, R.C. (1982). *Human sexuality.* Boston: Little Brown.

Matsumoto, D. (1996). *Culture and psychology.* Pacific Grove, CA: Brooks/Cole.

Matthews, D.B., Best, P.J., White, A.M., Vandergriff, J.L., & Simson, P.E. (1996). Ethanol impairs spatial cognitive processing: New behavioral and electrophysiological findings. *Current Directions in Psychological Science, 5,* 111–115.

Matthews, K.A. (1988). Coronary heart disease and Type A behaviors: Update on and alternative to the Booth-Kewley and Friedman (1987) quantitative review. *Psychological Bulletin, 104,* 373–380.

Maurer, D., & Maurer, C. (1988). *The world of the newborn.* New York: Basic Books.

May, J., & Kline, P. (1987). Measuring the effects upon cognitive abilities of sleep loss during continuous operations. *British Journal of Psychology, 78*(Pt 4), 443–455.

Mayer, F.S., & Sutton, K. (1996). *Personality: An integrative approach.* Upper Saddle River, NJ: Prentice Hall.

Mayer, J.D., & Geher, G. (1996). Emotional intelligence and the identification of emotion. *Intelligence, 22*, 89–113.

Mayer, J.D., & Salovey, P. (1997). What is emotional intelligence? In P. Salovey & D. Sluyter (eds.), *Emotional development, emotional literacy, and emotional intelligence.* New York: Basic Books.

Mays, V.M., Bullock, M., Rosenzweig, M.R., & Wessells, M. (1998). Ethnic conflict: Global challenges and psychological perspectives. *American Psychologist, 53*, 737–742.

McAndrew, F.T. (1993). *Environmental psychology.* Pacific Grove, CA: Brooks/Cole.

McAneny, L., & Saad, L. (1994). America's public schools: Still separate? Still unequal? *Gallup Poll Monthly, 344*, 23–29.

McBurney, D.H., & Collings, V.B. (1984). *Introduction to sensation/perception* (2nd ed.). Englewood Cliffs, NJ: Prentice Hall.

McCall, M. (1997). Physical attractiveness and access to alcohol: What is beautiful does not get carded. *Journal of Applied Social Psychology, 27*(5), 453–462.

McCall, R.B. (1979). *Infants.* Cambridge, MA: Harvard University Press.

McCann, U.D., Slate, S.O., & Ricaurte, G.A. (1996). Adverse reactions with 3,4-methylenedioxymethamphetamine (MDMA; "ecstasy"). *Drug Safety, 15*, 107–115.

McClearn, G.E., Plomin, R., Gora-Maslak, G., & Crabbe, J.C. (1991). The gene chase in behavioral science. *Psychological Science, 2*, 222–229.

McClelland, D.C., & Atkinson, J.W. (1948). The projective expression of needs: I. The effect of different intensities of the hunger drive on perception. *Journal of Psychology, 25*, 205–222.

McCloskey, M., & Egeth, H.E. (1983). Eyewitness identification: What can a psychologist tell a jury? *American Psychologist, 38*, 550–563.

McConnell, R.A. (1969). ESP and credibility in science. *American psychologist, 24*, 531–538.

McCormick, D.A., Clark, G.A., Lavond, D.G., & Thompson, R.F. (1982). Initial localization of the memory trace for a basic form of learning. *Proceedings of the National Academy of Sciences of the U.S.A., 79*, 2731–2735.

McCrae, R.R., & Costa, P.T., Jr. (1996). Toward a new generation of personality theories: Theoretical contexts for the five-factor model. In J.S. Wiggins (ed.), *The five-factor model of personality: Theoretical perspectives* (pp. 51–87). New York: Guilford Press.

McCrae, R.R., & Costa, P.T., Jr. (1997). Personality trait structure as a human universal. *American Psychologist, 52*, 509–516.

McDaniel, M.A., & Frei, R.L. (1994). Validity of customer service measures in personnel selection: A review of criterion and construct evidence. (Cited in Hogan, R., Hogan, J., & Roberts, B.W. [1996]. Personality measurement and employment decisions: Questions and answers. *American Psychologist, 51*[5], 469–477.)

McDaniel, M.A., Waddill, P.J., & Shakesby, P.S. (1996). Study strategies, interest, and learning from text: The application of material appropriate processing. In D. Herrmann, C. McEvoy, C. Hertzog, P. Hertel, & M.K. Johnson (eds.), *Basic and applied memory research: Theory in context.* Nahwah, NJ: Erlbaum.

McFarland, L.J., Senn, L.E., & Childress, J.R. (1993). *21st century leadership: Dialogues with 100 top leaders.* Los Angeles: The Leadership Press.

McGeer, P.L., & McGeer, E.G. (1980). Chemistry of mood and emotion. *Annual Review of Psychology, 31*, 273–307.

McGinnis, M. (1994). The role of behavioral research in national health policy. In S. Blumenthal, K. Matthews, & Weiss (eds.), *New research frontiers in behavioral medicine: Proceeding of the National Conference.* Washington, DC: NIH Publications.

McGothlin, W.H., & West, L.J. (1968). The marijuana problem: An overview. *American Journal of Psychiatry, 125*, 370–378.

McGovern, L.P. (1976). Dispositional social anxiety and helping behavior under three conditions of threat. *Journal of Personality, 44*, 84–97.

McGrady, A. (1996). Good news–bad press: Applied psychophysiology in cardiovascular disorders. *Biofeedback and Self-Regulation, 21*(4), 335–346.

McGuffin, P., Katz, R., Watkins, S., & Rutherford, J. (1996). A hospital-based twin register of the heritability of DSM-IV unipolar depression. *Archives of General Psychiatry, 53*, 129–136.

McGuire, W.J. (1985). Attitudes and attitude change. In G. Lindzey & E. Aronson (eds.), *Handbook of social psychology.* Reading, MA: Addison-Wesley.

McKay, R. (1997). Stem cells in the nervous system. *Science, 276*, 66–71.

McKim, W.A. (1997). *Drugs and behavior* (3rd ed.). Upper Saddle River, NJ: Prentice Hall.

McMillan, T.M., Robertson, I.H., & Wilson, B.A. (1999). Neurogenesis after brain injury: Implications for neurorehabilitation. *Neuropsychological Rehabilitation, 9*, 129–133.

McMurray, G.A. (1950). Experimental study of a case of insensitivity to pain. *Archives of Neurology and Psychiatry, 64*, 650.

McNamara, H.J., Long, J.B., & Wike, E.L. (1956). Learning without response under two conditions of external cues. *Journal of Comparative and Physiological Psychology, 49*, 477–480.

Mednick, A. (1993, May). Worlds' women familiar with a day's double shift. *APA Monitor*, p. 32.

Mednick, S.A. (1962). The associative basis of creativity. *Psychological Review, 69*, 220–232.

Meichenbaum, D., & Cameron, R. (1982). Cognitive-behavior therapy. In G.T. Wilson & C.M. Franks (eds.), *Contemporary behavior therapy: Conceptual and empirical foundations.* New York: Guilford.

Melamed, B.G., Hawes, R.R., Heiby, E., & Glick, J. (1975). Use of filmed modeling to reduce uncooperative behavior of children during dental treatment. *Journal of Dental Research, 54*, 797–801.

Melamed, S., Ben-Avi, I., Luz, J., & Green, M. (1995). Objective and subjective work monotony: Effects on job satisfaction, psychological distress, and absenteeism in blue-collar workers. *Journal of Applied Psychology, 80*, 29–42.

Meltzoff, A.N., & Moore, M.K. (1985). Cognitive foundations and social functions of imitation and intermodal representation in infancy. In J. Mehler & R. Fox (eds.), *Neonate cognition: Beyond the blooming, fuzzing confusion.* Hillsdale, NJ: Erlbaum.

Melzack, R. (1973). *The puzzle of pain.* New York: Basic Books.

Melzack, R. (1980). Psychological aspects of pain. In J.J. Bonica (ed.), *Pain.* New York: Raven Press.

Melzack, R. (1992, April). Phantom limbs. *Scientific American*, pp. 120–126.

Mershon, B., & Gorsuch, R.L. (1988). Number of factors in the personality sphere: Does increase in factors increase predictability of real-life criteria? *Journal of Personality and Social Psychology, 55*, 675–680.

Mersky, H. (1992). The manufacture of personalities: The production of multiple personality disorder. *British Journal of Psychiatry, 160*, 327–340.

Merzer, M. (1998) Some pilots admit to midair naps. Reprint from *The Spokesman Review*, June 21. **http://www.spokane.net/stories/1998/ Jun/21/S410433.asp.**

Metcalfe, J., Funnell, M., & Gazzaniga, M.S. (1995). Guided visual search is a left-hemisphere process in split-brain patient. *Psychological Science, 6,* 157–173.

Meyer, G.E., & Hilterbrand, K. (1984). Does it pay to be "Bashful"? The seven dwarfs and long term memory. *American Journal of Psychology, 97,* 47–55.

Michelson, L. (ed.). (1985). Meta-analysis and clinical psychology [special issue.] *Clinical Psychology Review, 5*(1).

Middaugh, S.J. (1990). On clinical efficacy: Why biofeedback does—and does not—work. *Biofeedback and Self-Regulation, 15,* 191–208.

Milgram, S. (1963). Behavioral study of obedience. *Journal of Abnormal and Social Psychology, 67,* 371–378.

Milgram, S. (1974). *Obedience to authority: An experimental view.* New York: Harper & Row.

Miller, G.A. (1956). The magical number seven plus or minus two: Some limits on our capacity for processing information. *Psychological Review, 63,* 81–96.

Miller, J. (1984). Culture and the development of everyday social explanation. *Journal of Personality and Social Psychology, 46,* 961–978.

Miller, J.G., Bersoff, D.M., & Harwood, R.L. (1990). Perceptions of social responsibilities in India and the United States: Moral imperatives or personal decisions? *Journal of Personality and Social Psychology, 58,* 33–47.

Miller, P.A., Kliewer, W., & Burkeman, D. (1993, March). *Effects of maternal socialization on children's learning to cope with divorce.* Paper presented at the biennial meeting of the Society for Research in Child Development, New Orleans, LA.

Miller, T.Q., Smith, T.W., Turner, C.W., Guijarro, M.L., & Hallet, A.J. (1996). A meta-analytic review of research on hostility and physical health. *Psychological Bulletin, 119*(2), 322–348.

Milner, B. (1959). The memory defect in bilateral hippocampal lesions. *Psychiatric Research Reports, 11,* 43–52.

Milner, B., Corkin, S., & Teuber, H.H. (1968). Further analysis of the hippocampal amnesic syndrome: 14-year follow-up study of H.M. *Neuropsychologia, 6,* 215–234.

Milton, J., & Wiseman, R. (1999). Does psi exist? Lack of replication of an anomalous process of information transfer. *Psychological Bulletin, 125,* 387–391.

Minton, H.L., & Schneider, F.W. (1980). *Differential psychology.* Monterey, CA: Brooks/Cole.

Mischel, W., & Shoda, Y. (1995). A cognitive-affective system theory of personality: Reconceptualizing situations, dispositions, dynamics, and invariance in personality structure. *Psychological Review, 102*(2), 246–268.

Mistry, J., & Rogoff, B. (1994). Remembering in cultural context. In W.W. Lonner & R. Malpass (eds.), *Psychology and culture* (pp. 139–144). Boston: Allyn & Bacon.

Misumi, J. (1985). *The behavioral science of leadership: An interdisciplinary Japanese leadership program.* Ann Arbor: University of Michigan Press.

Mitchell, E., Sachs, A., & Tu, J.I. (1997, September 29). Teaching Feelings 101. *Time,* p. 62.

Mitchell, R.W., Thompson, N.S., & Miles, H.L. (1997). *Anthropomorphism, anecdotes, and animals.* Albany: State University of New York Press.

Moffitt, T.W. (1993). Adolescence-limited and life-course-persistent antisocial behavior: A developmental taxonomy. *Psychological Review, 100,* 674–701.

Moghaddam, F.M., Taylor, D.M., & Wright, S.C. (1993). *Social psychology in cross-cultural perspective.* New York: Freeman.

Molineux, J.B. (1985). *Family therapy: A practical manual.* Springfield, IL: Charles C. Thomas.

Moncrieff, R.W. (1951). *The chemical senses.* London: Leonard Hill.

Monroe, S.M., & Simons, A.D. (1991). Diathesis-stress theories in the context of life stress research: Implications for the depressive disorders. *Psychological Bulletin, 110,* 406–425.

Moore-Ede, M.C., Czeisler, C.A., & Richardson, G.S. (1983). Circadian timekeeping in health and disease: I. Basic properties of circadian pacemakers. *New England Journal of Medicine, 309,* 469–476.

Morgane, P.J., Austin-LaFrance, R., Bronzino, J., Tonkiss, J., Diaz-Cintra, S., Cintra, L., Kemper, T., & Galler, J.R. (1993). Prenatal malnutrition and development of the brain. *Neuroscience and Biobehavioral Reviews, 17*(1), 91–128.

Moriarty, T. (1975). Crime, commitment and the responsive bystander: Two field experiments. *Journal of Personality and Social Psychology, 31,* 370–376.

Morin, C.M., Stone, J., McDonald, K., & Jones, S. (1994). Psychological management of insomnia: A clinical replication series with 100 patients. *Behavior Therapy, 25,* 291–309.

Morris, C. (1990). *Contemporary psychology and effective behavior* (7th ed.). Glenview, IL: Scott, Foresman.

Morrison, A. (1983). A window on the sleeping brain. *Scientific American, 249,* 94–102.

Moscicki, E.K. (1995). Epidemiology of suicidal behavior. *Suicide and Life-Threatening Behavior, 25,* 22–35.

Moses, S. (1990, December). Sensitivity to culture may be hard to teach. *APA Monitor,* p. 39.

Moses, S. (1991, April). New paradigms of science inquiry may help women. *APA Monitor,* p. 36.

Moyers, F. (1996). Oklahoma City bombing: Exacerbation of symptoms in veterans with PTSD. *Archives of Psychiatric Nursing, 10*(1), 55–59.

Mueser, K.T., & Glynn, S.M. (1995). *Behavioral family therapy for psychiatric disorders.* Boston: Allyn & Bacon.

Mumford, M.D., & Gustafson, S.B. (1988). Creativity syndrome: Integration, application, and innovation. *Psychological Bulletin, 103,* 27–43.

Murphy, J.M. (1976). Psychiatric labeling in cross-cultural perspective. *Science, 191,* 1019–1028.

Murray, H.A. (1938). *Explorations in personality.* New York: Oxford University Press.

Murray, H.G., & Denny, J.P. (1969). Interaction of ability level and interpolated activity in human problem solving. *Psychological Reports, 24,* 271–276.

Murstein, B.J. (1986). *Paths to marriage.* Beverly Hills, CA: Sage.

Muth, E.R., Stern, R.M., Uijtdehaage, S.H.J., & Koch, K.L. (1994). Effects of Asian ancestry on susceptibility to vection-induced motion sickness. In J.Z. Chen & R.W. McCallum (eds.), *Electrogastrography: Principles and applications* (pp. 227–233). New York: Raven Press.

Myers, D.G. (1992). *Social psychology* (4th ed.). Boston: McGraw-Hill.

Myers, D.G. (1996). *Social psychology* (5th ed.). New York: McGraw-Hill.

Narayanan, L., Menon, S., & Levin, E.L. (1995). Personality structure: A culture-specific examination of the five factor model. *Journal of Personality Assessment, 64,* 51–62.

National Advisory Mental Health Council. (1995). Basic behavioral science research for mental health: A national investment emotion and motivation. *American Psychologist, 50*(10), 838–845.

National Commission on Marijuana and Drug Abuse (NCMDA). (1973b). *Drug use in America: Problem in perspective. Technical papers—appendix*. Washington, DC: U.S. Government Printing Office.

National Institute of Health Consensus Development Conference. (1996). Integration of behavioral and relaxation approaches into the treatment of chronic pain and insomnia. NIH technology assessment panel. Reported in the *Journal of the American Medical Association, 276*(4), 313–318.

National Public Radio. (1997, July 16). *Group therapy and cancer.* (Transcript.) National Public Radio.

Neal, A., & Turner, S.M. (1991). Anxiety disorders research with African Americans: Current status. *Psychological Bulletin, 109*(3), 400–410.

Neale, J.M., & Oltmanns, T.F. (1980). *Schizophrenia*. New York: Wiley.

Neher, A. (1991). Maslow's theory of motivation: A critique. *Journal of Humanistic Psychology, 31*, 89–112.

Nehlig, A., Daval, J.L., & Debry, G. (1992). Caffeine and the central nervous system: Mechanisms of action, biochemical, metabolic and psychostimulant effects. *Brain Research Reviews, 17*, 139–170.

Neisser, U. (1967). *Cognitive psychology*. New York: Appleton-Century-Crofts.

Neisser, U. (1982). *Memory observed: Remembering in natural contexts*. San Francisco: Freeman.

Neisser, U. (1992). Amnesia, infantile. In L.R. Squire (ed.), *The encyclopedia of learning and memory* (pp. 28–30). New York: Macmillan.

Neitz, J., Geist, T., & Jacobs, G.H. (1989). Color vision in the dog. *Visual Neuroscience, 3*(2), 119–125.

Nelson, D.L. (1999). Implicit memory. In D.E. Morris & M. Gruneberg (eds.), *Theoretical aspects of memory*. London: Routledge.

Neugarten, B.L. (1977). Personality and aging. In I. Birren & K.W. Schaie (eds.), *Handbook of the psychology of aging*. New York: Van Nostrand.

Newman, B.M. (1982). Mid-life development. In B.B. Wolman (ed.), *Handbook of developmental psychology* (pp. 617–635). Englewood Cliffs, NJ: Prentice Hall.

Newman, P.R. (1982). The peer group. In B.B. Wolman (ed.), *Handbook of developmental psychology* (pp. 526–536). Englewood Cliffs, NJ: Prentice Hall.

Newton, P.M. (1970). Recalled dream content and the maintenance of body image. *Journal of Abnormal Psychology, 76*(1), 134–139.

New York Times. (1999, July 15). Doctor removes half of a patient's brain.

Nickerson, R.S., & Adams, M.J. (1979). Long-term memory for a common object. *Cognitive Psychology, 11*, 287–307.

Niehoff, D. (1999). *The biology of violence (How understanding the brain, behavior, and environment can break the vicious circle of aggression)*. NY: Free Press.

Nielsen, G.D., & Smith, E.E. (1973). Imaginal and verbal representative in short-term recognition of visual forms. *Journal of Experimental Psychology, 101*, 375–378.

Nisbett, R.E., Fong, G.T., Lehman, D.R., & Cheng, P.W. (1987). Teaching reasoning. *Science, 238*, 625–631.

Nissani, M. (1990). A cognitive reinterpretation of Stanley Milgram's observations on obedience to authority. *American Psychologist, 45*, 1384–1385.

Noga, J.T., Bartley, A.J., Jones, D.W., Torrey, E.F., & Weinberger, D.R. (1996). Cortical gyral anatomy and gross brain dimensions in monozygotic twins discordant for schizophrenia. *Schizophrenia Research, 22*(1), 27–40.

Nolen-Hoeksema, S., Girgus, J.S., & Seligman, M.E.P. (1986). Learned helplessness in children: A longitudinal study of depression, achievement, and explanatory style. *Journal of Personality and Social Psychology, 51*, 435–442a.

Noller, P., Law, H., & Comrey, A.L. (1987). Cattell, Comrey, and Eysenck personality factors compared: More evidence for the five robust factors? *Journal of Personality and Social Psychology, 53*, 775–782.

Norcross, J.C., Alford, B.A., & DeMichele, J.T. (1994). The future of psychotherapy: Delphi data and concluding observation. *Psychotherapy, 29*, 150–158.

Norman, D.A., & Bobrow, D.C. (1976). Active memory processes in perception and cognition. In C. Cofer (ed.), *The structure of human memory* (pp. 114–132). San Francisco: Freeman.

Norman, R. (1975). Affective-cognitive consistency, attitudes, conformity, and behavior. *Journal of Personality and Social Psychology, 32*, 83–91.

Norris, F.H., & Murrell, S.A. (1990). Social support, life events, and stress as modifiers of adjustment to bereavement by older adults. *Psychology and Aging, 45*, 267–275.

Norris, P.A. (1986). On the status of biofeedback and clinical practice. *American Psychologist, 41*, 1009–1010.

Nottebohm, F., & Barnea, A. (1994). Seasonal recruitment of hippocampal neurons in adult free-ranging black-capped chickadees. *Proceedings of the National Academy of Sciences of the U.S.A., 91*, 11217.

Novak, M.A. (1991, July). "Psychologists care deeply" about animals. *APA Monitor;* p. 4.

NTSB Accident Review, (1999, July 24). **http://www.afo.arc.nasa.gov/zteam/fcp/ FCP.current.NTSB.html.**

O'Connell, A., & Russo, N. (eds.). (1990). *Women in psychology: A bibliographic sourcebook*. Westport, CT: Greenwood Press.

O'Connor, N., & Hermelin, B. (1987). Visual memory and motor programmes: Their use by idiot savant artists and controls. *British Journal of Psychology, 78*, 307–323.

O'Leary, A. (1990). Stress, emotion, and human immune function. *Psychological Bulletin, 108*, 363–382.

O'Leary, K.D., & Wilson, G.T. (1987). *Behavior therapy: Application and outcome*. Englewood Cliffs, NJ: Prentice Hall.

O'Leary, S.G. (1995). Parental discipline mistakes. *American Psychological Society, 4*(1), 11–14.

O'Leary, V.E., & Smith, D. (1988, August). *Sex makes a difference: Attributions for emotional cause*. Paper presented at the meeting of the American Psychological Association, Atlanta, GA.

Office of Educational Research and Improvement. (1988). *Youth indicators, 1988*. Washington, DC: U.S. Government Printing Office.

Ogawa, S., Lubahn, D., Korach, K., & Pfaff, D. (1997). Behavioral effects of estrogen receptor gene disruption in male mice. *Proceedings of the National Academy of Sciences of the U.S.A., 94*, 1476.

Öhman, A. (1996). Preferential preattentive processing of threat in anxiety: Preparedness and attentional biases. In R.M. Rapee (ed.), *Current controversies in the anxiety disorders* (pp. 252–290). New York: Guilford.

Olio, K. (1994). Truth in memory. *American Psychologist, 49*, 442–443.

Olson, L., Cheng, H., & Cao, Y. (1996). Spinal cord repair in adult parplegic rats: Partial restoration of hind limb function. *Science, 273,* 510–513.

Oltmanns, T.F., & Emery, R.E. (1998). *Abnormal psychology* (2nd ed.). Upper Saddle River, NJ: Prentice Hall.

Olton, D.S., & Noonberg, A.R. (1980). *Biofeedback: Clinical applications in behavioral science.* Englewood Cliffs, NJ: Prentice Hall.

Olton, D.S., & Samuelson, R.J. (1976). Remembrance of places passed: Spatial memory in rats. *Journal of Experimental Psychology, 2,* 97–115.

Ones, D.S., Viswesvaran, C., & Schmidt, F.L. (1993). Comprehensive meta-analysis of integrity test validation: Findings and implications for personnel selection and theories of job performance. *Journal of Applied Psychology, 78,* 679–703.

Orlinsky, D.E., & Howard, K.I. (1994). Unity and diversity among psychotherapies: A comparative perspective. In B. Bonger & L.E. Beutler (eds.), *Foundations of psychotherapy: Theory, research, and practice.* New York: Basic Books.

Ortar, G. (1963). Is a verbal test cross-cultural? *Scripta Hierosolymitana, 13,* 219–235.

Oskamp, S. (1991). *Attitudes and opinions* (2nd ed.). Englewood Cliffs, NJ: Prentice Hall.

Oswald, I. (1973). Is sleep related to synthetic purpose? In W.P. Koella & P. Levin (eds.), *Sleep: Physiology, biology, psychology, psychopharmacology, clinical implications.* Basel, Switzerland: Karger.

Oswald, I. (1974). Pharmacology of sleep. In O. Petre-Quadens & J.S. Schlag (eds.), *Basic sleep mechanism.* New York: Academic Press.

Pace, R. (1994, July 28). Christy Henrich, 22, gymnast plagued by eating disorders. *New York Times,* p. A12.

Packard, R.G. (1970). The control of "classroom attention": A group contingency for complex behavior. *Journal of Applied Behavior Analysis, 3,* 13–28.

Paikoff, R.L., & Brooks-Gunn, J. (1991). Do parent–child relationships change during puberty? *Psychological Bulletin, 110*(1), 47–66.

Pakkenberg, B., & Jensen, G.B. (1993). Do alcoholics drink their neurons away? *Lancet, 342* (8881), 1201–1204.

Panksepp, J. (1986). The neurochemistry of behavior. *Annual Review of Psychology, 37,* 77–107.

Paris, S.G., & Weissberg, J.A. (1986). Young children's remembering in different contexts: A reinterpretation of Istomina's study. *Child Development, 57,* 1123–1129.

Parke, R.D., & Asher, S.R. (1983). Social and personality development. *Annual Review of Psychology, 34,* 465–509.

Parke, R.D., & O'Neil, R. (1999). Social relationships across contexts: Family–peer linkages. In A.W. Collins, & B. Laursen (eds.) *Relationships as developmental contexts. The Minnesota symposia on child psychology* (Vol. 30, pp. 211–239). Mahwah, NJ: Lawrence Erlbaum Assoc., Inc.

Parker, E.S., Birnbaum, I.M., & Noble, E.P. (1976). Alcohol and memory: Storage and state dependency. *Journal of Verbal Learning and Verbal Behavior, 15,* 691–702.

Parker, J.G., & Asher, S.R. (1987). Peer relations and later personal adjustment: Are low-accepted children at risk? *Psychological Bulletin, 102,* 357–389.

Parsons, H.M. (1974). What happened to Hawthorne? *Science, 183,* 922–932.

Patrick, C.J. (1994). Emotion and psychopathy: Startling new insights. *Psychophysiology, 31,* 319–330.

Patterson, C.J. (1994). Lesbian and gay families. *Current Directions in Psychological Science, 3*(2), 62–64.

Patterson, C.J. (1995). Families of the baby boom: Parents' division of labor and children's adjustment. [Special issue: Sexual orientation and human development.] *Developmental Psychology, 31*(1), 115–123.

Patterson, G.R., & Bank, L. (1989). Some amplifying mechanisms for pathologic processes in families. In M.R. Gunnar & E. Thelen (eds.), *Systems and development: The Minnesota Symposia on Child Psychology* (Vol. 22). Hillsdale, NJ: Erlbaum.

Patterson, G.R., DeBaryshe, B.D., & Ramsey, E. (1989). A developmental perspective on antisocial behavior. *American Psychologist, 44,* 329–335.

Paul, G.L. (1982). The development of a "transportable" system of behavioral assessment for chronic patients. Invited address, University of Minnesota, Minneapolis.

Paul, G.L., & Lentz, R.J. (1977). *Psychosocial treatment of chronic mental patients: Milieu versus social learning programs.* Cambridge, MA: Harvard University Press.

Paulson, P.C. (1990, November). The fine art of sleeping well. *University Health Service Bulletin,* pp. 1–2.

Pavlov, I.P. (1927). *Conditional reflexes* (G. V. Anrep, trans.). London: Oxford University Press.

Pearlin, L.I., & Schooler, C. (1978). The structure of coping. *Journal of Health and Social Behavior, 19,* 2–21.

Pearson, C.A.L. (1992). Autonomous workgroups: An evaluation at an industrial site. *Human Relations, 9,* 905–936.

Pedlow, R., et al. (1993). Stability of maternally reported temperament from infancy to 8 years. *Developmental Psychology, 29,* 998–1007.

Pedroarena, C., & Llinás, R. (1997). Dendritic calcium conductances generate high-frequency oscillation in thalamocortical neurons. *Proceedings of the National Academy of Science, 94,* 724–728.

Pekala, R.J., & Kumar, V.K. (1984). Predicting hypnotic susceptibility by a self-report phenomenological state instrument. *American Journal of Clinical Hypnosis, 27,* 114–121.

Pekala, R.J., & Kumar, V.K. (1986). The differential organization of the structures of consciousness during hypnosis and a baseline condition. *Journal of Mind and Behavior, 7,* 515–539.

Pellegrini, A.D., & Galda, L. (1994). Play. In *Encyclopedia of human behavior* (Vol. 3, pp. 535–543). San Diego, CA: Academic Press.

Peplau, L.A., & Cochran, S.D. (1990). A relationship perspective on homosexuality. In D.P. McWhirter, S.A. Sanders, & J.M. Reinisch (eds.), *Homosexuality/heterosexuality: The Kinsey scale and current research.* New York: Oxford University Press.

Perls, F.S. (1969). *Gestalt theory verbatim.* Lafayette, CA: People Press.

Perry, D.G., Perry, L.C., & Weiss, R.J. (1989). Sex differences in the consequences that children anticipate for aggression. *Developmental Psychology, 25,* 312–319.

Persky, H. (1983). Psychosexual effects of hormones. *Medical Aspects of Human Sexuality, 17,* 74–101.

Persson-Blennow, I., & McNeil, T.F. (1988). Frequencies and stability of temperament types in childhood. *Journal of the American Academy of Child and Adolescent Psychiatry, 27,* 619–622.

Pert, C.B., & Snyder, S.H. (1973). The opiate receptor: Demonstration in nervous tissue. *Science, 179*(6), 1011–1014.

Peskin, H. (1967). Pubertal onset and ego functioning. *Journal of Abnormal Psychology, 72,* 1–15.

Peterson, C., Maier, S.F., & Seligman, M.E.P. (1993a). Explanatory style and helplessness. *Social Behavior and Personality, 20,* 1–14.

Peterson, C., Maier, S. F., & Seligman, M. E. P. (1993b). *Learned helplessness: A theory for the age of personal control.* New York: Oxford University Press.

Peterson, C., Vaillant, G. E., & Seligman, M. E. P. (1988). Explanatory style as a risk factor for illness. *Cognitive Therapy and Research, 12,* 119–132.

Peterson, L. R., & Peterson, M. J. (1959). Short-term retention of individual verbal items. *Journal of Experimental Psychology, 58,* 193–198.

Pettigrew, T. F. (1969). Racially separate or together? *Journal of Social Issues, 25,* 43–69.

Petty, R. E., & Cacioppo, J. T. (1981). *Attitudes and persuasion: Classic and contemporary approaches.* Dubuque, IA: Wm. C. Brown.

Petty, R. E., & Cacioppo, J. T. (1986a). The elaboration likelihood model of persuasion. In L. Berkowitz (ed.), *Advances in experimental social psychology* (Vol. 19). Orlando, FL: Academic Press.

Petty, R. E., & Cacioppo, J. T. (1986b). *Communication and persuasion: Central and peripheral routes to attitude change.* New York: Springer-Verlag.

Pezdek, K., & Roe, C. (1995). The effect of memory trace strength on suggestibility. *Journal of Experimental Child Psychology, 60,* 116–128.

Phelps, L., & Bajorek, E. (1991). Eating disorders of the adolescent: Current issues in etiology, assessment, and treatment. *School Psychology Review, 20,* 9–22.

Phinney, J. S. (1996). When we talk about American ethnic groups, what do we mean? *American Psychologist, 51,* 918–927.

Pi-Sunyer, F. X. (1987). Exercise effects on calorie intake. *Annals of the New York Academy of Sciences, 499,* 94–103.

Piaget, J. (1967). *Six psychological studies.* New York: Random House.

Piaget, J. (1969). The intellectual development of the adolescent. In G. Caplan & S. Lebovici (eds.), *Adolescence: Psychosocial perspectives.* New York: Basic Books.

Pillow, D. R., Zautra, A. J., & Sandler, I. (1996). Major life events and minor stressors: Identifying mediational links in the stress process. *Journal of Personality and Social Psychology, 70,* 381–394.

Pion, G. M., Mednick, M. T., Astin, H. S., Hall, C. C. I., Kenkel, M. B., Keita, G. P., Kohout, J. L., & Kelleher, J. C. (1996). The shifting gender composition of psychology: Trends and implications for the discipline. *American Psychologist, 15*(5), 509–528.

Plomin, R. (1994). *Genetics and experience: The interplay between nature and nurture.* Thousand Oaks, CA: Sage.

Plomin, R. (1997). Identifying genes for cognitive abilities and disabilities. In R. J. Sternberg & E. Grigorenko (eds.), *Intelligence: Heredity and environment.* New York: Cambridge University Press.

Plomin, R. (1999). Parents and personality. *Contemporary Psychology, 44,* 269–271.

Plomin, R., & Rende, R. (1991). Human behavioral genetics. *Annual Review of Psychology, 42,* 161–190.

Plomin, R., Corley, R., DeFries, J. C., & Fulker, D. W. (1990). Individual differences in television watching in early childhood: Nature as well as nurture. *Psychological Science 1*(6), 371–377.

Plomin, R., DeFries, J. C., & McClearn, G. E. (1990). *Behavioral genetics: A primer* (2nd ed.). New York: Freeman.

Plomin, R., McClearn, G. E., Smith, D. L., Vignetti, S., Chorney, M. J., Chorney, K., Venditti, C. P., Kasarda, S., Thompson, L. A., Detterman, D. K., Daniels, J., Owen, M. J., & McGuffin, P. (1994). DNA markers associated with high versus low IQ: The IQ quantitative trait loci (QTL) Project, *Behavior Genetics, 24,* 107–119.

Plous, S. (1996). Attitudes toward the use of animals in psychology research and education: Results from a national survey of psychologists. *American Psychologist, 51*(11), 1167–1180.

Plutchik, R. (1980). *Emotion: A psychoevolutionary synthesis.* New York: Harper & Row.

Poe-Yamagata, E. (1997). Female participation in delinquent behavior is on the rise. *NCJJ in Brief (1)(2).* Pittsburgh, PA: National Center for Juvenile Justice.

Pontieri, F. E., Tanda, G., Orzi, F., & DiChiara, G. (1996). Effects of nicotine on the nucleus accumbens and similarity to those of addictive drugs. *Nature, 382,* 255–257.

Pope, K. S. (1996). Memory, abuse and science: Questioning claims about the false memory syndrome epidemic. *American Psychologist, 51*(9), 957–974.

Porkka-Heiskanen, T., Strecker, R. E., Thakkar, M., Bjørkum, A. A., Greene, R. W., & McCarley, R. W. (1997). Adenosine: A mediator of the sleep-inducing effects of prolonged wakefulness. *Science, 276,* 1265–1268.

Porter, L. W., & Roberts, K. H. (1976). Communication in organizations. In M. D. Dunnette (ed.), *Handbook of industrial and organizational psychology.* Chicago: Rand McNally.

Porter, L. S., & Stone, A. A. (1995). Are there really gender differences in coping? A reconsideration of previous results from a daily study. *Journal of Social and Clinical Psychology, 14,* 184–202.

Postman, L. (1975). Verbal learning and memory. *Annual Review of Psychology, 26,* 291–335.

Power, F. C. (1994). Moral development. In *Encyclopedia of human behavior* (Vol. 3, pp. 203–212). San Diego, CA: Academic Press.

Powers, S. I., Hauser, S. T., & Kilner, L. A. (1989). Adolescent mental health. *American Psychologist, 44,* 200–208.

Prager, K. J. (1995). *The psychology of intimacy.* New York: Guilford Press.

Prentice, A. M. (1991). Can maternal dietary supplements help in preventing infant malnutrition? *Acta Paediatrica Scandinavica, 374*(Suppl.), 67–77.

Prentky, R. A., Knight, R. A., & Rosenberg, R. (1988). Validation analyses on a taxonomic system for rapists: Disconfirmation and reconceptualization. *Annals of the New York Academy of Sciences, 528,* 21–40.

Prior, M., Smart, D., Sanson, A., & Obeklaid, F. (1993). Sex differences in psychological adjustment from infancy to 8 years. *Journal of the American Academy of Child and Adolescent Psychiatry, 32,* 291–304.

Ptacek, J. T., Smith R. E., & Dodge, K. L. (1994). Gender differences in coping with stress: When stressor and appraisals do not differ. *Personality and Social Psychology Bulletin, 20,* 421–430.

Puig, C. (1995, February 27). Children say they imitate anti-social behavior on TV: Survey finds shows influence more than two-thirds.

Pulaski, M. A. S. (1974, January). The rich rewards of make believe. *Psychology Today,* pp. 68–74.

Putnam, F. W. (1984). The psychophysiological investigation of multiple personality: A review. *Psychiatric Clinics of North America, 7,* 31–39.

Putnam, F. W., Guroff, J. J., Silberman, E. D., Barban, L., & Post, R. M. (1986). The clinical phenomenology of multiple personality disorder: Review of 100 recent cases. *Journal of Clinical Psychology, 47,* 285–293.

Quadrel, M. J., Prouadrel, Fischoff, B., & Davis, W. (1993). Adolescent (In)vulnerability. *American Psychologist, 2,* 102–116.

Rabinowitz, V.C., & Sechzer, J.A. (1993). Feminist perspectives on research methods. In F.L. Denmark & M.A. Paludi (eds.), *Psychology of women: A handbook of issues and theories* (pp. 23–66). Westport, CT: Greenwood.

Radford, M. (1996). Culture and its effects on decision making. In W.H. Loke (ed.), *Perspectives on judgment and decision making*. Lanham, MD: Scarecrow Press.

Radford, M., Mann, L., Ohta, Y., & Nakane, Y. (1990). Differences between Australian and Japanese students in decisional self-esteem, decisional stress and coping styles. Reported in Radford, M. (1996). Culture and its effects on decision making. In W.H. Loke (ed.), *Perspectives on judgment and decision making*. Lanham, MD: Scarecrow Press.

Raine, A., Lencz, T., Reynolds, G.P., Harrison, G., Sheard, C., Medley, I., Reynolds, L.M., & Cooper, J.E. (1992). An evaluation of structural and functional prefrontal deficits in schizophrenia: MRI and neuropsychological measures. *Psychiatry Research Neuroimaging, 45*, 123–137.

Rasika, S., Alvarez-Buylla, A., & Nottebohm, F. (1999). BDNF mediates the effects of testosterone on the survival of new neurons in an adult brain. *Neuron, 22*, 53–62.

Rastam, M. (1994). Anorexia nervosa: Recent research findings and implications for clinical practice. *European Child and Adolescent Psychiatry, 3*, 197–207.

Ravussin, E., Pratley, R.E., Maffei, M., Wang, H., Friedman, J.M., Bennett, P.H., & Bogardus, C. (1997). Relatively low plasma leptin concentrations precede weight gain in Pima Indians. *Nat. Med., 3*(2), 238–240.

Rayman, P., & Bluestone, B. (1982). *The private and social response to job loss: A metropolitan study.* Final report of research sponsored by the Center for Work and Mental Health, National Institute of Mental Health.

Reed, D.R., Ding, Y., Xu, W., Cather, C., Green, E.D., & Price, R.A. (1996). Extreme obesity may be linked to markers flanking the human OB gene. *Diabetes, 45*, 691–694.

Reed, S.K. (1988). *Cognition: Theory and applications.* Monterey, CA: Brooks/Cole.

Reed, S.K. (1992). *Cognition: Theory and applications* (3rd ed.). Pacific Grove, CA: Brooks/Cole.

Reed, S.K. (1996). *Cognition: Theory and applications* (4th ed.). Pacific Grove, CA: Brooks/Cole.

Reinisch, J.M., & Sanders, S.A. (1982). Early barbiturate exposure: The brain, sexually dimorphic behavior and learning. *Neuroscience and Biobehavioral Reviews, 6*(3), 311–319.

Renzulli, J.S. (1978). What makes giftedness? Reexamining a definition. *Phi Delta Kappan, 60*, 180–184, 216.

Rescorla, R.A. (1966). Predictability and number of pairings in Pavlovian fear conditioning. *Psychonomic Science, 4*, 383–384.

Rescorla, R.A. (1967). Pavlovian conditioning and its proper control procedures. *Psychological Review, 74*, 71–80.

Rescorla, R.A. (1988). Pavlovian conditioning: It's not what you think. *American Psychologist, 43*, 151–160.

Rescorla, R.A., & Solomon, R.L. (1967). Two-process learning theory: Relationships between Pavlovian conditioning and instrumental learning. *Psychological Review, 74*, 151–182.

Reyna, V.F., & Titcomb, A.L. (1997). Constraints on the suggestibility of eyewitness testimony: A fuzzy-trace theory analysis. In D.G. Payne & F.G. Conrad (eds.), *Intersections in basic and applied memory research*. Mahwah, NJ: Erlbaum.

Rhue, J.W., Lynn, S.J., & Kirsch, I. (1993). *Handbook of clinical hypnosis*. Washington, DC: American Psychological Association.

Richards, R., Kinney, D.K., Lunde, I., & Benet, M. (1988b). Creativity in manic-depressives, cyclothymes, their normal relatives, and control subjects. *Journal of Abnormal Psychology, 97*, 281–288.

Richardson, G.S., Miner, J.D., & Czeisler, C.A. (1989–90). Impaired driving performance in shiftworkers: The role of the circadian system in a multifactional model. *Alcohol, Drugs & Driving, 5*(4), 6(1), 265–273.

Riger, S. (1992). Epistemological debates, feminist voices. *American Psychologist, 47*, 730–740.

Riordan, R.J., & Beggs, M.S. (1987). Counselors and self-help groups. *Journal of Counseling and Development, 65*, 427–429.

Roberts, A.H., Kewman, D.G., Mercer, L., & Hovell, M. (1993). The power of nonspecific effects in healing: Implications for psychosocial and biological treatments. *Clinical Psychology Review, 13*, 375–391.

Robins, L.N., & Regier, D.A. (1991). *Psychiatric disorders in America: The Epidemiologic Catchment Area Study.* New York: Free Press.

Robins, L.N., Schoenberg, S.P., Holmes, S.J., Ratcliff, K.S., Benham, A., & Works, J. (1985). Early home environment and retrospective recall: A test for concordance between siblings with and without psychiatric disorders. *American Journal of Orthopsychiatry, 55*, 27–41.

Robinson, L.A., Berman, J.S., & Neimeyer, R.A. (1990). Psychotherapy for the treatment of depression: A comprehensive review of controlled outcome research. *Psychological Bulletin, 108*, 30–49.

Rodin, J. (1985). Insulin levels, hunger, and food intake: An example of feedback loops in body weight regulation. *Health Psychology, 4*, 1–24.

Rodin, J., Striegel-Moore, R.H., & Silberstein, L.R. (1985, July). *A prospective study of bulimia among college students on three U.S. campuses.* First unpublished progress report, Yale University, New Haven, CT.

Roediger, H.L. (1990). Implicit memory: Retention without remembering. *American Psychologist, 45*(9), 1043–1056.

Rogers, C.R. (1961). *On becoming a person: A therapist's view of psychotherapy.* Boston: Houghton Mifflin.

Roitbak, A.I. (1993). *Glia and its role in nervous activity.* Saint Petersburg, Russia: Nauka.

Romeo, F. (1984). Adolescence, sexual conflict, and anorexia nervosa. *Adolescence, 19*, 551–557.

Rosch, E.H. (1973). Natural categories. *Cognitive Psychology, 4*, 328–350.

Rosch, E.H. (1978). Principles of categorization. In E.H. Rosch & B.B. Lloyd (eds.), *Cognition and categorization*. Hillsdale, NJ: Erlbaum.

Rosenthal, D. (1970). *Genetic theory and abnormal behavior.* New York: McGraw-Hill.

Rosenthal, R., et al. (1974, September). Body talk and tone of voice: The language without words. *Psychology Today*, pp. 64–68.

Rosenthal, R., Hall, J.A., Archer, D., DiMatteo, M.R., & Rogers, P.L. (1979). The PONS test: Measuring sensitivity to nonverbal cues. In S. Weitz (ed.), *Nonverbal communication* (2nd ed.). New York: Oxford University Press.

Rosenzweig, M.R. (1984). Experience, memory, and the brain. *American Psychologist, 39*, 365–376.

Rosenzweig, M.R. (1996). Aspects of the search for neural mechanisms of memory. *Annual Review of Psychology, 47*, 1–32.

Rosenzweig, M.R., & Leiman, A.L. (1982). *Physiological psychology.* Lexington, MA: D.C. Heath.

Ross, C.A., Norton, G.R., & Wozney, K. (1989). Multiple personality disorder: An analysis of 236 cases. *Canadian Journal of Psychiatry, 34*, 413–418.

Ross, L. (1977). The intuitive psychologist and his shortcomings: Distortions in the attribution process. In L. Berkowitz (ed.), *Advances in experimental social psychology* (Vol. 10). New York: Academic Press.

Ross, L., & Nisbett, R.E. (1991). *The person and the situation.* New York: McGraw-Hill.

Ross, M.H. (1993). *The culture of conflict.* New Haven, CT: Yale University Press.

Roth, G. (1996, April 30). Eating less may bring longer life. *New York Times*, p. B8.

Rothbart, M., Evans, M., & Fulero, S. (1979). Recall for confirming events: Memory processes and the maintenance of social stereotypes. *Journal of Experimental Social Psychology, 15*, 343–355.

Rottenstreich, Y., & Tversky, A. (1997). Unpacking, repacking, and anchoring: Advances in support theory. *Psychological Review, 104*(2), 406–415.

Rotter, J.B. (1954). *Social learning and clinical psychology.* Englewood Cliffs, NJ: Prentice Hall.

Rouhana, N.N., & Bar-Tal, D. (1998). Psychological dynamics of instractable ethnonational conflicts: The Israeli-Palestinian case. *American Psychologist, 53*, 761–770.

Rowan, A., & Shapiro, K.J. (1996). Animal rights, a bitten apple. *American Psychologist, 51*(11), 1183–1184.

Ruberman, J.W., Weinblatt, E., Goldberg, J.D., & Chaudhary, B.S. (1984). Psychological influences on mortality after myocardial infarction. *New England Journal of Medicine, 311*, 552–559.

Rubin, K.H., Coplan, R.J., Chen, X., & McKinnon, J.E. (1994). Peer relationships and influences in childhood. In *Encyclopedia of human behavior* (Vol. 3, pp. 431–439). San Diego, CA: Academic Press.

Ruble, D.N., Fleming, A.S., Hackel, L.S., & Stangor, C. (1988). Changes in the marital relationship during the transition to first time motherhood: Effects of violated expectations concerning division of household labor. *Journal of Personality and Social Psychology, 55*, 78–87.

Ruffin, C.L. (1993). Stress and health–little hassles vs. major life events. *Australian Psychologist, 28*, 201–208.

Russell, J.A. (1991a). Culture and the categorization of emotions. *Psychological Bulletin, 110*, 426–450.

Russell, T.G., Rowe, W., & Smouse, A.D. (1991). Subliminal self-help tapes and academic achievement: An evaluation. *Journal of Counseling and Development, 69*, 359–362.

Russo, N.F. (1985). *A woman's mental health agenda.* Washington, DC: American Psychological Association.

Russo, N.F. (1990). Overview: Forging research priorities for women's mental health. *American Psychologist, 45*, 368–373.

Russo, N.F., & Denmark, F.L. (1987). Contributions of women to psychology. *Annual Review of Psychology, 38*, 279–298.

Russo, N.F., & Sobel, S.B. (1981). Sex differences in the utilization of mental health facilities. *Professional Psychology, 12*, 7–19.

Rutter, M.L. (1997). Nature-nurture integration: An example of antisocial behavior. *American Psychologist, 52*, 390–398.

Salthouse, T.A. (1991). Mediation of adult age differences in cognition by reductions in working memory and speed of processing. *Psychological Science, 2*(3), 179–183.

Samenow, S.E. (1999). *Before it's too late: Why some kids get into trouble—and what parents can do about it.* NY: Times Books.

Sanford, R.N. (1937). The effects of abstinence from food upon imaginal processes: A further experiment. *Journal of Psychology, 3*, 145–159.

Sarason, I.G., & Sarason, B.R. (1987). *Abnormal psychology: The problem of maladaptive behavior* (5th ed.). Englewood Cliffs, NJ: Prentice Hall.

Sarter, M., Berntson, G.G., & Cacioppo, J.T. (1996). Brain imaging and cognitive neuroscience: Toward strong inference in attributing function to structure. *American Psychologist, 51*, 13–21.

Satow, K.K. (1975). Social approval and helping. *Journal of Experimental Social Psychology, 11*, 501–509.

Sattler, J.M. (1992). *Assessment of children* (3rd ed.). San Diego: Jerome M. Sattler.

Saudino, K.J. (1998). Moving beyond the heritability question: New directions in behavioral genetic studies of personality. *Current Directions in Psychological Science, 6*, 86–89.

Saxe, L. (1994). Detection of deception. Polygraph and integrity tests. *Current Directions in Psychological Science, 3*, 69–73.

Scarr, S. (1993). Ebbs and flows of evolution in psychology. *Contemporary Psychology, 38*, 458–462.

Scarr, S. (1995). Inheritance, intelligence and achievement. *Planning for Higher Education, 23*, 1–9.

Scarr, S., & Weinberg, R. (1983). The Minnesota Adoption Study: Genetic differences and malleability. *Child Development, 54*, 260–267.

Schaefer, H.H., & Martin, P.L. (1966). Behavioral therapy for "apathy" of hospitalized patients. *Psychological Reports, 19*, 1147–1158.

Schaie, K.W. (1984). Midlife influences upon intellectual functioning in old age. *International Journal of Behavioral Development, 7*, 463–478.

Schaie, K.W. (1994). The course of adult intellectual development. *American Psychologist, 4*, 304–313.

Schanberg, S.M., & Field, T.M. (1987). Sensory deprivation stress and supplemental stimulation in the rat pup and preterm human neonate. *Child Development, 58*, 1431–1447.

Schiffman, H.R. (1982). *Sensation and perception: An integrated approach* (2nd ed.). New York: Wiley.

Schlenker, B.R., & Weigold, M.F. (1992). Interpersonal processes involving impression regulation and management. *Annual Review of Psychology, 43*, 133–168.

Schlenker, B.R., Weigold, M.F., & Hallam, J.R. (1990). Self-serving attributions in social context: Effects of self-esteem and social pressure. *Journal of Personality and Social Psychology, 58*(5), 855–863.

Schoenthaler, S.J., Amos, S.P., Eysenck, H.J., Peritz, E., & Yudkin, J. (1991). Controlled trial of vitamin-mineral supplementation: Effects on intelligence and performance. *Personality and Individual Differences, 12*, 251–362.

Schroeder, S.R., Schroeder, C.S., & Landesman, S. (1987). Psychological services in educational setting to persons with mental retardation. *American Psychologist, 42*, 805–808.

Schulz, D.A. (1984). *Human sexuality* (2nd ed.). Englewood Cliffs, NJ: Prentice Hall.

Schwartz, B. (1989). *Psychology of learning and behavior* (3rd ed.). New York: Norton.

Schwartz, G.E. (1974, April). TM relaxes some people and makes them feel better. *Psychology Today*, pp. 39–44.

Schwartz, J., Stoessel, P., Baxter, L., Martin, K., Phelps, M., (1996). Systematic changes in cerebral glucose metabolic rate after successful behavior modification treatment of obsessive-compulsive disorder. *Arch. Gen. Psychiatry 53*, 109–113.

Schwartz, P. (1994, November 17). Some people with multiple roles are blessedly stressed. *New York Times*.

Schwarz, E.D., & Perry, B.D. (1994). The post-traumatic response in children and adolescents. *Psychiatric clinics of North America, 17,* 311–326.

Schweickert, R., & Boruff, B. (1986). Short-term memory capacity: Magic number or magic spell? *Journal of Experimental Psychology: Learning, Memory, & Cognition, 12*(3), 419–425.

Schweinhart, L.J., Barnes, H.V., & Weikart, D.P. (1993). *Significant benefits: The High/Scope Perry Study through age 27* (Monographs of the High/Scope Educational Research Foundation, No. 10). Ypsilanti, MI: High/Scope Press.

Scott, C., Klein, D.M., & Bryant, J. (1990). Consumer response to humor in advertising: A series of field studies using behavioral observation. *Journal of Consumer Research, 16,* 498–501.

Scott, K.G., & Carran, D.T. (1987). The epidemiology and prevention of mental retardation. *American Psychologist, 42,* 801–804.

Scupin, R. (1995). *Cultural anthropology* (2nd ed.). Englewood Cliffs, NJ: Prentice Hall.

Seamon, J.G., & Kenrick, D.T. (1992). *Psychology.* Englewood Cliffs, NJ: Prentice Hall.

Sears, D.O. (1994). On separating church and lab. *Psychological Science, 5,* 237–339.

Seddon, J.M., Willett, W.C., Speizer, F.E., & Hankinson, S.E. (1996). A prospective study of cigarette smoking and age-related macular degeneration in women. *Journal of the American Medical Association, 276,* 1141–1146.

Seeley, R.J., & Schwartz, J.C. (1997). The regulation of energy balance: Peripheral hormonal signals and hypothalamic neuropeptides. *Current Directions in Psychological Science, 6,* 39–44.

Seligman, J., Rogers, P., & Annin, P. (1994, May 2). The pressure to lose. *Newsweek,* pp. 60, 62.

Seligman, M.E.P. (1995). The effectiveness of psychotherapy: The *Consumer Reports* study. *American Psychologist, 50*(12), 965–974.

Seligman, M.E.P. (1996). Science as an ally of practice. *American Psychologist, 51*(10), 1072–1079.

Seligmann, J., et al. (1992, February 3). The new age of Aquarius. *Newsweek,* p. 65.

Sell, R.L., Wells, J.A., & Wypij, D. (1995). The prevalence of homosexual behavior and attraction in the United States, the United Kingdom and France: Results of national population-based samples. *Archives of Sexual Behavior, 24,* 235–238.

Selman, R. (1981). The child as friendship philosopher. In S.R. Asher & J.M. Gottman (eds.), *The development of children's friendships.* New York: Cambridge University Press.

Selye, H. (1956). *The stress of life.* New York: McGraw-Hill.

Selye, H. (1976). *The stress of life* (rev. ed.). New York: McGraw-Hill.

Semrud-Clikeman, M., & Hynd, G.W. (1990). Right hemispheric dysfunction in nonverbal learning disabilities: Social, academic, and adaptive functioning in adults and children. *Psychological Bulletin, 107,* 196–209.

Shalev, A., & Munitz, H. (1986). Conversion without hysteria: A case report and review of the literature. *British Journal of Psychiatry, 148,* 198–203.

Shapiro, D., & Shapiro, D. (1982). Meta-analysis of comparative therapy outcome studies: A replication and refinement. *Psychological Bulletin, 92,* 581–604.

Shapiro, K. (1991, July). Use morality as basis for animal treatment. *APA Monitor,* p. 5.

Shepard, R.N. (1978). Externalization of mental images and the act of creation. In B.S. Randhawa & W.E. Coffman (eds.), *Visual learning, thinking, and communicating.* New York: Academic Press.

Shiffrin, R.M., & Cook, J.R. (1978). Short-term forgetting of item and order information. *Journal of Verbal Reasoning and Verbal Behavior, 17,* 189–218.

Shimamura, A.P., Berry, J.M., Mangels, J.A., Rusting, C.L., & Jurica, P.J. (1995). Memory and cognitive abilities in university professors: Evidence for successful aging. *Psychological Science, 6*(5), 271–277.

Shneidman, E. (1989). The Indian summer of life: A preliminary study of septuagenarians. *American Psychologist, 44*(4), 684–694.

Shriver, M.D., & Piersel, W. (1994). The long-term effects of intrauterine drug exposure: Review of recent research and implications for early childhood special education. *Topics in Early Childhood Special Education, 14*(2), 161–183.

Siegel, L. (1993). Amazing new discovery: Piaget was wrong. *Canadian Psychology, 34,* 239–245.

Siegel, R.K. (1982). Cocaine smoking. *Journal of Psychoactive Drugs, 14,* 271–359.

Sigman, M. (1995). Nutrition and child development: More food for thought. *American Psychological Society, 4*(2), 52–56.

Simon, H.A. (1974). How big is a chunk? *Science, 165,* 482–488.

Simpson, H.B., Nee, J.C., & Endicott, J. (1997). First-episode major depression. Few sex differences in course. *Archives of General Psychiatry, 54*(7), 633–639.

Singer, J.L. (1975). *The inner world of daydreaming.* New York: Harper Colophon.

Singer, J.L., & Singer, D.G. (1983). Psychologists look at television: Cognitive, developmental, personality, and social policy implications. *American Psychologist, 38,* 826–834.

Singh, G.K., & Yu, S.M. (1995). Infant mortality in the United States: Trends, differentials, and projections, 1950 through 2010. *American Journal of Public Health, 85*(7), 957–964.

Singular, S. (1982, October). A memory for all seasonings. *Psychology Today,* pp. 54–63.

Sinha, P. (1996). I think I know that face . . . *Nature, 384,* 404.

Sinnott, J.D. (1994). Sex roles. In *Encyclopedia of human behavior* (Vol. 4, pp. 151–158). San Diego, CA: Academic Press.

61% of Americans call drug use "immoral," survey reports. (1990, February 27). *Ann Arbor News,* pp. A1, A9.

Skaalvik, E.M., & Rankin, R.J. (1994). Gender differences in mathematics and verbal achievement, self-perception and motivation. *British Journal of Educational Psychology, 64,* 419–428.

Skeels, H.M. (1938). Mental development of children in foster homes. *Journal of Consulting Psychology, 2,* 33–43.

Skeels, H.M. (1942). The study of the effects of differential stimulation on mentally retard children: A follow-up report. *American Journal of Mental Deficiencies, 46,* 340–350.

Skeels, H.M. (1966). Adult status of children with contrasting early life experiences. *Monographs of the Society for Research in Child Development, 31*(3), 1–65.

Skinner, B.F. (1953). Some contributions of an experimental analysis of behavior to psychology as a whole. *American Psychologist, 8*(2), 69–78.

Skinner, B.F. (1957). *Verbal behavior.* Englewood Cliffs, NJ: Prentice Hall.

Skinner, B.F. (1987). Whatever happened to psychology as the science of behavior? *American Psychologist, 42,* 780–786.

Skrzycki, C. (1995, November 24). Is it pure or just pure nonsense? *Washington Post,* pp. F1, F4.

Smith, C. T. (1985). Sleep states and learning: A review of the animal literature. *Neuroscience & Biobehavioral Reviews, 9,* 157–168.

Smith, C. T., & Kelly, G. (1988). Paradoxical sleep deprivation applied two days after end of training retards learning. *Physiology & Behavior, 43,* 213–216.

Smith, C. T., & Lapp, L. (1986). Prolonged increase in both PS and number of REMS following a shuttle avoidance task. *Physiology & Behavior, 36,* 1053–1057.

Smith, D. N. (1998). The psychocultural roots of genocide: Legitimacy and crisis in Rwanda. *American Psychologist, 53,* 743–753.

Smith, E. P., & Davidson, W. S., II. (1992). Mentoring and the development of African-American graduate students. *Journal of College Student Development, 33(6),* 531.

Smith, G. P., & Gibbs, J. (1976). Cholecystokinin and satiety: Theoretic and therapeutic implications. In D. Novin, W. Wyrwicka, & G. Bray (eds.), *Hunger: Basic mechanics and clinical implications.* New York: Raven Press.

Smith, K. H., & Rogers, M. (1994). Effectiveness of subliminal messages in television commercials: Two experiments. *Journal of Applied Psychology, 79,* 866–874.

Smith, M. L., & Glass, G. V. (1977). Meta-analysis of psychotherapy outcome studies. *American Psychologist, 32,* 752–760.

Smith, M. L., Glass, G. V., & Miller, T. I. (1980). *The benefits of psychotherapy.* Baltimore: Johns Hopkins University Press.

Smith, P. B., & Bond, M. H. (1994). *Social psychology across cultures: Analysis and perspectives.* Boston: Allyn & Bacon.

Smith, S. M., Glenberg, A. M., & Bjork, R. A. (1978). Environmental context and human memory. *Memory & Cognition, 6,* 342–355.

Smollar, J., & Youniss, J. (1989). Transformations in adolescents' perceptions of parents. *International Journal of Behavioral Development, 12,* 71–84.

Snodgrass, S. E. (1992). Further effects of role versus gender on interpersonal sensitivity. *Journal of Personality and Social Psychology, 62,* 154–158.

Snyder, H. N. (1996). The juvenile court and delinquency cases. *Future Child, 6(3),* 53–63.

Snyder, M. (1987). *Public appearances/private realities: The psychology of self-monitoring.* New York: Freeman.

Snyder, M., & Cunningham, M. R. (1975). To comply or not comply: Testing the self-perception explanation of the "foot-in-the-door" phenomenon. *Journal of Personality and Social Psychology, 31,* 64–67.

Snyder, M., & Swann, W. B., Jr. (1978). Behavioral confirmation in social interaction: From social perception to social reality. *Journal of Experimental Social Psychology, 14,* 148–162.

Snyder, M., & Tanke, E. D. (1976). Behavior and attitude: Some people are more consistent than others. *Journal of Personality, 44,* 501–517.

Snyder, S. H. (1977). Opiate receptors and internal opiates. *Scientific American, 236,* 44–56.

Soloman, J. (1996, May 20). Breaking the silence. *Newsweek,* pp. 20–24.

Solomon, D. A., Keitner, G. I., Miller, I. W., Shea, M. T., & Keller, M. B. (1995). Course of illness and maintenance treatments for patients with bipolar disorder. *Journal of Clinical Psychiatry, 56,* 5–13.

Sommers, C. H. (1994, April 3). The myth of schoolgirls' low self-esteem. *Wall Street Journal,* p. 4.

Sommers-Flanagan, R., Sommers-Flanagan, J., & Davis, B. (1993). What's happening on music television? A gender role content analysis. *Sex Roles, 28,* 745–754.

Sorensen, R. C. (1973). *Adolescent sexuality in contemporary America.* New York: World.

Spanos, N. P. (1986). Hypnotic behavior: A social-psychological interpretation of amnesia, analgesia, and "trance logic." *Behavioral and Brain Sciences, 9,* 449–502.

Spanos, N. P., & Chaves, J. F. (1989). *Hypnosis. The cognitive-behavioral perspective.* Buffalo, NY: Prometheus Books.

Sperling, G. (1960). The information available in brief visual presentations. *Psychological Monographs, 74,* 1–29.

Sperry, R. W. (1964). The great cerebral commissure. *Scientific American, 210,* 42–52.

Sperry, R. W. (1968). Hemisphere disconnection and unity in conscious awareness. *American Psychologist, 23,* 723–733.

Sperry, R. W. (1970). *Perception in the absence of neocortical commissures. In Perception and its disorders* (Res. Publ. A. R. N. M. D., Vol. 48). New York: The Association for Research in Nervous and Mental Disease.

Sperry, R. W. (1988). Psychology's mentalists paradigm and the religion/science tension. *American Psychologist, 43,* 607–613.

Sperry, R. W. (1995). The future of psychology. *American Psychologist, 5(7),* 505–506.

Spiegel, D. (1995). Essentials of psychotherapeutic intervention for cancer patients. *Support Care Cancer, 3(4),* 252–256.

Spiegel, D., & Moore, R. (1997). Imagery and hypnosis in the treatment of cancer patients. *Oncology, 11(8),* 1179–1189.

Spiegel, D., Bierre, P., & Rootenberg, J. (1989). Hypnotic alteration of somatosensory perception. *American Journal of Psychiatry, 146,* 749–754.

Spitzer, R. L., Skodal, A. E., Gibbon, M., & Williams, J. B. W. (1981). *DSM-III case book.* Washington, DC: American Psychiatric Association.

Spitzer, R. L., Skodal, A. E., Gibbon, M., & Williams, J. B. W. (1983). *Psychopathology: A casebook.* New York: McGraw-Hill.

Spoendlin, H. H., & Schrott, A. (1989). Analysis of the human auditory nerve. *Hearing Research, 43,* 25–38.

Squire, L. R., Knowlton, B., & Musen, G. (1993). The structure and organization of memory. *Annual Review of Psychology, 44,* 453–495.

Squire, S. (1983). *The slender balance: Causes and cures for bulimia, anorexia, and the weight loss/weight gain seesaw.* New York: Putnam.

Sridhar, K. S., Ruab, W. A., & Weatherby, N. L. (1994). Possible role of marijuana smoking as a carcinogen in development of lung cancer at a young age. *Journal of Psychoactive Drugs, 26,* 285–288.

Stack, S. (1994). Divorce. In *Encyclopedia of human behavior* (Vol. 2, pp. 153–63). San Diego, CA: Academic Press.

Stancliffe, R. J. (1997). Community residence size, staff presence and choice. *Mental Retardation, 35,* 1–9.

Steele, C. M., & Josephs, R. A. (1990). Alcohol myopia: Its prized and dangerous effects. *American Psychologist, 45,* 921–933.

Steinberg, K. K. et al. (1991). A meta-analysis of the effect of estrogen replacement therapy on the risk of breast cancer. *JAMA, Journal of the American Medical Association, 265(15),* 1985–1990.

Steiner, J. E. (1979). Facial expressions in response to taste and smell stimulation. In H. W. Reese & L. P. Lipsitt (eds.), *Advances in child development and behavior* (Vol. 13). New York: Academic Press.

Steinhauer, J. (1997, July 6). Living together without marriage or apologies. *New York Times,* p. A9.

Steinhausen, H.C., Willms, J., & Spohr, H. (1993). Long-term psychopathological and cognitive outcome of children with fetal alcohol syndrome. *Journal of the American Academy of Child and Adolescent Psychiatry, 32*, 990–994.

Stern, L. (1985). *The structures and strategies of human memory.* Homewood, IL: Dorsey Press.

Stern, R.M., & Koch, K.L. (1996). Motion sickness and differential susceptibility. *Current Directions in Psychological Science, 5*, 115–120.

Stern, R.M., Breen, J.P., Watanabe, T., & Perry, B.S. (1981). Effect of feedback of physiological information on responses to innocent associations and guilty knowledge. *Journal of Applied Psychology, 66*, 677–681.

Sternberg, R.J. (1982, April). Who's intelligent? *Psychology Today,* pp. 30–39.

Sternberg, R.J. (1985). *Beyond IQ: A triarchic theory of human intelligence.* New York: Cambridge University Press.

Sternberg, R.J. (1986). *Intelligence applied.* Orlando, FL: Harcourt Brace Jovanovich.

Sternberg, R.J., & Kaufman, J.C. (1998). Human abilities. *Annual Review of Psychology, 49*, 479–502.

Sternberg, R.J., & Lubart, T.I. (1996). Investing in creativity. *American Psychologist, 51*(7), 677–688.

Sternberg, R.J., & Wagner, R.K. (1993). The g-ocentric view of intelligence and job performance is wrong. *Current Directions in Psychological Science, 2*, 1–5.

Stevens, G., & Gardner, S. (1982). *Women of psychology: Expansion and refinement* (Vol. 1). Cambridge, MA: Schenkman.

Stevenson, H.W. (1992). Learning from Asian schools. *Scientific American,* 70–76.

Stevenson, H.W. (1993). Why Asian students still outdistance Americans. *Educational Leadership,* 63–65.

Stevenson, H.W., Chen, C., & Lee, S.-Y. (1993). Mathematics achievement of Chinese, Japanese, and American children: Ten years later. *Science, 259*, 53–58.

Stevenson, H.W., Lee, S.-Y., & Stigler, J.W. (1986). Mathematics achievment of Chinese, Japanese, and American children. *Science, 231*, 693–697.

Stewart, R.H. (1965). Effect of continuous responding on the order effect in personality impression formation. *Journal of Personality and Social Psychology, 1*, 161–165.

Stiles, W.B., Shapiro, D.A., & Elliott, R. (1986). Are all psychotherapies equivalent? *American Psychologist, 41*, 165–180. (From Myers, 1992.)

Stock, M.B., & Smythe, P.M. (1963). Does undernutrition during infancy inhibit brain growth and subsequent intellectual development? *Archives of Disorders in Childhood, 38*, 546–552.

Stone, R.A., & Deleo, J. (1976). Psychotherapeutic control of hypertension. *New England Journal of Medicine, 294*, 80–84.

Stone, W.F., Lederer, G., & Christie, R. (1993). Introduction: Strength and weakness. In W.F. Stone, G. Lederer, & R. Christie (eds.), *The authoritarian personality today: Strength and weakness.* New York: Springer-Verlag.

Stoner, J.A.F. (1961). *A comparison of individual and group decisions involving risk.* Unpublished master's thesis, School of Industrial Management, MIT.

Strickland, B.R. (1989). Internal-external control expectancies. From contingency to creativity. *American Psychologist, 44*, 1–12.

Study links alcohol use to earlier death. (1990, October 2). *Ann Arbor News,* p. C1.

Subotnik, R.F., & Arnold, K.D. (1994). *Beyond Terman: Contemporary longitudinal studies of giftedness and talent.* Norwood, NJ: Ablex.

Sue, S., Zane, N., & Young, K. (1994). Research on psychotherapy with culturally diverse populations. In A.E. Bergin & S.L. Garfield (eds.), *Handbook of psychotherapy and behavior change* (4th ed., pp. 783–820). New York: Wiley.

Suedfeld, P.E. (1975). The benefits of boredom: Sensory deprivation reconsidered. *American Scientist, 63*, 60–69.

Suls, J., & Fletcher, B. (1983). Social comparison in the social and physical sciences: An archival study. *Journal of Personality and Social Psychology, 44*, 575–580.

Swaab, D.F., & Hoffman, M.A. (1995). Sexual differentiation of the human hypothalamus in relation to gender and sexual orientation. *Trends in Neuroscience, 18*, 264–270.

Symonds, A. (1979). The wife as a professional. *American Journal of Psychoanalysis, 39*(1), 55–63.

Tagano, D.W., Moran, D.J., III, & Sawyers, J.K. (1991). *Creativity in early childhood classrooms.* Washington, DC: National Education Association.

Takaki, A., Nagai, K., Takaki, S., & Yanaihara, N. (1990). Satiety function of neurons containing CCKK-like substance in the dorsal parabrachial nucleus. *Physiology & Behavior, 48*, 865–871.

Takami, S., Getchell, M.L., Chen, Y., Monti-Bloch, L., & Berliner, D.L. (1993). Vomeronasal epithelial cells of the adult human express neuron-specific molecules. *Neuro Report, 4*, 374–378.

Tan, D.T.Y., & Singh, R. (1995). Attitudes and attraction: A developmental study of the similarity-attraction and dissimilarity-repulsion hypotheses. *Personality and Social Psychology Bulletin, 21*(9), 975–986.

Tanner, J.M. (1973). Growing up. *Scientific American, 235*, 34–43.

Tanner, J.M. (1978). *Foetus into man: Physical growth from conception to maturity.* Cambridge, MA: Harvard University Press.

Tanofsky, M.B., Wilfley, D.E., Spurrell, E.B., Welch, R., & Brownell, K.D. (1997). Comparison of men and women with binge eating disorder. *International Journal of Eating Disorders, 21*(1), 49–54.

Taylor, S.E., Peplau, L.A., & Sears, D.O. (1994). *Social psychology.* Englewood Cliffs, NJ: Prentice Hall.

Telch, C.F., Agras, W.S., Rossiter, E.M., Wilfley, D., & Kenardy, J. (1990). Group cognitive-behavioral treatment for the non-purging bulimic: An initial evaluation. *Journal of Consulting and Clinical Psychology, 58*, 629–635.

Terman, L.M. (1925). *Mental and physical traits of a thousand gifted children: Genetic studies of genius* (Vol. 1). Stanford, CA: Stanford University Press.

Thelen, E. (1994). Three-month-old infants can learn task-specific patterns of interlimb coordination. *American Psychological Society, 5*(5), 280–288.

Thelen, E. (1995). Motor development: A new synthesis. *American Psychologist, 50*(2), 79–95.

Thomas, A., & Chess, S. (1977). *Temperament and development.* New York: Brunner/Mazel.

Thorndike, E.L. (1898). Animal intelligence. *Psychological Review Monograph, 2*(4, Whole No. 8).

Thurstone, L.L. (1938). Primary mental abilities. *Psychometric Monographs,* 1.

Tolman, E.C., & Honzik, C.H. (1930). Introduction and removal of reward, and maze performance in rates. University of California Publications in *Psychology, 4*, 257–275.

Tomarken, A.J., Davidson, R.J., & Henriques, J.B. (1990). Resting frontal brain asymmetry predicts affective responses to films. *Journal of Personality and Social Psychology, 59,* 791–801.

Torgersen, S. (1983). Genetic factors in anxiety disorders. *Archives of General Psychiatry, 40,* 1085–1089.

Torrance, E.P. (1954). Leadership training to improve air-crew group performance. *USAF ATC Instructor's Journal, 5,* 25–35.

Tower, R.B., Singer, D.G., Singer, L.J., & Biggs, A. (1979). Differential effects of television programming on preschoolers' cognition, imagination, and social play. *American Journal of Orthopsychiatry, 49,* 265–281.

Tranel, D. (1994). Memory, neural substrates. *Encyclopedia of human behavior* (Vol. 3, pp. 149–163). San Diego, CA: Academic Press.

Treaster, J.B. (1994, February 1). Survey finds marijuana use is up in high schools. *New York Times,* p. A1.

Treisman, A.M. (1960). Contextual cues in selective listening. *Quarterly Journal of Experimental Psychology, 12,* 242–248.

Treisman, A.M. (1964). Verbal cues, language and meaning in selective attention. *American Journal of Psychology, 77,* 206–219.

Trends in Education. (1995). *APA Education Directorate News,* Vol. II, (1), pp. 2–3.

Triandis, H.C. (1994). *Culture and social behavior.* New York: McGraw-Hill.

Trice, A.D. (1986). Ethical variables? *American Psychologist, 41,* 482–483.

Trotter, R.J. (1983, August). Baby face. *Psychology Today,* pp. 12–20.

Tulving, E. (1972). Episodic and semantic memory. In E. Tulving & W. Donaldson (eds.), *Organization and memory.* New York: Academic Press.

Tulving, E. (1985). How many memory systems are there? *American Psychologist, 40,* 385–398.

Tulving, E., & Schacter, D.L. (1990). Priming and human memory systems. *Science, 247,* 301–306.

Tulving, E., Kapur, S., Markowitsch, H.J., Craik, F.I.M., Habib, R., & Houle, S. (1994). Neuroanatomical correlates of retrieval in episodic memory: Auditory sentence recognition. *Proceedings of the National Academy of Sciences of the U.S.A., 91,* 2012–2015.

Tupes, E.C., & Christal, R.W. (1961). *Recurrent personality factors based on trait ratings.* USAF ASD Technical Report, No. 61-97.

Turk, D.C., & Salovey, P. (1985). Cognitive structures, cognitive processes, and cognitive behavior modification: II. Judgments and inferences of the clinician. *Cognitive Therapy and Research, 9,* 19–34.

Turkheimer, E. (1991). Individual and group differences in adoption studies of IQ. *Psychological Bulletin, 110,* 392–405.

Turnbull, C.M. (1961). Observations. *American Journal of Psychology, 1,* 304–308.

Turnbull, S., Ward, A., Treasure, J., Jick, H., & Derby, L. (1996). The demand for eating disorder care. An epidemiological study using the general practice research database. *British Journal of Psychiatry, 169*(6), 705–712.

U.S. Bureau of the Census. (1990). *Statistical abstract of the United States* (110th ed.). Washington, DC: U.S. Government Printing Office.

U.S. Bureau of the Census (1998). Current Population Reports, P60–200, Money income in the United States: 1997 (with separate data on valuation of noncash benefits). Washington, DC: U.S. Government Printing Office.

U.S. Merit Systems Protection Board. (1993). *Sexual harassment of federal workers: Is it a problem?* Washington, DC: U.S. Government Printing Office.

Uchino, B.N., Cacioppo, J.T., & Kiecolt-Glaser, J.K. (1996). The relationship between social support and physiological processes: A review with emphasis on underlying mechanisms and implications for health. *Psychological Bulletin, 119*(3), 488–531.

Uhl, G., Blum, K., Nobel, E.P., & Smith, S. (1993). Substance abuse vulnerability and D2 dopamine receptor gene and severe alcoholism. *Trends in Neuroscience, 16,* 83–88.

Underwood, G. (1994). Subliminal perception on TV. *Nature, 370,* 103.

Underwood, G. (1996). *Implicit cognition.* New York: Oxford University.

Unger, R., & Crawford, M. (1992). *Women and gender: A feminist psychology.* New York: McGraw-Hill.

Usher, J.A., & Neisser, U. (1993). Childhood amnesia and the beginnings of memory for four early life events. *Journal of Experimental Psychology: General, 122,* 155–165.

Vaillant, G.E. (1977). *Adaptation to life.* Boston: Little, Brown.

Vaisse, C., Halaas, J.L., Horvath, C.M., Darnell, J.E., Stoffell, M., & Friedman, J.M. (1996). Leptin activation of Stat3 in the hypothalamus of wild-type and ob/ob mice but not db/db mice. *Nature Genetics 14*(1), 95–97.

van der Pompe, G., Duivenvoorden, H.J., Antoni, M.H., Visser, A., & Heijnen, C.J. (1997). Effectiveness of a short-term group psychotherapy program on endocrine and immune function in breast cancer patients: An exploratory study. *Journal of Psychosomatic Research, 42*(5), 453–466.

Van Natta, P., Malin, H., Bertolucci, D., & Kaelber, C. (1985). The influence of alcohol abuse as a hidden contributor to mortality. *Alcohol, 2,* 535–539.

Van Yperen, N.W., & Buunk, B.P. (1990). A longitudinal study of equity and satisfaction in intimate relationships. *European Journal of Social Psychology, 54,* 287–309.

Vaughn, M. (1993, July 22). Divorce revisited. *Ann Arbor News,* p. C4.

Vgontzas, A.N., & Kales, A. (1999). Sleep and its disorders. *Annual Review of medicine, 50,* 387–400.

Vignolo, L.A., Boccardi, E., & Caverni, L. (1986). Unexpected CT-scan findings in global aphasia. *Cortex, 22,* 55–69.

Virkkunen, M. (1983). Insulin secretion during the glucose tolerance test in antisocial personality. *British Journal of Psychiatry, 142,* 598–604.

Vogel-Sprott, M. (1967). Alcohol effects on human behavior under reward and punishment. *Psychopharmacologia, 11,* 337–344.

von Hippel, W., Hawkins, C., & Narayan, S. (1994). Personality and perceptual expertise: Individual differences in perceptual identification. *Psychological Science, 5,* 401–406.

von Hofsten, C., & Fazel-Zandy, S. (1984). Development of visually guided hand orientation in reaching. *Journal of Experimental Child Psychology, 38,* 208–219.

Voydanoff, P., & Donnelly, B.W. (1999). Risk and protective factors for psychological adjustment and grades among adolescents. *Journal of Family Issues, 20,* 328–349.

Voyer, D., Voyer, S., & Bryden, M.P. (1995). Magnitude of sex differences in spatial abilities: A meta-analysis and consideration of critical variables. *Psychological Bulletin, 117*(2), 250–270.

Vygotsky, L.S. (1978). *Mind in society: The development of higher mental processes.* Cambridge, MA: Harvard University Press. (Original works published 1930, 1933, and 1935.)

Wachs, T.D., & Smitherman, C.H. (1985). Infant temperament and subject loss in a habituation procedure. *Child Development*, 56, 861–867.

Wadden, T.S., Vogt, R.A., Anderson, R.E., Bartlett, S.F., Foster, G.D., Kuebnel, R.H., Wilk, F., Weinstock, R., Buckenmeyer, P., Berkowitz, R.I., & Steen, S.N. (1997). Exercise in the treatment of obesity: Effects of four interventions on body composition, resting energy expenditure, appetite and mood. *Journal of Consulting and Clinical Psychology*, 65, 269–277.

Waid, W.M., & Orne, M.T. (1981). Cognitive, social, and personality processes in the physiological detection of deception. In L. Berkowitz (ed.), *Advances in experimental social psychology* (Vol. 14). New York: Academic Press.

Waid, W.M., Orne, E.C., & Orne, M.T. (1981). Selective memory for social information, alertness, and physiological arousal in the detection of deception. *Journal of Applied Psychology*, 66, 224–232.

Waldman, H.B. (1996). Yes, overall crime statistics are down, but juveniles are committing more criminal offenses. *ASDC J. Dent Child*, 63(6), 438–442.

Walk, R.D., & Gibson, E.J. (1961). A comparative and analytical study of visual depth perception. *Psychological Monographs*, No. 75.

Wall, R.P., & Melzack, R. (eds.). (1989). *Textbook of pain* (2nd ed.). Edinburgh: Churchill Livingston.

Walster, E., Walster, G.W., & Berscheid, E. (1978). *Equity: Theory and research*. Boston: Allyn & Bacon.

Walters, E.E., & Kendler, K.S. (1995). Anorexia nervosa and anorexic-like syndromes in a population-based female twin sample. *American Journal of Psychiatry*, 152, 64–67.

Wampold, B.E., Mondin, G.W., Moody, M., Stich, F., Benson, K., & Ahn, H. (1997). A meta-analysis of outcome studies comparing bona fide psychotherapies: Empirically, "all must have prizes." *Psychological Bulletin*, 122, 203–215.

Warr, P., & Perry, G. (1982). Paid employment and women's psychological well-being. *Psychological Bulletin*, 91, 498–516.

Warrington, E.K., & Weiskrantz, L. (1970). Amnesic syndrome: Consolidation or retrieval? *Nature*, 228(272), 628–630.

Washburn, M.F. (1916). *Movement and mental imagery: Outlines of a motor theory of the complexer mental processes*. Boston: Houghton Mifflin.

Watkins, C.E., Campbell, V.L., Nieberding, R., & Hallmark, R. (1995). Contemporary practice of psychological assessment by clinical psychologists. *Professional Psychological Research & Practice*, 26, 54–60.

Watson, J.B. (1924). *Behaviorism*. Chicago: University of Chicago Press.

Watson, J.B., & Rayner, R. (1920). Conditioned emotional reactions. *Journal of Experimental Psychology*, 3, 1–14.

Waugh, N., & Norman, D.A. (1960). Primary memory. *Psychological Review*, 72, 89–104.

Wauquier, A., McGrady, A., Aloe, L., Klausner, T., & Collins, B. (1995). Changes in cerebral blood flow velocity associated with biofeedback-assisted relaxation treatment of migraine headaches are specific for the middle cerebral artery. *Headache*, 35(6), 358–362.

Weaver, M.T., & McGrady, A. (1995). A provisional model to predict blood pressure response to biofeedback-assisted relaxation. *Biofeedback and Self-Regulation*, 20(3), 229–240.

Webb, W.B., & Levy, C.M. (1984). Effects of spaced and repeated total sleep deprivation. *Ergonomics*, 27, 45–58.

Wechsler, H., Davenport, A., Dowdall, G., Moeykens, B., & Castillo, S. (1994). Health and behavioral consequences of binge drinking in college. *Journal of the American Medical Association*, 272, 1672–1677.

Wechsler, H., Fulop, M., Padilla, A., Lee, H., & Patrick, K. (1997). Binge drinking among college students: A comparison of California with other states. *Journal of American College Health*, 45, 265–267.

Wedeking, C., Seebeck, T., Bettens, F., & Paepke, A.J. (1995). MHC-dependent mate preferences in humans. *Proceedings of the Royal Society of London*, B, 260, 245–249.

Wehr, T.A., Giesen, H.A., Moul, D.E., Turner, E.H., & Schwartz, P.J. (1995). Suppression of men's responses to seasonal changes in day length by modern artificial lighting. *American Journal of Physiology*, 269, 173–178.

Weinberger, D.R. (1997). The biological basis of schizophrenia: New directions. *Journal of Clinical Psychiatry*, 58(Suppl. 10), 22–27.

Weinstein, R.S., Madison, W., & Kuklinski, M. (1995). Raising expectations in schooling: Obstacles and opportunities for change. *American Educational Research Journal*, 32, 121–160.

Weinstein, R.S., Soule, C.R., Collins, F., Cone, J., Melhorn, M., & Simantocci, K. (1991). Expectations and high school change: Teacher-researcher collaboration to prevent school failure. *American Journal of Community Psychology*, 19, 333–402.

Weinstein, S. (1968). Intensive and extensive aspects of tactile sensitivity as a function of body part, sex, and laterality. In D.R. Kenshalo (ed.), *The skin senses*. Springfield, IL: Charles C. Thomas.

Weintraub, M.I. (1990). High-impact aerobic exercises and vertigo—a possible cause of vestibulopathy. *New England Journal of Medicine*, 323, 1633.

Weiss, B.A., & Reynolds, S. (1992). Generation of neurons and astrocytes from isolated cells of the adult mammalian nervous system. *Science*, 255, 1707–1710.

Weissman, M.M. (1993). The epidemiology of personality disorders: A 1990 update. *Journal of Personality Disorders* (Suppl.), 44–62.

Weissman, M.M., & Olfson, M. (1995). Depression in women: Implications for health care research. *Science*, 269, 799–801.

Wells, G.L. (1993). What do we know about eyewitness identification? *American Psychologist*, 48, 553–571.

Werker, F.J., & Desjardins, R.N. (1995). Listening to speech in the 1st year of life: Experiential influences on phoneme perception. *American Psychological Society*, 4(3), 76–81.

Werker, J.F. (1989). Becoming a native listener. *American Scientist*, 77, 54–59.

Werner, E.E. (1995). Resilience in development. *American Psychological Society*, 4(3), 81–84.

Wheeler, C.G. (1993). 30 years beyond "I have a dream." *Gallup Poll Monthly*, 337, 2–10.

Whisman, M.A., & Kwon, P. (1993). Life stress and dysphoria: The role of self-esteem and hopelessness. *Journal of Personality and Social Psychology*, 65, 1054–1060.

Whitam, F.L., Diamond, M., & Martin, J. (1993). Homosexual orientation in twins: A report on 61 pairs and three triplet sets. *Archives of Sexual Behavior*, 22, 187–206.

Whorf, B.L. (1956). *Language, thought, and reality*. New York: MIT Press–Wiley.

Whyte, W.H. (1956). *The organizational man*. New York: Simon & Schuster.

Wielkiewicz, R.M., & Calvert, C.R.X. (1989). *Training and habilitating developmentally disabled people: An introduction*. Newbury Park, CA: Sage.

Wiens, A.N., & Menustik, C.E. (1983). Treatment outcome and patient characteristics in an aversion therapy program for alcoholism. *American Psychologist, 38,* 1089–1096.

Wierzbicki, M. (1993). *Issues in clinical psychology: Subjective versus objective approaches.* Boston: Allyn & Bacon.

Wiggins, J.S. (ed.). (1996). *The five-factor model of personality: Theoretical perspectives.* New York: Guilford Press.

Wilder, B.J., & Bruni, J. (1981). *Seizure disorders: A pharmacological approach to treatment.* New York: Raven Press.

Will, G. (1993, April 6). How do we turn children off to the violence caused by TV? Wise up parents. *Philadelphia Inquirer,* p. A1.

Williams, J.E., & Best, D.L. (1990). *Measuring sex stereotypes: A multinational study.* Newbury Park, CA: Sage.

Williams, J.E., & Best, D.L. (1990). *Sex and psyche: Gender and self viewed cross-culturally.* Newbury Park, CA: Sage.

Williams, J.H. (1987). *Psychology of women: Behavior in a biosocial context* (3rd ed.). New York: Norton.

Williams, L. (1989, November 22). Psychotherapy gaining favor among blacks. *New York Times.*

Williams, L.M. (1994). Recall of childhood trauma: A prospective study of women's memories of child sexual abuse. *Journal of Consulting and Clinical Psychology, 62*(6), 1167–1176.

Williams, R.B., Barefoot, J.C., Califf, R.M., Haney, T.L., Saunders, W.B., Pryor, D.B., Hatky, M.A., Siegler, I.C., & Mark, D.B. (1992). Prognostic importance of social and economic resources among medically treated patients with angiographically documented coronary artery disease. *Journal of the American Medical Association, 267,* 520–524.

Williams, T.P., & Sogon, S. (1984). Group composition and conforming behavior in Japanese students. *Japanese Psychological Research, 26,* 231–234.

Williams, W.M. (1999). Peering into the nature-nurture debate. *Contemporary Psychology, 44,* 267–269.

Willis, S.L. (1985). Towards an educational psychology of the elder adult learner: Intellectual and cognitive bases. In J.E. Birren & K.W. Schaie (eds.), *Handbook of the psychology of aging* (2nd ed.). New York: Van Nostrand.

Willis, S.L., & Schaie, K.W. (1986). Training the elderly on the ability factors of spatial orientation and inductive reasoning. *Psychology and Aging, 1,* 239–247.

Wilson, G.D. (1987). An ethological approach to sexual deviation. In G.D. Wilson (ed.), *Variant sexuality: Research and theory* (pp. 84–115). London: Croom Helm.

Wilson, W., & Hunter, R. (1983). Movie-inspired violence. *Psychological Reports, 53,* 435–441.

Winerip, M. (1998, January 4). Binge nights: The emergency on campus. *Education Life (New York Times* supplement), Section 4A, pp. 28–31, 42.

Wing, H. (1969). *Conceptual learning and generalization.* Baltimore, MD: Johns Hopkins University.

Winn, P. (1995). The lateral hypothalamus and motivated behavior: An old syndrome reassessed and a new perspective gained. *Current Directions in Psychological Science, 4,* 182–187.

Winson, J. (1990). The meaning of dreams. *Scientific American, 263*(5), 94–96.

Winter, D.G. (1973). *The power motive.* New York: Free Press.

Witkin, A.H., et al. (1962). *Psychological differentiation.* New York: Wiley.

Wolberg, L.R. (1977). *The technique of psychotherapy* (3rd ed.). New York: Grune & Stratton.

Wolf, S.S., & Weinberger, D.R. (1996). Schizophrenia: A new frontier in developmental neurobiology. *Israel Journal of Medical Science, 32*(1), 51–55.

Wolpe, J. (1973). *The practice of behavior therapy* (2nd ed.). New York: Pergamon.

Wolpe, J. (1982). *The practice of behavior therapy* (3rd ed.). New York: Pergamon.

Wolpe, P.R. (1990). The holistic heresy: Strategies of ideological challenge in the medical profession. *Social Science & Medicine, 31*(8), 913–923.

Wood, J.M., & Bootzin, R.R. (1990). The prevalence of nightmares and their independence from anxiety. *Journal of Abnormal Psychology, 99,* 64–68.

Wood, N.L., & Cowan, N. (1995). The cocktail party phenomenon revisited: Attention and memory in the classic selective listening procedure of Cherry (1953). *Journal of Experimental Psychology: General, 124,* 243–262.

Wood, P.B. (1962). *Dreaming and social isolation.* Unpublished doctoral dissertation, University of South Carolina, Columbia.

Wood, W., Wong, F.Y., & Chachere, J.G. (1991). Effects of media violence on viewers' aggression in unconstrained social interaction. *Psychological Bulletin, 109,* 371–383.

Woods, S.C., Seeley, R.J., Porte, D., Jr., & Schwartz, M.W. (1998). Signals that regulate food intake and energy homeostasis. *Science, 280,* 1378–1383.

Woodward, K.L., & Springen, K. (1992, August 22). Better than a gold watch. *Newsweek,* p. 71.

Worchel, S., Cooper, J., & Goethals, G.R. (1991). *Understanding social psychology* (5th ed.). Pacific Grove, CA: Brooks/Cole.

Wright, J., Johns, R., Watt, I., Melville, A., & Sheldon, T. (1997). Health effects of obstructive sleep apnea and the effectiveness of continuous positive airways pressure: A systematic review of the research evidence. *British Medical journal, 314,* 851–853.

Wright, R. (1994). *The moral animal: The new science of evolutionary psychology.* New York: Pantheon.

Wundt, W. (1874). *Principles of physiological psychology.* London: Macmillan.

Wyatt, W.J. (1993, December). Identical twins, emergenesis, and environments. *American Psychologist,* pp. 1294–1295.

Wynn, K. (1995). Infants possess a system of numerical knowledge. *American Psychological Society, 4*(6), 172–177.

Wyrwicka, W. (1988). Imitative behavior: A theoretical view. *Pavlovian Journal of Biological Science, 23,* 125–131.

Yalom, I.D. (1995). *The theory and practice of group psychotherapy* (4th ed.). New York: Basic Books.

Yamamoto, K., & Chimbidis, M.E. (1966). Achievement, intelligence, and creative thinking in fifth grade children: A correlational study. *Merrill-Palmer Quarterly, 12,* 233–241.

Yanovski, S.Z. (1993). Binge eating disorder. Current knowledge and future directions. *Obesity Research, 1,* 306–324.

Yoder, J.D., & Kahn, A.S. (1993). Working toward an inclusive psychology of women. *American Psychologist, 48,* 846–850.

York, J.L., & Welte, J.W. (1994). Gender comparisons of alcohol consumption in alcoholic and nonalcoholic populations. *Journal of Studies on Alcohol, 55,* 743–750.

Zajonc, R.B. (1980). Feeling and thinking: Preferences need no inferences. *American Psychologist, 35,* 151–175.

Zajonc, R.B., Murphy, S.T., & Inglehart, M. (1989). Feeling and facial efference: Implications of the vascular theory of emotion. *Psychological Review, 96.*

Zametkin, A.J., Nordahl, T.W., Gross, M., & King, A.C. et al. (1990). Cerebral glucose metabolism in adults with hyperactivity of childhood onset. *New England Journal of Medicine, 323,* 1361–1366.

Zaragoza, M.S., & Mitchell, K.J. (1996). Repeated exposure to suggestion and the creation of false memories. *Psychological Science,* 7(5), 294–300.

Zaragoza, M.S., Lane, S.M., Ackil, J.K., & Chambers, K.L. (1997). Confusing real and suggested memories: Source monitoring and eyewitness suggestibility. In N.L. Stein, P.A. Ornstein, B. Tversky, & C. Brainerd (eds.), *Memory for everyday and emotional events.* Mahwah, NJ: Erlbaum.

Zigler, E., & Muenchow, S. (1992). *Head Start: The inside story of America's most successful educational experiment.* New York: Basic Books.

Zigler, E., & Styfco, S.J. (1994). Head Start: Criticisms in a constructive context. *American Psychologist, 49,* 127–132.

Zigler, E., & Styfco, S.J. (eds.). (1993). *Head Start and beyond.* New Haven, CT: Yale University Press.

Zucker, R.A., & Gomberg, E.S.L. (1990). Etiology of alcoholism reconsidered: The case for a biopsychosocial process. *American Psychologist, 41,* 783–793.

Zuckerman, M. (1995). Good and bad humors: Biochemical basis of personality and its disorders. *Psychological Science, 6,* 325–332.

Zuckerman, M., Miyake, K., & Elkin, C.S. (1995). Effects of attractiveness and maturity of face and voice on interpersonal impression. *Journal of Research in Personality, 29,* 253–272.

Zuger, A. (1997, August 19). Removal of half the brain aids young epileptics. *New York Times,* p. B12.

Zwislocki, J.J. (1981). Sound analysis in the ear: A history of discoveries. *American Scientist, 245,* 184–192.

PHOTO CREDITS

CHAPTER 1
Opener: Richard T. Nowitz/Photo Researchers, Inc.; p. 6 Zigy Kaluzny/Tony Stone Images; p 7 Mark Richards/PhotoEdit 9 Frank Siteman/Stock Boston; p. 12 (T) Photo Researchers, Inc., (B) Keystone Press Agency; p 13 (T) New York Public Library, (B) Osterreichische Nationalbibliothek, Wien; p. 14 Archive Photos; p. 15 (T) G. Paul Bishop, Photographer, (B) Yvonne Hemsey/Liaison Agency, Inc.; p. 21 (T) Philippe Brylak/Liaison Agency, Inc., (B) Cary Wolinsky/Stock Boston; p. 22 (left to right) Travelpix/FPG International LLC, Robert Caputo/Stock Boston, Arvind Garg/Liaison Agency, Inc., Index Stock Imagery Inc.; p. 23 Dinodia/Omni-Photo Communications, Inc.; p. 24 Jerry Bauer/Carol Gilligan; p. 27 (T) Breese/Liaison Agency, Inc.; (B) Jeff Greenberg/Index Stock Imagery, Inc.; p. 29 R. Lord/The Image Works; p. 37 From the film OBEDIENCE copyright 1965 by Stanley Milgram and distributed by Penn State Media Sales. Permission granted by Alexandra Milgram.; p. 40 Wade Bruton - UNC Charlotte.

CHAPTER 2
Opener: Roger Tully/Tony Stone Images; p. 51 E.R. Lewis, Y.Y. Zeevi, T.E. Everhart/E. R. Lewis; p. 52 David Young-Wolff/PhotoEdit; p. 56 Brad Markel/Liaison Agency, Inc.; p. 60 (T) Dan McCoy/Rainbow (B) Warren Museum, Harvard Medical School; p. 62 Mazziotta Et/Photo Researchers, Inc.; p. 66 (T) Richard T. Nowitz/Photo Researchers, Inc., (B) Howard Sochurek/Woodfin Camp & Associates; p. 67 Bruce Herman/Tony Stone Images; p. 71 Keith Brofsky/PhotoDisc, Inc.; p. 72 CNRI/Science Photo Library/Photo Researchers, Inc.; p. 73 Jean Claude Revy/Phototake NYC; p. 75 (T) PhotoDisc, Inc., (B) Hiller/Monkmeyer Press; p. 76 (T) Mike Mazzachi/Stock Boston, (B) PhotoDisc, Inc.

CHAPTER 3
Opener: John Berry/The Image Works; p. 88 Bob Daemmrich/The Image Works; p. 91 Don Wong/Science Source/Photo Researchers, Inc; p. 92 E.R. Lewis, Y.Y. Zeevi, F.S. Werblin. Brain Research 15 (1969): 559-562. Scanning Electron microscopy of vertebrate receptors; p. 94 Dr. Michael E. Phelps; p. 56 Pearson Education/PH College; p. 97 Fritz Goro/Time Life Syndication; p. 98 Hart-Davis/Science Photo Library/Photo Researchers, Inc.; p. 102 Mark Kelley/Tony Stone Images; p. 103 Dorothy Littell Greco/The Image Works; p. 105 Robbie Jack/Corbis p. 107 Sergio Dorantes/Corbis; p. 108 Steve Raymer/Corbis; p. 109 Ronald C. James; p. 110 (T) M.C. Escher's "Circle Limit IV" © 1998 Cordon Art B.V. - Baarn - Holland. All rights reserved, (L) Kaiser Porcelain Ltd.; p. 112 (a) Dr. Peter Thompson (1980) Perception 9, 383-384, (b) Pawan Sinha and Tomaso Poggio, Photo (c) Dirck

Halstead/Gamma Liaison; p. 119 Fred Charles/Tony Stone Images.

CHAPTER 4
Opener: Francois Perri/Liaison Agency, Inc.; p. 129 Haviv/SABA Press Photos, Inc.; p. 131 Will & Deni McIntyre/Photo Researchers, Inc.; p. 137 Marc Chagall (1887–1985), Russian, "Above the City". Tretyakov Gallery, Moscow, Russia. © 1999 Artists Rights Society (ARS), New York/ADAGP, Paris.; p. 144 Michael Newman/PhotoEdit; p. 149 Andrea Krause/Photo Researchers, Inc.; p. 153 Pierre Choiniere/Tony Stone Images; p. 155 The Granger Collection; p. 156 Will Hart/Will Hart; p. 157 Kal Muller/Woodfin Camp & Associates.

CHAPTER 5
Opener: Walter Hodges/Corbis; p. 167 Tom Bean/Tony Stone Images; p. 171 (T) Walter Dawn/Photo Researchers, Inc.; p. 173 Dubrowsky/Archive Photos, Inc.; p. 173 LeDuc/Monkmeyer Press; p. 174 David Turnley/Corbis; p. 181 Bob Daemmrich/Stock Boston; p. 182 Michael Newman/PhotoEdit; p. 183 Corbis Digital Stock; p. 187 Hank Morgan/Photo Researchers, Inc.; p. 188 Library of Congress; p. 189 Lawrence Migdale/Photo Researchers, Inc.; p. 190 Albert Bandura.

CHAPTER 6
Opener: Janeart/The Image Bank; p. 201 Bob Daemmrich/The Image Works; p. 202 Grant LeDuc/Monkmeyer Press; p. 204 A. Brucelle/Corbis Sygma Photo News; p. 209 Jeff Isaac/Photo Researchers, Inc.; p. 210 PhotoDisc, Inc.; p. 211 Michele Burgess/The Stock Market; p. 215 Stephen D. Cannerelli/The Image Works; p. 217 UPI/Corbis; p. 219 Andy Levin/Photo Researchers, Inc.; p. 220 Corbis Sygma Photo News; p. 221 Laima E. Druskis/Pearson Education/PH College.

CHAPTER 7
Opener: Courtesy BetzDearborn, A Division of Hercules Incorporated; p. 231 Joseph Van Os/The Image Bank; p. 233 Kal Muller/Woodfin Camp & Associates; p. 237 Bob Daemmrich/Stock Boston; p. 242 David Young-Wolff/Tony Stone Images; p. 247 Thomas Engstrom/Liaison Agency, Inc.; p. 250 (L) Forsyth/Monkmeyer Press, (R) Merrim/Monkmeyer Press; p. 253 Goodwin/Monkmeyer Press; p. 257 (T) Jeff Greenberg/Photo Researchers, Inc., (B) Jacques Chenet/Woodfin Camp & Associates; p. 258 Will Hart/Will Hart; p. 259 Russell D. Curtis/Photo Researchers, Inc.; p. 260 James Schnepf/Liaison Agency, Inc.; p. 263 Jake Lloyd/Photofest; p. 260 James Schnepf/Liaison Agency, Inc.

CHAPTER 8
Opener: Corbis; p. 277 PhotoDisc, Inc.; p. 279 (L) Camermann/The Image Works, (R) W. Hill, Jr./The Image Works; p. 280 AP/Wide World Photos; p. 282 IPI USA, Corp.;

p. 283 Michele Burgess/The Stock Market; p. 286 Skip Nall/PhotoDisc, Inc.; p. 287 Harlow Primate Laboratory; p. 288 Sylvain Grandadam/Tony Stone Images; p. 292 Rhoda Sidney/PhotoEdit; p. 300 Mark C. Burnett/Photo Researchers, Inc.; p. 296 Kobal Collection; p. 299 (all) Joe McNally Photography; p. 302 Jeff Greenberg/PhotoEdit; p. 304 Paul Ekman. Reprinted with permission.

CHAPTER 9
Opener: Rhoda Sidney/PhotoEdit; p. 312 Rose Hartman/Corbis; p. 313 Tom McHugh/Photo Researchers, Inc.; p. 316 Birnbach/Monkmeyer Press; p. 320 (top left) Spencer Grant/Liaison Agency, Inc., (top middle) Lew Merrim/Monkmeyer Press; (top right) John Eastcott/The Image Works, (middle left) Pearson Education/PH College, (bottom left) Sackman/Monkmeyer Press, (bottom right) John Coletti/Stock Boston; p. 322 Merrim/Monkmeyer Press; p. 326 D. Greco/The Image Works; p. 327 Nina Leen/Time Life Syndication; p. 328 Lawrence Migdale/Pix; p. 329 Will Faller; p. 332 Forsyth/Monkmeyer Press; p. 334 Byron/Monkmeyer Press; p. 339 Gabe Palmer/The Stock Market; p. 341 Ed Andrieski/AP/Wide World Photos; p. 344 Bob Daemmrich/Stock Boston; p. 345 Novastock/PhotoEdit; p. 348 F. Hoffmann/The Image Works; p. 350 Hiroji Kubota/Magnum Photos, Inc.; p. 352 Leinwand/Monkmeyer Press; p. 354 Michael S. Yamashita/Corbis; p. 338 Leo Cullum © 1997 from The New Yorker Collection. All Rights Reserved.

CHAPTER 10
Opener: Dante Burn-Forti/Tony Stone Images; Index Stock Images, p. 366. p. 367 (L) Erich Lessing/Art Resource, N.Y., (R) SuperStock, Inc.; p. 368 M. Grecco/Stock Boston; p. 370 (T) Culver Pictures, Inc., (B) Library of Congress; p. 372 (T) Laima Druskis/Pearson Education/PH College, (B) Greenberg, Jeff/Omni-Photo Communications, Inc.; p. 374 Bob Daemmrich/The Image Works; p. 380 Laima E. Druskis/Pearson Education/PH College.

CHAPTER 11
Opener: Carl J. Single/The Image Works; p. 392 Haruyoshi Yamaguchi/Corbis Sygma Photo News; p. 394 (L) Le Duc/Monkmeyer Press, (R) Schaefer/Monkmeyer Press; p. 395 David W. Hamilton/The Image Bank; p. 401 Paul Barton/The Stock Market; p. 404 Robert Harbison/Robert Harbison; p. 407 Christopher Bissell/Tony Stone Images; p. 410 Reininger/Contact/Woodfin Camp & Associates; p. 411 J. Pat Carter/AP/Wide World Photos.

CHAPTER 12
Opener: Alain Benainous/Liaison Agency, Inc.; p. 420 Ron Sherman/Tony Stone Images; p. 421 Library of Congress; p. 424 M. Gerber/Corbis; p. 429 Jacques Chenet/Woodfin Camp & Associates; 430 David Turnley/Black Star;

NAME INDEX

SUBJECT INDEX